Atlas of Digital Architecture

Atlas of Digital Architecture
Terminology, Concepts, Methods, Tools, Examples, Phenomena

Ludger Hovestadt, Urs Hirschberg, Oliver Fritz (Editors)

Birkhäuser
Basel

Preface 7
Chapter Gallery 15
Introduction 29

THE DESIGN I
Creating the Geometries of Architectural Artefacts

3D Modelling 57
Digital Data Acquisition 93
Digital Design Strategies 111
Computer Aided Design (CAD) 129
Generative Methods 145
Graphs & Graphics 175

THE IMAGE II
Visualising Architecture

Image & Colour 229
Rendering 255
Visualisation 285

LANGUAGE III
The Abstraction of Architecture

Text, Typography & Layout 327
Scripting 351
Writing & Code 369

MATTER & LOGIC IV
The Physical Representation of Architecture

Digital Manufacturing 405
Model Making 421
3D Printing 439

LOGISTICS V
The Dynamic Representation of Architecture

Virtual & Augmented Reality 463
Simulation 475
Geographic Information Systems (GIS) 491
Building Information Modelling (BIM) 507
Digital Cities 529
Big Data & Machine Learning 549

COEXISTENCE VI
The Interfaces and Modes of Collaboration
Between Information Technology and Architects

Being a 'Brand' 593
The Internet of Things (IoT) 613
Collaboration 629
Privacy & Security 643

In Conclusion: What Is Information? 693

Index of Terms, Companies, Software, Publications, Institutions 727
Index of People 737
Index of Architectural Objects 741
Sources for Quotations, Citations, and Statistics 743
Sources for Images & Graphics 747
Biographies 753
Colophon 759

Preface

rial team consisting of Ludger Hovestadt, Oliver Fritz (HTWG Konstanz – University of Applied Sciences), and Urs Hirschberg (TU Graz). Equipped with this, I would then schedule a one to two hour interview with the contributors, and based on my notes I would write their chapter.

This is more or less exactly what happened. Each chapter, once written, went back to the contributors, they gave notes or possibly arranged another meeting to deepen, refine, or edit the content, then, once they were happy, the text was sent to the editorial team for discussion and in some cases direct approval, or in others for further development involving the contributors.

Fittingly for an *Atlas* that has at its core digital technology, almost all of our work, including weekly editorial meetings, happened online. There has not, as yet, been any one occasion when everybody who was directly involved with this title has been in one room together; virtually all of our conversations were conducted by video call, and the only instances when interviews took place face-to-face were those when I happened to be in Zürich or Vienna anyway for some other reason.

In this manner, over the ensuing months, this book gradually took shape. As almost invariably has to be the case with a project of this size and scope, it took a little longer than originally planned, most if not all of the chapters grew a bit more expansive than the brief had foreseen, and with the creative ingenuity, tenacity, and immense patience and adaptability of our designers at Onlab, together we made this book.

AK:AI AND AN *ATLAS*

AK:AI (often styled ak•ai) stands for *Arbeitskreis Architekturinformatik*, which can perhaps best be translated as 'Working Group for Architecture and Computer Science'. Its members are a diverse collection of professors and lecturers who teach at architecture schools in the German speaking world – mainly Germany, Switzerland, and Austria – and many of whom are also practising architects or actively engaged in companies that operate at the intersection of architecture and the digital world. It was founded in 2003 and ordinarily meets once a year to discuss topics of common interest.

A recurring theme at these meetings had been the apparent lack of a textbook that is able to provide the foundations of the field its members are all engaged in. And usually the conclusion the group came to was that such a textbook could not be written: the range of topics is too wide, the field itself is constantly evolving, and the approaches to it represented in the group are simply too diverse.

Nevertheless, at the 2016 meeting it was decided to set out on the endeavour to write just such a book, an *Atlas* as it was soon called. There were two major factors that led to this change in perception. Firstly, digitality is by now firmly established. Information technology in architecture has reached a level of pervasiveness and maturity that makes a resource of this kind more necessary than ever: there is some confusion about the digital tools used in architecture and construction, and therefore also a growing need for a comprehensive text that addresses the bigger picture from all angles. The second factor is the method employed. To overcome the hurdles of disparity and their attendant potential for incoherence, the members of AK:AI took the bold step of allowing me, an outsider, to put into my own words *all* of their contributions, relinquishing control over how their chapters were going to be written, and giving me free rein in introducing my own at times wide-eyed perspective, my eclectic references, and my particular personal style. Whether this was a step worth taking is now for you, our reader, to decide.

HOW TO USE THIS BOOK

We explain in our Introduction why we think of this as an *Atlas*, giving you a brief overview of its structure. And we also say there that, as with any *Atlas*, we don't expect you to read it from start to finish. Beyond that, the book hardly needs a user's manual. But it is worth stating clearly and at the outset here that we have made a few categorical choices that are perhaps unusual in an academic tome. □ 29↘

We assume that you are conversant with your everyday digital environment and so we think you'll probably be able to look things up online. So for the sake of readability, we have done away with footnotes and endnotes. What you will find at the beginning of most chapters is a selection – in some cases very succinct – of recommended or relevant reading, and we give at the end of the book a full list of quoted references.

Also in the interest of allowing the text to flow, our designers at Onlab recommended to only place graphics, code samples, and thumbnails of pictures within its body. Larger versions of the images in black and white are grouped together at the end of each chapter, and colour images are displayed in the Colour Plates section at the end of each part, where appropriate always with corresponding captions.

There are a few conventions in place which bear pointing out. Because we assume that you will dip into and out of this book on any topic of your choosing, we treat each chapter as self-contained. This means that some concepts and significant people are mentioned repeatedly, as if for the first time. Where we deem it sensible to do so we refer to other chapters in the book that deal with a subject matter, and some technical or otherwise important terms are highlighted the first time they appear in a chapter with a reference to their previous and their next first appearance in other chapters. Where such a term is also the heading of a subsection, it is not specially highlighted. First mentions of individuals are almost always given with a brief describer and their dates, such as 'Italian artist, philosopher, and architect Leon Battista Alberti (1404–1472)'. These details are taken from their English *Wikipedia* entry and were last checked as we prepare to go to print in March/April 2020. Similarly, all links provided in this *Atlas* were last accessed then, and we appreciate, as we are sure you do, that by the time you follow any of them, they may no longer exist or point to altered content. While we have deployed due diligence in making sure that the information you find in this book is correct, we still encourage you to treat everything with the customary degree of caution and double-check facts, figures, and sources before citing them in your own work or study.

You will find links to online references and additional content such as coding samples or video lectures by following the QR code given for each chapter and on our website:

atlasofdigitalarchitecture.com

It remains for me as the writer to thank the editors Ludger Hovestadt, Urs Hirschberg, and Oliver Fritz, all the contributors, and the team at Onlab for their trust, their unwavering support, good humour, and generous spirit, all of which in combination has made it possible for us to offer you this work as a genuine, encompassing, and we hope for you in its utilisation as much as for us in its creation enjoyable collaboration.

Sebastian Michael
London, Good Friday 2020

Chapter Gallery

THE DESIGN
Creating the Geometries of Architecture

I

3D Modelling 57

Digital Data Acquisition 93

Digital Design Strategies 111

Computer Aided Design (CAD) 129

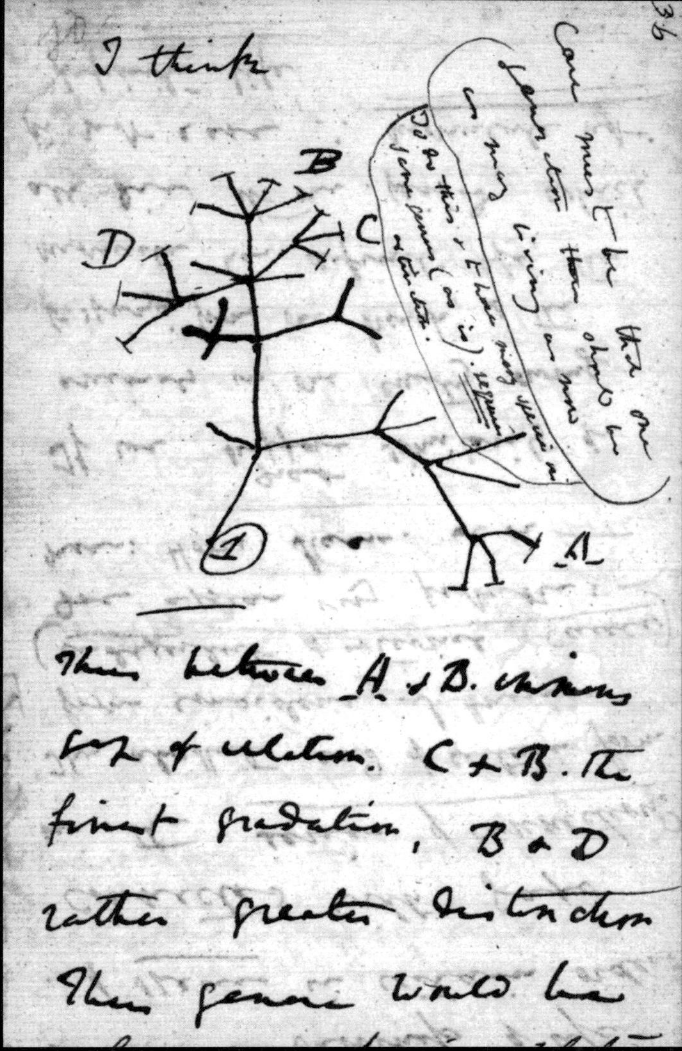

Generative Methods 145

Graphs & Graphics 175

Image & Colour

229

Rendering

Visualisation

The Abstraction of Architecture

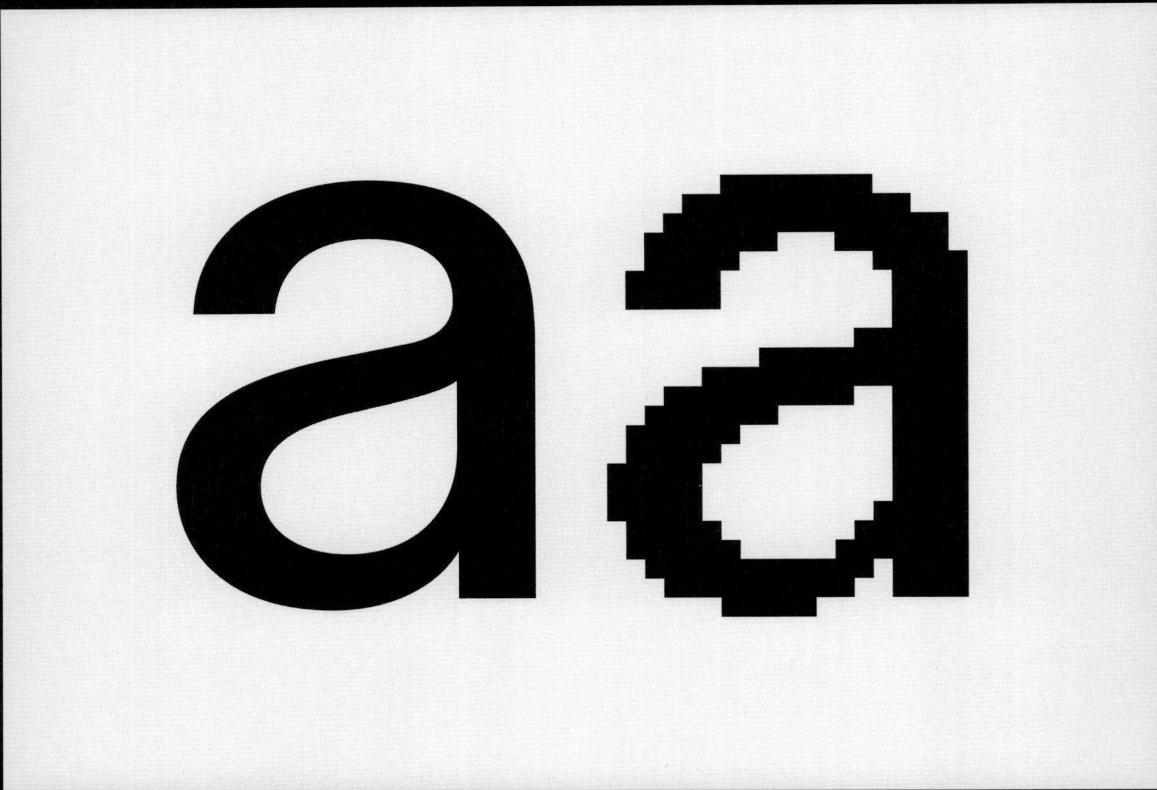

Text, Typography & Layout 327

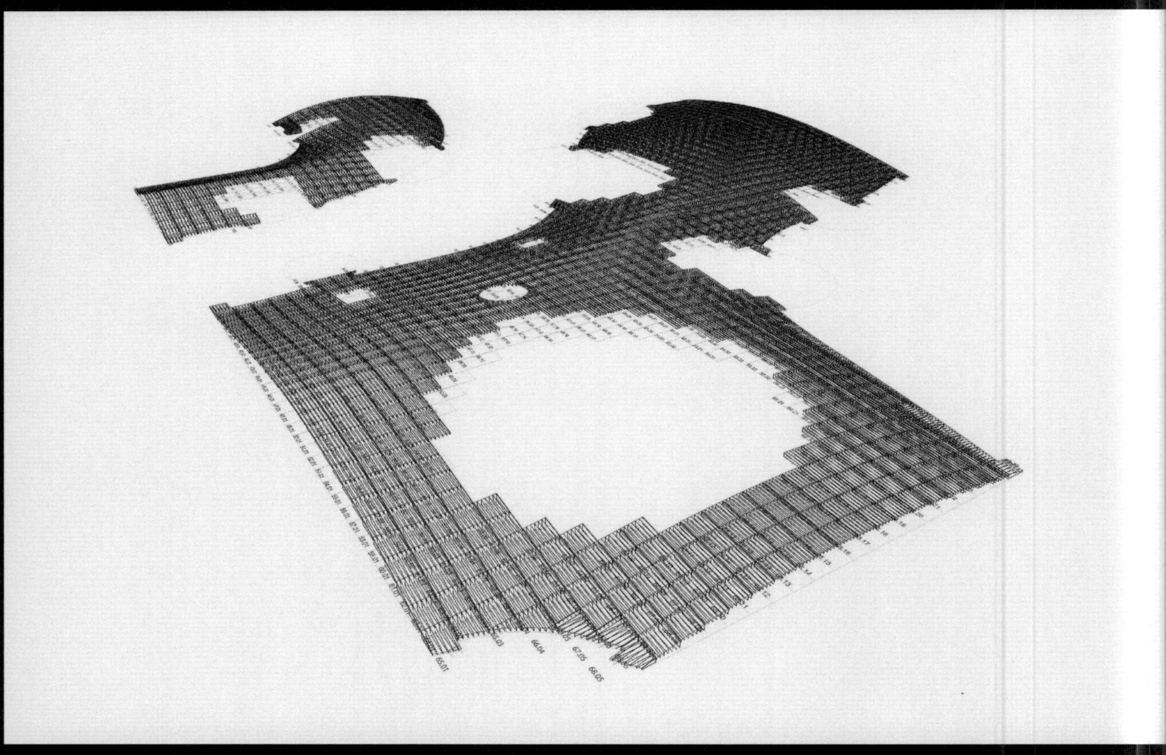

Scripting 351

UNIVAC

Digital Manufacturing

Model Making 421

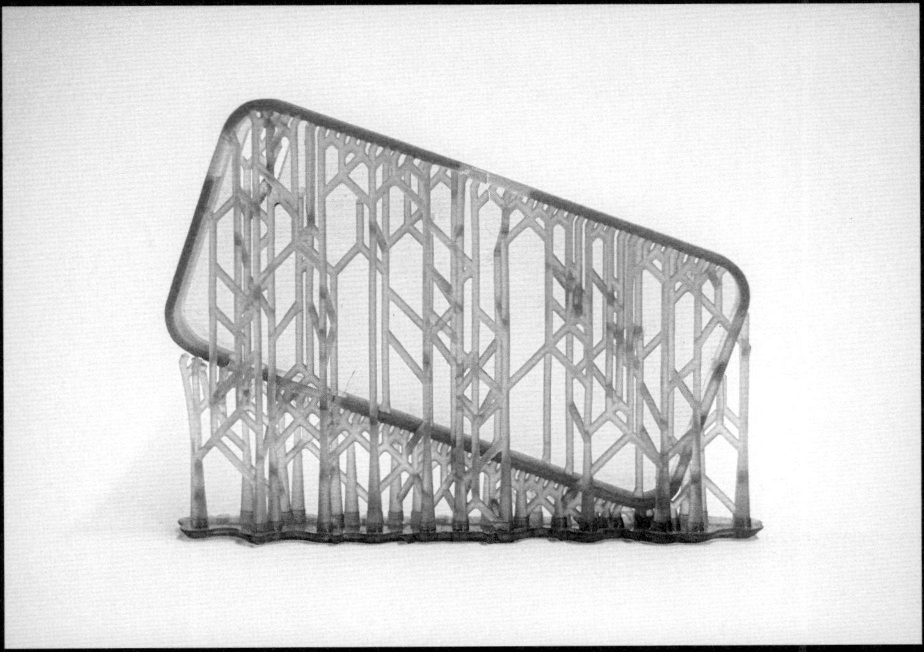

3D Printing 439

LOGISTICS
The Dynamic Representation of Architecture

V

Virtual & Augmented Reality 463

Simulation 475

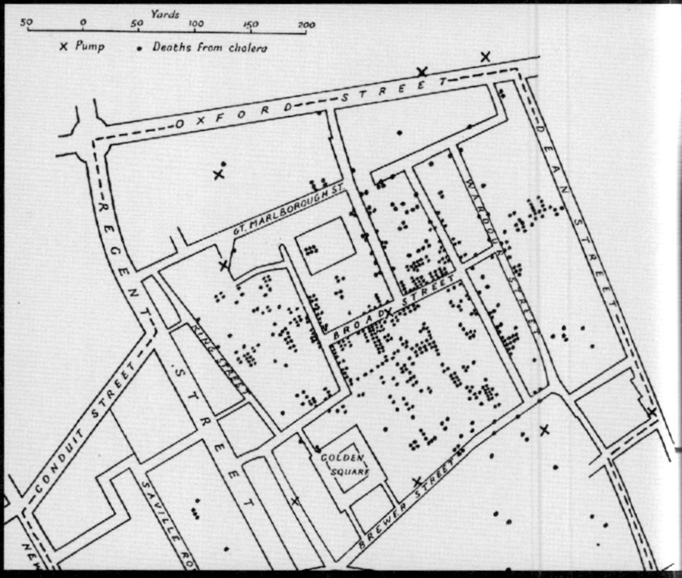

Geographic Information Systems (GIS) 491

Building Information Modelling (BIM) 507

Digital Cities 529

Being a 'Brand' 593

The Internet of Things (IoT) 613

Collaboration 629

Privacy & Security 643

Introduction

Ludger Hovestadt, Urs Hirschberg, Oliver Fritz

● Giovanni Pico della Mirandola: *Oration on the Dignity of Man*, 1496

Digitality and Architecture

AN ATLAS

What is it to be an architect today? Now, at the beginning of the third decade of the twenty-first century, well into an era that in the broadest term we might call one of *digitality*. What, indeed, is it to be human, a *digital human*, so to speak? And what then, specifically, is it to be a 'digital architect'? What is *Digital Architecture*?

If you are reading these lines with a professional interest, it is likely that you are an architecture student hoping to forge a career for yourself and to make your way in a field that – like so many others – is undergoing almost breathless changes, offering a bewildering choice of both charted and uncharted paths, and that finds itself in a constant state of technological flux: old traditions are disappearing or have already practically been lost, while new methodologies are opening up entirely new possibilities both in terms of what you can do, and crucially also in terms of how you can go about doing them.

With this book we want to give you a set of metaphorical maps to help you find your way around. Which is why we are calling it an *Atlas*. You could also think of it as a toolkit, though not one providing the manual tools that you can take out of the box and get to work with, or instructions on how to use them, but perhaps more some thought tools: knowledge on the one hand, and a theoretical framework on the other. But beyond these we want to convey also a *way of thinking*, a thought modus, if you will, that may equip you with the kind of mindset we believe can help you navigate this very open and therefore very exciting, but also at times daunting and possibly even disorientating, landscape. □ 175↘

Talking about 'thought tools' means talking about thinking, □ 369↘
and that means dealing with concepts at an abstract level. We start □ 549↘
doing so in earnest in [Graphs & Graphics], and then pick up the □ 643↘
thread intermittently in the theoretical chapters, [Writing & Code], □ 693↘
[Big Data & Machine Learning], and [Privacy & Security], conclud- □ 57↘
ing with [What Is Information?] at the end of the book. Other chap- □ 405↘
ters, such as those on [3D Modelling], [Digital Manufacturing], or □ 475↘
[Simulation], strike a more practice-oriented note, while others still, □ 327↘
such as [Text, Typography & Layout], for example, or [The Internet] □ 613↘

of Things (IoT), look at architecture and information technology in
☐ 593↘ a broader context. With Being a 'Brand' and Collaboration, mean-
☐ 629↘ while, we examine in more detail and at various levels the role of the architect as a 'digital human'.

The book is structured into six parts, which we hope are more or less self-explanatory; but it is appropriate to give a succinct outline here as a first aid to getting your bearings:

☐ ↖29 Following this Introduction, we proceed into the body of the *Atlas*, starting with:

☐ 55↘ Part I: The Design – Creating the Geometries of Architectural Artefacts. The six chapters in this first part, as the title suggests, all look at the digital methodologies, tools, and approaches that are available to the architect of today to generate the essence of their work: architectural design.

☐ 227↘ Part II: The Image – Visualising Architecture follows on from this both logically and sequentially, in that it looks at the visual representation of architectural design: the three chapters grouped together here cover the digital techniques that make architecture visible before it is built.

☐ 325↘ With Part III: Language – The Abstraction of Architecture we go a step further and delve into the realm of coding, its relationship with semantics and language, and how – as you will find us maintain throughout this *Atlas* – this has become fundamental to our understanding and practice of architecture in the 21st century.

☐ 403↘ In Part IV: Matter & Logic – The Physical Representation of Architecture, we draw an arc to the material reality of making architectural objects, and discuss the technologies – both contemporary and traditional – that are relevant to us in turning our concepts and their visual representations into tangible, haptic, three-dimensional objects.

☐ 461↘ Part V: Logistics – The Dynamic Representation of Architecture then broadens the spectrum to draw into the discussion the wide range of digital tools and informational contexts in which architecture is being realised.

Finally, in Part VI: Coexistence – The Interfaces and Modes of Collaboration Between Information Technology and Architects we conduct some differentiated reflections on where we stand and are likely to go as 'Digital Architects'. □ 591↘

The scope of this *Atlas*, then, is immense, and so in this brief Introduction we only really want to set the scene with the conceptual framework that we perceive to be in place for architecture. When we say 'a conceptual framework is in place', we immediately need to qualify this and add a note of caution. We are, like you, to some extent still finding our way. We are still developing the vocabulary: even just using a term like 'digitality' does not sit entirely easy with us, because the definitions are still quite blurry and in a process of taking shape. But that also makes a book like this timely, and the approach we are taking, we believe, essentially right. Not right as in 'correct' – which would suggest that there is a correct way of handling the subject matter, as opposed to any other, 'incorrect', way – but right as in 'workable and appropriate and suited to our own understanding and expertise'. □ ↖29

A WAY OF THINKING ABOUT ARCHITECTURE

We are keeping an open mind about virtually everything, including this book: it reflects not only a vast array of different characters and seats of knowledge, it also tries to tie these together into an intellectual outlook that seeks a dialogue, a correspondence, so to speak, both within the chapters that form this *Atlas*, and also with you, the reader, and the digital experience as it is forming 'out there' in the domain of architecture and in the world generally.

In this spirit, we are going to start here by inviting you to join us as we play through a couple of thought figures, as we like to describe them. You will find us do so now and then in this *Atlas*, and setting out this approach right here therefore serves a dual purpose. Firstly, we obviously want to share with you these thoughts, as we consider them relevant and helpful. Secondly, though, we also want to get into the *mode* of this *Atlas*, and help you understand, appreciate, and above all enjoy it.

Because chances are you may occasionally feel a tad bewildered by some of the things we do here, and some of the liberties we take. But our aim is not to alienate or scare you, we want to take you with us. Throughout this book, we depart from the stringent format and tonality of a traditional text book. This is deliberate.

We have decided, at the very outset of the project, that we want to create for you, our reader, a 'themescape' that comes replete with stories, anecdotes, metaphors, and parallels. Why? Because that is the reality of our existence today as digital human beings: the boundaries and strict delineations of disciplines are blurred, the clearly defined areas of competence that characterised the 19th and 20th centuries once again overlap, as they have done before, and much of what we are doing and dealing with today is fluid, malleable, and not at all settled or 'owned'.

So it makes sense to us to ease into our subject – which is after all expansive, as we have noted – with openness and curiosity, with a broad outlook, and a panoramic perspective. If therefore we talk to you, as we're about to, of Giovanni Pico della Mirandola, for example, and of master chefs, your instinct may well be to wonder: what on earth has this to do with my architecture? It will become clear. Possibly to some of you a little sooner, and to others a little later. Let that not worry you; it doesn't worry us. Come with us, go with the flow. Or if you don't feel like it now, use the *Atlas* as best suits you, and then □ ↖29 maybe come back to the following sections in this Introduction at a later stage. We are not on a course of instruction – 'this is how to do things!' – we are on an excursion of discovery and wonder; underpinned by solid foundations of factual expertise and decades of experience in the field. We are not going to get lost, we can assure you. And sooner or later we hope you'll find this exploration of our world as we find it: fascinating, stimulating, intriguing, and maybe also inspiring.

FROM RENAISSANCE MAN TO DIGITAL HUMAN

Here, then, lies a first parallel that we are keen to highlight, as others have done and continue to do: we find ourselves in a situation that is in many ways not dissimilar to Europe in the 15th century. With the beginning of the Renaissance, centuries-old certainties about the world we lived in dissolved, and new science, new art, new philosophies, and new perspectives, both literal and metaphorical, opened up an entirely new understanding of this world and therefore of going about interpreting and shaping it. Yet the term 'Renaissance' itself makes it clear that all was not 'new', that much of this new conceptualisation built on previously understood and used ideas. But the shift that took place then was categorical, far reaching, and ground breaking, much as the shift which had taken place two and a half thousand years earlier, when Western civilisation as we are able to recognise it today first emerged, and from which the Renaissance took so much of its inspiration.

C01 ● 050

With our move into the 'digital age' – our current era that is characterised by information technology or digitality – we similarly let go of many established certainties and 'ways of doing things', and are therefore not just called upon to adapt and adjust (though that too), but much more fundamentally we are given the opportunity to completely reimagine our own role in relation to the things we do, the materials we work with, the works we create, and the people we share our cities, our spaces, and our culture with. We can ask ourselves a whole different type of question, such as 'what is it I want to be today?', or 'wouldn't it be fantastic if I could design a building that understands me perfectly?', or 'where in the world do I want to be at home for the next hour or so?'

If we want to embrace this and open ourselves up in this way, we also need to become newly *literate*. In the Conclusion that mirrors this Introduction, What Is Information?, we postulate that □ ↖29
much as the thinker, philosopher, and architect of antiquity wanted □ 693↘
to become literate in reading and writing, so Renaissance Man (then almost exclusively man) found it liberating to become literate in a new mathematics and geometry that opened up scalable drawings and perspective to him: for the first time it was possible to rotate objects in space with proportional consistency. Today we, whom correspondingly we could call Digital Human, can acquire literacy in the language that defines our day: code. And in order to do so at a conceptual level, we need to understand at least the principles of the mathematics that make our world as it is today possible.

This may not be entirely easy, but it isn't entirely difficult either. In fact, it is less difficult than at first it appears. It requires a bit of patience, and it takes a degree of abstract thinking that doesn't always seem to 'come naturally' to us, but the effort and tenacity that you put in reap generous rewards, because what this thinking unlocks turns out to be an unprecedented abundance of possibilities, of potentials, of potentialities even, that without executing this conceptual shift are simply not available. We shy away from calling this 'progress' – a notion that is inherently problematic – because what we are looking at is not even in that sense a progression, certainly not a linear one, on a trajectory towards 'a better world' or a sought-for Nirvana. It's simply a new plateau, a next level of abstraction that is now within our reach.

Here, on this level, we can think in a way that is encompassing, immersive. It goes beyond analysing our 'problems' and trying to 'solve' them, and extends into sensing, absorbing, imagining, living. Maybe we can venture as far as suggesting that this is a *quantum way of thinking:* the kind of approach to our world that allows us to be the particle *and* the wave.

An analogy that may convey what we mean here is perhaps that of an ocean wave. Many today feel that they are being overwhelmed by technology and everything it enables, that too much is happening too fast, and that we are all in danger of drowning. If you find yourself literally on a beach and being washed over by a powerful wave, this can be a frightening experience. But what happens if you learn to swim? You may still not be strong enough to go against the wave, but you already feel a degree of confidence, possibly even pleasure, because you know that once the bulk of the wave is over, you can come up for air and orientate yourself and proceed in one direction or another.

Take this one level further and learn to surf: now you can ride the wave. You can experience the exhilarating sensation of being on top of it, even though you have zero control over it. Through practice you can master the wave and look forward to – even seek out – the next one.

And then go one step further still: forget thinking of yourself and the wave as two separate entities and *become part of* the wave: be the disturbance that troubles the water and allow from it to spring gorgeous white horses. Be the creative spirit that lets emerge from the spume something new. Un-separate your senses from your intellect and allow sense and sensuality to be one. This really scares people. Even writing a sentence like "allow sense and sensuality to be one" in an *Atlas of Digital Architecture* can, and by some people will, be seen as controversial. We have boxed ourselves into corners of disciplines and factual aloofness, and we are afraid to emerge from them because there are eggshells and mines all around. And it's impossible to tell which is which. Make one false move, say one charged word, use one loaded image and you might get blown up. The reasons for this are manifold and many of them are manifestly justified. Still, we think it is essential that we un-scare ourselves and be bold. Not wanton, or insensitive, but brave. To look at *everything*. Even at things that disturb us.

The fact is: we do live in scared and scary times, it's true. But who hasn't done so? The reason we are here where we are today is that as a species we are in fact spectacularly successful. Having to face the gargantuan challenges that we face is a luxury. Does that sound absurd? Only as long as we look at them through the lens of something alien, terrifying, imposed on us. If we recognise them as something we ourselves are a visceral part of, then we can enter a completely different type of discourse. One in which we don't have to be quite so afraid of everything – of opinions we don't agree with, of erotic connotations, of technology, of the future – or quite so angry about everything, and we can start to relax and say: we have creative potential. We can make beautiful things. We are this wave, and we are the particles it consists of too, and we love it.

002 ● 050

MASTERY

In this, in being the wave and letting from it emerge something new *and loving it* lies mastery. And intellectually, that's what we want to get to. Because what is mastery? It's being so technically accomplished, so dexterous, and so knowledgeable in what you do that what you do becomes 'second nature' to you. The English idiom itself seems to hint at this gap we want to bridge, where we no longer labour under the task, but inhabit it. Here we are in the realm of beauty, fecundity, abundance. We are, in the classical tradition, in the realm of the gods. What you call this today is up to you, but you realise: it's not Newtonian science alone. It's not facts and figures alone, it's culture, it's passion, it's connection; it exists beyond everything that is pedestrian and mundane, it's where love is and where words fail, it's *quantum*.

003 ● 051

Today, we have an abundance of images, indexes, references. Cultivating this abundance, that is what we want to do. Digitality is reaching omnipresence, and at breathtaking speed. Which is why we postulate that the real challenge today is not – as many a standard view has it – things becoming more complicated with computers, but rather that they are becoming extraordinarily simple. This is exactly why they are so successful: with their intuitive, easy interfaces, it is not us who understand computers any longer, it's computers that understand us. And now, with artificial intelligence and machine learning, even our problems can be formulated automatically, and automatically solved. What this leads to is not just an ubiquitousness of computing, with this comes saturation. There is now, you could argue, of everything not just enough, but *too much*: too much information, too much design, too much analysis, too much interpretation, too much confluence, too much speed. Everything is happening too fast for us, and we notice with alarm how everything has started to coalesce and look the same: our architecture, our cities, our environments, they seem to dissolve into a generic soup.

And so we think this is a good moment for us to take a step back, to pause and reflect on what this is now, architecture, on our networked planet. Who are we, 'digital humans', making, constituting, talking about this architecture. It's necessary now – and possible! – that we do *not* allow ourselves to be dragged along in an ever-accelerating current of time, running after our Warholian Fifteen Minutes of Fame, or shrugging our shoulders in a Beuysian resignation because really 'everyone is an artist' and everything therefore is probably somehow art and nothing at all matters. We can and need to take a position and formulate a point of view, declare who we are and what we are about. We need to, as we would say, master the generic.

In this context, and very much in the vein of what we said earlier about playing through some thought figures and this here being an excursion, we enjoy the analogy of a master chef. A person who, no matter where they are from, can delve into the sophisticated abstractions of a highly advanced culture, such as – in Europe – French cuisine, or in Asia Japanese cooking, and bring the methods, insights, and dexterity found there back to their own traditions and expand them, meld them together, to create new layers, new expressions, new iterations of their food culture. While Socrates may have thought of cooking as a mere skill but not an art, these are now methods that have been developed much like an art form, way beyond the levels of utility dictated by the need to feed people: they are conscious cultivations.

Take the *Netflix* series *Chef's Table*, for example. These are perfectly produced 50-minute portraits of creative culinary professionals from all corners of the world. What these people have in common is the passion with which they refine their practice and the efforts they go to to achieve something out of the ordinary. Struggle, in one form or another, seems par for the course, be this with their own personality, or, as very often is the case, with the expectations of the their parents, their friends, or the society they live in.

Our heroes come over as fearless, and they expose themselves existentially in their desire to become very, very good at what they do. And many of these portraits show that extraordinary things can come about only when you succeed at pushing through something that is fundamentally new. What is significant though is that, apparently throughout, these chefs attain their world class status and equip themselves with the 'vocabulary' they need for an international career by undergoing French-influenced training, and taking this into their regional cuisine, there to cultivate the ingredients – the plants, animals, and spices – they need to develop their own traditions. They in effect symbolise their home culture in a luxuriant, international, abstract language, which is capable of integrating all these local nuances, refinements, and levels of sophistication.

In this new self perception they are able to emancipate themselves and to establish new localised and differentiated processing and value chains in the concert of a global cuisine: flavour fusions that could never have been imagined, even within the complexity of a French cuisine. This enriches our planet: the world becomes a curiosity shop of colours, flavours, scents, textures, and tastes, medialised through the methods of orchestration: a panoply of attractions which we delight in being seduced, surprised, and challenged by. It allows us to feel sensually, emotionally, and intellectually refreshed and invigorated, inspired: reborn.

That's the stance we are taking, and since we are in such a fluid, evolving context, 'stance' is exactly the wrong word: because nothing stands still here, nothing is fixed, everything is in motion. Always. Our 'stance' is not static and not firm, it is an attitude, a gesture; our unafraid look into the eyes of the world, and what we want to say with it is: 'welcome to planet Earth!'

So, expressed in one more thought figure perhaps, we suggest: forget about the mediaeval geocentric world view, obviously. But also in a way forget about the heliocentric world view that emerged in the Renaissance with Copernicus, Galileo, and Kepler.

Because neither is wholly adequate any longer. Of course, the idea that we are at the centre of the universe and everything revolves around us has been conclusively proved wrong. But even if we think of everything on our world as being essentially fixed and us moving around our source of energy, the Sun, while observing how everything outside our solar system moves and evolves, we don't do our reality justice. Because what happens today is different again: things bend in space and time, they become active time capsules. They are electric, they read, store, process, and send data; they are globally networked; and so everything circles around a small point, which we call processor, of which there are trillions; they are able to turn back time or make it leap forward, they shimmer and vibrate. Think of Apollo – not the Greek god, but the American space mission – think of TV, cars, nuclear energy, aeroplanes; think of bubble gum, antibiotics, synthetic fertiliser; think of laser, the bikini, photovoltaic solar cells; think of the computer, of photocopying machines, think of the mobile phone... – These precious elements of time today are all connected and alive, and they are all like tiny planets that circle around each other. It is no longer possible to take one absolute standpoint and get an overview. You're part of the game. You have a standpoint and a perspective for a second, and the moment you change your position, the picture changes: it's like a Copernican reversal – it is fantastical.

004 ● 051

THE SHOCK OF THE 'OLD'

Sometimes nothing seems more surprising than the realisation that everything is not new. It is perhaps human nature to think of ourselves as inherently more brilliant than the generations before us. And with little else to believe in, maybe a faith in some kind of progression being possible for the human race is a comforting thought, which we don't want to demean. But the idea that we today are categorically cleverer, more clued up about our world, and therefore greatly advanced is fallacious. Yes, our understanding of the world has been broadened and deepened by science and technology, but looked at in the context of our respective realities, we are no different, and no 'further ahead', than the masters of yore. In order to make their own kind of 'progress', to discover, to learn, and to improve, they needed to have the same curiosity, the same intelligence, the same courage, if not indeed much greater than we have to muster, because while most of us can lead comparatively safe and comfortable lives most of the time in our pursuit of architecture, art, and wisdom, for many a creative and inventive mind of the past, the cultivation of their genius was a matter of life and death.

005 ● 052

GIOVANNI PICO DELLA MIRANDOLA

Let us introduce you to one character we particularly love for symbolising the boldness of spirit and intellectual panache of his era. Born in 1463 in the Italian town near Modena from which he takes his name, Giovanni Pico della Mirandola was very rich (he owned one of the largest libraries in the world), very well educated (he'd travelled extensively and studied at Europe's then most prominent universities, including Bologna and Paris), and very young indeed when he stamped his mark on the world.

006 ● 052

Aged 23, he compiled a catalogue of some 900 theses on what he considered to be the most important questions concerning religion and philosophy, and published them under the title *Conclusiones philosophicae, cabalisticae et theologicae* in December 1486.

He immediately found himself under attack for the outrageous ambition of his undertaking, and so he proceeded to invite any scholars inclined to do so to attend, at his expense, a public disputation in Rome of these 900 theses. In preparation, he wrote a short text – about 7,700 words in Latin – which he intended to give as his introductory speech and opening gambit. In it, he drew from a wide array of theological and philosophical traditions, voicing ideas that were nothing short of revolutionary at the time and that still strike us as daring, even radical, today. Two central themes stand out: that of human dignity, and the ideal of a universal harmony among philosophers and their schools of thought. Above all, Pico della Mirandola celebrates freedom. For him what truly distinguishes the human from any other being – animal or celestial – is our freedom to choose to become what we will. With this freedom comes great responsibility, but also our right to practise thought and to take our insights from wherever we want. (Equally emphatic is Pico's disgust with the commodification of education, and the prevailing, snide anti-intellectualism of his day. No wonder he speaks to us now...)

Pico never gave his address. Pope Innocent VIII suspended the event and set up a commission to examine his 900 theses for heresy. Pico promptly recycled the second half of his speech in an *Apologia* that he published three years later, in 1489, but this did not solve his problems: he faced years of persecution, and in 1494, two years after the death of his patron and protector, the powerful Florentine statesman Lorenzo de' Medici (1449–1492), Pico, together with his friend, Italian scholar and poet Poliziano (1454–1494), was murdered in Florence by arsenic poisoning.

Originally known simply as *Oratio*, and first published posthumously by Giovanni's nephew Francesco Pico in 1496, the title soon acquired the addition by which we generally refer to it now, and became the *Oratio de hominis dignitate* – the *Oration on the Dignity of Man* – which today ranks as one of the most influential texts ever written and is considered a 'manifesto for the Renaissance'.

TO SET US ON OUR WAY: A FUNDAMENTAL THOUGHT AND SOME COUNSEL

We don't expect you to read this book through from start to finish, and we don't even expect you to make sense of it all, certainly not in one go. Perhaps you may want to think of some of the things you find in this *Atlas* as references which, in isolation, seem like maps of remote islands, 'lost' in the ocean and populated mainly by strange creatures that are fascinating to behold, but have no immediate use to you as livestock or pets. Maps such as these in a geographical atlas don't come in handy immediately, certainly not when you're looking for the quickest route from Berlin to Paris, or want to check out the topography of the Andes. But they form part of the picture that makes up our world. Not knowing about these places or keeping them out of your consciousness would leave your view of the world not just incomplete, but distorted. You may not be able to step on a train at Zürich main station and get there in under five hours, but knowing that these places exist, and that there is a route that leads to them (perhaps by air, land, and sea, and then some hiking through thick jungle without a mobile phone signal and no further instructions) is in itself not just valid but necessary if you don't want to deprive yourself of a comprehensive understanding of your world.

So to set you on your way, and with our best wishes for an adventurous journey, we want to conclude this Introduction with one fundamental thought that we believe goes to the heart of 'getting' digitality, followed by a little advice. As with any advice, you can make of this what you will; advice primarily tells you a lot about the advisor, and so you can put this, too, in context and perspective: it gives you one more insight into where we're coming from and how we recommend you use this book and the technologies to which it aims to introduce you. You may wish to think of it, therefore, perhaps more as our 'counsel'. □ ↖29

COMPUTERS ARE NOT MACHINES

This is perhaps the most important point of them all. Accepting it opens up an escape from a whole raft of positions on information technology that we don't mean to critique here – nor are we going to discuss them – but to which we want to offer a conceptual alternative: the dystopias of French cultural theorist and urbanist Paul Virilio (1932–2018) and his 'philosophy of speed', the materialism of French philosopher and sociologist Bruno Latour (b. 1947) and his *Actor-Network Theory*, the sophism of French philosopher Jacques Derrida (1930–2004), the structuralist simplifications of American philosopher, historian, and activist Noam Chomsky (b. 1928), the aesthetic melancholies of French philosopher and literary theorist Jean-François Lyotard (1924–1998), or the shortcuts of American computer scientist and futurist Ray Kurzweil (b. 1948)... – We are listing them here as masters in their fields: they each have something to say and we recommend absolutely that you delve into what they are saying and examine how they are saying it, and why. But we want to add another take, still, on digitality.

We follow more the line of French philosopher Michel Serres (1930–2019), whose thinking affirms the constitutive importance of mathematics, science, and technology, and Dutch architect and architecture theorist Rem Koolhaas (b. 1944), who in fact offers the same affirmation, albeit with a degree of sarcasm.

Information technology is more powerful than anything we humans have ever brought about – cultivated – before. It not only touches, it infuses, *inhabits*, everything, and so nothing can shield itself, withdraw, or isolate itself, from this power. This is worth thinking through for just one moment: education, business, money, any contract, any art, any research, any project, any problem, any dialectic, any didactic, any design, any intention good or bad, any communication, any understanding, any travel, any health care, any experience: absolutely everything we do and have today is in one way or another possessed of digitality. Whether we want it to be or not. Whether we think so, or not. Even when we just meet up with a friend for a pint and we think: we're standing in a pub, glasses in hand, talking face to face. The world we're having this conversation in is one that is shaped, defined, made sense of by information. And the technology we have developed to handle it is of a kind that is all-pervasive. All intrusive, some would say, others would see it as the thing that gradually turns into the backdrop, the scenery or stage set, on which everything takes place, all present, but unnoticed other than as the thing that is of course there, has to be there, in order for there to be anything at all.

This is why you will hear us say, and emphasise: 'computers are not machines'. A machine is an apparatus that does a certain thing which it has been designed to do. Possibly a highly complicated, difficult, intricate, and sophisticated thing, like assembling a car that then – in itself a new machine – can take you from one place to another at considerable speed, in great comfort, while listening to Bach. That's extraordinary, but it is one thing. A computer is an information handling device that allows you to do *anything*. Anything that you can imagine, and anything that you can't. Which is exactly the reason why information technology is the technology that inhabits everything: because it can. It can be applied – literally, by means of applications – to anything at all. This is what makes it what it is, it is its chief characteristic, that it provides the potentiality for anything at all to be realised that we can or cannot yet think of.

That's extraordinary too, but it's also revolutionary on an exponential footing. It's an immense power that we have created for ourselves. And so it must also be something that we have to learn to handle. If many perceive this power as essentially a threat, then this is not because they're paranoid, it's because we are changing everything we've ever known about ourselves and our world. That's not banal. So with this power comes corresponding responsibility. We have, over the course of the twentieth century, become capable of annihilating in its entirety our planet and with it ourselves through the destructive force of the nuclear bomb, and we have at the same time and with the same technological and conceptual principles also become capable of creating anything we want. We have become as powerful as the gods we once believed in and whose stories we told when we first started relating, and then writing down, legends.

So, again, our situation is not really new. Any and all cultures speak of the whole: the universe they can perceive, and beyond what they can perceive, what they can imagine. The Ancient Greeks, with their deities whose foibles and misdemeanours were all too human, looked at everything, and everything was contained within their culture. Giovanni Pico della Mirandola and the many masters of the Renaissance looked at everything. And so it is not for us to either think ourselves exulted or damned. We are human. Maybe we are *only* human, but we are really capable of everything we have given ourselves the power to do. There's nobody else we can pass our responsibility on to. The only thing that we can do is meet it outright, upright, face-to-face: we have to – *have the opportunity to!* – accept, affirm, and cultivate it.

This is our world: it is immensely complex, at times breath-takingly infuriating and bewildering, and indescribably beautiful.

AND SO: OUR COUNSEL

Don't trust simple explanations

The world isn't simple. It's complex. If something or someone makes things look simple and straightforward, you can be certain of one thing and one thing only: you're not looking at the whole picture. You're either not availing yourself, or are being actively prevented from getting, all the relevant information. Once you accept that virtually everything has more to it than meets the eye, you can begin to make sense of the world. Until then, everything remains confusing.

Don't trust quick fixes

They are quick for a reason: they don't last very long and don't get you very far. The 'machine' is always faster than you are, and so to keep up with it you will find yourself forever running, and in doing so, you'll soon be running out of breath. If there appears to be an apocalypse on the horizon, this is the reason for it (the appearance of an apocalypse, not an apocalypse actually appearing on the horizon): as long as we're chasing bubbles we will be frustrated in our endeavours, and as long as we try to catch up with developments by hastily adjusting our actions whilst never addressing our thinking, we keep falling behind; and the more we fall behind, the more it seems to us that the cart, now driverless, is careering towards an abyss. Whether there actually *is* an apocalypse on the horizon, or the cart careering towards the abyss, thus ironically becomes immaterial. We have the wherewithal to create these immense challenges we are facing, and we also have the wherewithal to address them. Not with quick fixes, but with evolved thinking.

Don't trust prophesies and promises

It's a truism, but for that it is no less true: the only way to predict the future is to invent it. *Nobody* knows what's going to happen, and most predictions are extrapolations of projections based on current data and current thinking. But thinking, as we've just noted, cannot remain current, it has to evolve. And it does. We routinely do things today that our grandparents just a couple of generations ago would not only have thought impossible, they would not have been able to think it. So whenever you hear someone speak of an impending catastrophe because, 'if we continue doing this thing in this particular way, then by 2050 that will happen', you are entitled to ask: why on earth would we continue doing this thing in this way for another 30 years? We now have technology to do this thing completely differently, so the outcome you're predicting here is really unlikely. Unless of course we get stuck and do continue in the same rut for another 30 years. But that would be idiotic. And yes, there are exceptions to everything.

Do trust your intellect

Your feelings, your taste, your intuition: they're important, you wouldn't be human without them. But they are deeply unreliable, and inherently so. They are not bad and not bad for you, but they are not enough. Depending on them entirely renders you drunk on emotion: it may feel good, it may even feel right, but your discerning powers are diminished to the point where they become useless. If you want to know something so you can make sense of it, you have to make the effort to think it through.

Do embrace complexity

When things get complicated, you know you haven't thought them through properly. What you need to do is distance yourself and seek a higher level of abstraction to find a new order in things. This makes things more complex but less complicated, and that means they become easier to deal with. Not simpler: easier. It's a fallacy to think of systems as getting more complex with increasing numbers of components, as *systems theory* would suggest. An increase in the number of components makes a system more complicated, not, however, more complex. And so as we find greater levels of abstraction, our thinking becomes more complex, as has happened with *category theory* and information technology: here systems are not built around components, but the components themselves *are* the system.

Do get into mathematics

There is no need to be afraid of mathematics in general, or of the mathematics of the 20th century in particular: mathematics is complex, not complicated: it is a question of thinking complex thought, not of writing complicated formulas. They exist, yes, but they are misleading. The texts of Swiss mathematician and logician Leonhard Euler (1707–1783), for example, or those of French mathematician and philosopher René Descartes (1596–1650), or German mathematician Richard Dedekind (1831–1916), or those of the ancient Arabs, they are, in all their complexity, remarkably clear and easy to read, much easier even than their representations on *Wikipedia*, which tend to attempt to axiomatise mathematics. This, in turn, more often than not proves inadequate and renders mathematics cumbersome and unwieldy. Mathematics is neither cumbersome nor unwieldy: it is elegant, precise, and poetic.

Do love the world in its abundance

Bear in mind that the world has always been rich and beautiful, that, as the meme says, humans *are* awesome, and have always been. As we stated earlier: it is ridiculous to assume, and arrogant to boot, that just because we have more powerful technology today than ever before – and we do! – we are therefore cleverer, more intelligent, or understand the world *as it is*. We have more information, certainly, than ever before, and we process more of it faster, and our science is capable of things we could erstwhile at best have dreamt of, or not even that. But the world at any point in history is as differentiated as we can conceive it, as intricate as we can measure it, and as layered as we can fathom it, at that time. You may always marvel at its complexity and wonder about its mysteries, but you can never truly understand it in its entirety. What you can do is open yourself up to the world and ask good questions. Good questions are a good thing because they alone can produce good answers.

BECOMING LITERATE

And that takes us right back to where we started: what is it to be an architect today, what is it to be a digital human, what is Digital Architecture? You can't learn the 'fundamentals' of digitality: there is no cause and no effect. There isn't a set of rules or formulas that if applied correctly, result in the right outcome. There is no right outcome. The elements of information technology are causality in themselves: our age is one of fluidity and connections. Of dynamic nodes in the network and of potentiality. There are no straight lines and no calculable curves, or rather: there are, but they have no meaning above anything else, they lend no structure. That's why we say: let's learn to bathe in the digital ocean. Let's marvel at the colours and the patterns and the shimmering shapes. Let's be curious and let's trust both each other, and the thing itself, digitality.

If you keep yourself at a distance, with your critical faculties on high alert and a knowing, sceptical smirk about your lips, you can't do any of that. You can't be the wave and let something new emerge from its spume. Immersing yourself, you can. Whether you enter headfirst with a dive from a promontory, or by dipping in your toe cautiously and then seeing how it goes, that doesn't matter. But ultimately, you have to let go. Let go of the fear, push off from the land, relinquish the ground that you stood on and that felt so comforting, so secure.

And how do we do this? Once in the water, how do we 'become the wave'? We've already more than just hinted at this: there's a leaf we can take out of the book of the old masters, because they too had to let go of their rail and step into a new wave that may have seemed to many as if it were going to sweep them away to oblivion and that in fact landed them, and therefore us, on a new plateau: they didn't primarily learn to handle the tools of their age.

That, they treated as a given, and that was not what was new, and scary, and what deserves our great admiration today still, and also respect. The most important thing they learnt was to handle the symbols, the code of their age. They learnt to read and write. They became literate. They learnt to cultivate at an abstract level, and *that's* how they became different, more powerful people.

Becoming literate – whether you do so in your language as a child, or in your professional practice as a student; whether you do so in antiquity, in the Renaissance, or today – takes patience, practice, and perseverance. You just have to internalise the words, the sentences, the structures, the grammar. Practise, over and over again. Keep at it, repeat and repeat until you get good at it. There's no way around this. You have to do just as humans have done since the dawn of civilisation: learn the code of your age.

007 ● 053

008 ● 053

001 ● 035
Björk

002 ● 037
Alain Ducasse: a life worth eating... [Adam Goldberg]

003 ● 037
Jan van Huysum: *Still Life with Flowers and Fruit*, c. 1715.

004 ● 040
Children at play.

005 ● 041
Hurricane Katrina, 2005.

006 ● 041
Giovanni Pico della Mirandola painted by Cristofano dell'Altissimo, 1525–1605.

007 ● 049
Kisho Kurokawa, Nakagin Capsule Tower, 1970–72.

C08 ● 049
Somewhere in Cairo, 2014.

THE DESIGN
Creating the Geometries of Architectural Artefacts

I

3D Modelling 57
Digital Data Acquisition 93
Digital Design Strategies 111
Computer Aided Design (CAD) 129
Generative Methods 145
Graphs & Graphics 175

3D Modelling

Marco Hemmerling

- William J Mitchell: *Computer Aided Architectural Design*, 1977
- Robin Evans: *The Projective Cast – Architecture and Its Three Geometries*, 1995
- Mario Carpo: *The Digital Turn in Architecture*, 1992–2012 (AD Reader), 2013
- Helmut Pottmann, Andreas Asperl, Michael Hofer, Alex Kilian: *Architectural Geometry*, 2007
- Antoine Picon: *Digital Culture in Architecture*, 2010
- Patrik Schumacher: *The Autopoiesis of Architecture – A New Framework for Architecture*, 2011
- Frank P Melendez: *Drawing from the Model: Fundamentals of Digital Drawing, 3D Modeling, and the Visual Programming in Architectural Design*, 2019

Overview

CREATING SPACE

"I begin," Swiss-German artist Paul Klee (1879–1940) explained in his Notebooks, "where all pictorial form begins: with the point that sets itself in motion. The point moves off, and the line comes into being – the first dimension. The line shifts to form a plane, we obtain a two-dimensional element. In the movement from planes to space, planes give rise to a body (three-dimensional)."

This, as we shall see when we look at the actual processes further along in this chapter on 3D Modelling, not only describes one of the exact methods by which we can add a dimension to what we already have, namely by *motion,* it also elegantly sums up how we arrive at visual representations of three-dimensional objects generally: we build them from the elements that make up these three dimensions, and as there is no end to the possible ways in which these elements can be configured, there is no limit to the shapes an object may take. And it is really three dimensions we are interested in, because as architects what we do is create space. Whether we create it out of nothing – which, as we discuss in our chapter on Visualisation, is extremely rare – or whether we work with existing context and transform or reshape it, we always do something that creates a new space.

The evolution of dimensions, from point, to line, surface, and volume.

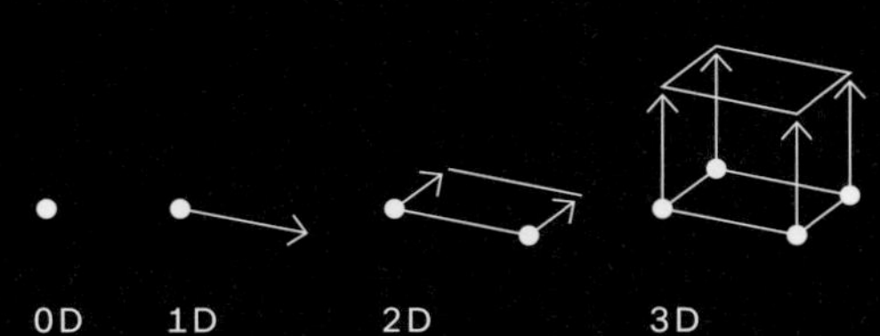

The purpose of 3D modelling, then, is to generate, and in the process describe, represent, and develop the objects that make up our space, as well as their attributes, so that we can understand the space we work with, and perceive as well as evaluate the architectural objects in it. Designing in and working with space means *manipulating* (adapting, changing, evolving) the objects and their attributes, and, if required, producing, manufacturing, or building them. Which in turn means sharing them, with the people we work with, with the people we work for, with the people who make the objects we design, and within our own teams.

Traditionally, with a two-dimensional approach to design, you had to make sure that any element that was changed on a plan, or any detail that was amended in a drawing, was also reflected in every other relevant piece of documentation. So if, for example, you decided to reposition the location of a supporting wall on one floor, because that would give you more usable space, then obviously you had to make sure that every plan and drawing, and every spreadsheet or table containing any type of calculation for this and every other floor followed this change through, otherwise you might end up with the type of an architect's nightmare that sounds great only as the name of a band: *Einstürzende Neubauten...* This makes keeping 2D design components coherent and intact throughout a big project genuinely vital and, because of its complexity, potentially very taxing.

By contrast, with a 3D model as the central reference, we can extract from this all 2D drawings and plans, and whenever we change anything in the model, no matter how big or how small that change, it is automatically and reliably reflected in all the other drawings and plans. And so the 3D model really sits at the core of what we create. From it flow all other relevant representations – every drawing, every plan, section, or detailed visualisation – and that means that the 3D model also becomes the link between what we can think and what we can build: with the 3D model we can simulate our design, test, and develop it; improve and perfect the thing that we create, which, as we have noted, is space. This particular facet to 3D modelling is also central to Building Information Modelling (BIM), on which we have a separate chapter in this *Atlas*, as you would expect.

□ ↖57

□ 507↘

There is also another aspect to 3D modelling that distinguishes it from 2D design: in two-dimensional floor plans and drawings, we invariably lack a perspective as experienced from *inside* the space. We therefore cannot perceptually follow through a spatial and atmospheric evolution of the design. What we essentially do is design in two dimensions and then keep our fingers crossed that the result, when it comes to its execution in three dimensions, will turn out just as desired. With 3D modelling we get an encompassing range of perspectives of the entire geometry: each detail, every feature can be made visible from any angle, because everything is virtually modelled. We are effectively building the object twice: first as a digital 3D model, and then on site for real. This means that while we are still in the design and planning phase, we can understand and manipulate even very complex three-dimensional constellations and relationships. As a result, we can take a categorically more holistic approach to our design with 3D modelling than was possible without.

□ 285↘

Drawing-based (left) vs model-based design approach (right). In the drawing-based approach the geometry of the building is described in 2D plans (floor plans, sections, elevations), while in the model-based approach all planning is done in 3D, and any required 2D plans are extracted from the model.

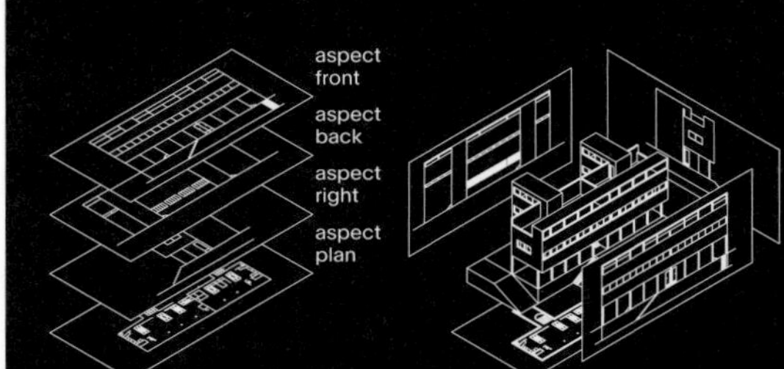

A CORRELATION OF METHOD AND ARCHITECTURE

The role that computing plays in all this is not peripheral to the job, but of defining importance. Since the 1980s, when the computer was essentially an electronic drawing tool that simulated the manual techniques which had been passed down the generations from the Renaissance onwards, the computer has matured into a fully-fledged design tool that doesn't just help us do our designing, but shapes the very way in which we design. It has become an integral development medium that brings with it its own qualities, its own potential, and also, of course, its own challenges.

Because of this, it has significantly changed architectural design, and it impacts not only on the appearance, but also on the experience of the architecture and space that is being created. What this means in turn is that if we want to take advantage of the full potential the computer has to offer, we need to acquire the skill and understanding to use it as what it is: an extension of our own creative intelligence. Not a tool, then, merely, but an augmentation of our own capability. This – a skilled and knowledgable professional approach to digital media – is what gives us the competence not just to retain (you might argue reclaim), but to cultivate an architectural quality as we see and imagine it, from design through to realisation. In doing so, it also at the same time allows us to influence the development trajectory of architecture and interior design in a much more emphatic, conscious (and also conscientious) manner.

If, as we think is essential, we treat 3D modelling as part of the design process and not merely as a virtual representation tool for geometries, then it naturally becomes constituent to our design strategy and forms part of the answer to the question: 'how do I arrive at my design?' This is fundamentally different from saying, 'I design, and I avail myself of some 3D modelling for the purpose of doing so'.

We like to draw a parallel here to the world of art in three dimensions. With 3D modelling, the architect or designer, like a sculptor, makes decisions that are informed by the design process itself: a sculptor shapes an object – either by chipping away at it or by bending, moulding, adding to, or otherwise transforming the material of which the object is made – and at any and every point is able to review the steps just taken and, based on these, consider the next ones. The object grows or emerges gradually through a process of repeating these two stages: generate and revise, generate and revise. 3D modelling allows us as architects to do the same, and that is why we don't think of 3D modelling as an interesting game of geometry, but as the design process itself.

The way in which the influence of digital methods on the conceptualisation, development, and realisation of architectural designs has increased over the last few years is evident wherever we look; and we often hear it said in relation to recently completed, spectacular buildings that they could not have been built without the latest computer technology. And so in this chapter we will not only be looking at the relevant methods and techniques in detail, but we will also be asking
361↘ ourselves the question: what exactly is the potential of 3D modelling technology for the architect's work today? As with so many a big, open question of this kind, we don't expect, in one chapter that forms part of a big *Atlas*, to find and be able to present all possible answers. But we believe it nevertheless to be conducive to our practice to be acutely aware of the question itself, and its many, and far-reaching, implications.

In his book *The Projective Cast*, English architecture theoretician Robin Evans (1944–1993) shows how the development of architecture historically bears the imprint of centuries of two-dimensional representation. According to Evans, the interrelation between how you can represent and conceptualise an architectural design exists because all activities of a building project occur by means of a projective transaction. This is true for all three of the following, successive steps:

- The designer/architect makes a sketch of their vision
- A perspective is drawn to explain the project
- The project is executed using orthographic drawings

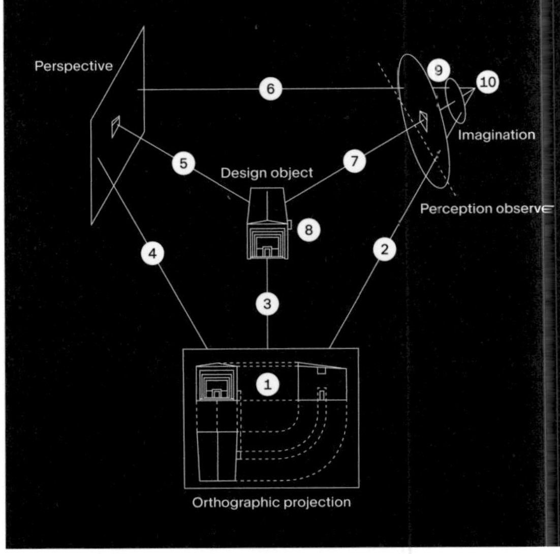

The interrelation between concept, design, representation and realisation of a project through visual projection (after Robin Evans).

Even in analogue design, the broad range of available representation methods (drawings, sketches, plans, elevations, among others) makes it necessary to familiarise yourself with the techniques and particularities of different tools, so you can deploy them appropriately and to their purpose. Digital methods offer a whole range of new possibilities on every one of the levels described by Evans:

- Illustration and conceptual design
- Presentation and communication within the planning team and with the client and stakeholders
- Project realisation, because data models can be directly transferred into physical objects

The upshot from which is that if we use the tools that we have available to us well, we can not only generate different shapes, but actually create new kinds of spaces that meet today's exacting demands for high quality built environments to work, live, and play in.

PARAMETRIC MODELLING

In essence, 3D modelling is digital form-finding and form definition, whereby we can differentiate between generating a 3D model entirely from scratch, and working with existing forms and adapting or amending them over any number of variations to achieve a 3D model.

Some widely used 3D modelling software, such as *Rhinoceros Grasshopper* for instance, is based to a large extent on geometric and parametric operations which, compared to standard Computer Aided Design (CAD) programs, offer a lot of freedom and allow for relatively rapid successes with a considerable degree of creativity and complexity. But, as we note in our chapter on Scripting, there are limitations to what we can do within its parametric structure. One of the authors of *Architectural Geometry,* a 700-page textbook on the subject is Austrian mathematician Helmut Pottmann (b. 1959). He notes the many challenges there are involving complex geometries that the computer simply can't handle on its own. Dealing with them requires strategic thinking and a grasp of the mathematical principles that lie at the heart of form definition itself. As we also suggest in our Introduction and in our chapter on Graphs & Graphics, among others, this ultimately means understanding the geometric constraints and mathematical definitions written in algorithm, in one other word: code.

Over the last twenty-odd years, parametric models have gained enormous importance in architecture. They offer fast and comprehensive manipulation of the overall object without the need to recreate the geometry. Its individual, project-relevant parameters are linked to a three-dimensional data model and are directly interdependent. If, for example, the wall thickness is changed, the model adapts to the change and automatically adjusts itself within the predefined limits. In terms of functionality it is therefore not dissimilar to an *Excel* or *Numbers* file: all the 'fields' (for which read data items and types) are logically interrelated to each other, so that if one input changes, all linked data items change correspondingly. The technique offers highly efficient and advanced model editing because the individual iterations of an object do not have to be saved separately. Instead, you save only those parameters that differentiate one iteration from another: the combination of the original object, its parameters, their limits, and the specified creation methods provides the framework for describing an infinite number of similar objects.

With a large project certainly, but even with comparatively small and straightforward architectural models, the complexity involved can be mind-boggling, wherein lies one of the chief challenges of the approach. If an object consists of multiple parameters, interferences can occur that have to be corrected either manually or automatically. And as we note in our chapter on Building Information Modelling (BIM), there is software available not only to do parametric modelling, but also to check the model for its own integrity. Having said that, putting a disproportionately high emphasis on certain parameters – whether this is intended or happens accidentally – can in fact open up whole new perspectives that may positively influence, even liberate, the design. **Parametrisation**, therefore, is also an important approach with which to adapt prototypes to new requirements.

During the design phase, the parametric model's possibly greatest strength is that, thanks to its dynamic data structure, it allows you to examine different variants of an object within one principle. The composition of the parametric **base model** defines the initial situation, from which you then play through as many versions or iterations of the concept as you want, or need, to get to the 'ideal' configuration. This makes the base model a foundation on which you rest your whole design process, and to □ 129↘ create it – as we hinted a moment ago and as we describe in much more detail in our chapter on the subject – you need some degree of programming knowledge, at least at the level of Scripting. □ 351↘

■ 353↘ **Scripts** are command chains of a programming language that define and connect certain processes and operational procedures. The basic geometry is supplemented with algorithms that make it possible to later influence the geometry and other aspects of the model, such as material choice and structure. More complex CAD programs offer the possibility to write your own scripts and algorithms. Based on this principle, the marginal conditions of the design □ ↖29 can be individually defined and manipulated, and □ 175↘ partial information in the form of 2D drawings can be automatically generated from the parametric 3D model: floor plans and cross-sections or cut patterns for individual building parts as well as formwork panel layouts and parts lists.

This automated process of generating graphic information from a 3D model is certainly much more efficient and faster than traditional planning methods used to be. And, as we also already pointed out but are happy to repeat because it is of such importance, the information relates to a single original model, which means that version conflicts or different interpretations can mostly be avoided.

At a similarly pragmatic level, parameters are particularly useful when defining and maintaining standardised components such as windows, doors, and stairs, and most CAD programs include parametrisation of simple objects as a routine function. Parametrised objects can (and in some cases have to) be supplemented with rules that protect the user from violating building laws or making structural errors. A parametrised stairway, for example, would typically feature rules about minimum and maximum number of steps, permissible and desired riser-tread ratio, required width, and the number and dimensions of intermediate landings.

PHYSICAL VS DIGITAL MODELS

What you know about an architectural space determines what decisions you can take about it, and these decisions may be multi-layered and, as we □ 507↘ have seen, very complex. It is therefore essential to recognise the different qualities that different kinds of modelling bring, not only so that we can deploy them appropriately and to the purpose, but also so that we can, as we have suggested before, use them to their full potential.

■ 361↘ Building a model, be this a physical one or a virtual 3D model, entails a continuous dialogue between the designer and the object. We are very familiar with this exchange from traditional, physical model building, where the tactile experience of handling materials and the way that different building elements fit

together constantly inform what we do. (In fact, we specifically refer to this dialogue in our chapter on
□ 421↘ Model Making.) It is in the nature of things that we often only really become fully aware of the composition and spatial order of a design when we begin to physically model it, simply because grasping their full complexity at the level of abstraction that we encounter in drawings and plans is practically impossible. So the physical model becomes a medium which allows us to test the characteristics of a design: just what we postulate the 3D model should be. But we argue that 3D modelling demands methods that are specific to
■ 407↘ the digital modelling process, as opposed to methods that simply simulate traditional ones, because the digital 3D model offers a compelling range of characteristics that differentiate it from the physical model, arguably as an advantage:

- □ 93↘ Much as we see in our chapter on Digital Data Acquisition, digital data, such as the measurements of a building or of its component parts, are recorded and processed as actual real life values, which means that we get a virtual representation of the building on a 1:1 scale. Zooming in to examine detail or out to get the overview is merely a matter of choosing view settings in the software: they can be freely and seamlessly adjusted to whatever is useful to us at the time for the task we are pursuing. A physical model, by contrast, will in its current iteration always be to scale and one scale only, for example 1:100. Of course, a 3D printer can produce the same physical model to any other scale, but it can do so only if the object has been digitally modelled.
- A digital model allows us to incrementally and suc-
□ 421↘ cessively add new information, which can then be represented either in context or separately. We can easily vary the level of detail within a model without affecting the basic content, since the concept of the design is always the same, no matter how much of the information we make visible. So even if we build a digital 3D model of great complexity, we can always contain and represent the relationships and dependencies between separate elements. It is this transparency in the construction of the model that gives us a holistic perspective on the entire process, integrating all its individual aspects.
- With a 3D model we can play through variations on a design theme and easily make different versions of principally the same concept. We can modify a 3D model in its appearance and geometry by a multitude of means, and stay in this constant dialogue and interaction that we seek with the model in a process of continuously testing our design decisions as a working method.
- Finally, the 3D model, being a dynamic digital representation of the proposed object, allows us to experience and evaluate the space from a first person perspective, for example by simulating a walk-through or showing you what a space will look like from your view point anywhere inside or around it.

None of which is to say, of course, that this renders the physical model obsolete. The opposite is the case: the 3D model that sits at the core of the design generating process can also be the source of the physical model that, in turn, can then be used to its full advantage when it is made, processed, or printed out. And even this does not do away with the hand-made physical model. Which is why we also dedicate a separate chapter in this *Atlas* to Model Making.

The Evolution of Digital Modelling

THE BEGINNINGS

□ 129↘ Whenever we talk about any aspect of Computer Aided Design (CAD) – on which we also have a chapter in this *Atlas* – and therefore by extension
■ 134↘ about Computer Aided Architectural Design (CAAD), we find ourselves back at one particular point in history: *Sketchpad*. CAD really starts there, in 1963, with the American computer scientist Ivan Sutherland (b. 1938). *Sketchpad*, as we narrate in a little more
□ 229↘ detail in our chapter on Image & Colour – though you will also come across it in several other chapters – was not anything like a contemporary 3D modelling program, but it marked the first time anyone successfully drew and worked with computer graphics. And although the results by our standards were not overwhelming, and the machine that was required to create simple line drawings cost around USD 100,000 when it was built in 1958 (which in today's money, depending on which measure you use, is anything from between about one to two million dollars), *Sketchpad* did lay the foundations for everything that followed, and if Sutherland hadn't done the development work he did at the Stanford Research Institute (SRI, now SRI International), then either somebody else would have had to do it elsewhere, or we would not have CAD, CAAD, and 3D modelling today.

We also on several occasions observe that it wasn't architects who were first to the table when it came to using CAD. But that is not to say that the idea didn't occur to people relatively soon. As early as 1977, Australian-born architect and urban designer William J Mitchell (1944–2010) in his seminal book *Computer Aided Architectural Design* made it clear that architecture and CAD had a future in common.

Taking computing in architecture a step further, Canadian-born American architect Frank Gehry (b. 1929) early on employed aerospace CAD and 3D modelling technology, specifically the *CATIA (Computer Aided Three-Dimensional Interactive Application)* software by French company *Dassault Systèmes*. *Dassault Systèmes* started out in 1977 as a 15 engineers-strong department of *Avions Marcel Dassault*, a French aeroplane manufacturer. Their software proved so versatile and adaptable that its founder realised there was potential not only for the aerospace industry, but for Computer Aided Engineering (CAE) and Computer Aided Manufacturing (CAM) generally. Founded in 2002, Gehry Technologies in partnership with *Dassault Systèmes* developed software applications, such as *Digital Project*, geared towards designing and testing complex architectural geometries. Gehry Technologies was subsequently acquired by the American software firm Trimble in 2014.

THE TURNING POINT

On 22 January 1984, some 72,920 spectators in the Tampa Stadium in Florida were watching the eighteenth Super Bowl encounter in American Football, between the Washington Redskins and the Los Angeles Raiders, together with a television audience numbering an estimated 77.62 million. During a break in the third quarter of the game, they were treated to a one minute film, by English director Ridley Scott (b. 1937), that would go down in history as the piece of advertising that – broadcast nationally only the once – heralded a new era of computing: entitled *1984*, it introduced to the world the *Apple Mackintosh* computer.

At a retail price of $2,495 – equivalent to about $6,000 at the time we write this in 2019 – it was hardly a snip, but it changed the way a generation of creative professionals did what they were doing. Being the first machine made for the general public that had a graphic interface and a mouse, it allowed people to do things on a computer they had never done before, such as draw. And although in the beginnings drawing on a computer was slow and painstaking work, it rapidly evolved and spawned the development of graphic design and design software that led from simple 2D drawing packages, via 2.5D to true 3D modelling software that we use today. (2.5D, variously known also as three-quarter perspective, or pseudo-3D, is a halfway house between two-dimensional and true three-dimensional representations that uses axonometric projection to achieve a 3D-like effect, without actually determining individual data points for the object in the third dimension.)

The Raiders beat the Redskins 38–9.

Dimensions: two-dimensional information can be represented in space by extending defined elements from the existing X and Y axes along a third Z axis. This stretches, for example, a square to a cuboid, or a circle to a cylinder. It gives an object the appearance of three-dimensionality, but only if the geometrical data of an object is individually defined for all three axes do you really have a 3D object that can extend freely in any direction.

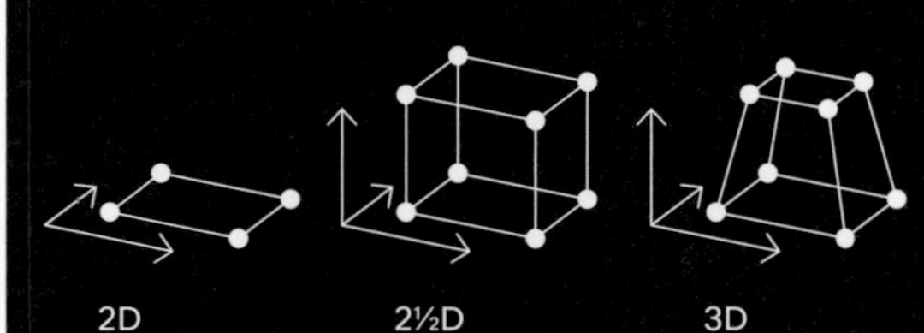

NEW FORMS

■ 409↘

As we have already noted, the architecture that has sprung up ('grown' may be a more appropriate way of putting it) since the beginning of the 21st century and that we see evolving today owes a great deal to computing. When the first chapter of computer aided design was mostly about getting lines and simple outline objects onto a digital platform where it would be possible to manipulate and develop them, and a second chapter had as its principal storyline the maturing of the graphic interface and making computational tools fit for general purpose in architecture, a third – and by this we don't mean to suggest final – chapter ushered in an era of form-finding that is not only enabled by technology, but driven by it.

It is not surprising that the possibilities opened up by freeform modelling blur the boundaries between architecture and sculpture – or form for form's sake – more than ever before. There is a powerful and deeply influential feedback loop at work, whereby the tools at our disposal shape the work we create, and the work we create informs the type of tools that are being developed. The American architect Greg Lynn (b. 1964) suggests that there is a design language that comes with the computer, and at the beginning you simply do what the software allows you to do. But the idea, of course, has to be, and surely is, that you go beyond what the software allows you to do and shape the tool to your own requirements and imagination.

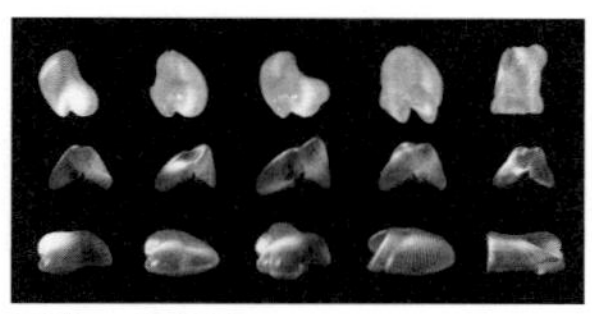

009 ● 078

■ 134↘

British-Iraqi architect Zaha Hadid (1950–2016) stands tall at this juncture. Rather than doing what 'the tools allow', she moved her expressive forms from the analogue plateau to the computer and used the computer to drive her own style forward. ■ 135↘ For many years she had to contend with seeing her work published and appreciated and even win prizes, but hardly ever realised as buildings. The good people of Wales and their political representatives brought this to a head for her, when, in 1994, she won the competition for designing a new Cardiff Bay Opera House against a field that sported entries from, among others, the Greg Lynn FORM firm, Dutch architect Rem Koolhaas (b. 1944), Japanese architect Itsuko Hasegawa (b. 1941), and Foster + Partners. Having beaten them in three rounds, she then had to stand by and watch as the politicians from South Glamorgan County Council and Cardiff City Council, as well as the purse-string administrators of one of the major funding bodies, the Millennium Commission, rejected her design and eventually ditched the entire project in favour of a less ambitious, and supposedly less 'elitist', general arts complex, the Wales Millennium Centre. (It is likely, but not provably certain, that Cardiff missed a winning trick there. Three years later, Frank Gehry's now legendary

Guggenheim Museum Bilbao opened its doors to the public. It quickly proved such a runaway success both in terms of its architecture and the impact this architecture is having on a once moribund conurbation, revitalising the whole area and boosting the city's profile and economy to the tune of, by now, billions, that it has given rise to the expression *'Bilbao Effect'.*)

Inseparably associated with Zaha Hadid is
■ 139↘ the term parametricism. Its coinage is attributed to London-based German-born architect Patrik Schumacher (b. 1961), who – then as now a partner in the firm – used it in 2008 to describe the practice's methodology. More specifically, Schumacher thinks of parametricism as an *autopoiesis*, meaning that
□ 507↘ it is a self-regulating system in which each part is connected to each other part, where a change to any part therefore will affect all other parts.

010A ● 078

010B ● 078

From the late 1990s onwards, a group of architects from the Netherlands start to become influential in architecture innovation. Finnish architect and historian Kari Jormakka (1959–2013) in 2002 refers to them in his book of the same title as *The Flying Dutchmen*. The book's subtitle, *Motion in Architecture*, yields an unmistakable clue as to the distinguishing feature of this style, which, similar to Zaha Hadid's, is characterised by fluidity and freedom from apparently any constraints of materiality.

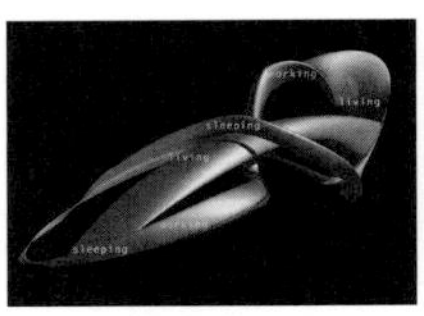
011A ● 078

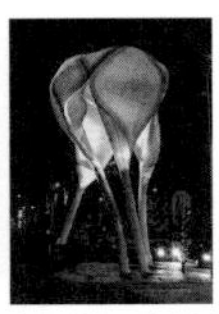
011B ● 079

Also much in common with Zaha Hadid, not all of their designs have ever been realised. Here, too, the delineation between sculptural form and practical
119↘ purpose is often deliberately and decidedly blurred, but there are some very notable exceptions, the Mer-
□ 351↘ cedes Museum in Stuttgart by UNStudio being a
□ 145↘ fine example.

□ 549↘

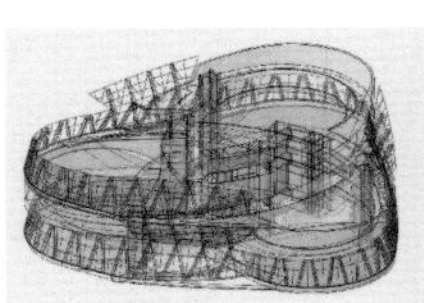
012A ● 079

012B ● 079

■ 157↘

FORM AND PERFORMANCE

If for some architects parametric modelling is very much about finding form and doing so in a free space
□ 351↘ that is not primarily concerned with function, but to which function in a sense yields and even adapts, there are also those architects who use the same or similar methodologies to the end of maximising a building's performance.

British architect Norman Foster (b. 1935) and his practice Foster + Partners could be said to fall into this 'category'. He uses computer algorithms not so much to find a form, but to model technological components of his designs, such as, for example, structural performance, air flow, or sun radiation. SOM (Skidmore Owings Merrill) employs similar techniques, and you also come across them at the intersection between architecture and engineering: we are looking here at an increasingly cross-disciplinary approach to 3D modelling, which also reaches into Building Information Modelling (BIM), as it happens.

013A ○ 216

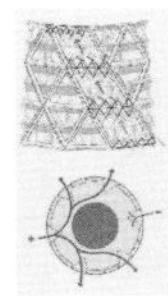
013B ○ 216

013C ○ 216

TODAY

By now, 3D modelling has firmly established itself as a design instrument in its own right.

The geometries generated – in some cases, you could say, 'conquered' – by people like Danish architect Bjarke Ingels (b. 1974) and his Bjarke Ingels Group (BIG) are good examples of this.

Meanwhile, at his studio, The Very Many, French architect and sculptural designer Marc Fornes takes this approach yet another step further, with his experimental pavilions and 'fantasy' structures that explore a spatial experience informed almost entirely by whatever form is possible in any given context.

014A ○ 217

014B ○ 217

SHAPE GRAMMARS

We come across *shape grammars* at various junctures in this *Atlas*, notably in our chapters on Scripting, Generative Methods, and Big Data & Machine Learning, and we don't want to pass them over entirely here either, because they play a significant and perhaps especially interesting role in the evolution of 3D modelling. Originally introduced by computational design theorist George Stiny and his colleague James Gips in a paper in 1971, they are artificial intelligence production systems used to generate two and three dimensional shapes, making it possible to use algorithms to not just modify, but actually create modular design components from scratch.

In a fascinating exercise, for example – and one not all dissimilar to the one we cite in our chapter on Scripting – Professor José Duarte of the Penn State College of Arts and Architecture analysed the work of Portuguese architect Álvaro Siza (b. 1933), to arrive at shape grammars which then produced entirely computer generated designs in the style of Siza. Shown both his original work and the versions using shape grammars, Siza is understood to have been unable to tell them apart.

015A ● 080

015B ● 080

Software

During the 1980s, the already mentioned *CATIA*, as well as *Pro/Engineer*, *Unigraphics* and *I-Dea* became the leading CAD software packages. All of them offered powerful 3D modelling systems, with their focus on industrial production rather than architecture, which is why they are often referred to as CAE (Computer Aided Engineering) or CAM (Computer Aided Manufacturing) programs, rather than CAD, with their main operating system being *Unix*. Meanwhile, on the PC platforms, Autodesk was gaining market share with its *AutoCAD*.

During the next decade, the 1990s, and with the explosion of personal computing, this new player made particularly strong headway, and by 1993, *AutoCAD* for the first time featured 3D solid modelling functions. *AutoCAD* continues to spread widely, but other packages, such as Bentley's *MicroStation* have become strong contenders in the mid-price market too.

Since then, the architectural community has seen a cascade of software debuts, including, in the Computer Aided Architectural Design (CAAD) bracket, *AutoCAD Architecture (ACAD)*, Graphisoft's *ArchiCAD*, *Nemetschek Allplan*, *Vectorworks*, *SolidWorks*, *AutoDesk Revit*; and, with their centre of gravity perhaps more in 3D modelling, visualisation, and animation, *Rhinoceros* and *Grasshopper*, *SketchUp*, *Maya/Alias*, *Cinema 4D*, *Blender*, and *3D Studio Max*.

CAAD

Computer Aided Architectural Design (CAAD) emerges in the 1980s, and throughout the 1990s establishes itself as a specialist area distinct – but borrowing heavily – from the existing Computer Aided Design (CAD) applications which, as we have seen, find widespread use and proliferation particularly in the automotive, aerospace, and shipbuilding industries, but also in military contexts. So while it is certainly true to say that architects took their time to embrace the technology, from around the launch of the first *Apple Macintosh* onwards, and with the attendant availability of prosumer priced hardware and software, this changes quite rapidly.

CAD systems started out in principle as expanded drawing boards: the method you applied to drawing on a computer at first was practically the same as you used on an analogue sketch pad; what was different was mostly the tool. These early systems used vector based technology, which, as we explore in detail in our chapter on Image & Colour, □ 229↘ has many advantages when it comes to processing power and data volumes, but also presents severe restrictions. Vector graphics ■ 232↘ are particularly good at handling points, lines, line sequences, curves, splines ■ 185↘ (on which more below), and surfaces, and these early drawings were entirely confined to two dimensions, graduating slowly towards the 2.5D intermediate step we've already encountered. 3D computer graphics became technically possible from as early as the late 1970s but, again owing to the cost of both hardware and software, took about another two decades before they found widespread use.

CAAD programs store geometric objects as numerical data. This construction model is based on vector algebra, ■ which defines geometries by mathematical functions: a circle, for example, would be defined by its centre and radius.

The coordinate system offers the frame of reference for this vector-orientated construction model and serves to precisely define the position of an object, be that in two or in three dimensions. Coordinate systems can be categorised along the following criteria:

- *Type* – is it a Cartesian, polar, cylindric, or spheric coordinate model?
- *Dimensions* – are the coordinates given on the plane or in space, in other words, are they two or three-dimensional?
- *Absolute or relative* – are the coordinates used based on a common zero coordinate and therefore absolute, or are they relative to the object?
- *Predefined or user-defined* – are the coordinates system-orientated (pre-defined), or are they user-defined and can their orientation and position therefore be set individually?

THE CARTESIAN COORDINATE SYSTEM 183↘

The coordinate system most commonly used in CAAD programs is the *Cartesian coordinate system*, named after the French philosopher, mathematician, and scientist René Descartes (1596–1650), who was first to publish on it as a concept in 1637, which is somewhat remarkable, considering how 'obvious' it seems to us now. It consists of three axes, X, Y, and Z, that are arranged orthogonally to each other to meet in a common point zero, called *origin*, and thus open up a three-dimensional space. Any point generated in this system can be determined exactly and unambiguously by noting its distance from the origin, for example X=3, Y=4, Z=5, which means that the position and orientation of any object that is defined by points on this plane or in this space can be numerically identified.

The Cartesian coordinate system in three dimensions:

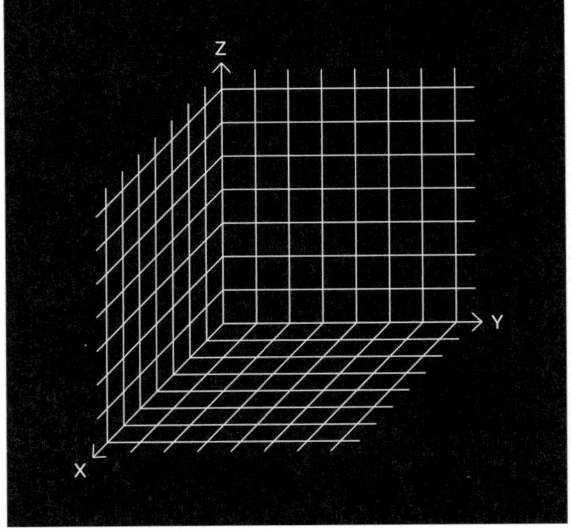

NAVIGATION

Possibly still one of the easiest and most common methods for navigating around a 3D model is with your mouse or trackpad and keyboard. 3D navigation tools allow you to view objects from different angles, heights, and distances:

- *3D orbit*: the target of the view stays stationary while the camera location or point of view moves around it
- *Zoom*: simulates moving the camera closer to an object or further away. As you would expect, zooming in magnifies the image
- *Pan*: enables you to drag the view horizontally and vertically

Historically, digital interfaces have been crafted to suit the hardware requirements of 2D screens, and designers have been fitting content and navigation inside the frames of displays, translating our real world experiences into icons and other user interface elements.

More sophisticated navigation tools, like 3D mice, digital pens, or force-feedback, eye tracking, and motion capturing systems provide a higher degree of freedom and a more intuitive, direct, and ergonomic way of modelling/designing.

■ 103↘ ■ 113↘ ■ 103↘ □ 507↘

Moreover, Augmented Reality (AR), Virtual Reality (VR), and Mixed Reality (MR) are changing how we design, create, and experience our spatial environment. These emerging technologies are certain to have a strong impact on the design practice of the future, as they offer more immersive scenarios to interact with space in real-time.

Apart from the dynamic navigation tools already mentioned, it is possible to define the details of a drawing as standard views – which are called up through keyboard shortcuts – or with icons in a program's navigation menu. For example, frontal and side views, but also spatial representations, such as isometric projections or perspectives can be shown directly. Most CAAD programs offer a choice of pre-defined standard views. Similar to the 3D orbit tool mentioned above, you navigate around and through your 3D model, changing your point of view, with the location of the model space remaining constant.

How to navigate in 3D: standard views (up) and object in space (down).

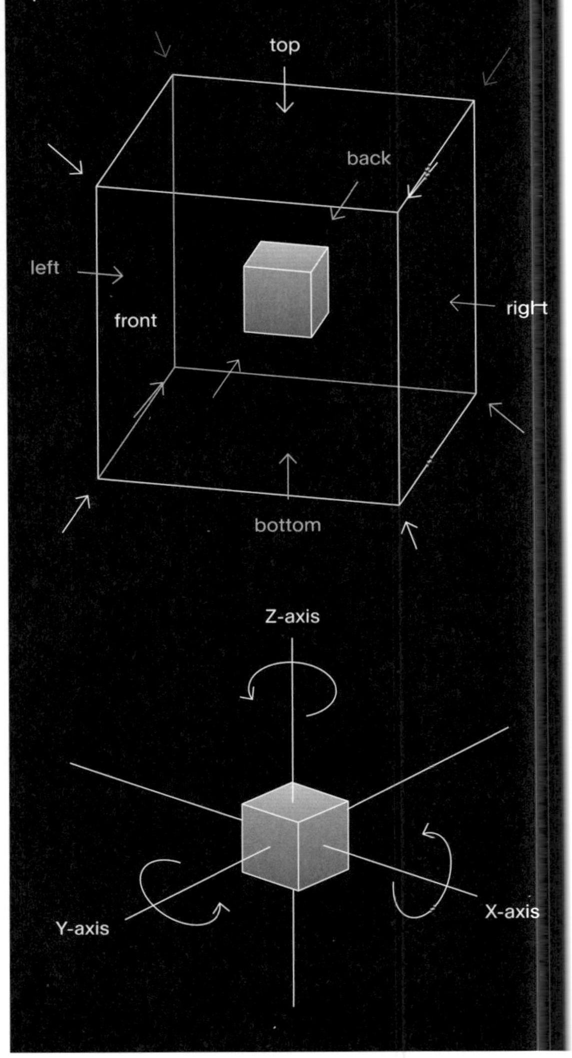

ORGANISATION

CAAD software programs organise drawings in layers and symbols and logically connect these individual elements into coherent designs. The individual elements (or building components) – such as walls, ceilings, windows – are either provided by the program itself in a library, or imported from different manufacturers, as is the case in Building Information Modelling (BIM); or the user creates them from scratch by themselves.

Because the logic that sits at the basis of this type of software is easy to understand, applications employing this principle are largely used for projects with manageable levels of complexity.

The addition of plugins – small software extensions – further expands the functionality of CAAD programs and allows for some (in certain cases considerable) degree of customisation.

USER INTERACTION

CAAD software already offers the architect a great deal of freedom in modelling geometries and modifying them, using versatile operators. As an extension of this, parametric 3D software – which was really pioneered in the film and gaming industries; notable examples being *SimCity* and *Minecraft* – enables an associative connection between virtual building blocks in an intelligently structured design. We are now in the realm of highly adaptable tools, where plugins and scripts enable very specific capabilities such as, for example, gradual changes in a support beam's cross section, depending on its expected loading conditions: if you connect your design interactively to a software that simulates compressions and tensions on the support structure, or climate parameters such as solar irradiation and wind loads on the facade, you can begin to optimise your project already during the design phase.

With these great many possibilities come some important purchasing decisions. We talk a lot in this *Atlas* about the different aspects of digital architecture and what they can do, or make possible, but it is worth pointing out every once in a while – and this is an opportune moment to do so – that not only do you as an architect or architect practice make an investment in the software you buy (quite apart from the hardware, which you're also bound to upgrade periodically), but you also, and particularly, make a big investment in the software that you *learn*. Most software programs require comprehensive skills if you want to use them to their full potential, and that means that you do not want to keep changing the software you use. The outcry and setback Apple suffered when it decided, in 2011, to radically revamp its by then industry-leading professional film editing software *Final Cut Pro,* and foisted upon editors worldwide entirely new workflows and practices serves as an object lesson in what happens when people who have been learning a software for many years and who have become experts at it are suddenly faced with big changes. Apple lost a great deal of faith from one of its most loyal communities of brand advocates, and substantial market share in the process, as users felt forced to adopt the *Adobe Premiere Pro* package, which largely emulated the program Apple had so rashly abandoned.

In architecture, which software you choose will similarly depend on a variety of personal and technical factors, which are likely to include geometry options and BIM compatibility, for example.

CAD AND BIM

As we've mentioned, we devote a separate chapter to Building Information Modelling (BIM) in this *Atlas*, and so we will not here go into any elaborations on it, but we do want to briefly point out the chief differences between CAD and this particular type of modelling.

□ 507↘

CAD works with individual drawings – plans, elevations, sections – which together form an architectural design. BIM, by contrast, integrates all individual elements into an interconnected whole, and stores each element together with its metadata: information about its materiality, colour, manufacturer, or unit cost, for example. Hence, graphic (geometry) and non-graphic information (metadata) is linked together.

If we were to employ a simple analogy: BIM is to CAD as a fully specified, three-dimensionally represented *Lego* brick is to a schematic drawing of that same object:

From 2D drawing to 3D model to fully-fledged BIM.

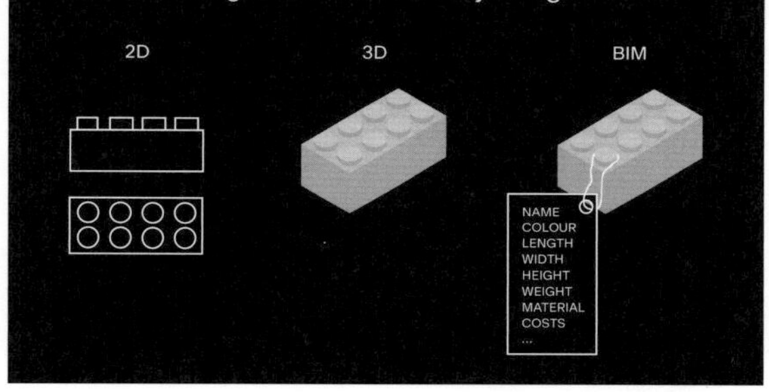

Generating and Transforming 3D Models

Over the following pages we are now going to look in some detail at the techniques and elements used in 3D modelling. They are, if you like, the basic components that lie at the heart of 3D modelling software, and the fundamental algorithmic operations the software uses to arrive at three-dimensional objects.

The tools that are available for 3D modelling are based on the same structures and workflows that we are familiar with from 2D drawing: an interplay between generating and modifying steps to construct the object. The main difference really is that the object does not come about on a two-dimensional plane, but instead references all three axes of the three-dimensional coordinate system: X, Y, and Z. Points, lines, surfaces, and volumes can all be precisely defined in this way.

Any similarities notwithstanding, 3D tools do require a greater knowledge and appreciation of geometrical principles and dependencies than drawing-based design methods, because geometry sits at the basis of any spatial design concept and offers a multitude of different forms to describe and represent a building or space design.

Regular geometries not only allow for exact definitions of dimensions and proportions, but because of their homogeneity and congruence, they often also integrate constructive aspects which may become important during the later execution stages of a building's realisation, for example when it comes to actually manufacturing the construction elements from wood, steel, or concrete.

For the simple manipulation of 3D objects, ordinary CAAD and 3D modelling software offers a range of tools to, for example, shift, twist, scale, copy, or mirror objects or individual elements that form part of an object. In addition to this, there are also tools to divide or join 3D objects, making it possible to generate a multitude of new geometries, and combine these into yet new objects.

In addition to these methods, there is also the dynamic modification of a geometry. This intuitive, model-oriented approach arguably has more to do with sculpting than drawing: it is possible to modify a 3D object's geometry by way of any of its component parts (point, edge, surface), or by way of its parameters (length, width, height, radius) and thus mould or shape the geometry into anything we want it to be.

TYPES OF MODELLING

361↘

We will examine specific 3D model forms in just a 269↘ moment, but first we want to summarise the two main categories into which 3D modelling can be grouped. (We say 'can be', because here, as in so many areas, there are not only overlaps, but also continuous flows 199↘ of evolution that make a categorical delineation almost impossible.)

In 3D modelling, a principal difference is made between a *solid* and a *surface*. A *solid* mathematically describes a geometry that has mass and that is closed in itself, while a *surface* describes merely the boundary conditions, shell, or envelope of a form. It is defined by surrounding planes rather than by massive volumes.

159↘ **Solid modelling** is therefore used to represent solid objects. A solid model is considered 'watertight' when the internal details of the modelled object are included. To generate a solid model, each of its parts is added one by one until the model is complete. A variant form of solid modelling is known as **assembly modelling** and describes generating a solid model from smaller constituent solids.

445↘ Correspondingly, **surface modelling** focuses on the external aspects of an object. You develop it by 'stretching' a surface over the object that is to be modelled, using 3D curves. This type of modelling is used to create and describe the external aesthetics of an object and tends to allow for a more free-form approach, which is also considered 'sleeker' by some. What it lacks is the mass quality of solid modelling, because if you were to cut into the model, you would find it to be hollow, with none of its interior characteristics specified.

This latter aspect gives solid modelling an advantage over surface modelling, because with it the object can be defined more intricately, giving you a better idea of how the building, product, or design will behave and perform in the real world.

That said, each type of modelling serves its own purpose depending on the kind of design you are working on, and so you will simply have to weigh the pros and cons of each approach in the light of what you are doing. Many different paths may lead to the same destination, and as you would not categorically declare one digital manufacturing or 3D printing technique to be 'the best', but would compare additive with subtractive procedures, for example, and select the one best suited to your needs, so in digital 3D modelling will you fare best if you choose the 'horse' most suited for your particular 'course'.

SOLID MODELS

Solid models are the most comprehensive representation of a three-dimensional object. They are closed virtual bodies which contain information about their volume, mass, centre of gravity, and textural as well as material qualities; and they allow for complex intersections.

There are two main categories of solid models:

- **BREP models**, also written as **B-rep**, which stands for **Boundary Representation**, the boundaries in question being those of the individual surfaces that together define the body of the object; and
- **CSG models**, which stands for **Constructive Solid Geometry**. CSG models consist of basic geometrical objects known as *primitive solids* or **primitives** – for example cubes and cuboids, spheres, cylinders, prisms, pyramids, or cones – which can then be combined or subtracted from each other to form new, complex geometries by way of **Boolean operations** (on which more below).

In constructive solid modelling we describe three-dimensional forms by purely mathematical methods. The construction of the model happens through combining self-contained geometries in various ways. (And note, of course, that constructive solid modelling does not, therefore, yield an object that is literally 'solid'.)

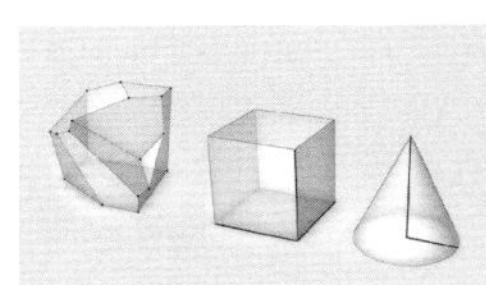

016 ● 080

PRIMITIVE SOLIDS

Primitive solids or *primitives* are the building blocks of CSG models. They include basic geometries such as the ones just mentioned – cubes and cuboids, spheres, cylinders, prisms, pyramids, or cones – and also some objects which are a little more complex, such as ellipsoids and toruses. 3D modelling and CAD/CAAD software usually offers these as ready to use objects that do not, therefore, have to be generated from scratch but can be deployed and manipulated 'off the shelf'. Since primitive solids are defined by mathematical formula, they can easily be customised by adjusting their dimensions and proportions.

Considering their importance in general, and to architecture in particular, calling them 'basic geometries' may sound a little prosaic. Swiss-French architect and architecture pioneer Le Corbusier (1887–1965), writing in his collection of essays *Vers une architecture (Toward Architecture*, or in English and more commonly known also as *Towards a New Architecture*) saw in them a more fundamental, indeed universal aesthetic:

"Architecture is the artful, correct and magnificent play of construction elements assembled under the light. Our eyes are created to see forms in the light: light and shade reveal the forms. Cubes, cones, cylinders or pyramids are the great primary forms that light makes apparent; their image appears to us pure and tangible, unambiguous. That's why they are the beautiful forms, the most beautiful. Everybody agrees with this, the child, the savage, the metaphysician."

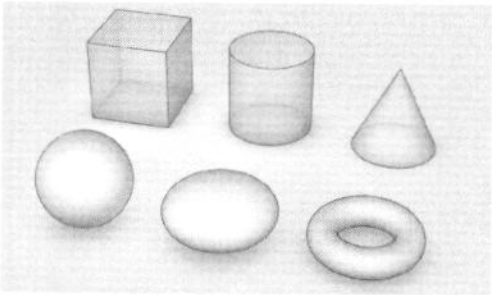

017 ● 080

REGULAR/PLATONIC SOLIDS
In general English usage, *regular solids* are treated as synonymous with *Platonic solids*. These are regular polyhedrons, made up of regular, congruent, polygonal surfaces. In other words: a Platonic solid object has a number of faces that are all of the same shape and size, and that are all in themselves regular, meaning that all angles and all sides of each surface are equal to each other. Furthermore, the number of surfaces that meet at each *vertex* (intersection of two or more lines) is the same.

Named after the Greek philosopher Plato (c. 425 – c. 347 BCE), who saw them as the building elements of the physical universe, there are, in that entire universe, exactly five such bodies: the *tetrahedron* (a four sided, trilateral pyramid), the *cube* (which has six faces), the *octahedron* (eight faces), the *dodecahedron* (twelve faces), and the *icosahedron* (twenty faces). The relationship between the surfaces, edges, and vertices in all five Platonic solids is the same, as defined by **Euler's formula** – *eix = cos x + i sin x* – named after Swiss mathematician, physicist, and logician Leonhard Euler (1707–1783).

Owing to their symmetry and regularity, which translates into a mathematical elegance that has been studied since the beginnings of civilisation, regular solids are not only considered to be inherently beautiful, they also find their way into mysticism and spirituality as objects possessing – depending on your beliefs – particular powers or, at any rate, symbolism.

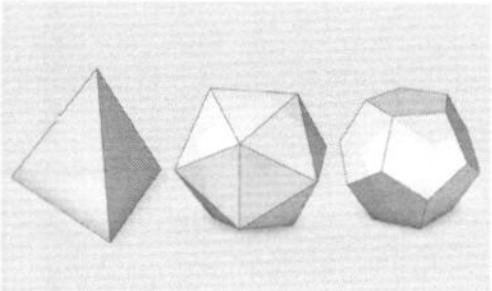

018 ● 080

POLYHEDRA
Apart from the five Platonic solids, all of which are polyhedrons or *polyhedra*, there are a literally infinite number of possible solids that don't fulfil the strict criteria of a regular solid, but that are still made up of flat surfaces with straight edges: the definition of a polyhedron.

Polyhedra are prevalent in architecture and interior design, on the one hand because they can be described geometrically with precision and are therefore comparatively easy to compute, and on the other hand not least also because they are easier and cheaper to manufacture physically than curved or dented geometries.

Within the category of polyhedra, there are some specific subgroups or classes, defined as follows:

PRISMS
A prism is polyhedron that has two identical polygonal bases (one upper, one lower) and a corresponding number of other faces, which are therefore all quadrilateral parallelograms.

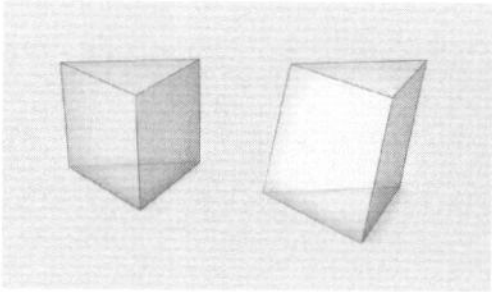

019A ● 081

019B ● 081

PYRAMIDS
In geometry, a *pyramid* is a polyhedron with a polygonal base and a corresponding number of triangular lateral faces meeting at an *apex*. Possibly the oldest and one of the most recognisable surviving architectural structures, and also the only one of the Seven Wonders of the Ancient World to remain intact, the Great Pyramid of Giza is a classic regular square pyramid. A pyramid is *regular* if it has a regular polygon as its base, and *irregular* if it has an irregular polygon as its base. Beyond that, a pyramid is considered *right* if its apex sits directly above the geometric centre or *centroid* of its base, and *nonright* if the apex sits anywhere else.

020A ● 081

020B ● 081

ARCHIMEDEAN SOLIDS
Continuing the tradition of neatly delimited geometrical bodies honouring Ancient Greeks, there are precisely thirteen *Archimedean solids*, named after the Greek mathematician, physicist, and astronomer Archimedes (c. 287 – c. 212 BCE) who, as far as we know, first described them. These are also polyhedrons, but unlike the five Platonic solids, which are made up of only one type of polygon each, these solids are composed of two or more regular polygons that meet in identical vertices, meaning that each intersection between two surfaces, irrespective of what type of polygon it belongs to, is of exactly the same length.

Probably the most widely used Archimedean solid is the *truncated icosahedron*, which consists of 20 regular hexagons and 12 regular pentagons: the football.

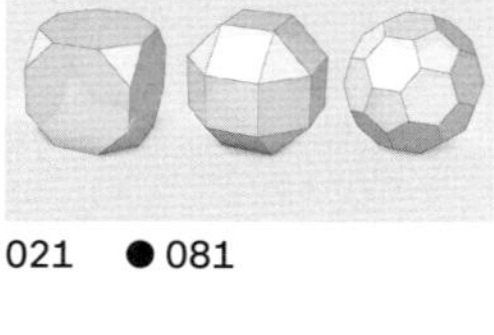

021 ● 081

FOAM STRUCTURES / 3D TESSELLATION

If you combine Platonic and Archimedean solids or polyhedra and prisms in the right way, you may end up with a foam-like structure. In nature, a foam is usually disordered, with a potentially large variety of different-sized bubbles making up an irregular system. But Irish physicist Denis Weaire (b. 1942), together with his student Robert Phelan, in 1993 came up with what is therefore now known as the **Weaire-Phelan structure**, which consists of perfectly equal-sized polyhedral bubbles, and which therefore yields a perfectly ordered, idealised, foam.

The concept of *tessellation* as we are familiar with from two dimensions can be extended also into three. Here, instead of tiling a plane with geometric shapes so that there are no overlaps and no gaps in the surface, you fill a space with geometric objects so that, similarly, there are no overlaps and no gaps in the volume.

Some geometries, such as the cube, any triangular, quadrilateral, or hexagonal prism, as well as a variety of other polyhedra, can be stacked into a regular crystal pattern to fill or tile three-dimensional space in such a way. (Among these, the cube is the only Platonic solid with which this is possible.)

American mathematician John M Sullivan (b. 1963) in his 2011 book *The Geometry of Bubbles and Foams* writes:

■ 290↘ □ 175↘ □ 351↘

"We consider mathematical models of bubbles, foams and froths as collections of surfaces which minimise an area under volume constraints. The resulting surfaces have constant mean curvature and an invariant notion of equilibrium forces. The possible singularities are described by Plateau's rules; this means that combinatorially a foam is dual to some triangulation of space."

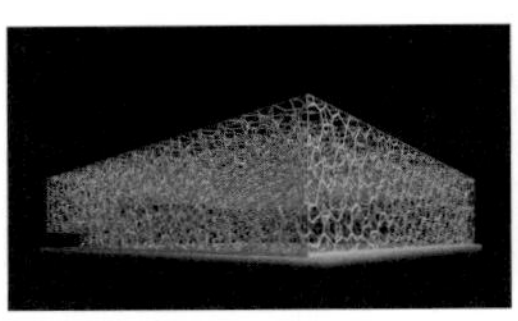

022A ● 082

022B ● 082

GEODESIC POLYHEDRA

■ 427↘

The most recognisable *geodesic polyhedra* in architecture, meanwhile, were built as **geodesic domes** by the American architect, systems theorist, and inventor Buckminster Fuller (1895–1983), who, taking a leaf straight out of the book of German engineer Walther Bauersfeld (1879–1959), developed and popularised the technique of using this geometry for self-sustaining lightweight (and often transparent) structures. He built the first one in 1949 and culminated his work in 1967 with the United States Pavilion for World Fair in Canada, which has since been turned into the Montreal *Biosphère*.

A geodesic polyhedron is a polyhedron made up of regular triangles that together approximate the shape of a sphere, which is why you'll also come across the term **geodesic sphere**. Each vertex on a geodesic polyhedron has the same distance from the solid's centre. You can arrive at a geodesic polyhedron by subdividing the surfaces of a Platonic solid into smaller triangles. Particularly well suited to this is the icosahedron (with 20 faces), because it consists of regular triangles whose vertices already lie on a common-sphere geometry.

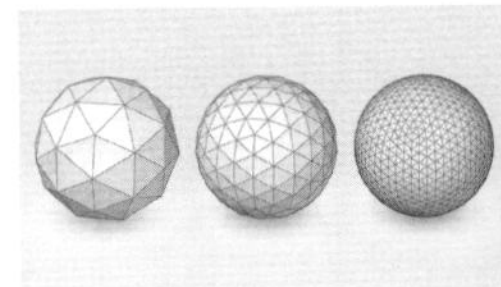

023A ● 083

023B ● 083

SOLID TRANSFORMATIONS

Having dealt with the basic types of modelling and introduced the most important kinds of solids in geometry, we now want to look at how these solids can be transformed to create new, possibly unique, geometries, and how these transformation techniques can be used in architecture, often to striking, even iconic effect.

BOOLEAN OPERATIONS

Boolean algebra is named after the English mathematician, logician, and philosopher George Boole (1815–1864), who formulated its principles in two books, *The Mathematical Analysis of Logic* (1847), and, in more detail, *An Investigation of the Laws of Thought on Which Are Founded the Mathematical Theories of Logic and Probabilities*, which was published in 1854 and is mercifully mostly known simply as *The Laws of Thought*.

The principal characteristic of **Boolean logic**, as we also discuss in our chapters on Graphs & Graphics and Scripting, is that rather than with numbers it works with **truth values**, namely *'true'* and *'false'*; and its operations, rather than for example addition or multiplication, are the **Boolean operators**, known as *conjunction* (*'and'*, denoted as ∧), *disjunction* (*'or'*, denoted as ∨), and *negation* (*'not'*, denoted as ¬).

In 3D modelling, these operations allow us to create new three-dimensional objects from basic solids, the primitives we encountered earlier. Applied to this end, the three Boolean operators correspond to three Boolean operations on solids:

- *Union* (corresponds to *conjunction* and is denoted as ∧): overlapping solids are united to form a new entity, whereby intersections inside the new solid are removed;
- *Intersection* (corresponds to *disjunction* and is denoted as ∨): a new solid is formed from the overlap between the two original solids, whereby any part of the original geometries outside the overlap is removed;
- *Difference* (corresponds to *negation* and is denoted as ¬): one solid is subtracted from another, whereby the order in which they appear determines which solid is subtracted from which, and this in turn affects the shape of the resulting new solid.

As famously illustrated in Danish architect Jørn Utzon's (1918–2008) design for the Sydney Opera House, Boolean operations can be carried out not just with two, but with several solids at the same time, which is why they present such a fast and effective method for developing complex geometries from existing regular solids.

024A ● 083

024B ● 083

DEFORMATIONS

Deformation tools manipulate the shape of 3D objects according to mathematical principles. To do this, you overlay the object you want to change with a simple deformation object, in the shape of a frame. The original 3D object and the deformation object are coupled in such a way that any change to the shape of the deformation object directly affects the shape of the original object. Among the most important deformation operations are:

- *Twist* – turns the top surface of an object in relation to the base surface, resulting in screw-shaped side surfaces
- *Taper* – reduces or enlarges the size of the top surface relative to the base surface, resulting in side surfaces that narrow or widen towards the top or the bottom respectively
- *Bend* – curves the object along a given radius
- *Shear* – shifts the position of the top surface relative to the bottom surface, resulting in a tilt or leaning shape in the side surfaces

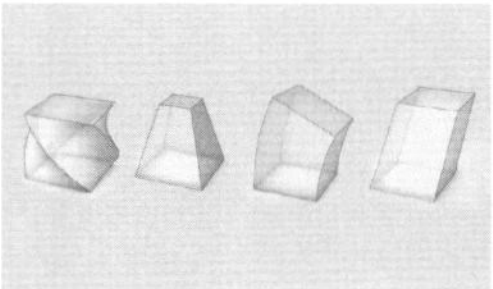
025A ● 084

025B ● 084

026 ● 084

Deformation tools can be combined with each other and they can also be applied multiple times to achieve desired shapes; they are equally applicable to solids and surfaces.

027A ● 084

027B ● 084

SURFACE MODELS

As we mentioned earlier, a *surface model* describes the geometry of a body by the surfaces which form its boundaries. For closed surface models, such as cuboids or spheres, the 3D model is comparable to a hollow body. You can carry out surface-related calculations and create simple intersections, besides of which it is also possible to allocate details about material qualities. Complex freeform geometries can be well represented by surface models, and they can be manipulated and modified in many different ways.

SURFACE NORMALS

The orientation of a surface is defined by its front and back, and any surface can be orientated in any direction in three-dimensional space. For the generation and manipulation of surfaces it is essential to know what their orientation is, and this is defined by a surface orientation vector, called the *surface normal*, or simply the *normal*, which is a vector that sits exactly perpendicular to the surface in question with its direction giving the surface orientation.

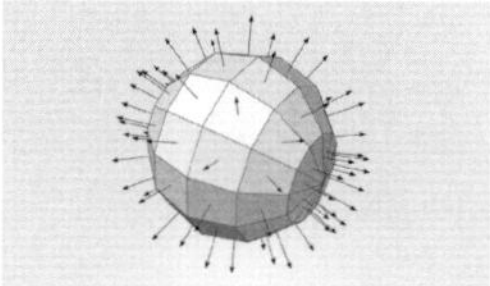
028 ● 085

UV MAPPING 190↘

In 3D modelling, the three-dimensional space in which the object is located is described by the three axes X, Y, and Z, much as you'd expect, and as we discussed when looking at the Cartesian coordinate system above. So if we want to project a two dimensional entity – such as an image, or a texture, for example – onto a surface that belongs to an object which sits within that space, we need a new grid with its own coordinates to describe that surface. This is our UV map: a matrix that is defined by two directions, U and V (so named purely because the letters X, Y, and Z are already taken to describe the space we're operating in).

The direction of the U and V axes adjusts to the direction of the generating boundary curves of this surface, meaning that if you have a cube, for example, that sits in your X, Y, Z space and you determine that the U and V axes of your UV map shall be the perpendicular edges of one of the cube's visible surfaces, then if you now rotate that cube, very obviously all visible surfaces change position, and consequently the U and V axes, which align with the edges of one of the cube's surfaces, change their orientation correspondingly.

In a 3D modelling program, or any other similar software, you can normally adjust the density and number of gridlines you want to display for your UV map. (We talk more about UV mapping in our chapters on Graphs & Graphics and Rendering.) □ 175↘ □ 255↘

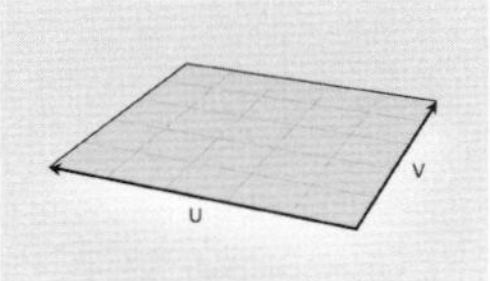

029 ● 085

SURFACE GENERATION METHODS

Classic surface types are based on kinematic generation principles and are also known as *analytic* surfaces. This is what we were referring to at the very beginning of this chapter: the geometry is generated by *moving* a basic shape along a defined path. A circle that is moved along a straight line generates a cylinder, a square moved along a straight line results in a cuboid, were the examples given. Analytic surfaces are classified according to the type of motion – linear, circular, or spiral – and their basic geometry.

EXTRUSION

The process we just described is called *extrusion:* an extension along a particular axis. You move a basis geometry, such as a circle, along a straight construction line which determines how long the extrusion is going to be. This way, a circle turns into a cylinder, as we have seen.

The process of extrusion always adds a dimension to the object you start out with. So while moving a one-dimensional geometry, such as a line, results in a two-dimensional one (here a quadrangle), moving a two-dimensional surface, such as a square, generates a three-dimensional solid (in this instance a cuboid).

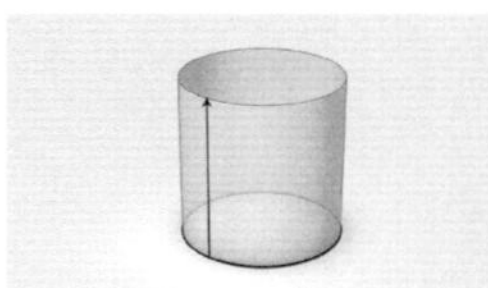
030A ● 085

030B ● 085

ROTATION

A *rotation* is a surface revolution generated by, unsurprisingly, rotating a flat or spatial curve around a central axis. Each point on the generating curve describes a circular geometry around the core of the rotation surface. Apart from the generating curve and the central axis, you can also define the angle of the rotation: a rotation angle of 360° leads to a completely enclosed surface, whereas a rotation of 180° will result in a semi-circular, open surface.

Depending on the basis geometry, a rotation generates a surface that is bent either once or twice. Straight lines result in simple bends, such as cylinder or cone shaped surfaces; already bent lines or curves result in double bent surfaces, such as spheres. Therefore, also the cylinder shown above can be generated by rotation.

Like extrusion, rotation adds a dimension to the basis geometry. Classic rotation solids which result from the rotation of regular surfaces include cylinders, cones, and toruses or tori.

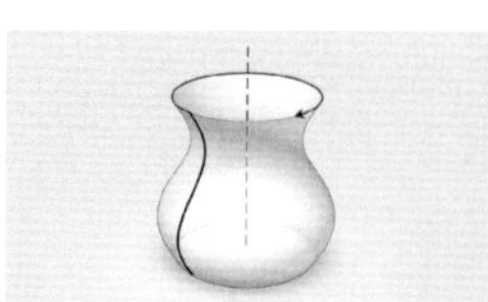
031A ●085

031B ● 085

REGULAR/RULED SURFACES

Regular surfaces are generated by moving a straight line along a curve: the resulting surface geometry can be understood as a tight sequence of parallel straight lines, which is why such lines are often shown in representations of regular surfaces, to make them more easily readable.

The great advantage of regular surfaces is that they can be generated without distortion, and they can be used as transitions between two- and three-dimensional geometries. Not all ruled surfaces are developable surfaces, but all developable surfaces are indeed ruled.

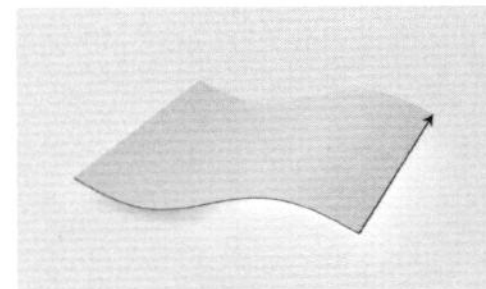
032A ● 086

032B ● 086

TRANSLATION SURFACES

A translation surface is generated by means of two *boundary curves* which meet at a single juncture. A parallel movement of one boundary curve along the second boundary curve creates the translation surface. (Moving the second boundary curve along the first boundary curve results in an identical translation surface.)

The method offers a simple way of generating complex surfaces from given boundary curves, and this principle is particularly easy to apply in architecture because it is only necessary to manufacture two sets of identical construction elements (for example beams) in order to arrive at a translation surface.

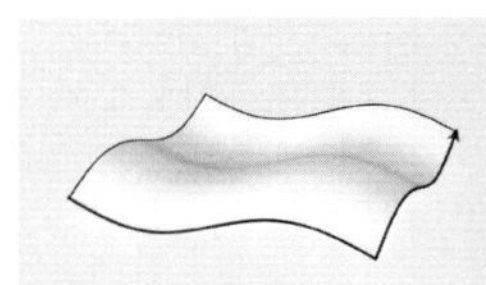
033A ● 086

033B ● 086

SADDLE SURFACES

Saddle or *HP (Hyperbolic Paraboloid) surfaces* are surfaces that are bent in two directions, and like regular and translation surfaces, they are normally generated by boundary curves.

Simple saddle surfaces feature straight boundary curves that sit at skewed angles to each other. They have the advantage that they can be easily reproduced in architecture with linear building components.

If the boundary curves are in themselves curved, their two main directions are *anticlastic*, meaning that their curvatures oppose each other.

Because of their stable static qualities, saddle surfaces are often used as shell or membrane structures.

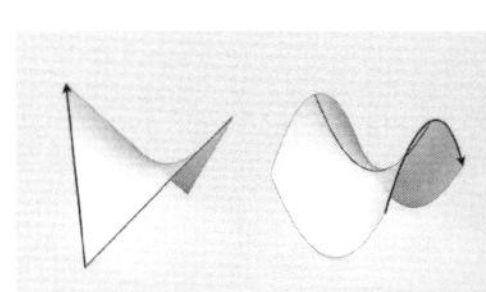
034A ● 086

034B ● 086

SCREW SURFACES

Screw surfaces are based on a helix or spiral shaped geometry. A helix geometry describes a consistent rising curve, guided along a cylinder surface. Spiral surfaces follow a similar principle in that they develop consistently around a core, but unlike helixes they also continuously approach or remove themselves from the core axis. A curve which follows either of these geometries generates a screw surface.

In architecture, you will find this shape for example in spiral staircases.

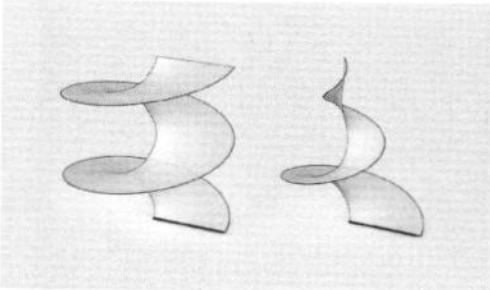
035A ● 087

035B ● 087

PIPE SURFACES

A *pipe surface* is generated as the envelope of a series of circles along a curve, which in this case is called a *directrix*. Strictly speaking, a pipe surface is such curve in which the circumference of the circle that describes the envelope is constant along the entire length of the curve. By varying the diameter of the circle along the curve, the pipe can be enlarged or reduced in size.

Applying different diameters along the same curve, the 'pipe' changes size over its extension. In this case it is no longer called a pipe surface, but a *channel* or *canal surface*.

Furthermore, it is possible to use varying diameter geometries such as ellipses or polygons to generate channel surfaces of different shapes.

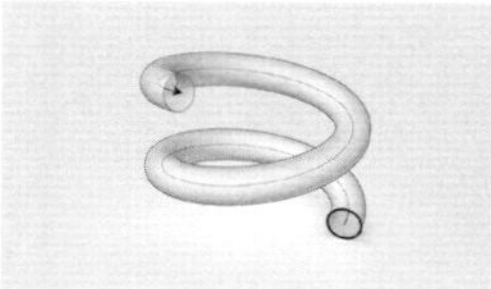
036A ● 087

036B ● 087

LOFT SURFACES

The **Loft function** uses a sequence of at least two cross-section geometries to create a homogenous surface area progression. Similar to an elastic membrane, the basis geometry is covered with a continuous enveloping surface. By means of a mathematical approximation processes, an optimal tangentiality is produced in the transition from one cross-section geometry to the other.

(Like 'spline' – which we will explain in a moment – the term 'lofting', has its origin in shipbuilding and aeroplane manufacture: 'lofting' describes the drawing of full-size templates or patterns for the production of curved shapes and bodies. These would typically be made in large lofts above a factory's main floor, hence 'lofting'.)

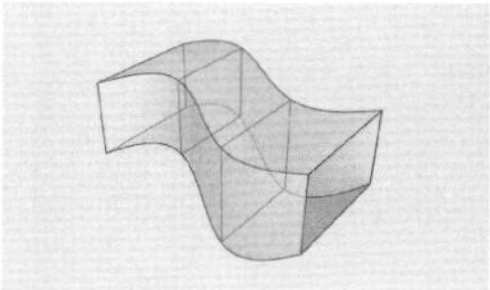
037A ● 087

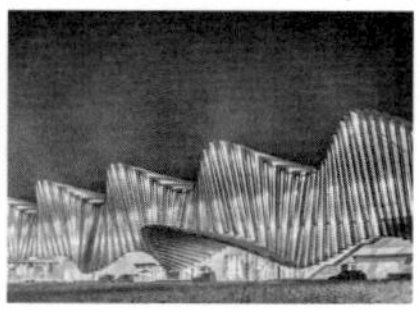
037B ● 087

FREEFORM SURFACES

Freeform surfaces are homogenous surfaces with soft transitions. They are an extension of classic surfaces, but allow for greater flexibility in their generation and manipulation. They are characterised as 'freeform' because they remove themselves from the strict boundary conditions of regular geometries, they are calculated by approximation methods, and they are built parametrically.

The ability of 3D modelling programs to generate these shapes in particular has had an enormous impact on architecture, as we have seen. Still, it is not the case that freeform geometries are simply a phenomenon of computer aided architectural design. You will find them as far back as 400,000 years ago, in the earliest dome-shaped arches of civilisation. But at least since the late 19th century, with the arresting shapes created by Catalan architect Antoni Gaudí (1852–1926), freeform surfaces have been very much part of the form repertoire of architects. (We discuss Gaudí's methodology in detail in our chapter on Model Making.) □ 421↘

FREEFORM CURVES

At the basis of freeform surfaces are *freeform curves*. There are three types of freeform curves which all follow the same principle in terms of how they are generated, but whose geometries are calculated using different algorithms:

- **Bézier curves** ■ 185↘
- **B-spline curves** ■
- **NURBS curves** ■

All these curve types are defined using control points that work a bit like an elastic band and determine the shape of the curve. The straight lines that connect these control points define what is known as a **control polygon**. In order to create a smooth, homogenous curve, the number of control points should be kept as low as possible, because the more control points there are, the more often the curve changes direction. ■

SPLINES

Splines are types of curves, originally developed for shipbuilding in the days before computer modelling. Naval architects needed a way to draw a smooth curve through a set of points.

The solution was to place metal weights (called *knots*) at these control points, and bend a thin metal or wooden beam (the spline) through the weights to arrive at a line that described the curve.

The physics of the bending spline meant that the influence of each weight was greatest at the point of contact, and decreased smoothly further along the spline. To get more control over a certain region of the spline, the draughtsman simply added more weights.

In computer graphics, the term 'spline' is therefore used to refer to a wide class of functions that are employed in applications requiring data interpolation and/or smoothing. Spline functions are normally determined as the minimisers of suitable measures of roughness (for example integral squared curvature) subject to the interpolation constraints.

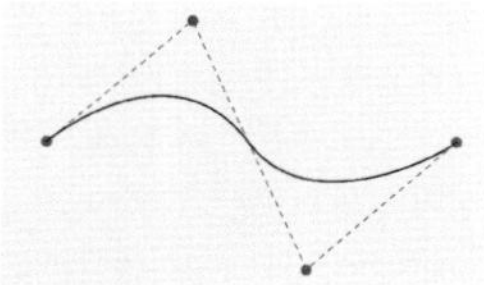
038 ● 088

INTERPOLATION & APPROXIMATION
There are principally two approaches to generating a curve geometry: *interpolation* and *approximation*. With interpolation you define the points which are to connect the freeform curve. The position of the control points is then deduced from the resulting curve geometry. Approximation reverses the pro-
134↘ cess: you first define the position of the control
□ 175↘ points and the geometry of the freeform curve is deduced from these.

BÉZIER SURFACES
French engineer Pierre Bézier (1910–1999) is not, as it happens, and as the name suggests, the inventor of the *Bézier curve* and therefore by extension the eponymous surface. The person who first developed an algorithm that made it possible to evaluate Bézier curves, then still nameless, was another Frenchman, Paul de Casteljau (b. 1930). He did so in 1959, whilst working at French car maker Citroën. Bézier at the same time was employed by Citroën's direct competitor, the equally French car maker Renault, where he was responsible for the company's Tool Design Office. Unsurprisingly, considering their common field, Bézier was working on very much the same thing as de Casteljau at more or less exactly the same time, and it was Bézier who developed the notation and particularly the use of node control handles that became associated with these curves through their adoption into *PostScript*, and then *Adobe Illustrator*, which is why engineers, designers, graphic designers, artists, and architects the world over know of Pierre Bézier, but few know of de Casteljau: the world of invention is not necessarily a fair place...

Today, Bézier curves are among the most
■ widely used freeform tools, and the **de Casteljau algorithm**, though nowhere near as famous, is also still an integral component of much of today's CAD software.

Depending on the number of control points they have, boundary curves for a Bézier surface are categorised into three groups:

- *Linear Bézier curve*: 1st order, 2 control points
- *Quadratic Bézier curve*: 2nd order, 3 control points
- *Cubic Bézier curve*: 3rd order, 4 control points

■ 97↘ The control points of a Bézier surface are positioned in a network constellation around the freeform geometry. The distribution of control points corresponds to the UV orientation of the surface, which in turn is defined by the generating freeform curves. Each point of the control grid has the same type of influence on the surface, which means that manipulating the shape locally is possible only within limitations.

B-SPLINE SURFACES
Much as Bézier surfaces are generated from Bézier curves, so *B-spline surfaces* are generated from corresponding B-spline curves. We talk about splines in a
□ 175↘ little more detail in our chapter on Graphs & Graphics, but let us here quickly point out that the term *B-spline* was coined by Romanian-American mathematician Isaac Jacob Schoenberg (1903–1990), with B standing for 'basis', and the word 'spline' referring to the type of
□ 175↘ function we discussed a moment ago under *Splines*.

A B-spline curve consists of two or more Bézier curves which are strung together with smooth transitions. Because you can adjust the curvature in both the U and V direction independently of each other, it is possible to achieve a finer grading of surface transitions than with other types of curves.

NURBS SURFACES
A *NURBS (Non-Uniform Rational B-Spline)*, which we also touch upon further in our chapter on Graphs & Graphics, is a special type of B-spline, and in some senses an extension of it. *NURBS surfaces* are based on these splines and follow the same principle as Bézier and B-spline surfaces, in that they are also defined and manipulated by a grid of control points. The difference between NURBS and other freeform surfaces rests in the fact that with NURBS surfaces it is possible to individually *weight* the control points, which means that you can exercise much more precise control over the surface. Also, NURBS surfaces can be both freeform and regular surfaces, which is not the case for Bézier or B-Spline surfaces.

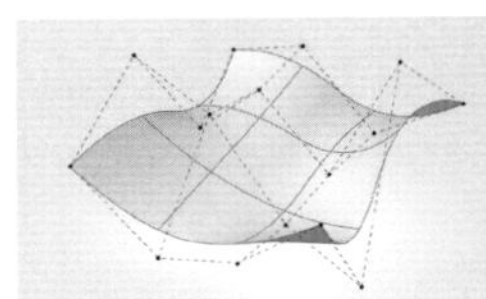
039A ● 088

039B ● 088

POLYGON NETS / MESHES
Complex freeform surfaces with soft edges, continuous gradients, and tangential transitions are expensive and difficult to realise in the manufacture of building elements and during construction on site. Which is why freeform geometries are often transformed into a *mesh* consisting of flat polygon surfaces. The polygons connect individual points of the basis geometry and create from it a faceted net which approximates the freeform surface. The more points are used in rationalising this type of geometry, the smaller the resulting polygons and the more accurate the representation of the freeform. A smaller number of points correspondingly results in a more rough approximation. *Polygon nets* are usually formed from one type of polygon, such as triangles, quadrangles, or hexagons.

Triangulation uses a division principle based on triangles and is especially well suited for the rationalisation of freeform surfaces, because three points always and necessarily are situated on the same plane. Areas which feature acute curvatures tend to be broken down into numerous small polygons, whereas for flat or near flat areas large polygons usually suffice. To obtain an even representation of the geometry, it is important that the side lengths of each polygon are equal or almost equal.

In transferring NURBS surfaces to polygon nets, you lose the ability to manipulate the surface with control points, which means that the free adjustment of the surface geometry becomes severely restricted. This is why the transformation of a NURBS surface into a polygon net should only ever really happen once the surface geometry has been defined.

(You'll also find more about polygons in our chapter on Graphs & Graphics.)

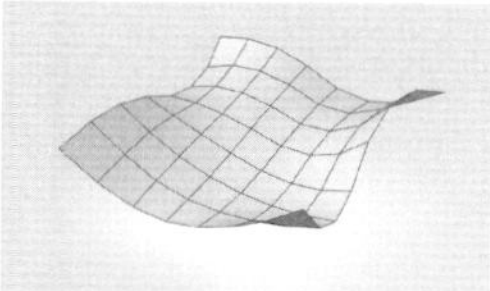

040A ● 088

040B ● 088

SURFACE TRANSFORMATIONS

As with our discussion of solid models, we now – having looked at the various types of surface models – want to also summarise the principal ways in which these can be transformed to generate new geometries. (CAAD and 3D modelling software offers special tools for generating surface transitions, automatically adjusting the border areas of surfaces as necessary.)

SPLIT, TRIM, JOIN

The functions *split* and *trim* are used to separate or remove parts of a surface. Two overlapping surfaces can be split or trimmed along their intersection, or by defining a partial segment using curves.

Splitting the surfaces means that both sections remain intact and can be used and manipulated separately, trimming a partial surface along its intersection with another surface removes that segment, much as we've encountered in the Boolean difference operation.

The *join* function, by contrast, unites two separate surface segments into a new unit.

041A ● 089

041B ● 089

FILLET & CHAMFER

The function *fillet* connects two surfaces that stand at an angle to each other, over a tangential ratio, to create a rounded transition.

The function *chamfer* connects two similarly angled surfaces by means of a bridging straight surface, creating a shaved corner effect.
In both cases, the size and angle of the connection can be defined by the user.

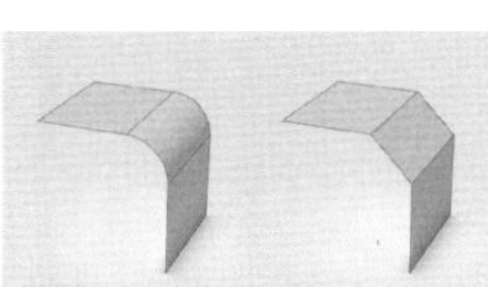

042 ● 089

BLEND & MATCH

The *blend* and *match* functions offer more complex transitions which can also be applied to surfaces that run parallel to each other.

Blend unites the two surfaces by means of a tangential transition, whereby the two original surfaces remain intact.

Match shifts one of the original surfaces towards the other and in the process reshapes it as necessary to create a transition.

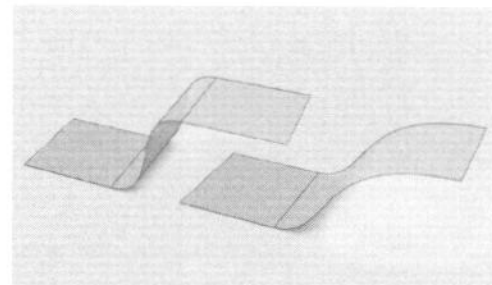

043 ● 089

OFFSET

A surface model describes the surface geometry of a form as it will be used in construction, but it does not, by itself, give any indication as to the thickness of the material. Using the *offset* function, it is possible to represent the strength of the material – for example the thickness of a concrete shell – in the 3D model: it generates a parallel surface in the direction of the surface normal at a consistent distance to the original.

Depending on the geometry of the original, offsetting a surface can create surface overlaps (with offset towards the inside) or gaps (offset towards the outside). These overlaps or gaps then have to be smoothed out, using the trim, fillet, or chamfer functions.

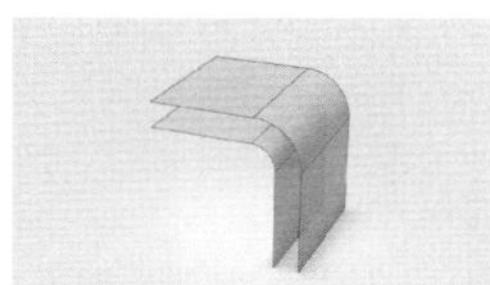

044 ● 089

DEVELOPABLE SURFACES

In 3D modelling as in mathematics, a *developable surface* is a surface in three-dimensional space that can be flattened out to the two-dimensional plane without distortion. A typical example of such a surface is the vertical side of a cylinder: it can be rolled out into a rectangular surface on the plane. Similarly, a cube can be 'unfolded' into its 'cutout' pattern without making any further adjustments to any of its sides.

Most bent surfaces can not be developed, including all complex freeform surfaces and also some regular, double-bent geometries such as spheres. There are some exceptions to this. We've already mentioned the cylinder, and to this we can also add cones and any regular surface that has been generated using a straight line.

The great advantage of developable surfaces to architecture is that they can be manufactured in one flat piece and then 'developed' or assembled into their final three-dimensional shape. The relevance of this to architecture is evident, and we look into applicable techniques more closely in our chapters on Digital Manufacturing and Model Making.

□ 405↘
□ 421↘

THE MAGIC CUBE

The *'Magic Cube'* is a particularly rewarding way of using developable surfaces to form an apparently complex spatial configuration. In this particular example, what looks like three intersecting cylinders 'drilled into' a cube in fact consists of planar shapes that can all be unrolled. The cutting patterns can then be processed from any flat material such as wood, paper, or metal, to arrive at a physical model.

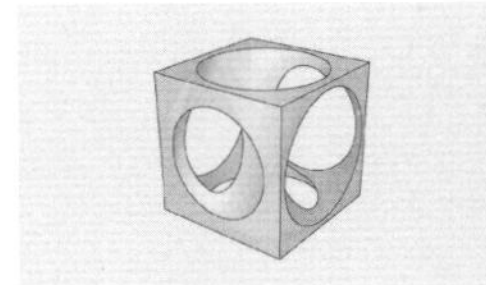

045A ● 090

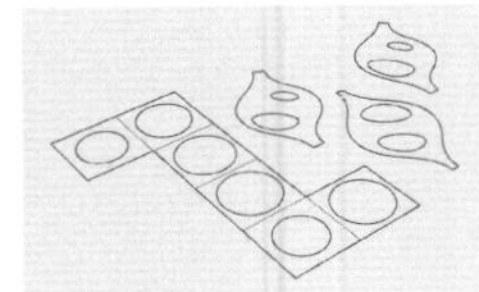

045B ● 090

The Outlook

In many ways, the most extraordinary thing about 3D modelling is perhaps that it is possible at all. And, in tandem with that most basic of all observations, how quickly it has become first useful, then important, and now indispensable. From the early beginnings – in the 1960s and 1970s – of helping aeroplane and car makers save time and very substantial costs by allowing them to test airflows and aerodynamic behaviours in a virtual environment, to the 1980s and 1990s when the film and burgeoning gaming industries started building entire digital cities because it was easier and cheaper to do so than to build them as physical sets and backdrops, to today when we routinely model and simulate every aspect of a planned development, took all of about half a century. Considering that during the previous century relatively little and during the millennium before hardly anything much changed in our design methodology as architects, the evolution we have recently gone through on the one hand, and the possibilities that are opening up as we write this sentence on the other, are fairly breathtaking.

In this *Atlas* we talk in various places about a convergence of disciplines and about the ways in which the language of the architect, the engineer, the urban planner, the programmer, and the digital manufacturer overlap and inform each other. But it is also worth bearing in mind that there are naturally great differences, still, between different application environments. How you model a car is fundamentally different to how you model a residential development, obviously. And it entails not only a difference in scale, but also a very different process. For us as architects it is important to be aware as much of the origins of 3D modelling and how far it has already travelled, as it is to recognise just how far it has yet to go. Because 3D modelling is by no means simple or easy: it can be fiendishly complex and – whether as a design tool or as a project management system – the 3D model can be both a fuel propelling you to great heights and a ball and chain around your ankle, dragging you down. Quite conceivably both at the same time.

It was Buckminster Fuller who is quoted as saying: "When I am working on a problem, I never think about beauty, but when I have finished, if the solution is not beautiful, I know it is wrong."

Creating anything – as an artist, writer, composer, filmmaker, inventor, architect – is a matter of getting things wrong. Of failing, repeatedly. Through failing, over and over again, we learn. As we learn, we modify our approach, we begin to understand why something we think should work doesn't, and we get better at what we do and make fewer mistakes until, ultimately, we may get it right. The idea of the genius who plants into the world perfection with the first throw and continues to do so with each subsequent one is a crazy fallacy. And this is one of the main reasons why 3D modelling is so useful and why, as an instrument of design, it will become more integrated, more pervasive, and more essential. Because it makes making mistakes a whole lot easier. With 3D modelling you can fail, fall flat on your face, and get up and do it all over, maybe better, maybe worse, in the relative safety of your virtual 3D environment, and you can do so over and over again, at no cost or damage, other than to your time, your nerves, and your sleep pattern.

The computer is not going to replace everything that has gone before, and nor does it do away with a need for expertise and sound judgement. We would argue – in fact we do, repeatedly – the opposite. As we note throughout this *Atlas*, with the unlimited potential of technology comes the big human question: what are we going to do with all this. Certainly, the distinction between what is hand drawn and what is computer generated will disappear. Partly it will disappear because the quality of computer generated design is so high and differentiated that it becomes indistinguishable from human drawing. Partly though it will disappear because the level of human input into the computer's generation process will – or at any rate can – become more subtle and more sophisticated.

What we do expect to happen also is that 3D modelling programs will smooth the bumps between different applications and combine the steps that lead from a design in the virtual space to an actual building in the physical reality. Right now, it is still mostly the case that as the architect I create a model in one program and when I send it to the engineering practice, they then have to convert it into something they can work with and make sense of. There needs to be, and we venture there will be, a coming together of these divergent requirements and approaches

How this coming together takes shape is another question though. On the one hand it can happen along the lines of BIM. This works with definitions, such as 'what is a door', 'what are the possible shapes a door can take', and 'what are the materials that are "valid" for a door'. The consequence of using this particular approach is that I end up with a very large ship that needs to somehow float on the creative waters and carry with it an almost infinite load of such definitions, covering absolutely everything the program might come across as a construction or design task in its lifetime. This makes the program bulky, and the solution, such as it is, to my design challenge inelegant and predictable, as it stems from an already existing set of 'possible outcomes' and is therefore interchangeable with other 'solutions' for other challenges.

Another approach is to eschew standardisation and instead look for simple transportation tools that will get me from A to B in the specific given situation; in other words: bespoke code. It means solving problems individually on a project basis, and it means programming. We see this as where we are heading: architects, designers, users of 3D modelling software, whoever we are, equipping ourselves with the ability to build our own tools. Since this means programming, even if at a basic level, so as to be able to write or adapt simple scripts for example, it also means I have to acquire an understanding of the basic principles of how I describe a shape, such as a cylinder, in geometrical terms, which is of course why we have given quite a bit of space in this chapter to such basics.

If this, as we expect, is going to be borne out, it brings about an interesting turn in the evolution of the role of the architect: historically, as the master builder, the architect had the overview over the project and, even if he (as it would invariably have been then) did not *do* everything by himself, he was *able to do* everything and he certainly *knew* everything. Over the course of modernity we have moved far away from that position, and as architects we can't, today, be comprehensively competent masters of the building process in its entirety, there are far too many areas where we rely on other people's professional expertise. But if we equip ourselves with the knowledge, skill, and understanding that we need not only to use a piece of computer software with its off-the-shelf elements and components, but to use it as our tool to build our own bespoke tools for designing and manipulating the three-dimensional geometry, then we can wrest back a great deal of influence and control over what we are building from planners, project managers, engineers, and administrators.

The computer, then, is, or at any rate can be, a source of empowerment for the architect. Because this kind of expertise that enmeshes the digital tool with the creative process cannot be farmed out to IT specialists. And we are in no doubt that this is not just desirable, but essential, because the alternative is a plug-and-play architecture which outputs physical instances of software libraries: standard blocks and elements that look like they've been designed by a machine, because they have.

We also need to be aware of another 'phenomenon' that is inherent in this kind of digital technology: the 'democratisation' effect. If these tools exist and are – at least at entry level – easy to use, then clients are able to use them too. Many pieces of 3D modelling software behave not unlike computer games. That means clients themselves can – and will – play. This may, and perhaps should, get some alarm bells ringing, for example at the horrifying prospect of a *'Comic Sans'* type approach to client-led architecture; but it also opens up avenues of greater, more dynamic end-user involvement in the creation of the spaces they are ultimately going to inhabit and work in, which, in many specific situations may be of great and tangible benefit to them. A school for children with special needs, for example, built with the particular requirements that these needs bring right at the forefront of the design imperative is likely to meet them more effectively than one built along standard school design principles with some adaptations made here and there, essentially as tinkering around the edges.

And this 'democratisation' perhaps also leads us to a final aspect we want to raise, here as elsewhere: the move towards open source and, more generally, Collaboration. We dedicate an entire chapter to this topic in this *Atlas*, and certainly we view this as a desirable development, and one that we may choose to position as part of a greater cultural change. What we can say with some conviction is that nobody generates architecture on their own, and so the moment I open up the process itself, I can manipulate it, work with it, make it mine own. This may seem paradoxical, but therein exactly lies its great and fascinating promise: by surrendering control I actually gain some; by sharing, I can define who I am, by not looking for solutions, but embracing processes, I can potentially get better results. □ 629↘

We see 3D modelling as central to a new architecture, the architecture of the 21st century. And that begs the question, immediately: 'what is – and what are the demands of – 21st century architecture?' Of course we don't have the answer to this for you, and we don't expect you to be able to come up with one just like that either. But if you have read the Introduction to this *Atlas*, you will know that we believe strongly that, "what you can do is open yourself up to the world and ask good questions." That statement is very much operational... □ ↖29

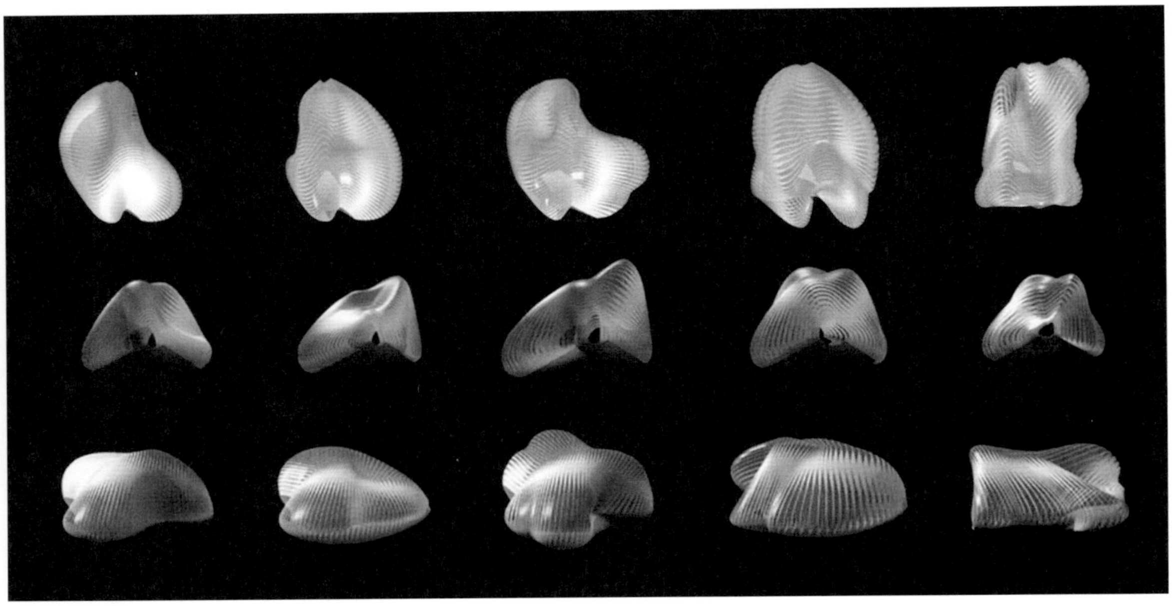

009 ● 063
Animate Form by Greg Lynn. [Greg Lynn FORM]

010A ● 064
Zaha Hadid: *Feuerwehrhaus*, Weil am Rhein, Germany, 1991 (analogue drawing).
[010A + 010B: Zaha Hadid Architects]

010B ● 064
Zaha Hadid: Guggenheim Museum, Taichung, Taiwan, 2004 (digital 3D model).

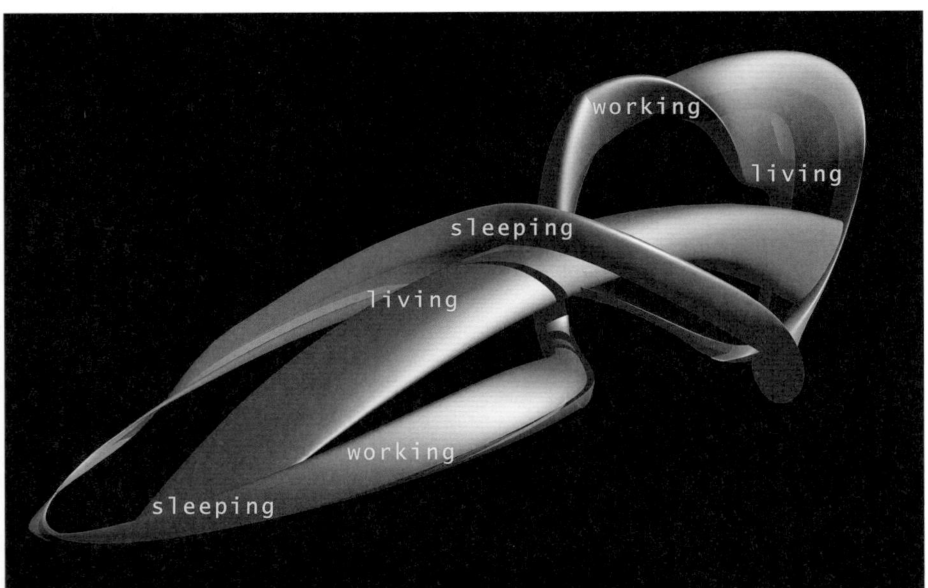

011A ● 064
Ben van Berkel/UNStudio: concept model for the Moebius House (1997). [UNStudio]

011B ● 064
Lars Spuybroek / NOX: D-Form, interactive installation.
[Lars Spuybroek / NOX]

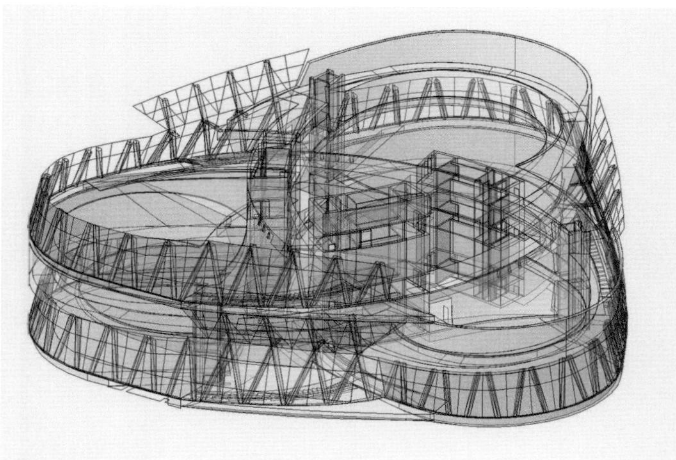

012A ● 064

012B ● 064
UNStudio: Model (012A) of the main exhibition floors of the Mercedes-Benz Museum, Stuttgart, Germany, 2006 (012B). [UNStudio | Julian Herzog]

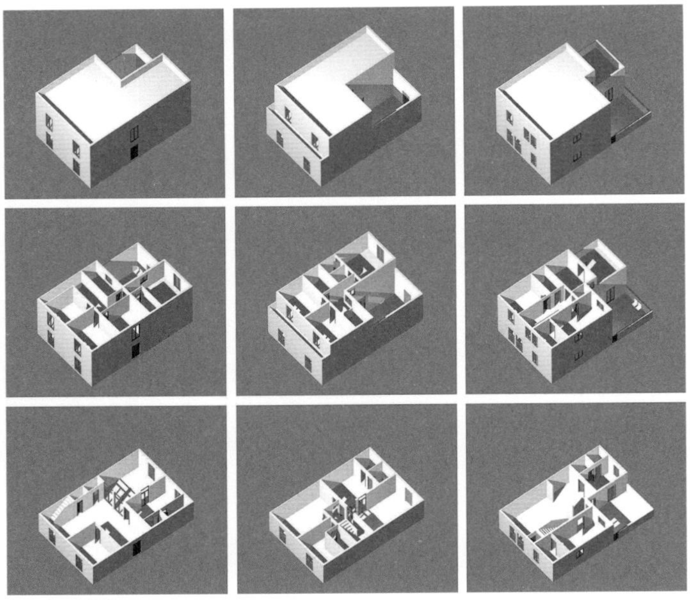

015A ● 065
José Pinto Duarte: shape grammar – research on mass customisation based on the Malagueira Houses by Álvaro Siza.
[015A + 015B: José Pinto Duarte]

015B ● 065
Álvaro Siza evaluating the shape grammar design of the Malagueira Houses, which he considered to be stylistically correct.

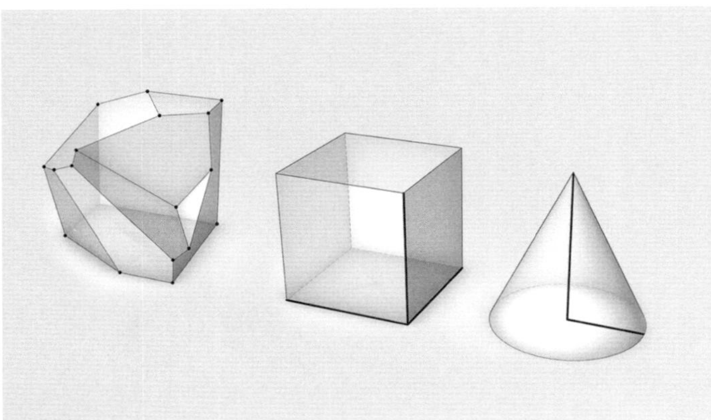

016 ● 068
BREP model (left), CSG models of a cube and a cone (centre & right).
[3D modelling illustration series: Marco Hemmerling]

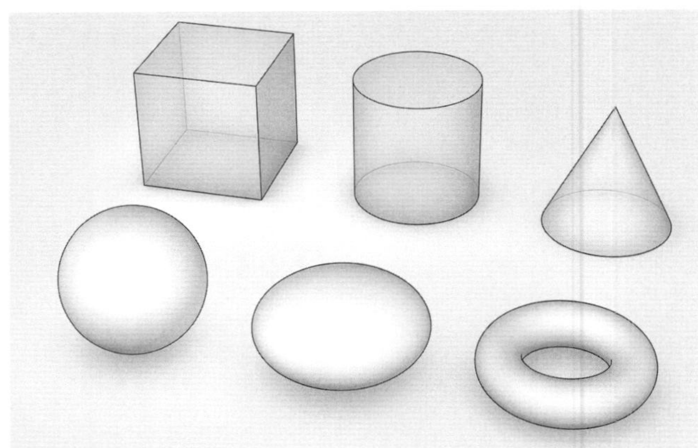

017 ● 069
Standard 3D geometries, based on simple mathematic definitions (for example length X width X height, or radius X height). [MH]

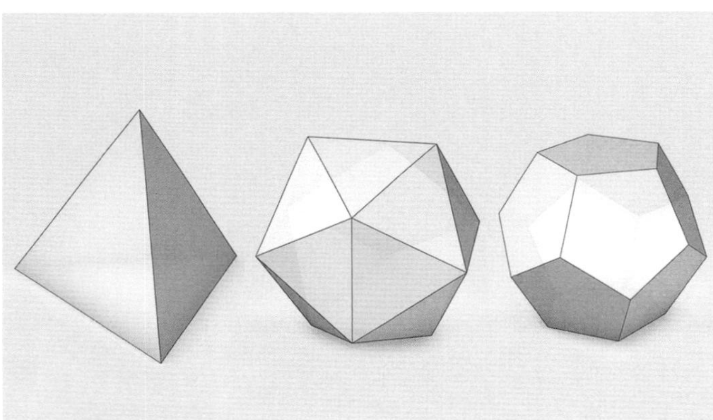

018 ● 069
Three of the five Platonic solids: tetrahedron, icosahedron, and dodecahedron. [MH]

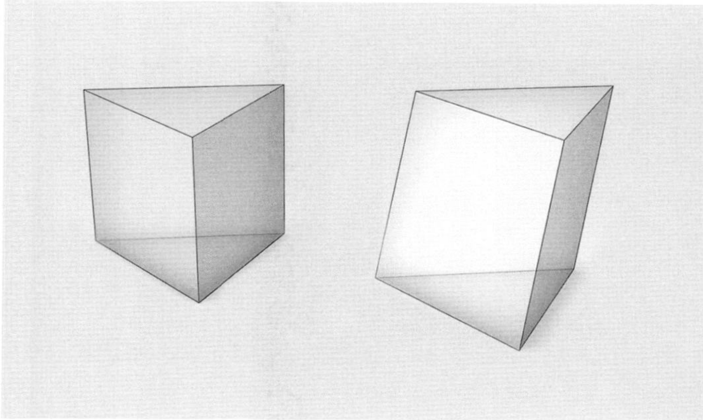

019A ● 069
Prisms with a triangular base (straight and sheared). [MH]

019B ● 069
Louis Kahn, National Assembly Dhaka, Bangladesh (1983). [John Pavelka]

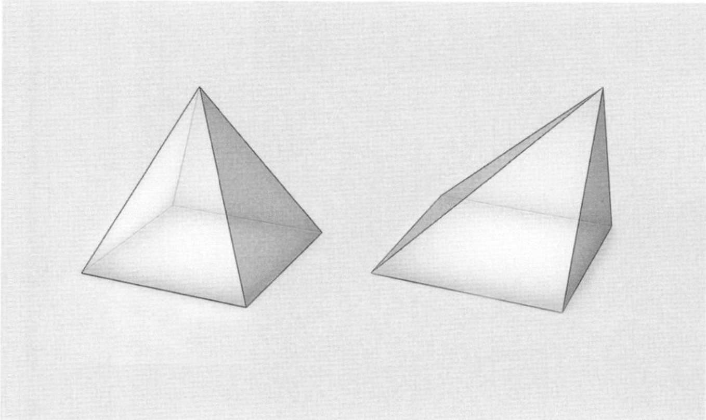

020A ● 069
Pyramids with a rectangular base (straight and sheared). [MH]

020B ● 069
Ieoh Ming Pei: Louvre Pyramid Paris (1989). [Beau Wade]

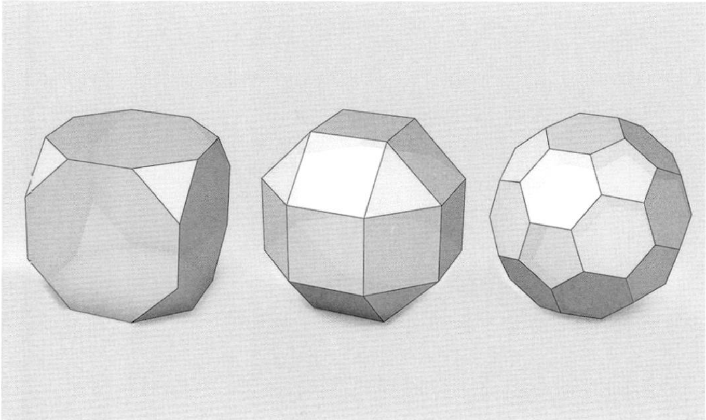

021 ● 069
Archimedean solids. [MH]

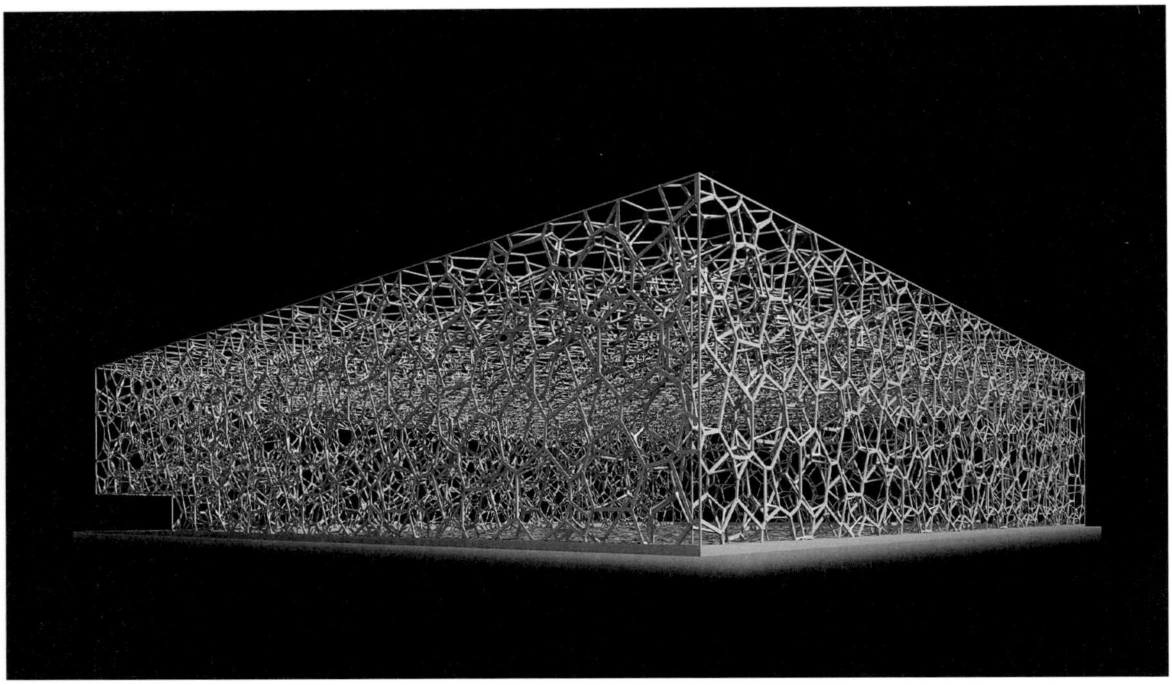

022A ● 070
Structural model of the Beijing National Aquatics Center (Water Cube), 2008. [ARUP (Sydney)]

022B ● 070
PTW Architects: Beijing National Aquatics Center (Water Cube) (2008) – facade detail.

023A ● 070
Geodesic spheres of incremental definition. [MH]

023B ● 070
Biosphere Environment Museum Montreal, featuring a geodesic dome designed for the Expo 1967 by Richard Buckminster Fuller.
[Cédric Thévenet]

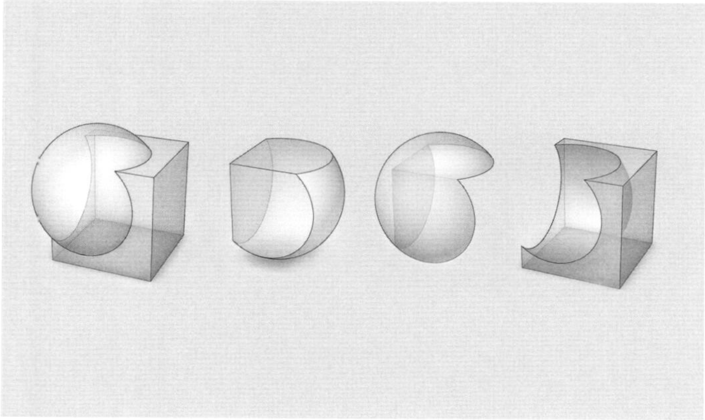

024A ● 071
Boolean operations (left to right): union, intersection and two versions of difference. [MH]

024B ● 071
Spherical solution: form-finding through Boolean operations for the Sydney Opera House by Jørn Utzon (1973).
[Enoch Lau]

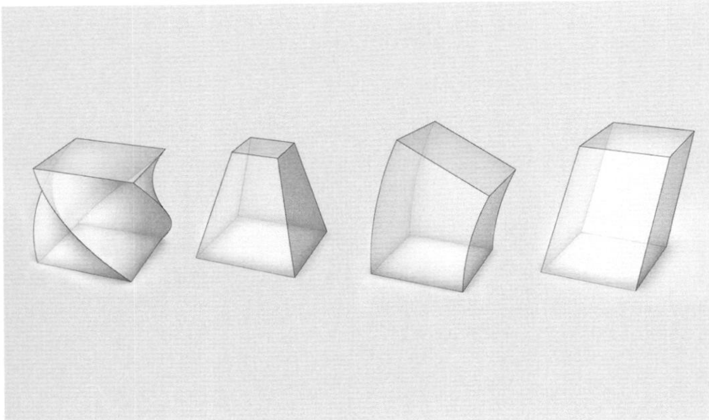

025A ● 071
Deformations: twist, taper, bend, and shear. [MH]

025B ● 071
Absolute Towers by MAD Architects, Mississauga, Canada, 2002. [Sikander Iqbal]

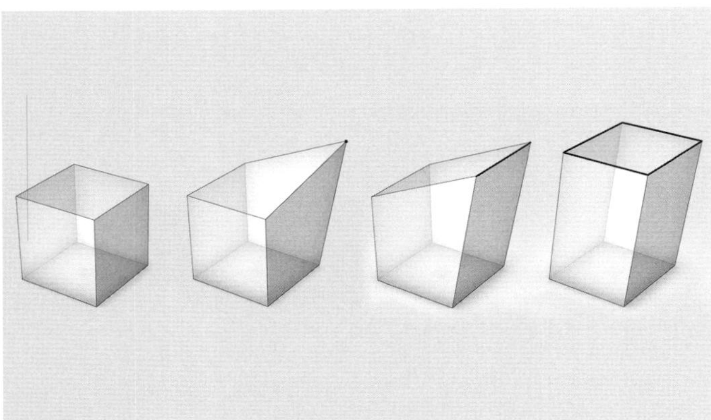

026 ● 071
Deformations: point, line, and surface transformation. [MH]

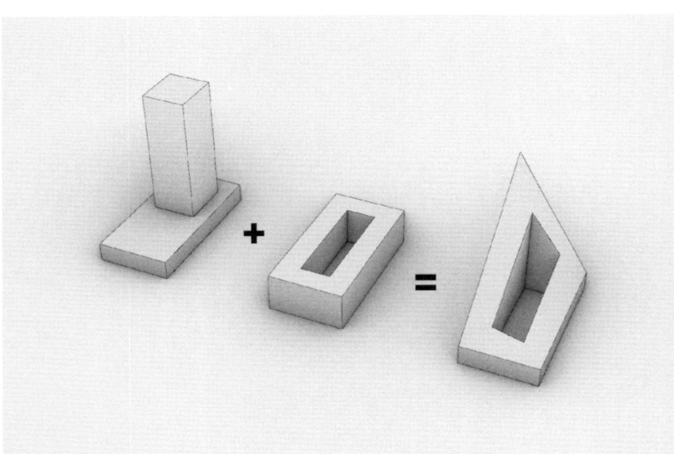

027A ● 071
BIG (Bjarke Ingels Group): design development, high-rise building Via 57 West, New York. [MH]

027B ● 071
Bjarke Ingels Group (BIG): Via 57 West, New York. [David Clay]

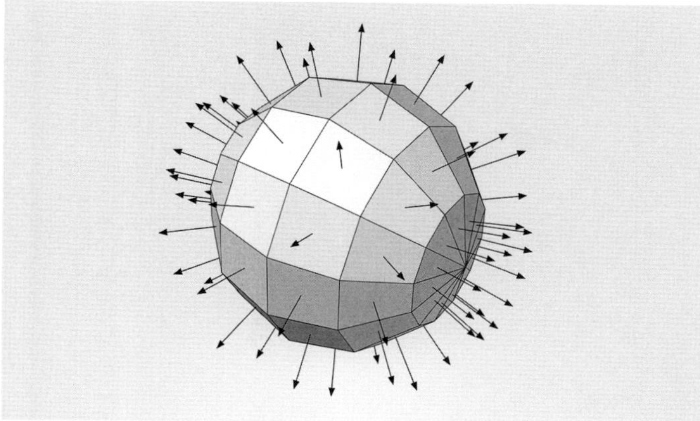

028 ● 071
Surface normals indicating the orientation of the surface towards the outside. [MH]

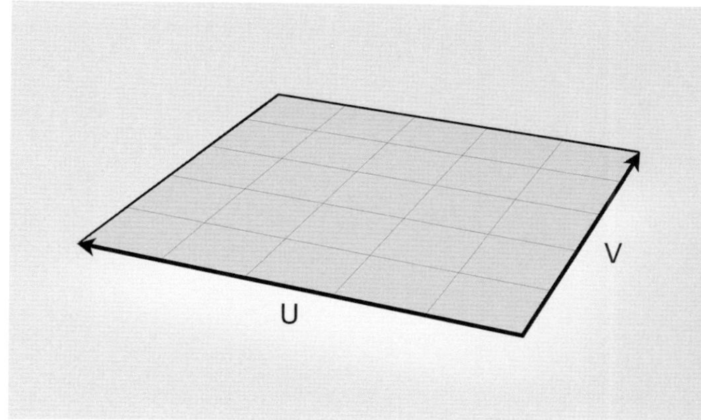

029 ● 071
UV directions of a planar surface. [MH]

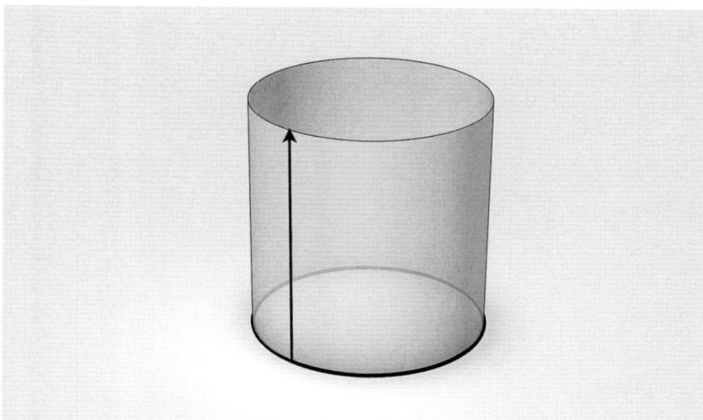

030A ● 072
Extrusion – a circle turns into a cylinder. [MH]

030B ● 072
Karl Schwanzer: *Hauptverwaltungsgebäude*, BMW-*Vierzylinder*, Munich (1973). [High Contrast]

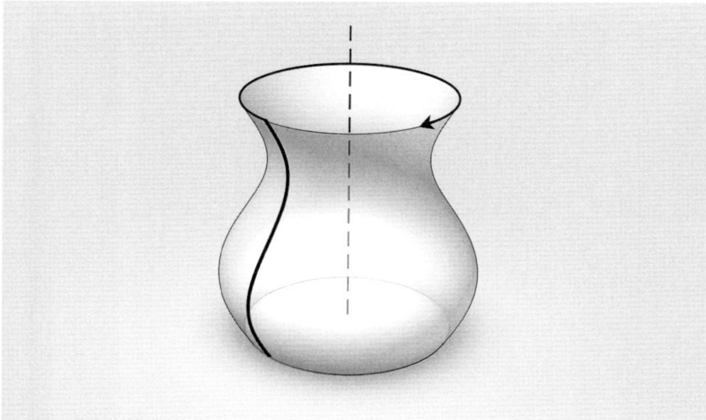

031A ● 072
Surface revolution: a curved line rotated around a central axis. [MH]

031B ● 072
Oscar Niemeyer: Cathedral of Brasília (1970). [Arian Zwegers]

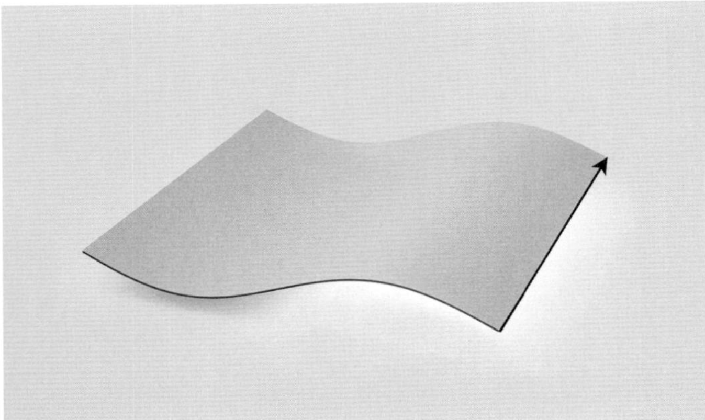

032A ● 072
Ruled surface generated by sweeping a curve along a straight line (or vice versa). [MH]

032B ● 072
ALA Architects / SMS Architekter:
Kilden Performing Arts Centre, Kristiansand, Norway (2012). [Carsten WT]

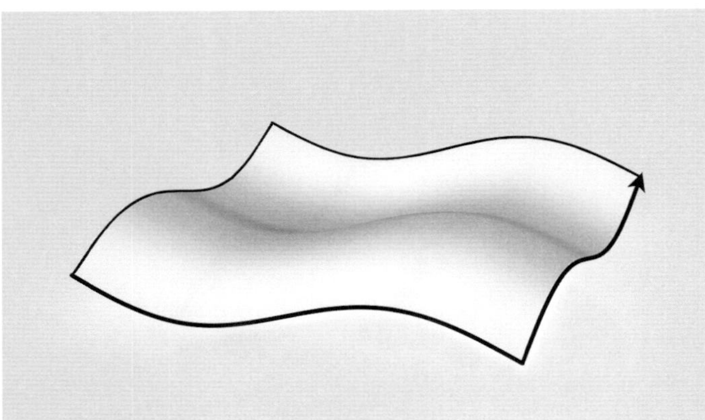

033A ● 072
Translation surface from two boundary curves. [MH]

033B ● 072
Bosjes Chapel, South Africa, 2016. Architect: Styen Studio, London. [Adam Letch]

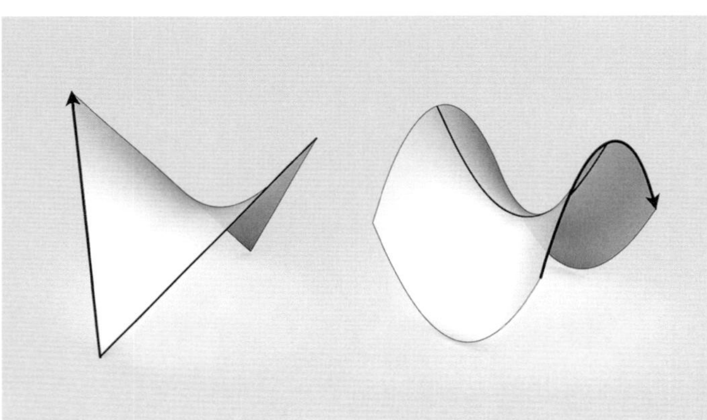

034A ● 072
Simple saddle surface (left), saddle surface with arc boundary curve (right). [MH]

034B ● 072
Erich Kaufmann (architect) / Ulrich Müther (engineer):
Teepott, Rostock, Germany, 2012. [An-d]

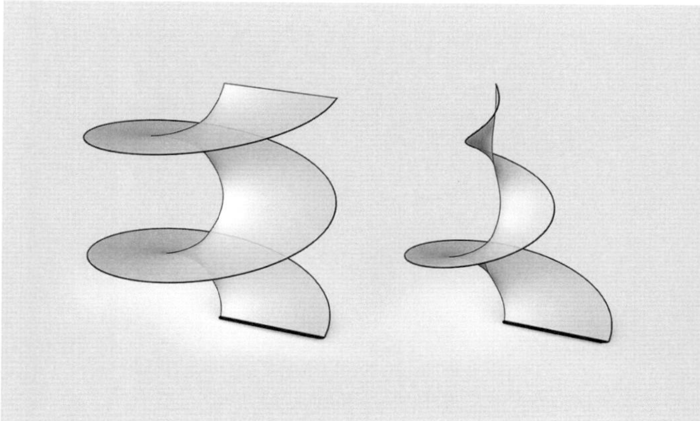

035A ● 073
Screw surfaces: helix, spiral. [MH]

035B ● 073
Frank Lloyd Wright: Solomon R Guggenheim Museum, New York, interior with spiral ramps. [Sérgio Valle Duarte]

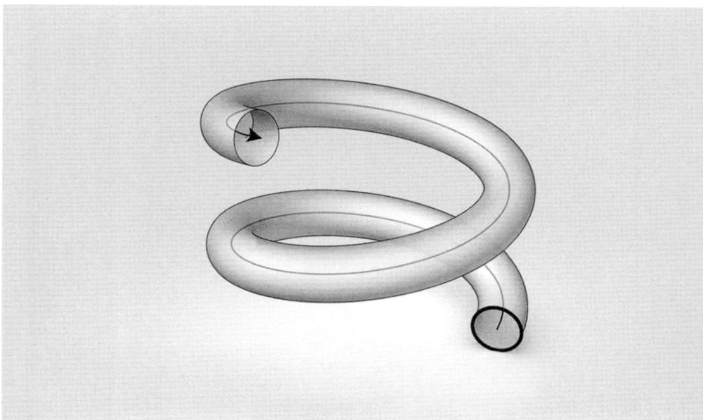

036A ● 073
Spiralling pipe surface. [MH]

036B ● 073
Renzo Piano, Richard Rogers: *Centre Pompidou*, Paris (1977). [pixabairis]

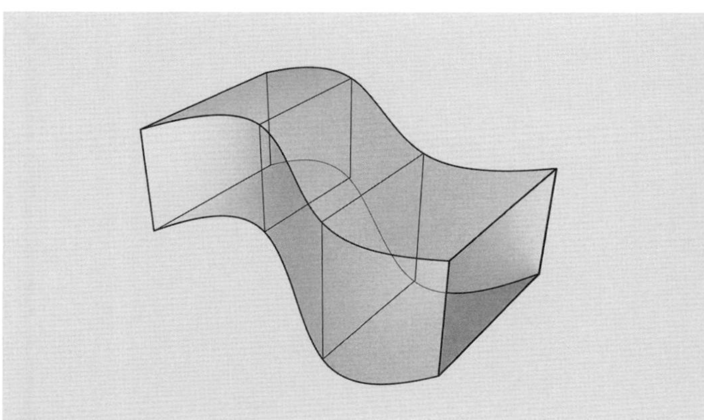

037A ● 073
Loft surface connecting different rectangular section profiles. [MH]

037B ● 073
Santiago Calatrava: *Reggio Emilia Stazione Mediopadana*, 2014. [Enrico Cartia]

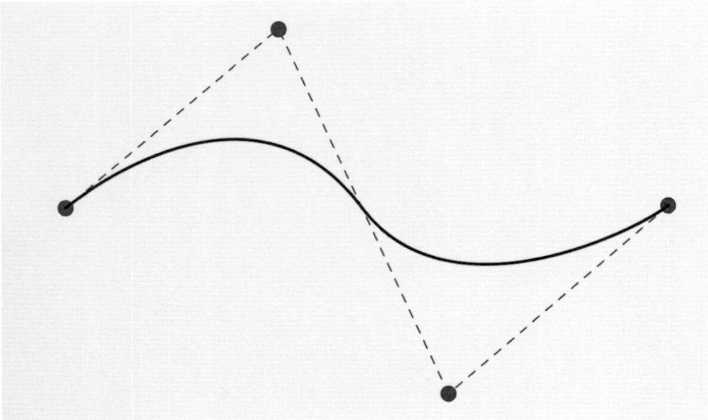

038 ● 073
Spline with control points. [MH]

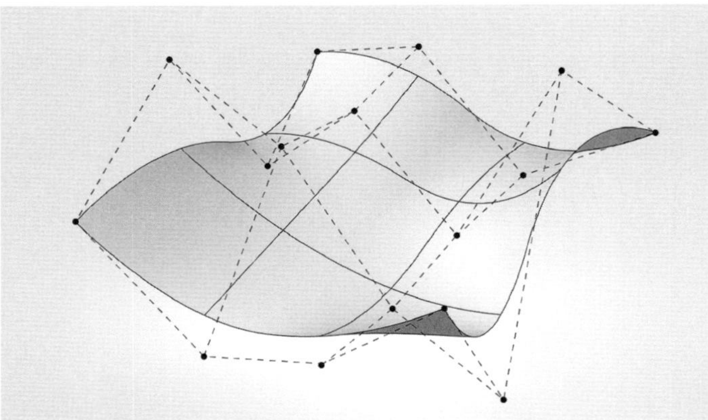

039A ● 074
Freeform surface with control points. [MH]

039B ● 074
Going Your Own Way. SANAA (Kazyuo Sajima & Ryue Nishizawa): Rolex Learning Centre, *École Polytechnique Fédérale Lausanne (EPFL)*, Switzerland, 2010. [Magdalena Roeseler]

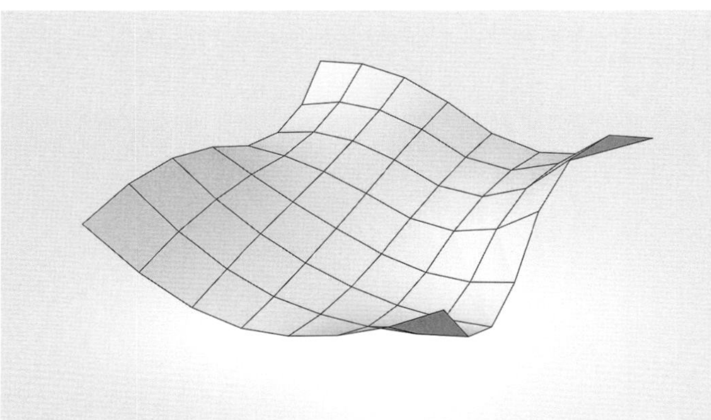

040A ● 075
Mesh from planar quadrilateral faces. [MH]

040B ● 075
Massimiliano Fuksas, *Fieramilano*: triangulated roof structure (2005). [Michele M. F.]

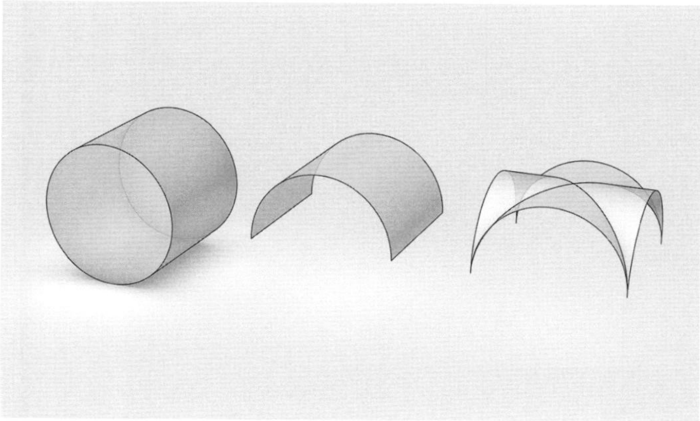

041A ● 075
Cross vault generation by trimming two intersecting cylindrical shells. [MH]

041B ● 075
Cross vault structure, Cologne Cathedral. [Thomas Robbin]

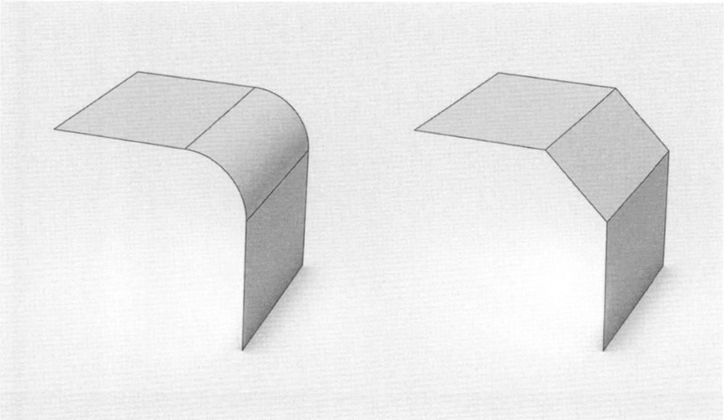

042 ● 075
Fillet, chamfer. [MH]

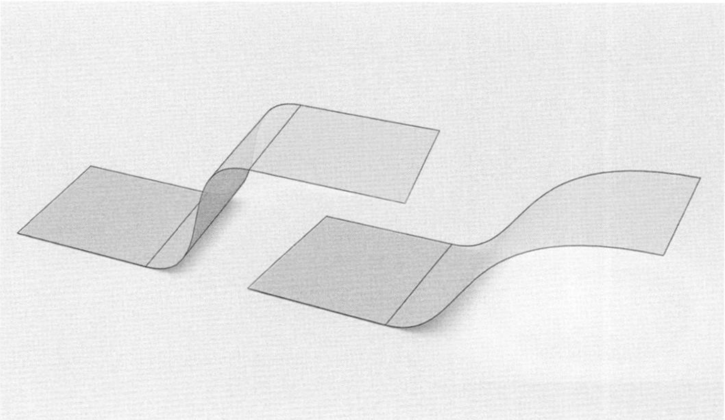

043 ● 075
Blend, match. [MH]

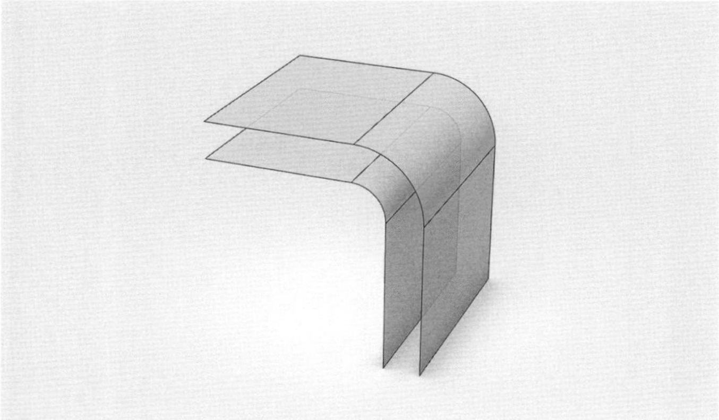

044 ● 075
Creating a material thickness definition using the offset function. [MH]

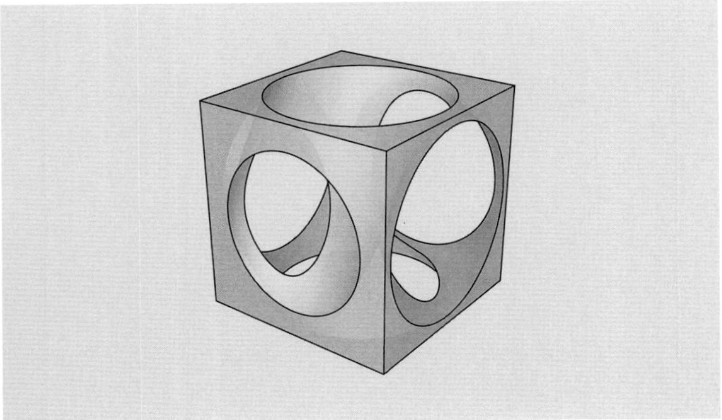

045A ● 076

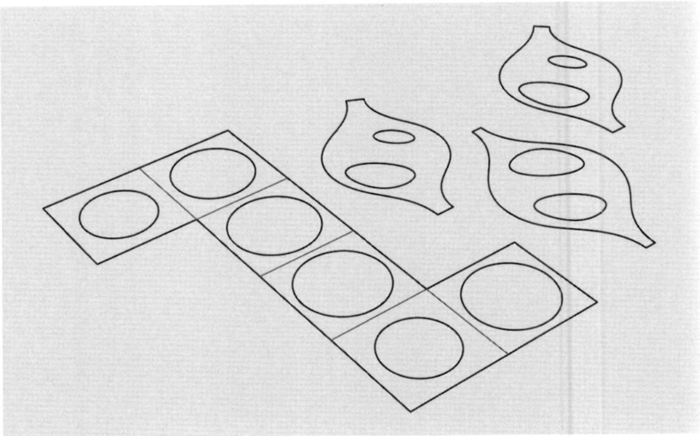

045B ● 076

The 'Magic Cube': 3D model (045A) and its constituent cutting patterns (045B). Using a combination of the 3D modelling strategies discussed in this chapter, you will be able to design and build one yourself!... [MH]

Digital Data Acquisition

Nikolaus Zieske

- Johannes Cramer: *Handbuch der Bauaufnahme*, 1993
- Ralph Heiliger: *Die Vermessung von Architektur*, 2016
- Luhmann/Schumacher (Eds.): *Photogrammetrie Laserscanning Optische 3D-Messtechnik, Beiträge der Oldenburger 3D-Tage 2016*

Overview

HOW TO CAPTURE THE BUILT-UP WORLD

"A man can do all things if he but wills them," is the positive take on life expressed by the Italian polymath Leon Battista Alberti (1404–1472), who very much practised what he preached and excelled, among others, as a poet, priest, linguist, artist, and philosopher, thus turning himself into the quintessential *Renaissance Man*. Mostly, though, he is today remembered as an architect, and very specifically as the first person of his era, the Renaissance, to *write* about architecture. Conceived as a textbook for craftsmen on the one hand, but also as an enrichment and education for, "anyone interested in the noble arts," *De re aedificatoria (On the Art of Building)* was written between 1443 and 1452, and in 1485 became the first printed book on architecture, pipping the work it was largely inspired by and based on, and which Alberti himself had translated from Latin into Italian, *De architectura* by Roman architect and engineer Vitruvius (c. 80–70 BCE – after 15 CE), to the post by one year. (*De architectura* first appeared in print in 1486.)

And why, apart from being in itself 'quite interesting', would that matter? If you read more of this *Atlas*, you will come across Alberti frequently. We mention him in several chapters, and for good reasons. Obviously, the fact alone that he translated the first standard work on architecture, making it accessible to his contemporaries who *practised* the art of architecture, and then wrote his own evolved version of it to drive the practice forward, marks him out as noteworthy.

But really there is a more fundamental and far-reaching aspect to the influence Alberti has had on architecture and how we approach it today: he was the first person to systematically, methodically survey Rome. It was his contention that in order to build in the city and create new architecture, it was essential to know and understand in detail what was already there. Rome being the centre of a then already two-thousand-year-old civilisation, there was a whole lot of antique masonry about the place that needed to be captured. And capture it he did, which is why it could be argued that, apart from everything else he is recognised for, archaeology, too, as we understand it today, started with Alberti.

Alberti realised that all you need to accurately record the position of an object in relation to another is to draw a circle on a piece of paper, papyrus, or vellum, divide it into equally spaced degrees, and attach a ruler that is also divided into equally spaced segments to the centre so it can swivel around the axis. By just using coordinates in relation to the centre of the circle – your anchor point – you can now locate any other point that is of interest to you.

046 ● 105

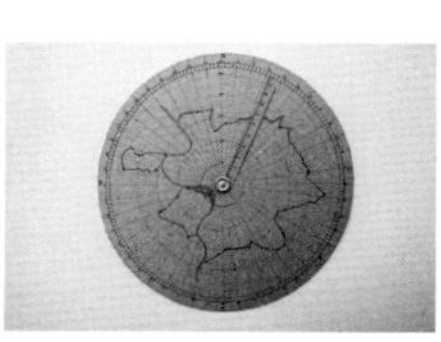

047 ● 105

If, at a time of extraordinary cultural change and radical shifts in technology, science, and thinking, Alberti found it both necessary and desirable to develop a methodology that allowed him to understand and handle the past, today we too, with the digital era putting us at a juncture that is no less significant than the Renaissance, have to develop and master methods appropriate to our age to understand and handle the past. 'The past', in architecture, is on the one hand what was there and has since gone, and it is – and here is where it all becomes patently relevant – what has been there and remains in place still.

It is no coincidence then that Alberti's first and most important commissions as an architect, and the works we can still admire today, such as the Palazzo Rucellai or the Santa Maria Novella church in Florence, were not buildings he designed from scratch, but adaptations of existing structures: transformations. And it is fair to say that since the beginnings – since long before the Renaissance and Alberti – architecture has gone hand in hand with taking, understanding, and transforming what is already there: the built-up world, or the remains of it.

Today we have the specialist field of Design and Construction in Existing Contexts, but really, how often does anyone get a chance to design and construct into non-existing context, into an *empty space?* That is, by far, the exception. And will continue to be, to an ever greater extent: the more architecture we do, the more 'existing context' there is; and the longer any of it exists, the more likely it is that some of it becomes at one point valuable in its own right for historical, heritage, or other reasons. There is, around the world, an ever growing stock of existing context that needs renovating, updating, securing, restoring, rescuing, modernising, adapting, preserving, rebuilding, or refreshing, or in some cases complete or partial dismantling (often in such a way that neighbouring buildings are not damaged or destroyed). Repurposing: how many an old warehouse or factory, church, or mortuary, public convenience, or power station has not been taken over and given a whole new look, feel, and meaning?

There are celebrated contemporary examples, such as the Tate Modern in London, or the *Musée d'Orsay* in Paris, or Gasometer City in Vienna. So if anything, working with, in, and around existing context is going to become more important, rather than less, not just because there is going to be more of it, but also because we are nurturing – so we would hope and venture – our awareness, sensitivity, and respect for the layers of cultural expression that are contained in architecture through the ages. And so if we are going to do work in any mature city in the world, or in many and varied rural and remote settings, we have to get to grips with what's already there. Either because we have to work with it, or because we have to work around it. And 'getting to grips' with it means understanding it and knowing its precise shape and composition, and that means capturing the built-up world. Today we almost invariably do this by digitalising it, by which we mean specifically: acquiring digital data on it, and therefore by extension also generating digital data where this is not yet available.

□ ↖93

Our chapter on Digital Data Acquisition therefore introduces the principal methods we have at our disposal to do so, and it also briefly looks at how we captured the built-up world around us before we had digital technology to hand, because, of course, the challenge or task here – as in many other chapters – is neither new, nor has it been brought about by our entry into the 'Digital Age'. It has simply shifted, and we do now what we have always done, but we do it using technology, and therefore methodology, that is quite radically different to what we used before.

What hasn't changed though is this: the physical world we inhabit is three-dimensional, and it is, in all its tangible physicality, complex, with many interconnected layers, materials, wires, pipes, tubes, supports, joints, pillars, beams, carriers, walls, windows, doors, ceilings, floors, and insulation; not to mention everything that's around the built elements, such as trees, mounds, rocks, streams, shrubs, bushes, and ponds; and everything that's built into the landscape, though it may or may not be part of the architecture itself, such as access roads, pathways, ramps, stairways, fences, perimeter walls, posts, and pylons. Everything that's there is the 'existing context'; it is also therefore the physical boundary we come up against, and as such it has to either be left alone, or changed, or removed, or in some other way dealt with: even if our decision turns out to be not to do anything with it at all, that is still a decision that has to be informed, and today we inform ourselves by looking at it, in all but the rarest of cases, on a computer.

The question, therefore, specifically is: how do we get the physical, three-dimensional world into our computer, where it then exists as a virtual 3D model on a two-dimensional plane, our screen? (Unless or until we print it out newly as a 3D model, for example, in which case it then becomes a newly three-dimensional object.)

BEFORE DIGITAL

One fine day in September 1858, a recently qualified governmental building surveyor called Albrecht Meydenbauer (1834–1921) was being hoisted up in a basket, along the outside wall of one of the turrets that adorns the romanesque, gothic, and baroque architecture of Wetzlar Cathedral, near Frankfurt in Germany, when something went wrong and this 24-year-old, with a whole lifetime of living to do still ahead of him, very nearly fell 25 metres to his near certain death. The incident remained a near-miss, but young Albrecht, shaken to the core, felt compelled to contemplate his mortality and, by some margin more useful to the rest of the world, to consider better, safer ways of measuring tall buildings.

French army officer and scientist Aimé Lossedat (1819–1907) today shares credit for the technology that Meydenbauer now developed and pursued over several decades, as he too, though in a much less dramatic fashion, realised that it should be possible to measure things that are at a distance from us, or high up, or in some other way difficult or dangerous to reach, by means other than actually, physically having to get to them. And so even though they worked individually, they are now jointly recognised as the inventors and founders of photogrammetry: the use of photography to measure and establish the distance to scale between measuring points, from which subsequently evolved stereophotogrammetry, which applies the same principle to the end of reproducing measurable visualisations of three-dimensional objects, and which we'll be looking at a little more closely in just a moment.

■ 270↘

Albrecht Meydenbauer's lucky escape not only tells us where one of the principal pre-digital methods for surveying existing context finds its origin, but also what we had before he helped invent it: physical, hands-on measuring tools, starting with, at the very beginning, the actual hand and other roughly 'standard' parts of the body, such as the thumb or the cubit or the foot. Then measuring rods, yard sticks, measuring chains, and measuring tapes. What they all have in common is that they require a physical presence and proximity to the object that's being measured, which makes them all, as methods, slow, inherently unreliable (especially on large projects), laborious and, as Meydenbauer was to find out, potentially life-threatening.

The other thing all of these methods have in common, and what neither photogrammetry, nor stereophotogrammetry, nor any of the other pre-digital methods we're about to mention changed, is that they *project* the three-dimensional world onto the two-dimensional plane, and in the process they also *reduce* it, quite significantly. This reduction is not necessarily a bad thing: take a large, elaborate structure, such as Albrecht Meydenbauer's near-nemesis, Wetzlar Cathedral, for example. It consists of hundreds of thousands – depending on how you count, millions – of elements and features, all of which are manifestly there, but all of which are not relevant to your purpose of defining the building *sufficiently*. And defining the building sufficiently is crucial, because define it insufficiently, and you may land in cataclysmic trouble, by accidentally knocking down the most important pillar, for example. Define it excessively though, and you may end up none the wiser, because you have so much detail that you can't make sense of it any more; or you can make sense of it, but you can't handle it, because the data volume is too large.

048 ● 105

An analogue projection of a building onto a set of sectional drawings, then, is on the one hand a simplification, it is also, by the same token and on the other hand, an abstraction, and quite possibly a welcome one too. Reducing real life information to its visual essence can make even a highly complicated structure easily and readily understandable, by representing it in a simple, schematic way. In order for this much simplified visual representation of the data in front of you to be useful and reliable though, you have to apply considerable expertise in selecting it: what you measure are exactly determined points. But if you choose them well, then a dozen or so of them may suffice: measure two corners of a room and then draw a line between them. The connecting line is defined by its start and end points, everything in-between is 'given' and requires no further definition or understanding. If you do this for all the relevant edges of the space, you get its dimensions, and those are your boundaries. What you are doing is use vectorised graphics in a selective, specific way. If you need to capture an ancient attic, you go there, look at it in detail, choose precisely which corners, beams, and joints are important to the roof staying up, and then you measure those and let everything else 'fall into place' around them, sure in the knowledge that if you do your job right, everything else will really just fall into place metaphorically, and not fall apart literally.

049A ● 105

049B ● 105

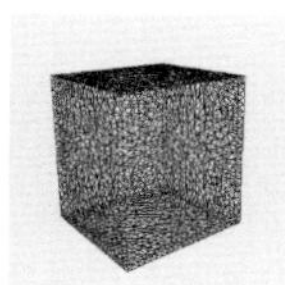

049C ● 105

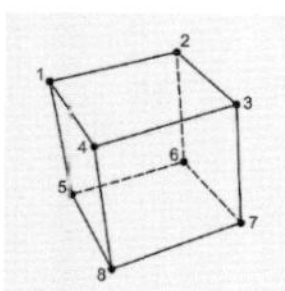

049D ● 105

The drawing or drawings that you get by necessity need to be to scale, and again you determine what scale is useful to you. A typical architectural drawing might have a scale of 1:50; but if it is a really large building you might go to a smaller scale, or vice versa.

And since all of this applies to all pre-digital existing context capture, these are therefore its main characteristics:

1 You spend time on site to analyse carefully the structure and sequence of the spaces you want to capture and then decide, based on your expertise and knowledge, what is important and what isn't and choose the important reference points to measure those, leaving out all the unimportant ones;
2 You use the very limited and selective data that you capture to create a strongly simplified abstraction of the physical object, whereby the very act of simplification and abstraction ideally helps you better understand the object, as it does away with irrelevant clutter;
3 Your abstraction on the two-dimensional plane of a sectional drawing renders the object to a predetermined scale that is fixed for this version of the representation. Creating a different scale version requires that you either replicate the process, or convert the existing scale to a new scale and then remake the drawings.

Apart from the physical manual measuring tools that we've already mentioned – the hand, the cubit, the yard stick, the measuring tape, to recap but those – what you had available to capture your existing context were principally the following instruments:

THEODOLITE
A *theodolite* measures angles on two planes only, but it can do so with great precision: on the vertical axis, where the position of a point is brought in relation to the *zenith* (the imaginary point directly above the instrument's anchor position) and/or any arbitrarily chosen reference points, and on the horizontal or *trunnion* axis, where the position of the same point is brought in relation to the position of one or several other reference points. With a little patience and using **triangulation** you can, by defining ■ ↖74 200↘
select positions of relevant points in relation to each other, get an accurate vectorised picture of your building or landscape features.

050 ○ 217

STEREOPHOTOGRAMMETRY
In nature, one of the most effective ways that allows an organism in position A to locate an object or another organism in position B with some degree of dependable accuracy, even if the former, or the latter, or both, should happen to be in motion, involves the principle that we recognise in *stereophotogrammetry:* our eyes continually look at everything from two slightly different positions and send the visual information to our brain, which then puts them together to form a three-dimensional image. It is not the only, but a good method to deal with things in three dimensions, and stereophotogrammetry mimics it by taking pictures from two (or more) different positions and then allowing us to work out the positions of any previously defined points relative to each other. The technique may be considered a forerunner of today's **multi-image photogrammetry**, ■ 270↘
which we'll also be discussing below.

051 ○ 217

LASER RANGEFINDER
A *laser rangefinder* uses a laser beam to measure the distance from the instrument to a given point. There are many different models on the market, both static on a tripod, and handheld, and their accuracy is dependent on the signal rate of the laser beam: the faster the laser pulses, the higher the precision.

The Swiss company Leica Geosystems pioneered the technology in the early 1990s, and with a retail price from around €100 to €1,500, their *DISTO* range of handheld laser scanners now uses Bluetooth and WiFi capable devices to communicate directly with smartphone or tablet apps to measure existing context both indoors and outdoors with an accuracy of up to 1/16th of an inch (about 1.6 mm).

TRANSITION TO DIGITAL

As the laser rangefinder shows, the world did not wake up one morning to decide, in one fell swoop: 'let's go digital.' And so digital data acquisition in the realm of existing context capture was not brought about by one single turnkey technology or in one decisive moment. Rather, there was a transition period, during which analogue technology gradually became more capable and started to communicate with computer programs, before purely digital methods of data capture became available.

TACHEOMETRY

In surveying, the *tachymeter* (also known as a *tacheometer* and not to be confused with either the tachymeter you find around the face of some more upmarket wrist watches, nor with the *tachometer* of a car that tells you how many rotations per minute the engine is doing) is an instrument not dissimilar to the theodolite, with the advantage that it uses the mathematics of the theodolite by itself and works out the distance of any given point in relation to its own position, without further input.

270↘

052 ○ 218

Tacheometry thus brings us one step closer to digitalisation, because it already does some basic computing on our behalf; but where it rests firmly in the 'old' methodology 'camp' is by still leaving the decision as to which specific points to measure with us. These would ordinarily be points that define things such as the edges of walls, the intersections between walls and ceilings and between walls and floors, or window fittings, thresholds, and steps, for example.

Like the theodolite and stereophotogrammetry, tacheometry is a *static terrestrial measuring method,* meaning that the surveyor, or geodesist, or architect, has to choose a fixed point on the ground from which to conduct a measurement, before moving on to another fixed point to obtain its coordinates in relation to the first one: the instrument itself can't be in motion while measuring. And it is also an optical measuring method, meaning that it requires a clear sight line between the point where the instrument is fixed and the point that is being measured.

For external surveying tasks, the tachymeter (as indeed, for a skilled geodesist, the theodolite) is a powerful and not overly problematic tool, because while it requires some expertise and a good deal of patience to choose your measuring and reference points (of which you need at least three) and to then traipse across the landscape from one point to the next to take your readings, there are usually plenty of options available to get a clear view and thus obtain a useful set of data. And (again as with the theodolite), if the process is carried out diligently, you get quite remarkable levels of accuracy, with a precision approaching around 1mm.

Inside an existing building, the method can be more troublesome, especially if you need to capture complex shapes or corners that are obscured by other parts of the structure, as you might find them in a narrow staircase, for example. Still, using tacheometry, it is possible to establish workable CAD drawings that show you where the walls, ceilings, floors, windows, and doors are, and an experienced team will know how to choose the minimum number of points required to yield practically applicable data sets. (Some care, incidentally, is required to create a clearly structured layering system from the outset, as you may otherwise end up with a confused mess of lines; so, for example, at the very least you would separate different floor levels out into discrete layers. And therein lies another drawback of the method: it requires a considerable degree of manual post-production that can be both time-consuming and tedious.)

FROM POINTS TO POINT CLOUDS

What today's actual digital data acquisition methods have in common is that they no longer expect you to select a few well-chosen points from which you can, by standard geometrical calculations, work out the shape of the object or structure you're looking at, but instead allow you to capture everything that's there, creating a three-dimensional image of what they can 'see'. Inversely, this also presents one of their principal limitations: digitalisation creates an *image*. A virtual version of the physical world that can then be analysed, understood, and worked with. But – with really just one or two noteworthy exceptions, which we'll look at – in the main, digitalisation captures only the *surface*. The virtual version we get of the physical reality is essentially 'hollow'.

053 ○ 218

This also nearly completes a parallel conceptual shift from *direct* to *indirect measuring* methods. Direct measuring methods are any of the methods we have so far discussed that entail you taking measurements directly on site from the object you are capturing. The use of measuring tapes and laser rangefinders are both direct measuring methods, because although one is manual and the other electronic, in both cases you actually measure the real life distance 'in the field' or inside the object itself to get your data. Indirect measuring methods, by contrast, are those that allow you to take an image (or several) of the object but require that you measure or calculate the distances between relevant points from this image, scaling them up to obtain their life-size values. Photogrammetry is an indirect measuring method, because although it predates digitalisation as we know it today by a hundred and fifty years, it relies on the accuracy and precision of the images taken to obtain applicable values. Today's digital data acquisition tools in the majority are indirect, since they mostly capture images – possibly very detailed ones – and work out the measurements from those images, rather than measuring any onsite distances.

The fact that digitalisation captures 'hollow' images that then provide the raw material for indirect measuring means that the work and the expertise of the person or team capturing the existing context shifts from preparation, job planning, and on-location execution, to post-production. The methods we're about to look at are fast on site, they can scan a room in minutes and a large building in a matter of hours, but they make it necessary for someone with an understanding of what they are doing to spend long hours at a computer afterwards, filling in the void, so to speak.

A *laser scan,* for example, will tell us with great precision where in the structure there is a wall. It will also tell us how thick the wall is and where it meets with the floor and the ceiling. It will tell us that there is a floor and there is a ceiling and just exactly how much empty space there is between them. But it will not tell us what the wall is made of: is it plaster board or brick? If it's brick, is it a standard 24 cm brick with 1.5 cm plaster either side, or is it an unusual, perhaps old or special type of slimmer brick with more plaster on either side. Or is it concrete? Where, behind the ceiling, are the beams and the joints? What are they made of? Granted, a theodolite doesn't tell us any of these things either, but it also doesn't 'pretend' to give us the whole picture. With a vectorised drawing we *know,* because we've already done a visual survey and selected our reference points, that we are getting a highly abstracted version of what's actually there. With a laser scan it looks, at first glance, as if we get a genuine representation of what's there, but that is deceptive.

This shift in effort towards post-production is not unique to architecture and digital data acquisition, of course. If you were an independent filmmaker in the 1970s or 80s, one of your greatest and most important budget items would have been film stock. It was expensive and therefore limited. So making your piece of avant-garde or *noir* cinema, you would need to spend a considerable amount of time and effort (and, if you had it, expertise), planning your shoot. You would be careful not only about choosing your setups, but you would also rehearse and then roll the camera only once you were quite certain that you were likely to get a usable take. Today, many a film school may recommend that you still do the exact same thing, but the reality is that you have no film stock: you can shoot everything. You can shoot rehearsals and alternative versions of the scene; you can improvise and go for extreme angles simply to try them out. As with so many other things we talk about in this book, being able to do any of this is not new: filmmakers have always chosen extreme angles, and many have improvised in the past. But you put much more effort and time into the preparation of the shoot, so you didn't run through your expensive film stock before you had everything you needed in the can. Now, you can delegate the effort to the edit suite. The only problem with shooting everything is that you then have to weed through all the footage and do all your selecting and pruning in post. Similarly, with digital data acquisition, you have to still at one point in the proceedings decide what *matters.* And now you do so after you've captured everything. While before, you selected points that you assumed (or knew) would matter, and then constructed from these very few points a picture that you already knew (or assumed) was relevant, now you end up with a *point cloud* which does not contain select, relevant points, but all the points that your instrument was able to 'see'. And these points are both 'discrete' – they are all separate from each other – and 'stupid': they are just there, they don't 'know' about each other, nor is their relationship with each other or anything else 'meaningful.' And you capture 1:1. That was not the case before either: before, as we have seen, you made scale drawings. Now, the data you capture is not scaled, it goes into your database or file straight from your measuring tool, and then you do with it whatever you please. If you look at it on your tablet, it will be one size, if you look at it on your desktop computer with its extra large external display, it will be a different size, and it absolutely doesn't matter.

And there then, in summary, lies the 'paradigm shift', if we want to call it that, which has occurred: you used to measure what you needed to know, which meant deciding beforehand what that was, so you could take accurate, relevant readings that contained very small sets of data from which you extrapolated all the rest. Now, you measure everything, which means deciding afterwards what, among the very large sets of data you obtain, is of use to you and relevant: you extract from what you have, which is everything, the information you actually need.

There are genuine advantages to this also: for example, it's difficult to miss something if you capture everything. You may only realise upon closer inspection of your virtual imagery that there is a particularly important feature that you simply didn't notice before. Since you have the data, you can zoom in on it and decide retroactively that this is exactly the one element that changes everything you thought you knew about this particular piece of architecture. Also, whereas the level of abstraction you needed to work with previously left out not only features and detail, but also colour and texture, contemporary capturing methods give you these as well. Depending on what you are dealing with, this can be tremendously useful to have to hand. Say you're digitalising the Alhambra in Granada, Spain: here, the mosaics and *mocárabe* form an integral part of the palace: capturing them completely and in every detail may be essential to doing any kind of restoration work that respects and reflects the original, for example.

DATA QUALITY

The usefulness of any data is dependent to some large extent on its quality. And as we have observed, more is not necessarily better. In fact, too much data can – not only, but especially if it is of poor quality – be an obstacle to insight, rather than pave the way towards it. But when we talk about the quality of data, we mean not only its inherent (or presumed) usefulness to any task we may have in mind (as in: very useful data equals 'good' or 'high quality'; not very useful data equals 'poor' or 'low quality'), but simply also what *kind* of data we have, because depending on what *kind* of data we have, we can or cannot do certain things that may or may not be important to us.

This means that different types of data and 'quality grades' lend themselves to different purposes or, if you like, applications. And while there is neither a clear-cut delineation between 'types of data', nor a standard way of grading quality levels, we can still make some broad observations. For example, high precision capture is capable of accurately reflecting amorphous forms which result in intricate meshes. These are large data sets with complex structures that are particularly useful when applied to extremely valuable heritage sites, where every detail is in fact of importance; in archaeology, where insights into very old structures can be gleaned from exact renderings of very small details; in architectural sculpture and for buildings from the romantic, gothic, and baroque eras where, much as with the Alhambra we cited above, decorative and structural elements in small detail may be critical to understanding the object as a whole.

054 ○ 218

Contrast this to a more generalised quality of data capture, where you accept a reduction in the level of precision towards the kind of tolerance you find in regular construction, because you are dealing with structured, standardised parts and decorative elements. This yields signally smaller data sets that consist of axes, grids, orthogonalities, and symmetries: the essential building blocks of BIM (Building Information Modelling). □ 507↘

This kind of data quality may not only be sufficient, but in actual fact more useful than the much higher precision quality described above when dealing with buildings of the Renaissance, or periods such as classicism, historicism, and modernity; their lines, patterns, and features being entirely suited to the method, therefore making faster, more efficient work possible, without any discernible loss in reliability.

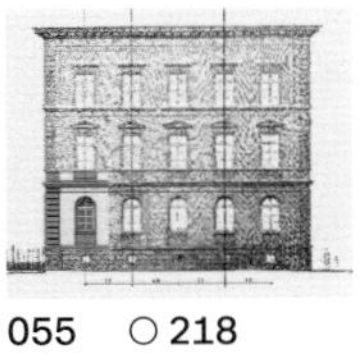

055 ○ 218

We have previously identified one of the challenges we face with contemporary digitalisation technology: a point cloud, for all its sheer data volume, does not give me any insights into what is behind the surface, let alone about the way in which this surface and what is behind it were put together. The speed with which I can obtain the data, its accuracy, and precision can be breathtaking, but the quantity of the data can also make it extremely time-consuming and difficult to get at the essence of what I need to know. And for much of what I need to know I have to analyse the data manually: there is no algorithm – as yet – to do it for me (although it may only be a question of time before there will be).

So if I'm interested in historical construction methods, for example, and I need to understand the various phases a building went through, the materials that were used, and the techniques that were employed to hold them together, then I have a lot of work cut out for myself, because I now have enormous quantities of data that I need to plough through and make sense of before I can do anything else. And not only do I have a lot of data that is pertinent, I also have a lot of incidental information that I may simply not need, because I have inadvertently captured every fence, every shrub, every lamp post, and, if I'm unlucky, every car that's parked out in the car park too.

And perhaps, before we go on to describing today's digital data acquisition methods in turn, there is one more thing that is worth bearing in mind: if I work with existing context – and we started out by positing that I almost invariably will – then in order to do this existing context justice I have to somehow try and get into the head of the architect or master builder who put it there. Because even if I want to radically change it, I still need to understand what it was that they were doing and why they were doing it, not only so that I can honour it and treat it with respect, but also so that I know what to expect when I start changing things. A defensive structure like a medieval castle will have been put there with completely different priorities in mind – and therefore been built in a completely different way – to an industrial factory in the 19th century. If that sounds a little obvious then that's because it is, but it nevertheless bears keeping in mind: we're not only talking about the building techniques and materials that were available in different eras, but about mindsets, cultural expression, and purpose. And to do this – to get into the architect's or master builder's head and understand what they were about – we still, in fact more than ever, need human knowledge, insight, and expertise.

METHODS

We have already described the theodolite, stereophotogrammetry, and tacheometry, as well as the laser rangefinder, these all being capturing methods that predate digitalisation as we understand it today, even though they are all still in use, and stereophotogrammetry has evolved into one of the main methods we're about to list, *multi-image photogrammetry*.

We also – a little in passing – mentioned the difference between *static* terrestrial and *kinetic* or *mobile* methods, static methods being those that make it necessary for me to find fixed points from which to take individual measurements, whereas mobile methods are those that allow me to roam while doing the measuring. It is somewhat in the nature of things that mobile methods are, to us today, quite a bit more interesting than static ones, and as you might expect there are some overlaps.

Finally, we have made a distinction between *direct* and *indirect* measuring methods, direct methods being those that measure distances directly on site in the 'real world', and indirect methods being those that measure distances in the image obtained from the data set. We can add to these any method that measures in a non-destructive, non-invasive way anything that cannot physically be reached.

056 ● 106

The difference between these indirect measuring methods lies mainly in the kind of electromagnetic waves that are being emitted and/or received: with **Ground Penetrating Radar (GPR)**, for example, they are in the invisible spectrum and therefore have to be translated into an image that we can visually interpret. If they lie in the visible light spectrum, we receive a picture or series of pictures that can then be assembled and thus become the source of information for a three-dimensional representation, as is the case with **image stitching**, for example, where individual pictures are lined up to form a large panoramic image to scale.

Which leads us to the following main methods for existing context capture by digitalisation, starting with those that only *receive* signals, in these cases light waves:

MULTI-IMAGE PHOTOGRAMMETRY / STRUCTURE FROM MOTION (SFM)
In *multi-image photogrammetry,* also known as *Structure from Motion (SfM)*, a series of photographs (numbering anything from dozens to hundreds or thousands) are taken of an object from different angles, and a computer software is then tasked with generating from these 2D images a virtual 3D model.

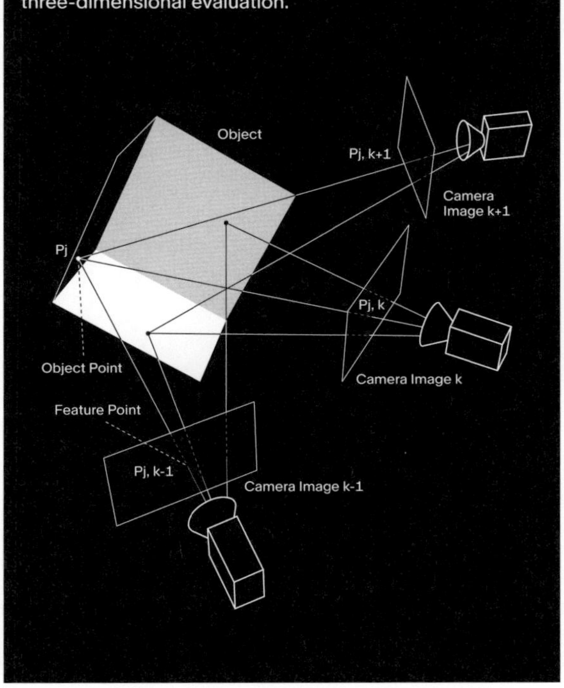

Photogrammetry using three digital images to determine the coordinates of select points for an object's three-dimensional evaluation.

What makes this method particularly interesting is that these source images do not have to have been taken with the purpose of photogrammetry in mind. As far back as 2009, researchers at the University of Washington were able to use some 150,000 individual pictures taken by tourists and posted by them individually to *Flickr* with the hashtag #Roma or #Rome to construct a working fly-through 3D model of Rome's principal landmarks, using, just as Alberti did in his survey of Rome, the Coliseum as their anchor point.

057 ● 106

LSD-SLAM: LARGE SCALE DIRECT MONOCULAR SLAM (SIMULTANEOUS LOCALISATION AND MAPPING)
Developed by the Computer Vision Group at the Department of Computer Science of the Technical University of Munich as an open-source project, *LSD-SLAM* uses a small camera to map and track objects of any size, building a virtual 3D model on a computer in realtime.

Having gone from 2D imagery to 3D point clouds, we can also reverse the process:

ORTHOIMAGING FROM A LASER SCAN
It is possible to arrive at a geometrically correct 2D image (meaning that it has the same accuracy as, for instance, a plan or a map) from a 3D image that has been generated by a laser scan.

058 ● 106

THERMAL IMAGING
Thermography uses infrared thermal imaging and thus offers one of few genuinely non-destructive methods capable of yielding insights beyond the surface and outline shape of a structure, giving clues as to the types of materials that have been used where, for example.

059 ○ 218

MOTION CAPTURE
Motion capture encompasses a range of methods that capture any kind of motion and translate it into a computer readable format that makes it possible to analyse, record, and manipulate these movements, and to use them to control applications.

Typical examples are the transformation of human movements to computer-generated 3D models, or head and eye tracking for the purpose of analysis or to control screen operations, or stereoscopic motion tracking.

060 ● 107

Performance capture is a specialist motion capture method that deals with human facial expressions, hand gestures, and other limb movements. This is widely used in the film industry to animate computer generated characters, such as Gollum, played by performance capture artist pioneer Andy Serkis in Peter Jackson's film trilogy of J R R Tolkien's *Lord of the Rings*.

MAGNETOMETER

A *magnetometer* measures the strength and, depending on the device, also direction of the magnetic field in a specific location, and is therefore capable of detecting magnetic material, such as iron. It lends itself particularly to *geophysical surveys:* the examination of a location for magnetic and gravitational fields, seismic activity, and *geophysical waves.*

GNNS/GPS SURVEYING

The GPS (Global Positioning System) is one – and
■ 493↘ possibly the best known – of several **Global Navigation Satellite Systems (GNNS)** that use satellite navigation technology to identify the exact location on planet Earth of individual objects, markers, vehicles, or people. These find their use also in archaeology (to map objects as they are being found, for example), land surveys, and road planning and construction, where electronic position markers are used to locate relevant coordinate points to within one centimetre.

DRAIN PIPE INSPECTION

Drain pipe inspection offers a specialist method to quickly capture the underground drain pipe outlets in a location. A pipe crawler, equipped with camera and satellite navigation, travels through the pipes and sends its location to a mobile receiver, such as a laptop computer. In Germany, the system can draw on a database of 50.5 million ground plans to immediately
■ show up every building in its immediate vicinity.

■

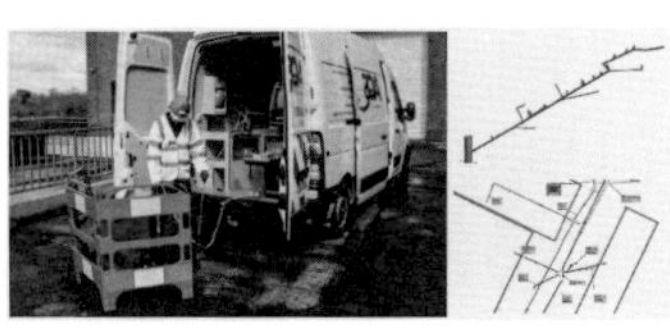

061 ● 107

The following are methods that send and receive signals, such as light beams or radio waves:

516↘ LIDAR/LASER SCANNING/3D SCANNING

Short for either *'Light Detection and Ranging'* or *'Light Imaging, Detection and Ranging', Lidar*, which you'll also find spelt as *LiDAR, LIDAR* or *LaDAR* (for *'Laser Detection and Ranging')*, is a method similar to radar, but using a laser beam rather than radio waves to measure the distance the signal travels, based on how long it takes to bounce back to the device.

A laser scanner is really a tachymeter that 'works on its own'. It can measure points at your desired density and then output a 3D image of everything it has 'seen', resulting in a point cloud.

Typically, the scanner 'reads' or scans the surface line by line, and there are variations both in the definition as well as in the instrument's capacity to not only register the shape, but to also measure the intensity of the reflected signal. Scanners that can do so are known as imaging laser scanners, as they produce photo-realistic planar representations of the given context.

There are static as well as kinetic/mobile laser scanners, and what they all have in common is that they scan the situation without discernment, meaning that they scan everything that is in their 'field of vision', whether it is relevant to the object being captured or not.

062 ● 107

063 ● 108

NAVVIS

NavVis is the name of a German capture system that uses small trolleys to scan large or complex indoor spaces.

064 ● 108

Ground based mobile systems like these quickly come up against obstacles though, such as staircases. The next logical step in the development is therefore:

AIRBORNE LASER SCANNING (ALS)

Airborne Laser Scanning (ALS) puts laser scanning technology onto small aircraft – typically a drone technically known as either a *UAV (Unmanned Aerial Vehicle)* or **UAS (Unmanned Aircraft System)** – to survey the topography of a defined area of land surface.

It combines on itself three elements: a GNNS (Global Navigation Satellite System) receiver records the spot position of the craft; an **Inertial Navigation System (INS)** determines the flight position (angles across, perpendicular, and along the flight axis); and a laser scanner sends out a laser beam at determined angles, measuring the time it takes to travel a given distance.

065 ● 108

TIME OF FLIGHT (TOF) CAMERA
A *Time of Flight (ToF) camera* is a 3D camera system that measures the *time of flight* that a light beam takes to cover a given distance. Since light travels at a constant speed, the camera is able to calculate the distance for each image point, and it can do so for many image points at once: this gives it an advantage over laser scanning, since it doesn't have to scan the scene line by line, but is able to take an immediate snapshot of the context.

Compared to other methods, ToF camera technology is still in its infancy, but as of 2017, available systems were able to cover a range from 20–30 cm to about 40 m, with a precision of about 1 cm. Image resolution is still low, but compared to other 3D scanning methods, image frequency, at up to 160 exposures per second, can be very high.

STRUCTURE SENSOR
Structure Sensor is a 3D augmented reality technology that can be used either with handheld devices (such as tablet computers or smartphones) or as wearable headsets/glasses, to scan or capture spaces or to create enhanced or mixed reality experiences. This makes it a crossover technology that is not specifically aimed at architecture and construction professionals, but also at a growing market in the creative, gaming, and entertainment industries.

■ ↖66 465↘

■ ↖66 431↘

066A ● 109

066B ● 109

GROUND PENETRATING RADAR (GPR)
OR RADIO ECHO SOUNDING (RES)
Ground Penetrating Radar (GPR) uses radar pulses to generate a visual representation of what lies beneath the ground and, as a non-destructive method, is particularly useful in archaeology and to establish a geophysical profile of a site, and, as *Radio Echo Sounding (RES)*, in the study of ice and glaciers.

APPS
There are a raft of consumer apps available for smartphones that are capable of measuring floor plans of rooms or entire buildings quickly, by tracking the movements of the device: you simply touch the walls with your phone and the app works out the dimensions of your space.

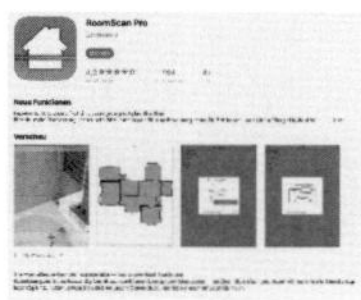

067 ● 109

The Outlook

Where we are most likely headed is towards a world which is digitalised in its entirety. This is not a utopian statement or wishful thinking, and we're not saying it's even by necessity a 'good thing', we just think it's likely. City planners, national governments, policy makers, international institutions, heritage organisations, and – quite possibly ahead of everyone else – leading commercial information technology players, such as Google, are working tirelessly, for different reasons and with varying ambitions, towards a fully captured existing context. And there is no reason to assume that this drive towards digitalising our cities, towns, and villages, our countrysides and our wildernesses is going to abate any time soon. Energy companies want to know where they can dig for resources or install power plant, environmentalists want evidence for why it would be better if they didn't. Investors want to know where they can convert sites into lucrative residential developments, neighbourhood associations want to prove that doing so will destroy their communities. There are an infinite number or reasons why we may want the built-up world around us, as well as the as yet untouched world, at our fingertips, ready to be analysed, understood, and either altered or protected from interference. Geopositioning systems and satellite scanning already achieve breathtaking levels of definition: from space it is now possible to capture the Earth at a pixel size of five centimetres across approximately. We are not far from reducing this to pixels that are one centimetre across. So full digitalisation is, we venture, the big picture outlook.

On a more applied, practical level, we can imagine that the as yet generally fairly weak link between digital data acquisition and digital architecture, and by extension digital manufacturing, will grow stronger. In our chapter on 3D Printing we mention medical uses for this technology and just how far advanced these are: it is no problem, today, to take a scan of a person's jaw, for example, and print a broken or missing part with a couple of teeth, to replace it. This is also imaginable in architecture: say you have an historically significant building that has been damaged by an earthquake but remains structurally intact, it may prove efficient and economical to draw on a digital scan of a similar or identical section in the same building and print this out on site to at least temporarily fix it. This may not satisfy as a lasting restoration, because heritage protection may require that original materials and craftsmanship are applied to treat a damaged site of significance, but as a prosthetic it may prevent the structure from collapsing and thus save it from much greater damage, while a more permanent solution is found. And there are, as we discuss in our chapter on Digital Manufacturing, any number of production methods (such as milling, lathing, shaping, or grinding) that

□ 439↘

□ 405↘

are perfectly capable of using authentic, historically appropriate materials, such as wood, stone, or metal on a large, 1:1 scale, directly from a virtual model, and therefore scan.

An at least partial convergence of 3D scanning and 3D printing machinery is likely too, and that means more people in more situations will be able to scan and print in one go, which makes the interaction between digitalisation and digital manufacturing faster, more natural, and more dynamic. And we predict a much greater fusion of augmented reality, experiential, and 3D capturing technologies, quite possibly with uses that we cannot, as yet, properly foresee.

In any case, the dedicated, specialist job of the geodesist is disappearing fast. Possibly not completely: government departments and city authorities may want to retain some highly specialist expertise for planning and preservation purposes, but in general, architects will not need to call on a professional to do surveys and inspections for them: all they really need is a smartphone with an app, or a handheld device that any of their juniors knows how to operate, because, as we've seen, the detailed analysis does not have to happen on site, it can happen back at the office, and take as much time as is required.

And it won't be just architects who will have digitalisation software on their devices as a matter of course. This is another development that we mention elsewhere in this *Atlas:* what used to be specialist tools for skilled professionals are turning into mainstream consumer level technologies that people just use, because they can. And so apps for the smartphone, such as *Structure Sensor* are likely to gain much wider distribution. This is not without potential problems. Take security, for instance. If all I need is a smartphone with an app to scan a space and get highly accurate, usable data about its windows, doors, access points, locks, wiring, and pipes, am I not making the space vulnerable? If a small drone can take not just aerial shots but do an in-depth laser scan of a building, such as a ministerial residence, or a defence installation, or a prison, or a power plant, or a royal palace, or a hazardous site, could someone with ill intentions not put this to unethical use?

Meanwhile, the data that is being captured, incessantly, in ever greater detail and definition, is not going away: it's being stored, and made accessible, to everyone. Whereas in the past, you might have been able to go to your local library or to your land registry to obtain the 2D ground plans or some drawings of the neighbourhood you were planning to design a new development for, now you have at your fingertips *Google Maps*, *OpenStreetMap*, *CityMapper*, and an array of public and private databanks that are either freely accessible or that can be purchased on the market.

And at a very fundamental level, all of this raises a question that we find ourselves confronted with over and over again: how do we edit our digital world and manage it? Can we manage it? Should we even attempt to? Or should we just swim in it, go with the flow, surf on it? How do I handle this abundance of data? In a world where everything is possible, what do I actually want to do?...

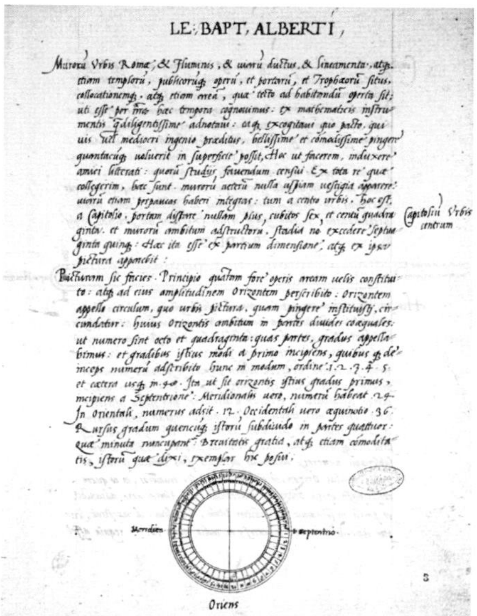
LE: BAPT. ALBERTI,

046 ● 095
Autograph from *Descriptio urbis Romae (The Delineation of Rome)* by Leon Battista Alberti.

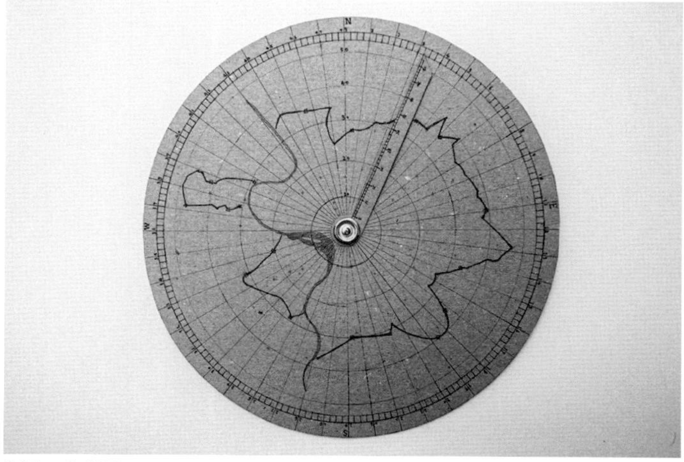

047 ● 095
The 'horizon' instrument that Leon Battista Alberti describes in his *Descriptio urbis Romae (The Delineation of the City of Rome).* [Zhongyuan Dai/McGill University]

048 ● 096
The south facing facade of Wetzlar Cathedral, after 1858. The arrow marks the spot where Albrecht Meydenbauer had his accident that led him to develop photogrammetry. [Albrecht Meydenbauer]

049A ● 097
A cube represented as: a raster dataset in a JPEG file. [Series 049A–049D: Nikolaus Zieske]

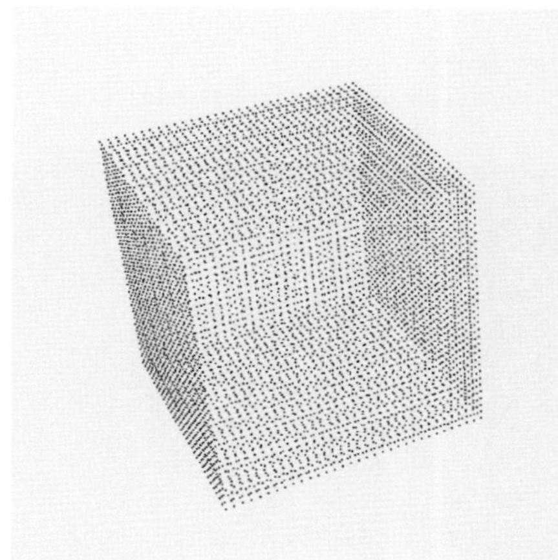

049B ● 097
A point cloud. [NZ]

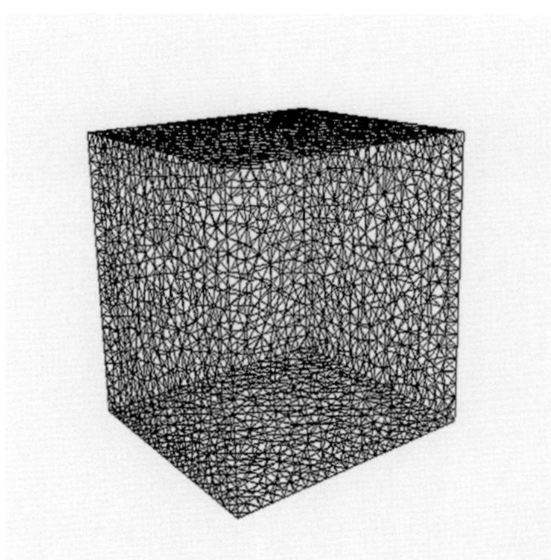

049C ● 097
A triangulated mesh. [NZ]

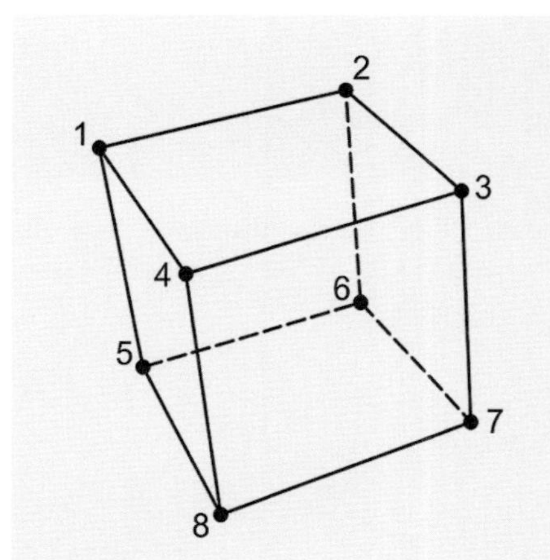

049D ● 097
And as a vector drawing, defined by only eight points. [NZ]

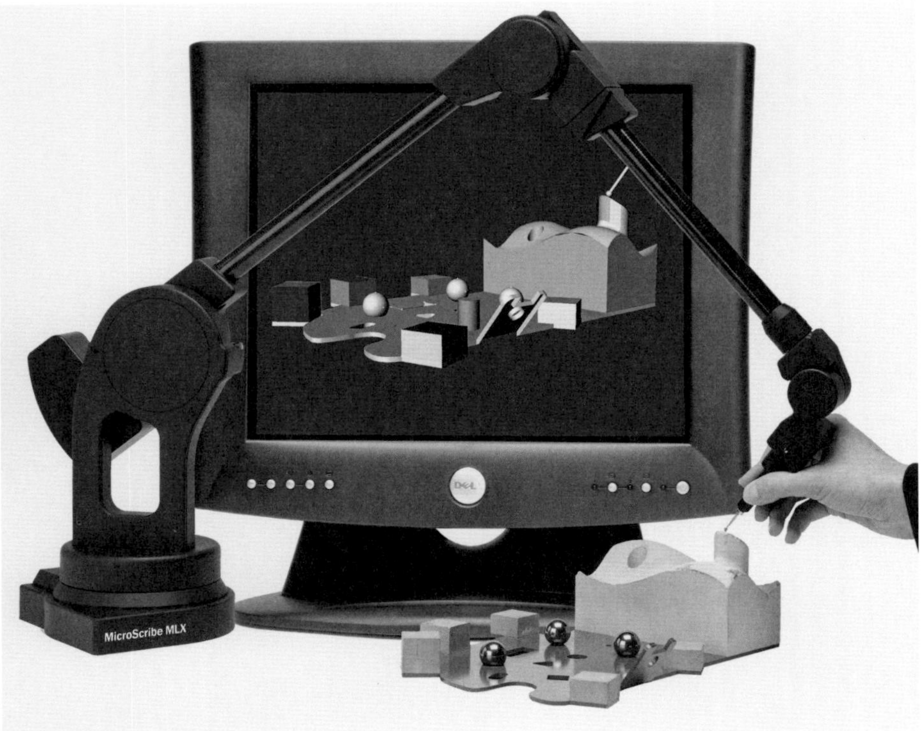

056 ● 101
Direct measuring of an object, using *Microscribe*. [Businesswire]

057 ● 101
Building Rome in a day: this digital model of the Coliseum was assembled by stitching together tourist photographs. [Nikolaus Zieske]

058 ● 101
Orthoimage, generated from a point cloud. [Nikolaus Zieske]

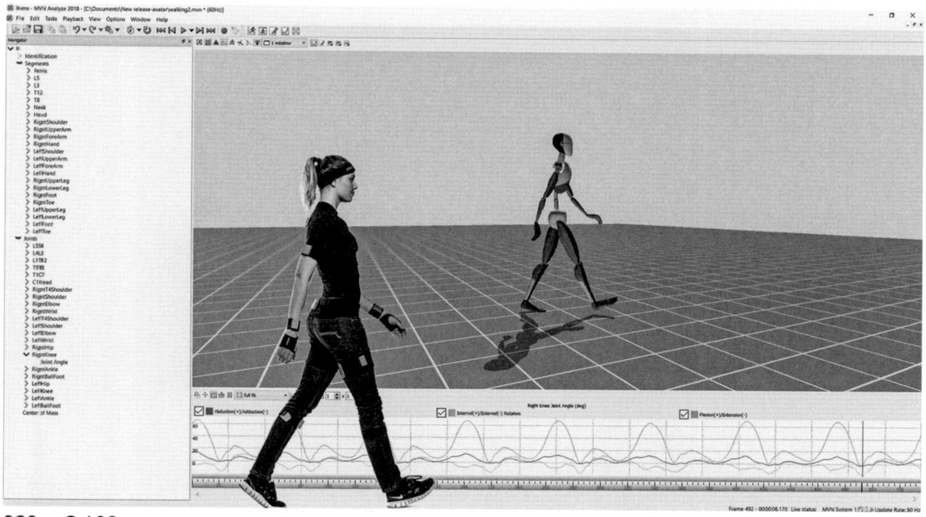

060 ● 102
Transformation of human movements to computer-generated 3D models. [Xsens]

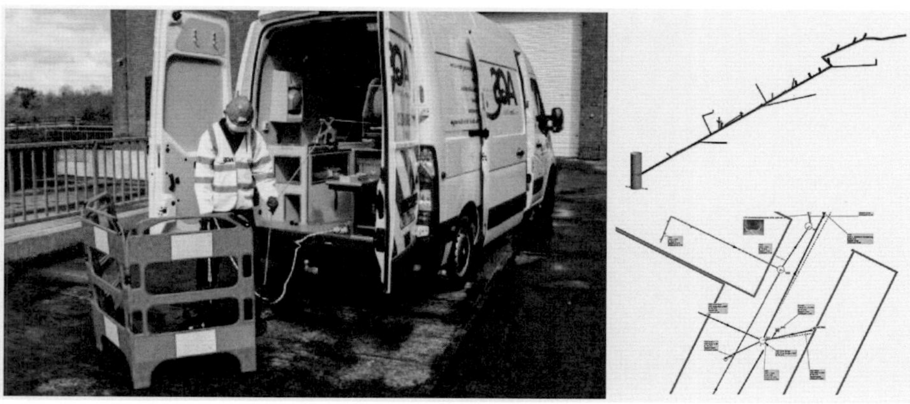

061 ● 102
Drain pipe survey and mapping. [Nikolaus Zieske]

062 ● 102
Static laser scanning with reference spheres. [Nikolaus Zieske]

063 ● 102
Static laser scanning with a point cloud scan image. [Nikolaus Zieske]

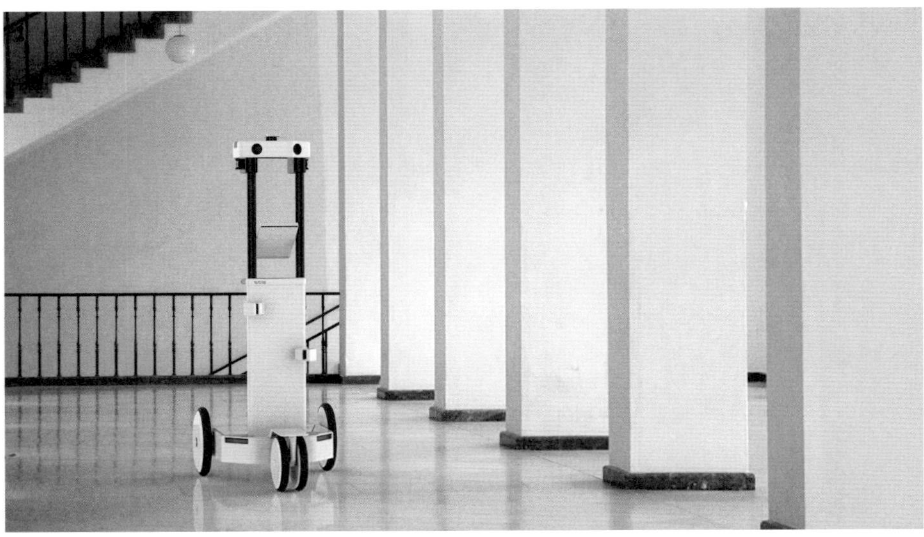

064 ● 102
NavVis – mobile indoor laser scanning. [*NavVis*]

065 ● 102
Unmanned Aircraft System (UAS) puts laser scanning technology onto a drone. [RIEGL]

066A ● 103
Structure Sensor is a 3D augmented reality technology that can be used with handheld devices. [Nikolaus Zieske]

066B ● 103

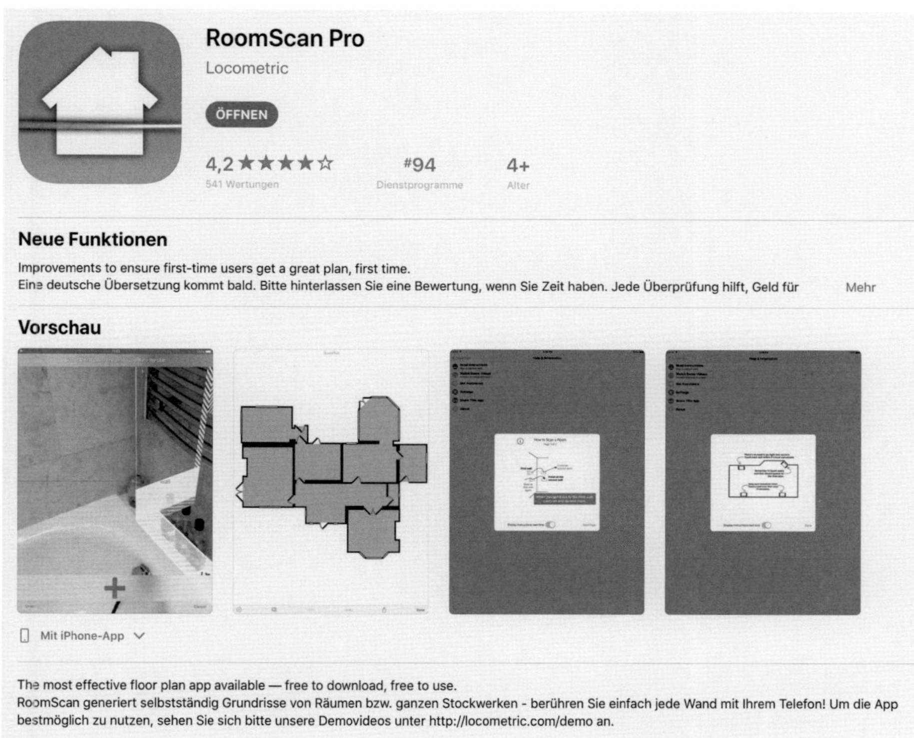

067 ● 103
RoomScan – capture by smartphone app.

Digital Design Strategies

Ursula Kirschner and Sven Schneider

- C Alexander: *Notes on the Synthesis of Form*, 1964
- J W Getzels & M Csikszentmihalyi: *Scientific Creativity. Science Journal, 3, 80–84*, 1967
- C M Eastman: *Cognitive Processes and Ill-Defined Problems: a Case Study from Design*, in: D E Walker & L M Norton (Eds.): *Proceedings of the Joint International Conference on Artificial Intelligence*, 1969
- A Newell & H Simon: *Human Information Processing*, 1972
- E Neufert: *Bauentwurfslehre*, 1973
- H A Simon: *The Structure of Ill-Structured Problems. Artificial Intelligence, 4, 181–201*, 1973
- H Stachowiak: *Allgemeine Modelltheorie*, 1973
- H W J Rittel & M M Webber: *Dilemmas in a General Theory of Planning. Policy Sciences, 4(2), 155–169*, 1973
- R Wittkower: *Grundlagen der Architektur im Zeitalter des Humanismus*, 1973
- W Hogarth: *Analyse der Schönheit* (facsimile of the First Edition, London 1753), translated by J Heininger, Dresden/Basel, 119 f., 1974
- W J Mitchell: *The Theoretical Foundation of Computer-Aided Architectural Design. Environment and Planning B: Planning and Design, 2(2), 127–150*, 1975
- G Stiny, W J Mitchell: *The Palladian Grammar*, in: *Environment and Planning B, 5 , 5–18*, 1978
- A D Radford & J S Gero: *Multicriteria Optimization in Architectural Design*, in: J S Gero (Ed.): *Design Optimization*, 1985
- Y E Kalay: *Computability of Designs*, 1987
- U Flemming: *Knowledge Representation and Acquisition in the LOOS System, Building and Environment, 25(3), 209–219*, 1990
- H W J Rittel: *Planen, Entwerfen, Design: Ausgewählte Schriften zu Theorie und Methodik*, 1992
- R E Oxman, R M Oxman: *Refinement and Adaption: Two Paradigms of Form Generation in CAAD*, in: *CAAD Future ´91 Conference Proceedings, Zürich, 322 f.*, 1992
- G Schmitt: *Architektur mit dem Computer*, 1996
- O Akin & R Sen: *Navigation Within a Structured Search Space in Layout Problems, Environment and Planning B: Planning and Design, 23 (4), 421–442*, 1996
- M Seraphin: *Das Maß der Dinge in: db 10/97*, 1997
- M Wigley: *Die Architektur der Atmosphäre*, in: *Daidalos 68*, 1998
- Y E Kalay: *Architecture's New Media: Principles, Theories, and Methods of Computer-Aided Design*, 2004

Overview

"Architecture," the Brazilian architect Oscar Niemeyer (1907–2012) is quoted as saying, "begins in the head. You think about a problem, imagine the building, and then you see the solution." And, notably, he continues: "Normally I develop a project in the head. The pencil then simply becomes the vehicle for transportation."

What is this process that gets us from the spark of an idea to a structure that stands in the world and that people can live, work, and move about in, watch a game of rugby in, or sit in to listen to a string quartet by Mozart? How do we get from the 'problem' as Niemeyer calls it – and as we, quite deliberately, will be discussing it in a moment – to the 'solution'? It may be the case that for some this does happen mostly in the head, and the pencil is merely a 'vechicle for transportation'. But for many others, the 'pencil' is clearly more than that. What exactly it is goes to the heart of the question we want to ask with this chapter on Digital Design Strategies.

Because either way – whether it happens in the head, or on paper, or elsewhere; and whether or not we view it as a case of solving a problem – if there is to be architecture, design needs to happen. Often it needs to happen whether we feel inspired or not. Mostly it needs to happen in a setting or context we may not or only partially be familiar with. Always it needs to happen to some sort of end, whether that end is a residential development, a sport stadium, or a concert hall, or a concept for our own practice and delectation. And so that begs the question: are there, or can there be, any *strategies* that help us make design happen? For us, writing an *Atlas of Digital Architecture,* the question most specifically arises: are there any *digital* design strategies? And in what way, if at all, are they different to any other strategies that may exist? And central to our whole discussion: to what extent do *digital,* as opposed to traditional or analogue, design methodologies and therefore strategies influence and shape the design and therefore the architecture that is being created? In short: what impact do digital design strategies have on us as architects and on the world we help shape?

In that fact alone, that architecture shapes the world we live in, lies the great importance we attach to design and anything that might be considered a strategy towards it: the process, the methodology; the exchange and development; the evolution of it. And there is no question that architecture does shape our world: it does so manifestly with actual physical objects that become part of our built environment, and it does so culturally as images, models, and ways of thinking. So design – specifically architectural design – really matters. Which means that how we get to this design matters too.

In late 2008 to early 2009, the *Architekturzentrum Wien* (the Austrian Museum of Architecture), ran an exhibition under the title *Architektur beginnt im Kopf [Architecture Begins in the Head] – The Making of Architecture* to show, "how individually architects use their tools to work, operate and design." The attendant description makes for fascinating reading:

> "While people in one Paris architecture office shoot at clay blocks, another office breeds orchids for inspiration and prefers to design using words. The architects concerned are R&Sie(n), and Lacaton & Vassal. Ben van Berkel says of himself that he is passionate about using tools, and describes the role of the architect as that of a John Cage-style conductor in the middle of an orchestra. Gary Chang (Edge Design Institute, Hong Kong) specialises in fast-track design and enjoys using colourful Lego bricks to build small models that can quickly be taken apart. In complete contrast to this, Atelier Bow-Wow in Tokyo makes 50 to 60 scale models per building that document every alteration in the development of the space with extreme precision. With 1,600 employees among the largest architecture offices in the world, the firm SOM Skidmore, Owings & Merrill talks about the design process and the difficulties with wind in the development of the tallest building in the world, the Burj Dubai (completion in 2009). While Lux Guyer, one of the first Swiss □ ↖111
> woman architects to have her own office, liked to design from her bed using a small wooden triangle, Lina Bo Bardi, who was originally from Italy before emigrating to Brazil after the second world war, always had her studio in a Portacabin directly on the construction site – where she solved technical details together with her craftspeople, sometimes entirely without plans. In 1973 Yona Friedman threw the computer out of his studio, saying that it dictated too much to him. The key design tools for Alvar Aalto, who developed his ideas in the drawing process, was his legendary 6B, a yellow Koh-i-Noor retractable pencil, and Finnish sketching paper made by Tervakoski that is still being produced today. An old Aalto sketch on the back of the Klubi 77 Klubb cigarettes he smoked incessantly is also among the exponents in the show."

So, for Niemeyer's 'pencil' above, read any number of possible means by which an idea may be 'transported' from the head to an expressed reality: sketches, drawings, models, and virtually anything else that helps it take shape and materialise, from a simple conversation to the fully immersive virtual ■ ↖66 272↘
reality experience. People use sewing machines to develop their ideas, not to mention the plethora of means that may not so much express as feed the design and thus become part of it: books, newspapers, films, pieces of music, natural features, the orchids we've encountered above... One way or another, what starts out in the head takes shape and needs to be shared and communicated. And today we take it for granted that at least part of this process – in some cases most or even all of it – is either achieved with or aided by computers.

Where, though, does digitality begin, and where does it end when it comes to design? As early as 1970, Greek-American architect and later founding investor of *Wired* magazine Nicholas Negroponte (b.1943) postulated a hypothetical 'design machine' which analysed specific construction tasks and, in an

interactive process, established for it legal and structural requirements to put out a series of possible alternatives. In a dialogue with the machine, the user would then choose from these a preliminary design, which was subsequently refined and completed. While we are not quite at that stage of automated design yet,
■ 135↘ we are, with parametric design methodology not really all that far off either. We touch extensively on
■ 164↘ Artificial Intelligence (AI) in our chapter on Big Data &
□ 549↘ Machine Learning, so our focus here will not be on this 'extreme' or extremely advanced end of digital design, but rather on digitally assisted *strategies* for design.

Even so, whenever we talk about 'machine learning', 'artificial intelligence', or 'automated design', we can almost sense a collective shudder go down the metaphorical spine of a creative community that is often, and often justifiably, wary of the computer 'taking over' from humans. German architect Oswald Mathias Ungers (1926–2007) expressed this, and a specific danger he saw in automated processes, back in 1985: "The primeval hut, for example, which was assembled from poles and brushwood, over the course of history has evolved into the most refined edifice of the temple, where each component draws on a once meaningful or simple combination of materials, but then acquires highest levels of quality and completion of the human spirit. That, in reality, is design. If you left this to the machine, you would forever rely on what already exists, you would never dare embark on the adventure of the new."

068 ● 125

This touches on the fundamental question we, as architects, or any artist using increasingly sophisticated – ultimately perhaps 'intelligent' or near 'intelligent' – software are bound to ask ourselves: what exactly is creation? Where does the new, the original, the extraordinary and inventive, actually stem from? To what extent can it, must, or should it draw from what has been done before? How much of it is evolution, learning over the generations, and adapting to changing realities, how much is it the fruit of a revolutionary mind, a radical departure from anything that's gone before, a rebellion of the creative spirit? Or, put simply: what *is* design?

That initial thought, of which Niemeyer speaks, of architects is mostly born within a given context: a brief, a commission, the outline for a competition and its specifications. And what triggers it may be yet another external element, either directly related to the challenge, such as a site visit, a meeting with the client, an impression of the neighbourhood or location, or, just as likely, completely unrelated and random: a chance encounter, a work of art, another building, a conversation… Both the context (the brief, the commission, the competition) and therefore also the first thought or idea for a design that serves this context are to quite some extent unforeseen and unpredictable. Yes, there are certain boundaries within which they are likely, but mostly the path of design leads from a set of unpredictable factors that are largely outside our control to a set of circumstances that we consciously create.

What we'll be doing in this chapter is explore, quite freely, the possibilities that exist for design, how these possibilities could be moulded into strategies and how these strategies have been broadened by digital technologies. We want to emphasise though that each design – if that's what it is, rather than, say, purely the application of a design principle – ultimately requires its own strategy, and so our ambition here is not to deliver the key to a universally applicable tool box or manual, but to encourage, and – if that's the right expression – help empower you to develop your own strategies.

We also want to stress that we will be thinking and talking in examples. Much as we can't and don't mean to attempt to serve up an off-the-shelf template or 'how to' guide to digital design strategies, we don't want to suggest that we're able or even keen, to cover everything there is to say on the subject. We will simply look at the question of what a design strategy can be considered to be – ways of defining what it is – and then we'll examine three particular examples of design strategies embedded in their historical context, to give us an understanding of how design strategies have evolved over time and how they have been shaped by the computer. What we hope to be able to show with this approach is on the one hand the extremely wide scope that there is for design strategies, and on the other where the strengths lie of digital technology, and where, perhaps, its weaknesses. Because some of the things we're about to look at, we'll find computers to be particularly good at. Others, perhaps not so much…

What Is a Design Strategy?

If we want to look at digital design strategies, we need to first of all establish what me mean by 'design strategy', so that we can then ask ourselves: what makes a design strategy digital. And that in turn means we need to ask ourselves: what is design?

There are three facets in design theory that particularly interest us and that may lead us to some answers:

- Complicating factors or finding solutions to wicked problems
- The set theory approach to design
- Generative models for creating solution candidates

THE CHALLENGE OF DESIGN: WICKED PROBLEMS

One way of looking at design is as a problem solving task: you have a current situation A (the situation as it is now, for example a derelict industrial site with nothing much in it that can be put to use any more), and you want a different situation B (the situation as you or someone who is tasking you with the design thinks it should be, for example a mixed purpose urban village with retail space, convenient access to transport, affordable living, some premium residential space to help finance the project, and a smattering of small business units to help regenerate the area). Your 'problem' now is that you don't know the path from A to B, and your design, when you have arrived at it, will be the 'solution' to your problem, because it will present you with that path and enable you to move from situation A to situation B.

If you do look at it in this way, the purpose of design then is to create an object – in our example a set of well grouped, interconnected buildings – that meets certain criteria which come specified with your desired situation B, for example efficient use of space to create as many decent size housing units as possible, agreeable common areas which enhance the sense of community in the new development, low energy consumption to meet statutory standards and make the development desirable as an investment, and overall high architectural quality at low construction and maintenance costs. In addition, the object or parts of it will have to fulfil certain very specific purposes: apart from living accommodation and work spaces, for example, it may have to provide a kindergarten, as well as parking space for at least one car per residential and small business unit. And there may have to be room for a new 200 seat cinema to replace an historic picture house in the neighbourhood that has to make way for the development, if the development is to be granted planning permission. The task, quite simply, is to somehow meet all these criteria in a satisfactory way.

As is patently evident though: this is not a simple task. Our example is, admittedly, fairly ambitious (and there's a reason for that), but even if only one or a few components were to be realised, the principle at work would be the same: you would go from an 'is' situation to a 'should be' or 'desired' situation by way of solving a design problem. But the 'problem' – here in a deliberately and explicitly complex example – is far from straightforward: it is entangled, interconnected, unpredictable. It is, essentially, and as so often is the case in applied architecture, a *wicked problem*.

The term 'wicked problem' was first coined in the late 1960s by the German design theorist Horst Rittel (1930–1990), which may account for the unorthodox use of the word 'wicked': it doesn't mean that the problem is 'evil', but that it is impossible or improbably difficult to solve, at least in a straightforward, linear manner. Rittel, together with American urban designer and theorist Melvin M Webber (1920–2006) later elaborated on the definition of 'wicked problems' in a paper of the same title in 1973, and contrasted them with 'tame problems', which confirms the notion that 'wicked' problems are really 'wild' or 'unruly' or 'chaotic', rather than morally defunct...

The difference between a 'wicked' and a 'tame' problem is that a 'tame' problem may well be fiendishly difficult to solve, but it does either have a solution, or a logically and rationally coherent set of solutions, or a pathway towards either. That's why a game of chess, for example, no matter at what level you play it, presents you with 'tame' problems throughout, since at any given stage the next move can be worked out in a way that makes sense and that reliably yields a certain outcome. A 'wicked' problem, by contrast, presents so many factors which you have little or no control over that it is virtually unmanageable, or needs to be approached as a complex set of challenges that are all interrelated in such a way that if you address one part of the constellation, this will either directly or indirectly affect some or all the other parts as well.

Rittel first introduced the terminology in social planning, but it was quickly and readily adopted in management science and can, in a more generalised sense, be applied to many other fields, including architecture and urban planning. A development project such as the one given in our fictitious case above very typically presents a decidedly 'wicked' problem. For example:

- The objectives may be vaguely defined to start with and then also change during the design period; for instance the concept of 'affordable housing' as defined by policy makers may be at variance to how it is defined by property developers. During the planning period, the cost of construction materials may suddenly rise due to a supply shortage, or a site survey may uncover an archaeological find, which makes preservation measures necessary that are both time-consuming and costly. In other words, the 'problem' itself is a moveable feast: as the project is being developed, it constantly changes, and anything I do about it may affect any other part of it. Say I downgrade my proposed triple glazing to a high quality type of double glazing to compensate for a price hike in materials elsewhere, then my energy efficiency rating will go down, which devalues my proposition overall.
- For any construction project, even much smaller ones than the one in our example, there are innumerable performance criteria that can be used to evaluate a possible solution. Many of these, though, can not be evaluated *objectively*, since they don't yield quantifiable values. How, for example, do you quantify whether a common area is 'agreeable' or not. What to your 12-year-old nephew who loves skateboarding whilst listening to Grime music constitutes a perfect afternoon spent on a smoothly surfaced square with low concrete benches may be a categorical nightmare to your grandmother who likes reading on her tablet device in peace and quiet in a nice shaded area whilst sipping tea under a tree. And you may have performance criteria that directly (or indirectly) contradict each other. For example, the perfectly agreeable canopied outdoor seating area for the new bar & grill which will be loved by late night diners and those who like to go out for a drink of an evening may cause a continuing headache to the neighbours opposite who want to go to bed at ten; and the built-in patio heaters which will keep night revellers happy and

warm will, by the neighbours who are already in a bad mood because they can't get any sleep, be considered an environmental abomination. What you end up with as a result is often not so much a solution as a compromise.

- Because the number of variables to generate a design is so large, there is neither a finite, countable number of possible solutions, nor is there even a clearly defined number of 'permissible' measures that can be taken into consideration. In other words: we not only don't have a finite set of possible outcomes, we don't even have a defined set of actual starting points.
- Characteristic of any 'wicked' problem is the inter-relatedness of factors. In architecture design and planning, there exists, between performance criteria and form variables a many-to-many relationship, meaning that each performance criterion will affect several form variables, and each form variable will affect many performance criteria. Say you look at the dimension of children's bedrooms in your proposed development and you find that they are really too small to comfortably accommodate a bed, a desk, and a wardrobe whilst also leaving some room for maybe playing, or practising an instrument, or pursuing a leisure activity. The moment you now re-dimension these bedrooms and make them bigger, you immediately affect the amount of space that's available for the other rooms in the flat. And if you make the flat bigger, you affect the amount of space that's available for all the other flats.

So there are a multitude of hurdles that have to be overcome to get from an 'is' situation A to a 'should be' or 'desired' situation B. And what makes this particularly tricky is that not only do we often not know the path to the goal, we may not even fully know the actual goal for certain.

A barrier that prevents us from knowing the path to the goal has been referred to as a 'synthesis barrier', by Dietrich Dörner in his 1976 text *Problemlösen als Informationsverarbeitung (Problem Solving as Information Processing)*. It can only really be overcome by looking for and examining possible solution candidates and charting their distance from the desired situation. Since the desired situation may in itself not be clearly defined, a barrier that prevents us from arriving at it (which in turn is sometimes called the 'dialectic barrier'), is overcome by employing the available solution candidates to obtain a clearer picture of what the desired situation really is. This makes the principle by which we search for a solution to our problem a cycle of generating and evaluating variants that impact on each other: a feedback loop, whereby the process of generating and evaluating the solution candidates is repeated over and over again until we arrive at a solution that meets all the criteria.

FINDING THE NEEDLE: SET THEORY

One of the most pervasive ideas of the twentieth century – although it probably dates far further back than that – is the *infinite monkey theorem*. It postulates that if you sat a monkey at a table in front of a typewriter, then given enough time (as in a very long time indeed, such as infinity) the monkey would eventually churn out the collected works of William Shakespeare. Or any other great writer for that matter. Or, in fact, since we are talking about time without limit, all the works ever written in any language that ever was or will be.

There is a mathematical proof for this, though the likelihood of it ever happening in real life, even if instead of a monkey (which would have to be an endless series of poor creatures thus mightily abused) you employed the world's most powerful super computers and simulated the typing action with them, is extremely small. The reason it is extremely small in real life (and thus in a time period that is at all limited) is that the combination of letters in the particular order that make up the complete works of William Shakespeare is really extremely specific. But because it is a possible set of arranged letters, words, sentences, and line breaks, grouped into scenes, acts, and plays, not forgetting the sonnets and the dramatic poems – so the theorem posits – this particular set would, at some point, *have to* materialise.

Which begs the fantastically interesting philosophical question whether a probabilistic theoretical possibility ('it is certainly *possible* that just by fluke this could occur') is also an *inevitability* ('it could theoretically occur, therefore it has to'), or whether, even in a universe where this is a possibility, the arrangement of letters required is so particular that even if the monkey or the computer were to go on typing forever, it would forever only put out random combinations that would never actually have to yield any deliberately formulated work of literature at all, no matter how long they continued to do so. In other words: without the specific instruction to play through *all possible* combinations of letters, however long this should take, but being allowed to keep on typing at random, would anything that to us makes sense in any language ever *have to* come about, or would it simply be an endless string of random letters. (Even if it did, it would still, of course, not be imbued with any meaning, since it would be an arrangement of letters that just happened to make sense in one particular language.)

A similar thought exercise can be carried out in the visual world: if you take a computer screen and use a software generator to allocate one of several million colours to each pixel (irrespective of how many there are), then by repeating the process over a long enough period – for which read infinity – you would end up with every work of art ever drawn or painted. In fact you would end up with every imaginable work of art as well as with every work of art never imagined, because over an infinitely long period you would arrive at *all* possible combinations of colours for each pixel on the screen and this by definition would include all images ever made or yet to be made visible, including the *Mona Lisa*, Picasso's entire Blue Period and everything that David Hockney has ever painted, drawn, or created on his iPad. And it would therefore also include every visual representation – ground plan, elevation, visualisation – of every building ever thought of or yet to be designed. We might call this an *infinite image theorem*.

This similarly raises the question: would a genuine random generator that is instructed to allocate colours purely by chance really play through all possible combinations and therefore by necessity hit upon all arrangements so ordered that they give us recognisable images, or would it simply keep illuminating the equivalent of static. In other words, without the instruction to play through *all* the possible combinations (which then is no longer a truly random generation but a ticking off of every possible instance on a very long list), would the *Mona Lisa* ever *have to* come about? If the *Mona Lisa* here were likened to a metaphorical needle, then the haystack of possible pixel combinations on your average computer screen is really quite extraordinarily big.

For a writer with words and for a designer with images, playing through an infinite number of random combinations, or even systematically playing through all possible combinations, is not an option. It's neither efficient nor, as we have seen, does it have meaning. So, much as a writer uses syntax and grammar to arrange letters and words in such a way that they are intelligible and also convey a certain sense and tone, the designer uses their syntax and grammar of visual and spatial elements to arrive at that which needs to be expressed. But, as any writer, or designer, or musician, or any other artist of any kind knows, understanding the syntax and grammar is not enough to arrive at a new creation. We use strategies to deploy these and any other available tools to our particular end, invoking our skill, experience, and imagination. The strategies, then, provide us with a 'space of variables', if you like: a thought room to play through different options, and test them for their viability.

Looked at this way, there is a *design space*, which is the set of all possible forms that a designer is able to create; there is a *performance space*, which is the set of all possible forms that fulfil certain given criteria, such as being capable of performing functions that are required of the object that is being designed; and there is the *solution space*, which is the set of all forms that are part of both other sets simultaneously.

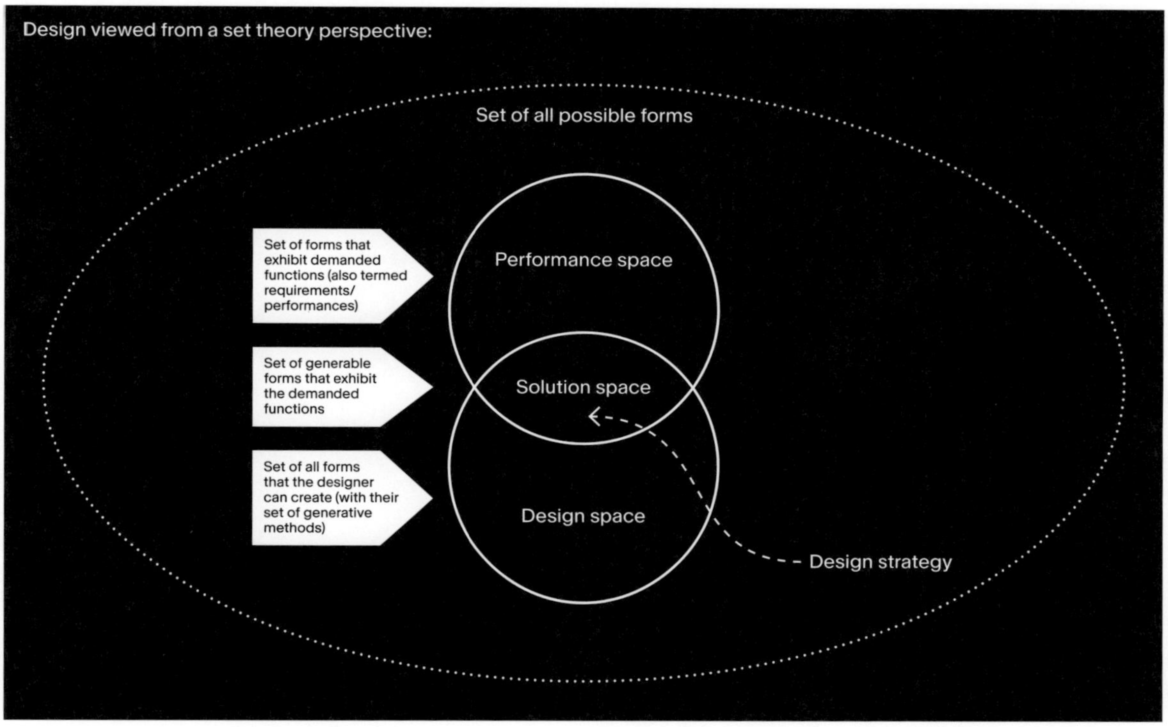

069 ● 125

In this approach, a design strategy is a way to arrive at the solution space by a process of comparison and elimination, and a particularly good design strategy is one that arrives at it by the most efficient route.

GENERATIVE MODELS

A model is a representation of an extant or possible reality, or, more often, of a segment or selection of such a reality. This selection does not contain all the characteristics of the reality that is represented, but those that are relevant for the purpose of the model in the given context. There are two chapters in this *Atlas* dedicated to models, 3D Modelling and Model Making, so we will not go into very great detail on this subject here. But models of all kinds can and do form part of architectural design strategies, and their great advantage over the reality they represent is that owing to their abstraction and simplified levels of detail, they tend to be easy and quick to change; in other words, it is nowhere near as difficult to manipulate a potential reality as it is to change a reality. As the Italian architect, poet, painter, philosopher, and polymath Leon Battista Alberti (1404–1472), whom we come across frequently in this *Atlas*, put it: "Here," – by which he means the model – "we can enlarge,

□ ↖57
□ 421↘

reduce, change, renew and completely redesign without penalty, until everything fits together and gains our approval."

This makes models and modelling systems powerful and versatile tools in design, and it is exactly what allows us to view modelling as a design strategy: playing through a number of variations that represent different assumptions about the form-function relationship of an object.

Computers still aren't really equipped to handle unquantifiable quantities, and the immense complexity of innumerable, vaguely defined variables in wicked problems flummoxes many a software because it expects concrete values that it can compare and set off against each other. But once a set of problems has been adequately defined, playing through numerous options or solution candidates that may perhaps vary only very slightly from each other is something that a computer can of course do particularly well.

Computers can also compare sets of data well and pitch them against certain criteria, finding overlaps between one set and another. But this presupposes that the sets are clearly, cleanly, and reliably defined, and it furthermore suggests that the design task is principally pragmatic: finding the most effective form for the given function within some given design parameters.

Computers are designed to handle programming languages, and so any approach that echoes (or, arguably, preempts) a scripting methodology, working along the principles of a language with its own grammar and syntax and following clear and interconnected sets of rules and corresponding outcomes is practically made for them.

And of course we can, and do, model with computers. It's not necessarily easy to generate a good model – it can be time-consuming and brings with it certain pitfalls, such as the temptation to limit yourself to what the software allows or provides by way of presets and templates – but, as we discuss elsewhere, computer modelling can be used as part of a design process, rather than merely as three dimensional representation of a finished design, to tremendous effect.

Three Design Strategies

All the above are really strategy approaches. But we are not only looking for approaches, we are also looking for some concrete strategies. For ways to tame the wicked problems, you could say; for efficient and at the same time creatively valid processes that yield up the *solution space* from the *design space* and the *performance space*.

The first of our three examples – and we stress again here that these are merely examples – falls into this category, dealing with *architecture as mathematical science*.

■ 164↘ Our second example looks at *architecture as a performative art*, where evolutionary algorithms and parametric design principles come into play, and therefore computing needs to similarly perform at an already much higher and more sophisticated level.

The third example might be labelled *architecture of the senses,* approaching, as it does, architecture as a process of thinking and designing through perception, which means that renderings, visualisations, and walkthroughs gain prominence here: computing at a virtual reality and real-time experiential level.

ARCHITECTURE AS MATHEMATICAL SCIENCE

In 1525, the Italian Franciscan friar and scholar of antique philosophy Francesco Giorgi (1466–1540) wrote a book called *De harmonia mundi totius (On the Harmony of the Whole World),* in which he expounds the notion of a cosmic harmony and the mystical power of numbers and their relationships to each other, drawing parallels between the ratios found in music and in architecture, for example by directly applying musical intervals to the ratio of the length and width of the nave of a church. Knowledge about these intervals goes back to the Greek philosopher and mathematician Pythagoras (c. 570–495 BCE) who had described them two thousand years earlier.

070 ● 125

The practice of identifying harmonious proportions and applying them to architecture stems from the desire to create buildings that are beautiful in a way that is universally understood and experienced. What matters here is not what I as the designer consider elegant or attractive, what matters is the mathematical principle that is *inherently good,* because universally (cosmically, even) in tune with itself, and therefore *incapable* of being anything other than beautiful.

The application of musical harmony theory to two-dimensional rules for architecture has always had its followers and it has always also had its detractors. Take French architect Philibert de l'Orme (1514–1570), in turn a scholar of Vitruvius, Alberti, and Palladio. In 1567, he still demands that: "an architect should not be a thoughtless, ignorant craftsman, but one who fathoms the causes and secrets of proportions," and goes on to explain how it is possible to, "transform a symmetry into a symphony, and a harmony for the ear into a harmony for the eye."

Give it two hundred years, until 1753, and the English painter, printmaker, and cartoonist William Hogarth (1697–1764) uses his own much noted treatise *The*

Analysis of Beauty to reject the prevalent theories of harmony and proportion, and instead of the relationship between numbers and lines points towards the beauty that is inherent in movement, the modulation of light and shade, atmosphere, and the character of the onlooker. We are now deeply into a subjective view of aesthetics, but even so Hogarth is also the man who comes up with the concept of the **line of beauty**, a serpentine (or S-shaped) line that in and of itself, according to Hogarth, conveys liveliness and activity, in contrast to parallel lines, which for him evoke stasis and death. ■

So aiming for regularly occurring proportions is certainly not the only strategy that can be employed to obtain harmony, but it is one that works. And being based on proportions, rather than on absolute values, it will work on any scale. Renaissance thinking is infused by this idea that there are proportional relationships which can be bundled into sets of universally applicable laws that are by necessity good. In the fifth book of his heroic poem *L'Italia liberata dai Goti (Italy Liberated From the Goths)*, the Italian poet, dramatist, and grammarian Gian Giorgio Trissino (1478–1550) demonstrates the relationship between a building and its detail as follows:

> *A cloister extends around the rectangle*
> *of the courtyard*
> *With lofty arches resting on columns.*
> *The shafts of the columns (viz., height) are*
> *of such height*
> *That the breadth of the circumference fully*
> *equals them.*
> *The thickness (viz., diameter) of these*
> *columns, though,*
> *Measures an eighth of such length,*
> *as does the height*
> *Of the silver bosses which crown them;*
> *The height of the metallic pediments*
> *Corresponds to half of this same*
> *measurement.*

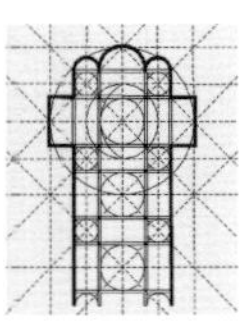
071 ● 125

Trissino completed his poem in 1527, although it was not actually published until twenty years later, in 1547. It is not, in all fairness, today considered a literary work of global significance, but in the intervening period something happened that made Trissino one of the most influential Italians of his era and for which he certainly deserves the recognition of the world of architecture.

In the second half of the 1530s, a young mason named Andrea di Pietro came to work on the Villa Trissino at Cricoli, Trissino's house near Vicenza, not far from Venice in Northern Italy. Trissino was a great admirer of Vitruvius and therefore immensely interested in architecture, and he saw in the twenty-something-year-old Andrea a talent that he took it upon himself to 'adopt' and nurture. He not only introduced him to the arts and sciences and enabled him to study architecture in Rome, he also gave him a new name, inspired by a character in one of his own plays, Andrea 'The Wise One', or, as he is now known the world over, Andrea Palladio (1508–1580).

Although it is by no means certain that the Villa Trissino was actually *designed* by Palladio, all Palladio's later works can be traced back to this time and the design principles at work here. It is viewed as something of a prototype, based on which Palladio went on to develop an exact geometry that aspired to putting the individual rooms of a house into a harmonious relationship with the ground plan – and therefore the locality – and also with each other. The logic and rule adherence applied here is so strong and consistent that more than four hundred years later, in the 1970s, the American design and computer theorist George Stiny, together with two colleagues, was able to develop a set of computational rules which not only systematised known Palladian architecture, but also allowed for the generation of 'artificial' new architecture that was, in proportion and character, exactly as Palladio himself would invariably have designed it. These **shape grammars**, as they are known, were so successful at emulating Palladio that they became indistinguishable from genuine Palladio designs. (We talk about shape grammars in several chapters in this *Atlas*, especially on Generative Methods and Scripting.) ■ ↖64 157↘ □ 145↘ □ 351↘

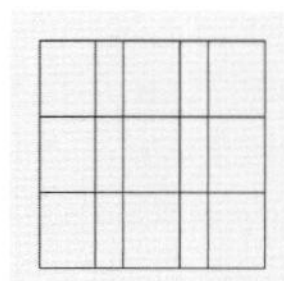
072 ● 126

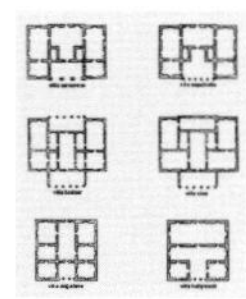
073 ● 126

Having studied Vitruvius, Giorgi, and Alberti under the aegis of his patron and sponsor Trissino, our newly named Palladio now develops his own theory of spatial harmony, in which he sets ground plans and elevations in relation to each other, strictly based on Pythagoras. In *I quattro libri dell'architettura (The Four Books on Architecture)* he explains his thinking thus: "Surely change and new inventions will delight everyone, but no-one should offend the rules of the art, or go against the commands of reason." This puts him firmly into the camp representing rational architecture in a battle of schools that has been raging across cultural eras and divides ever since, and pitches him directly against the postmodern deconstructivism of architects such as Canadian-born American architect Frank Gehry (b. 1929), British-Iraqi architect Zaha Hadid (1950–2016), or the Coop *Himmelb(l)au*, which rejects the classical rule book and seeks freer, more natural, and organic forms entirely, to express its own notion of beauty.

THE MODULOR

One of the proportions we are most familiar with, both from experience, as we encounter it all the time in our daily existence, and as concept, is the *golden ratio* (which you'll see referred to by any of nearly a dozen other names in English alone).

You can go as far back as the 'father of geometry', Greek mathematician Euclid (fl. 300 BCE) to find this fascinating number, ratio, relationship, and phenomenon studied, but in architecture it was really the Swiss-French architect, pioneer, and urban planner Le Corbusier (1887–1965) who most prominently based his designs on the golden ratio and went as far as inventing a method for scaling to harmonious proportions with it.

Heavily and directly influenced by the works of Vitruvius, Alberti, and the *Vitruvian Man*, by Italian Renaissance polymath Leonardo da Vinci (1452–1519), Le Corbusier took a male human figure as the basic dimensional 'unit', and, applying the golden ratio, derived from it 'valid' or 'pleasing' proportions that could then be scaled up or down, and would, because of their proportionality, always work. When first launched in 1943, the Modulor, as he called his creation, was originally based on the height of the average Frenchman, at 1.75 m. One of the principal motivations for Corbusier to develop the method had been the need to reconcile the French metric system, which was now gaining ground, with the previously dominant British system of inches, cubits, and digits that was based on the human body, and three years later, in 1946, Corbusier changed the ■ 338↘ base value from 1.75 m to 1.83 m, giving as his reason for doing so the fact that, "in English detective novels, the good-looking men, such as policemen, are always six feet tall!", six feet being 1.83 metres.

The German-born theoretical physicist Albert Einstein (1879–1955) was enthusiastic about the Modulor. He told Le Corbusier, "it is a measuring system that makes the the good easy and the bad difficult." Which more or less sums up the purpose of a measuring order, and would suggest that if ever there was a proportional, rule based design strategy that – as Corbusier no doubt expected – would soon take hold and become generally adopted architectural practice, then this would surely be it. Alas, it was not: the Modulor has since passed pretty much into obscure oblivion.

MODULE & TYPOLOGY

Many a student going to a university, college, or academy today will be pleased to find that their institution offers modular courses and will readily accept as normal that a module is a segment that is proportional to a bigger entity, and that modules are a direct or indirect measuring unit for the course of study they are undertaking.

Most, however, are unlikely to be aware that the word *module* itself, as a term to denote a proportional unit of measure, reaches right back again to our friend Vitruvius, who first mentions it in his *De architectura*. In ancient architecture, the *modulus* is the semidiameter of a column as measured at its base. Rather than running the risk – or the quite unnecessary effort – of having to design a temple with some random measurements that might lead to unseemly dimensions and awkward proportions, this simple but effective unit would serve as the basis for everything else, meaning that all the dimensions of the temple – column height, distance between columns, length, width, and height of the building – could be expressed in multiples or, should this become necessary, fractions of the module. This guaranteed that the building would have proportionality, and it made calculations remarkably simple.

In a wider sense, the module has been, and continues to be, used as a reference or literally as a unit of measure in architecture. It can be defined as the size of a handcrafted brick, for example, or the length of a wooden beam to determine the span and therefore size of a space covered by a roof, or a Japanese *tatami mat* which might determine the dimensions of a room.

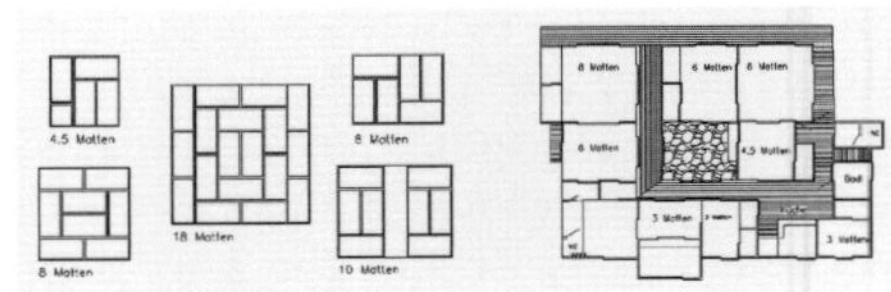

074 ● 126

The term *typology* was introduced to architecture by French architect and teacher Jean-Nicolas-Louis Durand (1760–1834). He used as modules geometric shapes, such as the circle, the square, simple axis systems, symmetrical arrangements, and primary building blocks to teach the basic elements of a design idiom, as an abstraction that prepares students for the creative process.

Taking this one step further in the pursuit of the ideal of affordable housing for everyone, Swiss architect Hannes Meyer (1889–1954) – who was the second director of the **Bauhaus** art school – developed catalogued typology in architecture to an industry norm product. Influenced by Meyer, German architect Ernst Neufert (1900–1986), who in turn was an assistant to the Bauhaus founding director, German architect Walter Gropius (1883–1969), produced the widely used and translated standard reference work *Architects' Data,* known in German as *Bauentwurfslehre* (literally: 'The Theory of Construction Design') and also simply by the name of its author, as the *Neufert.*

The rise of typology-based industrially fabricated and normed architecture in the post-war period comes as no surprise: following the destruction caused by Word War II, there was an acute housing shortage across central Europe, including East Germany, in what was then the German Democratic Republic (GDR). Since 1970, WBS 70 *(Wohnungsbauserie 70)* was the most widespread prefabricated building system of the GDR, based on a uniform slab grid of 1.20 m by 1.20 m, offering just a few floor plan types for the entire nation. This would ensure identical construction processes and also allow for even more rationalised mass production of other housing components, including furniture, such as the multifunction table *Mufuti (Multifunktionstisch)* and built-in furniture.

075 ● 127

THE GRID

In architecture as in other areas, working with industrially prefabricated components creates a need for standardisation, for which the grid offers a convenient tool: it allows the scaling up and down of structures, and this in turn ushers in an era of simple lines and plain surfaces: the 'emancipation of buildings from ornament', as it was often described. German-American architect Ludwig Mies van der Rohe (1886–1969) was a prominent proponent of this modernist style, embracing, as he did, the idea that 'less is more'. (We are simplifying matters a bit here, for the sake of brevity.)

076 ● 127

To use the grid in a three dimensional design process, American architect and pioneer in computer aided design Peter Eisenman (b. 1932) subjected the humble cube to a mathematical deformation process based on the theories of English mathematician, philosopher, and logician George Boole (1815–1864), for example for the Aronoff Center University of Cincinnati, USA. The geometrically complex modulation of the grid and the shape is the result of a computer-aided moulding process. His systemic approach was described by Swiss architectural theorist Werner Oechslin (b. 1944) in the architectural journal *Daidalos* in 1990 as follows: "He started with a 4-n cube, used it as a solid and as a frame, lined these up along the same rules and with progressive distances, transferred the lines to asymptotic curves and allowed these to overlap."

You may not find this description of a process immediately elucidating, and it may be hard to visualise just exactly what it is that Eisenman was doing, but it gives you a flavour of the theoretical foundations for designing with computers. We are just talking about a cube here, one of the simplest three dimensional objects available to us.

Carrying out digital design with 3D modelling has its roots in two-dimensional drawings. You move from the form grammar of the plane to a similarly applicable form grammar in three dimensions. There is a through line from the harmonious proportions of Palladio to those of Le Corbusier, who held that, "the plan is the generator," via another Swiss architect, Bernhard Hoesli (1923–1984), who contrasted Le Corbusier's assertion by insisting that, "in the cross section architecture is generated," both of whom agree, though, in their encouragement to designers to work in two dimensional drawings. This may be considered a route, perhaps, from the rule book of the Renaissance through the formalism of modernity to computer generated design today.

(We discuss 3D Modelling in detail in our dedicated chapter on the subject.)

ARCHITECTURE AS A PERFORMATIVE ART

Nature and architecture stand in a complex relationship to each other: how architecture fits into nature or stands up against it, how it uses nature's materials to at once protect the inside from nature while evoking nature within, how it emulates and pays homage to nature at the same time as it rebels against and tries to overcome nature, these are all part of that peculiar dynamic.

Bionics is the field of study that concerns itself with the transformation of analogies in nature into architecture, in other words, deliberately copying nature and applying how it works mathematically in buildings. Spanish architect, painter, and sculptor Santiago Calatrava (b. 1951), who may be considered one of the most successful architectural engineers of our time, is among those who are inspired by nature for their works, using in his construction many parallels to patterns found in nature, such as steel ropes that remind you of sinews, concrete structures that look like and also serve as skeletons, or columns that carry a roof like a tree carries its foliage.

The international architects studio LAVA (Laboratory for Visionary Architecture), meanwhile, carries out research into how future technologies relate to organisational patterns in nature, trusting that this will lead to an intelligent, friendly, socially and environmentally more conscious architectural future. The potential of self-evolving systems such as snowflakes, spider webs, and soap bubbles for new construction typologies and structures stems from a realisation – or at any rate perception – that in nature efficiency and beauty are in union with each other, and that emulating its principles will lead to a pleasing aesthetic that is also in tune with the environment. (In that sense it is, in terms of the stance that architecture takes, not all that far removed from the idea that harmonies such as they appear in the natural world are inherently pleasant to be surrounded by.) So LAVA combines a digital workflow with structural principles that are found in nature, and it pursues the development of cutting edge digital manufacturing methods with the explicit aim of achieving more (architecture) with less (money, materials, energy).

077 ○ 219

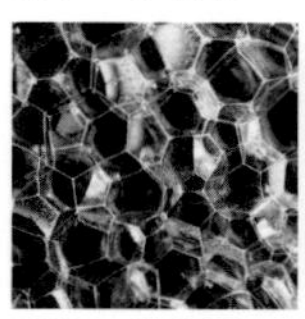

078 ○ 219

079 ○ 219

These couple of examples show perhaps how forms in nature can be applied to architecture: they demonstrate the possibility of using nature as a design generating element, and as a shortcut to create structurally stable and visually interesting solution candidates. □ ↖57

A different approach lies in using the underlying processes which have led to these shapes in nature and applying them to the design of buildings similarly as processes. This is something that can be simulated by computer, and the most famous example of it are Evolutionary Algorithms (EA). The basic idea is to imitate natural evolutionary processes which over numbers of iterations (generations) have brought about living creatures that are particularly well adapted to certain environmental conditions.

The principal sequence of a search for form by EA runs as follows: ■

1 You establish an initial population, generation t = 0. To this end, you use a generative model to randomly create a number of individuals.

2. A further number of individuals is generated by a process of recombination. Parts of the variable assignments of an individual are swapped with that of another.
3. The individuals that have been generated through these two steps are evaluated by an **Expectation-Maximisation (EM)** algorithm. This is a statistical method to find the best or maximum likelihood of certain outcomes within a set of given parameters.
4. On the basis of the tested fitness of individuals, a selection mechanism chooses a new number of individuals.

Steps 2 to 4 are then repeated until you either find a solution with an acceptably high degree of fitness, or until you have to abandon the process because you've run out of time. Crucial to this is that the search process – finding the best solution from the immense number of possible iterations – is left entirely to the computer.

An example of the use of EA is the optimisation of the roof structure of the Beijing National Stadium, for which the research collective *Kaisersrot* at ETH Zürich collaborated with architects Herzog & de Meuron. Here, a complex geometrical structure (the 'bird's nest' that has led to its colloquial name) was optimised in terms of its buildability, whereby the spaces between the beams needed to be minimised in size: "To do it 'by hand' you sit there for weeks, and whenever you introduce a new beam to limit the number of 'too-big red fields' you get too many 'too-small black fields' and so on. The software does not do it any differently, but the process is less tedious and much faster. And in doing so, it is able to optimise the ratio of big and small fields by using the evolutionary technique of genetic algorithms. The structure is increasing in 'fitness' and becomes optimised. It's an example of how to get a performative grip on disorder."

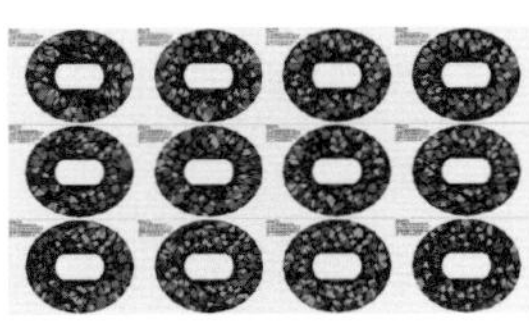

080 ○ 219

081 ○ 219

It's a process that could also be described as a 'bottom-up' strategy: you make only very few assumptions about which form best fulfils the required function. By comparison, traditional design methods are very much shaped by such assumptions. In the case of the Beijing National Stadium, a fit for purpose solution was bred within 5,000 iterations. Sadly, though, the result of the optimisation procedure was not actually realised. In the end, the building was constructed using regular methods, with a layer of non-functional, secondary beams giving it the iconic bird's nest look.

☐ 475↘
☐ 285↘
☐ 255↘

(We discuss some of these issues in more detail in our chapters on Big Data & Machine Learning and Scripting.)

☐ 549↘
☐ 351↘

ARCHITECTURE OF THE SENSES

"Architects may come and architects may go and never change your point of view," Paul Simon sang, somewhat cryptically, in his haunting *So Long,* to the American architect *Frank Lloyd Wright* (1867–1959), which was as much about his imminent break-up from singing partner Art Garfunkel as it was about any formative effect the grandmaster of 20th century American architecture may have had on him as a young composer. Frank Lloyd Wright had been dead for just over a decade by the time this particular tribute to him was released, but he might have appreciated the exquisiteness of the gesture, had he ever heard the tune: there is something about it. There are the multiple layers of meaning, some so hidden that even Art Garfunkel realised only much later that the song was as much about him as it was about the man of the title, and there is the instrumentation. The tune, of course. There's the whole, that is greater than the sum of its parts. It's what makes it, simple as it is, and as so many of Simon & Garfunkel's, a great song.

We know when that's the case. We may not be able to put our finger on it, and we may not even like everything that we know, instinctively it seems, to be extraordinary. It goes beyond just quality and taste. It has that extra dimension. In building terms, you could say, it has atmosphere.

How do you design an atmosphere? The thing that has no substance, but that is still somehow attached to the material. The 'feel' when you walk into a room. The thing that is not the texture of the wood and the colour tone of the floor and type of lighting, but what happens in-between them. The thing that is not the acoustic or the haptic or the look, but what they combine to. Frank Lloyd Wright understood himself to be an architect of atmosphere, and in his first essay, written in 1894 he states: "The sum total of 'house' and all the things in it with which we try to satisfy the requirements of utility and our craving for the beautiful is atmosphere, good or bad, that little children breathe as surely as the plain air."

Digital simulations, such as a rendering or a walk-through go towards helping us make the atmosphere of a building designable, similar to the way in which then new lighting techniques in theatre made it possible to transport the scenery of paintings onto the three dimensions of the stage at the beginning of the 20th century. If you are a strict follower of Le Corbusier, this kind of development in design might alarm you, as it marks a departure from the perfect reduction and abstraction of the drawing, and blind you with its visual impact and detail, whereas an adherent of Frank Lloyd Wright would most likely see 3D light simulations with more and more sophisticated detail in reflection, diffusion, and absorption as valuable tools towards an architecture of atmosphere. (We discuss these techniques in detail in our chapters on Simulation, Visualisation, and Rendering.)

The architecture firm Bjarke Ingels Group (BIG), well-known for their pragmatic utopian architecture that, according to their own website, aims to, "[steer] clear of the petrifying pragmatism of boring boxes" went new ways in finding a design solution for the Museum of the Human Body in Montpellier, France. Here they exemplified an approach which fuses atmospheric elements of urban and landscaping design in a shape that resembles two folded hands. Images of motion, such as cell division and the movement of populations guided the concept, while environmental factors determined the exact volume allocations.

The Outlook

> "The free sketch is the freest of all mediums. The sketch is free of gravity, free of regulations, free of determinations, edicts, costs and pressures. It is free of codes and as individual as the person who draws. The pencil is the fastest of all design tools, it is the Ferrari among them..."

Austrian architect and co-founder of Himmelb(l)au, Wolf Prix (b. 1942) may get himself into deep water with automotive enthusiasts, comparing one of the most through-engineered, designed, branded, and technologically sophisticated cars to a humble drawing stick that you can chew on, but this thought, which he expressed back in 1991, still says something about how architects, architecture, architectural design, and digital architectural design traditionally relate to each other and where, therefore, any such thing as a 'digital design strategy' fits in.

Swiss writer and dramatist Friedrich Dürrenmatt (1921–1990) considered the computer a logical evolutionary development of written language and numbers, and used for it the German term *Denkzeug.* 'Zeug' is a thing or stuff or a tool, and so a *Werkzeug* is a tool you work with generally, a *Schriftzeug* is a tool you write with, such as a pencil or pen, and a *Denkzeug,* consequently, is a tool you think with. And it's worth bearing in mind that Dürrenmatt shuffled off his mortal coil at a time when computers were much simpler tools than they are today.

So is a computer today a genuine design tool? Would an architect like Prix or a writer like Dürrenmatt today think of a well specced laptop and some crest of the wave software as *Entwurfszeug?* What scarcely anybody doubts or argues over is that your own creativity is what makes you a good creative designer. It even sounds like stating the obvious. But then obviously no amount of computing power and no software suite is going to either compensate for your own lack of vision or rob you of yours if you have it. Back in the late 1980s and early 1990s, many designers saw the computer not as a tool but as a threat. The German word *Zeug* on its own, interestingly, is also used to speak in dismissive terms about something non-specific that is of little value, pointless, mindless, or useless. *Dummes Zeug!* you might hear a German mother exclaim to her child who has just said something that is patently stupid or untrue. But a tool is a tool is a tool. It goes with you where you take it and makes with you what you make. The more sophisticated it becomes, the more it may allow you to be sophisticated, but the more it also demands that you understand it and are capable of handling it. But even that isn't new: if you put the Prixian Ferrari pencil into the hands of someone who is useless at drawing it will go exactly nowhere. Similarly, if you put someone who can't drive into an actual Ferrari and hand them the keys, chances are you're looking at a two hundred thousand euro write-off within half an hour or less.

What is certainly true though is that as any manual tool changes the way we work manually, and any think tool changes the way we think, so any design tool changes the way we design, and that means it changes *what* we design. And since the early days of graphic interfaces and CAD, since the infancy of the computer as, what it was then really, a drawing tool rather than a genuine design tool, not only has digital capability increased exponentially and beyond recognition, but something completely, radically new has happened: the network. We now design as creatives who are permanently enmeshed in a global context. Of course people have been influencing each other since they were able to walk outside their cave, but this state we are in, of being always on and always connected, of architecture practices as a matter of course maintaining offices in several major cities across the globe, of collaboration being possible in real time around the clock: that simply did not exist as recently as twenty years ago.

And not only have geographical boundaries melted into insignificance (certainly creatively speaking; what is happening in politics is not only another matter entirely but quite conceivably in parts a reaction to this precise phenomenon), but also the conceptual boundaries between disciplines and sciences: art, design, engineering; the environmental, physical, and atmospheric aspects. What used to be much more segregated areas of expertise are moving in both directions simultaneously. On the one hand, yes, even greater specialisation, on the other towards an inter-disciplinarian middle ground where architects, like other artists, become once again polymaths. We are, in this as in many other ways, in an era that echoes the Renaissance.

What we can say, or certainly in parts observe, in parts predict, is that our methods and methodologies are converging, and that across all art forms and disciplines digital tools give us ever greater flexibility and power to communicate, to collaborate, and thus to create as a process in which individual genius, as it were, is fed by the inspiration of a cultural context, nurtured by universally accessible but personally tailored learning, and enriched by a communal exchange of insights and ideas.

Hand in hand with this goes a similarly observable democratisation. These boundaries too are being blurred, and over and over we note that skilled and enthusiastic amateurs with time on their hands, patience in their minds, and the capacity to pick up expertise can, using professional tools, become masters in their own right. Or they may not, but still be using those same tools... As architects we may have to learn to handle this: working with non-experts. We need to hone our didactic skills because citizen involvement in planning has become part of the equation, as has customisation and the mix-and-match approach to product and solutions design. If you buy a new car, you will find it normal to go to your favourite manufacturer's website and virtually assemble your ideal specification and finish. With cars, this has been possible for some time. Now it's possible with your breakfast cereal, and we are not at all far away from it being quite possible and quite normal with architecture.

What we expect to see more of is design that employs strategies that are particularly enabled, and
□ 629↘ therefore also defined, by digitality. Collaboration (on which we have a chapter), networked creating, and the application of open source principles. Performative processes that find solutions over thousands of itera-
□ ↖29 tions, without prejudice or bias. In the Introduction to this *Atlas* we demand that we as architects ask good questions. This has to be part of a design strategy, surely: we may very often not only not know what the solution is, but also not know what it could be. And as we've seen, we may not even precisely know what the 'problem' or at any rate the challenge is. So describing the challenge becomes particularly important: this is formulating the question.

It has been suggested that in any given situation 20% of the effort yields 80% of the solution. This is the temptation of the mediocre, you could argue: settling at the point where you're 'nearly there'. A hell of a lot of bad art, bad design, bad music, and bad architecture arrives in the world at approximately this point. And it's easy to see why. If the proportions are even vaguely correct, then that by necessity means that for just the remaining 20% of the solution – the bit that gets you over the finishing line, including the all important and critical 'last yard' – takes up 80% or by far most of your effort. This is where good or excellent design, art, music, and architecture take shape.

Digital technology may not be able to 'do it all for you', but it can certainly help you accomplish a big chunk of the effort.

068 ● 114
Frontispiece of *Essai sur l'architecture* by Marc-Antoine Laugier (1713–1769), showing an allegorical representation of the Vitruvian primeval hut by Charles-Dominique-Joseph Eisen (1720–1778).

069 ● 117
Restricting the design space by using squared spatial modules only: *Der Technokrat (The Technocrat)* from *Ironismus*, 1989. [Ernst & Sohn]

070 ● 118
Pythagoras explores the relationship between ratios found in numbers and in sound. He experiments with bells and glasses of water. Wood cutting from: Franchino Gaffurio, *Theoria musica*, Milan, 1492.

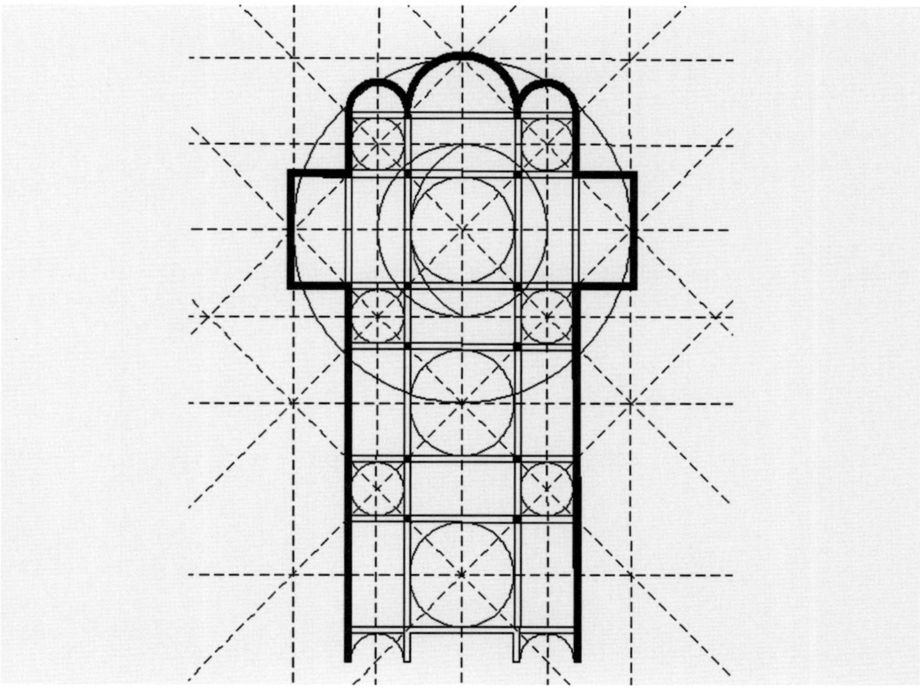

071 ● 119
The church of San Salvatore in Venice designed by Giorgio Spavento in 1506 and completed together with Tullio Lombardi by 1534. Karl von Freckmann has provided the plan with all the subsidiary lines needed for the design; his description, traced back to an axial measurement and two boom measurements, allows the development of the entire ground plan. [Ursula Kirschner]

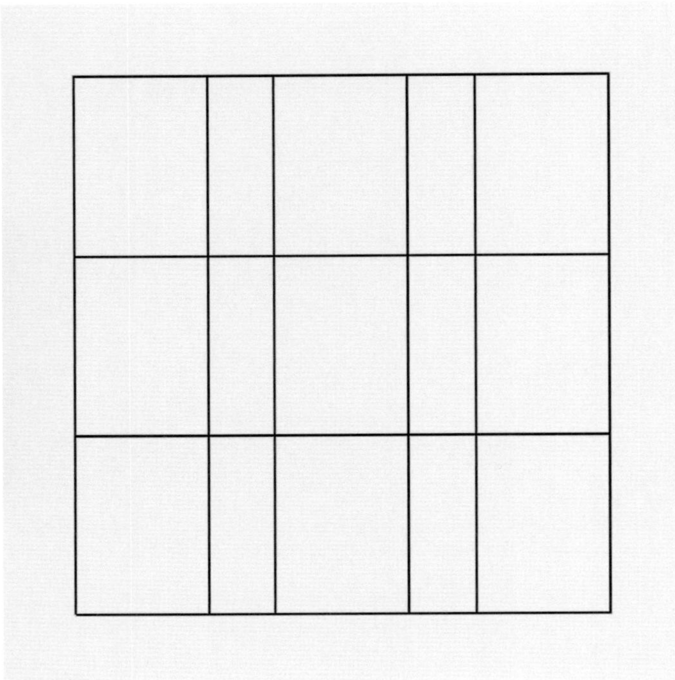

072 ● 119
Geometric key to Palladio's villas. [Ursula Kirschner]

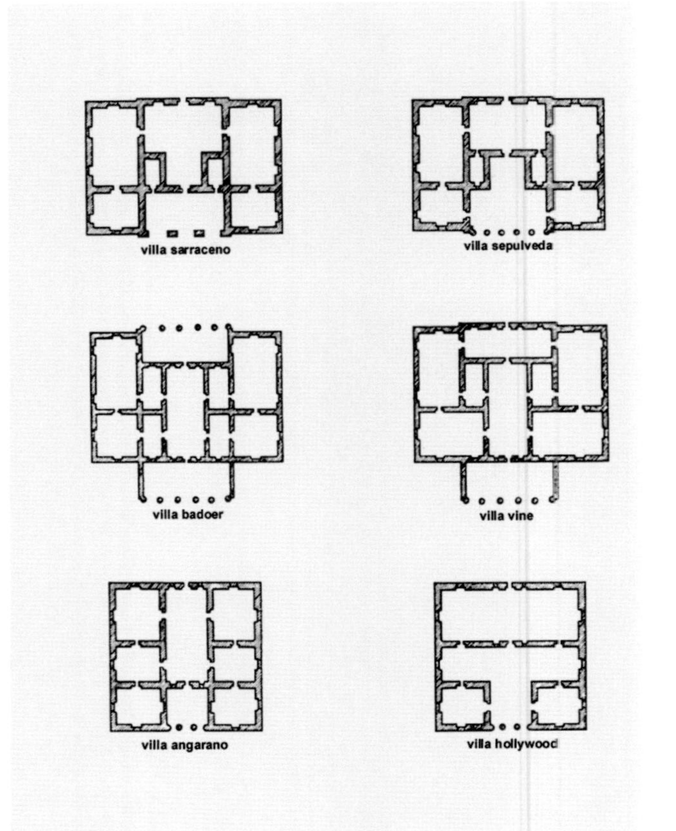

073 ● 119
Ground plans of Palladian villas, generated by shape grammars: on the left, ground plans that correspond to Palladio's original designs; on the right, entirely new variations. [George Stiny]

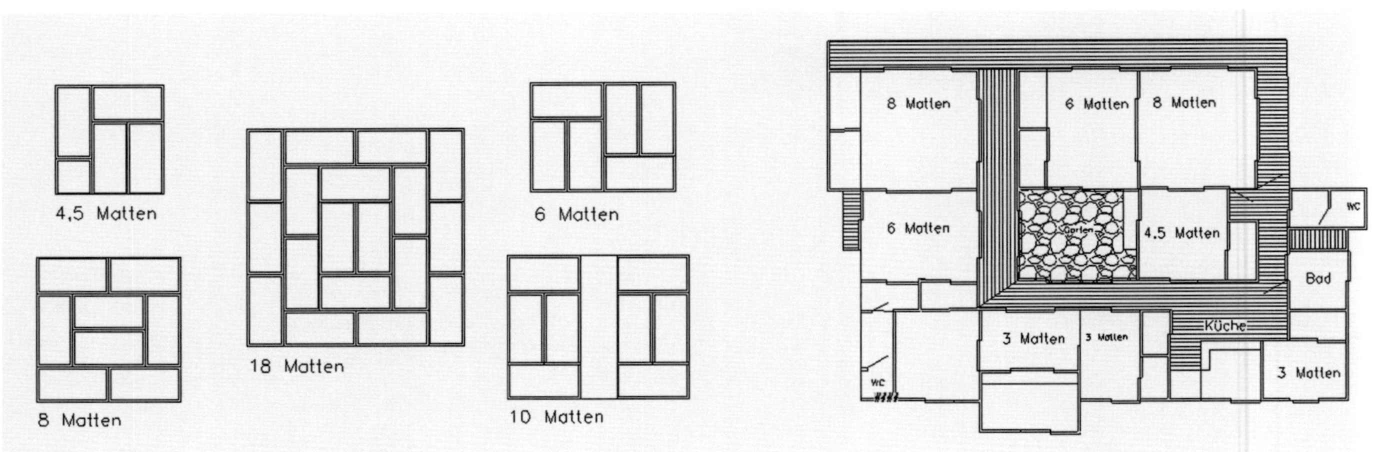

074 ● 120
The size of a room as determined by the number of tatami mats. [Ursula Kirschner, after Walzer: *Das Japanische Haus*]

075 ● 120
Weimar-West (2016). From 1978 until 1987, 3,660 flats were built in Weimar-West, using the prefabricated large-panel construction method. [Rouven Seebo]

076 ● 121
Seagram Building by Mies van der Rohe (1958). The detailing of the exterior surface was carefully determined to express the idea of the structural frame that lies underneath. [Noroton]

Computer Aided Design (CAD)

Harald Gatermann and Oliver Fritz

Overview

FROM HAND DRAWN SKETCH TO CAD

THE PROJECT IDEA

August Otto Rühle von Lilienstern is not a man widely known in the architectural world, and there is no obvious reason why he should be. Born in 1780 in Berlin, he was a Prussian army officer and writer on military subjects, and he was also a close friend of the German writer Heinrich von Kleist (1777–1811). Heinrich von Kleist is not an architectural figure either, but he is a significant dramatist, lyricist, and journalist of his era. In an essay published posthumously and most likely addressed to Rühle, entitled *Über die allmähliche Verfertigung der Gedanken beim Reden ('On the Gradual Formation of Thought Through Conversation')*, he counsels his friend that if he faces any problem that he can't solve through meditation, he should talk about it to someone. It doesn't even matter, so Kleist, whom you talk to and whether or not they are an expert on the subject, what is important is simply the process of conversing itself. "The idea comes through talking," as this brings to light and into focus the thought that already sits half-formed in your head as a vague notion.

This, you could argue, is really not so different to the process of design, in architecture and elsewhere: the 'idea' forms through an internal dialogue the architect is having with themselves. Using sketches, models, and other visual or physical iterations, it gradually takes on a more and more concrete shape until, at last, it is formulated in exact plans, elevations, and detailed scale models, and today also of course in fully-fledged 3D models.

In architecture, then, Kleist's 'gradual formation of thoughts through conversation' becomes a gradual formation of design through drawing and modelling, whereby the brain and the drawing are 'in conversation' with each other through the medium of the pencil or pen, so to speak. In the context of Computer Aided Design (CAD), this begs the question, can digital design tools replace pencil, ink, and paper? And if so, to what extent do they change the 'conversation'? Technically, they could have done so completely already, but it is interesting to note that analogue and specifically manual methods of 'communication' between brain and the visual representation of an idea are still very much in use a whole generation after the graphics card made drawing on consumer grade computers widely accessible and affordable.

One question that's at the core of all this and that we want to pursue in this chapter is: how does the idea for a project get from the head of the architect to a digitally communicable design? Because when we talk about CAD, it is generally taken as obvious that we are dealing with the implementation of planning ideas by means of digital media, with the aim of communicating these ideas to collaborators and stakeholders, and to ultimately realise the project. Whether the proposed concept refers to urban planning at one end of the spectrum (which would be considered the macro-level), to interior and detail design at the other (which, conversely, would be the micro-level), or to architectural or open space projects in-between does not strictly matter: the principles, broadly, are always the same.

So here we won't dwell on design theory and the origin of design, but take it as read that the idea exists and now has to be 'brought to paper'. This is the phase during which the architect (whether this now is an individual, a small team, or a large practice) has to communicate the project to everybody who is involved in it – colleagues, clients, authorities, specialist planners – by way of plans, models, words, and figures. And since sundry digital methods and approaches are the subject of many a chapter in this book, we also won't fan out into the wider areas of computer aided design or branch into 3D modelling, but limit ourselves quite narrowly to the computer as a 'drawing machine', in other words, to CAD as the digital application for generating first and foremost plans.

082 ● 140

THE PLAN

The classical medium for the type of communication we just referred to is the plan drawn or copied onto tracing paper, which contains all the relevant information as graphic elements and legends. And when we say 'classical' we mean this quite literally: this method of visual representation is almost as old as writing. As far back as 4,000 years ago, drawings were used in Mesopotamia to show planned three-dimensional buildings in an abstract, two-dimensional form. To what extent these were to scale is still subject of historical research, but what is certain is that a graphic language or convention had by then established itself and was being systematically employed, using simple single and double lines to represent walls, for example, with special symbols for doors and openings, not dissimilar to our standardised drawing technique today. □ ↖129

Over time we have made use of a wider and perhaps more nuanced range of symbols and conventions – for example hatching or shading – to indicate characteristics such as foreseen materials, and thus a contemporary graphic language has evolved in the construction industry which anyone with any interest in it can become familiar with, and which therefore allows everybody involved to deduce a three-dimensional construct from a two-dimensional representation, this being its exact purpose. ■ 262↘

It is important at this point to note that when we speak of a 'standardised drawing technique' and a 'contemporary graphic language', we mean just that: recognised common standards, which may vary a bit from region to region or country to country, but which are universally intelligible. It is a language that comes perhaps in different 'dialects', but that shares a common 'grammar' and can therefore be learnt. After all, the plans that come together during the process of design and execution of a building project are not only a communication tool, they also form part of a legally binding contract between the architect, the engineers and builders, and the client, and in fact everyone involved who has any say, including the authority responsible for granting a planning permission. These plans therefore need to be clear, exact, and dependable; not open to interpretation, but specific and unambiguous.

083 ● 140

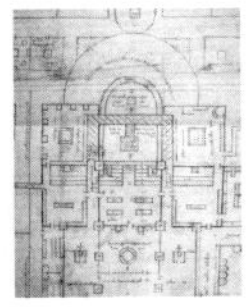
084 ● 140

■
□ 421↘
■
□ ↖57
■ 267↘
■ 204↘
■

PLAN CATEGORIES AND TYPES

A principal distinction can be made between design plan and project plan. A *design plan*, as we would expect, forms part of the design process, and on it therefore not everything has to be precisely defined or determined. There is an assumption that things may evolve, that the design phase is still in progress, and that materials, textures, details may yet change. A *project plan*, by contrast, is as much an instruction manual as it is an illustration. Things by this stage have been decided on, costed, and signed off. Contractors are bound by the details indicated on the plan and they really have to use the type of glass, the strength of steel, the thickness of wood as specified, and place them in the exact position foreseen, otherwise things will go badly awry.

One of the consequences of moving from hand drawings to CAD is that this differentiation between design plan and project plan has to some extent been lost, and today these two quite different categories of plan are all but indistinguishable.

We can also group visual representations more generally into three parallel categories:

- Analogue
- Symbolic
- Iconic

Analogue representations are hand drawn plans, which by necessity are always to scale, because they represent the object that's being designed or proposed in one particular iteration.

Symbolic representations are coded or digitalised or digitally generated plans, which do not have to be to scale, because in actual fact they do not physically exist until they are printed out. Before then, they are simply data on a computer and can therefore be scaled and manipulated at will.

Iconic representations use pictorial images that also do not have to be to scale, but that can be understood without further explanation, usually in the context of some plan or model.

With these principal categories established, we can now briefly look at the different types of plan that are commonly used.

Most prominent in the traditional repertoire are ground plans: horizontal sections through all relevant building elements. As standard practice for orthogonal buildings, these are taken at window level, to illustrate the windows' positioning along with the placement of any other openings, such as doors. Similarly, cross sections are used to communicate the height of the building, as well as other important construction elements, such as staircases, balconies, or roof overhangs; and elevations serve to show the outward aspect and appearance of the object from all its sides.

While, as we noted, it is not difficult to acquire a basic grasp of the visual language of technical drawings and plans, it is in the nature of things that this understanding is mostly limited to professionals. Laypeople often find it hard to orientate themselves simply on the basis of plans, sections, and elevations, and so to communicate a project to the general public, these graphic representations are usually complemented with illustrations and perspective drawings, and indeed models.

Model Making is a discipline in its own right, and we have a chapter on it in this *Atlas*, as well as on 3D Modelling, so we will not delve into these here. But on paper, the conventions used to achieve this less abstract level of communication are based on the principle of orthographic (or orthogonal) projection, which, as the name suggests, projects the three-dimensional object onto the two-dimensional plane. For simple structures, this method is comparatively easy to use, but more complex objects make it necessary to employ projective geometry; and in fact for a long time, while perspectives and shadows had to be drawn by hand, the umbrella discipline of descriptive geometry was a subject routinely taught at architecture schools.

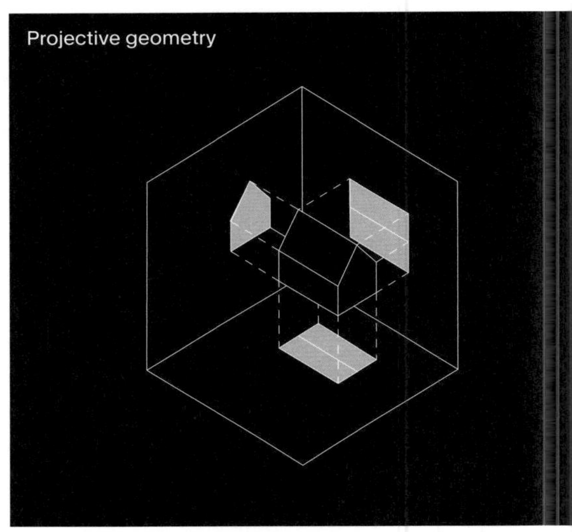

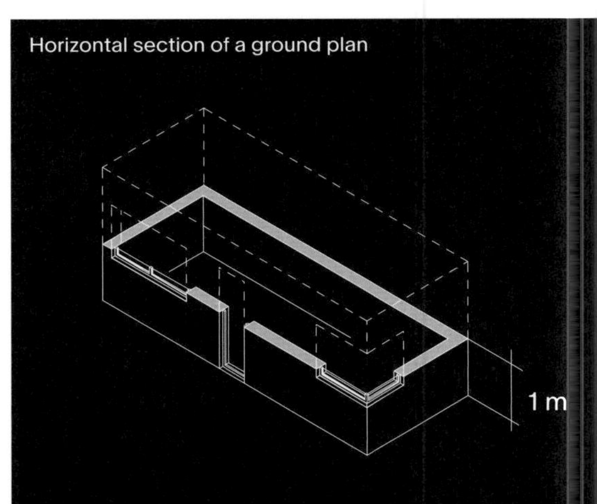

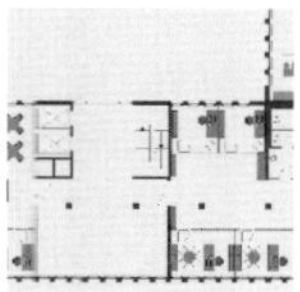

085 ● 141

Considering the extent to which plans today are being worked on digitally, and the strong drive – especially by public funding bodies and permission granting authorities – towards data exchange between architects and their collaborators and project stakeholders, the traditional paper plan still plays a remarkably important part as a communication tool and often remains on file as a dependable medium of documentation with a high likelihood of longevity.

LEVELS OF ABSTRACTION

Before we get into our topic of CAD in more depth, this may be an opportune moment to highlight the different levels of abstraction that are at work as we go from ground plan, through elevation and perspective drawing, towards CAD and 3D modelling.

If our starting point is a sketch or a manual drawing, then our level of abstraction is bound to be high: much detail is as yet unknown and left to the imagination; for as long as we are in black lines on white paper and monochrome shades of grey from various types of pencil or pen, we give not much of a hint towards any colour scheme, and even the materiality of a facade or construction element is – or at any rate can be – left open to speculation and future decision making.

What we show is the structure on its own, possibly with some additional elements of our choice if it's a perspective drawing, but nobody expects what they see to be what they get: there is much room for the design to develop, evolve, concretise, as we go further into the process.

Once we get into CAD and 3D modelling with contemporary software, the level of abstraction is markedly low. Now, we have the possibility to include exacting detail about every feature and element, about materials, colours, and even items that are strictly speaking extraneous to the design, such as pieces of furniture. When on a ground plan or elevation we might indicate where the bath tub goes, where the kitchen, and where any principal installations, in a CAD drawing or 3D model we'll be tempted to show what kind of bath tub, what design kitchen, and even include a photorealistic visualisation of the bed and wardrobe for the guest room.

This has its advantages as well as disadvantages, and we discuss them in quite a similar vein in our chapters on Visualisation and also Model □ 285↘
Making: the more detail you pack into your early □ 421↘
design, and the more realistic it therefore looks – the less abstract, conversely, your representation is – the more you commit yourself at that point. You push decision making towards the earliest stages of your design process, and once you show a client or a panel of decision makers your wood-topped cast-iron handrail for your staircase, that is going to be pretty much what they'll expect to see when the project is built.

What used to be a fairly open and therefore free early design phase where you might go into a competition with mostly a concept and many detailed questions as yet unanswered and possibly not even yet asked, now, with the ever more complex possibilities offered by digital tools, these early designs become more and more concrete, and therefore less abstract, and this is why we find ourselves conceptually in planning, as opposed to design, much earlier.

A Very Brief History of CAD

THE ORIGINS

Many technological developments initially adopt a form that emulates the technology they have evolved from. The car is a classic example of this: early cars were essentially motorised versions of comparably sized horse-drawn carriages. The computer keyboard is another: it would, at the time of its invention, have been easy enough to go for absolutely any arrangement of keys, but with the QWERTY keyboard having by then so firmly established itself, this was simply appropriated and slightly adapted. (We tell its story in our chapter on Text, Typography & Layout.) □ 327↘

In a similar vein, Computer Aided Design – which really considering its capabilities in those days ought to have been called Computer Aided Drafting – transferred traditional drawing techniques to a fairly basic new digital tool. The main purpose of this tool was to rationalise the drawing process, with the output still a two-dimensional plan, just as before.

As we note elsewhere in this *Atlas*, this method of computer aided drafting was originally used not first and foremost by architects, but by engineers in other sectors, namely the automotive, aerospace, and shipbuilding industries. It's what gave birth to the discipline of technical drawing, and so it is fair to say that the transition from manual to computer aided drawing began largely because of the evident advantages it offered in meeting engineering requirements, as opposed to answering design prerogatives. It is for this reason that early CAD programs were conceived as cross-disciplinary software. When architects first – and at first fairly tentatively – began to use CAD as a tool, architecture-specific features were appended to these existing programs as extensions.

So while in a laboratory setting new technologies were being developed that certainly pointed towards the future, in practice you had to cope with the fairly basic standards of the day for a while yet.

These entailed, for example, a separation of alphanumeric and vector-based input devices and monitors at one end, and also a separation of vector-based ink plotters and raster-based pinhead printers as output devices at the other. Since there were no scanners, and no conversion tools, you had to enter the coordinates of objects manually by keyboard, or trace them from existing plans on a graphics tablet.

086A ● 141

086B ● 141

■ ↖74 185↘ From 1982 onwards, software started to appear on the market that was actually geared towards architecture, now sometimes with the *Archi* prefix in the product name, as in Graphisoft's then groundbreaking *ArchiCAD*, to denote this specialisation.
□ 175↘ The early 1980s correspondingly also mark the era
■ ↖62 177↘ during which the term Computer Aided Architectural Design (CAAD) is first used to describe and develop the field of architecture-specific CAD.

By the mid-1980s the refresh rate on raster image monitors had become fast enough, and therefore their picture stable enough and at the same time their res-
■ ↖65 232↘ olution high enough, to comfortably display vector graphics as well as alphanumeric values, and so the need for two separate monitors fell by the wayside. Similarly, capturing existing plans no longer happened manually on a tablet, but by large-format scanner. On the output side, raster plotters and laser printers, which are roundly more reliable, faster, and more economical to run, replaced pen plotters, with one machine now capable of putting to paper text, figures, vectors, surfaces, and photos as standard. (Though it is perhaps worth noting that these pen plotters produced an output that was visually closer to traditional hand drawings than that of any new generation of printers.)

↖63 FROM 2D VIA 2.5D TO 3D

Continuing and accelerating technological evolution soon teased from the medium CAD new capabilities, and in terms of architectural representation the next logical step was to expand the two-dimensional plan into the third dimension, creating an elevation along a Z-axis. Before this was fully achieved, there was an intermediate phase, generally labelled *2.5D*. These programs were essentially hybrids that could depict an object or element two- or three-dimensionally, depending on which viewer you were using.

Another incremental stage towards 3D was held by wireframe models which gave accurate three-dimensional representations, but were fully 'transparent' and therefore often difficult to read, before finally 3D representations became possible, with those lines that would be invisible in a solid building actually hidden or covered. (More on this evolutionary stage and the issue of hidden lines in our chapter on
□ 255↘ Rendering.)

Classical ground plans were unable to represent unusual, specifically non-orthogonal, parts of an object, such as slanting or conic walls, freeform design components, or separate building elements, such as trusses, brackets, or beams. But the drive in the building industry towards modular and skeleton construction methods, which had started in the late 1960s and continued throughout the 70s, also prompted the development of CAD software that was capable of handling these types of three-dimensional elements, such as supports with cleats or plates, for example.

As a need grew in other fields – namely product design and machine building – for software that could manage smooth curves and similarly complex, non-orthogonal geometries, the programs that were being developed for these purposes found some pioneers who adapted and applied them outside their target market, gradually paving the way to freeform technologies such as NURBS (Non-Uniform Rational B-Splines) of the type that had been developed in the automotive industries, and which from about the 1990s onwards were integrated into architectural software and made usable there. (We talk more about these themes in our chapter on Graphs & Graphics.)

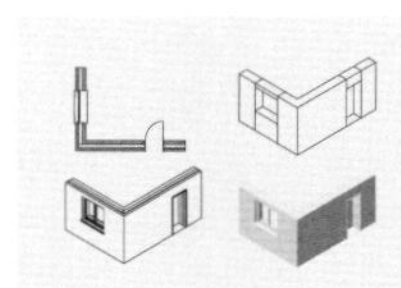

087 ● 142

SYMBOL LIBRARIES

With architecture-specific CAD software and the motion towards 3D we also for the first time get *symbol libraries*. These are libraries of symbols or blocks for construction elements that you need in day-to-day design tasks, such as trees, tables, chairs, showers, staircases: all the things that up until then you had to draw individually, and often very repetitively, since they appear in and around all kinds of buildings, all the time.

The great advantage of such libraries was that you now no longer had to spend time creating bespoke elements for every project. The great pitfall, or danger – and this is something we address repeatedly in this *Atlas* – is that with symbol libraries you are already nudging your architecture towards a *Lego* approach of using standardised, generic building blocks that you can swiftly and apparently effortlessly put together. Only, it isn't effortless, at least not if you take the task seriously. Because the off-the-shelf elements are all of a kind. They look, essentially, all the same. In order to make them specific to your project, you have to customise and individualise them – which you can, there are almost innumerable settings and specifications you can choose or determine – but that again takes a whole lot of time and effort, and a new kind of expertise.

Now, considering what we said earlier about the potential for, and also tendency toward, lower levels of abstraction and higher levels of detail in CAD and 3D modelling, this opens up a whole new challenge, which can be formidable: how much detailed customisation do you go for? If you leave things as they appear in the library, this may feel like keeping them open and therefore abstract, but in fact they may very well be quite detailed and precise, only not to your project, but for general purposes.

So these tools, as we see time and again, are certainly very powerful, but they can also be very limiting. Suddenly everything is super-concrete and specific, but it still all looks more or less like it's come off the shelf. Because it more or less has.

There are parametric elements, such as windows and staircases, for which you can adjust many different values to individualise the element, and there are static ones, such as tables or chairs, which you simply use as they are. And as you would expect you can build your own libraries, too. But in essence, this already is no longer drawing, it's mostly assembling. And from both the architecture student and teacher perspective, it raises the question: how do I learn or teach the art of how and why a window fits into a wall. How do I communicate 'windowness'? Who, indeed, is able or willing, or even keen, to think the window *afresh?*

It's not unlike using predictive texting: if it's effective, fast, and correct, then why not use it? But if you use it, then how do you develop your own language, your own tone even, let alone your own poetry?

PERSPECTIVE AND RENDERING

In parallel with continually improving capabilities which mainly served the purpose of accurately representing 3D objects, there was at this stage also a desire to be able to create more realistic visualisations as part of the design process. Crucial to this are central perspectives and shadows.

Drawing perspectives manually is demanding and labour intensive. If you want to draw a plausible central perspective, even as a sketch, within a useful timeframe, you have to be a skilled and experienced draughtsperson, and so a simplified method of spatial representation had established itself since antiquity in conventional drawings: axonometry. As a basic graphical projection it offered the advantage of being easy to generate with simple tools. But in view of the difficulties inherent in generating complex perspectives, any software that could make this possible with relative ease was bound to become attractive to architects, and so CAD now soon started winning over even diehard traditionalists simply because it offered this new solution to a generally taxing problem in design and planning.

It is worth noting here though that while rendering tools in CAD become mightier all the time, they are not as powerful as dedicated render engines, which in turn have also become bigger and more demanding to master over time. We talk about the various Rendering and Visualisation techniques in our respective chapters on these.

CAD AS A DEVELOPMENT TOOL

The 'perfect' renderings of CAD and render programs today can be truly impressive, but the 'fuzziness' of hand-drawn perspectives has its own charm and character, and a personal quality that in renders simply gets lost. Computer programs can fake this effect to some degree, but that is what you then have: faked imperfection, whereas the odd mistake or error, the mis-drawn line or the flourish, the personal touch that lends a drawing its 'signature appearance', these often appeal much more to the viewer's imagination than the clinical accuracy of a computer generated image.

While a computer requires exact data in order to handle a graphic representation of anything, a pencil drawing allows you as the designer to make simple and quick (also experimental) choices, for example about the hardness of your pencil and thus the thickness of your line, and therefore about the level of 'focus' your drawing is going to be in. In traditional drawing techniques, you would use a legendary 6B pencil for early sketches, because of its fat, soft stroke. As you started refining your drawings, you would move onto ever higher levels of hardness, leading to thinner, more precise lines and also requiring smoother paper. As a last stage, you would then use a technical ink pen and ruler and possibly a board-mounted drawing mechanism to bring your results to paper, but always in this order: first the design, then the detailed drafting.

The software industry was not originally interested in digitalising the design process, because the profitable market was not in design but in the effective, time and money efficient representation, production, and duplication of precise technical drawings and plans, which by their character are relatively invariant. Compare this to the difficulty in transferring to software the complex, intuitive, and imprecise design process, which undergoes many changes and corrections, and it is not surprising to find that software which made it possible to model in three dimensions, to control the design decisions visually, and to easily make continuous adjustments and corrections established itself only later.

088 ● 142

089 ● 142

■ ↖63

090 ● 143

PARAMETRIC DESIGN

↖114 149↘

□ 255↘
□ 285↘

The move from conventional design processes to one that is determined by mathematics marks a completely new departure in architecture, and you could say that CAD in the sense we have up until now understood it here ends and something else entirely begins.

While in classical design methodology form-finding and materials stood in the foreground, *parametric design* uses mathematically defined structures which are set by algorithmic rules and can be modified by varying their parameters.

This brings two major advantages: firstly it makes possible the generation of geometries which either can't be represented by traditional ground plans, or only with great difficulty; and secondly it allows you to then send the data that's required to manufacture construction elements and to realise the concept physically directly to the companies who are executing these jobs, for use with their digital manufacturing tools. (We talk about parametric design in various chapters in this *Atlas*, among them Digital Design Strategies, Digital Manufacturing, 3D Modelling, and Generative Methods.)

□ ↖111
□ 405↘
□ ↖57
□ 145↘

FROM CAD TO BIM

□ 507↘

The – possibly romantic – notion of the architect as a master builder or artist who dreams up a concept and moves it from their head, via hand drawn paper sketches, to CAD plans, and only thence, with the aid of their contractors and suppliers, to physical reality, is effectively a thing of the past. Where it does still exist, it is confined mostly to small construction projects. The bigger a project, the more demanding are the conditions that have to be met, and the more complex the factors that play into the planning, communication, and ultimately execution of the undertaking. Standards, laws, and the collaborative nature of large-scale projects make it necessary for stakeholders, specialist planners, and contractors to share reliable drawings, models, and data, which in turn makes it increasingly impossible for the architect to work in any kind of isolation, even during the design phase.

Which is why more and more architects find they have to leave the narrow horizon of the one-person studio or office behind and open themselves up to the world of complex planning. As we note in our dedicated chapter on the subject, there is immense pressure from large institutional clients, such as national and regional authorities, for the construction industry to adopt a seamless digital planning, execution, and maintenance lifecycle approach, for which read Building Information Modelling (BIM). We of course have a full chapter on BIM in this *Atlas* and so won't elaborate on it here; suffice it to say that the principal selling point of BIM is that it comprises one or several semantic data models that contain extensive and detailed information about building materials, characteristics, standards, and pricing, and therefore lend themselves to an integrated modelling process. This in an ideal case extends from conception to decommission of an architectural object, in other words, over many years or even decades, allowing for its continued and – so the aspiration – coherent management and maintenance regime.

Organisation of CAD Software

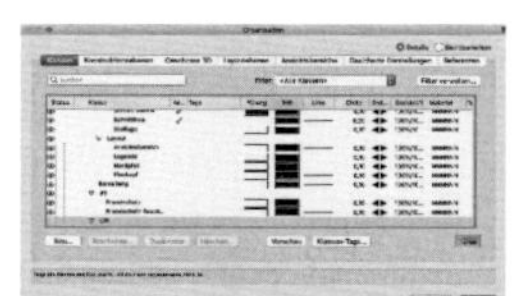

091 ● 143

LAYERS

We mentioned earlier how pen plotters yielded printed plans that came closest in appearance to hand drawn traditional plans, and although these machines have long since been superseded by faster and more versatile technology, the organisation of most CAD software programs owes its structure to these plotters, because in CAD software drawings are typically built in layers, and these layers more or less correspond to the layers you would print with pen plotters. It is fair to say though that there is no uniform system for this, with approaches varying from one piece of software to another, and in fact many programs feature several layer systems that are related to each other orthogonally.

Layers can be set to being visible or invisible or to any level of opaqueness in-between, they can be locked so as to prevent further changes being made to them, and they can be allocated to different drawing types and styles, such as stroke thickness, hatching, or colour. Together, these settings are sometimes referred to as drawing or style *attributes.*

Maintenance groups such as electricity and water supplies and different construction types can be classified and organised in layers, so that, for example, all electrical wiring and all pipework are kept separate from each other.

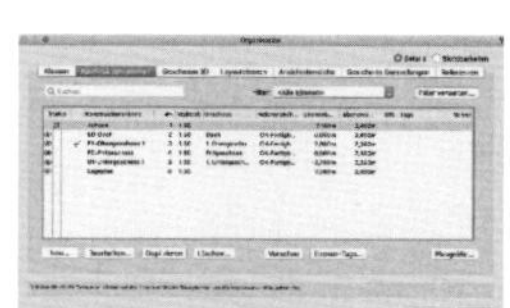

092 ● 143

Some programs furthermore have a layer system for the different physical levels of a building, namely floors or stories, and for different types of views, such as ground plans and elevations. To these, you can also then allocate different scales. And some programs separate a model modus at 1:1 scale from a layout modus, which might be to a scale of 1:100, for example.

WYSIWYG

Some CAD programs make your screen look effectively like a plan with a scale that is set from the start.

The style or drawing attributes appear on the screen as they do on paper, thus emulating the approach of a traditional analogue drawing board. As in other types of computer software, this is referred to as *What You See Is What You Get,* or *WYSIWYG* for short.

GROUPS

Different drawing elements can be grouped together. These groups correspond approximately to folders in data systems. The advantage of this is that you can then treat an entire group of individual elements in one go, by for example allocating a stroke colour to them or changing their size and position in the drawing.

SYMBOL OR BLOCK LIBRARIES

We already talked in detail about libraries: they form an important part of the CAD software structure.

The principle at work rests on symbols or blocks, or, more specifically, block definitions from which derive block references (block copies or instances) in the visible part of a drawing. Because these instances are linked to the block definitions, the amount of data that is required to work with these blocks is relatively small, no matter how often the item is deployed. And any time any alteration is made to the definition of a block, as long as this is saved under the original name, all block references – that is all appearances of the block as visible elements – will automatically be adjusted.

PARAMETRIC OBJECTS

Parametric objects are CAD symbols or blocks, such as staircases or windows that can be customised by adjusting often very detailed settings. They are mostly hybrid 2D and 3D symbols and form a stepping stone or development stage towards full Building Information Modelling (BIM). ☐ 507↘

SOFTWARE FORMATS

Most software formats for CAD are proprietary, including Autodesk's *Drawing (DWG)* and MicroStation's *Design File (DGN)* formats. Autodesk also developed the open-source *Drawing Interchange Format* – or *Drawing Exchange Format* – *(DXF)* to facilitate interoperability between its *AutoCAD* and other CAD systems, and since its first release in 1982 this has established itself in effect as an industry standard.

The Outlook

TEACHING AND LEARNING ARCHITECTURE WITH DIGITAL DESIGN TOOLS

We started our chapter with Heinrich von Kleist. Another seminal German literary figure (perhaps *the* seminal German literary figure), and contemporary of Kleist's, Johann Wolfgang von Goethe (1749–1832) in 1797 published a short ballad called *Der Zauberlehrling (The Sorcerer's Apprentice),* which for its simple archetypal story has entered popular culture and not only spawned several colloquial expressions in German and a classic Disney cartoon, but also lends its title to the long-running TV 'reality' show *The Apprentice.*

In the original story, the eponymous young hero takes advantage of the fact that the master sorcerer has left him alone in charge of the vault. Overestimating his own competence, he commands a broom to fill a basin with water for him, apparently so he can take a bath (or maybe his master has tasked him to do so for his own purposes when he gets back, the text does not further specify). The magic soon gets out of hand as the broom is so fast at fetching water that it threatens to flood the building, and neither will it cease when told to stop. When the despairing apprentice breaks it in two, both parts now go about their job of bringing in water, at twice the capacity, until finally the master returns and puts an end to the ill-fated proceedings. "*Die ich rief, die Geister, werd ich nun nicht los!*" the hapless boy wails at one point: 'the demons I've conjured up I can not now get rid of.' It's a cautionary tale of what happens when you unleash powers that you're not in command of yet. And we're happy to let it stand here as a none-too-subtle reminder that technology being applied with unintended, possibly sub-ideal consequences is absolutely nothing new.

CAD really stands at the beginning of digital design practice and in a sense you could say ushers in everything that follows. In this *Atlas* we largely eschew an altogether too celebratory tone and often note that actually much of what we do now with computers we have always been doing in one way or another, long before digital technology came about. We emphasise, in several places, that the masters of antiquity and the Renaissance were no less intelligent, or imaginative, than we are, and we even cite, in one or two places, those who at the time warned of bad practice or substandard technique, such as the Italian architect Sebastiano Serlio (1475 – c. 1554) who admonishes his contemporaries for not being on top of their craft. (See the conclusion to this *Atlas*: What Is Information?) ☐ 693↘

So with all the enthusiasm there no doubt is, and in many cases justifiably so, for the untold possibilities that come with computer aided design and, specifically, architectural design, we want to address here the for architecture students and teachers more principal didactic question of how to teach and learn architecture with these contemporary digital tools, and also highlight some of the pitfalls they bring.

We talked a bit already about the difference between drawing by hand and drawing or designing – often really assembling design – by CAD, and we mentioned the level of detail that CAD and indeed other digital design tools tend to foist on you, or at the very least encourage you to commit to, early on in the process.

There is another, perhaps more subtle, aspect to this, which ties into the overall question of how you learn to master architecture. And that is this: in the traditional analogue transition from rough sketches to pencil drawings to finished drawings by technical pen, you had to be really precise and conscientious about what you were going to commit to paper and what not. If you made a mistake in the technical drawing, you caused yourself real pain: it was difficult and time-consuming to make corrections, and so to avoid this pain you had to concentrate, and be careful, and 'rehearse' your metaphorical 'text'. Expressed somewhat prosaically, a mistake on a technical hand drawing would cost you about 7 euros in time and material. In CAD this falls off the cliff. If you make a mistake you simply correct it, a cost in material does not usually come into play unless you've already started printing out plans or models, and in terms of time the cost may be all of about 0.2 cents.

Similarly, the process in hand drawn design led from a very free, open, non-committal early phase through ever more concrete decision making to a finished set of plans and drawings that then were really 'there'. They existed and they were what was going to be built, if it was going to be built. Yes, changes could still be made, but they were costly and therefore considered very carefully. In CAD you can continue planning and designing until a couple of hours before the deadline, because at the end you just press 'print', and it's done. So your decision making process, having as we noted started so much earlier and become so much more detailed early on, paradoxically now also extends much further, with last minute changes being possible until almost literally the very last minute.

Fundamentally though, and this may be one of the most important aspects to bear in mind, the CAD generated drawing simply is a different species to its hand drawn predecessor. With its level of detail and parametric as well as semantic information, you could say it no longer asks questions. It only gives answers. And that, ironically, is in itself as much a loss as it might be considered a gain.

SOME PITFALLS

☐ 507↘

LOSING THE MEASURE OF SCALE

While it is possible to jot down hand drawn sketches on the corner of the proverbial napkin or in your sketchbook without much further immediate thought, in classical, analogue plan drawings – be they ground plans, situational plans, elevations, or cross sections – you need a defined, specified scale to which you are generating these drawings.

The scale you go for tends to be determined by the level to which the project has taken shape as a concrete idea. Starting perhaps with situational plans on a scale of 1:5000 to 1:500 depending on the size of the site, down to ground plans at may be 1:200 to 1:50.

The scale here determines not only the physical size of the plan, but in particular also the level of its execution. An experienced analogue planner will develop a sense for reading plans drawn up at different scales and for identifying from them at different stages in the project whether, for example, certain areas of the space are being given enough room or possibly not enough, or too much.

In CAD a sense of scale is a real problem, as often details are drawn much too precisely for even large scale drawings, or ridiculous font sizes are employed, which only become obvious once the plans are printed out. The attendant sense of proportion meanwhile is lost if ground plans are only ever seen as zoomed-in frames on a monitor during their generation, until finally the whole plan emerges in its entirety from a printer at the desired scale. Which is why you sometimes come across contemporary scenarios where a plan is presented in its 'full size' digitally too: either by means of oversized wall displays or on horizontal surface displays, such as Microsoft's *PixelSense* surface table.

LAZINESS

Among the harshest und most quoted criticisms levied against CAD (and, as it happens, BIM) is this: the ease with which it is possible to get hold of pre-defined, off-the-shelf construction and design elements – such as stairways, or bathrooms, or handles – leads to laziness. By inserting elements of this type into a plan or design unchanged and without further reflection, the very ethos of architecture to develop and use bespoke components in the creation of an edifice is offended, so the charge.

This siren call of standardised elements is getting louder, and not least for practical reasons. In traditional 2D design it was enough to draw an individual staircase in ground plan and cross section. In 3D or BIM this requires elaborate modelling with many attributes. The effort, therefore, of developing bespoke elements in 3D design is disproportionately greater and therefore the temptation of re-using existing components – whether self-designed previously or supplied with the software – is strong.

This too, though, is not entirely new: even back in the old analogue architectural practice, there were standard details which were often simply adapted, perhaps improved and recycled many times. The question therefore, here as in other areas, is not so much what is possible with the technology, but how do I use the tool and keep my integrity as an architect. As we note in our chapter on Building Information Modelling (BIM), there can be good reasons for using simple, easily manufactured, and time efficient planning components, such as where the primary objective is to put up a useful, good-enough-looking building at low cost, perhaps in response to an emergency situation. But it is difficult to build a really beautiful, unique museum, for example, from mostly generic blocks and symbols.

What we want to emphasise here once more is that you are dealing with a fundamentally different process and type of thinking if you start with perfect-looking components and refine these by and by, compared to starting with an idea and letting it grow organically with a long time being allowed to pass before the drawing has to make any claim to perfection.

A CONCLUSION ON CAD

The hand drawn sketch is and remains of importance. But in many ways the outlook for CAD is contained in the short section entitled From CAD to BIM above. We talk in a great deal of detail about what BIM has to offer and what criticisms are levied against it in our dedicated chapter on it, so there is no need for us to do so here. What seems entirely obvious though is that CAD as a 'computer aided drawing' tool has long been eclipsed by software that actually merits the label 'design', and that integrated, information-rich 3D modelling has become the norm.

Whether the route forward from here must by necessity entail BIM as we understand it today, or whether that presupposes a significant next evolutionary stage for BIM, or whether BIM will eventually be replaced by other, more contemporarily attuned types of modelling remains to be seen, and opinions vary widely on this matter. It would be rash for us to make any categorical pronouncements, therefore, not least also because BIM so much at the moment has the support of very large clients who therefore hold very big budgets.

What seems certainly significant in this context is that Autodesk, when it found its CAD software *AutoCAD* not ready for BIM in 2002, acquired *Revit*, which had been developed since 1997 and which is BIM '4D' capable. (We explain the somewhat idiosyncratic 'dimensions' of BIM in its chapter.)

CAD has established itself so squarely in architecture offices that, as we write this in 2018/19, without it nothing goes. This begs the question: what – in a world with or without BIM specifically – do we mean by CAD?

The increasing concretisation of which we spoke in non-standardised architectonic solutions entails an enormous amount of effort, which means that standardised solutions are strongly reinforced and encouraged. And that means that suddenly the 'kit' of available building blocks becomes very small, and architecture starts to look more and more the same, because small to medium size architecture offices just don't have the time and the resources to explore the sphere beyond standardisation, with only very large or prominent offices being able to form exceptions, because they can cultivate individual solutions with parametric designs.

We make the point in other parts of this *Atlas* – and several times emphatically so – that drawing as a literacy is being pushed into the background. We follow a through line from antiquity, where literacy concerned itself first and foremost with words, to the Renaissance, where the most impactful literacy pertains to drawing – specifically perspective drawing – and argue that today's literacy has to be one of code. If this thesis, such as it is, is correct, then that means that *drawing* is being supplanted by *coding*.

When, therefore, up until the beginning of the 'digital age' we thought of architectural design as principally an activity of visually drawing concepts and ideas, and consequently sought and were given software that would allow us to 'draw' digitally, now, as the digital era is reaching a first level of maturity, we realise that actually the chief element in architectural design of the future may not be the drawing but the *code*.

If this is even vaguely true, then our conception of what a CAD program does, or what CAD does within BIM, or what BIM does, will have to evolve. Currently, BIM is extremely complicated and often inelegant and counter-intuitive. But in languages such as **XML (Extensible Markup Language)** its approach ■ 336↘
can stabilise itself. With code, the tasks demanded by the huge data sets that BIM requires can be repositioned, and new approaches can be found.

Where CAD is right now – subsumed into BIM – it forms part of an approach to architecture in which everything centres around the data bank. The architect in this situation loses control over the building, as design has become secondary to economic, pragmatic, and regulatory priorities. The question then is, how do we, as architects, gain back control over what we do. Looked at in this way, BIM as well as in fact **parametricism** pose a challenge, a gauntlet to ■ ↖64 165↘
architects that takes the business of architecture out of our hands, and it is for us to assert our role and find conceptual and technological ways to state and practise what and who we are. CAD may well have a significant part to play in this.

So we would say, yes, CAD does have a future, but that future by necessity has to be tied in with 3D modelling. Yet the constraints of BIM, the deficiencies it has in terms of user-friendliness, and its factual hardness that requires users to commit to so many details so early on in the process, all open up a gap in the software market for a new 'soft' design tool: the digital equivalent, you could say, of the much loved 6B pencil. Something that requires no semantic data and that not just allows, but actively enables and facilitates freeform drawing, trial and error, experimentation, 'fuzziness', and few or late decisions.

This would, in a sense, bring us 'full circle', though here as so often, this is a complete misnomer, because it would much rather bring us, on this particular evolutionary helix, to a level above the one from where we set out – hand drawing – and allow the contemporary architect to work as creatively, as intuitively, and as fluidly as you would have done with your various pencils and ink pens and different types of paper, but do all of this from the outset in the digital environment, with no constraints or restrictions. That type of CAD tool would then truly deserve the epithet Computer Aided Design. And so perhaps it is not the case that working with software necessarily becomes easier, nor is that perhaps even desirable.

Maybe the job of the architect will indeed change and move away from drawing plans. But as we note in the conclusions to other chapters in this *Atlas*, there may be a motion for the architect of today 'back', or rather 'forward', but along a spiral figure of 'evolution', towards a more Renaissance style master builder who has the complete oversight on even the grandest of projects. And was it really the job of the Renaissance architect to draw plans? Or was it not much rather their job to think and express themselves in high concept and elegant abstraction...

082 ● 131
In 'conversation': hand drawings as a process to develop a design idea, for the whole project, or for a detail. [Anna Fedorov]

083 ● 132
The tipi tent: a structure that requires no plan or model. [W H Jackson]

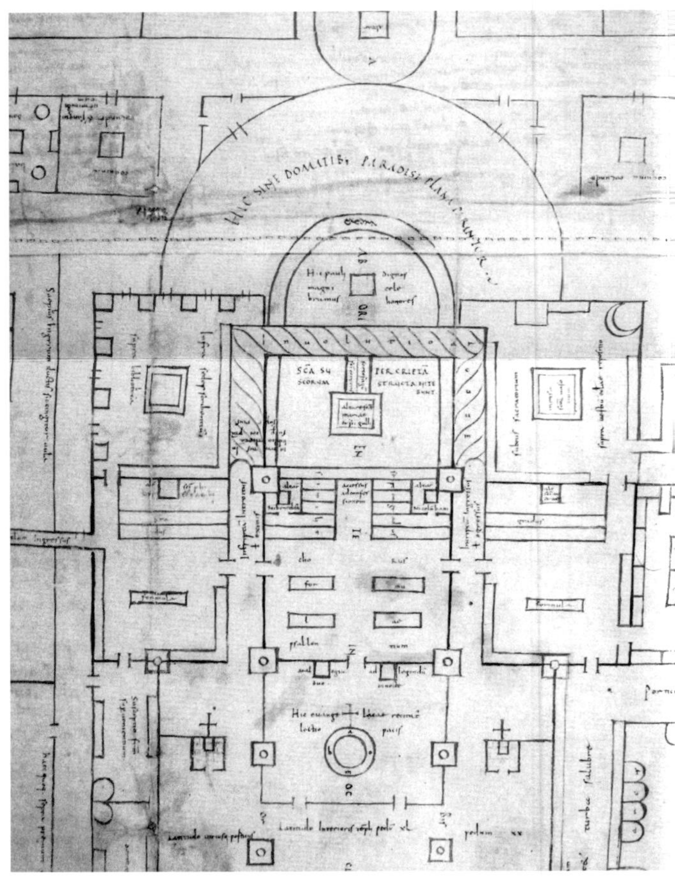

084 ● 132
The *Plan of Saint Gall* is a mediaeval architectural drawing of a monastic compound dating from 820–830 CE.

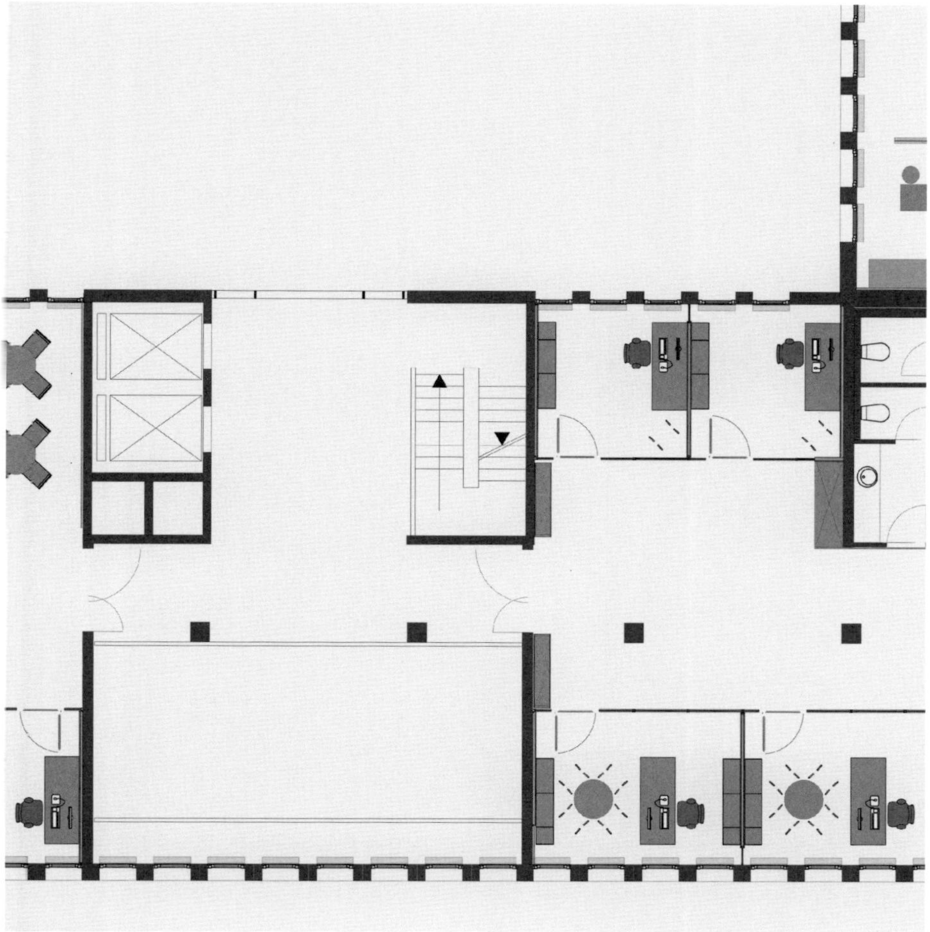

085 ● 133
2D ground plan. [Oliver Fritz]

086A ● 134
Separation of input devices: a graphics monitor next to an alpha-numeric monitor (with a pen plotter.) [Nemetschek]

086B ● 134
CAD work station with double monitor and digitising tablet as input medium. [Intergraph]

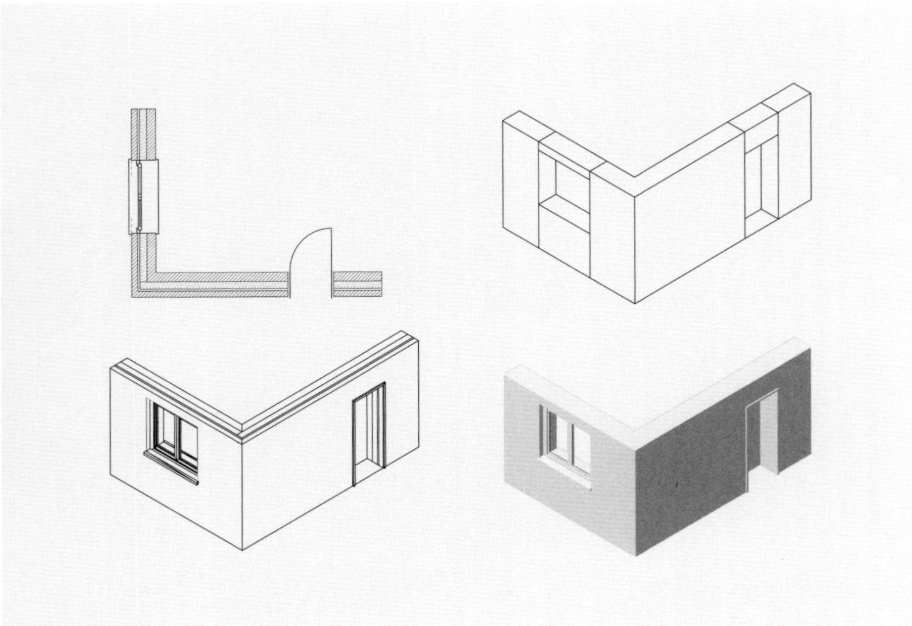

087 ● 134
The progression from 2D to 3D in traditional construction method and representation. [Oliver Fritz]

088 ● 135
Creative fuzziness with a soft pencil. [Oliver Fritz]

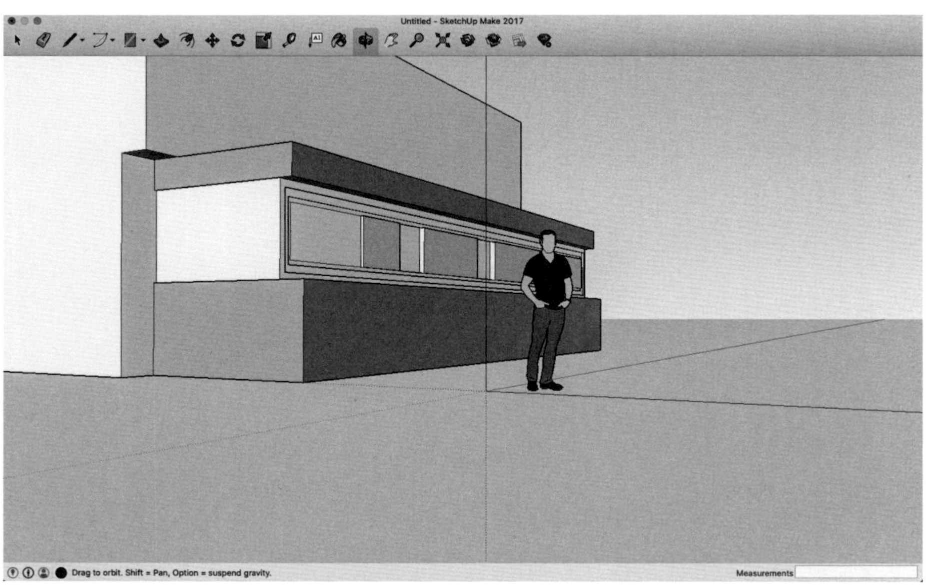

089 ● 135
3D modelling in CAD; here with *SketchUp*. [Oliver Fritz]

090 ● 135
Sketching and designing in the 3D space, here with *Google Tiltbrush*. [Katrin Günther]

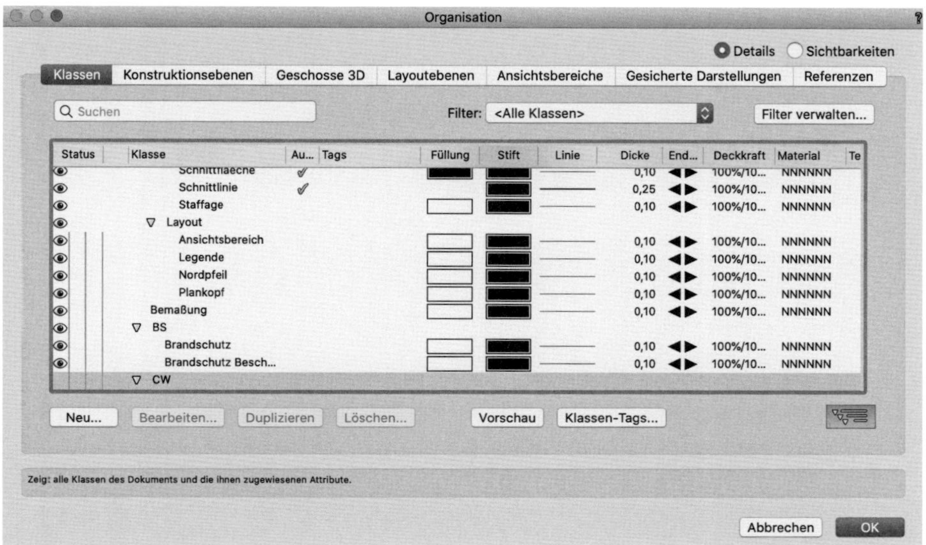

091 ● 136
Style attributes in *VectorWorks*. [Oliver Fritz]

092 ● 136
Layer settings in *VectorWorks*. [Oliver Fritz]

Generative Methods

Urs Hirschberg and Oliver Fritz

- Charles Robert Darwin: *On the Origin of Species by Means of Natural Selection, or the Preservation of Favoured Races in the Struggle for Life*, 1859
- D'Arcy Wentworth Thompson: *On Growth and Form*, 1917
- Ernst Haeckel: *Kunstformen der Natur*, 1899
- Alan M Turing: *The Chemical Basis of Morphogenesis*, Philosophical Transactions of the Royal Society of London. Series B, Biological Sciences, Vol.237, No. 641. (Aug. 14, 1952), pp. 37–72
- Christopher Alexander: *Notes on the Synthesis of Form*, 1964
- Nicholas Negroponte: *The Architecture Machine: Toward a More Human Environment*, 1973
- James Gips: *Shape Grammars and their Uses, Interdisciplinary Systems Research*, 1975
- John Holland: *Adaptation in Natural and Artificial Systems*, 1975
- George Stiny, William J Mitchell: *The Palladian Grammar in Environment and Planning B*, 1978
- Benoit B Mandelbrot: *The Fractal Geometry of Nature*, 1982
- Richard Dawkins: *The Blind Watchmaker: Why the Evidence of Evolution Reveals a Universe without Design*, 1986
- Przemyslaw Prusinkiewicz, Aristid Lindenmayer: *The Algorithmic Beauty of Plants*, 1990
- John Frazer: *An Evolutionary Architecture*, 1995
- Melanie Mitchell: *An Introduction to Genetic Algorithms*, 1996
- Michael Hensel, Achim Menges, Michael Weinstock: *Emergence: Morphogenetic Design Strategies*, 2004
- Axel Kilian, John Ochsendorf: *Particle-Spring Systems For Structural Form Finding in Journal Of The International Association For Shell And Spatial Structures*: IASS, 46 (148): 77–84, 2005
- Deussen, Oliver, Lintermann, Bernd: *Digital Design of Nature*, 2006
- P Müller, P Wonka, S Haegler, A Ulmer, and L V Gool: *Procedural Modeling of Buildings*. ACM Transactions on Graphics 25, 3, 614–623. (2006)
- Bernard Cache: *After Parametrics* in GAM.06 *Nonstandard Structures, Graz Architecture Magazine* Vol. 06, 2010

Overview

In July 1837, while compiling notes of his five year voyage round the world aboard the HMS Beagle as a gentleman scientist, the English naturalist, geologist, and biologist Charles Darwin (1809–1882) got to page 36 of his notebook B and drew on it a simple line diagram roughly resembling a tree, together with some scrawled annotations. Above it, practically as a heading to what followed, he wrote the words: "I think". It was his first 'evolutionary tree' and marked his rapid progression towards a fully fledged theory of evolution, which he completed formulating by the next year. Having embarked on his famous expedition with Captain Robert FitzRoy six years earlier, in 1831 aged 22, with just a bachelors degree to his name and preparing to become a parson, he was now laying the foundation to becoming one of the world's most eminent and at times also most controversial scientists.

Whether it was fear of upsetting his religious family and friends, or ill health, or the demands on his attention and time by his own ever expanding brood (his wife Emma gave birth to ten children, seven of whom survived beyond their early years), or whether it was just a desire to make sure his theory was correct and needing time to fully examine and test it, his era-defining work did not see the light of day until twenty years later, when, on 24 November 1859, it was published under the title *On the Origin of Species by Means of Natural Selection, or the Preservation of Favoured Races in the Struggle for Life* — what we generally know and refer to today as *On the Origin of Species*.

The book sets out a comprehensive theory of life evolving by mutation and natural selection, and postulates that we humans, as all species on our planet, are the result of a generative process, rather than of a fixed, preordained design. While in our great majority today we accept this as sound science, and although by then similar ideas had already been circulating and he was by no means the first person to think in this vein, it still flew right in the face of what in the 19th century was widely considered to be an incontrovertible truth: that God had created the world and everything that's in it; a view that we now call creationism. If the theory of evolution was correct, this meant that there was no Divine Architect who built the world and made every creature with a deliberate shape, meaning, and purpose in mind. Instead, life on Earth was simply there, and it multiplied, adapted, self-selected, and thrived, perfectly on its own accord.

The English ethologist, evolutionary biologist, and author Richard Dawkins (b. 1941) was, from 1995 until 2008, Professor for Public Understanding of Science at the University of Oxford and is to this date one of the best known public promoters of Darwin's ideas. In 1986 Dawkins published a book called *The Blind Watchmaker: Why the Evidence of Evolution Reveals a Universe without Design*. Dawkins' book discusses many aspects of the theory of evolution that Darwin couldn't have known about, but which have since been discovered. Still, to a designer the subtitle may at first sound just a tad categorical. Does Dawkins mean to suggest that design and therefore designers have no place in the universe? Or that what they purport to do does not exist? Not at all. What he does is compare design by a designer (here a 'watchmaker'), to 'design' by natural selection, in order to dispel the notion that complexity could not arise without the intervention of a 'creator'. And while Dawkins does not deny the existence of designers, he still humbles them to a degree by showing that evolution is capable of generating life forms of staggering complexity, arguably exceeding in elegance and finesse anything ever conceived by a designer.

Confirming Darwin's momentous theory, Dawkins shows that the natural world wasn't designed, that the the idea of a master builder of the world – in many religions synonymous with God – has no foundation in science, and that God, therefore, is not, after all, an architect. (Which may come as a bit of a blow to our profession, if not, perhaps, as a surprise...) He does, however argue – and this is of great relevance to us – that there are indeed Generative Methods □ ↖145
of design, because evolution by natural selection is just that: a generative method, albeit a particularly sophisticated one, as we shall see. And as we just noted, these methods are capable of arriving at objects and creatures that we ourselves would be unable to imagine, and this alone should pique our interest in the topic of this chapter.

093 ● 168

'EX NIHILO NIHIL FIT'

The term *generative method* is somewhat malleable, rather than a clearly defined, normed expression, and different people mean subtly different things by it, in different contexts. At its core lies the idea of a process: instead of viewing design as a fixed form, it is regarded as the result of several iterative steps. And while this sounds fairly obvious, the notion of process requires a different mindset and leads to a different way of thinking about design than we are generally used to. Just as Darwinian thinking resulted in a more fluid conception of different species, and led to the discovery of countless ways in which they are related, so the idea that forms are the result of generative processes leads to a new way of thinking about design, one that is more open to the notion of variation and optimisation.

And so from the outset, there are in fact two quite separate strands contained within the concept of 'generative methods': a method for creating complex forms, and a way of optimising design solutions. They both rest on the same initial premise, which is that you define a process based on a set of rules – an algorithm – and allow the computer to generate an output on its own, without any further creative input from you. (In architecture this would most likely be a digital 3D model.)

The big question is what happens next? In the first case, generative methods are seen as a formal game that enables a new type of design brainstorming. The result of the process is judged by a designer or group of designers who can make changes to the code or ■ 362↘ the parameters used, based on their preferences, and then go through the same loop again. In so doing, the designer is effectively creating an iterative process in which the design is improved until it fully meets expectations. This really isn't all that far from a traditional design process, which tends to go through many iterations as well. The chief characteristic and differentiator is algorithmic form generation: instead of the designer drawing evolving versions of the project, it's a computer program that does this job. This, incidentally, also means that many more variations are created, because running a computational process to generate a new iteration with today's tools is much quicker and easier than drawing one yourself. But apart from that it's still simply the designer's taste or preference or whim that determines the outcome. And if the algorithm isn't particularly good at coming up with interesting forms, the resulting project most likely won't be interesting either, just as would happen with an untalented designer, no matter how many iterations are drawn up. So, in this process the role of the designer shifts from coming up with a design to controlling the parameters or the algorithm that does so. But we will see that what used to be viewed as a complete change to the profession, namely that an architect has to become a computer programmer in order to successfully work in this way, no longer holds true. In fact, working in this fashion has become wide-spread among architects.

In the second case it is not only the generation of the model that is being done automatically, but also the iteration itself. So instead of a designer, it is another computer program that is responsible for deciding whether a result meets certain criteria or not, and to start another iteration with different parameters if it doesn't. This does not mean that a designer is not part of the process. But the designer's responsibility now includes the determination and quantitative specification of the desired criteria, as well as making sure that they can eventually be met, as otherwise the iterative process will never come to an end.

We will deal with both types of generative method in this chapter. With the first one, a designer tweaks a generative program either by manipulating the parameters or the code itself with the aim of generating appropriate forms. We will look at the tools and methods that enable this process.

With the second one, after each iteration what is known as a **fitness function** takes over the evaluation of the design. Here, we are looking at something that greatly resembles the evolutionary process Darwin discovered and described. We can call this second type 'survival of the fittest', as Darwin did or 'optimisation strategies for analytically unsolvable problems', as some researchers in this area will put it.

Both types of generative design strategy have their strengths and weaknesses, which we will discuss. As we shall see, the distinction between them isn't always simple, as there are many hybrids. It should also be noted that neither of them is completely unproblematic, and that there are good reasons for people to be sceptical of them. That said there are even better reasons to be really curious and excited. We are not assuming the mantle of prophets if we say that generative methods of both types will become more common in practice, and that we therefore do well to understand how they work and what their potential is.

In any case, what may look from the outside and at first as though you were allowing your computer to create something out of nothing is in fact still a mutual transaction. 'Nothing comes from nothing' is what the title of this section translates as, and this holds true here as elsewhere: you are not really creating *ex nihilo*. You are, at the very least, setting the rules, or, as we have otherwise phrased it, asking the question. The quality of your design, therefore, will be dependent on the quality of your rules: ask a good question, you may (there is no actual guarantee) get a good answer; or, if you apply the term 'quality' in its wider sense to mean 'type or character': the kind of answer (result) you get will by necessity be informed and defined by the kind of question (parameters) you set.

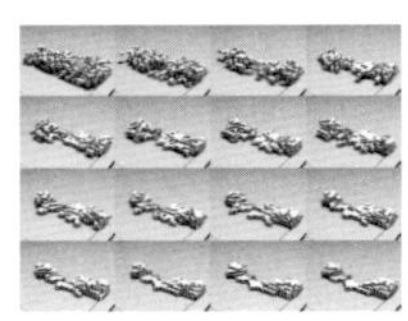

094 ● 168

Some Basic Concepts

Our general topic is fairly large and complex, and so we want to have a look at some basic concepts to begin with.

DESIGN SPACE

□ ↖111 In our chapter on Digital Design Strategies we introduce the term *design space*, which we define as the set of all forms a designer can create with their set of available methods. In the corresponding graphic we show the design space as a small area within the huge set of all possible forms. We will not repeat this discussion here, but obviously the concept is relevant. Any generative method constitutes a limitation, as it automatically rules out infinitely more forms than it is capable of generating. And critics of digital design strategies frequently cite this as a principal problem. The argument is that computers are limiting creativity because 'you only get out of it what you put in.' This is another way of saying what we just stated: that any generative method comes with its own, delineated design space. Arguably, though, this isn't a flaw, it can be the opposite. So generative methods are perhaps better thought of as strategies for form-finding. The more clearly defined the delineations of my design space, the better I am able to explore valid alternatives. The choice of a generative method is a declaration of what it is I am looking for. Choosing it is already an act of design. And don't forget that even a very well defined design space still normally contains infinite numbers of solutions. It's impossible to consider all of them, but there may be algorithmic ways to find some of the most appropriate ones amongst them. So: ideally the generative method I employ encodes aspects of my personal design intention and allows me to limit the design space in such a way as to make it easier for me to arrive at a valid design solution.

PARAMETRIC DESIGN

The term design space is often applied in connection with *parametric design,* which can be said to be the most widely used generative method in architecture. We will not go into too much detail here on this either, because we discuss parametric design in various other chapters of this *Atlas*, specifically those on 3D Modelling and the just mentioned Digital Design Strategies, as well as on Scripting. But since it is important for our context, let's reiterate the basics: a parametric model in essence is one in which dependencies are established between all of its parts. If this is done well, the model can be said to be 'intelligent': changing one parameter means that all affected parts of the model are adjusted accordingly. This enables us to study many alternative versions of a design quickly and easily.

Parameters can define many things. They can control the sizes or angles or curvatures of walls or rooms or stairs, or the numbers of floors, or the distances between openings, for example. From this short list you already see that parametric models can get complicated very quickly. Indeed, building a good parametric model is an art of its own, which constantly asks that you find the right balance: as few parameters as possible, as many as necessary. If there are too many, the model becomes unwieldy and hard to control; if there are too few, the design space will be too restricted for the model to offer the flexibility necessary to study meaningful alternatives. It takes a fair amount of practice and experience to get good at setting up parametric models, even with today's easy-to-use visual programming interfaces. But once mastered, the technique allows you to create powerful models with built-in proportional systems, capable of solving intricate geometric problems or of deriving complex compositions from simple curves and shapes.

Parameters can be seen as the equivalent to the genetic code of a design, and so they are prerequisite to any evolutionary design strategy, as we shall see. But its wide use notwithstanding, the term 'parametric design' is not in fact very clearly defined. It commonly refers to models created with a specific type of software, known as **parametric modellers** ■ 362↘. While there are lots of design strategies that can be pursued with such modellers, there are also many other algorithmic methods that can be used to generate forms. Confusingly, all of them involve some kind of parameters.

In this chapter we introduce and explain many different generative methods so that by the end of it you should have a good general overview of how they work and how they can be employed in practice.

RULES, LOGIC, AND RANDOMNESS

In everyday language, we principally associate the word 'rule' with a formally decreed or informally agreed set of laws that apply to a certain context, specifying on the one hand what is and what isn't valid or allowed, and also in applicable cases what the consequences are for any type of transgression. So in football, if you trip up your opponent in the penalty area, the referee under normal circumstances will find that an offence ↖135 181↘ has been committed which triggers a penalty kick as a punitive consequence. The same principle obviously applies to ordinary conduct in daily life, where these sets of laws collectively are known as the code of law.

In computing, the terms 'rule' and 'code' are similarly linked. Here the code tends to specify not so much what is 'allowed' (though that often too) as □ ↖57 what is required. It's principally a set of instructions. □ ↖111 But these instructions and their parameters follow a □ 351↘ set of rules that have the same conceptual structure: if this applies, then that shall be the consequence. (Mercifully, computers rarely have to deal with players flopping to the ground at the whiff of an opponent glancing at them, and rolling on the lawn screaming as if bitten by a tarantula. So deciding whether a consequence is warranted here tends to be a lot more straightforward and factual than in football...)

To help us appreciate the concept of generating forms with code, let's look at some simple coding examples that illustrate how we can define rules. (We cover the topic in considerably greater detail in our chapter on Scripting.) □ 351↘

The code in this example is written in *Mathematica*, the declarative **scripting language** ■ 354↘ we use throughout this book. But it could just as easily have been written in the scripting language of any CAD package, and it would look very similar.

Here is an array or field of cubes and the code responsible for generating it:

```
r={};
For[x=0,x<10,x++,
 For[y=0,y<10,y++,
  r=Append[r,Cuboid[{x,y,0}]]]]
Graphics3D[r,Boxed→False,Lighting→"Neutral"]
```

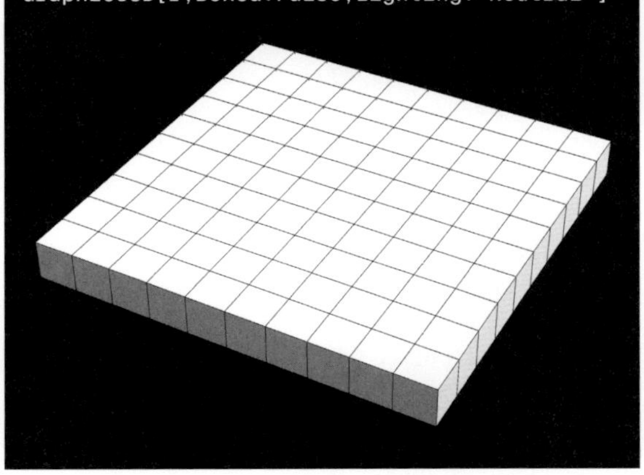

The array is generated with two nested *for-loops*. A loop is a structure that gets repeated a set number of times (in our case 10 times), typically using a counter variable (here *x* and *y* respectively) that gets incremented every time the code inside the loop is executed. In a nested loop, the code in the loop is itself a loop. In our example the outer loop increments the *x* values, the inner loop the *y* values, appending a cuboid to the array *'r'* with all possible combinations of the two variables, resulting in an array of 100 cubes. Up to this point there is nothing unusual. In fact, you could just as easily have used the array command that is built into every CAD system to create this field of cubes.

But now we want to introduce a rule. We do this by including a conditional statement in the code, starting with the operator *'If'*:

```
r={};
For[x=0,x<10,x++,
 For[y=0,y<10,y++,
  If[Mod[x+y,2]>0,
   r=Append[r,Cuboid[{x,y,0}]]]]]
Graphics3D[r,Boxed→False,Lighting→"Neutral"]
```

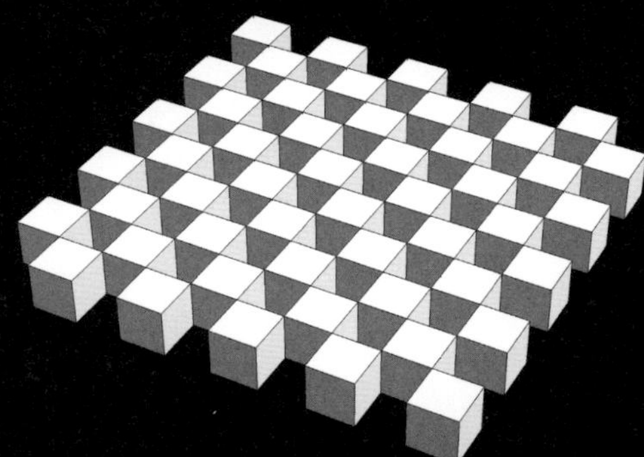

The moment we do so, we can handle our field of cubes in a way that with the standard array command wouldn't be possible.

What we are in fact saying is: 'if – and only if – the following conditions are met will a cube be placed at the specified location within the array.' Here we have generated a checkerboard pattern, by adding the condition that the box should only be placed if the sum of the values for *x* and *y* results in an
■ 179↘ odd number. The word *'Mod'* stands for the **modulo operator**. This finds the remainder in a division of two numbers. So the expression '7 mod 3' would return 1, since 7 divided by 3 is 2, with a remainder of 1. This is a convenient way to establish whether a number, specifically a whole number or integer, is even or not: the expression 'x mod 2' always either returns 0 if it is an even number, or 1 if it is an odd number.

What is of significance here, and to the non-programmer perhaps unfamiliar, is that in code the 'If' statement is evaluated not as a number, but as either 'true' or 'false'. Yet unlike a football referee who has to determine whether the condition of a player having been fouled is factually true, or whether this is just another case of a highly paid professional performing their antics, computers don't have to concern themselves with the concept of a differentiated truth. In computing, 0 usually equals 'false' and anything that isn't 0 equals 'true'.

So in our example a box is placed on the field if the result of the argument in parentheses after 'If' is *not zero*. And since *'Mod[x + y, 2]'* returns zero for all cases where the sum of *x* and *y* is an even number, it's easy to see how we can thus generate a checkerboard pattern.

A checkerboard may not be what we want. Luckily, just by making a small change to the condition, we can achieve something that looks quite different:

```
r={};
For[x=0,x<10,x++,
 For[y=0,y<10,y++,
  If[Mod[x,3]>0 || Mod[y,2]>0,
   r=Append[r,Cuboid[{x,y,0}]]]]]
Graphics3D[r,Boxed→False,Lighting→"Neutral"]
```

Here are some more patterns, each with the conditional statement – the rule – that defines it:

Rules and conditions result in different patterns.

```
r={};
For[x=0,x<10,x++,
 For[y=0,y<10,y++,
  If[x<6 || x>8,
   r=Append[r,Cuboid[{x,y,0}]]]]]
Graphics3D[r,Boxed→False,Lighting→"Neutral"]
```

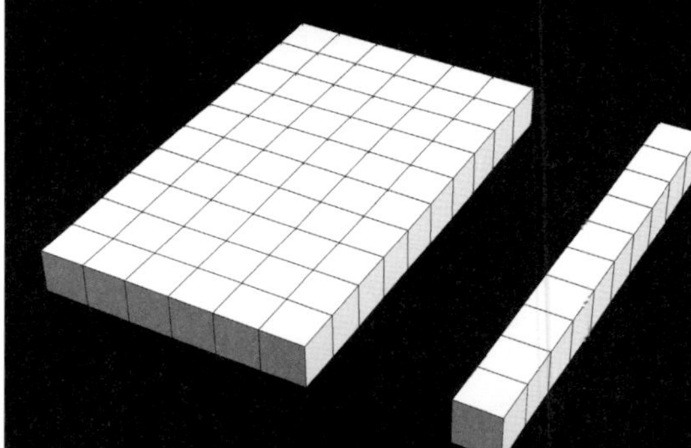

```
r={};
For[x=0,x<10,x++,
 For[y=0,y<10,y++,
  If[Mod[x+y,3]>0 && Mod[x-y,3]>0,
   r=Append[r,Cuboid[{x,y,0}]]]]]
Graphics3D[r,Boxed→False,Lighting→"Neutral"]
```

```
r={};
For[x=0,x<10,x++,
 For[y=0,y<10,y++,
  If[Mod[x+y,6]>0 && Mod[x-y,6]>0,
   r=Append[r,Cuboid[{x,y,0}]]]]]
Graphics3D[r,Boxed→False,Lighting→"Neutral"]
```

```
r={};
For[x=0,x<10,x++,
 For[y=0,y<10,y++,
  If[Mod[x,2]>0 || Mod[y,2]>0,
   r=Append[r,Cuboid[{x,y,0}]]]]]
Graphics3D[r,Boxed→False,Lighting→"Neutral"]
```

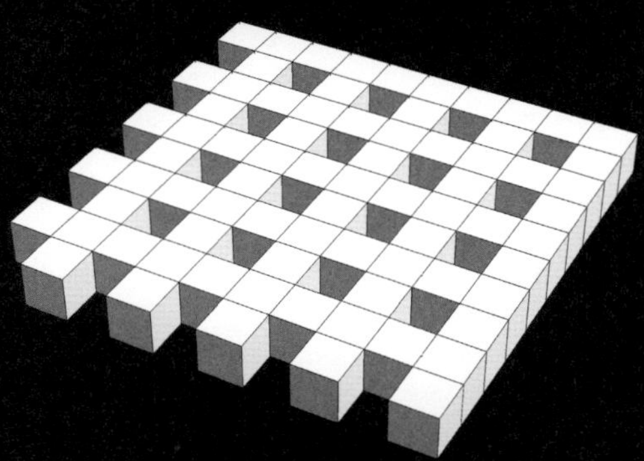

```
r={};
For[x=0,x<10,x++,
 For[y=0,y<10,y++,
  If[Mod[x-y,4]>0,
   r=Append[r,Cuboid[{x,y,0}]]]]]
Graphics3D[r,Boxed→False,Lighting→"Neutral"]
```

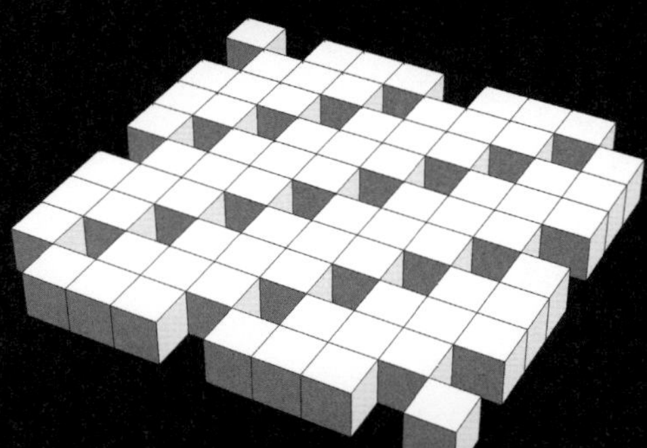

Interesting about these patterns is that they are defined procedurally. They have a mathematical logic that could be applied to fields of different sizes, and the pattern would look exactly the same every time the code is executed. But this mathematical predictability is also a bit sterile. One of the charming characteristics of nature is that no two things are exactly the same. There are slight variations and mutations in the gene code that have led to the wealth of living organisms that inhabit our world. So is there a way to mimic that diversity and differentiation on the computer? Can we write code that will produce slightly different results every time it is executed?

The simplest way to do so is by introducing random values. In our next example, we apply a random operator. The following code randomly generates a whole number (integer) in a given range (in our case 1 to 10). The statement checks whether this random value is greater than 3, which statistically will be the case about 70% of the time. The result of our nested loop with this randomised conditional statement now looks different every time it is run. But we should point out that these random patterns don't come about by 'accident': the rules are as precise as before, we just cannot predict the exact outcome for each case any longer.

Random function: only place cube if random value between 1 and 10 is greater than 3.

```
r={};
For[x=0,x<10,x++,
 For[y=0,y<10,y++,
  If[RandomInteger[10]>3,
   r=Append[r,Cuboid[{x,y,0}]]]]]
Graphics3D[r,Boxed→False,Lighting→"Neutral"]
```

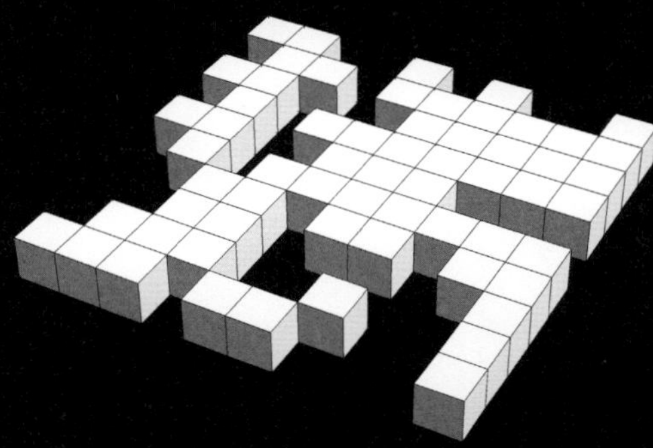

In the following series we see an array of patterns generated in this way. Note that the conditional statement – the rule that determines whether at a certain set of grid coordinates there will be a cube or not – is the same for all of them.

Random function: 10 × 10 arrays of cubes, with approximately 30% randomly selected cubes missing.

```
r={};
For[x=0,x<10,x++,
 For[y=0,y<10,y++,
  If[RandomInteger[10]>3,
   r=Append[r,Cuboid[{x,y,0}]]]]]
Graphics3D[r,Boxed→False,Lighting→"Neutral"]
```

We can also mix rules and randomness, and that is where randomness starts to become really interesting and useful. The following sequence uses one of the rule patterns, scaled up to a field of 20 × 20 cuboids. Then an additional line is added to the code, which ran-
■ 568↘ domly eliminates about twenty percent of the cubes. The result is a pattern that is both regular and irregular and will look different every time the function is called.

Combining a rule and a random function: approximately 20% randomly selected cubes from the regular pattern (first) are eliminated: the original pattern is still present, but now there is a random element to it (second and third).

```
r={};
For[x=0,x<20,x++,
 For[y=0,y<20,y++,
  If[Mod[x+y,3]>0 && Mod[x-y,3]>0,
   r=Append[r,Cuboid[{x,y,0}]]]]]
Graphics3D[r,Boxed→False,Lighting→"Neutral"]
```

□ 549↘

```
r={};
For[x=0,x<20,x++,
 For[y=0,y<20,y++,
  If[Mod[x+y,3]>0 && Mod[x-y,3]>0
   && RandomInteger[10]>2,
    r=Append[r,Cuboid[{x,y,0}]]]]]
Graphics3D[r,Boxed→False,Lighting→"Neutral"]
```

■ 540↘

```
r={};
For[x=0,x<20,x++,
 For[y=0,y<20,y++,
  If[Mod[x+y,3]>0 && Mod[x-y,3]>0
   && RandomInteger[10]>2,
    r=Append[r,Cuboid[{x,y,0}]]]]]
Graphics3D[r,Boxed→False,Lighting→"Neutral"]
```

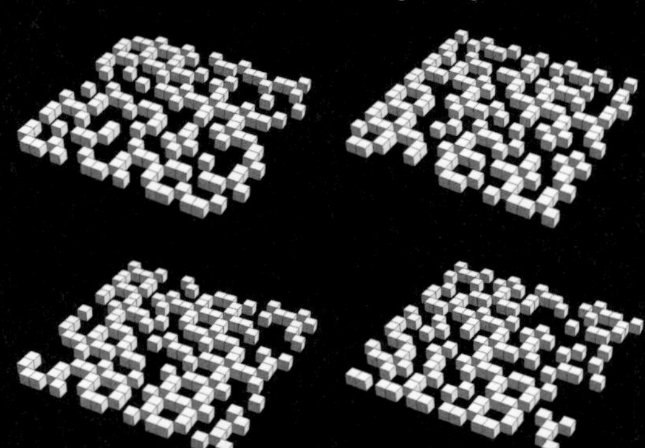

Our example is extremely simple, yet even at this level the use of random values leads to intriguing results. But it is worth pointing out that any impression of 'naturalness' that it may convey is misleading. It is nothing of the sort: the only thing random values can provide is a **stochastic**, a randomly determined process. But this is often used in generative methods to create the kind of variations we also find in the natural world, because as we have seen, it can soften the rigidity of rules and add a degree of fuzziness or variation, and also mutation. Random values are used for the distribution of particles in simulations of natural phenomena such as liquids or smoke, for example. Used intelligently and embedded in more complex sets of rules, random operators therefore can be very effective, and we will encounter examples as we progress through this chapter.

(We talk in some detail about stochastics and what differentiates them from statistics in our chapter on Big Data & Machine Learning.)

CELLULAR AUTOMATA AND THE *GAME OF LIFE*

While we are still in the conceptual overview of what generative methods are, we should take this opportunity to have a look at one of the most famous and also most curiously satisfying examples of a self-determining generative principle: the *Game of Life*, a strikingly simple computer program created in 1970 by English mathematician John Horton Conway (b. 1937). Just like the cube arrays we looked at in the previous section, it has nothing to do with optimisation, but it allows you to play through an amazing plethora of possible outcomes within the confines of a tiny set of rules, depending entirely on how you configure your starting elements. So while it is not a generative design method in the strict sense, it serves us particularly well here to illustrate how even in a very limited design space a set of very simple rules can yield infinitely complex outcomes.

The *Game of Life* is a **cellular automaton**, meaning that its universe consists of a regular grid of cells, each with the same dimensions and of an unspecified – in this particular case infinite – number, but with a finite number of states that each cell can be in. Here that number is two: a cell can be either 'alive' or 'dead'. (Similar states would be 'on' or 'off', or 'empty' or 'full'.) Conceived as a *zero-player game*, once it is set in action, there is no further human input: the program simply adheres to the rules it has been given until it either can go no further, or until it is stopped. All the 'player' does is determine the initial set-up and then observe what happens. (What happens can be surprisingly riveting, though...)

Whereas the rules for our cubes in the examples above were either fixed mathematical conditions or randomly generated values, the *Game of Life* demonstrates that rules can also be defined as references to the context, in other words the neighbourhood of 'living' or 'dead' cells any single cell currently finds itself in. It's this self-referentiality that makes the game so intriguing and so difficult to work out. Here, in the *Game of Life* (just as in life itself, arguably) nothing happens randomly, everything is governed by rules, and everything happens in context.

John Conway's *Game of Life*

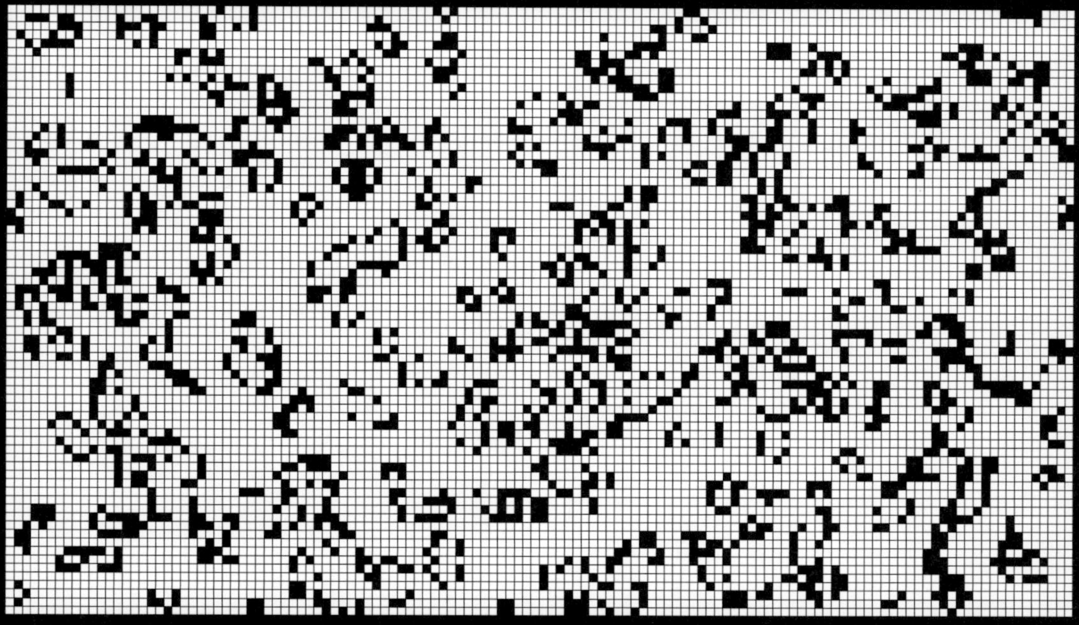

The rules Conway set for his game are finely configured to avoid extremes such as very fast population explosion or near-immediate extinction, and since they are so succinct, we can easily detail them here in full:

Taking place on a portion of an infinite orthogonal regular grid of cells which can only be 'alive' or 'dead', each cell always has eight neighbours, defined as any cell that lies directly adjacent to it, in any possible direction, horizontal, vertical, or diagonal.

At every step, all of the following transitions are carried out simultaneously:

1 Any live cell with fewer than two live neighbours dies 'of loneliness'
2 Any live cell with two or three live neighbours lives on to the next generation
3 Any live cell with more than three live neighbours dies from 'overpopulation'
4 Any dead cell with exactly three live neighbours revives and newly becomes a live cell

These rules don't change. The only thing that changes from one game to the next is the initial setup, which is called the 'seed'. The moment the rules are first applied – this is called the 'tick' – the first successor generation is created, and from then on in the game is left to its own devices.

What is particularly fascinating about this game is that it not only shows how a small set of rules can lead to many extremely different outcomes, but also, and perhaps in the context of generative design even more important, that many (though by no means all) of these outcomes are in fact unpredictable. So the notion that you only ever get out of a computer program what you put into it is proved wrong: even at this level, where the rules can be listed in four lines of text, the possible outcomes are not only infinite but also in many (but not all) setups quite unpredictable. (The only way to predict the outcome is by playing the game and then it is strictly speaking no longer a prediction.)

Conway initially didn't know, but it has since been proved, that from any number of different starting positions, there are some recurring patterns that then take on a 'life of their own', meaning that they no longer change until they come in contact with another live pattern. Among these, there are three principal categories or types: 'still lives' are static patterns that, although they contain 'live' cells, don't move and don't change. 'Oscillators' are patterns that stay in place but that oscillate between one shape and one or several others. 'Spaceships' and 'gliders', meanwhile, are patterns that not only change shape but also move across the grid for as long as their path is undisturbed, 'gliders' differing from 'spaceships' only in their smaller size.

The reason these patterns are of interest to us is that they are examples of patterns that *emerge* without further human input or control from the given set of parameters and the starting conditions. So even at this, most simple and basic, level of algorithmic generation, a computer program is capable of producing emergent shapes that are not, from the outset, designed, predicted, or even intended: they were part of the design space Conway defined with the above listed rules, but he was nevertheless completely unaware of them.

At the time Conway invented his game, he assumed that any possible starting configuration would eventually peak and thus come to an end, and he offered a cash prize of USD 50 to the first person or team to prove this conjecture correct or incorrect. In November 1970, a team at Massachusetts Institute of Technology (MIT) led by the then 27-year-old American mathematician and computer scientist

Bill Gosper (b. 1943) did so, which is why the *Gosper glider gun* is named after him. This is a starting setup that after a short while settles into a configuration that sits still on the grid, while producing a never-ending series of gliders.

The Gosper glider gun: produces gliders in eternity.

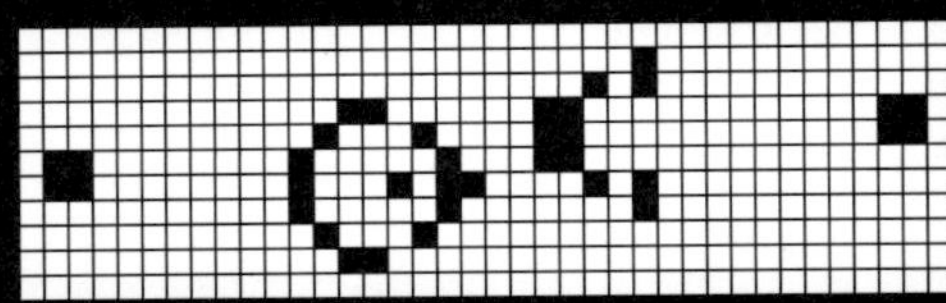

(There are several websites on which you can play with the *Game of Life* and try out the *Gosper glider gun,* as well as many other presets and different patterns of your own. One of these sits at playgameoflife.com.)

EMERGENCE

The concept of emergence is inextricably linked to the idea of generative design methods. It leans entirely on the principles we've discussed so far: you determine a set of rules and then play through a series of iterations from which a design may 'emerge'.

In generative methods generally, it is up to you how precisely you go about this, and so there are many possible ways in which a computer can generate a design. You either set stringent and differentiated rules to arrive at one or a limited number of possible results – this is in effect the principle at work in parametric design – or you set relatively loose rules and bank instead on a series of tests that help you determine which, out of a very large number of iterations, best fulfils your purpose or matches your style.

Philosophically speaking, the principal characteristic of emergence is that 'the whole is greater than the sum of its parts'. Emergent patterns are patterns that are the result of the interaction or coordination of many distinct elements. Though we should point out that not every phenomenon of this type should be called emergence. For example when cloud formations temporarily bear similarity with animals or faces, that's not what we call an emergent pattern. An emergent pattern is one that can be made explicit, that can be made to lock in, so to speak, and reveal previously unknown forces or relationships, such as in the case of the Gosper glider gun, where the emergent pattern is not only able to keep itself 'alive', but even to produce gliders indefinitely. In that way the emergent pattern offers a new reading of a set of elements and the rules that govern their interplay. This new reading is usually simpler and easier to describe than the description of all the individual elements would be. But it also depends on these individual elements. So emergence is characterised by increased complexity: it results in the simultaneous existence of different ways in which a collection of parts can be described. In emergence, an additional level of order is established, which is added to but doesn't replace the previous order.

Emergent triangle (after Gaetano Kanizsa):

You can also argue that emergence is, in a sense, a reversal of entropy: the degree of order in the system becomes ever greater, and thus seems to contradict the second law of thermodynamics according to which entropy and therefore the level of disorder in a system only ever and invariably increases. (It doesn't really contradict the law, though, as the law only applies when no energy is added to a system.)

Emergence isn't only interesting in the context of generative methods, it is relevant for any creative process. Australian author and professor John S Gero, who has worked extensively on the subject, defines it as follows:

> "A property that is only implicit, i.e. not represented explicitly, is said to be an emergent property if it can be made explicit. Emergence is considered to play an important role in the introduction of new schemas and consequently new variables. Emergence is a recognised phenomenon in visual representations of structure. It maps directly onto the concept of changing schemas since a new schema is generally needed to describe the emergent property."

When and under what circumstances new levels of order emerge in a system is a key question. Gosper found the patterns that were then named after him because he analysed the rules of Conway's game and actively sought to understand the mathematical puzzle they represent; he did not chance upon them by accident. And yet, in biological evolution, new species develop with characteristics that differentiate them from their forebears, without the guidance of a creator, but merely through trial and error. We are then looking at **self-organising systems** which produce new configurations from within themselves through self-referencing feedback loops. This is how apparently new things come about, which the original initiator seems to have had little to do with.

"All Things Are Number"

The natural world and the way it has evolved has inspired many of the generative methods we discuss in this chapter, in very different ways. What Conway called the 'Game of Life', is, as we've seen, just an array of grid cells that can be either 'alive' or 'dead', or which read 'on' or 'off'. So even though it seems to 'behave' as if it were organic, Conway's game doesn't actually look like the natural world at all.

A very different kind of legacy is one that traces the visual and structural patterns found in nature back to mathematics. This way of thinking has a long tradition. The ancient Greek philosopher and mathematician Pythagoras (c. 570 – c. 495 BCE) famously posited that "all things are number," and German astronomer, astrologer, and mathematician Johannes Kepler (1571–1630) wrote about the *Harmonices mundi (The Harmony of the World)* in his 1619 book of that title: they were both convinced that the universe was organised according to mathematical rules and proportions: an inaudible harmony that permeates everything. Both these great minds founded what to us sounds like a poetic notion on careful study of the natural world, and it remains fruitful and inspiring to architects to this day. The many proportional systems discussed in architectural theory from the earliest writings on architecture by Roman author, architect, and engineer Vitruvius (c. 80–70 – after c. 15 BCE) right through to Swiss-born French architect, designer, urbanist, and writer Le Corbusier (1887–1965) with his Modulor can be seen as an echo of this idea, as we also note in our chapter on Digital Design Strategies. By adhering to 'natural' proportions such as the *golden ratio*, architects try to imbue their designs with a timeless quality and make them resonate with this inaudible cosmic harmony. We have already mentioned parametric design, which is also founded on the notion of proportional systems, and we will explore the topic further when we introduce the term *morphogenesis* a bit further on. □ ↖111

But before that, we want to focus on one particular natural phenomenon which deserves its own section because it is the basis of a number of methods that are widely used in the digital generation of artificial plants and landscapes: *self-similarity.*

SELF-SIMILARITY

It is a well-known observation in nature: often basic shapes or patterns repeat themselves at regular or irregular scales. Think of patterns in leaves that look like trees, or coastlines whose dents and turns can be found at various scales. Or think of the short but famous documentaries *Powers of Ten* by Charles and Ray Eames: in combination they offer a trip from the molecular to the cosmic scale that shows that there are landscapes in our cells as well as on our planet, and highlights the similarities between molecules and celestial bodies.

The phenomenon was also taken up by mathematics: *fractals* and their algorithmic sibling, *recursion*, allow us to calculate and encode self-similar patterns that have an expanding or evolving symmetry based on a simple, repeating structure.

FRACTALS AND THE KOCH SNOWFLAKE 193↘

Among fractals, the *Koch snowflake* or *Koch curve* holds a special place, since it is one of the earliest fractals to be mathematically described, in 1904, by Swedish mathematician Helge von Koch (1870–1924), after whom it is named.

The Koch snowflake is generated by taking as the base shape an equilateral triangle, and applying to it the following three rules:

1 Divide each available line (3 to start with) into three segments of equal length
2 Taking the middle segment on each line as a new baseline, draw on each a new equilateral triangle, pointing outwards
3 Remove the segments that have served as new baselines in step 2 above

The first iteration of this process is still a simple and instantly recognisable shape: a regular hexagram. The second iteration, after the same process has been repeated, already begins to look to us a bit like a snowflake. From the third iteration onward, this snowflake never loses its six-pointed 'star' shape, but becomes ever more intricate around its edge.

In nature, fractals are famously found in anything from ferns to coastlines, to clouds, canyons, lightning, peacock feathers, and indeed snowflakes.

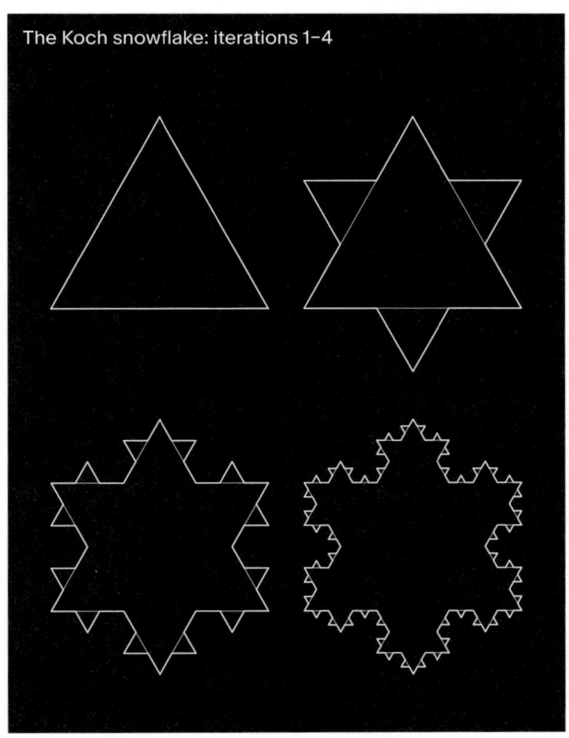
The Koch snowflake: iterations 1–4

(You will find a fully coded example of the Koch snowflake in our chapter on Graphs & Graphics.) □ 175↘

RECURSION

Strictly speaking, and in the context of computer science, the generation of most fractals does not involve iterative processes, but recursive ones. With recursion, you can define "an infinite set of objects by a finite statement," as Swiss computer scientist and designer of programming languages Niklaus Wirth (b. 1934) puts it in his 1976 book *Algorithms + Data Structures = Programs*. Among the defining characteristics of a recursive program or program component is that it is capable of calling itself up autonomously – that is without user input – to process specific functions. This is particularly useful in the computation of shapes, forms, and topographies as they appear in nature, such as snowflakes, plants, or coral reefs. The Koch snowflake is a classic example: depending on the number of recursions, it can become more or less differentiated. The principle at work in the Koch snowflake is also called a *rewriting system*.

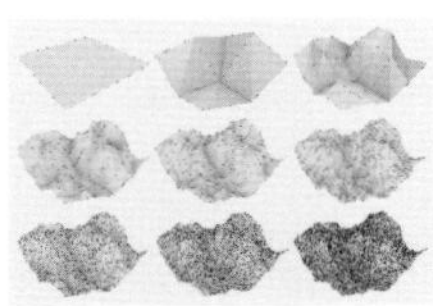

095 ● 168

ARTIFICIAL LANDSCAPES, LEAVES, AND TREES

This neatly brings us to landscapes and computer generated 'nature'. Fractals and self-similar patterns being such ubiquitous features in nature, they make for a mathematically simple (and therefore computationally cheap) method with which to create digital features that look like nature, not because they copy the patterns seen in nature, but because they apply the construction principle that nature applies, and let the program do the 'designing'.

Again, the process is that of a step-by-step increase in differentiation. Just as the Koch snowflake starts with a triangular line, which is then split up into increasingly finer segments, so fractal landscapes use the same principle with surface patches. The reason these landscapes don't all look the same is that a balanced level of randomness is built into the process, as you can see in the illustration above. There are a number of programs that generate procedural mountain ranges, for example, which can be used in virtual film sets and renderings of virtual landscapes.

096 ● 169

192↘

L-SYSTEMS

■ 192↘

In 1968, the Hungarian biologist Aristid Lindenmayer (1925–1989) developed a **formal language** – that is a language with a grammar or set of rules that is specific to itself – now called *L-systems* (or *Lindenmayer systems)* to describe the way in which algae, fungi, and other organisms grow fractal patterns.

L-System

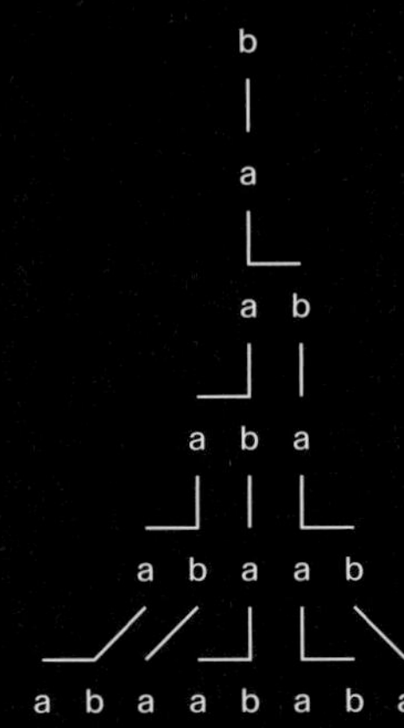

Lindenmayer used this simplest of L-Systems to model the growth of algae. Interestingly it is also a way to calculate the numbers of the Fibonacci sequence (after Prusinkiewicz).

Like fractals, L-systems in principle are recursive systems (or *rewriting systems),* as the following example of creating a fractal binary tree – featured on the English *Wikipedia* page on the topic – simply and compellingly illustrates.

Here, an axiom is fed recursively through a set of rules that determine how an input string is transformed into an output string:

- variables: `0`, `1`
- constants: `[`,`]`
- axiom: `0`
- rules: `(1 → 11)`, `(0 → 1[0]0)`

So if the axiom, as defined, is 0, then in a first recursion the rules determine this outputs as:

```
1[0]0
```

Applying the same rules now to this first recursion, a second recursion yields:

```
11[1[0]0]1[0]0
```

And again, in a third recursion:

```
1111[11[1[0]0]1[0]0]11[1[0]0]1[0]0
```

This can be continued infinitely. All that is required now to actually generate an image is to allocate graphic commands to each symbol, such as:

- `0`: draw a line segment in a leaf
- `1`: draw a line segment
- `[`: push position and angle, turn left 45 degrees
- `]`: pop position and angle, turn right 45 degrees

Which results in:

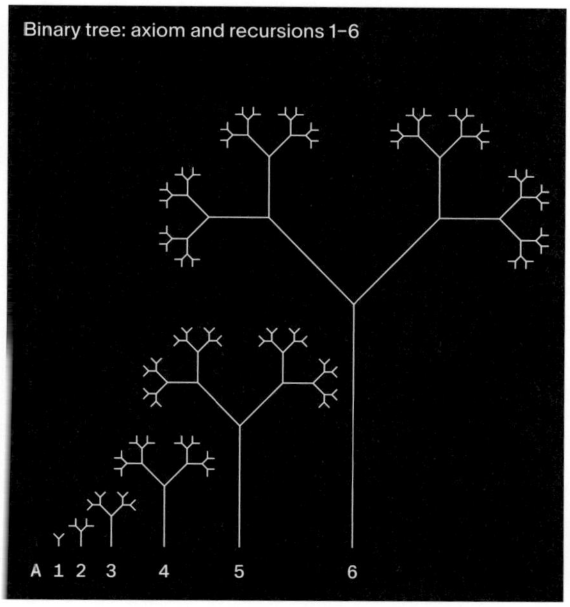

Binary tree: axiom and recursions 1–6

This rewriting system turns out to be extremely powerful. It is possible to 'grow' realistic botanical forms virtually, not just in 2D as in the classic example shown above, but in 3D, and thereby model artificial trees that are built and structured much like any organic tree. Ours is what's known as a DCFL example (for Deterministic Context-Free Language), there are also other types: stochastic grammars in which only a certain percentage of rewriting operations are executed (much as in the cube arrays we showed at the beginning of this chapter), or context sensitive grammars, where the context of a character (its neighbouring characters) determines whether a rewrite operation takes place or not. There are also parametric grammars, in which an element can be combined with a number of parameter values, which then become part of the rewriting procedure.

While it would go too far for us to discuss the implications of all of these types here in detail, it is worth pointing out their potency. Using these principles it is possible to generate practically any type of plant structure. With *XFrog* for example, you can model (for which read virtually grow) pretty much any plant known to botanists with astonishing fidelity and let them produce leaves and flowers at any stage of their virtual growth and ageing processes. *XFrog* is a 3D graphics software that takes its name from the acronym *X Window Finite recursive object generator.* It was originally developed by a team at the University of Karlsruhe, based on research into natural systems, as one of the earliest and most complex implementations of L-systems. Today the company of the same name that markets the product offers extensive plant catalogues to its users, and the vector models of its virtual plants can be found in countless CGI-animated films and games. Obviously ■ 263↘ they can also be used in architecture and landscape architecture models. While *XFrog* was among the first implementations of L-systems, they are now featured in many procedural modelling programs.

It is worth pointing out that while L-systems were invented to generate plants and nature-like patterns, you can also use them to 'grow' fantasy-structures or special types of architectural forms in this manner. The Iidabashi subway station by Japanese architect Makoto Sei Watanabe (b. 1952) is an early built example of an architecture that was not designed, but 'grown' on the computer. Watanabe uses the term *induction design* for his approach, in which the growing form also responds to a given design problem.

097A ○ 220

097B ○ 220

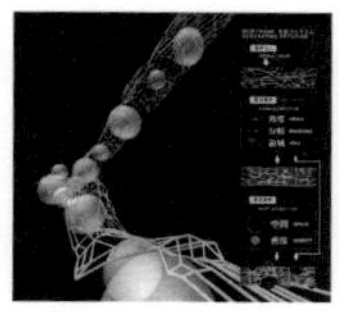

098A ○ 221

098B ○ 221

SHAPE GRAMMARS ↖119 540↘

We noted that while L-systems can be used to generate a multitude of other things, they were developed specifically to model the growth of plants. We might therefore wonder if there isn't a more general and at the same time less indirect approach, one that extrapolates a grammar directly from shapes, rather than through the processing and rewriting of strings?

Shape grammars, defined originally by American computer scientists George Stiny and James Gips in 1971, are just that: a way of formalising and abstracting the generation of forms by using geometric shapes. Shape grammars are similar to L-systems in that they are procedural and recursive, but they operate directly on shapes, which typically feature a marker to indicate at which point the next recursion will take place. A shape grammar is composed of virtual building blocks that specify a certain type of shape and how it may be transformed. Formally in computation they are a specific class of production ■ ↖64 systems that generate geometric shapes. They are strictly rule-based, and thus fall into the realm of algorithmic form generation. (We mention shape grammars also in our chapter on Scripting.) □ 351↘

Shape grammars (after Gerhard Schmitt):

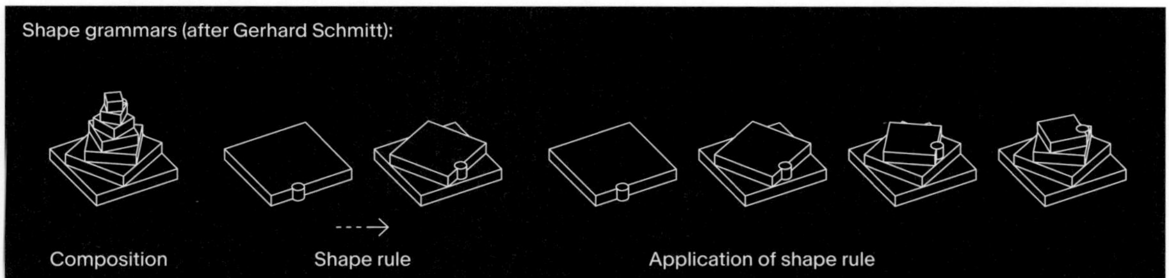

The method can be used to develop your own shape grammar, so that a set of designed shapes is applied over again, defining or contributing to the look and feel of a project without having to design each element from scratch, or they can also be used retroactively to analyse and reiterate a particular style of interest. Perhaps the most famous example of this to date (and one we also mention in our chapter on Digital Design Strategies) □ ↖111 is the analysis that Stiny did with another colleague of his, William Mitchell, of all of the ground plans of Venetian architect Andrea Palladio (1508–1580). Simply by analysing his architecture for its inherent rules and then applying these rules to the generation of new drawings, they presented 'Palladio-like' floor-plans which they argued might as readily have been designed by Palladio himself, as they were perfectly consistent with the grammar they had derived from the master's works, and by which they were also able to digitally generate all of his own originals.

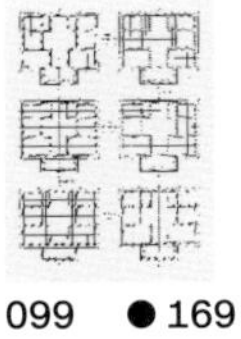

099 ● 169

Shape grammars are popular in academic circles, but they have had relatively little impact on architectural practice outside the research environment. One reason may be that working with them is actually quite complicated, and it's no accident that many of the best known applications (for example the grammar used for Palladio's floor plans) only work in two dimensions.

There are, however, some notable exceptions, where shape grammars have been successfully implemented into viable software systems. One of the best known cases in point is *CityEngine*. Developed by Esri R&D Center Zurich, which started life as a startup at ETH (*Eidgenössische Technische Hochschule*, the Federal Institute of Technology) Zürich under the name Procedural Inc, *CityEngine* is a professional 3D modelling software that is used in the creation of interactive urban environments, either based on real-world GIS data or to generate fictional urbanscapes. The first commercial release became available in 2008, when it quickly established itself as a powerful tool, particularly in the film and gaming industries, where it allowed the creators of both linear and dynamic narratives to effectively generate virtual settings for their stories at comparatively low cost. It is also used in city planning applications, for example to test the effects of proposed planning and zoning laws.

100 ● 169

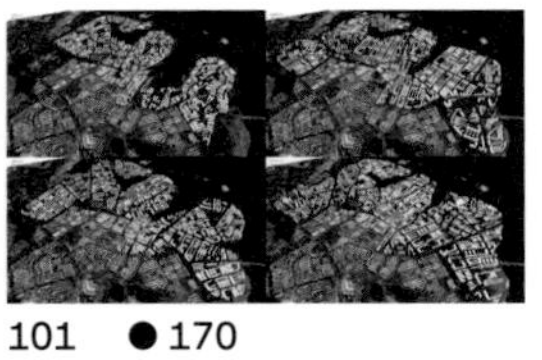

101 ● 170

MORPHOGENESIS

In 1904, the same year that Helge Koch first mathematically described his fractal snowflake, German zoologist, naturalist, and philosopher Ernst Haeckel (1834–1919) published his *Kunstformen der Natur (Art Forms of Nature)*, a work filled with beautiful and detailed depictions of biological forms. Haeckel, who discovered, described, and named thousands of new species was also an ardent admirer of Darwin, whose *Origin of Species* he tried to popularise by writing his own illustrated version of it, entitled *Natürliche Schöpfungsgeschichte (The History of Creation)*, published in 1886 in German and ten years later in English.

Most of the biological forms depicted in *Kunstformen der Natur* are sea creatures, and many of them so tiny that the sketches which provided the basis for the illustrations had to be done using a microscope. The hidden wonders of perfect symmetries that they revealed were presented to maximal visual effect, and unsurprisingly the wider public received Haeckel's book with great enthusiasm. It became influential to the Art Nouveau or *Jugendstil* movements in art as well as in architecture, and it also paved the way for *On Growth and Form*, a book written by Scottish biologist and mathematician D'Arcy Wentworth Thompson (1860–1948), first published in 1917. Which brings us to the title of this section: *morphogenesis.*

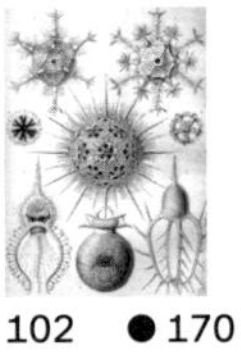

102 ● 170

Derived from the Greek *morphê* (shape) and *genesis* (creation), the word 'morphogenesis' denotes the biological process that causes an organism to develop its shape, whereby an emphasis is put on the notion of *process*. While the rules and regularities that can be found in the natural world have always fascinated curious minds, morphogenesis stands for a way of thinking that conceives of the world as being made up of processes, not fixed objects. The question of how these mathematical orders establish themselves in organic forms through growth wasn't touched upon until the twentieth century, when mathematical thinking started to take hold in biology, and Thompson's book is considered to be the first example of this way of thinking being laid out in this context. It introduces a mechanical and procedural approach to the study of form. He writes:

> "The form then, of any portion of matter, whether it be living or dead, and the changes of form which are apparent in its movements or its growth, may in all cases alike be described as due to the action of force."

> "Organic form itself is found, mathematically speaking, to be a function of time [...] We might call the form of an organism an event in space-time, and not merely a configuration in space."

On Growth and Form with its numerous illustrations had an impact on many different disciplines. Modernist architects such as Le Corbusier or his close German-American contemporary Ludwig Mies van der Rohe (1886–1969) were among its admirers. Thompson himself described the book as "all preface," and indeed in it he takes a broad swipe at all kinds of different topics, starting with a discussion of scale and magnitude, and of the forces that shape individual cells and their aggregations. He then describes and compares the spiral growth of various plants and shells, analyses the statics of horns and vertebrae and the inner structure of bones, and in the final chapter he also lays out a "theory of transformations or the comparison of related forms," which not only anticipates ideas that evolutionary developmental biology started working with a century later, but also formulates one of the most cited references for parametric design.

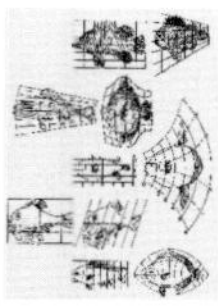

103 ● 170

It is worth noting that, unlike Haeckel, Thompson was not interested in evolutionary theory. His interest in the way forms were conditioned by natural forces was informed by a mechanical understanding of the world. Today, *The Chemical Basis of Morphogenesis*, a paper published in 1952 by the English mathematician, computer scientist, cryptanalyst, and theoretical biologist Alan Turing (1912–1954) is seen as the foundational text on the subject of morphogenesis in the modern sense. Turing, whom we encounter frequently in this *Atlas* and in different capacities, here presciently predicts a chemical mechanism of morphogenesis, entailing the diffusion of two different chemical signals, one activating and one deactivating growth, to set up patterns of development. Turing wrote his paper before DNA was discovered in 1953 and decades before the formation of such patterns was observed.

While Thompson's version of morphogenesis is one where organisms can develop different forms, based on the forces they are exposed to, but are fixed in their basic topology and thus unable really to evolve, Turing's theory opens up a new paradigm in generative methods, one where forms, based on their context, can be triggered to develop entirely new features. We shall get back to this important difference towards the end of this chapter.

PROCEDURAL MODELLING

As we have seen, L-systems and shape grammars are sophisticated ways of generating intricate forms. Yet, as we also noted, they aren't used very much in design. It could be the fact that they both involve recursions, which are inherently hard to wrap your head around, that has kept both shape grammars and L-systems from getting more of a following among architectural designers, but that's just a speculation. It may also be about to change, as what are known as *procedural modellers* are becoming more popular at some architecture schools.

At the time of writing (2019), the leading software for people interested in using generative methods in architecture is *Rhino Grasshopper*. Its chief attraction lies in the way it makes algorithmic tricks accessible to non-programmers while at the same time being fully procedural, yet also fully integrated into a standard 3D modelling environment.

There are a number of established parametric **solid modelling** programs that were originally developed for use in mechanical engineering, but have ■ ↖68
to some extent also entered architectural practice, the use of *Dassault Systèmes' CATIA (Computer Aided Three-dimensional Interactive Application)* by Frank Gehry and Associates being a famous example. Still: when architects talk about parametric design they nowadays more often than not refer to *Rhino Grasshopper* and its growing zoo of plugins (most of which are named after animals as well). We might add that the visual scripting environment *Dynamo*, which has similar features as *Grasshopper* and is developed by CAD market leader Autodesk, is also becoming more popular. (We mostly avoid mentioning specific software products in this *Atlas*, and when we do, such as here, we do so with a note of caution: we don't endorse any of them, and we name them simply to describe a current 'landscape' in computing, which as everything else in the digital technology realm is subject to dynamic flux and often very quick changes.)

The introduction of procedural modellers such as *Houdini* into architecture is a new and current development. Their origin is the special effects industry, where they are used to quickly generate landscapes and vegetation (which is why they include fractal landscape generators and L-systems), but filmmakers and games developers worldwide also have a constant need for smoke and explosions, and things generally breaking, splashing, or falling apart. To model these effects convincingly, procedural modellers include particle systems.

PARTICLE SYSTEMS

Much of the wizardry used for these types of visual effects is based on the simulation of natural forces applied to particle systems. Particle systems are computer generated distributions that emulate fuzzy phenomena such as you may find in nature: clouds, mists, fogs, turbulences, flames, hair, dust, or similar. While mostly used in special effects generation for games and films, they can also be of value in architectural modelling and parametric design if you want to generate a random pattern that looks natural.

104 ○ 221

Today, there is a vast array of procedural modelling tools that make these simulations fairly straightforward, which to some extent explains why they are so prevalent in Hollywood output.

A typical implementation of a particle system starts with an emitter (a point or object in 3D space) from which particles are spawned. Each particle has a given velocity, trajectory, and lifespan. (In the simulation of hair the particles are static and their travel paths are rendered all at once as curves.)

While particle systems are often used to create dissipating visual phenomena, they can also be turned into geometrically defined aggregate forms by replacing them with discrete elements. Converting the particles into *metaballs* – spherical shapes that are able to dynamically melt with their neighbours – allows liquids and liquid shapes to be successfully simulated and consequently also turned into static form. The fact that the forms resulting from such processes can be very unlike any conventional architectural shapes hasn't stopped architects from experimenting with procedural modellers. On the contrary: there is a lively scene of typically young designers who engage in producing virtual models of highly speculative architectural forms as videos and renderings.

105 ● 171

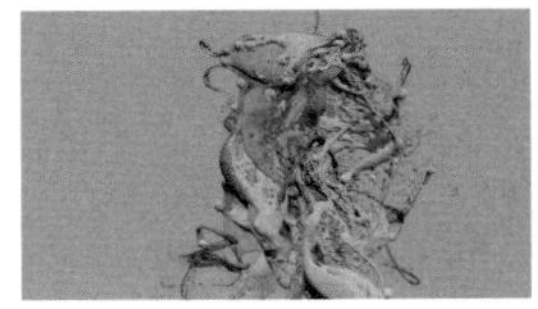

106A ○ 222

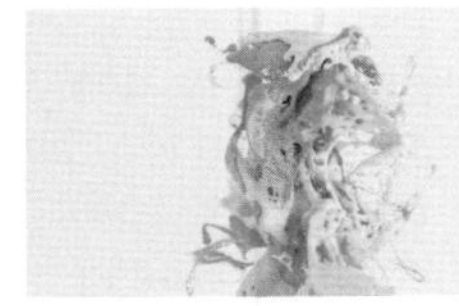

106B ○ 222

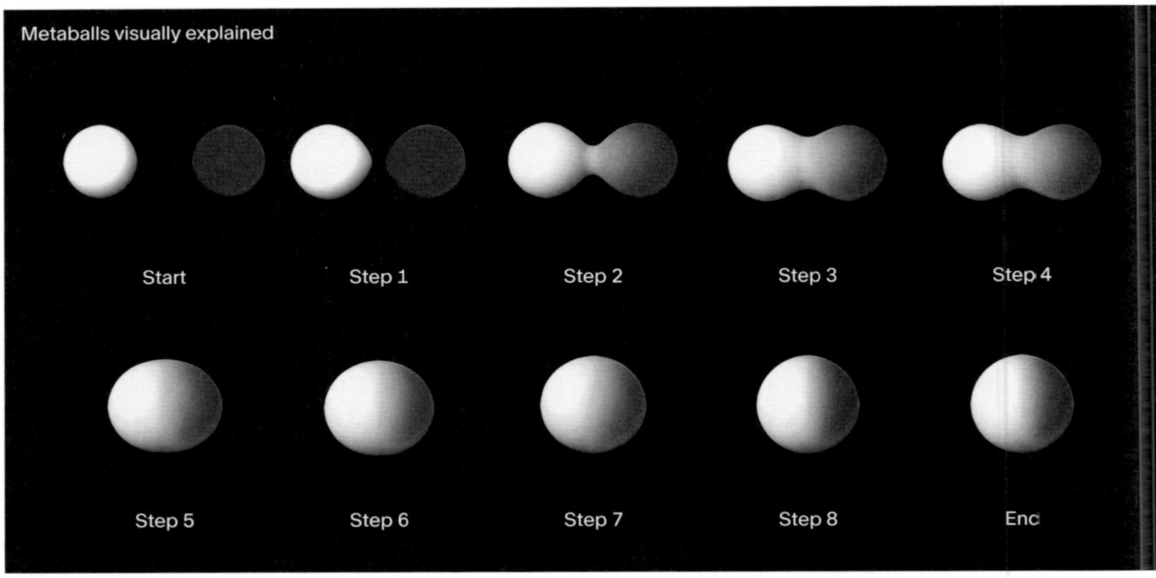

OTHER FORM-FINDING STRATEGIES

PARTICLE-SPRING SYSTEMS

We have just highlighted particle systems as a way to render special material effects from the natural world, such as smoke or explosions. *Particle-spring systems* are an extension of this principle. They have been used □ 475↘ extensively to address specific graphics problems, particularly to create realistic simulations for the animation of clothing and other fabrics. Particle-spring systems are based on lumped masses – called particles – which are connected by linear elastic springs. Each spring is assigned a constant axial stiffness, an initial length, and a damping coefficient. These systems can be used to model structural behaviours, and in a way they are the digital recreation of the famous ■ 424↘ hanging chain models by Catalan architect Antoni Gaudí (1852–1926), which we take a close look at in □ 421↘ our chapter on Model Making. Just as their analogue precedent, they can be used to determine the structurally optimal shape of arcs, vaults, and shells.

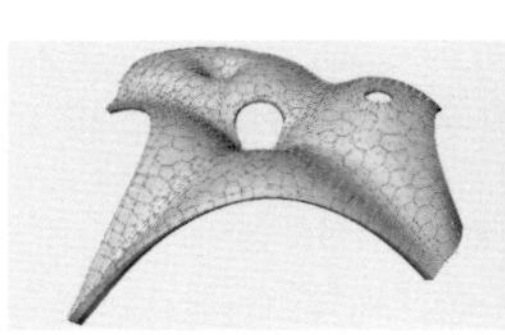

107A ○ 222

107B ○ 222

AGENT-BASED MODELS/SYSTEMS

Agent-based models have a long history in computing and are used in many settings. The simplest explanation of an agent is 'a robot without a body': a seemingly 'autonomous' entity that exists in software only. Agent-based systems or models are important in a variety of sciences, mostly in order to simulate complex systems. We mention them in our chapter on Simulation as a way to simulate crowds and to carry out path-finding studies in cities and buildings. Observing how people behave in a shopping complex or town centre can also make them useful in the design and arrangement of retail units and window displays, for example.

Swarms are natural agent-based systems, which lend themselves well for simulation. In architecture, a housing settlement can be described as a swarm, whereby its optimal constellation is then 'frozen' to generate a spatial context.

To a lesser extent agent-based methods have also been used as generative strategies in experimental architecture. What we stated in the section on procedural modelling above applies here as well: they are mostly used as part of speculative form-finding strategies.

TOPOLOGY OPTIMISATION

One of the best established and most widely used methods of form optimisation has become known as

■ 483↘
□ 351↘

topology optimisation. Its basis is the Finite Element Method (FEM), which can be used in applications such as structural analysis, heat transfer, or fluid flow. This is a mathematical method that is based on calculations done in spatial meshes, where each node in the mesh transmits information (simulating physical forces) to its neighbours. It is often applied to find the paths of forces through a shape, which can then be used to identify how the structural skeleton that is most efficient for a certain load case should be designed.

There are a number of plugins available for *Rhino Grasshopper* that support FEM-based topology optimisation, which have made the procedure fairly popular in design.

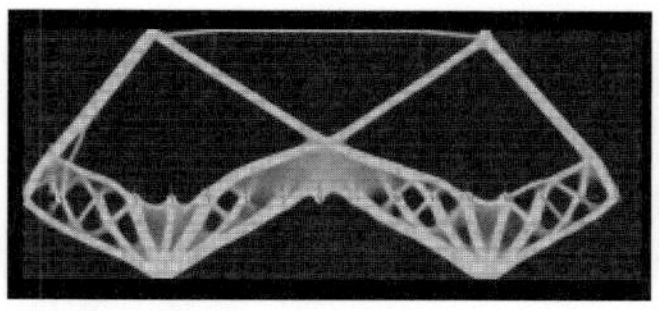
108A ○ 223

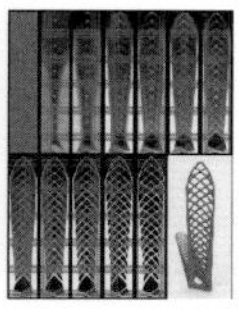
108B ○ 223

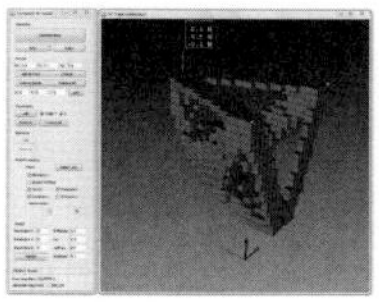
108C ○ 223

VORONOI DIAGRAMS

In architecture you often find yourself in a situation where you have to partition up a given surface area or plane into smaller sections. The *Voronoi diagram* (also *Voronoi tessellation*, and there are several other names in circulation) is a particular type of partition where the plane is divided such that each subsection defines the area from within which you have the shortest available distance to a predefined point that lies in that section. This sounds perhaps more complicated than it is: say you have a small town with a finite and currently set number of charging points for electric cars. These are unlikely to be exactly evenly distributed around town, so it can be interesting, useful, or even essential to know and be able to tell residents which is the nearest charging point to them. A Voronoi tessellation emerges by growing the radius from each set point until it meets with the boundary of any other point: the area so defined is the area most closely served by that point.

Voronoi tessellations are simple to calculate on a computer, and in design they make it seemingly easy to generate what resembles an organic look. For a while they were therefore a popular feature of many digitally generated designs. But as is the way with fashions: right now they tend be regarded as somewhat dated, which is not to say that their currency may not at some point rise again in the foreseeable future.

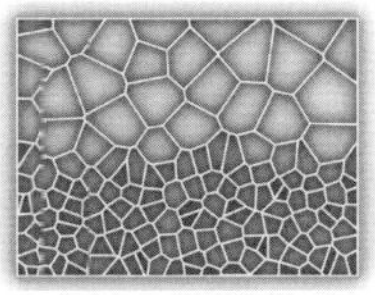
109 ● 171

THE CONSTRUCTION TREE

In our chapter on Scripting we discuss why the use of visual scripting environments is something of a mixed blessing, as it tends to keep the full potential of algorithmic design hidden from its users. Here we want to focus on the positive aspect. The fact that these visual scripting solutions have led to an ever more widespread use of parametric design really is a 'good thing', because what you create in this fashion perfectly fits the requirement for a process-oriented rather than static understanding of design. And the visual representation can in fact be seen as an essential part of this design method.

French author Bernard Cache (b.1958), in a piece published in *AA Files* in 2007 postulates:

> "If you approach new digital architecture in relation to older ideas of geometry, then you have to be aware of the tool in parametric software known as the 'construction tree'. In essence it is an interface, a device, which instead of showing forms, illustrates properties or relations. You model by dragging and dropping properties or relations onto a 'tree'. The more you master this tool the better and more interesting your designs will be. It should be something that all designers have to learn as a basic piece of knowledge. In a way it constitutes the mental aspect of any architectural project. I dream of the day when architectural reviews will look only at a student's symbolic 'tree', because this is the epistemological (rather than material) heart of parametric architecture."

This is a pertinent, if not entirely uncontroversial, thought, which you could counter with the question, 'is that not like writing a food review on the basis of a recipe without having tasted the food, or of a film on the basis of the script, without having watched the actual production?' Nevertheless, it highlights a contention we too consider significant: that for architects an understanding of the principles of parametric design is now indispensable.

The 'construction tree' here referred to, incidentally, varies enormously from one type of application to another. In the special effects packages mentioned earlier it will by necessity be very different to the 3D modelling plugins *Grasshopper or Dynamo*, for instance. Yet it is worth noting that the principle of the construction tree works remarkably well in both cases. And it is probably no accident that we are here still, or again, talking about a figurative tree, much as we started out with, back in 1837, with Charles Darwin.

Once you have created a parametric or procedural model, in which sizes and proportions are intelligently linked, you can not only very easily create variations, you also open the door to the optimisation procedures we already briefly touched on at the beginning of this chapter and which we now want to have a closer look at.

Optimisation & Design

"A design problem is not an optimisation problem," British-American architect and design theorist Christopher Alexander (b. 1936) writes in his book *Notes on the Synthesis of Form* – a treatise on how design processes can be made more rational. Rather than maximising certain characteristics, architecture just has to be 'good enough' on a vast range of topics, Alexander argues. And he has a point. The idea that a house is a machine for living in, as Le Corbusier famously and provocatively posited, and could thus be tweaked to become optimised in its performance, likewise is not one most architects nowadays would □ ↖111 subscribe to. We are aware of the many qualities a good building has that cannot be quantified (or only with great difficulty), and we prefer to take a holistic, multi-faceted view of architecture, one that doesn't easily square with the notion of optimisation.

Why then the title to this section? Put simply, because today there are a whole range of performance pressures put on construction projects of different types that can not – and nor should they – be avoided, such as maximising energy efficiency, for example. But also cost, use of materials, sustainability during and after its lifecycle, integration into an existing context: these are all factors that can't just be ignored.

We now have a sticker on every household appliance indicating its energy efficiency, but in many cases we are still unaware of the resource efficiency when it comes to our buildings, let alone their optimisation. This should change, and it can. And along the way designers will need some help from mathematical optimisation strategies. So when we argue here that optimisation and design in some cases can and should go together, we are really not subscribing to the idea that architecture as a whole is an optimisation problem. But being knowledgeable about optimisation strategies and informed about the consequences of design decisions in terms of their resource efficiency is something that is hard to argue against.

178 ↘

GENOTYPE VS PHENOTYPE, WICKED AND TAME PROBLEMS

For us to be able to optimise something, we first need to have clarity about the range of acceptable solutions: the design space we've already talked about, here to mean all the possible variations that can therefore be compared. Looking for the most suitable solutions within that space is also referred to as a Design ■ 362 ↘ Space Exploration (DSE). At the basis of design space exploration – much as we, in slightly different terms, suggested at the beginning of this chapter – lies a procedural understanding of design: a process or set of processes that will produce different results depending on the values of the given parameters.

In genetics a distinction is made between the hereditary information that is stored on an organism's genes – the *genotype* – and the observable and measurable ways in which the organism behaves in its environment – the *phenotype*. Similarly, in generative design we distinguish between the parameters that you set – equivalent to the genotype – and the characteristics of any given iteration – equivalent to the phenotype. The latter is something you can measure, observe, and therefore also evaluate, the former is a given input that may or may not yield usable results, as defined by yourself.

Since it is the evaluation that either prompts us to make amendments, or leads the program to introduce mutations of its own, evaluation is a critical aspect to this kind of generative design method. But evaluation towards an optimisation is not a simple or straightforward matter. In fact, it is a 'wicked' problem. We explain the difference between 'wicked' and 'tame' problems in our chapter on Digital Design Strategies, so we won't go into any great detail on this fascinating topic here, but in a nutshell, you are with a wicked problem looking at a situation where several, often very many, factors are connected to each other in such a way that when you solve one aspect of your problem, you create a new one elsewhere.

Architecture is awash with wicked problems, since in construction and spatial design a payoff in one area will almost certainly entail an expense, expected or otherwise, in another: say you have a residential development in which you want to maximise the quality of the space for the people who will be living there, while keeping that same space affordable, with a further priority being energy efficiency and use of natural daylight: the bigger you make your flats, the more living space you make available for your future residents, but the more expensive each unit will invariably become; the larger your windows, the more demand you put on their energy efficiency and safety rating, the higher you either put up the price of each unit or the lower your certification will be.

What therefore needs to drive the thinking is a concept from which I as the architect draw everything together, letting my individual decisions play in synch with each other so that, if I do this well – and with a bit of luck and fair wind prevailing – I arrive at an architectural solution that satisfies on all levels, or better still, that is in fact greater than the sum of its parts in its own way, because each individual element supports every other element, to the point where if you removed, added, or changed anything, the whole would instantly be less: a type of balanced perfection.

OPTIMISATION ALGORITHMS

There are available today many different optimisation algorithms that can help an architect or engineer find the best possible solution for a given project. The mathematics behind these algorithms is well researched and there are a number of software products on the market that make them available. *MATLAB* (for *MAtrix LABoratory*) by MathWorks, for instance, offers a whole range of optimisation processes that can be applied in engineering, science, and economic environments or tasks.

The problem with applying this type of optimisation in architecture is that all of these algorithms require large numbers of iterations to arrive at optimal solutions. And if the value that is to be optimised can only be determined with calculations that require long processing times (such as is the case for example for detailed lighting or structural analyses) an optimisation becomes practically unfeasible, as the thousands of iterations that are typically involved would take up way more time than is acceptable, especially during the design conception phase, when they would be most useful.

This is the main reason why these optimisations aren't more common in architecture. They only work for values that can be determined reasonably quickly, such as lengths of pathways, useable floorspace, or how much sunlight a facade will receive over the seasons. One way out of this conundrum is cutting down on processing time by using reliable rules of thumb or largely simplified algorithms. This can often yield very good results, which you can then verify with full calculations. There are also attempts to speed up the process by using machine learning algorithms that become good at 'guessing' the outcome of simulations, so to speak. This obviously is an issue in flux: the speed limitations that currently prevent a more widespread use of these approaches are being dismantled with each new generation of hardware, and so time here certainly works in the architects' favour.

Where the prerequisite fast calculations can be carried out, though, programs like these already allow for the integration of optimisation criteria – such as energy efficiency compared to the maximisation of living space, for example – into the design process. Thus 'optimal forms' can be generated that correspond to the performance simulation, incorporating all manner of factors, such as for instance solar irradiation: you set equations of what needs to be considered, and the algorithm churns out the best available answers.

THE PARETO OPTIMALITY

We've already mentioned wicked and tame problems, and here we want to delve just one step further into the limitations of optimisation: *'The Pareto Optimality'* may sound a bit like the title of an episode in the American science sitcom series *The Big Bang Theory*, but it is in fact the name given to the situation where in a system every criterion or preference that you have defined is at its optimal point *in relation to every other criterion or preference*, meaning that it is no longer possible, from this point onwards, to optimise any single criterion or preference without causing at least one other criterion or preference to lose out as a result. So although individual criteria or preferences may not be at their optimal point, they are at the optimal point in the given context, and the system therefore is, by the standards set with the specified criteria and/or preferences, at its most efficient and/or effective.

The terms Pareto frontier, Pareto front, and Pareto set are used interchangeably to describe the set of choices out of all available choices that are *Pareto efficient*. Say you have a range of possible options that you can plot on a graph, then the Pareto frontier includes all instances which are optimal, whereas any instance to either side of this line is sub-optimal or less than ideal.

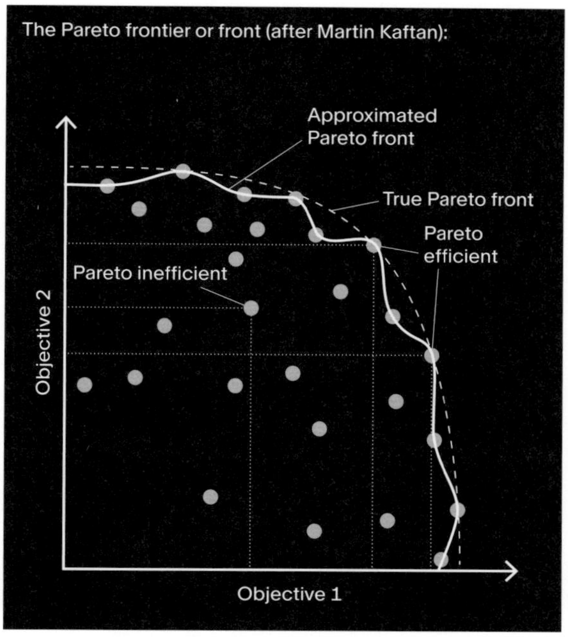

The Pareto frontier or front (after Martin Kaftan):

This delicate (because often difficult to obtain) state, also known as the Pareto efficiency is named after the Italian engineer, economist, and philosopher Vilfredo Pareto (1848–1923), who first formulated it, and who also came up with the *Pareto principle*, to which he similarly lends his name. Otherwise known as the *80/20 rule* or the *law of the vital few*, it observes and postulates that in many contexts and settings it is roughly 20% of causes that are responsible for 80% of effects. While not directly related to the Pareto optimality, it is a widely studied and recognised principle in business management, economics, and social science, and it plays an important part in computer science for optimisation purposes, where a standard school of thought says that you can solve 80% of software issues by fixing 20% of the most prevalent bugs, for example.

110 ● 172

Since it is impossible, in the real world, to get anything 100% right, the Pareto principle takes on such universal significance that it also matters to architecture: if you can identify the roughly 20% most important problems and concentrate your efforts on solving them, you should, by this route, arrive at an 80% perfect result, which by anyone's standards is likely to be very good. (This may also be, incidentally, where the difference lies between something that is to all intents and purposes 'very good' or even quite excellent, and something that is outstanding, genius even. The American singer Art Garfunkel (b. 1941), still best known for his turbulent creative partnership with singer-songwriter Paul Simon (b. 1941) in Simon & Garfunkel, is quoted as saying: "I'm a perfectionist.

If you're 99 percent toward a vision, to me, the gods live in that last 1 percent.")

■ ↖114 541↘

EVOLUTIONARY ALGORITHMS
& GENETIC ALGORITHMS

Among the optimisation algorithms mentioned, best known are probably *Evolutionary Algorithms (EA)*, of which *Genetic Algorithms (GA)* form the most common subset. They are used to generate solutions for analytically unsolvable problems. The problems are unsolvable because the number of unknowns is too large, or because the interdependencies between variables are intractable. They are, you could say, particularly difficult wicked problems, and as we have pointed out before, architecture is rife with these.

EA and GA emulate natural selection processes in nature, by evolving a starter generation of a representation – a design, or a model, for example – through several, often many, iterations to an optimised result, using a fitness function to evaluate each iteration, and learning *by itself* which specimens are the 'best' or 'most promising' from each generation, building this finding into its own structure, while allowing for random mutations to test possible unforeseen benefits or successes.

There are two components to any GA: a generative function, which turns a set of parameters (the genotype) into a design (the phenotype); and a fitness function, which evaluates the phenotype, that is it scores its properties and arrives at a number indicating its fitness. The series of steps these two components perform then looks as follows:

1 Randomly generate a population of individuals (designs, models, specimens)
2 Evaluate them against a specified fitness function or against specified design criteria
3 Select successful individuals for recombination
4 Generate a next iteration, allowing for one or several mutations: random alterations
5 Repeat steps 2–4 as often as specified or until the desired level of optimisation has been achieved
6 Select the optimal candidate(s) as the final result

111 ● 172

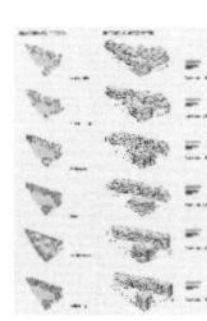

112 ○ 224

'AN EVOLUTIONARY ARCHITECTURE'

Genetic algorithms are mostly used to solve optimisation problems. If used in combination with a well-designed parametric model, they can help find optimal window distributions or structural properties, for example. But they also have the potential to become much more. In 1995, British architectural academic John Frazer (b. 1945), then a professor at London's Architectural Association (AA), wrote a

□ ↖111

book entitled *An Evolutionary Architecture*, chronicling his research group's efforts in this direction. As our understanding of generative processes and the

□ 549↘

speed of our hardware increases, this idea becomes

■ ↖114 182↘

more realistic. While much of the current thinking about parametric design seems to be inspired by a mechanistic conception of morphogenesis that we can trace back to D'Arcy Thompson, we can also conjecture that eventually the more fluid conception of morphogenesis introduced by Alan Turing will become prevalent.

Rather than having to start with a fully fledged parametric model, as is common today, you would then start with a much more open design space and use GA as a brainstorming tool to interpret a design brief. Say for example you were tasked with building a new municipal theatre with rehearsal, storage, and office space, as well as street level store fronts, bar, cafe, underground parking, and a generous foyer. You could of course take a sheet of paper and start by drawing sketches of the most beautiful building you can imagine. Alternatively, though, you can start with a set of parameters that you know simply have to be kept within: you know, for example, that the theatre requires a main house that comfortably seats 700 people with good sight lines, and a fully flexible studio space with up to 200 seats. You know you need temporary parking for 200 cars and a further 50 parking bays for staff. A statutory percentage of all of these have to be reserved for people with limited mobility. You obviously know the space into which the whole complex has to fit, and you know that the cafe/bar needs to be able to hold cabaret performances and podium discussions. The foyer will be used for art exhibitions. A decision may have been taken to use only sustainable materials, the building has to fulfil the city's ambition to provide carbon neutral services to its citizens, and there is bound to be a budget.

With a genetic algorithm you could describe accommodating all these requirements as your 'problem': you give some parameters that must not be breached and you set as your fitness function the best way in which your criteria are being met. You initiate the process with step 1 above and then run steps 2–4 maybe two thousand times, and what you will end up with may not be an absolutely perfect solution (in fact it never is with this evolutionary approach), but it should be a fairly good approximation to it. In all this, what is extremely important is that the algorithm throws in random mutations and doesn't just simply drive a straight line towards optimal configuration. As nature demonstrates: the real strength in evolution lies in unpredictability.

And this isn't a scenario from some distant future. Between 2001 and 2010, *Kaisersrot* was a research project at what was then the Chair for Architecture and Computer Aided Architectural Design (CAAD) – now renamed Digital Architectonics – at ETH Zürich. During that time it developed sophisticated architectural applications of GA which scored notable successes in ambitious projects that were realised in cooperation with some very well known and highly respected architect offices, most prominent among them perhaps Herzog & de Meuron for the Beijing National Stadium. (We reference this further in our chapter on Digital Design Strategies).

GENERATIVE ADVERSARIAL NETWORKS (GAN)

As we explain in our chapter on Big Data & Machine Learning, recent advances in Artificial Intelligence (AI) often make use of artificial neural networks, an information processing paradigm inspired by the way biological neural systems process data. In a nutshell, Neural Networks (NN) enable computer systems to learn. These networks have been around for some time, but they have recently gained in prominence, as they are at the heart of current advances in highly researched areas such as reliable computer vision for autonomous vehicles or speech recognition and real-time translation, where they're also referred to as deep learning or machine learning.

Generative Adversarial Networks (GAN), introduced as a concept in 2014 by American researcher Ian Goodfellow explore the generative potential of neural networks. They actually consist of two neural networks: one is referred to as the *generative network*, the other as the *discriminative network*.

This might remind you of the basic components of the Genetic Algorithms (GA) we discussed above, where there is a generative function and a fitness function that work together to evolve the 'fitness' of what is being generated. And indeed the basic idea is very similar. But here the part of the fitness function is taken over by a discriminative network: a ■ 649↘
neural network that has been trained to recognise a certain type of data, typically a category of images.

When we say 'trained' in the context of NN, what we refer to is a procedure that usually involves thousands of images and leads to the software being able to discriminate between them, by scoring how similar any image is to the statistics of that training ■
set; or put differently: to distinguish between real ■ 377↘
and fake images.

The task of the generative network, then, is to produce images that the discriminative network cannot distinguish from the training set. And because the generative network is a neural network and thus able to learn, it will get increasingly better at this task. After successfully completed training, the generative network will be able to produce fakes that the discriminative network cannot distinguish from the real thing.

Generative Adversarial Network (GAN) framework (after Thalles Silva):

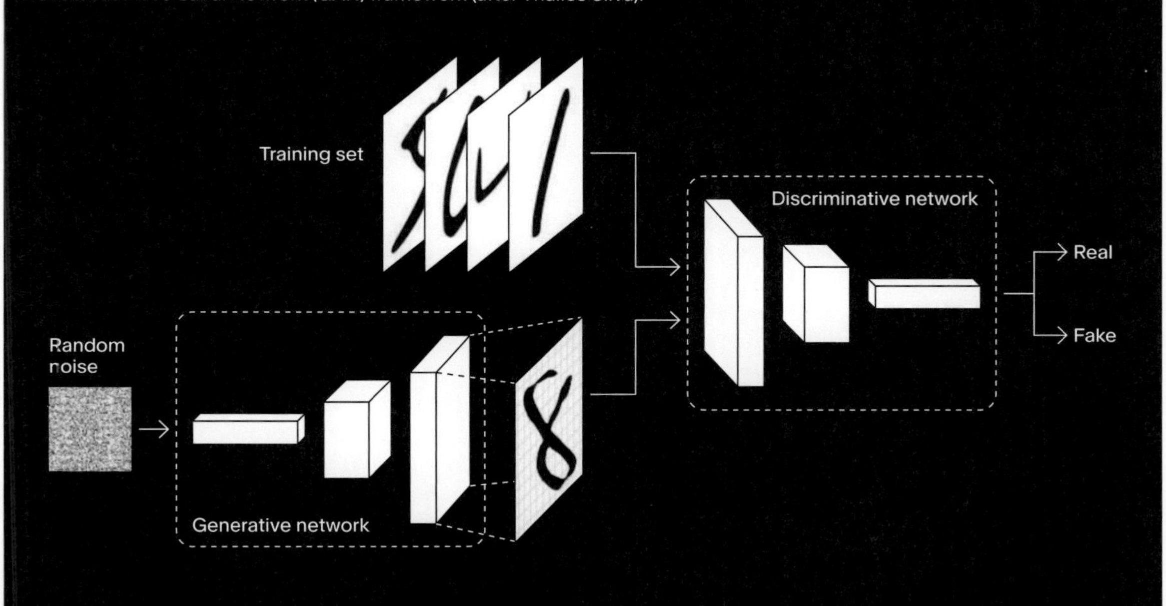

The generative network's training objective is to increase the error rate of the discriminative network.

French-American computer scientist Yan LeCun (b. 1960), one of the leading figures in machine learning and a Turing Award laureate, in 2017 when overseeing AI research at Facebook, called GANs, "the coolest idea in deep learning in the last twenty years." They have been used to produce artificial images of faces, but also to create architectural floor plans in certain styles. But unlike with shape grammars discussed earlier, the style here is not decoded analytically by a human, but automatically through a neural network that is trained with a training set. We expect to see many applications of GANs in the creative disciplines in the future.

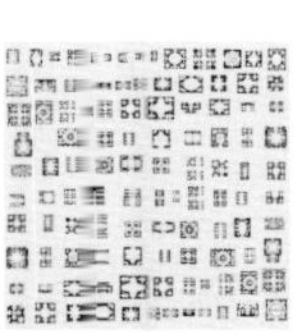

113A ● 173

113B ● 173

PARAMETRIC DESIGN – 'TOOL' VS 'STYLE'

It is impossible to talk about generative design methods without mentioning parametric design, and the moment you mention parametric design, as we have done a couple of times now, you also have to at least mention the term 'parametricism', coined by ■ ↖139
London-based German architect Patrik Schumacher (b. 1961), who as we write this is still head and sole remaining partner of Zaha Hadid Architects, following the death of Iraqi-British architect Zaha Hadid (1950–2016), who founded the practice in 1980.

At the Venice Biennale of Architecture in 2008, Schumacher put forward a 'manifesto' postulating 'parametricism' as "a new global style for architecture and urban design," as the title of an article he then published in *Architectural Design* phrased it. So, in effect, 'parametricism' is parametric design elevated to a theoretical concept and an architectural style. Reading this chapter, you will have realised that there are many different computational methods to generate form that involve parameters. And lumping them all together under the term 'parametricism' is not strictly helpful on a theoretical level. L-systems and topology optimisations have very little in common, either formally or conceptually. But 'parametricism' isn't only a theoretically imprecise term: the most problematic aspect of Schumacher's coinage is his intention to establish it as a style. Rather than explaining the manifold ways in which computational methods can in fact make a substantial contribution to the design process, the label 'parametricism' makes it easy to dismiss them wholesale as a mere fashion, something that will soon go out of style, as any 'style' invariably and ultimately must.

Parametric design is not just a fashion though, it is here to stay. Why do we say this? Because its essence is, as we've pointed out repeatedly, the establishment of links or dependencies between different parts and dimensions of a design. This is the basis of any proportional system and it is as old as architecture itself, certainly as old as architectural theory. It was in fact Bernard Cache, whom we mentioned earlier, who pointed out that parametric thinking is not in principle a novel idea. He convincingly shows that even Vitruvius – whom we also met before in this chapter and who crops up frequently in this *Atlas* for obvious reasons – thought and argued parametrically in his foundational work *De architectura* (known in English as *Ten Books on Architecture*). What has changed is simply how accessible parametric methods have become, and therefore perhaps how influential they are on architectural practice today.

And, on a more general note: as we saw when we were talking about morphogenesis, it is entirely possible in architecture to emulate nature and adopt natural forms. It is possible to simulate plants, for example, with striking accuracy both in two and three dimensions. What we shouldn't forget though is that these kinds of 'grown' forms are, in their structural make-up, subject to an entirely different logic to the one we use as architects when we are building things. Up until now at any rate, growing objects organically and constructing them have been two very different processes, and so while it may be interesting and aesthetically pleasing to use nature-inspired forms in architecture, it also only rarely makes sense to attempt a direct transfer of forms from one domain to the other.

SOFTWARE

Having spoken at such length about generative design methods, it may come as a surprise to find that there aren't actually a great many products on the market that support procedural design specifically for architecture. Researchers and developers at several universities have been working on generative approaches in architecture, and there are many successful programs that are used in an academic context, but there is little available on a commercial basis.

We've already noted the important exceptions: *Grasshopper* and – albeit with a much smaller user base – *CityEngine*. In fact, *Grasshopper* is currently the place where most of the (academic and non-academic) innovation in generative programming in architecture is taking place. This is due to the fact that *Grasshopper* has invited developers to create plugins, and this has really caught on: there are a large number of plugins available and usually they have an active community of users and developers that exchange questions and experiences in online forums. You will find *Grasshopper* plugins for most of the topics we have discussed in this chapter. (For example you could experiment with genetic algorithms using the aptly named plugin *Galapagos*.) The vast majority of these plugins have the additional advantage that they are available for free. That said they obviously also share the program's inherent limitations, which we have also pointed out.

The fact that so few of these plugins have the kind of user base that would warrant their survival as commercial software products supports our notion, ventured earlier, that the use of generative methods is not widespread in 'real world' architecture, but at least for now tends to be mostly an academic endeavour. And so as we write this in 2019, some individual architecture offices have their own, self-developed in-house solutions.

Nevertheless there are good reasons to expect that generative methods will become more and more common and that these types of programs will therefore become more widespread. This is already the case in other industries, such as in computer animation and special effects, where a number of procedural modellers are available. We mentioned one such programme, *Houdini* by Side Effects Software Inc, which seems to enjoy growing popularity among architects that use its features to develop experimental architectural imaginations.

All of which is simply to say: much as the topic of generative methods itself, so the software used in its application is at the more cutting edge of architecture. A lot of what you see generated is therefore far from utilitarian and may be regarded as 'fantasy architecture' that occupies a ground somewhere between the imaginary and the physical, that is either not very or not at all buildable, and that may not even make any claim to practicality. Architecture that is, if you like, deliberately 'out there'. Which is just as well, because innovation certainly needs the avant-garde, as without it the *'garde'* of the mainstream would never go anywhere at all.

Conversely, all of this is neither to say that you can *only* generate experimental objects with generative methods, nor that you *have to:* we are here mainly taking a snapshot of the current state of play.

114 ● 173

The Outlook

The outlook, then, for generative methods in architecture, is pretty much 'up for grabs': we expect that the tools that architects use routinely will gradually give us more options to integrate generative methods into our design, but we don't in fact envisage that these methods will 'take over' any time soon. So, while we think that generative methods will increasingly come to aid architects in dealing with the complexities of their profession, we do not share the notion put forward by some architects that generative design is or will soon be the architectural style of our day (nor that it should be thought of as a style). Neither do we think that the various algorithmic methods to arrive at novel forms should be regarded as a threat to the creative core of our profession. The threat to design exists, but it doesn't stem from the promoters of generative methods.

If you look at the United States, for example, some 95% of new buildings are 'designed' with standard templates that already exist anyway. So if anything, the real threat to the architectural profession isn't that clever computer programs might one day take over the design professions because they will outperform humans in terms of creativity and finding optimal solutions for conflicting briefs. The much more real threat to the profession is one of rampant banality: the simple copying of existing designs that allows developers to save money by not hiring qualified designers. The reality, and perhaps also irony, is that thinking away the architect does not actually require generative design.

So, even though we mention cases where computer programs can come up with evolutionary architecture, architects should not think of generative methods as their competition or enemy. On the contrary: they can be our friends! Generative methods can be extremely useful to solve complex or entirely new problems where some type or other of optimisation is sought, for example towards energy and material efficiency. This is the kind of thing that is difficult (if not impossible) to get right intuitively, but for a computer program it is comparatively easy. More to the point though: playing with generative methods – and we are using the word 'playing' here advisedly – can be excellent fun and very liberating. In many respects, generative methods have become a sandbox to experiment with form, from which have emerged, apart from many short-lived, 'unusable', and superficial specimens, also genuinely important ideas that do point towards an architectural expression of our age. And when we say we don't think generative methods will necessarily take over, we do think, certainly, that they will become more important and more prominent still. Generative methods will increasingly form part of the job of the architect and, no, they will not supplant or replace the architect.

We started our chapter with natural evolution and postulated that nothing comes from nothing. This is the crux of the matter: the real computational challenge, and also the real art of the programmer or programming architect, will be to invest in good rules. Also, at the beginning of this chapter and in one or two other places in this *Atlas* – namely in the Introduction and in Graphs & Graphics – we emphasise that if you want good answers (for which you might read 'solutions') you need to ask good questions. This certainly applies here: in order for parametric design, or any derivation of it including all variants of generative design, to yield results that are useful, or exciting, or revolutionary, or aesthetically striking, or any combination of these, the design parameters we set and the fitness functions we describe are both, and equally, of defining importance. The art then, or the challenge, is to find the right measure, the right balance, so to speak, between what is thrilling architecture and what can actually be built; between what ticks the boxes of efficiency and what makes for a beautiful place to live, work, or play in; between what we as architects and our clients and the end user feel comfortable with and what excites us and actually breaks new ground.

□ ↖29
□ 175↘

The future here is a fairly open book in which the space of possibilities is yet to be staked out.

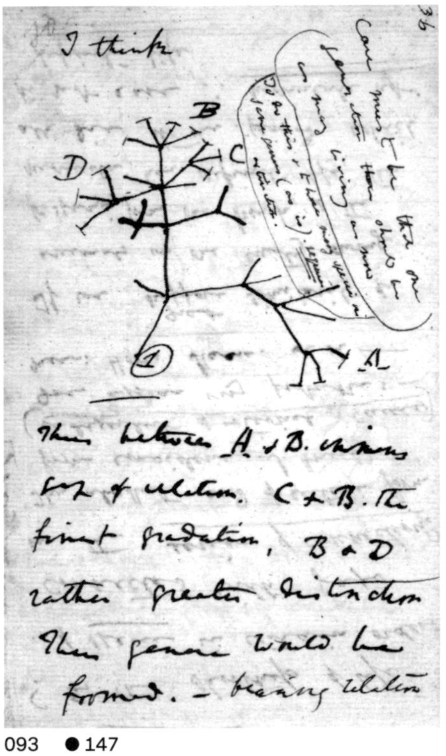

093 ● 147
Charles Darwin's first 'evolutionary tree' in his notebook 'B', from July 1837. The hand-written page says: "I think case must be that one generation should have as many living as now. To do this and to have as many species in same genus (as is) requires extinction. Thus between A + B the immense gap of relation. C + B the finest gradation. B + D rather greater distinction. Thus genera would be formed. – bearing relation" (continued on the following page with:) "to ancient types with several extinct forms."

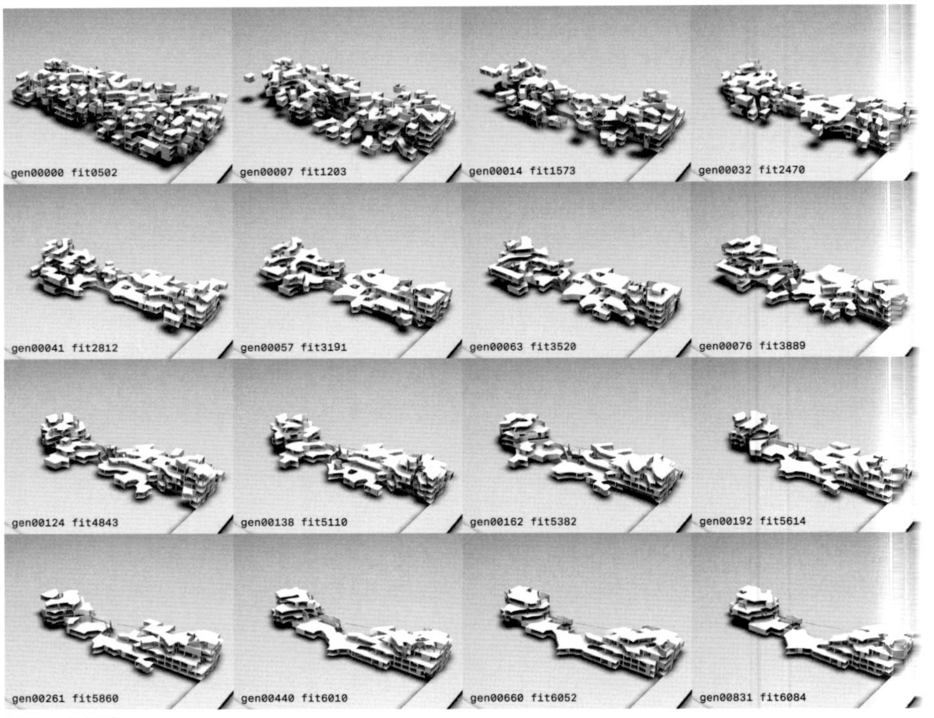

094 ● 148
Konsensmaschine: Genetic algorithms in architectural design. The *Konsensmaschine* is a competition entry for the redesign of the *Papierwerd-Areal* in Zürich, developed by the *Kaisersrot* research team of the chair of Architecture and CAAD (Computer Aided Architectural Design) at ETH Zürich. Taking into account room shapes and sizes, internal topology and infrastructure (hallways), construction, light exposure, and overall shape of the building, the *Konsensmaschine* used a genetic algorithm to optimise the 'fitness' of the design through hundreds of generations. The result was presented at the conference *Architekturbrennpunkte* in Zürich in 2004 alongside designs by Miroslav Sik, Dominique Perrault, Helmut Jahn, and Coop Himmelb(l)au. [*Kaisersrot*/ETH Zürich]

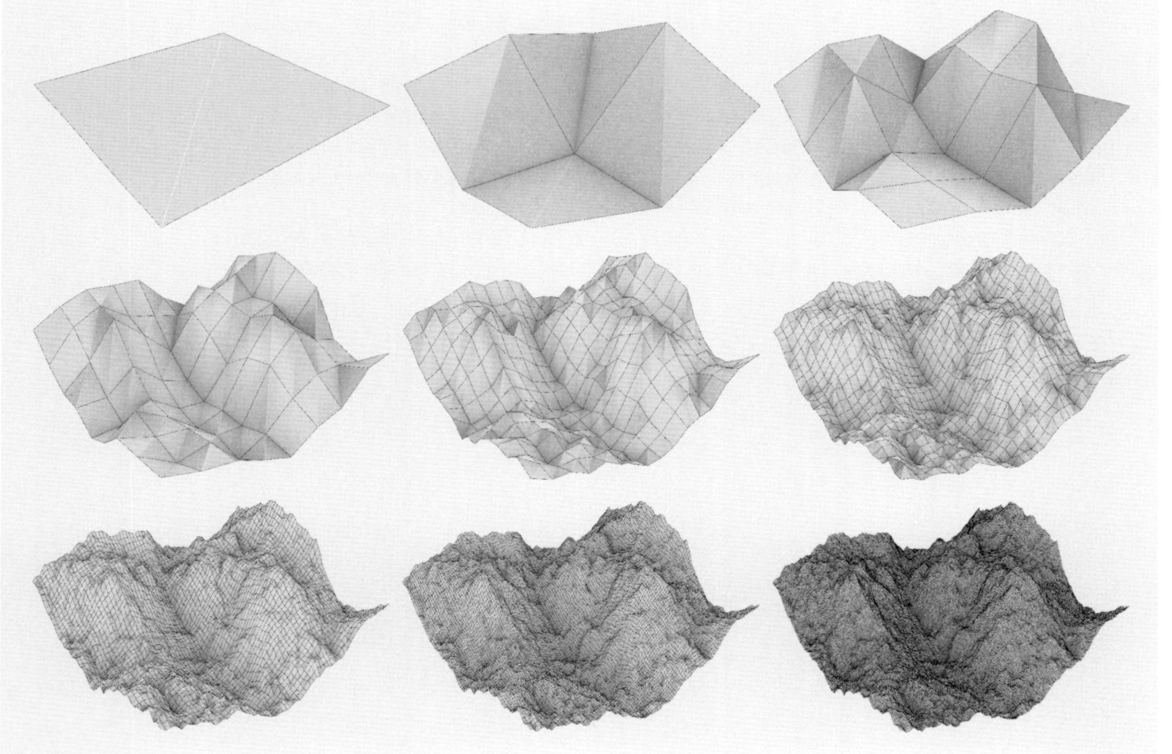

095 ● 156
Another example for recursion: fractal landscape generation. The initial landscape patch is recursively subdivided, the range of randomisation shrinks with the size of the patch. [Urs Hirschberg]

096 ● 156
Fractal landscape rendering. [Andi Mucke]

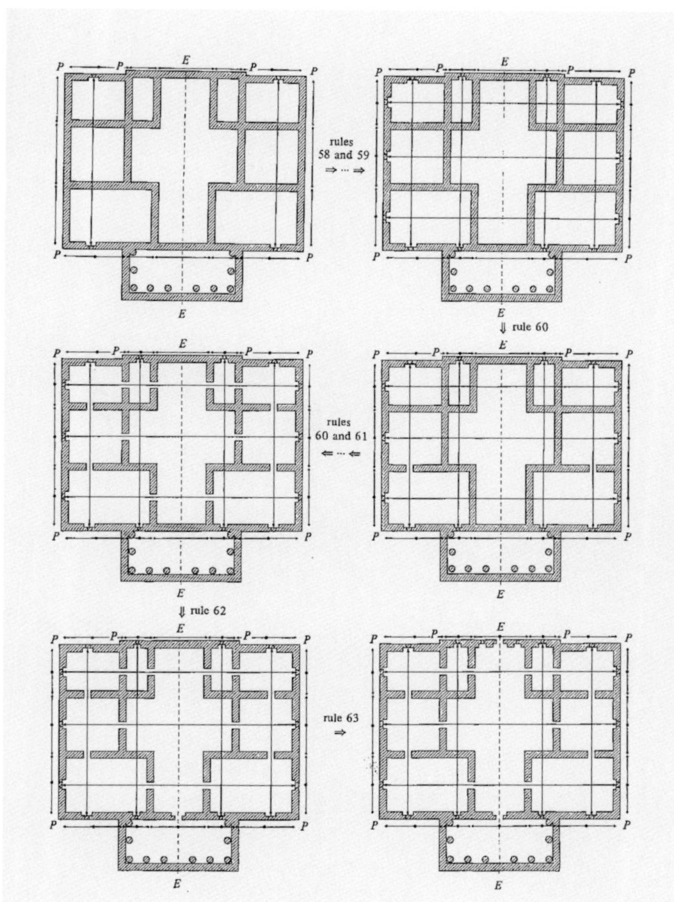

099 ● 158
Illustration from the seminal paper *The Palladian Grammar* by Stiny and Mitchell (1978). They show that their grammar is able to recreate the Villa Malcontenta. Shown here are the last steps of the process, the generation of the windows and doors. In a second paper published the same year, titled *Counting Palladian Plans*, they feature a catalogue of possible room layouts for Palladian villas, based on their grammar rules, including many layouts Palladio never designed. [George Stiny, William Mitchell]

100 ● 158
A virtual sci-fi city generated with *CityEngine*. This is a professional 3D modelling software that uses shape grammars in the creation of interactive urban environments, either based on real-world GIS data or to generate fictional urbanscapes. [Pascal Müller / Esri]

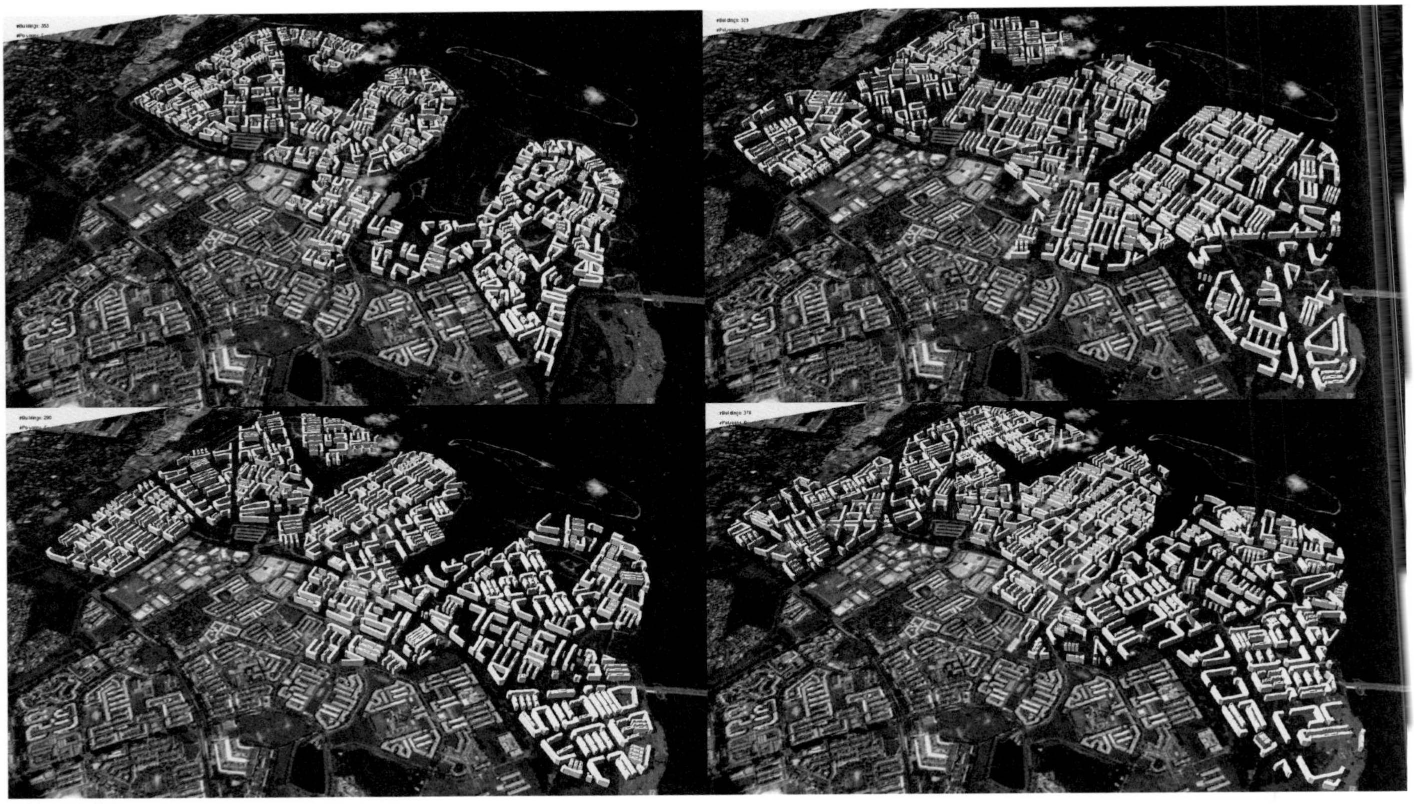

101 ● 158
Variations of city districts in Singapore, based on different zoning laws, created with *CityEngine* by the Future Cities Laboratory. [Singapore ETH Centre / ETH Zürich]

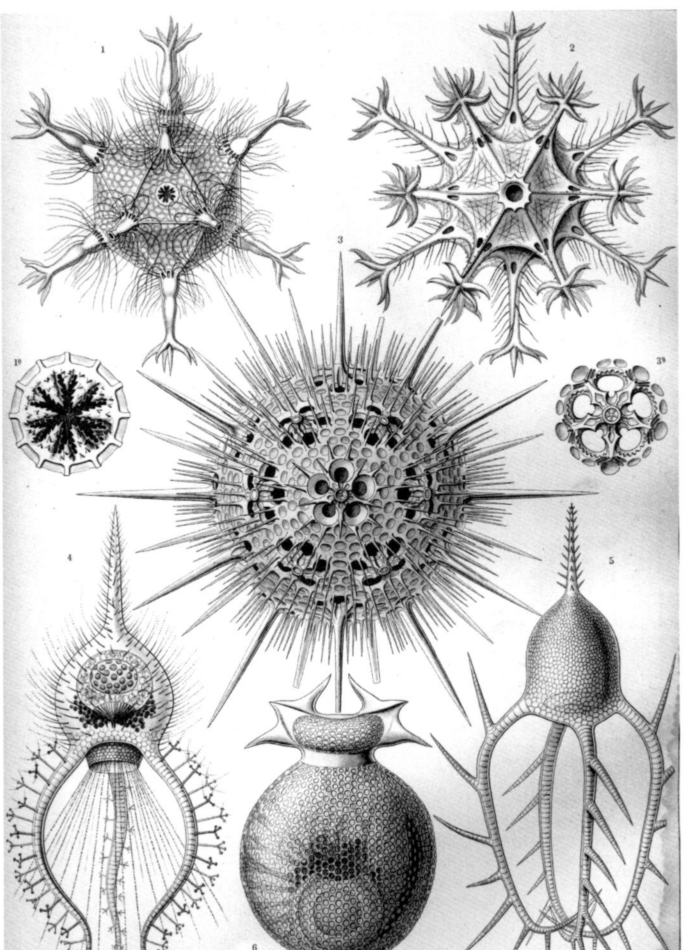

102 ● 158
Ernst Haeckel's *Kunstformen der Natur (Art Forms of Nature)*, 1904: a work filled with beautiful and detailed depictions of biological forms that was influential to the Art Nouveau or *Jugendstil* movements, and also inspired D'Arcy Wentworth Thompson for his *On Growth and Form*.

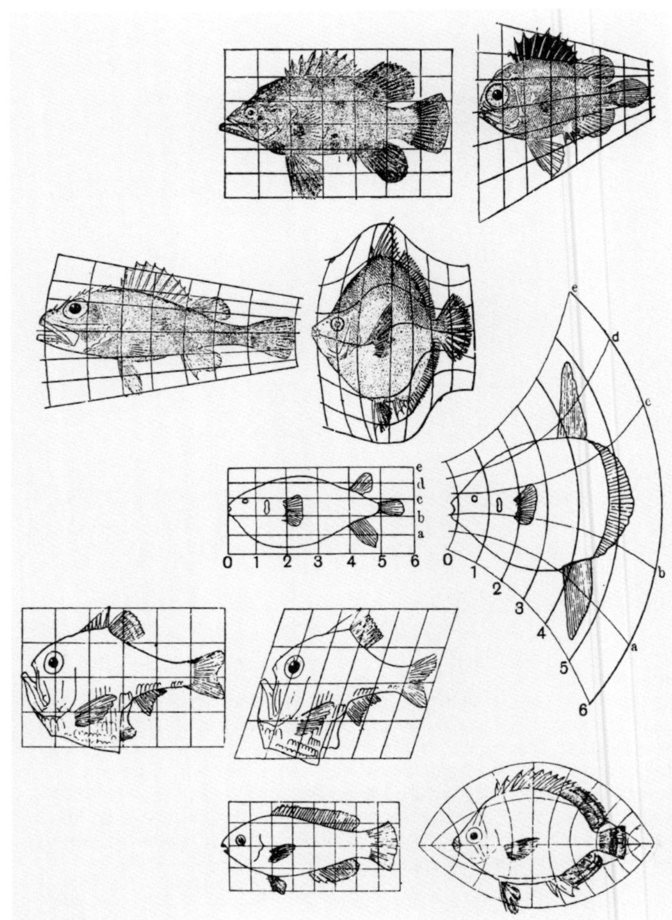

103 ● 159
Illustrations from *On Growth and Form*, D'Arcy Wentworth Thompson's influential book on the mathematical basis of organic forms, published in 1917. The final chapter, titled *Theory of Transformations or the Comparison of Related Forms* is a frequent reference in parametric design.

105 ● 160
Particle system rendered with billboards (left) and metaballs (right). Billboards are texture maps that are always turned towards the viewpoint. Here they create the illusion of fog. Metaballs, on the other hand, create the illusion of a liquid. Made with *Lightwave 9.0*. [Tcpp]

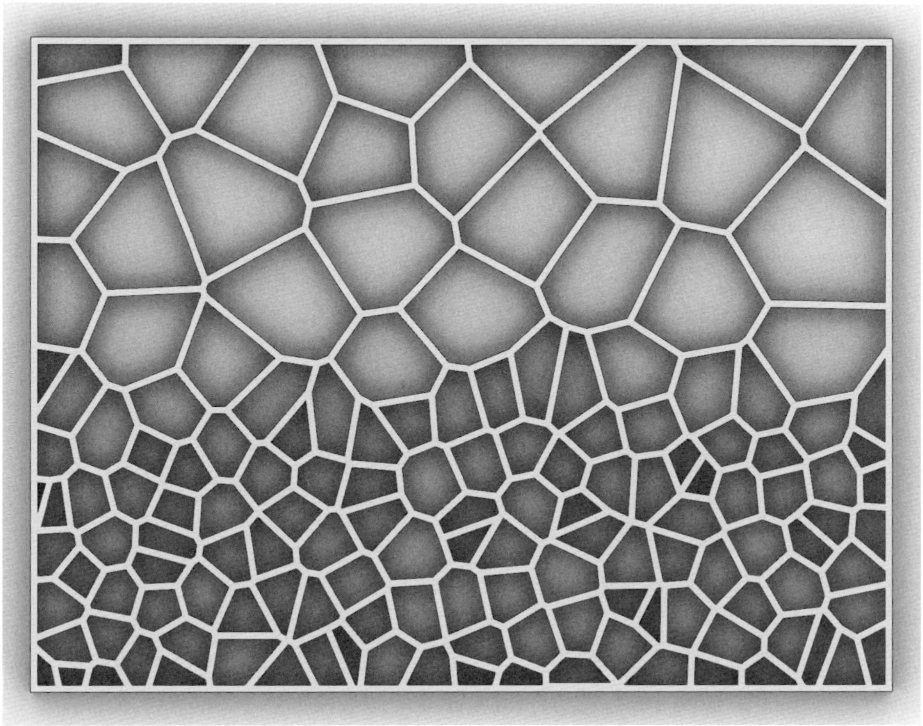

109 ● 161
Voronoi tesselations are a particular type of partition where a plane with a random distribution of points is divided such that each subsection defines the area from within which you have the shortest available distance to the point that lies in that section. It also creates decorative patterns that are sometimes used as architectural forms. [Milena Stavric]

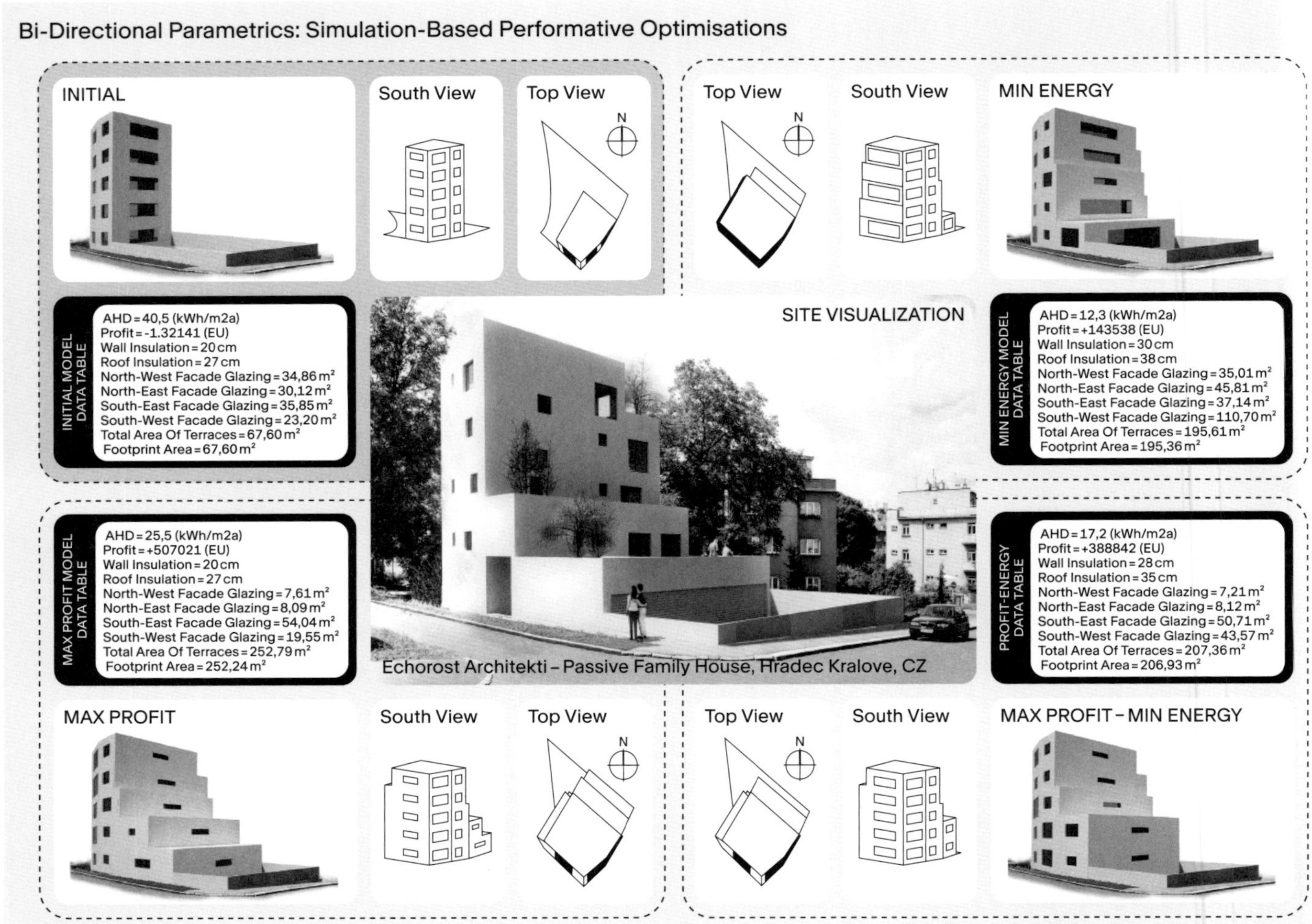

110 ● 163
The initial shape (top left) is optimised within the constraints of the parametric model: Maximising energy efficiency and maximising profitability lead to different results, as does the combination of the two. Case study done in the framework of the FWF (Austrian Science Fund) research project *Augmented Parametrics. Simulation and Expert Knowledge in Parametric Design.* (TRP 268-N23) [Jiri Pavlicek, Ioanna Simeonidou]

111 ● 164
Facade of the award-winning Kalkbreite project in Zürich, Switzerland. Designed wholly automatically, it was entered in the competition for which it won the prize anonymously. Developed by the *Kaisersrot* research team at the chair for Architecture and CAAD (Computer Aided Architectural Design) at ETH Zürich in 2009. The space modules of a layout are calculated for different qualities (view, path lengths, solar irradiation, vertical access, for example) and then tested and compared to other layouts. Depending on the weighting of these different factors, different architectonic layouts are generated, with one and the same space programme. [*Kaisersrot*/ETH Zürich]

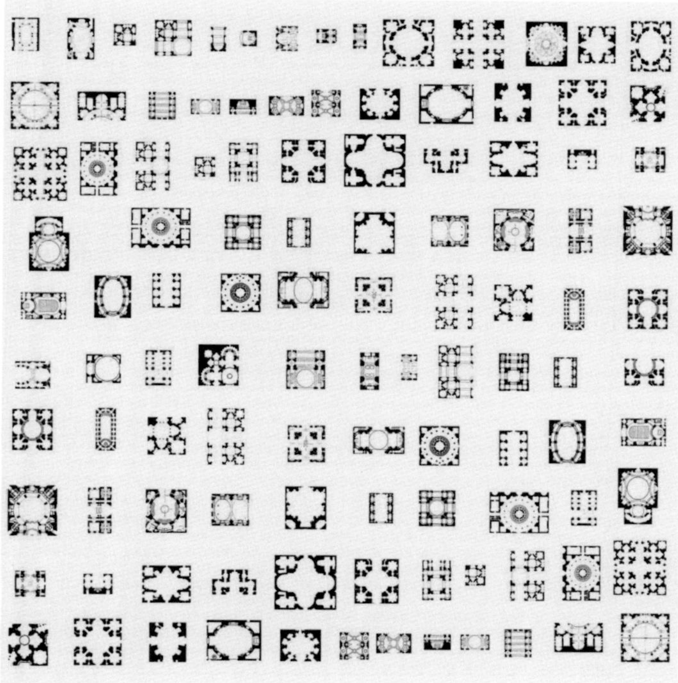

113A ● 165

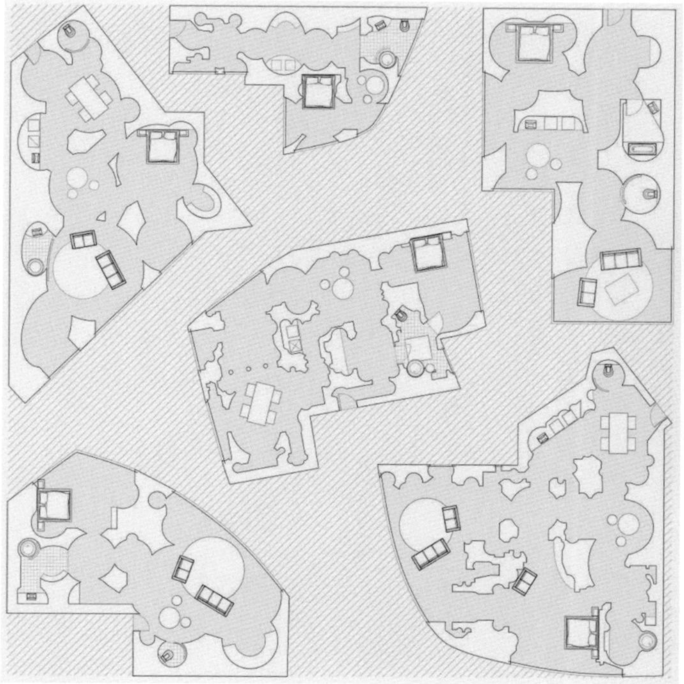

113B ● 165

GAN (Generative Adversarial Networks) Baroque style training set (113A) and generated units (113B). From Stanislas Chaillou: *AI + Architecture Towards a New Approach*, Harvard GSD Thesis, 2019. [Stanislas Chaillou]

114 ● 166

Skizoid by Joris Putteneers. Explorations with generative methods: procedurally generated speculative architecture that may not necessarily make a claim to buildability... [Joris Putteneers]

Graphs & Graphics

Ludger Hovestadt

The Queen's Garden Party

Imagine you receive an invitation to the Queen's Garden Party, because it's the Royal Institute of British Architects' anniversary, and on this particular occasion Her Majesty is interested in meeting and bringing together promising young architects from all over the world. (This is an unlikely scenario, by the way, but it serves a certain purpose, as we shall see...)

Alongside you, also invited are several hundred architecture students, as well as some really rather well known international figures who happen to be in town; say for example Jacques Herzog and Pierre de Meuron are mingling among the guests, as is Frank Gehry, Rem Koolhaas, and Norman Foster. There's The Queen and, because he has a special interest in architecture – although he may not see eye to eye with many of those present – also Prince Charles.

What you have in the gardens of Buckingham Palace is a collection of individual people, and the reason for them being there is that they should connect with each other. In its simplest abstract schematic, the people could be regarded as 'points' and the connections they either have or make with each other as 'lines'.

In **discrete mathematics**, and by application therefore in computing, a *graph* is a way of describing, and performing calculations with, sets of individual 'points' that are in one way or another related to each other: the 'lines' that connect them.

What makes graphs particularly interesting, versatile, and also complex is that, much as the human relationships between you, your peers, your professional idols, and the Royal Family at the Garden Party, the connections between individual points can not only be directional or non-directional, but also quite differently weighted.

So for example between the twelve hundred or so young people present, there might be a comparatively even mutual connection that is characterised by the fact that you are all aspiring to be architects. There is a non-directional relationship which allows each one of you to walk up to any other of you and say, 'hello, my name is Yasmin, where are you from?' and then continue the conversation along the lines of, 'how are you enjoying your tea, wouldn't it be nice to have a gin and tonic instead.'

This is not the case between you and The Queen. You cannot go up to The Queen and say, 'hello, my name is Yasmin, where are you from?' First of all because you already know where The Queen is from, and also because protocol requires that you only speak to her when you're introduced to her. Also, you might be taking your chances suggesting to her that it's really time to bring out the gin and tonic now. (You might get away with this though if you were talking to the Duchess of Cornwall, as she's supposed to have quite a good sense of humour...)

So not only are your relationships with these 'points' differently weighted, they are also directional: The Queen can say to you 'hello, where are you from?', but you cannot say this to The Queen. Similarly, you may really want to take this opportunity to talk to Frank Gehry, and zoom right in on him, but although you are extremely interested in him and know exactly who he is, he not only has no clue who you are, but also he has no time for you right at the moment, because he's busy explaining deconstructionism to Prince Charles. The connection that exists between the two of you is not mutual, it is directional, from you to him. And he is a considerably weightier 'point' at this stage than you are.

But even among your peers, where all of you are equally important, there may be directional and non-directional connections: for example, there may be Victor from Belo Horizonte, who's recently graduated and is now doing his PhD, and you just cannot get over how delightful he is. And how witty. And how reassuring and calm. And how incredibly handsome. And you may just fall a little in love with him and want to spend the entire afternoon talking to him, but to your dismay you have to realise that he has no eyes for you at all. He seems to be flirting away with Casper from Copenhagen, and this is all getting a bit much for you now. Again, we have a non-mutual, therefore directional connection, even though it exists between two equal points.

And the connections themselves can also be of a vastly differing nature and therefore weight or importance. No matter what you say or do to impress The Queen, you're unlikely to ever get as close to her as she is with Prince Charles, simply because he's her son. And no matter how much she's now part of the family, Camilla will never be able to be quite as fascinating to everybody else in the garden as Princess Diana was, when she was alive. ■

All of this is, of course, dynamic: if you replicate the same scene, with the same people, in five or let alone ten years' time, the weight of each point and the nature of each connection, as well as its direction, may have changed in many cases, while in others it will probably have remained largely the same. The Queen, for as long as she's around and able to attend, will always be the most important person at her own Garden Party. Even a revolution would find it difficult to change that. But you may since have built a strong reputation for yourself, and so people you have never met or heard of flock to you to seek your conversation. And as for Victor: well, the thing with Casper was never going to work out, was it, but you are now happily married to Paul and you and Victor have since become very good friends...

In graphs all these same things apply. You have connections between points, which can be directional or non-directional, and both the points and the connections can be differently weighted.

The points, in this example represented by people, are in mathematics and graph theory most commonly also called *vertices* or *nodes*; and the lines that connect them are called *edges* or *arcs*. And the reason any of this matters is that graphs form the backbone of information technology, and they are indispensable for Computer Aided Design (CAD) (to which we dedicate a separate chapter in this Atlas) and therefore □ ↖129 **Computer Aided Architectural Design CAAD**. ■ ↖134 359↘

115 ● 206

What Is a Graph

WHAT COUNTS AND WHAT MOVES

What we do in graph theory is 'count' and 'calculate' in a special way. Instead of viewing numbers as positive elements, such as the natural numbers

```
{1,2,3,4}
```

what we express in graphs are sets of positions, and we work with – it's not really accurate any more now to say 'count' or 'calculate' – the transitions or relationships between these positions:

```
{1→2,2→3,3→4}
```

So here, the numbers 1, 2, 3, and 4, instead of being expressions of magnitude or quantity (1 person, 2 people, 3 people, 4 people) may be viewed as positions or, in a vocabulary that is more unusual, but for architects adequate, *situations*: the person who happens to be in situation number 1, the person who happens to be in situation number 2, and so on. The arrows signal the connections between them, which in turn we can view as rules for moving, or transitioning, from one such situation to the next.

Thus, in the graph

```
{1→2,2→3,3→4}
```

we have four situations or *vertices* (1, 2, 3, and 4) with three *edges* between them.

The arrows indicate that these edges are directional; and if I am in situation 1, then the rule 1 → 2 tells me to move from situation 1 to situation 2. Once I am in situation 2, the rule 2 → 3 tells me to move to situation 3, and again, till I'm in situation 4. Much as there is no rule that leads to situation 1 (we simply took that as our starting point and accepted situation 1 to be in place), there is, in this example, no rule to
■ ↖162 move away from situation 4: we are here effectively at a dead end, and the movement stops.

■ ↖162 A set of vertices and edges, or of situations and rules, defines a graph:

```
g1={1→2,2→3,3→4};
```

Here is how to apply a graph to a situation and trigger a movement according to the first rule:

```
1/.g1
2
```

FORM VS STRUCTURE

An important thing to note is that a graph does not have a *form* as such; or rather, that it can have an *infinite number of forms* within its given *structure*. That is because graphs are defined exclusively by their structure, which is a *system of transitions* between situations.

The following are several representations of the exact same graph:

```
Graph[g1,VertexLabels→"Name"]
```

```
Graph[g1,VertexLabels→"Name",
      GraphLayout→"HighDimensionalEmbedding"]
```

```
Graph[g1,VertexLabels→"Name",
      GraphLayout→"CircularEmbedding"]
```

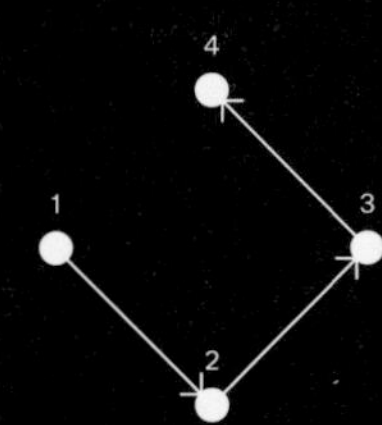

Forms with an identical structure are said to be *similar (homomorphic)* and can be *transformed (morphed)* into each other, such as the four examples above.

A *system of transitions* (that is, a *structure*, which in turn means a *graph*) can have many different *shapes* or *figures*. The term 'shape' or 'figure' is distinct from the term 'form': graphs, structures or systems have shapes, and shapes have forms.

You may think of a shape as a skeleton: for animals of the same species it is always the same, but it can yield widely different forms. But different species may still have the same structure. So shapes are an expression of the genotype – the principle or the idea of a species – forms are an expression of the phenotype, the instance or the individual. Shapes or figures are diagrammatic, forms are concrete. (We will come to the terms *genotype* and *phenotype* in more detail a bit further on in this chapter.)

We can also talk about these differences mathematically:

1 A *graph* is a structure in the sense of algebra;
2 The *shape* of a graph is an expression of the Euler characteristic (vertices - edges + faces == constant)
3 The *form* of a graph is the geometric form that preserves the structure and the Euler characteristic (what we call graphics).

In summary of the above, we have these three steps of concretisation:

```
g2={"graph"→"shape","shape"→"form"};
Graph[g2, VertexLabels → "Name"]
```

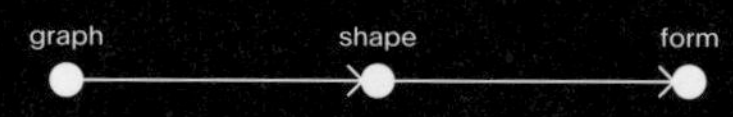

This is more precise than American architect Louis Sullivan (1856–1924) suggests when he famously postulates that "form follows function" in his highly influential essay *The Tall Office Building Artistically Considered*, published in *Lippincott's Magazine* in 1896. There, function makes no difference between the graph and the shape of our diagram.

There is also a game of concepts around these three levels that you might find interesting:

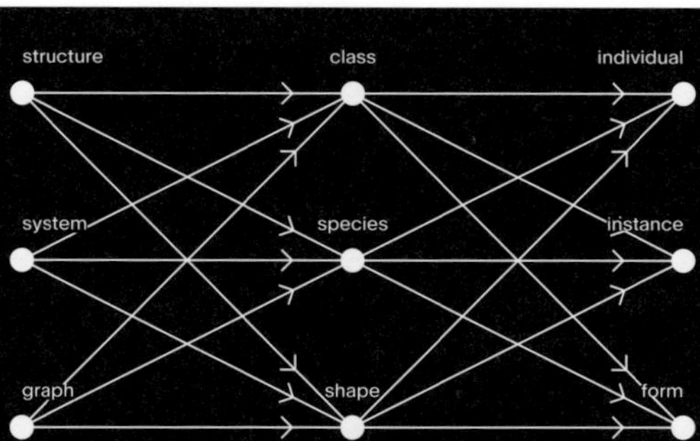

We here find ourselves in the realm of evolution, species, and varieties, most prominently articulated by the English naturalist Charles Darwin (1809–1882):

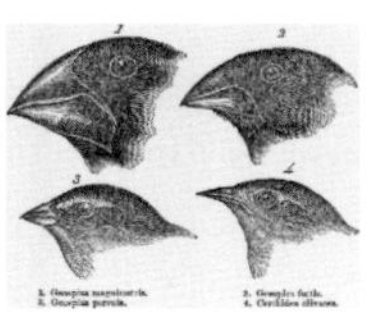

116 ● 206

Here is how these concepts are articulated with graphs. The following are two shapes or figures (or also '*classes*') of the same graph. And because they share the same structure (you could also say, because they share the same system), they can be morphed. What we are looking at is a diagrammatic form of the shapes:

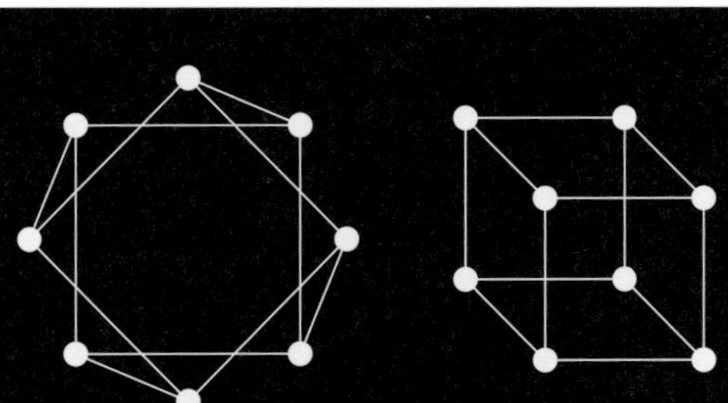

They have to be distinguished from their concrete forms: it's an example of a shape in two different forms.

Here are two different instances of a class, or two different individuals of a species:

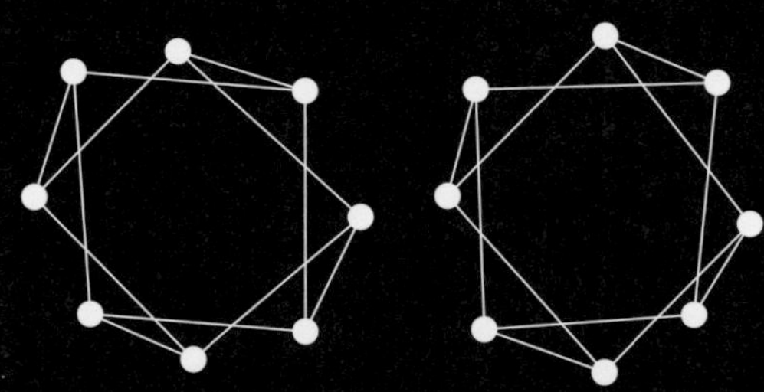

RINGS

Rings are special graphs which do not have dead ends:

```
g2={1→2,2→3,3→4,4→1};
```

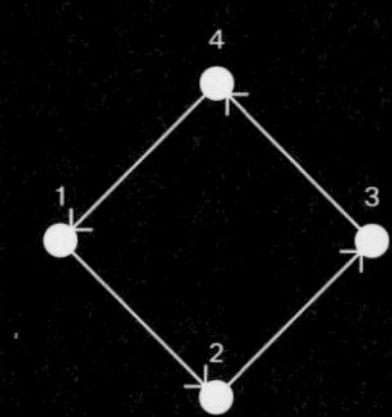

In this graph, for example, it is possible to keep on moving indefinitely:

```
3/.g2
4

4/.g2
1
```

Here is an illustration of a structure 'doing one round' through all available situations on the ring and back to the starting point:

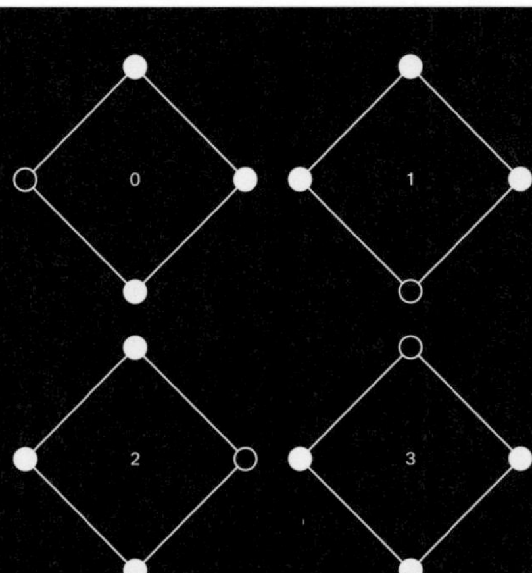

This corresponds to the **modulo operator** in mathematics, which identifies the remainder that is left over when you divide one number by another. So, for example, the expression '5 modulo 2' results in 1, because 5 divided by 4 equals 2 with a remainder of 1. ■ ↖150

```
Mod[5,4]
1
```

Number systems are organised in this way. Our example is a *ring* because you can add, subtract, and multiply, and you always find yourself in a situation of the structure:

```
Mod[5+2,4]
3

Mod[5-3,4]
2

Mod[5*2,4]
2
```

But you cannot do division in a ring. Which is why a mechanical calculating machine, such as the *Pascaline* – named after French mathematician, inventor and physicist Blaise Pascal (1623–1662) – for example, is capable of doing additions and subtractions directly, but, in this particular case, multiplication and division only indirectly, via processes of repeated addition and subtraction. Here, a digit is a circle of rotating numbers. You can similarly think of the
■ 329↘ Turing machine, which we discuss and describe in detail
□ 369↘ in our chapter on Writing & Code, as a ring rotating from one *internal state* of the machine to the next.

117 ● 206

THE ADJACENCY MATRIX

Graphs can be rendered as graphics, as we've seen above, but they can also be rendered as images. You start with an *adjacency matrix*, so called because it indicates whether or not the situations (vertices) on a graph are adjacent to each other, that is whether or not there is a line (edge) from one situation to the next.

Here is an example of an adjacency matrix, and it works like an image in numbers:

```
rules={1→2,2→3,3→4,4→1};
MatrixForm@AdjacencyMatrix@Graph@rules

(0 1 0 0)
(0 0 1 0)
(0 0 0 1)
(1 0 0 0)
```

The first situation and its relationships are noted on the first line. The presence of a directed edge is denoted by a 1, the absence of an edge by a 0.

The first digit in line 1 represents situation 1. It has to be labelled 0, because it can not have a connection with itself. Situation 1 does have a connection with situation 2, which is why the second situation in the first line is denoted by a 1, the 1 here standing for 'yes, there is an edge'. Situation 1 does not have any connection to situations 3 or 4, which is why the 3rd and 4th situation on the first line are labelled 0. Now the same principle is applied to situation 2, on line 2, to situation 3 on line 3, and to situation 4 on line 4.

Note that the direction of the relationship, indicated by the arrow, is significant: so on line 2 you see that for this situation there is a connection marked to situation 3, but not to situation 1, because the transitions go from 1 to 2, and from 2 to 3, but not from 2 to 1. (The same applies for the subsequent elements.) We here speak of directional or non-directional edges.

Here is the representation of this graph as an image:

```
ArrayPlot@AdjacencyMatrix@Graph@rules
```

And here, for comparison, is an image of the Cambridge University Network, in 2006:

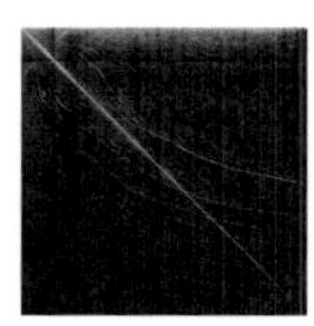

118 ● 206

This is a similar matrix of connections of web pages: white pixels indicate that these pages are hyperlinked, black pixels indicate that they're not.

A Parade of Graphs

So far, we have looked at graphs as basic, very simple structures and explained that the significant aspect to a graph is in fact the system of transitions within this structure. It is the graph's shape, we said, which can take on any number of forms, so long as that structure stays intact. While that's the case, and they have the same structure, these forms – we've also referred to them as 'figures' – are called 'similar' or 'homomorphic', and can be transformed or morphed into each other.

Of course, graphs can come in any number of shapes and their structure can have great complexity. Here we are going to show you some of them.

A really fine example of a fairly complex but eminently manageable and useful graph that allows millions of people to find their way around one of the great cities of our planet every day is the London Underground system. If you've ever been to London, you'll have seen – and most likely used – the official Tube map, as issued by Transport for London:

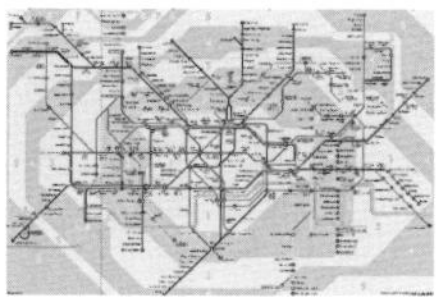

119 ● 207

Here is what the Tube map actually looks like when rendered to scale; it's still the exact same graph:

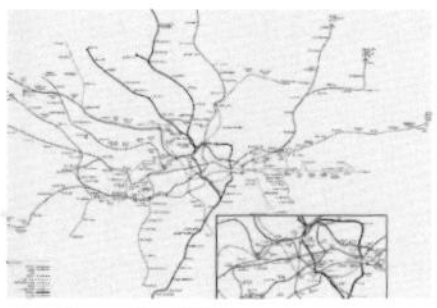

120 ● 207

And that is precisely the reason why graphs are so practically, applicably, useful. A graph is really nothing more, and nothing less, than an exact, but immensely flexible, representation of connections between points. So here are some other examples:

A Network of Friends on Facebook

121 ● 207

A Molecular Structure (Adrenalin)

```
ChemicalData["Caffeine", "MoleculePlot"]
```

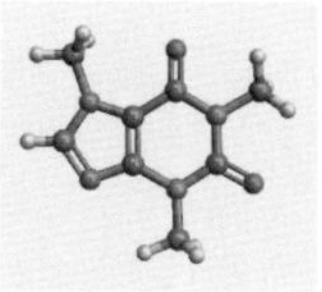

122 ● 208

Structures in Molecular Biology

123 ● 208

Streets in OpenStreetMap

124 ● 208

The Constitution of Graphic Objects in CAD

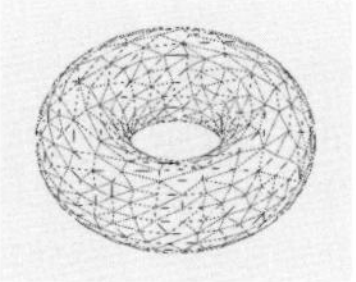

125 ● 208

The Constitution of Graphic Objects in CAD

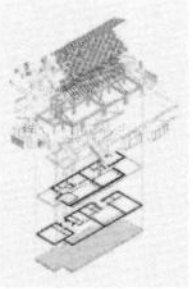

126 ● 209

In this last example, it is interesting to note that the diagrammatic shape and the concrete form at first glance seem to be the same, which is why this distinction is so unintuitive for people used to CAD. But as we know, **parametric design** makes exactly this distinction: you define a structure (for example in the schemes of *Grasshopper*), and you change the parameters to obtain the concrete form (for example in *Rhino*). ■ ↖149 359↘

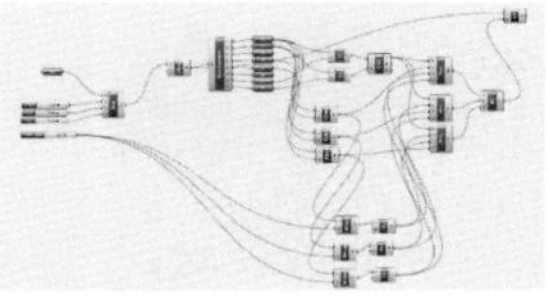

127 ● 209

Graphics or The Forms of Graphs

TOWARDS CAD

When we introduced graphs, we invoked the example of a Garden Party at Buckingham Palace to illustrate, perhaps a tad whimsically, the principle at work in a graph, and we've also seen and since reiterated that it is the structure of a graph that really matters. It's the structure that gives a graph its shape, and within that shape, it can take on any number of forms. When we now talk about forms, rather than shapes, we mean all the possible forms a graph can take with its structure.

We are, for this *Atlas*, particularly interested in graphs that yield meaningful *visual* representations, namely graphics. Some of the graphs we have looked at in our short Parade of Graphs above really don't need a visual representation to be meaningful: the visual representation helps us understand the graph and make use of its meaning, such as is the case with the map of the London Underground, but the trains on the Tube system can in fact work without us being able to look at a map and understanding which train goes where. The map is here to help us make use of the system, but the system – that is the graph – has its own purpose. Similarly, a molecular structure just exists in its own right, whether we draw it or not. And it functions – it has its purpose and that purpose is in place and plays itself out – with or without us as its witnesses.

There is no fundamental difference between this type of graph and a graphic. As architects, we tend to be fascinated by this, because we can morph forms into each other if they have the same structure.

We've also seen that structures can calculate. (We
□ 369↘ also refer you to our chapters on Writing & Code and
□ 549↘ on Big Data & Machine Learning.) Here we want to show you how structures can have concrete forms, and how we can model them in CAD systems. So when we'll be looking at the graphic of a rabbit soon, it is important to realise that this is not a dead form: it can move within its structure, which is what we then call animation; and it can 'talk clever', which is what we
■ ↖164 356↘ call Artificial Intelligence (AI). (It's quite a particular rabbit, this, and we'll tell you why in a moment.)

So now we want to concentrate on the forms of the types of structures as we specify them in CAD systems.

A FIRST GRAPHIC

Say we have a graph, g1, consisting of 4 individual situations, 1, 2, 3, 4.

```
s1:={1,2,3,4};
```

This does not as yet tell us anything about how these individual situations relate to each other: the graph has no structure and no form yet. By determining that the transition between the situations shall be a line, we can create a structure:

```
s1:=Line[{{1,2},{2,3},{3,4},{4,1}}];
```

Or simpler:

```
s1:=Line[{1,2,3,4,1}];
```

Now we know that our situations 1, 2, 3, 4 will relate to each other by a transition that is a line. And this means we are ready to set the coordinates for our situations to specify the form:

```
f1:={{1,1/2},{1/2,1},{0,1/2},{1/2,0}};
```

We now have a graph that we can output or 'draw', purely based on these parameters:

```
g1:=GraphicsComplex[f1,s1];
Renderer1@g1
```

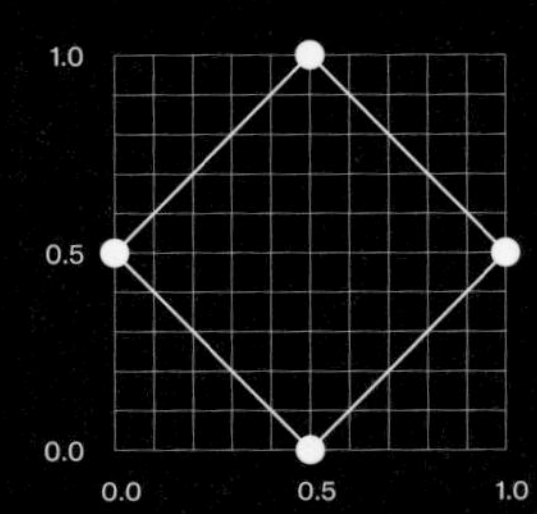

MORPHING THE GRAPHIC

Because of the distinction between structure and form, we can now change the form at will, simply by changing the coordinates of the points. The structure, meanwhile, and with it the overall type of visual representation, remains the same.

So with just the third coordinate changed from {0, ½} to {−½, ½}, the code generates a picture that looks noticeably different (remember, this is the same graph, morphed into a different form):

```
f1:={{1,1/2},{1/2,1},{-1/2,1/2},{1/2,0}};
Renderer1@g1
```

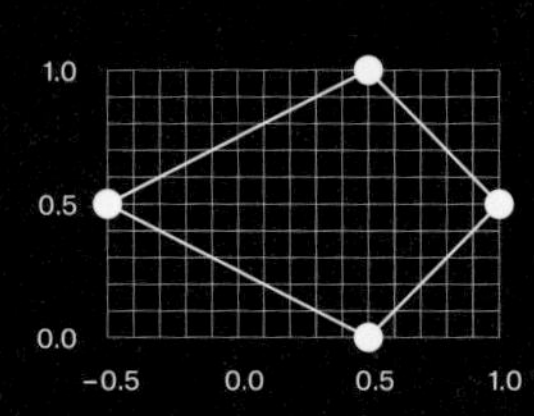

We can also morph or animate the structure from form 1 to form 2. Here this is done in 6 steps:

```
Row[(f1={{1,1/2},{1/2,1},{#,1/2},{1/2,0}};
     Renderer2@g1
    )&/@Range [0,-1/2,-1/12]]
```

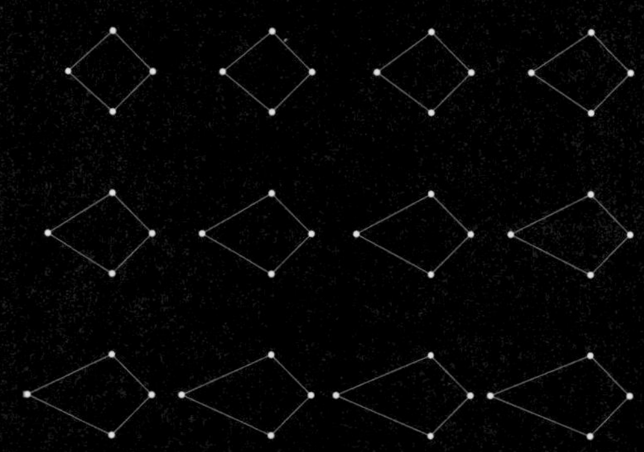

THE ELEMENTS OF EUCLIDEAN GEOMETRY
In *Euclidean geometry* (named after Greek mathematician Euclid (fl. 300 BCE) and generally regarded as the foundation of all geometry) the only elements available to us are points, lines, and circles.

We want to highlight a special self-reference of these elements. Think of a plane as a line along a circle, and of a cone as a circle along a line:

Now think of them as intersected in space:

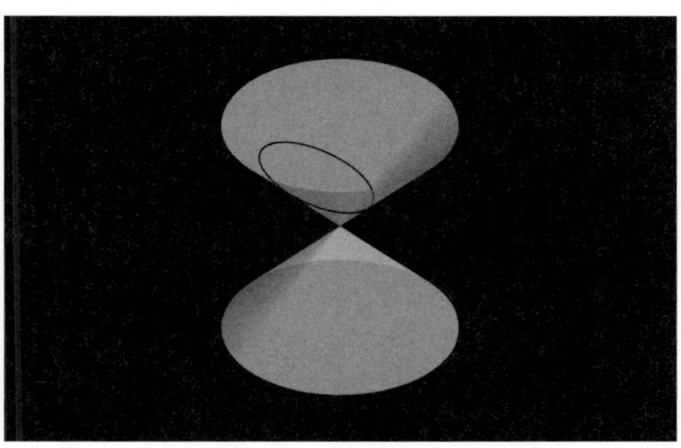

If this plane is parallel to the cone, the intersecting figure is a circle; if you turn the intersection plane by 90 degrees, the intersecting figure changes from ellipse via parabola and hyperbola to a straight line:

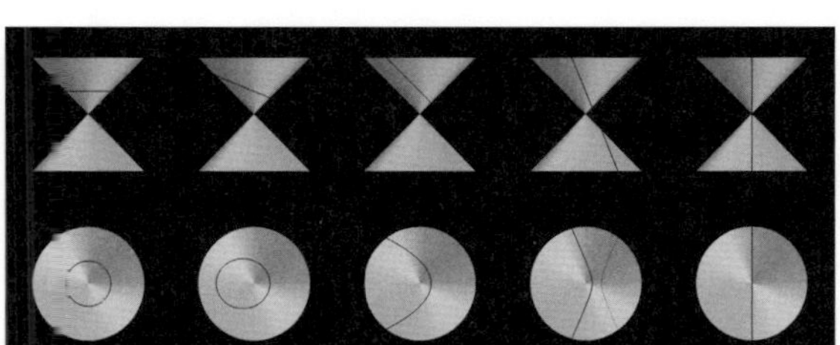

So line and circle are two different projections of one and the same constellation: the intersection of a circular line and a linear circle. And what's required to cover the translation between both is a rotation. A line is a *rational* link between two points, a circle the *irrational* part of the *real* link between two points. A line represents the *direction* within a circle, the circle represents the *distance* of a line. This might sound complex, and it is. But keep this in mind: don't think of circle and line as simple objects on a plane, they are *orthogonal* modes of thinking.

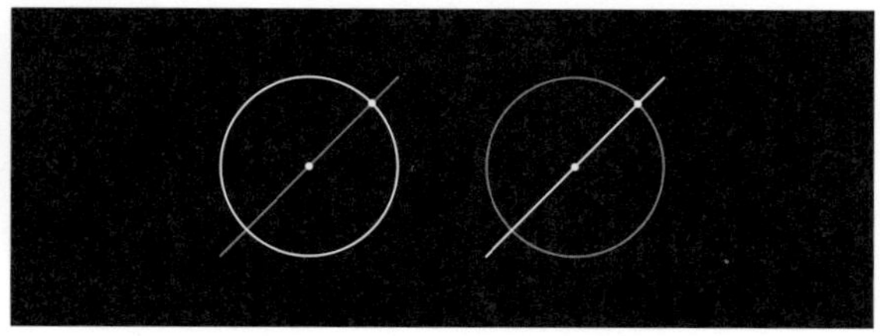

THE DIMENSIONAL CARTESIAN SPACE
It will not have escaped your attention that in order to define our points, we have used coordinates on a grid. Thus, the line

```
c2:={{0,0},{1,1}};
```

uses the coordinates `{0,0}` and `{1,1}` to define the placing of our vertices (points) 1 and 2.

We are here availing ourselves of the **Cartesian coordinate system** that was first established by French philosopher, mathematician, and scientist René Descartes (1596–1650) in his chief mathematical work *Geometry*, published in 1637 and also developed by his compatriot mathematician Pierre de Fermat (1607–1655) at around the same time. With this system, we can determine points and forms by sets of numbers. ■ ↖65 237↘

For example, here is how we define and notate points in one dimension:

```
p1:={-1,0,1};
```

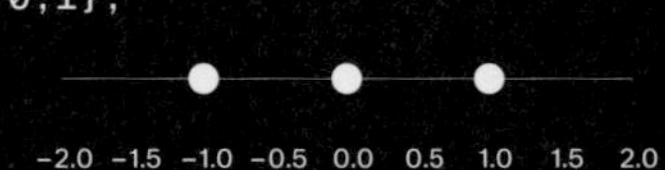

In two dimensions:

```
p1:={{0,-1},{1,1},{-1,1}};
```

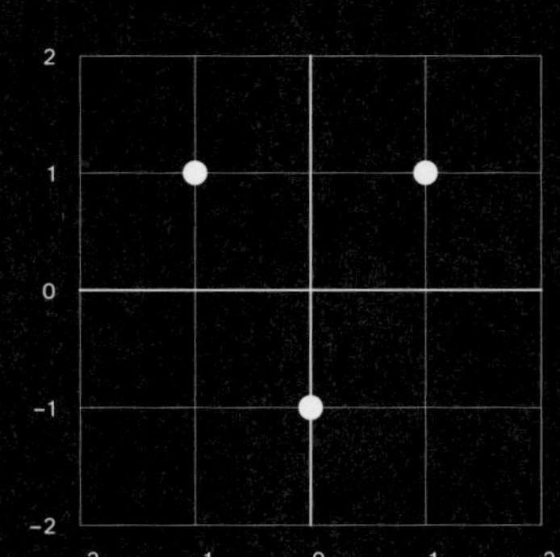

And in three dimensions:

```
p1:={{0,0,0},{1,1,1},{1,-1,1}};
```

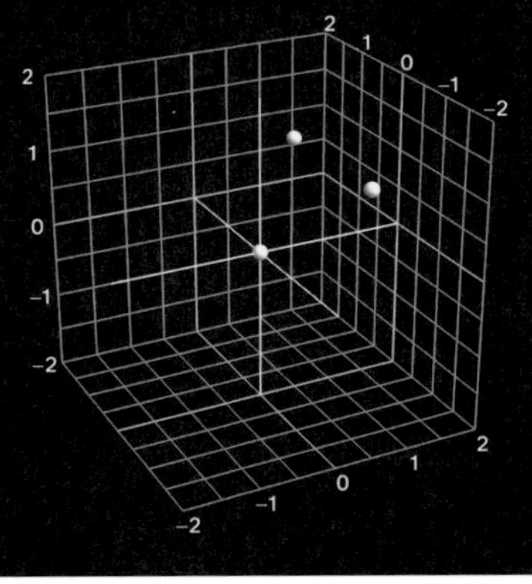

WHAT IS GEOMETRY

Surprisingly perhaps, the Cartesian coordinates system – unlike his geometry generally – has very little to do with geometry.

Geometry is about constituting elements. This is the very first definition in Euclid's *Elements:* "A point is that which has no part." Which means points, like all elements, are 'outside reality' and 'outside nature'. We cannot know them, we cannot understand them. They make no sense; you cannot touch them. Geometry puts these elements on a stage and lets them speak, in what we call *postulates*. Such as: "The extremities of lines are points." (Def. 1.3) And so we can have 'reasonable plays' with these elements on their metaphorical stage. In Euclid, they are represented as texts, from the Renaissance onwards, they are represented as drawings. Today, we represent them in code. (For an outline on our thinking on the relationship between written language in Greek antiquity, the perspective drawing in the Renaissance, and code in □ 369↘ the Digital Age, see our chapter on Writing & Code.)

Here, for example, is the graphic schema of part of a 'conversation' about the Pythagorean theorem:

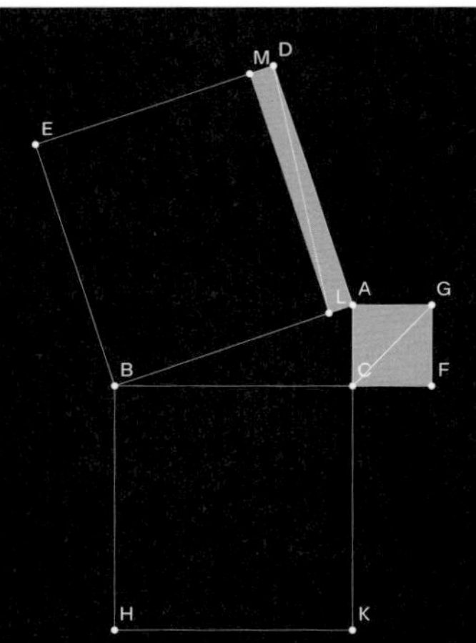

POLYNOMIALS AND THE CARTESIAN SPACE

In Euclidean geometry, straight lines run between two points, while curved lines are defined as sections of a cone: circles, ellipses, parabola, and hyperbola.

By contrast, in Cartesian or analytic geometry, a line can be defined by any number of points. The concepts used here are, for example, *function*, *figure*, *interpolation*, or *polynomial*, or specifically *Lagrange polynomial*, named after Italian mathematician Joseph-Louis Lagrange (1736–1813) for his contribution to the study of these types of functions.

Here, a line itself is a formula and it has a form such as

```
c3:={{-1,4},{0,2},{1,5},{4,6}};
```

whereby c3 gives the coordinates of the individual points, and the line is defined as an *interpolating polynomial*, which yields the resulting formula

```
polynom1=InterpolatingPolynomial[c3,x];
poly1[x_]=Simplify@polynom1
1/30 (60+34 x+75 x^2-19 x^3)
```

which in turn can be rendered like this:

```
Show[
 Plot[polynom1,{x,-1.5,4.5},
  PlotStyle→ {Thickness[.005],Black}],
 Graphics[{PointSize[.03],Point[c3]}]
 ]
```

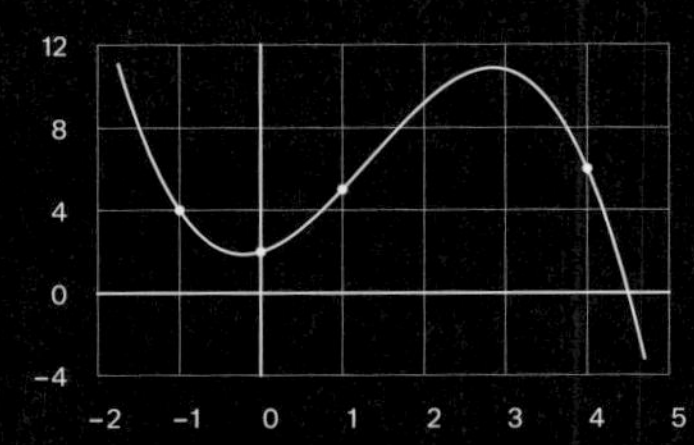

A line's individual formula, and with it its form changes drastically in absolute space, even if just one of its reference points is moved a little. Here, we're changing the coordinates of the third point slightly:

```
c3:={{-1,4},{0,2},{2,4},{4,6}};
```

Note how both formula and graph retain the same structure, but alter radically their appearance:

```
polynom1=InterpolatingPolynomial[c3,x];
poly1[x_]=Simplify@polynom1
1/5 (10-3 x+6 x^2-x^3)
```

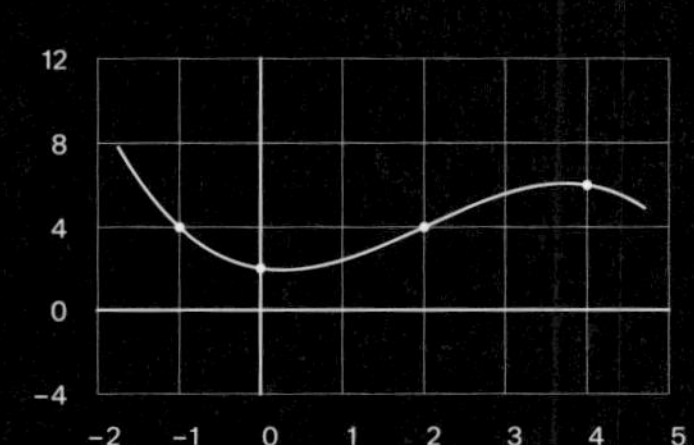

It might be a little complicated to explain what actually happens here, but let's try it anyway: In Euclidean geometry, a line follows a *proportion* between points:

$$(x-x_2)/(x_1-x_2)$$

In Cartesian geometry, every point contains proportions of all the other points (in this case 4 points). This is the *proportionality* of point 1:

$$((x-x_2)(x-x_3)(x-x_4))/((x_1-x_2)(x_1-x_3)(x_1-x_4))$$

This, of point 2:

$$((x-x_1)(x-x_3)(x-x_4))/((x_2-x_1)(x_2-x_3)(x_2-x_4))$$

The curved line in Cartesian geometry follows the sum of the proportionalities of all points.

MANIFOLDS, SPLINES, NURBS, AND THE NON-EUCLIDIAN SPACE

Things change when we work outside Euclidian and Cartesian geometries and enter the realm of **non-Euclidian geometries**, such as **Riemannian geometry** – developed by German mathematician Bernhard Riemann (1826–1866) in 1854 – and other **differential geometries**, about which to go into detail here would probably burst the parameters of this chapter, but which have in common that they emerged comparatively late – from the mid 18th century onwards – and concern themselves with non-Euclidean space.

A typical example of a non-Euclidean geometry is **spherical geometry**, where we encounter *manifolds*. A manifold is a **topological space** that in a small area resembles Euclidean space, but on a larger scale may not do so. From a human perspective, Earth is a perfect example of this, because while all spheres are manifolds, Earth is of a size that makes us experience it in our everyday existence as a Euclidean space: a rectangular acre, as far as we can tell, is a rectangular acre, and to all intents and purposes we can live and work with and on it. But globally speaking, we can not continue to treat the right angles of the acre as right angles or the parallel lines of its boundaries as parallel without running into serious trouble with our neighbours, or taking ourselves off the surface of the Earth.

Spherical, flat *(Euclidean)*, and hyperbolic geometry

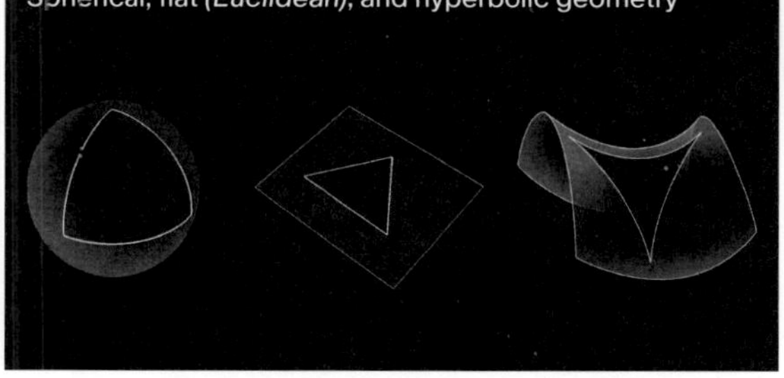

There is a striking difference between Euclidean and non-Euclidean geometry here. In Euclidean geometry, the total sum of the angles of a triangle always equals 180°, but this does not work on a sphere.

Imagine two points of a triangle on the equator, and one at the North Pole. The angles on the equator are 90° each, and the angle at the Pole can be of any size, depending on where on the equator you set your corners. But the sum total of these three angles is always greater than 180°. It's worth noting that we have been able to treat this observation geometrically only since relatively recently.

Obtaining an understanding of non-Euclidean geometry is quite difficult, and as an architect this may be frustrating for you, because there are a lot of complicated details you have to learn. But on top of that there are also many confusing misconceptions that abound.

The following analogy may help as an orientation: there is a symmetry between non-Euclidean, Cartesian, and Euclidean geometries. They are all perspective projections (as you know them from perspective drawings from the Renaissance, corresponding to Cartesian geometry), from a world governed by a linear circularity (like the cone in Euclidean geometry described above) on a rational plane, called non-Euclidean geometry. They each open up ↖65 363↘
a new way of thinking: Euclid projects the world of ↖134 363↘
things to thinking in space; Descartes projects the world of space to thinking in time; Riemann projects the world of time to thinking in 'life', we would suggest. And they all have to deal with the categorical distinction between that which is *real* (in Euclid, this is the circle) and that which is *rational* (in Euclid, this is the line). And while we are skimming the surface a bit here, we think that for you as an architect, this may probably suffice for the time-being.

As prominent applications of non-Euclidean geometry, we have *splines*, *NURBS* and **Bézier curves** at our disposal, and we talk about each of these in more detail in our chapter on 3D Modelling, so right now we shall simply proceed. ■ ↖73 □ ↖57

Here is how we suggest to read this instrument: we have seen above that the global straight lines in Euclidean space are multiplied and curved around the locality of the points involved to get an *infinitesimal* line in Cartesian space. With splines, we again multiply these infinitesimal lines and again 'curve' them around the points involved to get a *continuous* line in non-Euclidean space. (Note that the concepts of 'infinitesimal' and 'continuous' lines are ambiguous, but there is no simple categorisation in literature.)

Let's define, as an example, these coordinates as:

```
c4={{0,0},{1,0},{2,-1},{3,0},{4,-2},{5,1}};
sp=BSplineFunction[c4,SplineDegree→3];
```

And this is the rendering of its points and the graph. Note how the graph's line here does not go through the coordinates by which it is defined. They here act as 'anchor points' to which the line is, in a sense, tethered:

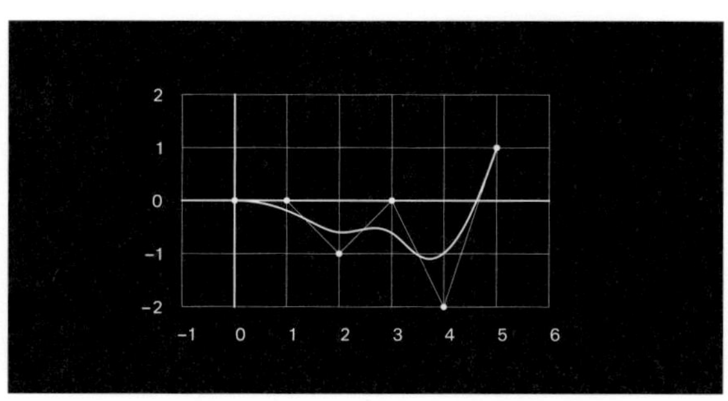

If we change only one of the points

```
c5=ReplacePart[c4,6→ {3,1}]
{{0,0},{1,0},{2,-1},{3,0},{4,-2},{3,1}}
```

the graph here now only changes around the last couple of points, while the first few points remain unchanged:

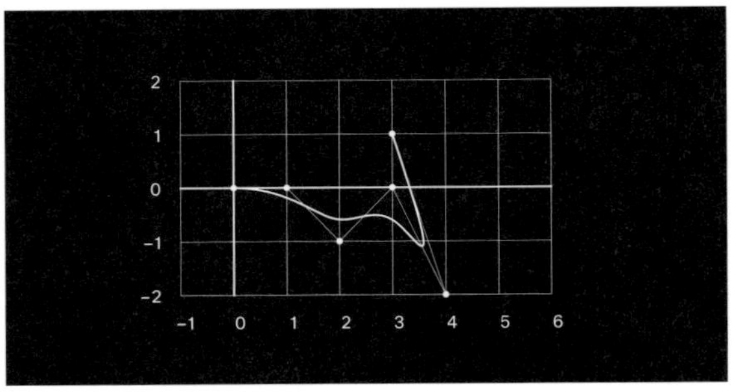

A small detail: we change the type of rendering with the spline function. Here is what we had with the *Lagrange polynomial*:

```
ip=InterpolatingPolynomial[c3,x];
Simplify@ip
1/5 (10-3 x+6 x^2-x^3)
```

We can take any value of the x-axis and get a corresponding single y-value:

```
ip /. x → 3.1
5.7138
```

Because each x value produces a single y value, a polynomial can never go back on itself or have loops. With spline functions this is different. It takes a parameter from 0 (first point) to 1 (last point) and returns two coordinates for all the points in between:

```
sp=BSplineFunction[c4,SplineDegree→3];
sp[.55]
```

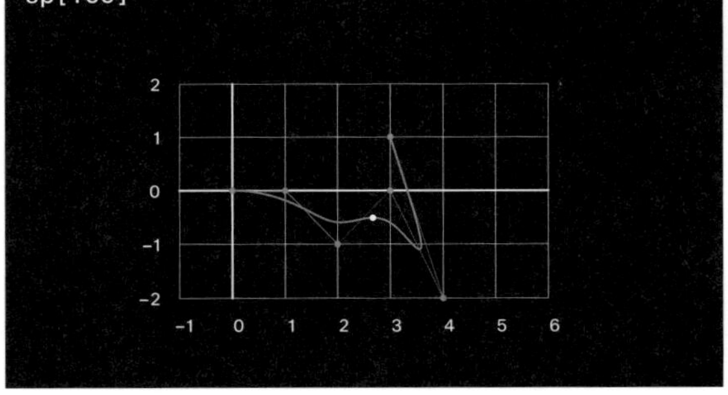

A spline is a dimension in itself, and it is projected into the two-dimensional Cartesian space. The spline is defined in non-Euclidean space and is projected to the Euclidean space to obtain the rendering.

A SUMMARY SO FAR

As this chapter shows: graphs and graphics are tricky. It is easy to throw concepts like 'form and structure' up in the air, or pull phrases like 'form follows function' out of a hat, but at a closer look it is not so simple. So to summarise our considerations thus far:

Graphs do not have any form, they are ideas. They exist in *absolute time*: you can think of them from the beginning to the end, or vice versa, you can rearrange them virtually, abstract, or detailed. You can image them running fast or slow, in or out; you can twist them and calculate them, but you *cannot see them*. They are not in space, they are in time. They are *real*.

Graphics are perspective projections of ideas from time to *generic space*. You can walk around these artefacts back and forth, look at them from different angles, close-up or from a distance. You can name them and you can leave them and return to them, but however you might try, you cannot be at two positions at the same time, and you cannot get multiple perspectives at the same time. In space *time is always passing by*. And *you cannot touch* the artefacts, because you do not have time in space. Therefore, a model, a form, or a graphic is visual and *rational*. And you need a lot of time to get an idea of an artefact: you are never sure of it.

Bearing all that in mind, we know three kinds of perspective projections of ideas into different realms of rationality:

- The *straight* lines of Euclidean geometry are lines in space.

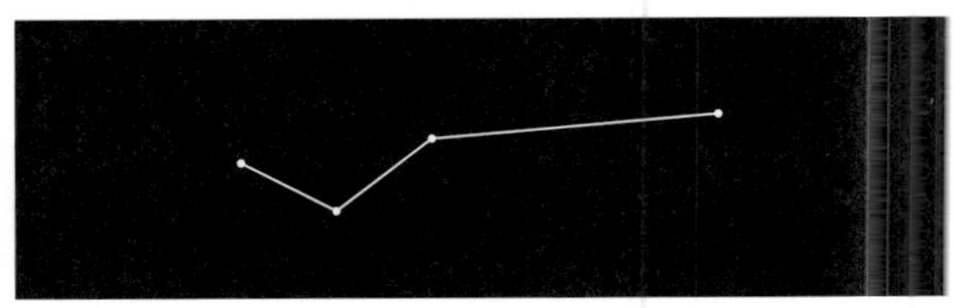

- The *infinitesimal* lines of Cartesian geometry are 'moving' lines in space or lines in time.

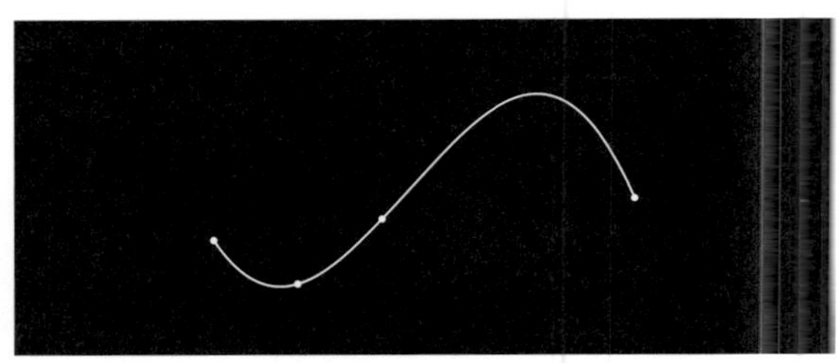

- The *continuous* lines of non-Euclidean geometry are 'moving' lines in time or 'live' lines in space.

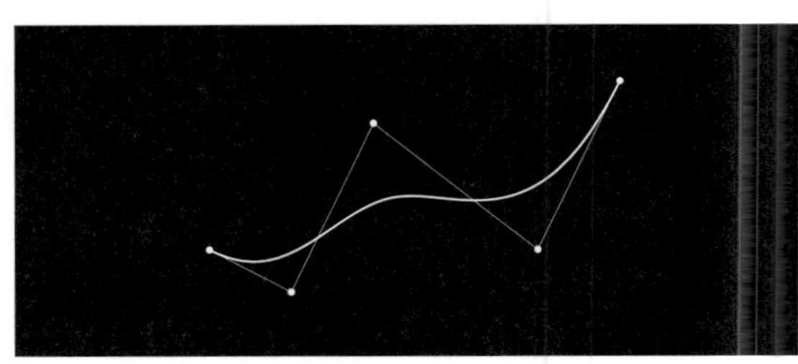

There is another interesting observation:

- Architects in the era of Euclidean geometry did not model with drawings, but with texts.

- Architects in the era of Cartesian geometry developed modelling with drawings, as we know it today. They also developed the drawings of Euclidean geometry as we know them today: they translated them from text to drawings.

- Architects of today are using computers to mimic the drawings inherited from Cartesian geometry. It is therefore really difficult to see that the continuous lines of today are not drawings at all. Technically you cannot bring them to paper with the drawing tools developed in Cartesian geometry. You have to code them and project this code onto paper with a computer.

So the technical medium to articulate an architectural model of today is not a drawing, just as it wasn't before the Renaissance. What we learn from this chapter is that your architectural idea needs to be developed on the side of the graph, which is about the selection and the composition of parts. It's like you imagine what to do at the Queen's Garden Party – how to dress, whom to speak to, how to move about – and the graphic is the projection of your idea onto the actual party: people talk, the corgis bark, Camilla's hat flutters in the wind, the band plays, people move about; stimulating or boring conversations unfold, time passes, and you take your chances...

You have the idea of the party in time, which you cannot see (graph).
You have the ratio of the party in space, which you cannot touch (graphic).
And you have your circular movements between space and time, which is interesting.

Graphs and Pathways

THE PRACTICAL USE OF A GRAPH
In the next few sections of this chapter we want to briefly look at some of the practical uses there are for graphs and graphics.

If you have ever found yourself relying on an app like *CityMapper* or *Google Maps*, the *iPhone's* native *Maps* or any other application that promises to get you from where you are to where you want to go, then you will know how eminently useful they have become and also how remarkably efficient they are at working out the fastest available route by your chosen mode of transport, even when the 'real world' vagaries of unforeseen obstacles are thrown into your path, such as closed transport links due to works being carried out, or congested roads, owing to traffic jams. In mathematical terms, this is a very common task for a graph, and highly typical, even if at urban living level it can become quite extraordinarily complex.

We saw earlier that a graph can be any number of things, and one of the most familiar things it can be is a map. (The graph really is all the nodes and all the connections of the map, rather than the map itself.) So when I ask an app, 'what's the best way for me to get from where I am to where I'm meeting my friends for a drink tonight?', I'm in fact asking a graph: 'what's the shortest connection between two points?'

The answer is a *path* and this path is in itself a graph; in fact it is a subgraph of the larger graph that is the map. You could say that the map is the graph of all possible paths, and the answer to your query is the subgraph of the shortest available path.

FINDING THE SHORTEST PATH
Here is a simple graph with 20 vertices and 30 edges, a dodecahedron, and the shortest route between two of these vertices marked in bold:

```
g=PolyhedronData["Dodecahedron",
"SkeletonGraph"];

FindShortestPath[g,13,7]
{13,2,5,11,7}
```

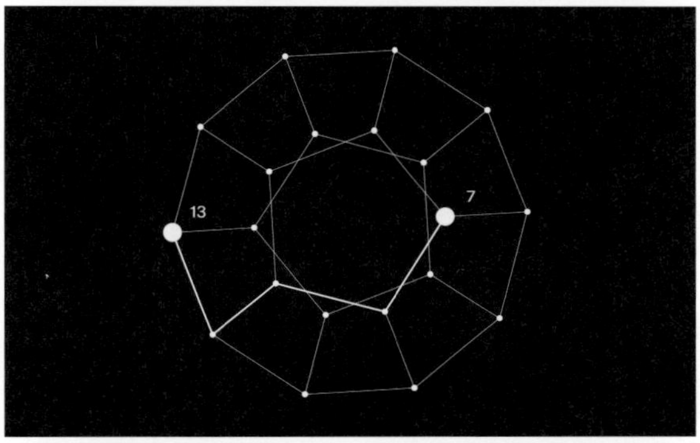

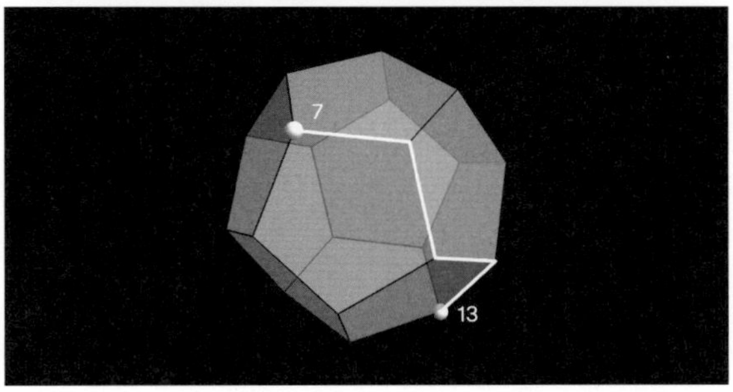

The exact same approach can be used for a more complex graph, for example to find the way out of a labyrinth:

WEIGHTED GRAPHS
You will remember the Queen's Garden Party, where we were talking about how both the points of a graph (the vertices or nodes) and the connections (the edges or lines) can be weighted.

In this next example, we are looking for the shortest *and* widest path between nodes 1 and 24 – the connections are weighted:

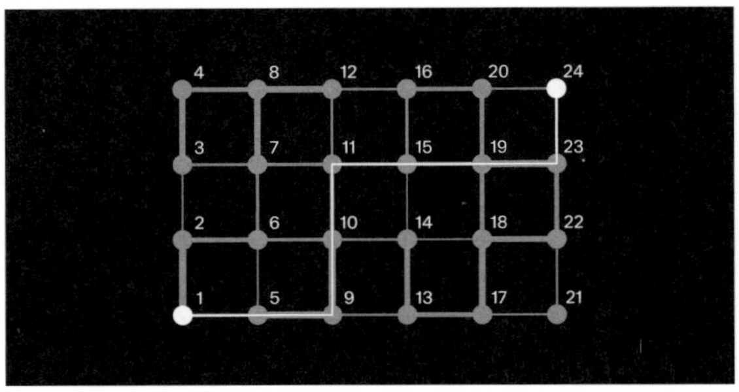

This is how navigation systems search for the most convenient route, weighting roads or transport links according to their average speed and reliability, and avoiding any known obstacles or delays.

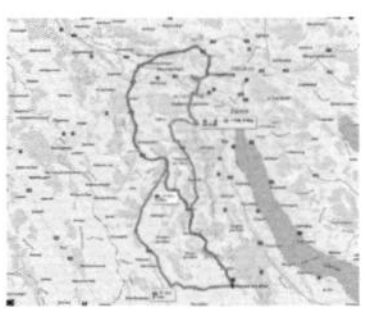
128 ● 209

And it is also how social networks search for your closest friends, how online bookstores find the most relevant reading material for you, and how spell checkers identify the likely most accurate suggestion for the word you're in the process of typing, even as you type it.

CENTRALITY MEASURES – GOOGLE'S *PAGERANK*
The centrality of a point can be measured, and a point is the more central, the more central neighbours it has. We know this measure from the Google *PageRank* algorithm. Named after its inventor and Google co-founder, American computer scientist and entrepreneur Larry Page (b. 1973), *PageRank* also obviously puns on the fact that it is the first algorithm used by Google to rank pages of the Internet according not only to the number but, importantly, also the *quality* of links pointing to them. Mathematically, this
■ 571↘ algorithm relates to the Markov chain, which we
□ 549↘ talk about in more detail in our chapter on Big Data & Machine Learning.

Here, the points or vertices are websites (specifically, their
■ 623↘ URLs), while the edges or connections are the links between individual pages.

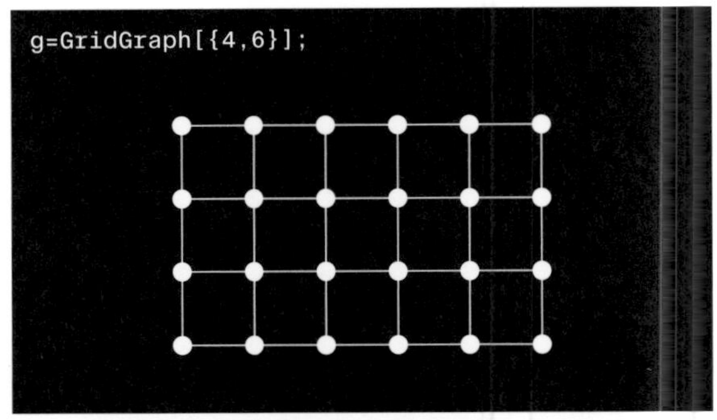

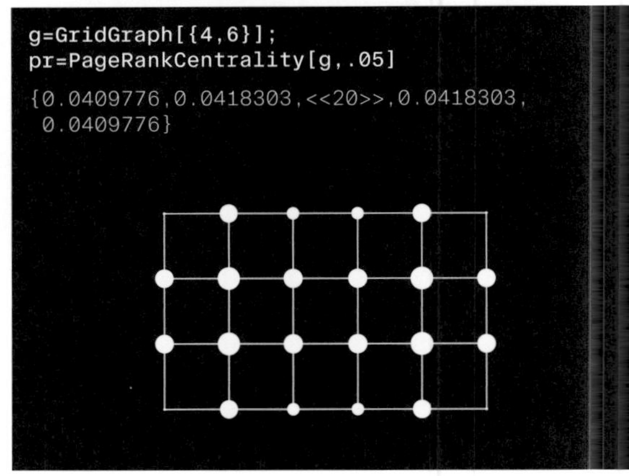

It looks significantly different on another graph, like this:

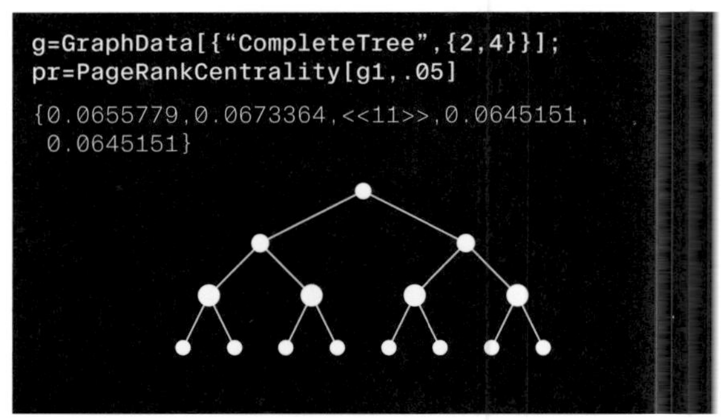

CENTRALITY MEASURES – SPACE SYNTAX
If we take the same graph and now measure instead of the centrality of the nodes the centrality of the edges, we get the following picture, which you will find referred to as *space syntax*:

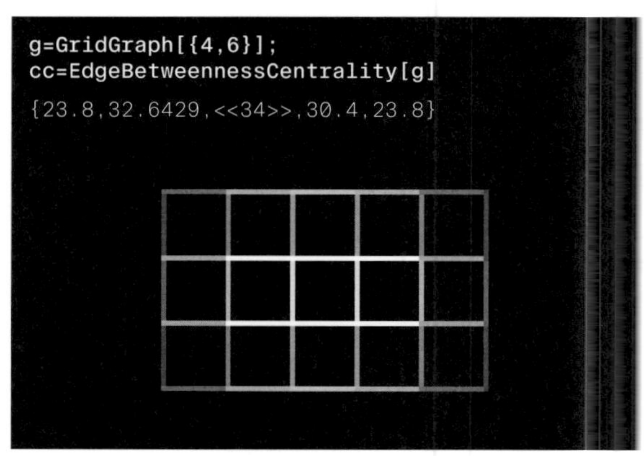

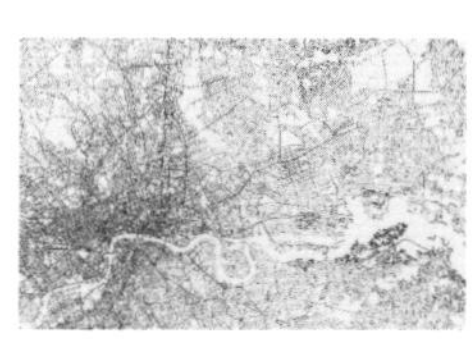
129 ● 209

Graphs and Surfaces

TALKING ABOUT THE FACE
We have so far only really mentioned geometrical planes briefly here and there, but never actually discussed them in any detail. But in computer graphics, the *face* is an element as significant as the point or the line, because faces are what allow us to not only generate 'line drawings' but to model two and three-dimensional objects and, as we will see in a moment, also give them texture, by very simple means in terms of coding.

In computer graphics, one of the most famous and oft-cited objects (which you'll find referenced in all manner of literature, and paid homage to in animated films, and which we've already mentioned very briefly in anticipation) is the *Stanford bunny*. It's a test model, developed in the mid-1990s at Stanford University whence it takes its name, and it was originally produced in the polygons (PLY) format, consisting, in its highest resolution, of 69,451 individual polygons.

130 ● 210

Since a graph can be as complicated as we want it to be, it is possible to 'make' virtually any object out of polygons, and the larger their number in relation to the surface area they need to cover, the smoother and therefore the more highly defined the object becomes.

Whereas in Euclidean geometry a plane is a two-dimensional surface that extends into infinity, in graphs a surface is read as a *cycle*. There are several different types of cycle, but for us in this context the most relevant one is the *closed walk*, which is a sequence of adjacent vertices that starts and ends with the same point but that has no repeating (or repeatedly occurring) vertices or edges other than the start/end point. It therefore describes a surface defined by these particular consecutive points. This is known as a *simple cycle*, and in CAD systems is then called a 'face'.

CYCLES AND FACES
This, for example, is the graph of an icosidodecahedron, rendered as a 3D graphic:

```
ph1=PolyhedronData[
   "Icosidodecahedron","GraphicsComplex"];
Graphics3D[{White,Opacity@.5,ph1}]


[…]
```

```
[…]
```

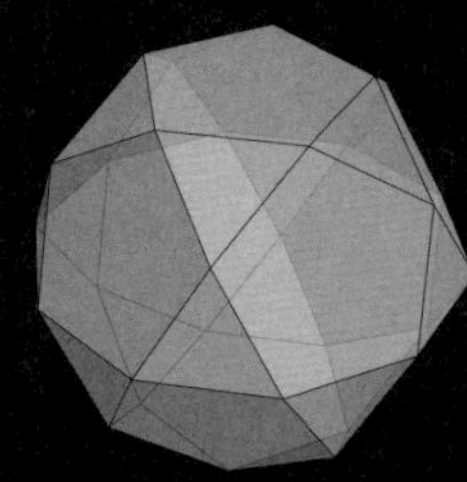

Remember how we said that a structure can have any number of different forms, into which it can morph? Here we have the same graph – that is the same structure – in a distorted 2D graphic or form:

```
ph2=PolyhedronData[
   "Icosidodecahedron","SkeletonGraph"];
```

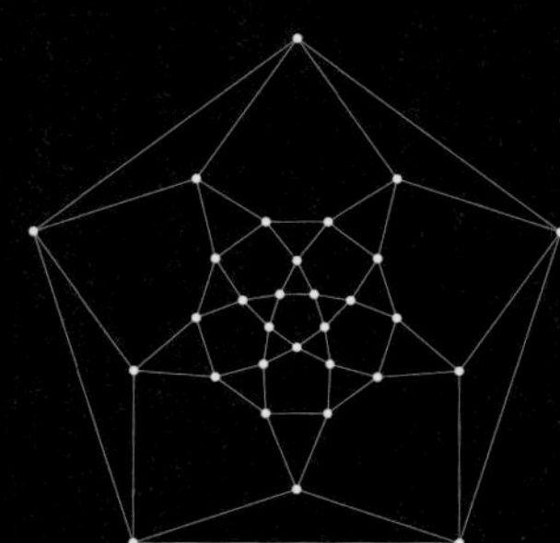

We can also render the same icosidodecahedron as an undistorted 2D graphic. Note how this is the same object, but a different graph: here we render it in its individual planes (forms), with a split graph (structure):

```
ph3=PolyhedronData[
   "Icosidodecahedron","NetGraph"];
```

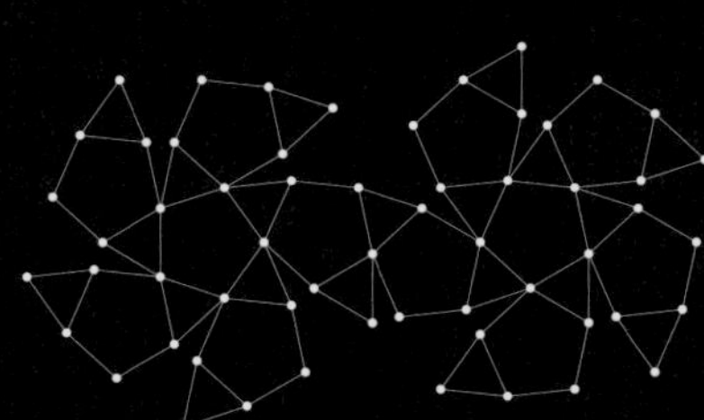

Now, a typical task is to find subgraphs as cycles of a specific size or magnitude. In this following example, we are looking for all the subgraphs – that is all the cycles – with exactly 3 reference points:

```
FindCycle[ph3,{3},All]
{{51↔54,54↔56,56↔51},
 {53↔55,55↔58,58↔53},
 <<16>>,{4↔8,8↔9,9↔4},{1↔3,3↔5,5↔1}}


[…]
```

```
[...]
```

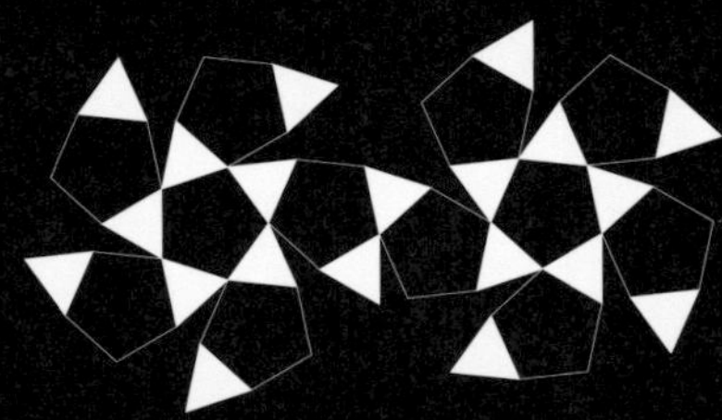

POINTS, LINES, AND FACES

☐ 693↘ In our conclusion to this *Atlas*, What Is Information, we witness the Italian architect Sebastiano Serlio (1475 – c. 1554) become indignant at the idea of a builder not knowing the difference between a point, a line, a plane, or a body. The distinction between them, specifically between points, lines, and faces is as rigorous and as systematic in graphics as it is important to Serlio: they are all different and independent perspectives on the exact same graph and the coordinates of its positions.

Here, for example, is a single representation of the same graph, as points, as lines, and as a face:

```
coords:={{1,1/2},{1/2,1},{0,1/2},{1/2,0}};
verts:={1,2,3,4,1};
gr2:=GraphicsComplex[coords,
   {Gray,Opacity[.5],Polygon@verts}];
gr3:=GraphicsComplex[coords,
   {Gray,Thickness[.025],Line@verts}];
gr4:=GraphicsComplex[coords,
   {Black,PointSize[.05],Point@verts}];
Graphics[{gr2,gr3,gr4}]
```

☐ 255↘

With these, we can now change attributes such as colour and line thickness:

```
gr2:=GraphicsComplex[coords,
   {LightGray,Opacity[.3],Polygon@verts}];
gr3:=GraphicsComplex[coords,
   {Gray,Thickness[.05],Line@verts}];
gr4:=GraphicsComplex[coords,
   {Black,PointSize[.1],Point@verts}];
Graphics[{gr2,gr3,gr4}]
```

And this is no different in 3D:

```
coords=PolyhedronData[
   "Icosidodecahedron","Vertices"];
verts=Range@Length@coords;
edges=PolyhedronData[
   "Icosidodecahedron","Edges"];
faces=PolyhedronData[
   "Icosidodecahedron","Faces"];

gr2:=GraphicsComplex[coords,
   {LightGray,Opacity[.3],Polygon@faces}];
gr3:=GraphicsComplex[coords,
   {Gray,Thickness[.01],Line@edges}];
gr4:=GraphicsComplex[coords,
   {Black,PointSize[.03],Point@verts}];
Graphics3D[{gr2,gr3,gr4}]
```

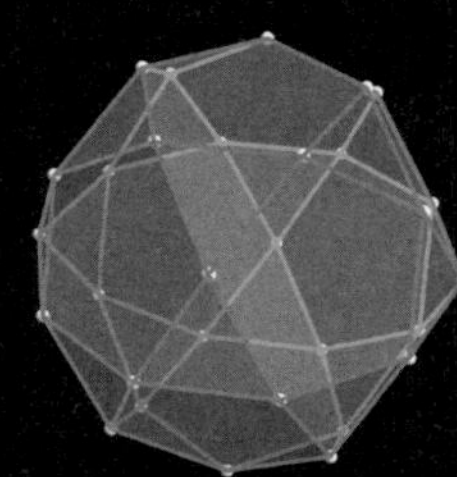

TEXTURE MAPPING

So as to cover the full scope of graphics systems, we want to also touch on the concept here of *texture mapping*. Texture mapping is an efficient way for us to add detail, such as shade, tone, or, as the term suggests, texture to a face and thus create far more realistic and natural looking objects in both 2D and 3D graphics than would otherwise be possible. (We come across texture mapping in several places in this *Atlas*, and discuss it in some detail also in our chapter on Rendering.)

To achieve texture mapping, a position of a graph is linked to two coordinate systems. The first of these two systems gives the coordinates of the picture that contains the texture.

(In this context, you will also encounter the
■ ↖71 term **UV mapping**. This is a particular method for texture mapping onto 3D objects, in which, much as in the example below, the texture map is a 2D source image. The letters UV in this case simply stand for the coordinates in this texture map, being used here instead of X and Y, to avoid confusion with the coordinates of the 3D object.)

In this following example, the texture image has a definition of 128 × 128 pixels:

```
texture = ;
Show[Graphics[{White,Circle[]}],texture]
```

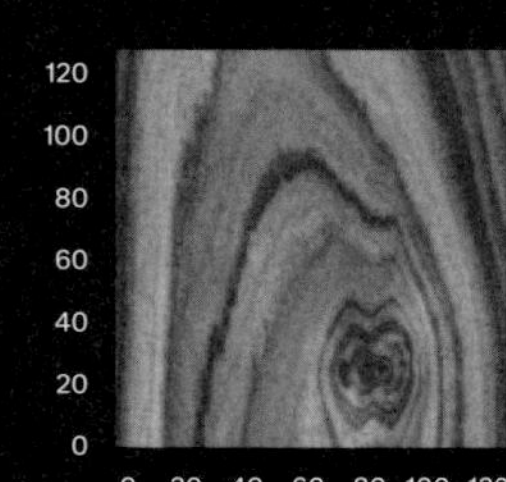

We now define a particular section of the image, by allocating coordinates within the image to the graph:

```
t1={{20,20},{108,20},{108,108},{20,108}};
Show[
  Graphics[{White,Circle[]}],
  texture,
  Graphics[{
   White,Point@t1,Opacity[.5],
   Line[Append[t1,t1[[1]]]]}]
]
```

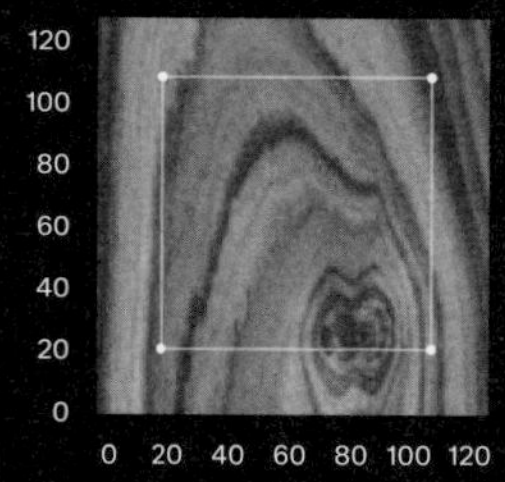

Note how `t1` defines four points by two coordinates, each within the image that is used as the map from which to 'scan' the texture. This is our first coordinate system.

A second coordinate system, `c1` below, is the one that defines the graphic into which this texture is rendered. In code, this expresses itself as follows:

```
g1:={1,2,3,4,1};
c1:={{1,1/2},{1/2,1},{0,1/2},{1/2,0}};
t1={{20,20},{108,20},{108,108},{20,108}};
gr4:=GraphicsComplex[c1,
   {Texture@texture,

Polygon[g1,VertexTextureCoordinates→t1/108]
    }];
Renderer1[gr4]
```

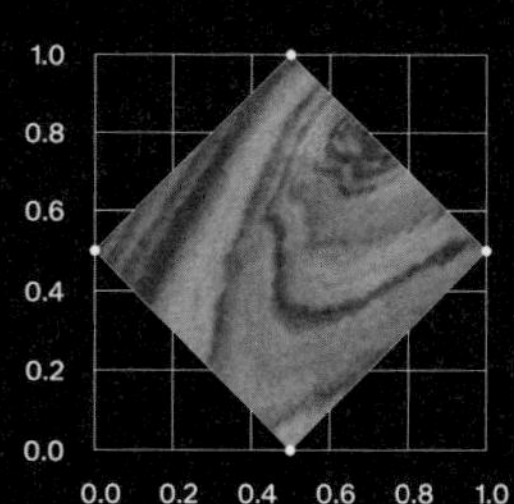

We can define the coordinates for our graphic in such a way that we get the pattern for a cutout:

```
ft=PolyhedronData[
   "Icosidodecahedron","NetGraph"];
svl=VertexList@ft;
scl=N@PropertyValue[ft,VertexCoordinates];
edges={#[[1]],#[[2]]}&/@ EdgeList@ft;
N@Max@scl;
sclN=(scl)/10.2 * 128;
Show[
 texture,
 Graphics[GraphicsComplex[
   sclN,{White,Point@svl,Line@#&/@edges}]]
]


[...]
```

```
[...]
```

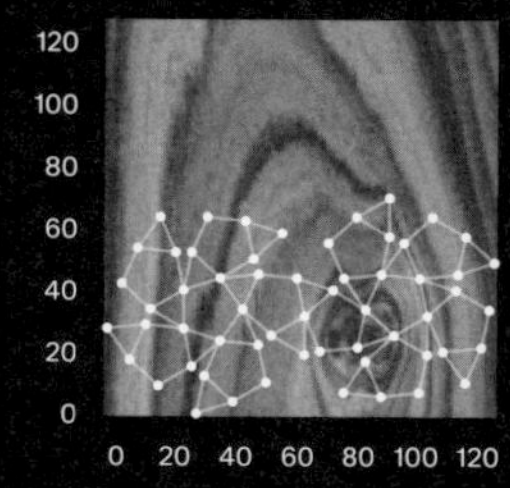


```
el3=FindCycle[ft,{3},All];
sl3=el3[[All,All,1]];
coords3=scl[[#]]&/@ sl3/10.2;

el5=FindCycle[ft,{5},All];
sl5=el5[[All,All,1]];
coords5=scl[[#]]&/@ sl5/10.2;

GraphicsComplex[sclN,{
   Texture@texture,
   Polygon[sl3,VertexTextureCoordinates→
          coords3],
   Polygon[sl5,VertexTextureCoordinates→
          coords5]
   }];
Graphics@%
```

Which we can then project onto the planes of a three-dimensional body with the same structure:

Our icosidodecahedron now has a plausible wood texture, achieved with a source image (the texture map) and five lines of code.

Graphs and Grammars

JOINING GRAPHS

You can read graphs as graphics, and you can also use them for the production of further graphs, which is then called a *grammar*.

Here is a simple graph:

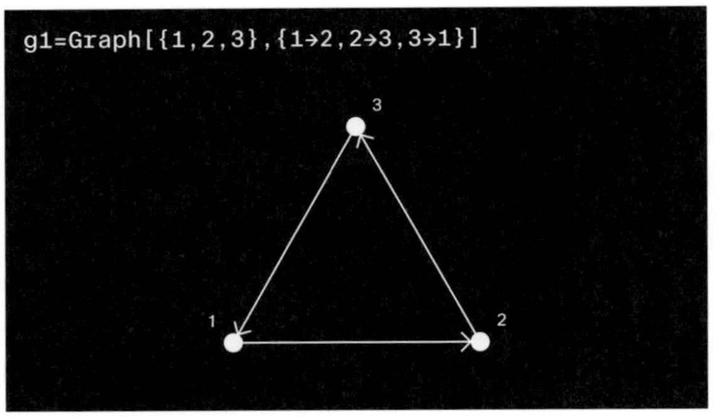

Now we join this graph with a second graph, in this case a copy of itself:

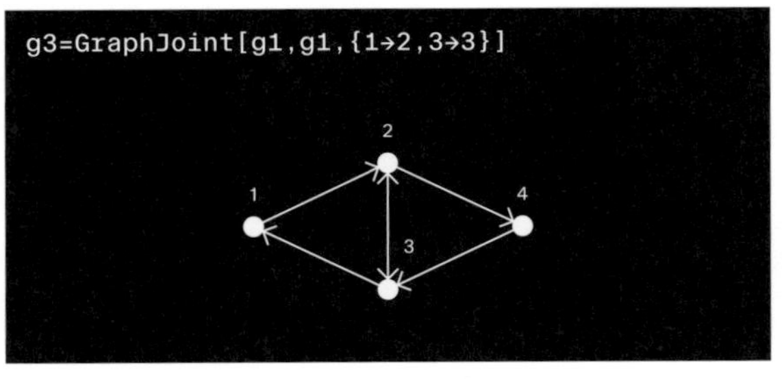

And repeat:

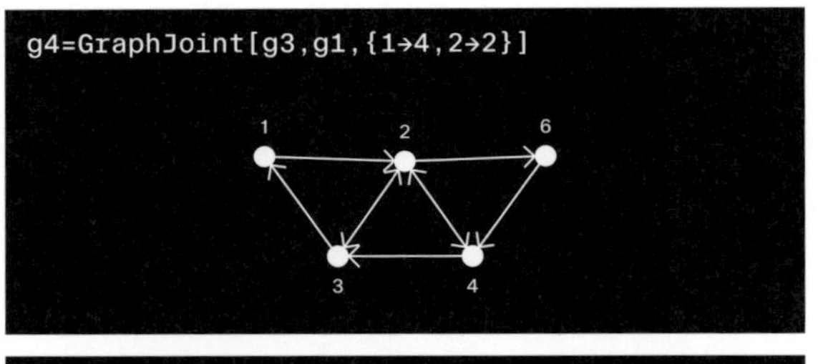

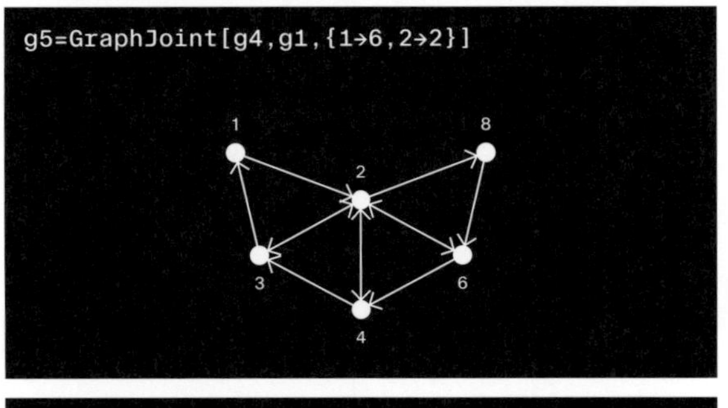

■ ↖156 540↘

■ ↖156 375↘

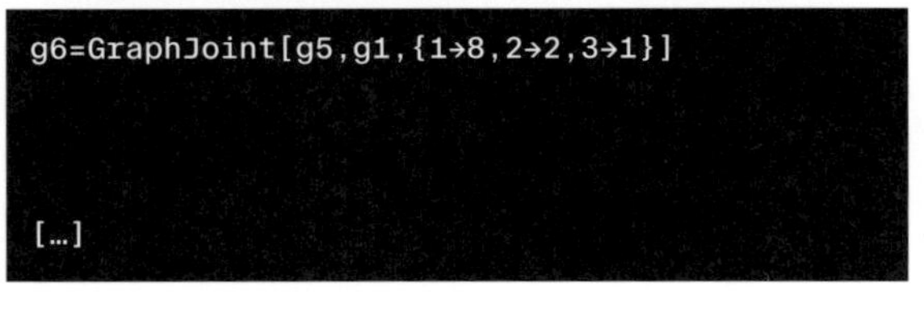

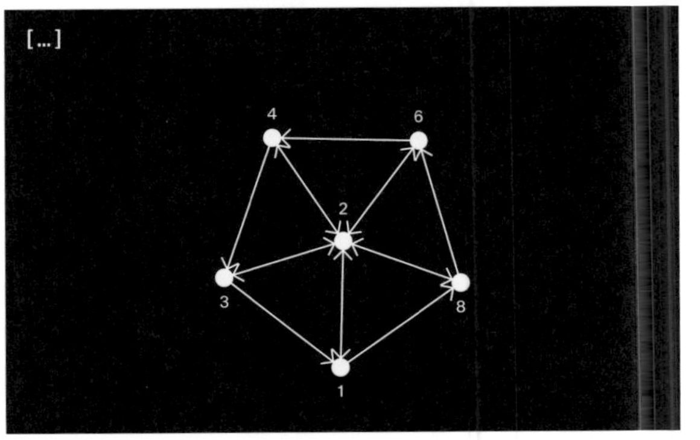

In two dimensions, we know these types of joint patterns from, for example, mosaics, tilings, and parquets.

131 ● 210

The same principle also works in three dimensions when the repeated arrangement of symmetrical elements creates a crystal ('crystal' here being a geometrical three-dimensional structure, irrespective of what type of material it is made of), and so the scientific reference for the 'art of joining' in the 20th century is crystallography.

We find them in structures such as those by German architect Konrad Wachsmann (1901–1980):

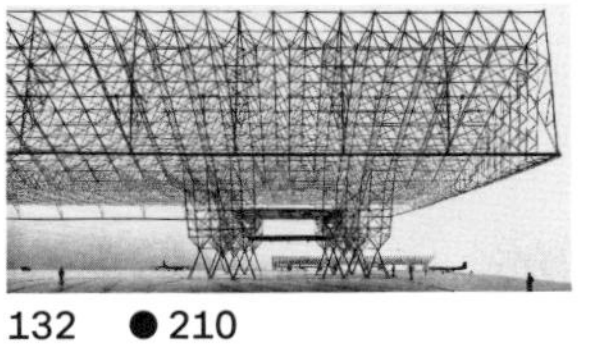

132 ● 210

Or in his *'Packaged House'* knot:

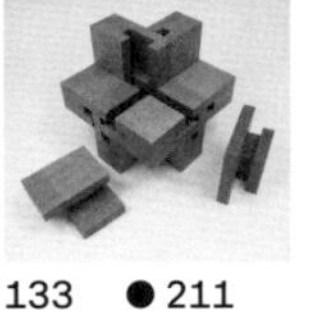

133 ● 211

The person to have advanced this particular aspect most in architecture is Swiss architect Fritz Haller (1924–2012).

134 ● 211

GRAMMARS

L-systems are named after the Hungarian biologist Aristid Lindenmayer (1925–1989), who developed them as a formal language grammar in which structures are repeatedly refined according to certain rules.

A well known example of this is the Peano curve, named after Italian mathematician Giuseppe Peano (1858–1932).

You start with a simple line:

```
play=Graphics[{Black,Line[{{0,0},{1,1}}]}]
```

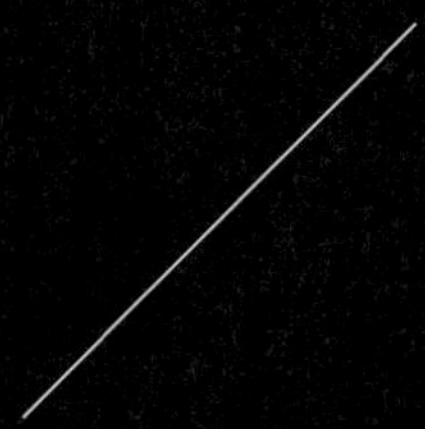

The rule subdivides the line and moves the centre point along the line's *normal*:

```
ruleL1 := Line[{p1_, p5_}] :>
   Module[{p2, p3, p4},
    {p2, p3, p4} =
     DiscretizeLine[p1, p5, {1/3, 1/2, 2/3},
      1/6 √[3]];
    {Line[{p1, p2}], Line[{p2, p3}],
     Line[{p3, p4}], Line[{p4, p5}]}
    ];

play = play /. ruleL1
```

And then this rule is simply applied recursively:

```
play=play/.ruleL1

[…]
```

This is the code in one line applied to a triangle:

```
Nest[#/.ruleL1&, △,3]
```

And to a square:

```
Nest[#/.ruleL1&, □,2]
```

This is a typical fractal and a simple example of a grammar. It is similar, in principle and in appearance, to the Koch snowflake, which we discuss in our chapter on Generative Methods.

■ ↖155
■ ↖155
□ ↖145

The Naturalisation of Forms

We now want to talk through an example of how we can get from a very basic graph, which has the simplest of structures and takes on a range of familiar forms, to a life-size structure in a few quite simple steps.

We start with a graph that consists of 12 situations:

```
tab=Table[i,{i,12}]

{1,2,3,4,5,6,7,8,9,10,11,12}
```

We choose as the structure for these situations a list, meaning that we simply create a table that contains the situations with no directional transitions from one point to another, nor any weighting or hierarchy, but simply an order:

```
tr=UndirectedEdge@@#&/@Partition[tab,2,1]

{1↔2,2↔3,3↔4,4↔5,5↔6,6↔7,
 7↔8,8↔9,9↔10,10↔11,11↔12}
```

Which so far, when represented visually, looks like this:

```
g3=GraphJoint[g1,g1,{1→2,3→3}]
```

Written as an adjacency matrix (such as we encountered earlier), it looks like this:

```
gr=Graph@tr

mf=MatrixForm@AdjacencyMatrix@gr

({
  {0,1,0,0,0,0,0,0,0,0,0,0},
  {1,0,1,0,0,0,0,0,0,0,0,0},
  {0,1,0,1,0,0,0,0,0,0,0,0},
  {0,0,1,0,1,0,0,0,0,0,0,0},
  {0,0,0,1,0,1,0,0,0,0,0,0},
  {0,0,0,0,1,0,1,0,0,0,0,0},
  {0,0,0,0,0,1,0,1,0,0,0,0},
  {0,0,0,0,0,0,1,0,1,0,0,0},
  {0,0,0,0,0,0,0,1,0,1,0,0},
  {0,0,0,0,0,0,0,0,1,0,1,0},
  {0,0,0,0,0,0,0,0,0,1,0,1},
  {0,0,0,0,0,0,0,0,0,0,1,0}
 })
```

What we can do now is calculate the distance, in terms of steps, from one point to another. This creates a **graph distance matrix**. Unlike the adjacency matrix, where each situation of the graph is given a row and on each row is labelled whether or not there is a transition (an adjacency) to any of the other situations, in this matrix, each situation on the graph keeps its row, but on it is given the number of steps this situation is removed from any of the other situations. So on the first row we see that situation 1 is 0 steps away from itself, 1 step away from situation 2, 2 steps away from situation 3, and so on. The same principle repeats itself for each of the 12 situations over 12 rows:

```
dm=GraphDistanceMatrix@gr;
MatrixForm@dm

({
  {0,1,2,3,4,5,6,7,8,9,10,11},
  {1,0,1,2,3,4,5,6,7,8,9,10},
  {2,1,0,1,2,3,4,5,6,7,8,9},
  {3,2,1,0,1,2,3,4,5,6,7,8},
  {4,3,2,1,0,1,2,3,4,5,6,7},
  {5,4,3,2,1,0,1,2,3,4,5,6},
  {6,5,4,3,2,1,0,1,2,3,4,5},
  {7,6,5,4,3,2,1,0,1,2,3,4},
  {8,7,6,5,4,3,2,1,0,1,2,3},
  {9,8,7,6,5,4,3,2,1,0,1,2},
  {10,9,8,7,6,5,4,3,2,1,0,1},
  {11,10,9,8,7,6,5,4,3,2,1,0}
 })
```

If we then calculate the sum for each row, we arrive at a number for each situation that tells us what the sum of the distance is to all other points in the system:

```
hl=Total@#&/@dm

{66,56,48,42,38,36,36,38,42,48,56,66}
```

And if we now plot these twelve newly derived instances of our situations as a graph, we get a very familiar shape:

```
ListLinePlot[hl]

[…]
```

```
[…]
```

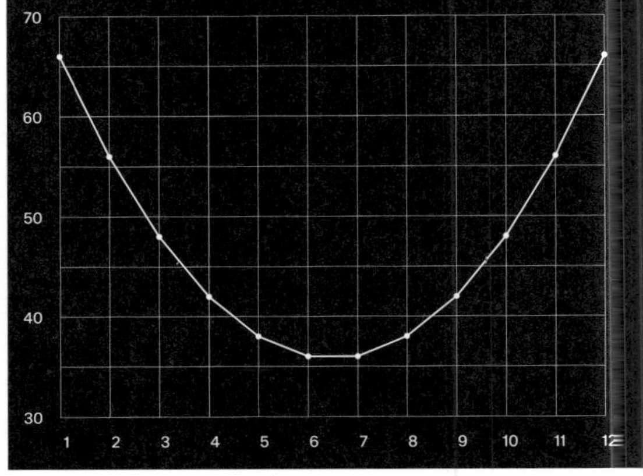

We can use the same method to create a slightly more complex shape, using a graph that, instead of 12 situations arranged in a list, consists of 12 situations arranged as a grid, 4 × 3:

```
gr=GridGraph[{4,4}];
```

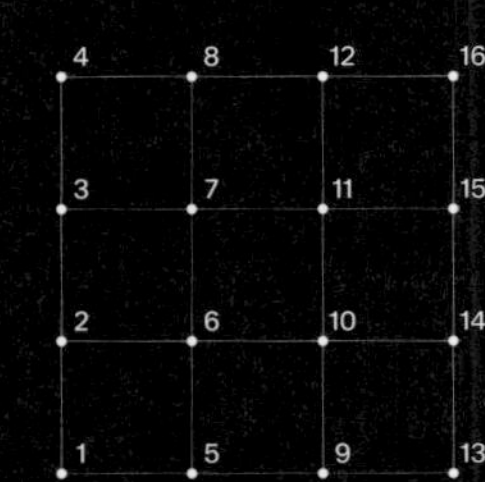


```
dm=GraphDistanceMatrix@gr;
MatrixForm@dm

({
  {0,1,2,3,1,2,3,4,2,3,4,5,3,4,5,6},
  {1,0,1,2,2,1,2,3,3,2,3,4,4,3,4,5},
  {2,1,0,1,3,2,1,2,4,3,2,3,5,4,3,4},
  {3,2,1,0,4,3,2,1,5,4,3,2,6,5,4,3},
  {1,2,3,4,0,1,2,3,1,2,3,4,2,3,4,5},
  {2,1,2,3,1,0,1,2,2,1,2,3,3,2,3,4},
  {3,2,1,2,2,1,0,1,3,2,1,2,4,3,2,3},
  {4,3,2,1,3,2,1,0,4,3,2,1,5,4,3,2},
  {2,3,4,5,1,2,3,4,0,1,2,3,1,2,3,4},
  {3,2,3,4,2,1,2,3,1,0,1,2,2,1,2,3},
  {4,3,2,3,3,2,1,2,2,1,0,1,3,2,1,2},
  {5,4,3,2,4,3,2,1,3,2,1,0,4,3,2,1},
  {3,4,5,6,2,3,4,5,1,2,3,4,0,1,2,3},
  {4,3,4,5,3,2,3,4,2,1,2,3,1,0,1,2},
  {5,4,3,4,4,3,2,3,3,2,1,2,2,1,0,1},
  {6,5,4,3,5,4,3,2,4,3,2,1,3,2,1,0}
 })
```

```
hl=Total@#&/@dm

{48,40,40,48,40,32,32,40,40,32,32,40,48,40,
 40,48}
```

```
c3D=Append@@#&/@Transpose[
    {GraphEmbedding@gr,(hl-48)/8}];
grD=Graph[
  VertexList@gr,EdgeList@gr,
  VertexCoordinates→c3D]
```

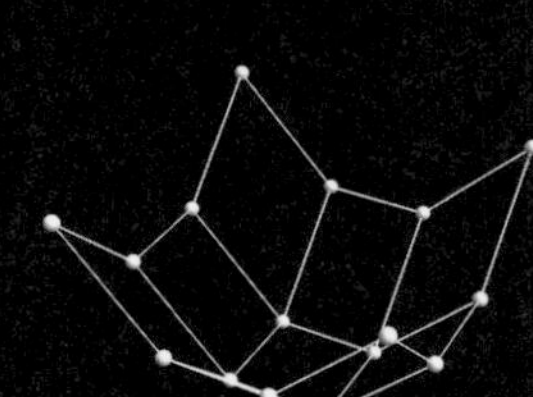

Here is the same process applied to a grid with 24 × 24 situations (n=m=24):

```
gr=GridGraph[{24,24},VertexLabels→"Name"];
hl=Total@#&/@GraphDistanceMatrix@gr;
c3D=Append@@#&/@Transpose[
  {GraphEmbedding@gr,(hl-48)/500}];
grD=Graph[
  VertexList@gr,EdgeList@gr,
  VertexCoordinates→c3D]
```

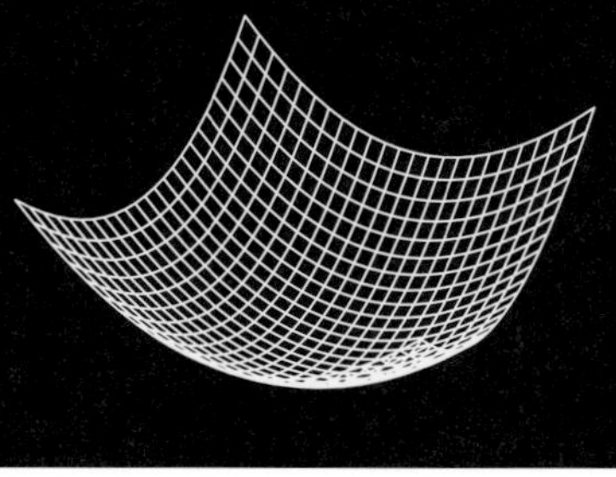

Let us emphasise though that this 'form' is not really a form as such, because it exists solely in formless mathematical structures. It's a diagram of a fictitious calculated world of connections, and thus no different to the schematic map of the London Underground or the computations of friend clusters on Facebook we've seen earlier.

That's why we prefer to speak of a shape that, rubberlike, can take on any form, just as long as the structure (the system of transitions) stays intact.

If a shape of this kind is rendered 1:1 as a life-size physical structure, we talk of a **naturalised form**. ■ We find this put into practice, for example, with Catalan architect Antoni Gaudí (1852–1926) – though to be sure, he did not arrive at his shapes with a computer – or German architect Frei Otto (1925–2015), as well as in many contemporary projects and experiments.

135 ● 211

136 ● 211

The Discretisation of Forms

TAKING THINGS APART AND PUTTING THEM BACK TOGETHER AGAIN

All of digital technology is predicated on the assumption – borne out in practice – that it is possible to break down continuous analogue entities (data sets, shapes, sound waves) into small enough individual components such that, when put back together, they are not only faithful to the source, but in fact, with today's levels of definition and the quality of our output devices, they often seem to 'improve' on the original.

In computer graphics, this process of breaking up a form into component parts that the software can handle is called *discretisation*. The term is derived from mathematics, where it describes the transposition of continuous functions into discrete counterparts, and so it is by no means unique to information technology.

The moment we draw a circle on a page, we present ourselves with a mathematical – and therefore digital – problem: we can easily draw a perfect circle. We may need a compass or saucer as a guide to do so, but the form we end up with fulfils in every necessary way the criteria for being a circle.

In mathematics, the formula

```
x2+y2==1
```

symbolises a perfect circle too. But in this instance it is an idea of a circle, because it is only ever possible to *approximate* the emerging shape. We will be talking more about this under the heading *Meshes* below.

And so on a computer screen – as in any other plotted drawing of a circle – to our perpetual vexation, we can never describe a *perfect* circle. We can come adequately, you might say more than sufficiently, close though; and to all intents and purposes, even with comparatively crude approximation, we soon are no longer able to tell the difference between a perfect circle and an imperfect one that is made up of a number of very short straight lines arranged in a circular pattern.

PIXELS

The most immediately recognisable and simplest form of these discretised communicative 'hubs' are pixels. As you know, and as we say elsewhere in this *Atlas*, pixels are picture elements (dots) on the two-dimensional plane, and so a cluster of pixels gives us a shape.

In the following example, we can see how the shape of a square becomes visible in the communicative interplay between individual pixels, which, in configurations of 8 × 8, 16 × 16, and 32 × 32, render the same, identical square, but in varying degrees of definition. It is an important facet of the concept at work here that we can talk of the square being the same, even though visually to us it appears quite different in each rendering:

```
c1:={{1,1/2},{1/2,1},{0,1/2},{1/2,0}};
gr2 :=GraphicsComplex[c1,{Black,Polygon@c1}];
Renderer2[gr_,res_]:=
 ImageResize[
  ImageResize[Image[Graphics[gr]],
   res,Resampling→"Gaussian"],
  96,Resampling→"Nearest"]
ImageAssemble[Renderer2[gr2,#] &/@ {8,16,32}]

[…]
```

```
[…]
```

Let us assume we now want to rotate the cube in its 16 × 16 pixel resolution anti-clockwise:

This following example shows us the discretising of what in Cartesian or analytical geometry is a mechanical twist and in Euclidean geometry is a formalised repositioning. The important thing to note here is that our digital pixels are entirely abstracted from any type of movement or form. They're just either there or not there. And through being there, they communicate the square at different stages of rotation, so although the square 'moves', the pixels don't:

```
c1:={{1,1/2},{1/2,1},{0,1/2},{1/2,0}};
gr2:=GraphicsComplex[c1,{Black,Polygon@c1}];
Renderer3[gr_,rot_]:=ImageResize[
  ImageResize[Image[Graphics[Rotate[gr,rot]]],
    16,Resampling→"Gaussian"],
    96,Resampling→"Nearest"]
ImageAssemble[Renderer3[gr2,#] &/@
  {0°,15°,30°}]
```

MESHES

Even more interesting, and also essential for working with CAD, is the problem of meshes. A polygon
■ 445↘ mesh in computer graphics is a graph consisting of a set of vertices, edges, and faces that defines a three-dimensional object, in the way that our familiar Stanford bunny is technically speaking simply a *polyhedral* defined by a mesh of 69,451 polygons.

To approach this topic, let's first of all adjust our understanding of the relationship between graphs and graphics. Because now we need to refine our premise. Our premise was that we have a graph, and we give coordinates to individual situations of this graph so as to obtain a graphic representation of it.

In analytical geometry, mechanical forms are determined by formulas. For example, the algebraic equation

```
x²+y²==1;
```

determines the form of a circle:

```
ContourPlot[x²+y²==1,{x,-1,1},{y,-1,1}]
```

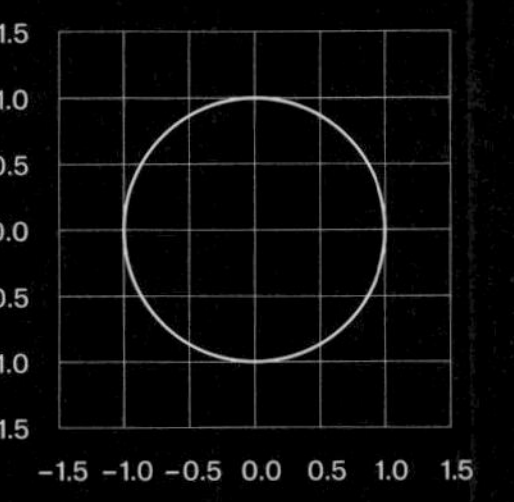

When we do this, we have to distinguish between the represented form of the circle and the formal idea, that is the formula, of the circle. The form is a rational fact: once it's there, it's there, and that's it; we can see it and make sense of it visually: it is therefore final.

The formula, by contrast, is in a sense fictional and therefore infinite. It exists as an abstract conception of all possible circles. In order for this fiction of the circle to become 'real', we have to discretise it in a system of points and in doing so specify to what resolution we want this idea to be iterated. Almost any are possible. Three or four specified points are clearly not enough: what we at this extremely low resolution see would be either a triangle or a square. But with just eight defined points we can already start to recognise the idea of the circle. With twenty, we are in no doubt. With four times as many, we don't even see the polygon any more. So the visual instances of this formula are very different in appearance and trigger in us quite different responses. But the circle itself, the formula, is exactly the same, we just specify varying parameters. We may also look at this as a mathematical rationalisation of the circle. Only through it do we arrive at the familiar graph for our graphic, here in three different resolutions:

```
res={.3,.09,.009};
Row[DiscretizeGraphics[Graphics[{Circle[]}],
    MaxCellMeasure→#]&/@ res]
```

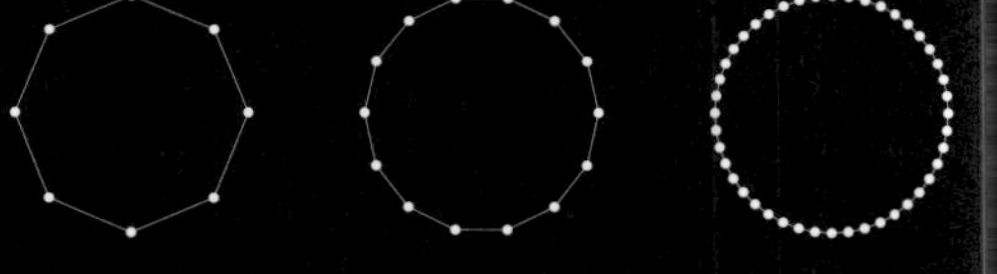

THE RATIONAL AND THE REAL

When we rationalise a circle we have a problem, because the perimeter of a circle can be defined only with irrational numbers. There are only very few rational points on the surface of a circle. Therefore a rationalised circle is not continuous: unlike a straight line it has 'holes'. And it intersects in very few cases with a straight line in rational number space:

```
mr=DiscretizeGraphics[Graphics@Circle[],
  MaxCellMeasure→.009];
pts=MeshPrimitives[mr,0];
Graphics[{InfiniteLine[{{0,0},{2,1}}],pts}]

[…]
```

```
[…]
```

Similarly, linear algebra also does not deliver any result for the intersection between a circle and this line in the rational number space, which corresponds to Euclidean geometry:

```
circle=x^2+y^2==1;
line=x==2y;
pts={x,y}/.
NSolve[{circle,line},{x,y},Rationals]
{x, y}
```

By contrast, in the *real number space*, that is in analytical geometry of modernity, circle and line intersect on the plane, because they can both be given coordinates in the same Cartesian X-Y grid, and as they are both basic shapes that are fully and sufficiently described as they are, they naturally and always intersect at the two precise points where the line meets the circle:

```
pts={x,y}/.NSolve[{circle,line},{x,y},Reals]
{{-0.894427,-0.447214},{0.894427,0.447214}}
```

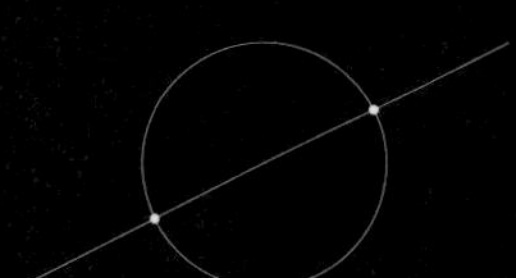

POLYNOMIALS
The *polynomials* we mentioned earlier – much as circles – are also, as we have noted, functions, and that means that in order for us to be able to present them graphically, they also have to be rationalised, for which read discretised.

Here we have a series of measurement points:

```
c3={{-1,4},{0,2},{2,4},{4,6}};
```

The idea of a linear relationship between these points:

```
ip=Simplify@InterpolatingPolynomial[c3,x]
1/5 (10-3 x+6 x^2-x^3)
```

The rationalisation of this idea in countable elements:

```
xl=Table[x,{x,-1,4,5/12}]
{-1,-7/12,-1/6,1/4,2/3,13/12,3/2,
 23/12,7/3,11/4,19/6,43/12,4}
```

```
yl=ip/.x→ xl
4,4835/1728,<<9>>,10465/1728,6}
```

And a graphic representation of the measurement points (white) and their interpolated graphic points (gray):

```
Graphics[{
  Thin,Gray,
  Line@Transpose[{xl,yl}],
  Point@Transpose[{xl,yl}],
  Black,Point@c3
  },Axes→True]
```

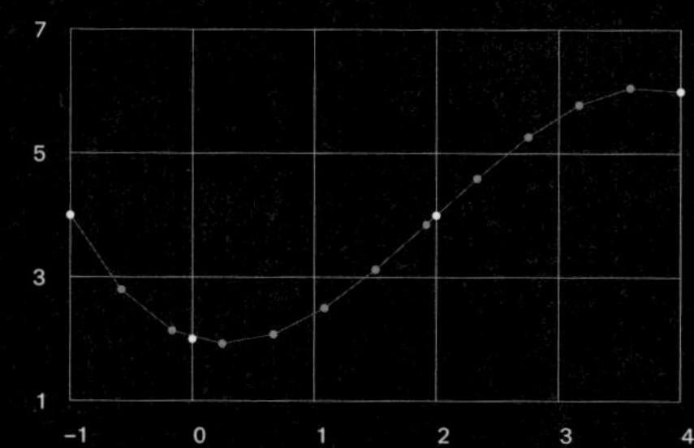

As we were able to do with the circle, we can again render this out in a series of different resolutions, here with 4, 12, and 48 elements, whereby only the white measurement points are shown as actual dots; the gray lines here are still discrete, but their connection points are not further highlighted:

This precise same principle is also applicable in 3D, with lists of interpolation functions in the X, Y, and Z directions:

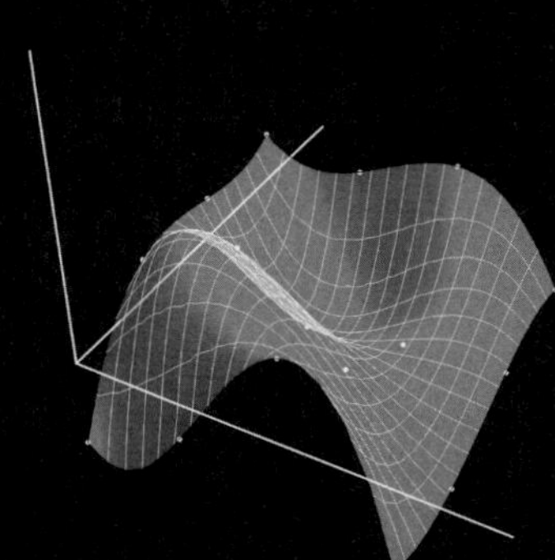

SPLINES AND NURBS
Splines and *NURBS*, which we also encountered earlier, similarly can have different resolutions. They express themselves in the degree of overlap of the areas of the different local interpolations, and so in the 'softness' of

the curve. Note how in the following four instances of the same graph, the curve goes from extremely edgy – this is not a spline at all yet, just the baseline function – to very smooth, while the points stay in exactly the same place: the smoothness of the curve is defined by the code element *'SplineDegree'*, labelled *'d'*.

```
pts={{0,0},{1,1},{2,-1},{3,0},{4,-2},{5,1}};
Row[Graphics[{
      LightGray,Line[pts],
      Black,Point[pts],
      Black,BSplineCurve[pts,SplineDegree→d]
      }]&/@{1,2,3}]
```

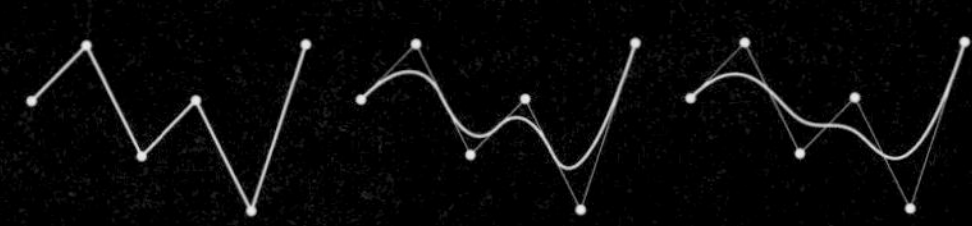

They can also be conceived in three dimensions:

```
cpts=Table[{i,j,RandomReal[{-
1,1}]},{i,5},{j,5}];
b=Row[Graphics3D[{
       PointSize@.02,Point@Flatten[cpts,1],
       Opacity@.5,
       BSplineSurface[cpts,SplineDegree→#]
       }]&/@{1,2,3}]
```

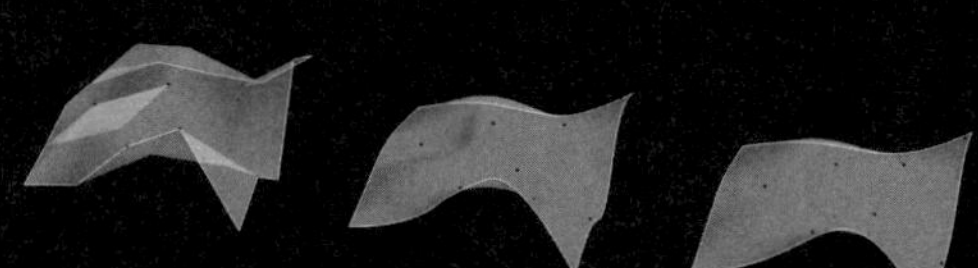

REGIONS

■ 362↘ In conventional CAD systems we are working on graphs with rationalised coordinates for the vertices. If, for example, we want to create a circle, we have to discretise the idea of a circle as described above.

This is the idea of a circle:

```
circle=x^2+y^2==1
x^2+y^2==1
```

These are the two functions, translating a line into a circle:

```
c=Solve[circle,y]
{{y→-√[1-x^2]{,{y→√[1-x^2]}}
```

This is the translation of a single rational point of the line to an irrational position on the circle:

```
c/.x→ 1/2
{{y→-(√[3]/2)},{y→√[3]/2}}
```

We can also work with angular instead of linear numbers to get the same result:

```
ϕ=30°;
{Sin@ϕ,Cos@ϕ}
{1/2,√[3]/2}
```

In both cases, irrational numbers are 'fictitious' and cannot be seen. They need to be rationalised or discretised with a certain resolution. Discretised numbers are called computational numbers.

```
c/.x→ 0.5
{{y→-0.866025},{y→0.866025}}
```

Conventional CAD systems, as all computing, use computational numbers, therefore a circle is a polygon of high resolution:

```
Graphics[{Thin,
  Line[{Sin@#,Cos@#}&/@  Range[0°,360°,30°]]
  }]
```

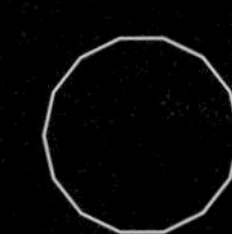

Now we can see a projection of the circle, but we've lost the idea of the circle. And if we want to, for example, intersect or connect elements, we always have to deal with errors: the fact that the rational element never meets the real element, or the artefact the idea. (These errors are a real pain in all CAD modelling!)

Solid modellers are a type of CAD system that do not work on a rational projection, but on the idea of the artefacts.

This is the idea of a circle:

```
c=x^2+y^2==1;
```

This is how to render this idea:

```
ContourPlot[Evaluate@c,{x,-1,1},{y,-1,1}]

d1=x^2+y^2<1;
RegionPlot[Evaluate@d1,{x,-2,2},{y,-2,2}]
```

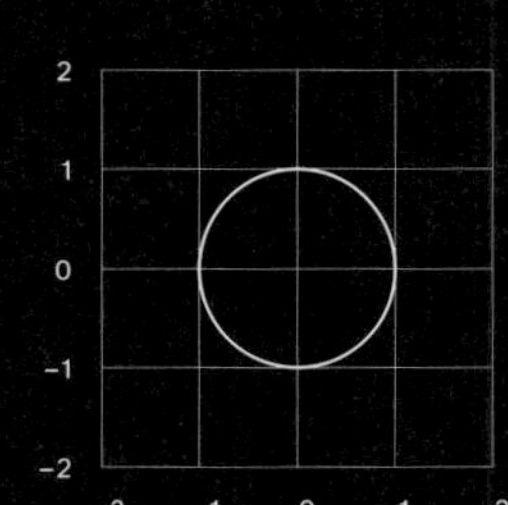

Instead of identities in space, this idea can define spatial relations, for example the insides and outsides of a circle:

```
d2=x²+y²>1;
RegionPlot[Evaluate@d2,{x,-2,2},{y,-2,2}]
```

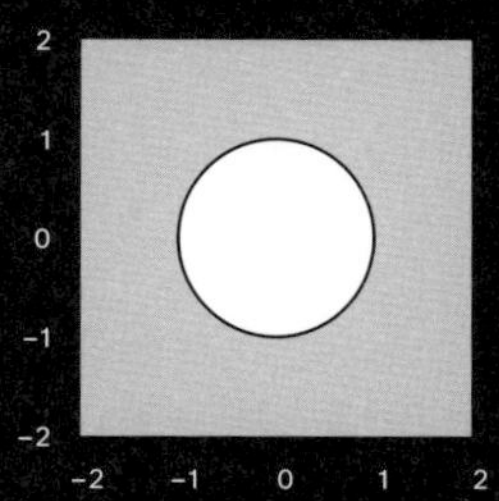

```
r1=x<0.5;
RegionPlot[Evaluate@r1,{x,-2,2},{y,-2,2}]
```

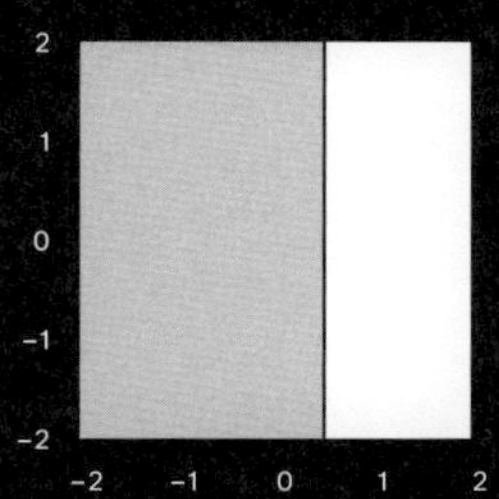

In the same way we can split sides:

```
RegionPlot[d1&&r1,{x,-2,2},{y,-2,2}]
```

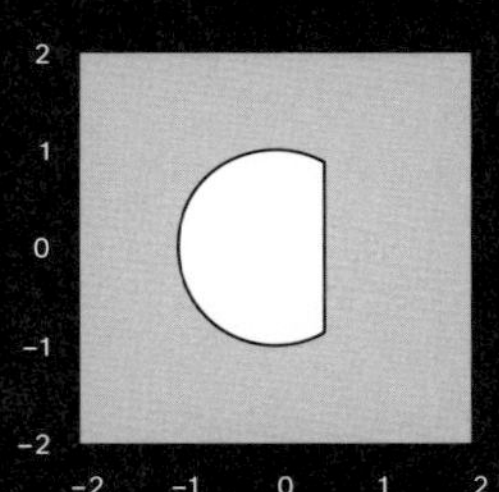

And we can combine these spatial ideas with **Boolean operations**. Named after the English mathematician, logician, and philosopher George Boole (1815–1864), these are logical expressions, such as 'true', 'false', 'and' (∧), 'or' (v), and 'not' (¬) that allow for a conditional flow of arguments, where a set of conditions being met results in an outcome that is different from the conditions not being met, or from a set of different conditions being met. We also come across them in our chapters on Generative Methods and Writing & Code.

■ ↖68 374↘

□ ↖145
□ 369↘

```
RegionPlot[d2&&!r1,{x,-2,2},{y,-2,2}]
```

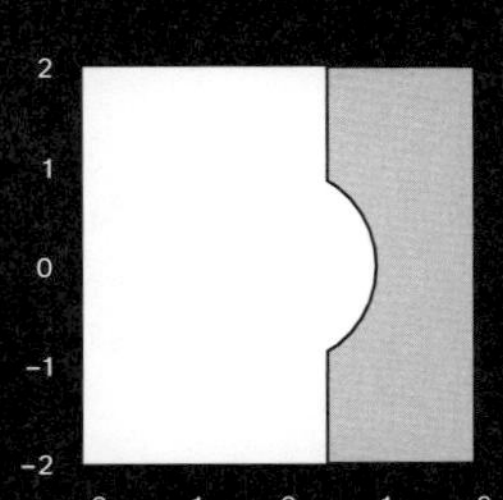

```
RegionPlot[!(d1&&r1),{x,-2,2},{y,-2,2}]
```

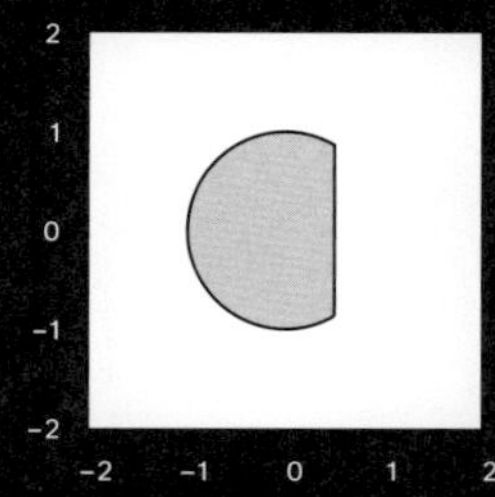

We can, as we would expect, also use Boolean operations to render 3D objects, though this is computationally a little more expensive (meaning more code and therefore more processing time and power is required), which in these tiny examples barely registers, but multiplied by the many elements needed for a complex visualisation starts to make a noticeable difference to how well your computer is able to cope. Today's computers don't consider this much of a challenge any more, but as recently as ten years ago, even the best machines would have struggled with comparatively simple tasks.

Here is the equation for a sphere:

```
sphere=x²+y²+z²==1;
ContourPlot3D[Evaluate@sphere,
 {x,-1,1},{y,-1,1},{z,-1,1}]
```

And for a cube:

```
cube=-1/2<x<1/2&&-1/2<y<1/2&&-1/2< z<1/2;
RegionPlot3D[ Evaluate@cube,
 {x,-1,1},{y,-1,1},{z,-1,1}]
```

And for a combination of the two:

```
RegionPlot3D[
 x²+y²+z²<1 && x < 0.5,
 {x,-2,2},{y,-2,2},{z,-2,2}
 ]

[...]
```

```
[…]
```

↖97 500↘

TRIANGULATION

In mathematics, a *region* is a concept that is notated in a formula such as, for example:

```
x²+y²<1
```

If we want to represent it graphically, it has to be rationalised to an acceptable level of accuracy, and a common solution for doing so offers itself in the shape of the triangle, because a triangle always forms a flat plane in space; in other words, it can be simply and unambiguously defined, always. This type of discretisation is called *triangulation*.

Once a triangulation has been applied, we only now work with these triangles: the idea of a circle or a sphere, or a square – whatever the shape was that we started out with – is forgotten, as discussed above. Also, the resolution of a triangulation, once set, can not be further refined: if you triangulate a sphere and you realise that it's not smooth enough, you have to redo the triangulation.

Below once more is a series of different rationalisations (discretisations), or forms, in each case of one and the same formula, but rendered in different resolutions, here not as points on a circle, but as triangulations of the plane. The level of triangulation is controlled by determining the size of the mesh and the precision of the form:

```
Row[DiscretizeRegion[
    Disk[],
    MaxCellMeasure→{"Length"→#},
    AccuracyGoal→1]&
  /@{1,0.5,0.2}]
```

```
Row[DiscretizeRegion[
    Disk[],
    MaxCellMeasure→{"Length"→.5},
    AccuracyGoal→#]&
  /@{1,3,5}]
```

And, correspondingly, the discretisation of a sphere to different levels of resolution:

```
Row[DiscretizeRegion[Ball[],
    MaxCellMeasure→{"Area"→#}]&
  /@{1,0.2,0.05}]
```

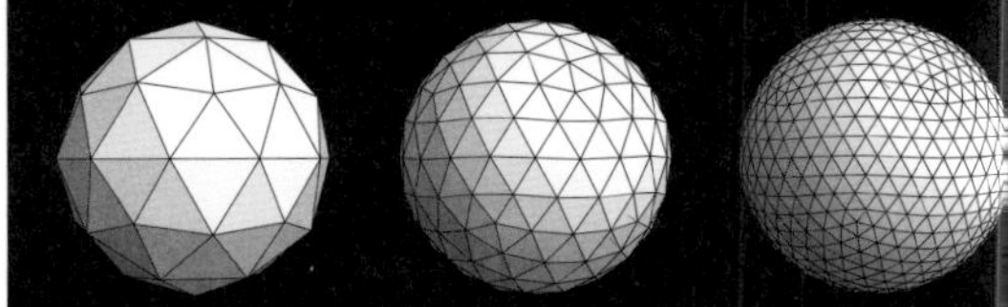

The discretisation of a Stanford bunny to different levels of resolution:

And as a Boolean operation:

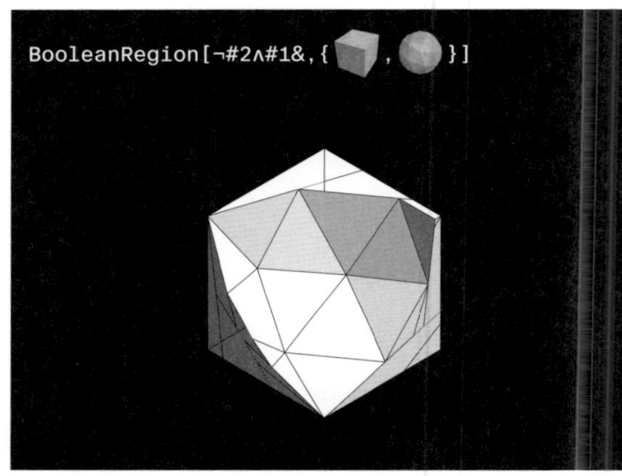

Today's modellers also offer modelling in what are known as *quads*: quadrangles instead of triangles. They give you as the user more control over the course of the lines of the discretisation, but unlike with triangulation, there is no common procedure that always and reliably works. So if, for example, you discretise a rectangle, it is adequate to subdivide this along the symmetries of the square. But doing so with 'free style' triangles is entirely inadequate.

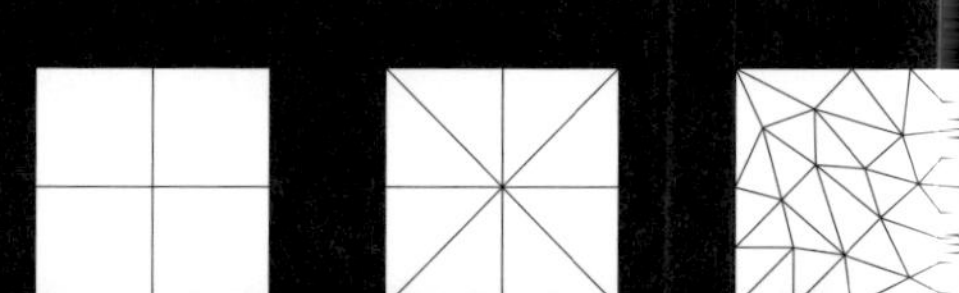

Also, on a sphere you run into problems with quads, especially at the poles:

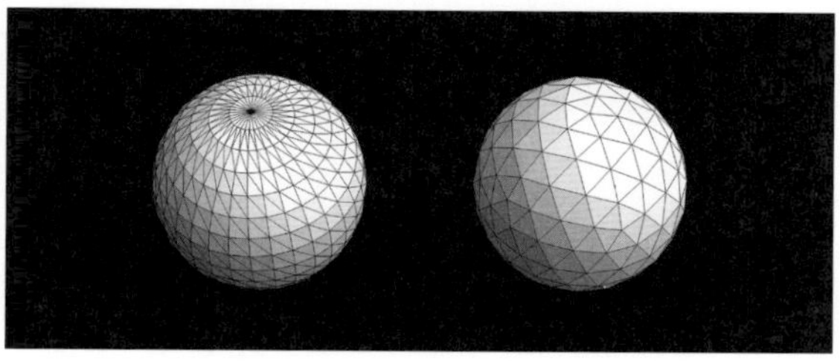

Therefore: if you are designing complex forms, you may use quads in areas where you want to control the edges, and triangles where you want to have smooth surfaces.

The Transformation of Forms

We have looked at how we can produce or generate objects. In many contexts we are dealing with parts of a harmonious whole. If the whole requires that it be a Stanford bunny, then the polygons by necessity will fit together in such a way as to produce the shape of a bunny. You could say that this process is about function, simulation, and optimisation: everything is geared towards a given and specified objective. We could also call this the 'design and production of objects', because that's what we are essentially doing with this process.

```
FindShortestPath[g,13,7]
{13,2,5,11,7}
```

Now, however, we want to turn our perspective around and think in the inverse direction: things shall be joined together not as parts of a whole, but as active and independent elements. They should not have to obey a predefined shape that we know we want to achieve; instead they shall be located in a way to constitute a space in-between: a generous space for things we do not know.

This, you could argue, is the difference between design and architecture. In design the whole is given (as in the Stanford bunny), and you organise parts in a way that best follows the idea of the whole. In architecture, on the other hand, designed elements are given and you constitute them in a way that allows you to make a strong architectural statement. You might think of the difference as 'top down' versus 'bottom up', but that would really be too simple, for the nature of the thinking is inverted between parts of a whole (axioms) and elements in open space (atoms). Assuming architecture to be the art of joining elements, there are two aspects of doing so: *translation* and *rotation*.

TRANSLATION AND ADDITION
Let's take an object and move it in space into any arbitrary position on our plane. Here is a square in its original position:

```
g1={1,2,3,4,1};
f1=Line@g1;
c1={{1,0},{1,1},{0,1},{0,0},{1,0}};

Graphics@GraphicsComplex[c1,f1]
```

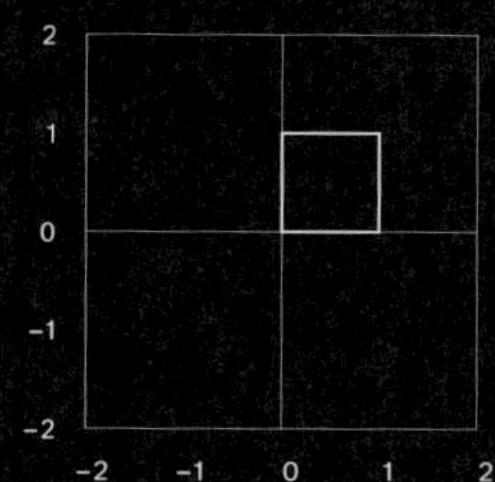

And here is the movement (d): an object is positioned by adding the vectors of all its vertices to the vector of the movement:

```
d={-1/2,-1/2};
c1=# + d &/@ c1
Graphics@GraphicsComplex[c1,f1]
{{1/2,-(1/2)},{1/2,1/2},{-(1/2),1/2},
 {-(1/2),-(1/2)},{1/2,-(1/2)}}
```

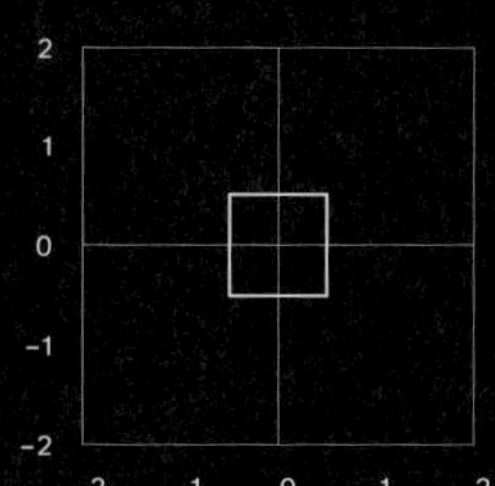

ROTATION AND THE MATRIX
Once an object is in a specified position, it also needs an orientation. An object is orientated by multiplying the vectors of all its vertices with the rotation matrix (in this case the *dot* or *scalar product*, that is the product of two Euclidian vectors a and b).

```
r=RotationMatrix[30°];
MatrixForm@r
c1=r.#&/@c1
Graphics@GraphicsComplex[c1,f1]
```

$$\begin{pmatrix} \frac{\sqrt{3}}{2} & -\frac{1}{2} \\ \frac{1}{2} & \frac{\sqrt{3}}{2} \end{pmatrix}$$

[...]

```
[...]
{{1/4+/4,1/4-/4},<<3>>,{1/4+/4,1/4-/4}}
```

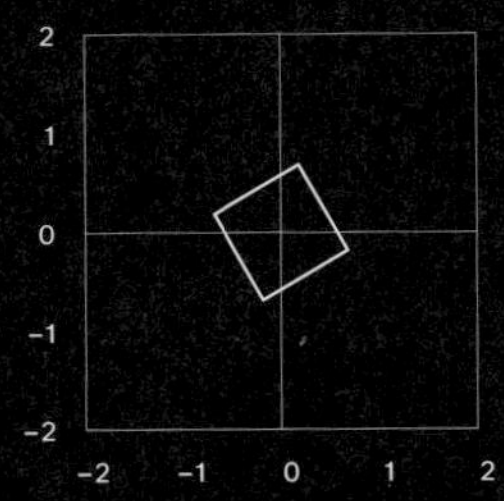

With these two transformations – translation and rotation – you can assemble all the architecture in the world!

SCALING AND MULTIPLICATION

CAD systems offer a multitude of additional transformations, such as scaling, mirroring, or skewing. Strictly speaking, we would argue that these are not architectonic transformations as such, because objects cannot simply be enlarged or made smaller, nor can they be mirrored; their design and the tools used to produce these objects have to be adapted in order to attain scaled or (with some exceptions, it has to be said) mirrored real-world objects. But of course, as long as we are in the virtual world – practising, planning, designing, or testing – we can do with computer software virtually anything we want.

An object is scaled by multiplying the vectors of all its vertices with a vector of the scale:

```
s={2,2};
c1=s*# &/@ c1
{{2(1/4+/4),<<8>>,2(1/4-/4)}}
Graphics@GraphicsComplex[c1,f1]
```

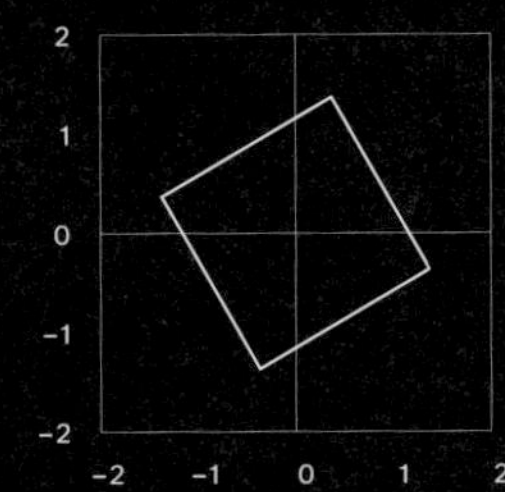

The Projection of Forms

PARAMETRIC DESIGN, LINEAR PROJECTION, AND ONE-OF-A-KIND PRODUCTION

We have been emphasising: graphs can take any form, the only thing that constitutes the character of a graph is its structure.

137 ● 212

It is for this reason that in *parametric design* and in digital manufacturing, products are not defined by form *and* structure, but solely by structure. Unlike traditional design methods where you arrive at your product and then either take it or its components to the site, there to be positioned or assembled, here now the form of a product is no longer absolute. In other words, it is not the same for all iterations, but dependent on the locality of its installation. A structural component, a steel frame, a window, or a type of cladding: as a graph it has one shape (for which read structure), but it may take any type of form (for which read onsite, real world iteration). The essence and the character, as we have seen and discussed, is exactly the same, all that changes and adapts to its specific environment is the iteration.

□ ↖145

You could argue, therefore, that conceptually the product – any architectural product so designed – is no longer made and then taken to the site of the installation, but rather that it is *projected*. (In real, practical life, terms, it may well have been physically made or printed or manufactured off-site and then taken as an object to the site, but there is a significant difference in how it is conceived and made to fit its destination, and that conceptual difference is what we are getting at here.)

What we would argue, then, is that in parametric design we do not just assemble an element at a given position (this is the act of translation) with a specific orientation (rotation), we also *project* it to a line or a face, and that would therefore be the equivalent of scaling and distorting.

Here now we have to reintroduce the terms *genotype* and *phenotype*. (We actually met them before, but there we rather skimmed over them.) They are borrowed from genetics and describe, respectively, the hereditary characteristics that are encoded on an organism's genes (genotype) and its observable behaviours (phenotype). (We also discuss them in our chapter on Generative Methods.)

The genotype can also be thought of as a 'prototype', or, to be a little more precise, as the prototypical element of an object, whereas the phenotype can then be thought of as its specific, localised iteration. What interests us here therefore is that in digital production, we think of the locality where an object is to be built and its outward, observable, and measurable characteristics as the *phenotype* onto which we can *project* the inherent *genotype* of our design, so that it works and makes sense.

```
genotype={{0,0},{1,1}};
phenotype={{3,7/2},{2,2}};
 Graphics[{
  LightGray,Rectangle@@genotype,
  Gray,Arrow [genotype],Point@genotype[[1]],
  Black,Arrow [phenotype],Point@phenotype[[1]]
  }]
```

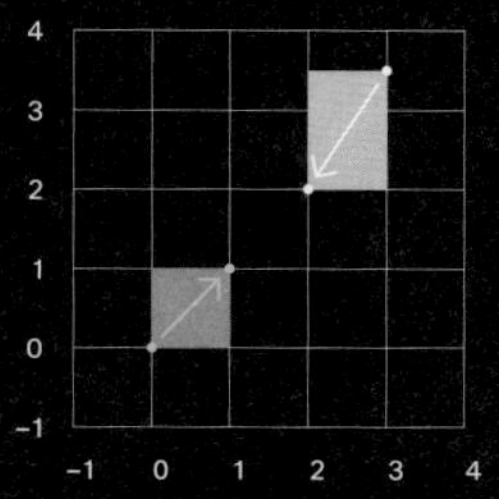

We calculate a transformation matrix between *genotype* and *phenotype*:

```
tf=Chop@FindGeometricTransform
   [genotype,phenotype]

{2, TransformationFunction[
 -0.769231 -0.153846 | 2.84615
  0.153846 -0.769231 | 2.23077
     0         0     |    1
]}
```

And then apply it to project the prototypical element to its specific location:

```
Graphics[{
  LightGray,Rectangle@@genotype,
  Gray,Arrow [genotype],Point@genotype[[1]],
  LightGray,GeometricTransformation[
   Rectangle@@genotype,
     InverseFunction@tf[[2]]],
  Black,Arrow [phenotype],
    Point@phenotype[[1]]
  }]
```

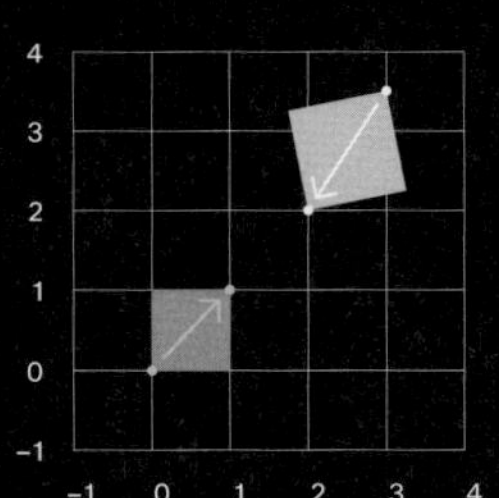

Think of whatever form you have, discretised and triangulated, as described above and think each triangle projected with these transformation functions, and you have the very principle of parametric design and one-of-a-kind production. It is literally the production of parts of a design, in strict conceptual distinction from its constituting elements. And that, to emphasise this distinction, leans more towards architecture than towards design. Design is done by linear projection, architecture needs a perspective projection. Which we want to introduce in the next section.

PERSPECTIVE PROJECTION

138 ● 212

There is a famous etching by German Renaissance painter, printmaker, and theorist Albrecht Dürer (1471–1528), called *Mechanical Creation of a Perspective Image* that depicts an artist at work, setting up a projection to create the perspective image so referred to in the title. (Perspective, which we don't want to go into here, was then, at the time Dürer produced his drawing, only about a hundred years 'old' – it had been known about and studied for several centuries in different cultures, but Western civilisation really started to understand the mathematical principles underpinning it only from the early 15th century onwards, in the revolutionary currents of the Italian Renaissance, which we refer – and draw parallels – to often in this *Atlas*.)

In order to achieve an accurate representation of a visual perspective in three dimensional space on his two-dimensional plane, the artist in Dürer's sketch sets up a frame that allows him to project the object on the table onto the screen held up by his assistant.

In graphics, projection is a special type of transformation of graphs that typically involves rendering an object or a shape onto another object or shape, either in the same or in a different dimension. This can be quite straightforward, such as simulating how a light source would throw the shadow of a piece of furniture onto a wall. But it can also become very complex, for example when round surfaces or reflections are involved.

Here is a simplified graphic 2D representation of a two-dimensional object (a square), a vantage point, and a screen between the two:

```
g1:={1,2,3,4,1};
f1:=Line@g1;
c1:={{1,0},{1,1},{0,1},{0,0},{1,0}};
screen:=InfiniteLine[{{-1/2,-1},{-1,1}}];
pa:={-2,-1};
gr2:=GraphicsComplex[c1,f1];
Graphics[{
  gr2,Thickness[.001],screen,
  Black,PointSize[.025],Point@pa
  }]
```

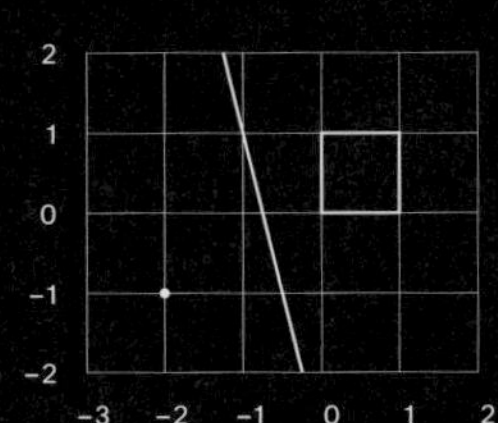

From the vantage point we draw a line to each coordinate point of the square and calculate the intersection with the screen. The projection comes about as the structure of the square is kept intact, while only the coordinates of the positions are transformed. What we get here is the transformation of a two-dimensional form in the plane into a one-dimensional form on a line:

```
lines=Line[{pa,#}] &/@ c1;
pts={x,y}/.
    First@Solve[{x,y}∈screen &&
       {x,y}∈ #,{x,y}]&/@lines
{{-(8/13),-(7/13)},<<3>>,{-(8/13),-(7/13)}}
```

```
gr2 :=GraphicsComplex[c1,f1];
Graphics[{
  gr2,Thickness[.001],screen,
  Black,PointSize[.025],Point@pa,lines,
  PointSize[.01],Black,Point@pts
  }]
```

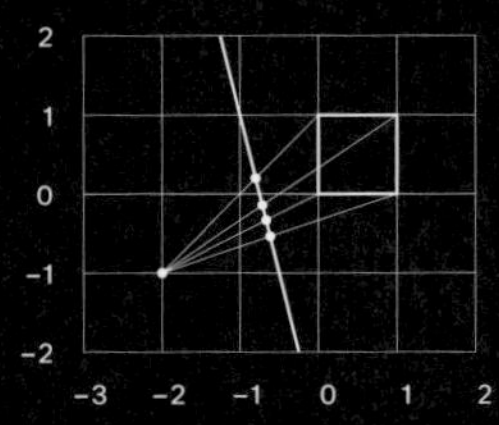

Using the same mathematics, we can transform an object from a three-dimensional form in space to a two-dimensional form on the plane. (The key element of this code is the solver of linear equations.)

■ ↖132

```
points={{9/2,-(1/2),-(1/2)},
         <<6>>,{11/2,1/2,1/2}};
cube=GraphicsComplex[points,
   Line[{{1,2},<<10>>,{7,8}}]];
screen=InfinitePlane[{{2,0,0},{2,2,0},
                    {2,0,2}}];
viewPoint={0,2,2};
viewLines=Line[{viewPoint,#}]&/@ points;
projPoints:={x,y}/.
     First@Solve[{x,y}∈screen&&
                {x,y}∈#,{x,y}]&/@viewLines;
projFig:=ReplacePart[cube,
                    1→projPoints[[All,1]]];
```

```
play :=Graphics3D[{
   cube,projFig,
   Gray,viewLines,
   Opacity@.2,EdgeForm[],screen,
   Opacity@1,Black,Sphere[viewPoint,.05]
   }]
play
```

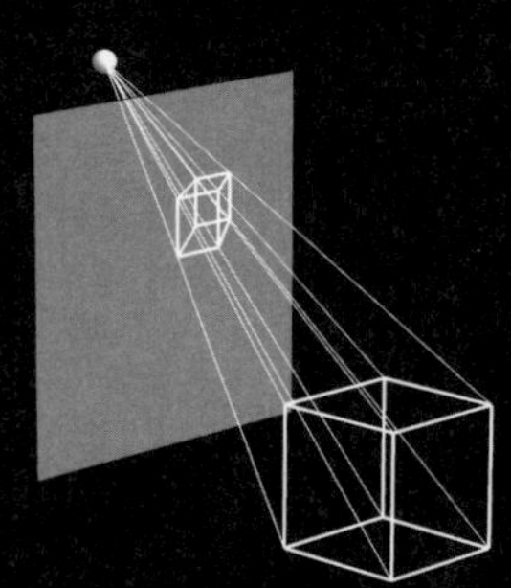

Or we can project to a curved image surface, where the projection lines do not intersect with an infinite plane (a x + b y + c z == d), but with a sphere (a x^2 + b y^2 + c z^2 == d). It is interesting to note that you only have to change the formula of the screen to get a spherical projection with the same code:

```
screen=Sphere[{0,2,2},3];
play
```

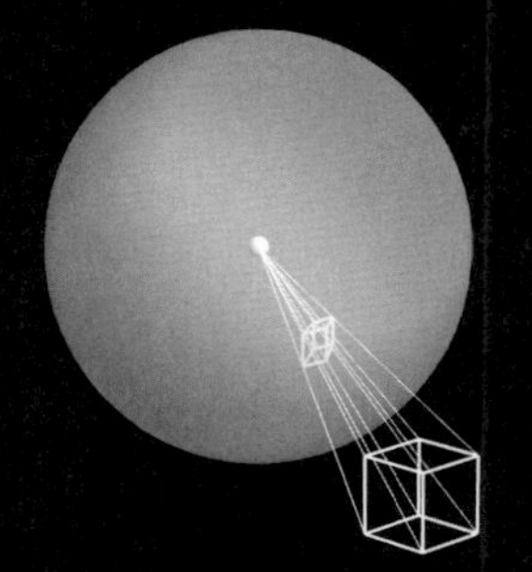

Of course, these examples are the projective geometry of the Renaissance onwards. We do not really know what a digital projective geometry of today looks like. But this is what we can learn:

One of the points we emphasise in this *Atlas* is that the architects of modernity and thereafter availed themselves of the architectural language of their day, and made themselves literate; the language of their day being the – specifically in terms of perspective – accurate *drawing*. It is of real significance therefore to note that with today's digital tools, all we need to create our architecture is an algebraic solver of linear equations, written as code. And as architects we can learn from the Renaissance masters who gained access to this projective geometry through drawing, and developed from it their architecture. Because we are confronted with the corresponding question: what does the architecture of a *digital* **projective geometry** look like? Which is why we have to go further with graphs towards computational active objects.

This is not comparable with parametric design. The elements of Italian architect Francesco Borromini (1599–1667), for example do not control the space; on the contrary: they are constituted to open up a space, as we have called it earlier, 'generous for things unknown'.

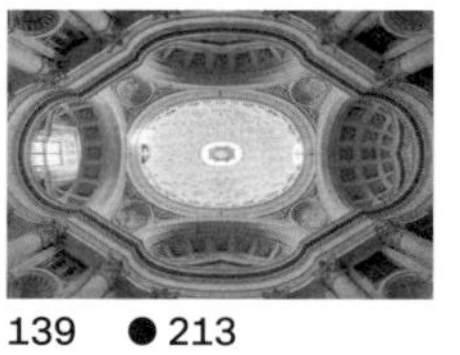

139 ● 213

Or look at a facade of Alberti's: his famous basilica is not an old structure rebuilt, it is really just an old structure given a modern face to speak to us in a new tongue.

140 ● 213

To follow these masters, we should think of our architecture today as active digital elements. It is good to see that with graphs we are able to mimic the models and constructions of the old masters, but it is important to realise also that graphs are the substance of computing itself. The things we describe in our chapter on Big Data & Machine Learning – the Turing machine, the Markov chain – are graphs that are connected to our world and activated. They need to be domesticated with a new architecture, much as the old masters domesticated their language with their architecture.

□ 549↘

115 ● 177
The Queen's Garden Party: all vertices and edges are not the same.

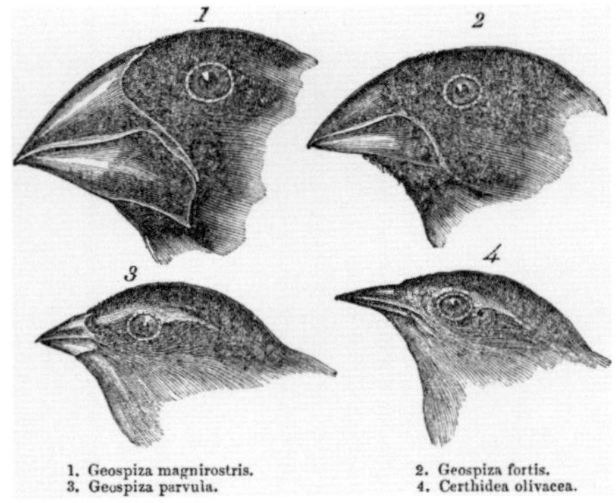

116 ● 179
John Gould, Galapagos finches, 1837.

117 ● 180
A six-digit version of the Pascaline, built in 1654.

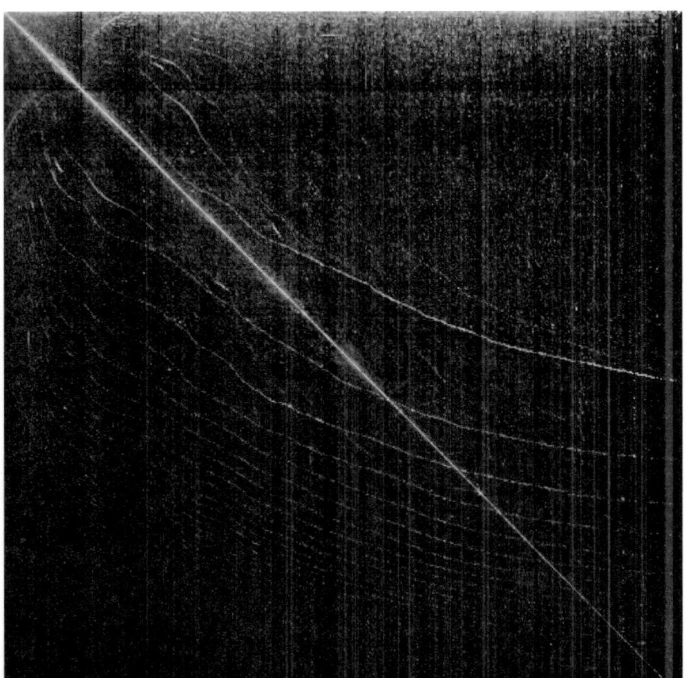

118 ● 180
Google matrix of Cambridge University network (2006).

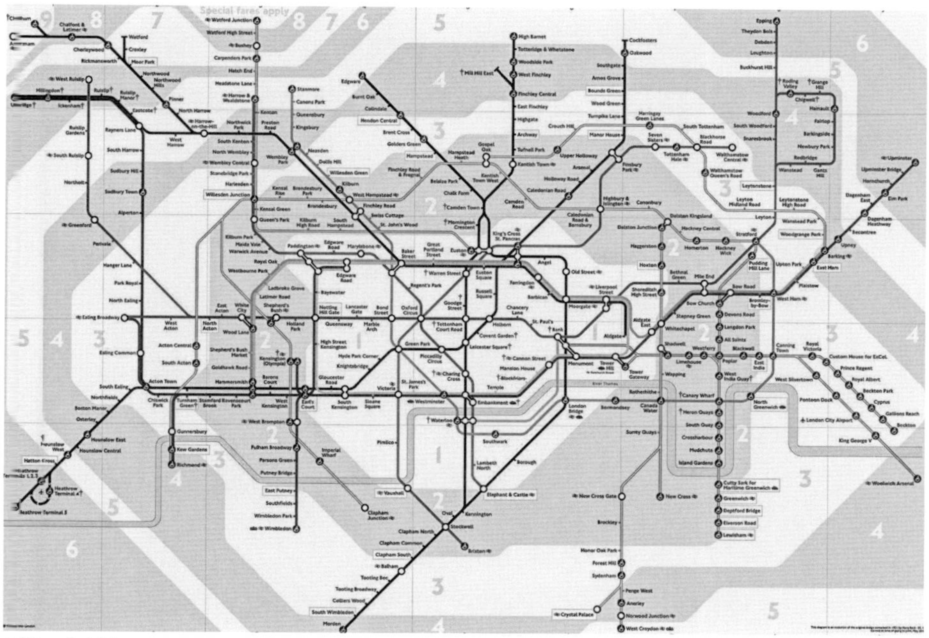

119 ● 181
The London Underground map. [Transport for London]

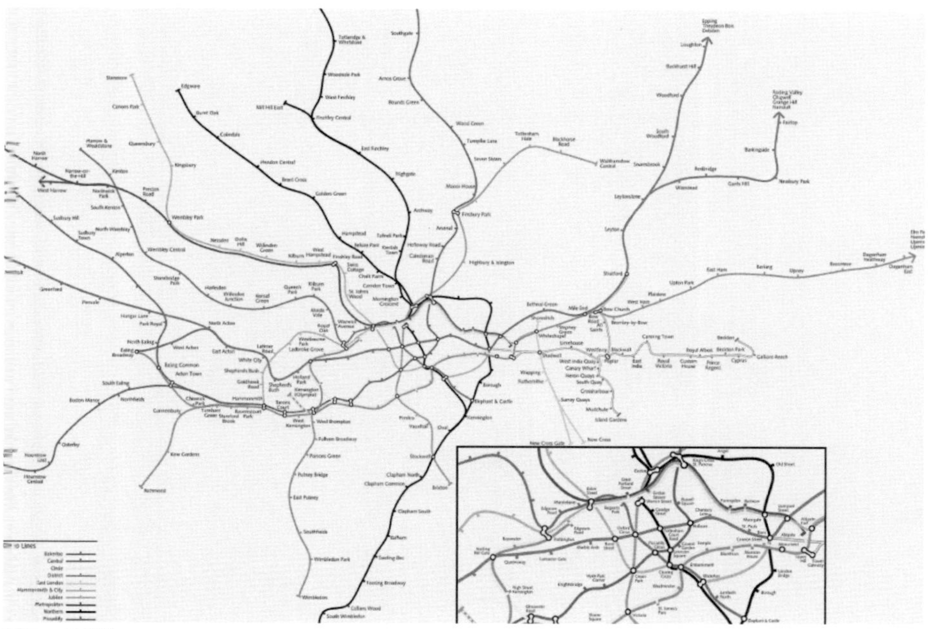

120 ● 181
Geographical map of the London Underground.

121 ● 181
A network of friends on Facebook.

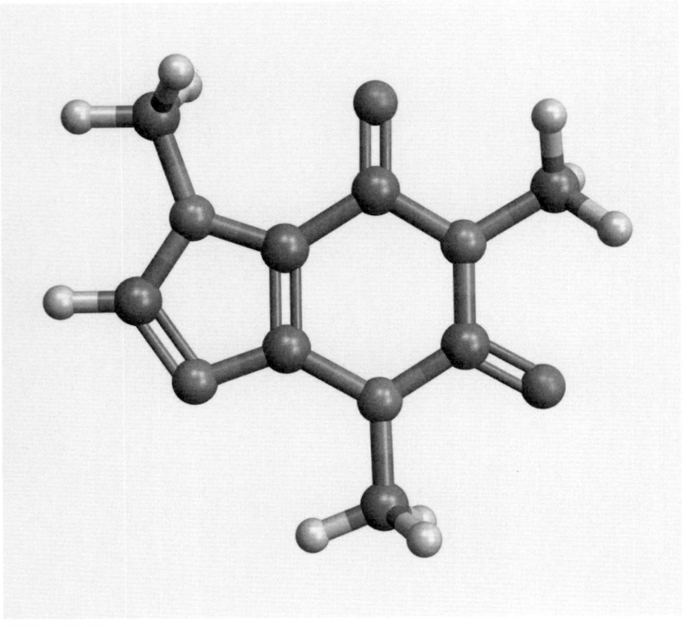

122 ● 181
A molecular structure (adrenalin).

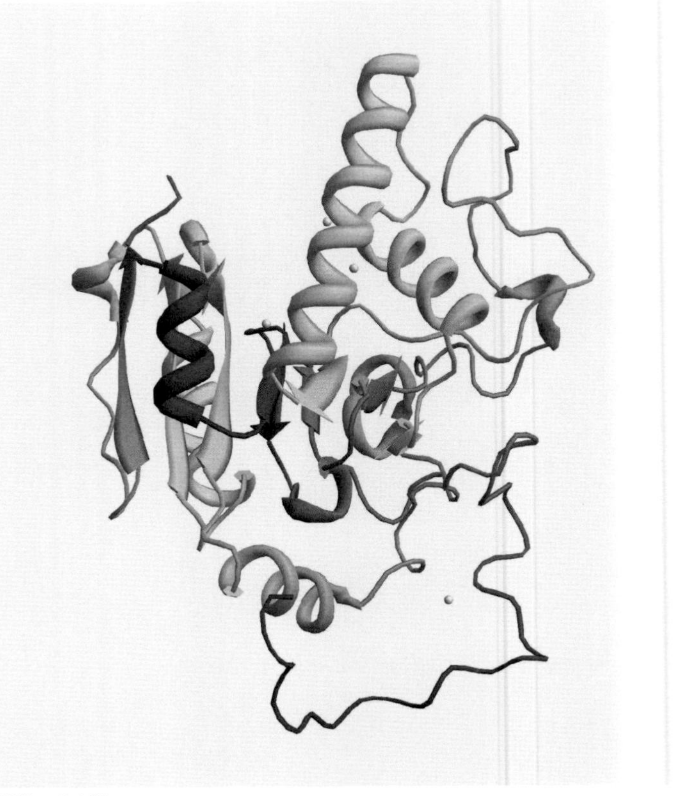

123 ● 181
Structure of a protein in molecular biology.

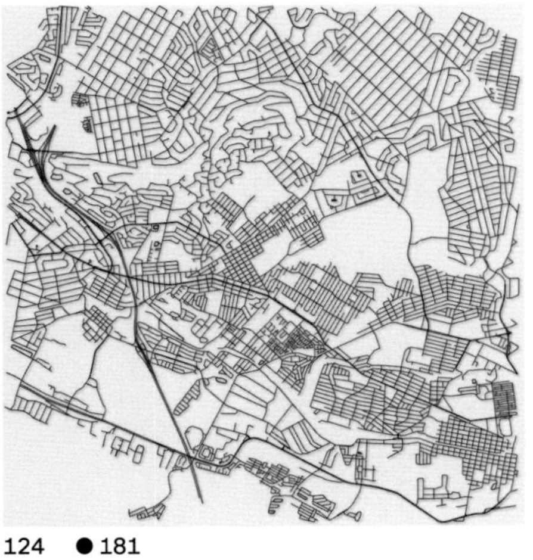

124 ● 181
Streets in *OpenStreetMap*.

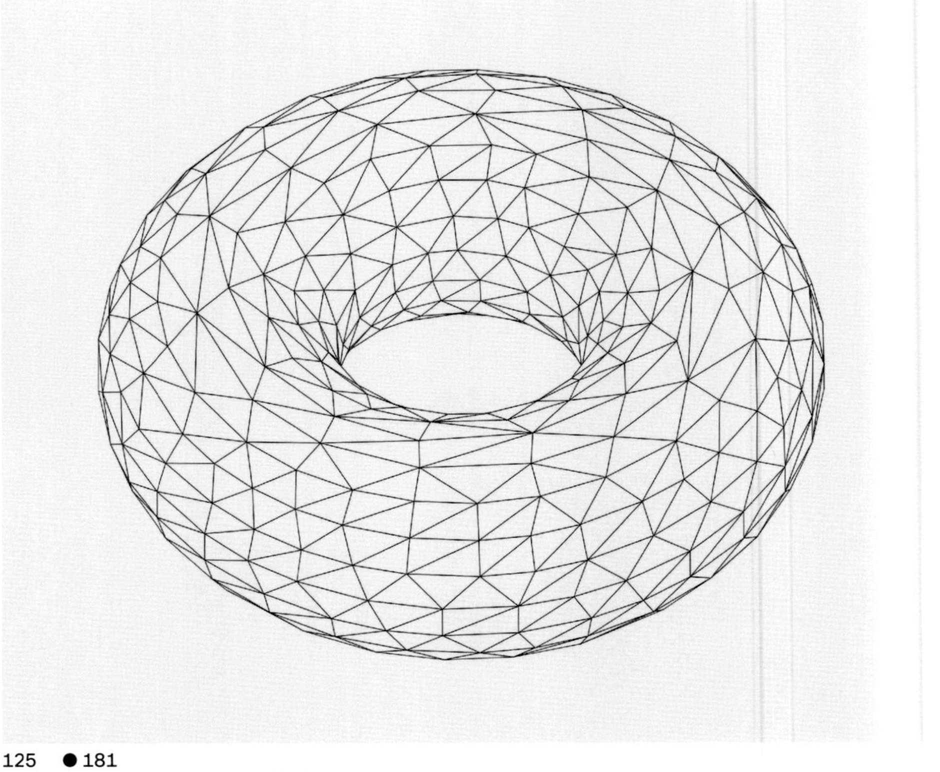

125 ● 181
Mesh of a graphic object in CAD.

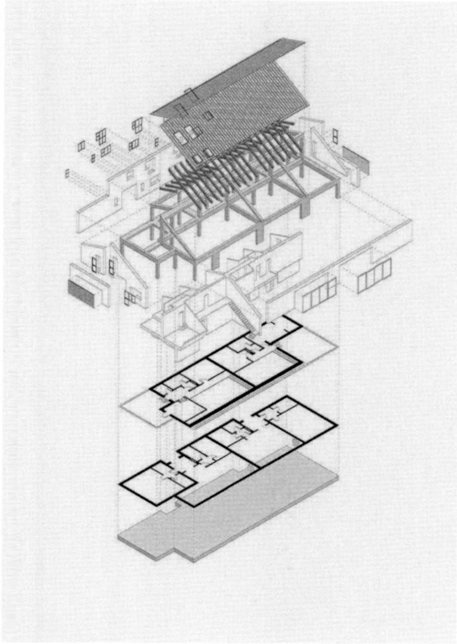

126 ● 181
A CAD drawing.

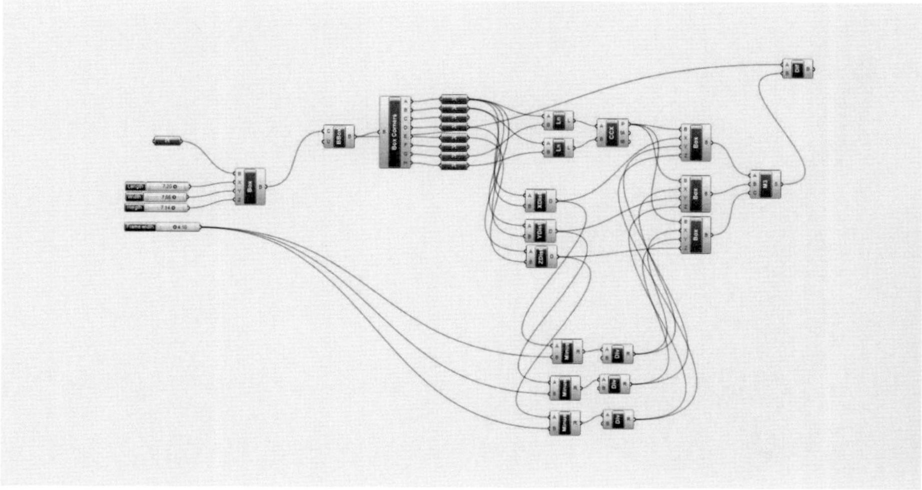

127 ● 181
Graph of *Grasshopper* commands in *Rhino*.

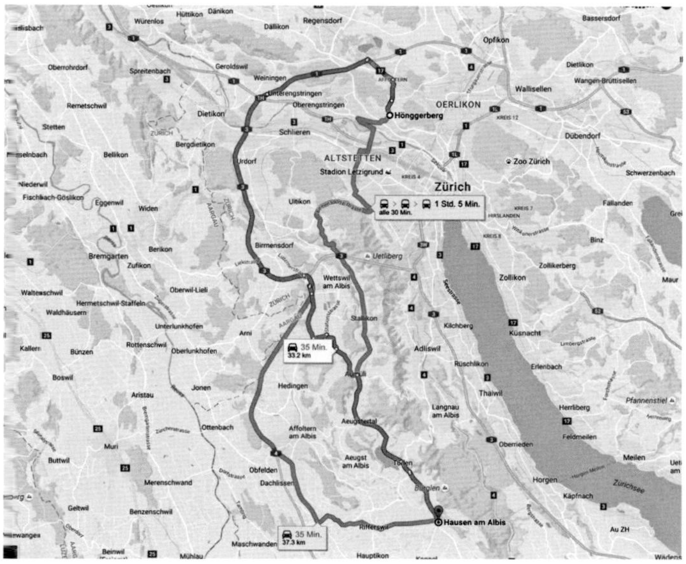

128 ● 188
A route on a map.

129 ● 188
A space syntax pattern of Greater London.

130 ● 189
The Stanford bunny.

131 ● 192
A Roman mosaic.

132 ● 192
USAF Hangar, Konrad Wachsmann, 1951.

133 ● 192
Reconstruction of three-dimensional knot for a modular office partition system by Konrad Wachsmann, 1943, by Marianne Burkhalter and Christian Sumi. [baumuster.ch]

134 ● 192
Fritz Haller (1924–2012)

135 ● 195
Gaudí's hanging chain models, 1889.

136 ● 195
Model of the bridge over the Basento river, scale 1:10; Institute ISMES, Bergamo, 1971.

137 ● 202
The Hungerburg funicular railway designed by Zaha Hadid Architects, 2007.

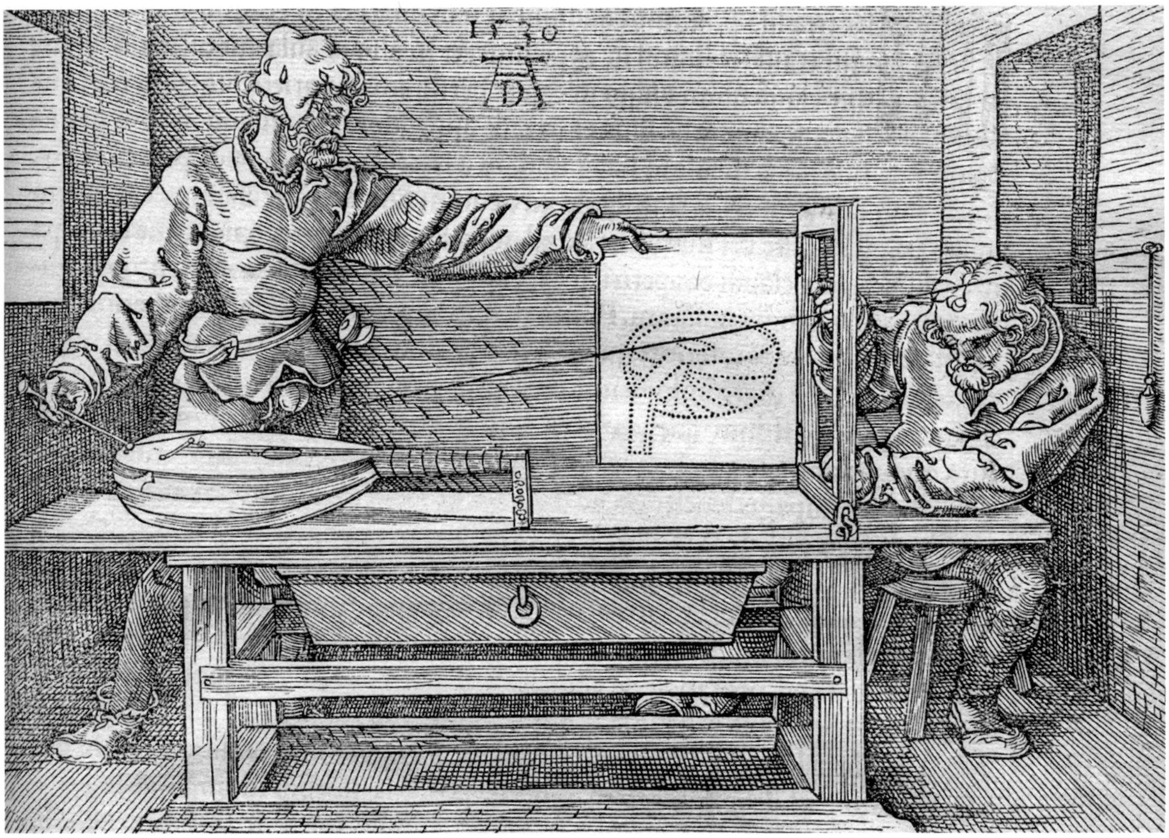

138 ●203
Albrecht Dürer: from *Underweysung der Messung (Four Books of Measurement)*, 1525: mechanical creation of a perspective image.

139 ● 204
Francesco Borromini (1599–1667): *San Carlo alle Quattro Fontane*, Borromini, Rome, 1646.

140 ● 204
Leon Battista Alberti (1404–1472): Facade of the Basilica of Santa Maria Novella, 1470.

Colour Plates

I

P. 55–213

013A ○ 064

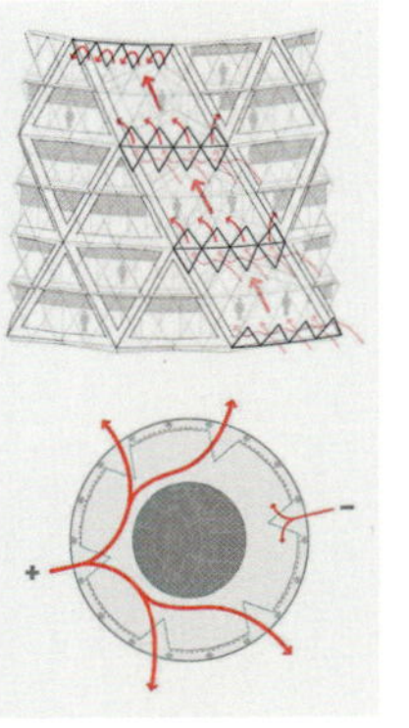

013B ○ 064

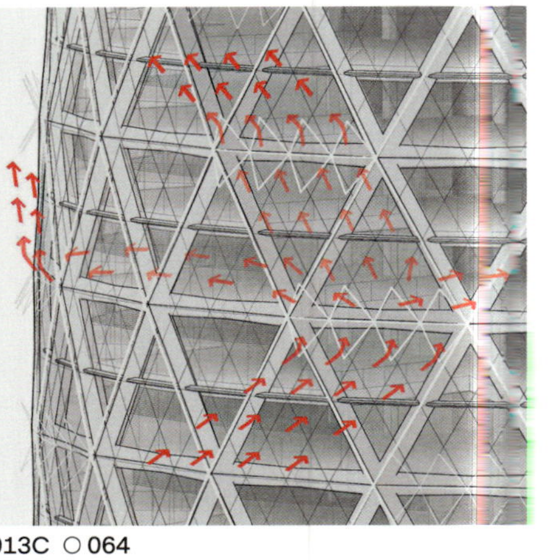

013C ○ 064

Foster + Partners: 30 St Mary Axe (formerly Swiss Re Building), known as 'The Gherkin', London, 2004 (013A) and performance diagrams (013B + 013C).
[Paste | Jonathan Massey & Andrew Weigand]

014A ○ 064 014B ○ 064

The Very Many: parametric design model, Minima / Maxima World Expo Pavilion, Astana, Kazakhstan, 2017 (014A) and the finished object (014B). [The Very Many | NAARO]

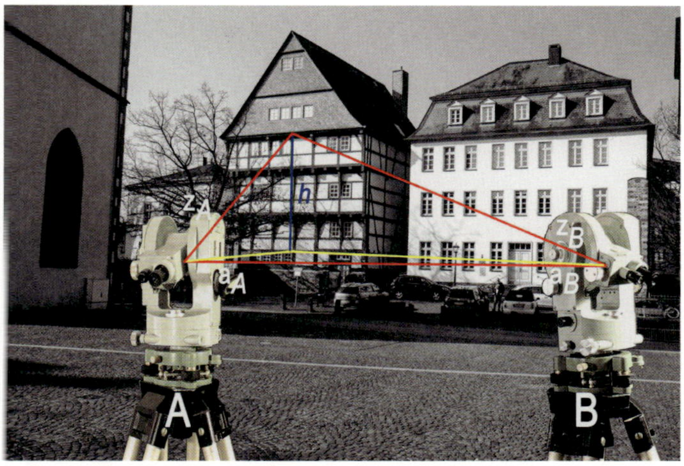

050 ○ 097

Triangulation by theodolite. [Nikolaus Zieske]

051 ○ 097

Point cloud using multi-image photogrammetry with the *PointSense Heritage* program. [FARO]

052 ○ 098
Tacheometry. [Nikolaus Zieske]

053 ○ 098
3D scan and data reconstruction of the Sir John Soane Museum. *A Museum Made Digital* by ScanLAB Projects, 2015–16. [ScanLAB Projects]

054 ○ 100
Amorphous surface structures can best be captured by precise digitalisation methods, such as triangulated mesh structures, here with different mesh width settings. [Nikolaus Zieske]

055 ○ 100
Partial generalised rebuilding of a classicism facade with the essential building blocks of BIM, using axes, grids, orthogonalities, and symmetries. [*Scan2BIM*]

059 ○ 101
A thermography image rendered as a raster dataset allows us to see behind an object's surface, for example. [Thomas Reinold]

077 ○ 121
The structure of the Beijing National Aquatics Centre, known as the Water Cube, is based on a unique lightweight construction, developed by China State Construction Design International (CCDI), PTW Architects, and ARUP, and derived from the structure of water bubbles in the state of aggregation found in foam. [Chris Bosse]

078 ○ 121
The structure of a foam, which the researchers around Juliette Pierre from the University of Paris-Diderot made visible by ultrasound and examined in terms of its acoustic properties. [Valentin Veroy]

079 ○ 121
The Water Cube model. [Chris Bosse]

080 ○ 122
Optimisation of the roof structure of the Beijing National Stadium.

081 ○ 122
The Beijing National Stadium by Herzog de Meuron, known as the Bird's Nest. [Peter23, edited by Ursula Kirschner]

097A ○157

097B ○157

Plants generated in *Xfrog*, a 3D computer graphics software first released in 1996 for the creation of branching structures that emulate organic plant branching behaviour using L-systems. [097A+097B: Jan Walter Schliep]

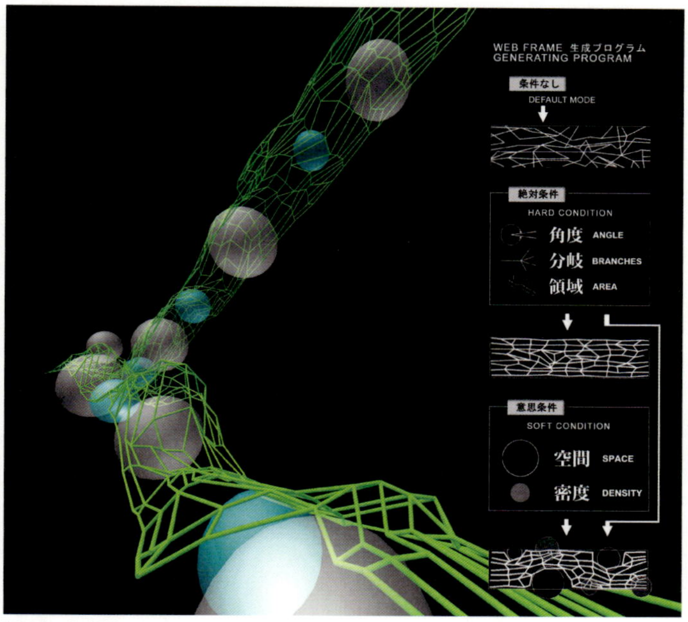

098A ○ 157

098B ○ 157
Induction design by Makoto Sei Watanabe: the *Web Frame* structure for the Iidabashi Subway station (2000) was not designed, but 'grown' in plant-like fashion, solving the problem according to a program developed by the architect. [098A + 098B: Makato Sei Watanabe]

104 ○ 159
Evocative architectural rendering of an evolving structure that overgrows and transforms a building. One of a series of images that SOMA architects contributed to the exhibition *Beauty Matters* in 2019 at the Museum of Estonian Architecture. The model was created with the procedural modelling programme *Houdini*. [SOMA Architects]

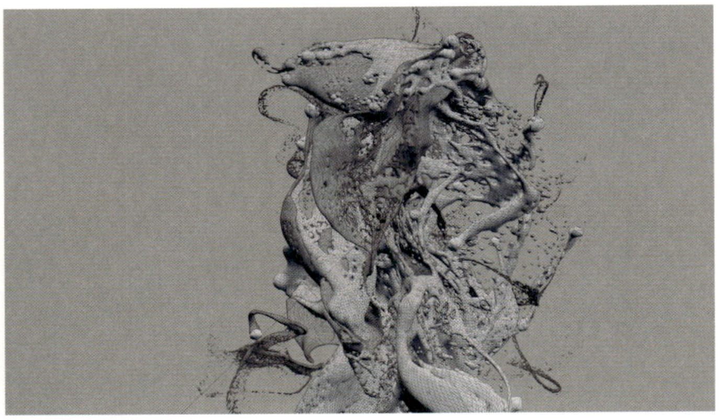

106A ○ 160

106B ○ 160

Paint Splashes by Gleb Alexandrov. Special effects as generative design tools: particles, smoke simulation, and metaballs in the 3D computer graphics software *Blender* were used to create this composition of liquid 3D forms, shown as shaded wire-model (106A) and rendering (106B). [Gleb Alexandrov]

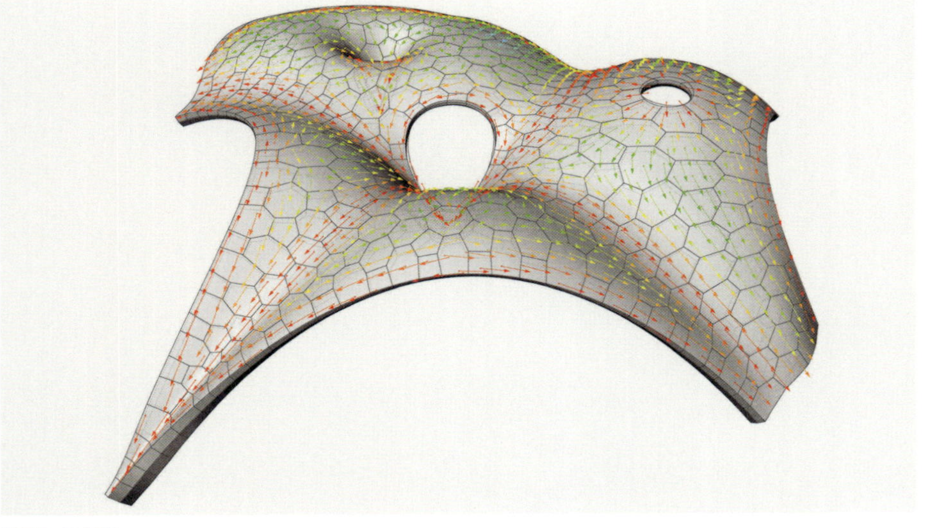

107A ○ 160

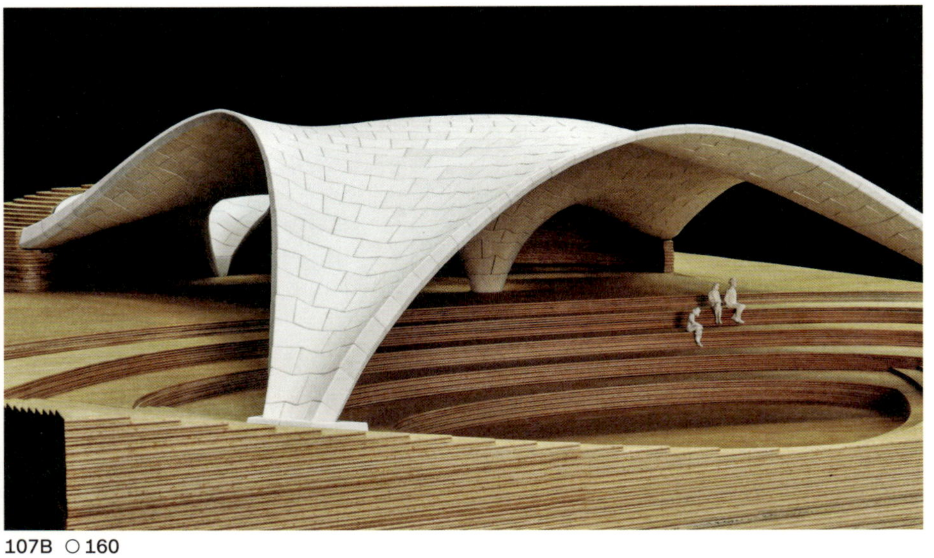

107B ○ 160

The MLK Junior Park Stone Vault project for Austin, Texas, is a unique unreinforced, dry-set, cut-stone masonry shell structure, developed by the Block research group of ETH Zürich. The structural form-finding was enabled by custom digital tools, which extend the particle spring system paradigm, using a method the authors call *Thrust Network Analysis (TNA)*. [107A + 107B: Philippe Block]

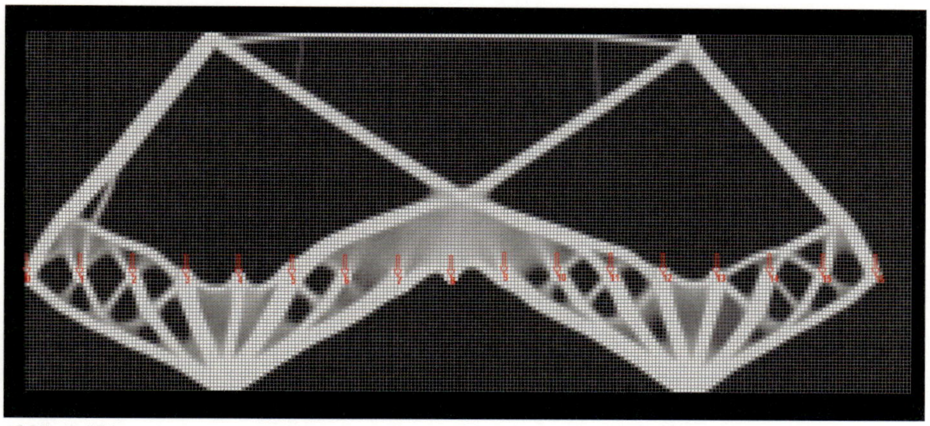

108A ○ 161
Topological optimisation of a bridge. Forces were applied at the locations indicated by the arrows. The finite-element based stress analysis identifies regions of low and high stress. On this basis it removes material wherever it is obsolete.

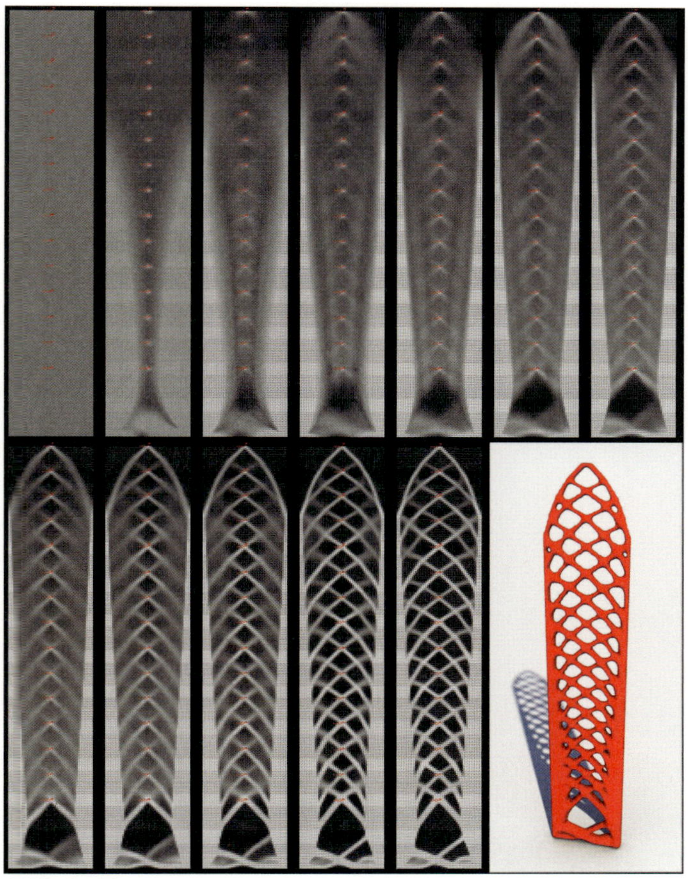

108B ○ 161
Topological optimisation of a tower under wind load. The upper left image shows a full block of material with wind forces applied. The subsequent images show the progression of material removal for regions of low mechanical stress. After several iterations, a distinct organic structure develops, which is also known as Michell truss.

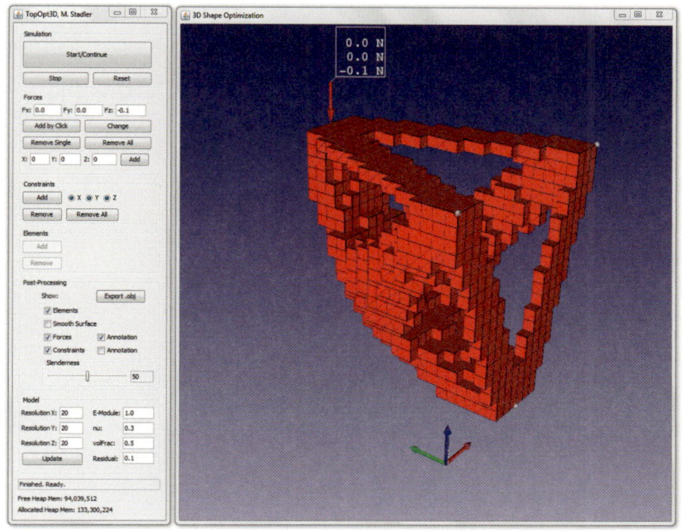

108C ○ 161
Topological optimisation in 3D. A filled block of material is loaded with a single force and suspended at three points in space (white dots). The finite-element based algorithm iteratively removes material in regions of low mechanical stress. The resulting structure is shown above.

Series (108A–108C) taken from the Seminar Simulationstechnik, *held by Michael Stadler at Graz University of Technology (TU Graz), 2006.*

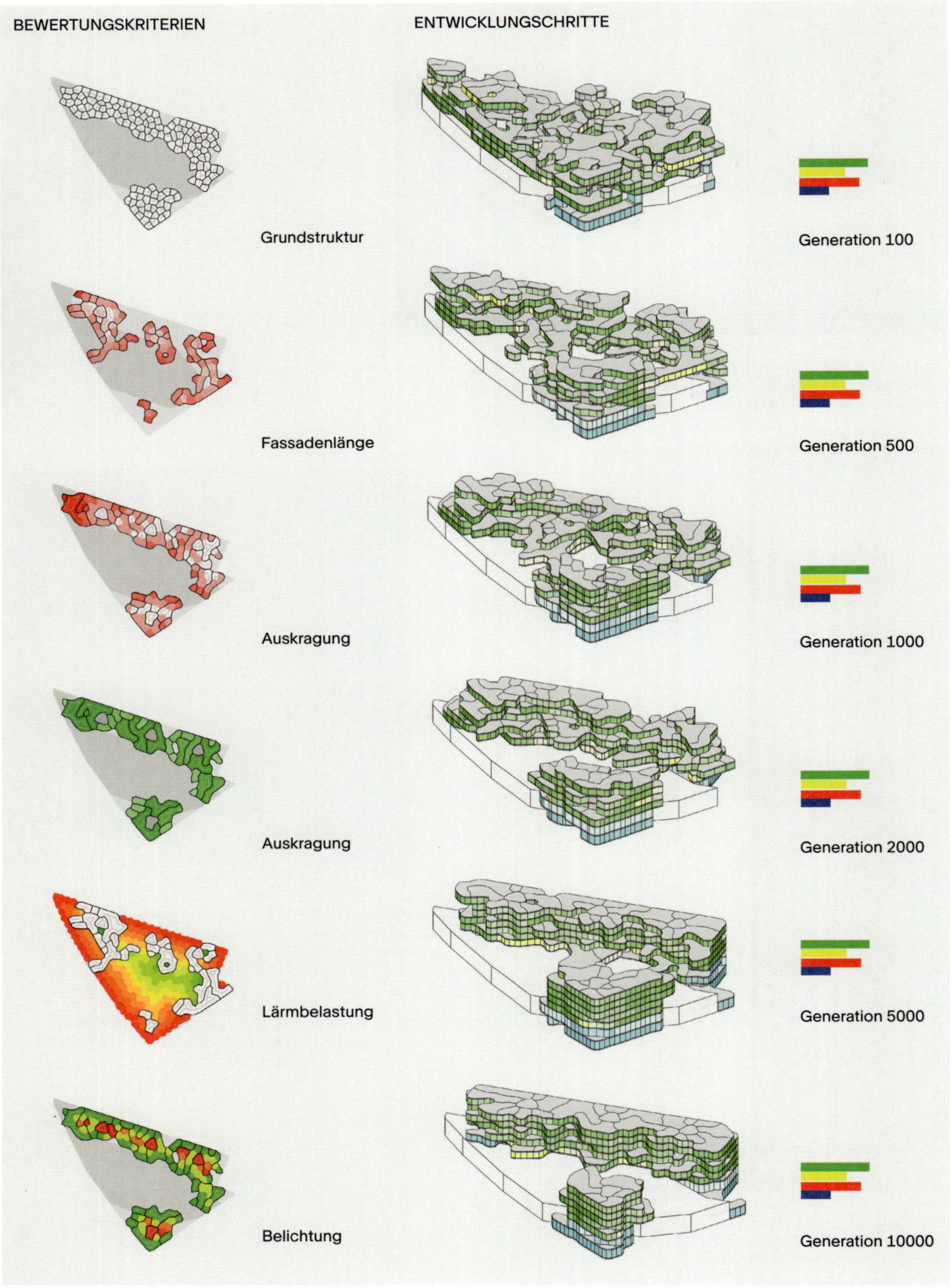

112 ○164
The room partitions of a layout are being calculated for different priorities, such as view, pathways, solar irradiation, vertical development, so that variant versions of the design can be evaluated and compared with each other. Depending on the weighting of individual qualities, different layouts are being generated, here already presented as 3D models. [*Kaisersrot* / ETH Zürich]

THE IMAGE

Visualising Architecture

II

Image & Colour 229
Rendering 255
Visualisation 285

Image & Colour

Harald Gatermann

- Nicholas Negroponte: *Architecture Machine*, 1970
- Nicholas Negroponte: *Soft Architecture Machines*, 1976
- Nicholas Negroponte: *Being Digital*, 1995
- Michael Friedewald: *Der Computer als Werkzeug und Medium: Die geistigen und technischen Wurzeln des Personal Computers*, 1999

Overview

MAKING IMAGES APPEAR

The Nobel Prize in physics for the year 1909 was jointly awarded to Italian inventor and electrical engineer Guglielmo Marconi (1874–1937) and German inventor and physicist Karl Ferdinand Braun (1850–1918), "in recognition of their contributions to the development of wireless telegraphy."

Marconi went on to effectively invent the radio and became a household and brand name for a while; and his "marvellous invention" was cited by the British Postmaster-General of the day as the sole reason anyone at all survived the sinking of the Titanic six years later, on 15 April 1912: it was thanks to radio communications that the RMS Carpathia was able to sail to the rescue and save at least some people from drowning in the icy waters of the North Atlantic Ocean. (Marconi himself had been invited to join the maiden voyage of the Titanic, but declined the offer, boarding RMS Lusitiana three days earlier instead, because he wanted to get on with some paperwork, and that vessel offered the services of a public stenographer. The Lusitiana made it to New York unscathed, but did not survive much longer anyway: she was sunk by a German submarine during World War I, on 7 May 1915). Karl Ferdinand Braun, meanwhile, is credited with inventing the **Cathode Ray Tube (CRT)**, which sits at the heart of the **oscilloscope** and all early generation television screens. Marconi and Braun together could thus be said to be jointly responsible for giving us 20th century media: radio and television. And Braun, specifically, is absolutely instrumental in paving the way towards computing with images.

From the perspective of a smartphone user today, who is carrying around a pocket-size device that is capable of professional quality photography and high definition video recording, as well as seamless integration with picture editing apps and social network sharing, all of which operated by touch screen, it is hard to imagine that computers, once upon a time and not that very long ago, did not have a user interface. At all. Not just maybe a very simple one, but none. You could, in the earliest days, set a computer off on its task and then wait until the computing was done, and that was it. 'Communication' was a one-way street of giving instructions (using keys, perforated strips and punch cards) and receiving results (on perforated paper strips, for example, or on printed paper). If the results were wrong because the input was incorrect, you just had to start all over again.

141 ● 244

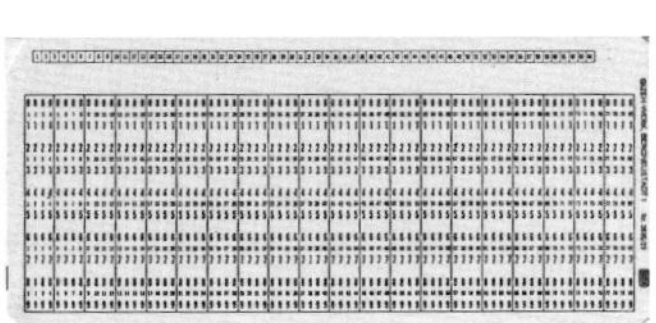
142 ● 244

So the idea of working with images did not cross the average person's mind, because there was nothing to see. By the 1960s, **mainframe** computers were equipped with **teleprinters**, a method that used a typewriter keyboard for putting in data, which was printed out simultaneously to make it visible. This was the prevalent technology in use until Phil Ray and Gus Roche, two engineers working for NASA (the United States National Aeronautics and Space Administration, which was at the time busy trying to put a man on the moon before the Russians would do so) started developing data input devices in combination with television screen technology. And that's what people who were using computers in the 1970s and early 1980s still remember, often fondly: flickering screens, usually green, with writing in crudely defined letters on them, and a blinking rectangular cursor that indicated where the next character would appear. ■ 355↘ ■

Being able to see immediately what you were doing obviously helped. At this point, though, and for a while longer, hardly any computers were able to actually process graphics. Some were. As far back as 1962, the American computer scientist Ivan Sutherland (b. 1938), then aged 24 and a PhD student at the Massachusetts Institute of Technology (MIT), had developed the first digital graphics program. *Sketchpad* ran on the transistor based *Lincoln TX-2* computer, which took up a significant amount of floor space at the Lincoln Laboratory and had a 64K 36-bit word **core memory**, meaning that it could handle 64 kilobytes worth of data in strings up to 36 bits long. For comparison: a single A4 page document, with ordinary formatting but without illustrations, in a normal word processing application, such as *Pages*, *Word*, or *OpenOffice*, takes up just about 65–70K of data. If you take out all the formatting and produce a **plain text file** with just the actual text, you can go to about sixty or seventy pages before you reach 64K. In 1958, when this machine was built at MIT's US Department of Defense funded and then world leading research institute, that was considered impressive, though it obviously limited the complexity of graphics that could be generated. Still, using an early light pen and a CRT **plotter display**, Sutherland was able to draw, store, and manipulate two dimensional technical drawings consisting of lines and curves, and in doing so he set the foundation for the **Graphical User Interface (GUI)** and all Computer Aided Design (CAD) technology that was to follow. ■ 287↘ ■ 334↘ □ ↖129

143 ● 244

The Lincoln TX-2 was one of a kind, and the personal computer had not yet made its appearance, so the machines most people used displayed 'images' – more image-like patterns – made of letters and numbers, the only building blocks available at the time. This was not without its charm: you could, by using, say, 20 × 30 letters and numbers, make an image that consisted of 600 individual characters, and if you chose them well, you were even able to give these images a sort of rough texture.

□ ↖229

Very early computer games employed this method of image representation to compelling effect, but it would be another fifteen years or so before the technology had sufficiently advanced, and refresh rates increased, enough to enable reasonably flicker-free white screen backgrounds. This is also the time when the mouse joins the keyboard as a standard input device, and the Graphical User Interface becomes widely available with the first consumer grade computer to feature both, the *Apple Mackintosh*, in 1984.

The scene is finally set for our chapter on Image & Colour.

144 ● 244

Dealing With Images & Colour

Sutherland's early achievements notwithstanding, up until about then – the mid-1980s – computing was of really very limited interest to architects. Architects live by inspiration, and much of that inspiration is, and has to be, visual. So while sketchbooks and photo cameras have long been the means by which we collect references and record architecture, and drawings and models have served us to make our yet-to-be-built projects visible, computing, for quite a while, seemed to have little to offer. (Computing was used by architect practices before then, but mostly in the preparation of item lists and budgets, and for word processing.)

From now on in though, from the moment affordable computers become capable of handling graphics, and computer screens capable of displaying them, information technology turns itself into a relevant tool for creative professionals. At first, and in the context of imagery, it does so perhaps more 441↘ to photographers than to architects, but with photography and architecture so closely entwined, the distinction soon matters little. CAD programs come into wide use (early ones, such as *AutoCAD* draw ■ ↖134 335↘ white lines on a black background, as the quality of monitors still isn't good enough to make it com- ■ 355↘ fortable for people to spend long hours in front of a bright screen) and architects start using computers to design and develop, and to manipulate images.

■
■

DISPLAYING IMAGES

VECTOR MONITORS

An early development in computer graphics came and went, leaving hardly any trace at all. Today, *vector monitors* are almost entirely a thing of the past, but at a time when computer memory commanded a premium, and when it was therefore of great practical advantage to be able to draw on-screen graphics with small amounts of data, they proved useful, because, as their name suggests, they do not have to address each point that makes up an image individually, but instead define the beginning and end points of lines as vectors.

Vector monitors were all based on CTR technology and thus worked like oscillographs; but here the cathode ray followed the path of defined lines, rather than tracing each available point on the display line by line horizontally, as it does in conventional monitors. Some types of vector monitors had the additional advantage (in certain contexts) that they used phosphors which stayed illuminated for several minutes after the electron beam had passed over them. This meant that they did not have to refresh many times a second, which in turn made them flicker-free and considerably brighter than ordinary vector displays. The downside of this was that the drawn image would stay on the display until the entire screen was wiped clean with a bright flash, which made the technology unsuitable for any type of application where images change often or constantly, such as in animation or CAD drawing in real time.

145 ● 245

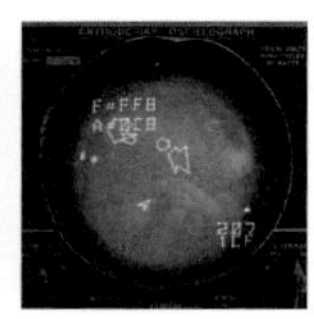

146 ● 245

RASTER GRAPHICS, BITMAPS, AND COLOUR DEPTH

The display technology we still use today – and have been using since the early 1980s – does not rely on **vector graphics**, but employs *raster graphics* as the principle by which it composes images on the screen. Up until the early 1990s, **VDUs (Visual Display Units)** had cathode ray tubes, of much the same kind as televisions did of the same era; and from about then onwards **LCD (Liquid-Crystal Display)** or **TFT LCD (Thin-Film-Transistor Liquid-Crystal Display)** technology took over, making possible the laptop by illuminating individual dots on a flat liquid crystal matrix. Either way, a raster graphics display treats each point that makes up the image on the two-dimensional plane as a separate *pixel* and defines that point to a given *colour depth*.

In order to handle a picture made up of pixels, the computer has to create a file that stores information about each one of them, which is why raster graphics images are data intensive: the more pixels they contain, the more data needs to be generated to define these pixels. And the same again is true for colour depth: the computer needs to tell the screen (or the printer, for that matter) whether the pixel has any colour at all or not, and if so, what the colour is. At the lowest, or shallowest, level of colour depth, the image has two colours only. Typically, these are (but don't have to be) black and white. The amount of data required for one pixel is precisely one bit: it can be either one colour (for example white), 0, or the other (for example black), 1.

One pixel though does not amount to much of an image. Depending on their size, a hundred of them can already constitute, if not perhaps a very intricate image, then a discernible pattern. But really if we want to be talking about pictures, even monochrome ones, we need to have a resolution of a few hundred pixels in each direction, horizontal and vertical. One such resolution in use with early VDUs was determined by the **VGA (Video Graphics Array)** standard at 640 × 480 pixels, back in 1987. This amounts to 307,200 pixels in total, which means that for a monochrome image consisting of strictly two colours only, the computer has to process and store 307,200 bits.

The file that the computer generates, or reads, is a *bitmap*: it records each pixel and for each pixel its colour. (It's really a list, but since the order in which pixels are listed is pre-defined and unvarying, it works just like a map). In this case, because we are dealing with a monochrome image, the bitmap contains one bit per pixel, making this simplest type of image file a *one-bit colour* image. Mathematically, this is an image that has 2 to the power of 1 (2^1) colours and therefore bits per pixel.

If we now want to add another colour, we have to do so in line with the 2 to the power of x table, because in binary computing (as opposed to, say, quantum computing) a bit can only ever have two options, 0 or 1, no more and no fewer, and so if we add to the bit that defines the first colour another bit that defines the second colour, then we necessarily have 2 × 2 = 2^2 = 4 colours. A two-bit colour image then requires 2 bits per pixel, so that our VGA image with 640 × 480 pixels now becomes twice as large in terms of data, while keeping exactly the same size on the screen.

In this same manner, colours can be added, and the colour depth increased:

- 1-bit colour: 2^1 = 2 colours
- 2-bit colour: 2^2 = 4 colours
- 3-bit colour: 2^3 = 8 colours
- 4-bit colour: 2^4 = 16 colours
- 5-bit colour: 2^5 = 32 colours
- 6-bit colour: 2^6 = 64 colours
- 7-bit colour: 2^7 = 128 colours
- 8-bit colour: 2^8 = 256 colours

256 colours yield an image we certainly recognise as 'in colour', and in fact the 8-bit colour depth is of particular significance, because for many years it marked the ceiling of what was achievable online, since the widely used and popular **GIF (Graphics Interchange Format)**, which was developed for the early American Internet software provider CompuServe in 1987, could not handle more than that. But the human eye is capable of discerning some ten million different hues and shades, and today's high quality displays have what is known as a **true colour** depth, which at 24 bits (2^{24}) gives each pixel a range of 16,777,216 possible colour tones. Correspondingly large is the file size and therefore data storage and processing requirement for this type of file.

2^{24} conveniently happens to be 256 × 256 × 256, which means that if each pixel on a screen is broken down into three sub-pixels, one for each of the three principal colours red, green, and blue, then each of these sub-pixels once again has a perfectly passable 8-bit colour depth on its own, combining with its fellow pixels for the other colour groups to true colour depth at 24 bits. Contemporary LCD screens use this subpixel principle.

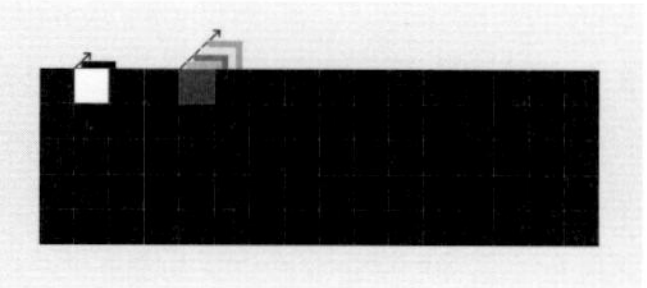

147 ○ 304

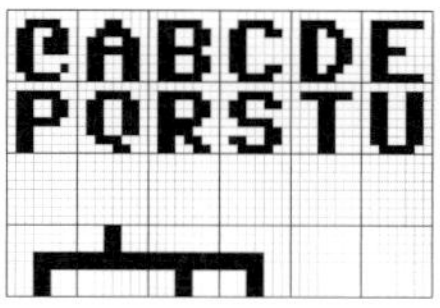

148 ● 245

149A ● 245

149B ● 246

149C ● 246

CREATING & CAPTURING IMAGES AND PRINTING THEM

Drawing directly with a computer is one of several ways of getting an image onto the computer to work with it. The first widely used interactive input method that made this possible was the mouse. But the mouse, for all its many obvious qualities, is a clumsy tool when it comes to intricate drawings, which is where the **graphic tablet** (or **drawing tablet**) comes in, as it allows the user to draw on a flat surface with an electronic stylus or pen, emulating the actions used in analogue painting and drawing. Similar, pressure sensitive, 'penabled' pens can also be used in combination with today's consumer gadget touch screens, to achieve much greater precision than is possible purely by hand. (Today we are so used to using smartphone touchscreen technology that we think it ordinary, but it wasn't until Apple released the first *iPhone* in 2007 that touchscreen technology really came into its own and became part of the average user's daily life, even though in professional contexts it had been around for a while.)

All these input methods – mouse, trackpad, graphic tablet, touchscreen – have their development roots in the middle of the twentieth century (some even earlier), but it was from the 1980s onwards that genuine strides were being made towards how we use them today.

150A ● 246

150B ● 246

THE FAX INTERLUDE

One afternoon in 1987, at the London offices of a well-established global newspaper and magazine publishing house, a group of dignitaries were shown the company's impressive, industrial-scale facsimile machine. The machine, it was explained to them, would take the full size newspaper page that was set there in London, and transmit it electronically, via international telephone cables, a few thousand miles across land and see to one of several printing centres dotted around the globe, where the page could then be printed out for that region on the same day, making international newspaper distribution not only fast and efficient but also highly cost effective. The dignitaries from politics and assorted royalty watched in wonder as the tray with said newspaper page on it slowly whirred into the machine, and, after a few short minutes whirred out again. 'Ah!' one of them exclaimed in admiration: 'and they send it right back again!'

The *fax* made a relatively short appearance on the technology horizon of general use: from the early to mid-1980s onwards it became omnipresent in offices, replacing telegraph and telegram as the preferred method for sending written communication at speed across a distance. Both these older, analogue, telephony based systems had the drawback that they could generally cope only with Roman characters, which is one of the reasons why fax technology found ready adoption and still remains in use today in countries that use logograms as opposed to alphabets, particularly in the Far East. Fax machines scan the page and then transmit it – as either an analogue or a digital signal – over the existing phone line to another fax machine, which *demodulates* the page and prints it out. A fax therefore is in principle a remote scanner, and it was a small step from making machines that could read written characters on a page and print them out in a different location, to making machines that could also read pictures (at first only black and white, soon also in colour) and print them out on the spot. (A fax machine reads the page line by line and then reconstructs it again at the other end line by line as well. To achieve colour you have to have at least three light sensors that scan the page for three colours, instead of just one, from which you then compose the output colours. We'll be talking more about colour profiles below.)

151A ● 246

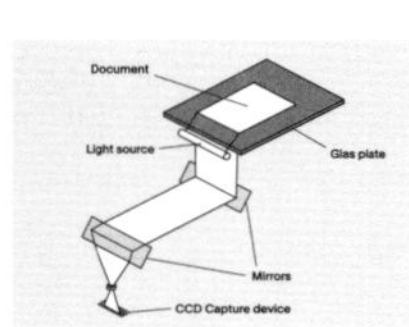

151B ● 246

SCANNERS & CAMERAS

Among the first people who wanted to be able to work with pictures on a computer were not only designers and pioneering architects, or anybody else wishing to draw by computer and then manipulate the drawings, but photographers. And for a while it wasn't digital photographs they were keen on handling, so much as their analogue pictures. (Digital cameras did not come into wide use until the mid to late 1990s, and in this area professionals were not necessarily first to the table: many photographers held on to their analogue equipment and working practices simply because they liked the quality, character and workflow of shooting pictures on film and developing them in the darkroom.) But if you create masterful photography on film, of which you then produce gorgeous prints, and you want to further manipulate these images on a computer you have to find a way of digitalising them.

There are two principal ways in which a two dimensional representation can be copied: either by photography (which then makes it possible to print the copy out as what it is, a photographically achieved duplicate, and photocopying machines have been doing this successfully since the American company Xerox introduced xerography to the mass market in 1959), or by scanning the page and breaking it down into individually addressable and manageable micro-components, namely pixels, which we can then manipulate and work with. In this precise basic difference lies the 'selling point' of a scanner over a photocopier or any other pre-digital camera technology. Because while scanning a page line by line – defining for each line a large number of individual dots by their hue and intensity – is time-consuming and requires processing power and a software component that can do so, it results in the kind of file we are already familiar with: a bitmap. And with a bitmap we can do anything we like. The other potential advantage of a scanner over a camera is that camera generated reproductions of flat images are prone to angle distortions, about which more in a moment.

(Today, most of us carry around with us a high resolution digital camera that's built into our smartphone, and so for quick practical uses taking a picture of a document may not only be as valid as scanning it, it may also quite simply be the only option available since not every plan, image, or other document can either be removed from where it is, or be adequately scanned by an app on your phone or a mobile scanner.)

Office scanners in turn have their own limitations, and as with any technology, you get the best results if you calibrate them to your particular use. To this date, most scanners have their own bespoke software, giving a relatively simple piece of basic machinery quite a range of optimisation settings. So here is a quick breakdown of the most important types of scan you may want to consider having at your disposal:

OFFICE MODE VS PROFESSIONAL MODE:

Some scanners distinguish between *'office mode'*, which is mainly for text-based documents or documents with non-critical illustrations, and *'professional mode'*, for high end photographic purposes.

SCAN SETTINGS: These are settings that directly affect the actual scan, such as:

- DPI (Dots Per Inch) value (controls resolution and therefore image size)
- Grid line removal filter
- Dust and scratch reduction filter
- Gutter shadow correction

Examples of settings that may be adjustable during a scan include:

- Horizontal and vertical resolution (image size)
- Brightness
- Contrast
- Gamma
- Histogram

All of which can also be further adjusted in post-production.

In the early days of scanning technology – the late 1980s – there was not as yet any software available to actually do anything with the scanned images. So in March 1989, the scanner company Barneyscan started shipping with its machines a software package it called *Barneyscan XP*. This was in fact version 0.87 of what barely a year later, in February 1990, hit the market as version 1.0 of *Photoshop* and then quickly became the industry standard in raster graphics based image editing, which it still dominates today.

What you also needed to work with your scanned image was an **Applications Programming Interface (API)** that could handle the communication between an image manipulation software, such as *Photoshop*, and the scanner, or any other imaging device, such as a digital camera. The authors of this software were a working group of industry programmers and developers, and they called themselves TWAIN, drawing on the rich tradition of idiosyncratic and often deliberately imaginative information technology nomenclature by referring to the poem *The Ballad of East and West* by English writer Rudyard Kipling (1865–1936), which happens to be one of the most mis-quoted and therefore misunderstood poems in the history of the English language. In it, Kipling says:

> *Oh, East is East and West is West, and never the twain shall meet,*

Which some people use to support an argument that the cultures of East and West are so different and incompatible that they can never get on with each other, ignoring the subsequent three lines which explain exactly the circumstances under which they can:

> *Till Earth and Sky stand presently at God's great Judgment Seat;*
> *But there is neither East nor West, Border, nor Breed, nor Birth,*
> *When two strong men stand face to face, though they come from the ends of the earth!*

The software programmers of TWAIN, unlike many politicians, social historians, and culturally segregative campaigners, understood Kipling perfectly and set about to make two things meet that were really rather different and that, at first sight, might look like they could never be working together to the same end: hardware and software. So they appropriated the word *twain* and spelt it in all caps, to make it more distinctive. In the process, they also made it look like an acronym, which bewildered those people who want their capitalised names to stand for something. This went so far that a competition was held to turn it into a 'backronym' and define its meaning retroactively. No winner was ever chosen, but the one that more or less stuck, and that is listed in some places as the 'official' definition of the term is: *Technology Without an Interesting Name* which, incidentally, makes it stop just short of becoming a recursive acronym, being, as it is, self-referential but not actually mentioning its own name...

152A ● 247

152B ● 247

152C ● 247

153A ● 247

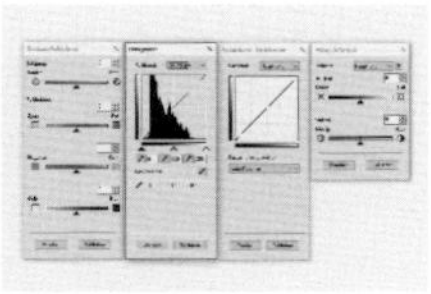

153B ● 247

■ 469↘

INPUT AND OUTPUT RESOLUTION – PPI (PIXELS PER INCH) / DPI (DOTS PER INCH) 441↘

You will find the terms *PPI (Pixels Per Inch)* and *DPI (Dots Per Inch)* used interchangeably, although they don't mean exactly the same thing. They mean such similar things though that the distinction is perhaps relevant here mostly for the sake of accuracy and to avoid confusion, as it isn't strictly necessary. Both denote image density or resolution by telling us how many individual raster elements there are along a given constant stretch, namely one inch (2.54 cm). For a high number of pixels or dots to fit along one inch, they have to be small, leading to a high image density and high resolution; whereas a low number of pixels or dots requires that these are comparatively large, which leads to a low density and therefore low resolution image.

This is exactly the same for both the PPI and the DPI measurements, the difference being solely that *pixels per inch* is really an *input resolution*, referring, as it does, to the number of pixels the input will result in once they are arranged on the screen, whereas *dots per inch* is an *output resolution*, telling us how many dots the printer will place on the page.

What a given PPI actually looks like on the screen depends entirely on the pixel density of the screen itself. Old CRT monitors, as we have noted, for years made do with a VGA resolution of 640 × 480 pixels. If you were to pack these into a tiny patch, then you would get quite a high pixel density, but your average VGA monitor had dimensions of maybe 12" × 9" (the standard aspect ratio then being 4:3), which meant that you had a pretty rough resolution. Today, it is absolutely common for a laptop to have a full **HD (High Definition)** display approximating 1920 × 1080 pixels (the standard ratio now being 16:9) which amounts to 2,304,000 pixels over an area that measures 15" diagonally; and a top of the range *MacBook Pro*, for example, in 2020 sports a native resolution of 3072 × 1920 or just shy of 6 million pixels over 16 inches diagonally.

PPI, then, does not give us any indication of the image size itself or its definition, but of how densely packed the image pixels are on the screen. The same full HD image that takes up a whole HD screen (no matter how big it is) will only occupy less than a quarter of the currently highest definition screens that are available to consumers: a **4K UHD (Ultra High Definition)** display packs no fewer than 8 million pixels onto the screen. (4K gets its name from the fact that along its longest side it has nearly four thousand pixels. The actual number is 3840 or, because of its wider aspect ratio, 4096 for **Digital Cinema Projection [DCP]**.)

A normal desktop display today is likely to measure no more than about 27" to 30" diagonally (they come in larger sizes too, but for a piece of equipment that sits directly in front of you to work with, these become impractical). So if a 27" screen has a standard HD resolution, then that means that along its baseline, which with an HD aspect ratio of 16:9 would have to be 23.5" long, it has 81.7 pixels per inch (which corresponds to 32 pixels per centimetre). This means that one pixel at this PPI is 0.3125 mm wide (and normally also as high, since pixels are usually square). In 2012, Apple registered the term *Retina Display* as a trademark, referring to very high resolution screens first used on the *iPhone* and then also its other product families. So called because at a normal viewing distance the human eye is no longer capable of identifying individual pixels on them, *Retina Displays* have a PPI resolution of around 300–400.

(You may wonder, in passing, how it is that up until the 4K display, screen and monitor sizes are given in diagonal measurements: the tradition stems from the early days of television. Those black and white TVs had round cathode ray tubes, so the relevant measurement for their size was the diameter. When broadcasters adopted 4:3 as a standard aspect ratio, this was close enough to a square to make it acceptable to still only keep the now slightly elongated 'diameter', the diagonal, as the single measurement, not least because it was a number that was easy to understand and bore a relation to what people were already used to. Though it is also possible that TV manufacturers found it convenient that the diagonal was always a bigger number than, say, the width of the box. Whether or not that was the case, it's a practice that has since been abandoned: 4K screens, as we just noted, refer to the baseline, not to the diagonal, even though the baseline is always shorter.)

With DPI, we no longer speak of pixels but of dots, and here as at the input end, DPI simply tells us how many dots line up along one inch. As with the display, the more dots fit, the smaller they have to be, the smoother and more highly resolved the picture becomes.

The two most common DPI (often spelt lower case 'dpi') values you will come across are 72 dpi, which is the de-facto Internet standard as it results in images of a density that is considered sufficient for everyday online use and allows for moderate file sizes, and 300 dpi which is the standard minimum density required to print photographic images to professional quality

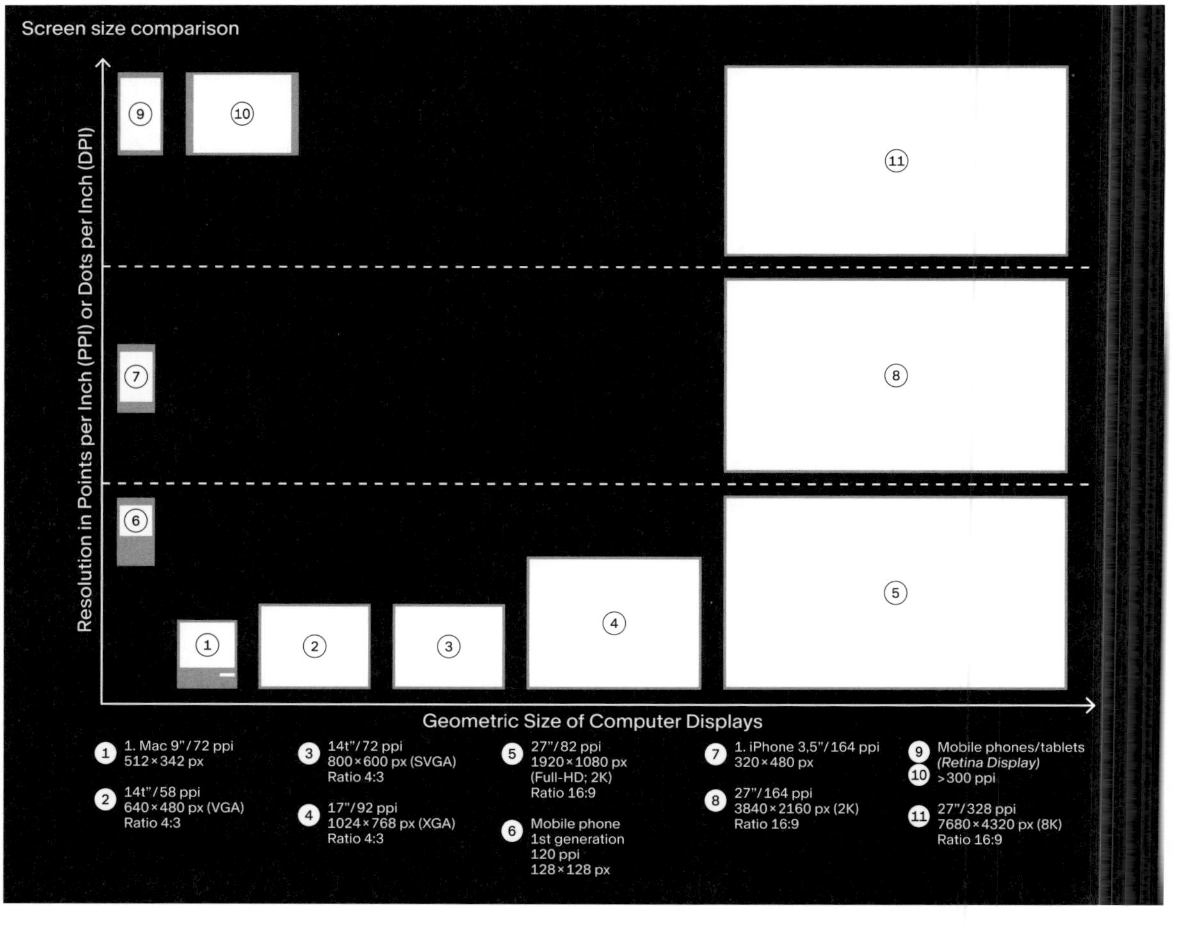

COLOUR PROFILES

Another, and in practical terms far more significant, difference between the image on screen and the printed image lies in the way colour is managed. Not the only available, but by far the most commonly used, colour model for digital cameras and computers of any kind is RGB, an additive colour model that takes its name from the three colours Red, Green, and Blue. When they appear as light, these can be added together to create virtually any colour the human eye is able to discern, including white, which results from all colours being added on top of each other at equal level. Black, here, is the absence of light and therefore does not have to be 'created', as the base colour of the un-illuminated screen is expected to be black or a close enough approximation to black.

Printing works not with light but with ink, and the background onto which the vast majority of documents and images are printed is expected to be white or an approximation to white. What's needed here, therefore, is a subtractive colour model, which takes away whiteness (or its equivalent, if you print on coloured paper, for example) from the page that is being printed on. The most widely used colour model of this kind is CMYK, which stands for the printing ink colours Cyan, Magenta, Yellow, and 'Key'. 'Key' tends to be black, which is why sometimes the model is also referred to as CMYB, with B standing for Black. In printing, the 'key' colour, or 'key plate', or 'key line' colour, is the colour that is used to give image contours sharp and clear edges.

The visual appearance of both profiles, RGB and CMYK, is very much device dependent, which means that the same image can look significantly different from one display to another (depending on their luminosity and calibration); and the same again is true for printed images, whose look will depend on the inks used and how the printer is calibrated. Furthermore, because the RGB profile can't be printed directly, any image created in it will have to be converted to a printable one such as CMYK, and as there is no standard conversion protocol, there can be great variations between the two colour profiles for the same image. Some, but not all, image post-production programs offer the user an option to save images with the CMYK profile.

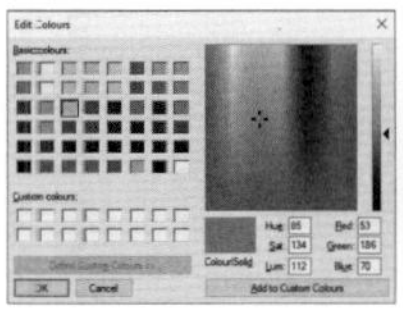

154A ○ 304

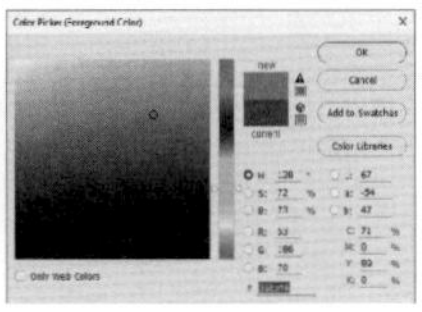

154B ○ 304

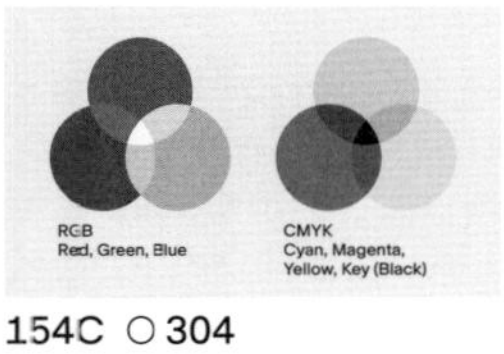

154C ○ 304

RASTER VS VECTOR GRAPHICS

As we saw when we briefly looked at the now obsolete vector monitor technology, there are two principally different ways in which a computer can treat an image. Either as a raster of a finite number of individual pixels or dots, each of which is discrete and can be addressed and manipulated separately, or as a set of vectors whose start and end points are defined, with all other pixels or dots in-between arranging themselves accordingly.

The advantage of a raster image is that because each point is treated individually, it can also be changed, manipulated, and erased individually. This is especially useful when dealing with photography and similarly intricate pictures. Creating graphics from scratch, however, is much more difficult pixel by pixel. Which is why CAD and other graphics programs, including some picture editing software, use the Cartesian coordinate system to define objects ↖183
which are then either saved as vectors or treated as vectors for as long as this is practical, before being converted into raster graphics. Similarly, entire vector graphics images can easily be converted into raster images, and the reverse is also possible, though less frequently applied.

The great advantage of vector graphics is that they allow objects (such as squares, circles, lines) to be treated as editable entities that can be scaled up without loss of definition or quality. By contrast, an element or layer that is defined as a group of pixels will, in scaling up, lose definition, because the computer has to 'invent' new pixels as the element grows in size, to fill in the previously undefined space. Also, and as we've already seen, as long as you're dealing with a comparatively small number of objects, vector graphics require much smaller data sets to be processed because you are defining only two coordinates for each vector, as opposed to all the pixels the object is made up of individually.

155A ● 248

155B ● 248

155C ● 248

ANTI-ALIASING

Because pixels on a screen and dots on a page are arranged orthogonally, horizontal and vertical lines always appear crystal clear and exactly as defined, both in raster and vector graphics, no matter how densely they are packed. Any slanted lines, curves, or circles though have to be composed of (normally) square pixels, which means that on all but the highest definitions there comes a zoom level at which these lines are no longer smooth. *Anti-aliasing* software compensates for this by filling the 'jagged' edges with pixels that have a colour tone that lies between the object line colour and the background. This makes them look smoother, but also less sharp.

The method is used not only in graphics but also in the representation of text on screen. In this case, it is called subpixel rendering, meaning that diagonals are first calculated at a finer resolution, and then the anti-aliasing effect is applied. Introduced in 2000, Microsoft calls its version *ClearType*, Apple does the same thing under the name *CoolType*. The technique takes advantage of the fact that, as we briefly mentioned above, on contemporary LCD displays each pixel consists of three sub pixels, in the basic colours red, green, and blue. (On most commonly used LCD screens for mobile phones, the sub pixels are arranged horizontally, which is why the effect does not work when the display is looked at from an acute angle.)

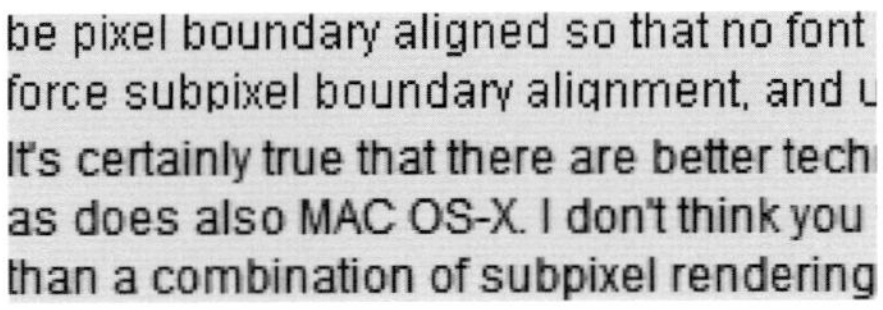

156 ○ XXX

HANDLING IMAGES

BITS & BYTES

Every piece of information that we can in one way or another interpret and do anything with – be that a letter, a number, or a pixel – has to be encoded in binary digits (1s and 0s) if a computer is to process it. (Again, we are here talking strictly about our ordinary, digital computing; what we are saying in this chapter does not apply to quantum computing, which is as yet in its infancy.)

This is why we refer to each individual 0 or 1 of computer code as a *bit*, a contraction of 'binary digit'. While it is possible to define a pixel with just one bit, most pieces of information require more than that, since one bit only allows for two possible options, but there are hundreds of characters and millions of colours. For example, and as we saw when discussing colour depth, to achieve a true colour image, we need 24 bits per pixel. Letters, numbers, and commands being so essential to computing from the beginning, a standard was agreed on in 1963, defining a first character set made up of the Roman alphabet, the numbers 0 to 9, the most frequently used punctuation marks, and some commands. This is the still familiar ASCII (American Standard Code for Information Interchange) table, of which we speak in more detail in our chapter on Text, Typography & Layout. As we also saw earlier, groups of bits have to come in numbers that are powers to 2, because one bit has two options and two options only: 0 or 1. Up until ASCII was agreed on, there were various smaller character sets in use, but ASCII defined 128 characters, which is 2 to the power of 7, making this a 7-bit code standard. This meant that any letter could be encoded with a group of 7 binary digits or bits.

■ 330↘ □ 327↘ ■

By this time, the word byte had already established itself to describe the group of bits which defines the smallest unit of information that both a human and a computer can understand. It was German-born American computer scientist Werner Buchholz (1922–2018) who had coined the term in 1956 while working for IBM (International Business Machines). He wanted a word that would be similar enough to the word 'bit' to allude to it, but different enough not to get confused with it, which is why he went for the spelling with a y. Non-specialists have confused the two ever since…

Today, we tend to define one byte as an 8-bit binary code, mainly because in the 1970s it was 8-bit microprocessors that began to dominate the market, while at the same time the universally accepted ASCII set was extended to 256 characters, which also required 8 bits, 256 being 2 to the power of 8.

Our true colour depth image with its 24 bits per pixel thus generates three groups of 8 bits or 3 bytes of data per pixel. This means that a standard smartphone picture today with a resolution of 2448 × 3264 pixels (note how the numbers are still divisible by 8), which therefore has 7,990,272 or just under 8 megapixels, would generate 24 megabytes (MB) of data that has to be stored, accessed, and processed. We say 'would', because it soon dawned on people that if computers were to do this at a practical speed, ways would need to be found of compacting these files to more manageable sizes.

157A ○ 305

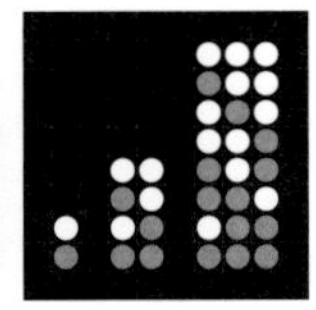
157B ○ 305

FILE FORMATS

UNCOMPRESSED

As far as the computer is concerned, a digital image, like any other set of data, is simply a string of bytes, each of which, we established nowadays tends to contain 8 bits; and a simple and effective method to store and process this set of data is as a bitmap. The bitmap is therefore not only a generic term for an image file, but it is also an uncompressed file format with the extension .bmp, and it could be considered to be the *urformat* for digital images developed by Windows in the 1980s.

Uncompressed file formats have the advantage that they preserve the image in its original quality without any loss either in colour depth or definition, and you don't have to spend processing time or power on converting the file. In situations where file size is not an issue these formats can therefore be entirely useful, especially where image quality and integrity are of paramount importance. This is also why professional image editing programs allow you to store uncompressed pictures in bitmap or raw formats.

Raw formats get their name from the fact that they are not yet (or only minimally) processed, which is why they are sometimes considered to be the digital equivalent of the analogue negative. A raw file is usually one generated by a camera or scanner, and it contains all the data captured by the device's sensor, together with some additional information, such as image metadata about the time and location of its capture, camera, and lens model, exposure data; also about the size and colour profile of the sensor, and possibly a densely compressed thumbnail image, among others.

There is no raw file standard, and so there are almost as many formats in use today as there are camera or scanner manufacturers, with a correspondingly large number of different file extensions.

In order to be able to actually work with a raw file and manipulate it in a post-production process, it has to be converted into a standard RGB profile, and there are numerous software applications and plugins available that can do this, both proprietary and open-source.

LOSSLESS THROUGH LINE COMPRESSION
It is possible to save on data volume by compressing blank and identical lines of bit code (for example where colours are repeated) for the purpose of storage, and then decompressing or expanding them again for the purpose of display, handling, and printing. A typical format that does this is the **Tagged Image File Format (TIFF)** with the file extension *.tif* or *.tiff*, which is one of the standards used in printing because it can handle printer-specific 'colour spaces' (the way in which colour is organised, for example as an RGB or as a CMYK profile), though less so online, as not all web browsers support it. (TIFF can also be used as a 'lossy' format to achieve greater reduction in file size.)

For example, consider a screen containing plain white text on a solid black background. There will be many long runs of black pixels in the blank space, and many short runs of white pixels within the text. A hypothetical scan line, with B representing a black pixel and W representing white, might read as follows:

```
BBBBBBBBBBBBWBBBBBBBBBBBBWWWBBBBBBBBBBBBBBBBB
BBBWWBBBBBBBBBBBBBB
```

With a **Run-Length Encoding (RLE)** data compression algorithm applied to the above hypothetical scan line, it can be rendered as follows:

```
12B1W12B3W20B2W14B
```

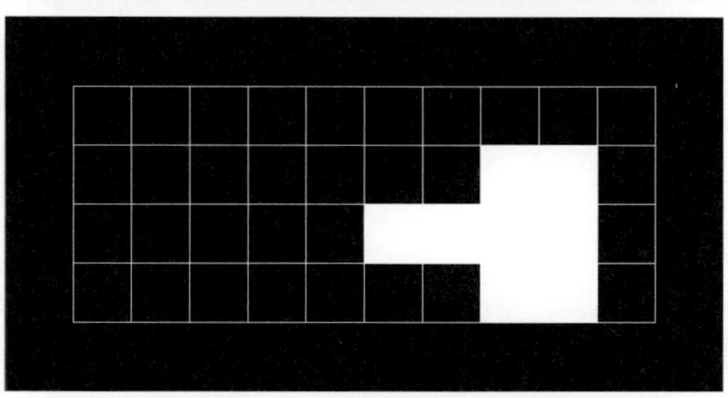

```
B B B B B B B B B B
B B B B B B B W W B
B B B B B W W W W B
B B B B B B B W W B
```

```
= 10B
  7B2W1B
  5B4W1B
  7B2W1B
```

WITH COLOUR LOSS
In the early days of the Internet, when a standard modem would connect you to the world at a speed of 56 kilobytes per second (compared to 50–60 megabytes per second that a decent WiFi connection achieves today), file size was a main issue that needed to be addressed, and the Graphics Interchange Format (GIF) developed by CompuServe with the extension *.gif* did so by limiting the colour depth to 256, which generates our familiar 8-bit image. GIFs, which its inventor Steve Wilhite insists should be pronounced 'jif', although the Oxford English Dictionary and many users consider both *'gif'* and *'jif'* acceptable pronunciation variants, is still widely used for animated online images, because of its compact file sizes.

LOSSY COMPRESSION
Not the only, but by far the most popular and most widely used file compression format for images was developed by the **Joint Photographic Experts Group (JPEG)**, which was a body set up by the International Organization for Standardization (ISO) and the International Electrotechnical Commission (IEC) in 1986, lending the format both its name and its extensions *.jpeg* and *.jpg*.

The compression algorithm used by JPEG leads to a loss of image quality that can be instantly noticeable, depending on the level of compression, but its great advantage lies in the fact that the user can set this level and thus adjust the image quality to the given context: a small picture online will require a far lower resolution than a poster size image that is actually going to be printed out and hung on a wall somewhere. Towards the upper end, an image compression to 'high' or 'best' level is often impossible to tell apart from the original, while still yielding substantial savings in data volume. Many digital cameras therefore also use the JPEG format to optimise their storage capacity.

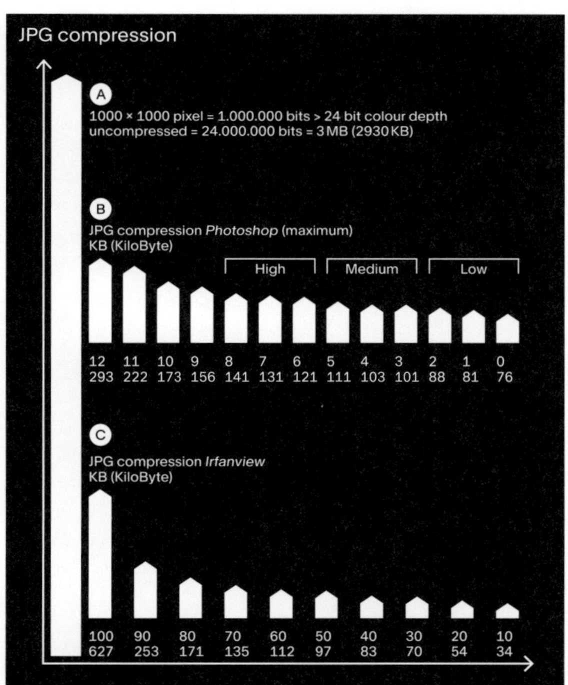

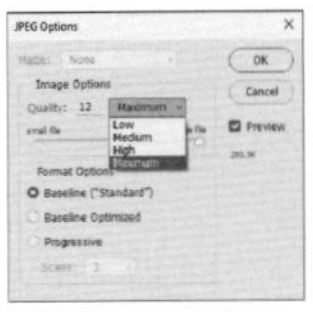
158A ● 248

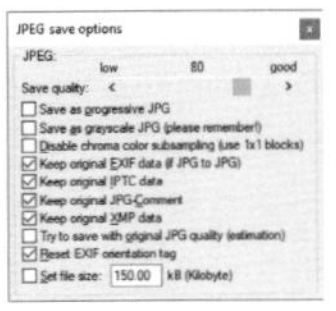
158B ● 248

158C ● 248

158D ● 248

158E ● 249

158F ● 249

IMAGE MANAGEMENT

Any image, whether generated on a computer, shot on a digital camera, or scanned, not only has to be processed and stored but also managed: filed, indexed, and sorted, so it can be retrieved and used in relevant contexts. Basic metadata, such as date and time when the image was created, when it was last edited, or its size and format, are all displayed in both *Explorer* and *Finder*: the respective native file management software for *Windows* and Apple *Mac* computers. But most image editing software contains management tools that allow the user to not only change the file name, but keep additional data, such as keywords or search terms and – this may be particularly useful in large image collections – image ratings.

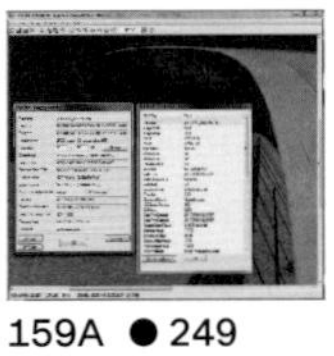
159A ● 249

159B ● 249

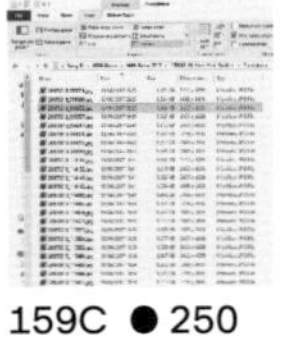
159C ● 250

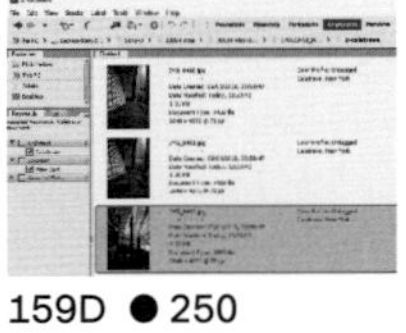
159D ● 250

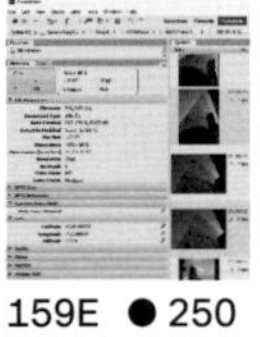
159E ● 250

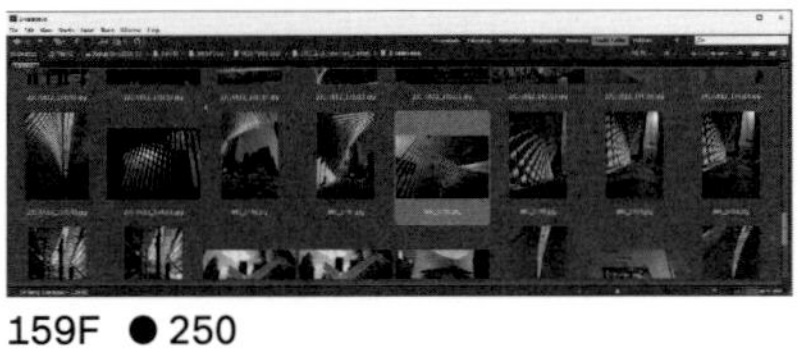
159F ● 250

FILE NAMING OF DIGITAL PHOTOS

Early digital cameras stuck to the old Microsoft file naming limitation of a maximum of 8 characters plus file extension (of normally three characters). Which is why to this date you will find digital pictures given names by their cameras like this:

□ 255↘

- DSC00001.jpg
- DSC00002.jpg
- DSC00003.jpg
- DSC04738.jpg

DSC stands for *Digital Still Camera* (as opposed to video camera). Other variants include:

- DSCN0007.jpg

With the N here denoting the camera manufacturer *Nikon*, or:

- P0000006.jpg

The P standing for *Panasonic*.

In the age of the smartphone, naming convention has moved on to a totally different principle, for example date and timecode, such as:

- 20180125_125801.jpg
- 20180125_132522.jpg
- 20180130_071805.jpg

The smartphone is also responsible for the inclusion of geodata (such as location and the direction in which the picture was taken) into the **Exif** data of picture files. *Exif* is really an acronym for **Exchangeable Image File Format**, and should therefore strictly be called *EXIFF*, but the body that originally specified it in 1998, the Japan Electronic Industries Development Association (JEIDA), which itself has since undergone a merger and is now known as JEITA (Japan Electronics and Information Technology Industries Association), apparently insists on spelling it *Exif*.

IMAGE EDITING

Entire atlases can be, have been, and continue to be written about working with images, but for architects, the most relevant categories of image post-production are probably these:

PHOTOGRAPHY: DISTORTION CORRECTION, DETAIL SELECTION, AND IMAGE RETOUCHING

DISTORTION CORRECTION: If you take a picture of a tall building and you do so from the ground up, your perspective will naturally distort the building, making it appear thinner the further away from your camera it reaches. Similarly, structures appear distorted on a horizontal line if they are pictured at anything other than a right angle. We're entirely used to this, and for many day-to-day uses, our brain simply compensates for it and we get the idea of what the building 'really looks like', even though we're looking at a distortion. But in architecture photography it may be important (or simply desirable) to have a correct proportional representation. This is where distortion correction comes into play: it allows you to adjust the image in any direction to eliminate optical distortions. (We also talk about this subject briefly in our chapter on Rendering.)

160A ● 251

160B ● 251

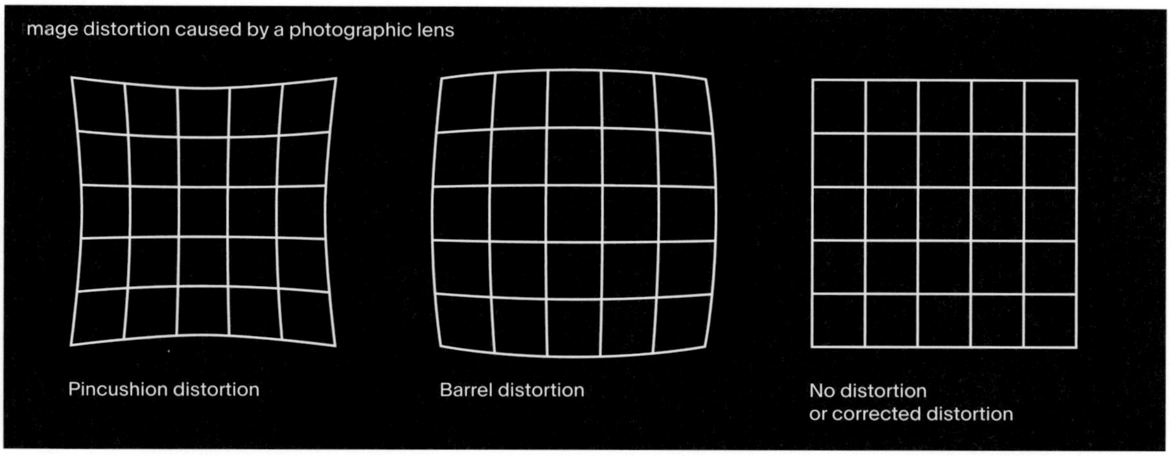

DETAIL SELECTION / FRAMING: It sounds like stating the obvious, but framing can make or break a picture. What you choose to show, and where within the frame you place it, radically affects how I as the viewer see the object. It's worth playing around with this and getting a feel for how big the differences are. Especially where your intention is on creating a striking image, your most effective tool above all else may often simply be framing: choosing an angle and a part of the whole that says something specific about the object.

161A ● 251

161B ● 251

IMAGE RETOUCHING: The reason 'to photoshop' exists as a verb is that the dominant picture editing software is, and has been since its launch, *Photoshop*. But of course it's not the only one, and even basic, free, or open-source applications will allow you to manipulate all manner of aspects of a picture.

Setting aside colour correction, light, and focus adjustments – which we'll come to in a moment – retouching may involve the removal of unwanted objects or elements, applying artistic filters to achieve a particular look or feel, changing or adjusting the background, or deliberately altering the appearance of the subject altogether. This can quickly veer into problematical areas where ethical and legal considerations play a part. In fashion photography, for example, making models look thinner and far more flawless than they can be in real life has given rise to extensive debates about body image and the culture of propagating levels of slimness that can become dangerous when aspired to by young people.

In architecture the question of truthfulness can also become relevant, although perhaps in very different ways. Removing traffic from a busy road, for example, or beautifying a neighbourhood, is potentially very dubious practice when you're trying to sell a property, but using the same manipulated picture in a book about the architect's style or their period might be a perfectly acceptable way of giving the publication itself an overall better appearance.

162A ● 252

162B ● 252

PHOTOGRAPHY:
LIGHT, COLOUR, AND FOCUS
All of these three elements can be manipulated to great effect in image post-production, but with varying ease. A badly lit picture – either vastly overexposed or way too dark – provides time-consuming challenges, because the editing software can only deal with the information that's stored in the image file, and where that information lacks contour and texture, it's really hard to get anything decent out of the picture. That said, even consumer level digital cameras and higher end phone cameras capture extraordinary levels of detail, even in bad lighting.

Similarly, focus can be corrected, and you can get some beautiful 'tilt shift' effects by deliberately blurring part of the picture you're not that interested in, to concentrate the attention of the viewer on the part of the picture that matters. But taking a good, in-focus picture in the first place is really the key to success.

Colour, on the other hand, is a breeze in post and can be added, adjusted, subtly or radically changed, at will and with ease. It's the simplest and most effective way to give a picture an immediate look, and to define an artistic style: super saturated, subtly faded, earthy toned, or in brilliant primaries: the same picture will take on many different appearances and communicate something completely different in each one.

163A ○ 305

163B ○ 305

163C ○ 305

163D ○ 305

□ 285↘
□ 255↘

SPECIAL EFFECTS:
STEREO, PANORAMA, AND HDR
(HIGH DYNAMIC RANGE) PHOTOGRAPHY

Contemporary digital cameras come with a range of photographic and lens effects that further widen the scope for creativity in visually representing architecture (or anything else, obviously).

STEREO EFFECT / STEREOSCOPY: This adds depth to the image by simulating a 3D or 3D-like appearance to an ordinary 2D photograph. The technique is not new (it dates back to the early days of photography, in the 19th century), and can be achieved either with a stereo lens (two lenses), as a digital camera effect, or digitally in post-production.

PANORAMA: Many cameras allow you to take super-wide angle pictures by effectively scanning the landscape from left to right. A similar result can also be achieved by physically or digitally 'sticking' together a series of individually taken pictures.

HDR High Dynamic Range photography also is not new (the idea can similarly be traced to the mid 19th century), and long before digital
■ 307↘ photography photographers have used **tone mapping** techniques to layer pictures taken at different exposures on top of each other, combining them to one image with ideal exposure throughout. The dynamic range here refers to the luminosity of an image: by increasing this, the image acquires a greater vibrancy and clarity than a standard dynamic range allows. Contemporary digital cameras mostly have an HDR setting that can simply be enabled or disabled.

CAD RENDERINGS (PERSPECTIVE)
– RASTER IMAGE

One of the most common visual tasks for architects is to show a client or the public what they are proposing in an existing context. Since the object we want to build doesn't yet exist other than in plans and visualisations, there has to almost always be a photomontage approach to integrating the proposed object into actual pictures of what's already there.

Although people will know they are looking at something that is as yet a fiction, it can be vitally important to get this right and make the generated object look real and natural. So perspective (the angle from which a real person would see the new building) and scale (the proportions of the object in relation to everything
□ 285↘ around it) are essential. What then also needs to happen is that light and shade, and the way surrounding elements, such as trees, pedestrians, cyclists, and cars group themselves around the object, are adjusted and where necessary added or repositioned. We cover many of the aspects involved in these processes in our chapter on Visualisation and to a lesser extent also in our chapter on Rendering.

CAD PLANS (ORTHOGONAL) – VECTOR IMAGE

More and more in architectural proposals or presentations, CAD drawings and plans get integrated with photography, for example by combining a ground plan with an aerial shot of the location, or showing elevations in their anticipated setting. Since photography post-production tools tend to be much more versatile than CAD tools, this is mostly done as image manipulation too.

The principal tasks here tend to be scaling (making the plan fit into the picture), and adding aesthetic touches such as shading. Nobody expects a CAD plan to look naturalistic in an image that is clearly a composite, but we are used to seeing even basic drawings given a degree of dimensionality, by shading and some simple light simulation, for example. This, in turn, can be easier to achieve in the CAD program than in the picture editor, since traditional photography and graphic design software is not geared to generating accurate architectural shadows.

164 ● 252

CREATING RASTER OR
VECTOR OBJECTS,
TEXTURES, PATTERNS

By now, both architectural and photographic/graphic image editing software comes with a raft of off-the shelf geometries, textures, and patterns that can be used to generate imagery from scratch or to complement pictures that have been either generated as photography or CAD drawings, or indeed as a combination of both. All of these objects, textures and patterns can normally be scaled, transformed, adapted, fine-tuned and generally customised; and the from-scratch generation of images is in itself an art form and a professional specialisation that is available as a career path.

165 ● 253

We talk in considerable detail about some of these techniques in our chapter on Visualisation.

The Outlook

The image in architecture has moved, apparently inexorably, towards a 'perfection' that is defined by its realism. Rendered images, just as much as photographs, can be – and are being – post-produced to the point where they are indistinguishable from each other and, whether they represent any kind of 'reality' or not, look 'real'. There has been, and will continue to be, a convergence of the rendered and the photographed image, as we also note in our chapter on Visualisation. ☐ 285↘

At the same time though we are now also beginning to notice a new move away from photorealism towards stylisation and abstraction. Analogue photography is making a comeback, as are hand drawings, not only because young architects rediscover the artistic freedoms these traditional methods offer, but also because trust in 'perfect' post-production is waning. Clients often find that, no matter how 'real' these images look, what they promise can not necessarily be delivered.

The quality of pictures – irrespective of how they have been generated or edited, how they are being displayed or disseminated – is technically so high now that often the human eye cannot discern any flaws, pixels, dots, or impurities any longer. And so as digital photography, image rendering, computer display, and print technologies reach maturity, we are looking in new directions, towards new visual languages that are newly abstract, newly stylised, and newly artistic. And this, though it may sound like a reversal of our journey so far, does not have to be either ironic or retrograde: digital technology has eclipsed analogue image techniques, but it has not made artistry and creativity obsolete. We therefore surmise that here lies the future: in pursuing the skills of photographic and architectonic tradition with the tools and the mindset of digitality.

141 ● 231
Computing without a monitor, early 1960s. [Rømevig]

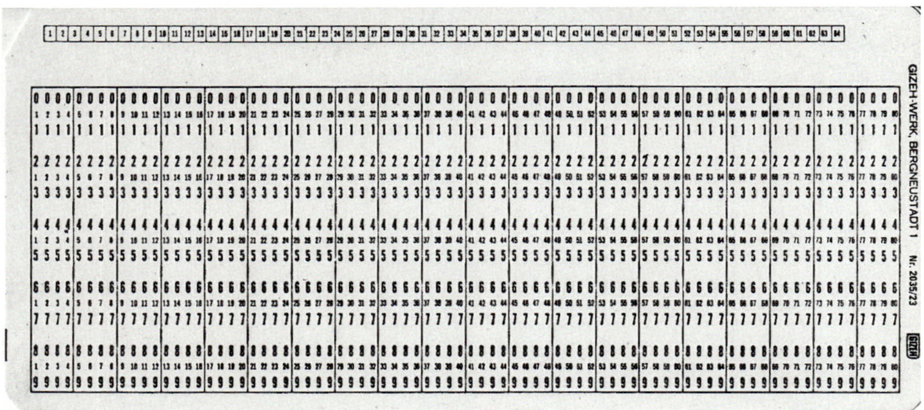

142 ● 231
An IBM-standard punch card in the 80 column format as input and output medium. [GIZEH *Werke*]

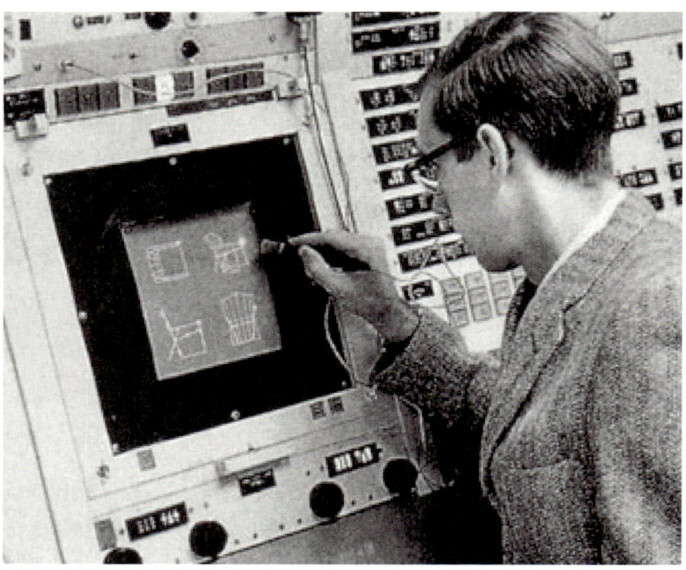

143 ● 231
Ivan Sutherland using *Sketchpad* on the *Lincoln TX-2* computer.

144 ● 232
Early computer games such as *Tetris* used raster image technology to generate simple geometric forms. [Cooljeanius]

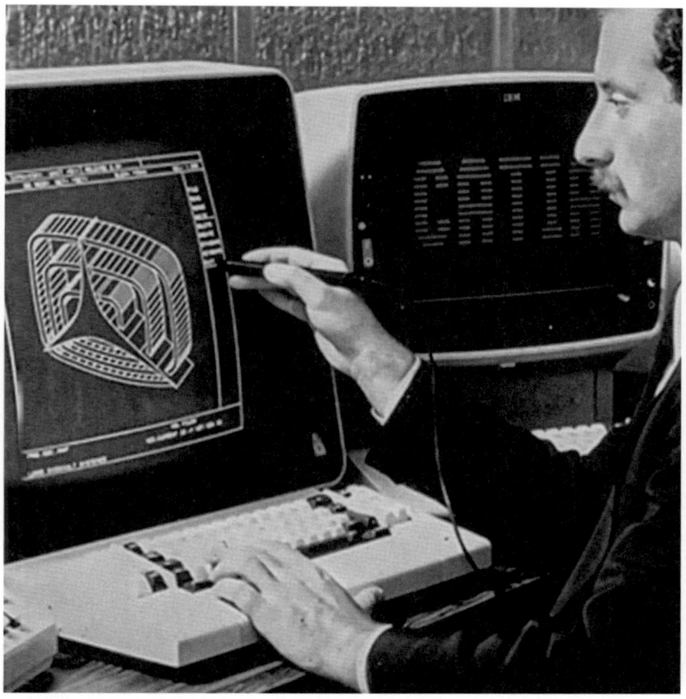

145 ● 232
A vector monitor with keyboard and light pen, part of the early *CATIA (Computer Aided Three-Dimensional Interactive Application)* system (first released 1977). [*Aero-Modelisme*]

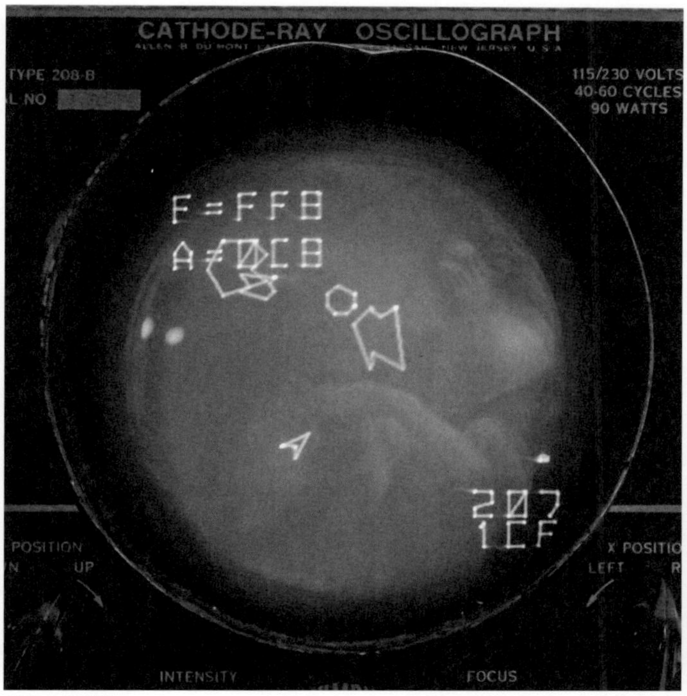

146 ● 232
A video game being played on a vector monitor. [Autopilot]

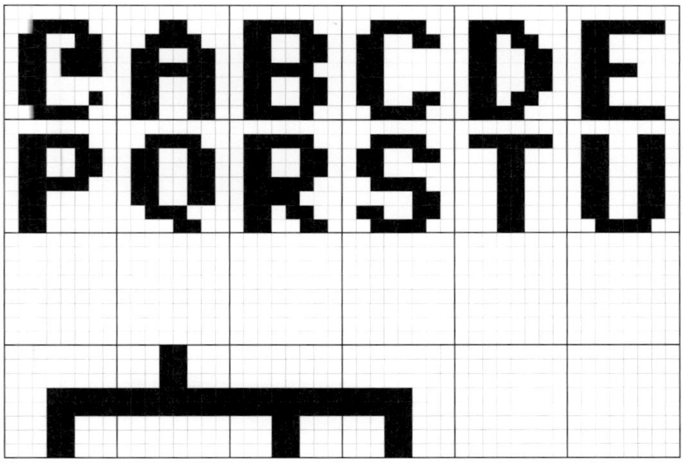

148 ● 233
The graphic representation of numbers, characters, and symbols was based on a raster; here, for example, of 8 × 8 pixels. [Harald Gatermann]

149A ● 233
An early raster monitor: green characters, numbers, and symbols are shown against a dark background.

149B ● 233
The first *Apple Macintosh* computer: black-and-white graphic display with a light background and a mouse as input device.

149C ● 233
The *Xerox Alto*: the first computer with a graphic user interface and a mouse, developed at PARC (Palo Alto Research Center) from 1972.
[Joho345]

150A ● 233
A simple raster image.

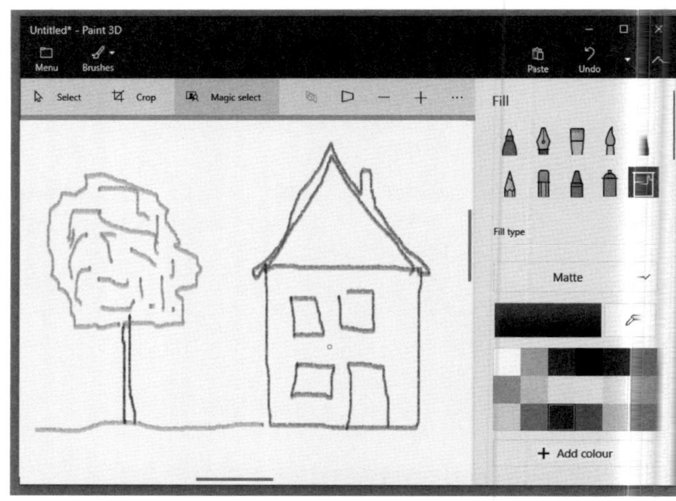

150B ● 233
A drawing created with a mouse or graphic tablet.

151A ● 234

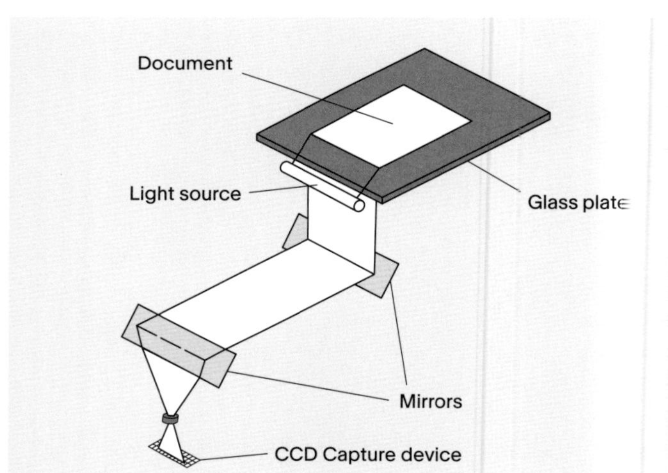

151B ● 234

Considering its relatively short flourishing period, the development of the fax machine goes back a very long time, to the mid 19th century, and many people have contributed to its genesis with their own incremental technology improvements; among them the Scottish inventor Alexander Bain (1810–1877), the English physicist Frederick Bakewell (1800–1869), the Italian physicist Giovanni Caselli (1815–1891), the English physicist and inventor Shelford Bidwell (1848–1909), the German physicist and inventor Arthur Korn (1870–1945), the French photographer and inventor Édouard Belin (1876–1963), the German inventor Rudolf Hell (1901–2002), and the American electrical engineer Elisha Gray (1835–1901).
[Miguel Durán | Oliver Fritz]

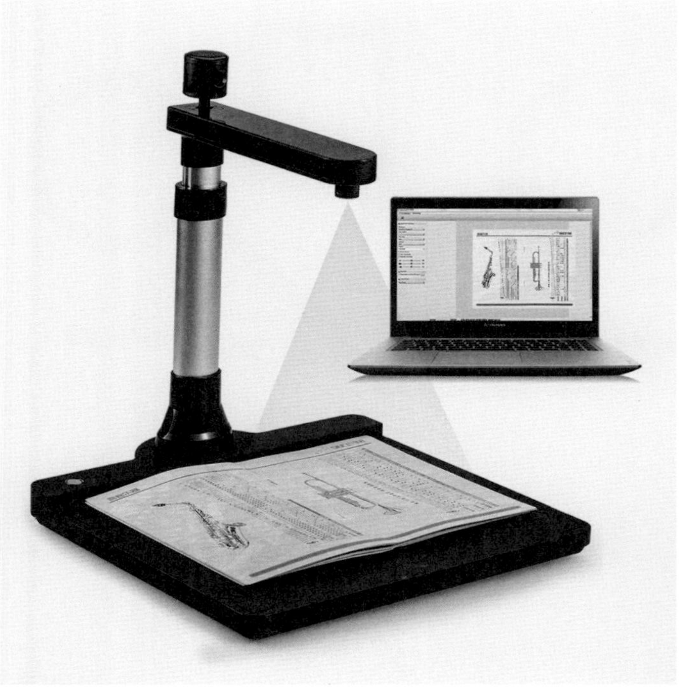

152A ● 235
Scanning methods.

152B ● 235

152C ● 235
Scanning with a smartphone. [Oliver Fritz]

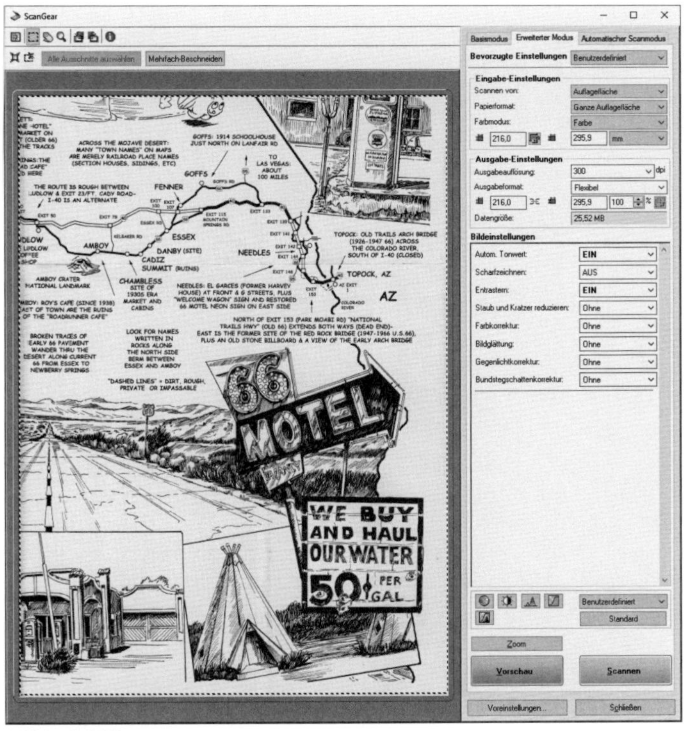

153A ● 235
The user interface of a scanner software which is linked via *TWAIN* to an image editing software. [Harald Gatermann]

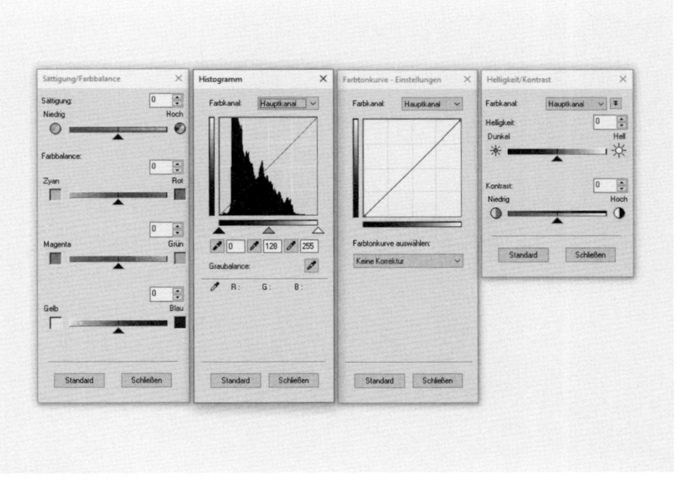

153B ● 235

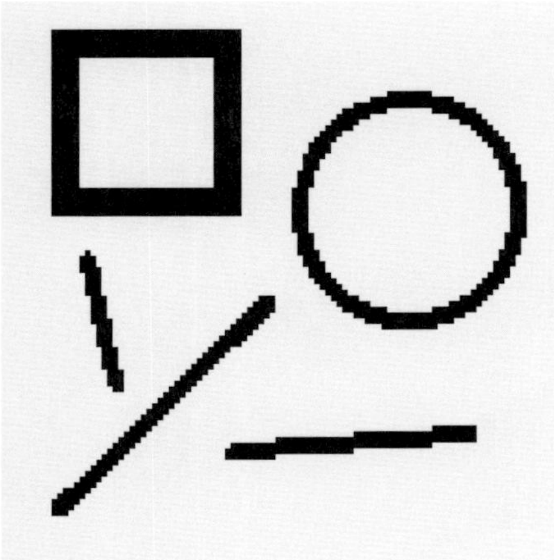

155A ● 237
Raster graphics.
[Series 155A–155C: Harald Gatermann]

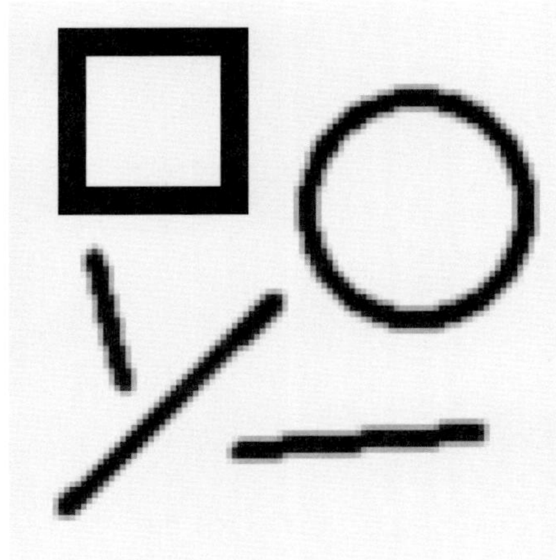

155B ● 237
Vector graphics.

155C ● 237
Anti-aliasing.

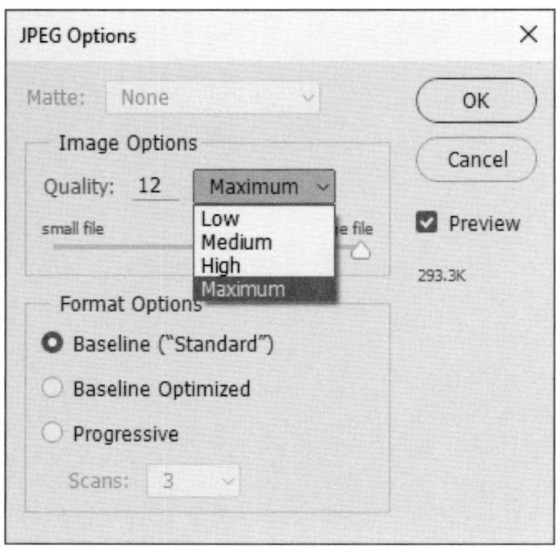

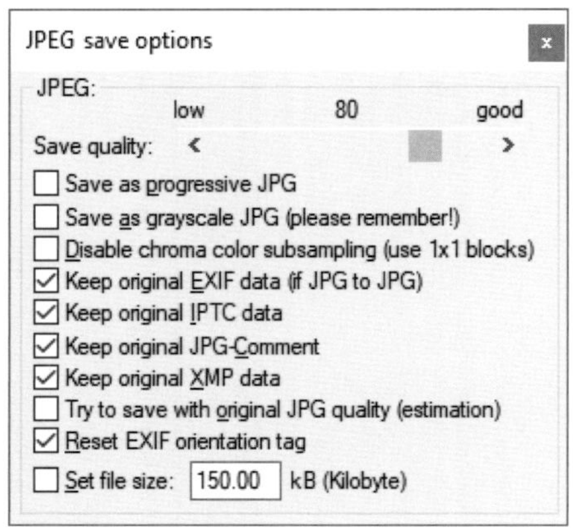

158B ● 240

158A ● 240
Quality vs file size in JPEGs. [Screenshot series 158A–158F: Harald Gatermann]

158C ● 240

158D ● 240

158E ● 240

158F ● 240

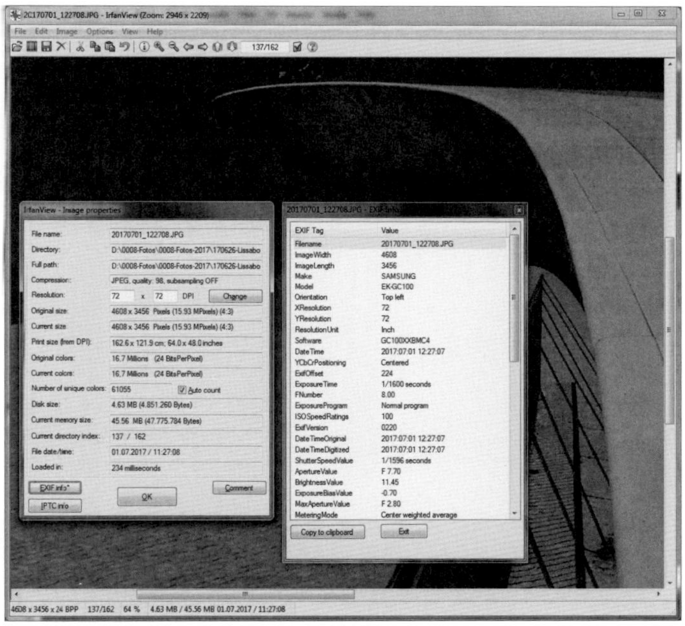

159A ● 240
Both *Windows Explorer* and *Mac's Finder* file management programs sort images by file name, and display them either as lists or as thumbnails in adjustable sizes. They also read and display the file's metadata. JPEGs. [Screenshot series 159A–159F: Harald Gatermann]

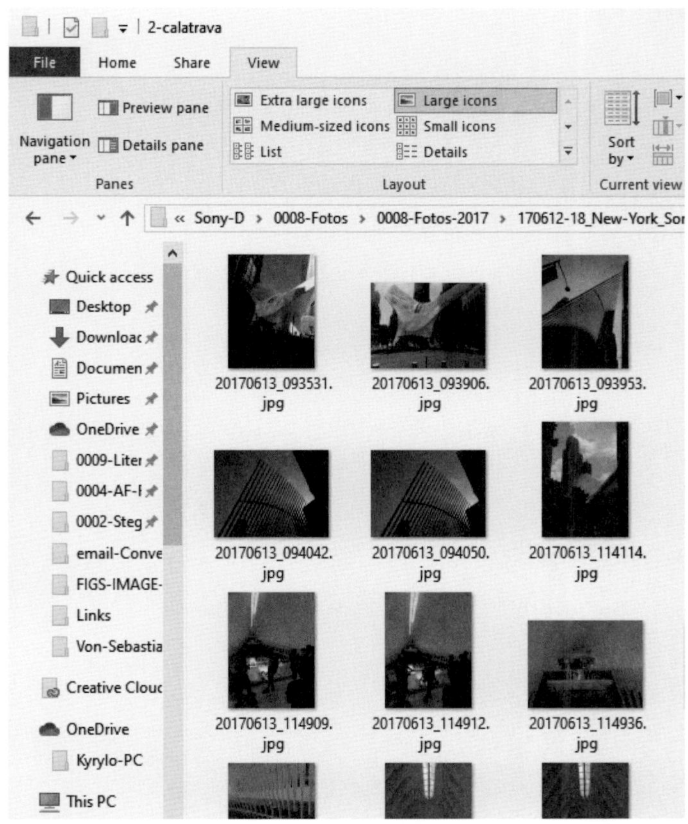

159B ● 240

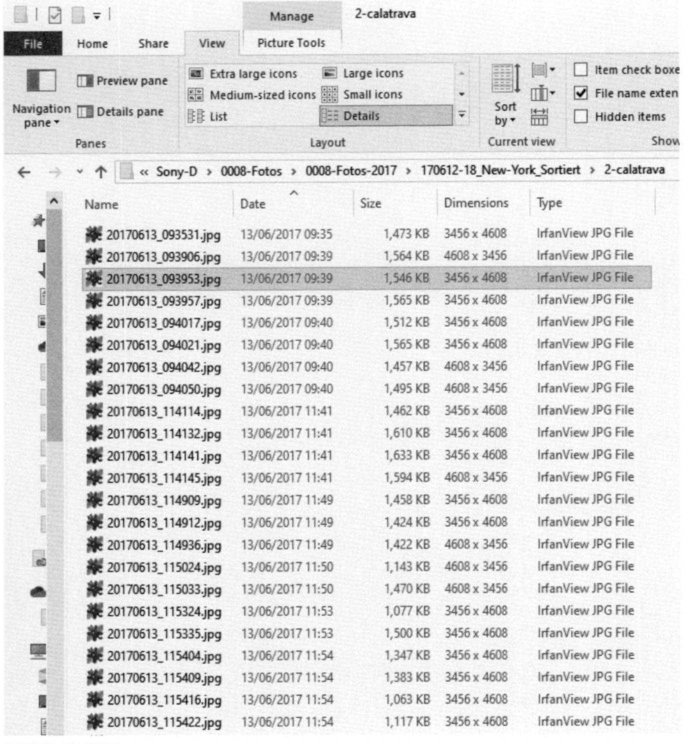

159C ● 240

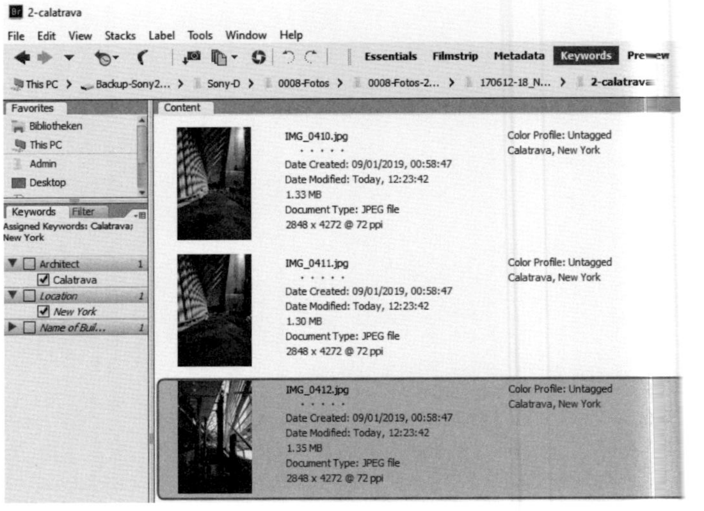

159D ● 240

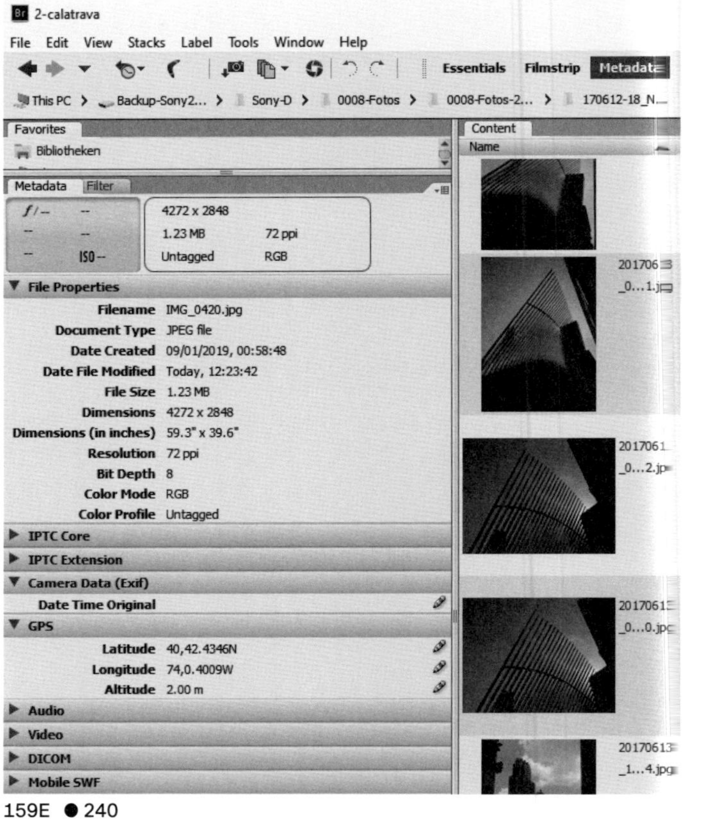

159E ● 240

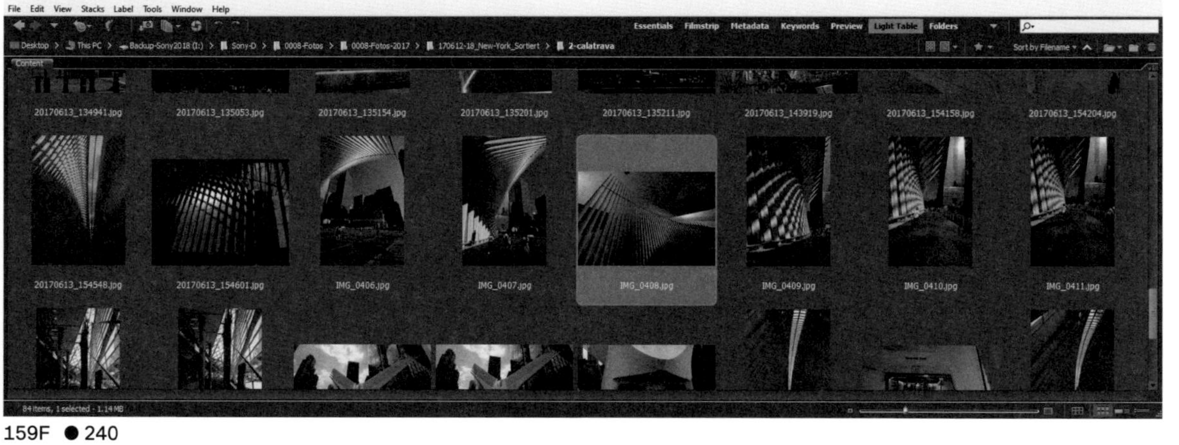

159F ● 240

160A ● 240
Image distortion corrected.
[160A+160B: Harald Gatermann]

160B ● 240

161A ● 241
Framing. [161A+161B: Harald Gatermann]

161B ● 241

162A ● 241
Retouching. [162A + 162B: Harald Gatermann]

162B ● 241

164 ● 242
Integrating CAD and raster image elements.

165 ● 242
Objects, textures, patterns.

Rendering

Urs Hirschberg

- Johann Heinrich Lambert: *Photometria*, 1760
- Andries van Dam, James D Foley, John F Hughes, and Steven K Feiner: *Computer Graphics Principles and Practice in C*, 2nd Edition, 1995
- Greg Ward Larson and Rob Shakespeare: *Rendering with Radiance: The Art and Science of Lighting Visualization*, 1998
- John F Hughes, Andries van Dam, Morgan McGuire, David F Sklar, James D Foley, Steven K Feiner, Kurt Akeley: Computer Graphics: Principles and Practice (3rd Edition), 2013
- Matt Pharr, Wenzel Jakob, and Greg Humphreys: *Physically Based Rendering: From Theory to Implementation, Third Edition*, 2017
- Tomas Akenine-Möller, Eric Haines, Naty Hoffman, Angelo Pesce, Michał Iwanicki, and Sébastien Hillaire: *Real-Time Rendering, 4th Edition*, 2019

Overview

Since 2016, the Bank of England has been busy replacing its existing paper bank notes with smaller, more durable, and more forgery proof polymer versions, starting with a £5 note featuring Winston Churchill, and followed by a £10 note in September 2017, dedicated to Jane Austen. A new £20 note is due for release in 2020. It will feature the self-portrait by a young J M W Turner (1775–1851) – widely considered the most important British artist to date – together with a detail from his famous 1838 painting *The Fighting Temeraire Tugged to Her Last Berth to Be Broken Up*, his signature, and his oft-quoted expression, "light is therefore colour."

Wherefore exactly light is colour, the bank note won't say, but dubbed 'the painter of light' owing to his exceptional use of this most insubstantial of 'tools', Turner introduced to art a whole new way of looking, of which he simply said: "My business is to paint what I see, not what I know." Yet, there is a blurred line between what the eye sees and what the imagination makes of it. Turner himself was not unaware of this and also noted that: "It is necessary to mark the greater from the lesser truth: namely the larger and more liberal idea of nature from the comparatively narrow and confined; namely that which addresses itself to the imagination from that which is solely addressed to the eye."

By which short excursion we have landed right in the middle of the two themes that are entirely central to our chapter on Rendering: light and 'reality'. And how light creates, but also distorts, enhances or sublimates, exposes and obscures, to any degree we are capable of imagining, any type of reality. In a visual context, the two are entirely entwined and inseparable from each other. Turner clearly was not the only painter who knew this, he merely serves as a fine example. Look at any great master of any era, and you'll be struck by the fact that once they learnt how to handle perspective and proportion, the absolutely most critical element to making a picture look 'real' or 'unreal' is light: how it behaves, how it illuminates surfaces, how it affects the colour and the appearance of texture, how it deceives as much as it reveals, how it lends contrast, dimension, depth, and atmosphere.

166 ○ 306

But before we go any further at all, let us briefly remind ourselves what rendering actually means. It's the processing of an outline image, "using colour and shading in order to make it appear solid and three-dimensional," as Oxford Dictionaries defines it. In other words: rendering is what architects do when they use pencil, crayons, or water colour to work over their drawings to make them presentable to their clients. The principle is the same as it is in what children do when they add colours to the black and white outline shapes of a colouring book.

The term 'render' has its root in Latin – *reddere*, from *re-dare*, 'to give back' – and has been in use in English since the Middle Ages, with various different meanings, such as 'translate', 'represent', or 'perform' evolving from then. Today it is mostly associated with digitally produced images, which is why to the above list of methods we now must add, at the top, any process involving a digital rendering tool. But it is useful to remember where the word came from, because while the means have changed by which we render, the painterly concerns with light and colour that lie at the core of rendering remain very much the same.

Considering its wide use and great importance to architecture, rendering does, as it happens, have something of a dubious reputation with many architects. This is because a well-made rendering can make bad architecture look good to uninformed clients, it can distort and distract, it can embellish and paper over cracks. But it can also serve a real and vital purpose: to give a better, more complete understanding of a proposed design.

'REALITY' AND 'REALISM'
A rendering is a simulation that allows us to assess a project before it is built. Naturally, therefore, the question of how 'realistic' a rendering can be is not only of great interest, but also of fundamental significance: we want to know to what level a rendering corresponds to the proposed reality. This is one of the reasons why, since its infancy, digital rendering technology has found itself on a practically consistent trajectory towards photorealism, aiming as much as possible to emulate reality as it would be photographed. In □ ↖255
many ways this makes sense, because at a time when Computer Graphics (CG) were rudimentary, flat, and ■
schematic, the ambition of rendering images in such a way that they would acquire naturalistic properties – contrast, dimension, depth, and atmosphere – was associated with achieving higher quality. But as we shall see, the term 'photorealism' is not without its own problems: the degree to which a photographic picture can be said to represent any given reality is entirely dependent on how we take that picture and what we then do with it in post-production.

In 1995 (still early days for rendering), the second edition appeared of a book that to this day is considered the 'bible of computer graphics' (not least on account of its hefty volume: at 1175 pages *Computer Graphics: Principles and Practice* outstrips even the book you're reading right now). In it, the authors defined visual realism as, "a picture that captures many of the effects of light interacting with physical objects."

It's a pragmatic statement, which makes the idea of realism sound simple enough, and which doesn't address Turner's distinction between 'what I know' and 'what I see'. The distinction is there, but implicit, and in a different sense: the focus here is on how we can capture and solve in algorithmic terms the effects of light interacting with physical objects, so that what we know about these effects can be made visible, and at what computational cost. It turns out that capturing these effects isn't simple at all: the book devotes over 200 pages to this quest for realism, chronicling the collective work of numerous researchers in computer graphics who have grappled

□ 285↘ with it. A chapter in an *Atlas of Digital Architecture* can at best communicate a fraction of the insight that a compendious work dedicated entirely to the subject achieves, but it is worth bearing in mind at this point that the principles described there have been developed scientifically and can be learnt and understood: all of the rendering programs available today draw on that knowledge and apply those principles in their algorithms and methodology.

Since the 1990s, photography post-production and rendering have both made spectacular strides, and today, photorealism may be both no longer defined in quite the same way, nor have the same aspirational lure as it did twenty years ago, let alone at the time when photography was invented. Back in 1840, not long after Turner first exhibited his *Fighting Temeraire*, the American writer Edgar Allan Poe (1809–1849) found himself moved to wax lyrical about the **daguerrotype**, a forerunner of photography invented and given its name by Louis Daguerre (1787–1851):

> "If we examine a work of ordinary art, by means of a powerful microscope, all traces of resemblance to nature will disappear – but the closest scrutiny of the photogenic drawing discloses only a more absolute truth, a more perfect identity of aspect with the thing represented. The variations of shade, and the gradations of both linear and aerial perspective are those of truth itself in the supremeness of its perfection."

Today we live in a world where manipulating photographs has become so easy and commonplace that Poe's words seem almost comical. But even when we don't deliberately manipulate photographs, the possibilities of advanced photographic techniques such as **HDRI (High Dynamic Range Imaging)**, for example, are capable of taking the concept of 'realism' to a level of the absurd, and quite a bit beyond, creating a whole new class of stylisation, straight from the camera. At the same time rendering has become virtually indistinguishable from photography. We talk a lot more about all this in our chapter on Visualisation, which for obvious reasons we recommend you read in close conjunction with this one.

What hasn't changed though is that whether you look at rendering as an art or as a skill, whether you liken it more to painting, drawing, or digital sculpting, its practice starts with looking, and the moment we start looking, we start seeing things that may or may not actually be there in the way our brain processes the information it receives from our eyes. Therein lies the discrepancy, highlighted by Turner between 'what I see' and 'what I know', and therein lies the great challenge of dealing with incredibly nuanced subtleties in an algorithmic way.

Instinctively we handle these nuances all the time. Take a white wall, for example: there's nothing extraordinary about it, and architecture is full of white walls. But no wall is genuinely completely white, ever, really. What our eye sees is a wall that has any number of shades of grey, blue, yellow, or any other colour that happens to be present in the current light spectrum, either reflected from other objects or generated from lighting sources; but what our brain interprets is 'white', because it knows that the wall is supposed to be white. What this means is that in an image a wall that is actually pure, uninterrupted white almost never looks 'natural'. Which takes us back to our challenge of 'realism': to make a white wall look real, we need to give it a shade that is congruent with its setting, which may have very little real white in it at all.

167A ○ 306

167B ○ 306

168A ○ 307

168B ○ 307

□ 327↘
□ ↖229

Towards 'Realism': A Brief History of Rendering in Technological Stages

□ 285↘ The history of rendering overlaps, unsurprisingly, with the history of Visualisation more generally, which we cover in our chapter on the topic, and we also mention some of the principal development stages that led from computers handling essentially numbers to them dealing with text and then images in our chapters on Text, Typography & Layout and on Image & Colour.

When it comes to computer graphics, which are at the root of anything to do with imagery in information technology, then no matter from which branch on the metaphorical tree we set off, the trunk always leads us back to Ivan Sutherland (b. 1938) and his 1962 *Sketchpad*, the root to all CAD programs. Together with David C Evans (1924–1998), who was also an American computer scientist and the founder of the Computer Science Department at the University of Utah, he set up Evans & Sutherland, which in turn was a leading and pioneering player in the development of rendering software and procedures.

This is where the move towards realism that we mentioned commences, and it does so with different and ever more sophisticated layers of shading.

In the course of this chapter you will frequently come across the term 'tracing'. And in fact various ways of tracing the lines of vision or conversely the paths of light rays into and through a scene are at the core of almost all algorithms that aspire to visual realism. The famous etching by German painter and printmaker Albrecht Dürer (1471–1528) featured in our chapter on Graphs & Graphics, in which he explains the construction of perspective, is also a perfect illustration of this type of tracing. The two gentlemen in the scene trace the line of vision using a string that goes from the point of view (a hook attached to the wall) to a lute, the object of which they want to create a perspective drawing. A simple device allows them to record the exact points where the line of vision (the string) intersects with the picture plane (a wooden frame placed on the table to which the actual drawing is attached with a hinge).

As a nod to the genius of Dürer and as a recurring theme you will see illustrations that are loosely based on this setting throughout this chapter. In order to show a more representative variety of 'effects of light interacting with physical objects', we have added a couple more items to the scene: a glass carafe filled with water, a knife, a rusty chandelier with a waxen candle, a piece of cloth, and a loaf of bread on a metal plate are placed next to the lute. They will allow us to go into some detail in exploring the most advanced procedures and tricks involved in rendering material properties. But the scene as a whole will also serve to illustrate many of the very basic principles we start out with.

169A ● 273

169B ● 273

170 ○ 307

VISIBLE SURFACE DETERMINATION

Before any shading of surfaces can take place in a meaningful way, the visibility of the surfaces has to be determined. This process is in many ways analogous to the hidden line removal problem: the need to remove, by algorithm, those lines in a computer drawn object that are not visible unless the object happens to be transparent, such as the edges of a cube that are obscured by its visible, front facing surface(s), for example. While for a cube this is a simple enough task, it can be challenging and therefore slow for complex or very large models, and finding ways to solve this problem has been one of the earliest concerns in rendering technology.

An effective way to address the issue is known as Z-buffering or depth buffering. The *Computer Hope* website describes this process clearly and succinctly thus:

> "When a scene is rendered, each pixel has an X and Y coordinate (horizontal and vertical orientation to the camera), as well as a Z coordinate (depth, or distance from the camera). The Z-buffer is a two-dimensional array (X and Y) which stores the Z-value of each screen pixel. If another object must be rendered at the same pixel location, the algorithm overrides the previous value if the new pixel is closer to the camera. This increases rendering speed for opaque objects, but transparent objects do not benefit since the distant objects are partially visible, and must be fully rendered."

Note that the Z-direction of the coordinate system is the third dimension that sorts elements in depth along the axis from the screen to the user's eyes (in the above quote 'the camera'), so to speak. This convention explains why the coordinate systems in typical computer graphics and rendering packages is different from the one used in Computer Aided Design (CAD) software, where the Z-coordinate is always the vertical, and why sometimes the data exchange between CAD and special effects programs will require conversion of the coordinate system orientation. □ ↖175 □ ↖129

The buffer in question occupies part of the computer's memory, and its efficacy is therefore hardware dependent. But the use of Z-buffers has become so widespread that almost all contemporary computers (including tablets and smartphones) now come with dedicated Z-buffer hardware installed.

171 ● 274

ILLUMINATION AND SHADING

The moment you introduce shading into outline drawings, you start adding depth, and you invariably face the issue of lighting generally. Once you deal with lighting generally, you approach, by degrees, reality as we perceive it, and so the story of rendering can almost be told in '7 Grades of Shade'. We say 'almost', because it's by necessity a potted history with several overlaps; and also, for the avoidance of doubt or confusion, we should stress that some of these methods and techniques are now mostly of an historical interest only and listed here to give an overall picture of the elements that make a rendered image, rather than to imply that you would use them in isolation any longer: contemporary rendering software will apply these effects for you at the push of a virtual button. ■

LAMBERT SHADING

The first type of shading that computers were able to handle as far back as the early 1970s is Lambert shading, named after Swiss mathematician, physicist, astronomer, philosopher, and pioneer Johann Heinrich Lambert (1728–1777), who was not only first to calculate and elaborate on perfect diffusion, now also known as Lambertian reflectance, but who was also the first person to prove mathematically that π is irrational. ■ 292↘ ■

Lambert shading and Lambertian reflectance describe an 'ideal' matte surface: one that reflects the light in an evenly diffuse way, irrespective of the viewer's angle or perspective. Put somewhat simply, the amount of light reflected on a surface with Lambertian reflectance is directly proportional to the angle at which the light reaches the surface, following Lambert's cosine law, which the English *Wikipedia* entry on the subject explains thus: "The radiant intensity or luminous intensity observed from an ideal diffusely reflecting surface or ideal diffuse radiator is directly proportional to the cosine of the angle θ between the direction of the incident light and the surface normal."

Lambert published his law in a book called *Photometria* in 1760. This, its Greek-derived title notwithstanding, was written in Latin, and it for the first time set down a complete set of photometric concepts, while also giving us the word photometry.

Lambert shading has the advantage that it is relatively easy for computers to calculate, and therefore to process and render; while its obvious disadvantage lies in its idealised 'flatness', which also means that it works comparatively well with even surfaces that have hard edges, whereas it does nothing for curved surfaces with no edges.

This play-off between a technique's effectiveness and the stride it makes towards photorealism on the one hand, and its computational expense – how much processing power and memory is required to render it – on the other is a constant tussle that characterises the entire history of rendering, as we shall see.

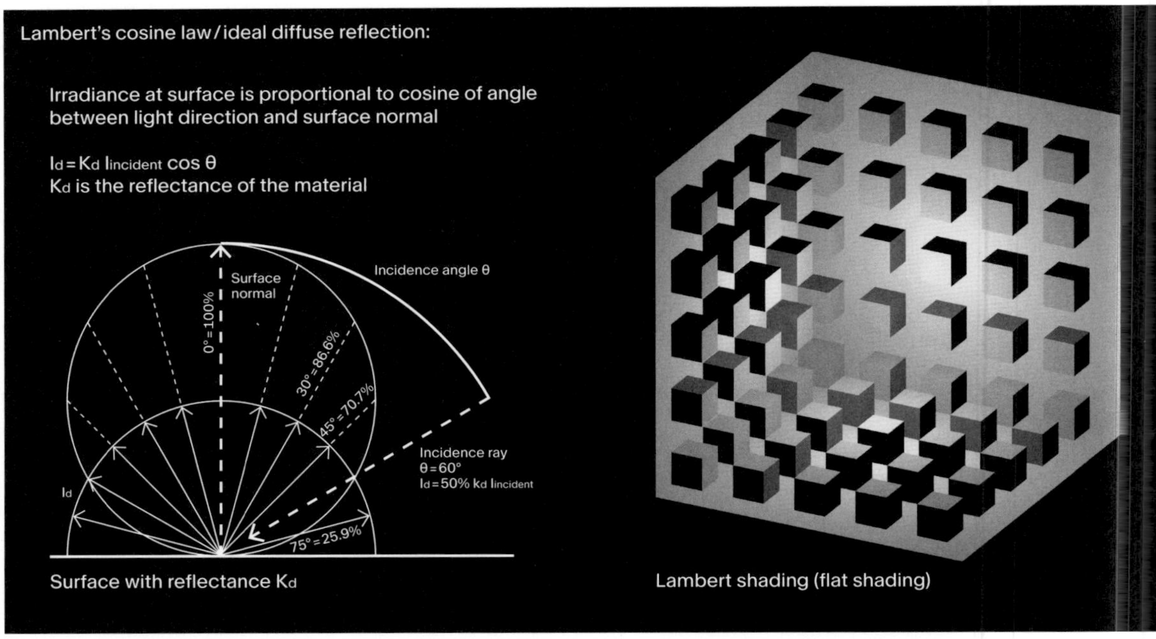

GOURAUD SHADING

The person to solve the problems posed by flat shading (such as Lambert's) was a French computer scientist named Henri Gouraud (b. 1944). In 1971, while working with David C Evans and Ivan Sutherland at the University of Utah, he wrote his doctoral thesis on the *Computer Display of Curved Surfaces*, in which he first published his approach, which was to interpolate the shade of each pixel covered by a polygon triangle based on the calculated values for each corner. Put differently: if you have a round surface that is really made up of a number of polygons (for example triangles), then you can treat each polygon as a flat surface, but rather than give it just the one shade – as you would do with Lambert's cosine law – you work out what each individual dot or pixel on that surface would be if it formed, as to our minds it does, a continuous surface with its neighbouring pixels. Although conceptually simple and computationally still manageable, the effect on the eye is striking: already a massive leap has been made towards what we might consider realism.

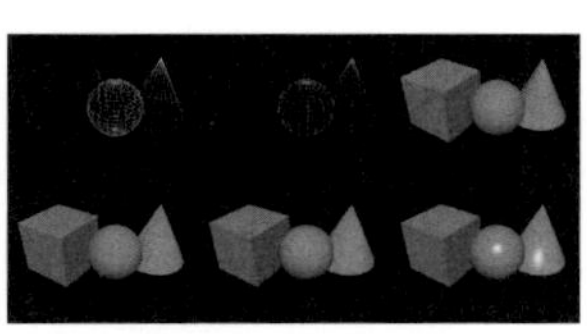

172 ● 274

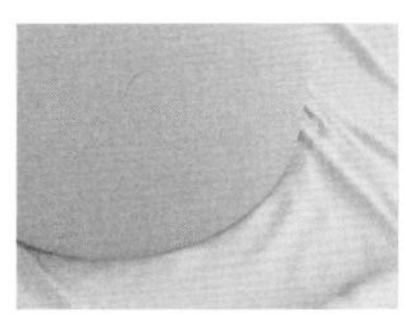

173A ● 275

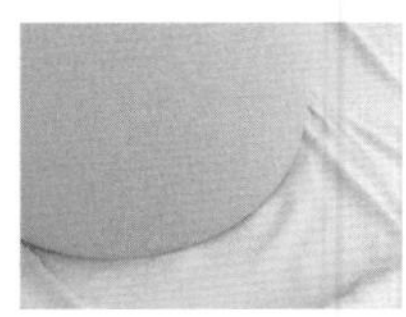

173B ● 275

PHONG SHADING

Another student working with Evans and Sutherland at Utah was the Vietnamese born French-American computer graphics researcher Bui Tuong Phong (1942–1975), who in 1973, then already terminally ill with leukaemia, improved on his colleague Gouraud's breakthrough, principally by refining the interpolation method to take into account small specular highlights. These are the white or very bright areas that you see on any reflective surface that has a strong enough light shining on it.

Because Gouraud used for his method the vertices of the surface polygons as references from which to interpolate the shading across the entire polygon, in cases where a polygon is sufficiently large, the spectral highlight may be absent from the calculation and therefore missing from the rendering. Phong managed to solve this by working out the surface normal for each pixel individually, rather than for each vertex, as Gouraud had done. This results in a yet more realistic image, but also comes at a higher computational cost.

PHONG E AND BLINN-PHONG SHADING

Utah continues to set the tone with two variations on the Phong theme: *Phong E*, which is a node offered by some softwares, which yields softer specular highlights than those on Phong surfaces, and also renders faster; and the *Blinn-Phong shading* or reflection model, which is the Phong model modified by a man named Jim Blinn (b. 1949), an American computer scientist who won his PhD from the same stable as Gouraud and Phong, but another five years later, in 1978. The differences between the Phong and the Blinn-Phong model are subtle and largely algorithmic.

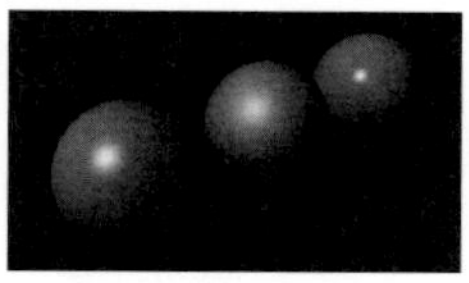

174 ●275

SHADOW MAPPING

From 1972 to 1977 – the exact period during which Phong and Blinn were at Evans's department at Utah University, and very shortly after Gouraud had published his paper – the American graphics researcher Lance Williams (1949–2017) was also studying there, before moving to the New York Institute of Technology (NYIT). There he invented a technique called **mipmapping** (where 'mip' stands for the Latin phrase *multum in parvo,* meaning 'much in little'), which to this day is used widely in computer games, flight simulation applications, as well as 2D and 3D imaging software, to speed up the render time for images: a *mipmap* is a sequence of the same image in progressively lower resolution. In a situation where a high resolution image would take a long time to load (too long, for instance, to make a gaming scene feel realistic), a lower resolution version of the same image can be loaded to cover for the delay. And mipmapping is also an important concept for texture mapping, a topic we will come to in a moment.

Williams's other major contribution to computer graphics and imaging was a paper entitled *Casting Curved Shadows on Curved Surfaces*, published in 1978, shortly after he arrived at NYIT, which introduced the concept and technique of *shadow mapping.*

Shadow mapping analyses the light source (or sources) in an image and calculates the shadows that an object would throw onto its surrounding surfaces. It therefore for the first time gives a rendered picture any kind of ambient lighting. Shadow maps as a concept are closely related to the Z-buffer we mentioned earlier: the shadow map does for a light source what the Z-buffer does for the view from a given viewer perspective or direction.

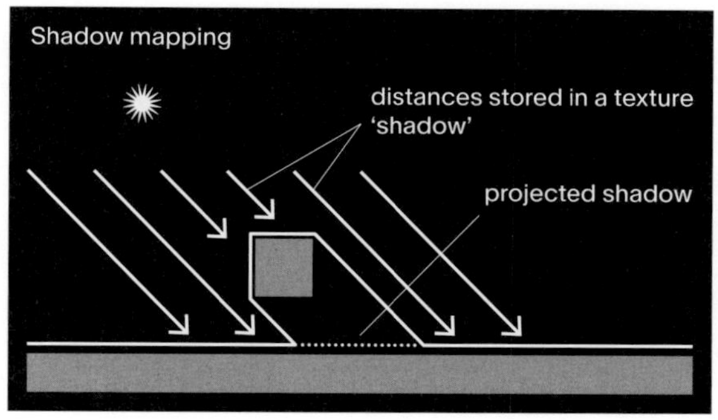

RAY TRACING 287↘

The next breakthrough followed shortly after, in 1979, when a man called John Turner Whitted published a paper under the title *An Improved Illumination Model for Shaded Display*, which, building on previously published research by other people, set the scene finally for *ray tracing.* (Ray tracing's precursor, **ray casting** – first introduced by Arthur Appel in 1968 – already used this method of following rays from the viewpoint into the scene, but unlike ray tracing didn't take any bounces into account, which made the result look flat and unrealistic by comparison.)

Contrary to what the name might suggest, ray tracing does not trace rays of light from a light source into a scene; rather, it traces the rays of vision from the spectator's viewpoint into the scene, and subsequently to its light sources. This makes sense when you consider that for the viewer to be able to interpret an image only the rays that end up at their eyes actually 'matter'. The physics of ray tracing remain the same irrespective of the direction in which you trace the rays: the path of light can be calculated both from the viewer into the scene and from the scene to the viewer. While this may sound self-evident, it actually isn't; yet it turns out to be the case.

Ray tracing principle: for every pixel on the picture plane a ray of vision is traced from the viewpoint (camera) into the scene. The more bounces, the more realistic the image, but also the longer the computation time.

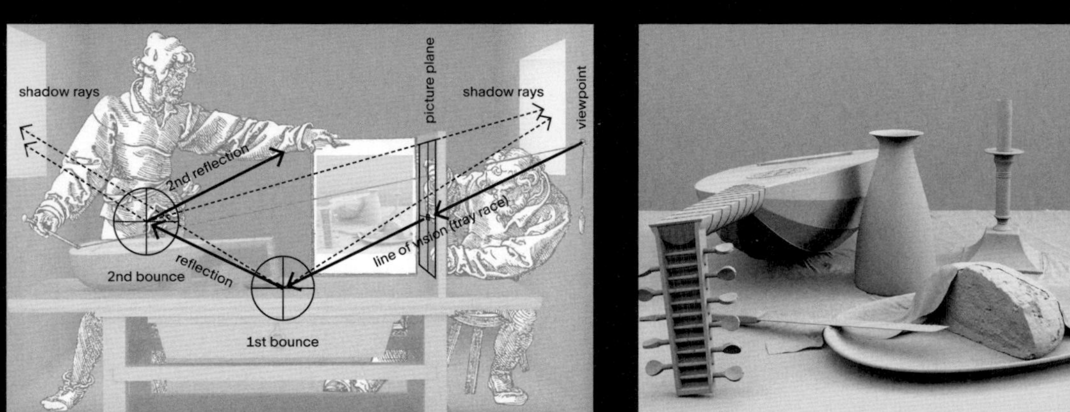

Whitted introduced to ray tracing a recursive process that spawns up to three types of rays every time light hits a surface: *reflection, refraction* (the change of a light ray's direction resulting from a material's properties), and *shadow.* The effect is repeated for every ray for as many bounces as the user specifies. Shadow rays, for example, go from a surface point to all light sources in the scene. So how realistic a ray tracing is
287↘ depends on the number of bounces that are pursued for each ray, but of course each bounce sets off separate processes to recursively follow each new scattered ray, and processing time thus increases exponentially with every bounce. The number of bounces therefore has to be kept at a level that the computer is able to handle.

Early ray tracing had no way of dealing with ambient light, that is light bouncing off other objects. Today's ray tracing techniques can accurately simulate optical effects as they occur in the real world, such as those already mentioned – reflection, refraction, and shadows – as well as *scattering* and *dispersion,* and so this nearly completes the range of light behaviours that we normally observe, including *transparencies.* And while ray tracing used to work
287↘ best for crisp shadows and reflections, more recent improvements of the method (such as **distributed** or **diffuse ray tracing**, **cone tracing**, and **beam tracing**) also allow it to render diffuse or soft shadows.

Ray tracing is computationally expensive, especially for the type of computer that was around at the time of its invention: the amount of data that has to be processed is defined by the number of pixels in the rendering that is being calculated. Therefore, render times for ray traced images increase by the square of their size (doubling width and height of an image results in four times the render time, tripling them takes nine times as long). For this reason, ray tracing to this day is not suited for real-time applications, although this may be about to change as more and more software uses
↖131 374↘ the **GPU (Graphics Processing Unit)**, or **graphics card**, for its purpose, rather than the computer's main chip or
354↘ **CPU (Central Processing Unit)**. We will get back to this particular recent development at the end of our chapter.

THE CORNELL BOX

Named after Cornell University, Ithaca, New York, where it was developed by a group of researchers in 1984, the *Cornell box* is a test which serves to establish the accuracy of a rendering method, by comparing a rendered scene to an actual photograph of that same scene. A simple set up is built as a physical model, this is photographed using what's known as a **CCD (Charge-Coupled Device) camera** – a particular type of digital camera – and the obtained settings, such as the emission spectrum, light source or sources, reflectance spectra from various objects, as well as the position and size of the objects, are then measured and used to reproduce the scene as a rendered image. The more capable the software, the more accurately it will render the image.

The Cornell box did an excellent job at highlighting the limitations of ray tracing. Ray tracing could only deal with direct lighting and was unable to capture effects such as *colour bleed* (objects taking on the colour of neighbouring objects) that we can observe in a photograph. And so it was clear that researchers had to up their game and develop advanced methods to arrive at what we now refer to as *Global Illumination (GI).*

175A ○ 308

175B ○ 308

GLOBAL ILLUMINATION (GI)

With very few exceptions, light bounces off any surface it meets, to a greater or lesser extent. Matt, dark, or porous surfaces will absorb much more light than glossy, bright, smooth ones, but there is hardly any material, texture, or colour that does not disperse some of the light that lands on it onto its surroundings. For developers of rendering techniques it was this ambient light – light scattered multiple times off multiple objects in all directions – that proved hardest to get to grips with. *Global Illumination (GI)* is the umbrella term for all methods that model the behaviour of ambient or indirect light.

RADIOSITY

Radiosity, much as virtually all the other techniques we are talking about here, has its algorithmic roots in research carried out as far back as the 1950s and 60s, but became useful and usable really in the mid-1980s. By addressing the problem of diffuse light it created a much softer, natural feel and look than was previously possible, and because it was able to produce soft shadows and the bleed effects of colour between objects in a scene, it was considered a game-changer when it was first introduced.

The key conceptual difference to what had gone before was that it treated all objects as light emitters. Letting the light bounce between all objects in the scene with progressive refinement, radiosity created light distribution models which were independent of the point of view of the observer. So, in order to also get the effects of reflections and refractions (which are directly influenced by the viewer's perspective), radiosity had to be combined with ray tracing. The radiosity solution was computation-intensive to create, but once it was there, it could be used in multiple ray-traced images. In fact, what is known as 'light-baking' – the pre-calculation of light-maps by radiosity methods – to this day is used to add realism to (the static parts of) real-time environments, such as first-person computer games.

Radiosity calculation: The geometry of the model is divided into patches. In an iterative procedure each patch is shooting and gathering radiosities from all other patches. The resulting ambient light distribution is viewpoint independent.

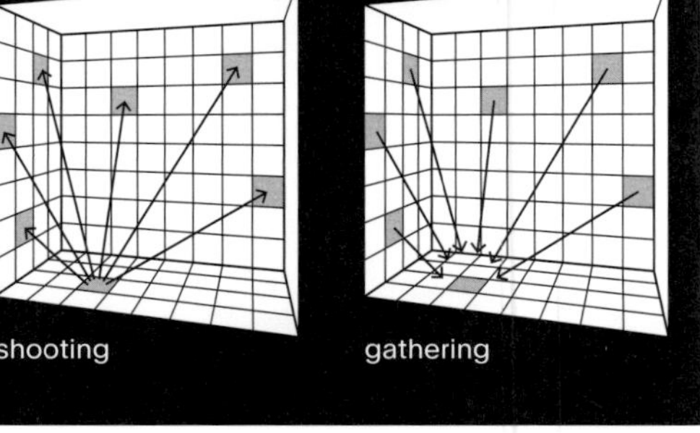

176A ○ 308

176B ○ 308

THE UTAH TEAPOT

You may have noticed, as we were talking about the early development stages of rendering, that in the 1970s the University of Utah was something of a hotbed for research in this field, with several breakthroughs happening there under the aegis of Sutherland and Evans. For the sake of completeness, and for the sheer pleasure it gives us to do so, we should mention one more Utah alumnus of that era: a British-born American computer scientist named Martin Newell, who is chiefly known for one particular object: the *Utah teapot*.

As recently as 2017, a writer for online magazine *Curiosity*, Joanie Faletto, called it, "the most important object in computer graphics." This may or may not be a touch hyperbolic, but it was certainly a pioneering work: Newell and his team at Utah played through innumerable test renderings of the teapot, continuously improving it, and over time it has become an immensely influential object that is often visually referenced in computer graphics, one prominent example being the animated feature film *Toy Story*.

177 ● 275

BIASED AND UNBIASED RENDERING

The radiosity algorithm was based on ideally matt Lambertian surfaces, and it has since been superseded by a whole range of other global illumination rendering methods, which can be divided into two types: biased and unbiased.

In a nutshell: unbiased rendering treats each ray with equal importance and makes no distinction between them in terms of priority. This results in extremely accurate (and therefore realistic) renders, but is also computationally very expensive.

Biased rendering introduces a process of several stages of calculation or pre-passes, which are then used as 'bias' or simplification of the GI solution. Examples of bias might include:

- Limiting the number of bounces of light that are followed through. By contrast, an unbiased render would follow each ray's bounce until it either leaves the scene or is completely absorbed.
- Adaptive sampling: this favours rays in areas of greater importance, for example where there is more light than in other parts of the scene;
- Suppressing or removing caustic rays: this is often used to reduce the volume of processing that needs to be done, as caustics are especially computationally demanding (we talk a little more about them in just a moment);
- Clamping or truncating secondary rays, for example to prevent spikes on very bright reflections (known as 'fireflies'). In fact, any type of tolerance threshold introduces a bias into the render. In practice, most render software works with some type of bias to optimise render time.

UNBIASED GLOBAL ILLUMINATION

Everything we just said notwithstanding, *unbiased global illumination* could be considered the 'holy grail' of rendering algorithms, as it takes no shortcuts to arrive at a physically correct light simulation. Here as above, 'unbiased' refers to the calculation method and signifies that this does not introduce any 'systematic error' or 'bias' into what is known as the **radiance approximation**. ■

Explaining this here in detail would probably go too far, but radiance approximation is a rendering equation developed in the mid-1980s, which calculates the amount of light that is emitted from any given point in an image along an observer's viewing direction. The rendering methods based on this theory are known as **path tracing**, **bidirectional path tracing**, **volumetric path tracing**, and **metropolis light transport**. ■ ■ ■ ■

While we don't want to go into the intricacies and subtle differences between these algorithms, it is important to understand that as a group they represent a new breed of rendering methods that take photorealism (for all the term is worth) to a new level. They can reliably model even very complex lighting situations and material effects, and unlike biased methods they don't require anywhere near as much expert knowledge. Rendering with biased GI software had turned into something of a specialist domain, because of the many intricate decisions that have to be made as to which settings to use for the **photon mapping**, for example, or when to use ambient occlusion. With these unbiased renderers, making successful renderings has become as simple as taking a photograph. (Or, as any serious photographer will tell you, as demanding.) Their downside is that they also take computation time to new heights, because until a sufficient sampling level is reached, unbiased GI renderings have a grainy look, and so depending on the task in hand, professionals will in most cases still prefer biased renderers for their work. ■

Owing to their intricacy and complexity, global illumination algorithms (both biased and unbiased, though the latter even more so) are computationally expensive, and therefore not of practical use in all settings. Yet the progress that has been made in recent years is impressive. **CGI (Computer Generated Imagery)** in films, for instance, can now be calculated so quickly that previews of scenes in which actors interact with CGI environments or creatures can be watched on set. Similarly, architectural stills imagery of digital 3D models can be generated with full GI in a matter of seconds where GPU rendering is performed on a fast graphics card. In 3D computer games too there have been notable advances in realism. Some games already feature raytracing effects for dynamic objects or changes of light, for instance. But given that 60 frames per second is now the standard for rendering 3D action sequences in ■ ↖157 interactive 3D games, full GI rendering will nevertheless remain an ambition for a while yet.

BIASED GLOBAL ILLUMINATION

In *biased global illumination* pre-passes are made to improve processing speeds for global illumination tasks. Depending on the software you use, these procedures go by different names: final gathering (or final gather), photon mapping, irradiance map, light-cache, for example. They provide approximations to the light distribution that are used to smooth over dispersed sample points and create a softer light distribution.

178A ● 275

178B ● 275

AMBIENT OCCLUSION

Another specialist biased global illumination technique, *ambient occlusion* calculates the level to which any given point in an image is exposed to ambient lighting, or rather, the level to which it is *not* exposed to light; in other words, the degree to which light is 'occluded' or blocked from a point in the image, or the point from light. A shelf or niche in a room, for example, or the underside of a table, would typically be more occluded than the wall or the top of the table. By identifying occluded parts of the model simply based on the geometry rather than the specific lighting conditions, ambient occlusion is used to boost the volumetric definition of a scene. And so, like all of the other biased methods, ambient occlusion is an elegant shortcut to arrive at more realistically rendered models without the long wait.

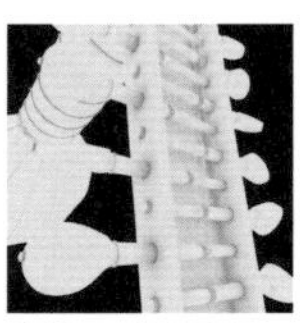
179 ● 276

CAUSTICS

Caustics deserve a special mention, simply because they present a particular, and particularly taxing, challenge in illuminating scenes. They are the light reflections and refractions produced by glass and water, for example.

180 ● 276

181 ● 276

With global illumination widely used and available, rendering has become very much like virtual photography, which is why it may be useful to also now talk a bit about what we have so far only referred to as the viewpoint or viewing angle, but what should really more appropriately be thought of as a virtual camera.

THE VIRTUAL CAMERA

The concept of a *virtual camera* seems a simple one: you have a point in space, a viewing direction, an up-vector (this specifies where, in relation to the camera, 'up' is: if the camera sits flat on a horizontal plane then that would normally be at 90° to that plane), and a viewing angle, which together define the viewing frustum: the field of view of the virtual camera and therefore the visible scene that appears on screen. Obviously that is not the end of the story...

DEPTH OF FIELD

In computer rendering you don't, by contrast to photography, actually have a *depth of field*. The term describes the extent to which a photographic lens is capable of showing an image in focus; in other words the distance from the nearest point to the camera to the point furthest away that the lens can focus on in one setting. Since there is no physical lens present in the generation of a rendered image, depth of field is technically irrelevant, as any point on the canvas can be rendered in perfect focus at will.

Although depth of field was unknown in painting and therefore is associated absolutely with photography, we are used, both in real life and in photographically created images, to see part of the picture in sharp focus and other parts blurred. Introducing an artificial depth of field therefore helps to make a rendered image more natural, or possibly, if the effect is exaggerated, more stylised.

Global illumination methods are able to render this effect perfectly. In some unbiased global illumination renderers, the size of the model compared to the size of the virtual camera lens is also taken into account. Just as in real photography, the depth of field effect is stronger in macro photography of very small objects, such as flowers and insects, than in, say, urban scenes. So unlike in most CAD applications where units and actual lengths can be assigned and where it wouldn't matter whether a building is modelled in metres or in millimetres, in rendering software, the depth of field effect for two models of such differing size would be distinctly different.

182 ● 276

183A ● 277

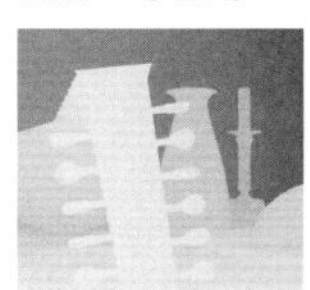
183B ● 277

183C ● 277

183D ● 277

TILT SHIFT

Tilt shift lenses in professional photography can, as the name suggests, be used for two effects: *tilting* and *shifting*. By tilting the lens, the light rays arriving at the camera are no longer perfectly perpendicular to the sensor (or, in analogue photography, film), and as a consequence a smaller portion of the image is in focus. It is therefore a depth of field effect. Shif refers to moving the lens along the image plane to create the effect of distance, for example to prevent the parallel line distortion of tall buildings, which we'll be talking about in a bit more detail next.

In digital post processing, the term *tilt shift* (or *tilt-shift)* is used to describe what is really a tilt effect that applies progressive blur filters to parts (usually the foreground and background) of a scene which was not shot with a physical tilt shift lens. This has in recent years become particularly popular, because it is easy to use and visually very effective: it tricks our mind into believing we're looking at miniatures, since we naturally associate scenes with a narrow depth of field with microphotography.

184 ○ 308

KEEPING VERTICALS VERTICAL

Among the elements that most easily distinguish professional architecture photography from amateur snaps are *verticals:* the vertical lines of buildings; especially tall buildings, since the taller they are, the more they converge in perspective distortion as they go up.

Geometrically, it's easy to prevent this effect: simply aim your camera exactly horizontally at the object, and all your verticals will appear parallel and look 'right'. The trouble with buildings is that they tend to be too tall to fit into our pictures unless we aim our cameras up. Professional photographers fix this by using the tilt shift lens: by physically shifting the lens they can move the centre of projection out of the centre of the image without having to change anything else.

Digital tools allow us to achieve the same effect without this expensive lens. In rendering, we can simply set up our virtual camera so that its line of vision is perfectly horizontal, and then use the shift function to move the centre of projection so that the entire building fits into the frame of vision. The distortion can in some cases also be corrected in photography post-production (with an image processing program), but it should be said that this isn't geometrically correct. (When the distortion is too big to begin with or when the scene contains too much depth, this type of image correction will not produce convincing results. Starting with a properly taken photograph or a rendering with a horizontal line of vision is in any case much preferable.)

While this 2-point perspective, as it is also referred to, is not strictly a more geometrically correct representation, it interestingly is nevertheless the more appropriate way to display a building from a human perspective. We know when lines are parallel, even if in the real world we see them converge, and so our minds, when we look at a building, perform the adjustment for us. But when we look at a picture of the same building, the distortion registers as unnatural.

185A ● 278

185B ● 278

BOKEH AND THE OPTIC DIAPHRAGM

At the extreme end of the continuing quest for photorealism, some professional renderers give the user access to highly specialist camera features such as the *optic diaphragm.* In a physical camera this is the – mostly iris shaped – aperture mechanism that sits between the lens and the film or the sensor chip and serves as the light gate that allows the photographer to control the amount of light that finds its way into the picture. It works exactly like the human iris, which dilates in darker environments to allow more light to reach the retina, and contracts in bright settings to limit the amount of light that enters the eye.

Aperture determines the size of the hole formed by the optic diaphragm and is expressed as a *focal ratio:* the proportion of this hole in relation to the overall size of the lens (f/1.4, f/2.0, f/2.8, for example). *Shutter speed* determines for how long the aperture is open and is expressed as a fraction of a second (1/30, 1/60, 1/125, for example). They are both standard settings in photography, and thus nothing unusual. Yet the idea of emulating them in rendering is in fact somewhat perplexing, since the physical constraints of lens sizes and shutter speeds have no bearing on images that are generated digitally. Some rendering programs go so far as to allow you to choose the type of diaphragm and determine the shape of the opening (whether it is circular or polygonal), and set the number of blades, thereby taking the idea of photorealism to its furthest – and, you might argue, most absurd – level.

Still, the reason the type of diaphragm and the shape of the opening it creates matter in photography is that they determine what is known as the *bokeh* effect. Bokeh derives from the Japanese word *boke,* which translates as 'blur' or 'haze'. It describes the blur specifically that is created by the photographic lens outside the depth of field. Different lens and aperture types result in subtly different blur shapes that to us can look more or less pleasing, and being able to choose the settings for the optic diaphragm therefore gives the user control also over the type of bokeh in the image.

Alternatively, the bokeh effect can be introduced in the post processing phase, where special filters (that require Z-buffer information) can be used to apply most of the effects that are achieved through lens settings, including those determined by the shape of the diaphragm. (Although some purists would say that bokeh effects are far more convincing when they are calculated as part of the rendering process, rather than in post-production.)

186A ○ 309

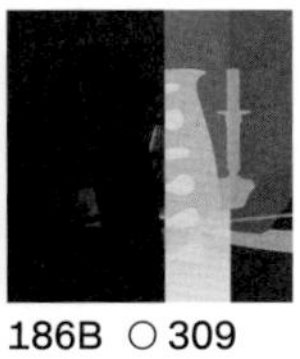

186B ○ 309

COLOUR CORRECTION AND FILTERS

We started this chapter with Turner and the old masters, and here now there's another leaf we can take out of their book when creating rendered images: to limit the colour spectrum.

There was an American painter, who, commercially wildly successful, went as far as trademarking the phrase, “Thomas Kinkade, Painter of Light,” the former being his name, the latter being a phrase hitherto as we’ve noted more or less universally associated with Turner. If you use your favourite search engine to look up Kinkade’s works (which we won’t reproduce here so as not to infringe his estate’s copyright), you’ll very quickly get an idea why, *alas!*, he is not ranked among the greats of this world. Apart from the fairy-tale pastoral ‘idyll’ of his subjects, his colour palette is so intensive and garish that you’d be forgiven for thinking you’re looking at a 1950s chocolate box, with chocolate of dubious taste in it...

Our world, even at its most colourful, is in fact rarely oversaturated. When it is, such as at a festival of light or in a garden in full bloom, we experience this as exceptional and intense. Reminding ourselves, therefore, that ‘light is colour’ and that there can easily be too much of a good thing will categorically contribute to keeping things ‘real’.

While in photography there are filters that can help us achieve a natural look, on the computer there are a vast range of colour correction tools to the same purpose. This is just as well, because there are also virtually no limits to the possible colour combinations and thus to potential pitfalls of unnaturalness. Generally, and unless you’re pursuing a particularly stylised look, the advice is to steer clear of violent concoctions and to err on the side of moderation by limiting the colour palette to a distinct spectrum that brings out the character of a project, rather than distracting from it.

187A ○ 309

187B ○ 309

DIRT

We’ve already touched on this phenomenon once or twice: much as our world is usually tonal rather than brilliant in colour, so it is almost always imperfect and to a greater or lesser extent grubby. Dust diffuses the light, scratches tarnish surfaces, patina settles on wood and stone, and wear and tear leave their marks on everything we touch. The only quasi spotless environments we are regularly confronted with are TV studios and, less frequently we hope, hospital operating theatres and mortuaries.

The computer, though, starts from a pristine canvas, which means that if we want our rendered image to look at all ‘realistic’, we’ll simply have to put some mess in it, by adding smudge and the natural traces of living.

Some of this can be applied in the same way as colour filters, during the image post processing stages. But there are also ways to introduce imperfections as part of the surface definition of a model, which brings us to the – by now long overdue – subject of texture mapping.

TEXTURE MAPPING

Texture is a major factor to every type of lighting and shading, and one we so far haven’t addressed in this chapter. *Texture mapping* describes the application of patterns or images to three-dimensional graphics to lend their surfaces a particular materiality or appearance. Since our world is full of objects that have surfaces with varying colours and properties, it’s easy to see that surface textures can be a useful feature. And indeed mapping textures onto surfaces is one of the oldest techniques in computer graphics.

The question a surface texture raises is not so much whether you want it – there’s normally a simple answer of yes, it’s appropriate/useful/adequate, or no, it doesn’t serve any purpose – but how you apply it: in what definition, for example, or at what scale.

When a texture is produced to specifically fit one single object, such as the facade of a house, we have to make sure that the proportions of the texture matches the surface it is mapped onto, as the result will otherwise be distorted or incomplete. While in practice this is not always entirely easy to achieve, conceptually it poses a fairly straightforward problem. But it also represents a special case. Often texture maps are used multiple times in a scene either because they are repeated across a surface, or because there are multiple instances of objects they are mapped onto. And here the problems become less straightforward. Repeating a pattern over too long a distance or too wide an area can have unintended consequences: a tile pattern, for example, may result in a diagonal line across the surface that makes what is supposed to look natural newly artificial. Even when no unwanted patterns emerge, it can still look silly when identical textures are recognisable in a rendering: a line of bookshelves, for example, in which the same collection of books appears over again. And a whole new set of challenges arises when the objects onto which textures are mapped do not have flat rectangular faces, but consist of curves, bends, holes, recesses, and branchings.

So while it seems obvious that finding the proper texturing solution is not always simple, this sadly means that the world of rendering is full of sloppy texturing: brick walls with bricks mapped in a way that would make a bricklayer’s hair stand on end, textures that are stretched beyond all proportion or that are altogether of the wrong scale, pattern repetitions that make what is supposed to be a sophisticated surface look like a cheap carpet... – When used correctly, though, texture mapping does prove extremely effective, as we are about to see when we look at some of its more advanced features.

188A ● 279

188B ● 279

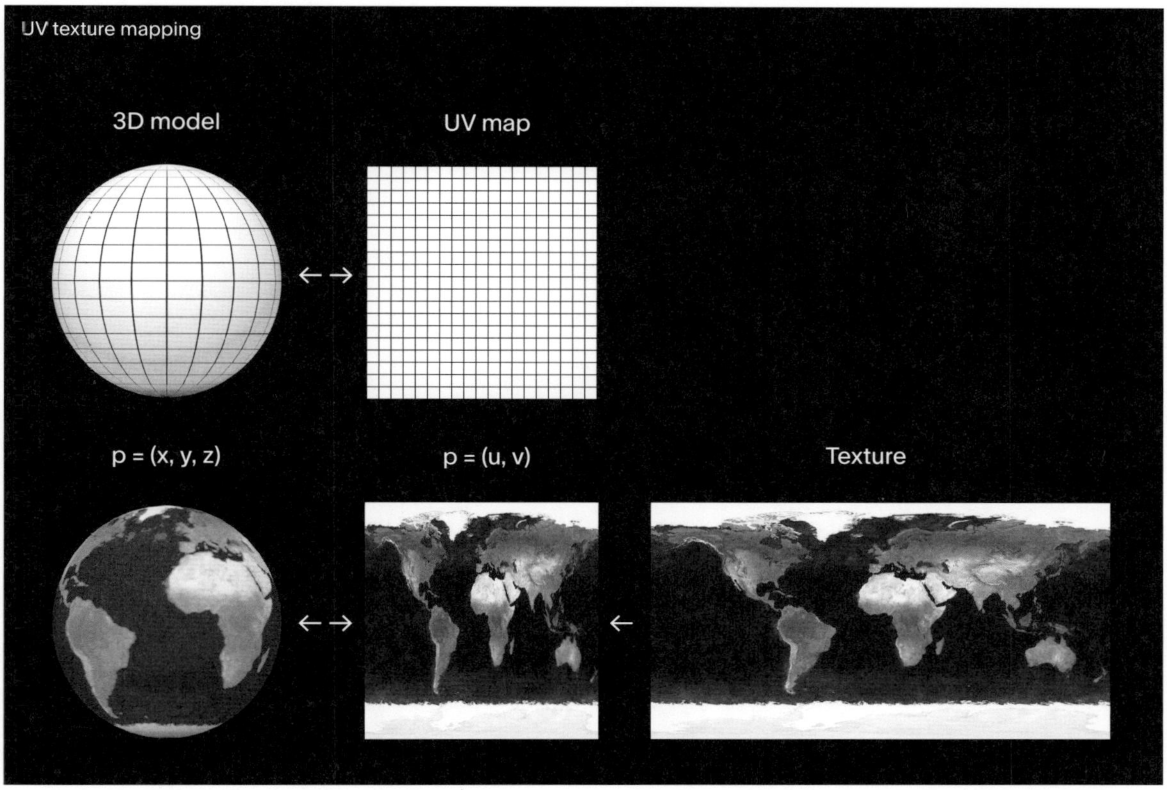

UV COORDINATES

Texturing is achieved by assigning corresponding coordinates between the pixel-space of the texture and the geometry onto which it is being mapped. This can be done by orthographic projection or by planar, spherical, cubic, or cylindrical projection. The highest level of control is possible by creating what's known as a UV-unwrap. U and V (in certain cases as we shall see also W) are the common names for the coordinates on the texture, respective to the 3D surface. This terminology allows you to distinguish texture/surface coordinates from the X, Y, and Z values used for Cartesian coordinates. U and V coordinates in the 3D model refer to points on a surface, even when this surface is bent or distorted. As visual construction aids to defining and working with UV textures, checkerboard patterns are commonly used.

STATIC VS PROCEDURAL TEXTURES

Textures are normally static images with a finite number of pixels in the U and V dimension. This leads to the potential problems with distortions or tiling patterns mentioned above. Alternatively we can use *procedural textures*, where each pixel value is the result of a mathematical function.

Instead of storing a data file with the texture and overlaying this on the geometry, they are generated algorithmically. Because of this, procedural textures tend to result in very clean patterns with mathematically defined, clear edges, which give them a look that for many uses is too sterile. To lend them a more natural look, you can therefore also introduce procedural disturbances, which are deliberately coded impurities. In fact there are procedural textures that manage to represent the irregular patterns of natural materials such as marble, wood grain, or human skin very convincingly.

One considerable advantage of procedural textures is that they allow you to avoid tiling effects. Some rendering programs also support *3D procedural textures* (or *solid textures*), which define UV as well as W values, thus making it easier to create convincing mappings for 3D objects made out of solid materials such as stone or wood. ■ ↖132

189 ● 279

BUMP MAPPING

Developed in 1978 by James Blinn of Blinn-Phong fame mentioned earlier, *bump mapping* is a technique that achieves similar results to surface textures, but by different means. Instead of applying an image pattern that is then repeated, the bump map recalculates an object's surface by 'perturbing' or distorting its surface normals so that the light now reflects and bounces off the surface as if it had bumps or irregularities in it which correspond to this map.

Since bump mapping only affects the surface normals, but not the surface itself, it does not change the overall shape of the object, nor the shadows it throws. It therefore has its limitations where these aspects are important, but on continuous surfaces bump mapping can be very effective. Bump maps are often used as overlays on textures, accentuating the grooves in a brick or tile texture or the like.

In real-time applications parallax mapping is used as a computationally efficient way to give more depth to bump maps.

DISPLACEMENT MAPPING

■ 484↘ *Displacement mapping* is also used to give structure to an object, but unlike bump mapping, it not only affects the object's surface, but actually changes its geometry. It can therefore be used as a quick ■ and efficient way to model intricate details. **Vector displacement maps** can even produce undercuts.

190 ● 280

ADVANCED MATERIAL DEFINITIONS

Today's GI rendering programs feature complex material definitions that employ any combination and/or layering of bump and displacement mappings imaginable to arrive at stunningly realistic, highly sophisticated material definitions, which strictly □ 463↘ speaking are not simply textures any more.

(See our image plates under *A Workflow Example* below for some insights into the high art of layering different types of textures to arrive at a hyper-realistic look.)

Contemporary 3D computer graphics allow you to not only represent diffuse colour information ■ through special types of texture map known as **diffuse map** or **albedo map** (from Latin *albedo,* mean- □ ↖255 ing 'whiteness'), but also:

- Reflectivity (specularity/glossiness/metallicity/roughness maps)
- Surface details, represented as lighting effects on the 2D surface (bump maps, normal bump maps)
- Surface details, represented as silhouette changes on the 2D surface (parallax maps)
- Surface details, represented as 3D offsets of the □ 285↘ surface (displacement maps, vector displacement ■ maps, **tessellation maps**)
- Indirect lighting/absorption potentials resulting from geometry (ambient occlusion maps, curvature maps, cavity maps)

The material definitions of leading rendering packages also include possibilities to render effects such ■ as **sub-surface scattering** convincingly. Sub-surface scattering is used to calculate the nonlinear effects of translucent materials such as resin or wax.

191A ● 280

191B ● 280

DYNAMICS

With some materials, texturing alone is not enough. For cloths, textiles, liquids, hair, or substances that are breaking apart, no amount of texturing will be enough to make them look realistic. The three major simulation methods known in computer graphics here are ■ **rigid body dynamics** (movement and fracture of a ■ geometry exposed to forces), **soft body dynamics** (deformation of a geometry exposed to forces), and **fluid dynamics** (behaviour of liquids and gaseous phenomena exposed to forces).

TEXTURING VS MODELLING

As we've seen, texturing is a powerful technique. It is not only a simple method to add flair, flavour, and complexity to a scene and enhance its realism, it can also be used to change the geometry. In fact, if used well, textures can be applied in such a way as to keep the geometric detail of a scene to a minimum. This is particularly useful in real-time applications such as games, where an excessive number of polygons would slow down the action, and where *'low-poly'* (as in low level of polygons) modelling is therefore a practical necessity. Yet players still want to experience environments that are rich with realistic detail. Luckily today's graphic cards are blazingly fast at rendering textures, and it's therefore in the realm of computer games that we encounter the most virtuosic use of texturing. As we explain in our chapter on Virtual & Augmented Reality, these techniques are becoming increasingly common also in architecture, and so it makes sense to be aware of the different approaches to modelling and texturing that are in use.

A WORKFLOW EXAMPLE

To round off our excursion into Rendering we want to give you a comprehensive example of the workflow involved in creating a rendered image. The cute scene we have pictured repeatedly in this chapter shall serve us to this purpose.

You may wonder though at this point why we would choose a still life for such an exercise: in terms of scale and geometry it is hardly typical for architectural renderings. One reason is that in our chapter on Visualisation we already discuss various approaches and considerations that come into play at the architectural scale. The other reason is that the smaller scale and the complexity of the objects in this scene allow us to address a number of advanced issues that are relevant in a real world setting. In CG projects for the film or entertainment industries, the techniques we are about to show are already standard procedures. As our appetite for higher levels of realism seems to be increasing in parallel with the technical possibilities of our hardware and software, these same techniques are also becoming more and more common in architectural renderings, especially when architectural interiors and their material properties are looked at in more detail.

(Most of the illustrations in this section are screenshots from the work process, though the interface elements have been eliminated, as we do not want to promote any particular software package.)

HIGH-POLY VS LOW-POLY MODELLING

When texturing of some complexity needs to happen, good control of the polygons in the model is of the essence. As mentioned a moment ago, for real-time applications such as games, where interaction and speed matter, the polygon count will be kept to a minimum, and textures will be used as much as possible to provide detail. In quality still images on the other hand, where a high level of realism is called for and details can be studied at length, high-poly models will be used.

Working with low-poly models, some authors will begin in a traditional modelling program and then use specialised tools to reduce the number of polygons. Others will keep the model compact and clean from the beginning. For high-poly models it might seem that these considerations do not matter, but a clean and easily manageable model geometry starts to pay off here as well, especially when textures are being applied. The most advanced technique for this simplified approach to modelling very detailed models is **Catmull-Clark subdivision surface modelling**.

One of its inventors is a name very much connected to texture mapping in general: the American computer scientist Edwin Earl Catmull (b. 1945). He studied – you guessed it – with Evans and Sutherland at the University of Utah and has many innovations and awards to his CV. Amongst others he is credited with inventing texture mapping, and one of the earliest examples of computer animation: *A Computer Animated Hand*. He later went on to become the head of Pixar Studios and even earned an Oscar, "for significant advancements to the field of motion picture rendering."

But back to subdivision-surfaces: they were invented for the purposes of digital animation as they allow for a combination of simplicity, efficient control, and high definition. Most of the elements in our scene were in fact modelled with a hard-surface high-poly subdivision workflow. A simple low-poly control cage is subdivided and smoothed generatively by means of Catmull-Clark subdivision. How exactly the smoothing of the geometry is performed is dependent on the topology of the control cage, the weight-values of edges and vertices, and the distances to the next edge.

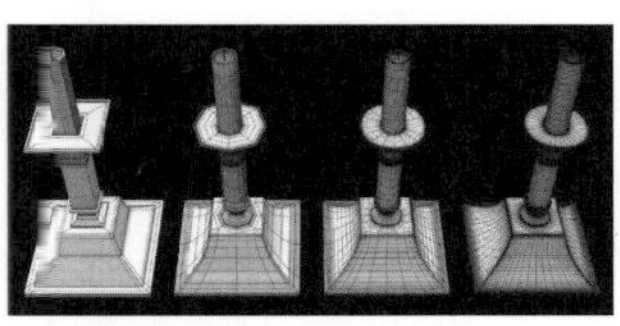

192 ● 280

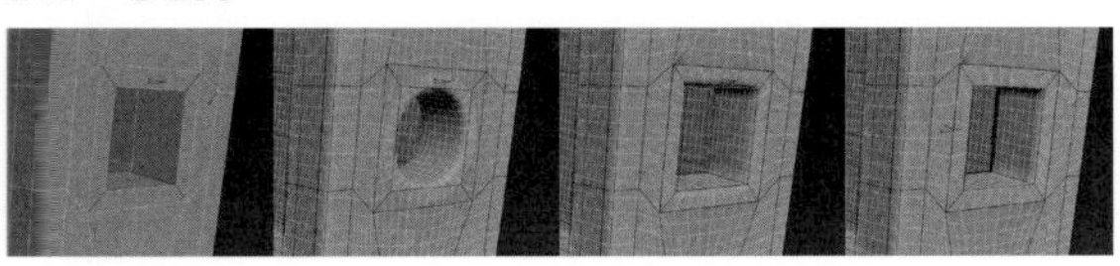

193 ● 281

POLE-VERTICES

High-poly models need to be monitored throughout the modelling process with relatively glossy materials in order to check for hitches in the smoothing of the geometry. Problematic points in the topology are pole-vertices, where either more (E-pole) or less (N-pole) than 4 edges meet in one vertex. Those poles can't be avoided, but they need to be introduced very carefully so as not to mess up the smoothing and shading. While it is all right to introduce triangular faces to solve certain geometries (such as a cylinder's flat cap, for example), polygons with more than 4 edges, known as N-gons, are generally considered to be bad practice. The quadrilateral faces (or simply: quads) are in any case triangulated for exporting or rendering the model, but throughout the modelling process, quads are used to achieve meaningful selections (loops and rings), UV-unwrapping (see below) and control of subdivisions and smoothing.

For these reasons, wireframe renders of quadrilateral topologies are often used in portfolios and showreels to demonstrate polygon modelling skills.

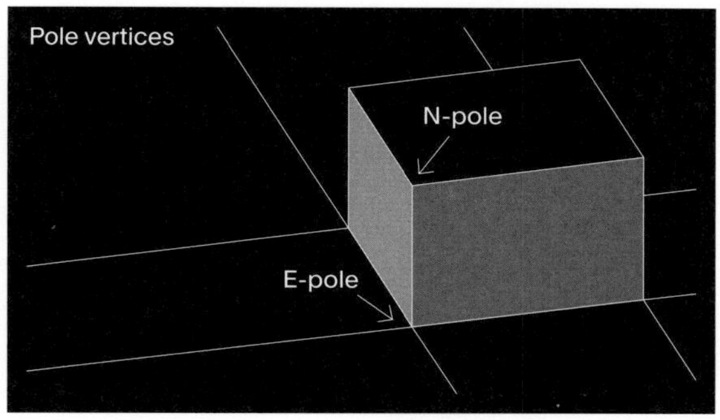

194 ● 281

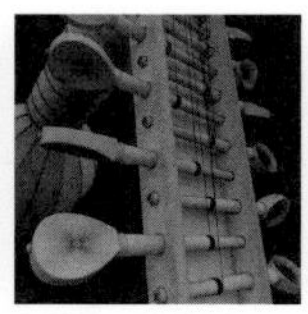

195 ● 281

196 ● 281

PROCEDURAL GEOMETRIC DEFORMATIONS

Just as procedural patterns can be used to create textures, so they can also be used to create geometric deformations. Depending on the scale/strength combinations applied, such deformation patterns will result in various forms of bulging and crinkling, which, if done with care, can add a bit of realism to an object. In our scene these methods were used to perturb the water surface in the carafe and the top end of the candle.

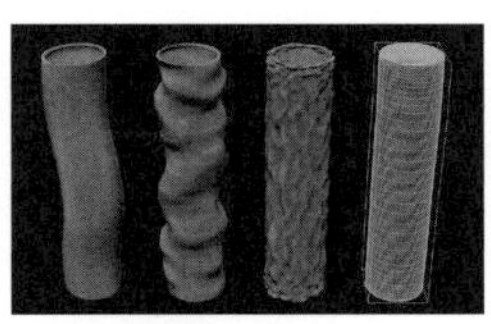

197 ● 282

UVW UNWRAPPING

As we noted before, the coordinates needed for texturing are defined in a different coordinate system than the vertex coordinates of a model. This space is called the UVW-space, to differentiate it from the local XYZ-space of the model containing the vertex coordinates. The UVW space is flattened to a 2-dimensional UV-space, which serves as the canvas for texturing.

For very simple shapes, the coordinate-transformation can be generated by a projection from **primitives** (plane, cube, sphere, cylinder). For more complex shapes, we need to do a UVW-unwrap, which is more or less a stitched and relaxed combination of several primitive projections. UV-unwrapping is in general considered to be a tedious but necessary step for proper texturing. Before starting the UV-unwrapping process, you have to make sure that the model is flawless and requires no further work, ■ ↖68 as any change in the vertex-count of the model will damage the entire unwrap. Checker-board textures are used to easily examine stretching and evenness of the texture resolution.

198A ● 282

198B ● 282

199A ● 283

199B ● 283

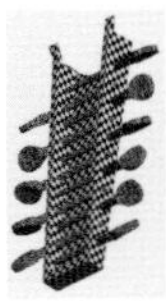
200A ● 283

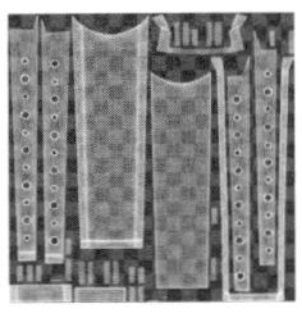
200B ● 283

LAYERED TEXTURING

For the texturing process, there are two possible approaches: You can work in the 2D texture-space and basically fill the UV-layout with image content. Alternatively you can work directly in 3D space and projection-paint the textures via the 3D model in the UV-space. For the first approach, an image processing program is sufficient (note that these software packages also include 3D painting capabilities). For the second approach, there are different stand-alone and plugin solutions available. These specialised tools offer the possibility to fluently combine working in 3D and in the 2D texture space with virtually unlimited layers and masks, while monitoring the shading effects in real time.

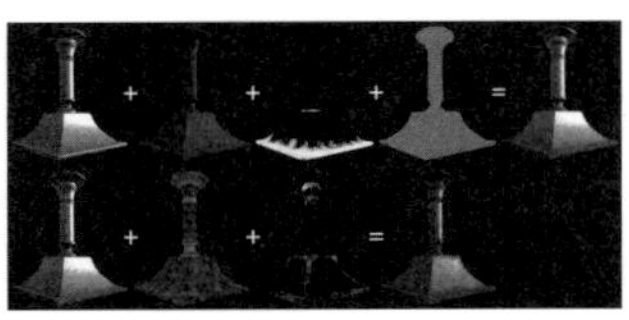
201 ○ 309

↖96 516↘ PHOTOGRAMMETRY

Even with all the layered textures and procedural geometric deformations described above, creating a detailed textured model of a loaf of bread for a close-up view is a daunting task. An alternative to modelling such a detail-rich object is to generate it by means of
■ ↖97 multi-image photogrammetry. Simply put, this pro-
■ ↖98 445↘ cess derives very dense point cloud data from a series of photographs of the physical artefact taken from different angles. (We talk about this also, and in a little
□ ↖93 more detail, in our chapter on Digital Data Acquisition).

From the point cloud, a dense mesh model can be derived, and diffuse textures can be projected from the original photographs. While the processing is more or less fully automated, the quality of the outcome is very much dependent on how exactly the photos have been taken. A perfectly static scene, sufficient parallaxation, minimisation of depth of field and motion blur, minimisation of artefacts (low ISO), around 30% overlap between the images, and a soft lighting environment to minimise burning directional shading in the diffuse texture are a few key aspects to the treatment.

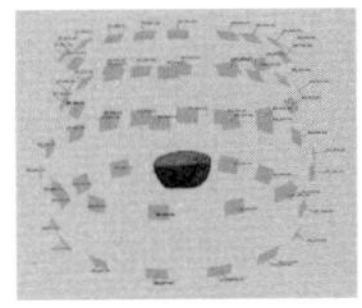
202 ○ 310

203 ○ 310

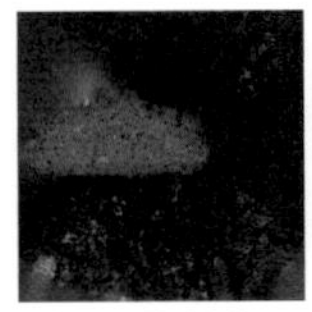
204A ○ 310

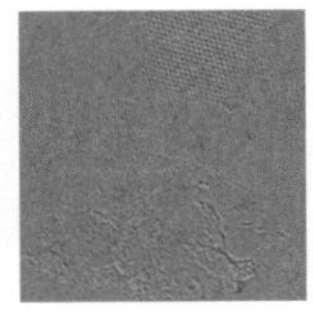
204B ○ 310

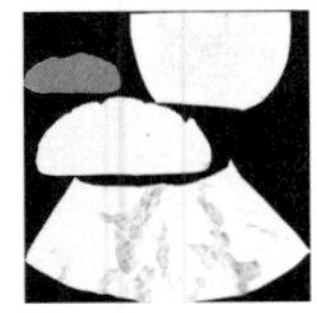
204C ○ 311

CLOTH SIMULATION (SOFT BODY DYNAMICS)

It is technically perfectly possible to manually sculpt organic geometry like cloth, but you need a considerable amount of artistic skill to do so successfully. Painters and sculptors through the ages have shown off their artistry by creating extravagant renditions of dresses and cloths. If you feel you might fail at drawing cloth naturalistically, it's relatively unlikely that you will be able to sculpt it in a 3D modelling software, because even the best digital artists master this only after years of study and practice. So in our example, the tablecloth was generated using a cloth simulation, based on what are known as *soft-body dynamics*. The resulting shape was then manually arranged to solve problems with the geometry.

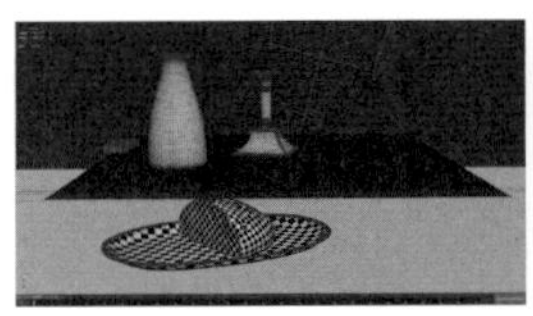
205A ○ 311

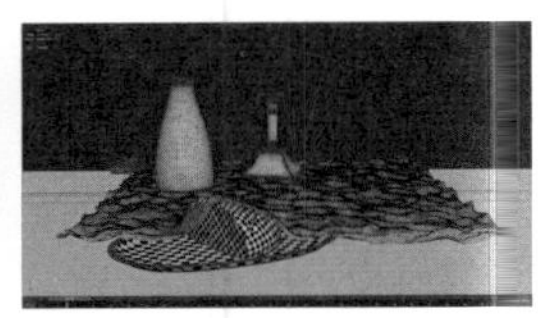
205B ○ 311

205C ○ 311

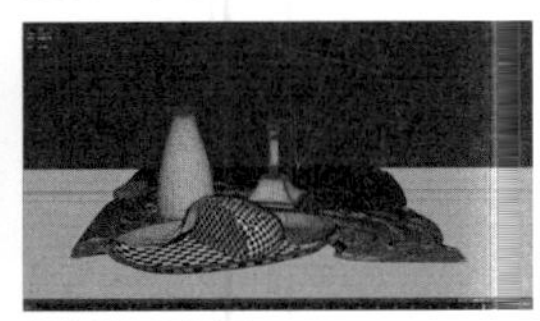
205D ○ 311

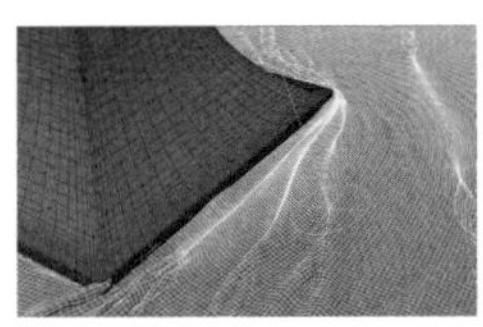
206 ○ 312

CANDLE FLAME SIMULATION (FLUID DYNAMICS)

Liquids and gaseous phenomena like fire, smoke, or magic effects are normally generated in computer graphics by using fluid dynamics simulations. Just like rigid or soft body simulations, fluid dynamics simulations use numerical models to solve systems of differential equations for the parameters in each cell for each frame. Fluid dynamics simulations are among the most expensive computations used in CG.

For the candle flame a grid-based simulation was performed to calculate how the temperature develops in each grid cell based on a heat source derived from the candle wick's geometry and a heat conservation model. With only 32,500 cells, the simulation in this case was very rough. The result is a voxel cloud (voxel stands for 'volumetric picture element') of the temperature parameters for each cell, which can be visualised directly in real time by the GPU.

By assigning a colour curve and opacity curve to the temperature values, we can render the cells as a flame/fire. At the rendering stage we can also decide whether the voxels are rendered directly, which results in a gaseous appearance, or meshed before rendering, which creates a more liquid appearance.

207 ○ 312

SCENE LIGHTING AND RENDERING
The objects in the scene are carefully arranged to reference the genre of the classical still life. All elements are visually connected by partially obscuring each other, giving depth to the scene. The tablecloth holds everything together, and by being draped over the bread loaf it also adds a narrative element: why is it arranged in this way? What happened here? The 'star object', the head of the lute, is closest to the viewer, but it is not in the centre of the composition, where instead the carafe, in fact slightly left of the image centre, is placed, reflecting the light from a window which we don't see. An upwards diagonal is established by the tops of the entities against the background, which is balanced by the line of the knife and the bread: together they break up the static perspective around the image centre.

Lighting also needs to support the mood of a classical still life: here we have a soft interior light, but with some distinct directionality to give the scene plasticity. Technically this was achieved by using a single spherical HDRI (High Dynamic Range Imaging) picture of a random interior, which fits the desired colour and luminance range. This image serves both as a global illumination light source and as a reflection environment. Important aspects of HDRI lighting are their colour space settings and the gamma/inverse gamma settings to control their exposure and contrast, which results in softer or harder shading.

208 ○ 312

POST-PRODUCTION
How much happens in post-production – that is after the image rendering is completed – varies a lot. As discussed in our chapter on Visualisation, some specialists work almost entirely in a painterly fashion, using but rudimentary renderings as the basis for their image processing and montaging work. In our example however we demonstrated a workflow that is fully computer graphics based. Thus there are no photographic elements collaged in, nor are there any matte-paintings in the final composite. So the post-production consists only of colour corrections and post lens effects like bloom and Depth of Field (DOF). Except for these, everything was done directly in the rendering program.

209 ○ 312

210A ○ 313

210B ○ 313

PHYSICALLY BASED RENDERING

When we said at the beginning of this chapter that the history of rendering can be told in 'grades of shade', that was of course something of a simplification. We wanted to show with these fundamentally incremental steps how at each stage of the development, rendering moved a little closer to what – by no means uncontroversially – could be described as 'realism'.

But there is also a fairly uncontroversial aspect to this realism that so far has not been mentioned. Realistic light simulation is not only used to produce good looking pictures, it is also a way to examine the light conditions in a space before it is built. Knowing about the lighting conditions of an environment is useful for any design project, but absolutely essential for projects such as museums and galleries, for example.

Radiance, the industry-leading program that lighting designers have been turning to for doing this type of physically based lighting simulation for many years now, was developed back in the late 1980s by Greg Ward-Larson at Lawrence Berkeley National Labs (LBNL) in California as an open-source application that anyone can download at no cost. It has been rigorously tested for predicting lighting conditions reliably and to this day is at the core of many professional lighting design solutions. Because of this, it was also, in some nerdier circles and at universities, a popular rendering program until the faster GI renderers came out. Ward-Larson, who was also an important figure in the development of the HDRI format, is continuing to work on it to this day. For more on this general topic see our chapter on Simulation. □ 475↘

REAL TIME RENDERING

We mention once or twice in this chapter, and also in our chapter on Visualisation, that the development of □ 285↘
rendering goes hand in hand with computer graphics for gaming, and that the gaming industry has played an instrumental role in advancing the technology. There the challenge is mainly one of speed, and we also touch on this repeatedly: if you create a computer game in which the aim is to give the player any kind of 'realistic' experience as they move through a setting – a landscape, a city, or a room – often in pur- □ 285↘
suit of something or someone, then you continually have to adjust the player's point of view, which means that every element that determines the lighting of the scene also has to change all the time.

If you're building a 3D simulation of a complex development or structure, with a walk-through or fly-through that takes you to any part of the building, you are dealing with much the same issue: in order for the user to experience anything that feels in the least bit 'natural', the rendering has to happen in real time, and that is very fast.

Today, this is obviously less of a problem than it □ 285↘ used to be, because of the exponentially advanced computing power that comes not just from computers' main processors (Central Processing Units or CPUs), but also, and here most significantly, from much improved graphics cards (Graphics Processing Units or GPUs), and data storage. As we noted earlier, the fact that many of the most recent GI renderers are now making use of the GPU has led to dramatic increases in speed.

On a concluding note to this section: with image rendering and photography being two very different sides of one extremely high denomination coin (if we think of the value imagery has to us in computing), it is not surprising that the trajectories of rendering techniques and photography manipulation have, since the 1960s, run in parallel curves of exponentially additive levels of sophistication. And as we see and also portray in our chapter on Visualisation, there are practitioners who approach the art of visualisation as principally one of digital painting, using an image processing program rather than working in 3D.

What doesn't change – and hasn't changed since the Renaissance – is that the creation of compelling imagery in two dimensions is an art, and that this art, whether it be drawing, painting, photography, or rendering, is one of composition, framing, and selection, and, arguably above all and enveloping everything else, lighting.

The Outlook

The concept of 'photorealism' is, in itself, deeply flawed. Strictly speaking, there is no such thing, as the moment you point a camera at anything, you are making a statement: the simple choice of your frame and where you position yourself in relation to □ 475↘ the object adds an individual, subjective input that defines the 'reality' you are looking at. If you then start to manipulate that picture in even the simplest way, be that by adjusting brightness and contrast, or be that by adding elaborate filters and touching up the picture in meticulous detail, you may be creating a more 'realistic' look, but that look is by definition an artifice.

Then again, as we have seen, photorealism is possibly no longer the watchword in rendering. The possibilities for image manipulation are limitless, and the power of rendering software now such that practically any up-to-date software and hardware combination is entirely capable of generating images that look like they were shot as photographs. The boundary that was really no longer exists.

This means that there is genuine room now for new visual languages. With anything being possible □ 285↘ and the need for emulating photography no longer □ ↖57 dominant, levels of abstraction become a matter of choice and style.

That being the case, it is hard to make any predictions as to where rendering will go next. Certainly we can observe as most recent developments more and more real time rendering, and, with advances in their capacity, more GPU rendering, which means that the task of rendering is delegated from a computer's own chip to a specialist chip, and therefore accelerated.

With rendering and simulation converging, and ■ ↖113 299↘ experiential virtual reality gaining importance also in architecture, we expect that there will be a move towards creating realistic space impressions, which are not just idealised versions of an object's design, but which come increasingly close to simulating what it will actually feel like to be in and move around a space once it is built. And again, we expect that more and more of these methods will be used simply to test the behaviour of light and materials in proposed settings, as part of the actual design and decision making process. (This is something we discuss in detail in our chapter on Simulation.)

As in so many cases, we observe two principal diverging trends: one towards a general 'democratisation' of technology – everyone now carries in their pocket a smartphone capable of taking perfect pictures – on the one hand, and towards specialisation on the other: the more everybody can do everything, the more people who are really exceptionally good at what they're doing are in demand.

As rendering has reached parity with photography, we don't really expect there to be magnificent strides in terms of the quality of pictures any more, but speed will still improve, which is particularly important in the film and gaming industries. In architecture, speed is of less significance, though here too it plays an increasingly important part in simulation settings, as we've noted. And with the continued proliferation of Visualisation and 3D Modelling there is also room for more services geared to large scale project realisations, such as render farms that do your processing for you while you keep using your computers for the purposes of design, for example.

There are highly specialist, commercial professional tools, which offer truly remarkable features such as sophisticated material and lighting libraries, but these are correspondingly expensive. And finally, here as elsewhere, there is continued and increasing potential for the open-source model to provide low cost rendering solutions for architects.

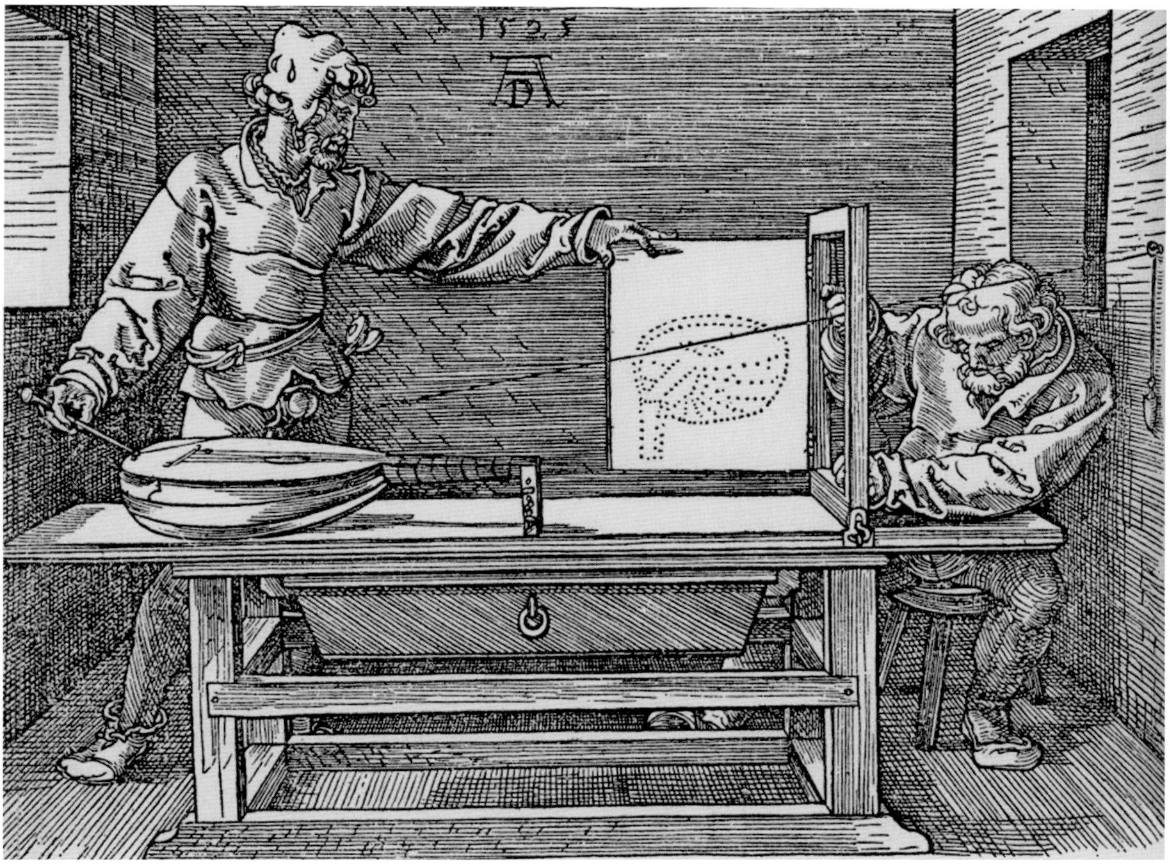

169A ● 259
A 1525 engraving showing a perspective drawing of a lute by Albrecht Dürer from his treatise *Underweysung der Messung (Four Books of Measurement)*. A string is used to trace the line of vision, intersecting with the image plane.

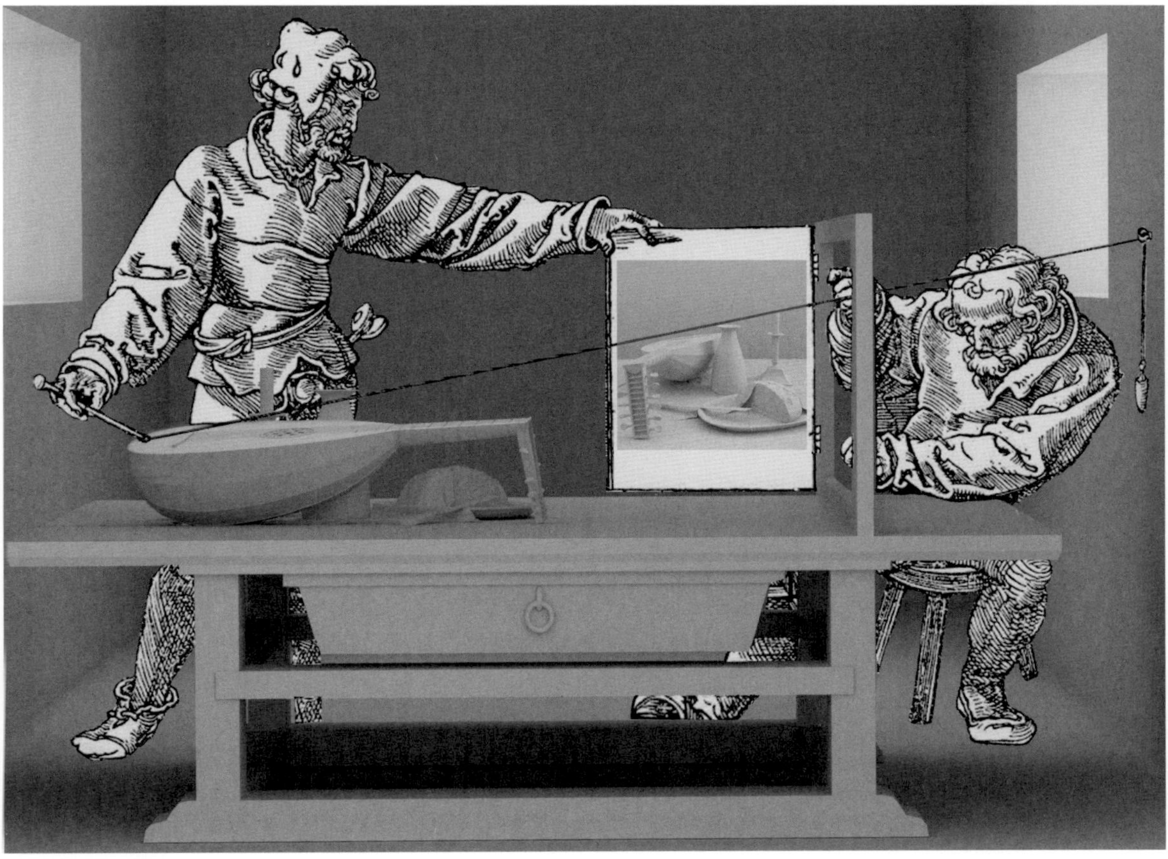

169B ● 259
The scene with lute and additional items, which is used repeatedly in this chapter, is a reference to Dürer's drawing.

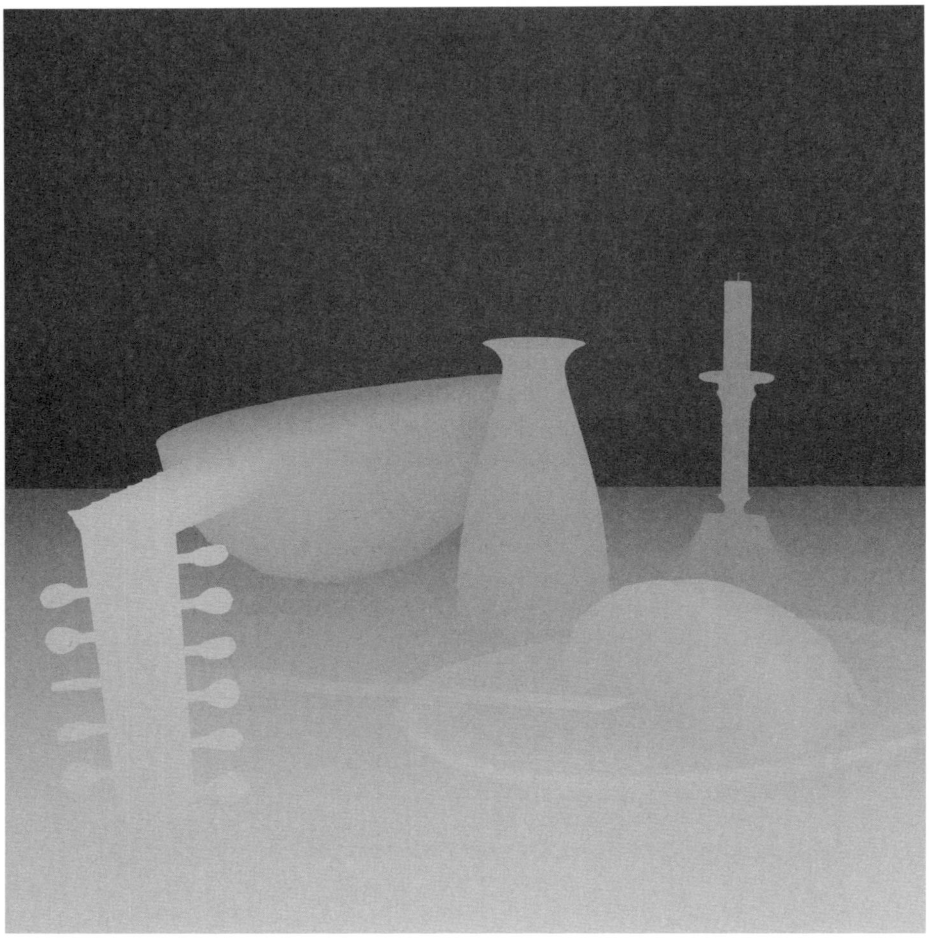

171 ● 259
Z-buffer image of the lute scene: the lighter the grey value, the closer it is to the (virtual) camera. [*Still Life With Lute* series and rendering samples: Ludwig Grimm]

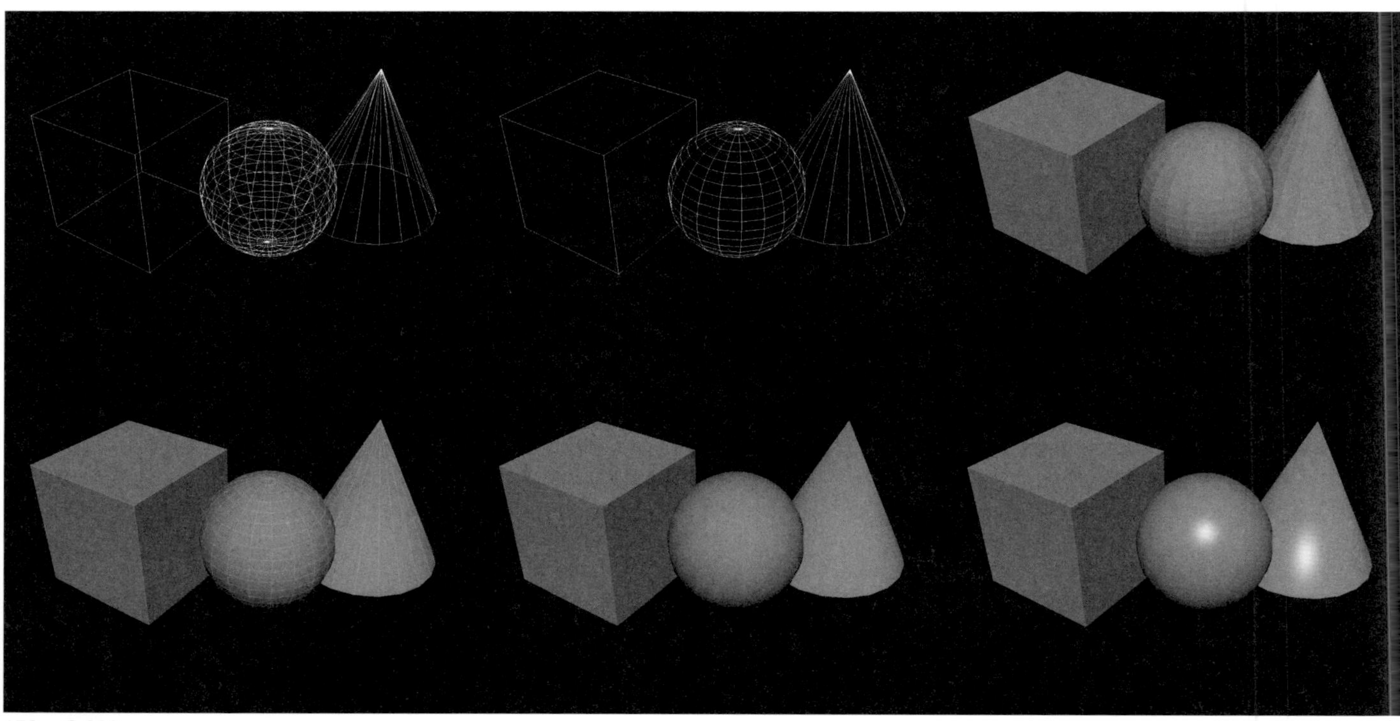

172 ● 260
The story so far: from a simple wire frame model (top left) to wire frame model with hidden lines (top middle), to flat (Lambert) shading (top right) to smooth (Gouraud) shading with and without edges (bottom left and middle) to Phong shading (bottom right). The continuous shading lets you forget that the objects are made up of individual faces. [Urs Hirschberg]

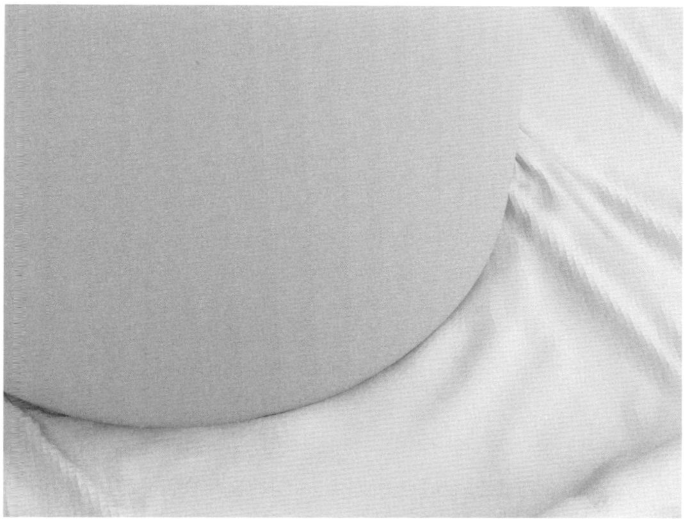

173A ● 260

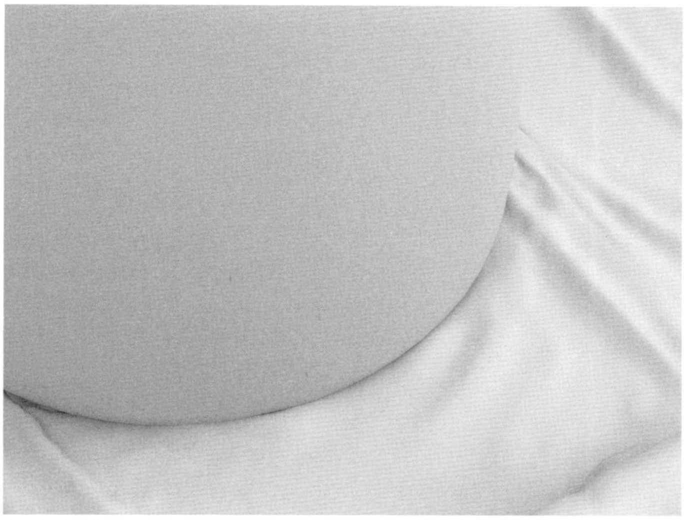

173B ● 260

Comparison between flat (Lambert) shading 173A) and smooth (Gouraud) shading (173B) on a high-poly model (a detail of the glass carafe in the still life). [LG]

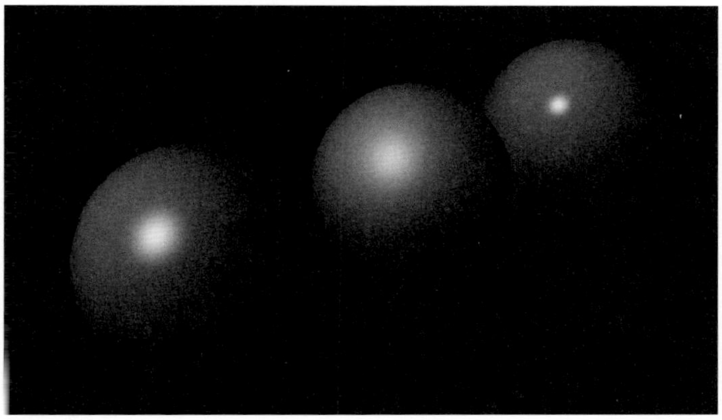

174 ● 261

Phong-E shading, Blinn-Phong shading, and Phong shading improved the rendering of specular highlights by working out the surface normal for each pixel. [Urs Hirschberg]

177 ● 263

A rendering of the famous Utah teapot using radiosity to handle diffuse illumination. [Dhatfield]

178A ● 264

178B ● 264

Scene comparison: without (178A) and with Global Illumination (178B). [LG]

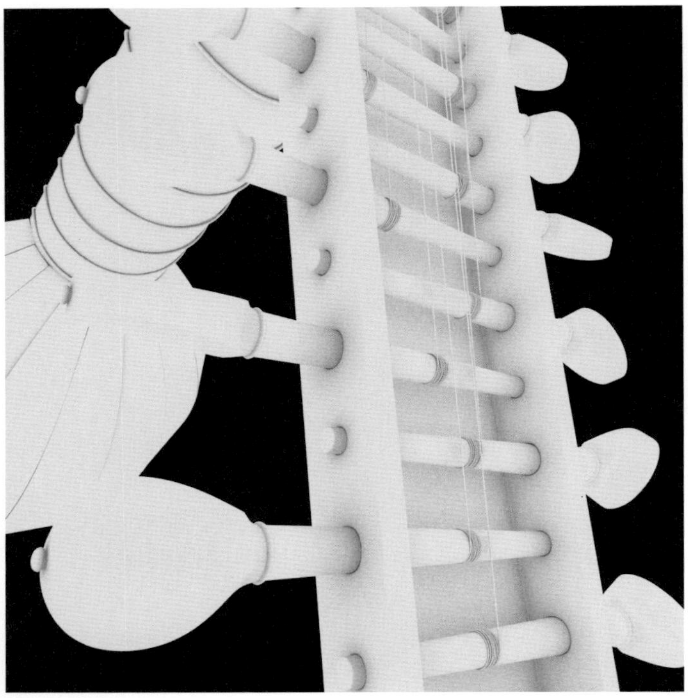

179 ● 264
Ambient occlusion calculated for tuning pegs of the lute. Ambient occlusion cuts down rendering time and accentuates the plasticity of the object or scene. [LG]

180 ● 264
Caustics in real life photography: reflections and refractions of light shining through a glass with water. [Eszter Katona / Urs Hirschberg]

181 ● 264
Subtle caustics in the lute still life. [LG]

182 ● 264
Exaggerated depth of field effect in photography: the twig of a peach tree with blossoms of which only those at mid-distance are in focus, creating a *bokeh* effect (from Japanese *boke*, meaning 'blur' or 'haze'): the aesthetic quality of the blur in the out-of-focus parts of an image produced by a lens. [Urs Hirschberg]

183A ● 264

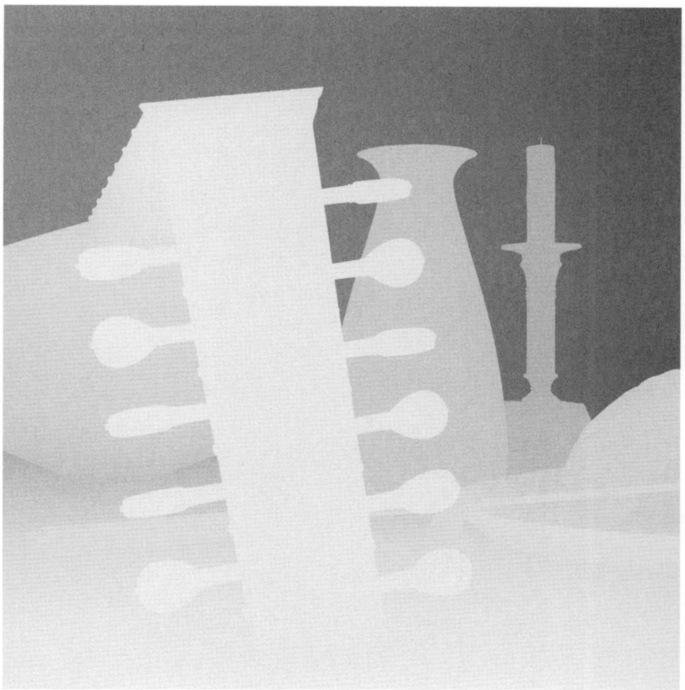

183B ● 264

183C ● 264

183D ● 264

Artificial depth of field creation based on a depth map in post-production: the rendered image without depth of field (183A), the depth map (183B), the processed image with focus on the lute head (183C) or the candle (183D). [LG]

185A ● 265

185B ● 265
Vertical lines: photograph taken with a shift lens (185A) and photograph taken from street level with a standard lens (185B). [Matthias Proske]

188A ● 266
Texture mapping describes the application of patterns or images to three-dimensional graphics to lend their surfaces a particular materiality or appearance. The image shows the basic concept as well as some of its pitfalls: a lot can go wrong with brick textures (top right). Procedural 3D textures (bottom right) avoid these problems. [Urs Hirschberg]

188B ● 266
Checker patterns are used to make the scale, direction, and distortions of textures in a model readily apparent. [LG]

189 ● 267
Procedural textures are mathematically defined patterns rather than fixed images. The procedures often make use of random functions to keep the patterns from ever repeating. Shown here are 8 of 32 procedural noise types found in the 3D software suite *Cinema 4D*. Similar procedural noise textures exist in most 3D modelling and imaging programs. The top row shows the noise texture as an image, below are applications of each noise type as displacement shaders to a sphere: normal, inverted, and at different scales, rendered with raytracing. [*Cinema4D*]

190 ● 268
Three spheres: one with simple texture, the second with bump mapping, and the third with bump as well as displacement mapping. The shadows show off the difference between bump and displacement mapping. [Urs Hirschberg]

191A ● 268 191B ● 268
Sub-surface scattering is used to calculate the nonlinear effects of translucent materials such as resin or wax. The left candle is rendered with sub-surface scattering, the right one without. The difference can be seen at the top, where the candle has a thin rim. [LG]

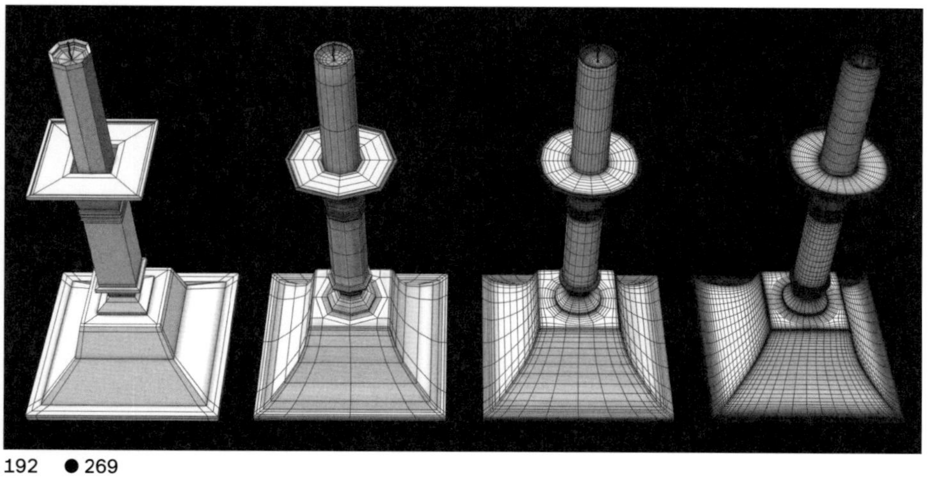

192 ● 269
Subdivision modelling of the chandelier: the original cage and 3 levels of iteration of Catmull-Clark subdivision are shown, each iteration multiplies the polygon count by 4, given a quad-based topology. [LG]

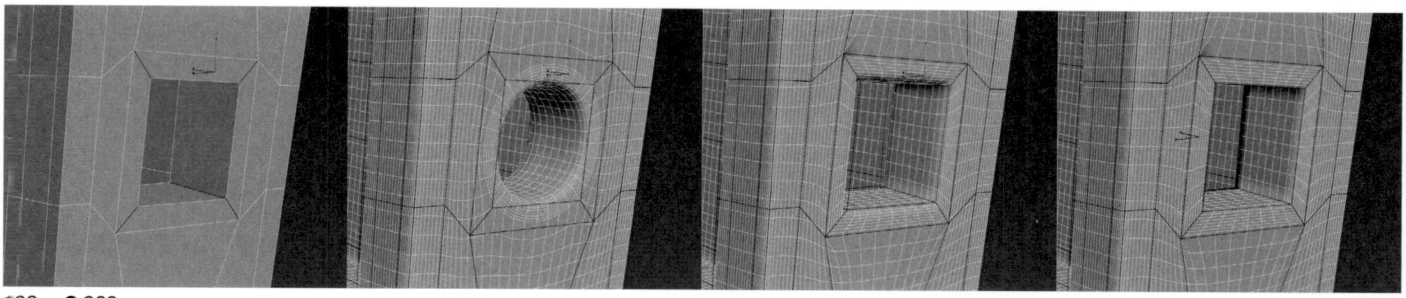

193 ● 269
Subdivision modelling of a peg-hole: With uniform spacing and weight-values of 0 for the inner edge ring of the cutout, a round hole is achieved. Setting the weights for the edge ring to 1 results in a square cut, but still its edges are chamfered. Setting the weights for the outer edge loop from 0 to 1 also sharpens the chamfer. [LG]

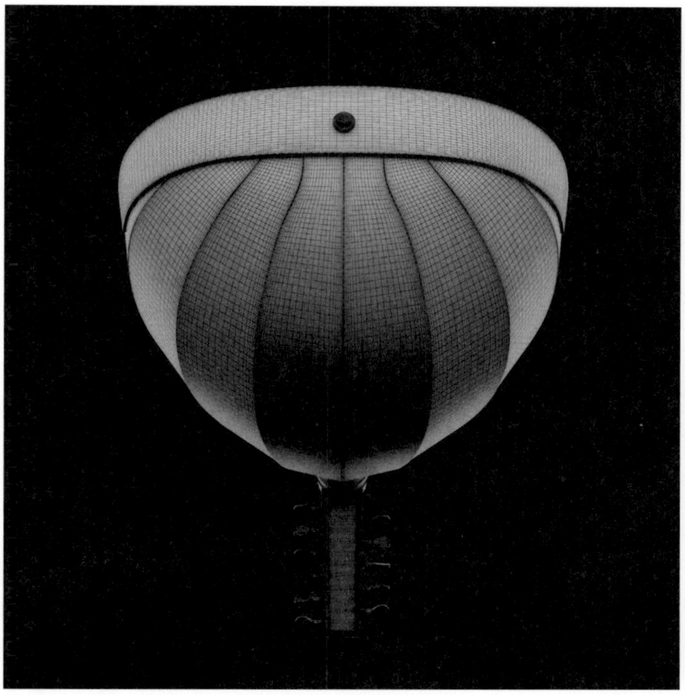

194 ● 269
Wireframe render showing the quadrilateral topology of the lute body. [LG]

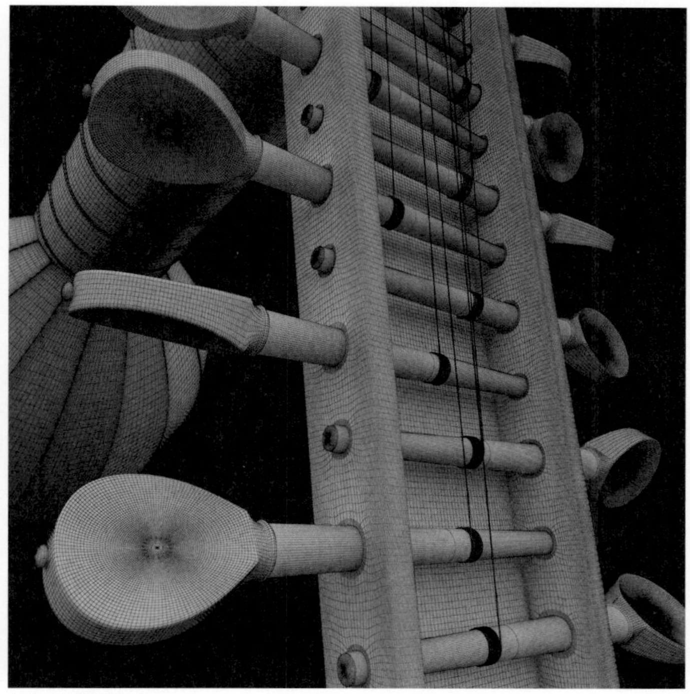

195 ○ 269
Wireframe render of the lute's head, showing the pegs with circular arrangements of triangular faces. [LG]

196 ● 269
Glossy rendering of the lute's head, to check for irregular surfaces. [LG]

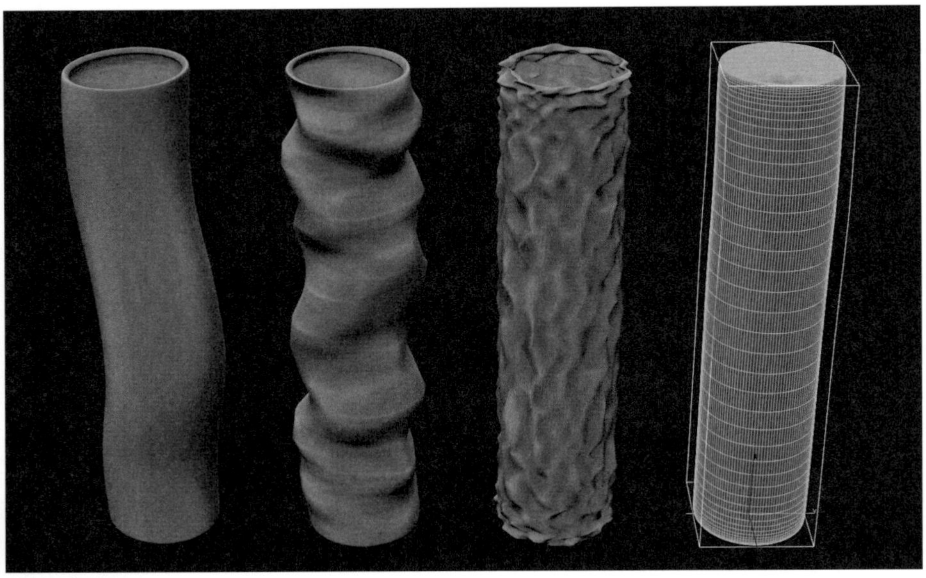

197 ● 269
Procedural geometric deformations: 4 different scale/strength combinations of noise deforming the candle geometry in X and Y, the final setting (right) gives just a subtle deformation to the overall shape. [LG]

198A ● 270 198B ● 270
UVW unwrap of the low-poly control cage. On the left you see the 3D model, on the right you see how all its faces are flattened and placed on a common 2D texture UV-field. As it is difficult to control the unwrap of a subdivided high-poly model, the underlying low-poly control cage is often used instead as a first step. [LG]

199A ● 270

199B ● 270

The smoothing of the subdivision can result in unwanted stretching when the unwrap is applied to the high-poly model, as can be seen in the checkerboard pattern on the left. To fix this, the unwrap needs to be 'relaxed', based on the subdivided topology. The result of this relaxation step is shown on the right. Now the texture of the wood pattern will be mapped without distortions. [LG]

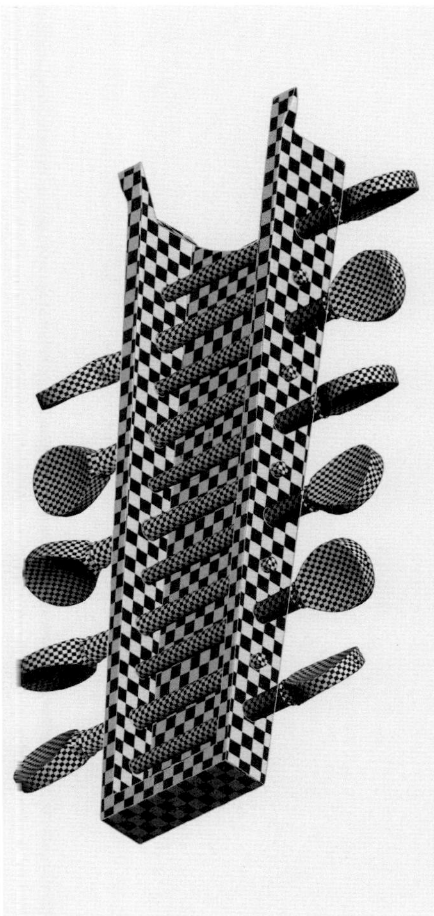

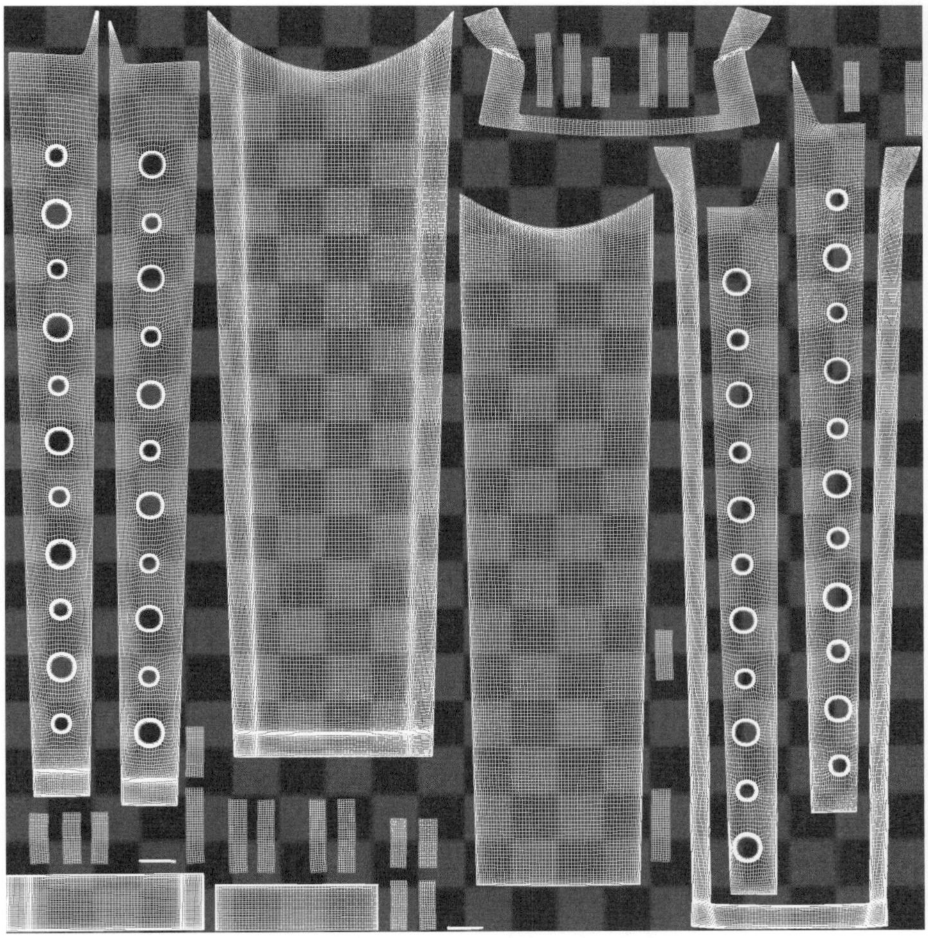

200A ● 270

200B ● 270

UVW-unwrapping completed: the final relaxed unwrap of the high-poly version of the head of the lute. [LG]

Visualisation

Dominik Lengyel, Philipp Schaerer

- Barbara Schock-Werner, Dominik Lengyel, Catherine Toulouse: *Die Bauphasen des Kölner Domes und seiner Vorgängerbauten. Cologne Cathedral and Preceding Buildings*, 2011
- Karla Kroeper, Sylvia Schoske, Dietrich Wildung (Eds.): *Königsstadt Naga. Grabungen in der Wüste des Sudan, Naga – Royal City*, 2011
- Excellence Cluster Topoi (Eds.): *Jenseits des Horizonts. Raum und Wissen in den Kulturen der Alten Welt*, 2012
- Ralf Grüßinger, Volker Kästner, Andreas Scholl (Eds.): *Pergamon. Panorama der antiken Metropole*, 2012
- Dietrich Boschung, Julian Jachmann (Eds.): *Diagrammatik der Architektur*, 2013
- Stefan Klösges, Eberhard Metternich (Eds.): *In aeternum cantabo. Zeugnisse aus 1300 Jahren kölnischer DomMusikGeschichte*, 2013
- Damian Dombrowski, Markus Josef Maier, Fabian Müller (Eds.): *Julius Echter. Patron der Künste: Konturen eines Fürsten und Bischofs der Renaissance*, 2017
- Bernd Nicolai, Jürg Schweizer (Eds.): *Das Berner Münster. Das erste Jahrhundert: Von der Grundsteinlegung bis zur Chorvollendung und Reformation (1421–1517/1528)*, 2019

Overview

"The height of sophistication," the American writer and diplomat Clare Boothe Luce (1903–1987) wrote in one of her novels, "is simplicity."

You may be forgiven for thinking that this is a truism, but perhaps that in itself makes it worth remembering as we talk about Visualisation. Because the subject of this chapter unites upon itself a myriad of techniques and a spectrum of approaches that allow for untold levels of sophistication and differentiation, as well as both artistic and technical detail, precision, and accuracy. At the heart of it though lies a simple premise and goal: to bring to life visually an object that for some reason or other cannot be pictured by capturing it on camera as it is.

Whichever technique you use – and there are dozens: drawing, sketching, collage, cartoons, photographic image editing/processing, modelling, and rendering, to name but these few – the moment you do any of these on a computer to the end of generating a new image, you are in essence doing a form of digital 'painting', whereby 'painting' here very broadly stands for 'creating a picture of the thing you want to represent *deliberately*.' This is what distinguishes it from, say, taking a snapshot of a building with your camera and just leaving it as it is, or allowing a computer to work out a pattern of lines, shapes, and surfaces based purely on some data you enter, to come up with an exact but otherwise uncharacterised image of what it knows.

What all visualisation has in common is that it interprets the object it portrays, and that it seeks to go beyond conveying mere information about it. It wants to trigger an emotional response and communicate something about the object that I as the person visualising it know and feel about it: what I consider important, how it sits in its context, what it was, is, or could be used for, what it means. Much as a painting conveys an artist's interpretation of a subject – whatever that may be: a person, a building, a still life, an abstraction, a fantasy, or a void – so a visualisation conveys an interpretation by the visualiser. As the visualiser, I have at my disposal exactly the same constituent elements that a painter or photographer has to give an image character and emotional impact: perspective, focus, and light; colour and setting; framing, detail, texture, and features, or indeed their absence.

A BRIEF HISTORY OF VISUALISATION

Before we go into the practice of visualisation, let us, as usual in this *Atlas*, briefly delve into its origins. It is not an entirely unexpected turn of events that has led us to visualisation as we know it today, and yet there are some fascinating twists in the tale.

Saying that architecture has always been visually represented is not only stating the obvious, it's also repeating ourselves, but we do so here simply to emphasise that visualisation in itself is neither new nor extraordinary: it's simply part and parcel of architecture. But across our spectrum of different techniques and approaches – we like to think of it more as a very large tent than a spectrum, covering, as it does, a very expansive area – digital technology has, as it has everywhere, made the image not only omnipresent and therefore more important, but also much more potent, in the sense of what the image itself can and does achieve.

The first steps from plans and drawings of projects towards digital visualisation were taken when it became possible to represent vectors and graphics □ ↖285 on computers. As early as 1954, the American computer scientist Douglas T Ross (1929–2007) wrote a program that was able to trace the movement of his finger, and display its vector – his handwritten name – on an oscilloscope ■ ↖231. He not only wrote the first hand-drawn graphics input program for a computer, he also developed the concept of the Automatically Programmed Tool (APT) ■ 409↘, a programming language and system that makes it possible for computers to control machinery, which therefore constitutes the principle behind Digital Manufacturing □ 405↘. And it was he who gave us the term Computer Aided Design (CAD) □ ↖129, without which architecture as we know it today would not exist. On both of these we therefore unsurprisingly have separate chapters in this *Atlas*.

By the late 1960s, the technique of ray tracing ■ ↖261 481↘ was under development, allowing for near-photo-realistic images to be rendered entirely on software. Ray tracing is so called because it traces the path of light from the viewer across the two-dimensional image plane to the light source, and simulates the effect it has on the objects it encounters. Ray tracing was by no means perfect though, its principal drawback being that it could not deal with diffuse light reflections, which the real world is awash with. But this alone – accurately representing how objects look under different, and differently arranged, lighting conditions – signalled a leap in computer generated imagery and paved the way for what we now recognise as visualisation, and also, as it happens, 3D Modelling □ ↖57, on which we also have a chapter in this *Atlas*.

The mid-1980s nudged both visualisation and 3D modelling further centre stage, with graphics interfaces becoming first more widely available and subsequently the norm on mass-produced computers, putting them into the hands of individual designers and small design studios at comparatively low cost. Before then, unless you were highly specialised and somewhat ahead of the curve, as an architect you had to colour and shade your drawings by hand.

Also dating back to the 1950s in terms of its origins, and achieving a breakthrough in the mid-1980s is the image rendering method known as radiosity ■ ↖262. This is based on a detailed analysis of how light reflects on diffuse surfaces, generating images that have a much softer light and shade gradation, making them therefore both more realistic and more artistic as well.

For all their various limitations, both ray tracing and radiosity marked significant steps towards Global Illumination (GI) ■ ↖262, which is the umbrella term used for all methods that model the behaviour of ambient or indirect light; and from about now onwards – the late 1980s and through the 1990s – computer graphics tools became ever more sophisticated and capable, making visualisation genuinely more interesting. A breakthrough occurred in April 2006 with the release of *Maxwell Render*, a commercially developed ray tracing-based software that was able to simulate diffuse lighting far beyond what had been possible with ray tracing before: this gave you lighting tools and features on your computer that were no longer dissimilar to what you might have at your fingertips in a real life photo studio. □ ↖255

Meanwhile, in 1987, a young American software engineer, Thomas Knoll (b. 1960), who was then a PhD student at the University of Michigan, encouraged and assisted by his brother John Knoll (b. 1962), who was working as a special effects supervisor for a visual effects company, sat down to create a piece of software which the following year, in 1988, they licensed to Adobe Systems, and which has since become the kind of household name that people use as a verb. To *photoshop* is something that has long ceased to be a purely professional pursuit, and many an image ingrained on our minds owes its qualities (whether they be memorable for the right reasons or not) to someone putting this particular application to use.

In this *Atlas* you'll find a dedicated chapter on Rendering, which covers in more detail the different (and incremental) lighting techniques that led us to where we are today.

211 ● 300

Visualising Now

We've pitched visualisation as a large tent, and one of the reasons for doing so is that under its metaphorical canopy come together such varied practices (or 'disciplines', if you like) as architecture, photography, archaeology; design of any description including urban, industrial, fashion, and consumer product design; and historical research; quite as much as science, fiction, and science fiction. Therein lies its rich potential, with which, of course, come potential pitfalls too.

Because whenever we are called upon to show something that either does not yet exist, or has once existed but has ceased to do so, or that does still exist, but is no longer intact, or anything that is simply too small, too large, too abstract, or too imaginary for us to employ purely reality based imaging techniques in its depiction, we are skirting, and quite often entering, the realm not only of interpretation but also of fabrication. In many situations we create an assembly of what we accept or assume to be knowable or possible facts. And that means there comes a considerable degree of responsibility with the act of visualisation, because we are planting images in people's minds that can be difficult for them to shed or ignore. This may be of little consequence if what we are visualising is a fantastical utopian world for the sake of a piece of entertainment; it may be gravely serious though if we are visualising an archaeological complex of historical significance.

Visualisation can and does use photography and photographic components and techniques (as we shall explore in some detail), yet the essence of visualisation is one of generating imagery artificially. And artificial though the process may be, it is far from automatic. If anything, it is the opposite: it requires manual skills that want to be acquired and honed. Because although digital visualisations are made mostly on computers, they're not made *by* computers. Nor can they be, if they are to have any claim to specificity and expertise, or to scientific or artistic validity, or any combination of these.

Be it an historic site that has long since crumbled to the ground but that you want to evoke fresh in the viewer's mind, or be it a project you want to conjure up for the first time in its as yet only imagined glory: if you furnish your visualisation with off-the shelf components, textures, finishes, and elements, then how can you possibly do it justice as an individual, even unique architectural entity? What you arrive at would be a generic fudge which may as easily be any other site or project. Applied to archaeology it can't begin to be historically or scientifically accurate; and applied to design it can't have any artistic integrity, unless in each case the elements that are being used have been made bespoke to the job in hand or adapted so as to suit it precisely.

As a serious visualiser you will learn to differentiate between what the algorithm can and can't do, and as you develop your style you will decide what you are going to use the tools, building components, and elements that are available to you for. But beyond this, you will need to understand some of the basic principles of photography, such as composition, focal length, aperture, and viewer perspective. Firstly because you may be taking pictures as your source material, but secondly, and no less importantly, because you are going to generate images that in one way or another resemble photographs, by virtue of the fact alone that they are two-dimensional representations of three-dimensional objects. The extent to which they resemble photographs is something you yourself can determine. Whether the approach you take is one of photographic realism or one of highly stylised conceptual abstraction is entirely up to you (or perhaps up to you and your client or employer). And even if you make a conscious decision that your visualisations should not resemble photographs at all, or paintings, or drawings, or any type of image known to humankind, but speak in an entirely new and individual visual language of their own, it will still be useful for you to know how this positions your pictures in relation to real life photographs.

Similarly, you'll want to know how lighting affects a scene, not just in terms of what is visible and what isn't, but also in terms of how it creates or changes the atmosphere of a space. And the same applies to the setting or environment: whether you are going to leave it blank and suggest that whatever there may be in the surroundings of your object is for the viewer to imagine, or whether you are going to paint a virtual picture of detailed landscaping, peopled with life-like figures going about their business under a summery sky, you will be making conscious decisions all along the way, because you are the director of the scene.

Visualisation then – and this can no doubt be said of any other digital creative process – is really a case of autonomous thinking: using the software of your choice to arrive at what you want to achieve, and understanding the principles of how the program helps you do this, even if you don't know the intricate workings of it.

THOSE PITFALLS

Digital visualisation has many obvious advantages over the purely manual techniques that preceded it, no question: speed, flexibility, incremental retouchability, expandability, transportability, versatility... – these all hardly need to be further expounded on at this point.

But there are also some dangers, the 'pitfalls' we mentioned earlier. Looming largest among them is one we've also already pointed out: that we 'fall victim' to, or at any rate allow ourselves to be seduced by, the convenience of automation; that instead of investing the time and effort it takes to acquire skill and experience, we think, 'the software can create this for me', and start doing things we wouldn't otherwise do.

Take for example *ArchiCAD*, the widely used commercial Building Information Modelling (BIM) software, launched by Graphisoft in 1984 (originally as *Radar CH*), when it effectively ushered in BIM as a modelling approach. (We naturally have a chapter on BIM in this *Atlas*.) In the version that was current as we first started writing this chapter in March 2017, when you opened a new project in 'photo realism' mode in a 3D viewer window, you as a default got a fresh spinach green ground and an immaculate blue sky to set you on your way.

There is nothing inherently wrong with either of these, except chances are you would not normally commence a new project with these two elements. But since they're there, you may understandably feel inclined to use them as your 'set' to start your composition. Being your 'set', they may or may not still be there by the time you're done, but they will certainly influence everything you do from the very beginning, even if subtly, subconsciously. And that means you've already succumbed to an automatism. That is no crime, but it's something you'll want to be aware of, because architecture that relies more and more on increasingly powerful rendering software is innately susceptible to what could be described as 'bad practice', where computer generated imagery acquires a degree of monotony which then is reflected in the architecture itself that is being built.

This can go so far as to turn into 'lazy architecture', when rather than using the available tools to develop and define an individual, recognisable style, it uses them to produce off-the-peg designs that are semi-prefabricated by the software itself. You can't, of course, blame the software for this: what the architect does with the available tools is really entirely the responsibility of the architect. And you can't blame the software developers either, because they obviously want to make things easy for you, helping you to get started as quickly and painlessly as possible, and then ushering you along a path of minimum resistance: that, to some extent, is their job. Yours is to put their work to good practice.

For the architect who uses visualisation in proposals and as part of the design process, there is one more thing to be at the very least aware of: if we put in front of our client a magnificent set of images that depict in captivating detail our vision for our project, with features, materials, decorative elements all beautifully rendered, we are making an explicit or implicit promise to deliver on this. Even if we make sure that our contract doesn't hold us to these earliest manifestations, we are putting these images in the minds of the people who make decisions and very possibly many others too, and almost no matter how experienced and intelligent they are, they will use them as their reference, if nothing else subconsciously. The great freedom we've enjoyed while creating the images can thus quickly turn into our shackles, as we risk leaving a trail of disappointment and frustration if we don't come up with what is now expected from us; and so we no longer have the leeway to pursue an incremental, explorative, emergent design process, because we've already locked our design into a fixed pitch.

A similar danger lingers for the visualisation of historical or archaeological architecture: if we are going to visualise the Metropolis of Pergamon, for example, whatever we put out there as an image then lives in the eye of the beholder. And once nested there, it may be almost impossible to erase the idea of it, should that become necessary. So we have to be circumspect not only in what assumptions we make about things we can't be sure of, but also how we use the reference material and data we have, and of which we think we are sure. If a picture speaks a thousand words, there may not be any guarantee that any of them are actually true. □ 507↘

One final flag we want to raise. Picture material, architectural references, the works of star architects whom we may be inspired by and even wish to emulate: all these are so accessible, so 'easy to grab' online, we can simply help ourselves to any components that they've come up with, and then rustle up our own creative soup with them. The 'stories' we tell today, with digital technology and constant, instant access to the global repository of the Internet, become very fast. We express ourselves mostly through imagery, but we don't necessarily have, or devote the time to find, our own social, political, and ecological position yet. But as architects – and not 'just' as architects, but also as contemporary human beings and digital citizens – we need to take a position, we have to claim the right to think as well as execute; to decide what is necessary, what is beautiful, what is excess and what is essence, what is scientific knowledge, and what is make believe, and then deal with these in whichever way we actively choose. (We discuss this particular phenomenon – the abundance of references in our age – and what to do with this abundance in our chapter on Being a 'Brand'.) □ 593↘

Two Examples, Two Approaches

We are uniquely placed to demonstrate this 'large tent' we have been speaking of, because our two topic experts for this chapter, Dominik Lengyel and Philipp Schaerer, are taking two really rather different approaches to visualisation, to two contrasting ends. This prompts us to make an exception in this case to all the other chapters in this *Atlas*. Whereas we disallow, throughout the book, that the topic experts of each chapter cite their own work, we here think that this would be missing an opportunity. Also, the work of both contributors is by its very nature visual, and so we are not in fact about to 'cite their research' so much as we are going to show examples of their work to illustrate what we mean when we explain their practice.

The two approaches have most of what we've so far been talking about in common. What separates them from each other more than anything else is that they visualise towards two quite different objectives. The techniques each use in their work are also different, but while not all methods are equally suitable for all purposes, it also isn't the case that the technique determines the approach. The whole point of visualisation, as we noted at the beginning, is that you make visible things that are either not yet or no longer there, or that are there but that cannot otherwise be seen. How you do this is to quite some extent up to you.

With the first approach, that of Dominik Lengyel, we find ourselves at the intersection of archaeology, architecture, and photography, where the objective of visualisation is to make explicit some, implicit other, facets of historical structures that either no longer exist or of which we now possess only the ruins or fragmented finds. This is a process of 'reconstructing' a once given spatial reality, and making it visible to the contemporary viewer in a way that on the one hand allows us to understand the building as it once was, while at the same time on the other hand also accepting that there are, in most cases, things we simply don't know for certain and that we therefore cannot visually represent with authority. This requires a great deal of scientific, even forensic, accuracy, and may, in traditional, purely archaeologically factual visual representations, lead to images that look 'incomplete' and abstract to the contemporary eye, because they deliberately omit any unknowns, leaving them to the imagination of the viewer. Here, the challenge of the visualiser is to honour the science and respect the limitations of what is known, and to what degree of certainty, whilst still 'painting' a picture that is compelling and engaging.

↖70 353↘

With the second approach, that of Philipp Schaerer, we find ourselves at the intersection of architecture, photography, and design, where the objective of visualisation is to demonstrate what is going to be, or could potentially be, built, but doesn't as yet exist. Since so much of architecture is 'consumed' – even long before it is made – in imagery that is proliferated in print (as it has been for centuries), and now exponentially also online, the consideration of what *kind* of images this architecture will spawn once it stands has moved to the core of its inception. This therefore also influences, even determines, to a very large extent the kinds of images that get generated as visualisations during the proposition and planning phases of a project.

In most cases, we are working with architecture that is going to form a new part of an existing context, and so visualising it in this context – perhaps even dramatising it – becomes crucial to the job: fleshing out detail, settling on materials, conveying the haptic experience, imagining how people will move, behave, and interact in the space, all these may in reality come further down the line (the project may not even yet have approval). But in order for it to capture the imagination of decision makers – who may range from individual clients to increasingly complex client-side boards and committees, to authorities which may have a plethora of regulatory and heritage restrictions to consider, right through to public opinion – the visualisation has to convince as a proposition, and sell a potential reality, irrespective of whether that reality then ever does, or does not, come about.

UNCERTAIN KNOWLEDGE – VISUALISING HISTORY

In 1965, the Azerbaijan-born, internationalist mathematician Lofti Zadeh (1921–2017) introduced to the world of mathematics the term **fuzzy set theory** to mean sets of defined objects that could have any degree of membership, rather than requiring that something either is or is not a member of a set, with no other options in-between. At the same time, he also coined the expression **fuzzy logic** to similarly describe a logic in which any real number between 0 and 1 may be true, unlike **Boolean logic**, which allows this to be the case only for either the values 0 or 1 (whereby in computing usually 0 is designated to mean 'false', and 1 'true', though it could also be the other way round).

The concept of fuzziness is a useful reference for us in the context of visualising the past, because the past comes to us through the haze of history and is therefore blurred, with its elements no longer clearly 'defined', even if they once were. History creates a haze because through time details get lost, physical substance is damaged or eroded; paper, papyrus, and vellum on which records were kept fall victim to weather, fire, and wilful destruction. None of this is a mystery. What turns into a part mystery is a vision of how things once really were. And we, trying to 'solve' this mystery, have to use what knowledge we have to build a picture of the past that is as accurate as it can be. This, it could be said, is a translation of a once physical experience into a visual representation, and because we are no longer able to actually experience the building physically, we are also no longer able to take pictures of it, which means we have to employ other means to represent the uncertain knowledge we have in a way that is clear enough for us to make sense of it.

'Making sense of it' here – in the historical, archaeological context of visualisation – is a critical factor. What we are really concerned with is arriving at a *scientifically valid* visual representation of what we know for certain. This means that we have to draw on all the available data and information (the 'hard facts', so to speak) and weigh up the, often many diverse, hypotheses and interpretations that have been produced on their basis by the community of archaeologists, historians, restorers, and architects who work with the given object, and then make something visually compelling of it. And this, 'making something visually compelling of it', gets to the nub of what we aspire to: often a diagram could easily represent the known facts. It could do so accurately and intelligibly. What visualisation wants to achieve though is to represent the known facts and the scientifically established hypotheses in a way with which we can readily connect, a way that makes sense not only intellectually and at an abstract level, but at an emotive level too, while leaving – and this is of immense importance – the facts and the hypotheses recognisably intact.

We have a wide array of methods available to do this, including all those already mentioned, ranging from traditional, pre-digital, to purely digital ones, in any combination. Here we want to concentrate on modelling, rendering, and retouching, simply because they are used in the practice of Dominik Lengyel and his partner Catherine Toulouse, whose work we are using as our example; and we'll also briefly highlight the role black and white imagery plays in this type of visualisation in particular.

As already mentioned, we dedicate separate chapters to both 3D Modelling and Rendering in this *Atlas*, so we will not explain these techniques in great detail here.

MODELLING

Digital 3D Modelling (as opposed to physical Model Making, which you'll also find a chapter on in this *Atlas*) today tends to form the basis from which practically everything else flows: it holds all the dimensions, the proportions, the data, and metadata that is known about an object. And so at the core of any visualisation that involves computer generated rendering, there has to be a virtual 3D model of the object that is being dealt with, in other words a data set that contains all the critical values and relationships that define it as a three-dimensional thing in space.

RENDERING

Rendering, in visualisation, very specifically is the generation of a two-dimensional image from a three-dimensional model. The model can be as simple or as intricate as it wants to be, it can be a very sparse, highly abstract, and 'skeletal' basic outline, or it can be an elaborately built scene with exquisite naturalistic detail, or anything in-between; the render process does to the virtual 3D model what a photograph does to a physical model: it transfers the object from three dimensions to two.

And much as a photo camera can only capture in an image what's there – leaving aside just for the moment the extraordinary extent to which the image, once captured, can then be manipulated in post-production – so a computer can only render information that it has. This means that anything we want to show up in the rendered image has to at some point be given to the rendering engine as an instruction. Where, how, and when this happens makes a great deal of difference to the result. The more care, therefore, I take in considering the type and character of detail I want to add to the model or scene, and the more diligently I handle things such as textures, lighting, and camera angle, the more refined the rendered image will be. The same, again, is true for a photographer and a physical model: the more thought that goes into the detailing and setup – the context and lighting, and the angle from which a picture is taken – the better the chances of a successful result.

Aside from the principal distinction that a rendering is a computer generated image of a virtual model as opposed to a captured image of a real-life object, the big difference between a rendering and a photograph is that the rendering software will come with a 'box' of tools and settings which can partly automate the process of image generation. As we discussed earlier when we looked at *'Those Pitfalls'*, depending on how I use these settings and how much I rely on patterns, textures, styles, and templates offered by the software, I may give a lot of control over to the program and end up taking very limited influence on the look and feel of the rendered image. But I absolutely don't have to: I can, and in our view should, customise, adapt, or in fact wholly eschew any of the off-the-shelf tools, and generate my render as a perfectly unique instance. And obviously, as with any photograph, I can then take the rendered image and work on it in as much detail as ☐ ↖57
I like in post-production. As we're about to see, this ☐ ↖255
is in fact an essential part of visualisation.

As a technique, rendering lends itself well to an incremental or evolutionary approach, whereby you refine the image with each iteration to the point ☐ ↖57
where it can be almost impossible to tell it apart ☐ 421↘
from an actual photograph. And because its basis is always the 3D model, you can generate any variety of pictures from the same source: you can change the lighting, camera angles, even animate camera pans, and thus render the exact same scene or object in as many different versions as you want or need.

RETOUCHING

'Retouching' simply means image post-production in one of any number of available image editing programs. As with photography, this part of the job is at least as important, if not in many cases more, than ☐ ↖255
the image generation itself. With the editing tools available today, there are virtually no limits as to how a picture can be transformed, which is why one of the most critical questions I, as the visualiser, have to consider during the entire process of visualisation is what I want to retouch in what way, and why.

The reason this is so important is that in truth *every* image is retouched manually. Normally you will at the very least adjust colour tone and grade, commonly using non-destructive settings, meaning that you can adjust, undo, and redo them freely as they do not affect the source image. The same techniques are used to generate, for example, background elements or an artificial gradient of the sky, intended to suggest spatial depth.

212 ● 300

Different brightness values in an object – and especially the levelling of brightness in the transition from object to sky – make careful fine-tuning essential. In order to get seamless transitions in rendered images, a pixel or colour depth of at least 16 bit is required, though you get better results with 32 bit depth, because the lower the bit rate, the rougher and more 'jagged' transitions become. (We talk in more detail about image depth and the technical aspects
□ ↖229 of raster imaging in our chapter on Image & Colour.)

What also makes retouching necessary is the integration of photographic elements in a rendered image. In this following example of the Cologne Cathedral interior, the sculptures you see on either side were photographed especially for the purpose of this visualisation. Capturing and adjusting them involved a process of several steps: first, the position of the sculptures in the virtual model was determined, to achieve a meaningful composition. Next – using ladders, a *Laser-DISTO* measuring device, and zoom lenses – the sculptures were measured and photographed in the highest possible resolution. This way, the perspective projection of each sculpture corresponded exactly to its rendered version in the image montage. And while it was then no longer possible to move the sculptures in the virtual model, you could still pan the camera to achieve an animation in which only the positions of the sculptures themselves had to remain fixed. (You will find a link to this if you follow the QR code on the title page of this chapter.)

213A ○ 313

213B ○ 313

DEPTH

We've already mentioned imitating the gradient of brightness in a natural sky to get a sense of depth in an image to serve its overall coherence. Another technique to the same purpose is the gradual fading of saturation and contrast, as happens in nature through mist and the haze of pollution, for example. In rendering, you can
■ ↖259 use the Z-buffer tool, which converts the entire scene into a greyscale image in which those elements nearest to camera appear white and those furthest away black. Using an image matte, you can then apply *Photoshop* effects such as fading into the distance as control channels in a corresponding settings layer.

In abstract representations you often have large flat surfaces (such as walls) that, left untreated, look unnatural. So for the sake purely of plasticity it may be necessary to use similar techniques as those just described to achieve some depth, and complement them with gradual progressions which would not result from a purely algorithmic lighting calculation. These do not, therefore, serve to correct the lighting conditions as such, but simply help the eye, which needs something to hold on to when it casts over wholly homogeneous surfaces that do not in reality exist. (You could say: depth technique here compensates for natural texture. – See Figure 211.)

BLACK & WHITE PHOTOGRAPHY

It is one of the great achievements of photography that we accept black and white images as just as realistic as those in colour. In visualisation we can take advantage of this when we want to avoid exposing the comparatively safe assumptions we can make about an object's geometry to the great uncertainty we may have about its colour scheme. Only an image that is kept entirely monochrome can solve this dilemma. We can't, for example, give in to the temptation of colouring the sky in blue, because that would add the dimension of colour and we would no longer be dealing with a black and white image: the buildings would suddenly 'be' white. But they may in fact have any kind of shade that we can't be sure of. To avoid this type of categorical falsification, the sky really has to stay grey, like the rest of the picture. And we know from many fine examples in photography that black and white pictures can evoke the brilliant blue sky of a sunny day just as powerfully as a colour photograph.

As noteworthy examples of the use of clear contrasts in black and white photography in an archeological context we would cite the work of German photographer, artist, and director Walter Hege (1893–1955), and in the context of reduced forms, such as we find them in classical modernity in architecture, the work of American architectural photographer Julius Shulman (1910–2009), whom we also encounter and quote further on in this chapter.

THE DILEMMA OF THE DIAGRAM

Speaking, as we were, of dilemmas: in the realm we are in – the one of the historically as-accurate-as-possible visualisation – we quite generally face this particular dilemma of how to reconcile scientific fact with evoking an emotional response. Our aim, after all, is to make experienceable something that can no longer be experienced. So we want our image to be more than a technical diagram: we want it to be experiential, even emotive.

There are some simple steps we can take to achieve this. We can, for example, choose our point of view. A ground plan or elevation drawing is clearly a visual representation of a building, but it is also an abstraction in perception. One we can read and understand, but one that doesn't in that sense give us a 'feel' for what we're looking at. We have to be quite expert to project from the diagrammatical picture in our minds a fully modelled image that has texture, detail, and atmosphere. But if we position ourselves where a human being might have positioned themselves in relation to the life-size structure, we already get a closer approximation to the experience of being there.

Another significant element we can introduce and control, and that we've already mentioned a couple of times, is light: by adding to the image everything we know about the way an object is lit – how the light enters through windows, where the sun is in relation to the building, what other light sources were available and how they were used – we immediately let it be much more 'alive'.

Neither of these solves our main dilemma though: that of the diagram. If we really use only the information and science we have, then in most cases we will still be restricted to a largely diagrammatical form of visualisation. And diagrams are notoriously bad at conveying emotion. So, if we stick at too abstract a level, we fail in our endeavour to communicate the full architectonic idea of a building as an experience. But if we begin to liberally sprinkle our visualisation with imagined colours, decorations, finishes, and textures, we remove ourselves from the scientific validity of our work.

This is a limitation we can embrace. We can say to ourselves: by keeping our visualisation at this level of abstraction we communicate not only what we know about the building, we also signal the fact that we don't know everything; and we even to some extent show what we don't know. In a historical or archaeological context, this is of real importance: a picture that purports to know more than it does is expressed in harshest terms, a lie. It may be a benign and well-intentioned falsification, but it nevertheless misleads. Whereas an image that admits that it is incomplete, because it has to be, may be visually unexpected, even surprising, and therefore demand more from the viewer, but it is an honest representation of what we know. And so where – for example for scientific reasons – this is the priority, the character of the visualisation has to correspond.

We could, then, say that visualisation of architecture in the context of archaeology occupies a place between that which is visible and that which is invisible, and tries to elucidate on this dynamic, rather than make that which is invisible visible, or obscure that which is visible to make it invisible.

Cologne Cathedral offers a good case in point. We know a great deal about its genesis: what stood on the site before the first church was built, what the shape and size were of this first church and its subsequent expansions and versions. But we also know very little. We have the remnants of the earliest baptistry, for example, from which we know its shape, and can deduce its size overall, but we really don't know how it was decorated. We don't know how it was painted or adorned with reliefs. Still, we can, purely from the architecture, make good assumptions about how the light fell into the space, even though we can't be certain how candles were used, for example, and how much they affected the 'feel' of the space at different times of the day. So if we were to add these details, including the ones we don't know, then we would be entering the realm of fantasy. And fantasy – randomly made up visual elements – unlike the imagination of both the creator and the viewer of the image, is exactly not where we want to be here, if we are trying to stay true to what we actually know.

Nevertheless: even imposing on ourselves these rigorous restrictions, we can, using only verifiable data and information, still arrive at a visually much more satisfying rendition than a simple diagram could do:

214 ● 301

This stands in contrast to **diagrammatic architecture**, ■ which, as a design method for the elements of a virtual model for example, can absolutely have its own advantages. It is diagrammatic structures which make it possible, for example, to model textures that illustrate the different development phases of a city such as Cologne as stereotypical buildings with different architectonic structures, but without individual characteristics.

These then are 'drawings' in the sense of the *Theory of Semiotics* developed in the 1860s by American philosopher, mathematician, and logician Charles Sanders Peirce (1839–1914). Explaining this here in detail would go too far, but at its core it concerns itself with the triadic relationship between an object, a sign that represents the object (here a drawing), and the person looking at the sign (or drawing). In Peirce's own definition, a *semiosis* is an, "action, or influence, which is, or involves, a cooperation of three subjects, such as a sign, its object, and its interpretant, this trirelative influence not being in any way resolvable into actions between pairs."

'VIRTUAL PHOTOGRAPHY'

If you want to create an image that not just captures but also feeds the imagination of the viewer, and communicates not just the known facts and the science, but also evokes an atmosphere and gives an impression of what it actually may have been like to be there at the time, then a purely technical rendering on its own will not suffice. Which is why Lengyel and Toulouse like to think in terms of what they call 'virtual photography'. By this (and not to be confused with **Virtual** ■ 486↘ **Reality photography** or **VR photography**, which refers to extreme wide angle, panoramic, or 360° photography that allows you to 'virtually enter' a picture and explore it from 'within') they mean an approach to visualisation that is in essence photographic, and takes the same care over the composition of a picture as a photographer would: a photographic commitment to the abstraction of a model so to speak, whereby the techniques of photography – lighting, exposure, camera angle, focus – are applied to creating an image that is, after all, not a photograph, nor pretends to be one, but offers an artistic vision all of its own.

Positioning an abstract geometry as hypothetical architecture carries its own risks, of course. But fortunately this method of visual representation does have its historical roots, and they in turn reach right into contemporary practice. It is still common today, for example, to make design models manually from white plaster or similar material, or to print them in 3D with monochrome resin. This connects us directly to the Renaissance where we find walk-in models made of wood, which were intended purely as geometrical references, where even their wood texture was not meant to evoke what would be the appearance of the structure once it was built in stone.

Abstraction of materiality then is part of our visual culture. And the same applies to architecture photography, which has developed methods of representing objects in a convincing spatial and atmospheric way even where it is only a perspective projection.

Visualising hypotheses combines both these traditions in a new visual language: an abstract geometry is 'photographed' as if it were real, thus fusing architectural modelling and architecture photography, but doing so virtually, whence 'virtual photography'.

IDEALISATION

When we speak of abstraction and highlight the fact that this necessarily entails leaving things out, we should emphasise that the important aspect to this here is not 'pulling things up' in the foreground, but working out what is essential. An idealised wall is really just an upright flat quadrangle: everything else there is to that wall – decoration, colour, texture, features – may serve all manner of purposes, but they do not add to its 'wallness'. The essence of being a wall is fulfilled by its shape and position alone.

You can apply this approach to a whole structure, as the example of the Berne Minster around 1550 demonstrates: here the surrounding elements are extremely idealised, as a townscape of gabled roofs. The statement is that the minster stood opposite the city hall in a medieval city, which featured a large number of densely packed, standardised buildings with this type of roof.

215 ● 301

But idealisation may also mean that an ideal was emulated in the realisation of one or many different buildings. German architect and erstwhile master builder at Cologne Cathedral Barbara Schock-Werner (b. 1947) examined the roughly four hundred churches that were constructed in the course of the Counter-Reformation by the prince-bishop of Würzburg, Julius Echter von Mespelbrunn (1545–1617), and found that this extraordinarily expansive project, which was intended to demonstrate the superiority of catholicism over Protestantism, must have been based on an underlying ideal. This hypothetical church, which existed only in her habilitation treatise as text, when translated into a visualisation, bears an uncanny resemblance to all four hundred of these churches, in differing but nevertheless strikingly similar ways.

216 ○ 314

ARCHITECTURAL FICTION – VISUALISING NEW REALITIES

AN IMAGE BASED CULTURE

We live, whether we choose to actively participate in this or not, in an image saturated world. On *Instagram* alone, its 800 million users (as at 2018) upload 95 million pictures and videos *each day*. Facebook, with an active monthly user base of 2.27 billion people or 30% of the world's total population (including those who have neither electricity nor access to the Internet), receives some 300 million picture uploads every day. Estimates suggest that roughly 90% of all data that exists in the world today has been generated over the last couple of years, and most of that data – though certainly not all – is digital.

We are not only inundated with images – contributing, in overwhelming numbers, to their abundance ourselves – we also, and as a direct result, have high expectations. We are used to seeing not only razor sharp, beautifully post-produced photography of actual things, we are equally at home with fantasy worlds, depicted in film and stills imagery in exquisite detail with life-like characteristics down to the sheen of a varnished table or the soft tuft of hair on a child's head. In fact, photography and computer generated imagery – with all the manifold ways in which we can enhance, edit, and adapt both – have converged to the point where they can be all but indistinguishable in their visual appearance, when the latter is at its most photorealistic.

All architecture being embedded in the cultural context of its day, and today's architecture thus being part of a world of pictures such as ours, architecture imagery has acquired an entirely new level of importance that far surpasses anything it possessed in the past. And so if architecture today has an outlook that is more than ever not just influenced by, but actually geared towards, its own visual representation, then that is hardly surprising.

ARCHITECTURE AS IMAGE

This dominance of imagery goes far: as architecture photographer Julius Shulman, whom we mentioned earlier, puts it: "Architects live and die by the images that are taken of their work, as these images alone are what most people see. For every person who visits a private house, there may be ten thousand who only view it as a photo."

Shulman spoke in a documentary that was released in 2008. *Instagram* did not even exist then (it was founded in 2010): he referred to photography *in print;* but today, with the proliferation of digital photography on the Internet, his observation holds true than ever before. Extrapolate from it the figures that would apply to a public building, let alone an *iconic* public building, such as, for example, the Sydney Opera House by Danish architect Jørn Utzon (1918–2008) and you are into millions and billions respectively: a few million people will, in its lifetime, visit or at least see from the outside the actual building, billions more will know it exclusively as imagey, and most of it online.

This creates a complex new dynamic. Buildings are static. With very few (and then spectacular) exceptions, they stubbornly tend to remain in the place where they've been put up. But they can only be fully experienced and therefore really known if you actually go there to experience them as three-dimensional real-life structures with all their characteristics, their atmosphere, the light as it arranges itself in the setting; the haptic feel, the smell, and the sounds. But in our media saturated world, the classic 'building inspector' – the expert who has been to the site and knows the building inside out – is being challenged by a far larger number of people who consume architecture purely through depiction: we all *think* we know the Sydney Opera House, and are quick to form an opinion on what we 'like' or 'dislike' about it as a piece of architecture, but very few of us actually have anything resembling a profound understanding of it as a building at all.

PICTURING THE UNBUILT

All architecture, no matter what period or era we are looking at, has at one point been imagined, textually, conceptually, and/or visually represented, and, if it still exists today, or we have any kind of record of it, most likely pictured; be that as drawings, sketches, plans, elevations, renderings, paintings, photographs, or what used to be called 'artist's visions'.

217 ● 302

To be sure, there are buildings in the world to which none of this applies: a favela in the outskirts of São Paulo, for example, may well have simply emerged with absolutely nobody ever putting so much as a pencil to paper, let alone using a computer to present their idea of an assembly of shacks for people to live in, but we don't think of this as architecture in that sense. When we talk of architecture as a process of designing, planning, and realising an architectonic vision, then – certainly today – one form or another of expressing this vision *before* the architecture gets built is inescapable. In fact, most architecture visualisation is an expression of the unbuilt: its aim is to communicate an as yet non-existent reality, be that on a site that has not previously been developed, or, as we've noted, and as we explore in more detail in our chapter on Digital Data Acquisition, much more often in an existing context, where therefore the proposed reality is not an entirely new one, but one that is being altered, albeit sometimes radically.

The two techniques used most in architecture visualisation today are computer rendering and image montage. They both have the same goal of communicating a fictional reality, but they achieve this by different means: Rendering, as we've seen above, does so by transferring a 3D modelled scene into a two-dimensional image; montage does so by arranging picture fragments to create a new image. And irrespective of which technique you use, you can avail yourself of all the possibilities and freedoms that image generation and image post-production offer, and do so in any style: whether you veer towards photorealism, or aim for a heightened level of abstraction; whether you dramatise the image with, for example, atmospheric lighting, or by choosing exaggerated perspectives and angles; whether you aim for a minimalist look by leaving out any extraneous or superfluous elements, or go in the opposite direction and populate your image with people, cars, dogs, plants, pylons, naturally occurring features, and human made debris: you as the visualiser are effectively the director of your scene; and much as the director of a film or of a play, or the painter of a picture, you therefore steer the attention of the spectator to what matters, and, more to the point still, what matters *to you.* (How much freedom you have in reality depends to a large extent on whom you are working with and for: the architect, the client, the project owner, the purse-string holder...)

218 ○ 314

DIGITAL COLLAGE

We've already mentioned 'image montage' as a visualisation technique and contrasted it to rendering. Image montage, which you will also see referred to as 'digital montage' or 'digital photomontage' was first employed commercially by advertising agencies in the 1990s. Philipp Schaerer – our co-expert for this topic and 'content owner' for this part of this chapter – was one of the people who adopted and then refined and developed it in the context of architecture, in his case while working at Herzog & de Meuron in the early 2000s, coining the term 'digital collage' for it. The method evolves directly from traditional analogue photomontage, transferring onto the computer those same processes of assembling into one image selective elements from two or several (often many) other source images.

Unlike rendering, which requires a 3D model or scene to be in place before any picture can be generated, digital collage starts directly on the two-dimensional image plane: you can begin with a blank layer, what for an analogue painting would be – and what we therefore still use as a metaphorical expression in English – an 'empty canvas'. Having said that, in order to make any kind of collage or montage, you will need some image components to work with, and so you'll want access to a large enough pool of suitable images that you can select elements or fragments from to build into the composite image as you go along, because that is the principal characteristic of digital collage: you arrange individual picture fragments (of whichever size) layer upon layer, and combine them to form your new fictional reality. Which image editing software you use for this purpose is up to you, but when we are talking about digital collage we are here always and only referring to pixel-based raster images, as opposed to vector-based ones, whatever the components that we choose from them may be: set pieces, textures, patterns, or indeed line drawings. They can be of any type at all, just as long as they can all be seamlessly interwoven and layered on top of each other. □ ↖93

219A ○ 315

219B ○ 315

And this is also what gives digital collage its vast scope in terms of styles: from highly abstract or conceptual approaches, right through to photorealism and hyperrealism, there are virtually limitless possibilities for defining the visual language of the image you are creating, with the use of as many or as few image components as you wish, going into as much or as little detail as you see fit.

COLLAGE BY INSERTION

Since really all architecture happens in some type of (built or unbuilt) context, most architecture visualisation of the unbuilt involves an act of insertion: the existing context can be photographed and used as a stage on which the new, altered scene is now built; in other words: into which the proposed architectural object is inserted. In order for this to work and look right, the insertion has to happen in such a way that the dimensions, proportions, and perspective make sense. Again, this technique is not radically different to what happened before the dawn of the digital age: architects would simply use analogue photography to take pictures of the existing context and then photograph a physical model from compatible angles, inserting this into the frame. (This is the same challenge as we came across in the section on archaeological visualisation, though in this instance reversed: whereas there we took photographs of individual items – in that specific case sculptures – and inserted them into the rendered object, we here take pictures of the environment and plant the object into this setting.)

220 ○ 316

221 ○ 316

Now, we usually have a digital 3D model which we can render with the correct perspective and proportions, and then we insert this rendered image into the photograph of the setting. Obviously, and as we have seen, with contemporary software it is entirely possible to process the whole visualisation in the render engine and do away completely with photography. But although this is possible, it is not necessarily efficient or even satisfactory: modelling and rendering complex objects and elements that form part of normal life, such as people, trees, plants, cars, bicycles, road signs and street furniture, water features, and the multiple and intricate light and shade patterns all these create on the ground, on each other, and on the object, is an extremely elaborate task. You can save yourself a lot of time and effort by concentrating the render on the architectural object itself, and using real life imagery to represent and augment the context in which you embed the object.

Assuming this is how you want to proceed, your first step would normally be to analyse your given context scene for its lighting conditions, and to choose your viewer perspective or camera angle. In a second step, you transfer these settings by means of virtual light sources and the virtual camera of the rendering software onto the architectural object, which you then, as a third step, insert into the base photograph.

222A ○ 317

222B ○ 317

222C ○ 317

222D ○ 317

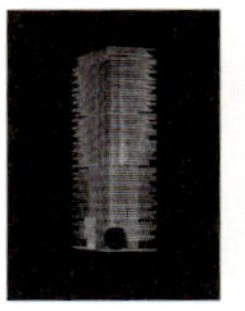
222E ○ 317

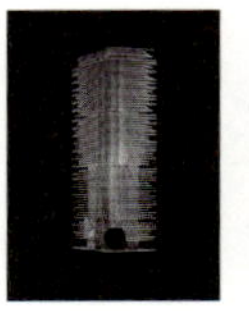
222F ○ 317

222G ○ 317

222H ○ 317

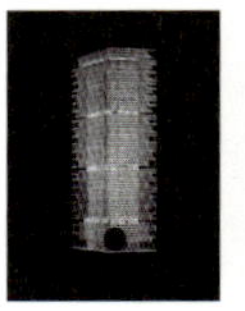
222I ○ 317

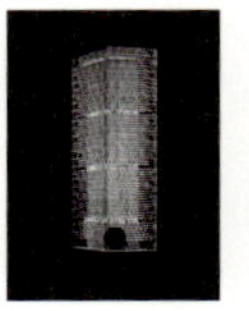
222J ○ 318

222K ○ 318

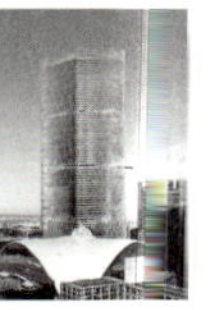
222L ○ 318

ALPHA BLENDING

In analogue photomontage, individual image fragments are tied to their carrier material – most commonly paper or sometimes photographic film – which makes weaving or blending them together difficult unless the montage is carried out with great skill: it is almost always possible to discern a cut or tear line and it takes a great deal of experience, time, and effort to eliminate all traces of where one fragment ends and another begins. Since digital images do not have any carrier material but consist purely of pixel data, blending fragments of all types and sizes seamlessly is comparatively easy in digital collage.

223 ○ 318

The process that makes this possible is called *alpha blending:* any computer graphic, apart from the colour channels, also has an alpha channel, which allows you to set the level of transparency or opacity for image pixels seamlessly from completely transparent (the layer is invisible) to completely opaque (nothing can be seen through the layer).

Alpha blending in itself would be interesting but not actually fuse our image. But standard picture editing software allows you to set this alpha value as a gradient across an area or border (the size or width of which you determine) of an image layer by means of a 'feather' tool, which defines how 'hard' or 'soft' the delineation ('feather') between two image fragments or between an image fragment and the background layer is going to be; in other words, how abruptly you go from transparent to opaque in the defined area: no feather at all means that the edge is completely hard and there is no overlap, whereas a wide feather is very soft with a large area of gradual overlap.

Not only does this make it possible to seamlessly blend together completely separate image fragments, it also allows you to treat different areas of an image with different levels of intensity, by adjusting, for example, hue, saturation, brightness, and contrast, and making these different areas smoothly dissolve into each other.

In architecture visualisation, this technique is now widely used, not only but particularly for the insertion of rendered objects into existing photographed contexts. Done well, and with a harmonious orchestration of light, perspective, and materiality between layers, the boundaries disappear, and the resulting image looks like a photographed reality that is already in place.

(We discuss these and other aspects of digital image manipulation, such as colour depth and colour space, in our chapter on Image & Colour.) □ ↖285

FULL-SURFACE COLLAGE

Not every architectural collage is meant for an existing context. In some cases – if comparatively few – a collage needs to be built from scratch, without using any type of photography as the base scene setting. There are several possible reasons for this: either because you are making a deliberate stylistic choice to show the architectural object *without* the existing context, or because the existing context has not been, or can't be, photographed in a relevant way, or simply because the planned architectural intervention is so all-embracing that it will obliterate all of the existing context and create a comprehensively new one.

While in such a case it no longer makes sense (or may just not be possible) to draw on photography as the starting point for the collage, this does not mean that no photography can be used at all: it may still be possible to draw on site photographs to extract from them certain features (skyline, landscapes, hills or mountains, for example), but rather than forming the basis for the scene, these are now simple picture fragments themselves, much as any other that are being used to blend into the image.

This type of digital collage from scratch gives you complete freedom as to what image component you now want to start with: you have a blank surface in front of you, and you can choose what you want to put in it, in what order. Often your starting point now may be rasterised line drawings, which here can serve as a skeleton to fix the perspective and geometrical structure of the image to. Similarly, a photograph of a basic physical model or an as yet incomplete rendering can serve as an initial layer, on which to build by adding detail, texture, materiality, objects, or people, or any combination of these.

224A ○ 319

224B ○ 319

224C ○ 319

224D ○ 319

224E ○ 319

224F ○ 319

224G ○ 319

224H ○ 319

224I ○ 319

224J ○ 320

224K ○ 320

224L ○ 320

224M ○ 320

224N ○ 320

224O ○ 320

224P ○ 320

224Q ○ 320

224R ○ 320

224S ○ 321

224T ○ 321

225A ○ 321

225B ○ 321

HANDLING IMAGE COMPLEXITY

Depending on the complexity of the image that is being created, a collage may consist of hundreds of individual picture fragments and components. Whether these are surface and material textures, figurative objects (such as humans and animals, equipment, trees and plants), or colour, contrast, brightness, and hue adjustments deployed to add plasticity and dynamics to the image: the possibilities here are again practically endless.

As we have implied, in most cases the image editing software will handle these fragments or components as individual layers (quite similar to the way you would use tracing paper to assemble multiple elements into a single image in a pre-digital world), and by far the most widely used software in this field, and recognisably the dominant force in picture editing more or less since its inception in the late 1980s, is and remains Adobe's *Photoshop*. Therefore, when, in the year 2000, Adobe increased the number of possible layers in the program's sixth edition from 99 to 8,000, the limitations for working with layered collages were all but removed. This meant that at a time when computer memory capacity and processing speeds still severely restricted the capability of 3D render engines, it was now already possible to achieve extremely high levels of complexity with digital collage in *Photoshop*. Rendering a large architectural proposition, such as Herzog & de Meuron's Beijing National Stadium – the 'Bird's Nest' – with wide camera angles, from an aerial perspective and including a surrounding cityscape with multiple light sources and a multitude of people, objects, and vehicles that bring a city to life, was at that time unthinkable, whereas a *Photoshop* collage could now quite easily handle this.

When we say 'could now quite easily handle this', we should qualify: handling high levels of image complexity with large numbers of fragment layers is not 'easy': selecting, layering, blending, fine-tuning are all done manually, and with dozens or hundreds of elements involved, organising these layers in such a way that you don't lose track of them and don't get lost in the plethora of different settings and adjustments they contain takes on a paramount importance.

IMAGE SOURCES AND SELECTION

Making digital collages presupposes that you have a resource of imagery that you can use to put together into a collage. Of course, all major picture editing programs have drawing tools which can be used to illustrate an architectural design, but if we are talking about collage or montage, we really mean that we take graphic, photographic, and picture fragments from existing image source materials and put them together to form a new picture, rather than drawing it, which would amount to a different technique altogether.

Right from the outset, certain criteria regarding the quality of the source material (or, as you may also hear them called, the *assets*) therefore have to be met. On the one hand, these are of a formal nature: the material has to have sufficiently high definition, for example, and it has to be available in a compatible raster format and colour space; on the other hand, they relate to content: can we bring these assets together into a coherent visual language and image logic. For instance, if you are aiming for a collage that has a certain degree of photorealism, you will want to choose source material that fits into the photographic perspective of your image. This means that the individual components are shot from a corresponding angle and in comparable lighting conditions. If these conditions are not met, and you use objects or people that are either distorted within the main image perspective, or lit from implausible angles or light sources, this will either quickly become obvious and the collage will look unnatural and flawed, or you set yourself up for an awful lot of additional work in making them fit artificially.

Image selection therefore is immensely important: as you go through your pool of possible assets, you'll want to apply consistent criteria for your preselection. And the greater the pool is, the more essential this becomes. Since our potential sources are now so numerous and so varied, our challenge today is greater in this respect than it has ever been before. And into this equation come issues such as copyright and ownership of the source material, which obviously also need to be considered.

MANUAL PROCESSING AND IMAGE AESTHETICS

What we have just said about preparation and selection notwithstanding, the bulk of the work in digital collage still consists of actually assembling the picture fragments. This, we've noted, is an almost entirely manual process: you have technology as input devices – a mouse or trackpad, a keyboard, a graphics tablet – but there is virtually no automation. Using selection and area delineation tools, you lift the individual components from their original picture and then align and fuse them with the new image, applying the blending methods outlined above to arrive at a smooth, seamless integration.

Digital collaging, then, apart from the quality of the source material, is largely reliant on the dexterity, skill, imagination, and artistry of the visualiser. This distinguishes the technique from computer rendering, where, once you've set the scene and the parameters, you hand over a significant part of the image generation process to the rendering engine. In digital collage, you keep control of each individual step, and this means you also absolutely define the style and visual language: your personal aesthetic.

Unsurprisingly, therefore, digital collage produces a much wider range of artistic styles than rendering, because the latter, in the end, rests on the range of available rendering algorithms, resulting in similar styles irrespective of who is the picture's author.

Considering that most architectural visualisation is generated during the planning phase of a project, digital collaging offers one further advantage over other methods: at this point in the proceedings it can be useful (in fact necessary) to steer the viewer's attention towards the elements or aspects of the proposal that are of particular significance, either because there is simply too much to take in in one go, or because not all aspects of the proposal are as yet fully worked out, and there are therefore parts of the image that can't as yet be shown with the same level of precision as others. A digital collage can help you make sense of a picture by, for example, selectively treating different areas of it in different ways: focus, transparency, density, brightness, contrast, and colour palette are all powerful means to direct a viewer's attention and to lift elements of significance, while letting those of less importance slip into the background of perception. (It is worth pointing out that you can also achieve this with computer rendering, but it is, once again, a much more elaborate process.)

226 ○ 322

PRESENTING THREE DIMENSIONS ON THE PLANE

As we've seen, a digital collage is an image construct in which – in the context of architecture – we combine picture fragments on the plane to represent three-dimensional structures. This spatiality we have to suggest, as any artist would, through line perspective and vanishing points that fix the shape and dimension of an object in relation to its surroundings and the picture plane, anchoring it in the viewer's eye. Since, unlike rendering, a digital collage does not rest on a 3D data model, this means that if, halfway through my image generation, I decide to change my viewing angle, I have to start all over again. In purely practical terms, this might be considered a genuine disadvantage compared to rendering, where the render engine can simply recalculate your image for you from any desired viewpoint. And it is also the reason why, unlike rendering, digital collage is not really suited to creating virtual walk-throughs for architecture, since these require constantly changing viewing angles, which with collaging would be extremely labour-intensive to generate.

The positive flip side of this particular coin though is that in digital collage, because you are working entirely on the plane – and unlike in 3D rendering, where a scene is modelled around virtual objects – each pixel can be individually edited, irrespective of what it represents: be it part of a tangible object, or an immaterial entity, such as a light texture or reflection, you can do with it what you will; and so, using the alpha blending technique explained earlier, for example, we can weave into our picture very smooth and subtle gradients, quite comparable to the *sfumato* technique, of which Leonardo da Vinci – whom, you may recall, we started our chapter with – was one of the principal proponents. He said that it is, "without lines or borders, in the manner of smoke," lending his pictures a particularly natural atmosphere and look. Which is why digital collages often are much softer in their appearance than rendered 3D scenes, which tend to be characterised by the sharp lines that come with vector based modelling.

227 ○322

The Outlook

Visualisation has come a proverbially long way, and most of that distance it has travelled from abstraction towards realism, to the point where photographed physical reality and visualised **virtual reality** can often no longer be told apart. This clearly isn't the end of the road for visualisation though, so where do we go from here?

Two possible, and possibly desirable, developments immediately spring to mind. One has to do with visual language, and one with process, and both break down into further, subtler evolutionary stages.

First, visual language. What we are really looking for now, in visualisation, is a style that stands up in its own right, that is specific and recognisable as an abstraction again, having come through the photorealism phase. Much as in other fields, where a new technique first tried to emulate its predecessors, before finding the ground for artistry on its own terms, we can imagine that as the technique of visualisation matures, visualisers will want to make it their own. Making visualisation look and feel like something that was shot 'for real' is not only not necessary, it also isn't really satisfying, seeing that it is so clearly an artefact. That visualisation underwent this photorealism phase is not surprising, and nor is it deplorable. Photography itself went through a similar phase: in its beginnings, photography mostly orientated itself at the then prevalent visual art form: painting. Only once the technology grew up did its artists and practitioners emancipate themselves from the old cultural framework and begin to help define the new one. By the middle of the 20th century, photography had evolved into an art form in its own right, not only not trying any longer to look like painting, but influencing strongly new generations of painters in search for their own language in turn.

Second, process. Visualisation programs are getting extremely good at their job and becoming extremely fast. At the same time, computer processing power still outpaces software demands, and so there is almost no doubt that before long the combined capabilities of software and hardware will make rendered ■ ↖272 465↘
imaging not only even more realistic and intricate, but beat photography 'at its own game' and start to yield technically 'better' results (say in terms of detail or resolution, for example) than we can get with a camera.

But perhaps most significant and of most consequence to the way we do things in architecture is the convergence of visualisation and 3D modelling techniques with virtual space technology: once you can construct as if by hand, light as if in real life, and move and manipulate objects in three dimensions, you are on the brink of going inside the object and moving around it in real time, finding out what it looks like, handling and shaping it. So here we may be looking at a technology that takes us onto its own meta-level: when a piece of software no longer just simulates the light in a space, but the appearance of light in that space, on its walls, floor, and the objects within the space; when the reality of a thing of the past or of a thing of the future is rendered so realistically that it just cannot be 'real', and when new abstractions, new stylisations, new artistic freedoms at one end, and new scientific anchors at the other become 'normal' for being extraordinary.

211 ● 288
Pre-digital visualisation: Oscar Nitzchke, *Maison de la publicité*, Paris, 1936. [MoMA]

212 ● 292
The *Circus Maximus* on Palatine Hill, Rome, circa 310 CE: the distant forest edge in the background and a subtle gradient of the sky are achieved in post-production with *Photoshop*. [Lengyel Toulouse Architects]

214 ● 293
Cologne Cathedral, 1320. [Lengyel Toulouse Architects]

215 ● 294
Berne Minster, 1529–1588: idealised townscape. [Lengyel Toulouse Architects]

217 ● 295
El Lissitzky, *Wolkenbügel*, 1924-25. Photomontage. [Verlag der Kunst]

Colour Plates

II

P. 229–302

147 ○ 233
Colour depth: a useful concept to imagine how each pixel can show a different colour. [Series 147, 154A–154C: Harald Gatermann]

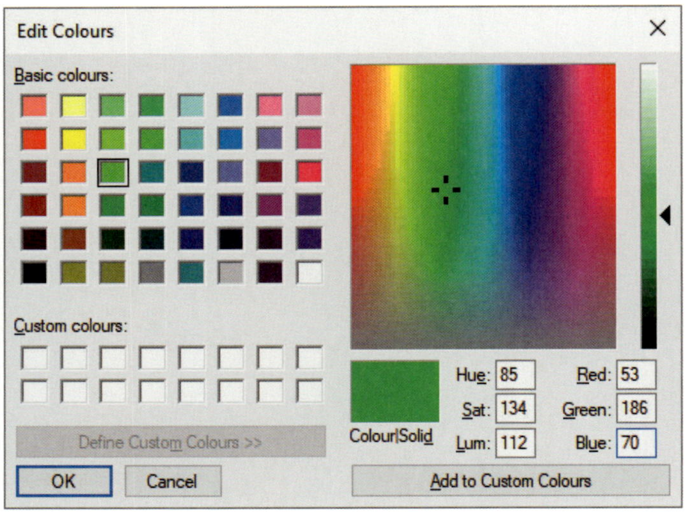

154A ○ 237

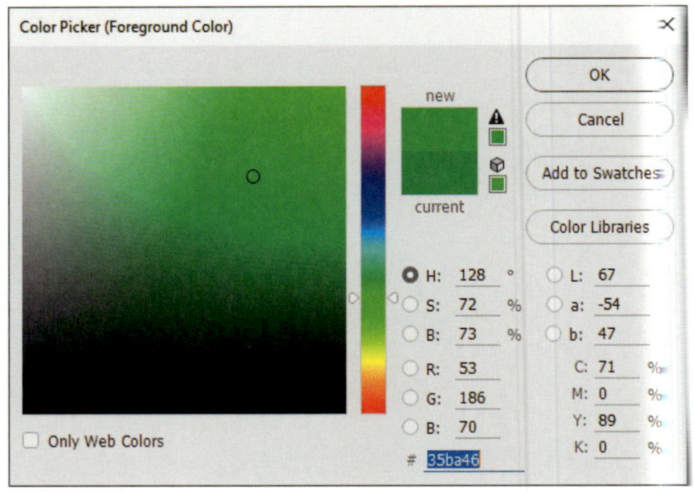

154B ○ 237

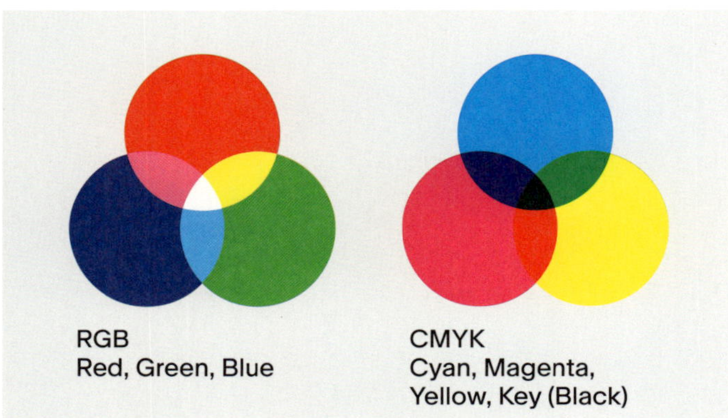

154C ○ 237
Colour models: RGB and CMYK.

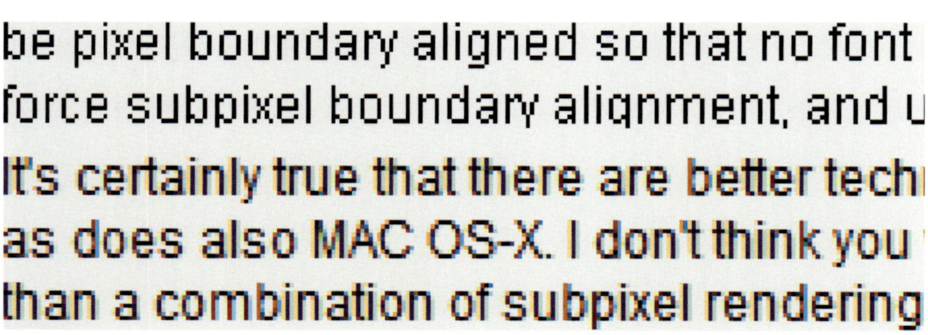

156 ○ 237
Anti-aliasing applied to text.

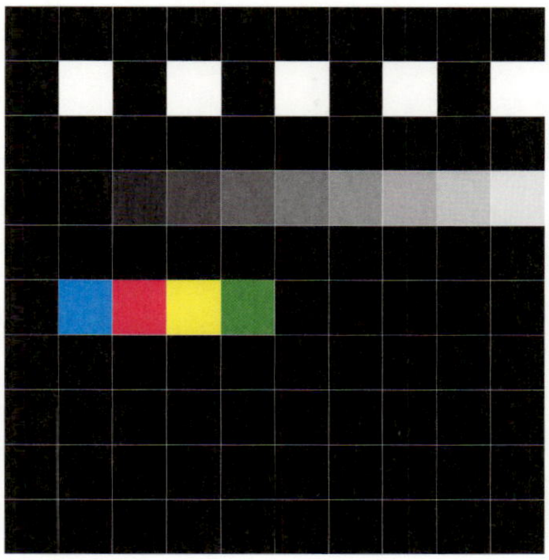

157A ○ 238
Example of 10 × 10 pixels in white, black, or colour. [157A + 157B: Harald Gatermann]

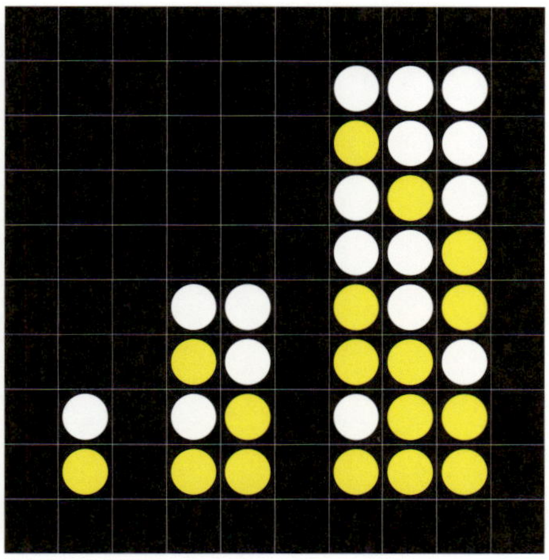

157B ○ 238
Schematic representation of 2, 4, and 8 bit colour depth.

163A ○ 241

163B ○ 241

163C ○ 242

163D ○ 242

Colour, light, and focus dramatically change the appearance of an image. [Series 163A–163D: Harald Gatermann]

166 ○ 257
"Light is therefore colour." J M W Turner's *The Fighting Temeraire Tugged to Her Last Berth to Be Broken Up*, painted in 1838 and first exhibited at the Royal Academy in London in 1839.

167B ○ 258

167A ○ 258
Vermeer versus van Dam: the second edition of *Computer Graphics: Principles and Practice*, written by Andries van Dam, James D Foley, John F Hughes, and Steven K Feiner, used a simplified rendering of the room depicted by Dutch master Johannes Vermeer in *The Music Lesson or Lady at the Virginals With a Gentleman* from 1662–65 as its cover.

168A ○ 258
Reality check: a photographic image with an HDR filter applied to it, combining the dynamic range of three images: one under-exposed, one 'normal', and one over-exposed. [Mariano Szklanny]

168B ○ 258
Tone mapping, the process by which an HDR photograph is rendered to a medium that has a more limited dynamic range, can also be used to create exaggerated contrasts and lighting effects, challenging the idea that photographs are by definition photorealistic. [Uli Herrmann]

170 ○ 259
Still Life With Lute. The making of this image allows us to explain various rendering techniques as well as ponder questions of realism and the "effects of light interacting with physical objects." [All renderings of the still life shown in this chapter, as well as all the images and graphics that explain the making of them, were created by Ludwig Grimm.]

175A ○ 262 175B ○ 262

The Cornell box is a test aimed at determining the accuracy of rendering software by comparing the rendered scene with an actual photograph of the same scene, and has become a commonly used test model. It was created by a team at Cornell University in 1984 and is designed to show diffuse interreflection. For example, some light should bounce off the red and green walls and onto the white walls, so parts of the white walls should appear slightly red or green. The right rendering shown here captures this subtle colour bleed whereas the left doesn't. [Urs Hirschberg]

176A ○ 263 176B ○ 263

Radiosity mesh model created with the software *Lightscape*, which, until 2002, when it was discontinued, was the leading radiosity program and popular with architects. The model is shown in wireframe (176A) and shaded mode (176B). The mesh is created during the radiosity calculation and has a higher density in areas of strong lighting contrasts. The diffuse lighting is 'baked' into the mesh model, which can be viewed and walked through in real time. Light baking is still used for real-time applications such as computer games. [*Lightscape*]

184 ○ 265

A real life vintage car convention looks like a miniature model with tilt shift applied. [Jay Lee]

186A ○ 265 186B ○ 265
Bokeh effect created in the post processing phase, using depth map and object ID map. [LG]

187A ○ 266
Is it art? There are clearly exceptions, but many great artists limit their colour palette. Dutch painter Jan Lieven's (1607–1674) *Still Life With Books* (187A) and a painting after the Italian artist Giorgio Morandi's (1890–1964) *Natura morta (Still Life)* series (187B).

187B ○ 266

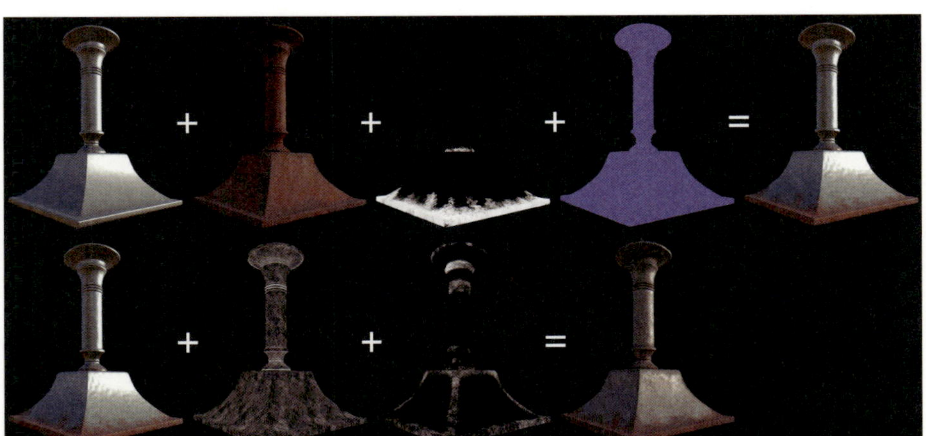

201 ○ 270
Layered textures: starting from a pristine metallic material, a combination of image-based, procedural, and painted texture layers result in the scrapyard metal look of the chandelier. [LG]

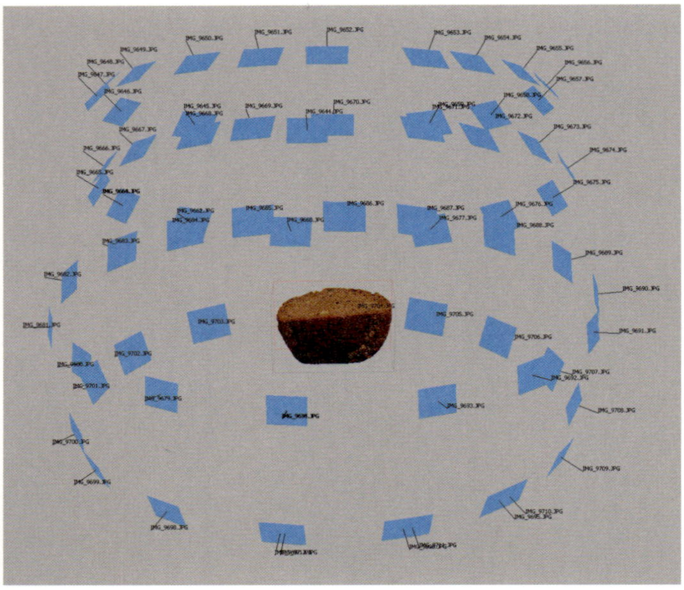

202 ○ 270
Multi-image photogrammetry: dense point-cloud data is derived from a series of photographs of the physical artefact taken from different angles in an automated process. [LG]

203 ○ 270
The point cloud can be turned into a high-poly model (here 1,600,000 triangles), which is usable for rendering. For real time applications the geometry needs to be rebuilt from an unstructured triangulated topology to a structured quadrilateral topology with a fraction of the original poly count (1,600,000 triangles to 9,200 quads). [LG]

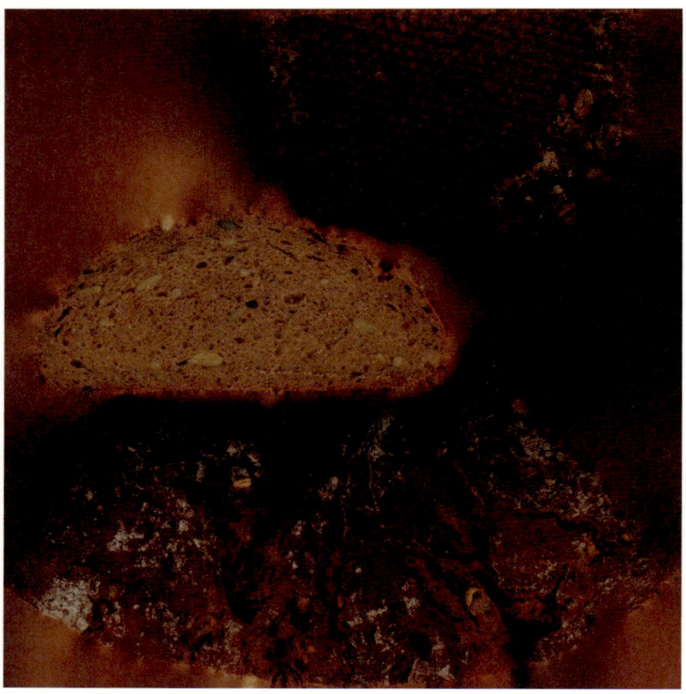

204A ○ 270

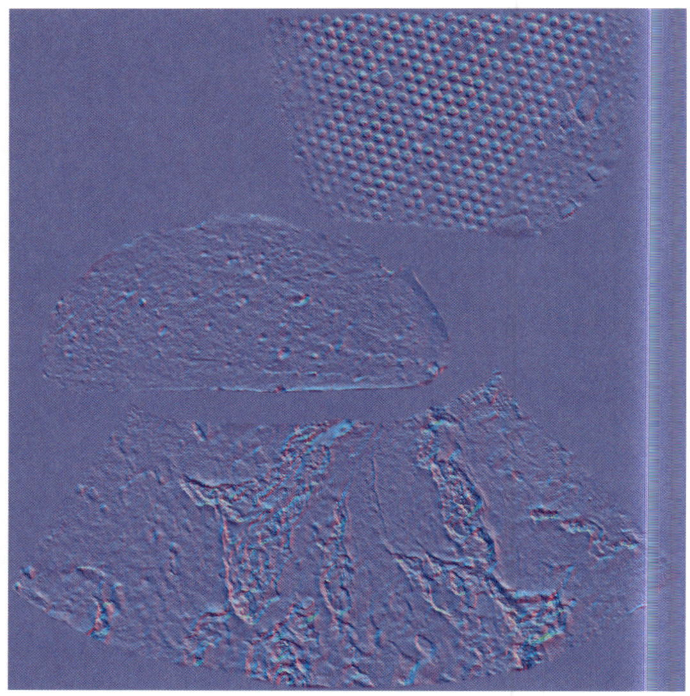

204B ○ 270

Texture maps of the bread. The diffuse map (204A) provides the colour information. While the high-poly model has enough detail in the geometry, for the low-poly version, surface detail is added with a bump map; a normals map in tangent space (204B); and an ambient occlusion map (204C). The red colour in the ambient occlusion map indicates ray mis-checks of the projection from the high-poly model, as the back side of the bread is missing due to the scanning setup. [LG]

204C ○ 270

205A ○ 270

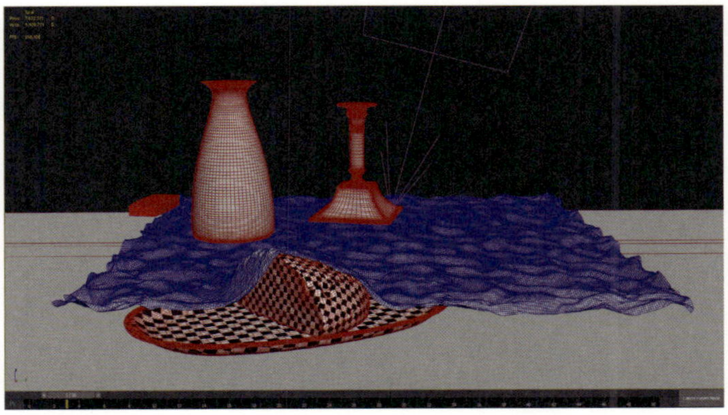

205B ○ 270

205C ○ 270

205D ○ 270

Cloth simulation setup: an overall gravity force works on all entities. *Blue:* soft body plane with 300 x 300 simulation elements. *Red:* rigid-body colliders with simplified colliders for the lute and the bread. *Purple:* a slight turbulent wind force to provide random wrinkles to the cloth. [LG]

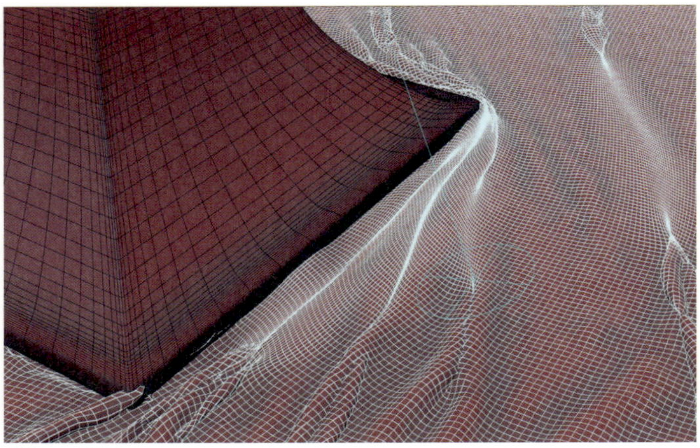

206 ○ 270
Relaxing and conforming the cloth by manual sculpting. [LG]

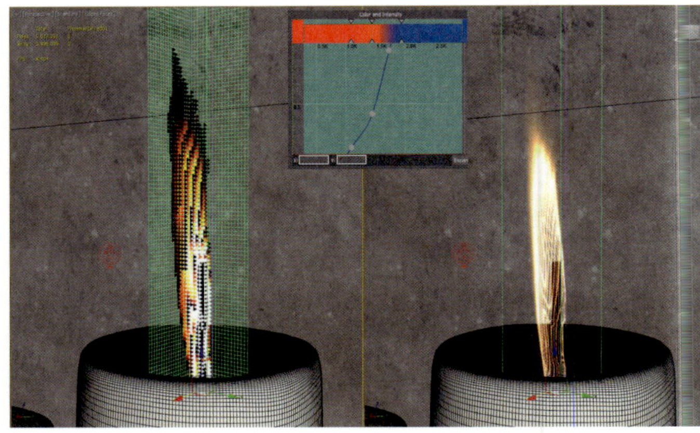

207 ○ 271
Candle flame simulation, using fluid dynamics: the result is a voxel cloud of the temperature parameters for each cell (left), which can be visualised directly in real time by the GPU (right). [LG]

208 ○ 271
HDRI picture used in the lute still life. It creates the desired soft lighting and has a compatible colour and luminance range. [LG]

209 ○ 271
Final image with colour correction done directly in the rendering package. [LG]

210A ○ 271

210B ○ 271

Final night version image: raw as resulting from the rendering package (210A) and with depth of field and bokeh added in post processing (210B). [LG]

213A ○ 292

213B ○ 292

Cologne Cathedral interior, 1856. [213A + 213B: Lengyel Toulouse Architects]

216 ○ 294
Julius Echter's hypothetical 'ideal church'. [Lengyel Toulouse Architects]

218 ○ 295
Meereshorst, 2009, Image Montage. [Philipp Schaerer]

219A ○ 295

219B ○ 295
National Stadium Beijing, China. Competition 2002, realisation 2004-2008. Architects: Herzog & de Meuron: basis image (219A) | final image montage – interior view concourse, 2004 (design development) (219B). [Philipp Schaerer / Herzog & de Meuron]

220 ○ 296
Hans Hollein: *Highrise Building*, Sparkplug, project, 1964. Photomontage. [MoMA]

221 ○ 296
Ludwig Mies van der Rohe and Edwald Mies, Bismarck National Monument, Bingen, 1910. Photomontage with model photograph. [MoMA]

"This work, one of Mies van der Rohe's earliest photomontages, seamlessly embeds his proposal for a national monument to the German statesman Otto von Bismarck (1815–1898) in a photograph of the Rhine landscape. Using the picture of the site supplied for the 1910 competition, Mies created a 'realistic' architectural scene through sophisticated photographic manipulation. His competition model was carefully photographed from below to match the perspective of the site image. In the resulting photomontage, the monument appears wedged into the hillside; its neoclassical colonnade and massive podium, overgrown with foliage, suggest that the building's existence is not hypothetical, but rather fact. The image, with its persuasive realism, is a precursor to contemporary rendering practices that merge fiction and reality."

(Gallery legend from *Cut 'n' Paste: From Architectural Assemblage to Collage City*, Museum of Modern Art, New York, July 10 – December 1, 2013)

222A ○ 296

222B ○ 296

222C ○ 296

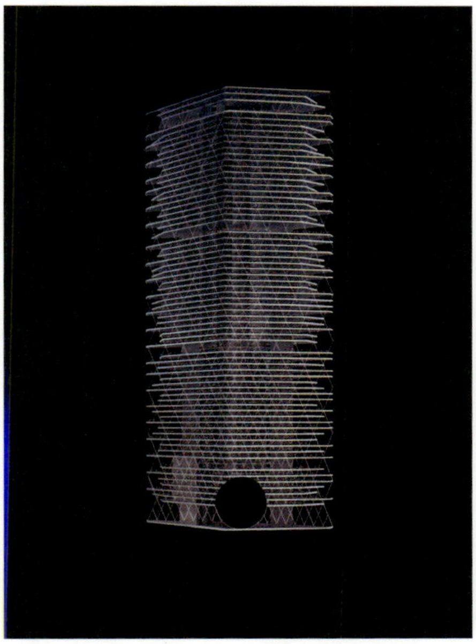
222D ○ 296

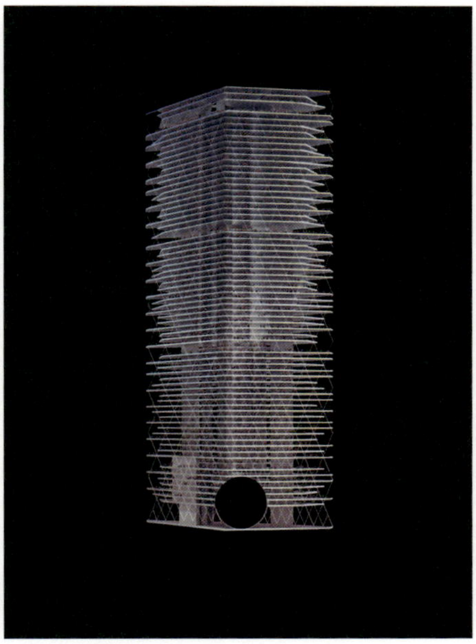
222E ○ 296

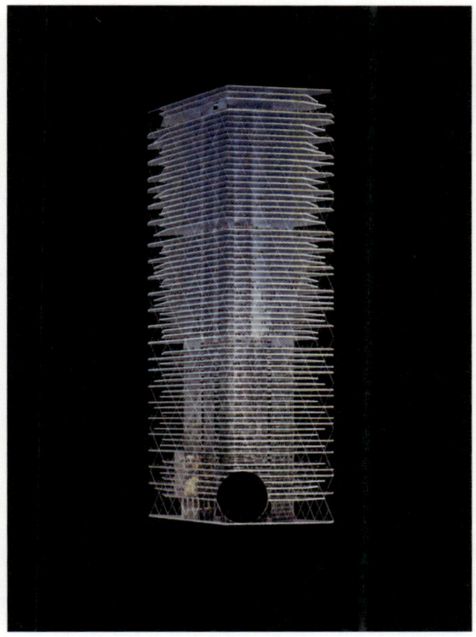
222F ○ 296

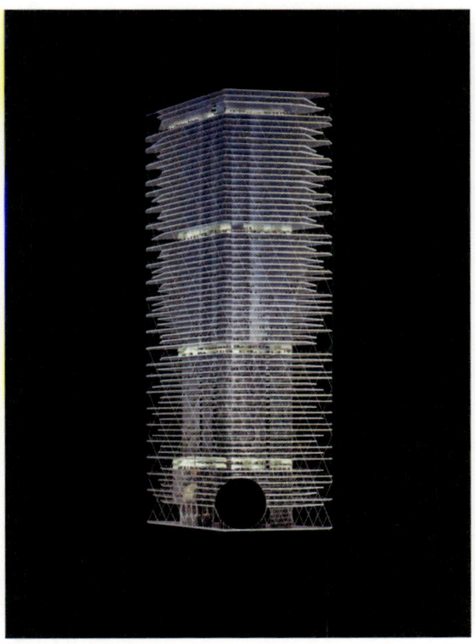
222G ○ 296

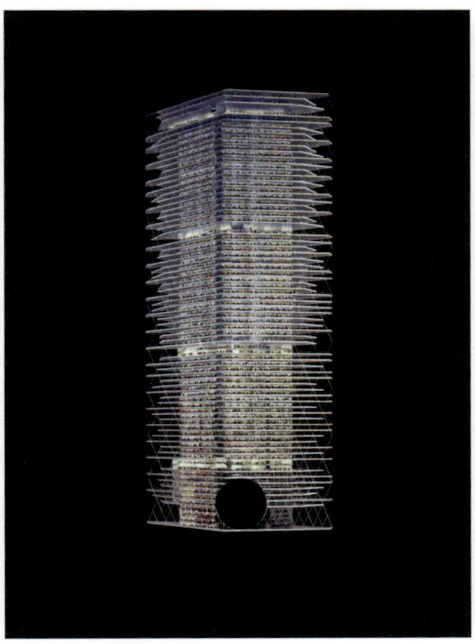
222H ○ 296

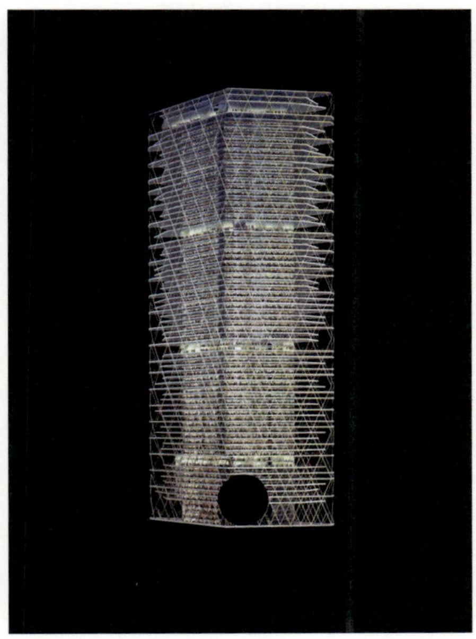
222I ○ 296

222J ○ 296

222K ○ 296

222L ○ 296

Collage by insertion, image montage, development steps (screenshots): *Tour Phare*, *La Défense*, Paris, France. Competition 2006. Architects: Herzog & de Meuron. [222A–222L: Philipp Schaerer/Herzog & de Meuron]

223 ○ 296

Ludwig Mies van der Rohe, Convention Hall, Chicago project, 1954. Analogue photomontage with model photograph. [MoMA]

224A ○ 297

224B ○ 297

224C ○ 297

224D ○ 297

224E ○ 297

224F ○ 297

224G ○ 297

224H ○ 297

224I ○ 297

224J ○ 297

224K ○ 297

224L ○ 297

224M ○ 297

224N ○ 297

224O ○ 297

224P ○ 297

224Q ○ 297

224R ○ 297

224S ○ 297 224T ○ 297
Development stages image montage (screenshots) example: *Bildbau No 5*, 2007 from the *Bildbauten Series*. [224A–224T: Philipp Schaerer]

The series of images entitled *Bildbauten* deals with the effect and the claim to credibility of images of architecture that appear to be photographs. Frontal views of fictional architectures serve as an example. All images try to reproduce a reality. They are not photographs; instead, they were newly designed and constructed from scratch by means of image synthesis and digital image editing.

225A ○ 297 225B ○ 297
Bildbau No 5, 2007, image montage, from the *Bildbauten Series*. [225A+225B: Philipp Schaerer]

226 ○ 298
Image montage, aerial view 2002 (design development), Forum 2004 Building and Plaza, Barcelona, Spain. Competition 2000, project 2001–2002, realisation 2002–2004. Architects: Herzog & de Meuron. [Philipp Schaerer/Herzog & de Meuron]

227 ○ 299
Image montage, exterior view 2002 (design development), *Allianz Arena*, München-Fröttmaning, Germany. Competition 2001–2002, project 2002–2004, realisation 2002–2005. Architects: Herzog & de Meuron. [Philipp Schaerer/Herzog & de Meuron]

LANGUAGE III
The Abstraction of Architecture

Text, Typography & Layout 327
Scripting 351
Writing & Code 369
Writing & Code – Elaboration 382

Text, Typography & Layout

Harald Gatermann and Oliver Fritz

- Adrian Frutiger: *Der Mensch und seine Zeichen*, 1978
- Peter Vollenweider: *EPS-Handbuch. Encapsulated PostScript*, 1989
- Friedrich Friedl, Nicolaus Ott, Bernard Stein: *Typography: An Encyclopedic Survey of Type Design and Techniques Throughout History*, 1998
- Harald Haarmann: *Geschichte der Schrift*, 2002
- Markus Wäger: *Grafik und Gestaltung: Mediengestaltung von A bis Z*, 2016

Overview

FROM NUMBERS TO TEXT

A computation is literally a calculation. In the English language, until the very late nineteenth century, a 'computer' was a person who carried out computations: mathematical calculations. There were calculators and calculating machines long before there were computers, and depending on what you count as a 'device' or a 'machine' you can easily go back five thousand years in history where you'll find the abacus, for example. But while the use of the word 'computer' to mean a calculating machine can be traced as far back as 1897, the first computers were actually referred to as **Turing machines**, after the English mathematician, logician, and pioneering computer scientist Alan Turing (1912–1954) whom we encounter repeatedly in this *Atlas*, because he advanced the concept of a machine that could execute programmable steps to the point where we now recognise it as the forerunner of the computer. (As we also point out elsewhere, he did not actually build a computer himself, nor did he name his theoretical machine after himself. We talk in much more detail about the Turing machine in our chapter on Writing & Code and its Elaboration.)

So, early computers were calculators. What distinguished them from ordinary calculating machines was that they were programmable, in the way Turing had proposed. And for several decades they really did nothing other than churn numbers. This they did well: their great advantage over humans, as many people would attest to at the time, was that they were fast and accurate at handling both large numbers and large numbers of numbers. Not only was there no need, therefore, in the beginning, for much of an interface, there also wasn't much need for words, since you would not give the computer anything to do other than what it was there for: to compute. You would then take the computations, and enter them into your report or your table or your presentation – which would be an actual document or slide show of pictures, or a series of acetate foils – and that was all that was required.

The problem this soon presented is that you do not need to go far with numbers before you chance upon words. Labels, categories, product ranges, shipping destinations, addresses, descriptions, tags, instructions: the moment you stray from pure mathematics into the world of things and people, you start using terminology, and so it was not long before people saw a need for computing with text. The first ones to do so were people in business, thus acting as a principal and powerful commercial driver for the advancement of the technology.

By now we are into the mid to late 1970s, and around this time computing becomes interesting also to the construction industry and therefore by extension to architects. Because now it is possible to do projections, for example of material and labour costs, as automated processes, and while hardly anybody yet expects computers to work as presentational tools, the idea of formatting numbers and text in a sensible and intelligible way already becomes relevant. But there is still, at this point, a clear division of labour between the person who does data processing and the person who uses that data and makes it presentable: Data Processor is a job, and one on which the usefulness of the company's computer hinges directly.

ELECTRIC TO ELECTRONIC TYPEWRITING AND THE QWERTY INERTIA

On 4 August 1891, the American entrepreneur and inventor George Canfield Blickensderfer (1850–1917) patented a typewriter design which two years later, in 1893, was unveiled to the public at the World's Columbian Exhibition in Chicago. By the end of that century, it was so popular that his eponymous factory was able to employ some 200 staff and put out 10,000 typewriters a year, making them best selling ■ ↖180 551↘ machines that were exported across the globe.

Particularly successful was the *Blickensderfer Model 5*, because it was lighter and more compact than its competitors, such as those from the Remington stable. What also set it apart from its rivals was a carefully, borderline scientifically devised keyboard layout, which featured three rows of keys. The bottom row – also known as the 'home row' – held letters which Blickensderfer through extensive study had found to be contained in 85% of all words used in the English □ 369↘ language: D, H, I, A, T, E, N, S, O, and R. They therefore □ 382↘ also were the 70% most used letters in the English alphabet. This meant that a typist could type almost everything they were ever likely to write without moving their fingers off that home row of keys. You would have considered it a safe bet, therefore, at the turn of the 19th to the 20th century, that if in future days any legacy from the typewriter would survive into a computer age, it would surely be the DHIATENSOR keyboard, invented by George Canfield Blickensderfer.

Alas, you would have lost. During World War I, sales of American made typewriters (particularly to Europe, where in the meantime there was strong competition also from the likes of Mr Olivetti, for example) declined, and Blickensderfer found himself manufacturing ammunition for the war effort at his factory, just to get by. When he himself succumbed to an illness a bit more than a year before the war was over, his company lost its captain and with him all direction, and soon it was sold, then sold off again, unsuccessfully, and finally dismantled, its assets being bought up by the Remington firm.

Blickensderfer had also been first to make and market an electric typewriter, the honestly named *Blickensderfer Electric*. We, however, know nothing of this today. What we do know of though is the **QWERTY keyboard**. ■ It was created by American newspaper publisher, politician, and inventor Christopher Latham Sholes (1819–1890) for the machine that was originally known as the *Sholes and Glidden* typewriter (also after his collaborator Carlos Glidden), but became famous as the *Remington 1*, when the fire arms manufacturer E. Remington & Sons decided to diversify precisely in the opposite direction to what Blickensderfer later was forced to do, from weapons into words. Remington acquired the machine and brought it to market as the first commercially successful typewriter in the world. Its keys were arranged in a not-quite random order, mostly so as to avoid letters that frequently followed each other in English being neighbours on the keyboard, because the metal keys, when hit in quick succession, would regularly jam if they sat right next to each other. Named for the first six letters of the top row, the QWERTY keyboard may have purely mechanical reasons for its existence, but owing to the success of the Remington brand, its arrangement was learnt as a ten-finger touch type method by so many people over so many years that to this day nobody has brought themselves to changing it substantially. (In other European languages, such as German, the Y and the Z have swapped places, making it a QWERTZ keyboard in some regions.) There is no ergonomic or scientific reason for its design, it has no intrinsic quality or benefit to the user, it's in use today purely because it would be too much hassle to change it, which is why it is there by inertia. (Technophiles fond of the 1980s may detect in this a premonition echo of the infamous VHS/Betamax calamity...)

From manual to electrically powered typewriters was a very small step, but from those to electronic ones that could remember some simple routines and store small amounts of data (such as frequently used phrases or a database of addresses) took a first leap into digitality. And so from the early 1970s onwards we see the convergence of the typewriter with the computer, when word processors make their entrance at first as massive, bespoke terminals that mostly emulate typewriter functions but combine them with text and data handling capabilities, such as file storage and merge fields that enable the generation of personalised documents and mail shots, for example.

228 ● 347

229 ● 347

The ten-finger touch type system allocates to each finger the nearest keys on the keyboard.

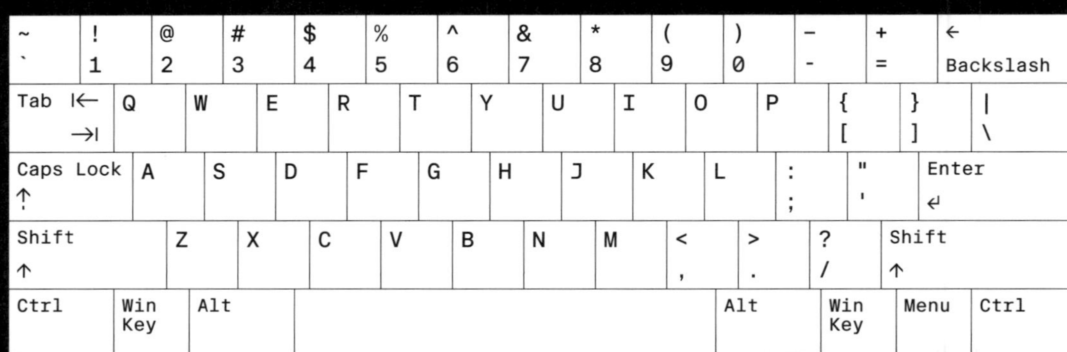

The computer keyboard expands the traditional typewriter set with navigation, function, and numerical keys.

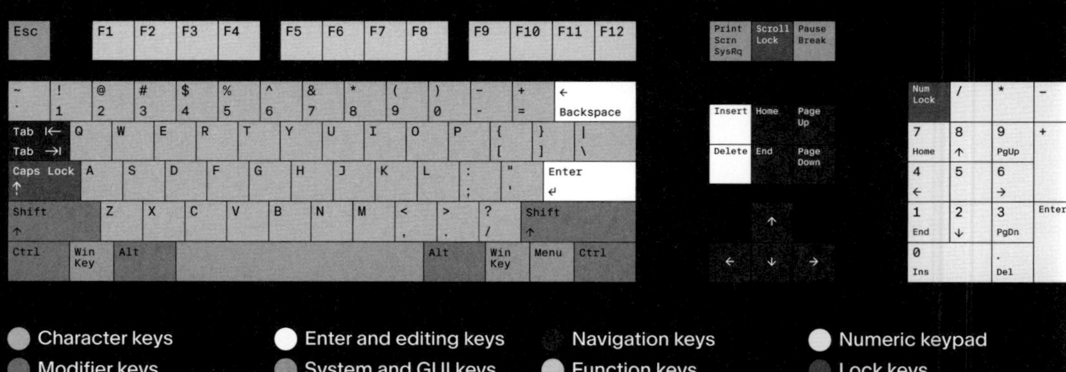

↖238

ENCODING TEXT: ASCII, ANSI, AND UNICODE

Whether numbers or letters (or later images, or anything else), in order for a computer to be able to work with it, it has to convert whatever it is dealing with into something it can process, which is binary code. For text and hybrid alphanumerical data that means converting all letters, numbers, and special characters, such as punctuation marks and symbols, into strings of ones and zeroes. And obviously it would help if different machines using different types of operating systems (of which at the time there were many) could read each other's software and files.

So as far back as 1960, the prosaically named American Standards Association Subcommittee X3.2 started officially pursuing a standard encoding system for the characters that seemed most relevant and useful to them, namely all upper and lower case letters that occur in the English alphabet (which is conveniently devoid of any accents, umlauts, o other quirkinesses found in most other European languages that use the Latin set as its base), the numbers 0-9 and a list of basic punctuation marks and operators. This was arrived at and first published three years later, in 1963, with the name *American Standard Code for Information Interchange (ASCII)*. It started out as a 7-bit encoding system for 128 specified characters, and then underwent several revisions over the next twenty-odd years, eventually turning into an extended 8-bit system capable of encoding 256 characters, although remarkably the second 128 code positions were never fixed, and so there is no actual official extended ASCII set, to this day.

ASCII built on the early teletype method of data entry, which relied on simple keyboards with no mouse, and allocated to each character a decimal number as an identifier. This could be used to input the character by pressing the ALT key together with the relevant number if no dedicated key was available, and it was this decimal number that was expressed in binary code. (As well as, incidentally, octal and hexadecimal code, both of which were particularly useful in early computing because they allowed the representation of binary code in a much shorter and therefore more easily readable way.)

The original ASCII table, with 128 lines numbered 0 to 127, reserved the first 32 positions for operators and instructions, such as 'Shift', 'Line Feed', and 'Carriage Return', and then listed punctuation marks before numbers, numbers before capital letters, and capital letters before lower case letters, with some more punctuation and the 'Delete' key completing the set.

The original ASCII character set (here shown with 8-bit binary code: note how the first digit of binary is a 0 in each case, so the entire set could also be written in 7-bit code).

Dec	Binary	Oct	Hex	ASCII
0	000 0000	0	0	NUL
1	000 0001	1	1	SOH
2	000 0010	2	2	STX
3	000 0011	3	3	ETX
4	000 0100	4	4	EOT
5	000 0101	5	5	ENQ
6	000 0110	6	6	ACK
7	000 0111	7	7	BEL
8	000 1000	10	8	BS
9	000 1001	11	9	HT
10	000 1010	12	0A	LF
11	000 1011	13	0B	VT
12	000 1100	14	0C	FF
13	000 1101	15	0D	CR
14	000 1110	16	0E	SO
15	000 1111	17	0F	SI
16	001 0000	20	10	DLE
17	001 0001	21	11	DC1
18	001 0010	22	12	DC2
19	001 0011	23	13	DC3
20	001 0100	24	14	DC4
21	001 0101	25	15	NAK
22	001 0110	26	16	SYN
23	001 0111	27	17	ETB
24	001 1000	30	18	CAN
25	001 1001	31	19	EM
26	001 1010	32	1A	SS
27	001 1011	33	1B	ESC
28	001 1100	34	1C	FS
29	001 1101	35	1D	GS
30	001 1110	36	1E	RS
31	001 1111	37	1F	US
32	010 0000	40	20	space
33	010 0001	41	21	!
34	010 0010	42	22	"
35	010 0011	43	23	#
36	010 0100	44	24	$
37	010 0101	45	25	%
38	010 0110	46	26	&
39	010 0111	47	27	'
40	010 1000	50	28	(
41	010 1001	51	29	)
42	010 1010	52	2A	*
43	010 1011	53	2B	+
44	010 1100	54	2C	,
45	010 1101	55	2D	-
46	010 1110	56	2E	.
47	010 1111	57	2F	/
48	011 0000	60	30	0
49	011 0001	61	31	1
50	011 0010	62	32	2
51	011 0011	63	33	3
52	011 0100	64	34	4
53	011 0101	65	35	5
54	011 0110	66	36	6
55	011 0111	67	37	7
56	011 1000	70	38	8
57	011 1001	71	39	9
58	011 1010	72	3A	:
59	011 1011	73	3B	;
60	011 1100	74	3C	<
61	011 1101	75	3D	=
62	011 1110	76	3E	>
63	011 1111	77	3F	?
64	100 0000	100	40	@
65	100 0001	101	41	A
66	100 0010	102	42	B
67	100 0011	103	43	C
68	100 0100	104	44	D
69	100 0101	105	45	E
70	100 0110	106	46	F
71	100 0111	107	47	G
72	100 1000	110	48	H
73	100 1001	111	49	I
74	100 1010	112	4A	J
75	100 1011	113	4B	K
76	100 1100	114	4C	L
77	100 1101	115	4D	M
78	100 1110	116	4E	N
79	100 1111	117	4F	O
80	101 0000	120	50	P
81	101 0001	121	51	Q
82	101 0010	122	52	R
83	101 0011	123	53	S
84	101 0100	124	54	T
85	101 0101	125	55	U
86	101 0110	126	56	V
87	101 0111	127	57	W
88	101 1000	130	58	X
89	101 1001	131	59	Y
90	101 1010	132	5A	Z
91	101 1011	133	5B	[
92	101 1100	134	5C	\
93	101 1101	135	5D	]
94	101 1110	136	5E	^
95	101 1111	137	5F	_
96	110 0000	140	60	`
97	110 0001	141	61	a
98	110 0010	142	62	b
99	110 0011	143	63	c
100	110 0100	144	64	d
101	110 0101	145	65	e
102	110 0110	146	66	f
103	110 0111	147	67	g
104	110 1000	150	68	h
105	110 1001	151	69	i
106	110 1010	152	6A	j
107	110 1011	153	6B	k
108	110 1100	154	6C	l
109	110 1101	155	6D	m
110	110 1110	156	6E	n
111	110 1111	157	6F	o
112	111 0000	160	70	p
113	111 0001	161	71	q
114	111 0010	162	72	r
115	111 0011	163	73	s
116	111 0100	164	74	t
117	111 0101	165	75	u
118	111 0110	166	76	v
119	111 0111	167	77	w
120	111 1000	170	78	x
121	111 1001	171	79	y
122	111 1010	172	7A	z
123	111 1011	173	7B	{
124	111 1100	174	7C	|
125	111 1101	175	7D	}
126	111 1110	176	7E	~
127	111 1111	177	7F	DEL

An extended ASCII character set:

0	NUL	0	0	63	?	111111	3F	126	~	1111110	7E	189	½	10111101	BD
1	SOH	1	1	64	@	1000000	40	127		1111111	7F	190	¾	10111110	BE
2	STX	10	2	65	A	1000001	41	128	€	10000000	80	191	¿	10111111	BF
3	ETX	11	3	66	B	1000010	42	129		10000001	81	192	À	11000000	C0
4	EOT	100	4	67	C	1000011	43	130		10000010	82	193	Á	11000001	C1
5	ENQ	101	5	68	D	1000100	44	131	ƒ	10000011	83	194	Â	11000010	C2
6	ACK	110	6	69	E	1000101	45	132	„	10000100	84	195	Ã	11000011	C3
7	BEL	111	7	70	F	1000110	46	133	…	10000101	85	196	Ä	11000100	C4
8	BS	1000	8	71	G	1000111	47	134	†	10000110	86	197	Å	11000101	C5
9	HT	1001	9	72	H	1001000	48	135	‡	10000111	87	198	Æ	11000110	C6
10	LF	1010	0A	73	I	1001001	49	136	ˆ	10001000	88	199	Ç	11000111	C7
11	VT	1011	0B	74	J	1001010	4A	137	‰	10001001	89	200	È	11001000	C8
12	FF	1100	0C	75	K	1001011	4B	138	Š	10001010	8A	201	É	11001001	C9
13	CR	1101	0D	76	L	1001100	4C	139	‹	10001011	8B	202	Ê	11001010	CA
14	SO	1110	0E	77	M	1001101	4D	140	Œ	10001100	8C	203	Ë	11001011	CB
15	SI	1111	0F	78	N	1001110	4E	141		10001101	8D	204	Ì	11001100	CC
16	DLE	10000	10	79	O	1001111	4F	142	Ž	10001110	8E	205	Í	11001101	CD
17	DC1	10001	11	80	P	1010000	50	143		10001111	8F	206	Î	11001110	CE
18	DC2	10010	12	81	Q	1010001	51	144		10010000	90	207	Ï	11001111	CF
19	DC3	10011	13	82	R	1010010	52	145		10010001	91	208	Ð	11010000	D0
20	DC4	10100	14	83	S	1010011	53	146		10010010	92	209	Ñ	11010001	D1
21	NAK	10101	15	84	T	1010100	54	147	“	10010011	93	210	Ò	11010010	D2
22	SYN	10110	16	85	U	1010101	55	148	”	10010100	94	211	Ó	11010011	D3
23	ETB	10111	17	86	V	1010110	56	149	•	10010101	95	212	Ô	11010100	D4
24	CAN	11000	18	87	W	1010111	57	150	–	10010110	96	213	Õ	11010101	D5
25	EM	11001	19	88	X	1011000	58	151	—	10010111	97	214	Ö	11010110	D6
26	SUB	11010	1A	89	Y	1011001	59	152	˜	10011000	98	215	×	11010111	D7
27	ESC	11011	1B	90	Z	1011010	5A	153	™	10011001	99	216	Ø	11011000	D8
28	FS	11100	1C	91	[	1011011	5B	154	š	10011010	9A	217	Ù	11011001	D9
29	GS	11101	1D	92	\	1011100	5C	155	›	10011011	9B	218	Ú	11011010	DA
30	RS	11110	1E	93	]	1011101	5D	156	œ	10011100	9C	219	Û	11011011	DB
31	US	11111	1F	94	^	1011110	5E	157		10011101	9D	220	Ü	11011100	DC
32		100000	20	95	_	1011111	5F	158	ž	10011110	9E	221	Ý	11011101	DD
33	!	100001	21	96	`	1100000	60	159	Ÿ	10011111	9F	222	Þ	11011110	DE
34	"	100010	22	97	a	1100001	61	160		10100000	A0	223	ß	11011111	DF
35	#	100011	23	98	b	1100010	62	161	¡	10100001	A1	224	à	11100000	E0
36	$	100100	24	99	c	1100011	63	162	¢	10100010	A2	225	á	11100001	E1
37	%	100101	25	100	d	1100100	64	163	£	10100011	A3	226	â	11100010	E2
38	&	100110	26	101	e	1100101	65	164	¤	10100100	A4	227	ã	11100011	E3
39		100111	27	102	f	1100110	66	165	¥	10100101	A5	228	ä	11100100	E4
40	(	101000	28	103	g	1100111	67	166	¦	10100110	A6	229	å	11100101	E5
41	)	101001	29	104	h	1101000	68	167	§	10100111	A7	230	æ	11100110	E6
42	*	101010	2A	105	i	1101001	69	168	¨	10101000	A8	231	ç	11100111	E7
43	+	101011	2B	106	j	1101010	6A	169	©	10101001	A9	232	è	11101000	E8
44	,	101100	2C	107	k	1101011	6B	170	ª	10101010	AA	233	é	11101001	E9
45	-	101101	2D	108	l	1101100	6C	171	«	10101011	AB	234	ê	11101010	EA
46	.	101110	2E	109	m	1101101	6D	172	¬	10101100	AC	235	ë	11101011	EB
47	/	101111	2F	110	n	1101110	6E	173		10101101	AD	236	ì	11101100	EC
48	0	110000	30	111	o	1101111	6F	174	®	10101110	AE	237	í	11101101	ED
49	1	110001	31	112	p	1110000	70	175	¯	10101111	AF	238	î	11101110	EE
50	2	110010	32	113	q	1110001	71	176	°	10110000	B0	239	ï	11101111	EF
51	3	110011	33	114	r	1110010	72	177	±	10110001	B1	240	ð	11110000	F0
52	4	110100	34	115	s	1110011	73	178	²	10110010	B2	241	ñ	11110001	F1
53	5	110101	35	116	t	1110100	74	179	³	10110011	B3	242	ò	11110010	F2
54	6	110110	36	117	u	1110101	75	180	´	10110100	B4	243	ó	11110011	F3
55	7	110111	37	118	v	1110110	76	181	µ	10110101	B5	244	ô	11110100	F4
56	8	111000	38	119	w	1110111	77	182	¶	10110110	B6	245	õ	11110101	F5
57	9	111001	39	120	x	1111000	78	183	·	10110111	B7	246	ö	11110110	F6
58	:	111010	3A	121	y	1111001	79	184	¸	10111000	B8	247	÷	11110111	F7
59	;	111011	3B	122	z	1111010	7A	185	¹	10111001	B9	248	ø	11111000	F8
60	<	111100	3C	123	{	1111011	7B	186	º	10111010	BA	249	ù	11111001	F9
61	=	111101	3D	124	|	1111100	7C	187	»	10111011	BB	250	ú	11111010	FA
62	>	111110	3E	125	}	1111101	7D	188	¼	10111100	BC	251	û	11111011	FB

In the 1970s it happened to be 8-bit microprocessors that pushed to the fore, precipitating the extension of the ASCII set to 8 bits, and because this then remained the standard for two very formative decades in computing, we today tend to define an 8-bit binary code as one *byte*. (We recount in our chapter on Image & Colour the good intentions behind this particular term's coinage.)

Meanwhile, though, the ambition of arriving at a universally adopted standard for character encoding remained just that, an ambition. With many more symbols and characters and an array of alphabets in use around the world to write in different languages, the 256 character 8-bit ASCII set was exhausted before it had been arrived at, and so further extensions were needed. By this time, the American Standards Association had been renamed twice, settling in 1969 to its current name, American National Standards Institute. Which is why ASCII revisions after 1969 carry the prefix ANSI, for example ANSI X3.4, in 1986; or the latest revision ANSI INCITS-1986 (R2012), whereby INCITS, pronounced 'insights', stands for International Committee for Information Technology Standards.

Rather than relying on the newly named ANSI to come up with a solution, internationally minded computer and printer manufacturers (notable among them Xerox and Apple), who wanted to sell their products worldwide, simply went ahead by themselves, looking for a global standard that would accommodate multiple languages with their special characters. It was a man called Joe Becker at Xerox who, in 1988, drafted a proposal for a 16-bit character set he suggested be called *Unicode*. There are 1,114,112 code spaces available in this system, the first 128 of which were occupied with characters identical to the 8-bit ASCII set, so that Unicode would be instantly backwards compatible. Although devised as a 16-bit set, Unicode can be encoded using 8-bit strings like ASCII, or even 32-bit strings. These different encodings are respectively named *UTF-8*, *UTF-16*, and *UTF-32*, with UTF standing for *Unicode Transformation Format*. UTF-8, as of April 2017, was used by 88.9% of all web pages on the World Wide Web, making it by far the most widely used character encoding system online.

☐ ↖229

Printing Text

FROM CONTINUOUS FEED TO THE SINGLE PAGE

If you are working mainly with numbers, and if what you are really interested in are the figures that come out at the other end of some computations, your priority is not the look and feel of your output. They are not only secondary, they are, at first, irrelevant. And your expectations from what you see on a screen (which in the very early stages of information technology is nothing, because there are no screens) right until the mid-1980s are not high, because monitors are capable only of displaying symbols, letters, and numbers, mostly as light green blinking characters on a dark background, and not formatted in any way as they would ever appear on a page.

Storage capacity being expensive and processing power limited, you also tended to print things out soon, so the computer would then be free to get on with what it was meant to be doing most: further calculations. And so what the printer industry came up with were printing machines that were capable of churning out large volumes of data quickly and cheaply, but reliably: the last thing you wanted when you depended on printed output in great quantities was a paper jam that held everything up.

The solution to this stack of priorities was continuous feed 'fanfold' paper that was fed into the printer by means of two perforated tractor strips, one on each side of the 'endless' strand. This kind of paper, often ruled with shaded lines to make it easier to read numeric tables across the page, allowed printers to handle large print jobs unsupervised, if necessary overnight, because they rarely failed. Special printing formats, such as address labels for mail-outs, used the same method, as did high volume form printing: invoices and delivery notes, bank statements, and even letters, if they were not considered terribly important, would be printed on perforated paper that could then be torn off into commonly used formats, stuffed into envelopes, and sent to people by mail. (Email, remember, did not yet exist.)

THE RISE OF A4

German scientist, satirist, and aphorist Georg Christoph Lichtenberg (1742–1799) was the youngest of seventeen children to a pastor and his wife near Darmstadt, and it was he who came up with the idea of a paper format that had a side to side ratio of 1 by √2, meaning that the tall side would be 1.414 times as long as its short side. The principal advantage of this (apart from yielding an apparently practical and pleasing proportion that is not far from the golden ratio of 1:1.618) is that when folded in half it results in two pieces of paper that have the exact same dimensions, which in turn means the format is easily and logically scaleable in both directions. This, as it happens, is the *only* ratio that does so: if the two sides stand at a right angle to each other in any other proportion, folding the page in half will lead to a new set of dimensions, and the process can't be repeated.

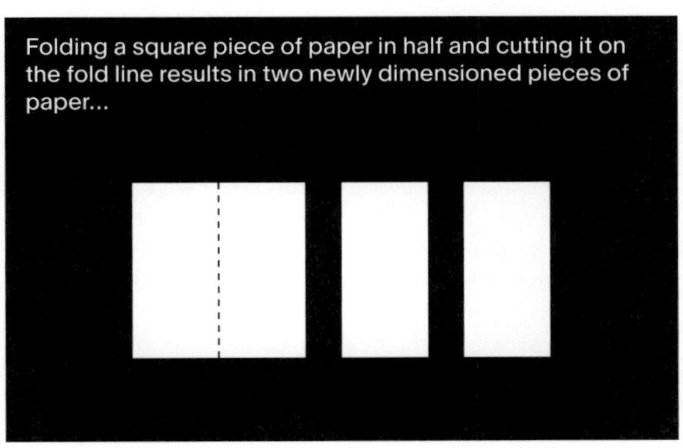

Folding a square piece of paper in half and cutting it on the fold line results in two newly dimensioned pieces of paper...

...whereas folding a piece of paper with the ratio 1:√2 in half and cutting it on the fold line uniquely results in two pieces of paper that retain the exact same ratio.

About 150 years later, in 1920, German engineer and mathematician Walter Porstmann (1886–1959) joined the then recently established *Normenausschuss der Deutschen Industrie* (Standards Committee of German Industry), having come to the attention of its managing director with a dissertation he'd written two years earlier on measuring systems. The *Normenausschuss* later became known as *Deutsches Institut für Normung (DIN),* but already in 1922 it published a set of standard paper formats developed by Porstmann. *DIN 476* was born, which is based on a piece of paper the size of one square metre, at the ratio Lichtenberg had proposed a century and a half earlier.

Porstmann called this square metre the *Weltformat (World Format),* labelled it A0, and deduced from it the sizes A1, A2, A3, A4, A5, and A6, by halving the sheet each time. The principle proved so compelling that other European countries readily adopted what German speakers still call DIN A4, what everybody else calls A4, and what, owing to its resounding success, in 1975 became ISO 216, a near global standard adopted by everyone, except the USA and Canada. (ISO being the *International Organization for Standardization.*)

■ ↖231 519↘

Folding a square piece of paper in half and cutting it on the fold line results in two newly dimensioned pieces of paper:

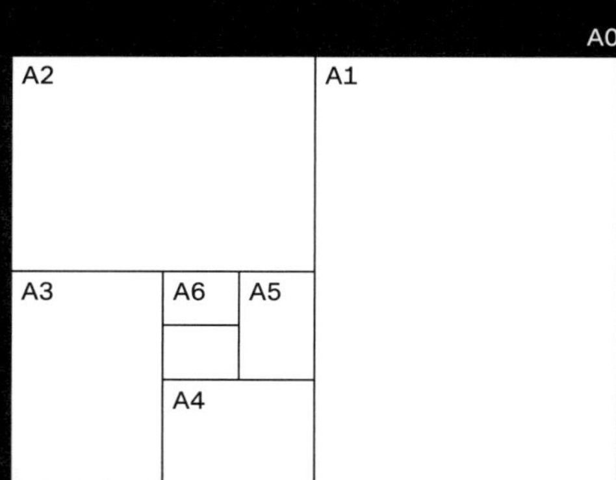

In the late 1970s and early 1980s, with the advent of word processing, and the attendant requirement for printing directly onto commonly used standard paper sizes, the single sheet printer now became commonplace, usually capable of handling A4, and in some cases also the larger A3 format. (A4 is the paper size that comes closest to the old British **foolscap folio**, which was the letter format most widely used in the British Empire and across Europe before A4 supplanted it.)

■ ↖327

230A ● 347 230B ● 347

PRINTERS & PRINT DRIVERS

Printing on single sheets of paper entailed page breaks and page formatting. Instead of just printing endless streams of data or text, you were now printing single pages that were meant to look like they had been typed up properly, and they soon would contain scalable fonts as well as images and graphics too.

In order to achieve this, you needed to tell the printer exactly what to do when, and that could be a matter of some complication, because each piece of software had to have a *print driver* that allowed it to communicate with the printer. With countless printer models hitting the market, using a plethora of different drivers, there were bound to be compatibility issues from the word go. Widely used software programs would have print drivers for the most commonly used printers built in, whilst specialist printers or less well known models had to supply their own print drivers, usually on a **floppy disk**.

POSTSCRIPT AND GUI OPERATING SYSTEMS

One solution to this issue was developed by Adobe Systems in the early 1980s, with a **page description language** they called *Postscript. Postscript* first came installed on Apple's *LaserWriter* printer in March 1985, two months after the launch of the first *Macintosh* computer in January of the same year, and it quickly established itself as a high-end standard for handling print jobs. The *Macintosh* was the first consumer grade computer to come with a **Graphical User Interface (GUI)**, provided by its operating system, the *Mac-OS.* This was swiftly emulated by the then much bigger and much more powerful Microsoft with their *Windows,* launched in November of that same year, 1985.

Postscript printers needed to be equipped with considerable processing power and memory capacity, as they did much of the data conversion required on behalf of the computer, and that made them costly. Too costly for many ordinary office settings, where plain numbers and simple text were still the bulk of everything that ever needed to be printed; but for graphic designers, artists, and indeed architects, the investment made sense. Still, the high 'onboard' implementation cost of *Postscript* meant that its days were numbered, and within fifteen years of its launch, by the beginning the 21st century, personal computers had caught up with enough speed, power, and memory to handle the graphics processing themselves. During the same time, alternative and much more economical printer technologies such as ink-jet printers had entered the market, making *Postscript* almost obsolete.

'Almost' being the operative term here: *Postscript* is still in use in professional settings where its ability to relieve a computer's processor can be a real advantage; and it also exists as a file format with the extension .ps or .eps, for **Encapsulated Postscript**

EPS), its compressed file version. An EPS file is a graphics file written in *Postscript*, which is used to deal with the requirements particular to embedding graphics elements in a document. Unlike *Postscript* generally, EPS always only describes *one* page. Adobe developed EPS in 1987 in collaboration with Aldus, developers of the early Desk Top Publishing (DTP) software *PageMaker*, and Altsys, which was developing vector graphics and typographic editors at the time.

Owing to its high implementation cost, *Postscript* catered mainly for the upper end of the market and people with serious professional graphics printing to do on a regular basis. But the GUI operating systems of both Apple *Macs* and Microsoft *Windows* compatible PCs were soon capable of handling printer management at the lower end on their own, which meant that the text or layout software now only had to communicate with the operating system's print driver, which then communicated with the individual printer. Printer manufactures, in turn, only had to deliver one compatibility touch point: *Windows* or the *Mac OS*. ■

With software and hardware in place to create text and graphics on screen, allowing the user to see what it looks like and define exactly how fonts, images, and graphics should appear on the printed page too, the stage was now set for the 'Desk Top Publishing Revolution', which we'll come to in a just moment. ■ ↖232 441↘

Until the arrival of *Postscript*, *Windows*, and *Mac OS*, a multitude of print drivers was required to print from different pieces of software with different types and makes of printer.

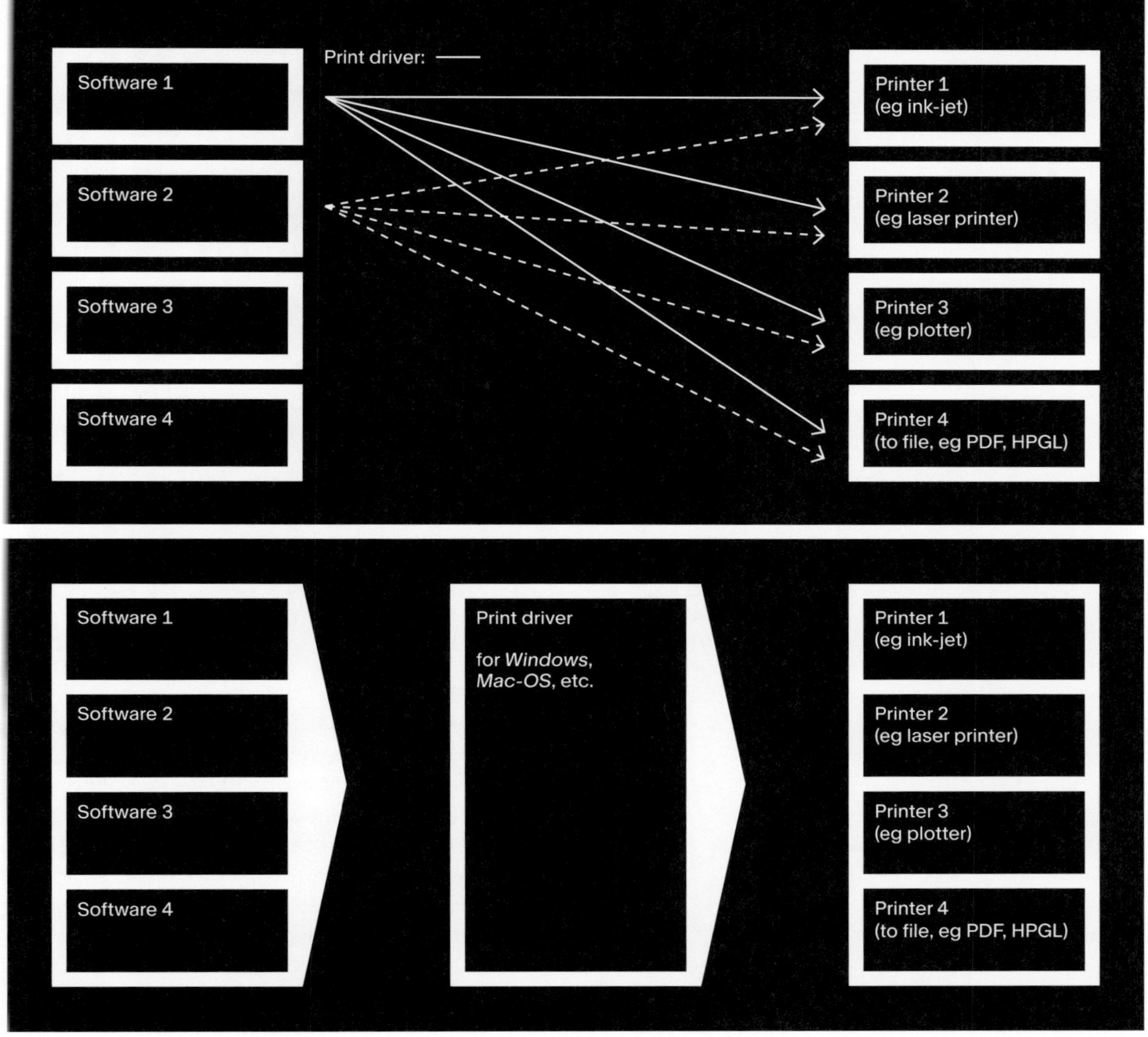

THE PDF

One of the main forces pushing *Postscript* out of the market was another Adobe invention emerging right from it: the *Portable Document Format (PDF)*. Released on 15 June 1993, it at a stroke resolved the majority of compatibility and formatting issues that had beleaguered computer users for the previous decade: keeping formatting intact from the screen to the printer and, importantly, from one piece of software or operating system to the next.

Major contributing factor to the success of the PDF and its very fast global adoption was the fact that while the software to *generate* a PDF, *Adobe Acrobat*, was licensed and therefore had to be paid for, the software to *read* a PDF, *Acrobat Reader*, was made freely available. This meant that the end user had no disadvantage or outlay from accepting a PDF, while publishers of any description or size were able to offer their content in a controlled format, and simply deliver the reader software with it, or provide a download link to it.

Also, early web pages on the Internet offered very limited layout options, and the PDF provided an easy and cost effective way to make magazines, newspaper articles, brochures, or prospectuses available for download in their original appearance. While this went against the then generally prevailing ethos of an open and free Internet – the PDF was, after all, still a proprietary format – its advantages were so compelling that it pushed through. In 2008, Adobe released PDF as an open format, and since then it has been adopted as an ISO standard worldwide.

(Microsoft's attempts at putting forward a competition to the PDF with its own **XPS [XML Paper Specification]** remained futile. The format exists, but it is nowhere near as widely adopted as the PDF. [XML
↖139 377↘ stands for **Extensible Markup Language**, which is the format XPS is written in.])

A PDF contains a complete set of metadata about itself, such as the fonts used – with these fonts embedded in the document – layout styles, and images. These are fixed at the time the document is generated, which is why PDFs provide a dependable guarantor of layout integrity in shared documents, as a file can only be annotated or specified fields filled in, but not in that sense edited with ordinary word processing software. (PDFs can be edited with professional programs such as *Adobe Illustrator*, for example.)

Furthermore, some PDF generators, such as *Adobe Acrobat Professional*, allow you to password protect your PDF or make it start in full screen mode, which turns it into a viable alternative to Microsoft's *PowerPoint* presentation software. There are also special types of PDF, such as the PDF/A format, designated for archiving purposes, which can't be changed by the user.

Significantly, a PDF can contain raster as well as vector data. This means that it is possible to edit a PDF (with a vector software illustrator program, for example), or to read it and separate it out into vector files or individual images (for example with *Adobe Photoshop*). PDFs can also incorporate interactive multimedia components or **U3D (Universal 3D)** elements, U3D being a compressed file format for 3D computer graphics.

Overall, it's this high level of versatility that makes the PDF particularly useful in architecture as a neutral data exchange program.

FROM WORD PROCESSING TO DESK TOP PUBLISHING

For anyone who hasn't experienced them it is hard to imagine that there were once mobile phones that could not send text messages, let alone take pictures, and that did not have any apps of any description, but were literally mobile telephones, made to the purpose exclusively of making and receiving phone calls on the hop. It is similarly somewhat strange to reflect on a computer that can do nothing other than process words. But early word processors did just that. A *Wang* word processor of the early 1980s occupied an entire desk space, weighed a ton (it actually weighed a few dozen kilos) and did no formatting to speak of. Data (for which read text) entry happened via an *MS-DOS* editor, which was capable of simple tabulation but otherwise gave you no control over how the text was arranged on the page: it simply put the words in paragraphs within set margins. You were able to set the margins.

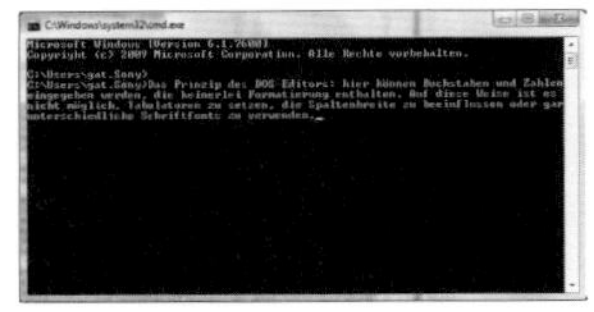

231 ● 348

RICH TEXT FORMAT (RTF)

In 1987, Microsoft introduced the *Rich Text Format (RTF)*, a proprietary cross-platform format that allowed for basic formatting such as bold, italics, and underlined text, and embedded fonts. It also, and importantly, made possible the integration of non-text objects, such as pictures, though they had to sit on a separate line.

RTF code was relatively simple and therefore, with a bit of knowledge and perseverance, also editable:

```
{\rtf1\ansi\ansicpg1252\deff0\deflang1031{\
fonttbl{\f0\fnil\fcharset0 Arial;}{\f1\fnil\
fcharset0 Calibri;}}
  {\colortbl ;\red0\green0\blue0;}{\*\
generator Msftedit 41.21.2509;}\viewkind4\
uc1\pard\hyphpar0\fi567\sl230\slmult0\qj\
tx760\tx1760\cf1\expndtw2\fs18 There comes
a point when not only those people are
interested who are directly affected…
```

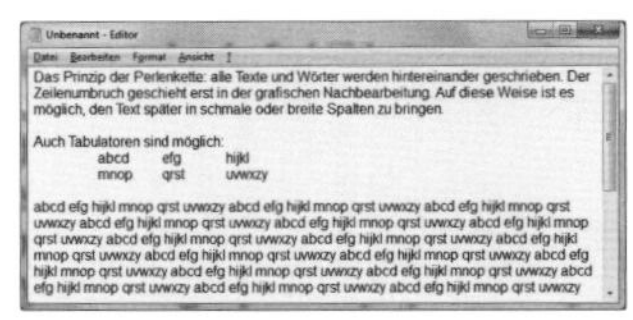

232A ● 348

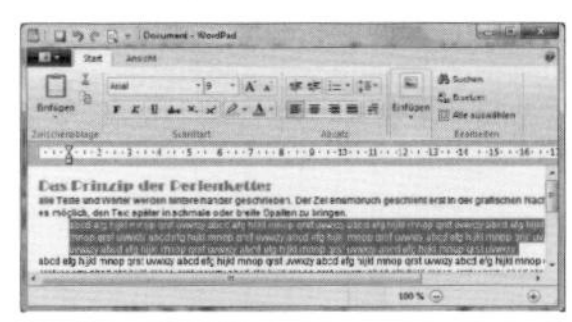

232B ● 348

WORDPERFECT VS *WORD*

If you asked anyone who took word processing seriously in the 1980s – because they spent their days and nights working with it, for example – about which word processor to choose, they would most likely have given you one word only: *WordPerfect*. It was a feature-rich application that, since 1982, ran on *MS-DOS* and that combined on itself two elements professionals most appreciate: user-friendliness and capability. Some would argue that it anticipated what later became associated mainly with Apple *Macs*: an intuitive interface and workflow. It therefore rapidly rose to the top of the pile and became the standard for word processing right up until *Windows 3* happened in 1990.

Windows 3 – Microsoft's 'answer' to the Apple *Mac* with its graphic user interface – and subsequent versions of *Windows* ran Microsoft's own *Word* word processing software, and with *Windows* dominating the PC market and *WordPerfect* slow to make itself compatible with *Windows*, *WordPerfect* quickly fell behind the far inferior Microsoft application, as *Word* took over and everybody simply made do with it. Not until 2001, when Apple released its *OS X* operating system which went out of its way to make *Windows* generated files compatible with its own equivalent versions, and *Word* documents became directly editable in Apple's own *Pages* word processor was there really any escape.

At almost the same time, in 2002, Sun Microsystems released the source code to the *StarOffice* suite it had recently acquired, thus creating the open-source *OpenOffice* (today known as *Apache OpenOffice*), whose *Writer* word processor is also now widely used across platforms, providing another viable alternative to *Word*.

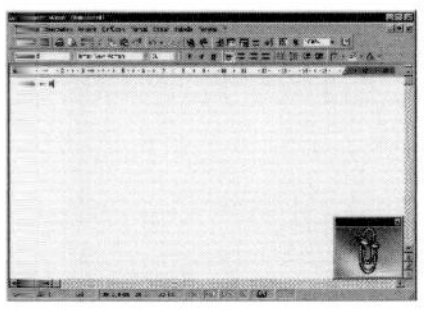

233A ● 348

233B ● 348

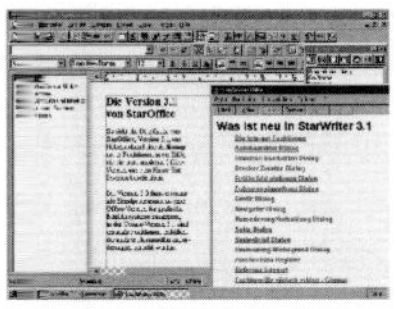

233C ● 348

DO-IT YOURSELF PUBLISHING

DTP stands for Desk Top Publishing, though it might almost as easily have been called DIYP for Do-it Yourself Publishing. This was a genuinely new thing. Before DTP, computing text was mainly a case of word processing, and word processing did what the term suggested: it processed words. The reason people used word processors were many and varied, but they had to do with text and handling it: writing reports, pitches, and essays or narratives of any sort was easier with word processors than with typewriters because you could correct as you typed without having to resort to physical means of erasion, and you could save and store documents and revisit them to review them. These sound like quaintly simple pleasures by today's standards, but they made a world of a difference. The step beyond getting the words right – creating layouts for books, essays, leaflets, proposals, magazines, and the like – was the realm of the professional graphic designer, and you would know if you had in front of you a student magazine or a neighbourhood newsletter, because they looked like they had been typed up and maybe cut and pasted together literally, physically, using paper and scissors, with some *Letraset* rub-on lettering for the titles and headlines.

DTP changed all that. With it, anybody halfway competent on a computer could produce documents using graphic elements, advanced formatting, and visually compelling typography. Standard word processors were not quite up to this task at first – and in the main still really aren't – but now you had programs like *PageMaker*, released by Aldus for *Mac* in 1985 and for *Windows* 1.0 in 1987. That same year, 1987, also saw the release by Quark Software of *QuarkXPress*, which over the next ten years pushed *PageMaker* off the perch of professional desktops and, in a competition for market share and territory, ultimately led to Adobe buying *PageMaker* and creating its own successor to it, *InDesign*, which it released in 2002.

What these specialist applications had in common was that they offered sophisticated, professional tools to place and manipulate text and graphics on the page, making layout and graphic design much more versatile and dynamic than it had been with manual type and analogue graphic elements. You could now adjust not just font sizes and line spacing but also for example kerning – the amount of space between individual letters – or letter width. (More on these below).

Few non-professionals would use these high-end applications though, and while they most certainly revolutionised the graphic design industry, it was possibly at the lower end of the spectrum that the DTP revolution became most visible and pronounced, as untrained computer users were suddenly able to deploy the more basic elements of graphic design in their documents, using consumer grade software.

WYSIWYG

Considering that for decades word processing was done without the typist or writer knowing what the page would look like before it was printed, it is remarkable how widely used and appreciated the technology really was, even then. But for the first twenty years or so, a document's appearance was determined not by them or by the word processing software, but by the printer.

Earliest printers borrowed print wheel or golf ball technology from electric typewriters, but this was soon followed by dot matrix printers. The printheads of these consisted of small needlepoints that planted individual ink dots on the page to make up the letters. This was fast and cheap, but also crude. Still, it allowed for shapes other than those set in fixed wheels or balls, and so it was possible now to print varying font sizes and basic shapes in monochrome.

The breakthrough again happened in the 1980s when laser and ink jet printers came to market, conveniently coinciding with the graphic user interface (GUI) mentioned earlier. These printers allowed for any kind of shape to be printed, also in colour, and that meant that for the first time you could work on screen on something that you could hope to print out to look just the same on the page.

WYSIWYG had arrived. It stands for *What You See Is What You Get,* and it requires that there is a point to point (actually pixel to point) correspondence between what's on screen and what the printer does. It also requires a fine enough resolution of the printed page, so it can emulate the screen resolution, at least in a good enough approximation. (We discuss this in more detail in our chapter on Image & Colour). □ ↖229

234A ● 349

234B ● 349

234C ● 349

234D ● 349

Layout

There is no special irony in the fact that an art school founded in Weimar in 1919 by German architect Walter Gropius (1883–1969) with a name that literally translates as 'House of Building' or 'House of Construction' and which soon became synonymous with an entire architecture and art movement, did not, at first, have an architecture department. The whole idea of Bauhaus was to bring together all art forms and disciplines and usher in an era of the *Gesamtkunstwerk* – the complete, and completely integrated, work of art – in which disciplines were indistinguishable, if nothing other than in terms of prominence and priority. Craft, design, and architecture were equal elements in an approach that also, and readily, encompassed graphic design and layout of posters, pamphlets, brochures, magazines, and proposals.

■ ↖120

235 ○ 400

It is perhaps unsurprising then that it is here, at this juncture, that our chapter starts to become really relevant to architects: from the point onwards where anyone with some aptitude can go about designing pages on their computer without having to call on a third party expert.

The page – we think of it normally as paper, but it can be a foil, it can be a projection slide, it can be a wall onto which we are going to print, or a floor – now is the canvas, and on it we arrange, today by computer, just as a hundred years ago by manual means, the elements that make up our design:

- Text (headlines, titles, captions, legends, descriptions, narrations, dialogue; from single words to sentences or phrases, to paragraphs)
- Graphics (lines, curves, frames, boxes, circles, bullets, icons)
- Images (photographs, drawings, scans, models)

These are the components we have at our disposal to express ourselves and to present our architecture in two dimensions, be that when we talk about it before it is realised, or after it has been built, or while it is in the process of being created. And today's word processors can all do the basics of what a dedicated desk top publisher can do: they allow you to liberally place and manipulate these elements; some help you with quick alignment reference lines that make it supremely easy to achieve a neat arrangement of text blocks and pictures, and they all allow you to scale and resize these elements and to move them about.

Professional software also allows you to decide whether to embed imported elements (such as images) or draw on them as file references while keeping the actual files outside the document you're creating (this can be useful if you have a data-heavy project, such as a presentation or a book with many images), and they will also give you much greater versatility in controlling individual aspects of each element.

All of them can output to PDF, which as we have seen is by far the most commonly used and therefore most useful format, certainly for preview purposes, as it is universally readable and viewable.

A typical Desk Top Publishing (DTP) workflow:

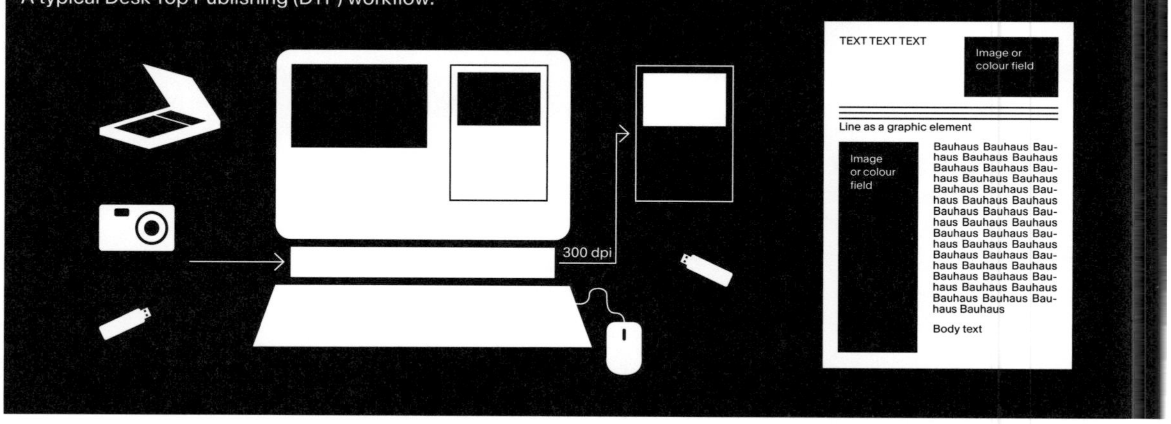

SOME LAYOUT PRINCIPLES

There is, as you would expect, not one right approach or let alone solution to the generic challenge of 'layout'. And while it is also true to say that some people are very capable of doing layouts more or less by instinct and with a 'good eye' for things such as proportion and pleasing presentation principles, there are some basic rules that can be learnt that will instantly improve your page design. (Here, again, we say 'page' whether we mean a page in a book or presentation, or a display or a plan.)

□ ↖29

In a way, you can look at this a bit like cooking. Generally, we tend to eschew the notion of 'recipes' in this *Atlas*, but we also in our Introduction speak of master chefs, and reference them as people who have acquired a skill to the highest level and thus are able to find in it their own creative expression and cultural freedom; and if there is one thing we can be fairly sure of, it is that they will have familiarised themselves at some point with some of the most relevant recipe books for their cuisine.

Here then we want to briefly touch on some of the learnable fundamentals to layout, especially with reference, for obvious reasons, to architects.

PLANNING THE PAGE

Still bearing in mind what we repeated a moment ago that we use the term 'page' here liberally, there are invariably some basic, often practical considerations to be made about the page layout, such as:

- Is there a format that particularly offers itself or that is in fact required? How much space do I need to accommodate my widest perspective, for example, or my biggest plan?
- Where and how is my layout going to 'live'? If it's a book, is there a standard shelf size at my department which this wants to sit on prominently? Or is the book aimed at a large audience, sold in general book stores and therefore required to fit well onto industry standard shelving? Is it a coffee-table publication that wants to take up its own space when laid out flat? What does a double page spread look like, and is this relevant?
- Say we are not talking about a book, but about a series of plans: where are they going to hang? How are they going to be viewed? How much room is there for them to be appreciated as well as understood?

These may seem like prosaic criteria, but they are eminently important, as they will inform the overall handling of the page and therefore the effectiveness of everything that's on it.

Generally speaking, in a book, document, or presentation, 'good practice' says that each layout page should have the same format, though there are obviously exceptions, such as when you need to include a panoramic pull-out, for example.

PLACING THE TEXT

If your page contains any text, you immediately enter the fascinating world of fonts, of which we will speak in a great deal more detail in a moment. But before then, there are again some very basic, principal considerations to be made that will greatly influence your presentation and its impact, such as:

- What is the relationship between graphics, pictures, and text? Both in terms of quantity – how much text is there – and quality, as in: what type of text is there going to be?

Which leads on directly to:

- The relationship between body text, legends or captions, and other visual elements: does the book, document, or plan have to 'work' without somebody being able to read some, all, or any of the text, or is the expectation fully, as with this *Atlas* for instance, that anyone genuinely interested will find time and leisure to read at least some of the body text?

As with any other visual or conceptual element, when placing text, a fundamental question to ask yourself is, what emotions do I want to evoke? Different fonts have very different effects on the reader, which is something marketers and designers know and exploit. A swirly, decorative font, for example, tells us something completely different about the author, the project, or the brand, than a sturdy, solid, sober one.

How, furthermore, should the text be arranged on the page: does the presentation call for fully justified blocks of text with both the left and right hand margins aligned, or is there a case for a less formal layout? In Western culture, the 'level of formality' could be argued to go, by degrees: full alignment, as you will find it in books, including this *Atlas*, to left alignment – standard for letters or other more personally voiced texts – to right alignment, which draws attention to itself as unorthodox and therefore possibly more 'creative', to fully centred which tends to evoke associations of ceremony, poetry, or declamation.

If your text is fully justified on both sides, then column width takes on a special relevance, because quite aside from the overall impact it may have on the look of your page, it will also affect the spacing of the words. If the relationship between the number of words and the width of the column goes out of kilter, then the text will be drawn apart with wide gaps between individual words that make reading it unpleasant or even difficult.

THE CASE FOR THE GRID

The body text – assuming you have any – will determine the horizontal grid size, because with it you will set the line spacing. We talk about line spacing a bit more under *Typography* below, but here we can already make the case for the grid: use it! Your desktop publishing software will feature a horizontal and vertical grid and they both come in eminently handy, because they allow you to snap objects to the grid lines and thus align them perfectly, even where the relationship between an object and text, or another object, is not immediately obvious, for example because they're not directly next to each other.

Just by virtue of this alignment feature, the horizontal grid certainly, but really to a lesser extent also the vertical grid are practically indispensable tools for creating order on the page, even if you set the page irregularly.

WHITE SPACE

One of the most powerful tools in the box of the layout designer is 'nothing'. Known as 'white space', it describes the area on the page – whether it be white or any other colour – that is left blank. How much white space you allow for on your page, and where you do so, can completely change the appearance and therefore character of your work, and tell your reader or viewer a great deal about it and therefore about you and the purpose of what you are doing.

Generally, and very simply, there is an 'ideal' relationship between visual elements and white space which makes the viewer feel comfortable about the page, not least because they are used to its proportionality. Allow for very little white space and you suggest that you have a lot of content to communicate but not much space or resources to do so, and you demand a certain amount of effort from your reader or viewer to work their way through that content. Allow for generous white space and you communicate a largesse of spirit, but also risk that the content may 'get lost' on the page, or that the arrangement of the elements gets more of our attention than the elements themselves.

THE HIERARCHY OF CONTENT AND THE STORY
Last in this section, but absolutely not least, is the consideration of what matters and in what order of priority it does so: the hierarchy of your content not only determines the heading levels, the font sizes for these and for the body text as well as any captions or legends, but also the order in which they appear. This ties into the arc of the story: what is the sequence of 'events' you want to take your reader or viewer through: where should they look first, where second, where last. Even a single page can thus be thought of as having a three act structure, though they be very short 'acts'.

Typography

Everything we said a short while ago in the context of the *Gesamtkunstwerk* notwithstanding, it will not have slipped past you that this chapter may on the surface seem somewhat tangential to architecture. And yet it isn't, because while architecture will always, and by its very definition, be either a physical manifestation of an object or its visual representation, we will also always need words to talk and write about it. And words that we write will be, in one form or another, set in type.

So whatever your relationship with architecture: digitality may have lowered many a bar and have made working with words easier and more accessible, just as it has made working with images and graphics and with all other creative elements easier and more accessible, but in all fields and all areas there is a limit to what the digital tool can do for you. Which is nothing so much as to say that while digitality has certainly all but eradicated the job of the physical typesetter, the jobs of the graphic designer and the expert typographer are far from obsolete. You may not be, or have any ambition to become, either, but having a grasp of the principles and fundamental elements that lie at the heart of typography will allow you to be a much more competent collaborator or client. Just as you may never be an engineer but need and want to grasp the principles of statics and physics in order to be able to understand what the engineer is doing and saying, so getting on top of the principles of typography may not turn you into an expert document designer, but it will make it a whole lot easier for you to communicate with one about what you want done.

Fortunately, the basic components of typography are refreshingly few. Typography is the art of arranging text on the page ('page' here as always meaning any kind of surface that the text will ultimately appear on, whether that is an actual paper page or anything else), and it encompasses the following principal elements, cascading down from the font:

THE FONT

In *The Third Man* – a post-war film directed by Carol Reed with a screenplay by the English writer Graham Greene (1904–1991), based on his own novella of the same title – Harry Lime, the character played by Orson Welles, finds himself standing on the steps of the *Prater Riesenrad* in Vienna, talking to his friend Holly Martins, who had just recently attended his, Lime's, supposed funeral. And it is here that Orson Welles comes out with one of the most quoted lines in film history, and one that people in the English speaking world have chuckled over ever since the film premiered in 1949: "You know what the fellow said – in Italy, for 30 years under the Borgias, they had warfare, terror, murder, and bloodshed, but they produced Michelangelo, Leonardo da Vinci, and the Renaissance. In Switzerland, they had brotherly love, they had five hundred years of democracy and peace – and what did that produce? The cuckoo clock."

Greene did not write that line, and he never took credit for it. Apparently, during the shoot, Welles ad-libbed it because they needed another sentence in the scene purely for timing purposes. He in turn attributed it to 'an old Hungarian play', though the most likely source of the sentiment seems to be an American artist named James Abbot McNeill Whistler (1834–1903), who mainly lived and worked in Britain, and didn't know very much about Switzerland.

Because droll as it is, it is also of course wrong, and on several counts. The Swiss did not invent the cuckoo clock, that was the Swabians, across the border, in the Black Forest, which is very much in Germany. Nor was Switzerland a particularly peaceful country during the era mentioned: the Swiss were known to be fearsome fighters and mercenaries, and between their first unilateral declaration of independence in 1291 with the *Rütlischwuur* and the adoption of the Swiss Federal Constitution in 1848 they went through numerous wars against the Habsburgs, the Emperor Maximilian I, and later against each other on religious grounds. There are even some famous Swiss people from that long period, but it is really in the 20th century that Switzerland as a place of creative and inventive ingenuity starts to come into its own, while the 21st century gave us Roger Federer and he alone makes up for everything.

But almost certainly the most widely recognisable and pervasively present Swiss thing around the world today is not Roger Federer, nor Swiss timing (be that watches or clocks or Olympic chronometry), nor cheese or chocolates, nor postcard tourism, nor the Large Hadron Collider near Geneva; it is, by some stretch, a font.

A font is a family of typefaces that all use the same design, whether they appear in bold, italic, light, or heavy type, and since everything we ever read in any kind of physical or digital 'print' (anything that is not handwritten) has to have a typeface, fonts are really exceptionally important to what the world we live in looks like and how we experience it. From the messages that you check on your phone first thing in the morning when you wake up, to the packaging on your breakfast cereal, to the signage on the road and on the Tube or on the bus, to everything you see in writing in and around your university or workplace, to obviously every book, every newspaper, and every webpage you ever come across: everything features at least one font.

We tend – graphic designers and typographers excepted – not to pay too much attention to fonts. They blend into our existence like water: we can't do without them, but we don't really think about how brilliant it is that we have them. But just as the fount of nature does not provide us with clean, instantly accessible drinking water, almost wherever we happen to be, without some nifty human thinking along the way, so the cornucopia of language does not come legibly and pleasing to the eye and mind without some outstanding design. The Swiss have claim on more than their fair share of excellence when it comes to architecture, design, and graphic design anyway, but when it comes to fonts from the 20th century onwards, they resolutely lead the way.

The father of the Swiss font is Adrian Frutiger (1928–2015). You will know his work better than you think you do, because you will have seen it a lot. If you go to Abbey Road in London to enact the famous Beatles album cover, the road sign there – as almost everywhere else in Central London – is in *Universe Bold Condensed*, a Frutiger typeface, part of the *Universe* font family. Motorway signs in Switzerland use *ASTRA-Frutiger*, a condensed version of the font named after the man himself. (*ASTRA* is the *Amt für STRAssen* – the department for roads in Switzerland.) The Dutch railways use a Frutiger font, as did Apple for its computer keyboards and Audi for its dashboards. But Frutiger's legacy lives on perhaps most prominently not in a font he designed himself, but one he heavily influenced and so, you could argue, spawned: *Helvetica*.

Helvetica started life as *Neue Haas Grotesk*, '*grotesk*' being the German spelling of 'grotesque', on which more in just a moment; Haas being the name of the type foundry, the *Haas'sche Schriftgiesserei* in the village of Münchenstein, just outside Basel, where the typeface was developed, and '*Neue*' simply meaning 'new'. A man called Edouard Hoffman was president of the Haas Type Foundry at the time, and while he is credited with having had 'input' on this new font, it was the Swiss freelance designer Max Miedinger (1910–1980) who is recognised as its creator, in 1957. It was renamed *Helvetica* (after *Helvetia*, the Latin name for Switzerland), in 1960 for marketing purposes, and it was a runaway success. Its simplicity and clarity and easy readability made it a favourite not only for contemporary print jobs and public signage, but significantly also on screen. It is one of the most widely used *sans-serif* fonts (which is the same as a 'grotesque' font, which we're just about to explain) in the world, and even if you create your documents in *Arial*, for example, you're really using a derivative of *Helvetica*.

Fonts are an evolutionary art and nobody designs a font entirely from scratch – *Helvetica* itself borrows heavily from an earlier font named *Akzidenz-Grotesk* – but *Arial* goes way beyond being 'inspired' by *Helvetica*. Designed in 1982 by a 10-person team around two font designers named Robin Nicholas and Patricia Saunders for Monotype Typography, it was especially created to be numerically identical in terms of character width and proportion with *Helvetica*, so that any document designed in *Helvetica* could be displayed on a screen or printed out without having to pay for the *Helvetica* licence fee. Robin Nicholas refutes it being a simple riff on *Helvetica*. In an interview with *MacUser* in 2005, he explained that it was, "designed as a generic sans serif; almost a bland sans serif," and this certainly is an advantage on the still not very advanced computer screens of the early to mid-1980s. There are also noticeable similarities to Monotype's own *Monotype Grotesque* font, which dates back to 1926. Still, the fact that it matches up precisely with *Helvetica* is clearly no coincidence. *Arial* found its wide distribution globally through being included on *Microsoft Windows 3.1* as a directly transferable alternative to *Helvetica*.

The furore around *Helvetica* and *Arial* runs deep and highlights this other aspect of typeface design almost everyone is simply unaware of: all these fonts are works of design. A lot of detailed creative thought goes into them, many considerations about how they work in different contexts and settings are being made, and each letter is carefully, individually crafted to fulfil a set of expectations associated with the font. And so they are – not always, but very often – proprietary works that carry licence fees. These licence fees, depending on the kind of use the font is put to, can be considerable. Licensing a very popular font such as *Helvetica* for an operating system that dominates ninety percent of the personal computing market, like *Windows*, for example, would be an expensive purchase.

Not only classic fonts, such as *Helvetica* or *Times New Roman* (one of the most widely used serif fonts), but any new font is somebody's creation and may therefore be copyrighted. The fact that you as a normal end user don't have to pay for any of them is purely down to the fact that they're mostly included, for your own personal use, in the software that comes with your computer. There are exceptions to this, and a very notable one is the *Courier* font by Howard Kettler, commissioned by IBM (International Business Machines) in 1955 and later redrawn by our friend Adrian Frutiger. It was deliberately never protected by copyright and so found wide use as a typewriter font, becoming effectively the typewriter standard for several decades in the second half of the 20th century.

And this also leads us on to one more observation about fonts very generally: a font being a piece of design, created by an individual or a team of expert typographers, you really should not mess with it. Most word processing, typesetting, or other graphic software allows you to treat text as any other image or graphic: you can stretch, condense, and distort a text box as you please. Strictly speaking, that's not 'allowed'. If you want to honour the integrity of the font design, you have to respect it and leave it alone and use it only in the versions it has been officially released, which very often does include light, condensed, bold, and italic variants of the design. You certainly must not distort it.

In 2017 there were estimated to be around 40,000 professionally designed fonts. That's according to *The 100 Best Typefaces of All Time*, a more or less self-appointed selection panel of German and American experts. Under the aegis of Monotype Germany – the company that brought you *Arial* – this chooses its favourites according to three criteria: sales figures (40%), 'historical significance' (30%) and 'aesthetic quality' (30%). *Helvetica* tops the list, followed by *Garamond*, by the early French type designer Claude Garamont, now mostly referred to as Claude Garamond (c. 1510–1561), with Adrian Frutiger's *Frutiger* coming in at number three. *Arial* doesn't make the list, but of course *Times* does (6), as does *Univers* (10), as does a curious font family called *Rotis*, in at number 32, by German typographer and graphic designer Otl Aicher (1922–1991). It is curious because unusually it combines on itself a serif, semi-serif, semi-sans, and sans version, and since its release in 1988 it has found widespread use in product packaging and also – this is the reason we point it out here – architecture.

High time, then, that we briefly touch on these font types.

(If you are keen on fonts, you can lose yourself for many an hour of fascinating diversion on the *Google Fonts* interactive website, where you can play with several hundred licensed and free-to-use fonts, learn about their creators, and even gain some insights into their usage data too.)

FONT TYPES

Fonts fall into two main categories: *serif* (also known as *Roman*) and *sans-serif* (also known as *grotesque* or *Gothic*). A serif is a small dash or line at the end of a stroke line in a letter, where in handwriting a quill or pen would naturally leave such a line as it touches down onto or is removed from the page. A serif gives a font a more 'classical' or traditional look, whereas sans-serifs are much more prevalent in contemporary use. Also, sans-serif fonts tend to be easier to read on a screen, while, either through habit or because of their visual composition, serif fonts can feel more comfortable on the page. Which is why serif fonts are still widely used in physical publications, whereas online publishing usually favours sans-serifs.

When choosing your fonts, you're normally well advised to stick to one or two fonts only. Here, as a rule of thumb, fonts that are very different – such as a decorative serif opposite a neutral sans – tend to combine well, whereas very similar fonts tend to look convoluted and disturbing on the page.

Times New Roman and *Helvetica*: two of the most widely used serif and sans-serif fonts respectively. Both are proportional typefaces. *Courier* is perhaps the most famous monospaced typeface.

Times New Roman

ABCDEFGHIJKLMNOPQRSTUVWXYZ
abcdefghijklmnopqrstuvwxyz
0123456789

Helvetica

ABCDEFGHIJKLMNOPQRSTUVWXYZ
abcdefghijklmnopqrstuvwxyz
0123456789

Courier

ABCDEFGHIJKLMNOPQRSTUVWXYZ
abcdefghijklmnopqrstuvwxyz
0123456789

TEXT PARAMETERS
Apart from the font family (the typeface itself) and the font type that it belongs to (whether it is a serif or sans-serif font), there are several additional parameters that matter to how a font appears in print, on page, on the facade of a building, in signage, or as projection. In summary, these are:

FONT SIZE
The standard basis for font sizes is 72 pt (72 points being equal to 1 inch). Most common in normal text on A4 pages and on webpages are 11 pt and 12 pt font sizes. In book print they can go as low as 9 pt or even 8 pt.

Fonts of different sizes often and naturally have to sit next to each other on the page, so as to create headings and captions for example, and here, as with font styles above, the rule of thumb is: don't mix font sizes that are very similar; so don't, for example, combine a 13 pt with a 14 pt font, as the differential is too small to properly register but already enough to get noticed and so unsettle the page, whereas a 12 pt against a 16 pt font works well and is in fact very common.

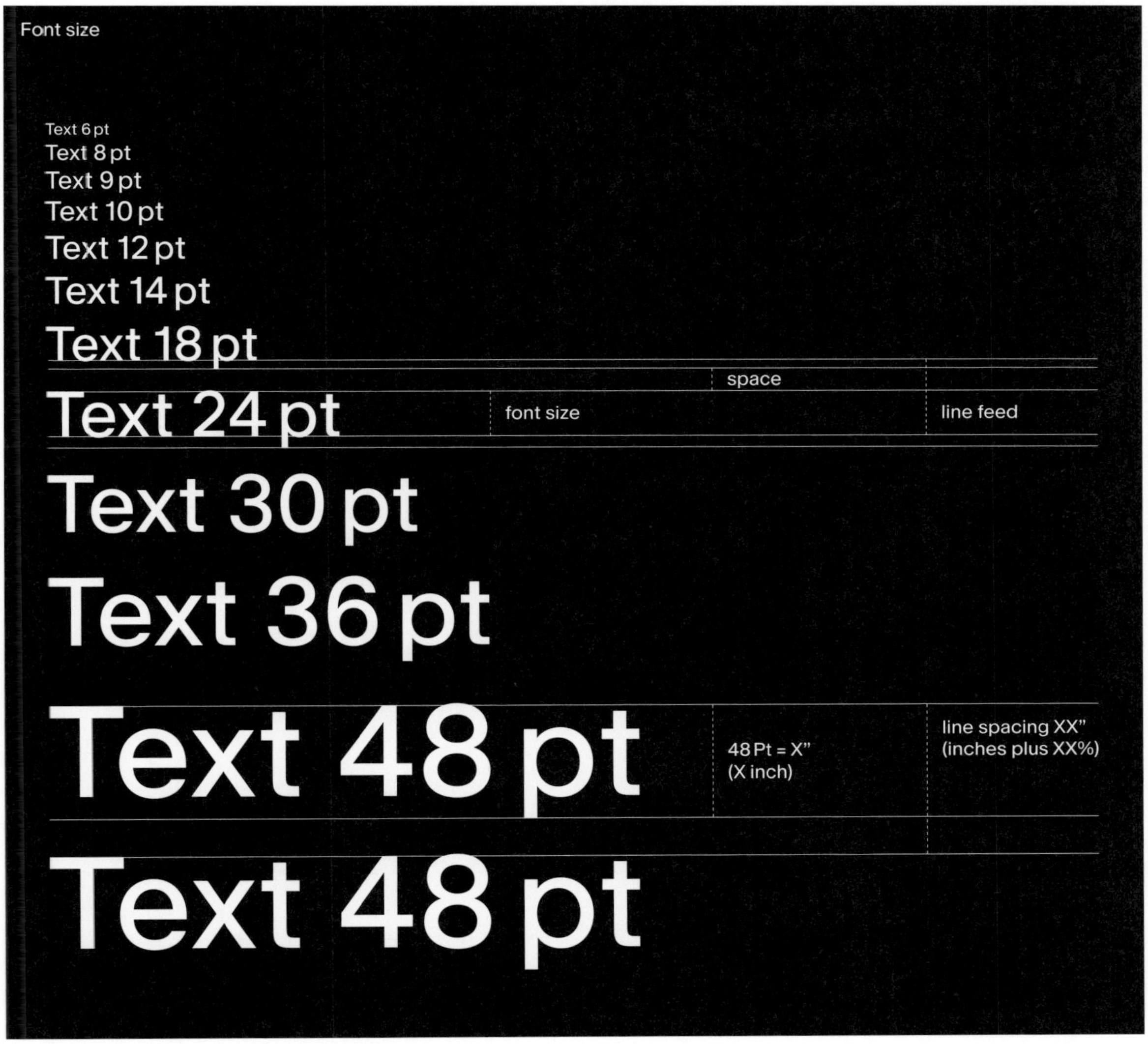

FONT COLOUR, TRANSPARENCY, MATERIALITY
Font colour is self-explanatory, but, particularly in graphic design and where text is used in architectural settings, transparency and/or materiality of the lettering can be used to great and often surprising effect.

LINE SPACING
This is the distance between lines; the basis here is usually 120% or 1.2 lines, though if you're writing a novel, you may well be asked by your agent or publisher to double space or 1.5 space your manuscript.

By spacing your lines 'properly' – that is in a pleasing and proportional manner – you can aid your reader greatly, while unusual line spacing draws attention to itself, and can make reading text difficult very quickly, both if the lines are arranged too far apart, and if they are squashed up too close together.

Generally speaking, large fonts can cope with more compact line spacing, whereas small fonts may need more space to allow the eye to keep lines of text apart.

LETTER PROPORTIONALITY
In *monospaced* type each letter takes up the same amount of space, as was common on mechanical typewriters; the most famous and still most cherished example being the *Courier* font, which is used in the film industry to this

day because in *Courier* 12 pt one A4 or US Letter size page of a screenplay formatted to industry standard tends to reliably result in one minute of screen time, which is a crucial factor to production and therefore cost. In *proportional type* each letter takes up as much space only as it needs. Most typefaces in use today are proportional.

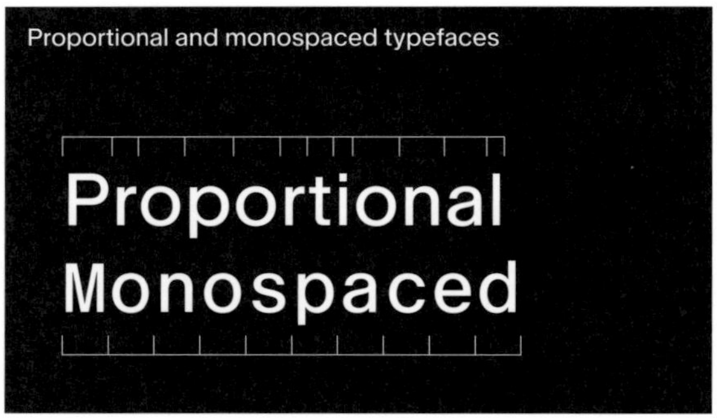

Proportional and monospaced typefaces

LETTER KERNING
Kerning refers to specifying the distance between letters, whether they are monospaced or proportional. This can be extremely useful when making minor, unnoticeable adjustments while setting text on a page, for example to avoid 'orphans' and 'widows' (single lines at the bottom or top of a page).

Similar to line spacing, letter kerning is immensely effective also in helping the reader get through a text with ease. If you're using a small font, you may want to choose slightly wide kerning, to make up for the letter size, whereas with very large fonts you can often 'squeeze in' a little more text by settling for a denser type.

OTHER ELEMENTS
At an advanced level, which is really where you would go only if you had a professional or otherwise particular interest in typography, you'll also find elements and terms such as:

- *Ascent and ascender height*
- *Cap height*
- *Mean line*
- *Median*
- *X-Line*
- *Baseline*
- *Descent*
- *Descender height*

As illustrated here:

Advanced elements in typography:

Cross Media Type & Layout

If the 1980s go down in IT history as the decade that brought us as general users graphic interfaces, 378↘ WYSIWYG word processing, and desktop publishing, in other words graphics, lifelike text, and widespread use of images on computers, then the 1990s was the decade that brought us the Internet.

There are several instances in this *Atlas* where we doff our metaphorical hats to the British computer scientist Tim Berners-Lee (b. 1955), because as the inventor of the World Wide Web (WWW) he made the 'Internet revolution' possible, and virtually everything we do online is in one way or another predicated on Berners-Lee's work. At the heart of that work lies the ■ 623↘ code he wrote for the WWW, the **Hypertext Transfer Protocol (HTTP)**, and the foundation he laid for the *Hypertext Markup Language (HTML)*.

HTTP is the set of rules that computers follow when they are in communication with each other to transfer text from one server to another, or from a computer to a server. We can think of this as the grammar. HTML is the language in which individual web pages are written, they follow that grammar so that the protocol can understand and handle them.

HTML

HTML, as its full name not merely suggests but spells out, is a *markup language*. A markup language is a programming language that uses human readable text and 'marks it up', by inserting annotations that tell the computer what to do with the text or object that is placed within it. In HTML, these annotations are called *tags*, and they are inserted in the HTML document in angled brackets. In HTML, many tags come in pairs, with their function applied to anything that lies in-between the opening and closing tag. The closing tag is the same as the opening tag, but with a forward slash. There are dozens of HTML tags; typical ones include:

```
<html> </html>     • tells the browser that this is a page written in HTML
<head> </head>     • denotes the part of the document that is invisible to the reader but
                     contains metadata about the document, such as its title and author,
                     for example
<body> </body>     • denotes the part of the document that is visible to the reader
<p> </p>           • denotes a paragraph
<br>               • denotes a single line break
```

The current version as we write this (2019) is HTML5. Compared to previous versions, it has more sophisticated document handling, and includes tags such as <video>, <audio>, and <canvas> to handle multimedia and graphic content without the need for additional plugins.

In the early days of HTML, many formatting tags were used to build web pages, such as <b> </b> for bold text, <i> </i> for italics, or <font> </font> for the type of font that was to be employed. While some of these are still in use and browsers can still read basic formatting tags such as for bold, italics, or to underline text, general practice has evolved to a separation of content and style, and for some time now the World Wide Web Consortium (W3C) has favoured and advocated the use of style sheets.

CSS

Cascading Style Sheets (CSS) is the name given to the style sheet language in use throughout the World Wide Web, in conjunction with HTML. It is employed to specify formatting and appearance factors of a web page, such as font style, font size, font, and background colours, among others. The style sheet acts like a 'manual' for the web browser to know what to do with different categories of text, such as titles, subtitles, body, quotations, legends, and tables.

Keeping the content separate from the style sheet has numerous advantages: if you are building a website purely with HTML, you will have to individually tag each element with its appearance instructions. This means that if you change your mind or want to update your website to a new look, or if your whole approach to the structuring of your content changes, you have to manually go through every single page and change the individual HTML tags. If, by contrast, you use a CSS, you can leave your many content pages untouched and just apply your changes to the one short style sheet to affect all the pages on your site.

This also makes it possible to use templates. Any web design platform – be it online, such as *Wix* or *Weebly*, or the widely used open-source *WordPress* – offers a range of professionally designed templates that you can simply apply to your content, with only minor adjustments then being necessary to make the website look right.

JAVASCRIPT

Along with HTML and CSS, *JavaScript* forms the third pillar of the World Wide Web today. JavaScript is used to handle dynamic web content, such as games, some more complex forms, and video and audio playback, and it is now universally supported by all web browsers.

Optical Character Recognition (OCR)

Since the early 20th century, attempts have been made – in some cases successfully – to convert written text into formats that machines can process. Originally, and in fact for quite some time, one of the principal objectives was to make text accessible to the visually impaired, converting type into telegraph code and later braille.

The American computer scientist and futurist Ray Kurzweil (b. 1948) in the 1970s became heavily involved in developing omni-font *Optical Character Recognition (OCR)* technology that would be able to cope with most kinds of typeface and convert text into spoken language.

Since the early 2000s, OCR has become available online as a web-based service (*WebOCR*), and there are now many apps for smartphones that not only read text but also translate it from one language into another. Similarly, OCR apps allow you to take a picture of some analogue text with your smartphone and convert this directly into an editable digital version. While until relatively recently this type of task would be accomplished – certainly in an office setting – with a scanner, some popular softwares such as *Adobe Acrobat* are now also capable to digitising a PDF using OCR.

The Outlook

Throwing around with blanket statements such as 'we live in a visual age' is, to our minds, inherently problematic, even though we do so ourselves sometimes. Because has there ever been an age that was not, in one way or another, 'visual'? Even if prior to digitality, it was not, perhaps, medial? And yet it is not far-fetched to suggest that thanks to the Internet □ ↖285 and computing, our relationship with imagery has □ ↖229 shifted a great deal, principally because of the sheer abundance of imagery there is, and the ease with which we can generate and disperse it.

□ 351↘ Far from doing away with text, this proliferation □ ↖175 of the image and of design has sharpened the need □ ↖327 for us as professionals of any description to understand the principles of type, layout, and design in relation to text, because text too has only multiplied in quantity and will continue to do so, without doubt.

Not only are our possibilities as architects for using and incorporating textual elements of any kind – letters, words, characters – into our objects greater than ever, also the bar for presentational purposes has risen to a level which sets expectations on a par with professional graphic designers: your proposal has to look good, and that means it not only has to come with inspired design for your architecture, but the packaging and delivery of your ideas is also expected to look and feel professional.

We don't anticipate this to change direction any time soon; if anything, we expect the convergence of disciplines to continue, and the professionalisation of presentation in all areas to increase. Partly, it will do so simply because it can: the technology is there, it's easy to learn and to use, and it produces (or can help produce) good-looking results; partly because we *do* live in an especially visual age where presentation and content are becoming inseparable, and where just having a fine idea is no longer enough to 'sell' it.

The whole concept of having to 'sell' ourselves as architects – be it in images or words – may well run counter to our intuition, and yet the culture we operate in at the time we write this book, towards the end of the second decade of the 21st century, is only just beginning to recoil somewhat from the brash commercialism of the late 20th century. There are alternative ways being sought and found, but these too need to express themselves, and they need to do so in an environment that has absolutely become digital. Therein, perhaps, lies the main point we feel is worth reiterating and emphasising here as we do in other chapters: you cannot, as an architect, be expected to be an expert at everything. But you can be expected to be literate. To know about the tools and the concepts at large in the 'digital world', and to be able to choose which ones to make your own and how to adapt them to your own needs and wishes.

On the surface, it may well be more obvious how topics such as Visualisation or Image & Colour (on both of which we have chapters in this *Atlas*) fit into this broader, overarching picture, but we advocate, as you will know if you have read other parts of this book, that you become as familiar with Scripting and Graphs & Graphics as you do with those, and with Text, Typography & Layout just as much: not because you are necessarily going to be called upon to design a book or be solely responsible for creating your own or your practice's website, but because you will, sooner or later, be dealing with people who do, and because architecture is inextricably enmeshed with all these fields.

We tend not to make many predictions in these *Outlooks* at the end of our chapters, and in this instance there is no obvious trend or technology that we feel needs highlighting: speech recognition is going to make further strides, no doubt, as is OCR, which we just touched on very briefly, to the level where it can recognise handwriting and old, historic fonts, as well as distorted manuscripts and damaged copy; and where it can read and translate seamlessly across major languages.

But when it comes to text in architecture – be that in online or physical publications about architecture, or be that as part of our architectural environment in signs, interfaces, and displays – we look towards an ever wider opening of the scope of possibilities, because technology is being ever more closely integrated with our objects; our environment itself is becoming medial and feature-rich, and that means that in all contexts and at all levels we will have more and not less text as part of the settings we create, whether at home, at work, or at play. The great and actually quite beautiful irony is that in our visual age and media saturated digital world, the written word is becoming only and ever more important.

228 ● 330
The Olivetti *Lettera 22* typewriter with the classic QWERTY keyboard.
[Matrobriva]

229 ● 330
An early alphanumerical keypad on a calculator.
[Stefan Vorkoetter]

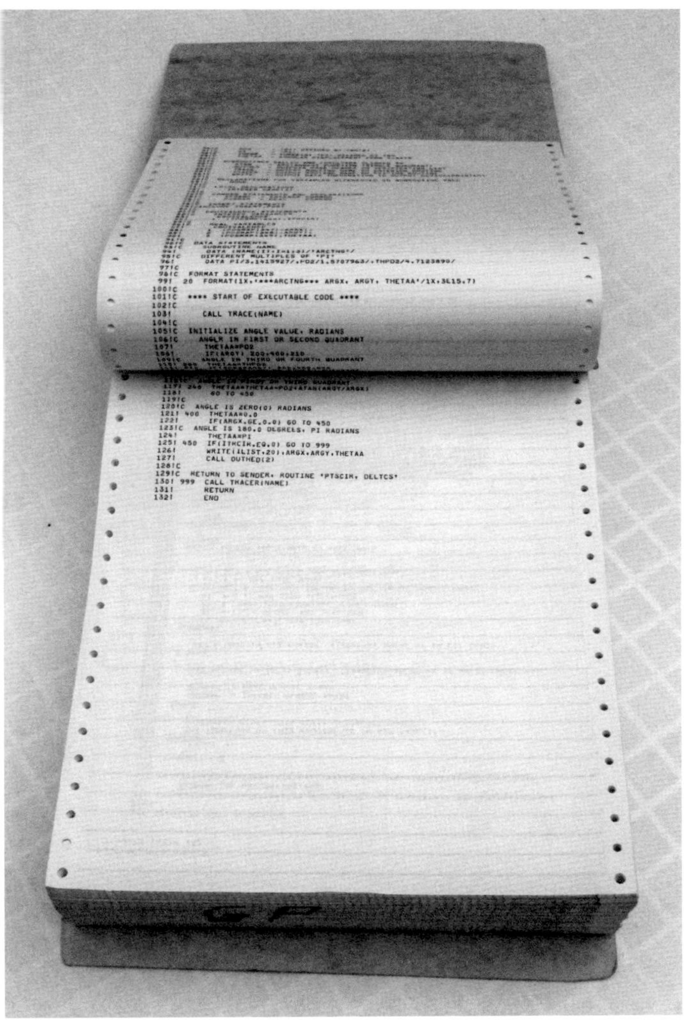

230A ● 334
From continuous feed paper (230A) to A4 (230B).
[230A: Arnold Reinhold]

230B ● 334

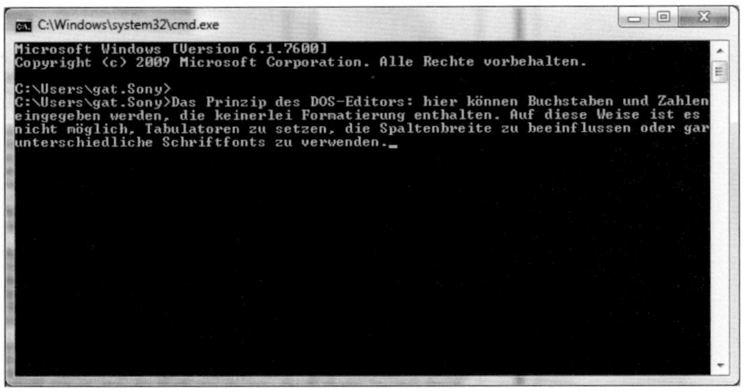

231 ● 336
The *MS-DOS* editor: only letters and numbers.

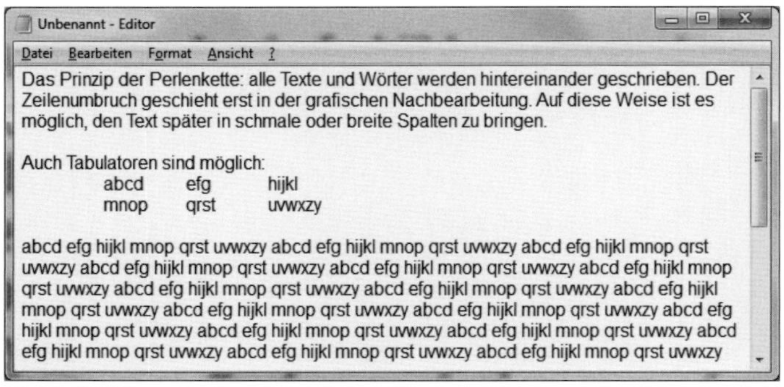

232A ● 336
Windows *Editor* and Microsoft *WordPad*: 'Rich Text'.

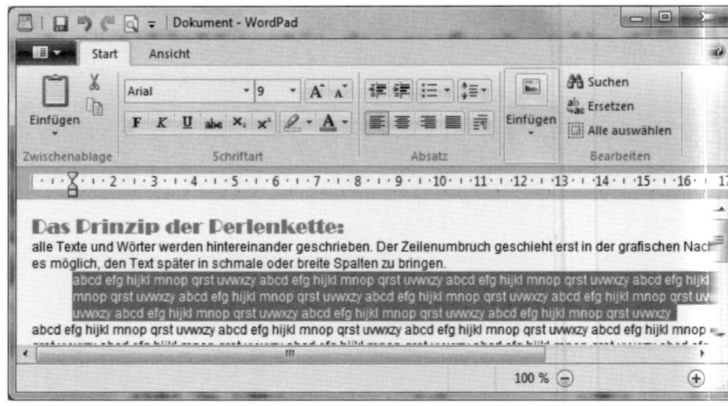

232B ● 336

233A ● 337
Microsoft *Word*

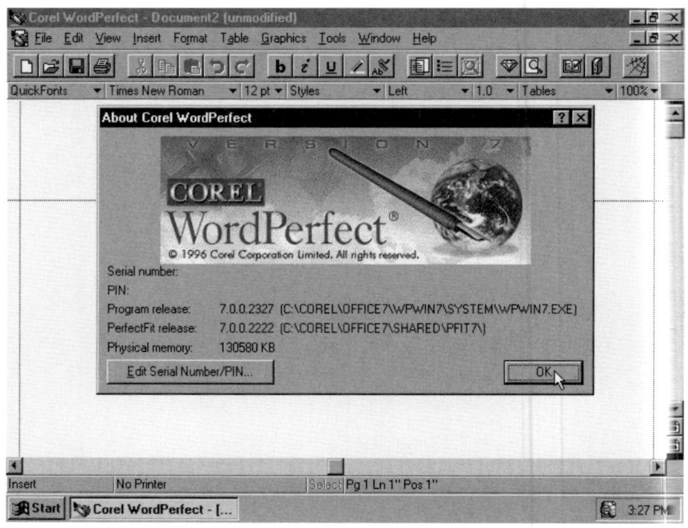

233B ● 337
Corel *WordPerfect*

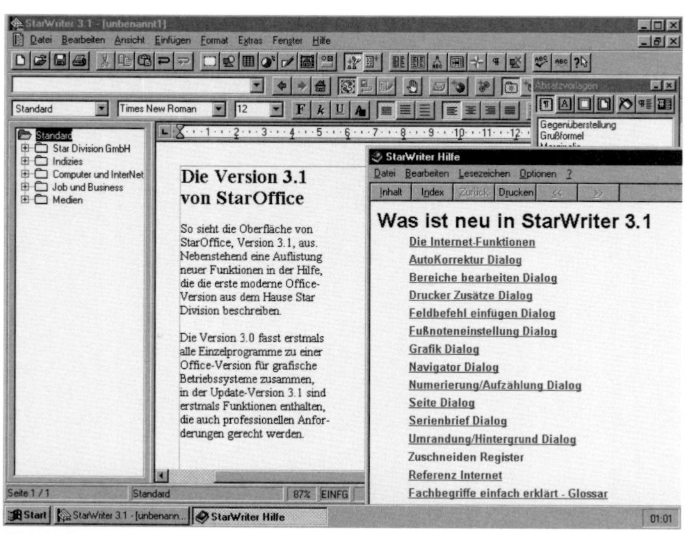

233C ● 337
Star Office

234A ● 337
A dot matrix print with its characteristic ink dots. [MikroLogika]

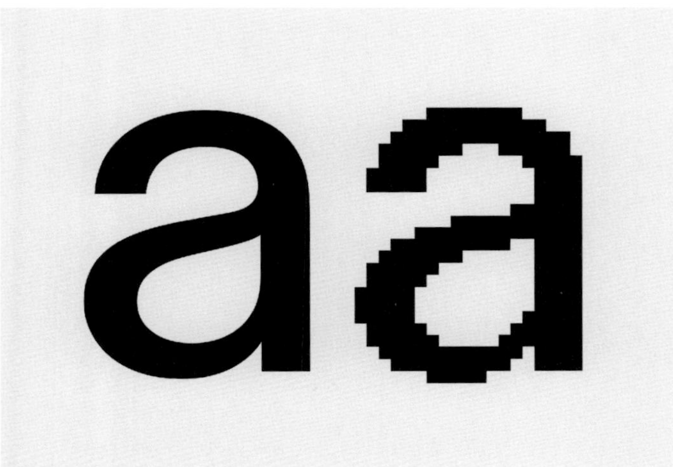

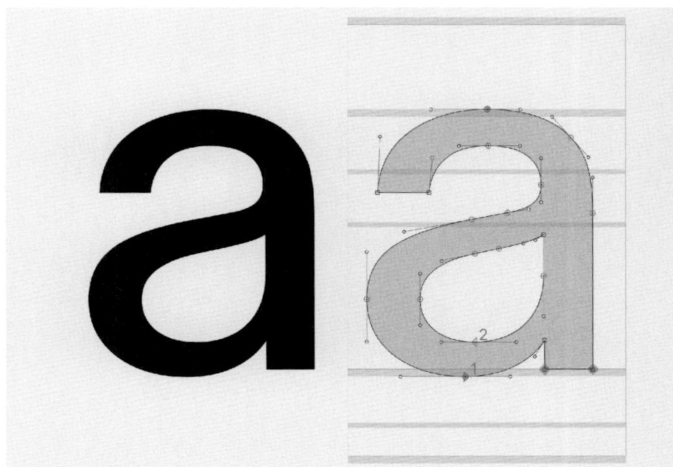

234B ● 337 234C ● 337
TrueType (234B left), bitmap (234B right). *TrueType* (234C) uses scalable vectors instead of pixels and thus produces sharp edges always, unlike pixel generated letters which on a screen can start to look blurred, depending on resolution. [Harald Gatermann / Onlab]

234D ● 337
[Harald Gatermann]

Scripting

Urs Hirschberg

- Seymour A Papert: *Mindstorms. Children, Computers, And Powerful Ideas*, 1980
- John K Ousterhout: *Scripting: Higher Level Programming for the 21st Century* in *IEEE Computer* magazine, March 1998
- John Maeda: *Design by Numbers*, 1999
- Casey Reas, Ben Fry: *Processing: A Programming Handbook for Visual Designers and Artists*, 2007
- Michael L Scott: *Programming Language Pragmatics, Third Edition*, 2009
- Bob Woodburry: *Elements of Parametric Design*, 2010
- H Pottmann, A Asperl, M Hofer and A Kilian: *Architectural Geometry*, 2010
- Mark Burry: *Scripting Cultures: Architectural Design and Programming*, 2011
- Tom Christiansen, Jon Orwant, Larry Wall, Brian Foy: *Programming Perl, 4th Edition*, 2012
- Wassim Jabi: *Parametric Design for Architecture*, 2013
- Arturo Tedeschi: *AAD Algorithms-Aided Design: Parametric Strategies using Grasshopper*, 2014

Overview

> "We are moving rapidly from an era of being aspiring expert users to one of being adept digital toolmakers."
>
> – Mark Burry: *Scripting Cultures: Architectural Design and Programming*, 2011

WHY SCRIPTING?

Scripting is child's play. Or rather, it should be. There is, objectively speaking, no reason why scripting shouldn't be as familiar – its concepts, its terminology, and its grammar as readily understood and to hand – as the fundamentals of arithmetic, or the principles of any natural language.

But as a 'language' – more accurately, a group of languages – scripting is still relatively new, and not yet something we naturally resort to in our everyday lives. This may be changing: the idea that children who are in the process of learning the rudiments of language and maths should also be taught the basics of coding has been around for almost as long as computing has been available to general users, and it is once more gaining traction. In 2012, then New York Mayor Michael Bloomberg announced to the world that he was going to 'learn coding'! This was to boost *Code Year*, an initiative by the interactive commercial educational platform *Codecademy*, to encourage people of any age to learn how to code. According to its *Wikipedia* page, *Codecademy* offers free coding classes in twelve different programming languages, and as of January 2016 had 25 million registered users. Meanwhile, in the United Kingdom, coding became part of the national curriculum, with a structured approach to the concepts of programming (learning what algorithms are, creating and debugging simple programs) being introduced in key stages from the age of five, right through to age 14 when children will be expected to program in two different languages and get to grips with **Boolean logic**, for example.

There are good reasons for all this, and for looking at it as a 'good thing'. If we define our current era as a 'Digital Age', or certainly as a time that in conceptual terms is characterised by information technology, we also have to accept that computer code lies at the heart of virtually everything we do. Much of the time this is deliberately hidden from our view: user-friendliness has become a pervasive goal, and software developers go to extraordinary lengths to shield us from coming into contact with the code that makes everything work. This may be well-intentioned and not in itself driven by anything other than a benign approach to us as consumers. But if we think of ourselves less as consumers than as human beings capable of creativity, invention, imagination, learning, and understanding the things we are dealing with, then gaining an insight into how things work and what the mindset or way of thinking is that goes into them not only makes sense, it also categorically emancipates and empowers us. And so the 'bliss' of ignorance in convenience notwithstanding, as free agents in a technological world we do well, in any case, to educate ourselves in code.

But what about your professional expectations? Do you, as an architect, absolutely need to be a competent coder? Probably not. Like most people in most professions, most architects get by using software that has been developed for them in such a way that simply mastering the user interface allows them to create and design, without ever so much as glimpsing a line of code. And there is nothing inherently wrong with this either. That being the case, then, is there even a need to be able to customise existing tools?

Very possibly yes. Take the widely used CAD application *Rhinoceros 3D*, for example. More and more people find that they can lend power to their elbow by extending its functionality. For *Rhino*, or *Rhino 3D*, as you may also hear it called, there is a free plugin called *Grasshopper*, which has enjoyed such popularity that with the release of *Rhino 6* in 2018 it became a fully integrated component of the program. *Grasshopper* gives you a graphical scripting interface, and rather than writing code, you drag objects onto a canvas and connect them with what look like elastic cables. In doing so, you effectively create parametric networks: dependencies between the various 3D objects in your scene. Your model quickly becomes more potent, opening up new ways to explore design alternatives. What you're in fact doing is adapt the software for your own individual purposes, because now you can move beyond the standard tasks it makes so easy for you to handle, and approach more complex tasks in a specific, targeted and – most important of all – personalised way. And you realise: you don't have to be a geek to make use of coding. With this approach, designers happily create scripts without ever actually *writing* any code at all.

We will come back to the question of how the power of scripting can be made accessible to designers, and whether graphical interfaces are indeed the best solution for this. For the moment we can simply observe that the fast growing popularity of *Grasshopper* shows that architects are eager to customise their tools to suit their way of working, if the threshold for doing so is low enough. This should come as no surprise: architects love their tools. Finnish architect, sculptor, and painter Alvar Aalto (1898–1976) is quoted as saying that "God created paper for the purpose of drawing architecture on it." His secretary had to prepare a stack of sketching paper, cut to size, waiting for him on his desk every morning. Other architects start with words and concepts, or with images that capture an idea or a mood they want to create in a new project. Others still start by building models. There are so many aspects to architecture that architects will develop their own personal preferences and their own set of tools that allow them to find and express their vision. So it makes a lot of sense to not only use the most potent programs you can lay your hands on, but to equip yourself with the ability to fit them to your personal needs. ■ ↖290

This may well be the strongest argument in purely practical terms for familiarising yourself with scripting: it puts in your hand a powerful tool that ■ 375↘ allows you to adapt your existing kit so you can do things your own particular way. You could almost consider scripting a meta-tool. If your ambition as an architect is not just to use what's out there in a generic way and follow the standard procedures that the available CAD software imposes on you; if, in other words, your ambition as an architect is to define your ■ 375↘ own signature approach to your work and to create architecture that breaks out of the boundaries of what everybody else can also do with the same generic tools, then by learning even the basics of scripting you can effectively design the way you design. And that is why we think scripting for architects is essential.

But there is also a more fundamental reason to embrace scripting. We would argue that scripting is the *lingua franca* of new media. If you acquire a workable knowledge of its concepts, grammar, and vocabulary, you become not necessarily a better ■ 375↘ architect, but you do become a better informed and ■ 375↘ therefore more powerful person in the 21st century, ■ 375↘ and as a consequence quite conceivably also an architect better equipped to get the most out of the plethora of digital tools on offer.

We will not attempt, in this chapter, to *teach* you any scripting. But we hope that we can entice you to look at scripting as a tool of tools that is particularly worth having in your bag of skills, and therefore to go out there and acquire it from the many sources that are available to you.

WHAT IS A SCRIPT?

Like any program, a script is a piece of code that tells a computer what to do. What computer programming and scripting have in common is that the code they are written in follows certain rules and conventions that are logical and coherent and that can be read and understood by any machine configured to work with it. This is why, appropriately, we think and talk of programming and scripting *languages*, since, much ■ 558↘ like any other written language, they each have their own syntax and semantics, which, though precise and specific, can often have many structural similarities to other languages.

The most fundamental and also most difficult ■ type of programming is known as **machine level** □ 369↘ **programming**, which uses numerical code that □ 382↘ a computer's **CPU (Central Processing Unit)** can ■ ↖262 374↘ directly execute. This kind of code can be virtually unintelligible to humans and is therefore extremely hard to develop. A step up from this comes **low-level programming**, which still offers little or no abstraction from machine-executable code and can be processed without needing any form of translation. It too, is largely numerical and not for the faint-hearted or inexpert coder.

But the vast majority of computer applications and their plugins or extensions are written in **high-level programming** languages, and this includes all scripting languages. A high-level language is one that is written in a code that is highly abstracted from machine-executable code, borrowing expressions and commands that are familiar to us from a natural human language we use ourselves, most prominently English. Because these languages are written in code that humans can relate to and understand, but that the machine cannot read, these high-level languages have to be made accessible to the CPU by either a **compiler** or an **interpreter** software.

A *compiler* takes the high-level language code and 'compiles' it into **machine code**, which, once this is done, makes the entire program executable by the CPU, as if it had been written in machine code in the first place. An *interpreter*, by contrast, 'interprets' the high-level language and carries out its instructions on its behalf each time it reads the code. This leads to the main difference between high-level programming and scripting languages: speed.

Scripting languages in their majority are *interpreted*, whereas high-level programming languages are usually *compiled*. As a result, scripting languages historically tended to be between 10 and 20 times slower in processing than programming languages, but because of their particularly high level of abstraction and much simpler syntax, they are also 5 to 10 times faster in being written. With improved interpreters the performance gap has since become much smaller, while ease of use still gives scripting languages a clear edge in development speed. This has made them increasingly attractive over time as processing power and speed continues to grow exponentially, still much in accordance with **Moore's law**, making processing time less of an issue, whilst the time and effort it takes to develop a piece of software in most situations remains a significant cost item. (We also talk about compilers and interpreters and give a coded example of an interpreter, in our chapter on [Writing & Code] and its [Elaboration].)

Here is a short comparison of a 'Hello World' program written in *Java* and in *Python* respectively:

Java code to print "Hello World":

```
class Hello {
public static void main (String[] args)
   {
    System.out.println("\nHello World");
   }
}
```

Python code to print "Hello World":

```
print "Hello World"
```

■ ↖149 375↘ A script, then, is a piece of computer code, written in a high-level **scripting language**. There are many different scripting languages; among the best known and most widely used are *Perl*, *PHP*, *Python*, and *Ruby*, ■ as well as *AppleScript*, all of which are also **glue languages**, because they can be used to 'glue' together other parts of programming that would otherwise not be compatible, drawing on existing software components written either in the same language or in some other scripting or programming language.

Glue languages are one of two main types of scripting language. The other major type – and there are overlaps, with languages being used for either or both purposes – are **extension languages**, which allow the user to extend an existing piece of software, for example by customising it. **Macros** are a typical example of this, as is *JavaScript*.

All of this makes scripts particularly useful in **application programming** (software development of user applications) and as interface between databases and web servers, and distinguishes scripting from **systems programming**, which is the software development of operating systems and other programs that enable a computer to run these applications and other software.

Today, many complex software programs are being developed in scripting languages, and some of these, for example *Python* and *Ruby*, are, in terms of their functionality, absolutely comparable ↖149 to programming languages, which is why they may also be termed **general purpose programming languages**. The historical distinction between *scripting* and *programming* languages is therefore gradually being blurred to the point where they have become almost synonymous. 'Scripting' today stands for an extremely broad range of possible uses and types of coding, and because of its versatility and great degree of user-friendliness and adaptability, scripting is sometimes considered the 'queen of programming disciplines'.

A Brief History of Scripting

THE ARRIVAL OF SCRIPTING LANGUAGES

Scripting, as distinct from 'traditional' programming, was first developed in the 1960s to automate certain tasks that until then had to be done manually on **mainframe** computer systems. IBM (International Business Machines) were a market leader in these large early computers, which used punch cards for data storage. Owing to the physical bulk of these cards and the slow speed of running them through a punch card reader, they would routinely have to be processed in batches, which is where the term **batch processing** stems from that we still use today. IBM developed a set of languages collectively known in the singular as **JCL (Job Control Language)** to automate this process, and this makes JCL one of the very first scripting languages ever used.

Scripting languages thus made their entrance just over a decade after the first high-level programming language, *Autocode*, was developed by British computer scientist Alick Glennie (1925–2003) for Manchester University's famous *Mark 1* computer. It is considered the first high-level programming language of them all, and *Manchester Mark 1* one of the world's first computers capable of storing a program on its own memory. (Glennie, incidentally, also bears the distinction of being the first human being to have played a game of chess against a computer program. Conducted over several weeks in 1952, it had been devised by the English computer scientist, mathematician, and cryptanalyst Alan Turing (1912–1954) whom we encounter frequently in this *Atlas*, but there was no computer in existence at the time that could execute the program, so Turing operated it manually, with pen and paper. Glennie won.)

Since then, the advancement of scripting languages has gone hand in hand with the development of information technology, consistently reflecting its major milestones.

MAINFRAME COMPUTING (UNTIL APPROXIMATELY 1985)

Automating processes made it necessary for the user to interact with the computer to exercise meaningful control over what it was doing when, and so scripting languages quickly proliferated in the design of interactive **shells** 377↘ for these mainframe machines, which until then had been non-interactive: they could simply do what they'd been programmed to do in their manufacture, and that was it. Now, through interfaces such as screens and keyboards, users were able to manipulate system commands, and this was ↖231 376↘ achieved through scripts, whereby the interaction between the computer's operating system, written in programming language, and the user happened through the shell, written in scripting language.

What rapidly followed were **time-sharing systems**, which allowed several users to gain access to the same mainframe computer simultaneously. This created a need for computer terminals: individual workstations typically consisting of a simple user 377↘ interface, such as a **VDU (Visual Display Unit)** ↖232 and a keyboard. These terminals were not functional computers in their own right, but again used shell programs to communicate with the mainframe machine.

Unsurprisingly, shell functions soon gained sophistication and complexity, and to this day system administration features among the most common uses for scripts, handling tasks such as generating automatic backups, for example.

PERSONAL COMPUTERS (APPROXIMATELY 1985–1995)

The PC ushered in a new era for information technology, as big, expensive mainframes were replaced by individual desktop (and later laptop) computers that were fully functional on their own and could be hooked up to servers to emulate the work pool behaviour of the erstwhile mainframes.

IBM had been at the forefront of mainframe computing and was keen to gain an edge on its competitors in this fast new development. In 1981, in a move that would define personal computing for the following two decades (and arguably beyond), IBM decided to allow two American programmers then in their twenties, Paul Allen (1953–2018) and Bill Gates (b. 1955) to supply their hastily assembled *Microsoft MS-DOS* as the operating system for its entire personal computer range. The term *IBM compatible* was born and Microsoft spent the rest of the century dominating personal computers, as virtually all other machines had to either also run on *MS-DOS* or act as if they did.

With PCs came user applications and this brought about a whole new spectrum of the general purpose scripting languages mentioned earlier, which could be used across applications and, as their name suggests, for a broad range of vastly different purposes.

To date, the most widely used scripting language is *Perl*, which was developed in 1987 by American computer programmer Larry Wall (b. 1954) for the *Unix* operating system, principally to facilitate report processing. Since then, it has evolved into a family of languages that are used, among others, in text processing, Common Gateway Interface (CGI) scripting, graphics programming, and system administration. A particular strength of *Perl* is pattern matching, which allows a user to search texts for specific words or character sequences, and replace them with others (find & replace functions), and it can be used interactively and respond to user input. This makes *Perl* a typical exponent of the general trend, starting with PCs, towards personalising the user experience, which has led to the development of numerous scripting languages capable of building or adapting user interfaces to suit individual users' needs.

(Although *Perl* is not originally an acronym, it is often given the 'backronym' or reverse acronym *Practical Extraction and Retrieval Language,* or any of several possible variants, such as *Practical Extraction and Reporting Language.* Wall really wanted to call his language Pearl, simply for this being a short name with positive connotations, until he realised that there already was a programming language called *PEARL*, which is in fact an acronym and stands for *Process and Experiment Automation Realtime Language,* and has absolutely nothing to do with *Perl*.)

THE INTERNET (SINCE APPROXIMATELY 1995)

The Internet, specifically the World Wide Web, has given scripting languages a significant further boost. A multitude of web applications use scripts both server-side and client-side. *Server-side* based software is software that sits on a web server and controls operations or tasks that either cannot, or, for pertinent reasons such as security or system integrity, should not ↖182 414↘ be performed on an individual's own computer, or that involve other machines on the network. The Common Gateway Interface (CGI) mentioned a moment ago is in fact a specification for such server-side applications: it defines how data can be passed from a client to a server and how programs that respond to these requests can be run on the server. *Client-side* software is software that, by contrast, sits on the 'client' machine, meaning the computer or device that is connected to the server via the Internet.

Scripts are instrumental in making server and clients talk to each other in a meaningful way that the user can understand and control. You may, for example, create a document, such as a project report, on your laptop with a piece of word processing software that sits on your computer, and then want to upload it or parts of it to your website as a case study. Handling either a PDF upload or importing text with a cut and paste command would be very basic and typical script tasks. And while there are many website builder applications that you can download and host on your own machine, the vast majority of websites are now built with server-based software which allows the use of server-based templates and themes. The code that enables the user to access all the functionality of the web-based software, assets, tools, and elements from their own machine is almost always written in script.

By late 2016 to early 2017, the most widely used scripting language server-side was *PHP*, originally created by Greenlandic-Danish computer programmer Rasmus Lerdorf (b. 1968), while client-side it has been for a long time and still is *JavaScript*, which was conceived in 1995 by American computer scientist Brendan Eich (b. 1961) as an extension language for HTML (HyperText Markup Language), in which practically all early web pages and applications were written, to enhance the user experience for the Netscape *Navigator*, which was the most successful web browser at the time.

Netscape and its *Navigator* just around then – towards the end of the 1990s – became central protagonists in what is now known as the First Browser War, which it fought and, although victorious in a major legal battle, lost against Microsoft's *Internet Explorer*. From the ashes of the *Navigator*, though, emerged the *Firefox* browser, and it in turn has been a major exponent ever since of the open source software movement.

Scripting has been and continues to be at the heart of this ethos, within which developers make their scripts, components, and libraries (software or script resources) freely available for other programmers to use, adapt, and build new software with, thus creating communities of programmers and users who jointly develop entire applications, application suites, and indeed scripting languages themselves.

Since open-source projects may draw on a vast global pool of users who themselves can become developers and contributors by giving user experience feedback and proposing bug fixes and optimisations, their scope of functionalities and applications is virtually unlimited. People who are able to solve a problem with a particular script can share that script to help other programmers, and scripting languages get steadily expanded through the addition of new, task-specific modules. *PHP* is an open-source language, as is *Perl*, which has a long list of modules for system management, web server and data banks, picture processing, image recognition, artificial intelligence, and many other uses. Whether you want to process or create PDFs, grab still frames from video clips, try your hand at MIDI (Musical Instrument Digital Interface) programming, or create an application that recognises items on your photographs, chances are that someone out there has already written most of the code you need and has made it available for free use as an open-source module or library in your preferred scripting language.

This is one of the strongest reasons why it is worthwhile to learn scripting: it puts a world of sophisticated digital tools and libraries at your disposal, free for you to benefit from. This open-source world is also reflective of a wider trend towards collaborative working, sharing, and joint creating, across distances and time zones; and the continuous exchange between user and developer communities makes it comparatively easy for beginners to get a foothold in coding and to find support in developing even complex new software applications.

THE ESSENTIAL GUIDE TO PROGRAMMING AND SCRIPTING ELEMENTS

Any programming or scripting language will feature *variables*, *operators*, and *control structures* as essential ingredients. Here, as an illustrative example, are variables, operators, and control structures as they are defined in *JavaScript*:

VARIABLE

- Boolean (0 or 1)
- Number
- String
- Array
- Object

Note: unlike most programming languages, *JavaScript* does not differentiate between *integer* and *float* and just uses the variable type 'Number' for both.

OPERATORS

Arithmetic Operators:

+	Addition
-	Subtraction
*	Multiplication
/	Division
%	Modulus
++	Increment
--	Decrement

Assignment Operators:

Assignment	x = y	x = y
Addition assignment	x += y	x = x + y
Subtraction ass.	x -= y	x = x - y
Multiplication ass.	x *= y	x = x * y
Division assignment	x /= y	x = x / y
Remainder assignment	x %= y	x = x % y
Exponentiation ass.	x **= y	x = x ** y
Left shift assignment	x <<= y	x = x << y
Right shift assignment	x >>= y	x = x >> y
Unsigned right shift ass.	x >>>= y	x = x >>> y
Bitwise AND ass.	x &= y	x = x & y
Bitwise XOR ass.	x ^= y	x = x ^ y
Bitwise OR assignment	x |= y	x = x | y

[...]

[...]

Comparison Operators:

==	equal to
===	equal value and equal type
!=	not equal
!==	not equal value or not equal type
>	greater than
<	less than
>=	greater than or equal to
<=	less than or equal to
?	ternary operator

Logical Operators:

&&	logical and
||	logical or
!	logical not

CONTROL STRUCTURES

- if – is used to specify a block of code to be executed if a specified condition is true
- else – is used to specify a block of code to be executed if the same condition is false
- else if – is used to specify a new condition to test if the first condition is false
- switch – is used to specify many alternative blocks of code to be executed

Loops:

- for – loops through a block of code a number of times
- for/in – loops through the properties of an object
- while – loops through a block of code while a specified condition is true
- do/while – also loops through a block of code while a specified condition is true

How to Get Into Scripting

The biggest challenge of getting into scripting, as with any language, is stepping over the first hurdle. For scripting, this hurdle is particularly high, because most of us are unfamiliar not only with the vocabulary, but with the way the language is structured – the grammar, so to speak – and even the 'tone' of it, what you get intuitively, without necessarily fully understanding it. Consequently, for most people, learning to script feels about the same as learning Chinese or Arabic feels to the average European language speaker: there's a new visual code, there's a different type of grammar, there is something inherently alien to the way of thinking. And that, in combination, makes for a high threshold to overcome. Luckily, once you do, things quickly become a lot easier, and quite a lot easier than you might expect at that. Easy enough for children to have a go and get good at it.

It is worth, at this juncture, to reconnect with this thought, which we put at the very beginning of our chapter, that really scripting ought to be child's play. As early as 1967, a team around South African born American computer scientist and educator Seymour Papert (1928–2016) and American artificial intelligence specialist Wally Feurzeig (1927–2013) developed an educational programming language called *Logo* (like *Perl*, not an acronym, but named after the Greek word *logos,* which here is taken to mean principally 'thought', although it can also mean many other things, among them 'reason', 'opinion', or 'word'). *Logo* used a graphical interface featuring a turtle icon which allowed the user to see on screen how their commands were being executed: you told the turtle whether to go straight ahead, turn left, or turn right, and by what angle, and then watched as it 'drew' the line for you on screen. The idea was to visualise the algorithmic thinking and thus make it easier and more entertaining for children to learn.

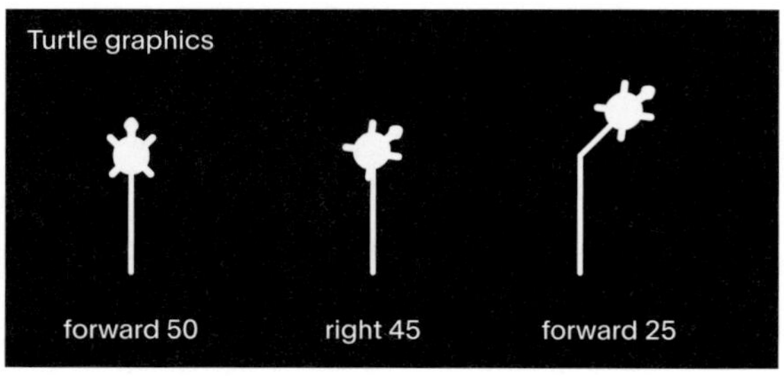

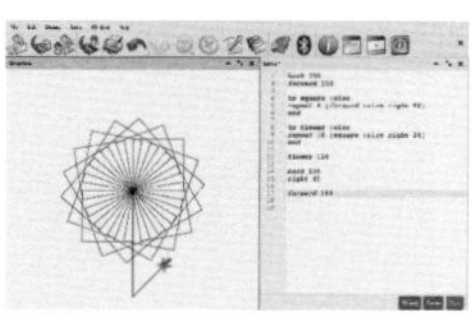
236 ● 365

This is an approach that has been adopted ever since: to bring dry code to life by means of graphical representations. Since 1998, *Lego Mindstorms*, originally developed as *Mindstorms Robotics Kits* by *Lego* in collaboration with the MIT (Massachusetts Institute of Technology) Lab have allowed children to programme the digital components of toy robots. Here, a scripting environment has been created in which the individual coding steps are carried out on a graphical interface in a way that is similar to assembling *Lego* bricks, and instead of coding with numbers, you put together individual digital parts such that the robot works.

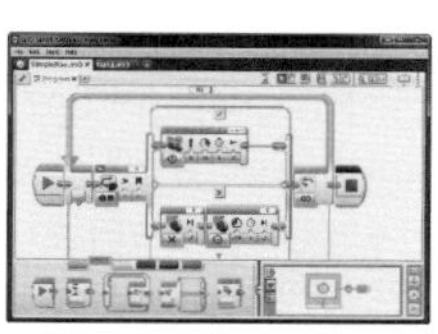
237 ● 365

THE APPEAL OF GRAPHICAL INTERFACES

There is a conceptual line that leads from this playful, user-friendly methodology of teaching children coding right through to *Grasshopper* for *Rhino*, which – though not designed for children but for professional designers – similarly tries to, and fairly succeeds in, making things easy and intuitive for the user. The key to this is the *Graphical Interface*, or GI.

Grasshopper is in fact a **Visual Programming Language (VPL)**. Developed by Dutch architect and programmer David Rutten in 2007, it was not the first, nor is it the only, popular VPL tool in architecture. *GenerativeComponents* (or *GC* as it's also often referred to) by Bentley Systems (makers of the CAD software *MicroStation*) has a similar philosophy and predates *Grasshopper* by a few years, having been introduced in 2003. *Dynamo*, developed by AutoDesk (makers of CAD market leader software *AutoCAD* and BIM software *Revit*), and termed by its makers a 'computational design BIM software' is more recent (it was launched as an open-source project in 2013) and also follows the VPL paradigm.

The popularity of VPLs in architecture is no accident. Many people prefer them to the more 'bare bones' scripting languages such as, for example *Python*, which is written in leaner code but more difficult to learn in terms of syntax. And this again will not come as a surprise: graphical interfaces imitate the process of modelling and allow the user to 'just get on with it' and design. And they're powerful tools in their own right. They make it comparatively easy to create shapes and alter them, to render versions and visualise objects ranging from the simple and compact the complex and vast.

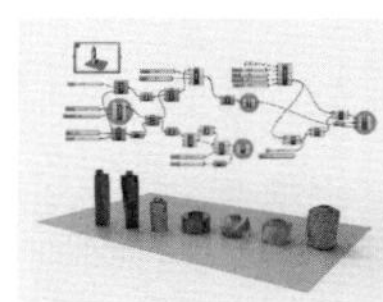
238 ● 365

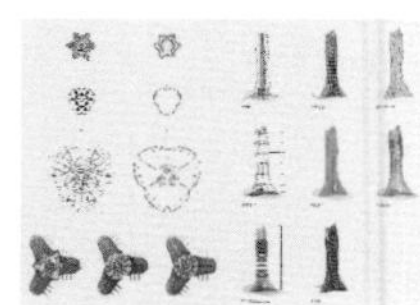
239A ● 365

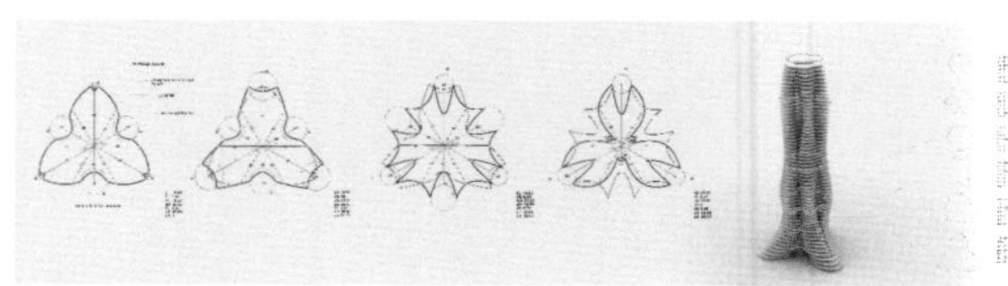
239B ● 366

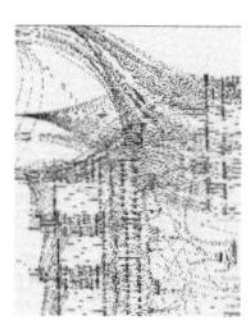
239C ● 366

By necessity any computing environment that makes things easy for the user also limits the user. This is something of an ongoing paradox: there is a liberating element to being able to 'just create' or 'just work'. The 'plug & play' concept was predicated on the idea that as a computer user you should be able to simply get started and not have to worry about setting up devices or learning software, and virtually the entire brand ethos of Apple is built on the notion that code is bewildering to most people and should therefore remain invisible. And up to a certain point this is extremely successful. Standard tasks and operations become super simple, and you as the user are able to achieve quick and satisfying results without any computer science whatsoever.

Conversely, though, with more complex and specialist tasks – those that fall outside the bandwidth of what the programmers have readily foreseen – you are liable to hit the buffers fairly quickly. Overcoming the limitations of the software within its own parameters then is either impossible or turns into a cumbersome and elaborate process of, essentially, dodging the code.

Grasshopper has enabled a particular type of geometrical design investigation to flourish. The Snowflake Tower by LAVA (Laboratory for Visionary Architecture) illustrates this: it is doubtful whether its design could have been accomplished by any other means. That said, as the example also demonstrates, *Grasshopper* can produce very unwieldy graphical charts when it is used in elaborate projects, thereby losing much of its elegance. Its saving grace is that it is built upon *Rhino*, a software that has extension languages (*Rhinoscript* and *Python*) and various developer tools and toolkits with which *Grasshopper* can interface. To control projects of the complexity of The Snowflake Tower effectively, users tend to resort to these means. Thus, *Grasshopper* (just as *GC* and *Dynamo*, by the way) is a software application that, in a sense, allows the user to get the best of both worlds: on the one hand a graphical interface that makes it easy to design standard procedures quickly, and on the other hand script windows which give the user scope to write more compact code or to extend the toolset, when the standard visual tools are not up to the task and become a nuisance rather than an asset.

This means though that in order to get the most out of a visual scripting environment like *Grasshopper* – to use it at an expert level – you need to know some conventional scripting too. And for the beginner, the first question tends to be: which language should I start with? The welcoming interface of *Grasshopper's* boxes and connecting cables offers a relatively low threshold for architecture students. But this intuitive, quasi-mechanical way of creating scripts can also become a problem. If you start on a graphical interface without ever learning to code, chances are you'll get stuck in that particular way of thinking. And this then once again limits you, because it obscures the mathematical principles of algorithmic modelling or design at work. It may even make it more difficult for you to understand them.

It took a while for it to become generally accepted that it is perfectly possible for artists to work directly with code rather than using some visual interface. In 1999, American designer and technologist John Maeda (b. 1966), then a professor heading the Aesthetics and Computation research group at the MIT Media Lab, led the way with his book *Design by Numbers*. It introduced a scripting language of the same name that was remarkable for its simplicity. (Incidentally *The Laws of Simplicity* is another book by Maeda, published in 2006). Maeda's MIT Media Lab students Ben Fry and Casey Reas in 2001 teamed up to create *Processing*, an easy to use programming language designed to help the electronic arts and visual design communities learn the basics of computer programming in a visual context. It has since become widespread and is also used at many architecture schools and in architectural research projects.

In this context it also is particularly interesting to note how *Swift*, which was launched by Apple as a learning tool for children in 2014 (it was subsequently turned open source with version 2.2 in 2015), does the direct opposite of what we generally associate with Apple's approach to computing: rather than basing itself on a graphical environment, it puts writing code at the heart of the experience. Children are encouraged to chat and share their programs with other users and treat scripting itself as an online game.

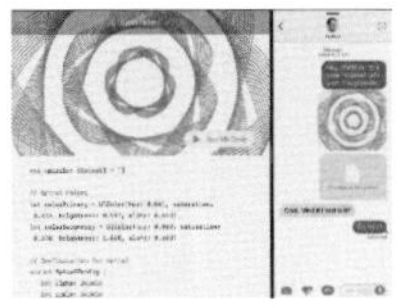

240 ○ 400

ARCHITECTURAL APPLICATIONS OF SCRIPTING

Now that we have a general idea of scripting, let's look more specifically at what its various uses in architecture are or can be. Earlier in this chapter we stated that scripting may be seen as a cultural technique, not unlike writing. And just like writing, there are many areas where it can be applied. Our chief example has been *Rhino Grasshopper*, because it is so widely used by architects.

What *Grasshopper* does is more generally referred to as **parametric design**: a way to set up relationships between individual parts of a geometry that allows for even complex models to be quickly adapted or adjusted, and for many different versions of a scheme to be tested and visualised with ease. (We will look at this particular application of scripting under the heading *Parametrisation* below.) Indeed, 'parametric design' has become something of a buzz word that has nudged itself centre stage in the discussion about what scripting can do in architecture. Yet scripting stands for much more than this, and we will try in the following sections to elicit some of the potential that it opens up to us as architects. ■ ↖181 428↘

AUTOMATION

We have spoken a lot about scripting as a tool that allows you to personalise your software and also about the advantage inherent (though perhaps sometimes less obvious) in understanding the concepts behind **Computer Aided Architectural Design (CAAD)**. What we've less focused on here – though we have mentioned it in more general terms – is the automation and simplification of workflows that are either repetitive or need to be executed often in slightly varying ways. ■ ↖177 424↘

Any repetitive task is potentially one that can be solved by scripting. A quick look around on the Internet will show up dozens of such simple utilities that allow you to, for example:

- Read from a spreadsheet
- Read from a database
- Read from a website
- Create a PDF document
- Count occurrences of a word in a document
- Replace specific words in a document
- Find duplicate files on your hard drive
- Compare entries in lists
- Find and list differences between different versions of files

And because these scripts are usually quite short, it's fairly easy to 'hack' them, in other words to create new versions of them that fit your specific needs.

The following is an example of a short *Perl* script that performs an everyday task, in our case the renaming of a bunch of files, possibly for archiving them. We've added some comments (marked by the '#' symbol) to explain the code, which makes the script look longer, but the essential commands are very compact:

```
#!/usr/bin/perl

$n = (@ARGV) || die (“usage: $0 FILES”);
print "\nGetting ready to rename $n files!";
while(@ARGV){
      #assign first element in array to variable $file and remove it from array:
      $file = shift(@ARGV);
      $old = $file; # assign original name to variable $old
      # change $file by using compact search and replace syntax: s/pattern/substitution/
      $file =~ s/\.JPG/\.jpg/; #if extension is JPG uppercase, make it lowercase
      $file =~ s/(\w+\.jpg)/pre\_$1/; #add ‘pre_’ at the beginning of Filenames ending in .jpg
      print “\nsetting out to change $old to $file...\n”;
      if (-e $file) { # make sure no file with new name already exists
            print “not changed! - $file already exists!\n”;
      } else {
            rename($old, $file) || die(“couldn't rename $old to $file”);
      }
}
```

Why do such scripts matter in architectural practice? Because at a practical level, a considerable portion of building and construction is ultimately about dealing with large quantities of things, typically specified in long itemised lists and voluminous catalogues. Scripts are extremely good at working with this type of data. And so scripting offers up very elegant ways of handling all kinds of large data sets relating to a project, to scan and analyse them, to hunt down errors, to adjust and update them. This can save serious amounts of time and – maybe even more importantly – prevent the kinds of mistakes we humans tend to make when we are forced to do repetitive boring tasks. Mistakes that can cost an awful lot of money, if not lives.

MODELLING

Another area where scripting may come in handy is modelling.

Most CAD programs support different modelling styles, and proficient CAD operators can be very fast at churning out 3D geometries. Yet sometimes scripting could make their lives easier. There are two principal cases when this applies:

1 Whenever a modelling procedure needs to be repeated many times, for example when you need to quickly create many versions or variations of a basic scheme;
2 Whenever a geometrical construction is too complex to be solved with common modelling commands.

In the first case, it can be useful to model one version, recording all the steps you took to create it, and then turn this into a script that performs the modelling operations with the possibility to incorporate variations. Some CAD applications make this easy because they create a transcript of all your modelling steps, which can then be saved as a script. In fact this type of transcript – a linear sequence of commands – is the most basic form of script: a finite number of steps that generate a certain result through a series of specified operations. (Which is, incidentally, the most general definition of an algorithm.) All you need to do, then, to alter the result is change values in this script, for example by introducing variables (or parameters, as they are normally referred to). The variations you need can now be introduced by calling up the procedure with different variables, or by making the script react to certain conditions.

The second case appertains to geometries that lie outside of what ordinary 3D modelling tools can do off the shelf. Things such as the panelling of a double curved facade or the exact make-up of a tensile structure, or an intricate curved staircase or ramp, for example. All these can be solved with scripts. Developing a script that generates a complex form forces you to think through your design and requires an in-depth knowledge of geometry. If this is your 'cup of tea', it can be a very enjoyable and rewarding thing to do. Though it's fair to say that some of the problems we just mentioned aren't readily solvable even if your knowledge of geometry is quite advanced. The research field of architectural geometry has sprung up in response to this type of challenge. It looks at architecture specifically as geometry and concerns itself explicitly with the mathematical foundations of architectural design, investigating the relationship between geometrical and constructive constraints. There are specialised firms or departments in larger and more ambitious architecture offices (such as the Specialist Modelling Group at Foster+Partners) that focus on these tasks. The *Centre Pompidou* in Metz by Shigeru Ban, or the Rolex Learning Center at the *École Polytechnique Fédérale de Lausanne*, EPFL, by SANAA, for example, could not have been built without the help of experts in architectural geometry and digital fabrication, who, essentially, wrote bespoke scripts for the purpose.

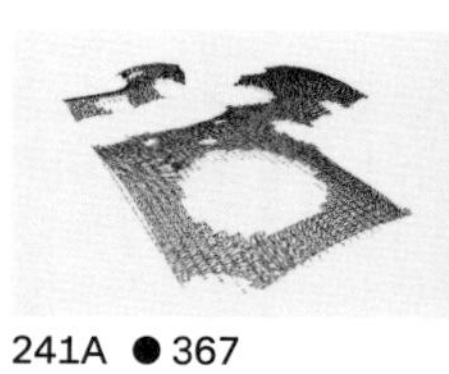

241A ● 367

241B ● 367

241C ● 367

PARAMETRISATION

In 3D modelling, we go through a series of steps to gradually build or design the object we want to create. As we have just mentioned, some CAD programs continually (or almost continually) write a transcript of your modelling steps, effectively recording your design process. And as we've also noted, it is then relatively easy to turn this record into a script. You now have an algorithm that can reproduce everything you've just modelled. And while it is sometimes tricky to record the picking and selecting that you do on screen as part of the modelling process, it's important to understand that all those modelling steps are just instructions to the CAD program, which it, in turn, processes as code. So, in theory, you could write a script that encodes *all* those modelling steps. Your script could then build the entire project that you've worked on over days or weeks in a matter of seconds. This is not something that is ever done in practice, though, for a number of reasons, which we will get to. It is nevertheless interesting to think about this for a moment: there is no limit to what can be modelled by scripts. In fact you could even go so far as to think of the file your CAD drawing is stored in as a sort of script: it contains all the elements you modelled, including all the 3D points, lines, faces, volumes, meshes, and whatever else it is you may have created as part of the modelling process. When you open the drawing, the program reads the file ↖61 and executes the instructions in it, recreating the model with all its objects and features. It doesn't do this in the sequence you modelled it, but the result is the same.

Calling a simple CAD file a script is a bit extreme, however, because it misses an important point: there is value in recording the actual sequential modelling steps that lead to a specific model. *Parametric* or *procedural modelling* is built around the notion that there is a stream of modelling commands that feed into each other. Modelling operations that are performed 'upstream' have consequences 'downstream'. If the process is recorded and can subsequently be modified, it is possible, for example, to replace a form upstream with a different one and to have subsequent modelling operations be performed on that form. The concept of **Constructive Solid Geometry (CSG)** that we talk about in our chapter on 3D Modelling has as one of its features what is known as a CSG tree, which works in this way. ■ ↖68 □ ↖57

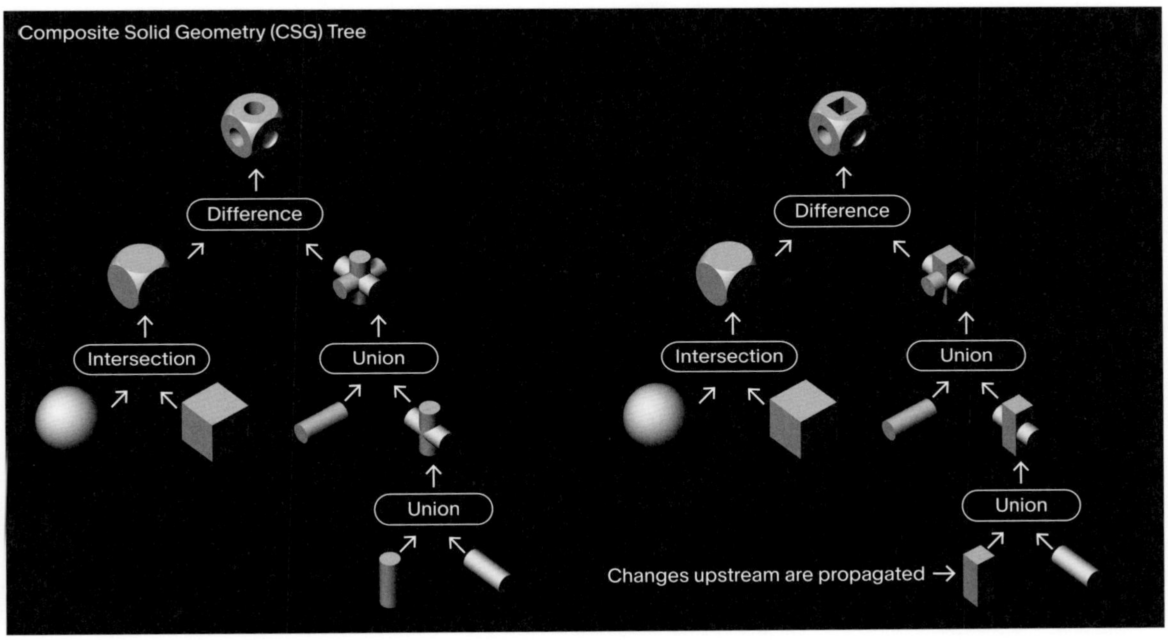

What, then, is a parametric model? It is a script that creates a model in a procedural way, but rather than having all the values 'hard coded', they are replaced with variables, which can be changed and adjusted. So compared to the simple transcript we just described above, the parametric model is much more flexible. If it is a well conceived parametric model, it contains dependencies between the variables that are carried through various modelling operations so as to allow you to create meaningful variations quickly, because changing one variable upstream automatically changes all dependant variables downstream and the whole model is adjusted accordingly. Its possibilities also far exceed those of a CSG tree, because in a fully parametric model you can establish connections and dependencies between variables on different branches.

In essence, that is what we mean by **parametric modelling**: you assign the parameters which characterise the sequence of modelling operations that lead to an object, and this means specifying relevant variables and absolute values, constraints for variables, and dependencies between variables. ■ ↖60 424↘

In practice most parametric models will *not* be models of entire buildings with all their rooms and staircases and lift shafts and the like. They will either be used to test variants of a scheme or to fine-tune a specific part of the building, such as the roof or facade. This is so because creating a parametric model takes time and effort: it is not a trivial task. So you only do this where you can expect significant benefits from it.

■ ↖148 The leading parametric modelling tools were initially developed for mechanical engineering, where models are smaller and constraints are more straightforward to formulate than in architecture. Parametric models with thousands of parameters, such as building projects would yield, are thinkable, but are not supported by today's parametric modellers, because these modellers focus on real-time user interaction. When too many parametric constraints are in play, they become sluggish and difficult to work with, even on fast computers. Though in all fairness, the manipulation of thousands of parameters is not only a computational issue, it provides little practical benefit for a human user. (We discuss algorithmic □ ↖145 form-finding strategies with more variables in play □ ↖145 in our chapter on Generative Methods.)

The art of parametric modelling, then, lies in how you set the parameters: how many of them, where they are, what relationship they have to each other, and what the permissible values are for each variable. In other words: finding the right measure. The rule of thumb for an ideal parametrisation tends to be, 'as few parameters as possible, as many as necessary'.

This can be a proper challenge: it's not always ■ ↖198 so easy to find the right parametrics. For some variables, there may be obvious ranges that make sense. Staircases are a classic example. Building codes in most countries are very explicit about what the minimal and maximal measurements are for treads and risers in any given circumstance. So it is straightforward to implement these codes as constraints into a ■ ↖149 **parametric modeller**. And while they don't necessarily come up with a solution that pays homage to the role a sweeping staircase plays in the architectural drama that unfolds as you enter the building, such parametric tools can prevent you from planning stairs that people trip over as they descend from the gallery, or that are simply not code-compliant.

In other cases even the first approximations to useful parameters are hard to come by, as default dimensions are much less straightforward to set. How wide a particular space needs to be or how many partitions a facade should be divided into is often more of an aesthetic than a technical consideration. Parametric models have the advantage of letting you test many variations very quickly, but if the parametric definition is not set up properly they also have the unpleasant side effect of precluding you from considering other – possibly more successful – options.

Finding the right sets of parameters is therefore fundamental to the design process, and as part of the parametric definition, you are at the same time explor■ ↖162 541↘ ing the design space. **Design Space Exploration (DSE)** is the term given to the practice of looking at possible or valid design alternatives. In applied prototyping and modelling, for example, it is essential that only 3D models that make sense in three-dimensional space are allowed. And this may require limiting the permissible values for variables, and their combinations, so that nonsensical or physically unachievable models are not possible.

When you're working with complex geometries, these limitations can quickly become difficult or even impossible to set manually, owing, for example, to the sheer number of variables you have to address. In such cases, it may be more effective to employ **fitness functions** to test relevant characteristics of the resulting model. These are functions that result in a value known as a *figure of merit* that indicates how closely an iteration of the model matches the desired objectives. So if, for example, wall thickness and the type of windows are variables, but the resulting model must attain a certain energy efficiency rating, then a fitness function calibrated towards energy efficiency will tell us whether any given set of variables has resulted in a model that passes that particular test, and if so by what margin. This makes fitness functions also a useful method for optimisation. (We talk about this too in more detail in our chapter on Generative Methods.)

Parametrisation can play a vital role also during design development. We have pointed to the popularity of *Grasshopper* and used The Snowflake Tower by LAVA as an illustrative example. But as mentioned earlier when we touched on the topic of architectural geometry, scripting and parametric models are also indispensable when it comes to making these new formal vocabularies buildable. Frank Gehry and Associates (now Gehry Partners) famously used the parametric **solid modeller** *CATIA (Computer-Aided Three-Dimensional Interactive Application)* not so much in the design as in the construction of the Guggenheim Museum Bilbao, and they have since continued to use it in virtually all of their projects. What convinced the firm's founder, Canadian-born American architect Frank Gehry (b. 1929), a self-described computer illiterate, to use the program was the vast cost savings it enabled in the construction process. *CATIA*, a program originally developed for the design of aeroplanes, was the perfect tool to streamline the construction of the steel skeletons that hold up Gehry's elaborate geometries.

FORMULA AS FORM

When looking for the most efficient way to build a form developed by designers, the specialists responsible for the rationalisation of construction usually end up re-building the entire 3D model they received from the design team. In what might be considered a sort of reverse-engineering, they try to find the simplest mathematical definition with which the geometric form can be described. Ideally this definition takes the form of a formula, because for guiding construction, the simplicity gained with a formula is extremely useful. And conceptually it is nothing but the direct application of the same parametric principles as sit at the heart of any user-friendly CAD software. So why is the reverse-engineering even necessary? Why don't architects work with mathematical formulae in the first place?

The idea of formula as form is quite straightforward, but it is very uncommon in architecture and not something we would recommend for most practitioners. If you want to use formulas as an actual design tool, you have to be really rather expert: what we are talking about here is to scripted architecture more or less as extreme ironing is to boules... Still, there are some architectural firms, such as IJP

Architects, that work in this fashion and they can certainly claim a degree of mathematical purity in their designs.

A program that allows you to work with formula as form perfectly is *Mathematica.* It was developed by British computer scientist and mathematician Stephen Wolfram (b.1959), who is now CEO of the Massachusetts-based Wolfram Research company and who also lends the *Wolfram Language*, in which *Mathematica* is written, his name. Originally launched in 1988, the software has since gained some favour with architects, and there are today architectural practices that use it directly in their design. We are in fact making use of the elegance of *Mathematica's* compact declarative style in several parts of this book, to illustrate fundamental algorithmic principles. While designing with formula is not for everyone and lends itself really mostly for some quite specific tasks, there is nevertheless a great deal to be said for it as a specialist tool. It is, as so often, a case of 'horses for courses': what gives you as the architect the greatest power is being able to use the best tool for the task in hand.

242 ○ 400

243 ○ 401

The Outlook

SCRIPTING: THE TRENDY SHAPE OF THINGS?

How do trends come about? How is it, for example, that as we write this book in the late 2010s, there is an identifiable look that 'cool' workspaces have: exposed brick walls, some post-disused industrial paraphernalia, comfortable but eclectic seating; a coffee bar – ideally staffed by one or two attractive but laid-back baristas of any gender – low heavy lounge tables, sparse but bold art and uncluttered lighting. And an assortment of young or young-at-heart people working on their *Macs*... – There is a feel to the age, and the age is reflected in the fashion of the day, not only as clothing, shoes, and hairstyles, but as a way of being and doing things.

In architecture, that's obviously the case too; and much as in other areas, the trend or the fashion is partly dictated by people who actively make choices about setting a trend or declaring something as fashionable, and partly it simply emerges from what's available: the materials, the technology. The software.

Among the most striking (and, some would say, beautiful) things that CAD software has unleashed into the world of architecture are curves. Organic shapes, undulating forms and waves; sweeping arcs and muscular bulges. Before CAD, they were the exception, because they were hard to design and harder to build. With CAD came NURBS, and that changed the whole aesthetic of architectural design. *NURBS* are Non-Uniform Rational B-Splines, and we explain them more in our chapter on Graphs & Graphics. Put simply, they are a tool within CAD programs that allows users to manipulate curves (mathematically: splines) just by moving handle points on a screen. Suddenly, curves of all kinds were no longer difficult, they were as easy as drawing a straight line. Unsurprisingly, then, they quickly became nearly as prevalent.

NEW LANGUAGES OF FORM

While neither organic forms nor parametric equations are new in architecture, there is no denying that digital tools, and specifically scripting and parametric design, have been instrumental in bringing about new languages of form in architecture. (We discuss these formal possibilities in more detail in our chapter on Generative Methods.) Arguably, some of the most spectacular buildings of recent date, such as the Guggenheim Museum Bilbao we just mentioned, the Metropol Parasol in Seville by German Architect Jürgen Mayer H (b.1965), or the Heydar Aliyev Center in Baku, Azerbaijan, by Iraqi-born British architect Zaha Hadid (1950–2016) were groundbreaking in the way they were designed and constructed. As such they can also be considered an expression of our time.

There is another aspect to how such new languages of form come about: yes, on the one hand the tools that are available shape the objects created with these tools, and the zeitgeist of an era finds its way into the expression – in art, fashion, music, architecture – of that era. Part of this zeitgeist phenomenon though is also how people communicate with, and influence, each other; and here the fact alone that computer languages are being developed by user communities as ongoing open-source projects means that there is a constant exchange of ideas, practice, problem-solving, and therefore naturally also of aesthetic and conceptual approaches within a generation of creative professionals.

Insofar as scripting has enabled these tools and continues to be integral to computer aided architectural design, scripting is instrumental in bringing about such new languages of form. But something being readily available does not, of course, give it validity in itself. There is an inflationary element to the use of architectural forms that may have very little or ■ ↖185
nothing to do with a project's actual design requirement, but effectively become a self-serving expression of what is possible with form. What we want to □ ↖175
emphasise, therefore, is that these two – scripting and form – are not contingent upon each other, meaning that scripting itself neither implies, nor does it suggest, any particular type of form or approach to form, ■ ↖185 673↘
such as the parametric variation of shapes.

Scripting is a cultural technique. We have referred to it as the *lingua franca* of new media, and pointed out its evolution in tandem with information technology as a whole. And so scripting in architecture is not tied to any particular stylistic or formal expression, but a tool to handle complex issues and challenges. And architecture today presents increasingly complex issues and challenges. While in other areas information technology has led to massive efficiencies and optimisations, in architecture this has not yet really been the case. We find ourselves confronted with more and more conflicting and pressing demands that often pitch society's needs for built environments against the requirements of environmental responsibility. The great potential of scripting as a design tool lies in the way it allows architects to delve deeper into these challenges and address them more rigorously. This, however, does not have to mean we do so more 'technically' or less individually. In fact the opposite: if you know some scripting, you can release yourself to some extent from the technical limitations of commercially available software and thus look at your design practice itself as a design project, by developing your own personalised design tools. And this means being able to lift architecture onto a new level.

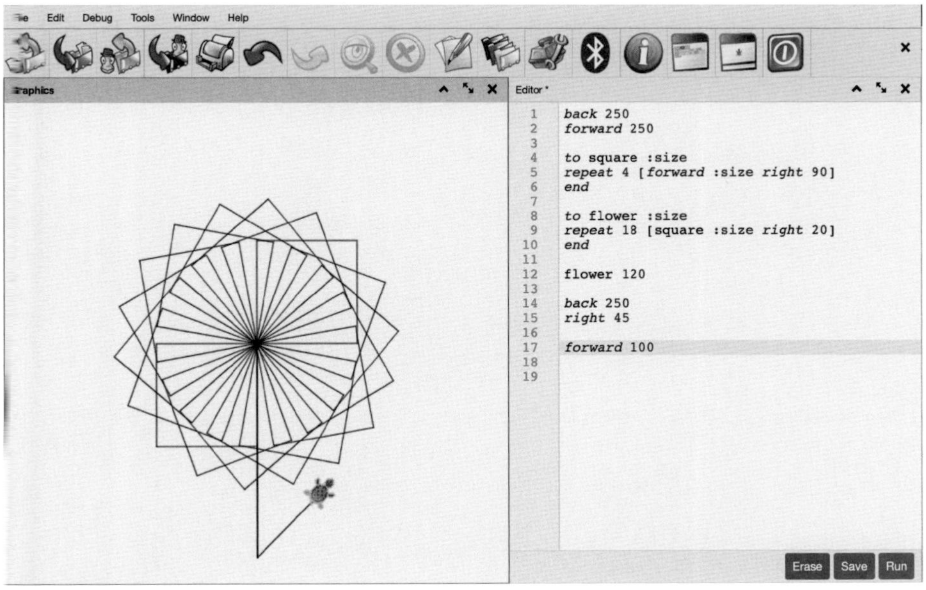

236 ● 358
Logo: coding by turtle. Since its debut in 1967 there have been hundreds of versions of *Logo*. The one pictured here can be tried out online at weblogo.terrapinlogo.com.

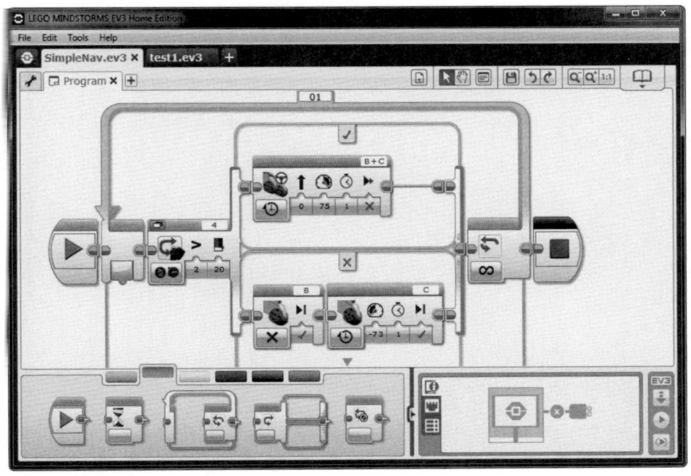

237 ● 358
Lego Mindstorms: coding by assembly in the spirit of *Logo*. (*Mindstorms* was in fact the title of a book by *Logo* inventor Seymour Papert).

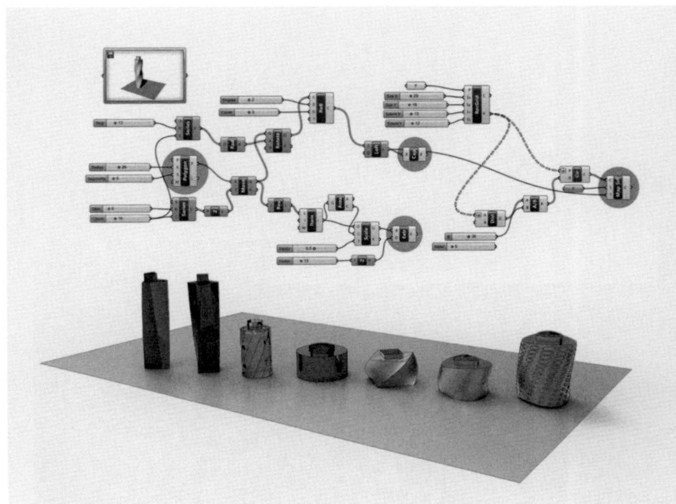

238 ● 358
Instances of a perfume bottle, created in *Grasshopper*. [Milena Stavric]

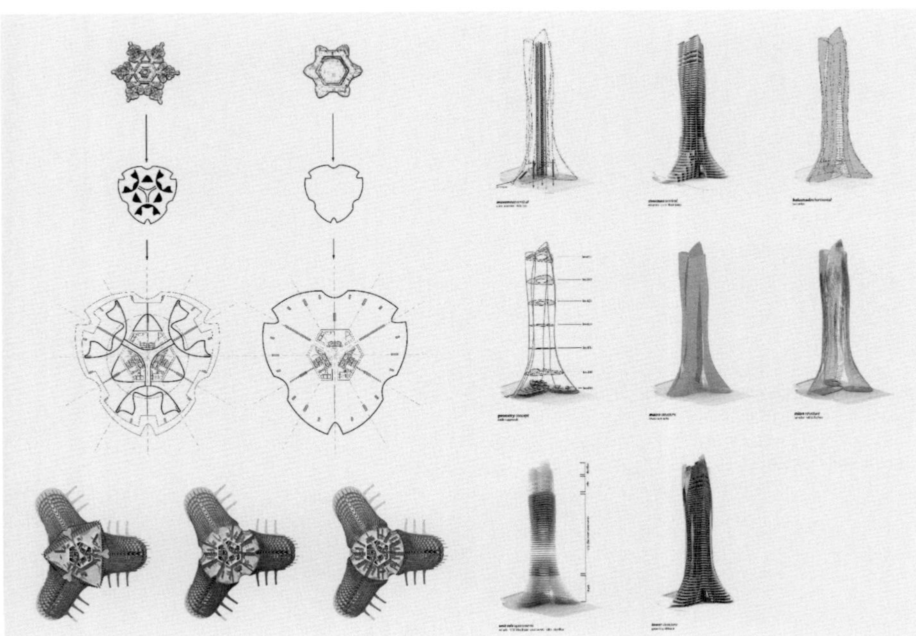

239A ● 358
The Snowflake Tower by LAVA (Laboratory for Visionary Architecture) is an unbuilt project for Abu Dhabi, inspired by the shape and structure of a snowflake. [Tobias Wallisser/LAVA]

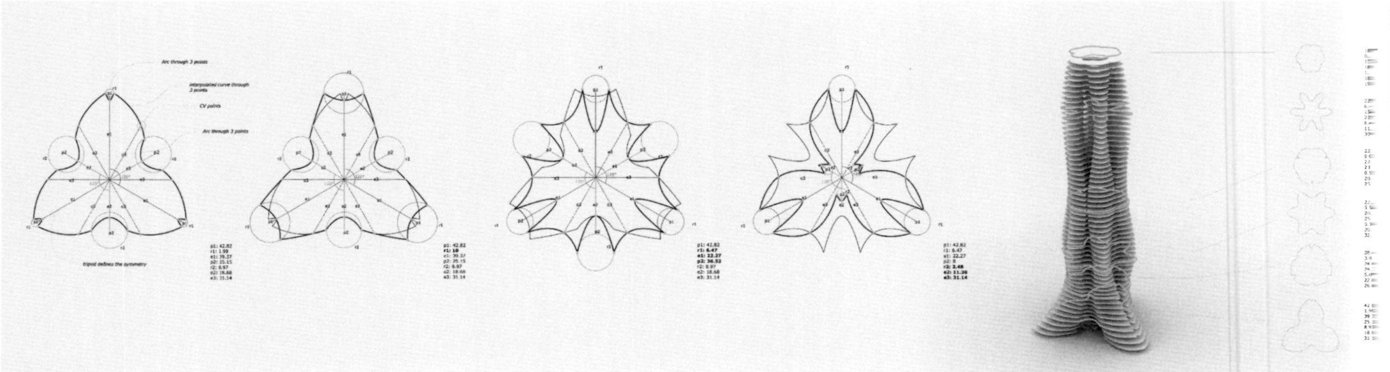

239B ● 358
Snowflake Tower geometry: the floor plans smoothly transition between different intricate geometrical shapes along the height of the Tower.

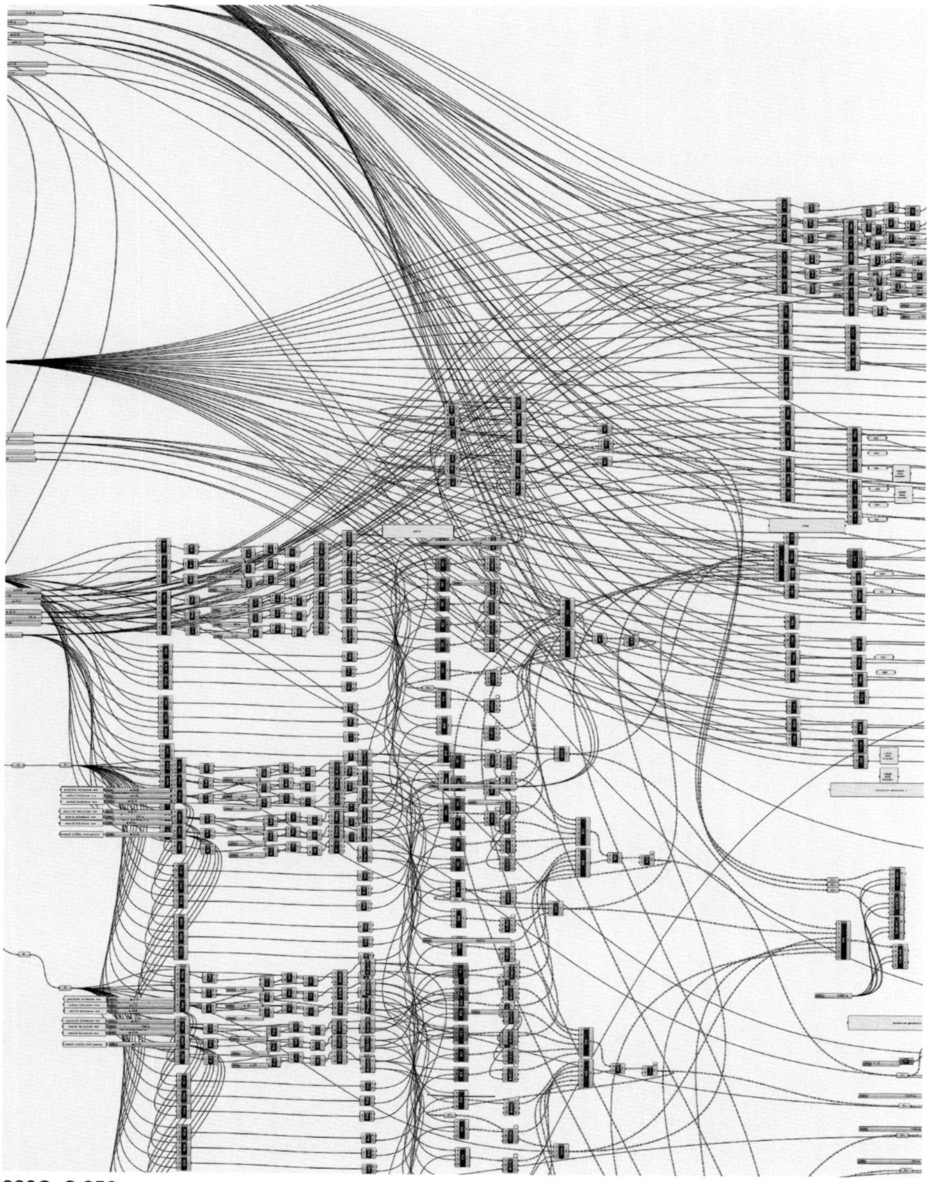

239C ● 358
Snowflake Tower *Grasshopper* code (detail): While it is doubtful whether the Snowflake Tower could have been designed by any other means than by using the Visual Programming Language (VPL) *Grasshopper*, it also highlights the inherent limits of VPL: with more complex designs the visual code becomes unwieldy. [239B + 239C: Tobias Wallisser/LAVA]

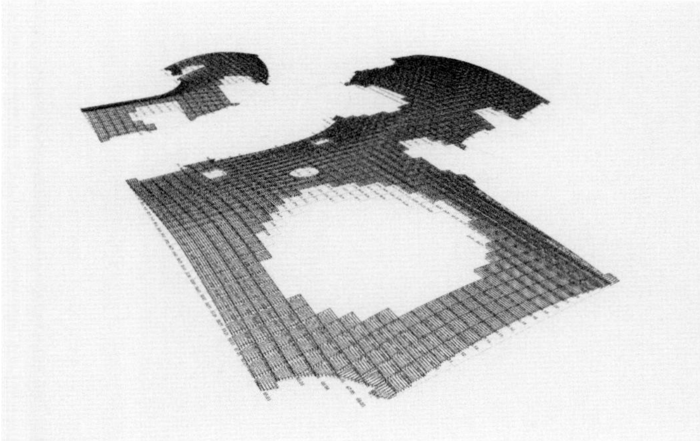

241A ● 360

241B ● 360

Digital model of the casting structure (241A) and concrete plate under construction (241B). [Design-to-Production]

241C ● 361

Finished interior space. [HP Schaefer]

The Rolex Learning Center at the *École Polytechnique Fédérale de Lausanne*, EPFL, designed by Japanese architecture office SANAA rests on a large, gently undulating concrete plate that and was challenging to construct. Specialists in architectural geometry from the firm Design-to-Production wrote bespoke scripts to facilitate the CNC-production of the non-standard double curved casting structure.

Writing & Code

Ludger Hovestadt

- Alonzo Church: *An Unsolvable Problem of Elementary Number Theory, American Journal of Mathematics, Vol. 58, No. 2 (April 1936), 345–363*
- Eric Vögelin: *Order and History*, 1956
- Friedrich Nietzsche: *Die Geburt der Tragödie Oder: Griechentum und Pessimismus*, 1878 (1872, 1874)
- Ferdinand de Saussure: *Mémoire sur le système primitif des voyelles dans les langues indo-européennes*, 1879

Words

THE PHONETIC ALPHABET, PERSPECTIVE & CODE

What is writing? What, indeed, is a letter? Start with any arbitrary letter of our alphabet, say T for example, and add another, R: you have two as yet unrelated symbols which, as you add more, can become anything you like:

> T R E E , T R A U M A , T R A N S L U C E N C E

It's fascinating and thrilling in equal measure: we can conjure up with letters absolutely anything we are able to imagine, whether it is natural, real, abstract, alive, dead, or yet to be created.

Take another couple: B, A – what shall they become:

> B A N D or B A N D I T ? B A C H or
> B A C H A R A C H ? B A R D or B A R B E R ?

Letters are cyphers, and letter sequences are like keys that unlock door upon door to any world of our choosing. An alphabet is nothing but a defined group of characters with a (more or less) agreed-upon sound, which we arrange to express what we think. The letters themselves are devoid of substance or meaning.

This is an important thought to hold on to early on in our reflection on Writing & Code: writing is about anything and everything, at all. And so in writing and reading lies immense power, because anyone who holds these keys can access anything that can be thought. Deploying that power therefore demands not just courage and imagination, but also caution and consideration. Words can build entire worlds, yes, but they can destroy them just as easily. One of the most influential books in our history starts with the sentence: "In the beginning was the Word, and the Word was with God, and the Word was God." Whether you are spiritually or religiously inclined or not, whether your faith, if you have any, is Christian, Jewish, Muslim, Buddhist, Hindu, or Universalist, whether you have a god or none, or many, whether therefore the *Old Testament*, from which this quote stems, has any specific meaning to you or not, you can take the sentence itself almost literally: the word can create anything.

THE ABSTRACTION OF WRITING

If words are keys that unlock the doors to the worlds we want to think and therefore speak or write about, then they are also the axis on which the world of our imagination turns: without words there can be no meaning; without meaning there can be no coherent thought; without coherent thought there can be no ideas we can share; and without ideas to share there can be no culture. Without culture there can be no civilisation; and without civilisation we wouldn't be writing this book and you wouldn't be reading it, because there would be no digitality and there would be no architecture, in fact there would be nothing of interest to any of us at all, because interest is thought, and in order to formulate thought we need words, and you see what we mean when we say that the world turns on words.

But we are here always and quite naturally talking about words that are not just written down *somehow*, or *any which way*, but that are written down *phonetically*. The reason we 'naturally' talk about words that are written down phonetically is that to us, as Europeans reared on the Latin alphabet with European languages, this is 'normal'. If you are reading this as someone whose first language is Chinese, for example, you may find that none of this is the case, that reading words that are written down phonetically is not second nature to you, but something you had to learn and that may at first have felt quite alien to you, and possibly still does so now.

In fact, our whole line of argument in this chapter stands firmly in the context of Western culture and could therefore be said to be Eurocentric. This here has to be the case, not because it couldn't be transposed onto other cultures, but because it is conceived from a European perspective and context. So if we do not write about other cultures here, this is out of respect for other cultures, rather than out of disdain, since in a book of this kind we can only ever really talk about things we are genuinely knowledgeable about and familiar with.

The first people in Western culture to use a phonetic script were the Ancient Greeks, who started doing so around 900–800 BCE. They took their cue from the Phoenicians, who populated the Northern African and Middle Eastern coastline around the Mediterranean from roughly 2500 BCE until 539 □ ↖369 BCE, when Persia's Cyrus the Great (c. 600–530 BCE) conquered them.

The Phoenicians in turn derived their alphabet from the hieroglyphic writing system of ancient Egypt, reducing about 1,000 symbols to 22. Consisting as it did of consonants only, the Phoenician alphabet marked a big step towards our abstraction of language, but it was not yet truly phonetic. The great contribution Greece made to writing was the *vowel*. Now you had a writing system that for the first time allowed you to spell words *as you said them*. By simply determining and agreeing how each letter should be pronounced, you could relate language reliably not only in terms of its meaning, but also in terms of its sound. You had, in effect, a 'recording device'.

The phonetic alphabet does not quite do the job of voice recorder, in that it does not of course capture and then by itself reproduce sound, but the effect it has on the recording and reproduction of language is not dissimilar to that of such a device: whereas before you needed to hear how a word was pronounced in order to reproduce it correctly, you now only needed to know the rules for the cyphers in front of you; and the cyphers themselves remained intact, they could be preserved and re-read. If you read them out loud – which you were able to do because you knew now what sounds to produce – the effect was the same as if they were being replayed.

Importantly, you can with a phonetic script read things out loud that you don't even understand. The more consistent the rules for the pronunciation, the better it works, obviously: If you don't speak Italian, for instance, this is a particularly rewarding language to try this out with, because its rules for pronouncing letter sequences are simple and extremely consistent, unlike English, which regularly baffles even native English speakers. So with their phonetic alphabet, the Ancient Greeks were able to write down and impart the wisdom that had come to them from the mouths of the even more ancient Egyptians and that were now in the keep of their priests, whether or not they were actually able to understand them.

It is not far-fetched to argue that the Greek alphabet marks a step change. It makes the Greek language 'transportable' across geographies and dialects, and so over the next four to five hundred years – and in no small measure precipitated by the startling success of Alexander the Great (356–323 BCE) with his conquests in the region – it becomes the *lingua franca* across the Eastern Mediterranean world. Koine Greek, which is mostly a fusion of Attic and Ionic Greek, and the language of the Hellenistic period, *The Bible*, the Roman Empire, and the early Byzantine Empire, is therefore not a purely 'natural language', it is a 'technical' invention, certainly in the sense of the Greek term *τέχνη* (Ancient Greek pronunciation: *ték*^{h}*nɛː)*, which means 'art' or 'craft': it is a civilisatory achievement, rather than a random evolution, a code deliberately defined so that all Greeks could understand and replicate it.

Not only does this have far-reaching consequences for the proliferation of Greek culture, it also leads to a radically new understanding of what it means to be Greek. Now, *anyone* who is able to read and write Greek is considered Greek, irrespective of where in the vast empire they live and how they talk: 'Greekness' comes to be defined by Greek *literacy.* And this literacy is the intellectual medium that stretches across the entire continent from Europe to India for more than a thousand years: it's a powerful invention.

DRAWING AS A FORM OF WRITING

Roughly two thousand years after the Greeks encoded language in such a way that it could be universally reproduced and that its sound as well as its meaning could be recorded and related, the masters of the Renaissance took a similarly momentous step. They were already able to read and to write – Latin had long since overtaken Greek as the most widely used language – but now they found a new way to medialise their skill. Quite suddenly, they were able to express centuries of tradition with just a few strokes of a pen or pencil on a piece of paper, and to funnel all their knowledge and insight onto a surface in a potent new form. Within a short period the new thinking and new technics of architecture expressed themselves most prominently in perspective drawing.

Perspective is what places an object in all its many facets in front of our eyes, even if it is not actually there, not there yet, or may in fact never exist. It's an achievement which today we clearly take for granted, but which prior to the 14th century just wasn't available to architects or artists, master builders or sculptors. What it amounts to is a new intellectual 'play' on a metaphorical 'stage': If the Greeks, with their phonetic script, were able to invent entire worlds in their theatres, now a new kind of 'theatre' opens up with the power to create something visually accurate out of anything, indeed out of nothing. Being able to do so is also a form of literacy. It's understanding how things work, getting on top of the structure, the principles and logic – the grammar – of this visual language, and knowing how to apply them, with mastery.

The impact this has is as categorical as was the invention of the phonetic alphabet. Because now you can represent in space not just buildings, but human bodies, plants, animals, machines: you can make accurate and meaningful representations of what your world is like *visually.* Think of the drawings of quintessential 'Renaissance Man', Italian polymath Leonardo da Vinci (1452–1519): they encompass technological inventions and the study of the human anatomy as much as sketches for his paintings. They transcend that which is actually there or that which is there on the outside, and especially also include proportionally correct visualisations of both his imagination and of the hidden workings of machines and organisms.

So the term Renaissance is perhaps only partially apt. It is, certainly, a re-birth of knowledge and of an aesthetic that has its roots in antiquity, but it is also an entirely new world that is being born here. And critical to its existence is the perspective drawing in particular. Now, what drives things forward is not just writing with characters (what we still call 'writing') but also writing with lines, what we call 'drawing'.

At the same time, traditional writing (with characters) also takes a categorical leap: we already had the alphabet and the literacy that goes with it, but now we get the printing machine that German printmaker Johannes Gutenberg (c. 1400–1468) introduces to Europe. Now, you could say, it is no longer the 'sequence in space' – the chain of letters that make up words and sentences – that *actually* matters, but the 'sequence in time': the fact that you can multiply the 'sequence in space' many times over and print a hundred thousand copies which you can then disseminate. Does it make the content of these pages meaningless? Of course not. But their power now lies in their multitude. The reason the authorities (in this case, the Catholic Church) can't control it any longer lies in their proliferation. And so the *95 Theses* published by the German reformer Martin Luther (1483–1546) are suddenly everywhere, and they change the face of Europe.

There is one more aspect to the Renaissance that goes hand in hand with this shift we are talking about: the emancipation of the vernacular. Up until the Renaissance, the two languages in Europe in which knowledge was codified were first Greek and then Latin. The Renaissance itself is possible partly because ancient Greek texts are rediscovered, translated into Latin, and newly taught. Our whole heritage of Greek philosophy owes its survival to this motion in history. But while this is happening, language also 'explodes', and thinkers, artists, architects, designers, theologians, and what will soon be described as 'scientists', start to write in their own dialects. Italian, French, Spanish; English and German: the idiom of the people.

Today, we are experiencing another shift of similar, if not in fact again much greater magnitude: the Internet and digitalisation do not substantially change the meaning of either the written word or of the image, but they explode their distribution and availability exponentially. Fact and fiction, 'real' news as well as 'fake'; videos of beheadings and of cute cats, images that are contrived and images that are constructed are all *everywhere.* And therein, in the situation alone that they are ubiquitous, lies their unmanageable potency, be this in any way positive or negative, or neutral.

In summary, then, you could say that the new method of writing of the Greeks is a new type of *mechanics,* much as the new method of drawing is a new type of mechanics in the Renaissance, and much as quantum mechanics is the new method of expressing our world today.

Similarly, you could say that the phonetic script of the Greeks is capable of *writing* any concept, that the printing machine of the Renaissance is capable of *multiplying* any script, and that the computer is capable of *operating* any kind of machine. Which takes us to the idea of 'digital writing' as a generic algorithm, or indeed any algorithm.

Algorithm

DIGITAL WRITING

If we are going to talk about the digital 'mechanics' of writing today, this has to start with a look at what coding is actually for: it is a way to make things computable – readable, manipulable, distributable, savable – by computer, as opposed to by human brain. And a computer is, as we just hinted, a universal or generic 'machine': a machine that is not controlled by its own physical mechanism, but by an algorithm. This is what makes it possible to put a computer to any use imaginable, if not in practice then certainly in theory. And so we arrive at the origin of what we understand as 'computing' today: the Turing machine.

THE TURING MACHINE

You will come across the Turing machine in several places in this *Atlas,* and we also explain it in some detail in our chapter on Graphs & Graphics (where we position it, not entirely unadventurously, as a graph).

The Turing machine is named after the English computer scientist, mathematician, and cryptanalyst Alan Turing (1912–1954), who proposed it as a mathematical model for the principle of digital reading and writing in 1936. While it is not, therefore, a computer, or even a prototype for a computer, it is universally regarded as having laid the foundation for computational thinking, and to this day an algorithm is considered to be computable if a Turing machine would be able to process it.

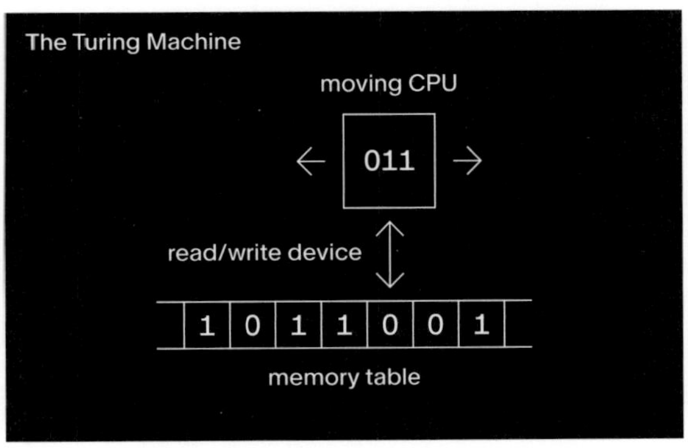

The Turing Machine

The Turing machine consists of:

- A potentially infinite *tape,* which can be read and written to;
- The *machine head,* which can move in either direction, right (forward) or left (backward), and which can read the tape, erase from it, and write to it; and
- A *program,* which controls the behaviour of the machine.

The program consists of a set of rules, which take into account:

- What is already written on the tape (what the machine reads); and
- The *'internal state'* the machine is currently in.

Based on these, the program instructs the machine to:

- Erase and/or write a symbol from or to the tape; and to
- Move the machine head either to the right (forward) or to the left (backward).

In the process of doing so, the program changes ↖329 551↘
the 'internal state' of the machine correspondingly.

Although it is crucial to the concept of the Turing machine – which, let us remind ourselves, is not an □ ↖175
actual machine but a purely theoretical model for one – this 'internal state' is not a clearly defined entity. Different people and successors to Turing take slightly different approaches to its interpretation. Broadly speaking, and mostly in line with Turing's own writings on the subject, it can be regarded as the overall state of the system, that is all the symbols currently on the tape, which therefore determines the state of progress the machine itself (and with it its operator) has made through the computation. In 'practice' it tends to mean the current or last accepted instruction the machine has received and been able to interpret.

Go to Writing & Code – Elaboration *for a theoretical walk through the Turing machine (page 382).* □ 382↘

THE VON NEUMANN ARCHITECTURE 649↘

Implementing the 'mechanics' of the Turing machine as a usable technology, the von Neumann Architecture is a computing model first described in 1945 – ten years after Turing formulated it – by Hungarian-American mathematician and computer scientist John von Neumann (1903–1957) in a paper entitled *First Draft of a Report on the EDVAC,* and it forms the basis for most computers known today. (EDVAC stands for *Electronic Discrete Variable Automatic Computer,* and is the name of one of the very first binary computers in existence. Proposed in 1944, it was approved by the United States military's Ballistics Research Laboratory in 1946, with an initial budget of USD 100,000 – equivalent to about USD 1.3 million today – and delivered three years later, in 1949.)

It is built like this:

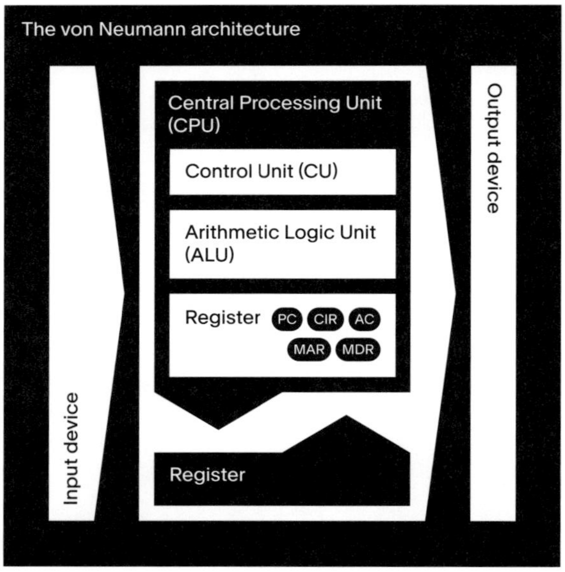

As you can easily recognise, the diagram directly reflects the structure of the Turing machine:

- Memory with input and output devices: this corresponds to the *tape* with the *data*
- ■ ↖354 618↘ ■ ■ The Central Processing Unit (CPU), consisting of a control unit and Arithmetic Logic Unit (ALU): the processor that handles the *program*
- And the machine itself: the *machine head* that reads and writes to, and moves along, the tape

- ■ ■ What makes direct and quick access to data possible in this set-up are the address bus and the data bus: they replace the slow and cumbersome step-by-step head movements of the Turing machine. The process here is much as you would find it in a big distributor's warehouse store: the symbols or characters are 'picked off their shelf' in the store, processed, and then either put back or moved to where they newly belong. Every now and then data come in (are read from the input device) and go out (are written to the output device).

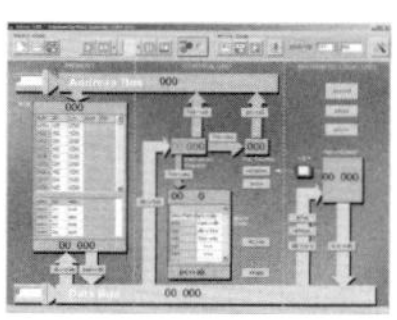

□ 384↘

244 ● 395

■ ↖262 470↘ □ ↖175 □ ↖351 ■ ↖199 383↘

Owing to the high demand for fast computer graphics and, more recently, for machine learning intelligence, an additional component has become prominent in today's computers: the GPU (Graphics Processing Unit). This is a specialised processor that features a very large number of ALUs working in parallel formation. A large screen, for example, is divided into hundreds or even thousands of individual tiles, and the information to be displayed on each tile is calculated by its own ALU. The same type of parallel processor is also very successful in carrying out the kind of operations that are required for large matrices in machine learning. They, too, are divided up into separate parts and then processed simultaneously in parallel.

245 ● 395

ASSEMBLY LANGUAGES

We said that inside a processor things work pretty much as in a large warehouse store: in order to retrieve a data packet, you have to know its exact location 'on the shelf', as it were. For 'shelf' here read 'memory'. This is a question of flow control: accessing the correct location in the correct order is absolutely prerequisite to the processor being able to carry out its job. Equally important is that you accurately determine the size of the data packet, which is a question of correctly identifying the data type, because if a data packet is too large for its 'shelf' or memory allocation, then neighbouring packets have to be moved aside and their addresses changed. This creates more work and therefore requires more processing time and power. In the world of a computer, where millions of data packets are moved every second, making this particular aspect efficient can spell the difference between a piece of software that works and one that doesn't. The programs that handle this part of data processing are written in *assembly languages,* and they are closely tied to the machine itself, since their operations are entirely dependent on the computer's architecture and the type and number of addresses it offers.

THE ADDRESS LOCATION

Both type and number of addresses that are available are similarly determined by the computer's architecture. Up until the late 1990s to early 2000s, the standard for personal computers was a 32-bit architecture, so called because its structure is based on 4 octets of 8 bits each. Because a bit can have one of two values precisely (0 or 1), a 32-bit architecture offers 2^{32} addresses, which corresponds to 4 gigabits or 500 megabytes (1 byte consisting of 8 bits). Since the early 2000s, 64-bit architecture has become common in consumer computing. This potentially offers 264 addresses or 2,000,000 terabytes.

Go to Writing & Code – Elaboration *for some code samples on Packet Sizes (page 383).*

THE ARITHMETIC LOGIC UNIT (ALU)

In our chapters on Graphs & Graphics and Scripting we discuss Boolean operations, which therefore we won't treat in any detail here. Suffice it to say that, introduced by the English mathematician George Boole

(1815–1864) in his 1854 work *An Investigation of the Laws of Thought on Which are Founded the Mathematical Theories of Logic and Probabilities*, they are simple logical operations that determine what happens if a certain condition is met or not met respectively.

Boolean operations are of relevance to us in computing because the processor retrieves a data packet from the memory and then processes it *logically.* This processing happens in the ALU, which we briefly encountered above: the Arithmetic Logic Unit. As it happens, for a computer to work perfectly well, only a very small number of logical operations are required:

- AND: 'true' is returned if both of two conditions are met
- OR: 'true' is returned if either one or the other or both conditions are met
- XOR: 'exclusive or' – 'true' is returned if either one or the other condition is met, but not both; and
- NOT: 'true' is returned if neither of two condition is met.

Go to Writing & Code – Elaboration *for some code samples on Boolean Operations and Binary Arithmetic (page 383).*

INTERPRETERS, COMPILERS, AND ABSTRACTION

When we were talking about assembly languages above, we were talking about the most basic kind of code that a computer's CPU can directly execute. This is called **machine code**, and it is either completely or almost completely numeric. It is the 'raw' code, so to speak, made up of the actual digits and symbols that the processor understands. Because it is almost entirely numeric, machine code, while most basic, is also most difficult for the programmer to work with, as to the average (even trained) human eye and brain it is practically unintelligible, which is why it is extremely hard to develop software in it.

One step up from machine code we find **low-level programming**. This is still basic enough for most processors to handle without further translation, and consequently still largely numeric, which means that it is still very difficult to write programs with, unless you have very advanced skills and a great deal of expertise.

Most programming therefore is done in what are known as **high-level languages**: programming languages that are highly abstracted from the machine code and work with expressions and commands a human being can readily understand or learn. This includes real words as they appear in a natural language, such as 'print', 'add', 'color', or, as you find them in the Writing & Code – Elaboration that follows this chapter, 'ImageSize', 'IntegerDigits', or 'ArrayPlot'. If you are new to programming, you may not immediately know what an 'ArrayPlot' is, but you can acquire the term and then remember it without too much difficulty, as you can words in any foreign language.

So now we have programming languages that humans can work with, but CPUs can't. What's required, therefore, is a bridge that leads from the human-intelligible, high-level language to the machine code. There are two such types of 'bridge' available: the *interpreter* and the *compiler.*

A compiler takes the high-level language code and 'compiles' it into machine code, which, once this is done, makes the entire program executable by the CPU, as if it had been written in machine code in the first place. An interpreter, by contrast, 'interprets' the high-level language and carries out its instructions on its behalf each time it reads the code.

In the majority, traditional high-level languages tend to be *compiled,* whereas the more recent **scripting languages** ■ ↖354 tend to be *interpreted.* The difference in practice expresses itself mostly in processing speed, and so, for as long as processing speed was a major issue in computing, the much faster compilers were preferred. Now that computer hardware even at consumer level reaches dizzying speeds, this is no longer such a priority, and so interpreters have gained a lot of ground, even though they are between five and ten times slower. This reflects the reality, also, that in computing you have to strike a balance between speed and flexibility. Often, therefore, the computationally expensive parts of a programme are turned into compiled functions, which can then operate in a more flexible interpreted environment. □ 382↘

(We also explain different level programming languages in our chapter on Scripting.) □ ↖351

Go to Writing & Code – Elaboration *for* The Brickwork Example *which illustrates an interpreter in action (page 384).* □ 382↘ ↖354

IMPERATIVE PROGRAMMING LANGUAGES AND THE PRIMACY OF FLOW CONTROL ■ ↖354 410↘

95% of today's programs are written in what are called *imperative* programming languages, such as *Fortran, Pascal, C, Java,* or *Python.* Based on the von Neumann computing architecture, their focus is on *flow control.* They describe *how* a program is supposed to work. They are clearly very successful, which is why they are so prevalent; and because they base themselves on traditional and familiar ways of thinking, ■ ↖354 they are considered intuitive and easy to understand. Their approach though tends to reduce the potential of digitality to a mechanical thought scheme or pattern.

Writing with imperative programs, we suggest, is therefore a bit like writing *prose,* but in the language of computing.

■ ↖354

DECLARATIVE PROGRAMMING LANGUAGES AND THE PRIMACY OF DATA TYPES

By contrast, *declarative* programming languages, such as *Lisp, Smalltalk,* or *Mathematica,* are based □ 382↘ on the **lambda calculus**, which is a **formal language** ■ 552↘ developed by American mathematician and logician ■ ↖192 554↘ Alonzo Church (1903–1995) in the 1930s. They are in a sense the inverse to imperative languages: instead of focusing on *how* to compute data, they focus on *what* to do with the data.

In the language of computing, declarative programs, we therefore suggest, lend themselves more to writing *poetry.*

And so, in a similar vein, if imperative programming languages represent the 'physics' and the 'geometry' of computing, then declarative languages are the 'chemistry' and the 'arithmetic'. Or, more metaphorically: imperative languages consider computers as physical 'bodies', declarative languages consider computing as a 'mental' play of symbols. ('Physics' expresses itself in hardware and in the way computers are built, the 'body'; 'chemistry' expresses itself in the interaction of symbols.)

This is how the Lambda calculus is defined:

A simplified definition of the Lambda calculus

$$FV(a) = \{a\}$$
$$FV(T_1\,T_2) = FV(T_1) \cup FV(T_2)$$
$$FV(\lambda a.T) = FV(T) \setminus \{a\}$$
$$B(a) = \emptyset$$
$$B(T_1\,T_2) = B(T_1) \cup B(T_2)$$
$$B(\lambda a.T) = B(T) \cup \{a\}$$
$$a[x\ T] = a$$
$$a[a\ T] = T$$
$$(T_1\,T_2)[x\ T] = (T_1[x\ T]\ T_2[x\ T]$$
$$(\lambda a.T')[a\ T] = (\lambda a.T')$$
$$(\lambda a.T')[x\ T] = (\lambda a.T'[x\ T])$$
$$B(\lambda a.T').$$

We want to stress here: the important thing is not for you to understand from this how the Lambda calculus works. What is important to realise is that it can be expressed in these very few but very abstract lines.

With von Neumann, then, we have an abstract machine, with Church we have a general procedure. Von Neumann in 1945 picks up on Alan Turing's work from 1936 onwards, Church develops his thinking during the 1930s. Together they form the nucleus for what we've seen in the development of programming languages during the 20th century. The foundations have hardly changed, they are remarkably invariant. What has changed over the last almost 100 years is their virtuosity in handling these techniques.

The Development Phases of Digital Writing

↖355 555↘

1960: MAINFRAMES – THE ABSTRACTION OF FLOW CONTROL

By the 1960s and 70s there was no longer a question whether computers could function at all, and if so how, and so the big questions in computer science no longer centred around individual operations and the basic data types in assembly languages. Now it was a case of controlling and optimising the program sequence. Typical examples of the kind of language used for 'structural programming' are *C*, *Algol*, *Pascal*, or *Ada*. It is from this era that we have flow charts (Petri nets, Unified Modelling Language (UML) or DIN 66001). This is the era of mainframes, where mostly male experts do the programming, while data entry and harvesting data output is done via terminals and on paper, by mostly female users.

It is estimated that the total number of mainframe computers built and installed worldwide lies in the tens of thousands.

246 ● 396

```
----------------------------------Setup Build---------------
Row 1 to 9 to 23
 COMMAND ===>
Scroll ==> CSR
    Build Highlevel:  P390A.OPENMAKE.COMSAMPL

    Project     ===>  MAINFRAME BUILD
DEMO                       / to Choose
    Search Path ===>  RE-
LEASE2                                    / to Choose
  Bldmake Options     / to Choose
       OM Options     / to Choose

  Actions: (A)dd, (C)opy, (D)elete, (E)dit, (B)uild and Build
(All)

     Target                       OS   Build Type
     load(asmhi)                  zOS  Assembler Load Module
     load(cblhi)                  zOS  COBOL Load Module
     load(cblhidb2)               zOS  DB2 COBOL Load Module
     load(cicimscb)               zOS  CICS IMS COBOL Load Module
     load(cmdprs00)               zOS  Assembler Ogj Load Module
     load(db2cobci)               zOS  DB2 CICS COBOL Load Module
     load(hic)                    zOS  C Load Module
     load(hicpp)                  zOS  CPP Load Module
     load(hicppdb2)               zOS  DB2 C Load Module
```

When we distinguish between *interface, program*, and *data* as the principal elements of an information technology system, we are looking, in the conception of high-level languages – and therefore of information technology of the 1960s and 70s – at *one* terminal with display and keyboard, an *arbitrary* number of programming steps, and *one* data model, which we may best picture as a structured table.

1980: PCS – OBJECTS – THE ABSTRACTION OF DATA TYPES

Object-oriented languages trace their roots to *Simula 67*, which was developed in the 1960s by two Norwegian computer scientists, Ole-Johan Dahl (1931–2002) and Kristen Nygaard (1926–2002) at the Norwegian Computing Centre, Oslo, and which, together with its immediate predecessor *Simula I*, is considered to have laid the foundation as the first object-oriented programming language. Most are closely related to the von Neumann languages, but have a much more structured and distributed model of both memory and computation. Rather than treating computation as the operations of a monolithic processor on a monolithic memory, object-oriented languages treat it as the interaction of semi-independent objects, each of which has both its own internal state, as well as sub-routines to manage that state. *Smalltalk* is the purest of the object-oriented languages; *C++* and *Java* are the most widely used; another example is *Eiffel*. It is also possible to devise object-oriented functional languages, the best known of which is the *CLOS (Kee89)* extension to *Common Lisp*, but they tend to have a strong imperative flavour.

In the object-oriented languages of the 1980s and 90s, we recognise an abstraction of data types towards functional units, the objects so referred to. With these, flow control drifts into the background, or rather, it is being implemented within the objects, as a general procedure. That's why it is now possible to assemble functional software elements arbitrarily, without having to expend too much thought on the program sequence. You can recognise this on computer screens, where interface objects are arranged to form large hierarchies of interactive surfaces. Each element is like a separate terminal, with which particular functions of a program can be freely accessed. This in turn is reflected in computer hardware, where, within very wide boundaries, many different building elements by all kinds of different manufacturers can be combined to a functional system. And so we are not surprised – in fact we expect – to find our *Logitec* mouse working absolutely fine with an *Asus* PC. It is no longer flow control, but the interface (or rather the definition of data types) that dominates computing.

247A ● 396

247B ● 396

In a way you could say that with this development, computers now go forth into the world: they become 'curious'. When with mainframes it was the programs that provided stability in a world of possibilities, our relationship with personal computers is inverse. Now the computer offers a spectrum of near unlimited possibilities, and in return the whole world is seen as a stable source. Hence the trend here towards infantilisation: a quest for the unspent, for original purity, for a basis on which we can depend in our informational needs with a clear conscience.

Similarly, it now no longer is about writing programs that are as fast as possible; instead the challenge has become to write programs as flexibly as possible. In other words – and entirely in line with what we observed earlier – the main question is no longer *how* to write programs, but *what* these programs are capable of doing. Which is precisely the reason why we no longer call these new object-orientated programming languages *imperative*, but *declarative*.

Here now, the interface is no longer the screen, but each individual element on the screen, enabling individual access to the different programs. There is no longer *one* terminal with a display and keyboard, an *arbitrary* number of programming steps, and *one* data model; we now have an *arbitrary* number of screen elements, an *arbitrary* number of programming steps, and *one* data model.

We also now have two kinds of 'master': on the one hand the *programmers*, deploying chains of letters that steer the machines, using high-level languages in a quasi aristocratic, mercantilist manner, and the *creatives* who line up with their machines in a quasi democratic, industrial manner. In this constellation now, the latter are disproportionately more powerful.

Currently, around 1.8 billion personal computers (laptops and desktops) are being built each year.

2000: THE INTERNET – BIG DATA – XML | MACHINE LEARNING – THE ABSTRACTION OF FLOW CONTROL

↖336 501↘
↖165 469↘

Scripting languages are an abstraction of von Neumann languages. They are distinguished by their focus on 'gluing together' components that were originally developed as independent programs. Several scripting languages were first conceived for specific purposes: *C shell* and *Bash*, for example, are the input languages of job control (shell) programs; *AWK* ■ ↖355 was intended for report generation; *PHP* and *JavaScript* are primarily intended for building web pages with dynamic content (with execution on server and client side, respectively). Other languages, including *Perl, Python, Ruby, and Tcl*, are more deliberately conceived for general purposes. Most place an emphasis on rapid prototyping, with a bias toward ■ 407↘ ease of expression over speed of execution.

Among the elements that make the Internet work at all are XML standards, whereby XML stands ■ for *Extensible Markup Language*. Developed by the World Wide Web Consortium since 1996, XML facilitates the exchange of information in many different types of document and application across platforms. While not, therefore, having any designated functionality of its own, a markup language distinguishes ■ ↖344 the operational instructions in a document from the semantic content. Much like the equally instrumental Hypertext Markup Language (HTML), developed by the English computer scientist Tim Berners-Lee (b. 1955), which lays the foundation for the World Wide Web as we know it, XML is generally annotated in tags, such as <to>, <from>, <body>, with corresponding closing tags (</to>, </from>, </body>).

■ ↖344

It is much more difficult to adequately and objectively assess this current development phase, since we are still right in the middle of it. Our outline sketch therefore here has to be much more speculative than for the previous phases, which are now part of computing history. But we have our method of symmetries and a framework of concepts. With these, we want to now have a look at what we can do today: computers are now *in* the world. When PCs were looking out to the world and exploring it curiously through their interfaces, aiming for stabilities for their program sequences, now, in the Internet, it is all about moving around the digital world in a controlled manner. New programming languages are once again concerned with flow control; object-oriented data types are considered to simply exist, in whatever form. New programming languages are also once again imperative, but on a higher level of abstraction. Computing now is neither primarily about *how* to write programs, nor about *what* these programs are capable of, but about *how we can use* these programs. The interfaces are no longer friendly hands extended to offer help, they are instead stimulating animations, encouraging us to *do* things.

248 ● 396

□ 613↘

Correspondingly, current development environments no longer operate one machine, but a whole spectrum of gadgets and computers, from TVs to laptops to smartphones to watches. The applications move with the user, they are no longer installed on a specific type of hardware; instead, they are fleetingly attached to a specific type of server in the Internet.

249A ● 397

249B ● 397

Now we no longer have, as with the PC, an *arbitrary* number of screen (interface) elements, an *arbitrary* number of programming steps and, *one* data model, we have an *arbitrary* number of screen elements, an *arbitrary* number of programming steps, and an *arbitrary* number of data models.

In the vast warren of probabilistic pathways of the Internet, computing has become a question of us finding our own personal way. Nobody is really concerned, any longer, with whether the interaction is intuitive or not, since operability is taken for granted, and so nobody is after comfort in that sense any more: the story has to be right, and it all has to work. With stability, rather than comfort.

Now we have three levels of mastery: 1) the *experts* of letter sequences who successfully implement logical truths, whom we willingly obey; 2) the *creatives*, who optimise our world within a functional framework and whom we would dearly like to belong to; and 3) the *paragons* of an improved life, whom we gladly follow. The pattern is once again: aristocratic, democratic, aristocratic.

The Internet of Things (IoT) will encompass more than 1 trillion devices.

A Synoptic Comparison

We have laid out with this chapter various strands of thought, explained the origins and some aspects of computing in detail, and offered some thought figures to draw parallels that we find of interest, without explaining them much further. We have elaborated on what letters are, what words – what, therefore language is – and what we want to be aware and cognisant of when we look at programming languages.

We are also conscious of the fact that not everything we have said (or are going to say) in this chapter will immediately strike you as obviously pertinent to architecture. But although we believe it is obvious that the thinking that underpins much of what we are talking about is relevant to all of information technology and therefore to everything that we do as digital citizens, and therefore also to architecture, we don't want to completely lose sight of the fact that this is an *Atlas of Digital Architecture*.

So we now would like to invite you onto one more leg of our proverbial journey together. By way of summarising many of the ideas we've already encountered, we want to steer towards a comparison of the language types we have discussed. We hope, and trust, that this will deepen further our understanding of writing and code in this, our digital age, and it will allow us to draw some links to architecture and architectural styles.

Let's start with what we said about mainframes, PCs, and computers in the Internet, and the number of programming steps, interface elements, and data models. (In the table below, we can also read 'global' for '1', because there is one shared unit for all participating individuals in the system, and 'local' for '∞', because there are one or more units for each participant individually):

Year	Environment	Language Type	Steps	Interfaces	Models
1960	Mainframe	Imperative	∞	1	1
1980	Personal Computer	Declarative	∞	∞	1
2000	Internet	Markup	∞	∞	∞

We can now look at this summary in architectural terms: in 1960 any kind of machine could be implemented, but form and structure needed to be specific. In architecture we have the corresponding International Style. The principal problem of this stage of technical development is combinatorial explosion.

This was 'solved' around 1980, when information emancipated from form. What we see now is many interconnected and explicit forms of information. Information becomes personal. In our field, this corresponds to postmodern architecture. The principal problem of this phase of technical development – as with any structure – is the frame problem: what to include and what to exclude. (We explain both *combinatorial explosion* and the *frame problem* in detail in our chapter on Big Data & Machine Learning.)

Since 2000, with markup languages and the success of the Internet, information has also emancipated itself from structure. And this is where we are today: we have technical consistency without form and structure. Which would seem like an idea of paradise. As an architect you principally can do what you want. This is what we observe today in many examples, but at a closer look and on second thought it becomes rather frightening: everything becomes amorphous by losing its form and structure. We are suddenly faced with non-architecture.

And so we are back where we started with this chapter: isn't this the same situation as when the Greeks invented their language with the technics of phonetic writing, or the situation the Renaissance addressed with the technics of spatial drawings? With these technics (and here, as in our Introduction, we use the term 'technic' deliberately and advisedly) our ancestors were able to describe everything and anything in the, for their time, most powerful ways, just because their new methods of writing and drawing had no given form and structure in the terms of the old world. Mastering these ciphers was their key to explore, domesticate, and cultivate a new world. This is the reason why, throughout this *Atlas*, we argue that to be an architect today we have to become digitally literate.

So considering our situation today and the, in effect, technical freedom of form and structure it offers us, it is at the very least interesting to note that the methodology of Building Information Modelling (BIM) and its Industry Foundation Classes (IFCs) that are being so forcefully propagated and even foisted upon architects across entire sectors sit absolutely in the scheme of 1960s mainframe architecture. Which means that, without any technical need to do so, they also foster schemes of global control of form and structure. As architects we may ask ourselves: why?

Go to Writing & Code – Elaboration *for a look at The Concepts of Computer Languages in Detail (page 390).* □ 382↘

■

HOW TO WRITE ■ 555↘

Wherefore all these considerations? The overriding question we want to ask is this: if we can express *anything* – first with text, then with drawings, now with code – then what are the forms of expression we can hold on to? This is a development that has started with the Ancient Greeks, that continued during the Renaissance, and that we today can confront with coding. And for us as architects, it is of particular significance, because if 'anything goes', then that may be fascinating at first, but it quickly turns into a challenge of the highest order: if every type of structure is possible, what form should architecture take? Hence our historical and theoretical interest in forms of expression that allow us to find stabilities for architectural forms which are not in themselves constructive or structural.

■ ■ 558↘ □ 549↘

Since Ancient Greek, we have grammar, logic, and rhetoric as forms of expression within phonetic writing. Since the Renaissance, we have *ichnographia* (which today we know simplified as 'ground plan'), *orthographia* (which today we know simplified as 'elevation'), and *scaenographia* (which today we know simplified as 'perspective') as forms of expression within spatial drawing. And we expect there will be a tripartite parallel once again for coding, since the advent of the digital era. □ ↖29

So as a final gesture, we want to try and create a scaffold or set of handles that we can hold on to as we find ways of talking about architecture. A *manner*, so to speak, that is adequate for our age. In order to do so, we need to now bring into the equation the Seven Liberal Arts of classical education. For the best part of about two thousand years, they have formed the framework within which people who acquired a higher education studied, and they are neatly divided into a *lower division*, which could be said to perhaps equate to today's bachelor degree, and the *higher division*, which correspondingly would therefore approximately equate to a master's degree today. The *lower division* is known as the trivium and encompasses *grammar, logic*, and *rhetoric*. Once you have mastered these and advance to the *higher division*, you are learning the quadrivium, which encompasses *arithmetic, geometry, music*, and *astronomy*.

■ □ 507↘ ■ ■ 501↘ ■

We are interested in the more basic *trivium*, and want to find parallels not only to the three modes of architectural representation *ichnographia*, *orthographia*, and *scaenographia*, but also, because they offer themselves and because we started our argumentation with a metaphorical stage, to the three principal forms of classical theatre, *satire*, *comedy*, and *tragedy*. What we want to do here is simply find other words to illustrate these symmetries and let them stand there, without further comment or explanation.

☐ ↖29 These following allocations then are neither obvious nor undisputed, and they may in fact meet with quite some resistance. So they can't be considered to be 'established' in any way. Still, we think they are important, and that's why we want to put them up here for discussion:

1 *Rhetoric:* The Art of Oratory

Satire: Criticises, mocks, and admonishes. (Until the 17th century, it was believed that 'satire' derived from and refers to the Greek mythological figure of the satyr. This has since been disputed and the word appears to stem from the Latin *satur* and the phrase *lanx satura* 'full dish' and thus refer in its origins to a medley or a rich offering of all kinds of fruit, for example.)

Dionysus: Intoxication, the nature of song

Epic: Descriptive literature

Ichnographia (ground plan) and, we would suggest, the competitive fertility of the automata.

2 *Grammar:* The Art of Writing

Tragedy: 'The Goat Song' (from Greek *τραγῳδία: trago-odia*, literally, 'goat song' – there are various possible explanations for this: a goat may have been the prize for the best play in the competition, or it may have been the sacrificial beast offered to the gods before the play; it could even be a misunderstanding and the word actually might be derived from *tyrgodia: tyrgos* being the harvest and again *odia*, song, simply because these tragedies and comedies were presented as part of harvest festivals? We really don't know...)

Apollo: The creative power of harmony

Drama: Text with allocated parts

Orthographia (elevation) and, we would suggest, the sacrifice of nature as a statue; optimisation

3 *Dialectic:* The Art of Conversation

Comedy: 'The Village Songs' or 'Revel Songs' (from Ancient Greek *κωμῳδία: kōmōidía*, a compound either of *κῶμος kômos* – revel – or *κώμη kṓmē* – village – and *ᾠδή ōidḗ* – singing)

Hermes, Aphrodite: The compelling forces of beauty, love, and deception

Poetry: Poiesis, mimesis

Scaenographia (perspective) and, we would suggest, the banquet of the rational

(We talk in a little more detail about our proposed parallels between *ichnographia, orthographia*, and *scaenographia* on the one hand and *satire, comedy*, and *tragedy* on the other in our Conclusion What is Information?)

WHAT TO LEARN

The subject of architecture in the digital world is not an easy one. And that is just as well, as there is no mastery without literacy. So as to the question of what programming language to learn, we suggest:

- *Processing* and *Grasshopper* belong to the game of *rhetoric*
- *Java*, and, more recommended today, *Python* belong to the game of *dialectic*
- *Mathematica* and the Lambda calculus belong to the game of *grammar*

We said earlier that we can't be sure about the correlations, but this will definitely help: if you want to *produce* things, follow the lines of *rhetoric* and *Dionysus* and learn, for example, *Grasshopper* to write 'epics'. If you want to *optimise* things and make them better, follow the lines of *dialectic* and *Apollo* and learn for example *Python* to write 'drama'. If you want to *create* new things, follow the lines of *grammar* and *Aphrodite* and learn for example *Mathematica* to write 'poems'. (We use these literary terms metaphorically, obviously.)

There are books and courses for all of these languages. But the same applies here as applies when you first learn to read and write at primary school: you have to go about it step by step, patiently, over many years. There are no shortcuts. But if you master this literacy, you will gain a new perspective on the world.

With *Processing* or *Grasshopper* you learn to build machines along sets of instructions. They are similar to predefined tool kits which allow you to build models, following the instruction manual. This is intuitive, because you learn how to build machines, and it is fast, but the perspective it offers onto digitality is distorted, because you think you've understood something that you really haven't mastered yet. You have to allow 3 to 4 weeks practice to be able to get first results.

With *Java* or *Python* you learn how to construct systems digitally. This is more general; there is no predefined problem and no concrete instruction. These languages are not tool kits, but offer the whole spectrum that comes with the power of expression of a programming language. You have to learn to specify problems digitally, and to develop solutions in this way. This takes time: realistically, you have to allow between 3 to 6 months to find a way in. In order to solve proper problems, you need about two years' practice.

With *Python* you become a digital system engineer. *Mathematica*, on the other hand, is a digital thought laboratory. If with *Python* you learn to write 'prose', with *Mathematica* you can create 'poetry'. With *Python* you learn a digital technique, with *Mathematica* you learn to think digitally. But with *Mathematica*, too, you have to allow for a 3-6 month learning curve to get the hang of it, and it will be about two years before you get to 'diploma' level.

(Of course, the languages proposed here are just examples, representative of their type. Although it is fair to say that as far as we know there is not as yet a sufficiently differentiated alternative to *Mathematica*. *Mathlab*, for example, belongs to the same language family as *Java*.)

Further Reading

If you are looking for a well-established, detailed and not too difficult to understand compilation of programming languages and their paradigms, we recommend this comprehensive book of 941 pages: M L Scott: *Programming Language Pragmatics* (Elsevier, 2009). It supports our theses in detail, even if the proposed order of concepts very much leans on established practice and historical development, and not, as we propose, on the principles and modes of thinking. This is especially the case for Chapter 6 on Flow Control, Chapter 7 on Data Types, Chapter 8 on the Abstraction of Flow Control, and Chapter 9 on the Abstraction of Data Types.

Elaboration

□ ↖369

Read these examples in conjunction with the introductory texts in Writing & Code.

Here as in the other Elaboration sections in this Atlas where we play through in-depth examples and experiments in coding, we use Mathematica*, written in the* Wolfram *programming language. This is a matter of preference, not compulsion: there are other programming languages that could do the same thing.*

THE TURING MACHINE

□ ↖373

Refer to Writing & Code*: The Turing Machine.*

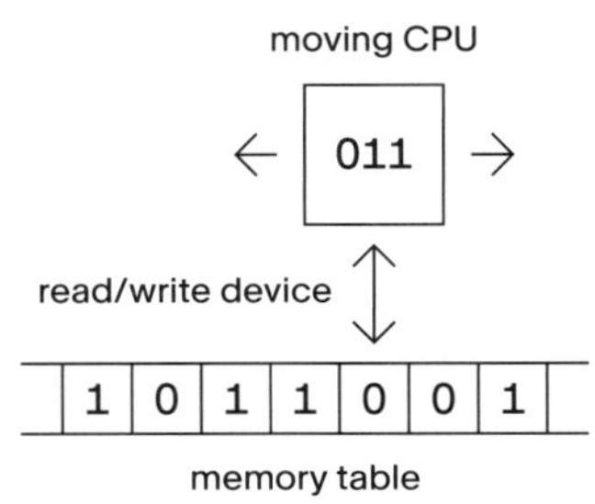

In *Mathematica*, we can write the rules of a Turing machine like this:

```
{1,1}→{0,0,-1}
```

It means that if the *internal* state of the machine is '1', and at the current position of the tape the machine reads a '1', then the instruction is to change the internal state of the machine to '0', write a '0' to the tape, and move one step to the left (–1). Here is how we can visualise this rule:

```
Grid[{PlotTuringRule /@ {{1,1}→{0,0,-1}}}]
```

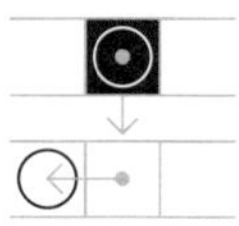

An actual program will consist of many such rules:

```
tCode={
   {1,1}→{0,0,-1},
   {1,0}→{0,1,1},
   {0,1}→{1,0,1},
   {0,0}→{1,1,-1}
   };
```

This is how they are visualised:

```
Grid[{PlotTuringRule /@ tCode}]
```

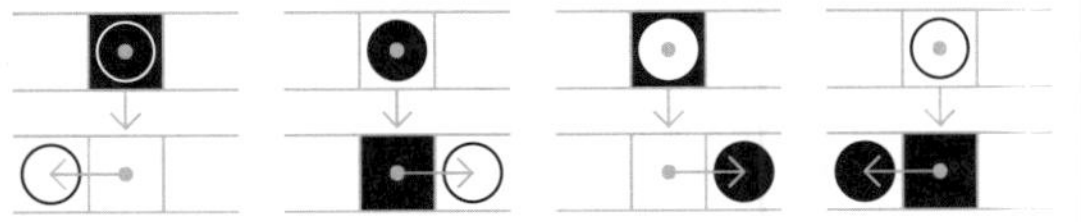

With the program in place, we now need a 'machine' to operate it. In *Mathematica*, this 'machine' is described by two numbers:

```
tState={1,6};
```

This means the machine has status '1' and finds itself at position '6' of the tape. We obviously also need a 'tape'. In this instance, we give it 12 'empty' cells:

```
tBand={0,0,0,0,0,0,0,0,0,0,0,0};
```

Here now is a graphic representation of the tape and the machine:

```
PlotTuring[tBand,tState]
```

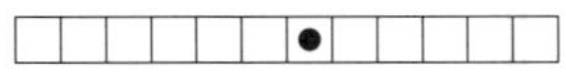

We run the program – rule 2 matches and is carried out:

```
rT:=
 {tBand,tState}=RunTuring[tBand,tState,tCode]
rT
{{0,0,0,0,0,1,0,0,0,0,0,0},{0,7}}
```

```
PlotTuring[tBand,tState]
```

At this next step, rule 4 is triggered:

```
rT
{{0,0,0,0,0,1,1,0,0,0,0,0},{1,6}}
```

```
PlotTuring[tBand,tState]
```

Thus the machine continues to run:

```
trace=Column@Reap[Do[Sow@rT,{n,12}]][[2,1]]
{
 {{{0,0,0,0,0,0,1,0,0,0,0,0},{0,5}}},
 {{{0,0,0,0,1,0,1,0,0,0,0,0},{1,4}}},
 {{{0,0,0,1,1,0,1,0,0,0,0,0},{0,5}}},
 {{{0,0,0,1,0,0,1,0,0,0,0,0},{1,6}}},
 {{{0,0,0,1,0,1,1,0,0,0,0,0},{0,7}}},
 {{{0,0,0,1,0,1,0,0,0,0,0,0},{1,8}}},
 {{{0,0,0,1,0,1,0,1,0,0,0,0},{0,9}}},
 {{{0,0,0,1,0,1,0,1,1,0,0,0},{1,8}}},
 {{{0,0,0,1,0,1,0,0,1,0,0,0},{0,7}}},
 {{{0,0,0,1,0,1,1,0,1,0,0,0},{1,6}}},
 {{{0,0,0,1,0,0,1,0,1,0,0,0},{0,5}}},
 {{{0,0,0,1,1,0,1,0,1,0,0,0},{1,4}}}
}
```

```
Column[PlotTuring@@@trace[[1]]]
```

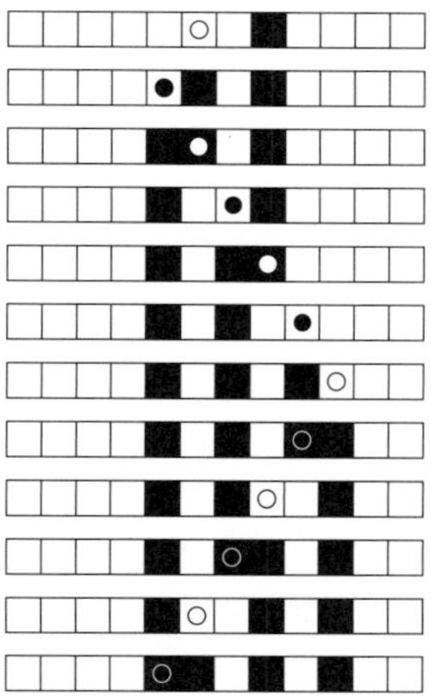

And that's the Turing machine. Fundamental to it is that any imaginable program can be written and processed in this way. And it is equally important to realise that there are exactly three components to this:

- The tape (the data)
- The machine head (the processor)
- The rules (the program)

PACKET SIZES

Refer to Writing & Code *: Packet Sizes.* □ ↖374

Data types and therefore packet sizes are clearly defined: for example, what's known as a *short integer* has 16 bits, which means it can count up to 65,536.

```
2^16
65536
```

An example:

```
n=32173;
IntegerDigits[%,2,16]
ArrayPlot[{%},ImageSize→128]
{0,1,1,1,1,1,0,1,1,0,1,0,1,1,0,1}
```

A *double* has 64 bits, which means that with it numbers can be calculated to an accuracy of approximately 30 digits.

A text character, such as a letter or punctuation mark, is allowed 8 bits, which means that up to 256 different characters can be identified:

```
2^8
256
```

Another example:

```
str="wo ist wendelin?";
Characters@str
ToCharacterCode@str
IntegerDigits[#,2,8]&/@ %
Flatten@%
Partition[%,16]
ArrayPlot@%
{w,o, ,i,s,t, ,w,e,n,d,e,l,i,n,?}
{119,111,32,105,115,116,32,119,101,110,100,
 101,108,105,110,63}
{{0,1,1,1,0,1,1,1},{0,1,1,0,1,1,1,1},
 {0,0,1,0,0,0,0,0},{0,1,1,0,1,0,0,1},
 {0,1,1,1,0,0,1,1},{0,1,1,1,0,1,0,0},
 {0,0,1,0,0,0,0,0},{0,1,1,1,0,1,1,1},
 {0,1,1,0,0,1,0,1},{0,1,1,0,1,1,1,0},
 {0,1,1,0,0,1,0,0},{0,1,1,0,0,1,0,1},
 {0,1,1,0,1,1,0,0},{0,1,1,0,1,0,0,1},
 {0,1,1,0,1,1,1,0},{0,0,1,1,1,1,1,1}}
{0,1,1,1,0,1,1,1,0,1,1,0,1,1,1,1,0,0,
 1,0,0,0,0,0,0,1,1,0,1,0,0,1,0,1,1,1,
 0,0,1,1,0,1,1,1,0,1,0,0,0,0,1,0,0,0,
 0,0,0,1,1,1,0,1,1,1,0,1,1,0,0,1,0,1,
 0,1,1,0,1,1,1,0,0,1,1,0,0,1,0,0,0,1,
 1,0,0,1,0,1,0,1,1,0,1,1,0,0,0,1,1,0,
 1,0,0,1,0,1,1,0,1,1,1,0,0,0,1,1,1,1,
 1,1}
{{0,1,1,1,0,1,1,1,0,1,1,0,1,1,1,1},
 {0,0,1,0,0,0,0,0,0,1,1,0,1,0,0,1},
 {0,1,1,1,0,0,1,1,0,1,1,1,0,1,0,0},
 {0,0,1,0,0,0,0,0,0,1,1,1,0,1,1,1},
 {0,1,1,0,0,1,0,1,0,1,1,0,1,1,1,0},
 {0,1,1,0,0,1,0,0,0,1,1,0,0,1,0,1},
 {0,1,1,0,1,1,0,0,0,1,1,0,1,0,0,1},
 {0,1,1,0,1,1,1,0,0,0,1,1,1,1,1,1}}
```

BOOLEAN OPERATIONS ↖374

Refer to Writing & Code *: The Arithmetic Logic Unit (ALU).* □ ↖375

Boolean AND operation: if all in a row are black, then black, else, white.

```
ArrayPlot[IntegerDigits[#,2,8]&/@
  {23,73}]
ArrayPlot[IntegerDigits[#,2,8]&/@
  {BitAnd[23,73]}]
[…]
```

```
[…]
```

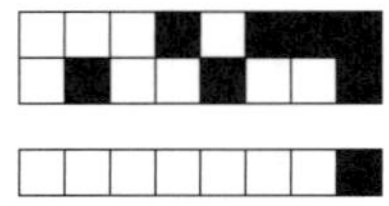

Boolean OR operation: if one in a row is black, then black, else white.

```
ArrayPlot[IntegerDigits[#,2,8]&/@{23,73}]
ArrayPlot[IntegerDigits[#,2,8]&/@
  {BitOr[23,73]}]
```

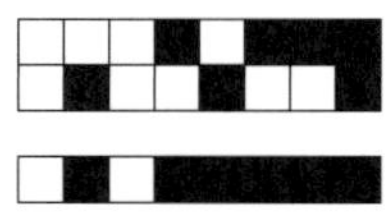

Boolean XOR operation: if all in a row are black, then white, else, black.

```
ArrayPlot[IntegerDigits[#,2,8]&/@{23,73}]
ArrayPlot[IntegerDigits[#,2,8]&/@
  {BitXor[23,73]}]
```

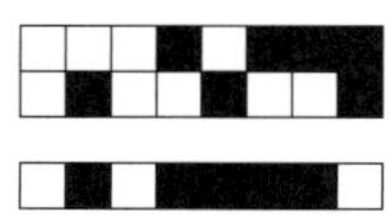

□ ↖375

BINARY ARITHMETIC

□ ↖374

Refer to Writing & Code *: The Arithmetic Logic Unit (ALU).*

Employing sequences of logical operators, the ALU is able to carry out arithmetic operations:

```
ArrayPlot[IntegerDigits[#,2,8]&/@{0,1}]
ArrayPlot[IntegerDigits[#,2,8]&/@{0+1}]
```

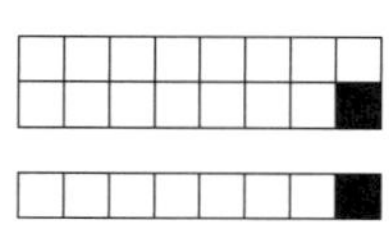

```
ArrayPlot[IntegerDigits[#,2,8]&/@{1,1}]
ArrayPlot[IntegerDigits[#,2,8]&/@{1+1}]
```

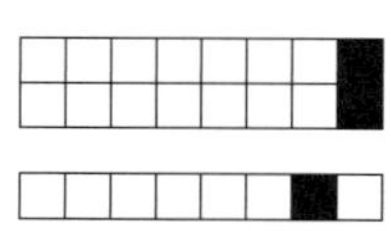

```
ArrayPlot[IntegerDigits[#,2,8]&/@{2,1}]
ArrayPlot[IntegerDigits[#,2,8]&/@{2+1}]
```

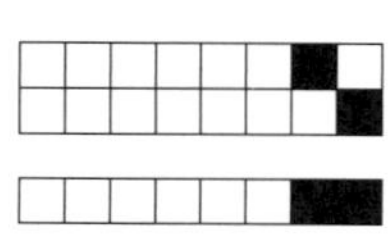

```
ArrayPlot[IntegerDigits[#,2,8]&/@{3,1}]
ArrayPlot[IntegerDigits[#,2,8]&/@{3+1}]
```

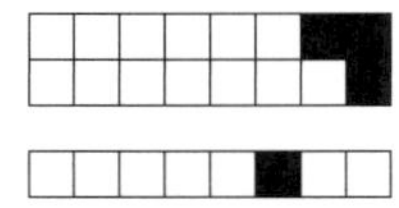

```
ArrayPlot[IntegerDigits[#,2,8]&/@{4,1}]
ArrayPlot[IntegerDigits[#,2,8]&/@{4+1}]
```

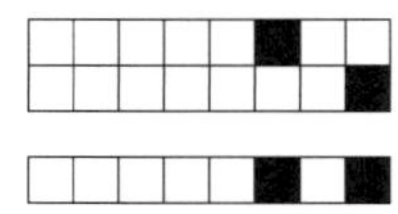

```
ArrayPlot[IntegerDigits[#,2,8]&/@{123,16}]
ArrayPlot[IntegerDigits[#,2,8]&/@{123+16}]
```

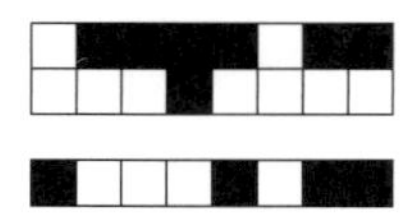

THE BRICKWORK EXAMPLE

Refer to Writing & Code *: Interpreters, Compilers, and Abstraction.*

The following provides an example of an interpreter in action with a 'special' (as in specially configured for this exercise) Turing machine.

THE SETUP
The status of this machine is determined by 6 attributes:

It sits at a position 'x, y, z' and has an orientation 'φ'. Furthermore, there is the last executed command 'c' and the width of any next step it is to take, 's'.

```
{{x,y,z,ϕ},c,s};
```

This, in our example, is the initial status of the machine:

```
pos:={{-2,-2,0,-π/2},SF,1};
```

Here is a graphic representation of this status:

```
AsPoints2D[pts_] := {
    Red,Thickness[.005],
    Arrow/@Partition[#[[1,1;;2]]&/@pts,2,1],
    Black, Disk[#[[1,1;;2]],1/6]&/@pts
    }
```

This is the stage – the plane that takes the place of the tape in the Turing machine – on which this machine will be operating:

```
gr2D:=Graphics[{
   Thin,Red,InfiniteLine[{0,0},{1,0}],
   Blue,InfiniteLine[{0,0},{0,1}],
   Black,play
   },
  PlotRange→{{-5,5},{-5,5}},
  GridLines→{Range[-5,5],Range[-5,5]}
  ]
```

And this is how we perform our first operation:

```
gr2D/.play→AsPoints2D@{pos}
```

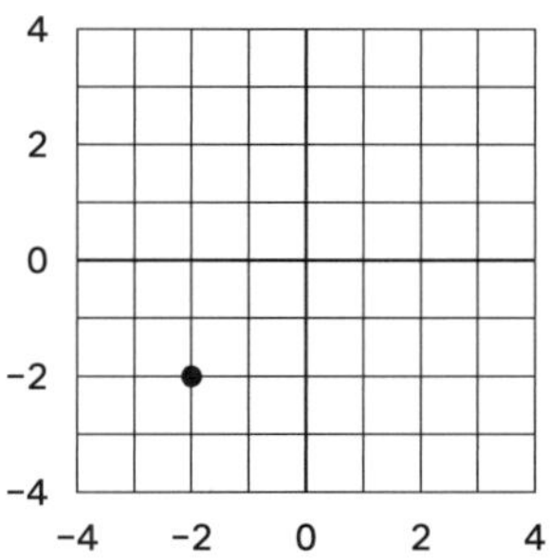

THE COMMANDS

Apart from the status of the machine and its stage, we also define rules or commands to change this status. For example, 'advance by one brick', called 'SF' (step forward):

```
SF[{pos_,cmd_,d_}]:={
  Join[pos[[1;;3]]+
    {d,0,0}.RotationMatrix[pos[[4]],{0,0,1}],
   List@pos[[4]]],
  SF, d}
```

```
SF@pos
{{-2,-1,0,-(π/2)},SF,1}
```

This gives us an initial track for the machine:

```
gr2D/.play→AsPoints2D@{pos,SF@pos}
```

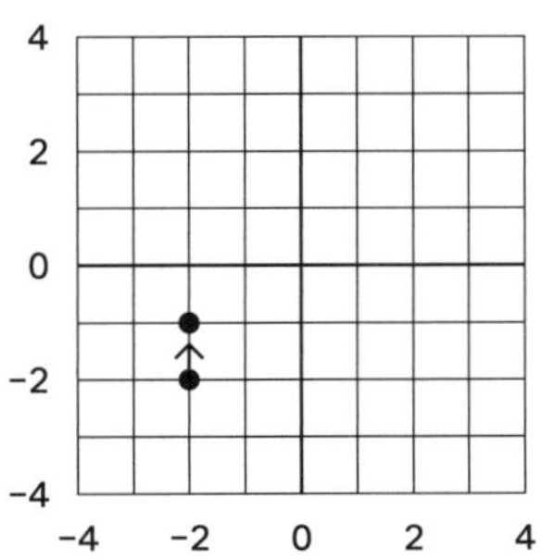

We can write corresponding commands for a whole set of commands: 'step left' (SL):

```
SL[{pos_,cmd_,d_}]:={
  Join[pos[[1;;3]]+
    {d,0,0}.RotationMatrix[
      pos[[4]]-π/2,{0,0,1}],{pos[[4]]-π/2}],
  SL,d}
```

```
SL@pos
{{-3,-2,0,-π},SL,1}
```

'Step right' (SR):

```
SR[{pos_,cmd_,d_}]:=
 {Join[pos[[1;;3]]+
    {d,0,0}.RotationMatrix[
      pos[[4]]+π/2,{0,0,1}],{pos[[4]]+π/2}],
  SR, d}
```

```
SR@pos
{{-1,-2,0,0},SR,1}
```

'Step back' (SB):

```
SB[{pos_,cmd_,d_}]:=
 {Join[pos[[1;;3]]+
    {d,0,0}.RotationMatrix[
      pos[[4]]+π,{0,0,1}],{pos[[4]]+π}],
  SB,d}
```

```
SB@pos
{{-2,-3,0,π/2},SB,1}
```

'Place half a brick' (SH):

```
SH[{pos_,cmd_,d_}]:={pos,SH,d}
```

```
SH@pos
{{-2,-2,0,-(π/2)},SH,1}
```

'Advance one step without laying a brick to create an opening in the wall' (SO):

```
SO[{pos_,cmd_,d_}]:=
 {Join[pos[[1;;3]]+
    {d,0,0}.RotationMatrix[
      pos[[4]],{0,0,1}],{pos[[4]]}],
  SO,d}
```

```
SO@pos
{{-2,-1,0,-(π/2)},SO,1}
```

Having defined a library of such commands, we now can put them into a sequence, which is the first step towards a new interpreted language.

This is the starting position for the machine, the code for the movements and a generic function, which translates the sequence of instructions to a sequence of positions:

```
pos:={{-2,-3,0,0},{},1}
code:={SL,SF,SF,SF,SF,SF,SR,SF,SF,SF, SR}
trace=Short@FoldList[#2[#1]&,pos,code]
{{{-2,-3,0,0},{},1},{{-2,-2,0,-π/2},SL,1},
 {{-2,-1,0,-π/2},SF,1},{{-2,0,0,-π/2},SF,1},
 {{-2,1,0,-π/2},SF,1},{{-2,2,0,-π/2},SF,1},
 {{-2,3,0,-π/2},SF,1},{{-1,3,0,0},SR,1},
 {{0,3,0,0},SF,1},{{1,3,0,0},SF,1},
 {{2,3,0,0},SF,1},{{2,2,0,π/2},SR,1}}
```

Here is what it looks like:

```
gr2D/.play→AsPoints2D@trace
```

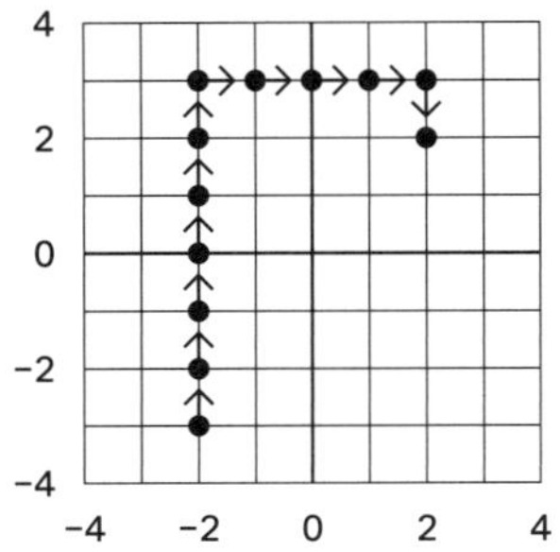

A LANGUAGE AND AN INTERPRETER

Now we go one step further and build an interpreter into a language which allows us to more adequately describe the paths. This, for example, shall be the code that instructs the machine to take 8 steps forward and 6 to the left:

```
codeC="7L5R7R4R";
```

The interpreter (in its own right a little 'machine') translates a new syntax into the command line above. To implement this, we use rules that expand the new code into the old one:

```
CodeStr2List[code_]:=
 Module[{cmd,par},
  cmd=Characters@
    StringReplace[code,_?DigitQ→""];
  par=ToExpression/@
    StringSplit[code,_?LetterQ];
  Transpose[{cmd,par}]
  ]

rules:={
  {"F",x_}:>(SF&/@ Range[x]),
  {"L",x_}:>Prepend[SF&/@ Range[x-1],SL],
  {"R",x_}:>Prepend[SF&/@ Range[x-1],SR],
  {"B",x_}:>Prepend[SF&/@ Range[x-1],SB],
  {"W",x_}:>Prepend[SO&/@ Range[x-1],SO],
  {"H",x_}:>SH
  }
```

And this is the interpreter at work:

```
codeC="7L5R7R4R";

codeL=CodeStr2List@codeC
{{L,7},{R,5},{R,7},{R,4}}
```

```
code=Flatten[codeL /. rules]
{SL,SF,SF,SF,SF,SF,SF,SR,SF,SF,SF,SF,
 SR,SF,SF,SF,SF,SF,SF,SR,SF,SF,SF}
```

Just as we've seen earlier, this code can be executed as both a graphic and as a calculation:

```
pos={{-2.5,-3.5,0, 0},SF,1};
spur:=FoldList[#2[#1]&,pos, code]
gr2D/.play→AsPoints2D@spur


[…]
```

```
[…]
```

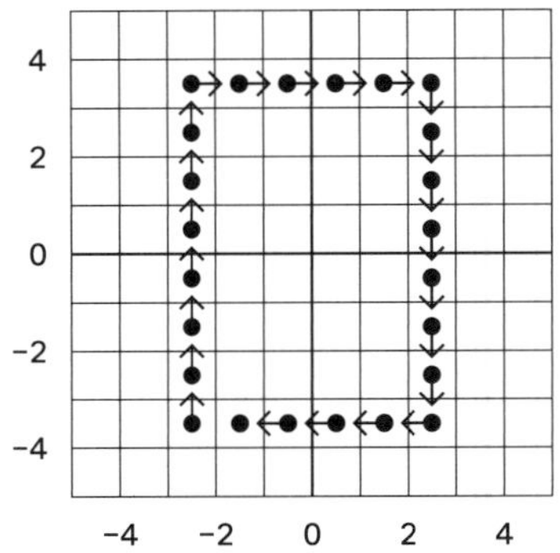

By counting the different steps, we get something of a 'bill of materials' for this construction:

```
BillOfMaterials[play_]:=
 Counts[#[[2]]&/@ play]
```

```
BillOfMaterials@spur
<|SF→20,SL→1,SR→3|>
```

We can now wrap these steps into a single function called 'Interpreter01':

```
Interpreter01[pos_,code_]:=
 Module[{codeL1, codeL2, rules},
  codeL1:=CodeStr2List@code;
  rules = {
    {"F",x_}:>(SF&/@ Range[x]),
    {"L",x_}:>Prepend[SF&/@ Range[x-1],SL],
    {"R",x_}:>Prepend[SF&/@ Range[x-1],SR],
    {"B",x_}:>Prepend[SF&/@ Range[x-1],SB],
    {"W",x_}:>Prepend[SO&/@ Range[x-1],SO],
    {"H",x_}:>SH};
  codeL2:=Flatten[codeL1/.rules];
  FoldList[#2[#1]&,pos,codeL2]
  ]
```

And, in a most compact and entirely suitable notation

```
pos={{-5/2,-7/2,0,0},SF,1};
codeC="7L5R7R4R";
pts=Interpreter01[pos,codeC];
gr2D/.play→AsPoints2D@pts
```

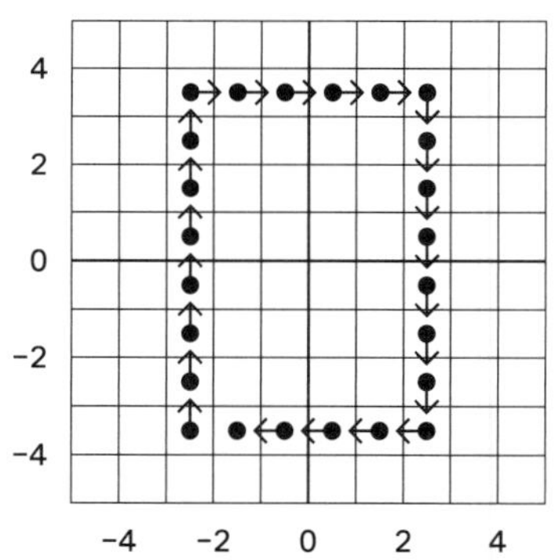

Now, instead of positioning the elements as central spots in each location, we want to place them so as to align with each other. The problem we now face are the symmetries of the corners. If we program a new actor we can get all the parameters of a step:

```
AsLines2D[pts_]:={Red,
  Module[{x1,y1,z1,l1,c1,a1,x2,y2,z2,
      l2,c2,a2,d,gr,tr},
     {{x1,y1,z1,a1},c1,l1}=#[[1]];
     {{x2,y2,z2,a2},c2,l2}=#[[2]];
     d=l1/4;
     gr=Polygon[{{d/2,-d/2},
        {d/2,d/2},{l1+d/2,d/2},
        {l1+d/2,-d/2},{d/2,-d/2}}];
     tr=FindGeometricTransform[{{x1,y1},
        {x2,y2}},{{0,0},{l1,0}}][[2]];
     {Disk[{x1,y1},1/18],
      Black,EdgeForm[{White,Thickness[.003]}],

Opacity[1],GeometricTransformation[gr,tr]
       }
     ]&/@ Partition[pts,2,1]
  }
```

```
gr2D/.play→AsLines2D@
   Interpreter01[{{-1.5,-2.5,0,0},SF,1},
    "5L3R5R"]
```

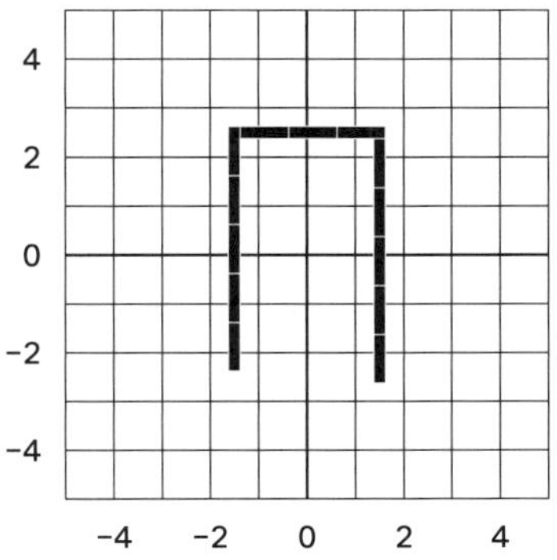

What's missing now is a fitting point:

```
AsLines2DP[pts_]:={
      Module[{x1,y1,z1,l1,c1,a1,d},
     {{x1,y1,z1,a1},c1,l1}=#;
     d = l1/4;
    {Black,EdgeForm[{White,Thickness[.003]}],
     Opacity[1],Black,Polygon[{
        {x1-d/2,y1-d/2},{x1-d/2,y1+d/2},
        {x1+d/2,y1+ d/2},{x1+d/2,y1-d/2},
        {x1-d/2,y1-d/2}}]
     }]&/@ pts}
```

And this is the code combined:

```
p1={{-1.5,-2.5,0,0},SF,1};
p2={{-2.5,-3.5,0,0},SF,1};
gr2D /.play→ {
   AsPoints2D@Interpreter01[p2,"7L5R7R4R"],
   AsLines2D@Interpreter01[p1,"5L3R5R"],
   AsLines2DP@{p1}
   }
```

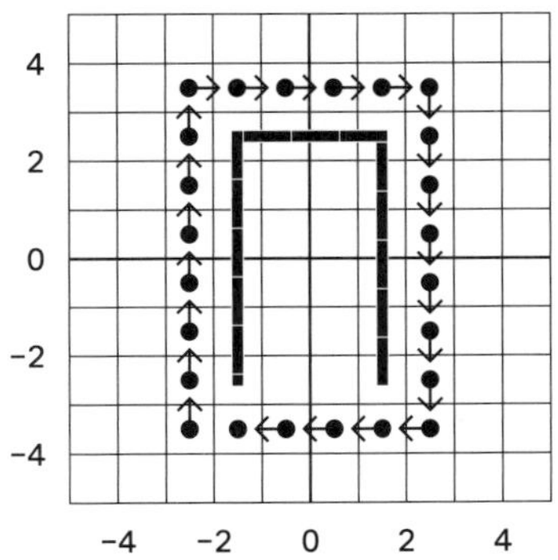

And now, on a reduced 'stage' and graphic (this is a bit like giving actors different costumes), but with the same logic and 'text':

```
spur={
   AsPoints2DR@Interpreter01[p2,"7L5R7R4R"],
   AsLines2DR@Interpreter01[p1,"5L3R5R"],
   AsLines2DPR@{p1}
   };
gr2DR/.play→ spur
```

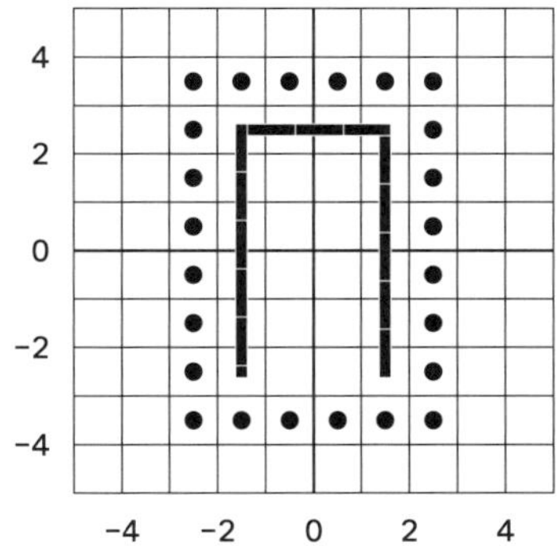

So far so good. We can now direct the proportions, add more details, even construct a building.

It is interesting to note, however, what we actually use to describe this little temple: we develop a simple but adequate language and implement an interpreter. We then get a very compact code of just a few bytes for our building: "7L5R7R4R" and "5L3R5R". That's it.

The hypothesis is that we can model any building like this: you can make a structured model and a compact representation of it by following the principles of a Turing machine and coding your object, instead of drawing it.

THE EXECUTION

You also get a whole lot more. We already had the 'bill of materials', which conceptually is just another rendering of the same structure, implemented as a different interpreter.

```
BillOfMaterials/@{
  Interpreter01[p2,"7L5R7R4R"],
  Interpreter01[p1,"5L3R5R"],
  {p1}}

{<|SF→20,SL→1,SR→3|>,<|SF→11,
  SL→1,SR→2|>,<|SF→1|>}
```

Or we can 'film' the stage play instead of taking a 'photo' of the finished construction. This just needs a step-by-step execution: no change in actors (for graphical reasons we choose simplified costumes), code or interpreter:

```
gr2DRS/.play→Take[spurF,#]&/@
   (Range@Length[spurF=Flatten[spur,2]]);
Row[%]


[…]
```

[…]

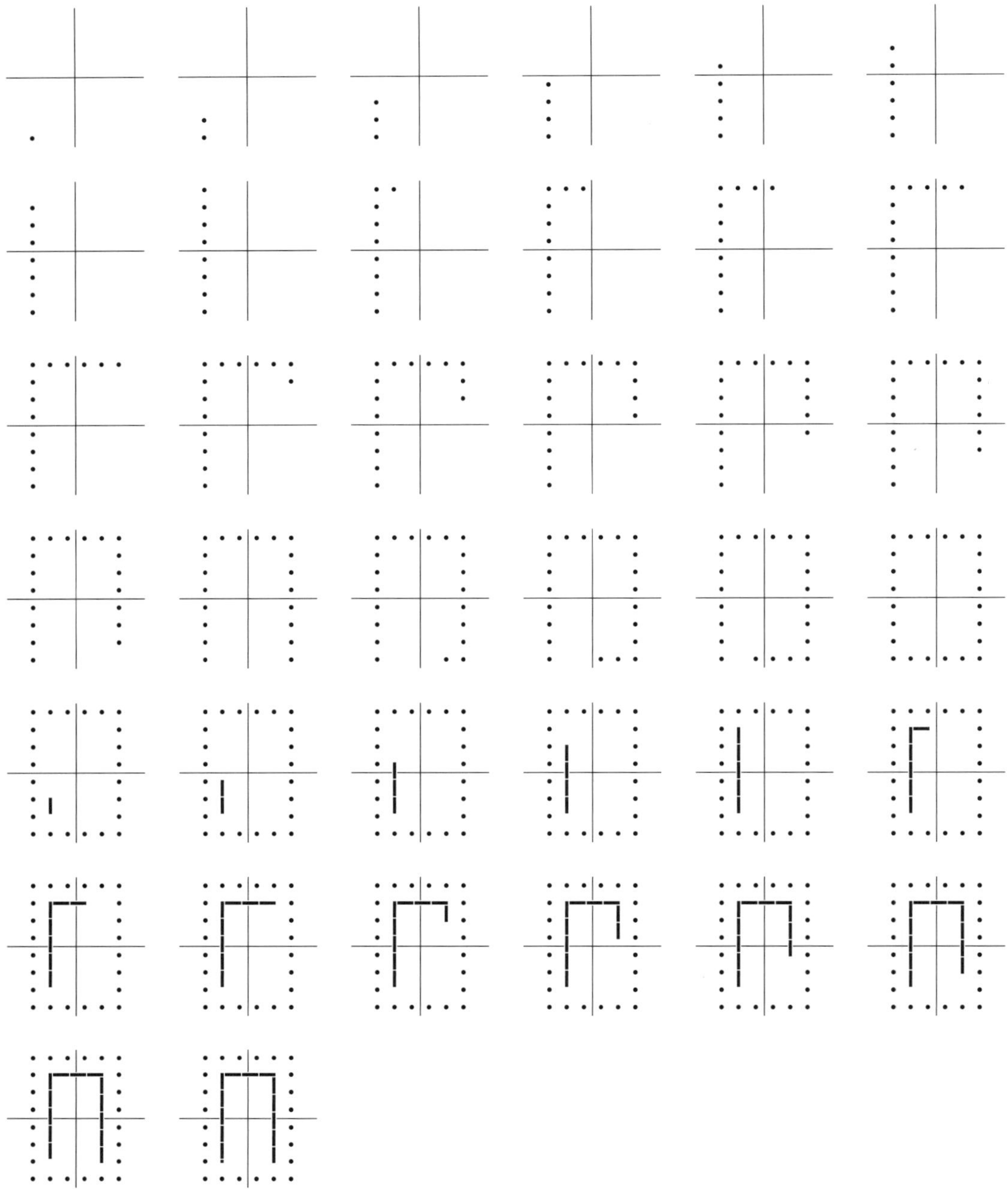

ASSEMBLY BY ROBOT

Let's have a look now at a machine that can actually position these elements. We don't need to change the structure of the building for this. We can immediately and simply specify a robot: it's a moveable structure with variable form. What we have to describe are the position of the robot (x, y), the lengths of the individual axes (translations), and the rotation angle of the joints. Subsequently, the points, the lengths and the rotations are assembled in the correct order, and that's all there is to it: we've just defined the movability of the robot:

```
L0={0,0,0};
P0=L0;

T1=TranslationTransform[{0,0,2}];
P1=T1@P0;

R1=RotationTransform[α,{0,0,1},{0,0,0}];
R2=RotationTransform[β,{0,1,0},{0,0,0}];
[…]
```

```
[…]
T2=TranslationTransform[{4,0,0}];
P2=T1@R1@R2@T2@P0;

R3=RotationTransform[δ,{0,1,0},{0,0,0}];
T3=TranslationTransform[{5/2,0,0}];
P3=T1@R1@R2@T2@R3@T3@P0;
```

The joints of the robot are now equations in linear algebra with the variables α, β and δ. But this is of no great concern to us in detail, because we have defined them in the simple form of the Lambda calculus:

```
struct={P0,P1,P2,P3}
 {{0,0,0},{0,0,2},
 {4 Cos[α] Cos[β],4Cos[β]Sin[α],2-4Sin[β]},
 {Cos[α](Cos[β](4+5Cos[δ]/2)-5Sin[β]
Sin[δ]/2),
  Sin[α](Cos[β](4+5Cos[δ]/2)-5Sin[β]
Sin[δ])/2,
  2-(4+5Cos[δ]/2)Sin[β]-5Cos[β]Sin[δ]/2}}
```

We can solve these equations and thus find the position of the joints by determining the angles:

```
param={α→π,β→-45°,δ→90°};
rp=struct/.param
{{0,0,0},{0,0,2},{-2√[2],0,2+2√[2]},
 {-(5/(2 √[2]))-2√[2],0,2-5/(2√[2])+2√[2]}}
```

This is the graphics of the robot:

```
robotG[struct_, param_]  :=
 Module[{rp=struct/. param},
  {White,
   GraphicsComplex[
    Join[rp,{
      rp[[1]]+ (rp[[2]]-rp[[1]])/3
      }],{
     Cylinder[{1,5}, 1],
     Cylinder[{1,2}, 1/2],
     Sphere[2, 1/2],
     Cylinder[{2,3}, 1/3],
     Sphere[3, 1/3],
     Cylinder[{3,4}, 1/5]
     }]}]
```

This is the graphic function of the stage (background):

```
Options[ShowRobot]={"points"→{}};
ShowRobot[struct_, param_,OptionsPattern[]]:=
 Graphics3D[{EdgeForm[],
   Red,InfiniteLine[{0,0,0},{1,0,0}],
   Green,InfiniteLine[{0,0,0},{0,1,0}],
   Orange,robotG[struct, param],
   Red,Sphere[#,.3]&/@ OptionValue["points"]
   },Boxed→False,ImageSize→256,
  PlotRange→{{-8,8},{-5,5},{-1,6}}]
```

This is the control of the robot:

```
Manipulate[
 ShowRobot[struct,{α→a,β→b,δ→c}],
 {a,0,360°},{b,0,360°},{c,0,360°}]
```

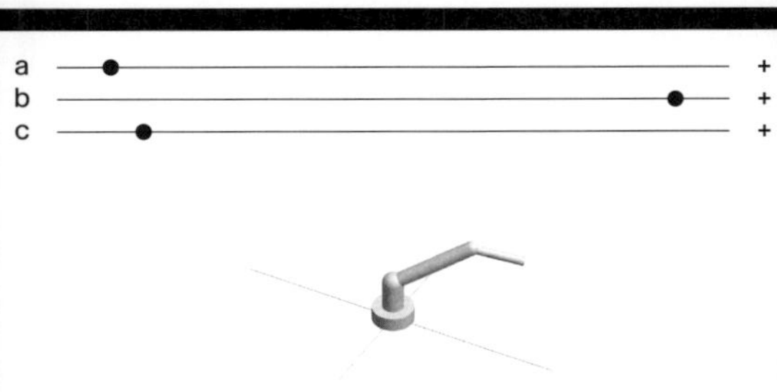

We also want to limit the range of motion for the robot. For example, a joint can only move within a specified angle:

```
robotConstr=
  {α,β,δ}∈Reals &&
   -π<=α<=π &&
   -π/2<=β<=0 &&
   0<=δ<=3π/4;
```

Now we can eliminate those angles that do not work mechanically – this would be the graphic:

```
param2={α→π,β→-60°,δ→-160°};
ShowRobot[struct,param2]
```

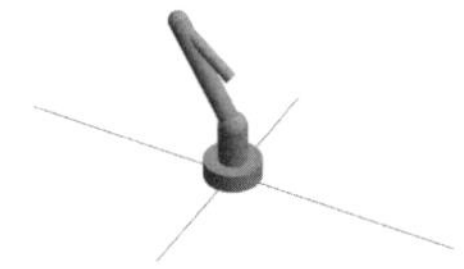

These are the tests:

```
robotConstr/.param
robotConstr/.param2
True
False
```

Now we determine the point on the 'artefact': the robot shall approach this position of the artefact; in other words, 'P5' equals the point at which the artefact is currently positioned. Now, the status of the robot is defined by the three angles α, β and δ.

This is our situation:

```
artefact={{-4,-3,0}};
ShowRobot[struct,param,"points"→artefact]
```

Remember the formula for the endpoint of the structure of the robot:

```
P3
{Cos[α](Cos[β](4+5Cos[δ]/2)-5Sin[β]Sin[δ]/2),
 Sin[α](Cos[β](4+5Cos[δ]/2)-5Sin[β]Sin[δ]/2),
 2-(4+5 Cos[δ]/2) Sin[β]-5/2 Cos[β] Sin[δ]}
```

It's a surprisingly simple process: we can just calculate the angles of the robot arm by equating the movability of the robot with the point of the artefact, in other words, by solving the linear equations. We see that there are several possible combinations for the angles:

```
sol=N@Solve[P3==artefact[[1]],
    {α,β,δ}]/.C[_]→0
{{α→0.643501,β→-3.06983,δ→-1.22653},
 {α→0.643501,β→2.30882,δ→1.22653},
 {α→-2.49809,β→0.83276,δ→-1.22653},
 {α→-2.49809,β→-0.07175,δ→1.22653}}
```

This is one solution that works:

```
robotConstr/.#&/@ sol
{False,False,False,True}
```

This is to select a solution that meets the constraints:

```
pos1=RandomChoice@Select[sol,
robotConstr/.#&]
{α→-2.49809,β→-0.07175,δ→1.22654}
```

This is to control the robot by this solution:

```
ShowRobot[struct, pos1, "points"→artefact]
```

Now we can work with a series of points:

```
artefact={{3,-2,0},{4,-2,0},{4,-1,0},
   {4,0,0},{4,1,0},{4,2,0},{4,3,0},
   {3,3,0},{2,3,0},{1,3,0}};
path=N@Solve[P3==# ,{α,β,δ}]/.C[_]→ 0&/@
   artefact;
params=RandomChoice@
    Select[#,robotConstr/.#&]&/@ path
{{α→-0.58800,β→-0.11852,δ→1.83640},
 {α→-0.46364,β→-0.11273,δ→1.48318},
 {α→-0.24497,β→-0.12413,δ→1.63333},
 {α→0.,β→-0.12527,δ→1.68353},
 {α→0.24497,β→-0.12413,δ→1.63333},
 {α→0.46364,β→-0.11273,δ→1.48318},
 {α→0.64350,β→-0.07175,δ→1.22653},
 {α→0.78539,β→-0.12158,δ→1.58329},
 {α→0.98279,β→-0.11852,δ→1.83640},
 {α→1.24904,β→-0.09042,δ→1.99599}}
```

And this is our robot working:

```
Magnify[Row[
  ShowRobot[struct,params[[#]],
     "points"→artefact[[1;;#]]
     ]&/@ Range@Length@path],1/2]
```

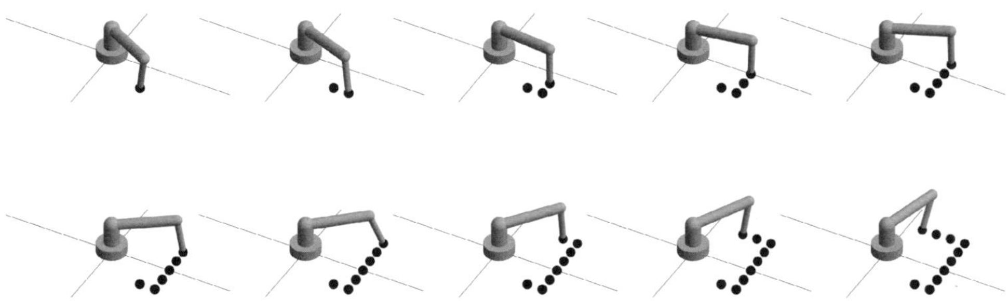

It's important to understand that the digital production is a rendering, and so the digital architectural model does not entail its own production. In this example we deduced the movement of the production of a model. But even with complex architectural models, this process is no different, nor does it have to be described much more comprehensively. All it took for the translation of a model into its production were about 2,700 characters.

THE CONCEPTS OF COMPUTER LANGUAGES IN DETAIL

□ ↖376

Refer to Writing & Code*: A Synoptic Comparison.*

HIGH-LEVEL (IMPERATIVE) LANGUAGES

Languages such as *Fortran*, *C*, or *Pascal* introduce an *abstraction* of flow control. We distinguish between geometric, logical, arithmetic and algebraic aspects of this abstraction.

THE GEOMETRIC ASPECT

In geometry, the 'points' of a flow are determined. High-level languages expand the sequential flow (the 'real line') of machine languages by the concepts of *iteration*, *selection*, and *recursion*.

ITERATION A repetition that is controlled directly by a variable:

```
Do[Print[i],{i,4}]
1
2
3
4
```

SELECTION A differentiation of cases which controls the flow of the program:

```
If[x<10,"small","big"]/.{{x→-1 },{x→2}}
{small, big}
Cases[{1,1,"a",2,3,"ball",2.3,9},_Integer]
{1,1,2,3,9}
```

RECURSION The result of a function is being newly processed by this function, until an abort criterion is met; for example, 'keep dividing by 2 until the result is no longer an even number':

```
NestWhileList[#/2&,123456,EvenQ]
{123456,61728,30864,15432,7716,3858,1929}
```

```
FoldList[Plus,0,{a,b,c,d}]
FoldList[Plus,0,{1,2,3,4}]

{0,a,a+b,a+b+c,a+b+c+d}
{0,1,3,6,10}
```

THE LOGICAL ASPECT:
THE STATE – ORTHOGONALITY,
NO SIDE EFFECTS

The logical aspect qualifies the geometrical point of a sequence (as above) with a variable. When in machine languages the data were almost physically tied to a certain address (we used the metaphor of a storage shelf), high-level languages use variables which either point to an address (in which case they are characters), or they potentially do so, in which case they are symbols.

The symbol 'x', in this following example, is anchored to a memory address which contains the number '3':

```
x=3
x

3
3
```

In high-level languages, variables have to be allocated to a *type* so that memory management – that is the reservation of sufficient bits for a variable – can be automated. In *Java*, for example, a variable has to be explicitly defined with a character:

```
int x=3;
```

In *Mathematica*, by contrast, this allocation is implicit, and happens by symbol. So the function 'Head' can ask for the current type of the symbol:

```
x=3;
Head@x

Integer
```

```
b="Der Baum";
Head@b
StringLength@b

String
8
```

Important about variables is that: 1) variables of the same type can be processed in the same way (*polymorphism* of points), and 2) their contents are independent of each other (*orthogonality* of points).

THE ARITHMETIC ASPECT

Through flow control and the introduction of variables, we can expand the concept of a function. While machine languages only know a few logical functions (such as AND, OR, XOR, NOT), and basic arithmetic operations (such as +, –,*) in high-level languages liberally assembled operations can be labelled as functions with a name:

```
Add[a_,b_]:=a + b
Add[3,4]
Add[5,3]

7
8
```

Or:

```
Absolut[x_]:=If[x<0,-x,x]
Absolut/@{-3,4}

{3,4}
```

Also, functions can call up other functions, creating nested functions:

```
Add2[a_,b_]:=Absolut[a] + Absolut[b]
Add2[-3,4]

7
```

Or, even nicer:

```
Add3[a_,b_]:=Add@@Absolut/@{a,b}
Add3[-3,4]

7
```

Because these functions can be nested, we determine the scope of application for the definitions of variables. There is a fundamental difference between *global* and *local* scope of application.

In this following example, a global variable 'c' is determined. We then define the function 'Add', which determines a local variable with the same name. We then call up the function 'Add' with the value of the global variable 'c'; the value of the local variable 'c' is printed, and as we leave the function, the global value once again applies to the variable 'c':

```
c=5;
Add[a_Integer,b_Integer]:=
 Module[{c},
  c=a + b;
  Print[c];
  c]
Add[c,c]
c
10
10
10
```

Similarly, we can typify the parameters of a function, so that, for example, in the following case an addition of non-integers is not carried out:

```
c=5.2;
Add[c,c]

10.4
```

THE ALGEBRAIC ASPECT
Not only can we assemble and label processes as functions, but data types too are assembled in high-level languages. Next to the basic data types of a machine language (integer, float, character), high-level languages also recognise composite types such as lists, arrays, enumerations and records:

```
p=<|“a”→2,“b”→1|>
<|a→2,b→1|>
```

```
p[“b”]
1
```

```
ReplacePart[p,“b”→ 5]
<|a→2,b→5|>
```

Lists:

```
a=List[2,3,4,5]
{2,3,4,5}
```

And there is always a set of functions which handles these composite data types appropriately, for example:

```
Append[a,6]
{2,3,4,5,6}
```

```
Extract[a,{{4},{1}}]
{5,2}
```

OBJECT-ORIENTED (DECLARATIVE) LANGUAGES
Remember: while the high-level (imperative) languages of the 1960s and onwards introduced an abstraction of the process, from about 1980 onwards, object-oriented (declarative) languages abstract data types. Imperative languages treat variables as characters and process them as rational, concrete tracks. They describe how a program should run. Declarative languages by contrast treat variables as symbols and concern themselves with what processes are to be carried out in order to achieve any particular goal. They describe what a program is capable of. Their basic concept is not to assemble functions that do the same thing, but to assemble functions that process the same things. Now the similarity of objects – whatever they happen to be defined as – stands at the fore.

THE ARITHMETIC ASPECT – THE MANY FUNCTIONS
From an object-oriented perspective we don't talk about variables and functions which are applicable either globally or locally, but about characteristics and methods of *objects* that are defined globally and locally. These objects therefore bundle characteristics and methods.

Here, for example, is an object that behaves like a counter. It has a state (variable 'n'), it can increase this state by 1 (method 'incr') and it can be reset to 0:

```
Needs[“Class‘Class’”];
Class [counter]:={
   n=0,counter
   reset[]:=This.n=0
   };
```

Here now we distinguish between a *schema* and an *instance*. The *schema* determines the principle of the object. This principle is expressed in concrete terms in the *instances*:

```
z1=New.counter[];
z2=New.counter[];
```

The two counters 'c1' and 'c2' now are in charge of the whole apparatus of the class 'counter'. Their data and functions work entirely independently of each other. They are *individual* counters:

```
z1.incr[]
z1.incr[]
z2.incr[]
z1.incr[]
z1.n
z2.n
z1.reset[]
1
2
1
3
3
1
0
```

THE ALGEBRAIC ASPECT
Schemas of objects form hierarchies. And here we talk about *heredity*. In this following example, we have an expanded counter which can count up and down. It is defined as an extension of the counter we saw above. Its instance inherits the status variable 'n' and the method 'incr' and in addition gets a method 'decr', which the two simple counters of the example above did not know:

```
Class[counterW,counter]:={
   decr[]:=This.n -=1
   };
z3=New.counterW[];
z3.incr[]
z3.incr[]
z3.decr[]
z1.decr[]
1
2
1
```

THE GEOMETRIC ASPECT – THE PROBLEMS – WHAT IS IMPLICITLY REQUIRED
Objects no longer follow the notion of an absolute time; objects formulate processes with specific temporal behaviours.

This following example shows what are known as *coroutines* (as in 'co-routines' or 'sub-routines'): a function is being invoked in four different processes which are carried out in parallel and their results summarised as a list:

```
fl[n_]:=2*n;
DistributeDefinitions[fl];
res=Table[ParallelSubmit[{i},fl[i]],
          {i,2,16,4}]
WaitAll@res
```

```
{ fl[2]  finished ,
  fl[6]  finished ,
  fl[10] finished ,
  fl[14] finished }

{4,12,20,28}
```

Events are a further manifestation of process control. In this following example, we see a process which is coupled to a graphic element (the plane framed in black), which awaits a mouse click to move the position of the circle to the position of the cursor:

```
DynamicModule[
 {pt={0,0}},
 ClickPane[
  Graphics[{Red,Dynamic@Circle[pt]}],
  (pt=#)&]]
```

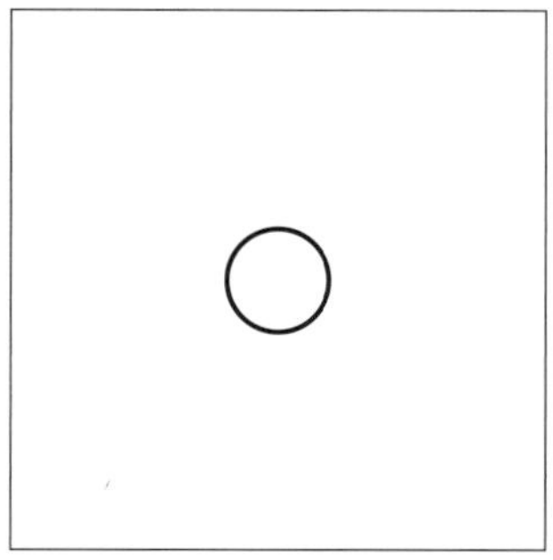

All known user interfaces are systems of objects whose processes await events that are triggered or instigated by the user.

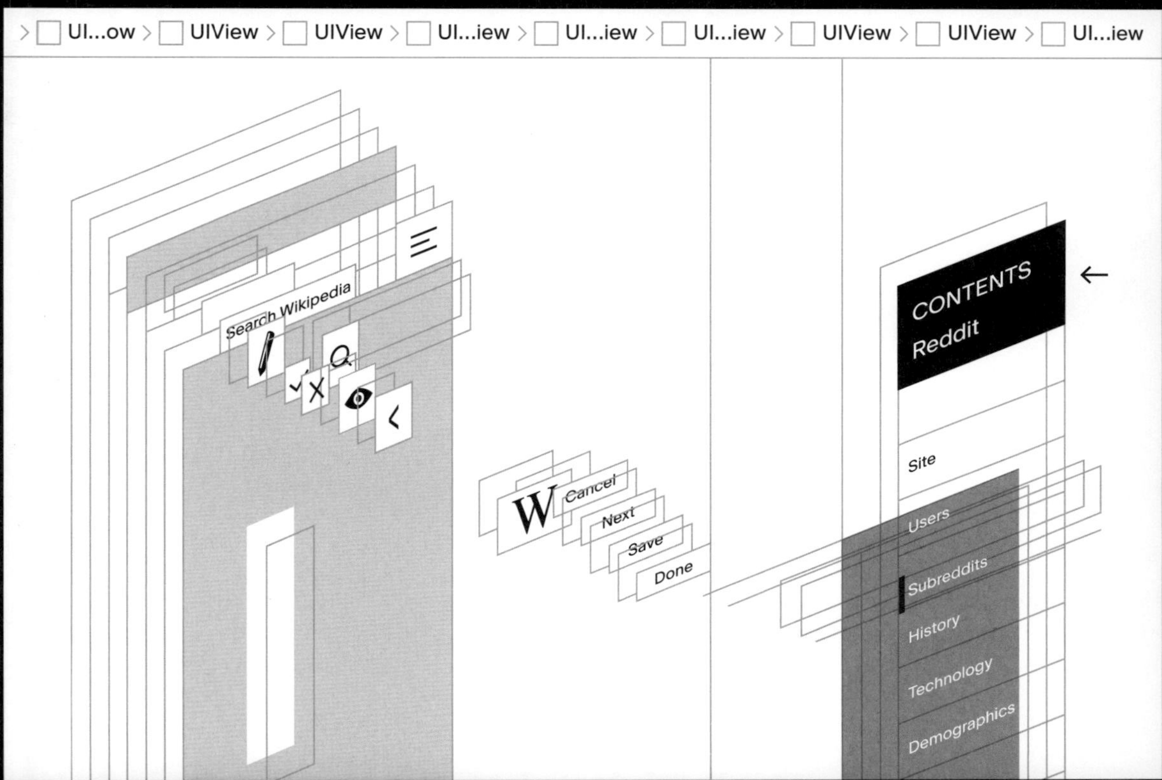

THE LOGICAL ASPECT
Here too we encounter the fundamental principle of *polymorphism*: the idea that systems of objects should have *interfaces* that are as consistent, even uniform, as possible, even if internally they work in very different ways. Here, we are really dealing with the state or *condition* of objects:

```
Class[counterR,counter]:={
   limit=1,
   counterR[l_]:=This.limit=l,
   Override.incr[]:=
    This.n=Mod[Super.incr[],This.limit]
   };

z4=New.counterR[3];
z4.incr[]&/@Range@12
{1,2,0,1,2,0,1,2,0,1,2,0}
```

This counter, which counts in even numbers, has the same interface as our first simple counter above, which keeps on counting:

```
z1.incr[]&/@Range@12
{1,2,3,4,5,6,7,8,9,10,11,12}
```

WRITING AND TALKING IN THE INTERNET (MARKUP LANGUAGE)

We now, with the near universal proliferation of access to the Internet, attain a level of saturation. The conception of a programming language is in essence structuralist, and therefore for our time probably no longer adequate. In the Internet, computing is neither about flow control, nor is it about the management of objects. It is much more about a fluid, general conversation: talking and writing, and that's what we use natural languages for.

In that sense the *markup languages* of the Internet are standardised exchange formats between programming languages. For example, it's standards around the markup language *XML (Extensible Markup Language)* that have asserted themselves for *instances*; while for *schemas*, they have done so around *XSL (Extensible Stylesheet Language)*. It's these markup languages that we use to describe things and their relationships in the Internet in the object-orientated manner we saw earlier. XML is used to describe data. Normally you need object-orientated applications to generate and process these data. *AJAX (Asynchronous JavaScript and XML)* is a standard of the XML family, which makes it possible to actively query the XML data of another application. The data of the Internet are formulated in XML. Since this standard integrates the schemas, these data can take any possible structure. Very large quantities of data with many possible structures form what today we mean by the term 'big data'.

This much about data types in the Internet. They do not represent any great novelty compared to object-orientated paradigms. The inventions of the Internet age lie in probabilistic flow control which, since approximately 2000, can be established with machine learning algorithms. And here, interestingly, it is not so much about giving programs an (imperative) form or a (declarative) structure, but to give applications an attractive stability within the endless data stream of the Internet. This, we would argue is no longer primarily a question of a language itself, but of talking and of the ability to speak in principle, in other words of literacy. Which is why we talk of computer literacy throughout this *Atlas*.

Colophon

EDITORS
Ludger Hovestadt
ETH Zürich, Department of Architecture,
Chair for Digital Architectonics

Urs Hirschberg
TU Graz, Institute of Architecture
and Media

Oliver Fritz
HTWG Konstanz University of Applied
Sciences, Chair of Digital Media
and Architecture

WRITER
Sebastian Michael

CONTRIBUTORS
Diana Alvarez-Marin, Jakob Beetz,
André Borrmann, Petra von Both,
Harald Gatermann, Marco Hemmerling,
Ursula Kirschner, Reinhard König,
Dominik Lengyel, Bob Martens,
Frank Petzold, Sven Pfeiffer, Miro Roman,
Kay Römer, Hans Sachs, Philipp Schaerer,
Sven Schneider, Odilo Schoch,
Milena Stavric, Peter Zeile, Nikolaus Zieske

COPY EDITOR
Sebastian Michael

ACQUISITIONS EDITOR
David Marold, Birkhäuser Verlag, AT-Vienna

CONTENT AND PRODUCTION EDITOR
Angelika Gaal, Birkhäuser Verlag, AT-Vienna

DESIGN AND LAYOUT
Onlab: Vanja Golubovic, Matthieu Huegi,
Thibaud Tissot

TYPEFACE
MH Archetype

LITHOGRAPHY
Andreas Gebhardt Reproduktionen

PRINTING
Holzhausen & Gerin Druck GmbH,
AT-Wolkersdorf

Library of Congress Control Number:
2020938918

Bibliographic information published by the
German National Library

The German National Library lists this publication in the Deutsche Nationalbibliografie; detailed bibliographic data are available on the Internet at http://dnb.dnb.de

ISBN 978-3-0356-1989-8 (Softcover)
ISBN 978-3-0356-1990-4 (Hardcover)
e-ISBN 978-3-0356-2011-5 (PDF)

P.O. Box 44, 4009 Basel, Switzerland
Part of Walter de Gruyter GmbH,
Berlin/Boston

9 8 7 6 5 4 3 2 1
www.birkhauser.com

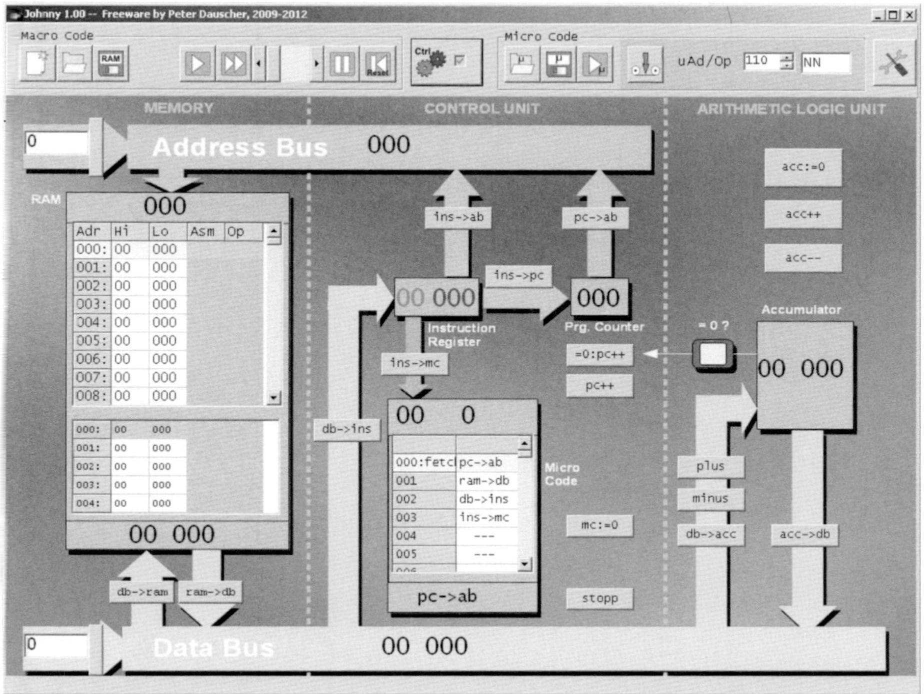

244 ● 374
A detailed simulation of a simple and virtual von Neumann computer.
[*Johnny Simulator*]

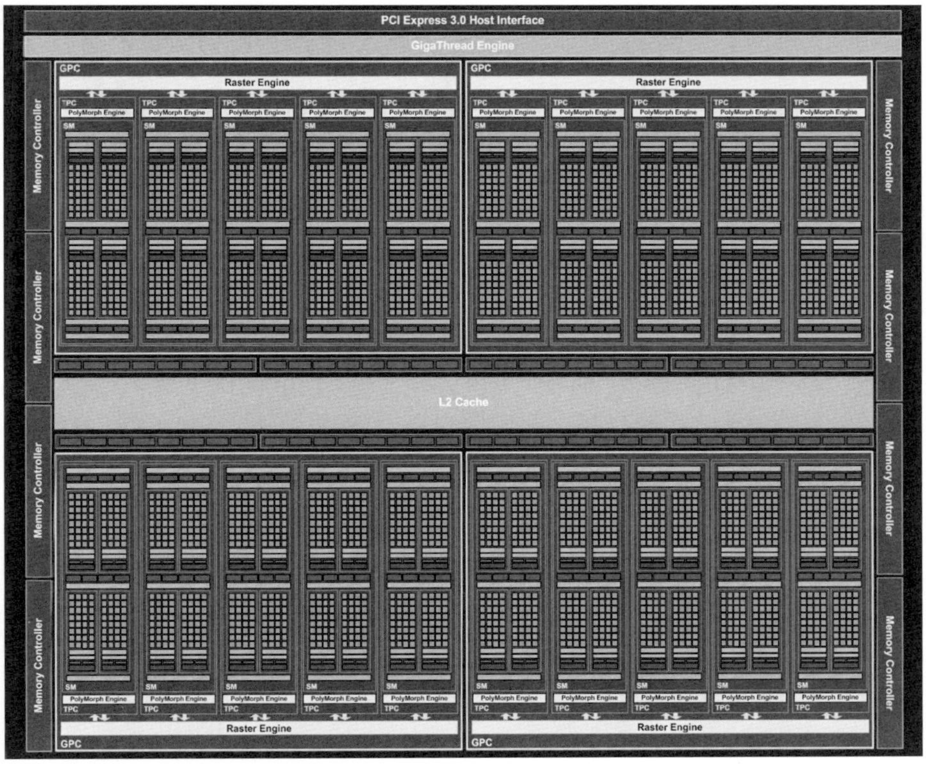

245 ● 374
A block diagram of the full *GP104 Pascal* GPU inside the *GTX 1080*.

246 ● 376
Mainframe computing 1960s.

247A ● 377
Personal computing 1980s.

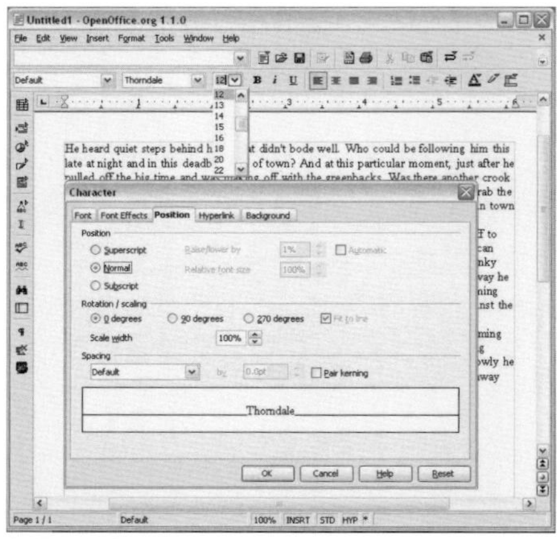

247B ● 377
Windows interface, 1980s.

248 ● 378
XCode programming environment for interfaces of mobile phones, 2000s.

249A ● 378
Mobile computing interfaces, 2000s.

249B ● 378
Mobile computing 2000s.

Colour Plates

III

P. 327–397

235 ○ 338
Bauhaus exhibition poster by Joost Schmidt, 1923.

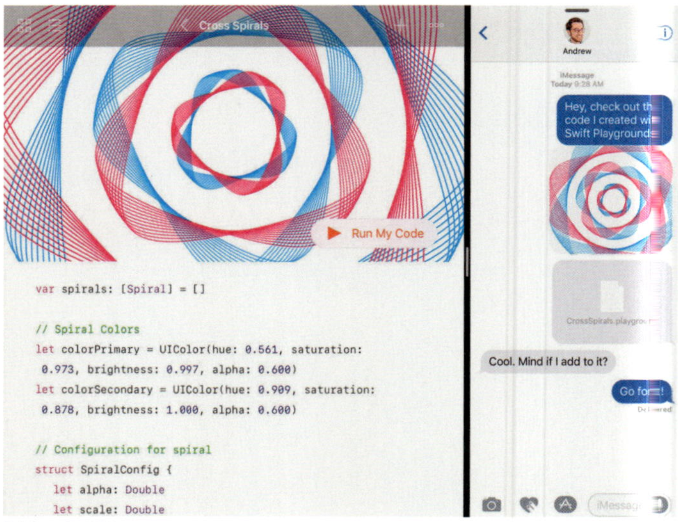

240 ○ 359
Apple's *Swift* combines scripting code with online chat to encourage collaboration.

242 ○ 363
Henderson Waves Bridge, Singapore: London-based IJP Architects used mathematical formulae in the design process. [Schristia]

243 ○ 363
Heydar Aliyev Centre in Baku, Azerbaijan, by Zaha Hadid. Parametric design has enabled a new language of form. [Wertuose]

Digital Manufacturing 405
Model Making 421
3D Printing 439

MATTER & LOGIC
The Physical Representation of Architecture

IV

- Conferences: ECAADE, ACADIA, ICCAD, Fabricate, Shape to Fabrication, Advanced Architectural Geometry, SmartGeometry
- Stephen Kieran and James Timberlake: *Refabricating Architecture: How Manufacturing Methodologies Are Poised to Transform Building Construction*, 2003
- Neil A Gershenfeld: *Fab: The Coming Revolution on Your Desktop – From Personal Computers to Personal Fabrication*, 2005
- Frank Barkow and Regine Leibinger: *An Atlas of Fabrication*, 2009
- Lisa Iwamoto: *Digital Fabrications: Architectural and Material Techniques*, 2009

Digital Manufacturing

Sven Pfeiffer

Overview

'A NEW UNIQUE'

What do a Jacquard loom, the Guggenheim Museum in Bilbao, the Cutty Sark, the Sagrada Família in Barcelona, and the Creative Commons all have in common? Indeed: Digital Manufacturing.

The term 'digital manufacturing' is in itself a misnomer: if we were to interpret 'manufacturing' literally and insist on manufactured objects being hand *(manu-)* made *(factured)* then we would have to concede that digital manufacturing does the exact opposite of 'what it says on the tin', and this, in fact, is one of its central characteristics: digital manufacturing is the production of physical objects directly from a computer generated design and code, with normally hardly any or no manual intervention at all in the actual fabrication. But this is a 'problem' inherent in the English use of the Latin-derived word 'manufacture', and one that we come up against in different guises also when we use it to describe industrial or other machine executed manufacturing.

In the context of architecture especially, digital modelling and digital fabrication are terms you will also encounter, and while there are big overlaps in their usage, we are here going to employ the slightly wider, perhaps more generic term *digital manufacturing.*

In what way, you may be wondering – and we rather hope that you are – does digital manufacturing connect these not only superficially but clearly also fundamentally very different entities named above? Rather than stepping into a linear explanation upfront, we propose to simply embark on this chapter that sits at the junction of so many different strands of exploration, and trust that by the end you will see precisely how they all tie together and also feed into each other.

The roots of digital manufacturing branch into many different sectors, among them aviation, defence, shipbuilding, and the automotive industries, where it therefore has long become standard procedure. In architecture though, while no longer in its infancy, it still finds itself in an early, perhaps establishing, phase. That said, it is now having a major impact on how we as architects do things, and beyond that on what we can envision doing: it not only changes the way we can model and construct, it very much also informs the way we can think; and that is why it is of such great significance to us. It sets a new framework for design and production and thus offers entirely new possibilities in project execution.

Until recently (bearing in mind we are completing this *Atlas* in 2019) the uses of digital manufacturing in architecture have focused principally on rapid prototyping for the production of models, and rapid manufacturing of construction elements (modules, walls, supports, shells, covers) for use onsite as actual building components, but here as elsewhere we are witnessing an acceleration of developments into wider and more varied applications of an expanding range of available technologies.

Arguably the most important of these technologies for architecture at this point is 3D Printing, otherwise □ 439↘ also known as additive manufacturing. In fact, we ■ 441↘ consider it important enough to dedicate a whole chapter to it. There are many other methods though that impact on our practice. We have grouped these into *subtractive processes*, *transformation* and *deformation processes*, *surface treatment*, *joining processes*, and *integrated processes*, and you will ■ find them summarised a little further down under *A Taxonomy of Digital Manufacturing.* ■ 636↘

Common to all digital manufacturing processes □ ↖405 is that they are not reliant on highly specialist, expensive tools and machinery. True, large 3D printers, for example, or big cutting and milling machines are not cheap. But within their capabilities, they are all-purpose apparatus that manufacture the object effectively from start to finish. Also – and this is the crucial point – they are not human operated: what they need to work is a set of software generated instructions. And that means they can easily be shared and put to all kinds of different uses on different projects by different studios or workshops for different clients. This is what gave rise, in the early 2000s, to what has been termed a maker ■ 430↘ culture, as exemplified by the FabLab set up by American computer scientist Neil Gershenfeld (b. 1959) at MIT (Massachusetts Institute of Technology), which facilitates and encourages the sharing of production ■ ↖62 430↘ facilities by small enterprises. Digital manufacturing is ■ therefore from the outset embedded in a sharing and collaborative approach to production, even though its origins conceptually lie in powerful industry sectors with major links to national defence structures.

What it also means is that upfront investment for the production of even short series or individual pieces can be kept low: there is no need to mass produce in order to amortise the hardware costs, because it makes no difference to the machinery whether it produces a number of different objects, or many objects that are identical. Consequently, digital manufacturing allows for highly individual, customised solutions specific to a given location, client, or design prerogative, and this in turn means that digital manufacture enables mass customisation: the production in great numbers ■ of fully customised items. For us this is of particular relevance, because in architecture it is more often than not the case that a bespoke element or part offers the best solution, or that only a very limited number of a given construction component is required.

Eliminating, as it does, human labour at the production stage, digital manufacturing dispenses with the need for highly specialised skills or craftsmanship: anyone who has access to the software and a relevant piece of machinery can make of an object a copy or an adapted version that in terms of quality is indistinguishable from any other of its kind made by the same process. Compare this to the differential in quality you are likely to get between an intricate ■ ↖377 514↘ wood cabinet made by the master carpenter and the ■ first attempt by the carpenter's apprentice, and you see how important this distinction can be...

Because it allows us to make adapted copies of unvarying quality, digital manufacturing lends itself perfectly to an evolutionary creative process: since the 'original' is a digital source code, it is not only easy and quick to make even minor or incremental adjustments without having to redesign the whole object from scratch, but teams of designers, even when spread over different geographical locations, can collaborate on projects and follow through the development process in real time.

By the same token, digital manufacturing offers previously unknown potential not only for collaboration, but also for the open source development of software code and sharing of applications both at the user and programmer ends. This opens up the architectural design process and makes possible approaches that rely on localised production, customisation, and personalisation of architecture that is held in the public domain or the Creative Commons, through projects such as *WikiHouse*, for example.

Within all of this, our focus lies in the seamless integration of digital data into a design and production process: it shifts control over materials and the manufacture of construction components directly into the hands of the architect and, by doing away with much of the reliance on specialist expertise and skill from master craftspeople and engineers, broadens greatly the scope of what is possible. Beyond that, putting production logic and the characteristics of different construction materials at the heart of the design process heavily influences that design process itself: as architects we find ourselves with a set of exceptionally versatile tools, which offer unprecedented scope for expression and a new authorial aesthetic, with which comes a near bewildering array of choices and possibilities that in themselves can absolutely present their own challenges.

This is why we don't consider it far fetched in this context to talk of an architecture of 'new uniques'. The architecture of antiquity and the Renaissance – really any architecture before the standardisation and mass production that typified the industrial age – was an architecture of 'uniqueness', which looked on the specifics of location, setting, purpose, cultural context, and client demands to create buildings that were created as singular instances of themselves. Similarly, we can now, with contemporary technology, approach architecture again as the creation of unique realisations of our vision, tailored specifically to the given set of circumstances and informed not so much by what materials, construction techniques, and the skills of our contractors allow us to do, but inspired by the potential we see in the given situation.

THE ROUTE TO TODAY

THE ORIGINS

■ 446↘
■

On 12 April 1805, the French Emperor Napoléon Bonaparte (1769–1821), accompanied by his wife, the Empress Joséphine (1763–1814), visited the city of Lyon, where French weaver, merchant, and inventor Joseph Marie Jacquard (1752–1834) introduced to them a mechanical loom, which he hoped would help French textile makers catch up with English factories that had pulled away ahead of them in the quality, quantity, and prices they were able to offer as a direct result of rapid industrialisation. Joseph Jacquard's loom presented something entirely new: it used sets of punch cards strung together in chains as a template for the fabric to be woven by the machine. Although Jacquard was by no means the first person to think of, or experiment with, automation (two fellow Frenchmen had done so more than half a century earlier), his was the first loom of its kind to work and yield usable, commercially viable results. The punch cards that rattled through his machine held the instructions, one row of weft per card, for the loom as to which warp threads to raise and what colour thread to shoot through the shed between the raised upper and the un-raised lower threads. In other words: they contained the programme for the pattern to be made.

Napoleon was duly impressed and, to his credit, recognised the potential. Just three days later, on 15 April 1805, he granted the city of Lyon the patent for Jacquard's revolutionary loom. Jacquard received a lifelong pension and a handsome royalty for each loom now bearing his name, sold over the next six years. Lyon swiftly not only regained a significant advantage over competing centres in making better, more intricate woven textiles faster, it also became a pioneering site for forerunners of digital manufacturing. Because while the conceptualisation of the patterns on punch cards was not as yet strictly 'digital', what Jacquard had realised and put into practice was that human manual labour processes could be codified and reliably repeated at improved quality and vastly accelerated speed by automaton.

So successful was the idea that the principle of storing data on punch cards was adopted by early IT manufacturers, chief among them IBM (International Business Machines), who used them in their development of electromechanical computers, such as the *Automatic Sequence Controlled Calculator (ASCC)*, known as *Harvard Mark I* in the 1930s and 40s. And although over time refined and much reduced in size, it was retained as a concept in computing right into the 1980s.

250 ● 417

While IBM and Harvard University were working together on making calculating machines that would eventually enable the first nuclear bomb, the American engineer and inventor John T Parsons (1913–2007) and his employee Frank L Stulen (1921–2010) became the first people specifically to use computer methodology to instruct machine tools, in their manufacture of helicopter rotor blades at the Parsons Corporation in Traverse City, Michigan, USA. In doing so, they became the inventors of **numerical control**, which still serves as the principle at work in the **Computer Numerical Control (CNC)** systems that sit at the heart of many digital manufacturing tools we use today.

251 ● 417

Parsons and Stulen's pioneering rotor blades for helicopters serve as a fine example for the strengths of digital manufacturing: they are exposed to extraordinary strains and stresses, so they need to be made of particularly resilient materials, yet their shape requires careful interpolation and precision engineering to make the craft lift off and stay in the air. Working this out separately for each blade can be done, but it is time-consuming and therefore expensive, it requires high levels of skill and expertise, and even minor errors can have fatal consequences.

They also offer a series of specific challenges that engineers are familiar with from shipbuilding: much as hydrodynamics, aerodynamics rely on finely configured curves that yield radically different performance with even relatively minor variations. Curving tough, durable material into perfectly shaped splines ranks among the great achievements of both successful ship and aviation engineering.

(This is where the Cutty Sark comes in, simply as an example: built in 1869 by Scott and Linton shipbuilders in Scotland, this was a cargo clipper that broke speed records on the trade route from Britain to Australia, in no small measure owing to the ingenuity of its wooden hull construction that allowed it to attain average long distance speeds of 15 knots, which equates to about 28 km/h or 17 mph.)

252 ○ 454

Parsons and Stulen – with the collaboration of IBM and MIT – started out just using computer calculations to arrive at their optimal blade design, with workers still carrying out these instructions manually. But by 1952, with the aid of a dedicated programming language called APT (Automatically Programmed Tool), they had succeeded in connecting the computer to the machine and allowing it to take charge of the servomechanism directly: CNC was up and running.

Military aircraft engineering continued to play a defining role in the evolution of digital manufacturing when, in 1977, the pendulum of invention swung back across the Atlantic to France where the aircraft manufacturer *Avions Marcel Dassault* (now Dassault Aviation SA) was working on the *Mirage* fighter jet and developed *CATIA (Computer Aided Three-Dimensional Interactive Application)*, an early Computer Aided Design (CAD) / CAM (Computer Aided Manufacturing) software that proved to have potential not just for aviation, but also for the automotive, shipbuilding, and consumer goods industries. This prompted *Avions Marcel Dassault* to create a new subsidiary company, *Dassault Systèmes*, who licensed the distribution of *CATIA* to IBM.

253 ● 417

In construction, it was artisan enterprises that spearheaded the path into digital manufacture, rather than architects and designers themselves. Positioned at the meeting point between artistry and skilled trade, they soon recognised and put into practice the advantages offered by processes that allow for ambitious creative expression with familiar materials, such as metal, wood, and stone, while saving on time and cost. Artis Engineering in Berlin, Germany, may be cited as an example and case in point: founded in 1994 as a traditional cabinet maker and carpentry workshop, it quickly latched on to the potential of CNC machinery and has since expanded into a firm employing a team of 30, specialising in highly complex and technically challenging construction projects particularly in exhibition stands and shop fitting where the boundaries between sculpture and utility are often blurred.

IN ARCHITECTURE

By the late 1980s and towards the early 1990s, experimental architects and studios, such as Greg Lynn FORM, Preston Scott Cohen, Coop Himmelb(l)au, and UNStudio, began to make use of graphics software – *Maya*, *Softimage*, *3D Studio*, for example – in the modelling of their architectural designs. This allowed them to work with forms that are inherently difficult to realise, and initiated a move towards geometric shapes and the appearance of materials that previously seemed impractical in construction.

At the same time, firms like Foster + Partners, SOM (Skidmore, Owings & Merrill), Gehry Partners, and ARUP began working with mathematicians and software developers such as Bentley, Autodesk, and the aforementioned *Dassault Systèmes* to develop the tools that would allow them to abstract and discretise these free geometries and make them buildable. Complex forms were rationalised and, by means of a 'file to factory' system, converted into tables for digital production methods. Supporting them in these endeavours, new companies such as Design-to-Production and Case offered themselves as service providers. ■ ↖287

■

254 ○ 454

RECENT YEARS □ ↖129

During the last ten years or so, the close collaboration between architects, engineers, IT specialists, mathematicians, and machine designers has led to a much greater integration of digital design tools into the production of construction elements, as more and more architecture practices tie them directly into their design process from the start. In tandem with this development, digital architecture production has established itself as a principal field of research into design and production methodology at universities around the world. ■ ↖63

■ ↖375

Designing for Manufacture

As we have seen, computing has not only opened up possibilities for design in architecture, it has also impacted greatly on our ability to make all manner of three-dimensional objects and spatial artefacts on all scales, from small fixtures to fittings and furniture, all the way through to fully fledged buildings. You could say that really it is the relationship between design and manufacture – or, quite generally, between idea and execution – that is being newly defined. So although 'digitalisation' is sometimes viewed as a threat to physical aspects of construction and to traditional skills and expertise – in fact to the entire cultural framework these are coached in – an ability by architects to work ever more closely and much more dynamically with master builders, carpenters, tradespeople, artisans, engineers, and construction specialists from various fields on ever more complex and challenging projects may in fact strengthen the historical ties between architecture and craft.

In this second part of our chapter we want to look in a little more detail at the continuum that stretches out between computer generated architectural design and its numerically controlled output, which is realised by means of a process chain of 3D modelling programs and CAD/CAM software.

THE PRINCIPLE

All digital manufacturing rests on the basis of information that describes the thing that is to be made and that can be read and interpreted by the machine making the thing as a set of instructions. This process entails several layers of abstraction that take the thing that is to be made from a state where it exists as digital media visualised on a computer screen – such as a virtual 3D model – to pure **machine code** that the machine acts upon to manipulate material, such as wood, resin, metal, ceramics, plastics, or concrete, for said thing to 'come about' as an actual physical object.

Obviously, the success of any such undertaking is wholly dependent on this process chain being uninterrupted, dependable, and precise. Only if there is a seamless exchange of accurate data between the design phase and the execution stage do you end up with the thing you're hoping to make. If at any point the chain is broken, or communication is inaccurate or incomplete, the project quickly falls apart.

The more complex and intricate the geometries that you are trying to achieve, the greater the volume of data, and with it the more relevant this seamless accuracy becomes. In a moment we will give a simple example of a set of data blocks that are required for a tool to carry out half a dozen moves. It's easy to see that generating a set of instructions that cut a cube out of a block of wood, and communicating this to a machine tool, offers comparatively few opportunities for error, and even where they occur, they can most likely be readily identified. But processing the code for a few hundred individually shaped, angled, and twisted curved braces that together will form an intricate domed truss, which has to support a roof that will withstand wind, rain, snow, and summertime sunshine for the next fifty or hundred years, yields up almost innumerable opportunities for both machine and human error that, if not caught in time, can lead to catastrophic failure with possibly dire consequences. And so while reading about digital manufacture can sometimes make it seem like it's mostly a case of clicking 'start' and leaning back to watch it all unfold, we want to highlight here the main elements that need to be in place for that click not to turn into a costly disaster.

So what are the individual steps, and which ones are being undertaken by the architect?

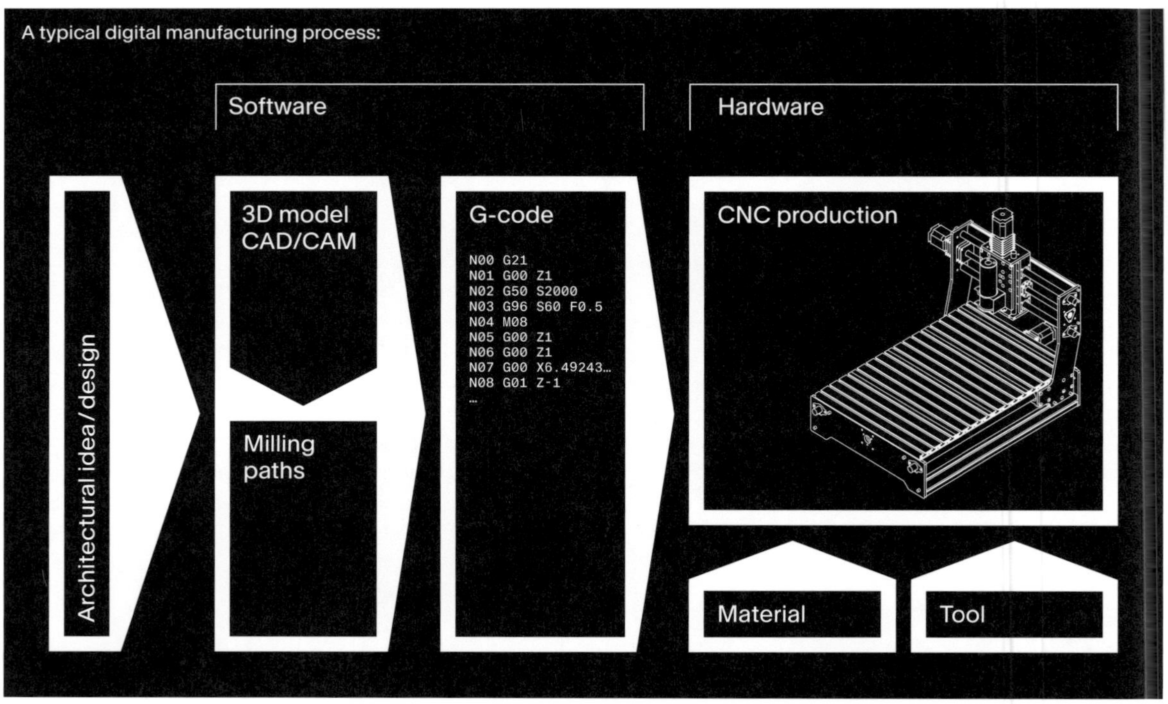

Anything that is going to be manufactured has to be described digitally first. In other words, we need a virtual 3D model of the piece that is to be made. (We keep specifying 'virtual' here when we talk of a 3D model, just to clearly distinguish it from a digitally manufactured physical 3D model, which may well be what we want to end up with.)

To create the virtual 3D model, we have a range of competing commercial software tools to choose from, some of which already foresee the manufacturing stage, or even incorporate it into their capability, depending mostly on their focus and orientation. Autodesk, for example, offers a suite of software applications that fully integrates the CAD/CAM workflow, as does 3D Systems, but their respective principal uses are likely to be quite different since the latter is a company specialising in stereolithographic 3D printing (on which more in our chapter on 3D Printing), while the former produces some of the most widely used architectural design software.

Once the individual components of the thing that is to be made have been defined as digital models – and this is really the design process, carried out with the CAD portion of the software package that as an architect you're most likely to be most familiar with – the CAM software works out the exact manufacturing action, such as the milling route a spindle or cutter has to take to extract from a block or stack of material the desired shape, and translates this into a numeric G-code which tells the machine precisely what to do, where, and when.

On any larger project that involves significant quantities of material or complex production line setups with their respective associated costs, the paths taken by the mill head, or any other tool of a similar scale, are simulated within the software environment first to detect any errors, and to fine-tune the instructions where necessary. Once the simulation is deemed satisfactory, the job is ready to be sent to the machine. (In most cases, and even after successful simulation, there will be a process supervisor in place to oversee the transmission and execution of data.)

As we shall see in a moment, there are a multitude of different types of CNC machines, with correspondingly different types of controls. Each type of control requires its own Numerical Control (NC) code. And although there is in fact a DIN/ISO (*Deutsches Institut für Normung*)/(International Organization for Standardization) standard numeric code, there are now also many 'dialects' that are at variance from it. Which is what creates the need for a post processor: once the CAM program has calculated the tool's paths, the post processor converts these calculated values into a CNC program, written in G-code. Specifically, it describes the tool paths as lines and curves for the tool head (or heads) to follow in relation to a fixed set of coordinates, and it defines the precise instructions relating to, for example, tool function, rotation speed, and feed rate, as applicable. The post processor, in other words, translates the design created by the user and digitised by the CAD/CAM software into an algorithm that the manufacturing machine understands.

This algorithm contains any number of program blocks. Each block forms a phrase or 'sentence' in programming language, which in turn consists of varying numbers of codes or 'words', each with a maximum of 80 characters. Thus, line by line, the algorithm delivers to the machine all the necessary instructions for any given step of the process.

As an example, in the following short program excerpt, we are looking at what a mill tool head is instructed to do at steps `N090` through `N140` of a particular sequence, within a work space defined by its X, Y, and Z axes:

```
N090 G00 X100 Y100
N100 Z0
N110 G01 Z-2 F10
N120 G01 X110 F20
N130 Y200 F15
N140 G00 Z10
```

The first line is the first block: ■ 442↘

- `N090` is the block identifier: as this script advances in steps of 10, this would therefore be the 9th block in the sequence that we're focusing on □ 439↘
- `G00` tells the machine to move the tool head in *rapid positioning* mode: this is a fast motion mode that simply shifts the head into position where it is next needed, without actually doing any work on the way
- `X100` and `Y100` are coordinates, so the tool head is moved to a point 100 millimetres along the X axis and 100 millimetres along the Y axis before carrying out the next instruction

Now we move on to the next block on line 2: ■ 446↘

- `N100` is the identifier, denoting here the 10th block
- The mode hasn't changed, so we are still in rapid positioning mode
- `Z0` gives the coordinate on the Z or depth axis, meaning the tool head is told to move to point zero, which is where it comes in contact with the material

And onto the next line:

- `N110` is the block identifier
- `G01` tells the tool to switch into *feed mode*
- `Z-2` tells it to advance in this mode by 2 mm into the 'negative' direction on the Z axis, meaning into the object, and
- `F10` tells it to do so at a speed of 10 mm per minute, which suggests that the new surface is sought 2 mm in from where it was before

Then:

- `N120` is the block identifier
- `G01` confirms the feed mode
- `X110` gives a new coordinate on the X axis that the tool head needs to move to now ■
- `F20` doubles the feed rate from what it was to 20 mm per minute

Then:

- `N130` identifies the block
- `Y200` gives a new coordinate on the Y axis
- `F15` splits the difference in the feed rate and tells the tool to now advance at 15 mm per minute

And finally:

- `N140` identifies the block
- `G00` puts us back into rapid positioning mode, and
- `Z10` tells the tool to withdraw to 10 mm above the Z axis

255 ● 417

CASE STUDY: CENTRE POMPIDOU-METZ
Centre Pompidou-Metz, the first satellite of the famous modern art museum of the Pompidou name in Paris, offers a good example of what can be achieved with CNC technology on a large scale.

256 ● 418

Designed by Japanese architect Shigeru Ban (b. 1957) and his French associate Jean de Gastines (b. 1957) and inaugurated in 2010, the building boasts one of the most complex wooden support structures attempted anywhere in the world in recent times.

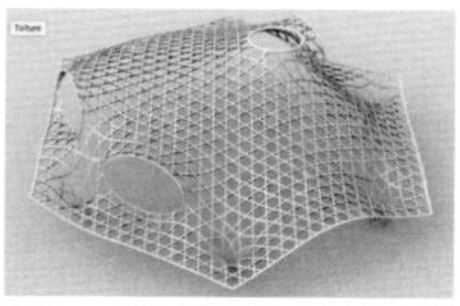

257 ● 418

Underneath a teflon finished fibre glass cover measuring approximately 8,000 square metres, it consists of almost 1,800 individual support elements made of glued laminated spruce timber, which, laid end to end, would reach some 18,000 metres in length.

The complex geometry of the beams was achieved through CNC processing, whereby the individual parts were prefabricated by a computer controlled mill and then assembled on location as a three-dimensional puzzle. Precision manufacture is prerequisite to this type of methodology, and the task of shaping these elements to within millimetres of their specification fell to German construction company Amman, who joined forces with Swiss timber specialist Hermann Blumer. Their approach rested on a principle of beams with cross sections at right angles, each made of three double layers of laminated timber.

□ 439↘
To keep the amount of data that had to be processed manageable, the individual parts were not modelled manually, but generated automatically as parametric models. These in turn were created by Design-to-Production, the company that specialises in the overlap between architecture and fabrication we mentioned earlier. The architects, in this case, simply provided a lattice model that served as a three-dimensional blueprint for the structure.

From a design perspective, the great achievement of the *Centre Pompidou-Metz* collaboration lies in taking everybody's requirements and priorities – from the planning engineer, to the carpentry firm, to the fitter on site – and extracting from these a set of wholly abstract rules, which can be formalised and formulated as a numerical computer program that then controls the manufacturing output to the most exacting standards.

258A ● 418

258B ● 418

258C ● 419

258D ● 419

On a more fundamental level, the project also exemplifies the change in significance of craftsmanship. Computer controlled manufacturing systems have shifted the focus of human expertise from operating construction tools towards conception and design: from the rear end of the process and the project's realisation to the front end and its planning. And so as production and construction become more automated, greater competencies are given to and also demanded of the architect if they are to communicate knowledgeably with contractors and engineers about the processes that make the realisation of their vision possible.

A TAXONOMY OF PROCESSES

Over the last fifty years, developments in numerical control technologies have given rise to an extraordinary range of manufacturing processes, which find use in all kinds of environments. Here we offer a brief overview of the principal methods, grouped into seven distinct approaches.

For all of these methods of digital manufacturing it is true to say that their efficiency, cost, and speed are determined not only by the technology itself, but also by factors such as the material that is being used, the level of precision that is required and therefore the tolerances that are available, as well as the desired finish and a job's complexity, and in tandem with this, the time required for machine set-up, operating times, and energy usage.

ADDITIVE PROCESSES / 3D PRINTING
Additive manufacturing, mostly referred to as 3D Printing, has become so significant to architecture that we have given it a dedicated chapter of its own in this *Atlas*. We are therefore not going to cover it here.

SUBTRACTIVE PROCESSES
Subtractive processes are so called because they literally subtract material from a given volume to arrive at an object of the desired shape. There are a multitude of available methods in this category, among them drilling, sawing, milling, punching, sanding, cutting, reaming, turning, and lathing.

These, in turn, variously employ processes such as machining or chipping, laser or electro beam subtraction, or chemical, electrical or thermic erosion.

PUNCHING
A tool forms holes of varying depth and circumference in a block of material, particularly metal. This is a fairly specialist method that finds application mainly in industrial contexts.

MILLING
CNC milling machines use rotating mill heads to remove material from a block or sheet. They are classified by the number of their axes; most common are 3, 4, and 5 axis machines, but large industry robots can feature 9 or more axes. CNC milling can be very fast, which makes it particularly effective on larger tasks with materials such chipboard, foam, and metal; but almost anything that lends itself to drilling or cutting is also suitable for milling. Standard size CNC milling machine trays are usually able to accommodate materials of several centimetres thickness.

LATHING
A workpiece is fitted into a machine that turns it on its own axis, with a sharp cutting tool sitting perpendicular to the object and removing material from it as it turns. There are some limitations to the use of CNC lathes, as they can only operate in circular motion, but the relative simplicity of the process makes it suitable and economical for some jobs, especially in wood and metal.

GRINDING
A grinding or sanding element is used to remove thin layers of material. This finds particular use in tool making and sharpening.

EROSION
Material is removed either by means of a laser or electro beam or through chemical processes – Electrochemical Machining (ECM) – or electric processes – Electrical Discharge Machining (EDM). ECM and EDM methods offer great precision and lend themselves especially to very tough materials, such as hard metals, which are difficult to work on with mechanical tools. Laser and electro beam cutters, meanwhile, use a laser or electro beam to cut materials such as chipboard, felt, wood, or acrylics (but not PVC) of up to about 1 cm thickness. They can vary the speed of the beam head as well as the intensity and resolution of the beam to achieve engravings, grid patterns, and cuts. Laser and electro beam cut objects are often used in the production of models and certain building components.

HEAT AND ELECTROCHEMICAL PROCESSES
An example of this is the CNC hot wire tool: a metal wire is heated to about 200 °C and guided across a block of material – principally foam or clay – to cut out of it the desired shape. This may be combined with a lathe system to obtain spiral ornamental shapes.

TRANSFORMATION PROCESSES
Here, rather than adding material or taking it away to achieve a particular shape, the material is transformed either through high temperature or by applying pressure to it. There are many types of material that can be used in transformation processes, including metals, glass, ceramics, artificial stone, and many polymers, which can be heated and then either poured or injected into casts, where they cool and solidify.

Processes include:

CASTING
A distinction is made between pressure casting and mould casting. In pressure casting, material (mostly metal) is forced into a cast under high pressure. This is an expensive procedure that is mainly used for the serial mass production of industrial parts. Mould casting is used to create negative copies of original positive shapes. This finds its use with almost any material for the production of prototypes, scale models of consumer goods, and all manner of other artefacts.

FORMING
Similar to casting, material is injected into a form or mould under pressure; the part then solidifies through compression, thermoforming, or in chemical reaction with solidifying agents.

DEFORMATION PROCESSES

Deformation processes give the material a new form without altering its molecular or chemical structure, but simply by applying physical force to it, possibly with the aid of high temperatures. Typically, materials start out in a semi-formed state (as blocks or sheets) and are then deformed through compression, extrusion, rolling, shaping, bending, or deep drawing.

Materials used therefore need to be either malleable, or deform under high temperatures and/or pressure, and this applies mostly to metals. Cold deformation requires more force, but often also yields higher precision and better surface finishes.

One of the main advantages of deformation over transformation processes is that they are efficient in terms of both labour and resources. The mechanical properties of objects produced in this way are often superior to those achieved by other methods, because the material's fibres are stretched but not broken.

Sequential application of deformation processes allows the manufacture of complex parts made from simple components, which is why deformation is often used in mass production.
Most important among these are:

LAMINATING
First the material is given the desired thickness by stretching it, before it is shaped under the pressure of two or more rotating rolls.

SHAPING
The object is shaped through pressure and bending.

FORGING
The object is pressed or beaten into shape.

EXTRUSION
The material is pressed through a template or tool that gives it its final shape.

SURFACE TREATMENT
■ ↖356 469↘ These manufacturing processes cause a change in the structure of the surface of the material. The most common practices are based on heat treatment, for example by heating up and then cooling down the material under controlled conditions. Other methods include mechanical processes (shot peening and sand blasting), electrochemical processes (galvanisation) or the application of metallic or organic layers through casting, immersing, rolling, or spraying.

JOINING PROCESSES
Mechanical, chemical, or thermic joining processes create a lasting or temporary joint between two or several separate parts to form an object of the desired shape, geometry, or characteristics. A key element here is the interaction between the materials and the energy that creates the union. In some processes the consolidating energy actually improves the structure or the properties of the material and therefore forms an integral part of the procedure.

Chief among joining processes are:

WELDING
Component parts are joined through progressive welding, using heat sources such as gas, electric arcs, plasma, or laser. The joint itself is achieved either by the addition of a welding agent or with the same material as the joined components.

BRAZING
A particular type of welding: component parts are joined by a material that has a melting point significantly lower than that of the materials that are to be joined.

SINTERING
The material comes in the form of a powder which is pressed into a form or mould and then hardened by the application of heat.

INTEGRATED PROCESSES
(AUTOMATION AND ROBOTICS)

On 25 January 1921, the theatre-going public of Prague was presented with the world premiere of a new play by the then 31-year-old Czech writer Karel Čapek (1890–1938) called *R.U.R.* which stood for *Rossumovi Univerzální Roboti*, which in turn translates as *Rossum's Universal Robots*. The eponymous creatures are made in a factory to serve their human masters, which at first they dutifully do. By the time the play is through though, they have become disenchanted with their lot, started a rebellion, and overthrown the human race.

Whatever the prescience of the playwright may or may not have been, it was the first time anyone had used the word 'robot' to mean an artificial person. Once coined, the term – borrowed from the Czech word *robota,* meaning forced labour or slavery – quickly gained currency and, having been introduced to the English language even before the play itself was translated and produced in London two years later, rapidly spread across the globe. Čapek's robots were not so much robots as we understand them today: made of inorganic, mechanical parts and equipped with artificial intelligence. They instead resembled more our notion of androids, but their conception still points at a relegation of menial tasks and production processes which previously were carried out by human beings to manmade 'machines', of a description. As it happens, in the last few decades more and more approaches have been developed that point not to a division of robotic and human work processes, but to their fusion and integration.

Strictly speaking, there are today still only a few robots in use in the construction industry, but this doesn't mean that there are no other forms of automated labour. Ever since machines have been controlled by computers, there have also been processes of automation. And automated machines are indeed robots: they not only carry out complex sequences of operations, but they are also capable of regulating their output, which means they are self-regulating and they even correct themselves as they go along.

For obvious reasons we here refer you also to our chapter on Big Data & Machine Learning.

CASE STUDY: SMART
(SHIMIZU MANUFACTURING SYSTEM
BY ADVANCED ROBOTICS TECHNOLOGY)
In Japan, where technological innovation carries a great deal of prestige and where labour costs are high, several integrative methods such as those mentioned above are currently being experimented with.

The Shimizu Manufacturing System by Advanced Robotics Technology (SMART) is a pilot project that integrates a series of production processes, among them montage and welding of steel frames, laying floors, internal and external casings, as well as the installation of various prefabricated construction modules.

The set-up of the system takes about six weeks. After this, the top floor and roof are put in place on four towers, which are used to raise the main construction platform, one floor at a time. The heart of the system consists of raising mechanisms and automatic conveyor technology installed on the platform. Overhead gantry cranes are attached to the roof structure so they resemble a built-in production facility. The whole process is computer controlled, with operators present to supervise it.

Once construction of a storey is complete, the structure is lifted onto the next floor where the process resumes. Simplified joints between individual components allow for quick assembly: self-centring columns, for example, require nothing more than a bit of adjusting with a torque spanner and a laser guided measuring tool. Next, a welding robot is used to accomplish the final joining of column ends. Prefabricated pipes provide another example of this type of rationalising production.

SMART represents a novel approach to computer integrated construction, which is expected to reduce the amount of labour required for the erection of an office block of several storeys by some 30%

The Outlook

Deployed intelligently and creatively, digital manufacturing, combined with feedback and simulation, can be the technology that may eventually erase a 500-year-old separation between design and construction. Boundaries are being blurred everywhere, not just in architecture, but here it is the integration of digital methodology that we expect to continue apace and that will move the competencies, skills, and approaches of the designer and the builder together to the point where they may become indistinguishable from each other, where design is achieved partly through a process of material-specific prototyping, testing, refining, and eliminating, and where construction becomes not so much an implementation of design as the tail end of a digital workflow.

This is not unique to architecture and construction. The simplification and perhaps ultimately elimination of transitional gaps between individual processes in the 'making of things' and a motion toward what is being called Industry 4.0 or the Fourth Industrial Revolution are all very much on the cards.

The concept of Industry 4.0 is interesting and in this context relevant because it envisions 'smart factories': networks of modular production facilities that communicate with each other, with their steering systems, and with humans through the Cloud. These **Cyber Physical Systems (CPS)** mark a logical evolution from the preceding industrial revolutions, which are commonly delineated as:

- *1st Industrial Revolution:* steam engine technology, mechanisation, and acceleration of production processes
- *2nd Industrial Revolution:* electricity, mass production, standardisation, and production lines
- *3rd Industrial Revolution:* information technology, automation, customisation

To which is now added:
4th Industrial Revolution: networked automated systems; machines that design machines, the Internet of Things (IoT).

This entails a much closer fusion of human and artificial intelligence, and previously human skill sets and expertise, leading up to much more hybrid approaches, where human creativity and design are augmented by machine capability that is defined not only by power and precision, but also by decision making and technologically 'enhanced intuition'.

This may, and almost certainly does, raise some questions, if not in fact ring alarm bells: are we as architects going to make ourselves obsolete? That is not a necessary outcome, nor is it desirable, of course. And a trajectory that may from the outset look as if it could obliterate all tradition, render human input surplus to requirement, and create a 'Brave New World' of a machine designed and built future could well lead elsewhere entirely. Take the restoration of historic monuments damaged through war or natural catastrophe, for example. Digital scanning, modelling, and manufacturing techniques are particularly well placed to achieve highly sophisticated results that with the best of existing knowledge and human craftsmanship simply would not now be achievable.

Work on the *Basílica i Temple de la Sagrada Família* – often referred to as the 'Gaudí Cathedral', although it is not in actual fact a cathedral – originally started in 1882, as a more or less traditional gothic church by Francisco Paula del Villar y Lozano. A year later, Villar resigned from his position as lead architect over some disagreements with the head of the client organisation. This paved the way for the then 30-year-old Catalan architect Antoni Gaudí (1852–1926) to take the helm and change everything we thought we knew about cathedral design completely. Not only was his vision and style radically different from anything that had been done before, he also largely eschewed more conventional architectural practice, such as drawing detailed plans, and instead made scale models by hand, which he shaped and refined in great detail as he went along.

The church was consecrated on 7 November 2010, a quarter of a century after it was designated a UNESCO World Heritage Site, and well over a century after construction first began. But it is far from complete. When Gaudí died in 1926, aged 73, the project was less than a quarter finished. Having reached midpoint in 2010, it is now (early 2020) expected to reach completion in 2026, a century after the architect's death. While this is still slow by most project's standards, it's a considerable acceleration compared to the first half construction phase, which took more than eight times as long. ■

There are many reasons why progress has sped up. The recognition and popularity that the building enjoys are no doubt a major factor: it now has an enviable status as a major landmark of global significance, and so funding is no longer quite as much of an issue as it has been. Also, the Spanish Civil War, lasting nearly three years from 1936 to 1939, and its legacy set the project back by more than a decade. But one significant reason work is now progressing faster is technology: CAD and CNC milling allow for stone elements to be shaped precisely in keeping with the design off site at not only a fraction of the cost, but also at much greater speed, than was possible with the manual processes of the twentieth century. □ 613↘

259 ● 419

260A ○ 455

260B ○ 455

260C ○ 455

260D ○ 455

With a view to automation and robotics, while in industry and trade automation processes have enabled highly integrated workflows, the unstructured, dynamic nature of construction and construction sites has so far to some extent held back their advance in this sector. As yet, fully integrated processes are limited to a small number of pilot projects, although in prefabrication and just-in-time delivery there have been significant developments.

The scope and the particular nature of the challenges it offers mean that it may be some time before we see integrated construction with robots as a matter of course. But in some fields, such as high rise building, it is possible that automation systems will be developed and refined gradually to the point where construction sites themselves resemble an assembly operation. Yet even though these new ways of working are at an early stage, and many problems such as the social and environmental implications are still waiting to be addressed in the discourse, the huge potential of combining computational tools and fabrication in design and building tasks of ever-increasing complexity is obvious.

One of the most relevant advantages of robotic manufacture for architecture may well be the possibility to develop construction elements for individual contextual solutions. Industry robots have of late become ever faster, more accurate, and – through implementation of new 'senses' (for example the 'sense of touch' or 'sight' with integrated camera systems) – also very much more flexible and easier to operate. With these developments we will soon reach a point where architecture and robot technology are much more closely related to each other, and we think that architecture and the construction industry will both benefit from this.

The motion towards automation in construction will appear on two levels: firstly there will be the 'real world' of construction, where humans and robots will work together and therefore interact; secondly there will also be the ever expanding virtual space where untold quantities of data and information will help conceive, design, and organise construction of the future.

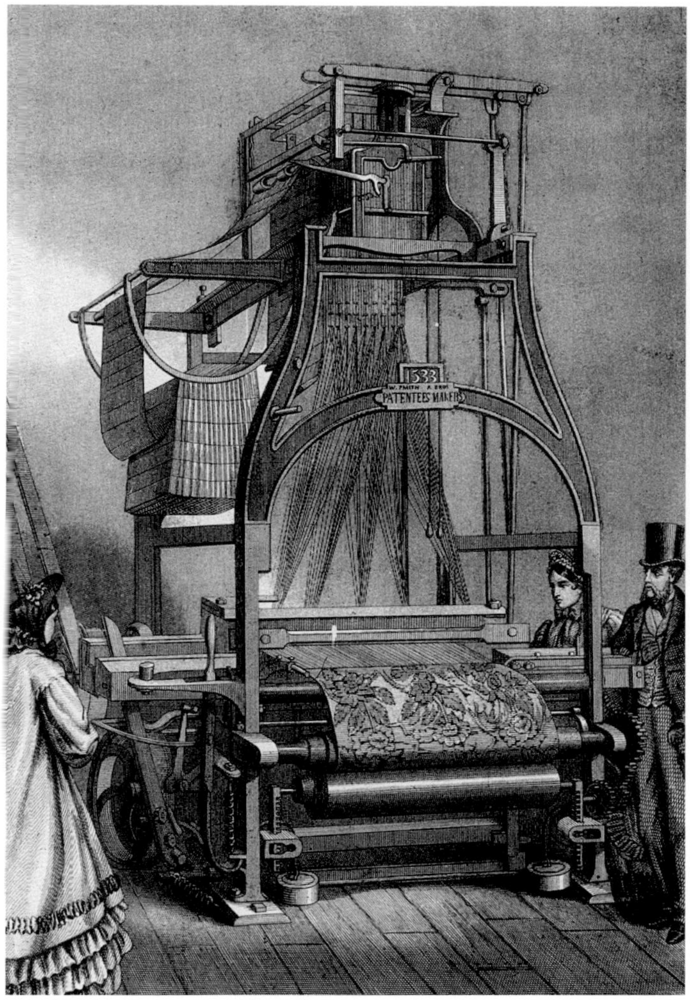

250 ● 408
The binary principle in use in the punch card operation of the Jacquard loom was the inspiration for early data processing machines. [Wellcome Collection]

251 ● 408
Pilot Fred Hill with John T Parsons and the Parsons Corporation helicopter at the Traverse City airport in the late 1950s.

253 ● 409
Lead developer Mike Muuss works on the *XM-1* tank in *BRL-CAD* on a *PDP-11/70* computer system, circa 1980.

255 ● 412
Example of a production line: *Hundegger K2i.* [Hundegger]

256 ● 412
Shigeru Ban, Jean de Gastines architects: *Centre Pompidou-Metz* (2010). [Shigeru Ban]

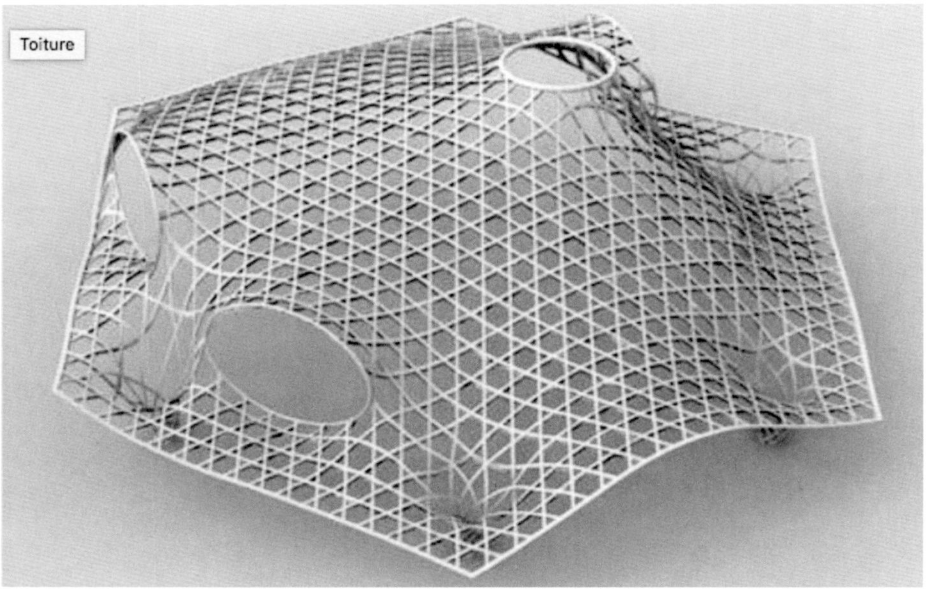

257 ● 412
The wooden structure supporting the roof of the *Centre Pompidou-Metz*.
[Design-to-Production]

258A ● 412

258B ● 412

Example of chamfer milling (258A), finger milling (258B + 258C), and cutting (258D). [Series: Hundegger]

258C ● 412

258D ● 412

259 ● 415
The *Basílica i Temple Expiatori de la Sagrada Família* in Barcelona. Gaudí's masterpiece is still being completed, using state-of-the art CAD and CNC technology.

- Albrecht Dürer: *Four Books on Human Proportions (Vier Bücher von menschlicher Proportion)*, 1532
- Gottfried Semper: *Die vier Elemente der Baukunst (The Four Elements of Architecture)*, 1851/ *Wissenschaft, Industrie und Kunst (Science, Industry and Art)*, 1852
- Valentin Kockel: *Rom über die Alpen tragen – Korkmodelle antiker Architektur im 18. und 19. Jahrhundert In: Rom über die Alpen tragen. Fürsten sammeln antike Architektur: Die Aschaffenburger Korkmodelle*, 1993
- Bernard Cache: *Earth Moves: the Furnishing of Territories*, 1995
- Bernd Evers: *Architekturmodelle der Renaissance: Die Harmonie des Bauens von Alberti bis Michelangelo (Ausstellung im Alten Museum, Berlin)*, 1995

Model Making

Hans Sachs and Milena Stavric

Overview

What is a model? And, more to the point, what is it for?

At first glance these may sound like rhetorical questions, but they are in fact fundamental to architecture and, even more to the point, our approach to architecture.

Though perhaps obvious, it's worth placing at the forefront of our minds that a model is not a reality, but an abstraction of a reality. That is, unless you build an object as a real life structure and then use that structure itself as a prototype or a model for something else, in which case your model is then both: a reality and an abstraction of yet another reality. In architecture, this happens all the time, as we shall see. And it brings us directly to this more significant and more interesting question: what is the model for? Because irrespective of how big or how small the model is, how detailed or how rudimentary, just how abstract or how life-like, and no matter how it was made, whether by hand or by a digital manufacturing process: the point of the model is what it is used for. Is it used merely to represent a proposed architectural reality, or is it used to develop a concept? Is it used to illustrate a design, or is it used to design? Is it used to demonstrate thinking, or is it used to think? Is it used to teach an audience an idea, or is it used to learn what the idea might be in the first place? Is it used to sell a product, or is it used to convey an experience.

As you go through this chapter, you will get a strong sense that we not only view, but actively propagate Model Making as part of a process, namely one of developing, designing, thinking, learning, and experiencing. To formulate it more precisely still, we see and advocate it as an *intuitive* learning process that helps us gain *implicit* knowledge: knowledge that we can't obtain simply from reading about, or studying, architecture, but that we internalise and absorb through all our senses. This means that whichever way you do it – be that by analogue or digital means – model making is something that takes practice, and it presupposes a dedication to the process itself, as opposed to a simple desire to finish the thing so it's done and can be shown to someone who needs to see it as quickly as possible.

Consequently, we further postulate model making as a process that *never ends,* at least not for as long as the project is 'live': there doesn't come a natural point where the modelling is done, and we can now get on with the job of building the 'real thing'. The idea of using modelling as a cyclical design process is that you improve complex systems in terms of their form, their material, and their function, continuously and for as long as this is practical, right until the project is up and can be handed over. And even then, depending on what kind of project we're dealing with, there is a good chance that the now built real life object is still a work in progress, and that the learnings and findings from how it behaves and functions in the real world and how it is used by real people will feed into its further development and management, or into future projects of a comparable nature.

If you do that, if you view model making as a learning process, then you can also argue that the point of the model is to help you 'trick' or outwit nature, because with a model you can work out how to do things that weren't possible before. If you want to learn how to fly, for example, you are going to have to build some models first: of your wings, your apparatus, your flying machine that will make you magnificent! If you want to build a tower that is taller than any ever built before, you could start by just constructing it, but your chances of success would be not much greater than those of the master builders at Babel. You really best find out if your dream is achievable by making some models to test the structure, the materials, the statics, the dimensions, the physics, let alone the aesthetics and economics of your undertaking. If you want to employ new materials in new combinations to achieve whole new spatial sensations, your path to fulfilment, more likely than not, will entail making many a model.

With the model you take a step outside nature and find out the mechanics of what it is you are trying to do: how the thing that didn't exist before could actually work. And that, we argue, is the real purpose of the physical model. Whichever way you arrive at it, be it by jointing pieces of wood, moulding clay, assembling metal, or by constructing your vision on a computer and then printing it out, or using any of the many other digital manufacturing processes available to you, if you don't learn anything from making your model, then your model is just a smaller, or simpler, more abstract version of a bigger, or more complex, more real-life thing: it may be pretty, it may be illustrative, and it may even have a point in existing □ ↖421
for the particular reason that it is either or both these things, but that then is all there is to it, and that's not very much, compared to what a model can be.

So while in the early to mid 1980s, as computer technology and CAD started to make themselves felt widely in architecture, it may have looked as if the physical model would soon be a thing of the past, the opposite turns out to be the case. The demise of the physical model has not only not materialised, but in fact since then there has been a veritable revival of physical model making, and to a degree never seen before. As a result of CAD and 3D modelling, the physical model has become more prevalent and more important and more integrated into the design process than possibly at any stage since the Renaissance.

There are many good reasons why this is so, some of which we're about to look at in turn, but one particularly relevant detail that we want to plant in your brain before we proceed is this: the computer generated 3D model does not have a scale. We highlight this in our chapters on 3D Modelling and Digital Data □ ↖57
Acquisition as a genuine advantage and selling point □ ↖93
of the technology: the data is handled on a 1:1 basis and we can zoom in and out of it at will. The physical model, again whether it is manufactured digitally or made by hand, anchors our object in a specific proportion relative to the real world, and nothing else so vividly, tangibly, and applicably communicates to us

■ ↖361 480↘ therefore scale and proportion in terms we can not just comprehend, but experience, as the physical model.

And there is one more principal point to the physical model that makes it as useful to us today as it ever ■ ↖359 479↘ was, if not indeed much more: better than anything else that we have available to us, a physical model is capable of immediately communicating complex physical phenomena and relationships concerning the object, its functionality, and its adaptivity to its environment. This includes essential factors such as materiality, colouring, discolouring under specific circumstances – for example when it gets wet – and touch. It gives us a particular insight into how materials behave: how they fold, bend, break, reflect, deform, even how they smell; and how any of this changes in different temperatures, with varying levels of humidity, and in different weather conditions and seasons. Because of this, the physical model initiates and then nurtures a dialogue of the senses that is simply not yet (and may never entirely be) achievable by purely virtual means.

MODELLING AS A PROCESS

Among the most striking buildings to have been taking shape over the last 135 years is the *Basílica i Temple de la Sagrada Família* by Catalan architect Antoni Gaudí (1852–1926) in Barcelona. (And counting: construction started in 1882 and completion is currently expected around 2026). It's a building we mention on several occasions in this *Atlas*, and that is hardly a coincidence: it combines on itself not only an immediately recognisable shape and a singular architectural vision, but it also stands out for the extraordinary efforts that have gone, and continue to go, into its realisation, and for the highly idiosyncratic methodology that sits at the heart of its design.

■ ↖160 One of these methods is the **hanging chain** or **catenary model**. It was not invented by Gaudí, but developed and perfected by him over several years. A *catenary* is the curve that a chain (or cable or rope) describes when fixed at two ends and left hanging, suspended between these two points under its own weight. It is an 'ideal' or 'idealised' shape that has its own specific mathematical properties, and it's one that we tend to perceive as inherently aesthetic, either through cultural assimilation, or possibly because it is one that the laws of physics dictate and that to us therefore seems 'natural'.

By hanging weights onto such 'chains' (which in fact he mostly made of string), Gaudí could not only change the shape of these curves and elongate the arches they formed, but he was able also to quickly, easily, and cheaply simulate the effect of minor adjustments in the mass and positioning of the weights on the overall structure, and therefore the look and feel of the project he was working on. Using mirrors or photographs to show him what the shapes looked like upside down, Gaudí achieved many of his signature designs.

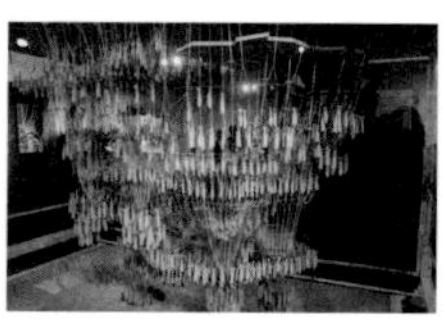

261 ● 434

Conceptually, what Gaudí was doing was to use analogue **parametric modelling** to arrive at a range of possible geometries from which to choose the perfect or preferred ones for execution.

Today we use parametric modelling in **Computer Aided Architectural Design (CAAD)** as a matter of routine, and it may seem tempting therefore to view physical model making as an increasingly obsolete practice that is principally now of historical interest. Clearly that is not the case. Instead, much as in other areas where digitality has given us new tools and new ways of working, there is now simply an additional overlapping circle: the Venn diagram that contains the sets of physical model, 3D manufactured model, and 3D model features union regions that are all of interest to us, because it is in these that the different skills and methods meet and inform each other, as we shall explain in more detail in just a moment.

We have seen similar developments in other fields before: in publishing, digital content has not done away with the printed book or magazine; in music, MP3s have not killed off vinyl, let alone the live music experience; and no matter how much money and technology the major film studios throw at digital 3D cinema, we still love the immediacy and thrill of theatre. And we find it normal that these technologies and approaches inform, complement, and support each other. There are millions of book titles available in print now, not in spite but because of digital technology: print on demand and simple design tool software have opened up what used to be a specialist industry to practically anyone who wants to make a book. Similarly, renowned live theatre producers such as Britain's National Theatre in London, are able to reach much wider audiences than ever before, by doing live broadcasts of their productions to cinema screens around the world. And much as we continue to enjoy the simple act of taking a record out of its sleeve and putting it on the turntable, waiting for the homely crackle when the needle settles on the disk, we of course don't rely on this in every situation. On a plane or while out running in the park, you'd obviously be much more likely to listen to your tunes collection on a smartphone instead.

At a basic level, the physical architectural model is not so different to the book or the vinyl record. It has something to offer that their digital counterparts simply can't: a materiality, a sensory experience, a connection with the content that is unique and uniquely material. But there is quite a bit more to it than that...

MODEL MAKING THROUGH TIME

THE ORIGINS

Physical model making has a history that may well be as old as architecture itself, though it is fascinating to note that this history is neither particularly well charted nor cast with a great many notable characters, and so we can't actually prove much of it. Nor is it even punctuated by more than perhaps two or three significant milestones. It is almost as if we had been taking the architectural model for granted, and in a sense continue to do so. This is not in itself all that surprising either: the idea that a miniature version of a greater object could help us understand the workings of this object makes perfect sense to us.

When we say that the history of model making is not 'particularly well charted', that does depend to some extent on where and how closely you look though. We do not know for certain how the architects of antique buildings before the Romans used models. But we do know that the materials to build temples, palaces and courts, government buildings and baths, and anything else that you might find in a city, costs money. We also appreciate that the more important a structure, the more important it is that it should stand up and not fall down. So chances are that even before we have any documented evidence of model making, models were indeed made. We also have some tantalising details that hint at model making in antiquity: we know, for example, that models for coffers were mentioned in the calculations for the Erechtheion, one of the temples of the Acropolis in Athens, built between 421 and 406 BCE.

We also know that humans have used physical objects to represent data for many millennia before then. This does not strictly fall under the umbrella term 'model making', but it does link to our understanding of the model as a physical visualisation of information. Here, as you would expect, the beginnings are even more diffuse, because much now depends on what you consider to be a deliberate physical visualisation. But as early as 5500 BCE, clay tokens were used in Mesopotamia to represent abstract concepts, long before the invention of writing and papyrus, for example.

262 ● 434

ARCHITECTURAL MODEL MAKING

Architecture as we know it in the Western world starts to be systematically and comprehensively documented with the Roman architect and engineer Vitruvius (c. 80–70 BCE – c. 15 BCE), whose treatise *De architectura (Ten Books on Architecture)* is the oldest surviving text we have on the subject and is therefore often cited as the 'beginning' of architecture. Both Vitruvius and roughly a century later the Greek-Roman biographer and essayist Plutarch (c. 46–120) make reference in their writings to models, and the preferred materials they mention appear to be wax and wood, which would go some way towards explaining why none survive, although we do have a marble model of a theatre dating back to that era. Possibly made as a votive piece, this is now being kept in the *Museo Nazionale* in Rome.

From the early Middle Ages onwards, we know of model making for certain, though again only through literature. But curiously then, from the High Mediaeval Period, there is virtually no mention of models at all. It is likely that either partial or even comprehensive models continued to be used, especially for structural tests, for example of pillars and arches, but making a complete model of a design presupposes that you know from the outset the exact shape your building is going to take, and this seems not to be the practice or approach adopted by the master builders of that period. Rather, they took geometries and tested them, implemented and repeated them, to arrive at a structure through evolution, replication, and expansion: you could liken this to an early generative, rule-based architecture.

This notion is somewhat supported by the fact that evidence of model making resurfaces precisely at the time when the conception of a comprehensive architectural vision is reborn: during the Renaissance. It coincides with the first appearance also of architectural perspective drawings, and so our contention that there is an overlap between the three-dimensional representation of architecture on the plane (when we are referring to the digital 3D model on the screen) and the three-dimensional representation of architecture in space (through the physical model) finds its parallel even here, in the period where we can more or less position the origins of model making as we understand it today (while being aware, always, that its roots reach far into the beginnings of civilisation).

263 ● 434

Now, during the Renaissance, we have some real riches: the Italian architect and sculptor Arnolfo di Cambio (c. 1240–1310) made models for Florence Cathedral; models of plaster, wood, and paper were made also for Bologna Cathedral in the late 14th and early 15th century – a wooden model from 1514 by Arduino Ariguzzi survives to this date – and from then on in there are increasingly numerous examples, including an eight-metre tall model of St Peter's Basilica in Rome, made by one of the most illustrious figures of the High Renaissance, the Italian sculptor, painter, and architect Michelangelo (1475–1564).

264 ○ 456

The Italian architect Antonio da San Gallo (or da Sangallo the Younger) (1484–1546) was in charge of construction at St Peter's Basilica from 1513 until the late 1530s, and during that time he too built a large 'walk-in' model, in his case of the entire project, which also survives to this day.

265 ● 435

From the Renaissance onwards, model making doesn't ever go away, but simply continues as part of architectural practice, with people like German architect Balthasar Neumann (c.1687–1753) using models not only to test the design and the static behaviour of his projects, but also as impressive presentation pieces of historical buildings for rich clients. One of his favourite architectural features was the rotunda, which he trialled extensively with models.

266 ● 435

MODELS IN MODERNITY

When next you bite into the succulent flesh of a banana, spare a thought for the man after whom, in all likelihood, it is named. William George Spencer Cavendish was born in 1790 in Paris, the son of William Cavendish, 5th Duke of Devonshire, and his wife, Lady Georgiana. Young William was only sixteen when his mother died, and five years later, when his father also passed away, 21-year-old William George acceded to the title, becoming the 6th Duke of Devonshire, and owner of no fewer than eight stately homes, together with some 200,000 acres of land: about 800 square kilometres, or roughly the size of the Canton Neuchâtel in Switzerland.

Cavendish never married, but he did leave a remarkable legacy. One fine day in 1823, as he was strolling through the extensive grounds at his Chiswick House, southwest of London, the improbably rich Duke, now in his early thirties and himself a keen horticulturalist, happened upon a young gardener working for his neighbours, the Royal Horticultural Society. So impressed was he with what he saw that he poached the 20-year-old and deployed him to one of his other properties, Chatsworth House in Derbyshire, some 150 miles away. There, the recruit immediately made his presence felt. On his first day, with the Duke himself absent on a trip to Russia, the keen new employee arrived at half past four in the morning, scaled the garden wall, explored the gardens, set the staff to work, took breakfast with the housekeeper, and met his future wife, the housekeeper's niece, all by nine o'clock in the morning.

Within three years, Joseph Paxton (1803–1865) was promoted to Head Gardener at Chatsworth, where he not only transformed the grounds, but also developed an interest in greenhouses. He spent a considerable amount of both his time and the Duke's money on developing them, building models and early prototypes of the kind of cast-iron and plate-glass construction that would soon make him world famous as the architect of The Crystal Palace, which housed the Great Exhibition of 1851 in London's Hyde Park. (Following the event, the structure was moved to the area that is now named after it, but was then known as Penge Peak in South London, where it stood until very sadly it burnt down in 1936.)

Paxton remained at Chatsworth until the Duke's death in 1858, and it was here that he cultivated a banana the Duke had brought home from his travels, naming it after his patron. It is this specimen that is the progenitor of the most widely consumed banana in the world today: the Cavendish. Cavendish's own great achievement, meanwhile, came after his election as president to the Royal Horticultural Society in 1838. This position allowed him to set up the Royal Botanic Gardens at Kew, generally known simply as Kew Gardens, which to this day is a major centre for research, a much loved visitor attraction, and UNESCO World Heritage Site.

Among the features that make Kew Gardens so successful, so attractive, and so noteworthy, are its spectacular greenhouses. The most iconic and famous of these, the Palm House, was built by English architect Decimus Burton (1800–1881) and the Irish iron founder and glasshouse manufacturer Richard Turner (1798–1881). It continues many of the design principles developed by Paxton in Chatsworth, as well, it has to be said, as work done by Scottish botanist and author John Claudius Loudon (1783–1843).

The similarities between the Palm House at Kew Gardens and its predecessor, the Great Conservatory at Chatsworth, as well as those between these two and The Crystal Palace are obvious, and it is fair to say that Paxton used his structure at Chatsworth as a life-size model for the much bigger Great Exhibition project in Hyde Park. Quite generally, Paxton's use of models exemplifies model making as a process: developing a building through modelling it, not just understanding its structure and static properties or the way it will look and come together, but evolving it through a series of iterations.

267A ● 435

267B ● 435

268A ● 436

268B ● 436

As is so often the case, the causes and effects of what is happening in a culture exercise mutual forces on each other. German architect Gottfried Semper (1803–1879) has several fascinating objects of fame to his name, among them the opera house in Dresden that carries his name, the Semper Opera, and one single barricade he built during the German revolution in 1848, of which he is quoted as saying: "It held, because it was practical; and as it was practical it was beautiful." His republican leanings and active part in the May Uprising of that year got him banned from the city, but that in turn led him to Paris and London, where he worked on several countries' sections of Paxton's Great Exhibition at the Crystal Palace.

During his time in London, and finding it difficult to secure any big projects of his own, Semper wrote and published two books that cemented his position as one of the 19th century's most influential architectural thinkers: *Die vier Elemente der Baukunst (The Four Elements of Architecture)* in 1851, and *Wissenschaft, Industrie und Kunst (Science, Industry and Art)*, in 1852.

Fundamentally, he noted that the industrial revolution, which had by now reached its peak, had changed the relationship between materials and architecture. Whereas prior to industrialisation, new materials would emerge slowly in response to a recognisable problem, this process had now been reversed, as industry flooded the market with new methods, machines, materials, and tools. These were all changing the way architecture could be conceived and realised. His work in Paxton's Crystal Palace would have given him the starkest example of this: it was purely industrial manufacturing processes and the new materials, which industry was able to provide in large quantities at low cost, that made these structures possible at all. Just as today's digital revolution is completely transforming all aspects of human life and endeavour, including architecture, so the industrial revolution brought about a new world that looked, felt, and behaved differently to any world before it.

But Semper also observed how traditional forms were retained through the ages. In his *Four Elements of Architecture*, he identifies four basic approaches to making things: weaving (textiles and patterns), moulding (pottery), carpentry (wooden structures, such as roofs, walls, and partitions), and masonry (constructing with stone). Now, with the technological advances that had been made since the mid-18th century, he added to these historical methods a fifth: working with metals.

It's this interplay of materiality and form, of aesthetic expression and the practical execution of what is possible that is of particular interest to us in model making: we can draw anything we like, and with our digital tools we can dimensionalise this into a spatial representation, but what the physical model alone can do is inform our thinking, our experience, our imagination *as we are working with it.* This is not to say that all form stems from the material (though as much has on occasion also been suggested), but it does mean that this process works in all directions, and that therefore the practice of physical model making is as important to our thinking as is our thinking to our eventual physical output: in fact, the techniques that Semper mentions – weaving, moulding, carpentry, masonry, and working with metals – are all being picked up and newly realised in digital manufacturing processes, as we expound in detail in our chapter on Digital Manufacturing.

THE 20TH CENTURY AND THE VISIONARIES

If we allow industrial era model making to be anchored and referenced through people like Paxton and Semper, then 20th century model making is really defined by the German architect and engineer Frei Otto (1925–2015), whose most famous and eye-catching object is the membrane roof of the Olympic Stadium in Munich, opened in May 1972.

Throughout his career, Frei Otto was interested in these lightweight tensile structures and, having to develop his techniques in an age before CAD was widely available, he did so to some extent with models. He himself talked about 'developing' architecture, rather than about 'design', and it is this process-orientated approach that makes him such an influential practitioner of adaptive, integrative model making: the innovative potential in his work, you could say, rests in the great interdisciplinary way of thinking between architecture, technology, art, science, and society. Recognising the 'modelness' of nature, he tried to make it useful for architecture and engineering, and thus for the people using the architecture.

Frei Otto's work has influenced contemporary architecture for well over half a century and continues to do so, not only through the structures that were realised and that can be visited and photographed today, but also through thousands of models, drawings, pictures, and sketches that are now in the treasury of architecture. From November 2016 to March 2017, the ZKM *(Zentrum für Kunst und Medien, Centre for Art and Media)* in Karlsruhe, Germany, for example, assembled 200 models, objects, tools, and instruments alongside more than a thousand pieces of visual media, ranging from plans to prints, pictures, and projection material, for an exhibition called *Denken in Modellen,* which, curiously, it translated as *'Thinking by Modeling',* rather than the more obvious *'Thinking in Models'* that the German suggested.

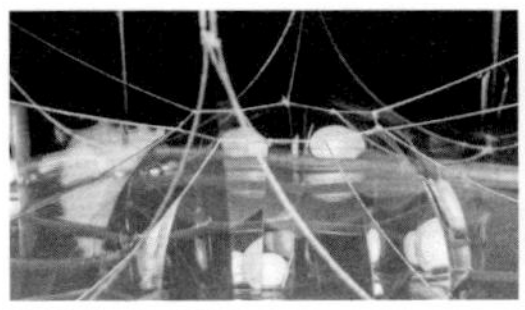
269A ● 436

269B ● 436

Other twentieth century exponents of model making who, through their systemic thinking, have paved the way towards digital methods include Swiss architect and furniture designer Fritz Haller (1924–2012), who was particularly interested in concepts such as 'universal solutions' as perhaps exemplified in his globally successful *USM Haller* office furniture system, or the 'Total City', which he developed while carrying out research at the University of Southern California under German-born American architect Konrad Wachsmann (1901–1980). Wachsmann in turn concerned himself with the universal usability of building components and the possibilities offered by industrial, prefabricated building elements.

None of these architects, thinkers, and pioneers would probably have been able to take credit for their respective life's work without at least a nod to American architect, systems theorist, and inventor Buckminster Fuller (1895–1983). He was extremely influential not just □ ↖405
as a designer, but particularly also as an architectural philosopher who cared deeply about human survival on planet Earth and pursued ways to make materials last longer and become more energy efficient. He coined the term synergetics to mean the study of ■
systems behaviour and systems transformation, and his most immediately recognisable (though also disputed) 'invention' is the geodesic dome, made from ■ ↖70
aluminium tubing and vinyl skin which, purely owing to its geometric structural properties, is capable of supporting its own weight without the need for any additional pillars, beams, or supports. (A principally identical structure by German engineer Walther Bauersfeld [1879–1959] actually predated it by some 20 years.)

270 ● 437

MODEL MAKING TODAY

We delved into our exploration of physical model making in architecture with Gaudí, and while the boundaries are always blurred, and it would therefore be foolhardy to attempt any clear delineations, he could be considered to represent a link between the methods of antiquity and the Renaissance on the one hand, and the methods of today on the other, by taking an empirical, experimental approach to what we have identified as analogue parametric modelling.

Travel *maestro-ponente*, or west-northwest, from Barcelona in a more or less straight line and effectively parallel with the French border and the Pyrenees until you hit the coast again, and you end up at another building we mention repeatedly in this *Atlas*: the Guggenheim Bilbao, by Canadian-American architect Frank Gehry (b. 1929). It's an outstanding exponent of **parametric design**, a method Gehry has been instrumental in developing; and his work is particularly relevant in the context of physical model making, because he employs a cyclical approach, starting out from a curve or a shape, then creating this as a physical model, digitising that form, adjusting it, and then printing it out and developing it further. This process is repeated, often many times, playing through variations on a theme, setting and then changing and adjusting the parameters to arrive at his shape compositions that are so distinctive and so compelling. In other words – and that's obviously why we acknowledge him here – his technique is a fine contemporary example of using models not for merely representational purposes, but as an integral part of the design process.

□ 475↘
■ ↖359 480↘

271 ○ 456

In such a cyclical process, the model represents a physical sketch, or perhaps a physical visualisation, or one of many developmental iterations, rather than the fulfilled vision of a design. And this is what we are particularly interested in with this chapter: the interplay between digital technology and the making of physical objects manually, and how the two approaches influence and inform each other; and also the particular – and particularly direct – access physical models give us to the haptics and materiality of an object while we are working on the design. As we have noted before, this is much quicker and more direct than by any other means, such as 3D modelling, for example, which thinks much more in routines than in an immediate material manifestation, and therefore has a much longer distance to cover between materiality and me.

In this context, we like to encourage thinking of ourselves as inventors: as people working at and with the intersection between cutting edge digital technology and the tangible, sensory reality of actual physical materials. This means we are operating also at the boundaries between what is imaginable (and, for example, drawable as part of a 3D model) and what is buildable: what the materials will actually bear. Such a spirit of invention and experimentation requires that we as model makers keep an open mind and use the model as an open medium. This, much as looking upon model making as learning, is an attitude we want to not only emphasise, but actively promote.

A particularly illustrative example of this interplay, and also one we discuss in some considerable detail in our chapter on [Simulation], where we cite it as a case study, is the *Elbphilharmonie* in Hamburg, by Herzog & de Meuron. Here, Nagata Acoustics, the Japanese firm tasked with creating the acoustic design for the entire project, built a 1:10 scale model of the large concert hall in order to be able to carry out actual physical acoustics measurements, which were then processed digitally; and from these simulations emerged the solution that was ultimately implemented: 10,000 bespoke panels that would line all of the surfaces in the hall other than the floor and the seats, each measuring 4–16 cm across and featuring on average a hundred microscopic divots or grooves, individually sized and spaced to maximise the desired effect of intimacy from the sound as it bounces off the surfaces at finely calibrated speed and intensity.

A similarly interesting and relevant reference is Japanese architect Toyo Ito (b. 1941), who works with medial surfaces, such as in his 1986 project Tower of Winds: in principle a fairly utilitarian structure, it serves as a ventilation shaft and houses cooling tanks for a shopping centre at Yokohama train station, but during the night time, sensors translate the ambient sound and wind into a dynamic light scape, feeding some 1300 lamps, 12 neon rings, and 30 flood lights at the tower's base. Testing, simulating, and developing this type of interactive, medial, and dynamic architecture also depends to some large extent on effective modelling and prototyping.

In fact, whenever you see contemporary constructions using vast expanses of glass, such as the Louvre Pyramid in Paris, by Chinese-American architect I M Pei (1917–2019), or 30 St Mary Axe in London, generally better known as the Gherkin, by Foster + Partners, you can assume that the engineering and glass manufacturing companies responsible for delivering the structure are using computer design and digital simulation in close and direct combination with physical models and real-life simulation to develop and test their concepts.

Model Making in Practice

THE EXPERIMENTAL SPACE

Considering that much, if not all, of your structurally critical modelling and simulation will be done digitally, the physical model is the free space of experimentation where you can explore through trial and error. This is where you can find out with your own senses which materials – foam, paper, plastic, wood, cork, glass, metal, stone, clay, sand, rubble, gravel, plants, string, cable, recycled rubbish – you want to deploy, and how. You'll need glues and a glue gun, cutters, cutting mats or some resilient surface to cut on, possibly some welding equipment, sticking tape both one and two sided; and there are micro-LEDs and glow sticks, wires, real and artificial moss and grass, cotton pads and sponges, varnishes, paints, and fixatives that may come in handy. You get the idea, and that's really as far as we want to go in telling you how to make a model: a practical course in model making is not on offer here, not least because the scope for experimentation, exploration, and doing what you enjoy, what interests and intrigues you, is so vast that your best bet is to simply go out, gather some stuff, and start making models. You have a plethora of guides and how-to resources both as videos and literature available online.

What we do want to offer is a manifesto, of sorts, for the physical model to be deployed in conjunction with digital technology. Because it's at these touch points, as we have encountered them in our examples, where digital and manual approaches meet and inform each other, that the most exciting things can happen. It's where traditional craft with its tangible manual skills meets abstract, digitally defined thought processes, where we can explore architecture in brand new ways, and ask ourselves the questions that help us define ourselves as architects: what is architecture to us, what do we want to achieve with it, how does it behave, and how do we do it, in our time.

That's why we advocate an integrative, inclusive, even holistic, approach to model making. A physical model, as we've seen with abundant clarity, is not only a compelling and instructive object for the representation of space, it is an indispensable development tool that in turn helps us make the most of our digital toolkit, as we shape our built environments. And because it is so easy to understand, so direct and sensory, it also forms a fundamental medium for collaboration and communication. This of course is true not just for architecture: in many other sectors, such as product design and manufacturing, mock-ups, prototypes, and physical simulations have for centuries now been integral to testing and trialling the handling, behaviour, and properties of anything from aeroplanes to cars to mobile phones and any household gadget you care to think of. Once an idea or concept has been materialised, it exists in the physical world, and this world then reacts and interacts with it in all its complexity, with all its physical and geometric limitations and possibilities, making these evident, visible, tangible, experienceable. That is the great strength of the physical model.

DIGITAL CRAFTING

Between 1512 and his death fourteen years later, the German painter, printmaker, and theorist Albrecht Dürer (1471–1528) extensively studied human proportions, much along the principles of Vitruvius, and the Italian Renaissance polymath Leonardo da Vinci (1452–1519), but expanding his research into physiognomy and movement too. Known as the *Four Books on Human Proportions* (*Vier Bücher von menschlicher Proportion*), Dürer's work became a cornerstone of the German Renaissance and highly influential in all subsequent European art.

Exactly five hundred years later, in 2012, a young PhD student called Pablo Garcia who, as we write this *Atlas*, is Associate Professor in the Department of Contemporary Practices at the School of the Art Institute of Chicago, took Dürer's drawings and created what he called a *profilograph:* this is a physical circular model that takes six of Dürer's 'archetypal' profiles and extrudes from them a continuous figure that seamlessly blends from one profile into the next. Projected as a shadow against a plain surface, the profilograph, when rotating, thus plays through all six profiles and all the intermediate stages in between.

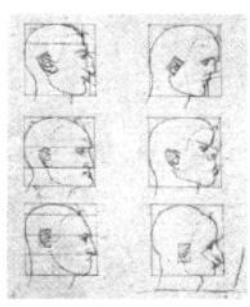

272 ● 437

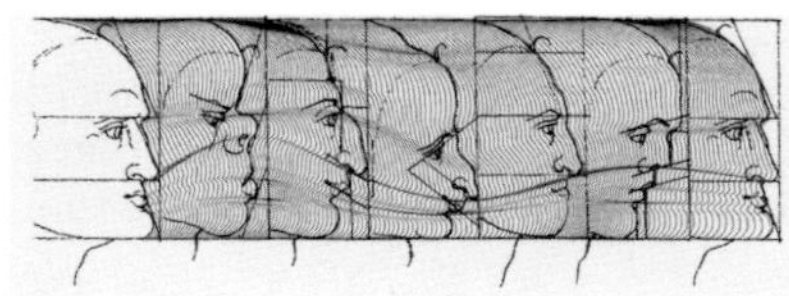

273 ● 437

This is a simple but especially charming instance of what we keep talking about in this chapter: the intersection between digital and analogue processes, where one informs the other, and something new and quite original emerges from their confluence.

We find a similar example in a small London-based setup called Robofold, founded in 2010 by Gregory Epps. His approach is one of using both manual and digital folding techniques of flat materials (principally paper and metal) in an evolutionary design process, whereby the folded objects are used as prototypes, then scanned, redigitised, recut, and refolded repeatedly until the desired shape is found.

We like to think of these approaches as 'digital crafting', as they combine the use of digital technologies with traditional skills towards the end of finding new geometries, and use materials in new combinations, often by a process of multiple reiteration.

Another noteworthy thinker and practitioner you come across in this area is the architecture theorist, furniture designer and associate professor at EPFL *(École Polytechnique Fédérale de Lausanne)* in Switzerland, Bernard Cache, who, in a 1995 book entitled *Earth Moves: the Furnishing of Territories* advanced the concept of **non-standard architecture**, which was picked up by French philosopher Gilles Deleuze (1925–1995) shortly before his death and given the label *'objectile'.* Cache in turn used this as the brand name for his own startup company the following year, which he founded together with his partner Patrick Beaucé to conceive and manufacture what they refer to as non-standard architecture components.

What these approaches have in common and what characterises them is that they emerge from the application of precision techniques in combination with the organisation of repetitive, adaptive processes to generate complex forms and freeform design through evolution and form-finding, rather than by traditional design methodologies.

MATERIALITY

We have been emphasising the materiality of the physical model, and this is clearly not limited to the 'sample', so to speak, that a model can give us of the material or materials that we are planning to use in a real world object. Often a model is made of materials that will never be used in the actual building, but still ■ ↖407 it will be able to communicate something about the relationship between different physical qualities, and it can form part of this iterative design process that we speak of when we refer to the model as a material, three-dimensional sketch.

Nobody is perhaps more strongly associated with materiality in contemporary architecture than Swiss architect Peter Zumthor (b. 1943), whose work ■ ↖407 442↘ is not only informed or shaped by the textures and visual as well as haptic qualities of the materials he uses, but almost literally seems to emerge from ■ them. If you've ever indulged yourself at his most famous – and probably most sensual – project, the Therme Vals spa in Switzerland, you will know how going deeper into the ever warmer, steamier, and □ 629↘ darker complex, and immersing yourself in its stone pools of varying sizes, feels like exploring a mysterious, and mysteriously simple, cave in the mountain itself. Obviously this is not coincidental: the building is largely constructed from locally sourced quartzite which defines its entire character.

An exhibition held in 2014 next door to another Zumthor building, the Kunsthaus Bregenz in Austria, put on display a large collection of physical models by Zumthor, showing just how much designing, working, thinking, and living with models is part of the architectural process for him.

274A ○ 457

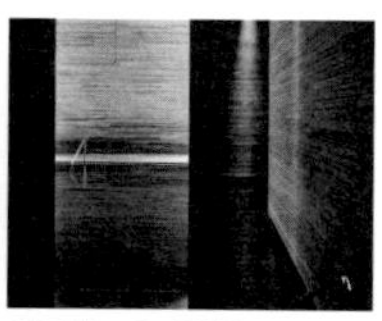

274B ○ 457

META-MATERIALITY

Taking the idea of material a step further, we can think of materials as not purely fixed, static substances, but as dynamic potentials in their own right: materials that are medial, responsive, that change shape, colour, consistency, texture, permeability, translucency – to name but these as possible examples – depending on time of day, temperature, rain precipitation, pressure exerted on them, amount of light they're exposed to, or any other factors that we can or maybe can't as yet think of. Materials themselves may then become useful applications, and we can begin to talk of a *'materiability':* material that has capabilities, that is intelligent, 'smart'.

275 ● 437

The physical model – irrespective of what materials we use to make it – in this context becomes part of a medial process, a continuous prototype that allows the architect or designer to keep trying out things, to test new combinations, to invent new materials, to make their own tools, and advance their own concepts, irrespective of what is supposed to be 'economical' or 'possible', or even, for as long as we are in the realm of creative exploration, 'safe' or 'responsible'. In conjunction with **digital modelling**, the design process does not, therefore, end with the materialisation of a virtual model; instead, a feedback loop is set in motion, where the physical model and the virtual model inform each other, and where the focus is on the intersection between virtuality and its physical translation, the object.

This spirit and approach to modelling fits with the **maker culture** that encourages and enables the sharing of open-source software as well as hardware, tools, machines, and facilities in what are known as **makerspaces** around the world, in other words: collaboration. (We discuss this and its equivalence in software design, for example the extraordinary story of the *Linux* operating system, in our chapter on Collaboration.)

BUILDING A DRAWING

We want to spin the thought of the model as a physical sketch just a little further, because it particularly interests us. We're used to the idea of drawing a building. But English architect and historian Jonathan Hill (b. 1958), in an article published in *Nordisk Arkitekturforskning* in 2002 entitled *Building a Drawing and Drawing a Building* invoked the reverse idea:

> "The two principal alternatives of architectural drawing are drawing a building or building a drawing, but great pleasure, and creative tension that has enormously stimulated architectural design, exists where they overlap, one feeding the other. A dialogue can exist between what is designed and how it is designed, between design intention and working medium. The selected 'drawing' medium is not just a means to represent, but a means to design, informing what is designed, and vice versa. If a building is to be made of artificial light, it can first be modelled in artificial light and drawn in photograms, so that the material of the building is also the material of the drawing. Similarly, a line drawing would make line architecture, not one of mass."

It is this interplay between what is being designed and the design process itself where the great power of the model lies.

MAKING ARCHITECTURE

In an information-saturated, fully networked, and consequently constantly dynamic world such as ours, it can be easy enough to lose sight of our senses. There is an irony perhaps in this, because virtual, augmented, and mixed reality experiences are entirely at the forefront of digital technology drives, and more than once in this *Atlas* do we point towards these as areas which are likely to play a much bigger role in architecture in the foreseeable future. This does create paradoxes: while nobody could accuse our current culture of being altogether too intellectual or even just cerebral, we are spending inordinate amounts of our time essentially 'in our heads', doing things on computers and interacting with screens and displays to create our digital realities.

But we are still physical, organic beings. We have acutely tuned senses that pick up the tiniest fluctuations in our sphere of perception, often long before we're able to tell what it is that we notice. We even call this our 'sixth sense', and although we don't have any precise metrics for it, we know that all the factors of our experience make for a whole that is signally greater than the sum of its parts. As architects, we cannot ignore this. Architecture is a sensory experience, and within it, many of the factors that make this experience what it is can't be separated out from each other, nor can they even be simulated. Some of course can (as noted earlier, we devote an entire chapter to Simulation), but if we are to succeed at making architecture that works for us as human beings, we have to, to some extent, take the word 'make' literally and allow ourselves to take things – objects, materials, tools – into our own hands and actually make stuff.

That way we can, as American sociology professor Richard Sennett (b. 1943) sees it, allow our head and hand to enter a dialogue and set the scene for an interplay between *homo sapiens* – here possibly seen less through the lens of the 'wise man' epithet that we have given our own species, than as a description of ourselves as 'thinking' or 'knowing' creatures – and *homo faber,* ourselves as 'the maker', in control of our own destiny, not through the power of our intellect but through knowing how to use our tools. Sennett is not the first nor the only person to suggest that treating 'head' and 'hand' as adversaries ultimately harms both and damages our understanding as much as our expression of ourselves, but that does not take away from what we think should be our ambition: to develop these two faculties of ours, 'head' and 'hand', into an indivisible union, and to become good at our craft, because that, in itself, is of value. As Sennett wrote in a piece entitled *Labours of Love* for *The Guardian* in 2008:

> "The carpenter, lab technician, and conductor are all craftsmen because they are dedicated to good work for its own sake. Theirs is practical activity, but their labour is not simply a means to another end. The carpenter might sell more furniture if he worked faster; the technician might make do by passing the problem back to her boss; the visiting conductor might be more likely to be rehired if he watched the clock. It's certainly possible to get by in life without dedication, but the craftsman exemplifies the special human condition of being engaged."

There is a well-rehearsed notion (which may or may not be strictly true) that it takes roughly 10,000 hours of practice to become a master at anything. Mastering a technique of any description and in any field ■ ↖103 465↘
according to this is principally a question of practice and dedication, of learning, experiencing, and experimenting with materials as much as with computer programmes, with physical tools as much as with digital ones. Beyond this, what Sennett speaks of fundamentally is a different stance towards much of what we're used and driven to today. Which is why we want to air it not just as a possibility or as an alternative, but as a principal choice of attitude that may well define how we understand ourselves as architects.

For decades now, certainly since the 1980s, we have found ourselves in a culture dominated by optimisation and efficiency: get as much out of everything as quickly as possible; after all, there are, somewhere along the line, profits at stake. This may be a brash generalisation, and clearly at the other end of the spectrum artists and craftspeople such as Sennett describes have not ceased to thrive or hone their skills, patiently and with great determination. But many artists and craftspeople, not just architects, continually come under pressure to 'get results', in as straight a line as possible from A (project initiation, contract being awarded) to B (project completion, ideally with a fanfare, to schedule and within budget). □ 475↘
And there are good reasons for this too, which we don't mean to negate: everybody has a budget and everybody wants their building to go up in good time. If you're talking about an Olympic complex, the whole multi-billion undertaking depends on it. But this efficiency and results driven – arguably 'corporate' – culture creates a mindset, and it permeates even academic institutions and places of learning, where the focus has shifted so much to churning out experts that will do well in business terms, with immediately applicable and sellable skills, that many an 'academy' has all but lost claim to that name as a place for the pursuit and practice of wisdom, knowledge, and the mastery of skills, for their own sake.

And yet here we are, at a time of extraordinary possibility and potential, with the most inspiring range of tools and technologies and a millennia-old heritage in skill and understanding. So why not make the most of this, and allow for cross-fertilisation of art and craft, of purpose and imagination, of precision and fancy?

An interesting example in this context is the Canadian architect and sculptor Philip Beesley who, according to his own website, has an interest in "responsive and distributed architectural environments and interactive systems, flexible lightweight structures integrating kinetic functions, microprocessing, sensors and actuator systems, with particular focus on digital fabrication methods and sheet-material derivations."

His works combine materiality and sensuality with crest-of-the-wave digital design and manufacturing technology that allows not only for incredible precision and accuracy in the creation of models and model-like objects, but also for these to take on medial behaviour. They illustrate just how wide the scope is for physical model making in the digital age.

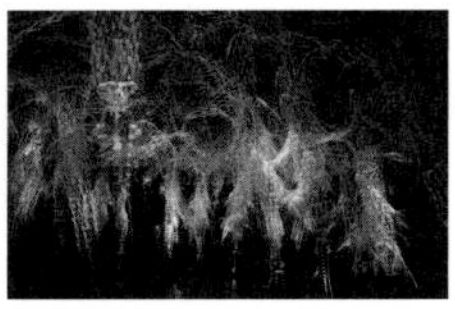

276 ○ 458

The French philosopher Michel de Montaigne (1533–1592) speaks of the healing power of failure. This is well understood not only at the personal, incremental level of little failures overcome turning into small triumphs of greater insight, but also on the grand, spectacular scale: those who have at one point failed miserably populate our 21st century 'hall of fame' across all disciplines, from Albert Einstein to Steve Jobs to Oprah Winfrey to J K Rowling. Patience and the right to fail and then to try, and try again, these are not luxuries, they are part and parcel of becoming excellent.

As a craftsperson or artist, you have to be able to take the limitations set by what is available – time, space, money – and turn them into your opportunities; the raw materials at your disposal themselves may prompt you to try new fusions, making for new metamorphoses. You are called upon to recognise coincidences that will help you burst your boundaries, to meet obstacles with improvisation to overcome them. If you're short of a tool to make the thing you want, you will just have to make your own tool. Therein lies invention, imagination: creation.

The physical model embodies this other, slower, more organic, arguably more human approach, and that's why it matters; but digital technologies open up a wide new field here that is directly connected to the manufacturing of real things, not just models, but mock-ups, prototypes, and indeed actual structures and architectural elements and objects.

The Outlook

□ 507↘

In his eponymous curve, the American architect Patrick MacLeamy (b. 1942), illustrates how Building Information Modelling (BIM) can help designers move the important decision making stages towards the earlier part of the process, when their influence on the whole project is still greater and the costs are still lower than they will be later on. This, as we describe in our chapter on the subject, is seen as a way of optimising architecture and reducing the potential for costly mistakes, and BIM puts a particular emphasis on it, elevating efficiency to a principal goal and beyond that to almost a design philosophy. Digital modelling in general tilts in favour of making decisions early on and determining from the outset the parameters within which variations and design alternatives are then played through. This is in the virtual 'nature' of things digital: you can layer objects and build them bit by bit, element by element. You can also experiment and treat digital modelling as a process, but you have to advance this to quite a considerable level before you are able, with a digital model, to communicate a 'feel' for the materiality and physicality you propose to be working with.

In that sense, digital modelling discourages you from treating the model as a 'sketch'. It doesn't make it impossible, but the emphasis lies much more on the result and on getting things right to achieve that result. A physical model, on the other hand, encourages you as the designer to explore your project more freely, in an open process that is not necessarily object or goal orientated, but that forms an organic part of a form-finding exploration from the inside out. The material, rather than the objective, leads the journey, and – perhaps paradoxically – by taking the process away from the abstraction of a digitised version of itself, it becomes easier to focus on the idea and to communicate it through the physical entity you're creating.

Another way to describe this difference of emphasis offers itself through looking at our role in the process. It is obviously important that you work with the materials that you are going to use, if you are to learn how these materials behave and fit together to create harmonies or tensions. In physical model making it is therefore not necessarily the form that comes first and dictates the materials, but instead the form develops from an amalgamation of processes; materials then inform the code and the manufacturing methods and machines that are being used in turn.

So it is not a case of either using traditional manual methods or digital technology, it is more simply the case that in this 'bottom up' configuration of all available techniques we can master what the machine does, rather than being dictated to by what it can do. And this is of the greatest importance, so much so that we stress it repeatedly in this *Atlas*: as architects we have to, in a way, become 'master builders' again, almost in a Renaissance sense; we have to understand what goes on 'behind the scenes' of computer programs and be literate in code; we have to know the physical properties of the materials we use in our buildings and continually demand of ourselves that we ask good questions. And that means going beyond the superficial banality of the goal, and actively investigating the processes and possible pathways that can get us there. The model is a perfect tool to this purpose.

So is there a future for physical model making? Unless you've skipped everything we've said in this chapter so far and jumped straight to the conclusion, you'll know that we're bound to say: yes. And emphatically so. Model making hasn't died out, and it isn't going to become extinct, and nor is the dedicated job of the Model Maker. Across the fully digitalised, networked world you will find individuals, studios, collaborative partnerships and new and old enterprises that devote themselves entirely to making physical models by one method or another. Many, of course, use digital modelling and manufacturing techniques that we have not touched on in this chapter, but deal with in the other, related, ones; others find ways of creating niches for themselves by working with particular materials, be that clay, or plaster, or wood, or plastics, or metals, or any combination of traditional or groundbreaking modelling bases.

As architects we always, repeatedly, continually, have to – want to – ask ourselves: what is it we are doing, how, and why? If ever there were any obvious, off-the shelf answers to these questions – which we don't truly believe there were – then by now they would have evaporated in a world of near-infinite possibilities. We advocate, as you know, an open minded and inquisitive approach. We are physical human beings with immense intellectual capacity. It's the combination of these two, not separate but fully entwined, aspects to our existence that has got us to where we are today: our experience of the physical world we inhabit is as much dependent on our understanding of it as our understanding is dependent on our experience of it.

If there is anything we need to be wary of, it is being sucked into a cultural vortex that could force us into losing our playfulness, our freedom to fail, our sense of adventure in being knocked down and getting up again, our curiosity about what that thing does to our skin, on our tongue, under our fingernails, and down our spine, our willingness to invest time and effort and brain space and muscle brawn to try out something that has never been tried before, our courage to risk everything for a brilliant idea; and to sacrifice all or any of these on the altar of efficiency, cost-effectiveness, and optimisation. Or to fall in with the crowd: to do just what everybody else is doing, because everybody else is doing it. To accept, unquestioningly, a *modus operandi* and think that in order to get anywhere, we have to fit in. Let that not be so: insist on your right to do it your own sweet way and find horizons completely different to the ones everybody else is looking towards. Do as the craftsperson does: focus on quality and improving your own practice above all.

The manually made model may seem a mere luxury, superseded by the greater efficacy of the digital toolkit. We say: get the best of both worlds and take an and-and approach to forge a creative space for yourself. Because it's in that space that amazing things happen. Become computer literate and learn to code, so you can not only use your digital tools, but adapt them, make them your own, make your own from scratch even. Learn the language of classic geometry: if you're not being taught it, demand to know. And roll up your sleeves, get your hands dirty, and make things from scratch, with whatever material that you find attractive. And who's to say that the processes can not be backwards and forwards reversed and exchanged: why would you *not* make a model of clay to get a feel for some kind of shape, then scan this shape, work with it on your computer, then print out a more intricate version of the model before moving on to define its parameters and creating a fully fledged 3D model, from which you draw visualisations, sections, and plans?

There is, as you can tell, a cultural aspect to this that we care about. As architects we have to – want to – collaborate with other people, with engineers, clients, contractors, craftspeople, the public. We want to be able to inspire and inform them, and we want to be able to learn from them. There are many digital and real world movements, tools, and platforms – from the makerspaces and open-source software we've already mentioned, to citizen participation, which we ■ 516↘
talk more about in our chapter on Digital Cities – that □ 529↘
shape and define this culture, which stands in stark contrast to the corporate, proprietary, control-driven culture that also exists and in many areas of the economy forcefully prevails.

As architects, then, we have to – want to – make quite fundamental, principal, ethical, perhaps even ideological, decisions that steer not only us ourselves but also the world we help build in one direction or another. When it comes to model making, this, among other things, entails taking a stance on whether we want to be service users and consumers, or co-creators. Are we going to layer a proposal in a convenient piece of software and then send it to the laser cutter and end up with our model, or are we going to work with an atelier or studio at eye level and develop the best possible model making technique that uses all the available and to us at the time affordable techniques and technologies in a creative, possibly even groundbreaking way?

We are interested in the exchange of disciplines and the new perspectives and impulses this exchange offers for model making and for architecture in general. And this is something we certainly see happening and expect to continue: a coming together of disciplines, a search for, and finding of, a common language. It used not to be the case that the architect was able to employ the same vocabulary as the IT specialist from the engineering firm. Now we can. We are working as directly with the web designer who makes our online presence as we are with the master carpenter who puts up the truss structure for the roof on the house we're building. There are many such touch points; and so we have much greater specialisation as people have to find their place in a complex, enmeshed professional world, but we also have a much greater coming together of specialists. We argue that we need to celebrate and cultivate this coming together, with workshops, factories, and shared spaces, both in the virtual and in the physical world.

First and foremost though – and this applies not only, but particularly, to physical model making, which is why we stress it here one more time – we need to articulate and communicate, through words and deeds, the inherent, for-its-own-sake value of creating. Creating is experimenting and experimenting is doing, for real.

261 ● 424
A 'hanging chain model' as used by Gaudí. [Milena Stavric]

262 ● 425
Physical visualisation: clay tokens in Mesopotamia, circa 5500 BCE. [Denise Schmandt-Basserat]

263 ● 425
Kryssvalv (Cross vaults) by Patrik Bergman, Per Erikson, and Åse Hagen [Carolina Menezes]

265 ● 425
Model of St Peter's Basilica by Antonio da San Gallo, measuring 7.36 m in width and 4.68 m in height. [arthistory390]

266 ● 426
The Würzburg Residence by Balthasar Neumann: a particularly fine example of German Baroque architecture, constructed between 1720 and 1744. [Rainer Lippert]

267A ● 426

267B ● 426

The Great Conservatory at Chatsworth (267A), designed by Paxton and completed in 1840, heavily influenced the design of the Palm House (267B) at Kew Gardens (1844–48). 84 metres long, 37 metres wide, and 19 metres tall, the Great Conservatory was the largest glass building in England until the construction of Paxton's Crystal Palace for the Great Exhibition at Hyde Park in 1851. [Godine | David Iliff]

268A ● 426
Model of Crystal Palace (268A) and the actual building (268B) by Joseph Paxton, 1851: the modular, on-site prefabricated glass and steel structure was revolutionary at the time. [Frank Dinger | Hulton Archive]

268B ● 426

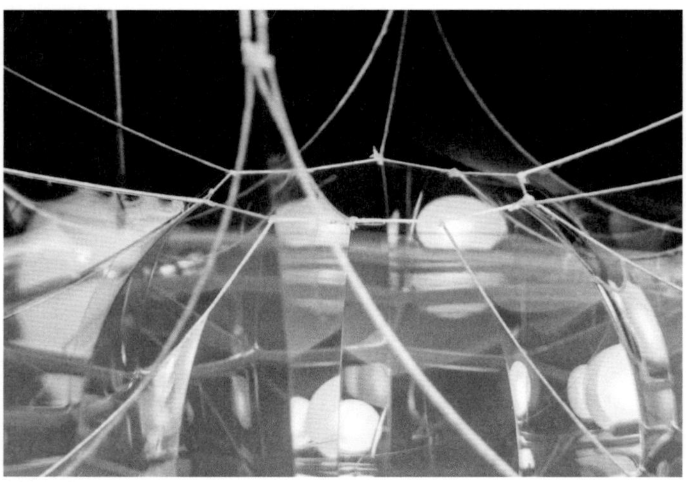

269A ● 427

269B ● 427

Frei Otto: soap bubbles model (269A) and lattice roof model (269B).
[SAAI *(Südwestdeutsches Archiv für Architektur und Ingenieurbau)* | Oskar von Miller Forum]

270 ● 427
Buckminster Fuller: the geodesic dome. [Milena Stavric]

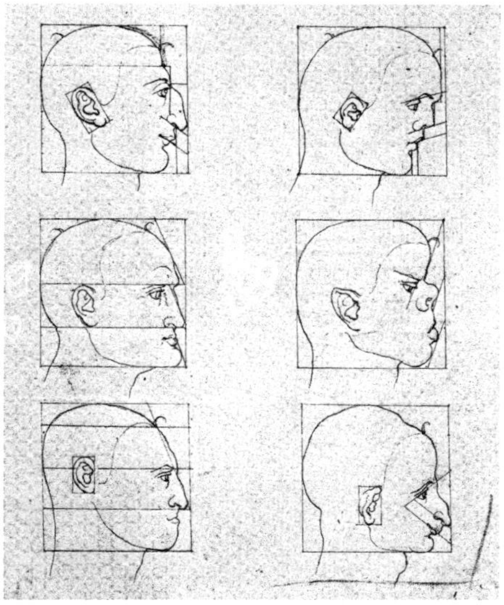

272 ● 429
Albrecht Dürer: six profiles from *Four Books on Human Proportions*

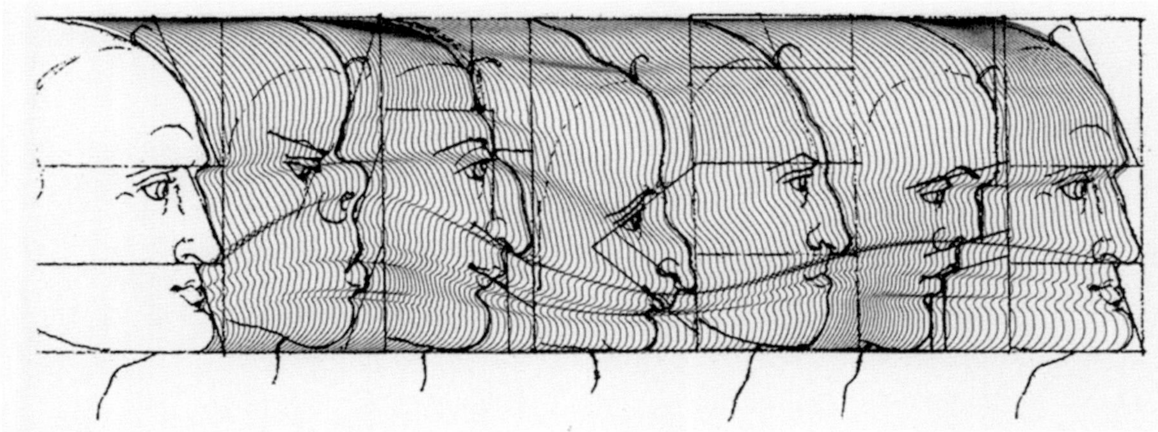

273 ● 429
Pablo Garcia: *Profilograph* after Dürer. [Pablo Garcia]

275 ● 430
'Materiability': liberating 'smart' materials. [Manuel Kretzer]

3D Printing

Oliver Fritz

Overview

3D Printing □ ↖439 isn't really printing at all. Then again, the more technical term additive manufacturing ■ ↖407 is only partially more accurate in describing the various methods that jointly fall under its widely used, and fairly wide, definition. With some technologies you add, with others it's more a case of subtracting, mostly it's a process that involves *melding* material to the end of forming an object (or a batch of objects) directly from a three-dimensional template or drawing generated on a computer. So what exactly *is* 3D printing? And why does it matter to architecture?

277 ● 451

We will describe the currently available 3D printing methods in some detail in a moment, but the principle for all of them is the same, even if they arrive at distinct results by decidedly different means. When in 2D printing you identify specific locations on a two-dimensional plane and furnish these locations with ink or a similar colouring agent to give you desired shapes – letters, images, patterns, maps – yielding visual representations of your two-dimensional original, in 3D printing you identify specific locations in three-dimensional space and similarly furnish these locations with material to give you a physical representation of an object that previously existed as a 3D drawing, plan, model, or design.

Since the arrival of digital technology, we have got used to think of such specific locations on the two-dimensional plane as *pixels*, and we expect an image or a font to be proportionally clearer and crisper – more highly defined – the smaller these pixels are and the more densely they populate the surface. This is where we get Dots Per Inch (DPI) ■ ↖235 as a measure of print definition from: the more dots there are on the page in a row per inch, the higher will be the definition of the resulting pattern or image. In three-dimensional space, the corresponding unit is a *voxel*, but as it happens, most 3D print processes don't in actual fact identify individual points in space and place them as discrete locations, but rather define and follow *vectors*. 3D printing therefore in that respect borrows more from vector graphics ■ ↖335 – where two-dimensional images are defined not by individual points either, but by vectors – than it does from pixel-based raster graphics ■ ↖232. (We discuss pixels and voxels in more detail in our chapters on Image & Colour □ ↖229 and 3D Modelling □ ↖57.)

So if the idea of print is one of imprinted copies of a pattern, multiplied quickly and in potentially very large numbers, then the term 'printing' here is maybe not so helpful. If the idea of print is simply a truthful representation of a thing, irrespective of speed or quantity (perhaps similar to a photographic print), then the term is already much more applicable.

What actually happens in 3D printing – and this again is principally the same irrespective of which method or process you use – is that minute particles of liquid, viscous, or dry pulverised material are fused, melded, or glued together to form a solid object; and what makes the technology famously versatile is that the methods and processes available to do so cover such a wide range of materials that virtually anything you can design or scan and therefore visualise in a piece of 3D software, you can then also 'print'. But when we say 'anything you can visualise you can print', we have to also, and immediately, add a major caveat, if perhaps not so much in theory as in practice. In *theory* it is entirely true to say that you can print anything that you can design on a computer. In practice, however, even top of the range 3D print technology does not yet in all settings and reliably always deliver satisfactory results, and it is by no means certain whether it ever will, particularly in life-size architecture.

The challenges you face with 3D printing are still legion, for example when it comes to haptics: many digitally printed materials – such as resins and plastics – simply don't feel as good to the touch as wood, metal, or stone. You can 'print' metal or ceramics, and even wood-derived materials, but doing so well is neither simple nor quick: it can be messy, laborious, wasteful, and expensive. Or take durability: there are (as we mention a little further below under *A Very Brief History of 3D Printing)* aerospace manufacturers now who use digital printing techniques to produce engine parts, because they are tougher and more efficient than those made by traditional methods, but that is the exceptionally high end of 3D printing. Towards the middle and lower ends, a printed material's reliability and stability may not always compare well with those manufactured by other methods.

The point we are making here, therefore, is not a blanket statement about quality or let alone the aesthetics or more intricate aspects of 3D printing, but a distinction between something that you 'print' and something that you 'construct'. In 3D printing, there's no 'building' in the traditional sense: you don't have to solve any problems of engineering systemically. In fact, 3D printing allows for the exact opposite approach to how engineers used to think: rather than starting with building blocks and working out how they can be configured into a complex structure, with 3D printing you set out with a structure of whatever complexity you seek, and the material *becomes* this thing: no tools, no assembly, no screws and fixtures required. For most of the available methods, there isn't even a bonding agent, since the particles themselves 'stick' together: the 'glue' is the material itself. What you effectively do in 3D printing is *render* your design physically.

278 ● 451

THE CONCEPTUAL SHIFT

If you can render in material anything you can design, then you can make anything you can imagine. (In our context here, we'll keep calling it 'print', because accurate or not, the term has established itself, and this chapter is entitled '3D Printing' after all.) And you can do so by a fully or near-fully automated process that requires no specialist skill or attendant expertise. In this respect, 3D printing is different to any other way of making things that we've known before. And because of this, we are with 3D printing looking at a step change: what we might cautiously label a 'conceptual shift'.

3D printing therefore is worth examining briefly at conceptual level. Before it became viable, you could build or construct or assemble anything you were able to build or construct or assemble. This sounds obvious, but what it means is that you could make what your building elements – bricks, beams, screws, joints, fillers, girders – and your skill or expertise at putting them together allowed you to make. The limitations, setting aside cost or brief, were dictated by the materials you had available on the one hand and by your engineering capacity on the other. Thus, making a highly ornate, delicately patterned relief ceiling panel, for example, would require not only a particular type of wood, stone, clay, or plaster that could take on and durably hold your design, it would also presuppose a level of craftsmanship and technical know-how that would allow you to actually produce this design. If you were an architect, builder, artist, or designer, you had
■ ↖411 to learn your craft and master it.

With 3D printing, you can use a vast array of materials, from cheap polymers to exceedingly strong metals like titanium, and yet your limitations, such as they are, are dictated mostly by your imagination; and perhaps by the fundamental laws of physics. Within these, you can do more or less whatever you want: if you have mastered it as a *concept* – a design, an idea that you are able to visualise three-dimensionally as a computer drawing – you can most likely also produce it as a physical object. There is comparatively little expertise involved. It would be disingenuous to say 'none', since most 3D print processes require some degree of post-production, which to do well is not necessarily easy and may in turn have to be learnt. But there is no construction work, no calculation, not even really in that sense any trial and error. And in this particular point lies one of the most practical and applicable uses and therefore advantages of 3D printing: you can do whatever you want and then change a detail here, a parameter there, a set of rules or attributes elsewhere, and the printer will render out another version, altered in line with your amendments.
■ ↖430 Your 'trial and error' turns into play: variations on your theme. And as 3D printing matures, you can now do this with increasing delicacy and precision, down to molecular level, or right up to an inhabitable 1:1 scale.

This has many implications, in terms purely of practicality (what can be built in the first place), in terms of cost (how expensive it is to generate and develop a particular design), and in terms of workflow (how you arrive at your final object or building from your design). But sticking with the notion of a conceptual shift for one moment longer, it also has some fairly far-reaching consequences for our understanding of 'making things'. Because if you can generate complex forms without tools in one go, then that means *everything* can become complex, multi-layered, in a sense sophisticated. You can integrate functionalities into textures, electronics into layers, dynamics into design. This is not to say that you *have to* do so, or that it even necessarily makes sense to do so, but it opens up a new range of possibilities, which are characteristically different to what you had available before as a designer, and therefore as an architect.

3D printing, then, has the potential to give you new freedoms. And with new freedoms, of course, come new and very different types of challenges and responsibilities. Because fundamentally it means you are your own boundary. And with unlimited options, which ones do you choose? According to which criteria? What are your priorities? If 'anything is possible', what, if anything, is 'necessary'? What 'good'? Or 'beautiful'? Or 'interesting'? Or 'relevant'? Or even just 'desirable'? 3D printing is not alone in this, but rather it is part of a technological development that demands of us new, but basic decisions. It asks, as other digital technologies ask: 'What do you want to do, if you can do whatever you like?' And that's what we mean by a conceptual shift.

A VERY BRIEF HISTORY OF 3D PRINTING

Speaking to an interviewer on *Good Morning America* in a science segment that was broadcast on 30 January 1989, the American inventor of stereolithography, Chuck Hull (b. 1939), explained what his machine did by saying: "I think a good way to describe it is to call it a three-dimensional printer." It is highly probable, though not certain, that as well as 3D printing by this particular method, he thus also introduced the term '3D printing'. The patent for his invention, which he had developed in the early 1980s, had been granted in 1986, and by the end of the 1980s, stereolithographic 3D printing had become commercially available. It quickly yielded great competitive advantages to car manufacturers in particular, because theirs is the kind of industry that puts a lot of effort into research and development, with modelling an essential and up to this point especially time-consuming and costly part of the process.

As expensive machines that were able to quickly, easily, and relatively cheaply produce fully bespoke individual pieces, 3D printers soon also formed an ideal offering for FabLab, founded at the Massachusetts Institute of Technology (MIT) in 2002 by Neil Gershenfeld. This allowed people to share a space and facilities and, as its motto proclaimed, "make (almost) anything," which in turn marked the beginning of a maker culture or movement that was characterised by small companies and individuals similarly sharing resources to pursue their own individual projects.

Soon after, in 2004, the English mathematician and engineer Adrian Bowyer (b. 1952) published an essay which sketched out the development of an open-source, cost effective 3D printer. This led to the establishment of the RepRap Research Foundation, which had the purpose of developing these plans as a not-for-profit organisation. Following the great demand for RepRap, from this emerged MakerBot

Industries in 2009, which to this day makes desktop 3D printers under its own brand.

279 ● 451

In 2006, Hull's patent on stereolithography expired, and this turned 3D printing over to the public domain. As a result, prices quickly tumbled, making the technology readily accessible at consumer, prosumer, and boutique level.

Fast forward another ten years to 2016, and Mattel brings to market a printer called *ThingMaker* at a retail price of USD 299, putting 3D printing at everyone's fingertips. Meanwhile, at the other end of the spectrum, the range of materials that printers are capable of shaping has grown and begun to include serious manufacturing bases such as steel, bronze, titanium, and porcelain. In August 2016, USA's NASA (National Aeronautics and Space Administration) announced that it would be using 3D printing in the manufacture of its new *Space Launch System (SLS)* rocket, because it found that printed injectors tested up to ten times more efficient than traditionally manufactured ones.

So from environments where weight, reliability, and performance make the difference between success and failure of a mission (to Mars, no less, for example), to those where cost is permanently at the forefront of feasibility considerations (such as in the manufacture of cars), right through to consumer level, where ease of use and affordability are the main selling points, 3D printing technology has been chalking up notable breakthroughs over its short but impressive history.

THE IMPACT OF 3D PRINTING

On 15 February 2016, *Nature Magazine's* biotechnology website published an article called *A 3D Bioprinting System to Produce Human-Scale Tissue Constructs With Structural Integrity*. The following day, Tyler Koslow, a writer for the *3D Printing Industry* website reported this under the marginally more evocative headline: *Bioprinting Breakthrough: Researchers 3D Print Living Tissue for Functional Implants*.

Nowhere appear the advances in 3D printing more striking – and more strikingly *useful* – than in their medical context. We are on the point of being able to print *functional implants with living tissue*, and this has immeasurable implications. We are already successfully printing fixed and mechanical parts for our bodies, with obvious benefits for patients. Bone replacements, skull patches, joints, nose cartilage, vertebrae: replacing a damaged or lost portion of a person's body cheaply and quickly with a purpose-made component that fits perfectly can change their quality of life for the rest of their days. We're about to take this one step further, with, in the longer term, printed organs ready for transplant: spare parts for humans, bespoke and produced on demand.

3D printed body parts for human beings are at one end of the spectrum, occupying the place where 'design' (so to speak, or at any rate their shape) strictly follows their function, which is to augment or replace an existing purpose. At the other end of the spectrum, 3D printing is well placed to liberate design from functionality and allow the designer of an object to put their imagination above all else and so create completely at whim: you can print a guitar that looks like it's made of chocolate, and there's nothing to stop you from printing chocolate to look exactly like a guitar. Whether or not there is any point to doing so is a different matter entirely. But once upon a time, a rose was a rose was a rose; now you can print a rose that is actually an inhaler. Or a screwdriver. Or, quite conceivably, a rose.

None of this, incidentally, is entirely unheard of: Catalan artist Salvador Dalí (1904–1989) in 1936 presented the world with his aptly named *Lobster Phone*, which unsurprisingly is a phone in the shape of a lobster. What *is* new, and what's different, and what is likely to have a great effect on our understanding of 'manufacture', is that virtually anything is possible in almost any material, essentially at the push of a button. And this at domestic, creative studio, and industrial level. Which is why 3D printing will continue to grow in terms of the impact it has on all spheres of life, even when it comes to very mundane, day-to-day matters.

Say the swivel bit that connects the hose to your vacuum cleaner breaks. Before the Internet, you would go to the hardware store or the manufacturer's outlet and hope they still stock the part you need, so you can purchase it. Or you might phone up the manufacturer and order it from their catalogue. Since the Internet, you've been much more likely to order it from the manufacturer's website and wait for it to arrive in the post.

3D printing allows you to download the part from your manufacturer's website and print it out for yourself today, probably at a fraction of the cost. Though what is important here is not so much the cost benefit to you as the consumer, nor even the time it will take you to get back to your spring clean: neither of these make for a breathtaking change in the quality of your life. What really matters is that manufacturing as we've known it throughout the industrial age is changing and possibly coming towards an end.

When for nearly two centuries the best way to make things of a decent quality at an affordable price was in standardised mass production, shipped to large warehouses, and distributed through immense logistical apparatus, what we'll find more and more is that we can get the part that we need just from our own printer, or, if we don't have or want a printer ourselves, from the local print shop. And even if it isn't us who carries out or specifically orders the print job, the part may still be printed individually, at the manufacturer's own facility. Just-in-time delivery morphs into decentralised production-on-demand, while serial, standard mass production is becoming less and less relevant in more and more areas. Because another thing all of the currently available 3D print methods have in common is that it makes no real difference whether you print a thousand pieces of one design, or one piece of a thousand different designs each, and that is something that absolutely does not apply to industrial manufacturing processes.

Our mindset can thus take a new step: when throughout antiquity and the Renaissance our manufacturing tradition was rooted in literally making things by hand, modernity moved away from the small workshop and the specialist artisan to the factory with industrial mass production, generating, in the process, not only previously untold material 'wealth' but also unimaginable quantities of rubbish, waste, and excess. 3D printing makes possible something of a 'return to craft', you could say, except of course it is not a return at all, it's a progression to a completely new type of artisanry: one enabled, informed, and fed by digital technology.

New as it is though, it has similar characteristics: we can move away from making generic products in large quantities that conform to simple standards in return for obtaining affordability and convenience, and instead newly embrace bespoke design. If this allows us to make objects while in the process generating less waste, requiring less packaging, involving shorter delivery paths, and much reduced logistical infrastructures, then that too may amount to a significant impact.

3D PRINTING IN ARCHITECTURE

As we write this at the end of the second decade of the twenty-first century, there is a palpable sense of excitement abroad in the world of 3D printing in architecture, because people are beginning to 'print' actual houses. Up until very recently, the main applications for 3D printing in architecture had been confined to prototyping and model making, where the speed, comparative ease, and undeniable versatility with which ideas could be rendered as tangible objects has transformed practice. When previously a small atelier may have had to devote its entire staff for a whole week to the task of making just one scale model, now a skilled CAD designer can do so in a day and print a near flawless specimen. (The 'near' here may be an operative term: depending on a model's intricacies and the 3D print method used, a model may still be in need of a fair amount of manual cleaning up and detailing before it could be called 'flawless', as we've hinted before.)

280 ● 452

☐ ↖145

Especially in conjunction with other approaches in digital architecture, such as Generative Methods, which we briefly touch on in *The Outlook* below and cover in its own chapter, one of the strengths of 3D printing lies in allowing for a workflow that is not just computer aided but genuinely information technology driven. If we said before that anything you can imagine in three-dimensional space can now be rendered as a physical object, then that still holds true in the context of architecture; and because of the range of available print materials, this really opens up new horizons for what is achievable. There is a sense that if we now start printing multi-layered, in time even technology enhanced, structures or structural components that then form a building, we are entering a phase in architecture where we no longer really 'build'. Instead, we 'orchestrate'. And we can do so in a manner that is largely informed by our design priorities, in other words: our imagination.

281 ● 452

How architects the world over will put this potential – and with it its many new challenges – into their practice very much remains to be seen. In 2015, in Suzhou, near Shanghai, China, engineer and entrepreneur Ma Yihe received a lot of attention for building a 'luxury villa' in two days with a large printing machine that uses a specially (and secretly) formulated type of concrete. Meanwhile, in Amsterdam, Hedwig Heinsman and DUS Architects were in the process of outputting their first printed canal-side townhouse, using a prefabrication method: components are printed offsite and then assembled on location. Also in the Netherlands, a live project to print the first pedestrian bridge across a narrow canal was underway by 2016. These are eye-catching developments, using very different approaches not only in terms of printing technology deployed, but also in terms of their architectonic ambition and purpose.

As is typical for any technology that is advancing from a nascent and highly specialised phase to a mature and broadly applicable one, its actual uses and, more to the point, its actually useful applications need to be tested and found out, and this is happening even as we speak. Does the fact alone that we can print internal partitions that have their wiring and light switches built into them mean that we should actually do so, when perfectly decent and handsome light switches are readily available for a few cents or euros, and when a piece of flat material that is well insulated and easily capable of housing basic technology can be made efficiently and cost-effectively on a production line?

Leaving aside the questions of efficiency and cost, what do printed building elements and structures look and feel like? What kind of finish to we want to live or work in, and is there anything in the array of printable materials that comes close to the warmth and texture of a hardwood floor, for example, or the sheen of an exquisite veneer? Architecture is clearly more than mere design: haptic, aesthetic, and atmospheric aspects play as much into the architect's consideration as structural and practical ones.

Many would argue therefore, and we feel inclined to agree, that the really exciting developments in 3D printing for architecture do not lie in building entire houses, nor even large building components such as walls, girders, pillars, or supports, but in printing intricate bespoke components that would be expensive and difficult to make otherwise: joints and brackets, glass frames and cladding, for example, or transitions and multi-layered elements consisting of several different materials that may have to be positioned with micrometre precision. It is no coincidence that 3D printing is proving so successful in medicine, as indeed it is in high tech engineering: both involve calibrating 3D printing machines for individually produced objects with incredible accuracy. But scaling this up to the macro dimensions of a house or a building complex is a whole different ball game.

So for you as an architect, there may be no definitive answer to the question, 'what is 3D printing for, and what does it mean to me?' But it is certainly the case that 3D printing is having – and will continue to have – a ground-shifting influence on the way you can conceive, sell, plan, test, model, develop, and ultimately put into the world your architecture.

3D SCANNING

Anything you can print in 3D you can potentially also scan in 3D, and vice versa. As you would expect, a 3D scanner creates a digital representation of a real-life physical object, and it does so by generating either a point cloud, which references positions in three-dimensional space as locations on an X, Y, Z grid, or a polygon mesh, surface model, or solid CAD model, each of which does much the same thing.

This means that while there are still at this point many pitfalls and hurdles for 3D scanners to overcome, a situation is entirely foreseeable in which someone whose washing machine breaks down opens it up, removes the offending part, scans it, prints out a new one and substitutes it for the old one: 3D scanning may well therefore mark another shift towards decentralised, on-demand home or small workshop manufacture that, for obvious reasons, goes hand in hand with 3D printing.

COPYRIGHT & PIRACY

If you can print anything you can design or scan in 3D, then that means anyone with a 3D printer can, theoretically, print anything they can get their hands on. Perhaps not quite 'anything' yet, there are, as we have pointed out, still limitations to what 3D scanners can do, and the more intricate and sophisticated an object is, the more quickly you will reach these limitations. But besides scanning, the fact alone that you can share the software and files you need for 3D printing means that here as in other areas where digital technology has shifted the proverbial paradigm, copyright and intellectual ownership enter a new phase.

To the music industry – as a particularly prominent example – this looked for a while like the end of the world; and for several years the wholesale collapse of music and musicianship was gloomily predicted, most vociferously perhaps by people who had built themselves bountiful revenue streams based on the then traditional business model. But the world did not end, and music did not die. It changed, and substantially so. The industry adapted, at first reluctantly, and eventually (within a few years), it managed to move the great majority of illegal and unpaid downloads to legal, paid downloads and streaming, by offering easy to use download and streaming platforms with reasonable pricing structures.

That does not mean that everything is sorted and hunky-dory just yet in the world of music: many musicians, for example, complain that they see next to nothing by way of royalties of the revenues that big platform providers generate. At the same time though, far from a decline in music production, there has been a proliferation of artists, styles, genres, and niches that cater for vastly differentiated tastes and give artists the opportunity to create their own work and find their own audiences on their own terms. Meanwhile, the availability of free or next-to-free music on users' devices has not dampened their enthusiasm for live music; in fact the opposite has been the case: festival attendances and live concert ticket sales have soared and the indie scene is thriving.

Copyright is perhaps not really the big issue then. It may not really be an issue *at all* for that much longer. Because in a post-industrial, for want of a better word 'digital', economy and culture, of which on-demand production, cross-fertilisation, open-source development and knowledge sharing are integral features, there are good arguments to support a view that our understanding of 'intellectual property' can and should change. And that may mean redefining what an 'idea', a 'design', or an 'invention' is legally, in proprietary terms, let alone philosophically, in conceptual terms.

■ ↖270 516↘
■ ↖196
■ ↖68
■

A particular issue in the wider context, not so much of copyright as of legality generally, presents itself with the printability of controlled devices, such as weapons. It is now possible – and has been put into practice – to make available online the file you need to print a gun that can kill someone. This may not be big news in countries where people consider owning a gun that can kill someone to be a constitutional right, but it is a big problem in parts of the world where a view prevails that putting lethal weapons into just about anyone's hand is essentially asking for homicide rates that are way out of proportion.

So 3D printing – much as many other technology – also throws up big and far reaching ethical questions. The very fundamental one that we've come across before, 'does the fact that I can do something mean that I therefore should or let alone have to do it?' here acquires a whole different set of meanings. And while this is not something we can or want to solve in this *Atlas*, or pretend to have ready answers for, it is certainly something we need to be conscious of when we discuss the technology.

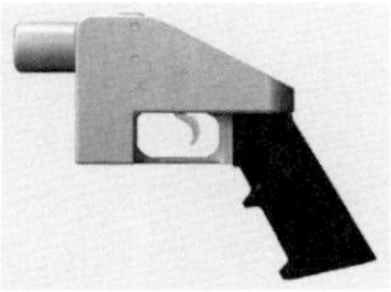

282 ● 452

MATERIAL MATTERS

As we have seen and highlighted, a defining characteristic of 3D printing technology is that you can make almost anything out of anything: plastics, metals, ceramics, even edibles. Any material that can be pulverised and then glued or melded together, or any material that can be liquefied and then caused to harden into a defined shape is in principle suitable for some type of 3D printing. Which method or technology you choose will largely depend on extraneous factors such as the strength, durability, precision, look, and feel you require, and how these stand in relation to cost and time as a framework: they will set the parameters. What you're really interested in though is the result, the object. The thing you'll be holding in your hand or putting up to stand in the space, or that may in fact *be* the space.

And this means that what you're really interested in is the material. Because it's the material that dictates the printing method, and beyond that, the material ends up being the object. The thinking is, and has to be: if I want to print an ultra-light but unbreakable wing flap for my new solar plane, what material has the properties that I'm looking for; and on from that follows the method of printing that works with this particular material to this particular end.

Material is also the most interesting aspect from a business perspective: if you've ever owned a laser or inkjet 2D printer, you will know from experience how manufacturers grab you with the machine and then milk you with the ink. You may well pay the same again as you paid for your machine just to replace your first whole set of ink cartridges, but without them your printer is useless, and so you buy them anyway, even if you curse the brand for having duped you into thinking you had a good deal.

If this is true for 2D printers, as a principle it is bound to hold true for 3D printing, even if perhaps for different reasons. Because while only an expert will really notice the difference between one manufacturer's ink and another's on a piece of 2D print, in a 3D printed object, the quality and texture of the substance makes all the difference. And once you start talking about objects that sit in people's bodies, or that keep people up in the air, or that people live in, then the material you make things from becomes a matter not only of sensory experience and style, but of life and death. And so material matters.

It is also why from a research and development perspective materials are the most important thing to focus on, the thing from which others – such as future print technologies and advances in speed and complexity – will emanate. And it leads on to another issue that has to play a big part in the manufacture of structures, objects, and mechanisms that have critical functions: certification.

In the building trade, in medicine, in aerospace, in food production, in any area really, regulators and authorities certify materials for safe and proper use to prevent accidents that could easily turn into calamities. This does not change with printing. The fact that something is printed does not automatically make it safe or fit for purpose, and it remains the responsibility of material suppliers and printer manufacturers to seek compliance with regulatory standards; and the task of supervisory bodies to ensure it.

3D Print Processes

■ ↖411
■ ↖408

3D printing is an umbrella term which – as we briefly noted right at the start – is mostly applied synonymously with *additive manufacturing* to describe several different processes that can be used to render or synthesise a physical object from a 3D map, model, or drawing.

SOFTWARE

Irrespective of which specific method you use, the printer receives instructions telling it what to print from an **STL file**. (STL here stands for *STereoLithography*, the method originally developed by Chuck Hull for 3D Systems and now widely used across all types of 3D printing.) File generation can happen in any 3D modelling or CAD software capable of outputting in the STL format.

The printer then uses another piece of software, known as a **slicer** to process the STL file, virtually 'slicing' the 3D computer model into layers. In the three-dimensional print space this is also referred to as the **Z resolution** (or **Z-axis resolution**). Layer thickness may range from about 100 µm to 16 µm, which corresponds to a Z resolution of approximately 250 dpi to 1,600 dpi and is thus comparable to 2D printer pixels.

The slicer outputs a file in **G-code** – a **numerical control** programming language – which the printer reads as its set of instructions.

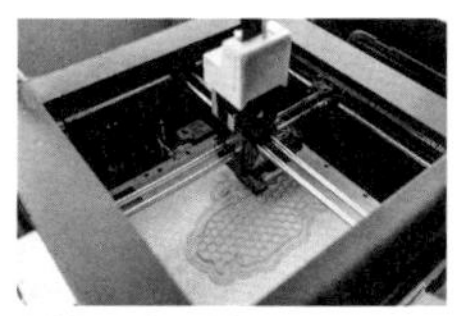

283 ○ 458

METHODS

At the time of completing this *Atlas* in 2019, there are some eight principal 3D printing methods, which fall into three major categories:

METHOD	PROCESSES	PRINTABLE MATERIALS
Light polymerisation	Stereolithography (SLA)	Photopolymers
	Multi-Jet Printing (MJP)	
Extrusion	Fused Deposition Modelling (FDM), also known as Fused Filament Fabrication (FFF), Fused Layer Modelling (FLM), or Plastic Jet Printing (PJP)	Thermoplastics, eutectic metals, rubbers, plasticine, clay, edible materials
	Direct Ink Writing (DIW), also known as Robocasting	
	Multi-Jet Printing (MJP)	
Powder bed	Selective Laser Melting (SLM)	Thermoplastics, metal alloys, metals, ceramics; and with glue practically any pulverised material
	Selective Laser Sintering (SLS)	
	Electro-Beam Melting (EBM)	
	Inkjet Head 3-Dimensional Printing (3DP)	

STEREOLITHOGRAPHY (SLA)
Stereolithography uses light polymerisation to cure or harden liquid photopolymers into objects.

The build platform rests in a vat, initially at the top, exactly one print layer (equivalent to one voxel) below the surface. The vat is filled with photopolymer resin: a liquid polymer that will harden upon contact with light. Above the build platform, laser beams focus UV light onto the liquid's surface in the exact place required to create the first layer of the object that's to be printed: polymer exposed to the UV light cures and solidifies, everything else stays liquid.

The build platform is then lowered by one layer, and the process repeated: gradually, the object takes shape, layer by layer, as the build platform descends into the vat. Once the object is complete, surplus resin is drained off and the object cleaned and finished. (Some stereolithographic printers are able to add resin layers to the object even if its overall height extends above the vat surface.)

Contemporary SLA printers expose a membrane from beneath and pull the object from the resin bath.

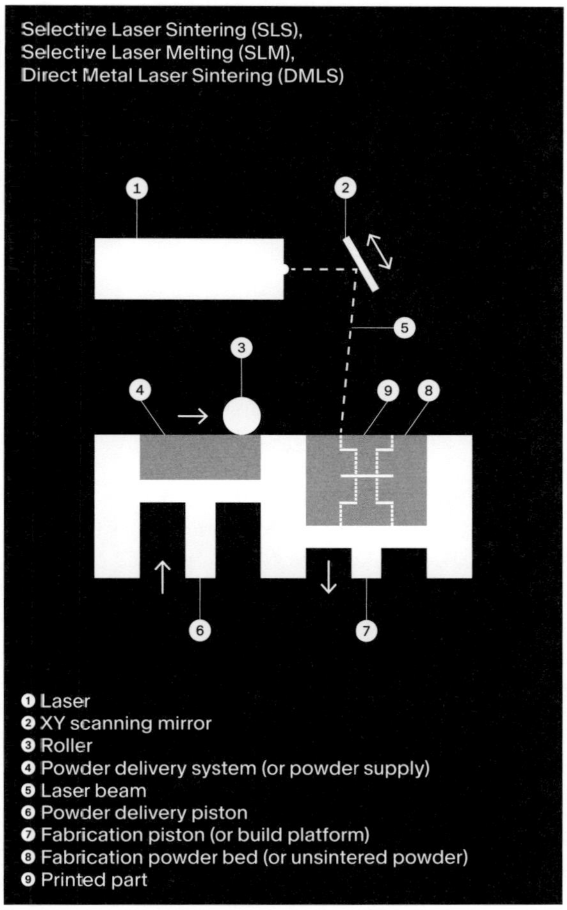

Advantages:
- High definition and quality finish
- Good build size, with standard machine output up to approximately 50 × 50 × 50 cm, and top of the range models achieving up to 210 × 70 × 80 cm
- Relatively high speed

Disadvantages:
- Supports are needed to avoid deflection and to create overhangs
- Elaborate clean-up / post-processing
- Cost

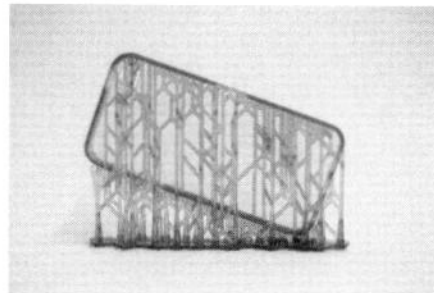

284 ○ 459

MULTI-JET PRINTING (MJP)
Also an extrusion method, *Multi-Jet Printing (MJP)* can be looked at as a process that combines the principles of *Stereolithography (SLA)* and *Fused Deposition Modelling (FDM)* in so far as it deposits different kinds of photo-curable plastic resins or casting wax and then immediately dries the material with UV light.

The print platform in this instance is a dry stage, with a printhead carriage moving across it. Print material is supplied as liquid photopolymers, with casting wax serving as fill material. A piezo inkjet printhead uses several nano jets to deposit print and fill material onto the print platform, placing one layer at a time; the layer is then instantly smoothed and exposed to UV light to cure it. Once a layer is complete, the printhead rises by one 'notch' (one voxel), and the process is repeated layer by layer until the object is complete. Support wax is removed and the object cleaned up and finished.

Advantages:
- Very high precision and quality, with Z-layer resolution as high 1,600 dpi equivalent: a layer thickness of 16 μm
- Multiple materials can be used in one go
- Mostly no supports needed as gaps are filled with wax
- Easy and quick post-processing

Disadvantages:
- Limited range of materials (photopolymers)
- High cost

FUSED DEPOSITION MODELLING (FDM)
Fused Deposition Modelling (FDM), *Fused Filament Fabrication (FFF)*, and *Plastic Jet Printing (PJP)* all label the same extrusion process, but *FDM* is a term trademarked by Stratasys Inc, with the others having been suggested as legally unencumbered alternatives.

Printable materials include thermoplastics, eutectic metals, rubbers, plasticine, clay, and edibles. (Eutectic metals are metal alloys that change from solid state into liquid or vice versa at temperatures significantly lower than the temperatures at which their components do so individually.)

Here, the print platform is a dry stage around which the print head moves, dispensing a thin flat filament or paste as the print material. This is run through a print head nozzle, which heats the material to the point where it liquifies and deposits small droplets to form a layer. Upon extrusion, the material solidifies and the process is then repeated layer by layer until the object is complete, at which point, depending on its intricacy and shape, it may need cleaning up and finishing. Support or fill materials can be deployed during the print process to deal with small overhangs.

Advantages:
- Wide choice of materials available in different colours
- Low cost

Disadvantages:
- Supports needed for overhangs
- Slow speed
- Print quality

285 ○ 459

Fused Layer Modelling (FLM),
Fused Filament Fabrication (FFF),
Fused Deposition Modelling (FDM)

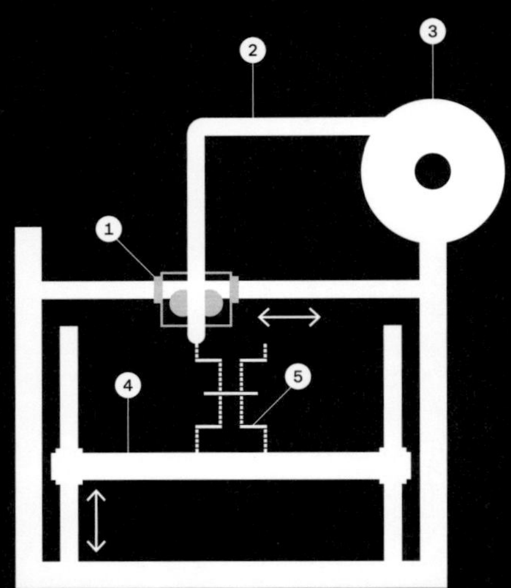

❶ Extrusion head (feeding mechanism + heater + nozzle)
❷ Filament
❸ Filament spool
❹ Build platform
❺ Printed part

DIRECT INK WRITING (DIW)
OR ROBOCASTING
Direct Ink Writing (DIW) or *Robocasting* uses an extrusion process that is similar to FDM/FFM/PJP, but takes advantage of the rheological properties of some ceramic pastes or slurry to retain their shape before drying.

The process was first developed specifically for the purpose of using additive manufacturing in the production of 'green bodies' (objects made of clay); materials used are therefore principally ceramics.

As in FDM/FFM/PJP, the print platform is a dry stage around which the print head moves, in this case dispensing a ceramic paste. Again, the nozzle deposits small droplets to form a print layer, but here the material does not dry immediately, but instead retains its shape owing to its pseudo-plastic behaviour. The process is repeated layer by layer, resulting in an object that is in a soft and fragile condition and has to be dried and/or sintered to acquire its final, stable state. Support or fill materials can be used to deal with small overhangs.

Advantages:
- High level of precision
- Use of specialist materials, for example biocompatible substances in medical applications

Disadvantages:
- Supports needed for overhangs
- Slow speed
- Elaborate post-processing (drying, sintering) required

SELECTIVE LASER MELTING (SLM)
A powder bed method, *Selective Laser Melting (SLM)* is one of several processes that bond fine powder particles into a solid substance. Print materials can include almost any type of metal or metal alloy.

The print platform is a powder bed, on which a layer of fine pulverised print material is laid out. A laser beam moves across the surface of the powder bed and heats particles where required to melting point, joining them together to form a solid substance on cooling. The platform is lowered and a new layer of powder added and printed. This process is repeated layer by layer until the object is complete; then unused powder is removed and the object cleaned up and finished.

Advantages:
- Very high print quality with extremely strong materials possible
- Several objects can be printed simultaneously in one process, depending on size
- Large print dimensions
- No support materials required for overhangs

Disadvantages:
- Elaborate and messy clean up
- Cost

SELECTIVE LASER SINTERING (SLS)
In practice, there is today not much of a difference between *Selective Laser Sintering (SLS)* and SLM. It's also a powder bed process that causes particles to bond by applying a laser beam to fine pulverised material. Unlike SLM, SLS does not heat the material to the point where it turns liquid and melts, but instead where it sinters: particles bond with their neighbouring particles without going through a liquid state. For this reason, SLS lends itself to printing thermoplastics and ceramics, as well as metals and alloys.

The print platform is a powder bed, on which a layer of fine pulverised print material is laid out. A laser beam moves across the surface and heats particles to the point where they sinter with adjoining particles to form a solid substance on cooling. The platform is lowered or the print head raised and a new layer of powder added and printed; the process is then repeated layer by layer until the object is complete; unused powder is removed and the object cleaned up and finished.

Advantages:
- Very high print quality with a wide range of materials possible
- Several objects can be printed simultaneously in one process, depending on size
- No support materials required for overhangs

Disadvantages:
- Elaborate and messy clean up
- Cost

ELECTRON BEAM MELTING (EBM)
Electron Beam Melting (EBM) is a powder bed process similar to SLM. The main difference lies in the delivery method of energy to melt the powder. Here, rather than laser, an electron beam is applied to the print surface. The process is carried out in a vacuum at very high temperatures (up to 1000 °C), which makes it possible to use materials that react strongly with oxygen, including metals and metal alloys such as titanium.

The print platform is a powder bed, on which a layer of fine pulverised print material is laid out within a vacuum chamber. An electron beam moves across the surface and heats particles where required to very high temperatures, at which they melt and join with neighbouring particles to form a solid substance on cooling. The print platform is lowered or the print head raised and a new layer of powder added and printed; the process is repeated layer by layer until the object is complete. Unused powder is removed and the object cleaned up.

Advantages:
- Very high density resulting in high manufacturing quality
- Multiple parts can be printed simultaneously
- Few supports needed
- Reliability

Disadvantages:
- Can only be used with conductive materials
- Cost
- Limited size
- Clean-up

INKJET HEAD 3-DIMENSIONAL PRINTING (3DP)
Also a powder bed method, *Inkjet Head 3-Dimensional Printing (3DP)* uses a binding agent to glue particles together. This makes the process versatile, with a wide range of possible print materials, including sand, plaster, plastics, and ceramics. By adding dye to the binding agent, different colours can be achieved within one object during the same print process.

The print platform is a powder bed on which a layer of fine pulverised print material is laid out. An inkjet printhead moves across the surface and deposits small droplets of glue onto particles where required to bond them into a solid form. The print platform is lowered or the print head raised and a new layer of powder added and printed. The process is repeated layer by layer until the object is complete; unused powder is removed and the object cleaned up.

Advantages:
- High levels of precision
- Wide range of hard and soft print materials available
- By adding dyes it is possible to print multi-coloured objects
- No support needed for overhangs

Disadvantages:
- Depending on materials used, high cost
- Elaborate and messy clean-up
- Additional post-processing is often necessary as objects may be brittle or fragile

Stereolithography (SLA)

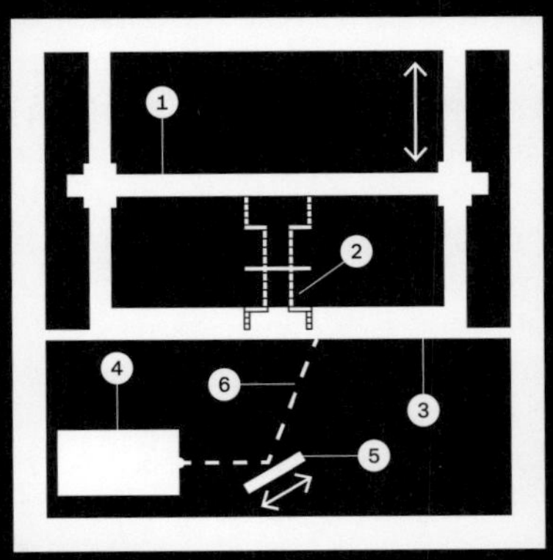

❶ Build platform
❷ Printed part
❸ Resin tank and resin
❹ UV laser
❺ XY scanning mirror
❻ Laser beam

The Outlook

When high quality 2D printers became readily affordable, the floodgates opened on what was until then an almost non-existent, or at any rate extremely niche activity: do-it-yourself design. It was one thing traipsing to the stationer's and buying a few sheets of *Letraset* to create headings for a school paper or a birthday party invitation, it became quite a different matter using *TextArt* on your word processor and then printing out your creation at home. *Comic Sans* was born, and village fetes never looked the same again...

While access to technology is no guarantor for quality, there is no doubt that it can, and does, unleash potential, and people who have never before thought of themselves as creative or artistic are suddenly given tools to experiment and practise, at no risk and with very low entry thresholds to overcome. The 'arrival of digital' has launched entire photographer, musician, filmmaker, writer, and designer careers; not to mention the multitude of hobby or spare time activities it allows people to pursue from their own homes.

There is no reason to assume that 3D printing may not have a similar effect on the design and manufacture of objects. A domestic quality 3D printer now can be yours for three hundred euros, and that means anyone with a bit of creative flair, some patience, and a modicum of technological curiosity to acquire the basic software skills can now produce quite extraordinary 3D designs and make them happen.

Meanwhile, at a professional level, 3D printing becomes a companion tool for generative design: if you are going through an evolutionary process in which you allow algorithms to do the design for you based on your conceptual brief, often through numerous generations or versions, then it is of obvious value to have an output device that allows you to quickly, cheaply, and with no additional expertise produce prototypes or models of different iterations to assess and compare.

Of similar importance are likely to be developments in materials, their combination, and their integration with technology. It is already easy to print in two or three different materials, sturdy as well as flexible, to make life-size technology prototype models that look and feel very much like the object – the camera, the hair dryer, the remote control – that the user is ultimately going to hold in their hand. Once it becomes possible to print, for example, virtually unbreakable, crystal clear transparent materials, or casings with embedded electronics, all in one go and at high speed, then production by printing may open up interesting new avenues, particularly in specialist or highly individualised technology sectors.

Speed is a crucial aspect to all this. At the moment, precision and speed sit at opposing ends of an inverse value equation: the higher the precision, the slower the printing process, and the more expensive. If print technology advances to a level where – much as in industrial robotic production – it yields up both precision *and* speed, then there can be yet another gear change in manufacturing.

For the architect, the thing of most interest, beyond model-making, is most likely scale. And with scale comes the principal question we've already discussed:
☐ ↖405
what does it mean for architectural practice if we are able to print – and digitally manufacture in general – life-size objects, components, and materials. Does it make sense to print a whole building? Or even parts thereof? When it's easy, cheap, and convenient to produce prefabricated walls or tiles or floorboards, is there any point to making these things with a printer? The answer may well depend on the situation, and the type of architecture you're pursuing.

By traditional means, if you want to integrate air conditioning, media, and general home or office technology into your structure, you need walls that are maybe 10 to 20 cm thick, and you do so by assembling pieces with a whole lot of cabling, connectors, switches, and other, mostly very basic, technical clutter tucked away behind clean surfaces. For most ordinary settings, such as family dwellings or standard office spaces, this may suffice and be a cost effective way of building new houses and work places. But there may also be settings where it makes sense to let these components become part of the fabric itself and print them directly into the walls, not only allowing for a simplification of the planning and building processes, but also opening up possibilities as to how you then deploy these structural elements.

Much will no doubt depend on cost: if, as has been the case in other areas of digital technology, the expense of using large and fast printing machines comes down, and it no longer makes much of a difference to your budget and the time it takes to erect a structure whether your walls are eight inches thick, straight, and stand at right angles, or one inch thick, curved, and undulating through your organic space, because they are going to be printed anyway, then you are faced with actual design choices, and these in turn may well then inform how you approach your project.

Our hunch is that – eye-catching though they are – machines and processes that 'print' entire houses are not really where the future or the real strength of 3D printing in architecture lies. Much rather, we think that where 3D printing will make most of a difference is in the manufacture of things that other manufacturing processes can't do or can do only slowly and expensively. That means bespoke and intricate components, for example, or elements with moving parts and electronics, as well as precision layering of several different materials.

That said, Digital Manufacturing, on which we also have a chapter in this *Atlas* and of which 3D printing is a well-established and technologically fairly mature exponent, is clearly here, and here not just to stay, but also to make significant strides yet.

277 ● 441
3D scanned busts reproduced in 3D print. [Hannes Thalmann]

278 ● 441
A print head creating construction elements layer by layer. [Hannes Thalmann]

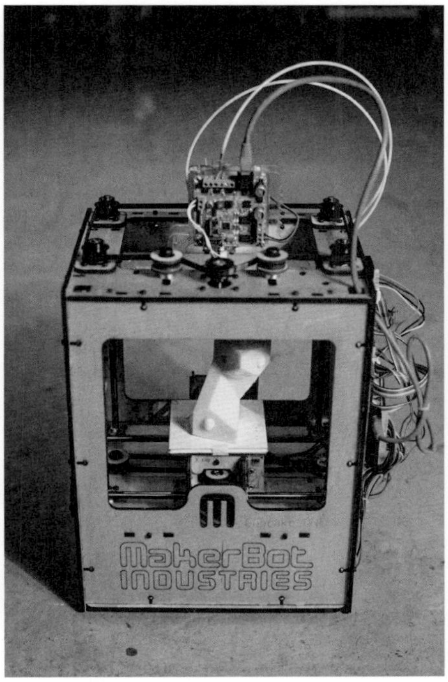

279 ● 443
Cupcake CNC by MakerBot: This 3D printer was sold as an assembly kit: the circuit boards were already soldered up, so the buyer only had to do minor soldering at non-critical points to make the machine operational. [Bre Pettis]

280 ● 444
3D printed walls of a structure. A Building on Demand (BOD) printer developed by COBOD International in action. [3DPrinthuset]

281 ● 444
A 3D printer nozzle putting down a layer of concrete on site. [3DPrinthuset]

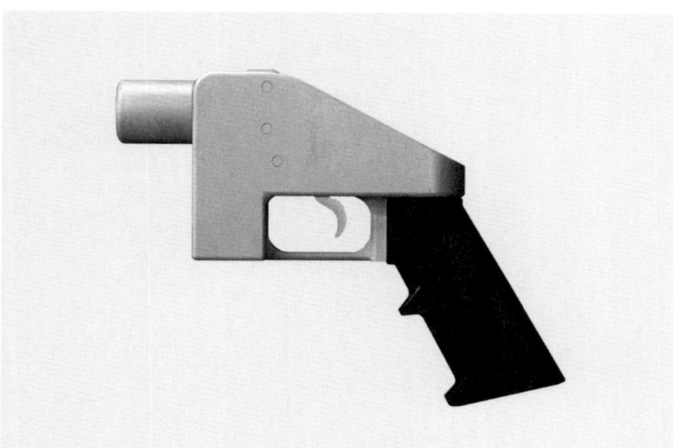

282 ● 445
A printable single-shot handgun. [NotLessOrEqual]

Colour Plates

IV

P. 405–452

252 ○ 409
The Cutty Sark at its purpose built museum in Greenwich, London. [Jeff Wallis]

254 ○ 409
The Guggenheim Museum Bilbao (opened in 1997), designed by Frank Gehry: one of the most famous early exponents of free geometry architecture.

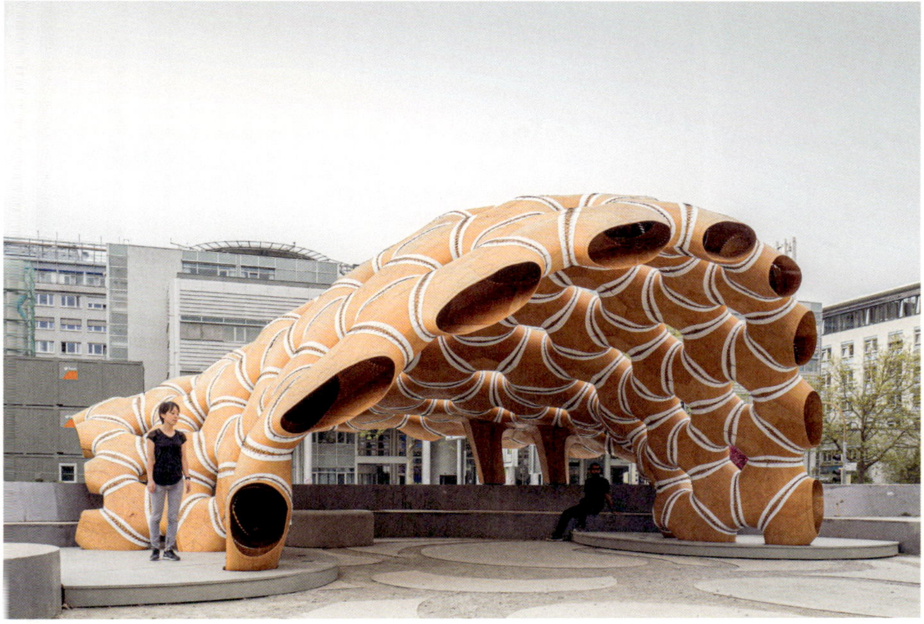

260A ○ 415
The Research Pavilion of the Institute for Computational Design (ICD) at Stuttgart University is an annual project led by Professor Achim Menges that allows researchers and students to experiment with digital manufacturing processes from design through realisation.
[Series 260A–260D: ICD/ITKE *Universität Stuttgart*]

260B ○ 415
Assembly process of 36 lightweight fibre composite components on site.

260C ○ 415

260D ○ 415

264 ○ 425
1:20 Scale Model of St Peter's Basilica dome by Michelangelo.

271 ○ 428
Physical sketches: the models of Frank Gehry. [Bettina Matthiessen / Vitra Design Museum]

274A ○ 430

274B ○ 430
Peter Zumthor: the model as a way of working (274A). | Sensory materiality: Therme Vals (274B). [*Kunsthaus Bregenz* | Markus Tretter]

276 ○ 432
Hylozoic Soil by Philip Beesley: "implements a distributed sensor network driven by dozens of microprocessors, generating waves of reflexive responses to those drawn into its vast array of acrylic fern stalagmites." [Philip Beesley]

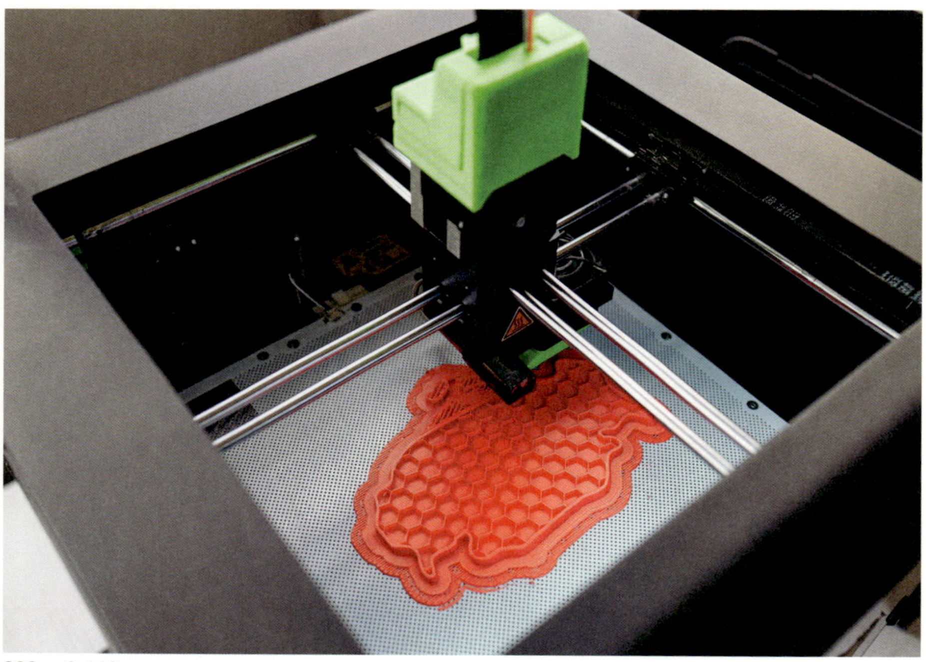

283 ○ 446
Apart from using supports, a slicer can also generate infills with structures of varying stability. [Hannes Thalmann]

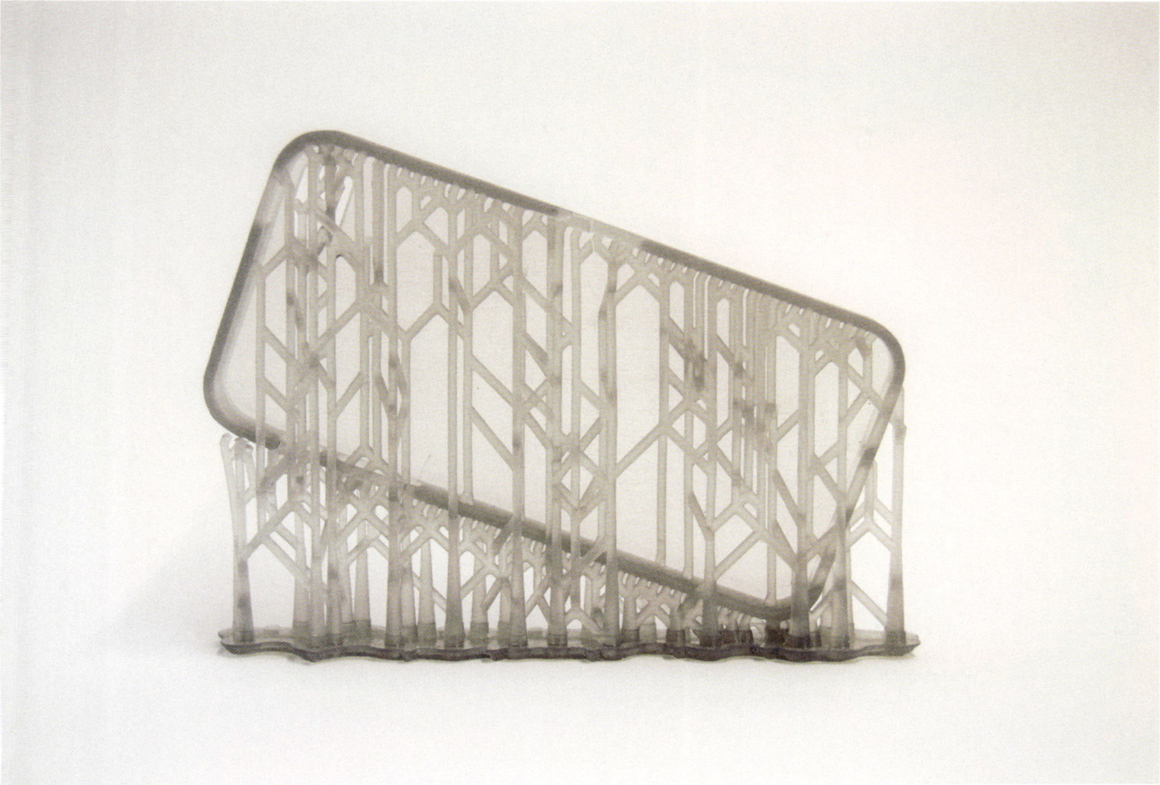

284 ○ 447
A mobile phone case printed from flexible material by stereolithography (SLA). [Open Innovation Lab HTWG]

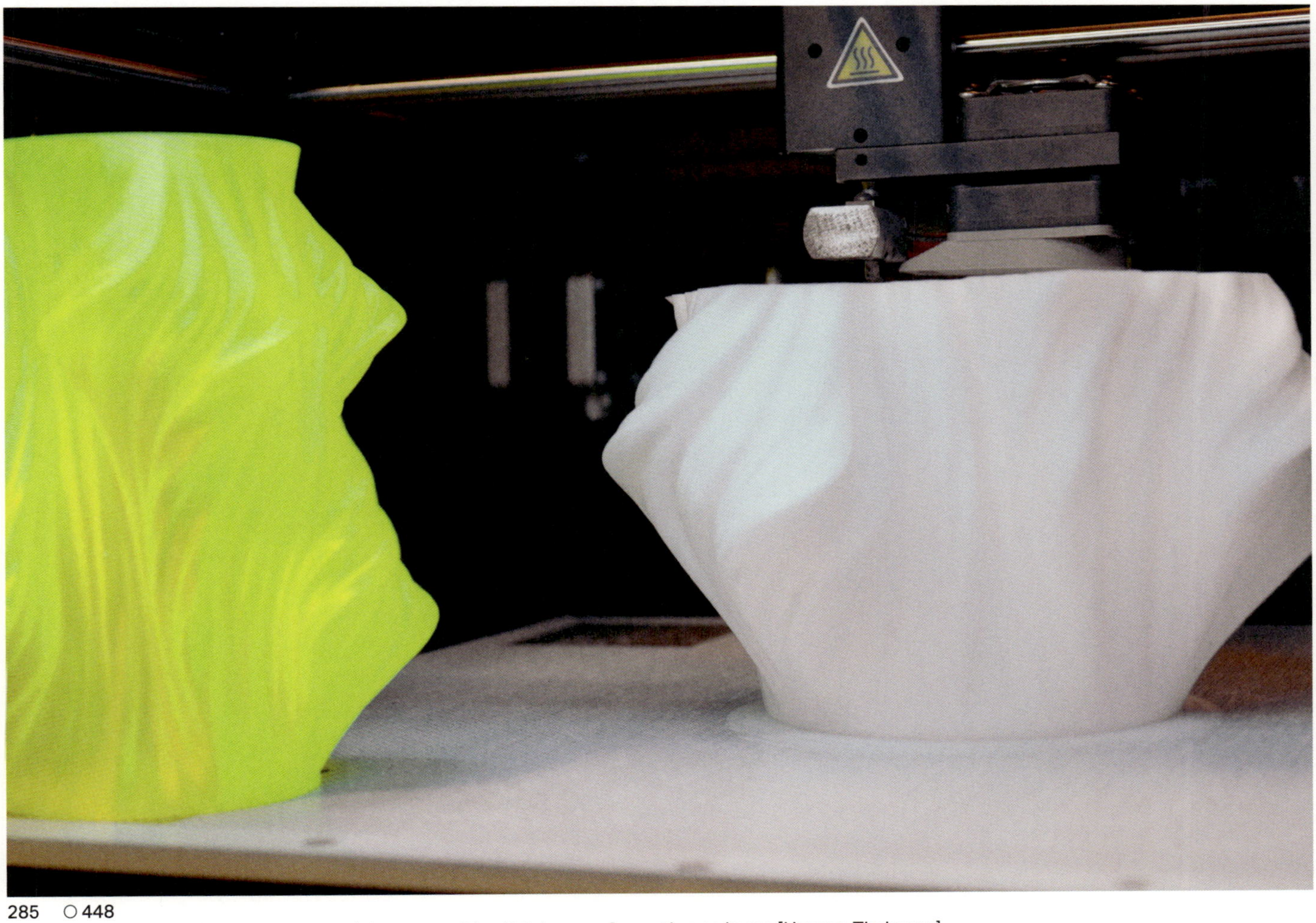

285 ○ 448
With FDM, a spiral path process can print a wrap with a thickness of exactly one layer. [Hannes Thalmann]

Virtual & Augmented Reality 463
Simulation 475
Geographic Information Systems (GIS) 491
Building Information Modelling (BIM) 507
Digital Cities 529
Big Data & Machine Learning 549

LOGISTICS V
The Dynamic Representation of Architecture

- Multimedia: *From Wagner to Virtual Reality*, by www.artmuseum.net based on the book of the same name, co-edited by Randall Packer and Ken Jordan, 2003
- Oliver Grau, Roger F Malina, Sean Cubitt: *Virtual Art: From Illusion to Immersion*, 2003
- Jason Jerald: *The VR Book: Human-Centered Design for Virtual Reality*, 2015

Virtual & Augmented Reality

Sven Pfeiffer

Overview

"Why," the English writer Virginia Woolf (1882–1941) asked in one of her essays, "should a real chair be better than an imaginary elephant?" She put the question in a literary context, wondering, "why should the final test of plot, character, story, and the other ingredients of a novel lie in their power to imitate life?"

It's a pertinent question that goes to the heart of our chapter on Virtual & Augmented Reality. Because the point of both (and we will often be referring to them in this chapter as one 'thing', even though they aren't, and we shall also explain why) is one of storytelling in a created or manipulated reality. What that story is, and what the reality, is really up to us. And this applies to both Virtual Reality (VR) and Augmented Reality (AR), much as it does to literature.

In the 1982 film *The Draughtsman's Contract* by British director Peter Greenaway (b. 1942), Mr Neville, the artist referred to in the title, is contracted by a Mrs Virginia Herbert to make a dozen drawings of her husband's country estate, ostensibly for said husband, while he is absent, pursuing some business in Southampton. The artist so employed dictates to Mrs Herbert's lawyers terms that compel his client to meet with him in private and to "comply with his requests concerning his pleasure" with her, but as the story progresses and the drawings take shape, the world that Mr Neville finds himself in transpires to just never be quite what it seems. In his endeavour to achieve a three-dimensionality in the 'reality' that he sees, he uses a wire frame to accurately gauge proportion and perspective, and as he glances at the house and its grounds through this device, objects begin to appear that seem to tell their own story. Being concerned, as he is, with capturing the Herberts' estate exactly as it presents itself, he finds he has no choice but to record what he sees, and so when a drowned Mr Herbert is found in the moat and a picture emerges of a murder, the artist's role as an observer and also partaker of the life on the estate can, and will, suddenly be used against him…

286 ● 472

What is the 'real world'? And how – for the purposes of this chapter, at least – does it relate to the 'virtual world'. Is the virtual world any less 'real' than the 'real' world? French philosopher Gilles Deleuze (1925–1995) thought not: as early as 1968, he declared that, "the virtual is opposed not to the real but to the actual. The virtual is fully real insofar as it is virtual."

Today, as the technological concepts of virtual and augmented realities are approaching a degree of maturity in their realisation, our experience bears this out. Even at the simplest level, say that of our online presence or our engagement with social media, our interactions, our presentation and our 'staging' of ourselves, our conversations and our flirtations, our arguments with, our admiration for, and our disapproval of other people, turn out to be every bit as real as they are face to face in the physical world. So much so that not only do we have wildly successful online dating platforms, but also the serious and in some cases deadly issues of cyber bullying and trolling. Of course this is not actually what Virtual & Augmented Reality as a subject is about. Nor is it about drawing an accurate representation of a Wiltshire country estate in a fictional, sensual power entanglement. The reason these brief considerations are relevant here is that they put into some context the notion of 'reality'. □ ↖463

Also, it is useful to recognise that our desire to both represent and manipulate reality to create for ourselves a different type of experience to that which is already available from 'reality' such as it exists, is far from new or inherently tied to digitality. ■ ↖299 As *The Draughtsman's Contract* – a narrative set in the late 17th century – illustrates, and as we shall ■ ↖103 further find out: artists and visionaries, writers and architects have all been 'inventing' virtual realities long before any of us had access to the electron.

Before we take a look at the historical timeline, though, we want to define what we mean by 'virtual' and 'augmented' reality respectively, and set out just why they are of significance in architecture today.

VIRTUAL VS AUGMENTED REALITY

Everything we just said about the pre-digital age notwithstanding, today we mean, by both virtual and augmented reality, a creation, or an extension of our perception, of a reality by *digital* means. Obviously, you can augment your reality by any number of other, non-digital means too. In fact, if you step into a dark space, then the moment you light a candle you could be said to be augmenting your reality. But to all intents and purposes the definition, today, of a virtual or augmented reality is a reality that is being manipulated digitally.

This is what they both have in common. The difference between virtual and augmented reality is largely one of degree: a *virtual reality* setting is completely isolated from the outside world. This means that I, as the user, *immerse* myself in a wholly digitally generated and therefore in that sense 'artificial' world, where my sensory experiences – with today's technology first and foremost vision and audio, but increasingly also gesture and touch – all belong to that reality, while everything without is irrelevant and ideally does not register, as that would be experienced as an interference with the virtual reality I'm immersed in.

Augmented reality, by contrast, is a crossover between our physical reality and a digital reality that overlaps to enhance or, as the name more precisely suggests, augment it. It is therefore also known as a Mixed Reality (MR). ■ ↖431

A MEDIUM & DESIGN TOOL

Neither virtual nor augmented reality is in that sense a 'technology'. There are any number of technologies that can be used to create a virtual reality or to augment an existing one. But rather than as a bunch of technologies we like to think of them severally and jointly as a *medium*. It's a complex medium that requires a broad set of creative and technical skills, and some considerable knowledge to be able to communicate with it successfully.

We are already widely familiar with virtual and augmented reality techniques to let us experience imagined or planned built contexts, for example in simulations or walk-throughs of proposed projects, and of course in gaming, where the whole point of VR is to 'escape' the 'real' world, and dive into the world of the game to face its challenges and get absorbed in the adventures it has to offer. The former shows us what a physical design that has so far not been realised will look and feel like, the latter never once concerns itself with the physical, built-up world, as it needs to exist and function solely on the virtual plane. And there are overlaps: virtual experiences of real-life buildings and real-world settings of virtual games.

So beyond a medium, virtual and augmented reality technology can also be a tool that's of use both to ourselves and to the people we work with or for, such as clients, stakeholders, contractors, engineers, or partners. It allows us to communicate aspects of a design that are not visually perceptible, such as the behaviour of materials, temperature fluctuations under different conditions, or the flow of static forces in complex structures. It allows us to play through different scenarios in, or versions of, a built context and to not only illustrate these, but actually simulate them.

This amounts to a step up that virtual reality offers compared to other forms of representation. As ☐ ↖255 we explore in more depth in our chapter on Rendering, it is by now common in architecture to render planned spaces, but until relatively recently we didn't have any technology that would allow us to experience a space from *within* as well as from the outside before it was ☐ ↖285 built. Visualisation was really restricted to flat images ☐ ↖421 and videos, and Model Making to static models. A ☐ ↖57 shift towards virtual reality comes with dynamic 3D ☐ 507↘ Modelling and Building Information Modelling (BIM), where we can already manipulate perspectives, zoom in or out, and turn the object on various axes to look at it from different angles. Virtual reality takes this onto the next level by 'wrapping the screen around us', so to speak. Instead of us being outside the computer and looking at its display, we now effectively step into the digital world created by the computer: it surrounds us and we interact with it directly, not through a structured user interface, such as a keyboard, trackpad, or mouse, but through our own body, including eye movements, expressions, and gestures.

To us as architects, these two aspects – communication and simulation – are of critical and ever increasing significance. They on the one hand facilitate, while on the other hand also responding to, a democratisation in construction, which sees more and more participation of people who are affected by a project, but who may not have much, or in many cases any, expertise at all. The importance of this can scarcely be overstated: If your undertaking is dependent on a large and varied number of people 'getting it' to the point where they allow it to happen, even embrace it, then communicating it to them, allaying their fears, enthusing them about its prospect, can easily make or break it. Clearly there are no guarantees that even the most gorgeous 3D simulation or lifelike virtual reality experience will convince doubters and usher a project through the warren of hurdles and obstacles it may face. But being able to give stakeholders a comprehensive idea of what is planned also enhances the feedback quality, so we're really using different technologies to create a continuous and ideally beneficial loop to drive a project forward.

With this in mind, and taken another step further, VR opens up a compelling range of possibilities not only for communicating design, but also for the design process itself; and perhaps the greatest, and as yet least realised, potential for virtual and augmented reality in architecture lies here exactly: as a design tool. The iterative process of design, which looks at the problems or challenges a project poses and then tests out different approaches to possible solutions can, and we think will, benefit greatly from VR, because the effect a building will have, how it 'behaves', so to speak, and importantly also how it prompts us to behave, can be far more fully explored with VR than could be without. This is not just about detail and design intricacies, but very much about responding to and interacting with the design.

The history of twentieth century post-war architecture in particular is littered with examples of designs that look good 'on paper' (or indeed as models), but that people just don't use in the way the urban planners and architects foresaw, even though an awful lot of thinking has gone into them. This does not even have to result in disaster or the building being knocked down, it can simply be a gigantic missed opportunity.

The Barbican Centre in London is perhaps not a bad example of this. Opened in 1982 after a lengthy planning and construction phase, Europe's biggest performing arts centre immediately gained a reputation for being impossible to find. It's huge, you can see it for miles, but people just couldn't get to it. Whatever the architects had imagined would happen by plonking the vast complex in midst a densely assembled residential estate, the Barbican's first function for the visitor became that of a labyrinth. With no direct or even otherwise clearly delineated access routes, it instead offered various pedestrian 'pathways' and one largely hidden and for pedestrians forbidding principal road that led to a car park and an obscure taxi rank and drop-off point. Labyrinths can be fun, if you have time on your hands and don't actually need to get anywhere quickly. But most people in London lead busy lives, and when they go to the theatre or the symphony, they really want to be there at the scheduled hour: late coming is deeply disruptive and correspondingly frowned upon. So the Barbican drew yellow lines on the ground to guide visitors from various possible Tube stations into their centre. Being British, they also appreciated the funny side of the situation: in the first few years of its operation, the venue's gift shop sold pin badges with the Barbican's double B logo and a yellow labyrinth printed on them.

287 ● 472

Today, the Barbican is doing well and the architecture still divides opinion, as it did 35 years ago, with some loathing every one of its several hundred thousand bricks, others loving the amazing auditoria and the surprisingly pleasant lake feature in the middle of it all. The missed opportunity, such as it is, lies in the execution and bringing to life of an architectural vision: since 1982, there have been two major and numerous minor attempts at making the place somehow more user-friendly. This means that apart from the main structure and facade, almost every element has at one point or another undergone some tinkering. And there are clearly spaces that are not fulfilling their purpose – whatever that may have been – to this day. There's a whole patch of empty no-man's land wedged between a low-covered pedestrian flyover, some loftily named residential towers (Shakespeare, Tennyson), and a staircase leading down to the almost pretty square. You can sense a bit what probably should have happened here: there's room for a cafe, there are some lonely trees, and there is plenty of space for people to congregate. Except people don't congregate, the unit where there should be a cafe is a nondescript shop that changes hands every few months but is mostly closed the rest of the time, there's nowhere to look at or to focus on, and no ease to rest your mind. There aren't even any benches, now, though possibly at some point in the past there were or were meant to be. It's a non-space, surrounded by what could be a haven but feels like a bunker. Until you get inside. There, although the design has equally been tampered with in many ways over the decades, and hardly any of the architects' original concept has been left untouched, you immediately feel much more at home. For a start you know where you are. True, it can still be mildly confusing, trying to get to grips with an idiosyncratic levels hierarchy and oddly positioned lifts, but somehow you know now that your seat, your nearest loo, and your much needed drink are all never further away than a few dozen yards. And there are friendly staff dotted all over to help you, who couldn't be lovelier if they tried.

It is impossible to know what would have happened if... – that's a rule we have no way yet of breaking. The parallel universe is and remains pure speculation. But some in-depth virtual reality testing of the concept could hardly have thrown up a weirder and on oh so many levels more maddeningly unsatisfactory solution to what clearly is in essence the problem of a great idea. That, the Problem of the Great Idea, could well be the thing that digital architecture in general, but virtual and augmented reality most particularly, are best placed to tackle: the closer we can get to a 'real world' experience of that idea before it is actually implemented, the better our chances of making it truly great, not only on paper, but also in practice.

THE HISTORICAL TIMELINE

We suggested a little earlier – and you could argue somewhat adventurously – that virtual reality is not strictly 'new' (as in a product of the digital age and thus the 20th century), but that the idea of augmenting our reality and, by means of technology, creating entirely artificial environments that are designed to have a particular impact on our senses and make us experience certain things in a certain way, stretches right back in history. How far is obviously open to conjecture, since it depends entirely on how you define not just one but several of the associated concepts, such as 'manipulation', 'reality', 'artifice', and even 'experience'. It's very likely that we can draw a line back to the dawn of civilisation if we really put our minds to it, but maybe that's going a little too far, and unnecessarily so.

But certainly from about the Renaissance onwards, we can discern deliberate techniques that are designed to transform not just our space but also the perception of reality within that space to a particular end. Enhanced perspectives, *trompe l'oeil* effects, and dimensional 'distortions' are now being used to make buildings and the rooms inside them appear bigger, more impressive, or simply more elegant than otherwise they would be.

A walk through VR history

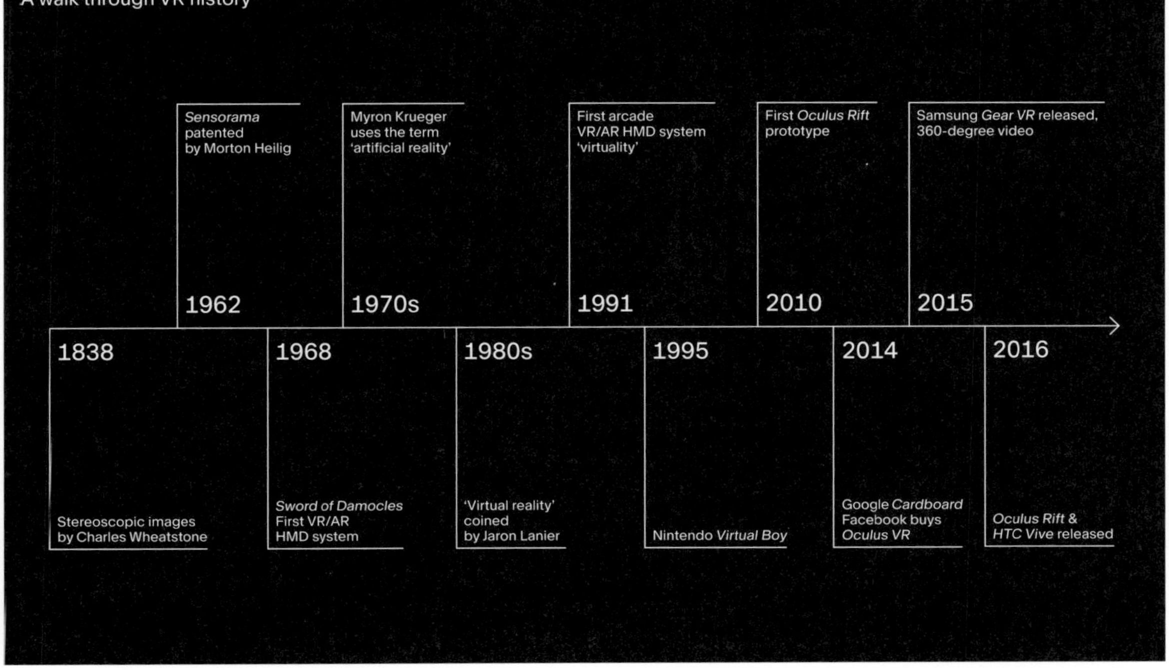

A pertinent example of this is St Peter's Square in Rome. Here, the Italian sculptor and architect Gian Lorenzo Bernini (1598–1680) uses the two giant colonnades that define the square not only, as he puts it, to embrace, "the Catholic faithful like a mother with open arms to strengthen their faith; the heretics to reunite them with their church; and the faithless to convert them to the one true faith," but also to make the facade of the imposing St Peter's Basilica look less stout.

The opening between the smaller *Piazza Retta* directly in front of the church, and the bigger, elliptical *Piazza Obliqua* is kept narrower than the width of the building. From the perspective of the visitor in the square, this doesn't register. What registers instead is that the facade appears narrower than it is, and thus more proportional to its height. Similarly, by making the 'round' square not a true circle but an ellipse, the church appears to come closer more quickly to the visitor who approaches it from a distance. These are simple but extremely effective methods to 'augment' by architectural methods the reality that is being created.

288 ● 472

In 1745, while spending time mostly in Venice, the Italian artist Giovanni Battista Piranesi (1720–1778), who would later become famous mostly for a long series of highly detailed and in their accuracy almost photographic *vedute* or 'views' of the city of Rome and its buildings, began work on another, very different series of drawings, 16 in total, which were published for the first time
□ ↖129 in 1750 under the title *Le carceri d'invenzione*.

In English they are known either simply as *The Prisons* (which is doing them something of a disservice) or as *The Imaginary Prisons*, which comes a great deal closer to the Italian *'invenzione'*, and in fact somewhat surpasses 'invention' in accuracy, because these sixteen drawings, which in their artistry augur the precision and attention to detail that would establish Piranesi's name, are not of actual, real life prisons, but of prisons of the imagination. It's a lively, and in no small measure disturbing imagination, depicting seemingly limitless dungeons of cavernous vaults with ladders, steps, bridges, spiked wheels, sculptural heads and lions, torturers, and the occasional prisoner being mercilessly abused.

They look, in fact, not unlike the story board or sketches for a contemporary virtual reality game: there is no reason why you couldn't use these drawings as a starting point to design an entire self-contained world that could keep a player immersed and busy, helping, or freeing, or in a plethora of unpleasant ways killing prisoners, or fighting prison guards and trying to get out alive. Yet these images and the stories they might inspire stem from the imagination of the artist. True, there were – and continued to be for many centuries, in parts of the world to this date – truly gruesome places where human beings were and are detained and tortured and put to death, and it is entirely possible that Piranesi had been to and seen some of them. But the reality he creates is virtual. And that doesn't actually make it seem much less real to us…

289 ● 473

From the end of the 19th century onwards, photography offers increasingly interesting and sophisticated methods, at first not so much for distorting or manipulating reality, as for capturing it, and soon lays the groundwork for film and therefore cinemas.

Cinemas could be said to be the first photomechanical immersion chambers, and by the time we have full widescreen projection and surround sound, we are almost in a virtual reality that has been created for us on celluloid (later digitally), and that can be conjured up in any properly equipped theatre, anywhere in the world.

290 ● 473

Virtual reality as we understand it today doesn't get its name until the late 1980s, but the technological approaches that we recognise and have built on ever since they were first experimented with start in 1966 with the American computer scientist Ivan Sutherland (b. 1938), whom we encounter repeatedly in this *Atlas* as a pioneer in computer graphics with his groundbreaking program *Sketchpad*. This set the foundation for much of what became Computer Aided Design (CAD), and many years later, in 1988, it won him the Turing Award, which is the highest accolade available in computer science, named after the English computer scientist and cryptographer Alan Turing (1912–1954), whom we also meet regularly in this *Atlas*.

Following his breakthrough with *Sketchpad*, Sutherland set to work on Head Mounted Displays (HMDs), and by 1968, together with his student Bob Sproull, he had put together the first iteration on a long route to what they called the *Ultimate Display*. It was so heavy that it needed to be suspended from the ceiling, which earned it its nickname *Sword of Damocles*. And it was far from ultimate: the virtual environment, such as it was, consisted of wireframe rooms, but the system was already able to track the user's head movements and change the experienced perspective based on this. And as a developmental experiment it started to map out the path to the concept Sutherland had in mind, which was far reaching:

> "The ultimate display would, of course, be a room within which the computer can control the existence of matter. A chair displayed in such a room would be good enough to sit in. Handcuffs displayed in such a room would be confining, and a bullet displayed in such a room would be fatal. With appropriate programming such a display could literally be the Wonderland into which Alice walked."

291A ●473

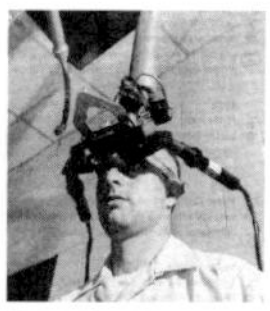
291B ●473

We cannot know without asking them whether American film directors The Wachowskis (Lara, b. 1965 & Lilly, b. 1967), then known as the Wachowski Brothers (Larry and Andy), were inspired by, or even just aware of, the ideas proposed by Sutherland, namely that in the *Ultimate Display* a bullet would be as real as a bullet is to us in the physical world, but in some of the most arresting visual sequences in their 1999 film *The Matrix*, we as the audience experience time at the speed of a bullet, and those characters that are also capable of doing so are therefore able to dodge them. The Wachowskis were certainly influenced by the English writer, mathematician, and logician Lewis Carroll (1832–1898), whose 1865 children's fantasy *Alice's Adventures in Wonderland* Sutherland referred to, and also by the French philosopher Jean Baudrillard (1929–2007), whose treatise on symbols, reality, and society, *Simulacra and Simulation*, they made their leading cast read before even handing them the screenplay.

The Matrix stands our conception of reality on its head by creating a world in which everything we perceive as real is actually a virtual reality created by an artificial intelligence which feeds on humans' bodies as a source of energy: we are kept in a comprehensively immersive VR simulation of our own lives so that we will never notice that we are being used as living batteries for the machine that needs us.

By the time The Wachowskis were writing *The Matrix* in the early 1990s (they sold the rights to the film together with two others in 1994), the term 'virtual reality' had barely entered the vocabulary. Its roots in other, non-computing specific contexts go back a bit further (and it is therefore impossible to say with precision who coined the term: its first published use in the English language appears to be in a translation of a French book on theatre), but for our purposes the person most widely credited with popularising it to describe a digitally generated concept is the American computer scientist and musician Jaron Lanier (b. 1960), who, together with a man called Thomas Zimmermann, in 1985 co-founded VPL Research Inc, a company that pioneered the production of virtual reality gadgets. Among these, and perhaps most notable as an invention, was the *Dataglove*, which allowed users to manually manipulate objects in the virtual space. The *Dataglove* was sold at about USD 9,000, and they also created an HMD they called *EyePhone*, which retailed just a bit higher at USD 9,400, and an *EyePhone HRX* version for which you'd have to fork out a cool USD 49,000. It was in the marketing of these devices that, from about 1987 onwards, the term *Virtual Reality*, or *VR* for short, gained traction.

As with Artificial Intelligence (AI) and Machine Learning (ML), the early promises of the 1960s were not soon fulfilled, and even a company like VPL Research was not able in the mid to late 1980s to successfully tap into a mass market. This was not for a lack of imagination or ambition: mainly it was simply a case of the hardware not yet being up to what the concept foresaw. VPL Research went bankrupt in 1999 – the year *The Matrix* was released – and it would take about another decade before VR started to come into its own, because while it had been advancing steadily, especially in the games industry, it was really in the second decade of the twenty-first century that miniaturisation and price drops started to reach critical mass. (We talk in more detail about this in our chapter on Big Data & Machine Learning.) □ 549↘

In April 2012, the then 20-year-old American entrepreneur Palmer Luckey (b. 1992), founder of Oculus VR launched a crowdfunding campaign to raise USD 250,000 to finance the development of the *Oculus Rift* virtual reality gaming headset, in collaboration with the wider developer community. Oculus raised nearly ten times their target, USD 2.4m, and barely two years later, in March 2014 Facebook bought Oculus for almost one thousand times as much again: $2.3 billion. The consumer product hit the market another two years later, in March 2016.

At the same time, Taiwanese consumer electronics firm HTC launched its *Vive* headset, and Microsoft its *HoloLens*, which had an introductory price of USD 3,000. (By comparison, the *Vive* had an introductory price of USD 800 and the *Oculus Rift* launched at USD 600, all of them in the year 2016.)

Meanwhile, in 2014, Google launched its *Cardboard* ultra-low-cost self-assembly kit, made, unsurprisingly, of cardboard, which works in conjunction with a mobile phone and an app and retails for as little as USD 5 a piece. The *Samsung Galaxy Gear* is not in that sense a fully-fledged virtual reality device, but a wearable watch that has some VR functions such as gesture recognition built in, which it uses in conjunction with a smartphone.

These very recent developments (they all fall well within the second decade of the 21st century), point towards a wide opening of the market with extremely dynamic startups quickly being recognised for their potential and gobbled up by the world's largest players for outlandish amounts of money: tell-tale signs that there's movement in this sector now, and VR is coming of age.

Hand in hand with this we have also seen a palpable democratisation of the technology, with major development projects being shared among the developer community, and the original funding often coming from a broad fan and supporter base of donors and investors, rather than the big corporations (who, owing to their purchasing power, may well still end up owning the property and cleaning up large profits).

PROGRAMMING TECHNOLOGIES FOR VR

Here, without going into detail, we want to reference three programming technologies that are freely available as we write this in 2018/19, and that are compatible with contemporary VR headsets, such as *Oculus Rift*, *HTC Vive*, or *Google Cardboard*, just to give you an idea of the spectrum.

In development since 2014, *WebVR* is an Application Programming Interface (API) that is being developed in an open-source environment and that offers an accessible, compact piece of software whose goal, according to its own website, is, "to make it easier for everyone to get into VR experiences, no matter what device you have," by connecting the headset with a compatible browser.

■ ↖235 496↘
■ ↖414 512↘
■ ↖377 486↘

□ ↖57 *Unity* is a proprietary cross-platform games engine developed by Unity Technologies. First launched in 2005 for Apple's *OSX* for *Mac*, it now works on over two dozen operating systems. *Unity* supports 2D and 3D graphics and, although suited to much more complex and demanding tasks than *WebVR*, still offers a comparatively low entry point, with a strong focus on plug & play functionalities. Most VR applications currently in development for *Oculus Rift* and the *HTC Vive* rely on *Unity*.

Unreal Engine by Epic Games traces its history back to 1998 and has established itself as a widely used industry tool. Its code is written in *C++*, which makes it particularly portable, and it uses the third party *Blueprint* editor to visually represent and define the behaviour and rules of the virtual world that is being created. Compared to *Unity*, *Unreal* offers a higher degree of graphics quality and more flexibility in detailed fine tuning, but it also requires more expertise.

Generally, as we write this, it is still true to say that if you want to make a VR scene immersive and allow the user to 'really' enter the digital world and walk around in it, you do need experts. In architecture, the workflow is not optimised yet for the demands of this technology. For example, the data you might create in programs such as *SketchUp*, *Autodesk Revit*, or *Vectorworks* still have to be transferred manually to the 3D engine and there be optimised for VR. But there are now tools in development – such as *IrisVR* – which will make these processes a lot easier. In the longer term, as we've already mentioned and as we'll explain in a bit more detail in *The Outlook* below, we anticipate that architects will design and plan at least some of their objects directly in the virtual world.

FROM GAMES TO ARCHITECTURE

The great driver, not only in virtual and augmented reality, but here even more than in other digital disciplines touching on architecture (□ ↖475 Simulation and 3D Modelling being obvious and obviously related examples) have been games. Games developers have been more inventive, more dynamic, and more agile than those in any other industries, and their tech-friendly consumers have been more ready to spend, and to explore uncharted experience territory, than most others. In 2016, the gaming industry breached the one hundred billion US dollar mark in terms of market size, of which a bit more than a third was spent on products for mobile devices.

In this context, it is fascinating to note that the most successful of all 'virtual reality' games in terms of sales is *Minecraft*. Created by Swedish video game programmer and designer Markus Persson (b. 1979) and first released by his own company Mojang Specifications in 2011, *Minecraft* stands out because it does almost the opposite of what most virtual reality projects aim to do. Rather than make an artificial reality that is as 'lifelike' as possible by going for the most naturalistic look that can be achieved with the technology, *Minecraft's* world is kept deliberately simple. The player uses blocks, slabs, and other *Lego*-like virtual elements to create the world they want to inhabit, with no pretence being made that this is anything other than a game and a very abstract, simplified reality. (Mojang fell into the hands of Microsoft in 2014, for USD 2.5 billion. Persson and his two cofounders Carl Manneh and Jakob Porsér left the company at that point.)

In architecture, we were comparatively slow to adopt the techniques and technologies that the gaming and also the film industry developed for simulation, 3D modelling, and visualisation, and we are also not strictly at the cutting edge of virtual and augmented reality. But as in those other digital spheres, this is changing, and more rapidly so. There is now software that you can use with standard architectural design tools, such as *Rhino3D* – similar plugins for *AutoCAD* and *ArchiCAD* are also being developed – which allow you to create VR experiences without much previous knowledge.

The Outlook

"Die Zukunft hat schon begonnen," the German writer and futurologist Robert Jungk (1913–1994) famously
□ ↖463 proclaimed in his 1952 book of the same title. Jungk was not talking about virtual reality so much as about the acutely felt perils of the Cold War and its attendant nuclear race, but the question of what kind of a reality
■ ↖374 the 20th century would leave behind was foremost on his and many other people's mind and, four years after the publication of that almost era-defining dystopia by English writer George Orwell (1903–1950), *Nineteen Eighty-Four*, Jungk's was a warning, really, rather than an expression of unbridled joy: 'the future
■ ↖377 has already begun.'

We can more or less take this sentence as the subtitle for our century. Tomorrow is always already here now. Technological developments are so fast that as we type this sentence today, we already know that by the time you read it, so much will have happened in digital technology, and therefore also in architecture, that some of the things we say will already be out of date, and many will soon need updating. And while this is certainly true for the whole *Atlas*, it is particularly true for this chapter on Virtual & Augmented Reality, because here we see things moving at an especially keen pace. Mostly because they can: the technology has caught up, and the processor and graphics card speeds are now so good, the display resolutions so high, and the components so small that virtual reality is now, as we move into the third decade of the 21st century, becoming an actual reality all in its own right. Combine this with the advances that are being made in artificial intelligence and machine learning, and we have very little reason to doubt that over the next ten, fifteen years the use of virtual reality in many spheres of our lives, and in all kinds of industries, will mushroom. Architecture, we think, is no exception to this; in fact if anything we envisage that in architecture in particular, virtual and augmented reality tools will prove immensely useful.

This is not without its potential pitfalls and drawbacks. As a demonstration, simulation, and presentation tool, VR is today still quite clumsy and rudimentary. You do not as yet have, and it will be some time before you can get (if ever, and this is by no means certain), the haptic, real-life sensory qualities in a virtual reality experience that you can easily get from a physical model. But the gap is closing, and with the audiovisual experience we're almost there.

But we see – as we've mentioned once or twice before, but as is important here now to emphasise – the real impact of VR in architecture not in presentation, but in design. This 'branch' is as yet in its infancy, and our hunch is therefore to some extent speculative. But there are many advantages that designing from 'within', so to speak, can bring, with the user experience explored from the beginning, and in a constant exchange between architects, designers, engineers, manufacturers, clients, and stakeholders. It offers – somewhat ironically perhaps – a much more 'organic' process, one of almost 'growing' a building out of the experience that we aim for, rather than imposing one on it.

This, too, is not without its problems, of course. Quite apart from the principal question as to how much does an architect really want to surrender their artistic vision and creative control to a committee of collaborators, with VR, much as with other toolkits that shift the decision making forward in the process (we note this in BIM, for example) we may find ourselves in danger of fixing things too soon, of walking our client through a near life-like experience of a concept that we then can no longer change or evolve in harmony with what the physical reality suggests, because we've made an 'unalterable' promise that we'll be held to.

The more powerful the medium – and we've called VR and AR a medium more than simply a technology or a tool – the more incumbent it is on us to find ways to master this medium, and not allow ourselves to become its slave. This is – and that is no coincidence – the exact same challenge that Robert Jungk talks about in his book for society as a whole and that pervades our technological present now: how do we master our inventions to our own greatest benefit.

ARCHITECTURAL STORYTELLING

For us as architects, there is another interesting element that we are really only beginning to latch on to: the narrative. Our era is defined by storytelling. Much more than other periods, during which abstract and conceptual thinking stood at the fore, we are constantly called upon to tell 'the story', and if it doesn't as yet 'exist', then to create it. As architects, we tend to be good at representing space in two or three dimensions: it's what we're trained to do. What we have little experience in, and hardly any training for, is representing character (the user, the client, the worker, the inhabitant, us) in space (the object we're proposing to build), and time (as and how things happen, what we do, how we behave). But this is now a facet of architecture. Not one that any person or any group of people have sat down and deliberated on, it's just happening: the technology is there, the overlaps are flowing into each other and blurring the boundaries, we live in a fully medial age, we are called upon to master storytelling as well. And so we do well to learn from the masters of storytelling: the makers of films and games. They really do have training and experience in creating stories with characters in space and time, that is their primary concern, night and day. There are people in these industries who will literally spend eighteen, twenty hour days in darkened rooms sitting at a computer, working out just that: how to tell the story as an experience.

APPLIED REALITY

How, then, in more concrete terms, should we imagine this? We are, as you know, inclined towards caution when it comes to predicting the future, but here are some examples of what we imagine virtual and augmented reality tools may enable, some of which we've already hinted at:

- Much more seamless processes between architects, engineers, and contractors; for example being able to stand together in a room that is yet to be built, look at where things are and where they need to be, and to draw lines, or to 'insert' components, to mark and to change elements, all while in the virtual space, all just by using gestures.
- Similarly, and later in the process, being able to manipulate machinery (such as in 3D manufacture) through gestures and thus generating highly bespoke, precisely detailed objects for a project.
- Generally, the further integration of design and manufacture/modelling: we are not far from being able to design a room in the virtual space and to then print it out as a physical object.
- Quality control and the examination of existing contexts: surveyors can now already wander about an object – be it a newly built one, or one that needs to be changed or added to or dismantled to make room for a new one – and their headsets can immediately record measurements and any flaws or features they want to note.
- The incorporation of ourselves as human beings and ultimately users of the space into its design; for example by employing the services of a dancer and motion capture to design a space.

All of which presupposes and in a way demands of us a certain command of the medium, a literacy. We say this repeatedly in our *Atlas*, because it's relevant in so many respects. It is maybe neither possible nor necessary for us as architects to become fully-fledged VR experts. There are now, and there will be in future, more people who will specialise in this field and push the boundaries for us. Whether I as an architect want to do this is, ultimately, really up to me. I may not: I may be much more inclined to work with other methods. But as a contemporary professional I need to at least know what the tools are, how they work, how other people use them, and how I can use them if I want to: give myself the freedom to design as I choose.

If you're skeptically inclined, you could – as some people absolutely do – predict the end of architecture through digital technology. We think different. We think a medium such as virtual and augmented reality can give architecture a shot in the arm, invigorate and renew it: empower and embolden us to create a new architecture of the imagination...

286 ● 465
Distorted reality: *The Draughtsman's Contract*. [BFI]

287 ● 466
The Barbican Centre viewed from above. [Suttonpubcrawl]

288 ● 468
St Peter's Square, Rome by Gian Lorenzo Bernini, drawn by Giovanni Battista Piranesi (1720–1778).

289 ● 468
Giovanni Battista Piranesi: Imaginary Prisons – *Carceri Series, Plate XIV.*

290 ● 468
Chronophotography, 1886: between photography and the moving image. [Étienne-Jules Marey]

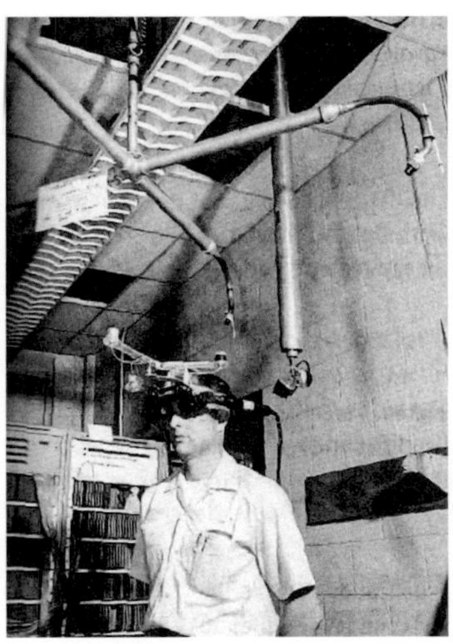

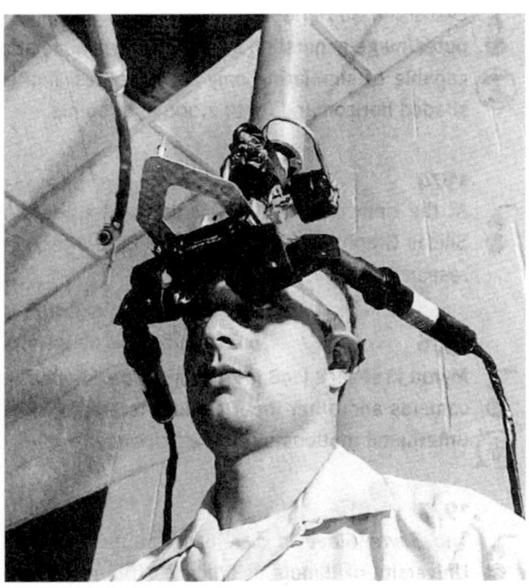

291A ● 469 291B ● 469
The Damocles Sword – the first Head Mounted Display (HMD) developed by Ivan Sutherland and Bob Sproull. [H Quinten Foster and Don Vickers]

- Antero Markelin and Bernd Fahle: *Umweltsimulation*, 1979
- Ernest Burden: *Design Simulation*, 1985
- Stephen R Sheppard: *Visual Simulation*, 1989
- Angela Schönberger: *Simulation und Wirklichkeit*, 1991
- Claus Dießenbacher: *Computersimulation und -visualisierung in der Architektur*, 1998
- Jan L M Hensen, Roberto Lamberts (Eds.): *Building Performance Simulation for Design and Operation*, 2011

Simulation

Bob Martens

Overview

If you drive through Switzerland on one of its pristine country roads or sensibly financed motorways, or travel on one of its proverbially punctual and impeccably timetable-coordinated trains, you will at one point or another come across an empty or near empty field or garden where there may be a barn or an old family home, or pass some other plot of land with or without an existing structure on it, and you will notice that someone has planted some wooden (or, more recently, also metal) poles into the scenery, each with small, right angled bars at the top. In some cases it will be fairly obvious, in others less so, that these curious, often quite elaborate temporary marker constellations have been put there to stake out the dimensions of a new building that is proposed for the site, so that neighbours and other locals affected by the plans can gauge the impending change to their environment and, if necessary, file with the authorities any objections or concerns they may have.

What you are looking at is a most basic, simple form of 1:1 analogue [Simulation]. Which already demonstrates how broad a field of activity the term encompasses, because from this to an intricate 3D computer model that addresses every aspect of a new development's workings, there lies a wide and varied spectrum across many layers of technology and methodology, both analogue and digital. This being an *Atlas of Digital Architecture*, we will largely focus on digital methods, and these alone cover several specialised areas such as statics, light, acoustics, energy, air flow, and the movement of people and traffic, as well as evacuation procedures and emergency situations.

292 ● 487

Irrespective of what is being simulated and how, what all simulation has in common is that it is *measurable*, and that the given parameters or values which determine the simulation are *specific*. That is what defines a simulation and possibly distinguishes it from other, more random or experimental modelling methods, although there are of course large areas where they intersect. Still, we speak of simulation principally when we aim to obtain some findings that are useful to us for a particular purpose, for example to know how certain design elements work together, or to analyse an identified aspect of a building (how natural light falls into different floor areas and how it combines with artificial light, for example), or to optimise its construction (what are the minimum material requirements to keep a structure safe under all foreseeable circumstances). The overall purpose of simulation, then, is to get a representation of a reality in given conditions, whereby simulation expressly lays claim to being *verifiable and consistent* within these conditions.

You are, however, with simulation working in a 'laboratory' situation, and that means there are limits to how dependable any findings can be. On 10 June 2000, the aptly named London Millennium Footbridge opened to the public, spanning the river Thames between St Paul's Cathedral and Tate Modern, the art museum housed inside the former Bankside Power Station. The public was keen: completion of the bridge ran about two months behind schedule, and so now, on a fine summer Saturday and with The Queen cutting the ribbon, Londoners flocked to the new structure in droves for its long anticipated inauguration. 90,000 of them visited and crossed the new bridge on that day alone, with some 2,000 individuals on it at any given time.

This triggered a phenomenon no-one had foreseen. The Millennium Bridge is an elegant suspension bridge, and the static workings of this kind of structure under various conditions are well known: engineers had anticipated, and accounted for, all kinds of pressures, stresses, movements, and behaviours, but what nobody knew was that once a certain number of people were walking on the bridge (you could call this a critical mass), its horizontal sway would reach an extent at which people instinctively and without noticing fell into step with that sway, and therefore □ ↖475
with each other: in order to stay upright and stable they would ever so slightly correct the placing of their foot in the direction of the movement, and since everybody did so at the same time, the effect was similar to two thousand troops marching across the bridge in step. Bridge builders know that this can do serious damage to their structures, and so a few miles upstream, at the Albert Bridge, which opened in 1873, you can still find the old iron sign that instructs any military that might be crossing: "troops must break step".

The Millennium Bridge overnight acquired the epithet 'wobbly' and today is still often referred to as 'The Wobbly Bridge', even though it was closed on the 12th June that year, and not reopened until eighteen months later, on 22 February 2002, after 89 dampers had been installed, at a cost of some additional GBP 5 million. The problem, which at first had mystified the architects and engineers, was identified by running real life 1:1 trials – simulations – with hundreds of volunteers walking to and fro on the bridge for several days after it was closed to the public.

293 ● 487

Since the turn of the century, computer simulation has moved on considerably, and today it is far more easily accessible even to small architecture practices; so it is entirely possible that a digital simulation with today's computing power and software might have prevented the flaw from ever occurring. But it is by no means certain: a much more recent building, 20 Fenchurch Street, also in London and known as the 'Walkie-Talkie' owing to its clunky curved shape, was still under construction in 2013, when people noticed that the parabolic glass facade to its south side was reflecting sunlight at concentrations capable of melting paint on cars or burning window sills. Or frying an egg on the pavement...

☐ ↖421 ☐ 507↘

DIGITALITY & SIMULATION

Since the late 20th century, digital design tools have enabled architects to come up with and implement ever more adventurous geometries, and in the process simulation has acquired ever greater significance in architecture across the board. Today we can broadly divide this board up into two main areas:

- *Design simulation:* form-finding and presentation of space
- *Performance simulation:* testing the behaviour of, for example, structure, light, or energy

We will discuss them in more detail and give examples under *Applied Simulation,* further on in this chapter.

In both of these – and there are naturally considerable overlaps – a dynamic interplay between the demands of a physical reality and the conceptual ideas that are meant to lead to this reality is in force. In design simulation it may be a case mainly of the representation of space, such as we also discuss in ☐ ↖57 ☐ ↖421 ☐ ↖285 ☐ ↖57 our chapters on 3D Modelling, Model Making, and Visualisation: what are the shapes that work best visually, and what materials, textures, and finishes should I use? In performance simulation it may be much more a case of aesthetics and stability: how much material can I remove before the structure becomes unstable? Where do I need to put fire exits and staircases to be able to evacuate a large building quickly, without ruining my design?

The bigger, more ambitious, and complex a project, the more important simulation becomes. And if you look at something like the Palm Islands in Dubai, or, also in Dubai, the Burj Khalifa tower, or even, staying in the region, at something like the Convertible Umbrellas by German architect Bodo Rasch (b. 1943), which cover vast areas in several cities of Saudi Arabia: all these offer significant challenges not just in their construction (though that too), but particularly also in their maintenance and operation: they find themselves in extreme situations where water, wind, and sunshine, respectively and jointly, exercise pressures and forces on materials, mechanisms, and the people on, in, and underneath them, which would not only be costly to leave to trial and error in the physical world to sort out, but also untenably dangerous.

294A ○ 582

294B ○ 582

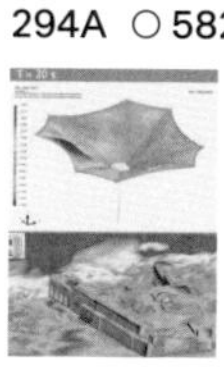
295A ○ 582

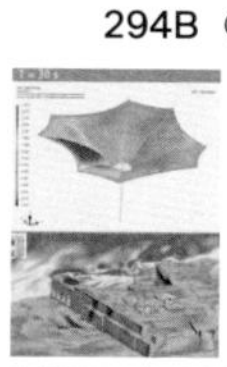
295B ○ 582

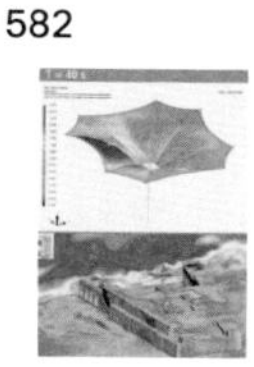
295C ○ 582

As we have seen in many other areas, both in architecture and elsewhere, digital technology, even where it doesn't necessarily invent a new process or methodology, often shifts decision making further down the line of a creative or conceptual process. (It also in certain respects does the opposite, as we note and discuss in our chapters on Model Making and Building Information Modelling (BIM), for example.) We may invoke a typewriter analogy here: back in the days before word processing, you really had to plan your text carefully before you sat down and started to type it, because once you committed it to paper, that's where it was. And quite often what you were typing would also go on one or even two carbon copies straight away, all of which were permanent physical imprints of what you were doing. If you made a mistake, it was on there. So naturally, people would often write text in long hand first, then rewrite it, make corrections, rework it, and only finally, when they were sure they were saying what they wanted to say, would they reach for the typewriter (or hand over to a typist). Today, that's not the case any more. You compose your text on your computer or pad from scratch and tinker with it till the last moment, and beyond. Even once you've printed it out, the effort it takes to make a minor correction and then send it to the printer again is minimal. Only once you go into publishing your book or releasing your text to the public, do you really have to decide: this is it, final version, 'good to print'.

With digital technology and architecture, a similar phenomenon comes into play, and it applies to simulation as much as it applies to 3D Modelling, for example, and straightforward design: the computer moves your point of no return down the line. And with simulation you can learn a lot about your object to help you make sure that you sail past that point smoothly, towards the destination you actually want to get to.

A BIT OF BACKGROUND

It is said that the Italian architect and sculptor Gian Lorenzo Bernini (1598–1680) used 1:1 scale mock-ups in his work on the St Peter's Basilica in Rome and possibly also for the colonnades in front of it, so the idea of simulating a building before putting it up is certainly not new. Even some of the more tangential connections between simulation and other fields of expertise have precedent in history. Much of the computer software, for example, that is used in 3D modelling and that therefore also underpins programming and coding principles for simulation software was pioneered in the film industry, where realistic 3D renderings of scenes and settings have been developed since the early 1990s. But back in the late 1920s and very early 1930s, immediately before the Nazis came to power in Berlin, the German *Reichskanzlei* (the Chancellery, equivalent to today's *Kanzleramt*), originally an 18th century palace, was comprehensively refurbished, with the local film industry providing scenery as mock-ups to simulate and visualise what the new building would look like when complete.

So, both as a communication tool and as a method to avoid mistakes, simulation predates digitality by a very long stretch. And simulation has always been, and will continue to be, a practice that may produce very different results, depending on who does it and with what goal in mind: a property developer will simulate their project to the public and the authorities in possibly a quite different manner than, say, a neighbourhood association or environmental protection group might simulate the exact same thing.

The history of computer simulation itself is brief and aligns entirely with the evolution of computing in architecture in other areas: up until about the mid-1980s it is mainly in the automotive industry and in aerospace and military environments that computing power and software sophistication are capable of producing useful studies. The Hungarian software developer and entrepreneur Gabór Bojár (b. 1949) can be credited with advancing the technology sharply in the direction of architecture, with his groundbreaking *ArchiCAD* software, which he launched with his company Graphisoft in 1987 as one of the first of its kind to be designed for a personal computer, the original *Apple Macintosh*. But even by this stage, computing power and processing speeds were still very limited, which is why analogue simulation methods involving models and drawings at a much higher level of abstraction continued to prevail.

From the mid-1990s onwards, computer hardware gets smaller and faster, and software more capable, and so Computer Aided Architectural Design ■ ↖424 512↘ (CAAD) begins to take hold and make itself felt in the creation of architecture, by facilitating more complex, lighter, and more ambitious structures. Because of this, a new engagement with materiality emerges: the question of what is buildable and what isn't. Meanwhile, the arrival of the Internet gives rise to collaborative practices and open source development, and much wider and faster sharing of insights and information.

The mid-2000s usher in the era of tablets and smartphones, of big data and cloud networks, and what we refer to as ubiquitous computing ■ 536↘ (about which much more in our chapter on The Internet □ 613↘ of Things (IoT)). We are now in an era that allows for highly complex, real-time simulations to be carried out by anyone who has access to a half-decent machine, some professional software, and a degree of technical know-how, but potentially also a fair bit of time and patience, because simulation can be an elaborate business, as we shall see.

Applied Simulation

We've already identified the two principal areas into which simulation broadly falls, and we're about to give you a few examples to illustrate them. Across these areas, we use different types of simulation to accumulate snippets of information that we can then piece together to form a comprehensive picture of a reality. This can be applied both as a forward projection, testing objects before they are built, and retroactively, analysing processes that have occurred, for example to improve them or to learn from problems or catastrophes. (This can happen on all kinds of levels: since the 9/11 disaster in New York, for example, many independent experts have used simulations not so much to find out how skyscraper design can be improved to withstand similar attacks, but to establish the exact nature of the damage that was caused and, in many cases, to attempt to disprove the official version of events.)

There are some specialist areas of simulation that we won't cover in this chapter, since they really form fields of research and study in their own right, most prominent among them earthquake simulations, which are of absolutely critical importance to architecture and engineering in areas prone to seismic activity, such as Japan or the American West Coast, but also for example simulation aiding reconstruction or restoration of damaged or destroyed cultural and/or sacred buildings, where considerations such as historical accuracy, faithfulness to the original concept and meaning of a structure, and the authenticity of its materiality all acquire major significance.

DESIGN SIMULATION

Simulation in architectural design mainly focuses on the representation and, where relevant, the correction of the intended effect of a yet to be built architectural reality and the elements that characterise it. Here therefore is our strongest overlap with 3D Modelling □ ↖57 and Visualisation □ ↖285, on both of which we have dedicated chapters in this *Atlas*, which is why we will not dwell too much on this particular field here. But in all of these – simulation, 3D modelling, and visualisation – we are confronted with the question: where does that reality begin and where might it end, or, perhaps more likely, 'seep' into the realm, purely, of the imagination.

In other words, is a simulation advanced to perfection so as to maximise its impact as part of a selling process, or is it kept to its most pragmatic version, to come as close as possible to the building that is most likely to be released. Are the 'ideal' vision and the buildable reality the same, or are they at odds with each other? And what is there to be said, if anything, for simulation that is perhaps efficient and practical, but composed of essentially superficial set pieces that the software facilitates, but that neither manage to generate genuinely good architecture, nor fail completely by putting out architecture that is truly awful?

Design simulation, then, apart from everything else, involves a judgment call on what that simulation is meant to achieve far beyond practical terms; it is part of the design process and, as such, also a conceptual tool.

296 ○ 583

297A ● 487 297B ● 487

297C ● 487

■ ↖424
■ ↖428 524↘
□ ↖57
□ ↖175
□ ↖111
□ ↖145

In this context parametric modelling takes on increasing significance as part of a parametric design process overall. We deal with this in several chapters in this *Atlas*, including, among others, 3D Modelling, Graphs & Graphics, Digital Design Strategies, and Generative Methods, and so this is also an area we won't need to delve into further at this particular juncture. Suffice it to say, therefore, that parametric modelling allows the simulation of complex geometries and forms that can not be achieved with standard design tools. A well known example of a parametric modelling software is *Grasshopper.*

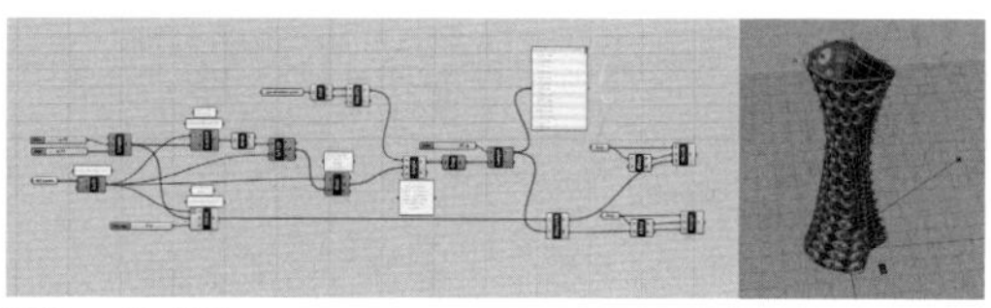

298 ● 488

PERFORMANCE SIMULATION

Performance simulation encompasses a wide range of tests and analyses that examine certain aspects of a building, whether this is a project that is yet to be realised or an object that's already in existence but needs modifying. It is of particular interest to us as architects, and not covered elsewhere in this *Atlas*, which is why we lend this the bulk of our attention here.

It is worth noting at this point that performance simulation is a playground for experts: you need a strong technical background and high levels of skill that aren't acquired quickly. Which is to say: you don't become a performance simulator overnight! You can, however, get an idea of what is involved within a few paragraphs, and that's what we are hoping to convey in what follows.

ACOUSTIC SIMULATION

Within performance simulation, acoustic simulation is a field still largely applied in specialised contexts only, such as in the construction and fitting out of concert halls and live performance venues or recording studios, where acoustics play an obviously essential part and are considered central to the building's purpose and therefore its construction process.

The fact that it is still confined as much as it is to settings where aural perception lies at the core of our experience can be explained partly by a degree of neglect in contemporary architectural culture of sound generally. But it also has a lot to do with the particularly great challenges that acoustic simulation poses, and their attendant demands on time and budgets. These same challenges though are also what make acoustic simulation especially interesting and useful for us to be looking at in more detail, since similar processes – often very time-consuming and demanding – are involved in many other types of performance simulation.

Take a music venue that is designed for different types of performance, some amplified (such as jazz), others not (such as chamber music), or a venue which from the outset has a multi-purpose functionality and needs to be suitable for music as much as for the spoken word, for example. These different activities all produce different sound patterns that reflect off surfaces in different ways, and therefore require different levels and types of reverberation. The shape of an auditorium contributes dramatically to how sound behaves. As we shall see in more detail shortly, whether you build a traditional shoebox (such as the famous *Musikverein* Vienna, world renowned for its acoustics), or – generally more favoured today – an arena (such as the *Elbphilharmonie* Hamburg of our case study below) makes a great difference to how music is heard by an audience.

299 ● 488

Even though far less deployed in other areas, acoustic simulation can (and arguably ought to) be integral to the design of any space where people spend time, since acoustics contribute so much to the atmosphere, be it a restaurant/cafe/bar or a class room, a railway station or a museum. Or a workplace: a large open plan office, for example, is a space where hundreds of people spend long hours of their working day, many of them in conversation either face-to-face or on the phone, so how noisy it gets, how easy it is to understand the other person, and how much privacy the setting affords for staff to be able to conduct sensitive exchanges are all relevant to how well a building functions.

There are, within acoustic simulation, several specialised subdivisions. Salford University, for example, lists no fewer than eight areas of current or recent research:

- Geometrical room acoustics modelling
- Boundary element modelling
- Time domain boundary element modelling
- Finite element modelling
- Finite difference time domain modelling
- Modelling for outdoor sound propagation
- Modelling for acoustical materials
- Modelling of active noise control

As regards software, it is in some cases possible, but rare, that you would import existing 3D CAD data into an acoustic modelling program. Rather, you use specialist acoustic modelling software to build an abstract (therefore simplified) model which describes the dimensions of the space, as well as any other parameters that may be relevant, depending on the complexity of the task and the time and budget you have available

Examples of acoustic modelling software include *CATT (Computer Aided Test Tool)*, *Odeon*, or *EASE (Enhanced Acoustic Simulator for Engineers)*.

MODELLING A HALL WITH *CATT ACOUSTIC*
CATT Acoustic is a software package that is used to simulate acoustic parameters of spaces during the design phase in a calculation model. It was originally conceived for the design of room acoustics of larger spaces, such as theatre auditoria. The calculation core of *CATT Acoustic* applies different methods, including **ray tracing**. ■ ↖287

We come across ray tracing in several chapters of our *Atlas*, mostly in the context of visualisations where the rays refer to light. In acoustic modelling, ray tracing is a calculation method in which the individual paths of sound waves – the rays referred to here – are modelled. Depending on the geometry, the objects present in the space, and the properties of all surfaces, the waves in the model will reflect and change direction. By customising individual waves, very often the acoustics are stochastically determined at all locations in the space. Beams are sent from an input source or sources, and the beams' properties, such as direction and volume, recorded at various receiving points. Also taken into account during the simulation are diffusion factors, which can be entered per octave band for each material.

THE INPUT MODEL: The input model is a three-dimensional scale model of the space in which diffusing and absorbing properties of surfaces and objects are introduced. Here, a sound source can be placed at any location, and similarly receiving points can be set anywhere. Creating an input model is usually done on the basis of CAD data.

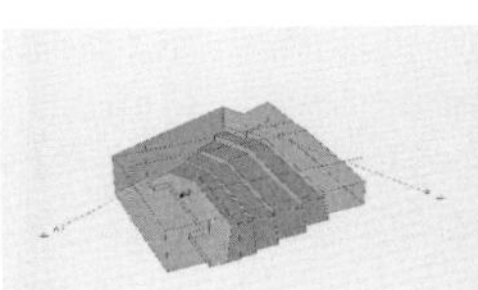
300A ○ 583

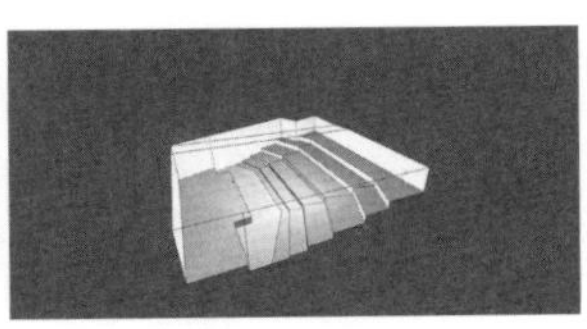
300B ○ 583

TIME TRACE: The following image series depicts fragments of a time trace plot to give an impression of the calculation method. It shows how the sound rays of a certain frequency – in this case 1000 Hz – move from the source through the model at different moments, here after 5 ms (milliseconds), 25 ms and 40 ms.

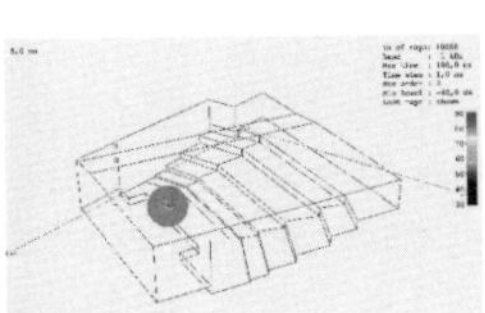
301A ○ 583

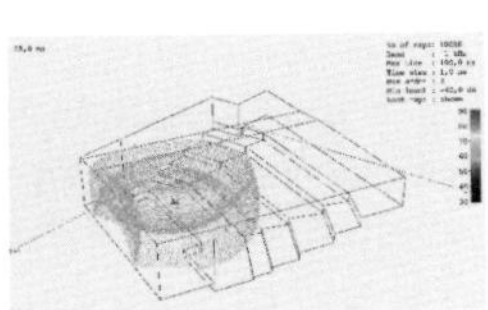
301B ○ 583

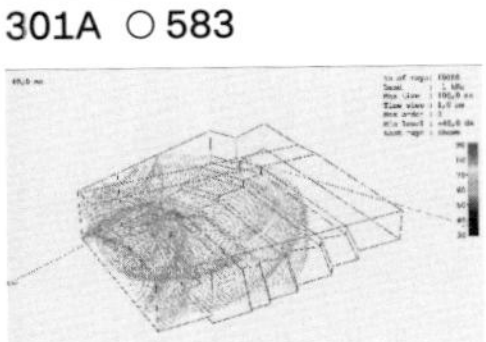
301C ○ 583

SOUND PIXEL RENDERING: With *CATT Acoustic* it is possible to determine both *how* and *how much* the sound in a room decreases, and what influence objects in the space have on the 'distributions' of sound across the room. This is visualised with a colour scale and gives an indication of the decreasing noise level in the space. In this example, the noise level decreases from 90 dB on stage to 60 dB in the auditorium:

302 ○ 583

CASE STUDY: *ELBPHILHARMONIE* HAMBURG
One of the most striking buildings in Germany's second largest city, and certainly one of the most expensive, is the *Elbphilharmonie* Hamburg, affectionally known as Elphi. It's 26 stories tall and provides 120,000 square metres (1,300,000 sq ft) of floor space, on which it houses 45 luxury flats, a hotel with 244 rooms, conference facilities, restaurants, bars, a car park, and a spa. Plus three concert venues: a 170 seater studio, a 550 seat *Kleiner Saal* (small concert hall) for chamber music, jazz concerts, and recitals, and the flagship *Grosser Saal* (big concert hall) which seats an audience of 2,150 music lovers for symphonic concerts.

For all three concert venues, architects Herzog & de Meuron employed the services of Nagata Acoustics, who joined the project in 2004, shortly after its inception, and worked on it for 12 years, providing, "all acoustical consulting services from the design phase through construction and project completion," as their website recounts.

Chief acoustician Yasuhisa Toyota (b. 1952) cites two principal factors that informed his approach to the acoustic design: the room's shape and its interior design materials. A major challenge for large concert venues is achieving a sense of intimacy between the audience and the orchestra. For this reason, 'closeness' stood at the forefront of the team's priorities, and by the time Toyota got involved, the decision had already been taken that the architects would go for a 'vineyard' or arena design of the auditorium, in an attempt to bring as many members of the audience as close to the orchestra as possible:

> "For our room acoustics design, achieving acoustical 'intimacy' most importantly meant how to obtain effective and valuable early sound reflections and, to do this, how to create acoustically effective walls around and in the vicinities of the sections of audience seating. Our design solution involved creating small groups of audience seats and designing effective, sound-reflecting wall surfaces for every group of audience seating."

303A ● 488

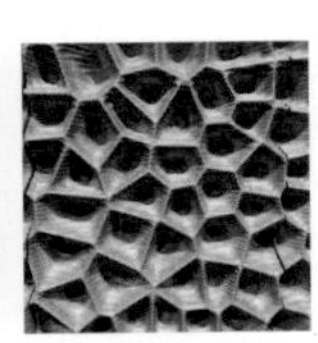
303B ● 489

Principal Consultant Keiji Oguchi takes up the thread and explains how physical scale models – commonly used to conduct analogue measurements of sound reflection prior to the digital era – were used here in combination with computer models to measure sound reflections:

> "The audience seating blocks and ceiling height, as well as the placement of a hall's walls determine how reflections reach different locations within a hall. To study these basic shapes in the 'Grosser Saal', we began by using computer simulation based on the geometrical acoustics to study how the reflections would distribute. With these studies we had intensively discussed about the basic room shape with the architect.
>
> "In the next phase of our room acoustics design after fixing the basic room shape, we built a 1/10 scale model of the hall interior and conducted acoustical experiments in the scale model to study more details about how sound would behave in the space. Our first step in scale model testing was to check for detrimental echoes and, if an echo was found, to solve how to eliminate it."

Of the various options available to eliminate echoes – changing the angles of reflective surfaces, adding sound absorption materials, or adding sound diffusion elements – the architects favoured the latter, and so Nagata built 1:10 scale models of finely 'seashell'-textured diffusion elements to simulate and test the efficacy of this method.

304A ● 489

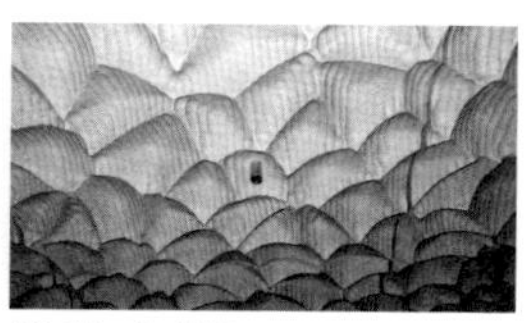

304B ● 489

Through extensive trials both with the physical models and computer simulations, the solution was arrived at: 10,000 bespoke acoustic panels that would line all of the surfaces in the hall other than the floor and the seats, namely ceiling, walls, and balustrades. The panels would measure 4–16 cm across and average a hundred microscopic divots or grooves, individually sized and spaced to maximise the desired effect of intimacy from the sound as it bounces off the surfaces at finely calibrated speed and intensity: some panels need larger divots to absorb more sound because they are further away from the source and so the echo is more pronounced, whereas panels closer to the orchestra have a subtler texture.

The effect of a million such divots covering the hall's interior is not dissimilar to that of the neoclassical decorative elements used in the great hall of the *Musikverein* Vienna mentioned earlier. This concert venue, built by Danish architect Theophil Hansen (1813–1891), was inaugurated in 1870, long before there were any established techniques – let alone digital tools – for acoustic simulation. Its success as a building is largely down to the architect's instinct and experience, and a fair portion of good fortune.

Back at the *Elbphilharmonie*, the ten thousand individually shaped and uniquely grooved panels were made by bespoke geometric computation specialists One to One, whose founding director Benjamin Koren explains that the acoustic, aesthetic, and practical requirements put together supplied the parameters for the design: "Once all of that is in place, I hit play and it creates a million cells all different and all based on these parameters. I have 100 percent control over setting up the algorithm, and then I have no more control."

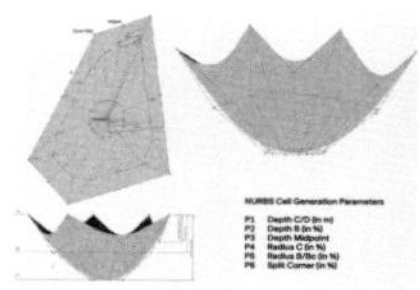

305A ● 489

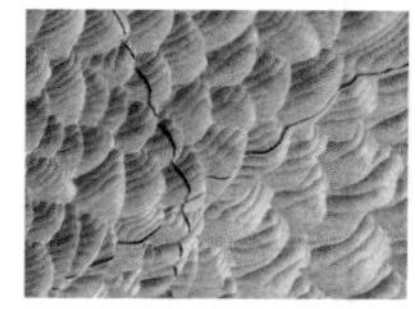

305B ● 489

The immense effort of planning, assessing, and simulating the concert hall's acoustics does not, however, mean that the venue immediately 'feels' perfect. Toyota points out that the first rehearsal of an orchestra in a new setting is the worst time to judge its acoustics, because they will all not be used to the new sound yet, they will not be working as one, but concentrating on the unfamiliar surroundings, and they will not yet have made the building's acoustics their own:

> "At a minimum, an ensemble should spend 2 to 3 months rehearsing in its new hall and, when possible, rehearse for 6 months in the hall before the hall officially opens. In keeping with these guidelines, the Elbphilharmonie project schedule gave the NDR Elbphilharmonie Orchester 4 months of rehearsal time in the new 'Grosser Saal' before opening night."

This example is, of course, particular in many ways, and it's a high-profile project with especially demanding end use, but any sizeable undertaking – and it is really sizeable undertakings that benefit most from elaborate simulation – will present its specific and often formidable demands and challenges. As we have already noted: it is in the nature of things that the larger and more complex the building, the more sophisticated and taxing will be the simulations: a computer model may have to play through tens of thousands of variants, using millions of data points to arrive at a set that it can evaluate with any usable kind of result. Simulation is therefore not only time consuming and labour intensive on the part of the people conducting the trials – they have to continually assess the process and refine the parameters to hone in on those findings that are of real relevance – but also requires substantial amounts of computing power and processing time. Simulation at this level, whether this be of acoustics or any other performance element of a structure, is therefore really not for the faint-hearted...

STRUCTURAL SIMULATION

As we would expect, structural simulation concerns itself with the simulation of an object's structural system. Once the architectural design is done (in most cases this is the sequence of events, though there can be exceptions), the structural properties with their relevant stresses and loads are worked out; in other words: you calculate the forces that will bear on the structure and examine their effects on it.

To this end, current technology uses – for either the entire structure or parts of it – what is known as the **Finite Element Method (FEM)**, which is a mathematical procedure to carry out a corresponding **Finite Element Analysis (FEA)**. The two terms are often used interchangeably and both refer to the principal concept of breaking down very large, possibly *infinitely* large problems with very large, possibly *infinite* numbers of factors into manageable, finite, and therefore calculable portions, which are used as the basis for the simulations. (Although structural simulation is largely done by computer today, manual calculations are still being used as well, but mostly now only as estimates in the early stages of the design development.)

We mentioned elsewhere that contemporary architecture tends towards lean, delicate structures that seem suspended in space and appear to defy the laws of physics. At this point in the proceedings, these laws make themselves unmistakably known, and so there is often a conflict here that needs to be resolved between the priorities of the design and the realities of what is after all a material world.

Much as the level of detail in design increases as the project progresses, so the level of detail and refinement in structural planning normally grows over a project's development. Often, therefore, projects start with relatively crude initial versions, on the assumption that it is always possible to arrive at more elegant and more perfect iterations by a process of refinement and optimisation, and so make better use of the materials and their qualities at an advanced stage.

What, then, do computer based structural calculations look like and how do they work in practice? At the core of this process lies the relationship between architect and structural planner: after all, the type of CAD software normally used by architects is built differently to the type of software a structural engineer uses, yet at some point they have to work together on the same model, and so there are a number of plugins available that bridge this gap and enable the exchange of data between these different types of software. (There are also approaches which try to integrate the two types of software from the outset, Building Information Modelling [BIM], on which we have a separate chapter, being one.)

It is possible, for example, to take a project that has been designed by the architect using *Autodesk Revit*, and import it into *Dlubal RFEM* (surfaces and supports) or *Dlubal RSTAB* (supports and frames only) for structural analysis, whereby the data model undergoes a process of abstraction during the transition.

Once this is done, you or your structural engineer can add to the geometrical properties those of the material and include in the data set the construction elements' critical load and stress bearing properties. There are norms for these, which can be drawn from standard sets, such as **Eurocodes**, which has become the *de facto* construction code for the European Union, or indeed from any other relevant literature.

Generally, we speak in this context of the horizontal and vertical load transfer that needs to be accounted for. Apart form the structure's own weight and that of the building's interior, there will be a range of additional loads and forces that a structure will need to withstand, and these vary greatly, depending on the purpose of the building and its use, and, very obviously, its size. A concert hall or a sports stadium
will naturally have to cope with much greater com- ■ ↖161
plexity than, for example, the residential living room ■
of a semi-detached house in a garden suburb.

Also, any building anywhere in the world will be exposed to temperature fluctuations, wind and weather, to greater or lesser amounts of precipitation and possibly snowfall, quite apart from any potential seismic activity, which, as we mentioned before, requires its own type of specialist analysis. Any and all of these factors can, and to quite some extent do, cause tensions and even deformations in the material, and so these too will form part of the structural simulation. Any corrections that are required can at this stage be made and the entire simulation process repeated until the structure is safe and sound.

306A ○ 584

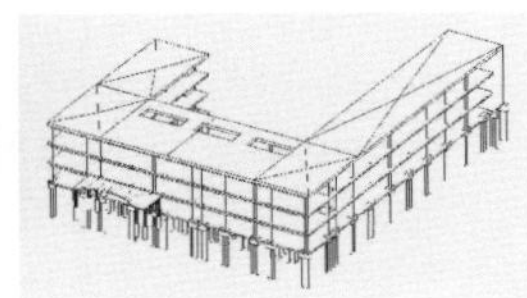
306B ○ 584

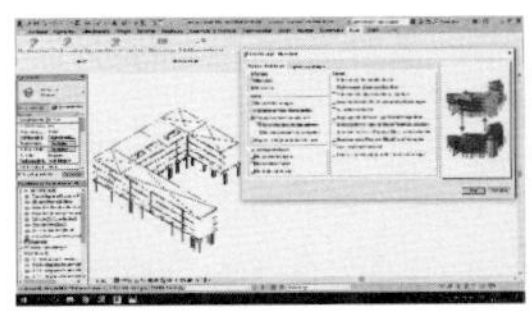
306C ○ 584

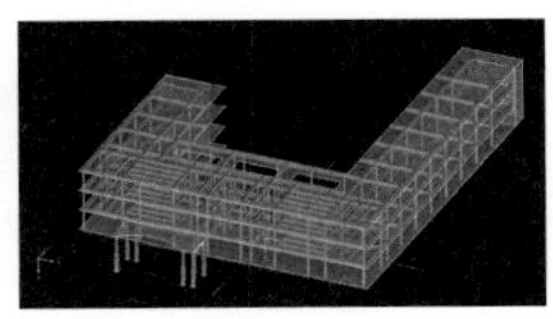
306D ○ 584

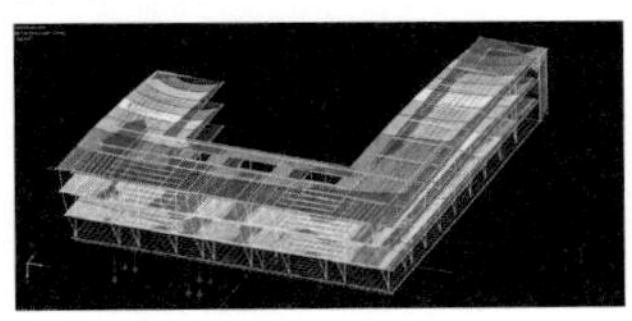
306E ○ 584

LIGHT SIMULATION

Light simulations include all aspects of light flow, light generation, and light management in and also around a building: how natural light behaves throughout the daytime in different weather and seasonal conditions, how artificial lighting design complements and, during the night time, replaces natural light; but also the light,
light reflections, and shadow creation of a building □ 507↘
and therefore its light impact on the existing context and environment are all subject of light simulations.

307 ○ 585

308 ○ 585

Although light has no material substance and therefore cannot be 'touched', we are highly susceptible
to even slight variations in lighting, and the human ■
eye reacts extremely sensitively to differing constellations, registering changes within seconds.

Today, when computer-assisted representations dominate the 'market' of visual simulation, it is interesting to note that full size simulations conveying the – especially artificial – light configurations of a project still have a major stronghold in architecture. The standard procedure for light simulation often consists of the trial positioning of lighting objects on location, in other words setting up a 1:1 simulation on the construction site. In view of the great deal of effort that goes into this approach, any methods of gaining similar results by means of at least partial computer representations are certainly worth pursuing. The degree of abstraction involved, however, may be too high to make observations that can as yet lead to conclusive results and therefore genuinely informed decisions.

309 ○ 585

310 ○ 585

CONTROL OF DAYLIGHT AND ARTIFICIAL LIGHT (ILLUMINATION ENGINEERING): The essential purpose of lighting control is to provide the exact right amount of light needed for whatever activities take place in a space at any given time. This implies that there may well be several different types of activities – each with their own specific lighting needs – going on in a space, all of them supported by appropriate lighting control.

The same variability holds true for daylight, although primarily owing to its changing incidence (or lack thereof) into a space or room
↖268
during the course of the day. This incidence is ultimately controlled by openings in the building envelope, but light openings of the same size may have very different effects, depending on their position in the structure and the direction in which they face. Incident light is routinely reduced by means of shading – with blinds, shutters, or curtains, for example – but more sophisticated means, such as dynamically activated or adjusted glass tints, are also now available.

Despite constant technological advances, artificial lighting still cannot replace daylight, precisely because it is characterised by perpetual change. Therefore in lighting design for new buildings, synergies between both types of light should be considered and taken advantage of where this is possible.

ENERGY SIMULATION

Across the EU and the USA, buildings account for roughly 40% of all energy use: nearly half. (The rest is split about equally between transportation and industry.) So energy management in buildings is a big deal: the bigger the building, the bigger the deal; and not only are there environmental and therefore increasingly also regulatory factors that architects, planners, engineers, and clients need to consider, but also simply cost: lighting and heating an energy-inefficient building is a complete waste of money, because it's unnecessary. And for existing, particularly historical, buildings of heritage value, energy solutions can make the difference between terminal decline and a continued, even revitalised existence.

Obtaining reliable predictions about a building's energy performance is therefore essential to a productive and efficient design process. In this context, the development and timely application of computational building performance simulation tools is an established area of research in building-related disciplines and professions, such as architecture, civil engineering, mechanical engineering, and environmental physics. But sustained efforts are still needed to fully integrate this type of simulation in the practice of building design and operation. Recent global discussions and developments that highlight the need for better eco-efficiency in building construction and maintenance underline the critical importance of such efforts.

Energy simulation covers a broad range of simulation topics. Apart from a building's energy performance (which could be said to be the most obvious area of application), other important aspects include heat and mass transfer in building materials and between the building envelope and the environment, indoor climate regulation and thermal comfort, hygro-thermal building performance and moisture, and internal air flow and ventilation.

311 ○ 585

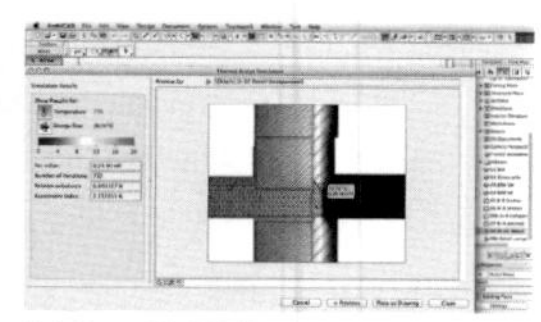
312 ○ 586

AIR FLOW AND CFD (COMPUTATIONAL FLUID DYNAMICS) SIMULATIONS

Melting cars and burning window sills were not the only problem London's 'Walkie-Talkie' building that we mentioned earlier caused. Another complaint about it is that it apparently creates a wind-tunnel effect at street level, and in this it is by no means alone: large construction projects can have entirely unintended consequences for their neighbourhood, as well as themselves show phenomena that can be systematically simulated and thus predicted or prevented.

Air flow and *Computational Fluid Dynamics (CFD)* simulations create models of local air flow, air temperature, and air pressure conditions to help prevent such unintended consequences, or to solve existing problems. These calculations are data intensive and require a lot of computing power, and so very often only short periods are actually studied, with findings extrapolated from those.

In this field, **interactive modelling** is especially relevant and useful: here, predefined buildings are positioned and repositioned within a simulation to get an immediate visual representation of air flow changes, making clear what effects variations in building shapes have on the environment. This method can be employed on individual buildings, as well as on a large scale, for example to aid urban or rural planning. CFD can thus be used as a strategic planning tool, capable of yielding usable insights within seconds when otherwise computations might take several hours. (It is worth reiterating, though, that the computing power required and the time spent on processing is entirely dependent on the quantity of data that's being generated. Obviously, the more detailed and complex a model, the greater the computing task.)

Commercial software available to this purpose at the time of writing (2018/19) includes *Ansys CFD, Autodesk CFD, and the* open-source *OpenFOAM.*

313A ○ 586

313B ○ 586

EXAMPLE: LARGE SCALE AIR FLOW SIMULATION HERRENBERG

The town of Herrenberg, in the picturesque corner of south western Germany that is Baden-Württemberg, used CFD simulation to compare air flow in the local area with particulate measurements. This, however, had its limitations, as Uwe Wössner from the High Performance Computing Centre *(Hochleistungsrechenzentrum,* HLRS) Stuttgart highlights:

"We wanted to measure particulate concentrations on location, and compare these with the simulation. What we learnt from this is that the quality of the 3D town model is not really enough for an exact 3D simulation. We still needed to do a considerable amount of fixing before we were able to extract from the data any usable insights."

314 ○ 586

315A ○ 586

315B ○ 586

315C ○ 587

315D ○ 587

315E ○ 587

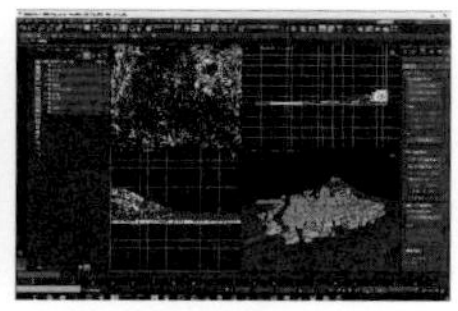
315F ○ 587

FIRE AND EVACUATION SIMULATION

Fire, airflow, and evacuation simulations all tie together into an area that is of literally vital importance in large, complex structures where thousands, in some cases tens of thousands of people work, live, and socialise. Whether or not they make it out on time in an emergency can rapidly turn into a matter of life and death in any large building or complex, be that transport (underground and/or train stations, car parks), shopping centres, office blocks, schools, universities, residential housing, or mass event venues such as theatres, concert halls, and sport stadiums.

Evacuation simulation is based on modelling the expected movement of people, and calculates different escape scenarios. What matters most here are possible emergency causes (fire sources and fire expansion, smoke, threats - such as from explosive devices - or building failure, such as flooding), and the width and length of escape routes, the number of doors (thickness, material, and type) along those routes, and in each case where and how these entities are or may be situated.

Evacuation simulation is important not only in new buildings, but equally where an existing context is being redesigned or repurposed: escape routes, fire exits, and measures to keep these free from smoke and obstacles or congestion may have to be reconfigured, especially if the number of users has changed significantly since the building's originally intended purpose. A building's fire resistance and - absolutely critical for a safe evacuation - overall timings can be worked out using dynamic temperature calculations, for instance in case of a fire, in relation to its source.

(The actual software used for this type of simulation may be dependent on national/regional construction regulations.)

316 ○ 587

317 ○ 588

The Outlook

All architects have to communicate their vision somehow, and so to some extent you could say all architects have to do simulation, even though we may often stay more in the realm of visualisation and modelling than simulation as such. But even at a very basic level, it is entirely common for an architect to produce credible 3D imagery to show someone what the loft conversion they are dreaming of would look and feel like.

From a certain level of complexity and project dimensions upwards though, turning a vision into reality becomes technically and structurally very demanding, and that's where simulation experts come in. As we have already hinted, this is a specialist field that is covered by a range of very different kinds of 'players'.

On the one hand, there are some big companies, such as UNStudio (United Network Studio), a global architecture, design, and urban development company with offices in Shanghai, Amsterdam, and Hong Kong; the London based Foster + Partners which also operates worldwide and has particular experience in light simulation; the London headquartered, global engineering and consultancy group Arup, who have a spectacularly wide range of projects to their credit; or the Frankfurt based international engineering firm Bollinger + Grohmann, to name but these as examples.

On the other hand, there are in simulation also opportunities for very small, down to one-person, enterprises which can forge an identity and existence for themselves by specialising on certain areas. Based in Graz, Austria, Michael Stadler with NIn-sight, for example, offers "parametric technologies with high-end simulation algorithms," his "covered domains" ranging "from mechanical to fluid, biological, pharmacological and thermal effects." Similarly, in Innsbruck the Uto collective, founded by Ursula Frick and Thomas Grabner, "focuses, along with the generation and analysis of complex geometries, on the development of formal strategies, data driven design approaches and generative structures." This just to show the immense scope there is in simulation as a field of activity; and we can expect this to remain the case, even to proliferate further, as visualisation,
■ ↖465 513↘ modelling, and **virtual reality** technologies mature.

Fundamentally, simulation could be regarded as the link between what we can think and what we can build. Whatever it is you're going to build, during the process of realising your project you need pre-
■ ↖293 cisely formulated ideas of what you want to achieve, and accurate representations of these ideas: pretty pictures alone won't suffice. With the current desire by architects worldwide to build ever lighter, more aerial, even ethereal, structures and work with forms that reach into geometrical complexities which can not be grasped, let alone analysed, by conventional methods, simulation in architectural design will
■ ↖469 517↘ only gain in importance. There is still a strong trend towards building bigger, more ambitious projects that require proper staging – for which read simulation – before they can be constructed, both for public and client relations reasons and for purely practical, test-related reasons: *buildability.* And all this is true for architects working in all different visual styles.

□ ↖57 Form-finding sits at the intersection of 3D
□ ↖285 Modelling, Visualisation, and Simulation, and in
□ ↖475 all these areas we believe to witness a move away from off-the-peg software solutions towards libraries which have been and are being developed open-source in the community. A good example of this is *Modelica,* an object-oriented open-source language for the creation of physical models.

While a shift towards collaboration, cloud computing, and open-source software development is one side of the outlook, the other side sees established architecture offices develop their own soft-
□ 549↘ ware tools. An early and pioneering example of this is Gehry Technologies, an offshoot from its parent company Gehry Partners.

Coding, scripting, and customising your software for your own purpose will gain in importance we believe, as will possibly in tandem with it a search for a new, more abstract visual and conceptual language, away from the current 'gold standard' of photorealism.

With denser populations making more demands on especially urban space, aspects such as materials, materials technology, ecology, and energetic behaviour will become ever more important, as will health and safety, building health, and the elimination of inherent structural vulnerabilities.

Architecture and the construction industry are very substantial contributors to the economy, and there is, and will continue to be, growing interest in how simulation can add value to a building project for example by maximising its operational efficiency and reducing construction and maintenance costs. Speaking of costs: across the developed world labour costs continue to rise, and so the better you simulate and anticipate problems, and the more efficient you make your processes and workflows, the more cost effective can be your build.

Users and clients will want to be involved in the process more, as they come in contact with visualisations and simulations more, and they often take decision-making as you go along for granted, not just at major project level, but even when it comes down to a young family building or adapting their first home.

In terms of technologies, we see panoramic photography, **VR (Virtual Reality) photography**, and virtual reality moving closer together.

Meanwhile, in the areas of earthquake research damage prevention, and extreme weather contingencies, both the level of sophistication and the demands on protection from adverse conditions and events will increase, and thus gain significance.

Finally, across the board we expect great strides to be possible through **machine learning**. If a computer program can learn the simulation stages it needs to go through by itself, it does not then have to keep calculating them from scratch, and that means it can complete certain types of very elaborate analyses up to five thousand times faster than is possible by traditional means: a simulation that would ordinarily have taken five days to process now takes five minutes. And so overall, thanks to faster computing generally on the one hand, but very specifically also thanks to more intelligent computing on the other, increasingly complex tasks, such as conducting the manifold simulations required for a large urban multi-purpose development for example, no longer take exponentially more time to accomplish, the more complex they get, but simply increase in volume in a linear fashion. And that means that simulation will, we expect, become more and more effective. We talk in a great deal more detail about these developments in our chapter on Big Data & Machine Learning.

292 ● 477
11 real world analogue simulation Swiss style. [Planerwissen]

293 ● 477
The Millennium Bridge: wobbly no more. [Bob Martens]

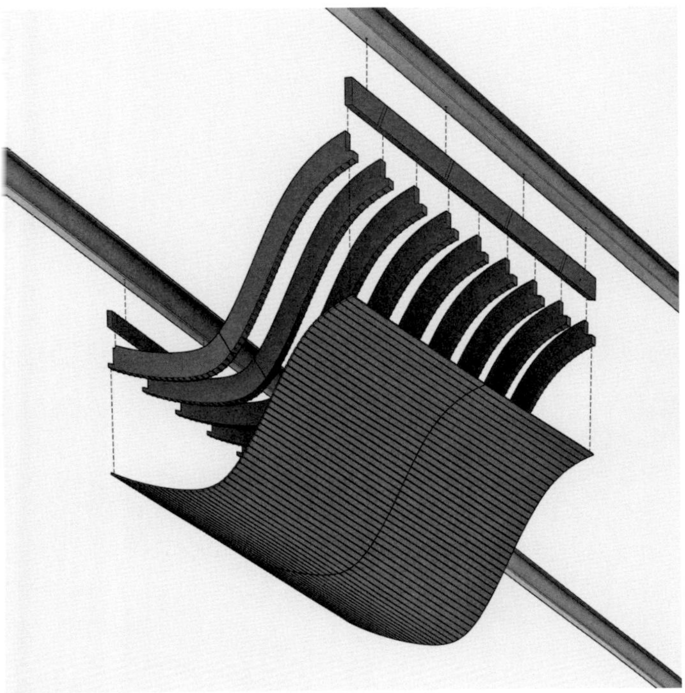

297A ● 480

297B ● 480

297C ● 480
Simulation of highly complex geometries to test viability/buildability and material optimisation. [Series 297A–297C: Fabian Scheurer]

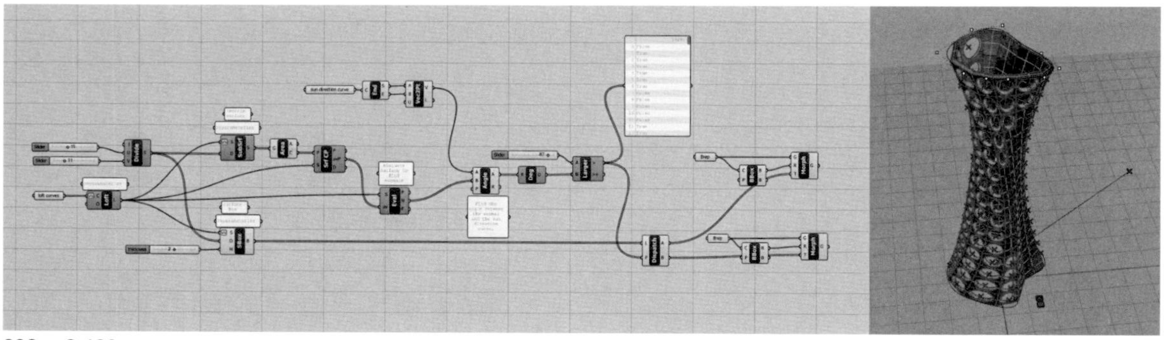

298 ● 480
Grasshopper (plugins: *Ladybug, Honeybee, Caramba*). [Glen Wilcox/University of Michigan]

299 ● 480
Musikverein Vienna: legendary acoustics. [Bob Martens]

303A ● 481

303B ● 481
Elbphilharmonie Hamburg by Herzog & de Meuron.
[303A + 303B: Bob Martens]

304A ● 482

304B ● 482

1:10 Scale Model and 'micro-shaping' on the ceiling to achieve sound scatter. [Nagata Acoustics]

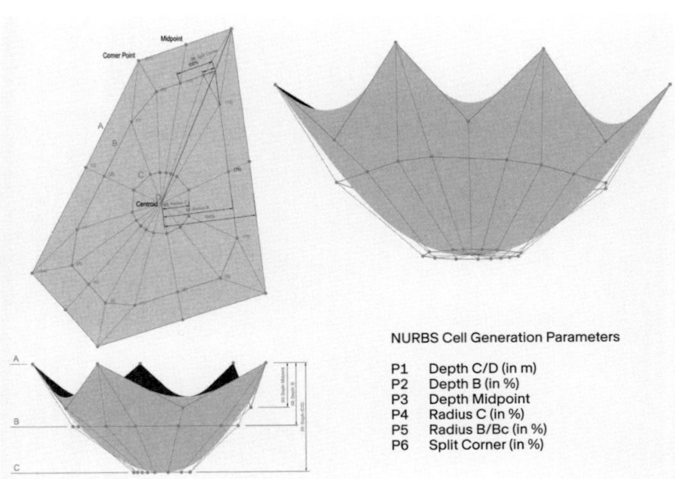

305A ● 482
Parametric design of bespoke acoustic panels.
[305A + 305B: One to One]

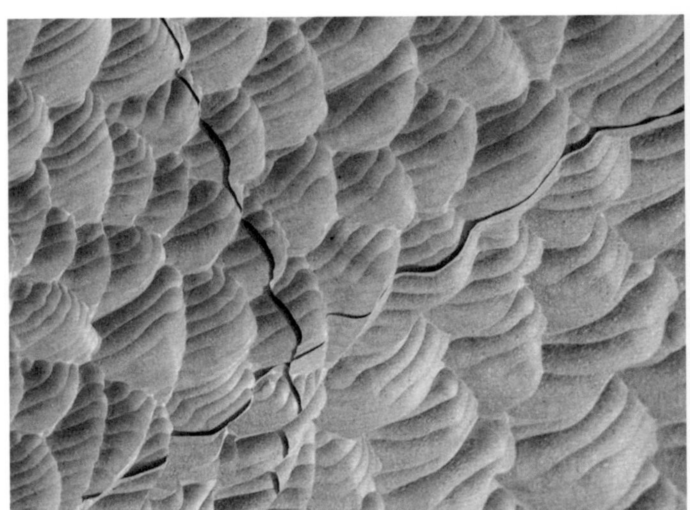

305B ● 482

- Frederik Ramm, Jochen Topf: *OpenStreetMap: Die freie Weltkarte nutzen und mitgestalten*, 2010 (3rd Edition)
- M Martino, R Britter, C Outram, C Zacharias, A Bidermann, C Ratti: *Senseable City – Digital Urban Modelling and Simulation*, MIT Senseable City Lab Working Paper: 1–15, 2010
- B Resch, M Mittlböck, S Lipson, M Welsh, J Bers, R Britter, C Ratti, T Blaschke: *Integrated Urban Sensing: A Geo-sensor Network for Public Health Monitoring and Beyond, International Journal of Geographical Information Science* (Paper 268): 1–19, 2011
- Bernd Streich: *Stadtplanung in der Wissensgesellschaft: Ein Handbuch*, 2011 (2nd Edition)
- K Kloeckl, G Di Lorenzo, O Senn, C Ratti: *LIVE Singapore! – An urban platform for real-time data to program the city*, MIT Senseable City Lab Working Paper: 1–17, 2011
- Ralf Bill: *Grundlagen der Geo-Informationssysteme*, 2016 (6th Edition)

Geographic Information Systems (GIS)

Peter Zeile

Overview

19th century Soho in London was a far cry from what it is today: a colourful, cosmopolitan beating heart of town, bustling with good restaurants and cafes of all hues, chic shopping, few (and increasingly discreet) reminders of its relatively recent red light past, some major West End theatres, and a great many pubs offering very fine ales. One of these pubs now carries the name of a man who made history on the very spot where it stands: the English physician John Snow (1813–1858).

In 1854, Soho, then one of the poorest districts in London, suffered yet another cholera outbreak, and a particularly calamitous one at that, claiming the lives of 616 people. The general school of thought at the time was that cholera was an airborne disease, and so any attempts at containing it hinged on that perception. It was not a view that John Snow shared. He surmised that contaminated water carried the bacteria responsible for cholera, and in order to test and prove his theory, he investigated the locations where cases had occurred. In a series of now celebrated and since then often reproduced maps, he plotted the incidents of deaths and found that they clustered around one particular well on the corner of what was then called Broad Street – today's Broadwick Street – and Cambridge Street, which no longer exists: today's location of the John Snow pub. But even affected families living a little further away, when asked about their water consumption habits, revealed that they drew water from the Broad Street well, rather than from any of the wells closer to their homes, for reasons of personal preference and convenience.

Equipped with his data, John Snow convinced the authorities to remove the handle of said well, and the death toll promptly declined. It turned out the well had indeed been polluted by waste seeping into it from a nearby cesspit. Snow himself treated his evidence with considerable caution and admitted that the outbreak had already started to abate before action was taken. Still, John Snow today is credited with several significant achievements: first and foremost the linking of cholera epidemics to drinking water contamination, which we now know to be correct. But also, and for us in architecture of particular interest, the systematic association of data with geographical locations, and their effective analysis. John Snow is not only a pioneer in epidemiology, but also a trailblazer for Geographic Information Systems (GIS).

318 ● 504

WHY GIS?

Today, the health sector is just one of several in which GIS plays an increasingly important, if not in fact indispensable, role: urban planning, gaming, environmental and social management, even the development and deployment of UAVs (Unmanned Aerial Vehicles, or drones) are all tied in with geographic data, as are app-based ride share and taxi services such as Uber and Ola, or indeed location-based dating and hookup apps. Many of our great (and small) real world challenges can be identified, analysed, visualised, and therefore addressed by using digital models.

As far back as 1998, in a talk titled *The Digital Earth: Understanding Our Planet in the 21st Century,* the American environmentalist and then Vice President, Al Gore (b.1948) declared: "I believe we need a Digital Earth. A multi-resolution, three-dimensional representation of the planet, into which we can embed vast quantities of geo-referenced data." The point of doing so has not changed all that much since John Snow: if you have data about what happens on Earth and where, you can deal with it in a targeted, informed, specific and therefore – so the hope and fair chance – effective way.

The term *geographic information system* itself can be dated and attributed precisely to the English geographer Roger F Tomlinson (1933–2014), who, while working at Spartan Air Services in Ottawa, Canada, in 1963, initiated and developed what became the Canada Geographic Information System (CGIS). As a vast country with immense natural resources and environmental treasures, Canada was among the first to recognise the need for a nationwide land inventory and management system that would be capable of quickly and efficiently handling large amounts of data. That is what GIS – even at a time when computing was still in its infancy – offered, which is why Canada became its earliest and historically significant adopter. ■

Tomlinson's ambition then is still the main purpose of GIS today: to capture, organise, analyse, and present spatial data. Thanks to the combined forces of immensely increased computing power compared to the mid-20th century, the Internet, smartphones with their multitude of apps, and Global Navigation Satellite Systems (GNSS) such as the universally known GPS (Global Positioning System), as well as the Russian GLONASS (Global Navigation Satellite System), and the European Space Agency (ESA) led Galileo satellite navigation system, we are now able to do this with unprecedented quantities of data from all over the world. (We will talk a little more about GPS in particular a bit further down.) ■ ↖102

While John Snow had to obtain his information himself by going around the (as he rightly assumed infected and highly contagious) location in person to manually plot data points on paper, we now draw on an array of data sources, from official statistics, land registry entries, and routine surveys, to installed urban and environmental sensors (measuring traffic, air pollution, or footfall, for example), right through to 'volunteered data' that comes from individuals allowing their mobile devices to feed information about their movements or behaviours into a system of statistical observation: what *Wired* magazine journalists Gary Wolf and Kevin Kelly in 2007 referred to as the "quantified self." This, in a comprehensively networked society, is of increasing importance, and it naturally overlaps and interweaves with other sources all the time. The term Volunteered Geographic Information (VGI), □ ↖491 ■

meanwhile, was coined in 2007 by British-American geographer Michael Frank Goodchild (b. 1944) in a paper called *Citizens as Sensors: the World of Volunteered Geography* published in *GeoJournal.*

The Uber-developed and recently (2018) turned open-source geospatial analysis tool *Kepler* offers an interesting example of how user-generated data can provide insights into, and striking visualisations of, human activity. Uber habitually collects quantities of data about passenger journeys, including pick-up and drop-off times and locations, and thus is able to show these movements and analyse them for strategic and logistic purposes.

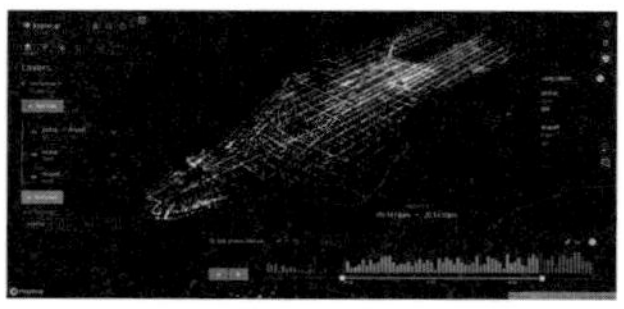

319 ● 504

Another example in a similar vein comes from *LIVE Singapore!*, a project by the MIT (Massachusetts Institute of Technology) Senseable City Lab [sic]. It provides, as its own website puts it, "people with access to a range of useful real-time information about their city by developing an open platform for the collection, elaboration and distribution of real-time data that reflect urban activity," expounding that: "giving people visual and tangible access to real-time information about their city enables them to take their decisions more in sync with their environment, with what is actually happening around them."

Wherein lies the principal advantage of a real-time GIS: rather than having to rely on static information that may or may not be relevant at any given moment (is the road blocked due to traffic? Is there heavy demand on taxis owing to a tropical downpour? Does the store have the item I'm after in stock right now?...), a GIS that taps into multiple data sources and keeps these open and up to date around the clock can be used not just for planning and management purposes, but directly by end-users themselves in the running of their everyday lives.

320A ● 504

320B ● 504

Like everything else, tracking people's movements can have unintended consequences: personal exercise monitoring website and app *Strava* – based in San Francisco and operating globally – tracks users' athletic or sporting activity, particularly cycling and running. Founded in 2009, by 2017 it was able to claim on its website that it could draw on "nearly a trillion GPS data points." In January 2018, it was reported that *Strava* users were inadvertently revealing the locations of secret US military bases they were stationed at, just by jogging around them, as suddenly the app-generated paths drew the outlines of defence installations that were not marked on any other map.

Sadly we can't show you the map, because *Strava* don't like you to know about this case. Instead, a member of their legal team responded to our request for image rights with an arch rejection, stating that: "We do not give permission for academics to write about the global heatmap press in January 2018 as most of it was incorrect information. Strava did not inadvertently disclose anything. Our members choose to make their location public and contribute to the heatmap. If they do not wish to contribute, they have a suite of privacy controls they can use to keep their activity private."

Inadvertent or 'intentional', the example provides a fascinating insight into user volunteered graphic information and its potential effects (be they desired or not), and even without *Strava's* permission you can read all about it by using your favourite search engine or looking up Alex Hearn's entertaining piece in the *The Guardian.* (You'll find a link to it by following the QR code at the beginning of this chapter.)

OPENSTREETMAP

As we complete this *Atlas* in 2019, probably the most used and best known Internet map globally is *Google Maps,* with its ubiquitous owner investing large sums and considerable human resources in its development. (By 2012, Google was reported to be employing 1,100 full time staff, and drawing on the services of some 6,000 contractors, to generate its mapping.) But Google also relies on a number of regional and local map companies dotted around the world for its source data, and so its copyright and licensing model is neither entirely clear nor let alone straightforward. Because of this, and because it is impossible to export and then work with Google's geographic data, it is difficult to employ *Google Maps* for the production of situation plans; and there are similar issues with competitor mapping services, such as Microsoft's *Bing Maps* or *Apple Maps.*

A viable and eminently usable alternative to these proprietary systems is *OpenStreetMap,* at openstreetmap.org. Founded by British computer scientist Steve Coast (b. 1980) in England in 2004, the project was a direct response to the unavailability of freely accessible map data both in the UK and across the world. *OpenStreetMap* emulates the concept and success of *Wikipedia* and understands itself as, "a map of the world, created by people like you and free to use under an open licence," as its website introduction puts it. Owned and run by the Open Street Map Foundation (OSMF), with hosting supported by, among others, University College London (UCL), Imperial College London, and a company called Bytemark, *OpenStreetMap* is built and maintained by a community of voluntary contributors, drawing on VGI.

OpenStreetMap is not the only, but certainly the leading open-source mapping service as we write this; and while VGI has its own potential drawbacks – data reliability and quality being cited as issues, for example – open-source map data has the real advantage that not only is its user licence free of charge, but also the maps can be adapted and tailored with scripting or program-native tools and methods. Generating a figure-ground diagram from *OpenStreetMap* data using the free open-source tool *Maperitive*, for example, requires no more than a dozen lines of extremely straightforward code that you can borrow as a ready-made rule for your data query.

Here is a sample code that generates a figure-ground diagram (*Schwarzplan* in German) in *Maperitive* from *OpenStreetMap*:

```
//      Rules for Maperitive by ABRob
//
//      Schwarzplan
features
        areas
                building : building
properties
        map-background-color : #FFFFFF
        line-style : none
rules
        target : building
                define
                        fill-color : black
                draw : fill
```

21 ● 504

So, while applications such as *Strava* and studies such as the one by Senseable City Lab may be considered 'high end' and highly complex – both in terms of their data sources and the way they utilise that data – using GIS at this far more basic level can be directly applicable to the work of an individual architect or architecture student. Obtaining a reliable land registry map for the proposed location of a new project has often been a problematic and longwinded process in the past. Local councils and municipal authorities can be slow in responding, the records kept may be inaccurate and/or incomplete, or simply out of date, and while it is time-consuming and therefore costly to generate a morphological analysis of an area by way of a new figure-ground diagram, it is easy and quick to bypass these issues with data obtained from *OpenStreetMap*, for free. For large parts of Europe – Germany, Austria, and Switzerland included – there are now near-exhaustive data sets available, containing comprehensive information about buildings, streets, and points of interest.

What makes a ground plan generated in this way particularly interesting and different to one produced by traditional means is that each individual drawn element has its own unique ID, which can be linked to (in theory unlimited volumes of) information. This brings GIS into close conceptual proximity with other data-rich planning and visualisation methods, such as Building Information Modelling (BIM), to which we dedicate our next chapter in this *Atlas*, and about which we will also talk some more further along in this one.

THE SHAPEFILE FORMAT

A common file format for handling GIS data is *shapefile*, developed and regulated by Esri, which in turn takes its name from its original founding name Environmental Systems Research Institute. While Esri is a privately owned company, it operates shapefile as a largely open standard.

'Shapefile' as a name may suggest that you are dealing with one single file, which is exactly not the case. The format is in fact a conglomerate of at least three mandatory file types (and, as many a student finds out the hard way, for the shapefile to work and not crash it's essential that all its components are kept in the same directory folder under the same name before the file extension):

- *.shp – the shape file for the geometry itself
- *.shx – a positional shape index file linking the geometry to attribute data
- *.dbf – the attribute file, holding attributes for the geometry, in dBase IV format ■

Apart from these, there are about a dozen additional optional file formats that can be used in combination with each other to handle, for example, various spatial, attribute, and geocoding indexes.

GIS VS CAD

From an architect's perspective, one of the first questions GIS may well raise is 'why?' – why would you learn GIS when you can draw plans that quite possibly look better with any industry standard CAD program that's also much easier to use, or even with *Illustrator* or *Photoshop*? And that may well be true, especially at the beginning, and for small projects. But as soon as the dimensions of the space that is being represented reach a certain level, the data analysis and management strengths of GIS start to come into play. Which means that very broadly speaking, city structure planning lends itself well to GIS, while the more you get into urban design and object architecture, the advantages of CAD are likely to win out.

Much will therefore depend on what you want to achieve, and how. GIS is categorically different in its approach to CAD: in CAD, you can simply start drawing what you imagine, whereas with GIS you have to first of all have your data in place. The quality of anything you are going to produce with a GIS depends to a very large extent on the quality and integrity of the data from which you set out. So the process in itself is not simply a matter of designing or creating, but rather one of assembling data sets, and taking from them insights that then inform your design.

As we shall see when we look in detail at *How it Works* and *The Components of GIS* below, there are, in GIS, point, line, and polygon layers, which can't simply be combined or 'put on top of each other', as you would in purely visual design software. Rather, every element you work with has to have one or several attributes, and these elements can only be connected □ 507↘
to each other and to the geography they're in by way of operations. Having said that, everything that can be an element can have 'intelligent data', with information about its size, materiality, costs, characteristics, age, and measurements, for example; and this information can be exchanged between software that handles two, three, or indeed four 'dimensions', the latter incorporating temporal factors, such as the development or behaviour of an element or material over its lifecycle.

Furthermore, unlike in classic CAD systems, in GIS, individual elements can feature attributes which, through their geographic coordinates, also know what is happening in their neighbourhood: this relational data is known as an element's topology, and we'll be talking about it in a little more detail shortly.

GIS is also a core component of what are known as **Planning Support Systems (PSS)**. First described in 1993 by Britton Harris and British urban planner and geographer Michael Batty (b. 1945) in a paper entitled *Locational Models, Geographic Information and Planning Support Systems*, they are a type of **Decision Support System (DSS)** that use a combination of tools and methods to help political and administrative bodies in their (here particularly planning related) decision making about urban developments and large scale projects by bundling calculations, workflow management, and GIS functionalities, which is also why they are often the focus of research, and cited as examples for the power of GIS.

As we already ventured, the advent of Building Information Modelling (BIM) to some extent closes this 'informational gap' in CAD, and BIM may be regarded as a bridge that links the two methodologies represented by CAD and GIS, if perhaps as yet not quite seamlessly. Meanwhile though, none of these technologies is standing still, and the possibilities for design and graphic fine-tuning within GIS have improved a great deal since the early days when, compared to CAD, they were at best rudimentary.

A POTTED HISTORY OF GIS

In the 109 years between John Snow's cholera map of Soho in 1854 and Roger Tomlinson's Canada Geographic Information System (CGIS) in 1963, GIS, although not yet named, was not entirely unthought of. The history of GIS develops roughly in tandem with the history of computing generally, which is hardly surprising, seeing that the concepts and technologies so very much entwine, and here as elsewhere the milestone advances come with the Internet in the early 1990s, and with smartphones, since 2010.

The two people who can be credited with igniting a conceptual drive towards GIS are Charles Leslie Miller and Robert Arthur Laflamme who, while working at the Photogrammetry Laboratory of MIT developed their *Digital Terrain Model* and published a paper on it with the same title in 1958. This set the tone and framework for what followed and is certain to have influenced and informed Tomlinson in his work.

■ ↖469

During the 1960s, and on the back of the CGIS, some rapid strides were made: in 1964, the American architect, city planner, and educator Howard T Fisher (1903–1979) set up the Laboratory for Computer Graphics and Spatial Analysis at Harvard Graduate School of Design, shortly to be followed by American entrepreneur Jack Dangermond's (b. 1945) Environmental Systems Research Institute, which, as we've noted, is now known simply as Esri and dominates the market for GIS worldwide, with a share of it in 2014 of 43%.

The 1960s also saw advances in image and graphics processing (we deal with this in much more detail in our chapters on Visualisation and Image & Colour), and the 1970s ushered in early breakthroughs in CAD printing and cartography, as well as marking the advent of **Land Information Systems (LIS)**, which formed a subset of GIS, specifically used for cadastral or land-use mapping, as carried out by local authorities to record legal domain boundaries and ownership details.

□ ↖285
□ ↖229

In 1982, the US Army Construction Engineering Research Laboratory (USA-CERL) started development of a land management and environmental planning software, which it called *Geographic Resources Analysis Support System* (*GRASS*, also known as *GRASS GIS*), whose source code it made freely available from the outset, and which it continues to offer as a multi-platform modular program in many different languages.

The 1984 *Apple Macintosh* breakthrough in consumer level computer graphics, which ushered in a step change in how computing was used in architecture generally, is also mirrored in GIS, although GIS software is not, in fact, particularly geared towards *Apple Macs*: as we write this, still only one major GIS program, *QGIS* (developed in 2002 as an open-source platform by Gary Sherman, originally under the name *Quantum GIS*), works on *Mac*'s current operating system, *OSX*, while Esri's market-leading *ArcGIS*, for example, either requires a *Mac* to run *Windows* (which for many a *Mac* user is anathema and entirely defies the purpose of having a *Mac* in the first place), or is limited to their first *Mac*-native *ArcGIS Explorer*, which offers a range of map viewing and visualisation options, but not the full capability of its mother software.

We've mentioned Global Navigation Satellite Systems (GNSS): their arrival in the 1990s gave GIS an enormous boost, and 1992 saw the publication of American writer and game designer Neal Stephenson's (b. 1959) sci-fi novel *Snow Crash*. This features an 'Earth' software, developed by the fictional Central Intelligence Corporation, which is said to not only have influenced various subsequent real life virtual globe programs, but inspired the research 'branch' of German design and media development firm Art+Com to create *Terravision*, which on its own website it describes as, "an isochronous realisation of Neal Stephenson's literary idea in the novel 'Snow Crash' as well as a prequel to Google Earth."

In 2002 – the year Sherman launched *Quantum GIS* – NASA (the US American National Aeronautics and Space Administration) started developing *NASA WorldWind*. Not an application, but a **Software Development Kit (SDK)**, it was launched two years later, in 2004, as an open-source **Application Programming Interface (API)**, providing users with a free tool to create their own geospatial data visualisations; and in the following year, 2005, Google bought *EarthViewer* from the indirectly US Central Intelligence Agency (CIA) funded Keyhole Inc, renaming it *Google Earth*. A *Google Earth Pro* version, which until 2015 cost four hundred US dollars a year to subscribe to, is now also free and offers enhanced GIS functionalities, making possible the handling of shapefile formats, and allowing the assignment of design rules to draw elements. 2011 saw the launch of *CesiumJS*, which describes itself as "an open-source JavaScript library for world-class 3D globes and maps," and, because it is free to use and based on common *JavaScript*, may be considered something of a hot favourite in the 3D Earth community at the time of writing.

Since around 2007 – this in turn is the year Goodchild published his paper on VGI – there has been an effort by professionals in the industry to arrive at a standard set of methods that could be applied across GIS disciplines, platforms, and applications. At a workshop on *Spatial Concepts in GIS and Design* in Santa Barbara, California, hosted by principal partners Esri and the National Center for Geographic Information and Analysis at the University of California in December 2008, the foundations were laid for what would become known as Geodesign. Michael Flaxman, who later founded the company Geodesign Technologies, defined this at the GeoDesign Summit held in 2010 as, "a design and planning method which tightly couples the creation of a design proposal with impact simulations informed by geographic context." Both, the Scottish landscape architect Ian McHarg (1920–2001) and Carl Steinitz, emeritus professor of Landscape Architecture and Planning at the Harvard Graduate School of Design, are credited with setting the theoretical framework for Geodesign.

In July 2016, American start-up Niantic in a collaboration with Japanese games giant Nintendo bestowed upon an unsuspecting world their location based augmented reality game *Pokémon Go*, which quickly topped the download charts and became something of a global phenomenon, sending children and adults alike in search for virtual creatures in the real world, sometimes to the chagrin of the real people and creatures already there, and occasionally at unreasonably high risk to themselves. Within less than a year, by June 2017, the game's own website, in a post it titled *Celebrating the First Anniversary of Pokémon GO!* declared 750 million downloads worldwide.

■ ↖465

Meanwhile, Ralf Bill, who is Professor at the Institute of Geodesy and Geoinformatics at the University of Rostock, in the late 1980s for the first time published his book *Grundlagen der Geo-Informationssysteme (Basics of Geo-Information Systems),* which, currently in its 6th edition, is considered a standard work on the subject in the German-speaking world.

How it Works

THE COMPONENTS OF A GIS

There are a wide range of different kinds of information systems – typical ones would include management, corporate, bank, airline, library, public authority, and private institutions information systems – and they all, in common with geographic information systems, tend to be built on the principle of the extremely straightforward 'four pillar model'. This consists of:

- Computer hardware (a processor and periphery components, such as input and output devices, display and data storage)
- Computer software (the rules and programs that determine the functions and processes that can be carried out)
- Data (the quantitative and qualitative information that is being handled)
- Users (the people who actually use the information)

What makes a GIS 'special', or at any rate different to other information systems, is that it is spatially orientated, meaning that it contains and deals with information about phenomena that either directly (through primary metrics) or indirectly (through secondary metrics) relate to the position and situation of a place on Earth.

This geographic information normally falls into one or more of four distinct categories:

- Global (referencing the position of a place in relation to the world as a whole)
- Regional (referencing the position of a place in relation to the region it finds itself in)
- Local horizontal (referencing the position of a place in relation to the locality on the ground)
- Local vertical (referencing the position of a place in relation to the locality beneath or above the ground)

These four categories offer considerable scope: it is estimated that between 60% and 80% of all administrative, logistic, strategic, and service oriented activities of a company, institution, or governmental department are in some way or other related to space.

But what is so 'special about spatial'? Geographic information covers a very broad spectrum of data volumes, from a few gigabytes per object to petabyte quantities. A lot of this has to do with the nature of spatial data itself: coordinates present a formidable challenge for algorithms and databases because they can, and very often do, consist of a range of entirely different metrics that have no obvious 'common denominator'. For example, the way an energy supplier views a customer and their location (as a point on a supply network) will be at great variance from the way a local authority views the exact same property (as a two-dimensionally delineated land parcel), while a land use statistic will have yet another metric, and view the same location as a place where two adults and two children live, though unaware, perhaps as yet, that there's a third one on the way...

In passing, we mentioned primary and secondary metrics: *primary metrics* are those that directly and unequivocally describe the specific and precise geographic location of an object or element. Typically, these are coordinates that are clearly defined in the given context. As *secondary metrics* we encounter data that references the location of an object or element indirectly, but not necessarily, therefore, less systematically. Examples of secondary metrics might include post codes, street names, addresses, place names (village, town or city, but also district or neighbourhood names) or even kilometre or mile markers along open roads and motorways.

Everywhere on Earth is somewhere, and that somewhere can or, more often than not, has to be spatially defined. This makes geographic information not just prevalent but omnipresent. Owing to this and its very great variety, geographic information is used and needed in applications of all types, to all kinds of purposes, across disciplines.

Because most geographic information – though □ ↖229 not all – is tied to built environments and permanent installations, and by definition to geographical locations, it tends to have a long shelf life: from the moment a project enters a concrete planning phase until the building ceases to exist, it usually stays in the same place. From the perspective of anyone using GIS, this is maybe just as well, because by and large, geographic information is also expensive: it's time-consuming and elaborate to assemble and maintain, and so, as a consequence, it is also valuable and traded highly. Just how valuable depends to a large extent on how and how much it is used. And the spectrum here is vast: from top end urban management through to citizens' own personal use, the range of applications geographic information can be put to is practically unlimited. It's information, so it's easily shared globally across networks, but it's also diffuse: because of its many different types and sources, and its 'transportability', it is difficult to control. With these combined characteristics come a range of pertinent issues, of which high levels of data storage (the sheer volume of data) and high security requirements (the need to protect the data, both for its own integrity but also to prevent it from being misused) rank among the most important.

RASTER VS VECTOR DATA

In GIS as in other visual representations of physical (or any other type of) reality, a distinction is made between raster and vector data, and from this distinction stem two of the principal challenges in GIS too: the conversion of one data type into another, and the use of both data types in combination with each other.

Raster data mostly comes from imagery that either starts out as raster files, such as aerial or satellite photography, or that has been digitised into raster images, such as drawings, photographs, or other picture material that has been scanned or re-photographed; while vector data tends to originate from drawings and plans that have in most cases been generated as vector images, for example in CAD software, or land registry information that is recorded as vector data.

Using both raster and vector data in combination is inherently difficult, because the data structure is so categorically different: raster data defines individual pixels, and all image or graphic elements are made up of these pixels to a specified density and colour depth, whereas vector data defines image and graphic elements as points, lines, polygons, or planes, resulting in generally much smaller quantities of data that are also, however, in some respects less versatile.

Converting vector data into raster data by rasterising it is a comparatively easy process, whereas vectorising raster data is much more difficult and complex. But the difference between an ordinary raster image and a raster-based GIS is that in a raster-based GIS each pixel may not only contain information about its colour and colour depth, for example, but also additional details, such as about its geographical location or its relationship to other points (pixels) in the image. This is what makes handling and especially converting GIS raster data a particularly tricky task.

(We talk in some detail about raster and vector imaging generally in our chapter on Image & Colour.)

OBJECT BASED VS SPACE BASED DATA MODELS

Another, similarly important, distinction is made between *object based* and *space based data models*.

In an object based data model, the (usually architectural) object itself is the focus and starting point of the observation: you have a building of any description, and this will be defined by a set of data points in the form of either vector or raster data. Individual elements of the object will have their own attributes, and they will relate to each other in space in a certain way, all of which makes for GIS data that can be stored, manipulated, and analysed.

With a space based data model it is the environment that gives the starting point and therefore the initial focus of the analysis. A satellite image of a geographical area, for example, generates a space based data set, where the observation does not at first focus on one individual object, nor even a group of objects, but on the area covered, and into this are placed reference points that relate to objects, and that relate these objects to the space.

Both models, then, offer data sets that can yield insights not only about the object or the space respectively, but about how the basis of each set – the object in one case, the space in the other – relate to any other components and thus other parts of the observation.

In view of these differences and their attendant challenges, knowing and understanding what the data model is that you're using is obviously of paramount importance.

TOPOLOGY

Apart from information about the characteristics of individual elements – their materiality, size, composition, texture, colour, price, to name but these as examples – GIS, as one of its potentially most useful capabilities, can store and handle information about the *topology* of elements and objects in space: the relationship between them, such as what is next to what *(adjacency)*, what, if anything, is inside or contains what else *(containment)*, and also how close one object or element is to another *(proximity)*.

THEMATIC DIMENSIONS

In GIS, the term 'dimension' is used not only for the three spatial dimensions we're familiar with from geometry (resulting in 2D or 3D visual representations) and the temporal 'dimension' that we can add to observe objects and elements over time (which we've already briefly mentioned), but also to topology, as outlined directly above, and to a 'thematic' dimension, which relates to the number of object classes or 'layers' we are dealing with, in other words: the category of an observable entity.

Thus, a GIS is considered to be thematically

- one-dimensional, if just one object class or layer is being examined
- two or more-dimensional, if two or correspondingly more object classes or layers are being examined

The following chart shows examples of thematic dimensions, from top to bottom: natural water features, settlements, road and other traffic, precipitation, geological relief, 'the real world' (after Franziska Klügl):

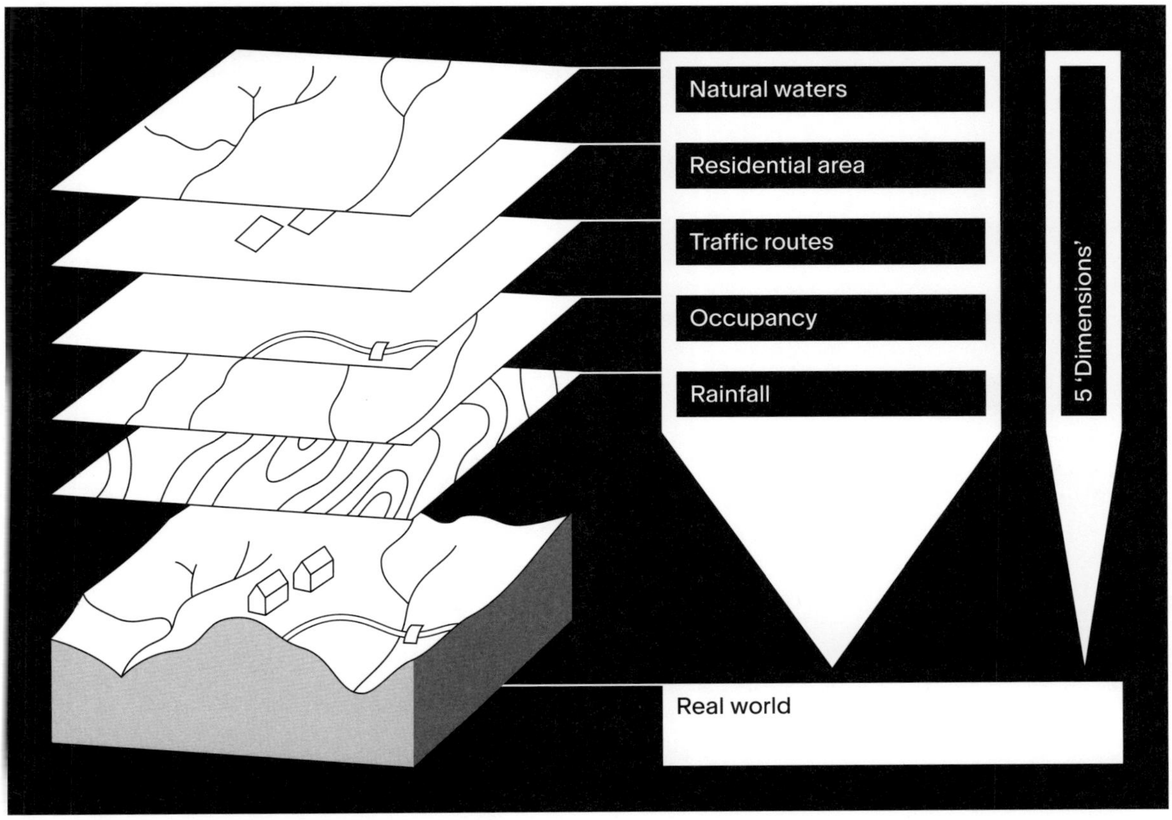

WHAT TO DO WITH A GIS

We've already mentioned some of the many and varied possible purposes of a GIS, and given some examples to illuminate at least part of the spectrum.

What in concrete terms you can do with your GIS depends first and foremost on the type of data you have available, and on how it is modelled: raster or vector data, object or space based, what are the thematic dimensions (the number and type of object classes or layers) you want to study. According to its data make-up and composition, a GIS can yield a very wide range of different possible types of analysis, for example:

- The kind of ground plan generation from land registry or *OpenStreetMap* data outlined earlier
- Citizen or user behaviour analysis, such as we've seen in the Uber and Senseable City Lab studies above
- Historical, social, etymological, and similar analysis
- Straightforward statistical evaluation, for example a population's distribution in terms of age, gender, household size, educational levels, and other demographic data that is either publicly available or can otherwise be captured
- Spatial analysis, for example how much of a buffer zone there is in an area between the streets and its buildings, how many green spaces or recreational areas there are, how they are spaced, how easy or not it is to get to and from specified locations (amenities, shops, hospitals or health centres, schools, kindergartens, parks, leisure centres, public services); journey times from and to individual objects or feature points by various modes of transport (can the residents of a new development walk to all their most essential services, how long does it take a pedestrian to get to their nearest bus stop, do the cycle paths link up into a coherent network), how long does it take the average resident to get to their place of work and back
- Energy and other resources usage analysis, such as where, how, and when people in certain areas use power, water, modes of transport; air pollution patterns and other environmental observations
- Climatic, thermal, and geological analyses, such as how seasons, weather, climate, seismic activity, or similar phenomena affect objects and people in an area of observation
- Generation of maps, plans, virtual globes, and visualisation, as well as animation of past, present, and future developments in an area of observation, over time

The list, very clearly, is not exhaustive.

A CASE STUDY
During the first half of 2015, eight bachelor students at the Department of Computer Aided Planning and Design Methods at the University of Kaiserslautern, Germany, embarked on a project to which they gave the title *Track Me if You Plan!*

With themselves as subjects of their study, they used their smartphones and a combination of apps to observe their own movements for four weeks. The resulting data set (including information on where they went, why they took a certain route, or how long they spent in a given place) was then analysed and visualised with a view to answering one question in particular: how do movement and behaviour patterns differ between people who are familiar with a city and those who aren't?

The study is interesting for a couple of reasons: ↖200 firstly, it serves as an example of using people as sensors. (Here the data was volunteered by the researchers themselves, though it was in fact also complemented with the findings from some 346 questionnaires that were completed by other people.) Secondly, it illustrates a deployment of GIS methodology on a principally very simple and inexpensive basis, at 'entry level' so to speak, but still capable of yielding useful insights and results.

Starting point for the eight students was an article they found published in *Wired* magazine in June the previous year, 2014, written by Alex Davies, entitled *Strava's Cycling App Is Helping Cities Build Better Bike Lanes.* The piece opens with the sentence: "Oregon wants to make its roads safer and more convenient for cyclists, but has a problem – it has very little data on where people ride and what influences their choices." The writer does not specify which of the one and a half dozen Oregons in America he is thinking of, but the point of interest, for the young Kaiserslautern researches, was that city and town administrations in general, irrespective of where in the world they are, face a challenge of finding accurate, relevant, and usable data to help them plan infrastructure and services for their citizens. In the case of this particular Oregon, a solution was offered by *Strava,* who, unlike the department of transport, had *lots* of data on people's cycling behaviour.

Inspired by this case of user generated and volunteered data assisting urban planners, the *Track Me if You Plan!* team used their own smartphones to, as the title of their project suggests, track themselves. For this, apart from the phone camera to take pictures and an audio recorder to capture interviews and memos, they used an app called *Moves,* which was first developed by Finnish firm ProtoGeo in 2013, and has since been taken over by Facebook. There are, as the team acknowledges, a whole range of apps available that work in a comparable way and that like *Strava* or *Moves* avail themselves of the smartphone's built-in GPS technology, which in turn uses **trilateration** to locate the device at any given time in relation to at least three, for additional accuracy mostly four or more, satellites.

In principle, trilateration is not dissimilar to the broadly familiar **triangulation**. Put simply, the main difference is that while *triangulation* measures angles, *trilateration* measures distances. What both methods have in common is that they use fixed reference points to determine the geographical or relational position of a specified point, in this case the user's smartphone. Most of these apps then are able to export their data in either the widely used **Comma Separated Values (CSV)** or the more specific **GPS Exchange (GPX)** file format for the researchers to conduct data analyses and visualisations, or indeed in the **Keyhole Markup Language (KML)** format, which allows for data to be displayed in two-dimensional maps and 3D Earth browsers, such as *Google Earth* for which it was originally developed.

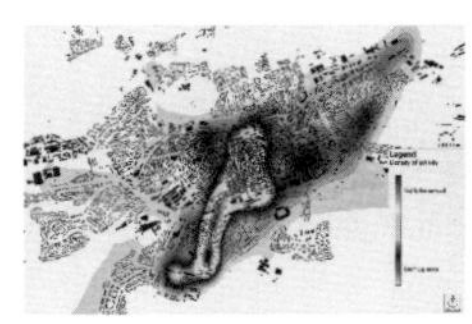
322A ○ 588

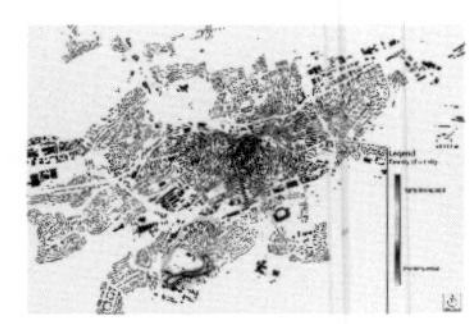
322B ○ 588

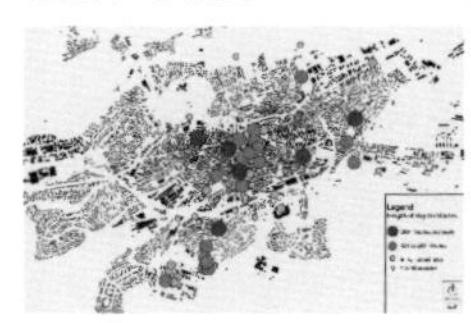
322C ○ 588

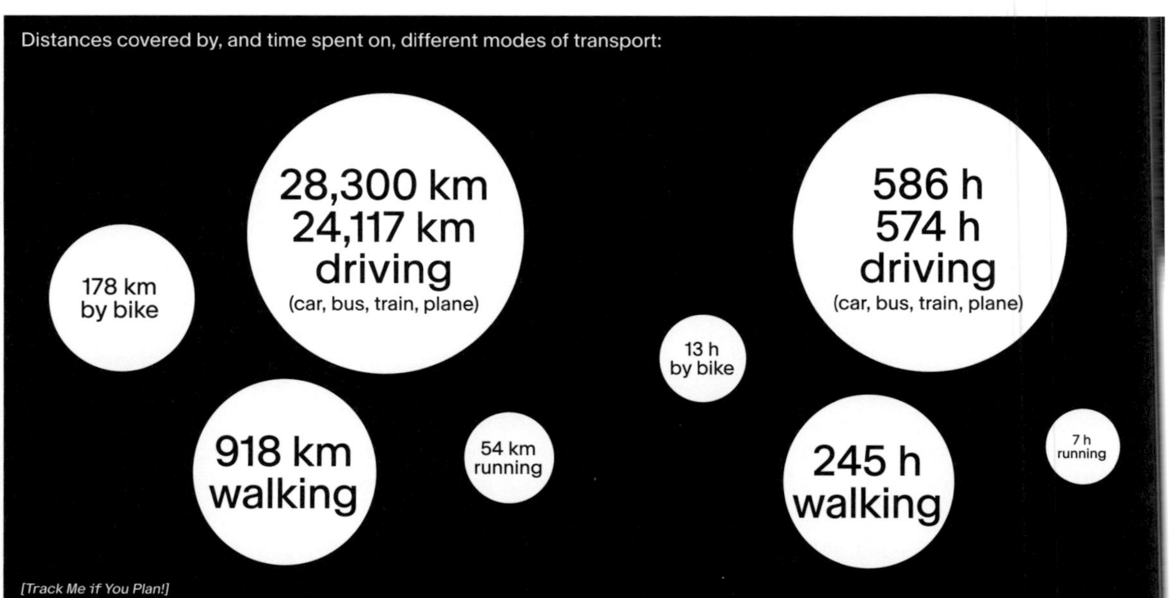

To round off our chapter on GIS, and before we get to the usual *Outlook*, we want to position GIS in a bit more detail in relation to other software programs and applications, which it often is or can be used in combination with, and then also briefly list some of the most commonly used and widely available tools.

GETTING TO GRIPS WITH THE INITIALISMS AND ACRONYMS: GIS, BIM, IFC, KML, GML, CITYGML, XML, AND INSPIRE

As we've already mentioned, we devote a full chapter in this *Atlas* to Building Information Modelling (BIM), so we don't want to go into any detail about it at this point, but we should touch here on the convergence of BIM and GIS, as that is becoming increasingly important.

The whole concept of BIM is based on the systematic assembly, management, maintenance, and exchange of semantic information about every component, construction element, and locational aspect of an architectural object. This includes the materials that a building is made of and their many individual properties, but also geographical, topological, 'ontological', and 'taxonomical' data. (In the world of BIM, which pretty much makes up its own language, 'ontological' information refers to various 'concepts', 'attributes', 'relations', and 'knowledge' that can be exchanged between human beings – as opposed to machines – and 'taxonomy' to different types of information and how it is presented, in other words: what kind of document/table/model features what type of data and to what end this data is used.)

Considering the scope, therefore, that BIM offers for data that is or can also be relevant to GIS applications, it is unsurprising that we are looking at increasing areas of overlap between the two, since GIS similarly concerns itself with the geography, topology, 'ontology', and 'taxonomy' of built environments and, especially, how people use these.

In BIM, the standard format for information exchange is called IFC, which stands for Industry Foundation Classes, and is set by buildingSMART, which used to be known as the International Alliance for Interoperability (IAI). It is the organisation whose main purpose is the alignment of standards across BIM applications. Having started out as a consortium founded by Autodesk in 1994, the Alliance was constituted as a not-for-profit body in 1997, with IFC made an open standard that has since also become an official ISO (International Organization for Standardization) standard.

In GIS, the principal standard is known as GML, which stands for Geography Markup Language. First developed in the late 1990s by a man called Ron Lake, the standard allows for geographic data to be managed, analysed, and visualised. It is defined and maintained by the Open Geospatial Consortium (OGC), a body consisting of some 500 plus commercial, governmental, not-for-profit, and academic organisations, whose purpose it is to develop and promote open standards for GIS, the Internet of Things (IoT), and geospatial content generally. Like IFC, GML is also an ISO recognised standard. The Keyhole Markup Language (KML) we encountered a moment ago also became an open standard in 2008 under the aegis of the Open Geospatial Consortium.

The main difference between KML and GML is that KML is largely focused on the presentation of spatial models, whereas GML is able to tie these into topologies, 'ontologies', and 'taxonomies', as understood also in a BIM context. Like KML, GML is notated in XML, which stands for Extensible Markup Language, which is an open standard developed by the World Wide Web Consortium. ■ ↖377 511↘

Also in 2008, the OGC adopted CityGML as an official standard and became its guardian and steward. This GML based data model and exchange format is used to store digital 3D models of cities and landscapes and was originally developed by the Special Interest Group 3D (SIG 3D) which in turn was part of an initiative called *Geodata Infrastructure North-Rhine Westphalia (GDI NRW)* in Germany. ■ 537↘ □ 507↘

Meanwhile, in 2007, the European Union, taking the concept of the 'acronym' to new levels entirely, launched INSPIRE, the *Initiative Infrastructure for Spatial Information in the European Community,* which seeks in the longer term to create a Europe-wide unified geodata infrastructure, so as to secure interoperability across national borders.

Apart from the two different file standards, there are some conceptual differences between the approaches in GIS and BIM, which need to be gradually overcome. One way of expressing these differences is as modelling approaches: with BIM this starts with the object that is to be built, and the first and main purpose of the digital model is an accurate and as comprehensive-as-possible representation of this object. In other words: the starting point is the planned, yet to be created reality of the proposed building. This has been referred to as a 'top-down' approach, assuming that the basis or bottom is the existing reality and the target or top is the planned reality. GIS approaches the model from directly the other direction: you have a real world environment which you measure, observe, assess, analyse, and then visually represent in a model: the prime objective of the GIS model now is the representation of the existing reality, into which an imagined reality will be built. For this reason, the GIS approach has also been called, in the same configuration, a 'bottom-up' approach. ■ ↖379 510↘

A second principal difference between GIS and BIM is the scope and content of the data model: with BIM this is confined to a detailed capture of a specific object. Depending on what kind of object you're talking about, this may be very detailed indeed. We note in our chapter on the subject that BIM is being pushed particularly for large-scale, public sector projects (for which, in some countries, the use of BIM is now compulsory). A new airport or train station, for instance, will contain vast amounts of building information that needs to be modelled. Still, the BIM concerns itself with that complex, and nothing else, whereas GIS concerns itself with *all* objects, as well as roads, landscaping, power and water supplies, vegetation, even climate, and of course population of a whole area, village, town, city, region, country, continent, or the globe. The potential scale of a GIS is therefore unlimited, while the potential scale of a BIM may be vast, but remains confined. ■ □ 613↘

These fundamental differences between BIM and GIS, and their inherent compatibility issues notwithstanding, the two modelling approaches still feed into each other, and GIS data often serves as an important basis for architectural object and infrastructure planning, which means they have to be somehow integrated into the BIM. Similarly, much of a BIM's data has direct or indirect consequences for the GIS data set and therefore also needs to be fed back into the GIS for the relevant location accurately and reliably, if the GIS is to retain its value and functionality.

GIS AND GPS

We have already touched, in broad outline, on the important role Global Navigation Satellite Systems (GNSS) play for GIS. And we've also pointed out that for most people by far the most readily recognisable of these is the Global Positioning System (GPS), which in common usage has become quasi synonymous with GNSS. GPS – one of several GNSS – is owned by the United States and operated by the US Air Force Space Command (AFSC).

Founded in 1973 by the US Department of Defense, GPS launched its first satellite in 1978, and today as we write this forty years later in 2018, it has 31 satellites in orbit at a height off the ground of 20,180 kilometres (12,540 miles), positioned in such a way that from any spot on Earth there are always at least 4 satellites above the horizon, capable of locating a GPS transceiver on Earth to within about 5 metres. (Actually, GPS through its Standard Positioning Service [SPS] for civilian use with a single transceiver guarantees an accuracy of only about 15 metres. But by using a network of fixed, ground-based reference stations, what is then called **Differential GPS** can increase this accuracy up to about 10 centimetres, which is why ordinary consumer level car navigation systems for example are so unnervingly precise.)

A GPS tracker can deliver data in various output formats, including traditional geographic coordinates described in degrees, minutes, and seconds. Most common though is the **Universal Transmercator (UTM)** coordinate system, which divides the Earth into sixty zones of 6° longitude in width, though there are several exceptions, with segments as narrow as 3° and as wide as 12° to accommodate particular geographic features, most notably the shape of Norway. Each zone is then divided into 20 latitude bands of 8° 'height', which are labelled with Latin letters C to X (omitting A, B, I, O, Y, and Z). Any point on Earth can therefore be located by giving the zone and the *easting* and *northing* reference, which is the distance given in metres from the intersection between the equator and the zone's *central meridian*. There are some historic variations, but the reference ellipsoid used today for UTM is the **World Geodetic System (WGS)**, which is generally referred to as **WGS 84**, whereby the '84' stands for 1984, the year of its latest and therefore current revision.

GIS software doesn't tend to handle traditional geographic coordinates well, which is why the data usually has to be converted into the UTM format. The John Snow Pub in Soho, where we started our excursion into the land of GIS, and which finds itself at 51.513274 latitude and -0.136593 longitude (51° 30' 47.7864" N, 0° 8' 11.7348" W) thus has UTM coordinates of 30 N 698681 5710793.

TOOLS

We've also already mentioned some of the most commonly used GIS tools, but it is worth summarising them here, with a view, specifically, to how relevant they are for architects:

Perhaps among the most immediately and obviously useful tools for architecture students as well as for small to medium size architecture firms whose main focus and area of expertise is not first and foremost strategic urban planning but the design and development of individual architectural objects and object groups within given settings, are the small, in some cases open-source tools that are freely available and easy to use, such as:

- *Google Earth* (earth.google.com)
- *Google Maps* (maps.google.com)
- *OpenStreetMap* (openstreetmap.org)
- Based on *OpenStreetMap* data, *Maperitive* (maperitive.net) offers a free to use open-source tool to generate maps
- *QGIS* (qgis.org) is a fully-fledged free, open-source GIS that draws on a large, global, and very responsive community and is available in multiple languages with extensive data libraries
- *GRASS* (or *GRASS GIS*), developed by the US Army, is similarly open-source and free to use
- *ArcGIS* by Esri may be considered the benchmark GIS application in the commercial sector: it holds roughly the position in GIS that *Photoshop* holds in graphic design and image manipulation, but it is, correspondingly, not free – at the time of writing, a typical installation may cost in the region of EUR 5,000–6,000
- Trimble's *SketchUp*, available in a free to use *'Make'* and a paid for *'Pro'* version, offers an interesting bridge between 'ordinary' 3D modelling and GIS, as it gives you access to some GIS functionalities even though it is not primarily a GIS software
- *NASA WorldWind* is a free development tool to create geospatial data visualisations
- *Maps.Me* is a multi-platform app for smartphone and tablet devices that also uses *OpenStreetMap* data. Originally developed and released independently in Zürich, Switzerland, in 2012, it has since been bought by the Russian Internet giant Mail.Ru.
- *CityMapper* is a multi-award winning multi-platform transport planning app, which started life (and is still headquartered) in London, and at the time of writing covers major cities in Europe, the Americas, Australia, and Asia (but not, as yet, Africa). It relies on public, open, and user-generated data to steer its users through major cities by any mode of transport in the most efficient and/or the desired way.

The Outlook

We expect low-end, smartphone app based ways of using GIS – or variants of GIS with a similar approach – to become more relevant and more directly attractive not only, but especially, to architects in the near foreseeable future. GIS can still be very time-consuming and costly, particularly if you have to generate your own data, or radically reformat, restructure, and reorganise diverse existing data sets, but GIS approaches that use readily available, free technology and data analysis methods that are not particularly hardware intensive can offer not just a 'way into GIS', but also create entirely new and fresh uses for GIS.

At the high end, professional, level, we expect both CAD and GIS, and BIM and GIS, to move closer together and to ultimately more or less converge. As with other areas, rather than radical differences between individual software applications, the main factors for deciding what program to use will be ones mostly of personal choice: which product or product group do you find easiest to get on with, where is the centre of gravity of your work, what do you already know and use frequently, and what would entail learning an entire new suite and its unfamiliar workflows.

Also as in many other areas – and as we keep coming back to in this *Atlas* – a certain, even if basic, level of knowledge about, and competence in, scripting/coding and programming is likely to be more, not less, necessary in the coming years: the questions for most architects using GIS are, 'where do I get the data I need', 'how do I use it', and then, 'how can I get the most useful results from the data?' This third question may well be answered: 'by tailoring the software to your needs, by adapting or even creating your own bespoke tool for the exact purpose you have in mind.'

We believe there will be an increasing convergence also between real world data and the digital models that exist of the real world, down to increasingly accurate detail, in real time. If, as we expect will be the case, the wealth of data we keep on all elements of all objects in our built environments increases, and we expand the databases and computing power for this data to be used more and more widely, and to be updated in a dynamic exchange between data keepers and data users, then we can begin to envisage a situation in the not too distant future where – for the large part of our globe – inhabited regions exist as virtually one-to-one digital copies of their real world iterations: what Al Gore talked about in his vision for a Digital Earth, and what we talk about in more detail also in our chapter on Digital Cities. □ 529↘

Hand in hand with such a development, we would expect that GIS programs and their operations will become easier to use and more intuitive, and that therefore also their use will spread. Planning and designing our cities – and indeed all our inhabited environments – in an intelligent and considerate way means using good data well. We would expect GIS to play a major, and growing, part in this.

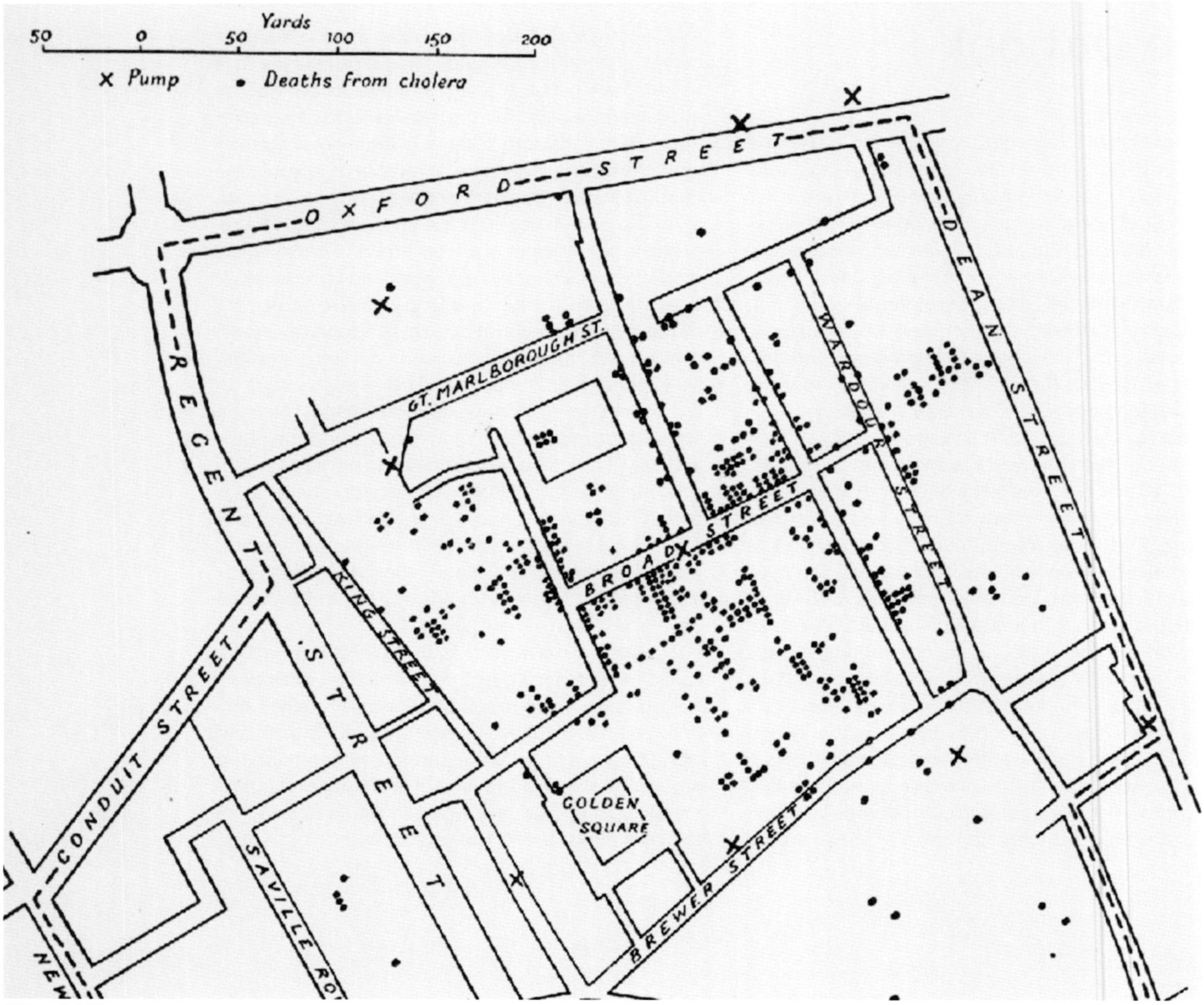

318 ● 493
Pioneering map: John Snow charted deaths caused by the cholera outbreak in London's Soho in 1854 with black dashes, showing a clear cluster around the pump on the corner of Broad Street and Cambridge Street.

319 ● 494
Manhattan as seen through Uber rides: pick-ups and drop-offs mapped during the course of one day. [Uber/Mapbox]

320A ● 494
Singapore: isochronal (cyclical, periodic) representation of journey times. [320A + 320B: MIT Senseable City Lab]

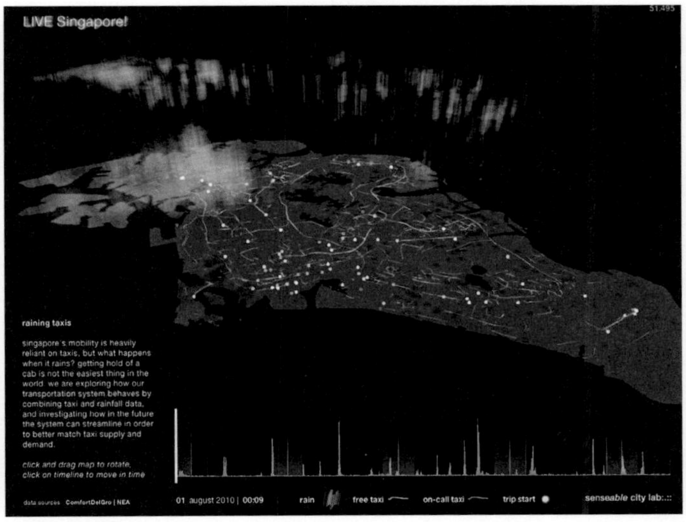

320B ● 494
Rain cloud and taxi stop points in realtime.

321 ● 495
A figure-ground diagram of the city of Konstanz, Germany, generated using *OpenStreetMap*. Only the 'building layer' is inked in black. The map is almost literally up to date at any time the data is retrieved. [Peter Zeile]

Building Information Modelling (BIM)

Jakob Beetz, André Borrmann, Petra von Both,
Frank Petzold, Odilo Schoch

Overview

On 13 November 1961 London Heathrow Airport opened its first terminal dedicated to long-haul flights by international carriers. It was an age when air travel still had a lustre of glamour about it: there was a helicopter service straight from the terminal building to the centre of town, and since the majority of the routes from here headed across the Atlantic Ocean for America or towards the Indian and Pacific Oceans for Asian destinations, it was named 'Oceanic Terminal'. By 1968, it had been renamed to the prosaic Terminal 3 it is known as today, and although during its first expansion in 1970 it became the site of the UK's first travelators (or moving walkways), the building now appears to have few claims to fame, unless you count the achievement of handling some 17.7 million passengers who arrive or leave on nearly 90,000 flights here each year.

For architects, though, the comparatively unspectacular building holds one more point of interest that hardly anybody else knows about. Between 1987 and 1990 it was refurbished again, at a cost of some GBP 110 million – approximately EUR 2 billion in today's money – and this vast project goes down in history as one of the first to systematically use what we now understand as Building Information Modelling (BIM). Since then, BIM has steadily grown in importance, and its use has spread ever more widely. Today it plays an increasingly prominent part in planning and architecture, especially for large, public sector and Public-Private Partnership (PPP) projects. It hasn't reached this position without controversy, and so in our chapter on this topic we want to look not only at what BIM is, at its potential, and its 'added value', so to speak, but also at some of the worries that it elicits from its critics, and at the shortcomings they highlight.

THE DEFINITION
– WHAT BIM IS AND WHAT IT ISN'T

Possibly the most basic and important thing to establish is that BIM is *not* a software and it is *not* a tool, or even a set of tools. Building information modelling encompasses three principal aspects:

- *A semantic data model,* which may in fact consist of several models that are linked to each other through a reference model
- The *modelling process,* which may stretch over extended periods and involve contributors and collaborators from many different fields, and
- *Management of the model:* the planning and coordination of data and information flows.

It is, in short, a methodology: an approach. The distinction is important, because under the BIM banner there are many different tools – software packages and suites, applications and programs, by a range of different developers – of vastly varying character and quality, and they all, in one way or another, serve this method.

Their range being so wide, they do so with greater or lesser success, and with subtly different priorities. Some of these tools, for example, handle open-source, non-proprietary data formats to aid interoperability, while others don't and are therefore tied into a software maker's own system; but the purpose of any BIM is in essence the same: a structured, seamlessly data-supported collaboration between professionals, contractors, and stakeholders on a construction project. Ideally, from a BIM perspective, this reaches across the entire lifespan of the object, from the first initial design and planning stages, through the regulatory, licensing and permission processes, to construction, and then also, importantly, beyond, into and throughout the object's use and maintenance, right to the point where it is either dismantled or converted, or in some other way brought to the end of its intended existence.

In order to be able to achieve this purpose, a building information model – much as the term suggests – needs to be rich in accurate and detailed semantic information about itself and every component in it. Therein lies its chief characteristic: that it is not only a digital or visual or physical representation (as a drawing or a sophisticated 3D computer model or a physical model of a building might also be), but that it contains a wealth of data that is useful – arguably essential – for the object's developers to have to hand and be able to share.

The National Institute of Building Sciences in the United States, on its *National BIM Standard – United States* website, gives a succinct and certainly □ ↖507
applicable explanation:

> "Building Information Modeling (BIM) is a digital representation of physical and functional characteristics of a facility. A BIM is a shared knowledge resource for information about a facility forming a reliable basis for decisions during its life-cycle; defined as existing from earliest conception to demolition.
>
> A basic premise of BIM is collaboration by different stakeholders at different phases of the life-cycle of a facility to insert, extract, update or modify information in the BIM to support and reflect the roles of that stakeholder."

In this – the inclusion of stakeholders, and offering a management and coordination method from the beginning right through to the end of a building's lifecycle – lies one of the main 'selling points' of BIM. Other methods of digital planning and 3D Modelling (on which □ ↖57
we have a separate chapter in this *Atlas*) can do many things that BIM can do (and some of these arguably better), but if and where comprehensive data sets are created and maintained systematically, they can be used to assist in updating, changing, renovating, and managing, over many years, highly complex structures.

The 'added value', in other words, of a well-kept BIM is a cross-discipline data integration that, in an ideal case, will facilitate the seamless collaboration of dozens, in some cases hundreds, of different (and different kinds of) professionals, contractors, and personnel, over several decades. And one of the fundamental ideas behind BIM, and advantages brought forward in its favour, is that it be able to do these things at a lower cost, and susceptible to fewer errors, than would otherwise be possible.

Building information modelling rests on a consistent use and loss-free reproduction of a digital construction model throughout its entire lifecycle.

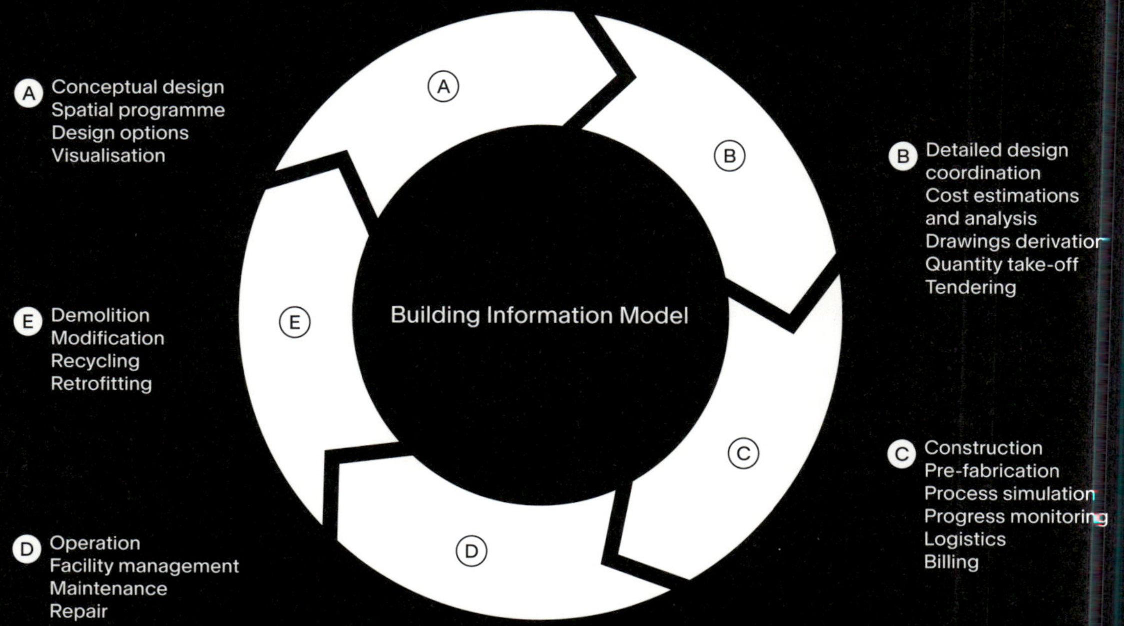

SEMANTICS AND STANDARDS

Like other 3D modelling techniques, BIM uses a digital 3D model or referenced set of models as the source for all drawings, plans, and elevations, which means that any change that is made to any of the core models automatically and immediately gets translated into every other iteration or rendition of the building or parts of it.

Also in common with other 3D modelling methods, BIM gives efficient access to a wide range of simulation and analysis tools, which offer synergies between the construction and other industries that use comparable methods.

What distinguishes BIM from other techniques is its particular focus on semantics: the meaningful information that is stored with each object. For example, a simple BIM element such as a door may have in the region of 60 internationally accepted parameters just to describe its most essential characteristics.

A BIM typically – and this is one of the most persistent and most argued over bones of contention – draws on a catalogue of pre-defined, but adaptable and customisable, elements, such as walls, windows, doors, or supports; and these elements in turn combine what is usually a parametric geometrical 3D representation with their own descriptive characteristics, such as size, thickness, fire resistance, price, colour, material, and their relation to any other element that is part of the architectural object. Similarly, statutory requirements, such as planning regulations, safety standards, and building norms can be incorporated into the model, which consequently delivers plans, elevations, and sections that conform to these externally given requirements, without having to go through separate compliance processes.

■ ↖501

■

Critical to the success of such an approach (whether this now entails one single model or, as you would find on a large project, a whole set of interlinked models) are therefore standards and standardised interfaces. If you want engineers, craftspeople, suppliers, regulators, and architects all to be able to work together and to store, access, and manipulate data about the model or models, then very obviously they all have to have a compatible understanding of what things are. BIM is thus closely tied into a concerted effort by parts of the construction industry on the one hand, and by government bodies and agencies on the other, to define standards that can be agreed on and therefore become universally applicable.

One of the driving forces behind BIM, and also its *de facto* standard and norm setter, is buildingSMART, which used to be known as Industry Alliance for Interoperability, a function it still holds today. Originally initiated by Autodesk as a consortium between it and eleven other, invited, companies in 1994, the body was opened up to interested parties generally about a year later, in September 1995, and it developed what is still today the most widely used set of standards for BIM components, the **Industry Foundation Classes (IFC)**.

These in turn have their roots in what today is known as ISO 10303, but started life between 1984 and the mid-1990s as **STEP**, for **Standard for the Exchange of Product Model Data**. Much as this earlier, more descriptive (and still informally used) name suggests, it provides a standard that aims to assist in what the ISO's official title for it also elucidates as "Automation systems and integration – Product data representation and exchange."

In 1997, following demands from Autodesk users that IFCs should be non-proprietary, the organisation was renamed International Alliance for Interoperability, and reconstituted as a not-for-profit, industry-led body. In 2005 the name was changed to today's brand-like buildingSMART, as members came to the conclusion that their former name was not comprehensible or catchy enough.

Both buildingSMART and its approach to standardisation are not without their critics. Among the problems that have been identified with IFCs is that they are at best moderately fit for purpose during the design phase of a project, and then only really in the construction of buildings. Efforts to expand them also to lifecycle management and to infrastructural projects, such as bridges, railways, tunnels, and roads, for example, are very recent. And even in the normal design of buildings, IFCs don't manage to fully reflect real world construction methods in their data concepts. Most serious though is perhaps the charge that working with IFCs is still, to this day, understood to be tinkering with defined data sets. As recently as March 2018, buildingSMART decided against a more Cloud-based approach that would have been more dynamic and contemporary.

On a brighter note, since 2010 buildingSMART has been working towards a format to facilitate data exchange between different BIM software packages. As their own website explains:

> "Before 2010, endusers, who wanted to exchange issues, proposals and change requests in BIM-data-models, always had to exchange the whole BIM-model as a bulk data. The receiver had to compare different releases of the BIM-model in order to filter the requests from the sender. As a much more efficient way to support this effort the idea of developing an open standard to enable BIM-workflow communication between different software tools had been proposed to buildingSMART."

The result of this initiative was the **BIM Collaboration Format (BCF)**. This, from an end user's perspective, is by some margin the greatest success so far in the history of BIM standards. It makes it comparatively easy to use many of the advantages of digitalisation, such as the unambiguous naming of construction parts, or server-based, location and time independent access to information. It is a flexible, **XML (Extensible Markup Language)** based standard, which is far easier to implement than IFC. Apart from that, buildingSMART has also developed what it calls a 'simple ifcXML' which, it explains, is conceived to "provide use case specific IFC model definitions," enabling a reduction in complexity and thus helps "to simplify implementation." Furthermore, it reduces files size, therefore leading to "lower resource requirements."

BIM AND GOVERNMENT POLICY

Across the globe, in the developed as well as the developing world, governments and societies face extraordinary challenges that we are all too aware of: demographic shifts, particularly urbanisation and the inherent changes in infrastructural requirements this brings, the rapid changes in behaviour that are associated with new technologies, and of course population growth, to name but these as examples. Many industry sectors are by now well into the ongoing process of digitalisation, pursuing optimisation and with it improved efficiency and higher profits as chief ambitions; and entire national and pan-national strategies have been developed to structure and facilitate these transitions, always under the assumption, of course, that its goals be beneficial and therefore desirable.

In the United Kingdom, since April 2016, all centrally procured construction projects have to achieve what the government's *2011 Construction Strategy* defined as BIM 'Level 2' (we spell out these levels in full a bit further down). Germany Trade & Invest, the foreign trade and inward investment agency of Germany, has launched what it calls *Industrie 4.0* and describes as "the German strategic initiative to establish Germany as a lead market and provider of advanced manufacturing solutions." It goes on to say: "One of 10 'Future Projects' identified by the German government as part of its High-Tech Strategy 2020, the 'INDUSTRIE 4.0' project represents a major opportunity for Germany to establish itself as an integrated industry lead market and provider." Similarly, and directly inspired by *Industrie 4.0,* China's *Made in China 2025* plan encapsulates an even broader set of objectives to upgrade China's very varied and divergent manufacturing industries and bring them to world-leading status in the context of digitalisation. In the United States, meanwhile, the state of Wisconsin in 2010 passed a law that obliges all public projects with a budget of USD 5 million or more, and all construction projects with a budget of USD 2.5 million or more to incorporate BIM.

Governmental departments and agencies committing themselves to BIM, and in some cases, such as Germany and the United Kingdom, not just promoting it but legislating towards its use in publicly funded projects, has far reaching consequences and pushes BIM as an approach right to the fore, making it increasingly integral and ultimately inescapable for architect offices and engineering firms alike. The German ministry for transport and digital infrastructure, BMVI *(Bundesministerium für Verkehr und digitale Infrastruktur),* has set up a phased implementation plan that aims at "helping BIM in Germany to a breakthrough" by 2020, and that it says is "primarily applicable to construction in infrastructure and infrastructure related projects, but can also be used as a model in other areas." While this means that this initial drive affects mainly large undertakings such as national roads or airports, the idea – and the intention – clearly is to usher in BIM as a general approach.

■ ↖501 537↘

The reasons why policy makers and public purse string holders are keen on BIM are manifold, but among the most weighty ones are these:

- The realisation of big building projects anywhere requires that a large number of people from different areas and with varying levels of expertise work closely together, often never having done so before, but having been effectively 'thrown in' with each other through a competitive tendering process. So instead of an architect office being able to execute its plans with a couple of engineering firms it has a close rapport and understanding with, it may suddenly find itself collaborating within a corporate culture that it not only doesn't know, but very possibly doesn't share, simply because the client has decided that this combination would offer the best cost-yield configuration. And this in itself is not as arbitrary as it may sound: in many countries, Germany and the UK being typical examples, any public money that is being spent needs to go through a rigorous process of tendering and selection, to guarantee an open playing field and to combat corruption.

- Also characteristic of the German (as indeed Austrian and Swiss) construction industry in particular, but reflected elsewhere, is its high level of fragmentation, and a tradition of many small and medium size companies working in both planning and supplier roles to a project. This means that portions of a project's execution are by necessity dispersed over a wide range of miniature management structures, and therefore need to somehow be roped together into an overriding methodology.

□ ↖129
■ ↖479 536↘
□ ↖57
■ ↖469 532↘
□ ↖491
□ 529↘

There is an explicit strategic goal, then, to the implementation of BIM, which is to increase the efficiency and reliability of not just individual construction projects, but of the construction industry as a whole. This is, again, of extraordinary significance, because it closely and directly associates a technological approach, BIM, with stated government policy ambitions, and directly manoeuvres an entire industry sector towards its adoption. The then Chief Construction Advisor to the UK government, Paul Morrell, is quoted as telling the domestic construction industry to either adopt BIM or be "*Betamaxed* out," which, as a policy stance in a pluralist democracy may be seen as inherently problematic. The imposition of BIM especially on smaller architecture practices which often do not have the resources to invest in the technology, and, more importantly and in terms of cost much greater, in the training of their limited staff on how to use it, can and does cause real anguish and operational difficulties.

Also, many architects may feel instinctively that as creative, independent professionals it should be up to them what methods and technologies they employ in their work, rather than be told to toe the line or be pushed off the perch, even if it is the reality of a digital economy that in order to do any type of business, the vast majority of people will at one point or another simply have to start using one of very few available software products that dominate any given market.

Getting hold of this evolving reality and responding to it has become an existential challenge for architects worldwide. Stefan Behnisch, a German architect with offices in Stuttgart, Munich, and Boston, expresses this in an interview with *Bauwelt* magazine: "The discussion around BIM at the moment is led by project managers, not by architects. But if we don't contribute anything to the topic ourselves, we architects will soon be on the outside."

CHANGES IN PLANNING METHODS

How did we get to 3D modelling and BIM? To help us grasp the scope and significance of BIM today, it may be useful to chart, in outline form, the route that has taken us here from a methodology perspective.

THE HISTORICAL BACKDROP

At the time of the Heathrow Terminal 3 renovation, the term BIM did not yet exist. The reason this particular project is so strongly associated with BIM is that two people, a Simon Ruffle in 1985 and a Robert Aish in 1986, wrote about the software and approach that was used for it in separate papers and called this a 'building model' in the sense that we use BIM today: an information-rich, digital model that could be shared collaboratively. The software in question had been given the endearing name *Really Universal Computer Aided Production System (RUCAPS)* by its developers John Davison and John Watts, both graduates from the University of Liverpool. They subsequently marketed it to the industry through GMW Computers Ltd, an offshoot of Gollins Melvin Ward (GMW) Architects in London. It would take another few years, until 1992, before two researchers, G A van Nederveen and F P Tolman, published a paper called *Modelling Multiple Views on Buildings – Automation in Construction*, in which they appear to have coined the term *building information modelling* itself.

Being intrinsically woven into the history of Computer Aided Design (CAD), Computer Aided Architectural Design (CAAD), and 3D Modelling, the roots of BIM entangle with these and stretch back to pioneers of computing in architecture and Artificial Intelligence (AI), such as American computer scientist Herbert A Simon (1916–2001), Greek-American architect Nicholas Negroponte (b. 1943), and Scottish landscape architect Ian McHarg (1920–2001), who in his 1969 book *Design With Nature* set out the principles of what were to become Geographic Information Systems (GIS), which in character are not dissimilar to BIM, and which we discuss in a separate chapter, as well as in our chapter on Digital Cities.

Here as in many other places in this *Atlas* we are also bound to mention the American computer scientist Ivan Sutherland (b. 1938), who with his legendary 1962 program *Sketchpad* pioneered (so as not to say 'invented') computer graphics, and the American university professor Charles Eastman, who as we write this teaches Building Information Modelling at the Georgia Tech School of Architecture, having effectively created the forerunner to BIM, then called *Building Description System (BDS)* in the 1970s: the "first software to describe individual library elements which can be retrieved and added to a model," as writer Vanessa Quirk puts it in her *Brief History of BIM* on the *ArchDaily* website.

BDS was an experiment and found no widespread practical, let alone commercial use, and so it fell to American software company Autodesk, since 1982 makers of the widely used *AutoCAD* software, to propagate the term *Building Information Modelling* (in their case spelt with an L short of the British/international style) in a white paper published in 2003. This set out a comprehensive strategy for using BIM in the construction industry and is worth a read (there's a link to it from the QR code at the beginning of this chapter), not only because it fires the starting gun in what appears to be a deliberate and headlong race towards BIM, but also because in just under seven succinct and quite clear pages it explains the point of BIM, while at the same time framing it into something of a sales pitch. This has been noted and levied as an explicit or implicit criticism of BIM ever since: that it and its origins are inextricably linked to commercial interests.

FROM CAD TO BIM

The CAD programs of the first generation were really drawing tools: they generated (supported, if you like) two dimensional geometries which therefore consisted of their basic elements: lines and planes. Consequently, what you were able to create with these programs were essentially discrete plans or elevations, meaning they were flat drawings that contained no or little additional 'intelligence' or semantic information, that were unrelated to each other, and that therefore had to be amended manually every time any single aspect of the project changed.

A second generation of now 3D CAD systems was already capable of making complex 3D models. These were, by definition, no longer plan-based but model-based, which made it possible to automatically deduce from the core 3D model perspective drawings and plans, elevations, and sections, which would therefore correspond to the model. It was now no longer necessary to manually update individual drawings: these outputs were connected and related to each other. This, obviously, made for a leap in reliability and accuracy: both vital in any design and engineering project.

BIM systems take a principally different approach to design. No longer is it either plan-based or model-based, but *object*-based, 'object' here referring to construction elements or objects, rather than to the overall architectural object. The model now is generated with either predefined or user customised construction elements as the building blocks for the design: the walls, windows, ceilings, floors, pillars, staircases become the 'assembly kit', simply put, from which the project is put together. As we've emphasised, these elements are not just geometries though, they are endowed with information about themselves, much of which is not merely useful, but in fact essential for the building to be able to stand up and fulfil its purpose: material qualities, strength, physical characteristics, static properties are all integrated and therefore part of the planning and design process. Before and outside BIM, it would often fall to a structural engineer to retrospectively work out whether an architect's design actually held up. If it didn't, changes to the choice of materials and their positioning would have to be made, which would naturally affect everything else in the project. This approach can lead to lengthy and costly delays and also may greatly compromise a designer's vision at a point in the proceedings where considerations about time and money are already reaching critical stage.

To make possible the use of information-rich construction elements as building blocks, BIM draws on extensive pre-defined libraries that contain the relevant data. Commercially, this offers an attractive access point for manufacturers to supply planners and architects with such libraries of standardised, normed, and appropriately appointed digital versions of their physical products that they hope to sell into the project. It is this 'kit' aspect to BIM that has earned it, arguably a touch unjustly (though opinions diverge widely on this subject), the epithet '*Lego* Architecture'. Unjustly, because not only has *Lego* become an incredibly versatile and faceted treasure trove of modelling toys, but also because, as we keep pointing out, some BIM systems, quite unlike *Lego*, do allow for the adaptation and **parametric modelling** of its components, which means that a steel carrier beam, for example, can be specified to its geometric dimensions and strength according to a given set of rules or parameters, and then be scaled and made available in a range of different sizes and strengths from a bespoke catalogue. In other words, there is some scope for customisation and flexible modelling in this kind of kit.

CHARACTERISTICS OF THE BIM APPROACH

We have already touched on some of the characteristics that distinguish BIM from other digital (or indeed analogue) planning methods, and that may be considered its principal advantages over these, in relevant contexts. They can be summarised as:

- Generating a consistent set of models for everyone working on a project, so there are no discrepancies between different versions and iterations emanating from them and the reference model that links them to each other.
- Tying together all the involved software applications into one overriding system, so that, for the entire duration of a building's lifecycle, the information stored and handled in relation to it remains intact, complete, and accurate. (This presupposes that software applications on the one hand and data on the other are continuously and flawlessly updated and maintained over anything up to fifty, seventy, or a hundred years. The project leader of London's Crossrail – a fantastically complex railway project running east to west underneath London and slotting seamlessly into the existing Underground and Overground public transport network – declared during a BBC documentary that their work needed to last for another hundred years. That is a very long time in information technology, which, in itself and in its entirety, has barely two thirds that age as we write this...)
- Providing a basis for timely validations and simulations to test the building for its structural, functional, environmental, and economic strengths, and to play through design options. (For example lifecycle analysis, energy simulations, or collision detection.) This in itself, at least in theory, has the potential to be an augmenter of structural and functional quality: if potential problems can be caught early, they can be addressed effectively and without incurring the kinds of delays or costs that can cripple a project at a later stage.
- Facilitating the decision making processes through a single information basis. Again, it may not always work in practice, but conceptually, it sounds almost like stating the obvious: the better the information you work with, the better informed your decisions will be; therefore, in theory, the better and more dependable should be the decision.
- Being able to demonstrate and visualise the impact a building will have, and then also to show how requested changes are being implemented. In complex projects that involve not only a wide range of professionals but, significantly, also a large number of very diverse stakeholders (neighbourhood associations, environmental action groups, for example), this can acquire make-or-break importance. Creating 3D visualisations, **virtual reality** walkthroughs,

■ ↖480
■ ↖486

■ ↖407

and physical prototypes (rapid prototyping) can all assist the discussion and dialogue between interested parties and aid their understanding of what they are dealing with.

- Reducing the need for retroactive changes. (Assuming that there is accurate and detailed quantitative as well as qualitative modelling, a consistent coupling of planning and execution, and ultimately the generation of a reliable and complete building documentation that can serve as the basis for running the place once it's up.)
- Optimising a construction project for cost and energy efficiency. About 40% of all our energy consumption goes into buildings. Both their construction itself, but then in particular regulating the temperature inside them – keeping them warm during cold periods and cool during hot periods – uses an enormous amount of energy, which expresses itself in cost. In a world where energy and its sources are major (and rapidly changing) factors, it does not really make sense to design a building and then see how much energy it uses; BIM allows these factors to be considered from the outset.

Looked at in this way, there are, both from a client and from a designer or architect perspective, benefits in taking a collaborative approach that puts information, and therefore an integrated 'intelligent' workflow, at the centre of the construction process. We might then think of the information as a 'digital clay', from which you shape the building you want to make.

A SHIFT IN EMPHASIS

BIM, with its focus on integrated, cooperative planning, shifts the effort and therefore emphasis towards the early stages of the project, compared to other approaches. In conventional planning, the biggest effort goes into the later phases of planning and design, when the overarching creative principle and rationale have been sought, found, and approved, and when the detail of the execution is now worked out and tested. This means that most in-depth analysis, simulation, and evaluation tools that try the project for its structural and functional integrity can only really be applied towards the end of the process, because only then will all the relevant factors that determine things such as energy consumption, people flow, light distribution, or similar be in place. But by that time making changes to the design is not only much more difficult than early on, but also signally more expensive.

A founder member and as we write this still chairman of buildingSMART is American architect Patrick MacLeamy (b. 1942), after whom the *MacLeamy Curve* is named. This is a more contemporary version and slight elaboration on the older *Boyd Paulson Curve,* named after the American civil engineering professor at Stanford University, Boyd Paulson (1946–2005), who in 1976 was most likely the first person to describe the relationship between design stages: the level of influence a designer has on the design, and the cumulative cost of the project. Both Paulson's curve and MacLeamy's adaptation of it illustrate the inverse relationship between the level of influence and level of cost over time: the further along the design process you go, the lower the level of influence you have on the project, and the higher expenditure climbs. What Patrick MacLeamy added was simply two more waveforms that illustrate this shift of emphasis and effort in a BIM workflow compared to a conventional one:

BIM shifts the emphasis and therefore effort of planning and decision making processes towards the earlier phases of a project, compared to conventional approaches.

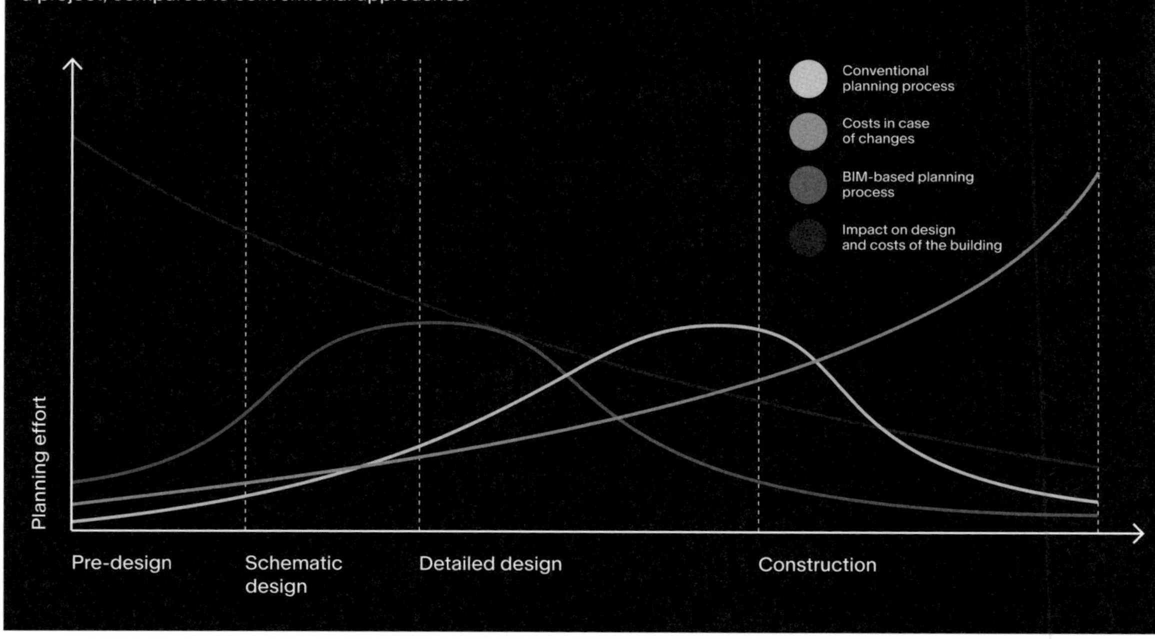

There are advantages to this: it makes analyses and simulations possible much earlier, which means that different design options can be examined and compared to each other, which in turn may well improve the overall quality – certainly in terms of functionality – of the design. When by conventional methods many of the significant calculations can only be carried out once the design process is complete and all the relevant pieces of information have been compiled, BIM starts with the compilation of all the relevant pieces of information (or plausible placeholder units, where the actual information is not yet known), which means calculations can be made from the beginning, and the building adapted and shaped accordingly.

BIM AND COMPETITIONS/ AWARDING OF CONTRACTS

There can be little doubt that big, powerful clients want BIM. If that weren't the case, government departments with billions to spend would not, in search of cost savings and efficiencies, develop BIM implementation strategies and legislate in favour of BIM. The reason big clients like BIM is that the projects they have to award tend to be extremely complex and very expensive. So anything that allows them to keep a handle on budgets, and nudges (in some cases coerces) architects and engineers to work together towards optimising their use of materials and tailoring their designs towards saving on running and maintenance costs is obviously seen as welcome.

By associating detailed information on materiality, durability, energy efficiency, maintenance requirements, and costs with any and all types of components and elements used in a building project, BIM seeks to allow planners to establish with great precision and early on how much a building is really going to cost in all these terms. When by traditional methods such costs would have to be worked out manually in long-winded calculations which would always be prone to human error (chief among them simple data inputting) and computing mistakes, BIM offers a considerable degree of accuracy and reliability. This means the teams generating a proposal can be more certain of their figures and the client can more easily assess a proposal's efficacy.

BIM, PROJECT EXECUTION, AND A WEIRD WORLD OF DIMENSIONS

The moment you start reading BIM literature or familiarise yourself with BIM websites, you will notice that you have entered a world with a vocabulary entirely of its own. This is not altogether surprising, since BIM is steeped in formalised processes and standardised entities, so people dealing with these day in, day out, and having to communicate them, will naturally develop their own jargon. For the uninitiated, one of the more perplexing quirks of BIM nomenclature is its use of 'dimensions'. (Interestingly, we come across a similarly fanciful, but different, riff on the concept of 'dimensions' in the closely related area of GIS, as we note in our chapter on the topic.)

BIM considers a model that has a temporal component to it – such as described just a moment ago, where the model incorporates information about the project execution plan – as a *4D model*, which is easy enough to appreciate, since in common usage 'time' is often (though contentiously) considered to be a 'fourth dimension' too.

Including time as part of the modelling process can be of extraordinary significance, as it means that the various project stages and their schedules are integrated into the BIM, so that any discrepancies or location specific clashes, such as part of the site being required for conflicting purposes, for example, can be caught and ideally avoided.

Earlier, we briefly mentioned London's Crossrail. Here, and although we can assume that BIM is very much in use, it became obvious towards the later stages of the execution that at Farringdon station the rapidly advancing track laying team, which was on schedule, was about to be held up by the more slowly progressing station building team.

Farringdon, like many other stations on what will, once opened, be known as the Elizabeth Line (after the current monarch, Queen Elizabeth II), required a delicate balancing of multiple priorities and meeting of simultaneous challenges: during the week, a station that in a normal year serves nearly 24 million Tube and about 12 million rail passengers had to remain open as much as possible; local residents and traffic had to be as undisrupted as could reasonably be expected; and into an already tightly packed hub that was built roughly a century ago, there had to be woven and wedged a brand spanking new station with new platforms, new escalators, new ticket hall, and new tracks. The tracks, incidentally, just around here, needed to be laid down with specially designed shock absorbers and silencers, because they lie within earshot (and will a few yards down the line be directly underneath) one of London's most prestigious art centres with the Barbican Theatre and the home to the London and the BBC Symphony Orchestras, Barbican Hall.

If the track laying team now at this critical juncture had to wait for the station building team to finish their work before they could load their supplies through the station and continue laying their – right here particularly sophisticated – tracks, this would have held up the entire project at exorbitant cost. So, purely because of a location specific space collision, the project management decided, more or less on the hop, to dig a twenty-odd feet wide supply well on the Farringdon Tube station platform, so materials could be sent down this shaft onto track level, bypassing the Crossrail station that was still under construction. Building that 'emergency well' in itself took several weeks, but was deemed worthwhile because the consequences of the delay otherwise would have been so grave and costly. (Incidentally, and all that said: as we are about to go to print in Spring 2020, Crossrail has gone over budget by approximately GBP 3.45 billion and its opening been delayed by several years...)

While most people would agree that the three spatial dimensions together amount to 3D, and with the question whether or not time is a 'fourth dimension' already subject to some debate, in BIM now 'cost' is not looked upon as simply a baseline component that – as in any project of any kind in any industry – requires a budget, but as a 'fifth dimension', whence the idea that a model which also covers cost components is therefore a *'5D model'*. (It is really a 3D model with time and cost factored into it.)

BIM AND LIFECYCLE MANAGEMENT

We've already cited lifecycle management as one of the major selling points of BIM. There are advantages to being able to hand over a construction project to the client together with a complete data set of everything that might be important for the building's management and maintenance. A large public project with multiple tenants and high footfall functions, such as a railway station or an airport, but also special use objects, such as a hospital or an opera house, will have a lifecycle of many decades, and during that time is likely to clock up in maintenance costs many times what it cost to put up.

In this case, and where a BIM has been brought up to the latest and most accurate state with any □ ↖93 alterations or additions logged and captured, we speak of an *as built model*, which you also find referred to as a *'6D model'*, whereby the 'sixth dimension' here is meant to be simply the information that ■ enables said lifecycle management.

■ ↖270 536↘ Such information may include details about ■ ↖102 built-in machinery, electrical and other installations and connections, wiring, plumbing, maintenance schedules, warranty terms and conditions, special instructions, and indeed expected lifecycle of individual building components, such as lighting units, air conditioning, heating, refrigeration, or similar. This level of modelling integration can obviously be extremely useful. But that usefulness is heavily dependent on constant servicing of the model. In other words: any change, update, alteration, repair, or replacement that happens on the real life object has to be systematically, rigorously replicated in the BIM for it to retain its relevance. Considering the untold number of factors that play into a complex site, such as an airport or even just a shopping centre, and what we know about the fallibility of human nature, that is a tall order indeed: if the caretaker of your school decides to nip out to the hardware store to replace that wobbly door handle on the boys' loos, but does not enter this purchase in a standard conform way into the BIM, then the BIM is already out of synch with the building it models.

Where a BIM is meticulously maintained in tandem with the actual building though, the BIM can then, when the building comes to the end of its lifecycle and needs to be dismantled or repurposed, give very exact details about the types of materials that have to be disposed of, what is recyclable and how, what the value is of any apparatus or machinery that is still of use, and how the impact of dismantling or demolition on the environment can best be mitigated.

With more and more architecture becoming □ 613↘ 'intelligent', and the Internet of Things (IoT) slowly turning into something of a reality, an additional potential opens up for BIM to be useful. As an information-rich virtual model of a real-world building, the BIM can contain all 'intelligent' components that the building itself will feature, such as sensors, automated functionalities, and connected built-in devices, which means they in turn can be tested and fine-tuned in the virtual model ■ ↖445 to catch any glitches or inadequacies before they are actually, and much more expensively, put in place. Similarly, aspects that have a great impact on the running costs of a real-life building, such as heating efficiency, actual room temperatures (as they present themselves with machinery, sunshine, or people factored in), air flow and fluctuations owing to weather conditions, can be continually monitored and analysed on the virtual model, and the actual building correspondingly cali- □ ↖475 brated. (See also our chapter on Simulation.)

↖433

BIM AND EXISTING CONTEXTS

More and more of construction, be it for residential, business, or mixed use, takes shape in existing contexts. This is an issue particularly in Europe. In Germany, it accounts for over 80% of residential construction. Much of this existing context, however, is not in the state it was in when it was first built, and so although in most cases there will be some documentation about these buildings, that documentation is very often incomplete, as alterations were either not, or only partially, recorded.

As we discuss in our chapter on Digital Data Acquisition, there are various methods for capturing and digitising existing contexts and thus creating usable 3D models or indeed fully-fledged BIMs to work with these contexts, such as manual measurements, **tachymetry**, **photogrammetry**, or **laser scanning**, for example. But up until now, BIM has been primarily used for new construction outside existing contexts, and this is reflected in the currently prevailing BIM software, which often makes assumptions, for example about wall surfaces running in strict parallel to each other, or walls and floors sitting at true right angles. In existing contexts, we frequently encounter deviations from these ideals. Either for aesthetic reasons, or because of geographical peculiarities, or simply because over time a building has moved and settled, many old structures are not as a BIM would expect them to be. And that means that in order for existing contexts to become workable with BIM, there is often a compromise that has to be reached between the level of precision that the program expects, and what the reality can offer. In other words: a BIM may have to be complemented with vague and incomplete elements, because it is only possible to capture the surface dimensions, for example. The reconstruction of the existing context then is a matter of surveys, diagnostic procedures, and the diligent application of historical and scientific expertise, which means it is always a case of interpretation, rather than of absolute certainty.

When we are dealing with the renovation of ordinary buildings, it is possible (and usual) to make generalisations during the process of digitisation, to reach a close enough reflection of the real world situation, which is then also represented in the semantic data set. Elements that are affected by the renovation are tagged or labelled according to their condition, and any required action (for example repair, restoration, or removal and replacement) referenced in a relevant BIM object catalogue. But as soon as we move into heritage stock and historical construction research, the level of required accuracy rises dramatically. This makes reconciling the existing context with the generalisation of a BIM incompatible, and so where a generalisation or simplification becomes necessary, it is also necessary to chart and protect the detail of, for example, the measured or captured **point cloud**, such as it might result from a laser scan.

All that said, where it is possible to adequately represent old building stock in a BIM system, the BIM can become a useful tool for information handling and processing of existing contexts, and, given the right conditions, may serve to provide a great level of security in planning and ultimately also cost stability in renovation and restoration projects.

BIM AND CITIZEN PARTICIPATION

Big construction projects are rarely uncontroversial. Whether it is a new shopping centre or an airport expansion, a skyscraper, an urban village, or a new high speed rail link, even a new bridge, or a football stadium; whether this is in a big city or in the country, or on the edge of a town: there will be objections, invariably.

There will be people who will be directly affected by the plans and resist the changes they bring. There may be people who will have to be relocated, perhaps against their wishes. There will be environmental, heritage, cultural, and sentimental factors. Taste: what to an architect or planner looks awesome, to a local resident committee may look like an insult. And vice versa. And so what becomes ever more important is that the people who are affected by a construction project are drawn into it. They have to be allowed to voice their objections, and have reason to feel that these objections are taken seriously. Crucially, they have to be kept informed and involved, so they themselves 'buy into' the project, rather than protesting against it, or filing objections with the local authorities, or, perhaps in a worst case scenario, depositing lawsuits against it. Not only can local resistance delay a project or escalate its costs, a well organised campaign can rapidly sink it.

When the award-winning Artistic Director of London's Southbank Centre, Jude Kelly, unveiled plans for what was called the *Festival Wing Proposal* in March 2013, she did not reckon with just how much people would value a thing that they had got to love and cherish, and how hard they would fight to keep it, even though technically or legally it was never 'theirs' nor their supporters' to 'own'.

Underneath the existing structure of the large complex, there is an empty space that has become known as The Undercroft, which is where skateboarders have made their home since the 1970s. In order to help finance her ambitious project, Kelly proposed moving these skateboarders, and using that location for retail units and cafes. Reasonably enough, she thought, she offered them a new and similar sized, purpose designed skatepark about 120 metres upstream underneath the Hungerford Bridge. To no avail. The skateboarders argued that The Undercroft was the birthplace of British skateboarding and the hub of their culture. Many people who have never skated in their lives recognised and supported their claim to a space that was not originally designed for them, nor had ever been officially been 'given' to them, but that, over time and through permanent use, they had come to call their own.

Also, the campaign to save The Undercroft from development successfully highlighted the unique character and value of a perfectly un-monetised space that was not commercially polluted through sponsorship or advertising, and not curated by any authority, but simply used by people in a way that best suited them. Within months the skateboarders had collected tens of thousands of signatures, garnered 150,000 statements of support, and encouraged some 33,000 official objections to the project, so that by early 2014 the then London Mayor Boris Johnson declared that he would not endorse a removal of the skateboarders from The Undercroft to the new site some four hundred feet away. It was a triumph for citizen power, and the Festival Wing has not been built: if you walk along the South Bank from the Hungerford Bridge towards the National Theatre, you will find to your delight that the skateboarders are still there, day and night, pursuing their activity in The Undercroft, untroubled and free.

A BIM does not guarantee that you won't incur the wrath of a long established local culture if you threaten them with eviction or relocation, but good 3D models and simulations as well as Virtual & Augmented Reality experiences or demonstrations can help you communicate what the vision is and how it will – but also how it will not – affect the locality and the people attached to it. Aspects that are of common concern, such as noise intrusion, light and sightline obstruction, or pollution can be simulated and illustrated in a way that non-experts can understand and process. □ ↖463

Citizen participation is thus facilitated and what has been termed the social sustainability of the project moves centre stage. The more prominent and impactful a construction project, the more significant this becomes. ■

'A MARCH OF THE BUREAUCRATS' – THE CRITIQUE OF BIM

It is impossible to discuss BIM without running into its detractors, and quickly. The subject may be a quarter of a century old now, but it is still just as controversial as it has been since the word go. There are many criticisms that are levied against BIM, and many of these have to do simply with its functionality: unwieldy databases, unintuitive user interfaces, uncreative workflows. It is fair to say that this smoke is not without its fire and that BIM – as anything that involves technology – finds itself on a development curve which did not start at a point of perfection. Other types of digital methods have similarly gone through longer or shorter teething phases, though it is also pertinent to observe that BIM has long since left the pram and is now, as technological approaches go, a fully fledged adult, and should therefore have its own adequate bite, which perhaps it does not in every aspect, still, have.

For an *Atlas* of this nature it is appropriate that we acknowledge the fact that BIM is not without its failings, but our task is not so much to debate technologies and approaches, as it is to present them, dispassionately, and to allow you as the reader to inform yourself further and to find your own position towards anything we talk about here. But BIM isn't just a technology, or a technique, or a tool, or a software. It is, as we have called it, an approach, and one that goes hand in hand with far-reaching policy decisions that determine, for example, which architecture firms can and cannot bid for public projects (such as in the UK where those who are 'Level 2' BIM compliant can, whereas those who aren't, can't). And because BIM as a conceptual approach goes right to the heart of who we are as architects, and touches on the ethos, practice, and nature of our profession, it is also incumbent on us to highlight the reasons this is seen as so problematic by so many people.

We are used, in architecture and construction, to apply, and comply with, standards; there are safety regulations and building restrictions at every turn, so working with and within these can hardly be the issue. Also, it seems astonishing, even from a non-BIM-oriented stance, that the same quarter century into CAD as we are into BIM, we should not be using, and using much more routinely, semantic information about the elements we're designing and ultimately building with.

As regards standards, an argument can and is being made that with the global indexation of products and construction elements, such as provided by Google, and machine learning algorithms, ■ ↖486 536↘
standards are in fact no longer necessary to achieve

the aims of BIM, and that therefore, while the ambition of seamless collaboration and information-rich, intelligent modelling is absolutely worth pursuing, the methodology of BIM is simply out of step with techno-
□ 549↘ logical developments. (We talk more about Big Data & Machine Learning in our chapter on the topic.) Still, this does not sound like the fundamental problem.

What, then, is the problem?

The problem is of a principal, and therefore political nature. BIM, one side will argue, offers a path towards transparency and collaboration, cost efficiencies and standards, not at the expense of creativity or design, but through cutting waste, eliminating laborious routines, and minimising the potential for error or wilful mismanagement and corruption. The other side argues that BIM imposes an old-fashioned, already outdated paradigm on an entire industry, not in the public interest, but in the interest, mainly, of commercial operators who from all this have much to gain. Rather than allowing for a cultural, self-determined pace of change towards a digitality that keeps itself dynamic, alive, and in tune with what is happening at every level – on the Internet, in apps, in small startups, in the 'real' virtual world – BIM forces itself upon practitioners and makes everybody obey big corporate and institutional clients who are, correspondingly in a big corporate and institutional mindset. 'BIM,' we have heard one voice say, 'is an unashamed march of the bureaucrats, and all the smaller offices and organisations are being forced to fall in line: that's breathtaking.'

So the views that people hold on BIM are strong, and as convinced as are its proponents, as passionate are its objectors. And that is worth bearing in mind as we look at the application of BIM in practice.

BIM in Practice

LEVELS OF BIM

BIM being an approach rather than a single technology, there are, unsurprisingly, many different ways in which it can be implemented. And also different levels or degrees to which this is done. In the UK – according to Ishveena Singh in *Geospatial World* as at April 2017, "the undisputed BIM champion of the world" – the government has spelt out 4 levels to usher in a phased alignment with BIM, as we've already seen. Because they are simply formulated and therefore summarise well the various degrees to which BIM may be in use in any given setting – whether in an area where these levels are official policy or not – we are happy to list them for you here in full:

> *LEVEL 0*
> Projects will use only 2D computer-aided design (CAD) drafting. There is very little collaboration. Any data that is exchanged is typically done so via paper or print.
>
> *LEVEL 1*
> Projects will use a mixture of 2D and 3D CAD drafting. They will use a common data environment for the electronic sharing of data. This will often be managed by the main contractor and may be shared among team members. Projects may also use some standard data structures and formats.
>
> *LEVEL 2*
> Projects will use intelligent, data-rich objects in a managed 3D BIM environment. All parties working on a project are able to combine their BIM and design data to collaborate and share information through the use of a Common Data Environment (CDE). The CDE enables users to carry out checks against data validation strategies to make sure they are on target.
>
> *LEVEL 3*
> Projects at this level are fully collaborative. They use a single, shared project view for data integration, which all parties can access and modify as allowed through process and security controls.

TYPES OF BIM

Similarly, there are broadly speaking four different types of BIM, as follows:

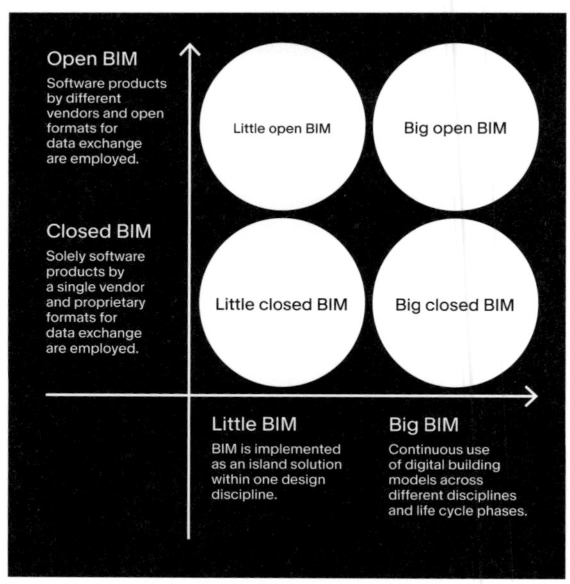

LITTLE BIM VS BIG BIM

A first distinction is made between 'little' BIM and 'big' BIM.

'Little BIM' involves the application of BIM as an 'island', meaning that BIM software is used to

accomplish one particular goal, within only one discipline and over one or few project phases only. In other words, it's the use of BIM by a single practitioner or practice within the parameters of a specific design/development task.

'Big BIM' refers to the use of BIM software across disciplines, over several or many phases or indeed the entire lifecycle of a project, and involves the systematic communication between all project participants throughout.

CLOSED BIM VS OPEN BIM

At any level, and whether big or small, BIM can be divided into two further major categories, 'open' and 'closed'.

'Closed' BIM is the use of a single proprietary software platform with native data exchange formats, meaning that only the software products of this manufacturer can be used, and that data exchange is possible only over the proprietary, software-specific, interface.

'Open' BIM denotes the use of multiple software products, including open-source programs and open, model-based information exchange formats, such as, for example, IFC, which are not platform or manufacturer dependent.

BIM SOFTWARE TYPES

While Graphisoft's *ArchiCAD* may be regarded as the first full implementation of BIM, there is, as we have noted, not one single BIM software. In fact there is not even one single type of BIM software, as the program you may find yourself using will be very much dependent on the actual use you have for it.

Dan Taylor, in a *Construction Management* blog on the business software research and review site *Capterra*, summarises several basic types of – in this instance specifically free and/or open-source – BIM software tools, which are fairly representative of the scope that's available (examples as at May 2017):

BIM VIEWER

A BIM viewer does not allow you to make a BIM, but, as the name suggests, it allows you to view a 3D model and customise or tweak its presentation options. (It is, perhaps, what an *Adobe Reader* is to *Photoshop*.) Examples include *BIMx* by Graphisoft and *BIM Vision*.

STANDARD OFFICE APPLICATION-BASED BIM

This is the use of BIM with standard office applications such as Microsoft's *Excel* or the free *OpenOffice Calc* to view and manipulate BIM data as simple spreadsheet tables, in the non-proprietary COBie (Construction Operations Building Information Exchange) format.

BIM AS A BOLT-ON FOR CAD SOFTWARE

While many would argue that the whole point of BIM is that it offers a fundamentally different approach to 'ordinary' CAD, the reality is that many architects are familiar with CAD and hesitant to 'dive into' BIM headlong. A 'bolt-on to CAD' is a program that offers BIM functionality within the familiar CAD setting and as such presents something of a compromise or entry point for people who find themselves needing, rather than particularly wanting, to use BIM, for example *FreeCAD*.

BIM SOFTWARE TOOLKIT

As Dan Taylor puts it: "A software toolkit can be adapted or used to build a variety of BIM solutions, including extensions to existing applications. However, that means possessing or having access to the relevant software programming skills." Examples include *xBIM (eXtensible Building Information Modelling)* and *BIMServer*.

BIM FROM THE START

This is software that has been purpose-designed for building information modelling and offers full BIM functionality. Examples include *B-processor* and *4BIM*, and, of course, any of the commercial proprietary offerings on the market, including *ArchiCAD*.

BIM CATEGORIES

Much as there are different types of BIM software, so there are several different categories, into which some or any of these may fit. Commonly identified BIM categories as at 2018 include:

- *Architecture*
- *Sustainability*
- *Structures*
- *MEP (Mechanical, Electrical and Plumbing)*
- *Construction (simulation, estimating, and construction analysis)*
- *Facility management*

CDES AND CDE

The actual data of a BIM is usually shared in what are known as *Common Data Environments (CDEs)*. Stefan Mordue, a writer on the Chartered Institute of Building's *BIM+* website calls the CDE, "the digital space where BIM data flows," and explains:

> "The Common Data Environment (CDE) is simply a digital place in which the information comes together. With vast amounts of digital data being created and shared during a project's lifecycle, the CDE becomes an ideal environment in which to promote a collaborative working culture. It should be the foundation from which you facilitate, manage and disseminate data and project information between multi-disciplined teams in a managed process throughout the project lifecycle."

To make things just that bit less straightforward, there is also a piece of software called *Common Desktop Environment*, which therefore is also known as *CDE*. This started out as a proprietary *desktop environment* – the generic term used for software that enables different programs to run with a shared Graphical User Interface (GUI) – developed by Unix, but has since been released as open-source. *CDE*, as in *Common Desktop Environment* is used to handle specific purposes, such as claims management, ↖334 for example, or IFC files. It is therefore possible to find yourself both in a Common Data Environment CDE and in a *Common Desktop Environment CDE* at the same time, though for different reasons and to different ends.

DATA MODEL AND CONTENTS

We have, throughout this chapter, emphasised the use and value of semantic information that is the cornerstone of a BIM. Even so, the purpose of the BIM is not simply to accumulate as much data as is possible in any and every case. The amount of data – the *data level,* as it is known – wants to be in tune with the purpose of the model. It is therefore not necessary a case of integrating all the data there is, but of selecting the right data to integrate at the right level, and this depends very much on what the BIM is intended for.

So determining what a BIM is going to be used for is essential if it is to be useful at all. Here are some – by no means all – of the common uses of BIM:

Technical visualisation	The visualisation of a 3D model as the basis for being able to talk about it in project discussions and showing it to the public.
Coordination of specialist trades	Bringing together specialist trade models in a coordination model for the purpose of collision evaluation and systematic conflict resolution.
Plan derivation	Deriving design and execution plans from the master model.
Cost estimation and calculation	Establishing quantities (volumes, surfaces) based on the model for the purpose of producing cost estimates and calculations.
Specification, tendering, awarding of contract	Defining model-based specifications in the contexts of tendering and the awarding of project contracts.
Structural planning	Using BIM for the purposes of structural calculation and verification.
Work flow modelling ('4D' modelling)	Tying the 3D model into the project work flow and timeline.
Time-based simulation of cost ('5D' modelling)	Tying the '4D' model into the cost calculations for the production of relevant construction elements.
Project progress control	Using the model to monitor and evidence actual construction progress.
Accounting	Using the model for financial and budget control and final accounting.
Deficiency management / snag lists	Documenting deficiencies and snags, and their resolution.
Operation and maintenance	Adoption of data sets for the purpose of long term site operation and maintenance.

The German company *Hochtief ViCon*, which describes itself as "one of the leading service providers in the field of virtual construction and Building Information Management," to celebrate its 10th anniversary in 2017, published a 'hit list' of the top ten uses their clients put BIM to. While this has to be seen for what it is – one particular company reporting on its own activities – it offers an idea of what the most popular uses of BIM are in this market:

1 3D visualisations
2 3D modelling
3 3D quantity evaluation
4 3D planning coordination
5 3D planning evaluation and approval
6 '4D' construction process planning
7 '4D' construction progress audit
8 '5D' cost planning and budget supervision
9 3D stock documentation
10 Mobile data capture

EXCHANGE REQUIREMENTS
AND LEVELS OF DEVELOPMENT

Which types of use you put your BIM to may not be primarily down to you, but may well be dictated by your client, particularly if they demand BIM integration as part of their terms. In such a case, there will be a cost-benefit analysis for the project in question, from which follows a set of *exchange requirements,* which specify what the contents of the BIM are to be, for various processes.

In practice, and as borne out by experience, the different elements of a BIM will be at different stages of development at any given time, and so for each element there is therefore the need also to specify a *Level of Development (LOD),* whereby a distinction is made between *geometrical* information and *alphanumeric* information. The former is further labelled as **Level of Geometry (LOG)**, the latter simply as **Level of Information (LOI)**, and both may have their own – at times potentially vastly varying – development trajectory.

The international geometric level of development standard that has established itself ranges from LOD 100 to LOD 500. The BIMFORUM (The US Chapter of buildingSMART International) *2017 Level of Specification* documentation comes in two parts plus a guide, all in all encompassing several hundred pages, but in summary, LODs may be structured, for example, as follows:

LOD 100
The element is represented very simply by means of a symbol or a generic marker. Some essential properties, which are necessary for the conceptual pre-planning phase are also defined.

LOD 200
The element is represented with its approximate position and geometry, together with the most important characteristics, especially information relating to cost.

LOD 300
The element is represented with its exact position and geometry, to the level required for construction. Based on this level, the project's execution can be planned and prepared. Normally, this level is also used to establish quantities and service specifications.

LOD 400
The element contains all the geometric and alphanumeric information that is necessary to produce, build, manufacture, or change the element. This includes assembly instructions and any specified building procedures.

LOD 500
The element fully represents the real building element as regards position and geometry, and contains all the necessary data and specifications as well as information and data that is used for the long term supervision and management.

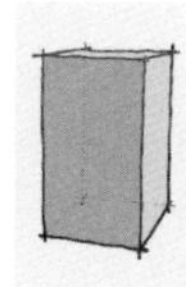
323A ● 526

323B ● 526

323C ● 526

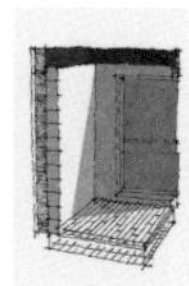
323D ● 526

323E ● 526

Levels of Information (LOIs) tend to be defined on a project basis, as there are no national or international standards for this as yet.

PROCESS MAP AND EXECUTION PLAN
The more or less final piece in this very large jigsaw puzzle is the BIM *Execution Plan*, which is pretty much self-explanatory: a timeline that lists all the relevant roles, processes, data exchange points, and deadlines with agreed specified Levels of Detail (LODs).

Also in this context, you come across the process map, which acts as a flowchart for the various modelling and data capture and handling processes.

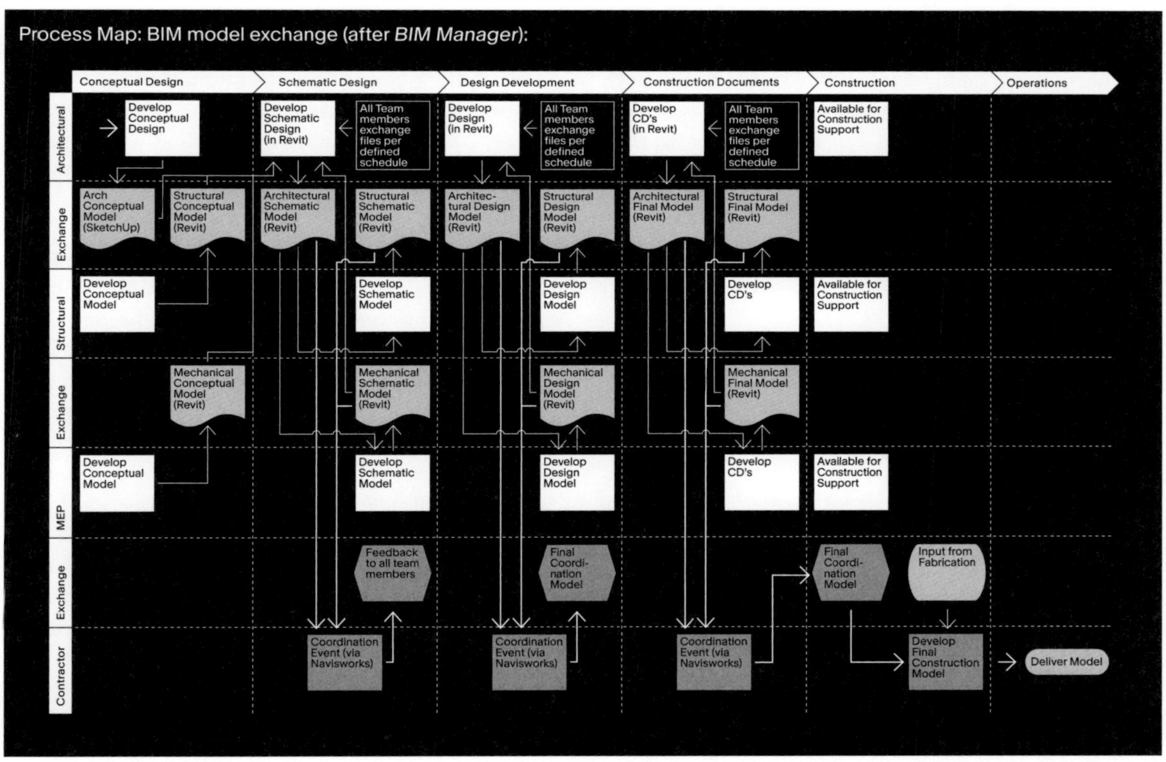

Process Map: BIM model exchange (after *BIM Manager*):

CLASSIFICATION
Similarly important for the BIM to work is a consistent and by all project participants agreed-upon system of classification, which structures and standardises terminology. This prevents misunderstandings and disallows the same type of element or component being called different things by different people working on the same project. The two most commonly used classification systems are, from the United States Omniclass, and from the United Kingdom Uniclass. In Germany, DIN276 is partly in use as a classification system, but this is not comprehensive, concerning itself mostly, as by origin it does, with cost.

MODEL CHECKING
With so many pieces of information contained in one

model (or set of models), and so many factors depending on this information being correct, checking the entire system for accuracy becomes vitally important. For this purpose, there are specialist model checker tools, which are able to not only check conformity with standards, classes, levels, and conventions, but also to detect errors such as geometric overlaps or gaps.

EMPLOYER'S INFORMATION REQUIREMENT (EIR)
The employer in question here is the client who awards the project. Spelling out and specifying in detail what their information requirement is from all involved parties should help to ensure that everybody knows what kind of information they need to supply and feed into the model, and at what level. This can also be important during the tendering phase, where parties pitching for a contract can be held to a clear set of conditions that are to be met in order to be eligible for a contract.

A typical EIR should cover points such as:

- Which phase of the project do the EIRs relate to (in Germany these will correspond to the *Honorarordnung für Architekten- und Ingenieurleistungen [HOAI] Leistungsphasen)*
- Aims: what is the employer/client aiming to achieve by using BIM?
- Application: what are the specific applications for which BIM is being used?
- Scope: which parts of the project are to be modelled compliant with BIM?
- Basis of modelling: which digital and analogue materials will be made available by the employer/contractor for the generation of the model? Are there BIM construction element libraries whose use is compulsory?
- Geometric level of digitalisation: which Level of Geometry (LOG) is required for individual construction elements?
- Semantic level of information: which Level of Information (LOI) is required?
- Classification: is there a classification system in use? Which attributes do construction elements have to have?
- Coordinate systems in use
- Data exchange formats in use
- Data exchange points: which type of information has to be made available when and how?
- Quality control: how will quality control be carried out both on employer/client side and on contractor/employee side? (The employee here being the entity that is carrying out the project.)
- Shared data environment: how will the shared data environment be realised; who carries responsibility for it (employer or employee), whose naming and status conventions are operational?
- Roles and responsibilities: which roles and responsibilities are being filled/covered by whom?

BIM JOBS

BIM is a 'growth sector' and there are, as we write this, a great many opportunities for people who are skilled and experienced in using BIM. In many instances, particularly in smaller offices, there will be an overlap between BIM and other types of design and project management software that a young architect will encounter and be expected to be able to use, but there is also a steadily expanding job market for BIM specialists.

The following are three examples of BIM jobs, pitched in ascending order of seniority and therefore responsibility:

BIM MODELLER
Typically, a BIM Modeller's role will include tasks such as:

- Developing BIM execution plans (usually with support from a BIM Manager)
- Setting up new project models in accordance with given project standards
- Working with the Project Manager and various discipline engineers to define deliverables schedules, and implementing these within the model
- Supporting the project team with technical delivery using specialist BIM software
- Producing structural models
- Coordinating models
- Producing drawings of models

A BIM Modeller will usually have to be skilled and experienced to some specified level in using BIM software such as *Revit* or *AutoCAD* in the preparation of drawings and models, and have some knowledge of structural systems and how to coordinate them.

Qualifications required will normally lie in the fields of engineering, construction, management, or architecture, and most openings are likely to presuppose a familiarity with industry standards, BIM execution plans, and command of some programming skills.

BIM COORDINATOR
A BIM Coordinator is responsible for the coordination of the processes of generating and managing the digital models that are generated and maintained as part of a BIM project.

They therefore need to have an in-depth understanding, knowledge, and experience of the role of BIM Modeller and be able to draw on a high level of expertise in construction and architecture generally, as they will also find themselves on site, monitoring progress on the project compared to the BIM, and need to be capable of adjusting, updating, and overseeing the maintenance of the model.

BIM Coordinator is usually a mid-weight supervisory role and therefore requires the attendant personal, communication, and management skills that come with working in a collaborative setting and being responsible for other team members.

BIM MANAGER
The BIM Manager oversees BIM Coordinators and BIM Modellers and is responsible for the development and maintenance of the BIM throughout a project's lifecycle.

As a senior role, the BIM Manager is tasked with identifying – ideally anticipating – any problems, clashes, complications, or difficulties before they escalate into a crisis, and they have to be actively involved in finding solutions for any issues that do arise. They are responsible for the BIM being aligned with the BIM execution plan, and obviously they need to be fully conversant with the processes and software involved in setting up, developing, and successfully managing a BIM.

Since BIM Managers work closely with other senior members of a project's delivery team, and have direct contact and communication with clients, subcontractors, partner firms, suppliers, and their own teams, they are expected to be good communicators and in possession of leadership skills.

A Conclusion and Outlook

As far back as 1974, Charles Eastman – he of BDS fame mentioned earlier – wrote in his paper entitled *An Outline of the Building Description System*:

> "Architectural drawings have many inherent weaknesses. They are highly redundant, describing the same part of a building at several different scales. Since drawings are two-dimensional and a building three-, at least two drawings are required to characterize any part of the building arrangement, and on these, at least one dimension must be depicted twice. Thus information on drawings is inherently redundant and a design change leads to changes in a whole set of drawings. A large amount of effort is directed at keeping the various drawings consistent."

Hardly anybody would argue with that. Or that 3D modelling is the way forward, and in fact has been for nearly half a century now. Yet still, no other chapter in this *Atlas* raises quite so many questions that are quite so directly politically charged as BIM. This is no coincidence. As we have said at the very beginning, BIM is an approach, a methodology, and with this comes a mindset – a way not only of doing things but also of looking at the world – and therefore a cultural statement. The one thing everyone seems to be in agreement on is that BIM goes beyond the confines of an architectural solutions toolkit and that it has vast, long-lasting implications for urban planning, civic space development, and the role of the architect today and into the future.

For these reasons, we are treating these final pages in this chapter as both, something of 'a conclusion' (this is in itself a misnomer, since nothing, at this point, can really be concluded about BIM: it is very much a thing in flux and progress), and the usual 'outlook'.

If we go back to the strongest criticisms levied at BIM – that, in an age of Cloud computing, it is cumbersome and old-fashioned and liable to produce '*Lego* architecture', giving commercial interests, project management, and the bureaucracy of very large and therefore mighty clients the upper hand over architects as space creators, we have to ask ourselves the question, to what degree is any of this justified and does BIM by necessity stifle creative, organic, artistic building? Put somewhat simply: can you create art with BIM?

The Royal Academy of Arts in London seems to think so. Its annual *Summer Exhibition* traditionally dedicates the Large Weston Room to architecture, and in the 2017 edition the focus was on 'construction coordination drawings'. Featured prominently, and thus sharing the gallery with works by, among many others, Anthony Gormley, Tracey Emin, Anish Kapoor, Anselm Kiefer, and Gilbert & George, were parametric X-ray projections of the Battersea Power Station redevelopment and an X-ray projection of the BIM for the Crown Sydney building.

At the basis of BIM are parametric methods, which allow for forms of architecture that would previously have been simply impossible. This suggests that the argument that BIM limits design and creates '*Lego* architecture' is, if not strictly unfounded, then also not strictly solid, and not likely to remain valid in the medium to long term.

Clearly there are commercial interests that encourage, even entice, planners to use pre-defined construction elements, and there are similarly commercial interests associated with the software products that are used in BIM, but as we have noted, these pre-defined elements can be customised and there are open-source BIM tools available.

What BIM does, above all, is change the way we work, specifically the way we work together. Yes, there are technological foundations, yes standards and specifications are being established, but what you do with these as an architect is, if not entirely, then to quite some extent up to you. The point of BIM is not simply to introduce into your workflow digital tools: for BIM to be successful, the way in which studios and practices on the one hand, and projects on the other, are organised has to adapt, and this by necessity presupposes that people working with BIM embrace the collaborative culture it entails. Therein lie some of BIM's principal advantages: that it integrates and encourages the coming together of different fields of expertise very early on. It means that mistakes or flaws can not only be detected earlier, or responsibility for them allocated, but that weak spots or links in the model can be identified before actual mistakes or errors are made: that it helps identify those areas on a project which in collaboration between the various experts involved still have to be further, and more deeply, developed.

So, yes, of course, it is possible to 'do' BIM on the cheap and cobble together lazy architecture; it is equally possible to use it to your creative advantage. And even the notion of 'lazy architecture' may need to be qualified. In certain contexts, architecture just has to be quick, inexpensive, and functional. If you are a city authority and you suddenly find yourself in need of fifty thousand accommodation units for newly arrived refugees, then a solution that allows your appointed architects and their contractors to quickly put up decent housing is most likely welcome. Similarly, at the less extreme ends of a very wide spectrum: not every building is a flagship development, a world class museum, or the new terminal building for an international airport. Some projects are just residential housing, with maybe a creche or a kindergarten, for people who need to be able to afford to live somewhere. And here, at the lower, less spectacular end that we might call the 'bread and butter', as opposed to 'fine dining', level of construction, the ability to optimise and extract the highest possible efficiencies can actually improve the quality of the architecture and therefore of life for its users. In other industries, this is sometimes referred to as 'individual serial production'.

If you look at the work of someone like British-Iraqi architect Zaha Hadid (1950–2016), who features frequently in this *Atlas,* and for good reasons, you can hardly describe it as lacking in creativity or originality. It may or may not be to somebody's taste, but that is an entirely separate matter, and evidently true of any architecture anywhere in the world. At the end of the day, a tool is a tool, and a toolkit a toolkit. You can take a pencil and draw some gorgeous curves on a sheet of pristine paper, or you can stab someone in the eye with it: mostly, it comes down to your own personal disposition…

Also, it is not necessarily the case that BIM is only relevant to big projects and therefore big architecture and engineering practices. In the right hands, BIM can enable a single person to pursue their own ambitions and grow their niche business, as perhaps the example of AEC *Architectes* Rotzer & Kaempfer in the French speaking part of Switzerland might illustrate. Originally strong-armed into buying BIM software, what started out as a one-man band doing bespoke wooden objects, the office has since grown into a successful architecture, interior design, and
■ ↖480 637↘
furniture business. In a context like this you could argue that BIM, rather than limiting the architect, allows the architect to lead and flourish.

Where BIM can make the life of the architect easier in particular is in taking dull, repetitive tasks, such as generating and maintaining item lists and costing proposals, off their hands. These are often exactly the points at which human error creeps in, and many a marvellous design has suffered serious setbacks through relatively minor calculation mistakes that, by the time they were recognised, could no longer be rectified.

The question, then, that primarily poses itself as we look towards the coming years is: why should architects suddenly do everything differently to how they have done things before. It is, in other words, one of cultural change. And cultural change tends to meet with resistance, for very understandable reasons. If you have spent years, possibly decades, getting good at what you are doing, and a combination of pressure from clients and the mere availability of new sets of tools imposes itself on you to start learning new approaches, you may well feel less than ecstatic about the prospect. Add to that the fact that quite objectively much of the software is far from perfect at this stage. Many applications are still complex and difficult to use, and they are often what you might call counterintuitive, especially to the creative mind. Then again, when CAD first appeared on the architectural scene, it too was far from perfect, and many people felt it would hem in architects' freedom, yet today hardly anyone would consider CAD an imposition. A lot of that has to do with the software having improved and become infinitely more capable. A lot too though has to do with people simply getting used to it and over the years investing not just money but also time and effort into learning how to handle it, and getting good at doing just that.

So it may help to think of BIM neither as a given situation nor as an all-or-nothing proposition. It's a technology in progress, and a methodology in development, and it is not necessary to say a categorical 'yes' or 'no' to BIM. Rather, you have to think about why you would use BIM and in what ways it may make your life easier, and then work out your own process, depending on the kind of project you want to apply it to.

Working with libraries and catalogues of pre-specified elements may not be your thing. To the architect who understands themselves as an artist it may well be anathema. On the hills a few kilometres southeast of Basel, Switzerland, near the village of Dornach, you'll find a rather extraordinary building, the *Goetheanum*, designed by the Austrian philosopher, architect, and esotericist Rudolf Steiner (1861–1925). Here, no two windows are exactly the same, each door handle looks like it's been designed and made *especially* for that particular door, right angles are virtually absent from the concept, and the whole thing comes as close to a *gesamtkunstwerk* as you probably could in the early 1920s with the then revolutionary method of visible cast concrete. It's worth a visit, because if BIM is, as we ventured early on in this chapter, working with digital clay, this is almost literally formed out of actual physical clay models, in almost the exact opposite process of what you get with **parametric design**.

But nearly a hundred years have passed since that object was created, and today, many would consider it a luxury to think of window frames as individual design elements. In truth, for a very large building with very large glass surfaces, it is really not necessary to do so. Having said that, if you want to achieve something like the 30 St Mary Axe (better known as The Gherkin) building by Foster + Partners, you will end up again with highly specific demands on the shape, size, and strength of your window panels. It is, as in so many spheres of life, the proverbial swings and roundabouts.

What we are suggesting, then, is that there is no conclusive statement to be made, either about BIM or about any other architectural approach. What we would hope is that many of the things that today present so many obstacles will gradually fall by the wayside. As BIM becomes more user friendly and more intuitive, resistance to it should dwindle. That means the user interface of some of the software will need to become more welcoming and easier to get on with for visually minded people, as most architects are. That said, we keep reiterating in this *Atlas* that we expect architects to become code literate; we even go so far as to suggest that it will not in fact be by drawing and by visual representation that the milestone architecture of tomorrow will be created, but by scripting and code, though, for sure, neither will go or happen without the other.

And finally, there is a strong argument to be made for using standards – without which BIM is unthinkable – but in the right way. There has been, over the last few years and maybe decades, a drive towards Europe-wide norms, with an implicit (sometimes explicit) view to aligning look, feel, and practice of many things, not just architecture, across the continent. This does not tend to go down well, nor is it sensible. A building on a Greek island is and should look and feel, actually *be,* different to one on a Scottish isle. The way Italians use their piazzas is different, inherently, culturally, historically, climatically, from the way Norwegians use their town squares. A villa on the Côte d'Azur does not want or need to have the same characteristics as a chalet in the Alps.

We started this chapter with the origins of BIM at Heathrow's Terminal 3. There have been both success stories and also cautionary tales for BIM since then. That BIM is no guarantor for a smooth operation is self-evident, and exemplified nowhere perhaps as comprehensively as in Berlin's Brandenburg Airport. Scheduled to open in October 2011, it is currently (2020) still under construction and tentatively expected to get ready by 2021. Nobody, of course, is suggesting that the project's abject failure so far and to date should be blamed on BIM. It is entirely possible that BIM has already and continues to prevent a much greater construction calamity. But neither is it as simple as saying: BIM is just a tool, how successful it is is down to how good you are at using it; and nor is it possible (or let alone fair) to say that BIM will either categorically make or break a project. Clearly, the factors that play into how useful BIM is in any given context are numerous (so as not to say innumerable), and each project will have its own prerogatives that determine the approach that we take to it.

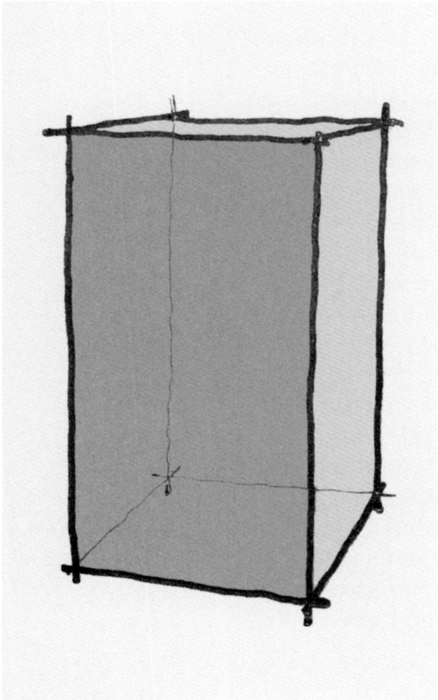

323A ● 521

323B ● 521

Levels of Development (LOD) 100 to 500 (323A–323E). [AI AR TUM]

323C ● 521

323D ● 521

323E ● 521

- Michael Batty: *Defining Geodesign (= GIS + Design?)*, in *Environment and Planning B: Planning and Design*, *40* (1), 1–2, 2013
- Markus Braach: *Solutions You Cannot Draw*, 2014
- Anthony M Townsend, Alissa Chisholm: *Making Sense of the New Urban Science*, 2015

Digital Cities

Reinhard König and Sven Schneider

Overview

"We are living in the age of cities. It is an urgent time, and an uncertain one. Never before have human beings built so much with such haste. Yet we understand so little about how our urban world grows and – sometimes – declines." Thus wrote Anthony M Townsend, then a Senior Research Fellow at the New York University (NYU) Rodin Centre for Transportation & Policy Management, in a paper entitled *Making Sense of the New Urban Science*, which he published in 2015. By the time you read this in 2020 or sometime thereafter, his observation will not have lost its relevance.

The city is without a shadow of a doubt the most important environment we now live in. And it's an environment that is almost entirely human made. Even nature in the city – the parks, the beaches, the riverbanks, the gardens – is carefully designed, adapted, managed, controlled, cultivated. And while there are perhaps not many certainties in an ever, and ever more rapidly, changing world, one thing we can say with some considerable degree of confidence: the process of urbanisation is going to continue.

By the middle of the twentieth century, in 1950, some 30% of people lived in cities. Since then, this proportion has increased steadily, breaching 50% for the first time in 2008, continuing to add just under half a percentage point each year, topping 55% by 2018. That's an average across the globe. In some parts of the world the proportion is much higher, both in emerging economies, such as Brazil (86%), and mature ones, such as the USA (82%). Arguably, even what many people in Europe regard as 'country living' is no longer in that sense rural. It may not be exactly urban either, but it exports the convenience of the city to the greenery of the countryside or suburbia: easily reached by regular transport link and permanently connected by broadband Internet and telephony to everywhere else in the world. And some of the cultural offerings that are specific to the city can now also find their way into the local village or small town cinema, in the form of live-streamed performances from the metropolitan theatres or opera houses, for example. Meanwhile, the fast and accelerating emergence of mega-cities since the second half of the 20th century is not a function of nature, it's a phenomenon of culture. And so, all their problems, their vast iniquities, and gargantuan challenges notwithstanding, they, like all cities, are an expression of civilisation.

And yet, dominant as the city has become, there are in fact no globally accepted standards that spell out what exactly a city is. This, too, is not so surprising, since what defines a city in Western Europe may differ greatly from what defines a city in South East Asia, for example. We're just about to look at some of the physical and social aspects that characterise the city, but what cities across the world largely do have in common is that they offer – or at any rate offer the promise of – lifestyles which are defined by education, economic opportunity and mobility, communication, social exchange, and cultural wealth. And, as in everything else, information technology plays an increasingly significant role in all this.

PRE-DIGITAL CITIES:
THE HISTORICAL BACKGROUND

Accepting that there is no standard definition of the city, we can still identify characteristics that are typical of the city as opposed to a small town, a village, or the remote countryside.

Chief among these is the relative spatial density of a large number of people. This is what makes it possible for overarching urban functions to come about: a hospital, a university, a theatre or concert hall, a sports stadium, a public bath, a stock exchange... – they all become feasible as soon as, and only really when, population density reaches a certain level (you could go as far as to say 'critical mass'), because they are all to a greater or lesser extent dependent on economies of scale, on the availability of support staff and skilled professionals to provide a service or offering, and on sufficient numbers of people needing or wanting that service for it to be both functional and viable. We speak in this context of a **spatial economy**. ■

Similarly, there are social aspects to living amongst many people in close proximity, which may be experienced as great cultural enrichment and opportunity, but can also become alienating or isolating. It is no coincidence that the fear of being surrounded by people is called *agoraphobia:* the fear of the open square, where, for example, traditionally busy markets would be held. By the same token, the city affords a degree of anonymity and with it much greater personal freedoms than can be had in small, tightly-knit communities where fitting in with the approval of your peers and not falling foul of spoken and unspoken rules may be tantamount to survival. Depending on your choices and lifestyle, it is entirely possible, in a big city, to live in a neighbourhood for decades without ever getting to know, or being known to, anyone.

URBAN MODELS

Building on this principle of central locations and functions, the first urban models were being developed from the early 19th century onwards, attempting to explain the formation of cities and the distribution of people in them. An example of this is *The Isolated State*, by German economist Johann Heinrich von Thünen (1783–1850), in which he postulates his very own model of land use with a set of now famous **Thünen rings**. In an age before refrigeration, realtime logistics, rail freight, or motorways, these rings spell out the ideal positioning of agricultural activity in zones around the city so that perishable goods and fuel for cooking and heating would get to the people most quickly, whereas the growing of crops, for example, could be done further away from the most populated areas. ■

About a hundred years later, German geographer Walter Christaller (1893–1969) set out his **central place theory**, the main tenet of which is that settlements ■

function as central places to serve surrounding areas. In 1964, the Argentinian-born American planner and economist William Alonso (1933–1999) published his work *Location and Land Use* in which he built on the Thünen rings model and elaborated further on the rent yields certain types of land could achieve.

Again, it is worth noting – emphasising, even – that the way cities 'happen' or come about varies enormously from one place in the world to another, and from one historical period to the next. In Europe, it is not at all uncommon for a city to reach a 'critical mass' density that allows it to own and provide a plethora of cultural offerings and social amenities from as few as 100,000 inhabitants, which is why European travellers often find it perplexing when they go to emerging economies such as China or Brazil to find cities of two or three million people or more with hardly any advanced urban infrastructure. And in parts of Africa vast agglomerations have formed over the last hundred years that really do not yet possess the characteristics of cities, but rather present quasi-urban sprawls that simply grow because people move towards them from under-resourced rural areas, with no urban planning in place to accommodate and cater either for those who are already there, or let alone for the new arrivals.

TRANSFORMATION

One universal and defining phenomenon of cities is that they not just form, but continually *transform* too. From the very initial stages of becoming a settlement, they change. First they may change from village to city, then from city to metropolis; the influx of people from different cultures and communities will transform them within themselves: neighbourhoods get gentrified, others suddenly acquire a specific ethnic or cultural flavour as people move into parts of town where they have family and friends, and entire areas get repurposed, as economic or industrial settings fall into disuse.

Inescapably, this means also that the models and guiding principles of city planning change. And quite obviously there is no consensus as to what makes a 'good city', neither over time nor across geographies in any given era.

Brasília, the capital built from scratch in the middle of the Brazilian highland plateau, was inaugurated on 21 April 1960 and in 1987 became a UNESCO World Heritage Site. If you go there, you will immediately be struck by the really rather outstanding buildings of its Brazilian architect Oscar Niemeyer (1907–2012) who, together with urban planner Lúcio Costa (1902–1998), almost uniquely among twentieth century architects was able to realise an entire urban vision on a metropolitan scale. The next thing you'll notice is how spaced out it is. And not only are the distances huge, what connects everything are roads with no footpaths. The urban 'ideal', here, that was implemented with absolute rigour, is one of wide open spaces, excellent road connections from one place to another, tiny, self-contained leafy neighbourhoods with local amenity clusters of shops, cafes, and restaurants, and no regard for pedestrians whatsoever. The result is as impressive as it is infuriating, because while you are in a little paradise as long as you drive your car, the moment you try to go places on foot you are done for. This does not mean that it is categorically unpopular: many people who live in Brasília absolutely love their city. It just exemplifies how easily one person's urban utopia can turn into another person's nightmare.

■ ↖512 551↘

On what we may assume to have been a fine summer day in July 1933, a group of architects who made up the fourth *Congrès International d'Architecture Moderne (CIAM)* embarked on a ship called S S Patris in Marseilles and sailed together to Athens, holding on board their conference on urban planning. The unorthodox choice of venue had offered itself after the political situation in Moscow had become too unsteady for the *congrès* to be held there, as originally planned. Top of the 'agenda', as it were, was the concept of the Functional City, which had preoccupied them since their previous meeting in Brussels, three years earlier. Once in Athens, the architects exhibited their studies at a show that was opened by the Prime Minister at the National Technical University of Greece, and then went back on their ship to return to Marseilles, failing, however, to come to any agreement over the merits or otherwise of said functional city.

Probably the most influential member of the congress was Swiss-French architect Le Corbusier (1887–1965), and he, ten years after this event, in 1943, published the *Athens Charter*, in which he built on his own 1935 work *The Radiant City* and the principles of the Functional City presented in Athens. This document had an immense impact on city planning in the post-war years, and Costa and Niemeyer both took many of its findings to heart and implemented them in their designs for Brasília.

With its extreme emphasis on order and structure, and very little room for organic growth or random development, the concept was not without its detractors. One of them, Australian art critic Robert Hughes (1938–2012), minced no words in his 1980 TV documentary series *The Shock of the New* when he declared: "Nothing dates faster than people's fantasies about the future. This is what you get when perfectly decent, intelligent, and talented men start thinking in terms of space rather than place; and single rather than multiple meanings. It's what you get when you design for political aspirations rather than real human needs. You get miles of jerry-built platonic nowhere infested with Volkswagens." Clearly, city planning never has been, nor is it ever likely to be, a matter of straightforward and universally applicable solutions...

THE DIGITALISATION OF CITIES

Digitalisation accelerates transformation. It does so in every sphere of our lives, it does so in the city. Many transformation processes that would constitute extraordinary changes each on their own are currently taking place simultaneously: working methods, artificial intelligence, energy generation and distribution, jobs and the labour market, transport systems, and of course architecture are all undergoing fundamental and extremely rapid shifts. That may be stating the obvious a bit, but cities are not just susceptible to these changes, they are drivers to them. And if that's the case, if cities and what we do with them power these very far-reaching, radical changes that affect every aspect of our lives, then that puts us as architects, much as it does strategists and urban planners and politicians, very much on the spot. It demands of us that we take a stance and that we make informed, even wise, choices that are not only aesthetically compelling and technologically impressive but also ethically sound.

As an example: one of the aspects that puts these developments into particularly sharp relief is the fact that with our current methods for generating energy, and with our prevailing consumer behaviour, we are using way too many resources, and for the wrong things. Although here too a shift is underway and accelerating, we are still largely tied into a model and mode of thinking that treats energy as resources, and consequently we push against the limits of what these resources can do for us. Indeed, right now there is a major disconnect between how we use our resources and what the planet as a whole can provide under current conditions.

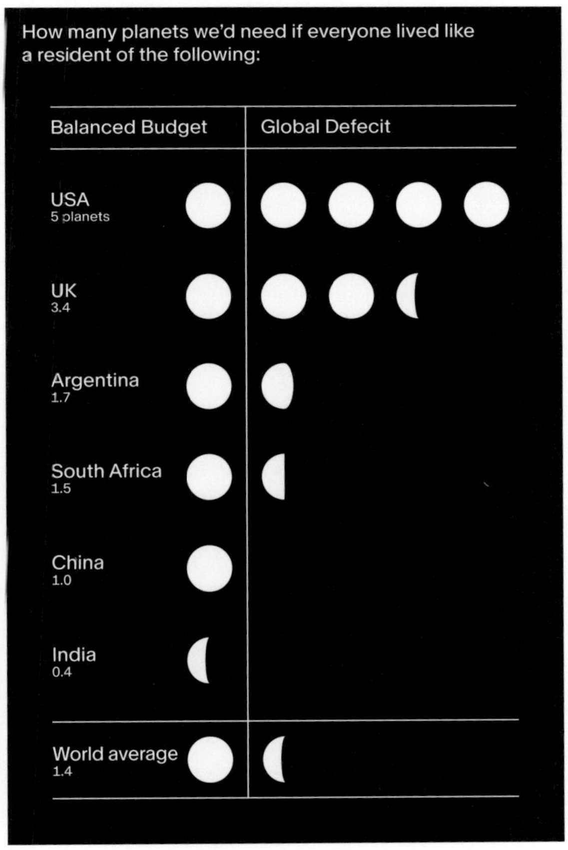

This has prompted the United Nations to define 17 *Sustainable Development Goals*, which were published in September 2015, and of which Goal No 11, *Sustainable Cities and Communities* is defined as: "Make cities and human settlements inclusive, safe, resilient and sustainable." But what is not obvious from Goal No 11 is what exactly we mean by 'inclusive, safe, resilient, and sustainable', nor what kind of questions any of this raises for ourselves both in the post-industrial, fully connected, digital world, and in the developing or emerging world.

Take for example cultural heritage: a Gothic cathedral is not a 'sustainable' building. It makes no sense economically or ecologically. It's a cultural extravagance, and, from a purely utilitarian standpoint, unnecessary. The costs to maintain it are exorbitant, heating it effectively is impossible, and it serves no discernible use on which lives depend. But nobody we take seriously and certainly not we ourselves would argue that the cathedrals of Europe should be closed, repurposed, torn down, or reduced in size so they become 'sustainable'. And that is one specific example. There are millions of instances large and small where we have to weigh one priority against another, where we have to – not just as architects, but as citizens – adapt to the changes, rise to new challenges, and invent ourselves and our lifestyles afresh; decide who we are and what we want from our cities. What's the point of bringing together 70,000 people every other weekend so they can watch twenty-two individuals kick a leather sphere around for 90 minutes, throwing themselves to the ground at regular intervals in pretend agony for being breathed at? None, you could argue: 'that's a complete waste of infrastructure, energy, transportation, emotion, and time, and it's entirely unsustainable!'

As we're about to see and discuss in some detail: in the city today almost literally everything is possible. And that means we have to keep defining what we mean by the city, what, in concrete, real life terms, we want our cities to be, and what we want them to be about. None of this is entirely new, but it's entirely urgent, owing in no small measure to digitalisation. Because in view of these ever faster transformation processes and an obvious need to respond to them with agility and imagination, stringent master plans or design rules for urban spaces are really no longer adequate, if they ever were. Instead, what we are seeing emerge, and what is much more capable of dealing with these dynamic situations, are self-adjusting models which are able to continually respond to evolving circumstances: adaptive urban planning and design models. They, however, require a mindset of fluidity and openness, and an imaginative generosity of spirit.

This is in itself not without its new challenges and conflicts of interest, as we mean to illustrate with the example of 'smart cities'.

SMART CITIES

Hand in hand with the desire to make our urban existence more sustainable, while allowing for its economic potential to be fulfilled and its cultural richness to flourish, goes a need for our cities to become 'smart', because with *smart cities* we do in fact stand a chance of being able to address many of our pressing environmental and social issues. But with the technology for smart cities come vested interests. The high end products that make them possible and that therefore have a very large impact on how we do things are being sold to urban administrations by technology companies which may have priorities that are very different to those of us citizens (let alone to those of us architects), and many a corporate idea of what makes a good neighbourhood solution may be decidedly at odds with what the neighbourhood itself thinks. Also – as recent examples involving 'disrupters' such as Airbnb and Uber have shown – a tech startup may simply have little or no regard for anything resembling a local or regional culture, long established work practices, employment rights, health and safety concerns, or indeed anything at all, other than their own rapid growth and profit.

So before we go any further, we should perhaps address what we actually mean by 'smart cities'. The expression is somewhat flexible and open to interpretation, but the English *Wikipedia* entry offers a serviceable and simply-worded definition, which we are happy in this instance to adopt, if nothing other than to lay out the territory:

> "A smart city is an urban development vision to integrate information and communication technology (ICT) and Internet of Things (IoT) technology in a secure fashion to manage a city's assets. These assets include local departments' information systems, schools, libraries, transportation systems, hospitals, power plants, water supply networks, waste management, law enforcement, and other community services. A smart city is promoted to use urban informatics and technology to improve the efficiency of services."

What this already makes clear is that, although the concept of 'smart cities' is often used in direct conjunction with specific technology developments that are propagated by big players with the primary goal of placing their products, smart cities are not in fact only, and perhaps not even primarily, about technology itself, but about using technology to improve people's lives, for example by creating new social relationships, such as between the well-to-do middle and upper layers of society and disenfranchised ones, for example refugees, by making services accessible and understandable to people irrespective of where they are from or what their educational level is.

A good example of the ambition of a smart city comes from Vienna. Developed by the city authorities together with urban planning experts, it was adopted by the city council on 25 June 2014 and sets out a long-term strategy for Vienna's future. Its own website tells us that:

> "The Smart City Wien framework strategy defines goals for the development of a city that assigns priority to, and interlinks, the issues of energy, mobility, buildings and infrastructure. The framework strategy defines one meta goal for 2050: 'The best quality of life for all inhabitants of Vienna, while minimizing the consumption of resources. This will be realized through comprehensive innovation.'"

Specifically, *Smart City Wien* lists a number of premises on which the development of Vienna as a smart city should proceed:

- Radical preservation of resources
- Holistic planning approaches
- A high level of socially balanced quality of life factors
- The proactive deployment of innovation and technology

What we therefore expect in smart cities – or, for that matter, in digital cities generally – and what we very much witness, is a proliferation of new business models, a reconfiguration of urban services and a rapid progression driven by digital invention. And with these, we are of course seeing the kind of deliberate disruption and reinvention of economic practices and traditions that are not by necessity 'bad' or unwelcome, but that certainly change things. The already cited examples of Uber and Airbnb are particularly pertinent in this context, seeing as they are still quite new (they were both founded in 2008), and have both had a disproportionate impact on their respective industries – private transport and private accommodation – considering their actual size. Rather than owning car pools or premises, or employing large numbers of people to provide their services, they both act effectively as enablers for ordinary people to be economically active in their sector. While this causes upheaval and obvious challenges, it also does create opportunity and potential.

What both these business models have also in common is that they are app driven. And it could be argued that the defining technology component of this early part of the 21st century is in fact the app, and by extension the app-like website, usually tied into it. We say this with no guarantee or even prediction as to how long it will continue to be the case, since we don't know what lies around the corner in terms of inventions and technology. But from dating to casual hookups, from restaurant or chef-prepared meals delivered to your home to perfectly calibrated recipe boxes that you can cook for yourself; naturally any and all kinds of online shopping, car sharing, coach surfing, and banking; the sharing or gig economy, instant connectivity, and the astonishing accuracy of apps such as *CityMapper*, which don't just show you where in a city you are, but dependably work out public transport links for you, taking into consideration temporary obstacles and going as far as advising you in which part of an underground train you are best off riding: these are all potent indicators that we are well and truly leading digital lives and that the principal instrument allowing us to do so is the app. And that was just not the case before the arrival on the scene of the smartphone, just over a decade ago as we write this in 2019.

Throw into the mix concepts such as **eParticipation** and **eGovernment**, by which local, regional, and national authorities enable their citizens to do anything from requesting rubbish clearance to reporting a problem with dog fouling, to filing their tax returns, or registering to vote online, and you have an increasingly comprehensive coverage of all aspects of our urban existence. This goes much further and into quite different territory too: today, there are an estimated 210 million surveillance cameras in operation worldwide. Large global cities, such as London and New York, have particularly high camera to human ratios: in London it is one camera for eleven citizens, which means that on an average day about town in London you are likely to be captured on surveillance cameras more than 300 times.

But that is only the tip of a very substantial iceberg. Through our smartphones we continually let our service providers and app makers know where we are, what we are doing, whom we're talking to, and what we are looking at. We may be adding to congestion in our cars, but at the same time we're also helping to ease that congestion, because mobile networks know where the bottlenecks lie and alert us to them. Obviously, there are any number of weather stations, air pollution monitors, traffic surveillance systems, and security installations that are permanently observed by professional staff, and we are moving towards having our emotions and wellbeing monitored too, with ease.

The multiple award-winning *Sentiment Cocoon* by designer and architect Moritz Behrens and lighting designer Konstantinos Mavromichalis is a charming example of a relatively low tech, but engaging sculptural installation. Originally on display at the Arup headquarters in London and subsequently in an adapted installation in Australia, it responds to how people feel through a simple interface. It's a playful example that was carried out as an experiment. But as technology advances become rapidly and vastly more sophisticated, real time emotional maps of an entire city, for example, are no longer an outlandish idea. (See also our chapter on Big Data & Machine Learning.)

324 ● 544

The implications all of this has for our lives are immense and we ignore them at our peril, because while the convenience of most of these apps and services is forever attractive, the infringement they signify on what we once used to consider our private sphere is also staggering. We are all of us familiar with Facebook and *Instagram* and we may or may not have misgivings about their reach and the pictures and personal data they mine, but once again, this is just the 'friendly' side of us becoming the product. Every Google search, every email composed on their platform, every tweet, every comment, every 'like', and every app downloaded, obviously every website we visit and every place we go using something like London's *Oyster* card or the amazingly end-to-end integrated *SwissPass*, everything we buy using our store or loyalty card, or our bank or credit card for that matter, and anything we buy or pay for with our phone, is registered, processed, and will, invariably, be used in one way or another. Perhaps not strictly against us – providers such as Facebook and Twitter are at pains to convince us that all they are doing is make our online experience 'more relevant' to us – but most likely not only with our best interests at heart.

Much of this erstwhile 'privacy' we surrender voluntarily. We 'check in' at restaurants and bars to let our circle of friends know we're having a splendid time, we sprinkle our newsfeed with pictures of ourselves in all manner of joyous situations, we allow ourselves to be found by friends in the vicinity, and we naturally use the electronic passport gates which recognise us from our stored photograph, even if it's nearly ten years out of date: it takes an astonishingly small amount of data to positively identify a person from a picture; forty pixels between the eyes is the figure that has been quoted to us by a technology expert.

At the developer conference *Build 2017*, Microsoft introduced their not uncontroversial *Video Indexer*. Sold to the tech community as a democratiser of surveillance technology, this online platform allows absolutely anyone to upload their video footage and have it analysed by the algorithm for individuals featuring in them, for keywords, and searchable themes.

It is now not only possible, but also in some companies already practice, to microchip employees. We've been doing this with pets for years, and the technology is clearly safe. It also brings us ■
another step closer to a melding of ourselves with technology. And again, the practical advantages of □ 549↘
being able to gain access to your company building and using the photocopier without having to flash a badge will in many people's minds far outweigh any squeamishness they may have about carrying a chip under their skin. And the question of course with all these developments is where, if ever, does it end? Does it even have to end? Maybe it doesn't. Maybe we are on a trajectory to becoming fully fledged hybrids; this is entirely possible, and who's to say that it would necessarily be a bad thing. If cancers, dementia, blindness, deafness, severe disability, and straightforward ageing can all be alleviated or eradicated by doing so, what's not to like?

None of this, you may argue, has anything directly to do with urban planning or let alone architecture. Except of course it does, because it delivers the backdrop, the stage, so to speak, on which we will have to do city planning and architecture into the immediate and intermediate future. If – as will very shortly be commonplace – much of urban traffic is made up of autonomous vehicles, does this make the urban road situation better or worse? Will we be safer, or more at risk? All this data at our disposal: what are we going to do with it? How will we define our ideal urban spaces: vast and abstract like Brasília, or compact and characterful like Basel?

The American founding executive director of *Wired* magazine Kevin Kelly (b. 1952) used the title *Out of Control* for his 1994 book about "the new biology of machines, social systems, and the economic world," and it is perhaps not entirely hyperbolic of him to have done so. Certainly, we are relinquishing control on a grand, unprecedented scale. And that's what we have to be acutely aware of as we go on making cities for our 21st century and beyond.

So, having set the scene, as it were, let us delve more deeply then, and in more concrete terms, into digital urban planning.

Urban Planning and Design

Among the first people to look into the way information technology can do urban design was the Greek-American architect Nicholas Negroponte (b. 1943), who in 1967 founded the MIT (Massachusetts Institute of Technology) Architecture Machine Group to study human-computer interaction. In 1970, he published a book called *The Architecture Machine*, in which he looks forward to a time when, "genuine ■ ↖512 562↘ man-machine dialogue is achieved, when man and machine will act together on something closer to equal terms toward a common goal, each contributing his-its own characteristic faculty." This was followed ■ in 1976 by *Soft Architecture Machines*, which offered something of an update and a radical extension to the thinking: "The general assumption of this new book is that the architect is an unnecessary and even detrimental middleman between individual, continuously changing needs and the continuous incorporation of those needs into the built environment. The book proposes a new kind of architecture without architects, and even without surrogate architects." In the intervening period, there was also a title called *Urban 5: A Machine That Discusses Urban Design*.

The idea that the architect can be thought out of the equation entirely, moreover that they are, if anything, an obstacle to design may send a shiver of considerable discomfort down the spine of anybody who is studying architecture, and not everybody, obviously, would agree with him. It is nevertheless interesting that these far-reaching pronouncements were made at a time when CAD was in its infancy, when the vast majority of architecture offices weren't even using computers yet, and when the concepts of ■ ↖479 581↘ ■ ↖517 **ubiquitous computing** and **machine learning** were still being treated as theoretical notions, rather than as imminent realities.

A quarter of a century later, in 1996, Australian-born architect and urban designer William J Mitchell (1944–2010) uses his book *City of Bits* to formulate a vision of a digital city that by now is informed by a technological context in which computing has learnt to walk, and where the Internet, though still young, heralds an era of the connected city.

DIGITAL URBAN PLANNING

Before we consider the more advanced methods available for urban analysis and synthesis, let's take a look at the basics of collecting and managing digital urban data.

GEOGRAPHIC INFORMATION SYSTEMS (GIS)

□ ↖491 ■ ↖270 We dedicate a whole chapter to Geographic Information Systems (GIS) in this *Atlas*, so we don't want to delve into any great detail here, but clearly they play a significant role in digital urban planning, and so a brief summary overview will not go amiss.

GIS were originally developed to manage large, space-related data sets, and although there have been moves towards integrating GIS into the design process, it is currently still quite a laborious task to create for instance an urban development proposal with a GIS, which is why these systems are not often used for actual design purposes. Instead, they principally serve the purpose of doing evaluations and urban analyses.

Technologically speaking, a GIS is in essence a databank in which each entry relates to a specific real life location on Earth. In order to give these spatial relationships unambiguous definitions, they are normally referenced using global coordinate systems with exact values for longitude and latitude. By contrast, ordinary **CAAD (Computer Aided Architectural Design)** systems tend to work with local coordinates that are unrelated to global positioning. Also specific to GIS is that, unlike CAAD, the data sets are not organised in layers, but in **feature classes**, whereby a feature class will contain, for example, all polygons or all points, or lines, or captions in a particular region.

Popular GIS include *QGIS* – the Q here stems from '*Quantum*', as the program was previously known by the name *Quantum GIS* – which is a well-developed, free open-source software, originally released in 2002. The leading commercial (and correspondingly expensive) product is *ArcGIS* by Esri.

For the type of urban analysis examples we're about to discuss, there are various GIS implementations or plugins, and apart from numerous spatial analysis methods, GIS also offer integration of web services, which allow the user to access GIS data banks online via a dedicated website. This means that most GIS functions can today also be used through web interfaces. Map applications, such as *Google Maps* and *Google Street View* draw on GIS data banks; in fact, the calculation of routes is a particularly good example for a GIS web service. *OpenStreetMap (OSM)*, meanwhile is an open GIS data bank that aims to make spatial data for the whole world accessible and therefore allows anyone to download entire data sets for free.

If you think concepts such as *Google Street View* or *Google Earth* through to their next level and beyond, you ultimately arrive at a complete digital copy of the real world. Depending on how many sensors (for example smartphone platforms such as Google's *Tango* or the on-board cameras of autonomous vehicles) capture and measure our physical world, we can have a quasi realtime virtual version of it, together with the multitude of possibilities (and also potential dangers) this brings. (German sci-fi and crime writer Tom Hillenbrand [b. 1972] conjures up an intriguing scenario in his novel *Drohnenland*, which has investigators move in such a virtual copy of the real world, able to intervene and interact with it, while remaining invisible to it.)

URBAN 3D MODELS

Apart from 3D models such as *Google Earth*, which are generated algorithmically, using **photogrammetry** from satellite imagery, there are also 3D models which are created manually. These are often better suited for planning purposes, because they consist of simple planes and solids, and they are capable of varying levels of detail:

325A ● 544

325B ● 544

325C ● 544

325D ● 544

Today it is possible to create urban 3D models simply by analysing ordinary pictures harvested online, and contemporary digital urban models have the ambition to integrate as much geographically referenced data as possible; in other words, they complement geometrical elements with semantic information about what their function or meaning is, and how they are used.

As we write this, a lot of work is being put into developing open formats for urban 3D models that contain all relevant details, such as the energy consumption of a building, for example. One such model that is well known and forms the basis for most German urban 3D models is CityGML, where GML stands for Geography Markup Language, which is an XML or Extensible Markup Language developed by the Open Geospatial Consortium (OGC), which in turn is a global voluntary consensus standards organisation.

Digital urban 3D models are at the core of simulating such factors as microclimates, wind, noise, traffic, and solar irradiation, which makes them a particularly useful tool during the planning process. (See also our chapter on Simulation and several links to online examples, which you'll find by following the QR code on the title page of this chapter.)

326 ● 544

Virtual Singapore is a good example of a research and development project that tries to unite the two digital models of GIS and BIM (Building Information Modelling), on which we also have a chapter in this *Atlas*. Both approaches fuse geometrical data with semantic information and store these in a database. The main difference between them lies – simply put – in their respective visual representation method: BIM represents elements through solid geometry, while GIS shows spatial elements through plane models. But we expect that these two types of modelling will continue to move closer together and in due course become an integrated digital model type capable of representing all objects and object elements on all scales.

WHAT-IF AND HOW-SHOULD-IT-BE APPROACHES

In urban design and planning, it is not uncommon to use analysis and simulation to evaluate finished designs and to proof their quality and robustness. But these same methods have the potential to lead the design process right from the beginning. So in this section we want to look at the 'what if' approach to forecasting, and compare this to 'backcasting', which asks the reverse question: 'how should it be?' With this latter approach, you define what performance your design solution needs to achieve and get the software to automatically query the project and generate a set of best possible solutions. This kind of computational planning offers a built-in mechanism to test that you as the designer meet the stated requirements of the original design brief.

URBAN SIMULATION AND LARGE SCALE URBAN MODELLING (LSUM)

As their name suggests, what-if models run through simulations of what happens if I do this or that to the ■ ↖501
setup in my model. They are among the most widely ■
used types of modelling, and they are similar to what ■ ↖511
SimCity does for its players: they are used to predict the development of urban regions and systems – for example demand on transport infrastructure, internet usage, variations to the labour market – based on scientific insights into the way their subsystems work. They therefore allow for a detailed examination or analysis of the dynamic effects individual parts □ ↖475
of the system have upon each other. Since urban simulations tend to cover a whole urban system (as illustrated in the scheme below), they are also called *Large Scale Urban Models (LSUM)*. One of the most comprehensive LSUMs is *UrbanSim*, which, on its own website, describes itself as follows:

> "Regardless of which geographic representation is used, the model structure is similar. Households and businesses (jobs) move and make location choices as the regional economy grows, and real estate developers add housing and nonresidential buildings in □ ↖507
> response to changes in demand, and subject to local development constraints. Price and rent models predict the pricing outcomes in the real estate market, and adjust to reconcile shifts in demand and supply. A simplified flowchart illustrates this process below."

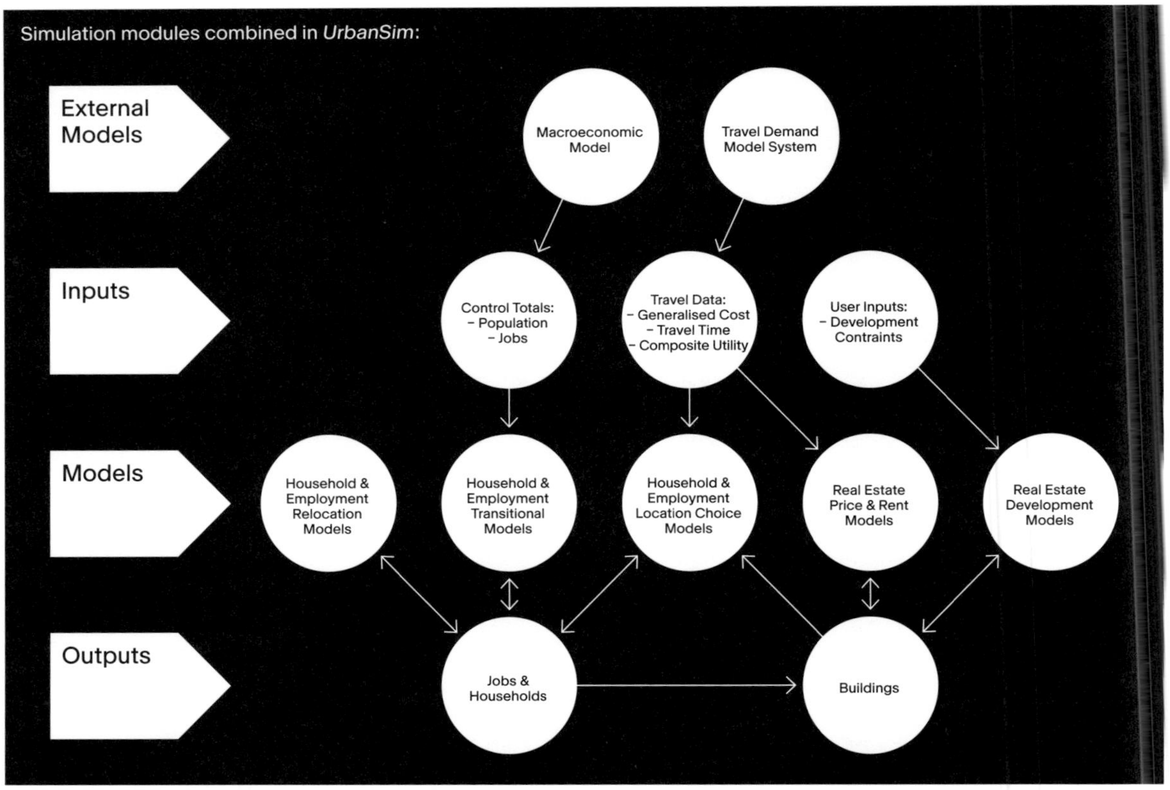

LSUMs such as *UrbanSim* also include many urban analysis methods, which we'll discuss separately a bit further down in this chapter. The main difference between these methods is that analysis is primarily used on a bigger scale, for whole cities, regions, and countries, as opposed to individual objects, and that therefore the spatial representation is abstracted into a cell-based resolution. Furthermore, the timescale for LSUMs is typically given yearly, in 5-year steps. This means that one iteration of a simulation represents the changes of one year in reality.

Standard urban simulation models cope well with scenarios such as, 'what happens if I lay down a new railway line to this area', or, 'how will a large investment of public housing affect this part of the city', whereas less spectacular interventions, such as greening a residential street or connecting cycling paths, often don't yield many great insights with these models. (We will consider methods for spatially more granular analyses in the section that follows).

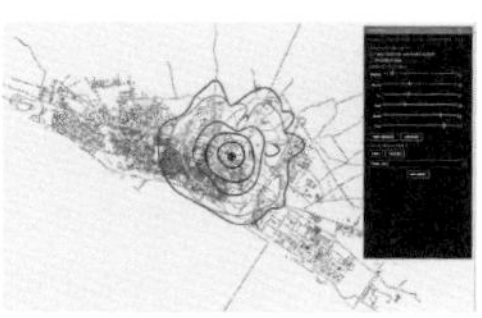

327A ● 545

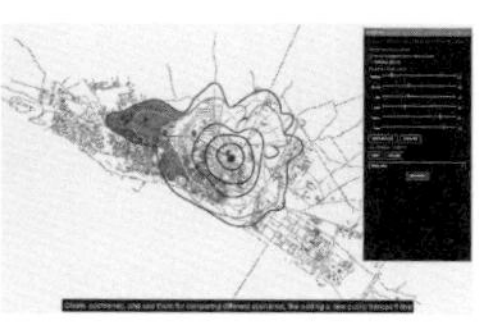

327B ● 545

Another sophisticated and therefore data hungry and complicated approach that is nevertheless widely used comes in the form of **agent-based simulations**, such as land use transportation models. The focus of these is to either simulate traffic based on a land use map (demand), or the other way round, to simulate potentials for new land use based on current traffic. A well-known exponent of this type of model is *MATSim*:

Inherent in any type of urban modelling or simulation is the principal difficulty that it cannot factor in technology that has not yet been developed. The pace of technological advancement is such, though, that even over a relatively short stretch, such as five or ten years, certainly over twenty years – in urban planning terms not an unrealistic time-frame – game-changing new inventions may enter the frame which render any previous forecasts or predictions effectively obsolete. What-if models may help us evaluate all kinds of imaginable future scenarios, but that smartphones would lead to a service like *FourSquare*, for example, was really not foreseeable for most people only fifteen twenty years ago.

URBAN ANALYSIS

URBAN MORPHOLOGICAL ANALYSIS

Urban morphology is the geometry of streets, plots, and buildings. Understanding morphology is essential for urban planners, since, once built, it persists over long periods of time and thus has a long term influence on the urban user: the citizen.

There are different criteria that can be computed, based on a given urban morphology. For example:

DENSITY

At its most basic, density refers to the number of people that are living in an urban area (people per hectare: P/ha). But it also concerns itself with land consumption: the amount of surface area that is used by the population. The denser the population, the less land needs to be consumed for habitation and can therefore be used for other things, such as agriculture.

Density is also a measure for the authorities or government to regulate urban developments: an investor, for example, may want to build residential units for as many people as possible, but this might overstretch the local infrastructure or lead to overcrowding.

ACCESSIBILITY
Accessibility indicates how easy it is to access goods or people in an urban location. It can be assessed by applying network analysis methods to streets and buildings. Basis for this is the transfer of a city model to a graph: streets and houses become vertices, their relationship to each other edges (a house connects to a street, the street to another street, that street to another street, that street to another building – see also our chapter on Graphs & Graphics).

From this type of graph, it is possible to measure different types of centrality, for example which is the street with the shortest access routes to all other streets. The same approach is also used in social network algorithms and analyses. So by asking how many contact requests someone needs in order to be connected with all other members of a network, I could find out who the person is with the smallest number of 'degrees of separation' from the largest number of people: that would be a very 'important', or at any rate 'popular' person.

You can also calculate the distance between vertices by different metrics, for example surface distance, acuteness and number of angles, or incline of the territory. While surface distance gives you a good idea of how far you'd have to walk to get from one place to another, an analysis of the angles will tell you how easy it is to reach a particular location: the less often you have to change direction and orientate yourself, the easier it is. This is known as cognitive distance.

Applications that use this type of method include *Space Syntax*, developed at UCL (University College London) and *City Form Lab* at MIT, which allows for the analysis of the correlation of the use of buildings (especially commercial usage that is concentrated in central locations) and the use of urban spaces (such as identifying locations that have the potential for social interaction).

VISIBILITY
Visibility is important for evaluating how easy it is to navigate the city: can you see landmarks, what is the signposting like?

It also concerns the visual impact of a building: how well is it visible from a certain vantage point, does it obscure any major landmarks? (In London, for example, there is a clearly defined radius within which any new building may not obscure St Paul's Cathedral, to preserve at least part of the historic skyline for future generations.)

The ground plan area that is visible from a particular point is known as the isovist. Isovist theory concerns itself with the methodology and analysis of visual impact and visibility of objects in architecture.

With an established isovist it is possible to calculate form factors, such as how big an area is, how diffuse or how compact, how far it is possible to see from a building, or from how far it is visible; and draw conclusions about the human spatial experience and the emotional impact a building will have. It may also soon be possible to combine this methodology with smart citizen data (for example emotion cards) in realtime, to make predictions about which type of urban form is experienced as agreeable or disagreeable by the people who use it. □ ↖175

SOLAR ANALYSIS
Solar analysis calculates the amount of solar irradiation a surface area receives, as both energy and light, for example to avoid dark interiors in large buildings.

It also has various possible applications for photovoltaics and thermal solar installations. Google's *Sunroof* project, for example, helps you calculate the potential energy your roof could generate and even connects you to your local suppliers.

Solar analysis also serves as the basis for further analyses, such as the identification of urban heat islands (densely populated urban areas tend to be warmer than the surrounding countryside, as the city's building stock retains much more heat), or a straightforward energy usage analysis (buildings with high levels of solar irradiation receive a lot of heat energy, which is a real advantage in cold or temperate climates, but not ideal in hot climate zones).

SYNTHESIS

GENERATIVE METHODS, FAST PROTOTYPING, PROCEDURAL MODELLING, ALGORITHMIC URBAN DESIGN AND PLANNING

In today's urban planning practice, urban analysis methods are used usually only to evaluate finished design proposals. The potential that these methods have for informing urban planning processes in the early stages is rarely used. This means that there is a gap between analysis and synthesis of urban designs. As a consequence we see considerable room for cost reduction and increased planning efficiency by improving computational support in the early planning phases.

A corresponding argument was made by American civil engineering professor at Stanford University, Boyd Paulson (1946–2005), who was probably the first person to describe the relationship between design stages, the level of influence a designer has on the design, and the cumulative cost of the project. In a now famous diagram published in 1976, he illustrates this relationship with a couple of curves representing the inverse relationship between influence and cost over time: the further down the design process you go, the lower the level of influence you have on the project, and the higher expenditure becomes. □ ↖351 (A more recent version of the same graphic is the MacLeamy curve, which has been used to argue for the deployment of BIM.)

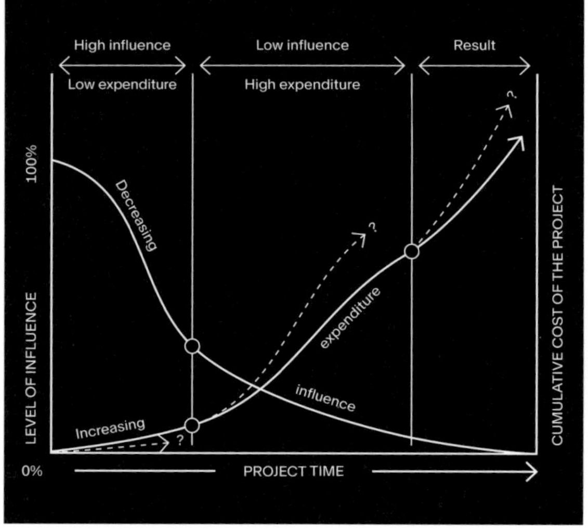

Boyd Paulson's curve shows the relationship between the designer's or planner's influence on a project and the corresponding expenditure across the project time line.

Although the Paulson curve was originally developed in the context of building design, it can similarly be applied to urban planning projects. Here we encoun-
■ ↖152 ter the same fundamental issue of the significance of the early design phase, during which important decisions pertaining to urban fabric, density, networks, land use, and many of its defining components are made, all of which rely on sound information.

■ We use the term **spatial configuration** to describe the geometric and topological representation of the urban fabric. For spatial analysis, we usually need geometric and topological information, and planning synthesis methods likewise need to cover both: geometry and topology. This means we work not only with (parametric) geometry models, but also with the topology of a configuration (the number of components and their relation to each other). Anything, ranging from a city, a district, neighbourhood, building, down to an individual object's floor plan can be denoted as a spatial configuration, regardless of scale: what matters is only the relationship of spatial components to each other.

A simplified approach to the modelling of urban
■ ↖157 557↘ structures uses additive **shape grammars** for the creation of road networks, the definition of land use, and the parcelling and placement of buildings on a
■ ↖192 plot of land. Based on what are known as **L-systems**
■ **(Lindenmayer-systems)**, **dividing grammars** are then used to create spatial configurations of a predetermined outline shape, by, as the name suggests, dividing it up. The first work on dividing methods,
■ using **subdivision trees** was carried out in the early 1970s, initially by George Stiny. It was Stiny who, together with a colleague of his, James Gips, created the concept of shape grammars and subsequently, in 1978, with William Mitchell, applied the principle of L-systems to the study of architectural forms, using simple initial shapes as axioms and transforming them with operators (such as rotation, scaling, moving, copying, mirroring) into more complex forms and configurations. (For more on shape grammars and L-systems, see also our chapter on Scripting.)

A comparatively comprehensive model, which generates urban structures such as streets, blocks, and abstract buildings with life-like rules and restrictions based on the techniques of L-systems and shape grammars is called *The Induction Cities*, by Japanese architect Makoto Sei Watanabe (b. 1952), first released in 2002. Particularly interesting about it is that here a model has been implemented which delivers results that are useful for architects and designers in the early design stages, compared to previous models that were either aimed at larger systems (as discussed above under *Urban Simulation*), or that were 'merely' capable of generating abstract spatial structures.

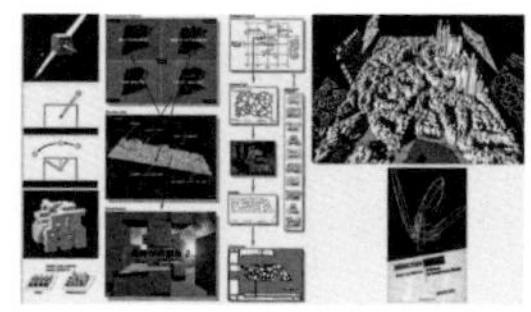
328 ● 545

First attempts at automatically generating urban structures were made in around 1970 – the time when Nicholas Negroponte published *The Architecture Machine* – with experiments on automated and relatively abstract cellular models, not unlike what children play with in *Minecraft* today. At their base is the technique of **cellular automata**.

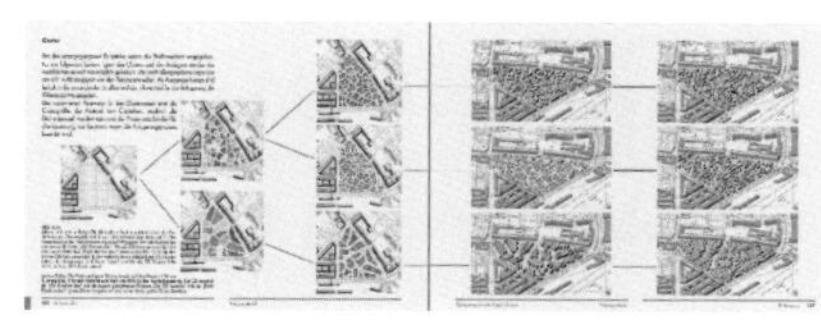
329 ● 545

Most shape grammar studies and software prototypes have remained stuck in the domain of pure research and not found any commercial implementation. A notable exception to this is *CityEngine*, which we want to introduce in a little more detail here, because it is quite unique.

Developed at the Computer Vision Lab at ETH *(Eidgenössiche Technische Hochschule)* Zürich by a team around Pascal Müller, and now part of Esri, *CityEngine* uses a relatively new approach known as *procedural modelling*, which makes this a rules based software that can model large scale urban environments in great detail. It was the first commercially released application of its kind for generating city models and spatial configurations, including streets, blocks, plots of land, buildings, and facades. Originally aimed at the film industry, it has since become widely used in urban planning, architecture, archaeology, and cultural heritage, as well as game and entertainment design.

330 ● 545

While *CityEngine* is a very powerful tool for the procedural modelling of cities, and its wide range of uses notwithstanding, it has not established itself in urban design practice. The reason for this is likely to be the relatively complex implementation of its procedural rules, which are set by means of its own script language, CGA shape grammar.

The process is similar to any classical shape grammar, in that you start with an initial shape and then, based on this, apply various rules in a particular order. For designers, this is not an intuitive approach, as it requires you to think backwards from your design idea and divide your shape up into a sequence of transformations.

An easier option for designers is using procedural models that are integrated into normal parametric/algorithmic design software. The small developer company DecodingSpaces, for example, has released a number of components that plug into *Grasshopper*, to the end of generating an urban fabric. Thus, there are now separate components for creating road networks, land parcels, and building volumes, which can all be controlled parametrically. This means that the length of a road segment, for example, or the dimensions of a land parcel, or the height of a building, can be regulated through parameters:

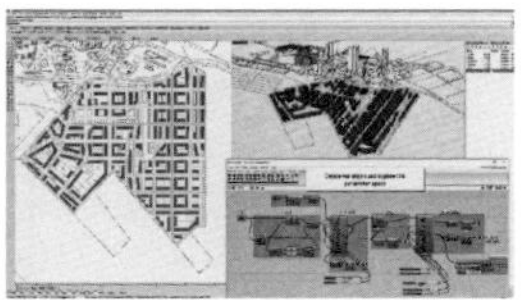

331 ● 545

AUTOMATION OF DESIGN,
AI IN DESIGN,
COGNITIVE DESIGN COMPUTING,
OPTIMISATION IN DESIGN

The final step in the automation of the design process lies in the development of autonomous design agents. This may be seen in the context of a general technological drive towards automation in all areas of our lives and therefore touches upon major questions, such as our own role in a fully dynamically digital world.

We still wouldn't hold with Negroponte's ambition of doing away with the architect. For us it is and remains a case of giving the architect and urban planner new possibilities. And there is a lot to be said for that, because it means being able to control things at a much higher level.

So, based on the generative/procedural models described above, we now want to consider how the power of computation can be harnessed by combining Generative Methods with urban analysis methods to close the gap between the analysis and synthesis of urban designs.

For this purpose, heuristic search methods are normally employed, and among the most useful ones in this context are Evolutionary Multi-criteria Optimisations (EMO), which allow us to explore a multidimensional design space, providing a basis for the designer to evaluate contradicting requirements: a task urban planners are faced with frequently.

EMOs are algorithms that automatically generate spatial configurations. Following rapid advancements over the last decade or so, algorithms for problems with two or three objectives are now well established, and current research has since turned to problems with four and more objectives, usually called many-objective optimisation. So algorithms are now available that can deal with a large number of objective functions, in which the accuracy of estimates and the available computing resources can be traded off against one another. ■

We expect that in order to take advantage of these programs, designers will need to surrender control over some parts of the design process to computers, but in exchange they will get a new, powerful level of command over complex computing processes. It also means that designers have to explore the potential of their role as commanders of partially automated design processes. The idea of autonomous design agents is to enable an urban planner to treat planning as a backcasting problem by defining what performance a design solution should achieve and to automatically query or generate a set of best possible solutions. This kind of computational planning process offers proof that the designer meets the original, explicit design requirements.

For the management of synthesised design and planning variants during an urban planning process, we use Design Space Exploration (DSE), which is an active research field that covers various disciplines. DSE is, "about supporting humans to do design work such that the overall system engages in patterns of exploration that are beyond unaided human capability," as Rob Woodbury and Andrew Burrow put it in their 2006 paper *Whither Design Space?* ■ ↖362

A major issue here is that current generative methods are not linked to the design space. They produce individual solutions without analysing their relationships with each other, such as how similar they are with respect to their geometry, topology, or objective values.

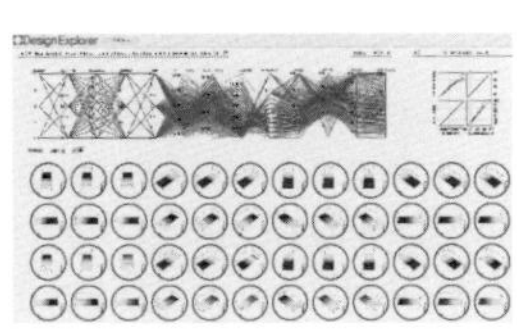

332 ● 546

In practical and technical terms, automation is based on the following procedures, which, as is evident, are really combinations of well-established methods:

- *Optimisation:* the combination of urban analysis (everything you can measure) with procedural approaches (generating spatial configurations)
- *Data bases* of myriads of existing solutions (GIS, BIMs), which can be adapted and customised for your own specific use □ ↖145
- Evolutionary algorithms as the basis for playing through, and searching for, good solutions ■ 555↘ ■ ↖164 ■

Conceptually we want to ask ourselves: what is the definition of the vision? What do we want to achieve? Optimisation shows possible paths towards this vision. This invites us to turn around the 'what if' questions we looked at earlier and ask instead 'what do we want' questions, which are the kind of question that automation methods as yet struggle to answer.

Nevertheless, machine learning algorithms can observe human designers in their use of these tools and adopt their problem solving strategies: they can watch us and learn from us what we consider to be good design, or an ideal city, and as a result become better assistants to us, offering us a solution before we have even formulated the problem.

All of which, then, really leads us to asking a different kind of question. We emphasise at various
□ ↖29 points in this *Atlas*, starting with the Introduction, that critical to any kind of success we as architects, designers, or urban planners may have, is an ability to formulate good questions. And what this technology and its use allows us to do is formulate good questions. Instead of restricting myself to saying, 'what do I want to design today?', I can cast the scope bigger and wider and ask: 'what is my idea of a future city, or of an urban project?' This is quite categorically different to the 'what if' question. Instead of playing through 'little' or even 'larger' scenarios, I say to the system: 'Here is my vision, show me how to get there and how to do it. That's a fundamentally new approach, and one you might – somewhat idealistically – term 'a common search for a better world for us to live in'.

□ ↖111

E-PARTICIPATION, CITIZEN DESIGN SCIENCE

In general, there are two ways to integrate citizens in urban planning processes. The first one is passive, taking data from people without enabling them to influence the planning process directly. Corresponding methods are crowdsourcing or using citizens as sensors. Data can be collected via websites (for example by allowing people to report on problems, damage, or waste in the urban environment), or by using sensors of mobile devices such as smartphones or wristbands that allow the tracking of movement patterns and people's responses to the environment.

The second approach is more active. Technically this can be done with new web interfaces, which allow people to submit urban design proposals. Another possibility is to establish a collaborative design platform, for example in the shape of an interactive table with integrated screens or projections. Such systems require the development of bespoke software that integrates simulations and customised control methods. Controlling the scenarios can then be done with physical objects such as *Lego* bricks, foam blocks, or other individual elements.

A particularly interesting interface for this kind of experimental design process is the *Interactive Simulation Table*, developed at the Technical University (TU) Munich.

333A ● 546

333B ● 547

Any future-oriented computational design support still needs to be aware of the human designer's role. What we are looking for is an approach that combines the excellence of human cognition with the power of modern computing technology in a productive manner. Because the automation we have discussed works best for what we know as *tame problems*, not, however, for solving *wicked problems*, for which human brains are still essential. (We explain in some detail the difference between *tame* and *wicked* problems in our chapter on Digital Design Strategies.) In a nutshell: 'tame' problems are problems that may well be very difficult and complicated to solve, but that can be approached with straightforward rational thinking and therefore also straightforward rational computing. 'Wicked' problems, by contrast, are complex and dynamic, and they don't have one single solution, because each intervention affects other parts of the system of interrelated problem areas.) We therefore call this approach cognitive design computing. The computational part aims to mimic the way a designer's brain works by combining state-of-the-art optimisation and machine learning approaches with the available simulation methods. The cognition part respects the complex nature of design problems by providing models for human-computation interaction. This means that a design problem is shared between computer and designer.

In Summary

Since so much of this chapter has been about developments that are either underway or that we can expect in the near foreseeable future, it makes little sense to now conclude on an 'outlook', as we mostly do in these chapters.

Instead, we just want to reiterate a couple of things we have already said but that to our minds merit being emphasised, because they are so significant. First of all – and this really is possibly the most eye-catching take-home from this chapter – urban planning, urban research, and the science of the city are becoming more and more important, the world over. With the global trend towards urbanisation continuing unabated, cities will matter more, not less; they will become bigger, not smaller; and they will be 'more digital', for certain.

It is absolutely no coincidence that over the last twenty years or so, the world's leading universities have embarked on something of a development spree for urban research:

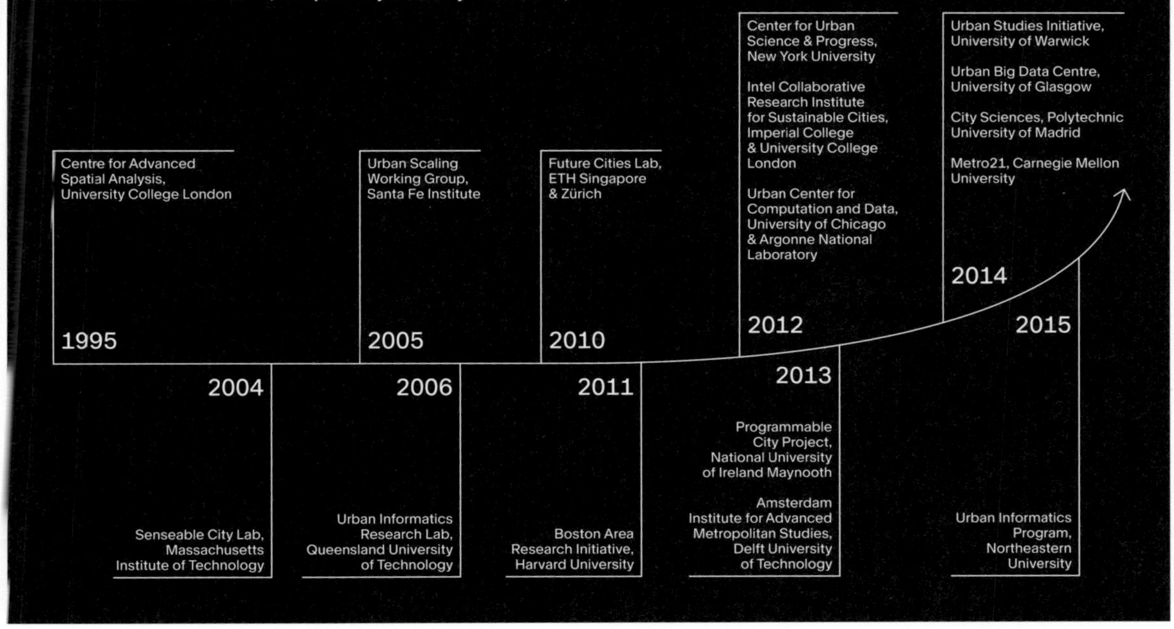

Urban research on the rise (compiled by Anthony Townsend):

And these cities that are continually evolving and that are springing up or melding together from smaller or looser settlements, they will be dynamic, responsive, and fully connected. They will be more, and more autonomously, adaptive; and ultimately they may well be able to largely plan themselves at functional level, leaving you as an architect to get on with creating and designing your vision.

324 ● 535
The Sentiment Cocoon by Moritz Behrens and Konstantinos Mavromichalis. [Sebastian Michael]

325A ● 537

325B ● 537

325C ● 537
Digital model with different levels of detail.

325D ● 537

326 ● 537
Screenshot *Virtual Singapore*. [*Virtual Singapore*]

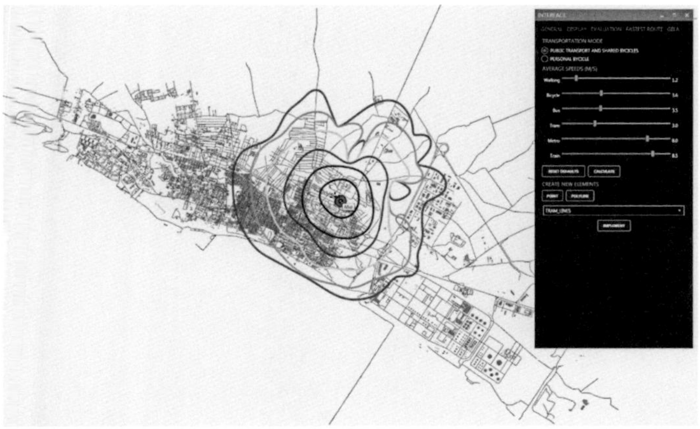

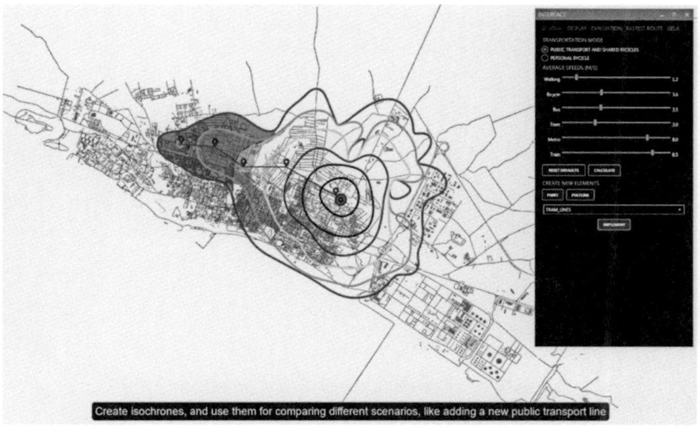

327A ● 538

327B ● 538

Screenshots: infrastructure planning tools developed by the Austrian Institute of Technology (AIT). [AIT]

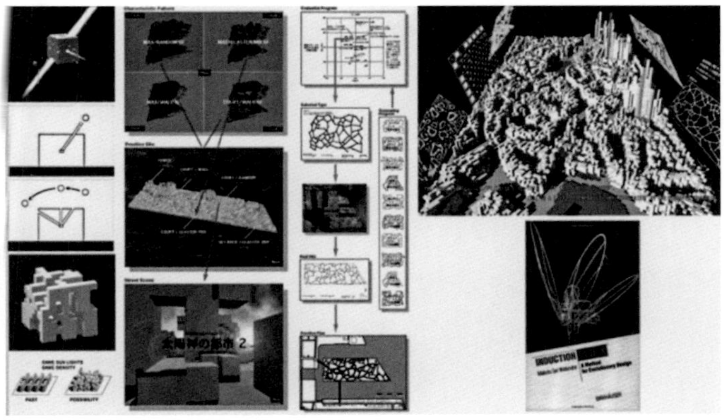

328 ● 540

The Induction Cities, Watanabe 2002.
[Induction Design Project]

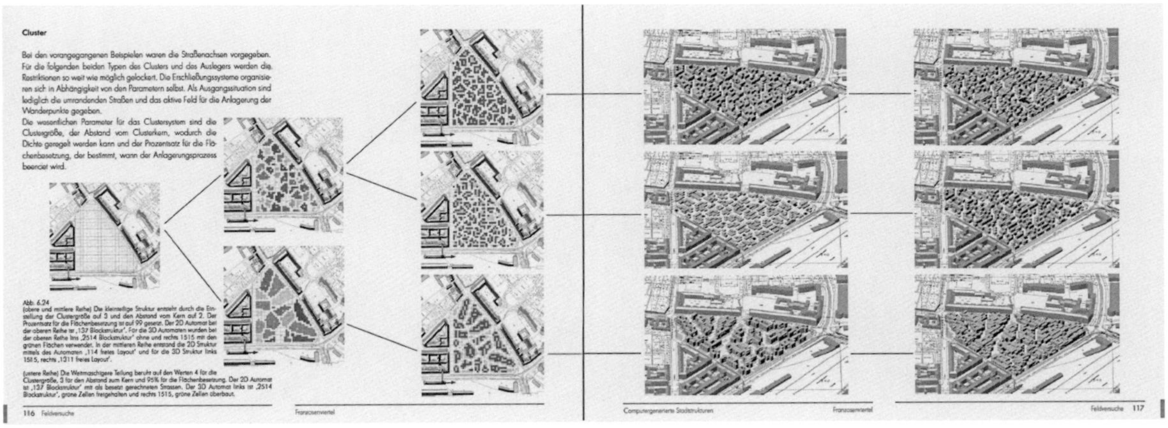

Cluster

Bei den vorangegangenen Beispielen waren die Straßenachsen vorgegeben. Für die folgenden beiden Typen des Clusters und des Auslegers werden die Restriktionen so weit wie möglich gelockert. Die Erschließungssysteme organisieren sich in Abhängigkeit von den Parametern selbst. Als Ausgangssituation sind lediglich die umrandenden Straßen und das aktive Feld für die Anlagerung der Wanderpunkte gegeben.

Die wesentlichen Parameter für das Clustersystem sind die Clustergröße, der Abstand vom Clusterkern, wodurch die Dichte geregelt werden kann und der Prozentsatz für die Flächenbesetzung, der bestimmt, wann der Anlagerungsprozess beendet wird.

Abb. 6.24
(obere und mittlere Reihe) Die kleinteilige Struktur entsteht durch die Einstellung der Clustergröße auf 3 und den Abstand vom Kern auf 2. Der Prozentsatz für die Flächenbesetzung ist auf 99 gesetzt. Der 2D Automat bei der oberen Reihe ist ‚137 Blockstruktur'. Für die 3D Automaten wurden bei der oberen Reihe links ‚2514 Blockstruktur' ohne und rechts 1515 mit den grünen Flächen verwendet. In der mittleren Reihe entstand die 2D Struktur mittels des Automaten ‚114 freies Layout' und für die 3D Struktur links 1515, rechts ‚1311 freies Layout'.

(untere Reihe) Die Weitmaschigere Teilung beruht auf den Werten 4 für die Clustergröße, 3 für den Abstand zum Kern und 95% für die Flächenbesetzung. Der 2D Automat ist ‚137 Blockstruktur' mit als besetzt gerechneten Strassen. Der 3D Automat links ist ‚2514 Blockstruktur', grüne Zellen freigehalten und rechts 1515, grüne Zellen überbaut.

116 Feldversuche

Computergenerierte Stadtstrukturen

Feldversuche 117

329 ● 540

Cellular Automata from *Generating Urban Structures: A Method for Urban Planning Supported by Multi-Agent Systems and Cellular Automata*. [Reinhard König]

330 ● 540

Screenshot *CityEngine*. [Esri]

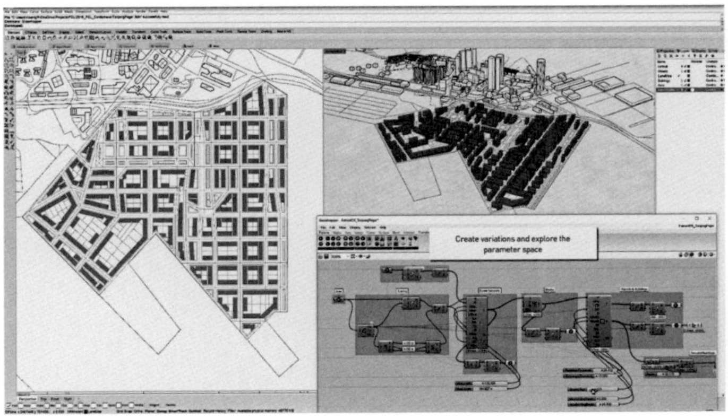

331 ● 541

Screenshot: *DeCodingSpaces* Toolbox. [Reinhard König]

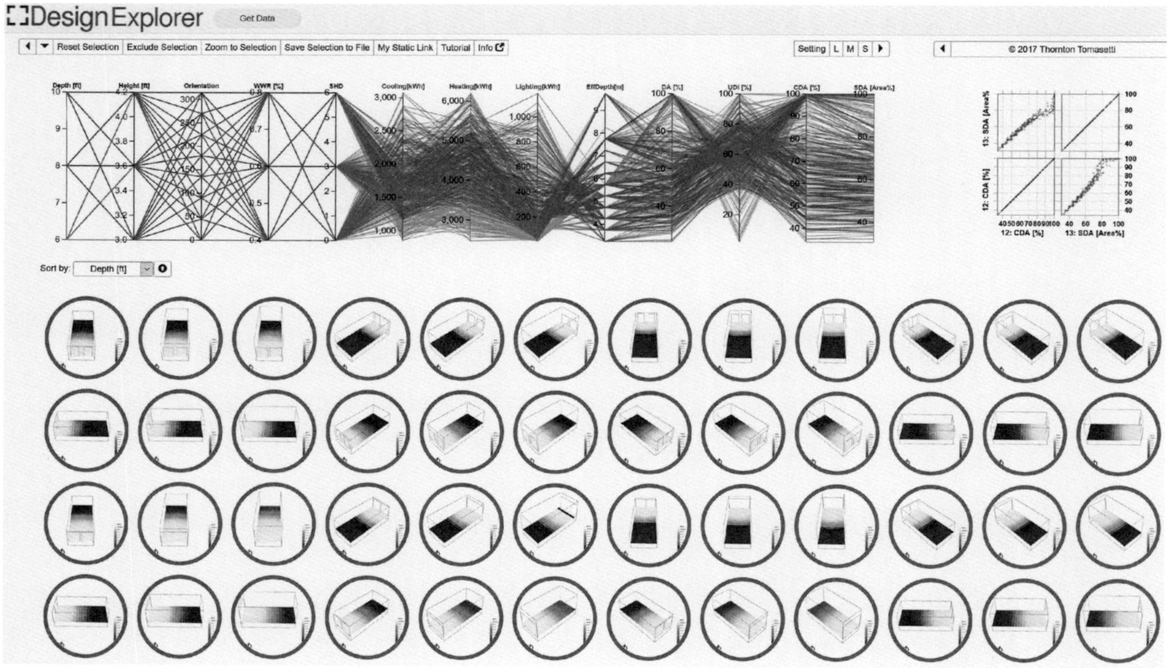

332 ● 541
Screenshot *Design Explorer*. [Reinhard König]

333A ● 542
The *Interactive Simulation Table* by TU München. [333A + 333B: Collaborative Design Platform, *Technische Universität* (TU) München]

333B ● 542

- George Boole: *An Investigation of the Laws of Thought on Which are Founded the Mathematical Theories of Logic and Probabilities*, 1854
- Alan Turing: *Computing Machinery and Intelligence in Mind*, LIX (236): 433-460, October 1950
- Ray Solomonoff: *An Inductive Inference Machine. Dartmouth Summer Research Conference on Artificial Intelligence*, 1956
- Douglas R Hofstadter: *Gödel, Escher, Bach. An Eternal Golden Braid*, 1979
- Hubert Dreyfus, Stuart Dreyfus: *Mind over Machine: The Power of Human Intuition and Expertise in the Era of the Computer*, 1986
- Ulrich Flemming: *More than the Sum of Parts: The Grammar of Queen Anne Houses*, 1987
- Michel Serres: *Le contrat naturel*, 1990 (*The Natural Contract*, English translation by Elizabeth MacArthur and William Paulson, 1995)
- Stuart J Russell, Peter Norvig: *Artificial Intelligence: A Modern Approach*, 2003 (2nd edition)

Big Data & Machine Learning

Ludger Hovestadt

Artificial Intelligence

INTELLIGENCE

In the 1982 film *Blade Runner*, directed by English director Ridley Scott (b. 1937) and written by Hampton Fancher and David Peoples, the fictional Tyrell Corporation uses what it calls the Voigt-Kampff test to establish whether someone is a replicant or a human being. Set in a bleakly retro-futuristic Los Angeles in 2019, replicants are artificial beings created and programmed by the Tyrell Corporation for use in work colonies in space, and the need for such a test stems from the fact that some of these beings have returned to Earth and started to infiltrate and disrupt the social order controlled by the corporation. The Blade Runner of the title is a person whose job it is to hunt them down and 'retire' (or, depending on your take on synthetic humanoids, 'kill' them). The Voigt-Kampff test uses a series of questions designed to elicit an emotional response, which is not only observed, but also biometrically assessed, and the more advanced and sophisticated the replicant, the higher the number of questions that are required to arrive at a positive identification.

334 ● 574

Philip K Dick, whose 1968 novel *Do Androids Dream of Sheep?* the film is based on was perhaps a tad optimistic in his proposed time-frame: as we complete this *Atlas* in the actual year 2019, we are not quite yet at the point where we can bio-engineer creatures who act, think, look, and display emotions so human-like that simple perception is no longer adequate to distinguish them from humans. But depending on whom you listen to, we may not be that far from it either.

The fascination we have with non-human, but human-made, intelligence dates back many centuries, but only in the last couple of decades or so has the prospect of making a creature that could pass a Voigt-Kampff test moved within anything that resembles conceivable reach. The very familiar real-world **Turing test** sets the reverse challenge, to create an artificially intelligent entity that – in a purely natural language conversation – cannot be told apart from a human being. Opinions as to when we will get to this milestone diverge widely, from those who believe never, to those who think of it as imminent, to those who say this has already happened. American futurist Ray Kurzweil (b. 1948) was willing to place a USD 20,000 bet on *Artificial Intelligence (AI)* being genuinely indistinguishable from human intelligence in a Turing test setting by 2029. But predicting the future is an inherently tricky business, and it's worth noting that most forecasts that were made in the early days of computing about how things would go in AI – including, it should be said, by pioneers of AI – turned out to be wrong. ↖532 647↘

Today, artificial intelligence finds application in fields such as reasoning, problem solving, knowledge representation, planning, learning, natural language processing, perception, vision, motion and manipulation, and social intelligence; and we can be sure that this list is not exhaustive. In fact, we can apply AI to virtually any sphere of our lives at all. This may strike us as both surprising and somewhat unsettling, because up until relatively recently, AI was considered to be the stuff of science fiction. Now we find that not only does it pervade our daily lives, it really also signals a new kind of understanding of our world.

How we got to this point, and what this understanding is of our world – not just for architects, but for all of us – those shall be the main subjects of our brief exploration of [Big Data & Machine Learning] in this chapter. □ ↖549

WHAT IS COMPUTING?

In 1854, the English mathematician, philosopher, and logician George Boole (1815–1864) published a book entitled *An Investigation of the Laws of Thought on Which Are Founded the Mathematical Theories of Logic and Probabilities*, more generally known as *The Laws of Thought*. It's the work that laid down the foundation for everything that followed in computing and information technology, because while it does not talk about either, and nor does it talk about **machine learning**, it does set out a type of logic that makes both possible. ■ ↖536 597↘ A few years before writing his book, in 1849, Boole had become professor of mathematics at Queen's College Cork, Ireland. The college is now known as University College Cork, and in 2015 it went to some lengths to mark Boole's 200th birthday, stating:

> "Boole's legacy surrounds us everywhere, in the computers, information storage and retrieval, electronic circuits and controls that support life, learning and communications in the 21st century. His pivotal advances in mathematics, logic and probability provided the essential groundwork for modern mathematics, microelectronic engineering and computer science."

Most people agree that computing itself starts with the English computer scientist, mathematician, and cryptanalyst Alan Turing (1912–1954) who lends his name to the aforementioned Turing test and whose ■ 553↘ **Turing machine** is seen as the forerunner of all comput- ■ ↖373 647↘ ers today. The A-machine, as Turing himself called his invention (where the 'A' stands for 'automatic'), was not a working computer, but a theoretical model for one, providing a precise definition of an algorithm, and with it of 'computability'. This was a critical achievement, because the very first step you need to take before you can begin to compute is to understand what can and what can't be computed. (We talk in a lot more detail about the Turing machine, and walk through a coded example of one, in our chapter on [Writing & Code].) □ ↖369

At exactly the same time as Turing was working on his machine, in 1936, the American mathematician

and logician Alonzo Church (1903–1995) was working on the same problem of computability and came
■ ↖375 711↘ up with the **lambda calculus** (or **λ-calculus**), which Turing on sight recognised as another valid universal model of computation. Together, Church and Turing
■ are therefore now credited with the **Church-Turing thesis**, which in mathematical terms defines as computable anything that is computable by a Turing machine.

□ 643↘ In our chapter on [Privacy & Security] we also introduce Turing as a pivotal figure in the Second World War, where he was instrumental in breaking the supposedly 'unbreakable' Enigma code used by the Germans and the Axis powers to encrypt their communication. Shortly after the war, by 1948, Turing had joined the Computing Machine Laboratory, set up
■ 617↘ two years earlier by British mathematician and fellow codebreaker Max Newman (1897–1984) at the Victoria University of Manchester, where he helped develop the now legendary *Manchester Mark 1*, the first usable stored-program computer, and the *Ferranti Mark 1*, the first commercially produced general purpose computer. Around the same time, in 1951, a former fellow student of Turing's, British computer scientist Christopher Strachey (1916–1975), was working on a computer version of the board strategy game draughts, which he was able to adapt for the *Manchester Mark 1*, so the computer could play, as he himself put it, "a complete
■ game of draughts at a reasonable speed." Strachey therefore is credited with writing the first successful artificial intelligence program.

On the other side of the pond, towards the end of the same decade and while employed at the development campus of IBM (International Business Machines) in the charmingly named town of Poughkeepsie, New York, the programmer and AI pioneer Arthur Samuel (1901–1990) in turn created his own version of the same game, which, being American, he referred to as checkers; and it was Samuel who appears to have coined the term 'machine learning' in his paper entitled *Some Studies in Machine Learning Using the Game Checkers*, which was published in the *IBM Journal* in 1959.

335 ● 574

Samuel worked with IBM's first commercial scientific computer, the *IBM 701*, which had a memory of 2,048 words at 36 bits each, which gave it a total capacity of 73,728 bits or just over 9 kilobytes, expandable to twice its size by adding another 72 Williams tubes. These tubes, in themselves the first instance of a **Random Access Memory (RAM)**, had a diameter of three inches each. You'll be hard pushed to identify a single file on your computer now as small as the entire memory of the *IBM 701*, and its 72 standard tubes would have taken up most of your office, but even so, Samuel's breakthrough piece of programming was recognised as so significant that when word about it got out, IBM's shares leapt by 15 points overnight: the future, investors knew, had already begun.

In 1966, German-American computer scientist Joseph Weizenbaum (1923–2008), while working at the Massachusetts Institute of Technology (MIT), developed a **Natural Language Processing (NLP)** program to which he gave the name *ELIZA* (which, although not an acronym, seems to always be written in capitals), after the character Eliza Doolittle in the play *Pygmalion* by Irish writer George Bernard Shaw (1856–1950). This had just recently, in 1964, been turned into the multiple award winning film musical *My Fair Lady*, and in both the play and the musical, the fictional Professor Henry Higgins tries to teach the Covent Garden flower girl Eliza to speak 'proper' English, so he can pass her off as a society lady. (What starts out as a social experiment invariably turns into a romantic love story, of course, with a satisfactory ending for both parties involved.)

ELIZA, Joseph Weizenbaum, 1965. ELIZA was able to functionally converse in English with a person. (See also *Before Siri and Alexa There Was ELIZA* on *YouTube*. You'll find a link by following the QR code at the beginning of this chapter.)

```
Welcome to

                    EEEEEE  LL      IIII  ZZZZZZZ   AAAAA
                    EE      LL       II       ZZ   AA   AA
                    EEEEE   LL       II     ZZZ    AAAAAAA
                    EE      LL       II    ZZ      AA   AA
                    EEEEEE  LLLLLL  IIII  ZZZZZZZ  AA   AA


Eliza is a mock Rogerian psychotherapist.
The original program was was described by Joseph Weizenmann in 1966.
This implementation by Norbert Landsteiner 2005.


ELIZA: Please tell me that's been bothering you.
YOU:   The weather is awful.
ELIZA: I'm not sure I understand you fully.
YOU:   I hate the current weather.
ELIZA: You say you hate the current weather ?
YOU:   Yes, that's what I said.
ELIZA: I understand.
YOU:   Great.
ELIZA: Please go on.
YOU:   I would say it's your turn now!
ELIZA: Why are you concerned about my turn now ?
YOU:   █
```

Weizenbaum's challenge with ELIZA was not quite so ambitious: it was mainly intended to demonstrate the superficiality of communication between human and machine, being, as it was, not a learning or an artificially intelligent program, but one that simply emulated conversation patterns based on stored stock responses. He still was reportedly surprised to find that when his secretary was interacting with ELIZA – fully aware that this was merely a simulation – she asked for privacy, as she felt she was having a personal conversation. Despite its severe limitations, ELIZA is therefore considered by some to be one of the first programs to pass the Turing test, as this does not evaluate artificial intelligence or the validity of a program's responses themselves, but simply determines whether or not a human being interacting with a program is able to distinguish its responses from that of another human. (It is this aspect of the test's definition that makes it so difficult for scientists to agree whether or not its criteria have genuinely been met.)

336 ● 575

Thirty years later, in 1996, the then reigning world chess champion, Garry Kasparov, sat down opposite IBM's *Deep Blue* chess computer in Philadelphia for a match pitching man against this highly specialised machine. Kasparov won the match four games to two, but a milestone was nonetheless reached, as this was the first time that a reigning champion was beaten in a chess game under tournament regulations by a computer, twice. IBM updated its 'player', and the following year in New York, Kasparov lost a match by three games to two with one draw. Although symbolically *Deep Blue's* victories were significant, they in actual fact still did not really signal a conceptual breakthrough in machine learning and artificial intelligence, since its success was largely due to its processing power and ability to play through millions of possible moves in quick succession before choosing the optimal one, rather than to any more advanced or let alone 'creative' kind of computational thinking.

But *Deep Blue* without a doubt paved the way to an arguably much greater marker, which was set in 2016 when young British startup company DeepMind Technologies, founded in 2010 and since acquired by Google, set its *AlphaGo* computer against 18-time Go world champion Lee Sedol. *AlphaGo* won the match, as a first against a professional Go player, four games to one. Quite apart from being able to draw on formidable processing power, *AlphaGo*, unlike *DeepBlue*, used **Artificial Neural Networks (ANN)** and **reinforcement learning** to work its way through the $2.08168199382 \times 10^{170}$ legal game positions of Go. That number – roughly 2 times 10 to the power of 170 – is considerably larger than either the Shannon number, which estimates the number of possible chess games at 10 to the power of 123, or even the number of atoms in the observable universe, which is estimated at around 4×10^{80}.

Meanwhile, in 2011, IBM pitched its natural language question answering system *Watson* against two previous winners of the long-running American quiz show *Jeopardy*, where it proceeded to win and take home a USD 1 million cash prize. *Watson*, while not connected to the Internet, had access to 200 million pages of stored content, both structured and unstructured, including the then current full text of *Wikipedia*.

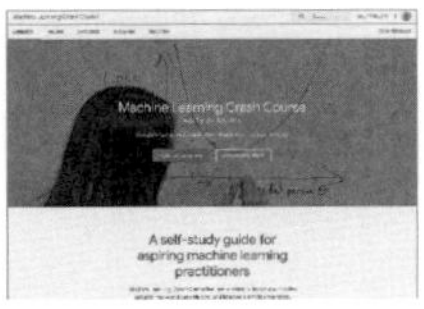

337 ● 575

Today, machine learning has become so much integral to our lives that we can scarcely imagine our existence without it. From the finger print scanner on your laptop to gestures you perform on your tablet, or any personal assistant such as *Siri* or *Cortana*, *Google Now*, or *Amazon Alexa*: they all depend on machine learning processes. Jack Clark, then technology journalist at *Bloomberg*, reported that in 2015, there were 2,700 artificial intelligence projects at Google alone. When, in 2011, German and American computer scientists Sebastian Thrun (b. 1967) and Peter Norvig (b. 1956), then both at Stanford University, decided to offer their *Introduction to Artificial Intelligence* course online for free, 160,000 people in more than 190 countries signed up, which prompted the foundation, a year later, of Udacity, a for-profit online academy that today delivers mainly vocational courses for professionals, and what it calls 'nanodegrees'.

This pervasive omnipresence of artificial intelligence and its deep, though often superficially unnoticeable, enmeshment with our daily existence has profound implications for us all, in all different areas: politics, business, education; from the obviously practical application to the highly conceptual framework, we face entirely new challenges that we are not yet truly equipped to deal with in terms of either our culture or our technology. Take the complicated case of Cambridge Analytica, for example, which in 2018 found itself at the centre of a scandal that involved the technically legal, but ethically highly dubious and ultimately illegitimate appropriation of personal data from some 87 million Facebook accounts. (We describe this case and enter in more detail on the questions it raises in our chapter on Privacy & Security.) ☐ 643↘

One of the most striking, and for many people still most unsettling, developments in artificial intelligence and machine learning may well be the autonomous or self-driving car. Thrun also happened to lead the development of Google's self-driving car project, having previously won the DARPA (Defense Advanced Research Projects Agency) Grand Challenge 2005. This is a 212 km (132 miles) off-road course for autonomous vehicles, which he'd entered with *Stanley*, a driverless car he had developed with his team at Stanford University. By 2016, Google had created the company Waymo for its self-driving car project, and by the beginning of 2017, its test fleet (including pre-Waymo drives) had clocked up more than 600,000 miles in fully autonomous mode.

By the same time, road testing of self-driving vehicles had become legal in just over a dozen US states, with one, Michigan, allowing for these to be driverless, that is without a driver capable to be in, or take control of, the vehicle if necessary. But self-driving vehicles are barely the tip of a gigantic proverbial iceberg. And we're not just talking private cars: in fact, taxis, vans, and lorries are likely to be among the first to go fully autonomous – because wherever there is a paid driver involved there is by consequence a substantial cost that can be saved – and especially also tractors, because they perform monotonous, simple drive patterns away from pedestrians, cyclists, and other traffic. Thrun says: "I think that artificial intelligence is almost a humanities discipline. It's really an attempt to understand human intelligence and human cognition." This is always worth bearing in mind: artificial intelligence is not an alien force, it is human-made. The (as we write this) current CEO of IBM, American businesswoman Ginni Rometty (b. 1957) is one of many who agree that, "the reality is this technology will enhance us. So instead of artificial intelligence, I think we'll augment our intelligence."

Whether you find yourself fearful and pessimistic, or enthusiastic and hopeful about AI, or anywhere in-between, most people concur that the challenges it offers are as formidable as the opportunities are spectacular, and so maybe the last word in this introductory section of our chapter should go to the English writer Douglas Adams (1952–2001). He is most famous for his radio series and book trilogy *The Hitchhiker's Guide to the Galaxy*, but in another humorous work of his, *Dirk Gently's Holistic Detective Agency*, he comes up with the following suggestion, motivational and
■ ↖375 sensible at once: "Let us think the unthinkable, let us do the undoable, let us prepare to grapple with the ineffable itself, and see if we may not eff it after all."

CREATING INTELLIGENCE

"Let me put it this way, Mr Amer: no 9000 computer has ever made a mistake or distorted information," declares HAL 9000, the computer in charge of the Discovery One spaceship in *2001: A Space Odyssey*, before it starts seriously malfunctioning and tries to kill off the ship's human crew, succeeding in all cases but one. American director Stanley Kubrick's (1928–1999) 1968 film of the screenplay and simultaneous novel by British futurist and writer Arthur C Clarke (1917–2008) is a celebrated work of science fiction, but the spectre it paints is not unique. The man-made intelligence who is supposed to serve us but then destroys us has been with us since antiquity. For as long as we have been able to think of ourselves as conscious, sapient beings, we have also been able to think of beings just like us, made by us, and the thought has both fascinated and terrified us, through the ages, in equal measure.

In our culture, the most compelling instance of this is surely Frankenstein's creature. Grotesquely iconised by Hollywood and since spun off in all manner of directions, it was originally dreamt up by the then 18-year-old English writer Mary Shelley (1797–1851) on a road trip through Europe with her lover and future husband Percy Bysshe Shelley (1792–1822) and their friend Lord Byron (1788–1824), both now celebrated poets who did 'rock'n'roll' long before it existed, by living fast, loving hard, and dying all too young. The novel's full published title, *Frankenstein; or, The Modern Prometheus*, not only signals that we are firmly in the modern era now, but also compares Dr Frankenstein to the Greek god who created mankind and gave it fire by stealing it from the gods, incurring the wrath of Zeus in the process.

George Boole was still a child when Shelley and Byron left behind their earthly woes, aged 30 and 36 respectively, and Mary Shelley, who reached the age of 54, also died just before *The Laws of Thought* was published. So neither of them could have known directly of the thinking that was about to be introduced to the world. But the Industrial Revolution was well underway, and Shelly did sense that it would be the then still somewhat mysterious yet unquestionably enormous force of electromagnetism that would allow her experimental scientist to imbue his creature with life. Also, this creature is not a machine: it gets any intelligence it has from the brain that sits in the head it is given as a hand-me-down from a deceased human being.

Yet by the time Shelley writes her tale of recycled human parts being brought to life by the spark of electricity, people such as French philosopher and mathematician René Descartes (1596–1650), English philosopher Thomas Hobbes (1588–1679), and German philosopher Gottfried Wilhelm Leibniz (1646–1716) have all, in their own ways, started to plant the seeds for seeing intelligence as a rational formalisation of thought that could be processed symbolically and systematically, therefore not only by the human brain, but also by any machine capable of calculation. Leibniz went as far as to imagine a **formal language** that would be so universal and in itself logically coherent that, using it, two philosophers would have no further need for disputation amongst each other, but would be able to sit down at a table and say to each other instead: 'let's calculate'.

With the scene thus set, let's look at how we went from being able to think machine learning, to actually make it.

THREE PHASES

Artificial intelligence as we understand it today can be dated back with almost unnerving precision to the summer of 1956. That's when the Dartmouth Summer Research Project on Artificial Intelligence, otherwise simply known as the Dartmouth Workshop took place at Dartmouth College in Hanover, New Hampshire, USA. It was organised by a man in his late twenties who was then Assistant Professor of Mathematics there, American computer scientist John McCarthy (1927–2011). Together with American cognitive scientist Marvin Minsky (1927–2016) and two others, he sent out a proposal in September 1955, suggesting that, "a 2 month, 10 man study of Artificial Intelligence be carried out during the summer of 1956," at his college. In doing so, he coined the term 'Artificial Intelligence', encompassing within it various fields of study that had hitherto been pursued under varying names; and he was able to make it stick.

At Dartmouth, Newell and Simon presented the *Logic Theorist*, which they had developed together with a man called Cliff Shaw. It was the first program to be specifically designed to mimic human problem solving skills, and they were the first programmers to use both the method and the term heuristic in programming, to describe an algorithmic approach that sacrifices optimality or completeness in problem solving for speed by approximating solutions, for example by comparing search results and ranking them in order of relevance and then following only those that are most likely to provide an acceptably useful result fastest.

From here on in, the evolution of artificial intelligence and machine learning can be broadly, but quite adequately, structured into three phases.

1 THE GOLDEN YEARS (1956–1974)

Largely in tandem with the period of mainframe computers, which we discuss in our chapter on Writing & Code, what followed Dartmouth is considered to be a first 'golden era' in the development of artificial intelligence, which saw great advances being made and considerable amounts of government funding being poured into the field, especially in the UK and the US. Correspondingly high, also, were expectations. In a 1970 interview with *Life Magazine*, Minsky said: "In from three to eight years we will have a machine with the general intelligence of an average human being." He was wrong, of course, and spectacularly so, but not alone; and nor was he first to make such wildly ambitious predictions: The American economist and cognitive psychologist Herbert A Simon (1916–2001), five years earlier, in 1965, had already declared, "machines will be capable, within twenty years, of doing any work a man can do."

The rapid breakthroughs in algorithms that could handle taxing computational problems, such as solve mazes and play chess, went hand in hand with first successes at working with natural language, such as Weizenbaum's ELIZA, or American computer scientist Daniel G Bobrow's (1935–2017) *STUDENT* program, which, written in 1964 as a PhD thesis, was capable of solving high school algebra problems. But computer hardware at the time quickly reached its limitations, and by the mid-1970s the metaphorical steamroller had shuddered to a halt, with funding drying up and the anticipated and much heralded artificial intelligence revolution simply not materialising. By 1973, the British Science and Engineering Research Council (SERC) – at the time the body responsible for funding science research in the country – had commissioned a report into the efficacy of its AI development grants. Signed by British applied mathematician James Lighthill (1924–1998), this report, entitled *Artificial Intelligence: A General Survey*, turned out to be something of a death knell for free-form, open-ended research, prompting the British government to end funding for AI projects at all but three universities.

One of the main reasons Lighthill cited for his damning verdict was the problem of *combinatorial explosion* that AI had come up against, and that computers of the 1970s were incapable of overcoming. We feel inclined to say 'yet', but in fact computers will always face this problem, as it only and always becomes bigger and more taxing. And so although computer hardware is getting faster and more powerful at an exponential rate, it will always be in a sense catching up with what we expect of it.

COMBINATORIAL EXPLOSION ↖379 703↘

Combinatorial explosion describes the way in which a mathematical problem very quickly becomes vastly more complicated when the given parameters increase by even an apparently small order. A beautifully simple and impressive example of a combinatorial explosion is the Latin square. This is an arrangement of numbers in which a given set of *n* order of fields is filled so that numbers appear once and once only each per column and per row:

■ ↖541
■
■ ↖376
□ ↖369

A Latin square of the order n = 3

1	2	3
2	3	1
3	1	2

What matters for the conditions of the Latin square to be met is not the value of the entries, but their combination. We could, instead of the numbers 1, 2, and 3, also use the letters A, B, and C, or any others, or make up some symbols of our own: the combinatorial complexity and therefore computational task would remain the same. (If we made up symbols of our own and expected the computer to represent these graphically, then the computational task would not in fact be the same, it would be quite considerably larger, but this simply because of the graphic representation of these symbols, not owing to the square's mathematical structure.)

If the Latin square were to consist of only one field, then in order for its conditions to be met, there would be only one combinatorial possibility: as soon as we put a number or letter or symbol in that field, the one 'row' and 'column', consisting of the one field, is filled with a value that appears once and once only. If the square consists of two fields across and two fields down, this only doubles to 2: there are still only two possible combinations with which the conditions can be met. At the order of three, though, as in the example illustrated above, we witness a first small jump, from 2, not to 4 (double) or 6 (three times), but to 12: there are precisely 12 different ways in which you can complete the above square for its conditions to be met.

But look what happens as you grow the square, in each case by one row and one column only:

Combinatorial explosion in the Latin square:

1	1
2	2
3	12
4	576
5	161 280
6	812 851 200
7	61 479 419 904 000
8	108 776 032 459 082 956 800
9	5 524 751 496 156 892 842 531 225 600
10	9 982 437 658 213 039 871 725 064 756 920 320 000
11	776 966 836 171 770 144 107 444 346 734 230 682 311 065 600 000

It is not even necessary to express this as a graph: the table itself acts as one. Except the curve, if you were to plot this, would be much, much steeper.

□ 567↘ *(Go to* Big Data & Machine Learning – Elaboration *at the end of this chapter for a coded walk through.)*

In artificial intelligence, this combinatorial explosion appears everywhere, all the time: a modelled natural language processing task involving, say, a test vocabulary of ten known phrases becomes not just ten times more complicated or even exponentially more complicated when a hundred such phrases are used, but much, much more complicated. In the 1970s, this meant that artificial intelligence tasks that on paper, and therefore in the confines of theoretical laboratory settings, looked and perhaps even were logically easy enough to solve, when applied to real-world challenges almost immediately outstripped all available computing power.

□ 693↘ □ ↖175

THE FIRST AI WINTER (1974–1980)

With funding having dried up on both sides of the Atlantic, and criticism of the research that had been carried out tagging itself onto a broader disillusionment about what had been achieved compared to what had been promised, a period that came to be known as a *First AI Winter* settled over the scientific community. The British philos-
□ ↖369 opher John Lucas (b. 1929) was among those who felt, and expressed, doubts that the approach that had been taken was likely ever to produce the kinds of results expected. One of the reasons
■ 700↘ he cited for this were the two **incompleteness theorems** posited by Austrian-born American mathematician, logician, and philosopher Kurt Gödel (1906–1978) back in 1931.

Put somewhat simply, they state, in the case of the *first incompleteness theorem*, that in any consistent formal system within which a certain amount of arithmetic can be carried out, there are statements of the system's language which can neither be proved nor disproved; and, in the case of the *second incompleteness theorem*, that such a formal system cannot prove that the system itself is consistent, assuming that it is indeed consistent. This means that if you have a set of computable axioms which are capable of dealing with the laws of arithmetic, then this set of axioms cannot be both consistent and complete: if it is consistent then there will be contained within it statements that are true, but not provable.

Put even more simply, it means that there are always some things that are true but that you cannot prove. Truth, it transpires, cannot be absolute: it has its practical limitations and depends on the settings of the boundaries that are set for it. It is local. This has far-reaching and profound consequences for science, mathematics, philosophy, and our understanding of our own existence, because if it is proved that there have to be things that are true that can't be proved practically, then that makes any science, mathematics, philosophy, and understanding of our own existence resting on positive proof as a prerequisite for a conception of truth suddenly unsound and demands a fundamentally different approach. (We also touch upon these questions – though not specifically on the incompleteness theorems – in What Is Information and Graphs & Graphics.)

II: EXPERT SYSTEMS & THE KNOWLEDGE REVOLUTION (1980–1987)

If the first of the three phases, the Golden Years, corresponds roughly to the era of mainframe computers, then this second phase – following the interlude of the First AI Winter – aligns itself with the era of personal computers or PCs, as described in our chapter on Writing & Code.

In 1978, a man called John P McDermott, who was then at the Carnegie Mellon University in Pittsburgh, Pennsylvania, USA, was tasked with writing a program that would help American computer manufacturer Digital Equipment Corporation (DEC), best known under its trademark *Digital*, automate and streamline the ordering systems for its *VAX* line of 'mini-computers', so called because although one of them could easily take up the space of several fridge-freezers, it was small when compared to some of the computers ordinarily available at the time, which occupied entire basements in large companies.

McDermott originally called his creation *XCON*, which was short for *eXpert CONfigurer*, but later changed the name to *R1*, apparently referencing a little joke that was already widely circulating among engineers and other professions at the time, along the lines of: 'three years ago I couldn't spell knowledge engineer, now I are one.'

R1 was not the first, but possibly the first truly successful rules-based **expert system**, and it quickly

■

proved of great practical use to its client company, because it fulfilled tasks with extraordinary accuracy levels of 95–98%, by far exceeding the performance of human 'experts', and it did so considerably faster. Having gone live in 1980, by 1986 it was saving *Digital* an estimated USD 40 million a year. Small wonder then that private sector industries latched on to the idea and started investing heavily in this new and much more narrowly defined sector of artificial intelligence.

Far from the lofty ambitions of yore to emulate common sense knowledge, which, as the name suggests, covers the often seemingly simple but in fact in terms of potential combinations and therefore data volumes vast problems of everyday living, these projects now concentrated instead on small, manageable, and highly focused pockets of expert knowledge that the computers of the day could actually handle. This led to the insight that knowledge-based systems could, if not become truly 'intelligent', be truly useful, since they allowed the user to quickly access information that was stored and categorised in a systematic and therefore reliable way. It also separated the coding and therefore 'thinking' that a computer had to do from the information it used as its knowledge base.

Some representative items from the *R1* database:

```
RK711-EA
    CLASS: BUNDLE
    TYPE: DISK DRIVE
    SUPPORTED: YES
    COMPONENT LIST: 1 070-12292-25
                    1 RK07-EA*
                    1 RK611
RK07-EA*
    CLASS: UNIBUS DEVICE
    TYPE: DISK DRIVE
    SUPORTED: YES
    FLOOR RANK: 8
    DEPTH: 28 INCHES
    WIDTH: 24 INCHES
    HEIGHT: 42 INCHES
    UNIBUS MODULE REQUIERED: RK611*
    PORTS: 1
    VOLTAGE: 120 VOLTS
    FREQUENCY: 60 HERTZ
    CABLE TYPE REQUIRED: 1 070-12292 FROM A DISK DRIVE UNIBUS MODULE
                         OR 1 070-12292 FROM A DISK DRIVE UNIBUS DEVICE
```

A sample rule of the configurator for the *DEC VAX* computer:

```
DISTRIBUTE-MB-DEVICES-3

    IF: THE MOST CURRENT ACTIVE CONTEXT IS DISTRIBUTING MASSBUS DEVICES
        AND THERE IS A SINGLE PORT DISK DRIVE
                THAT HAS NOT BEEN ASSIGNED TO A MASSBUS
        AND THERE ARE NO UNASSIGNED DUAL PORT DISK DRIVES
        AND THE NUMBER OF DEVICES THAT EACH MASSBUS SHOULD PORT IS KNOWN
        AND THERE IS A MASSBUS THAT HAS BEEN ASSIGNED AT LEAST ONE DISK DRIVE
                AND THAT SHOULD SUPPORT ADDITIONAL DISK DRIVES
        AND THE TYPE OF CABLE NEEDED TO CONNECT THE DISK DRIVE
                TO THE PREVIOUS DEVICE ON THE MASSBUS IS KNOWN

    THEN: ASSIGN THE DISK DRIVE TO THE MASSBUS
```

In architecture we also have these kinds of rules, called shape grammars: we discuss them in our chapters on Generative Methods, 3D Modelling, and Digital Cities.

■ ↖540
□ ↖145
□ ↖57
□ ↖529

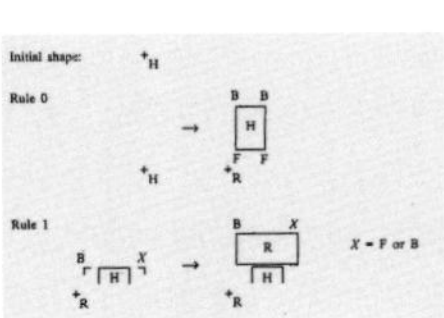

338 ● 575

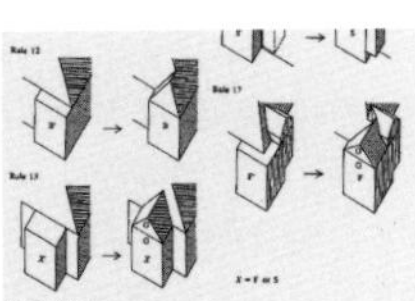

339 ● 575

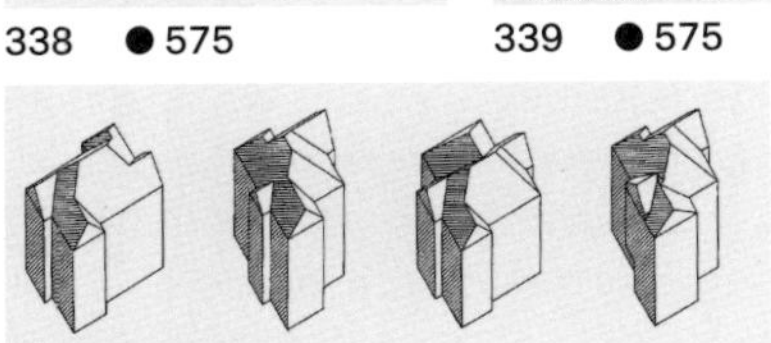

Figure 19. Basic Queen Anne houses.

340 ● 576

The era coincided with a decision by the Japanese government to invest the equivalent of some USD 850 million in their *Fifth Generation Computer* project, which started in 1982 and mapped out a ten-year plan to create an 'epoch-making' computer capable of holding conversations, translating languages, and reasoning like a human being. Alas, all was not plain sailing...

THE SECOND AI WINTER (1987–1993)

Once again, the expectations and promises were simply pitched too high, and once again, while progress was made, it was not as breathtaking as the people spending millions on the research were led to believe would soon be the case. Fifth generation computers were being built, but they were far wide of the mark of

□ ↖369 holding conversations or translating languages fluently, let alone reasoning like human beings.

The programs available, though perhaps 'expert' and useful within their given parameters, were also incapable of learning, or of overcoming some of the fundamental problems of intelligence, such as the **qualification problem** and the **frame problem**. The *frame problem* was first defined by our friend John McCarthy and British computer scientist Pat Hayes (b. 1944) in a paper entitled *Some Philosophical Problems from the Standpoint of Artificial Intelligence* and describes the problem of 'framing', as it were, a robot (or artificial intelligence) existence in a natural environment, using **First Order Logic (FOL)**. Specifically, it describes the problem of finding a comprehensive enough set of axioms to adequately describe the robot environment, thus enabling it to make sound decisions within it. The *qualification problem*, on the other hand, concerns itself with the impossibility (real or imagined) of listing without exception all the conditions that are required in a real world situation for an action to have the intended consequences.

■ ↖379 704↘ ■ ↖354 619↘

None of this was entirely new: it was a 20th century technical formulation of a conundrum famously posited in 1814 by French scholar Pierre-Simon Laplace (1749–1827) in what he didn't call, but what is now widely known as, **Laplace's demon**:

"We may regard the present state of the universe as the effect of its past and the cause of its future. An intellect which at a certain moment would know all forces that set nature in motion, and all positions of all items of which nature is composed, if this intellect were also vast enough to submit these data to analysis, it would embrace in a single formula the movements of the greatest bodies of the universe and those of the tiniest atom; for such an intellect nothing would be uncertain and the future just like the past would be present before its eyes."

III: GENERIC ARTIFICIAL INTELLIGENCE (2000–NOW)

Following the interlude of a Second AI Winter, the third phase of AI development is the one we are in today, and it corresponds to the third phase we describe in our chapter on Writing & Code, there called *The Internet – Big Data – XML | Machine Learning – The Abstraction of Flow Control*.

Deep Blue's victories against Kasparov in 1996 and 1997 and *Stanley's* win of the DARPA Grand Challenge in 2005 both were defining moments in the evolution of artificial intelligence, and both of them were possible not so much because the thinking had matured (although that too), but because computing power had finally caught up with programmers' and computer scientists' ambitions. *Deep Blue's* processing speed, after all, was not a little faster than the *Ferranti 1* computer on which Christopher Strachey had played draughts. It was ten million times faster.

With computing capability following **Moore's law** and doubling every two years, a 'chink in the curve' was finally reached, where every couple of years this doubling made such a big difference that from the beginning of the decade to its end, computing changed beyond recognition. In this *Atlas*, whenever we talk about the big changes that happened in digital technology, and in how digital technology is being used in architecture, we come back to the same period: mid-1980s to late-1990s. This is when computing really gets on its feet and starts to walk. And because Moore's law continued (and still to quite some extent continues) to be in effect, it wasn't so long before computing started to run.

Aside from the still accelerating computer speeds, we have had two developments since the beginning of the 21st century that have given us more progress and a better outlook on artificial intelligence than we have ever had before, and that have moved operational AI applications not just closer but actually into the realm of our everyday existence, with the kind of examples we've already mentioned: navigation, personal assistants, or driverless cars. One of these is the Internet, and with it the fact that we are now connected and therefore able to do things such as exchange information and update our geographical position in real time; the other – as a direct consequence of being connected – is constant and immediate access to previously unimaginably large data sets: big data.

We are about to look at what exactly big data sets mean for our ability to make accurate predictions, but before we do so, let's set out briefly what we are now really dealing with.

Who Are We?

BEING HUMAN

Artificial intelligence is not, we would argue, about a new technology, or even about a bunch of technologies. AI is about us as human beings and about how we use technology, what we understand technology to be. And this has always been the case: our own inventions have always been about who we are.

IN SPACE

We can, if we want to (and we clearly do), span an arc here over three levels or layers, which we might call *space*, *time*, and *life*. Within this schematic, you could say that we evolve (or 'graduate', or 'transition', depending a bit on how judgmental you want to sound) from the origins of our Western culture – and we are very much looking at this here as elsewhere from a Western perspective – where we find ourselves expressing ourselves 'in space'. The classic Greek sculpture is an example of this: it is three-dimensional, undeniably beautiful, even life-like, but static. It idealises to quite some extent the human form (particularly the male human form) and sets it on a par with the form of the gods: it elevates the human being, if not in thought and words, then in his representation to a status of perfection.

341 ● 576

IN TIME
With the Renaissance and scientific examination and therefore our first real understanding of anatomy, sculpture begins to 'move': the interplay of the body's muscles, the way it balances, suspended during an action, the tension it captures before an imminent act, all of this, you could say, puts sculpture into time as well as space.

So when we look at the studies of Renaissance artists such German painter and printmaker Albrecht Dürer (1471–1528) or Italian polymath Leonardo da Vinci (1452–1519) today, we have nothing but admiration for their intricacies, their detail, their accuracy. But it is worth remembering that da Vinci carried out his research in secret, as it was forbidden to dissect human bodies in his day. From the perspective of his elders – which was shaped by the middle ages – what he was doing was sacrilegious.

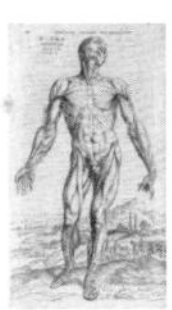

342 ● 576

By the eighteenth century, we have moved another step further, and while it would possibly be adventurous to suggest that Renaissance sculpture has ever yet been 'improved' on, into the equation come precision mechanics that attempt to create life-like machines which not only seem to be 'alive' because of their dynamic poses and anatomical as well as emotional authenticity, but because they actually move. An example of this are the automata by Swiss-born watchmaker Pierre Jaquet-Droz (1721–1790), who among many other wonders managed to build a mechanical boy that could write pre-programmed phrases in real ink with a real quill onto real paper.

IN 'LIFE'
Today's sculpture, then, goes beyond 'space' and 'time', and aims at emulating 'life'. In 2009, French artist Zaven Paré (b. 1961) spent a month and a half 'shut in', as he calls it, with *Geminoid HI-1*, the *Actroid* robot alter-ego of its co-creator, Japanese robotics engineer Hiroshi Ishiguro (b. 1963), conversing with it 8 to 10 hours a day, in an attempt to forge a relationship and, as he puts it, "build the personality of the character."

343 ● 576

And so whether it's Mary Shelley's *Frankenstein* or, 150 years later, Richard O'Brien's riff on the theme, *The Rocky Horror Show*, which, shortly after the sexual revolution of the 1960s and just as punk was getting ready to scandalise popular culture in London and New York, had a transsexual Dr Frank'n'Furter make a creature with the physique of a bodybuilder principally for his own delectation in the pursuit of "absolute pleasure" and "sins of the flesh," we make in every given era of 'technology' what we seem to be most in need of...

With AI – no different than with anything else we've come up with, only perhaps, because of its far reaching impact, more so – we experience how the concept of technology gets newly defined as we move deeper into its uses. We begin to understand ourselves as human beings differently with and because of it. And this means that alongside these new technologies, we develop a new language, a new mastery, and also, certainly, a new architecture.

ON ARCHITECTURE

You may by now be wondering, what has any of this got to do with architecture? And you'd be forgiven, even though it has more to do with architecture than at first glance meets the eye.

Firstly, on a purely pragmatic level, it does so because we can already design, and will move further towards designing, objects algorithmically. And these objects are not, and will not be, just static structures, but they are already and will increasingly be 'intelligent' buildings. In fact, we can now quite easily conceive of something along the lines of an 'architectural Turing test', which simply asks, can a human being distinguish a computer generated design from a human generated design? And there would be many a design already out there that could pass that test, not least because the boundaries between what is computer generated and what is human generated with the aid of, not just computing, but artificial intelligence as we understand it today, are now so blurred.

But secondly, and on a more fundamental level, because whenever a new reality is being created through whatever development – be that an industrial revolution, a cultural step change, a political earthquake, or a technological explosion – architects are called upon to constitute locations of meaning, which understand and reflect the (today globalised) world around them.

Architecture embodies our culture. It does so at a specific location, and wherever this location is, and whatever the culture that frames it, the architecture has to take a stance within it. Its point is not to achieve a harmonic coexistence with what's already there: it's about challenging as much as representing culture. It is about articulating an active stance with an architectural identity. Thus, architecture is reflected in our culture and our culture in reflected in architecture: one shapes and informs the other. And what is true of 'culture' generally is necessarily true also of 'technology', since technology and culture, too, are inseparable, as we have seen. Or, as the author of our oldest surviving treatise on architecture, *De architectura*, Roman architect and engineer Vitruvius

(c. 80–70 BCE – after c 15 BCE), puts it: "Architecture is a science arising out of many other sciences, and adorned with much and varied learning; by the help of which a judgment is formed of those works which are the result of other arts."

NATURE, TECHNIQUES, INTELLIGENCE, AND MASTERSHIP

And so, without feeling a need, at this point, to go into architecture-specific examples, let us examine a little more closely these two core terms, as *nature* and *technology* converge:

Nature comes from Latin *natura*, *nasci*: 'being born, coming about, to emerge'. The Greek semantic equivalent to this is φύσις (*physis*, from which we get our 'physics'). It describes, therefore, the principle of the world as it is.

Technology is Greek in origin, from the word τεχνικός (*technikós*, which in turn derives from τέχνη *téchne*) and roughly corresponds to our 'art, craft, skill': a particular aptitude in any area of human endeavour. It describes, therefore, the principle of *human beings mastering the world*.

Going one step further, French philosopher Michel Serres (1930–2019) argues that all things in nature – organisms, formations, plants, phenomena, and human beings – speak as independent, active, even intelligent subjects. Through writing, we humans enter a 'contract' not with each other 'about' these things in nature, but *with* all things in nature and so in fact with nature itself: the process of encoding and decoding in writing systems involves an exchange during which we cannot understand each other absolutely, but we can 'make friends': we can learn to communicate and to develop and agree on the terms of our mutual contract. This was the case in ancient Greece with the invention of phonetic script, it was the case also during the Renaissance with accurate technical and anatomical drawings, and it is the case today with code. Each time we enter a new phase of 'contracting' nature with a new kind of 'writing', this opens up a new world: we are reborn, it is another renaissance.

When we develop radical new ways of thinking, we use them to 'stage' the elements of nature, in a way that from the at that point traditional perspective seems outrageous. In the new form of thinking we make the old form newly explicit: the old form does not cease to exist, but we dissect it and articulate it anew. In a sense, these articulations – irrespective of the technology used, and no matter when they occur – can be described as a way of making nature 'artificially intelligent': we *think* nature as *intelligent*. The new thinking emancipates itself from old nature, which is why it can write about old nature. That, Serres argues, is the principal characteristic of technology: it's a dexterity, a trick, a pact, a contract with nature; something new beyond nature in a new world; a new physics, just as we often see it used in descriptions of the Renaissance.

Going at it from this particular philosophical perspective, all we really have to do then is learn to 'read' this 'intelligence in nature', in order to be able to 'write' new things. But 'reading' and 'writing' here are not merely two sides of the same coin. If I want to be able to speak and write with the voice of a master, the 'reading' has to be internalised. It's not unlike swimming, or riding a bicycle, or playing the piano: as long as you have to think about what you're doing, you keep catching up. The mastery lives in what you do becoming second nature, in the light touch, and the easy, playful gesture.

□ ↖369

TECHNOLOGY TODAY

In his paper back in 1959, Arthur Samuel defined 'machine learning' as computers' ability to learn without being explicitly programmed. If you go to the *Wikipedia* portal on the subject, you will find a great many procedures discussed there that can in their multitude, be quite bewildering. We don't think it is necessary or even useful for architects to lose themselves in detail here, not least because the field is now again undergoing extremely rapid development, and we anticipate that anything we expound on from a technical angle will soon – most likely by the time you read this in print – be out of date.

So we will keep our chapter at the conceptual, 'big arc' level; and here there are two things we want to qualify:

1 Often, even mostly, where it says machine learning 'on the tin', there is in fact little or no machine learning 'inside': in most cases when people talk about 'machine learning' and 'big data', what they really mean are 'a lot of data' and superstatistics, such as Principal Component Analysis (PCA) and K-means clustering, which is a particular form of data mining. What they all have in common, and again without wanting to go into any detail about them, is that they are not actual machine learning processes, but very advanced statistical procedures.

2 What we need to be mindful of when discussing artificial intelligence and machine learning is that intelligence itself cannot be visualised. It is not a case of taking a brain scan or finding ingenious diagram drawing or mapping techniques that show us what intelligence 'looks like' and therefore what it is: intelligence is by its nature intangible and invisible. What we see and what we get is *the effect* of intelligence, always.

That latter point brings us right back to Michel Serres. Our principal thought is both simple and complex at the same time: intelligence has to be written down in this 'contract' between nature and physics. And with artificial intelligence today, the symbols (not the characters or signs we use to represent these symbols!) of this 'contract' have neither the structure nor the form of the old world: they are really new.

This distinction between that which is symbolised, the symbols themselves, and the signs or characters used to represent these symbols takes us to the American mathematician and philosopher Norbert Wiener (1894–1964) whose most famous pronouncement and insight is that information is neither matter not energy, but needs matter for its embodiment, and energy for its communication.

We have a couple of times in this chapter referred you also to our chapter on Writing & Code and the progression we sketch out there from mainframes, to PCs, to ubiquitous computing and the Internet. Again, this pattern turns out to be relevant here too, because:

1 With information technology between the early 1960s and the early 1980s, and mainframe computers as the 'shape' of intelligence, the idea was pursued that computers are really machines that imitate geometrically, graphically, whatever the program execution demands. This, straightforwardly put, is the concept of the computer as *matter*: a crude imitation of nature, chasing after points in space and time. It could be likened to a search for the 'ultimate deal', rather than a 'contract' about something new.
2 With information technology since the early 1980s, and PCs as the 'mode' of computing, and then the emergence of expert systems and intelligent structures, the idea has been pursued that computers are movable apparatus. Now they are not models of the world, but structures in the world. Programs don't describe how computers should work, but what they should do: these are, therefore, predictions. This correspondingly is a conception of computers as *energy*. The search for a new cause of the cosmos; the diligent, analytical interpretation of a cosmological order. The laying down of lines in space and time, from secure positions. The search for the 'right' commission, instead of a contract about something new.
3 Today, with the Internet, computing is probabilistic in the sense of category theory and quantum physics: things appear as you ask them. If you ask for a wave (the connections, the energy), you get the wave, but you lose the particles (the locality and identity – the material). If you ask for the particles, you lose the wave. So, with Google, for example, it makes no sense to search for the reasons behind the answers to a question, because each question changes the probabilistic constellation: I principally get new answers to the same questions, each time. ■ ↖536 615↘

Where, then, in this setting, does meaning come from, or purpose? We have our Internet, and we can find meaning neither in material nor energy, neither form nor structure. We find significance only in our questions, and this is a fundamentally different relationship we have to intelligence and the world around us, compared to what we had two or three hundred years ago; and it is also entirely characteristic of artificial intelligence today: that it is probabilistic. But big data is not big statistics. Big data is data that is unstructured, unwieldy and possibly incomplete. The only way to deal with it is with probabilistic AI. In other words: rather than sitting down to analyse the data and draw statistical conclusions to prove or disprove your point, you allow the algorithm to find *all* patterns in their probabilities. It indexes all the 'treasures' and all 'truths', and that's why these don't make any sense. Everything is possible and impossible at the same time. Only if we ask questions, which means intelligently localising these global approximate truths, do they turn into a concrete reality. So the machines know everything, but everything to them has no meaning. And this is the part that falls to us architects: to configure meaningless global elements meaningfully in a concrete location.

A New Writing in a New World

On that note, let's proceed now to the craft of information. To put it succinctly: today, it is about everything. In the last 20 years, we have learnt to generate multitudes of everything, and our challenge now is to deal with this multitude, what, elsewhere in this *Atlas*, we refer to as the 'Big Plenty'.

And when, in the companion part to this chapter, Big Data & Machine Learning – Elaboration, we talk you through some examples, perhaps the most interesting, most striking point we want to make and illustrate is this: that's all there is to it. There is some complex thinking, but it results in really remarkably simple, penetrable, and, as you will see, quite extraordinarily short code. We encounter this same insight also in our chapter on Being a 'Brand': the amount of coding that's required to work with this overwhelming wealth of data is extremely compact and, unlike the data itself, manageable. So while this chapter does not set out to teach you coding – and it wouldn't succeed, because there is more to it than in this *Atlas* we can or want to cover – what it can and wants to do is show you how simple, even elegant, and concise the coding is that's involved in genuine machine learning and artificial intelligence processes. Yes, you have to be (or become, at least somewhat) code literate, but you do not have to be above average intelligent to understand it.

And when we say 'understand', we don't even want you to worry if you don't immediately follow each and every step in detail: allow yourself to absorb the thinking, and it will, in its own time and manner, start to percolate.

□ 567↘

IT ALL MAKES NO SENSE ANY MORE

Everywhere we care to look – the Internet, the supermarkets, the magazines, the films and videos, the designs – we recognise that there is plenty of everything. There is not just enough, there is more than enough. This is the 'Big Plenty' we mentioned just a moment ago. And this is what we consider to be a fundamental problem. How to make sense of it. Or rather, as it turns out: how to distinguish between 'creating sense' and 'making meaning'. □ 593↘

In the 'old world', before information technology, and also in nature as we find it today, things always seem to make sense. We see the immense variety, and we can taste it, feel it, or measure it with our instruments. We can trace it, analyse it, discover it; establish from it functions, schemes, or classifications. All of this is based on our senses: there is one nature and within this nature we create sense with our senses.

Information, however, is not of this nature. Yes, we can see the shadows of information on our screens, or we can touch its manifestation as a 3D print, but we cannot see or grasp the information itself. We cannot sense it: information does not create sense. Here we remind ourselves of Norbert Wiener: information is neither energy nor matter. Even so, or perhaps exactly because of this, we are obviously able to twist and change our world in uncountable ways. Which is not just interesting but also of greatest importance to understand our time.

We may summarise our situation in this phrase: 'Information creates no sense, but we can talk about it'. Or to put it programmatically: there is a flood of no-sense and we have to learn to talk about it in a new way, to make information meaningful to 'save our planet'. This sounds like a bold assertion, but it looks to us very much like that it is exactly the mood of the global discussion today.

■ ↖536 Let us bring this back to **Computer Aided Architectural Design (CAAD)**. In a combination of grammars and parametrics we can, with very little code, generate a practically infinite number of architectures, as many examples over the last 20 years illustrate. And we are in a way quite helpless with this: the architecture seems at once athletic and drunken; caught up in a competition for as many forms and colours as possible. This, you could say, is a Dionysian design principle at work: irrational, chaotic, emotional, and instinctive.

The more pictures we have in front of us to look at, the less sense a single picture creates. The more theories we have available to draw on, the less sense one single theory creates. The more empathy we can give, the less our empathy makes a difference; the more design there is, the less that design gets noticed. We find this summarised for example in the concept of 'junkspace' invoked by Dutch architect, theorist, and urbanist Rem Koolhaas (b. 1944), whose thinking you could perhaps summarise as: 'you can't improve by doing better.'

Our contention is that if we want to actually make meaningful architecture, we have to engage in a different type of game, and that's what we now want to look at.

344 ● 577

UNDERSTANDING NATURE

In the *Elaboration* part that follows this chapter we play through a few simple mathematical examples that illustrate the thinking of the 18th and 19th century. This is what we mean by 'creating sense'.

The relationships described there are fundamental and their significance can hardly be overstated, so we have to examine them carefully: producing events that create sense is a way of predicting a *future*. This is how we understand nature, and we align ourselves with nature. In mathematics we call this *analytics*, introduced in our *Elaboration* by *stochastics*. It was developed primarily in France in the 18th century, and we need to delineate this from the counting of events in the past, which we call *statistics*. Summarised in a simplistic form, statistics could be said to be the pragmatic English answer to the French stochastics.

All of our analytical, classical, scientific world is described in these terms; this is how things are differentiated from each other, how they are being classified. It is how predictions are made, it's how the steam engine works, how industrial plant are built, it's how the politics and the economy of the 19th century play themselves out.

In art we can look at the work of Prussian artist and architect Carl Friedrich Schinkel (1781–1841) to see the orchestration of all parts of our world equally in time and nature. In his *Landscape with Pilgrim*, for example, the clearly delineated typical objects are arranged, in many repetitions, into a single, revealing motion towards the light.

345 ● 577

ENTROPY OR THE FINAL STATE OF ANY SYSTEM

This brings us to the challenge we face today, and so we now want to discuss the principal limits of all analytics, or of creating sense, which has been explicated in mathematics between around 1880 and 1920, and which is the basis for the developments in the 20th century, most prominently articulated in quantum physics and information technics. (It is really more precise to speak of 'technics' here, rather than of the more commonly employed generic term 'technology'.) This discussion requires a little patience – we will follow a string of concepts from systems, to energy, to entropy, through negentropy to information – but the effort will be worth it.

In our line of argumentation we can describe a *system* as an 'interplay of parts within a predicted pattern with nature', and everything in the 18th and 19th century is in tune with the concept of the system. It does three things:

1 It delineates an inside from an outside
2 It describes the interplay of its parts
3 It anticipates the future

When we talk about an *interplay of parts of a whole*, and of *stochastics* and the prediction of the future with systems, then *energy* describes the *interplay of the workings* or the *liveliness of a whole*.

So energy can express itself in different ways; it can take on different forms, such as, among others, potential, kinetic, electrical, thermal, or chemical, but it is a basic principle of physics that energy – against our instinct perhaps – cannot actually be 'used up'. It cannot be destroyed, it can only be transformed. This is what the *first law of thermodynamics* states, which is why it is also known as the law of conservation of energy.

What changes over time, then, is not the 'amount of energy', it is the *form the energy takes*. And this transformation of energy goes in one direction only: from a state of great order or low entropy to a state of great disorder or high entropy. This is what the *second law of thermodynamics* states, and in a way it is most reassuring: energy over time always 'loses' its 'shape', going from more highly structured to more random forms, unless we do something to it to halt or reverse the process. We can illustrate this 'loss of shape' by releasing a drop of ink into a glass of water. The drop, which starts out in theory as a perfect sphere and in practice as a tear shape will over time invariably dissolve into a random distribution which ceases to create any kind of sense. This process is called *dissipation*.

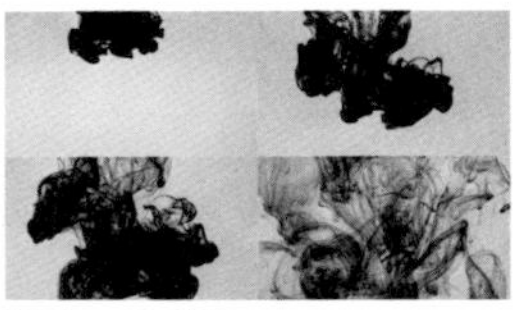

346 ● 578

Entropy then is a measure of the absence of sense – senselessness, even nonsense: forms that create sense, in which the individual parts contain *few possibilities*, have a low entropy; whereas random, nonsensical forms, the parts of which contain *many possibilities*, have a high level of entropy.

If we put the laws of thermodynamics on a cosmic scale, then time starts with a big bang with zero entropy, and a single necessity, and ends with the heat death and maximum entropy at the 'thermodynamic equilibrium', where all physics is in balance and the world is in a state of pure contingency.

This is the fascination of a Sherlock Holmes in the dark street corners of London, it's the energy of *Frankenstein*, it's Darwin's evolution. It plays in Sigmund Freud's id, ego, and super-ego; it's industrialisation, it's what we call capitalism today, it's landscape gardening, and the picture of Dorian Gray... – As an example we can take *The Great Western Railway* by English painter J M W Turner (1775–1851): here we see forms of energy dissolving in a space of contingencies, with a single energetic engine just off centre, drawing our focus, creating sense.

347 ● 578

NEGENTROPY, INFORMATION – OR THE ROLE OF THE INTELLECT

What is the 'solution' to this 'problem'? What can we do in the face of inescapable death? We would argue that it lies in our conception of information. Often, we tend to adopt a defeatist, dystopian position: we yield to nature, we allow ourselves to be governed by the senses alone, we eschew the use of our intellect. But why not take a look at the realm of physics, to see how we can leap across this 'finite' boundary:

Maxwell's demon is the name of a thought experiment dreamt up by Scottish mathematical physicist James Clerk Maxwell (1831–1879), which demonstrates how – in theory at least – the second law of thermodynamics could be overcome. It goes like this:

We have a container filled with a gas. The gas molecules move about in it randomly, driven by thermal energy. We now divide this container into two chambers and install a gate between them. At the gate, we place a little demon who watches the movement of the molecules. Those with a high velocity, he directs through the gate into the chamber on the right, those with a low velocity he directs into the chamber on the left. Thus sorting the particles, he creates a difference in temperature: the right-hand chamber will heat up, whereas the left-hand chamber cools down. If implemented in practice, this would create energy, which could power a steam engine for example, out of nothing. In actual physics, this is not 'allowed', for which read not possible, which is why the figure at the gate is thought of as a 'demon'.

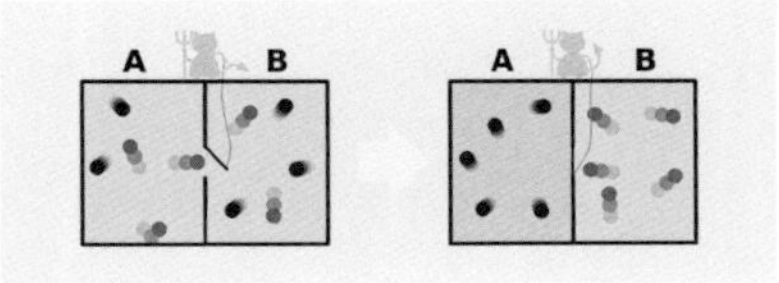

348 ● 578

What's interesting to us is the question: what is this demon? He observes the white noise at elementary level and sorts particles. All nature is the motion of these particles. The demon sits outside, observes nature and does not touch any particle: he is super-natural. If the motion of the different particles is the natural sense of the world, then the demon is without sense, but intervenes with nature. Which is indeed demonic.

We also know this thought experiment in a somewhat different form as the *evil demon* in the context of Cartesian doubt, after René Descartes: Descartes asks, what if all our senses were being deceived by a demon, as in the Wachowskis' 1999 science fiction feature *The Matrix?* What, in such a world, can we rely on, what can we know?

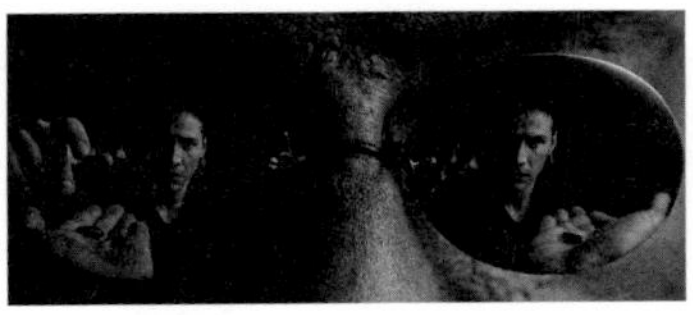

349 ● 579

Descartes' answer is as simple as it is famous: *cogito ergo sum.* – I think, therefore I am. I am the sorting demon. That's the only thing I can rely on: the rational decision. Opening or closing the door. This is what abstracts me from nature and from the senses, which can be deceived.

Descartes and Maxwell both affirm the thermodynamic end, in which everything is senseless. This stabilises the intellect as 'supernatural', and it is the intellect which constitutes meaning beyond the thermic death.

We introduced the concept of *entropy* to show that creating sense inevitably ends in thermodynamic death. The concept of *negentropy* is defined as negative entropy, or reverse entropy. What we want to highlight here is that entropy is an analytical and thermodynamic term: with it, we leave an old world behind. Negentropy is a term from quantum mechanics: with it, a new world is born. In this world, the focus is not on analysis and creating sense. Instead it turns to something like 'writing a stageplay' from out of the principal contingency, or the plenty of no sense: it's what we think of as a 'making of meaning'.

We can illustrate this 'making of meaning' like this: imagine your are the Maxwell demon and instead of entropic energetic particles in a container you have random pixels on your screen. And now you take your mouse and turn the pixels 'over' one by one to form an image of your choosing, for example of Clint Eastwood. Like the demon, you are out of nature and you *make* your new reality.

□ 567↘

350A ● 579

350B ● 579

This picture no longer 'creates sense' like the exposed silver crystals of a photograph: it is not natural in that it does not have any relation to a physical or any other cause out there. It does not follow the natural lines of necessities. It has been made 'out of the blue', from contingencies. It establishes new meaning, because it is actually made. And we should affirm: its primary character is not sensory, but intellectual.

We can witness this progression from the sensory to the intellectual realm around 1900 in mathematics, in physics with the advent of quantum physics, and also in art. Take French painter Claude Monet (1840–1926). His *Nymphéas* emerge intellectually from a dead entropic 'mist'.

351 ● 579

It is this process that we think of as negentropy, which, as we have noted, is a key concept in information technics. Information plays together with negentropy: it 'captures' and 'circulates' entropic processes – just like Maxwell's demon – towards vivid meaningful elements.

In thermodynamics all consistency dissolves. With information, forms are made quantum mechanically. The thermodynamic thinking of the enlightenment and classicism is orchestrated around concepts like functions, reality, sensitivity, analysis, creativity, beauty, the individual, or classification. This thinking projects into the future and dissolves itself in time. Information, by contrast, is rational: it looks upon time, bundles time into forms and draws a new present.

If you get this twist in thinking, the technical implementation of the demon is not too complicated. (See Big Data & Machine Learning – Elaboration: *The Markov Chain and Machine Learning*.) If you can define a meaningful context in time (for example a game of chess, a search engine, a book shop, a self-driving car) and if you are connected to all of the parts of this context, you can take a probability image with an eye on each part of the whole system. You have as many images of the system as parts (which, by the way, is a classical multiplication). The 'pixels' of these images are white if the part is looking at a 'closest friend'; it is black, if it is of no interest. Now you can turn this package of images in the real world like a hologram towards any situation within the meaningful context, which means you obtain a good next move in chess, you get relevant answers to your search questions, the book shop sells you the right book, and the car takes you to your destination without human intervention. And that's it.

Reflection

Here then perhaps a concluding consideration, rather than our usual *Outlook*. Ours is an adventurous thesis, and that's more or less all there is to it: AI is not a technological problem. Quite the opposite: it substitutes complicated technology with simple but complex algorithms. And that's why the implications are truly enormous.

Ray Kurzweil, in tune with English theoretical physicist Stephen Hawking (1942–2018) among many others, points out the enormity of the potential pitfalls and downright danger, as they see it, of AI. And while it would be ridiculous to suggest that there are not issues of great magnitude that we need to be aware and conscious of, we want to emphasise here also, and particularly, the sheer potential. For architects, for inventors, for artists, for entrepreneurs, for educators, for engineers, for environmentalists, for visionaries. If we can show you, over a few pages of simply written text and about 150 lines of code, the principles of applied AI, then think what you can do if you devote just a slim part of your studies to learning it.

When our civilisation started to read and write, the first instinct of the powerful was not to leap for joy and set up schools to teach every child as quickly as possible. Their first instinct was to guard this new skill, and therefore power, closely and jealously. The idea that just about anyone could avail themselves of knowledge was greeted not with open arms and celebrations, but with dismay. At every single juncture of our development as a species you will find people – well informed, serious, genuinely concerned, and highly intelligent people – predict the end of the world, more or less, or at any rate the grave danger inherent in whatever happens to be around the corner. Giving women the vote was going to end the species, as children would no longer be born. Abolishing slavery was going to end all economic activity as no more work would be done. Factories were going to end all human craft. Video was lamented to have killed the radio star long before it could have done so (it never really did), and of course the Internet was going to end all social life, all literacy, all human interaction, and all culture. You can pick virtually any moment in history and you will find someone fretting about something or other spelling the end for humanity, quite imminently. 'The end is nigh.' Always has been, always will be.

Should you blithely ignore all warnings and dismiss any critical voices as doom-mongers or Luddites? Absolutely not. Just take things with a pinch of salt and look upon your world with a sense of perspective. And nor do we mean to suggest that you embrace every new thing with unbridled, unthinking enthusiasm. We're human beings: we're capable of differentiating, of being selectively smitten. Not everything is what it seems, and not everything turns out as intended. The fact that an algorithm, such as Google's *PageRank* for instance, takes a whole new approach to a whole new problem does not by necessity mean that it is conceptually revolutionary. Google's world view and business model are remarkably orthodox: find ways to control the traditional markets, open them up on a global scale, don't talk too much about the quantum nature of the techniques used but explain them as 'understandable' mechanical tools, and turn everything possible into profit in an established economy. And we don't blame Google for this. It's the environment Google operates in – our culture, our society, our world – which has to understand this 'quantum nature of information' we have been talking about, and learn to domesticate and cultivate these powerful techniques.

Google is now so big, so overbearing, and so all-pervasive that you'd be forgiven for thinking there is nothing that can be done to resist it. But if you don't want to be a minion to Google, you can always be a mini-Google and start beating the titans at their own game: you don't need more than a small computer and a short bot script. For example, create your own news feed: you can define a personal profile of your interests and then let the computer crawl the Internet for you continuously – as Google does – to curate a personal news feed from sources you can trust. And when we say 'you don't need more than a small computer' to do this, we mean that literally. Any ordinary laptop will do just fine, but if you don't want your main machine's processor to be kept busy on a task like that, a *Raspberry Pi 3 Model B* is perfectly capable of searching 50,000 news items a day. As we write this in 2018, you can buy this current version of the popular palm-sized educational single-board computer for 35 euros. (We exemplify this thinking and approach in our chapter on Being a 'Brand'.) □ 593↘

Obviously, if you can do this, then so can anyone else: the technology is available and the programming skills required are fairly basic. And that raises all kinds of questions about privacy and security, because there is a comparatively small step from systematically searching published web content for the purpose of finding relevant information to building AI programs with serious ulterior motives. (And we are discussing these issues in detail in our chapter on Privacy & Security.) □ 643↘

All of which means that the really big questions raised by Big Data & Machine Learning, the □ ↖549 challenges we are facing and therefore having to deal with, are no longer primarily technological, but political and economical ones. They concern our privacy, the integrity of data; they involve the new power bases and the commodification of information. You've heard it said before: for Facebook and Google, you are the product. Not because they make you, but because they mine you, for every bit of information they can get about you. Every term you search for, every item you like or comment on, every picture you post, every email or message you send or receive through any of their channels, everywhere you visit, every direction you get, every time you 'check in' or leave a review: you're continually, voluntarily giving them a clearer idea of who you are, so they can pimp you to their advertisers, with astonishing precision. And we are talking here about two companies that may be vast and excessively powerful, but that, on all the evidence we have, are essentially 'benign'. (There are whole separate debates that can and need to be had about what constitutes, in this or any other context, a 'benign' corporation, involving a raft of issues such as a company's willingness to pay fair levels of tax, for example, but this is clearly not the place for them.) Suffice it to say that given these extreme concentrations of power, we need to look at the political dimension and realise that not every 'big player', let alone every big government agency, secret service, or organised crime outfit does necessarily have our best interests at heart.

And on a fundamental, final note, it's worth bringing back to mind: if everything is connected to everything else, data really has no meaning, because there is a 'sensible reason' for everything: we don't assume any structure, we simply take what we can get and group things together into meaningful relationships. And whatever this sheaf happens to be, machine learning allows us to stabilise it.

To see what we can – and also have to – expect, ■ 596↘ and what intelligent questions we will be able – and also have – to ask, we need look no further than history. Just as the Renaissance developed a new archaeology – as exemplified by the survey of Rome conducted by Italian architect, poet, philosopher and polymath Leon Battista Alberti (1404–1472) – so we today see that the great digitisation projects are expressions of a new 'archaeology' that we use to create a stability for something new: it is a basis for artificial intelligence and for a new type of 'writing'.

□ ↖507

It is now possible – and we know this because we are doing it – to download, from open data sources, hundreds of thousands of ground plans for all the buildings in Switzerland, for example. Once you have all these ground plans, you can then classify all these buildings into, say, 30 or so different 'prototypes'. These prototypes you can then turn into Building Information Modelling (BIM) classes, and, if you feel so inclined, use (or share) these BIM classes to design new buildings that from the outset sit within the conceptual environment you are working in. This means you – and for 'you' here read 'your software' – can 'learn by doing'. And that is exactly why all the analytical disciplines – machine building, medicine, any form of analysis, engineering, theory, 'reading', skills – today find themselves in a crisis and why a new, stabilising architecture is needed.

Elaboration

Read these examples in conjunction with the introductory texts in Big Data & Machine Learning.

Here as in the other Elaboration *sections in this* Atlas *where we play through in-depth examples and experiments in coding, we use* Mathematica, *written in the* Wolfram *programming language. This is a matter of preference, not compulsion: there are other programming languages that could do the same thing.*

COMBINATORIAL EXPLOSION

Refer to Big Data & Machine Learning*: Combinatorial Explosion.*

The following (right hand column, top) is a Latin square, in which each row and column yields the same sum, 6:

A Latin square of the order n = 3

```
Grid[{{1,2,3},{2,3,1},{3,1,2}}]

1 2 3
2 3 1
3 1 2
```

☐ ↖549

These are all 12 possible Latin squares of the order 3:

```
Row[MatrixForm/@LatinSquares[3]]

(1 2 3)(1 2 3)(1 3 2)(1 3 2)(2 1 3)(2 1 3)
(2 3 1)(3 1 2)(2 1 3)(3 2 1)(1 3 2)(3 2 1)
(3 1 2)(2 3 1)(3 2 1)(2 1 3)(3 2 1)(1 3 2)

(2 3 1)(2 3 1)(3 2 1)(3 2 1)(3 1 2)(3 1 2)
(1 2 3)(3 1 2)(1 3 2)(2 1 3)(1 2 3)(2 3 1)
(3 1 2)(1 2 3)(2 1 3)(1 3 2)(2 3 1)(1 2 3)
```

☐ ↖555

Here is the explosion of possibilities, depending on the order of squares:

```
{
{1,1},
{2,2},
{3,12},
{4,576},
{5,161280},
{6,812851200},
{7,61479419904000},
{8,108776032459082956800},
{9,5524751496156892842531225600},
{10,9982437658213039871725064756920320000},
{11,776966836171770144107444346734230682311065600000}
}
```

COMBINATORICS

Let's start with a system consisting of four different parts, which can be arranged in 24 possible *combinations*:

```
per=Permutations[
 {GrayLevel@0.0,GrayLevel@.33,
  GrayLevel@.67,GrayLevel@1.0},4,4}];

Length[per]

24
```

```
ch3={
     #[[1]],Rectangle[{-1,-1}],
     #[[2]],Rectangle[{0,-1}],
     #[[3]],Rectangle[{-1,0}],
     #[[4]],Rectangle[{0,0}]
     } &/@ per;
ch4=Partition[ch3,12];
lines=Fold[
 Translate[{#1,#2},{3,0}]&,{},#]&/@ch4;
lines=Fold[
 Translate[{#1,#2},{0,3}]&,{},lines];
Graphics[lines]
```

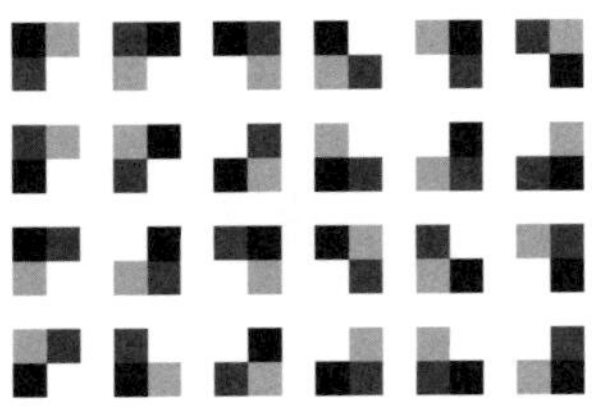

If we dismantle the unit into 6 parts, we already get 720 possible combinations. Because of combinatorial explosion, any system has to be constructed as compact as possible. A system is characterised by how logical and error-free it is, as it excludes the world at large with the exception of few select parts.

```
per=Permutations[
     GrayLevel/@{0,1/5,2/5,3/5,4/5,1},{6,6}];
Length[per]

720
```

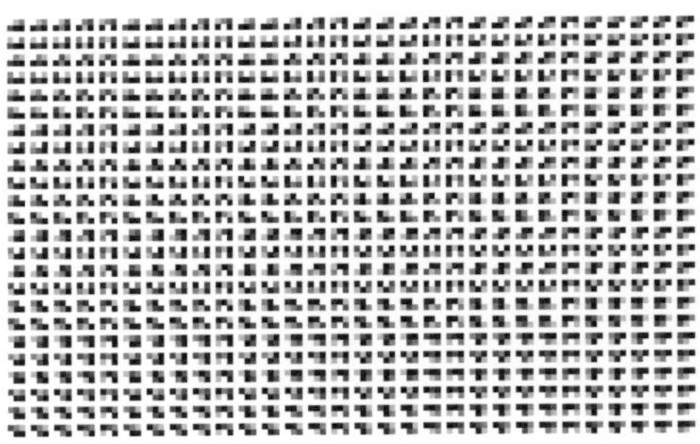

RENDERING OF COMBINATORICS

A system is always the fictional interplay of its parts. It has no form, so it can't be seen until and unless it is rendered into a concrete form. A system can take on an arbitrary number of forms, and it can be translated between these forms, as the following example shows.

Here is a state of the system we've just described, consisting of 6 parts, represented as a list of 6 coloured panels:

```
per[[1]]
{■,■,■,□,■,■}
```

These are the rules for the translation of the colour panels into numbers or letters:

```
rule={■→1,■→"A",■→"B",□→2,■→3,■→4};
{1, A, B, 2, 3, 4}
per[[1]]/.rule
{1,A,B,2,3,4}
```

This is another state of the same system:

```
per[[100]]/.rule
{1,4,A,2,3,B}
```

This, another way of representing it:

```
per[[100]]/.rule2
```

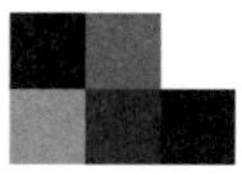

GRAMMAR AND GROWTH

Grammars constitute a principal procedure to model architecture. These, too, are systems, as defined above, but here it is not the parts that are being positioned in a combinatorial way, but instead the whole system is being read as a self-referential, that is recursive, branching process.

The following example replaces the character '1' with the character sequence '{1,{−1,1}}'. This rule is now applied to its own result several times, and we quickly recognise a growing character sequence of the 1st, 2nd, 3rd, and 4th iteration or order.

```
BR2[len_,rot_,ite_]:=
 Module[{},
  If[ite==1,Return[len]];
  {len,{-BR2[len/1,rot,ite-1],
        BR2[len/1,rot,ite-1]}
   }]
Column[(δ1=NormalDistribution[2,.01];
    δ2=NormalDistribution[6,.01];
    LinkLength [len_]:=len/RandomVariate@δ1;
    LinkRotation[rot_]:=π/RandomVariate@δ2;
    BR2[1,π/6,#]
    )&/@ {1,2,3,4}]
{
 {1},
 {{1,{-1,1}}},
 {{1,{{-1,{1,-1}},{1,{-1,1}}}}},
 {{1,{{-1,{{1,{-1,1}},{-1,{1,-1}}}},
  {1,{{-1,{1,-1}},{1,{-1,1}}}}}}}
}
```

The traces of this branching process can also be represented graphically:

```
BR2[len_,rot_,ite_]:=
 Module[{},
  If[ite==0,Return[]];
  {Line[{{0,0},{0,len}}],
   Translate[{
     Rotate[{BR2[LinkLength@len,rot,ite-1]},
            LinkRotation@rot,{0,0}],
     Rotate[{BR2[LinkLength@len,rot,ite-1]},
            -LinkRotation@rot,{0,0}]
    },{0,len}]
   }]
Row[(δ1=NormalDistribution[2,.01];
    δ2=NormalDistribution[6,.01];
    LinkLength [len_]:=len/RandomVariate@δ1;
    LinkRotation[rot_]:=π/RandomVariate@δ2;
    Graphics[BR2[1,π/6,#]]
    )&/@ {1,2,3,4,5,6}]
```

□ ↖145
□ ↖175
□ ↖529
□ ↖351

(See also our chapters on Generative Methods, Graphs & Graphics, Digital Cities, *and* Scripting*.)*

↖152

STOCHASTICS & STATISTICS

□ ↖561

Refer to Big Data & Machine Learning*: A New Writing in a New World.*

Let's now move from the writing of systems to reading them.

When we were writing systems we faced the problem of realising the conception of a system with as few parts as possible, so that it will function in a stable and flawless manner as planned. This is what we call 'construction' or 'design'.

Reading systems, we face the problem of establishing whether the elements that we can see and measure are in fact part of a system or not. It is important here to appreciate that we cannot see or know the system, we can only measure individual states or characteristics. And we don't even know whether the measurements we obtain are the expression of one system, several systems, or in fact no system at all.

With this question we arrive at Swiss mathematician Jacob Bernoulli (1655–1705) and the area of stochastics.

THE LAW OF LARGE NUMBERS

Here is a throw of three dice:

```
n=3;
series:=RandomInteger[{1,6},n]
series
{2,4,4}
```

As we would expect, we get a random sequence of numbers. If we throw the dice again, we may get a completely different sequence:

```
series
{6,3,3}
```

We can, however, view these sequences not as a quantity of individual elements, but as connected parts of a system, by, for example, identifying the mean value of all throws of the dice we have carried out so far:

```
n=12;
series
N[#[[1]]/#[[2]]&/@
 Transpose[{Accumulate@%,Range@n}],3]
```

```
{1,5,2,5,2,2,3,5,2,1,6,6}
{1.00,3.00,2.67,3.25,3.00,2.83,
 2.86,3.13,3.00,2.80,3.09,3.33}
```

```
series
N[#[[1]]/#[[2]]&/@
 Transpose[{Accumulate@%,Range@n}],3]
```

```
{2,3,6,1,2,3,6,5,4,4,1,5}
{2.00,2.50,3.67,3.00,2.80,2.83,
 3.29,3.50,3.56,3.60,3.36,3.50}
```

We can see now that individual throws are random, but the sequence of accumulated mean values shows less and less variance: they converge.

Here are different sequences of 1,000 throws. At the start of each sequence, its pattern is very individual; but over time they always converge towards the value 3.5.

```
n=1000;
Row[Show[
    ListLinePlot[Accumulate@
     RandomInteger[{1,6},n]/Range@n],
    Graphics[{Red,Line[{{0,3.5},{n,3.5}}]}]
    ]&/@{1,1,1}]
```

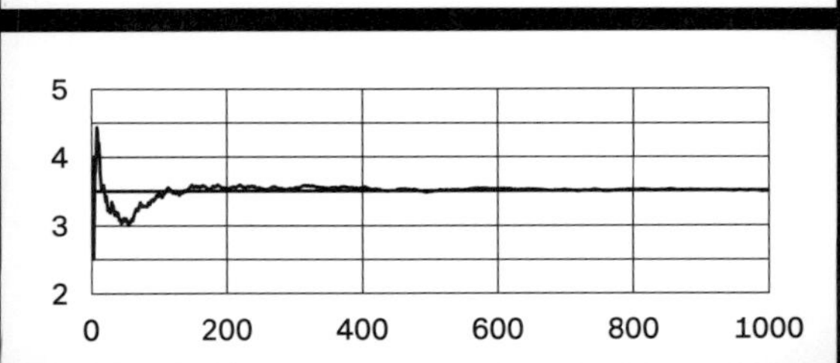

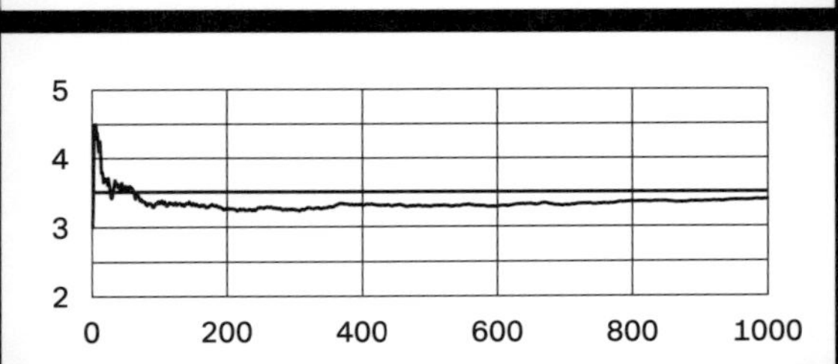

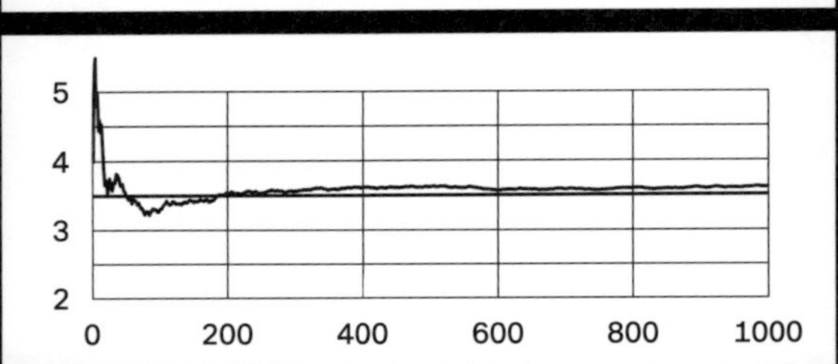

This phenomenon is known as the **Law of Large Numbers (LNN)**, first formulated by Bernoulli, in his groundbreaking work on probability, *Ars conjectandi*, published eight years after his death, in 1713. According to it, the bigger the quantity you deal with, the closer the actual real life data curve gets to the ideal.

So we can say: if the readings or measurements converge to a number, they are systematic. In this case, they are always the throws of dice, which, like any system, are connected and will not be influenced by their environment.

One additional thought is also important: we can say about these measurements that they are of a system without knowing how the system itself is constructed. Thus, Darwin can classify living creatures in accordance with individual characteristics, without having to know or explain how they work. And so *species*, *classes*, *types*, or *styles* are all pure fiction, which results from the stochastic of individual characteristics.

CHANCE OR EVENTS WITHOUT SENSE

Let's go one step further:

A die has 6 sides. Instead of examining a system by identifying the mean value of the throws, we can also count how often a number has been thrown:

```
pln=100;
plt=RandomInteger[{1,6},pln]; Short@plt
pct=SortBy[Normal@Counts@plt,First]
pctN=#[[2]]/pln&/@(List@@#&/@pct)
ListLinePlot[pctN,PlotRange→{{1,6},{0,.2}}]
```

```
{4,5,2,1,2,2,1,3,3,6,5,2,5,2,
 <<72>>,6,5,1,1,1,4,2,5,3,3,6,1,2,2}
{1→19,2→20,3→16,4→14,5→19,6→12}
{19/100,1/5,4/25,7/50,19/100,3/25}
```

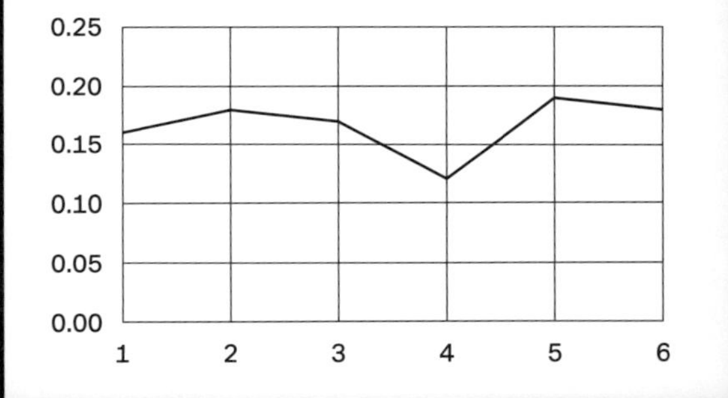

Now we carry out the same exercise with 100,000 throws:

```
{5,5,1,6,4,1,6,5,5,1,6,5,3,
 <<99974>>,1,5,2,2,3,1,4,3,3,5,3,6,5}
{1→16630,2→16538,3→16835,
 4→16825,5→16529,6→16643}
{1663/10000,8269/50000,3367/20000,
 673/4000,16529/100000,16643/100000}
```

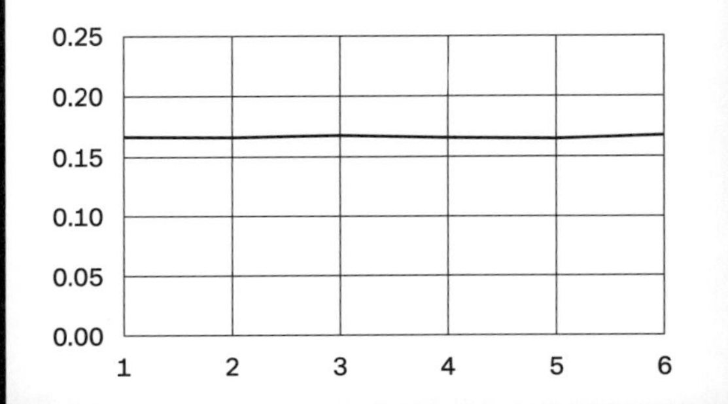

Again we note: the distribution of throws evens out with the number of throws. The even distribution means that the events are not connected to each other. We can't make any prediction, there is no cause and effect; the throws make no sense, they are accidental. In mathematical terms, we are therefore talking about a *set*.

Here is another graphic representation of accidental events; what we call white noise, much as we may encounter it on an old analogue TV that receives no signal:

```
pts={RandomInteger[600],
     RandomInteger[450]}&/@Range@1000;
Graphics[Point@pts]
```

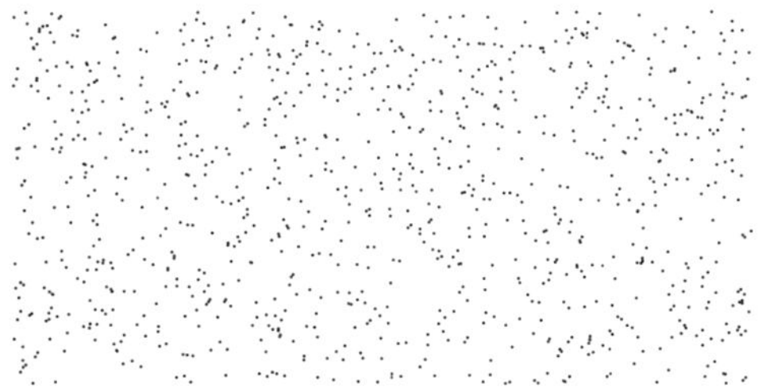

And here is yet another representation of accidental events: not points on a surface, but the direction and length of the next step in each case, in movements from one point to another. This is called **Brownian motion**, after Scottish botanist Robert Brown (1773–1858).

```
Graphics[{BezierCurve@Accumulate@
         RandomReal[{-1,1},{60,2}]}]
```

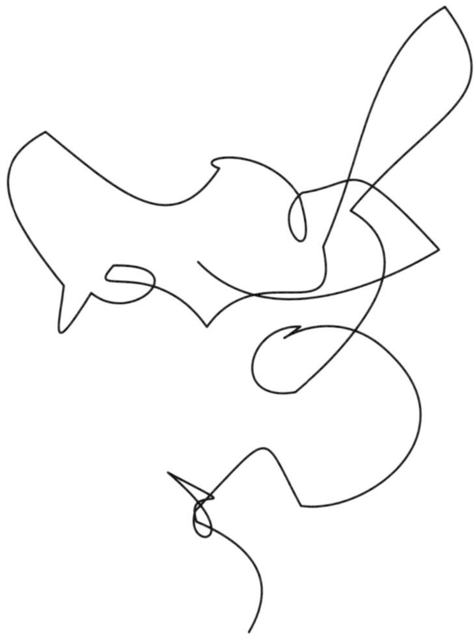

SYSTEMS OR EVENTS THAT MAKE SENSE

We can also think about throwing dice differently, and not look at doing so as a sequence of individual, isolated events, but as a sequence of accidental events. We no longer now look at the throws individually, but as part of a whole, as a system.

Let's start with a simple 3-part system:

```
pln=1000;
series=RandomInteger[{1,6},{pln,3}];
Short@%

{{2,2,6},{5,6,6},{1,2,6},
 <<994>>,{1,6,4},{1,3,6},{5,2,4}}
```

We now have 1,000 *individual* systems of a *species*. Let's work out the sums of each individual and count the *frequency* of the sums:

```
tot=Total /@ series;Short@tot
counts=SortBy[Normal@Counts@tot,First]
ListLinePlot[List@@@counts]

{10,17,9,9,11,12,6,7,7,14,
 <<980>>,15,12,16,13,11,11,8,11,10,11}

{3→3,4→12,5→22,6→42,7→60,8→100,
 9→107,10→136,11→131,12→129,13→84,
 14→68,15→37,16→39,17→22,18→8}
```

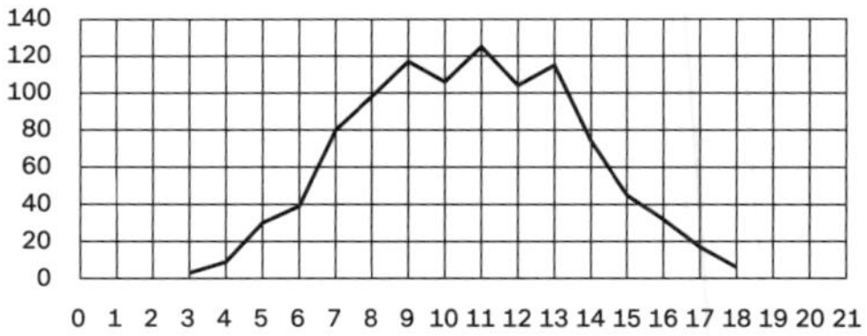

This distribution of frequencies is entirely different to the random distribution of individual chance events. What's known as *normal distribution* shows itself whenever random elements stand in systemic relationship to each other, such as in our example of the sum of three elements. It appears in cases, in other words, where we can look for a common cause. Where the distribution of events appears as a bell curve, they make sense: they are individual events of a *type* or *species*.

THE PRODUCTION OR PREDICTION OF EVENTS

Just as the measurements of elementary events which are independent of each other converge towards a single value, so connected events converge towards the bell curve. The ideal curve is determined by the mean value:

```
mean=Mean@plt

21/2
```

And here is what is known as the *standard deviation* – that's the width of the bell curve:

```
sDev=StandardDeviation@plt
```

$$3\sqrt{\frac{42}{43}}$$

This now is the function of the normal distribution, which consists of mean value and standard deviation:

```
nd=PDF[NormalDistribution[mean,sDev],x]
```

$$\frac{1}{6}\, e^{-\frac{43}{756}\left(-\frac{43}{756}+x\right)^2}\sqrt{\frac{43}{21\pi}}$$

```
Plot[nd//Evaluate,{x,0,21},Filling→Axis]
```

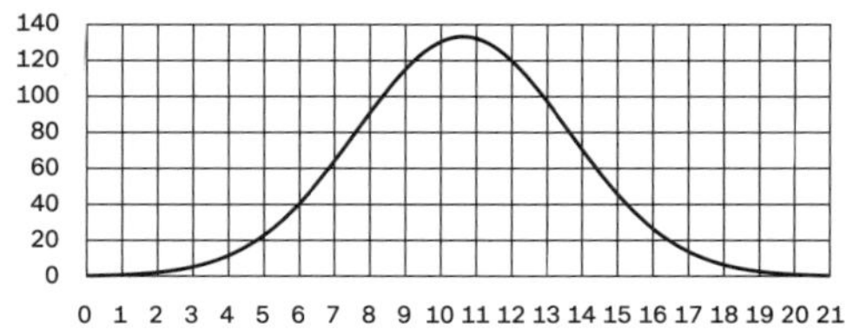

Any system, or any species, thus is *defined* and *specified* by its mean value and standard deviation.

Any concrete quantity tends to have a distribution similar to this ideal, as French mathematician Abraham de Moivre (1667–1754) postulated with his Central Limit Theorem (CLT), which establishes that in most cases involving random variables, their sum aligns broadly with a normal distribution, that is a bell curve.

Here is another graphic representation: a normal distribution arrangement of points as it may come about if we shoot arrows from a bow at a target disk, for example:

```
pts=RandomVariate[NormalDistribution[0,.1],2]
     {600,450}&/@Range@1000;
Graphics[Point@pts]
```

In contrast to a random distribution arrangement without any form, the individual elements here produce a common form; they are not freely movable and we can make arguments and predictions about it, because there's something to look at: the arrangement makes sense. The measurements are systematic and we can assume a system behind them that is characterised by a mean and a standard deviation.

PARAMETRICS AND INDIVIDUALS

Let us then now use mean and standard deviation and individualise the 'tree' that we generated earlier.

A system may, as we discussed, take on many forms. And this leads us to the second significant technique of architectural modelling: with a combination of grammar (for the generation of a structure) and parametrics (for the generation of form) we can, for example, produce many individuals of a certain species, or different instances of a class.

```
BR2[len_,rot_,ite_]:=
 Module[{},
  If[ite==0,Return[]];
  {Line[{{0,0},{0,len}}],
   Translate[{
     Rotate[{BR2[LinkLength@len,rot,ite-1]},
            LinkRotation@rot,{0,0}],
     Rotate[{BR2[LinkLength@len,rot,ite-1]},
            -LinkRotation@rot,{0,0}]
     },{0,len}]
   }]
δ1=NormalDistribution[2,.1];
δ2=NormalDistribution[6,1];
LinkLength[len_]:=len/RandomVariate@δ1
LinkRotation[rot_]:=π/RandomVariate@δ2
tree :=Graphics[BR2[1,π/6,6]]
Grid@Partition[Table[tree,{i,1,16}],4]
```

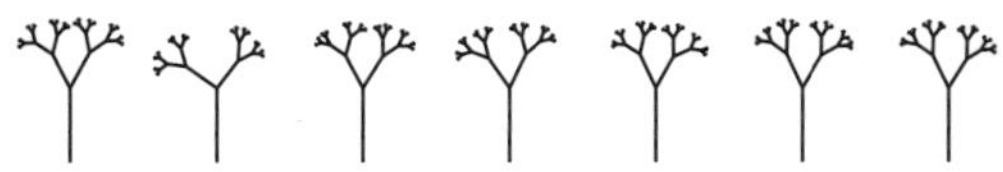

THE MARKOV CHAIN AND MACHINE LEARNING

↖188

Systems have a principal characteristic: expressed positively, they work the same everywhere; expressed negatively, they are never complete or detailed enough for any concrete case; in other words, they are never adequate. Or, as Gödel notes and as we explain in the main body of this chapter, a system cannot be complete and consistent at the same time, it can only ever be complete and inconsistent, or incomplete and consistent at the same time.

With the *Markov chain*, named after Russian mathematician Andrey Markov (1856–1922) who researched it in the early part of the 20th century, and machine learning we can overcome this limitation of stochastics and systems. The procedure is as simple as it is baffling and abstract, and we like to think of it as a 'global locality'.

Say we have a series of three different, individual events:

```
series={1,2,1,1,2,1,2,3,2,1,1,2,3,1,2};
```

This is the list of possible events:

```
states=DeleteDuplicates@series
{1,2,3}
```

These are the transitions between these events (the sequence in which they happen):

```
transitions=Partition[series,2,1]
{{1,2},{2,1},{1,1},{1,2},{2,1},{1,2},{2,3},
 {3,2},{2,1},{1,1},{1,2},{2,3},{3,1},{1,2}}
```

These are the sets of follow-up events that happen after each event; in the first set you have all the events that follow 1, in the second all the events that follow 2, and in the third all the events that follow 3:

```
follow=#[[2]]&/@Extract[transitions,
       Position[transitions,{#,_}]]&/@states
{{2,1,2,2,1,2,2},{1,1,3,1,3},{2,1}}

C1[fol_,states_]:=
 (Length@Position[fol,#]&/@states)/Length@fol
```

From this, we get the predicted probabilities from one event to the next, in other words: the probability that a particular event will happen after the previous one:

```
pm=C1[#,states]&/@follow
{{2/7,5/7,0},{3/5,0,2/5},{1/2,1/2,0}}
```

These are the numerical values represented visually:

```
ArrayPlot@pm
```

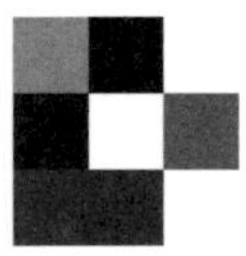

Now we encode the Markov process:

```
P=DiscreteMarkovProcess[1,pm];
```

■ 597↘

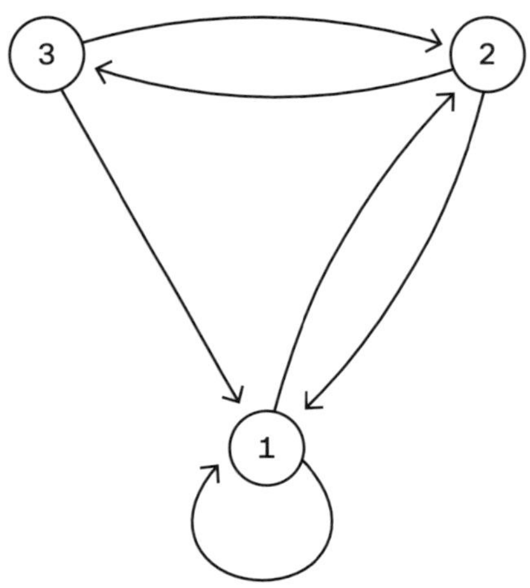

This process is now capable of making predictions which correspond to the profile of transition probabilities:

```
data=RandomFunction[P,{0,20}];
ListPlot[data]
```

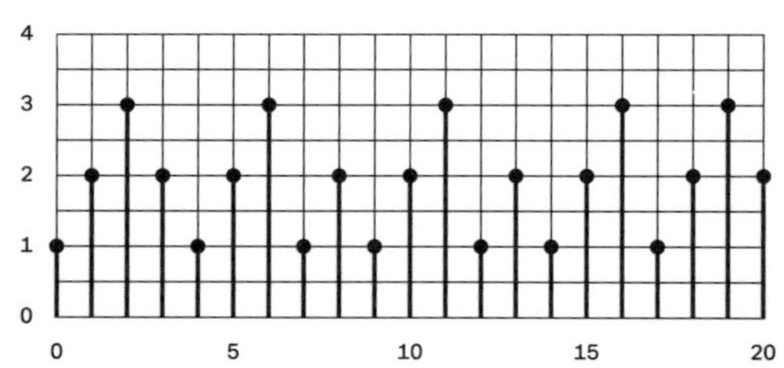

The movement of these predictions corresponds to the movement of the individual measurements, without having to make any global assumptions about them. The movement has the character of the measurements, whatever they are, and this 'whatever they are' is the critical point: we do not need to make any further assumptions about the system or understand anything about it. We just need a series of measurements and we can, for example, make weather forecasts.

We describe as an event the weather in one location and the weather in various neighbouring locations. Then we take readings for the weather over a certain period of time. From this, we work out transition probabilities for the weather over that period, and from this, we in turn work out transition probabilities for this particular location. Now we can read the probabilities for a certain kind of weather at this particular location for tomorrow.

Or we can go online, take hyperlinks of webpages, follow people and predict their movements: welcome to social media.

And that's it! Everything else is merely a question of big data sets, fast processing, and large networks. And that's the important point that we want to emphasise once more: inside the overall complexity, things are strikingly simple.

AN EXAMPLE DRIVER

Here then, to conclude, an example on the subject of autonomous driverless vehicles. (In this case we are using a Self-Organising Map [SOM]).

Here is a list of events that are characteristic of good driver behaviour when approaching a traffic light; what you would normally do when you are driving along the road and you see a set of traffic lights on either green, amber (yellow), or red, depending on your current speed and the speed limit on that stretch of road. It is principally a choice between brake or accelerate:

```
green=100;
yellow=50;
red=0;
eventList={
   {"tLight"→green,"limit"→50,"speed"→10,
    "break"→0,"gas"→20,"eval"→100},
   {"tLight"→green,"limit"→50,"speed"→20,
    "break"→0,"gas"→40,"eval"→100},
   {"tLight"→green,"limit"→50,"speed"→15,
    "break"→0,"gas"→40,"eval"→100},
   <<15>>
   {"tLight"→green,"limit"→100,"speed"→100,
    "break"→0,"gas"→30,"eval"→100}
   };
```

Here is a visualisation of one of these events: the traffic light is red, the speed limit is 50 km/h, the current speed is 20 km/h, we are braking, and everything is fine.

Now we create a driver:

```
driver=IDcreate[6,6,6];
```

This is a visualisation of the driver's 'brain'. As it has not yet been trained, what we see is 'white noise':

```
Image3D[Partition["weights"/.driver,6]]
```

```
Row@IDslices@driver
```

Now we train the driver with a list of events:

```
vecList=#/100.0&/@{"tLight","limit","speed",
         "break","gas","eval"}/.eventList;
driver["weights"]=
 IDtrain[driver,vecList,100,12];
```

The 'brain' acquires some structure:

```
Image3D[Partition["weights"/. driver,6]]
```

```
Row@IDslices@driver
```

And already we can let our driver loose on its own, by getting it to make predictions. In this case: if the light is green, the speed limit 30 km/h and the current speed 0, what are the predictions for acceleration and brake? Based purely on what it 'knows', the driver accelerates a bit, which is correct: it is handling a situation it has never encountered before, with a 'brain' that has never even tried to analyse what driving is:

```
situation1={driver,green,30,0};
DisplayDrivingEventSensors@@%
```

```
Drive@@situation1
{"break","gas"}/.%;
DisplayDrivingEventActuators@@%
{{break→0,gas→10,eval→100}}
```

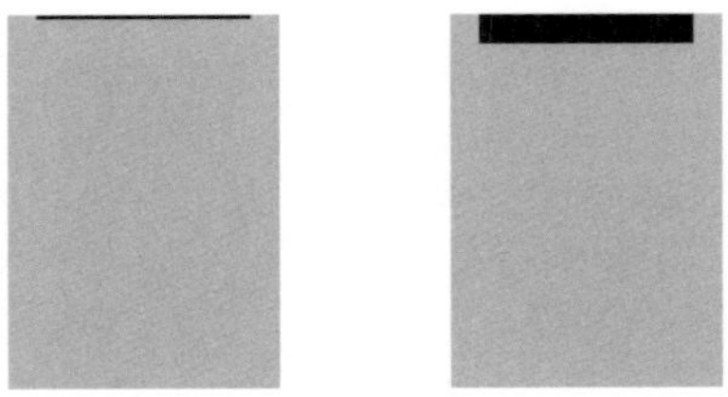

Of course, this is only one single event, out of possible millions on a long car journey. But as we say: the truly fascinating thing here is not so much that our artificial driver can make a correct decision, but that it can do so with a few short lines of code and a wealth of data to draw from. And that's all we really want to achieve with this exercise: to show that big data and machine learning are complex, but not very complicated, and you need very little code to work with them.

334 ● 551
LOS ANGELES, NOVEMBER 2019
...
HOLDEN: You're in a desert, walking along in the sand when all of the sudden –
LEON: Is this the test now?
HOLDEN: Yes. You're in a desert walking along in the sand when all of the sudden you look down –
LEON: What one?
HOLDEN: What?
LEON: What desert?
HOLDEN: It doesn't make any difference what desert, it's completely hypothetical.
LEON: But how come I'd be there?
...
From *Blade Runner*, 1982. [The Blade Runner Partnership]

335 ● 552
Playing checkers on the *IMB 701*, 1956. [IBM]

336 ● 553
Kasparov makes the first move. – Garry Kasparov, then world chess champion, opens the first of six games against IBM's *Deep Blue* computer, in 1996. [*The Atlantic*]

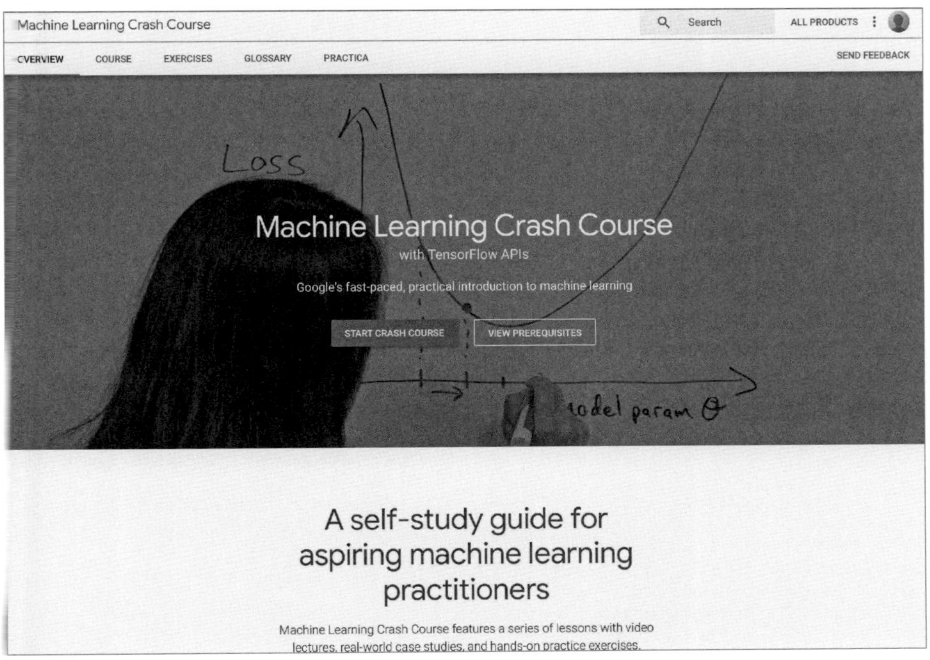

337 ● 553
Google offering online crash courses in machine learning, 2018. [Google]

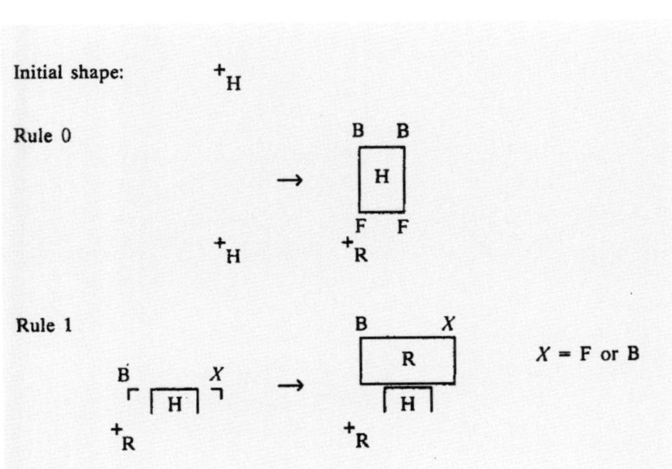

338 ● 557
The initial rules for a shape grammar for houses in the Queen Anne Style. Ulrich Flemming, 1987.

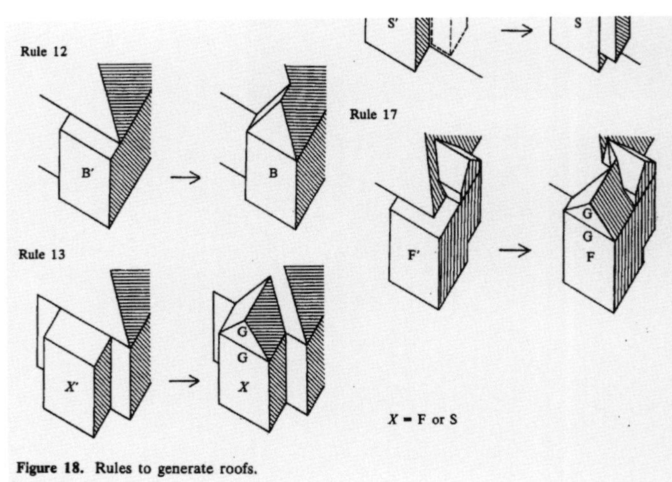

339 ● 557
Detailing the rules for a shape grammar for houses in the Queen Anne Style. Ulrich Flemming, 1987.

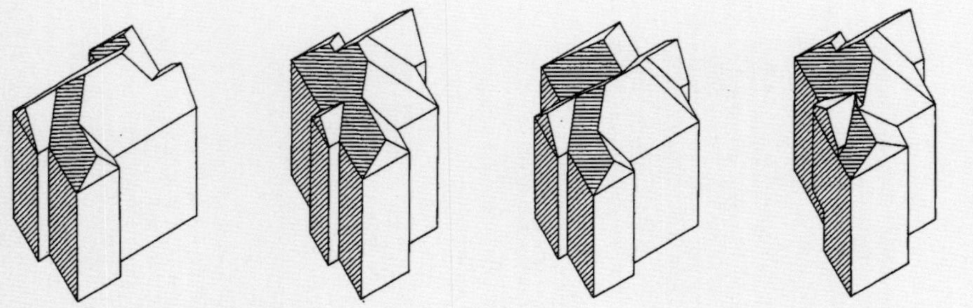

Figure 19. Basic Queen Anne houses.

340 ● 557
Some examples of the results of this grammar. Ulrich Flemming, 1987.

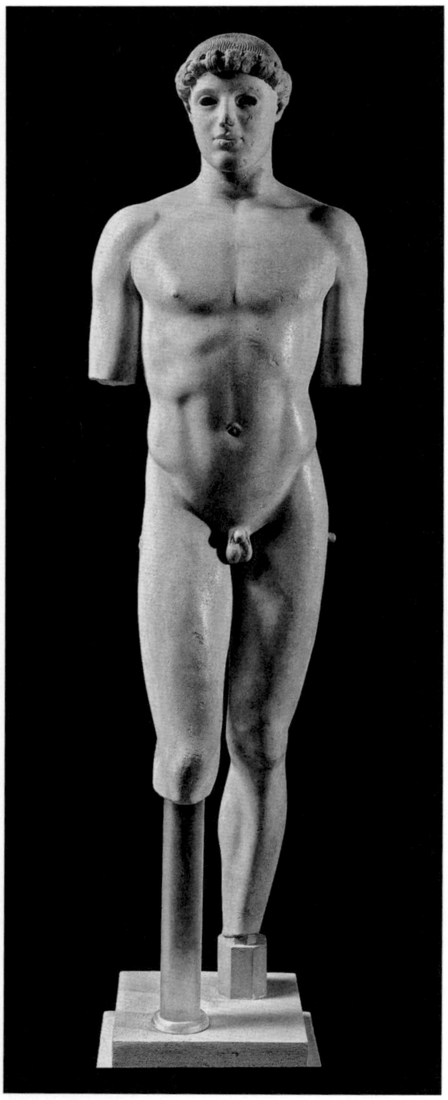

341 ● 559
Greek sculpture 'in space': *Kritios Boy*, c. 480 BC.

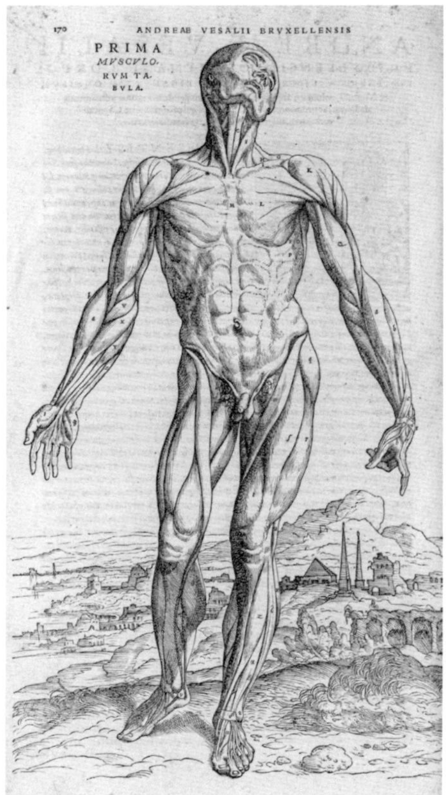

342 ● 559
Renaissance sculpture 'in time' – a study of motion from *De humani corporis fabrica libri septem (On the Fabric of the Human Body in Seven Books)* by Flemish anatomist and physician Andreas Vesalius (1514–1564).

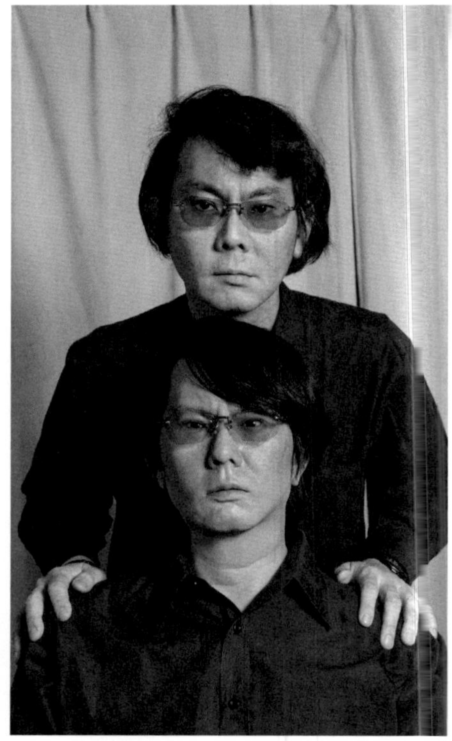

343 ● 559
Today's sculpture 'in life': Hiroshi Ishiguro.

344 ● 562
Jennifer Chang & Belén Gándara: *Synesthesia Pharma-Huasca*, 2011: “We remap consciousness to break the notion between awareness and delirium.” [Jennifer Chang & Belén Gándara]

345 ● 562
Landscape with Pilgrim by Carl Friedrich Schinkel, 1813.

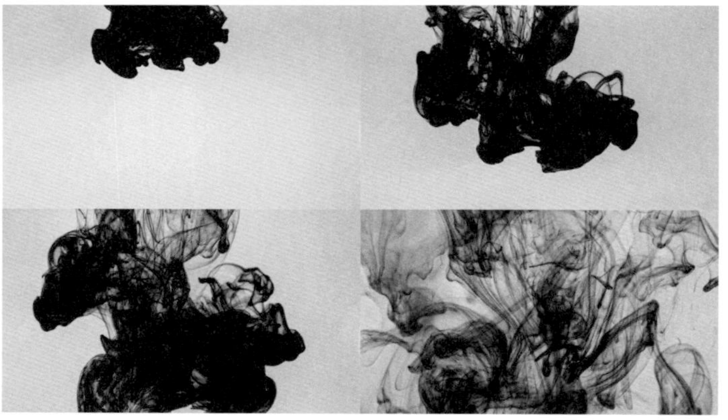

346 ● 563
Distinct forms of energy and low entropy over time always develop to dissipated forms and high level of entropy.

347 ● 563
J M W Turner: rain, steam, and speed – *The Great Western Railway*, 1844.

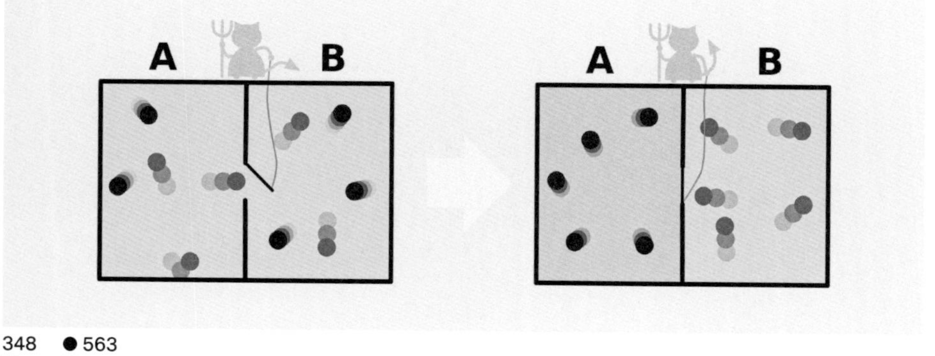

348 ● 563
Maxwell's demon looks at the particles in each chamber and sorts them by type.

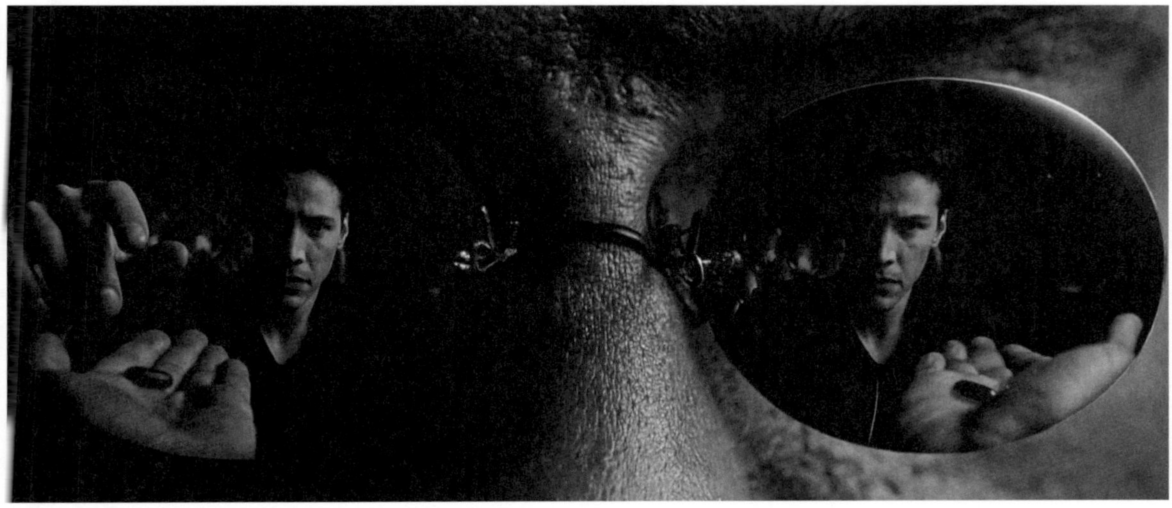

349 ● 563
The Matrix (1999): "You take the blue pill, the story ends: you wake up in your bed and believe whatever you want to believe. You take the red pill, you stay in Wonderland, and I show you how deep the rabbit hole goes."

350A ● 564
Information is negentropic and always made by rational decisions from out of the entropic white noise.

350B ● 564
Clint Eastwood.

351 ● 564
Nymphéas by Claude Monet, 1906.

Colour Plates

V

P. 463–579

478A ○ 478
The outside areas of the Prophet's Mosque in Medina are covered by 260 convertible parasols designed by Bodo Rasch. The total spanned area amounts to 145,000 m². The height of the parasol constructions, when open, is 21.70 m, the size of the pre-stressed parasol membranes is 26 × 26 m each. [294A + 294B: str.ucture]

294B ○ 478

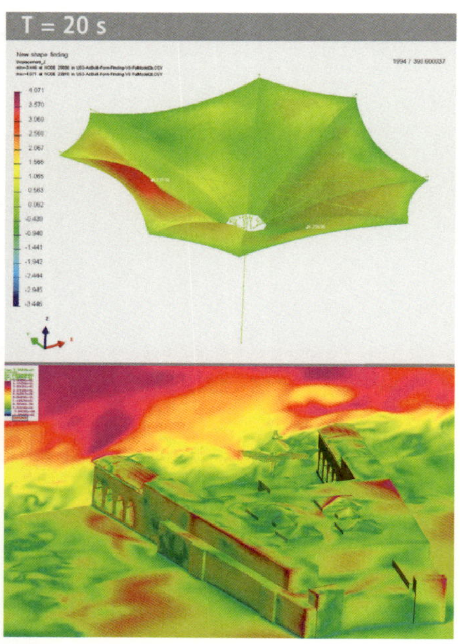

295A ○ 478

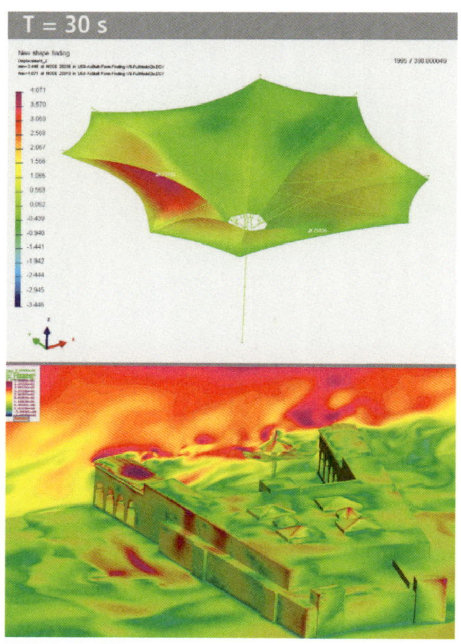

295B ○ 478

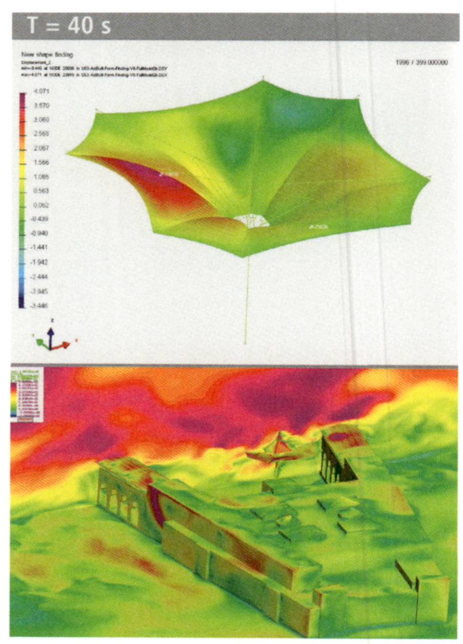

295C ○ 478

Fluid structure interaction simulation of the critical configuration when completely open: analysis of wind-induced oscillations and cut sizes, vertical membrane distortion, and wind speeds. [str.ucture]

296 ○ 479
Seductive pictures can simulate a reality that may be less likely to come about than it is capable of selling a project. [Mir]

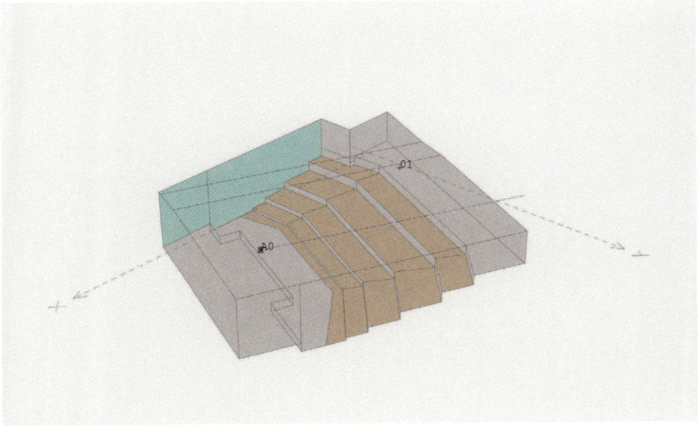

300A ○ 481

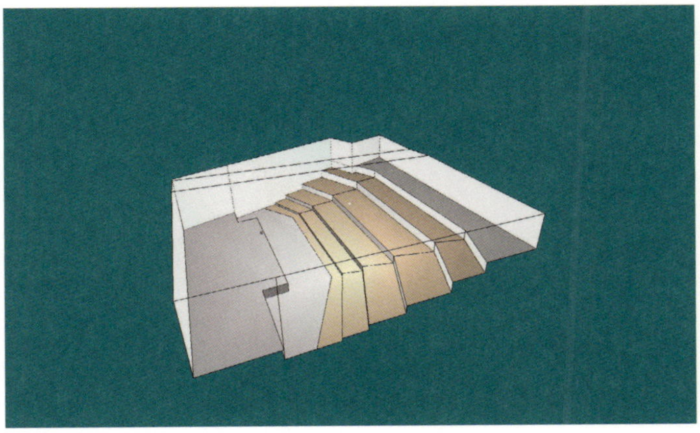

300B ○ 481
Input model with sound source on stage and reception points in space. [moBius Consult]

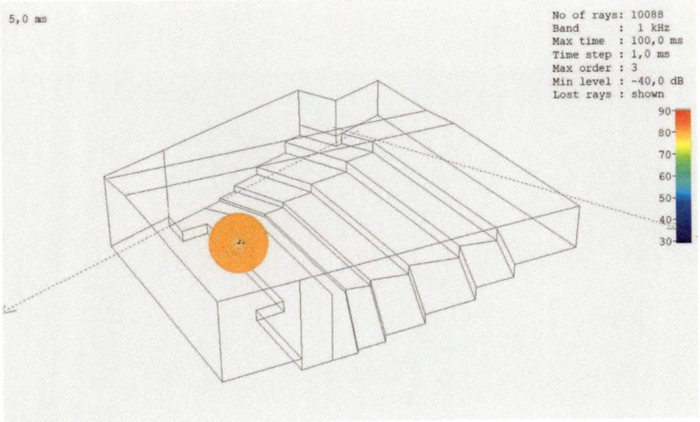

301A ○ 481

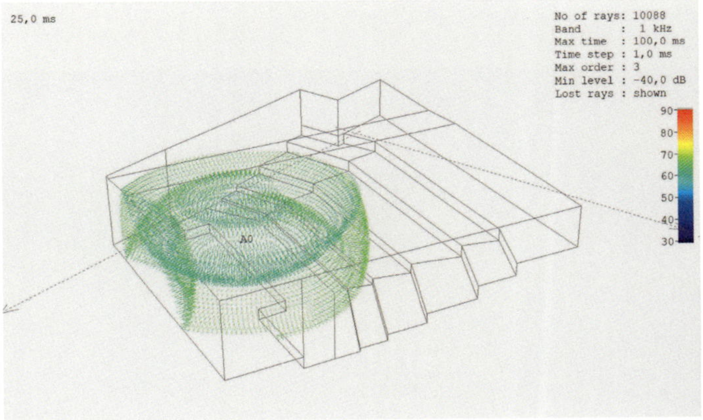

301B ○ 481
Time trace: sound expansion from sound source on stage after 5, 25 and 40 milliseconds. [Series 301A–301C: moBius Consult]

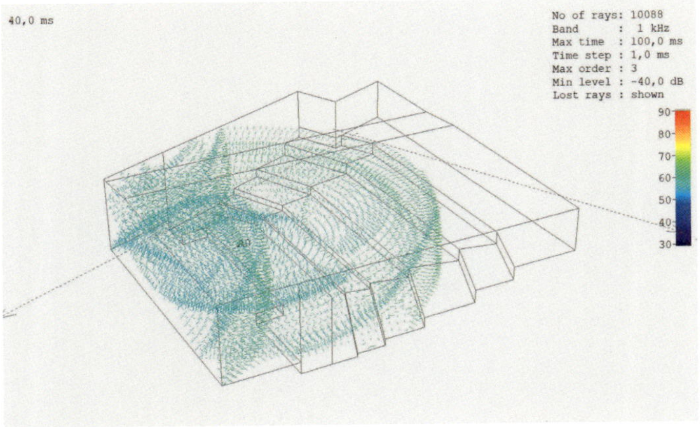

301C ○ 481

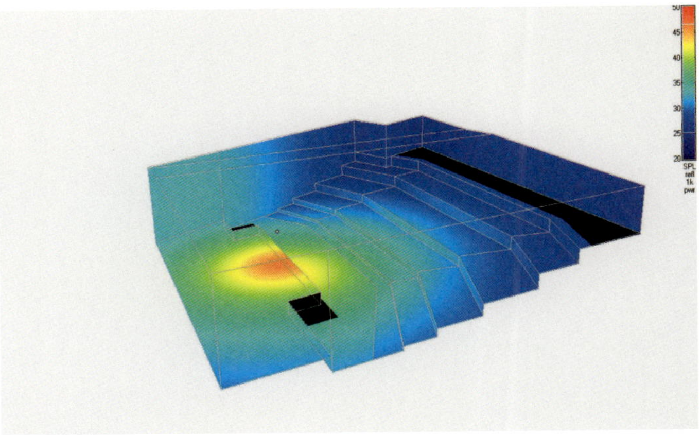

302 ○ 481
Decreasing noise level in a room. [moBius Consult]

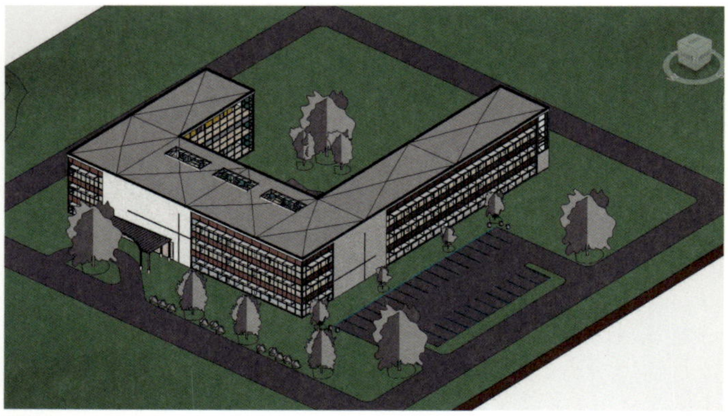

306A ○ 483
Architectural representation. [Series 306–306E: Paul Hechinger]

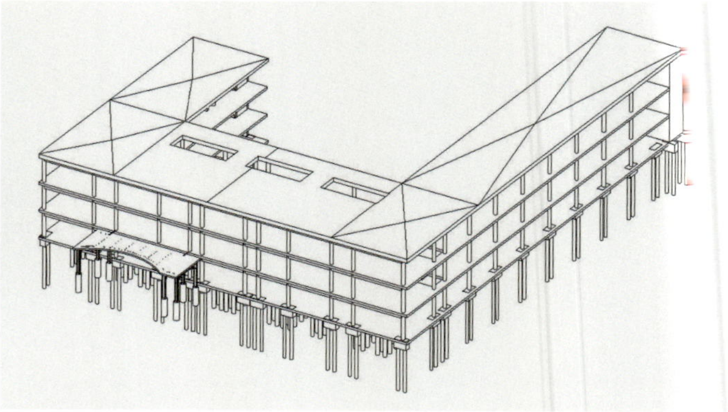

306B ○ 483
Representation that shows the structural elements in the same model.

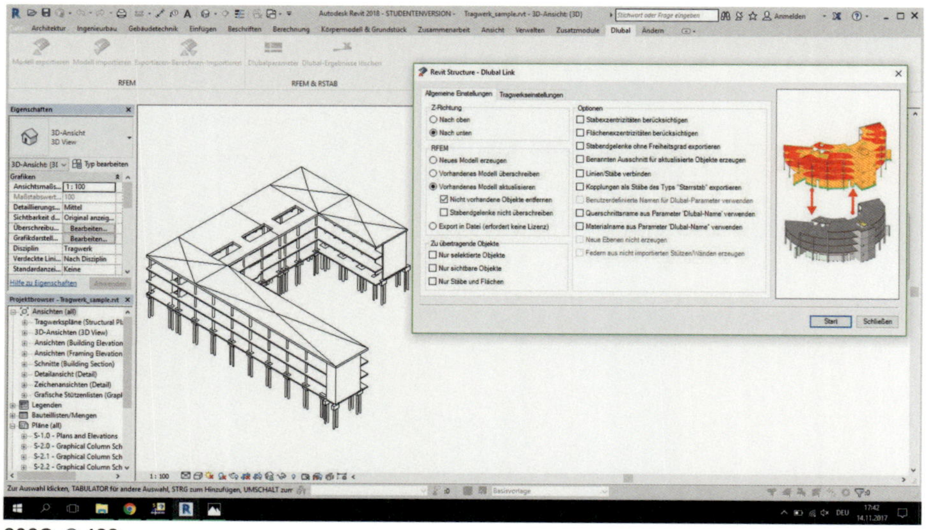

306C ○ 483
The project is ready to be exported, in this case, from *AutoCAD Revit* to *Dlubal RFEM*, and the plugin equipped with relevant data.

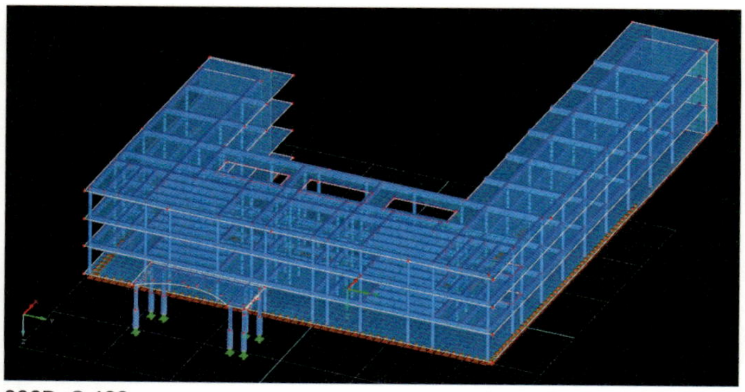

306D ○ 483
The model has been imported into *Dlubal RFEM*. Load and other relevant data can now be added.

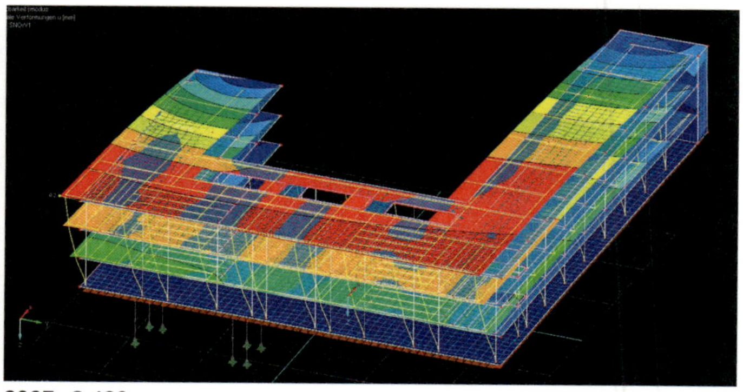

306E ○ 483
The simulation shows the overall deformation of the structure and highlights which parts of it need to be improved.

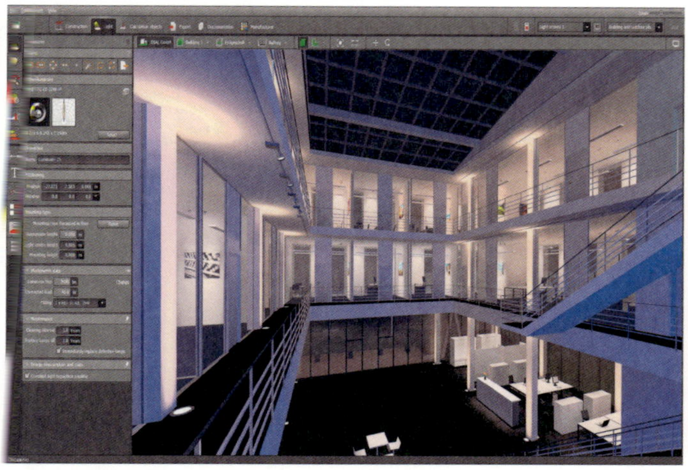

307 ○ 483
Interior light simulation – *DIALux*. [DIAL GmbH]

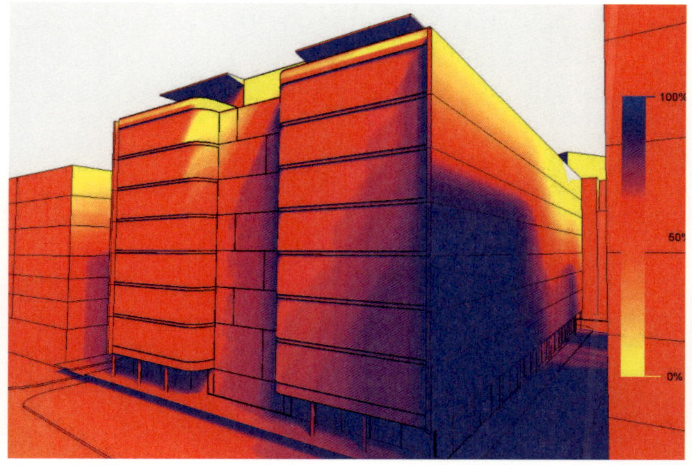

308 ○ 483
External light simulation: shadows cast by a new building on existing objects. [Max Tillberg]

309 ○ 484
Light simulation: radiance. [Greg Ward and Judy Lai, Lawrence Berkeley National Laboratory]

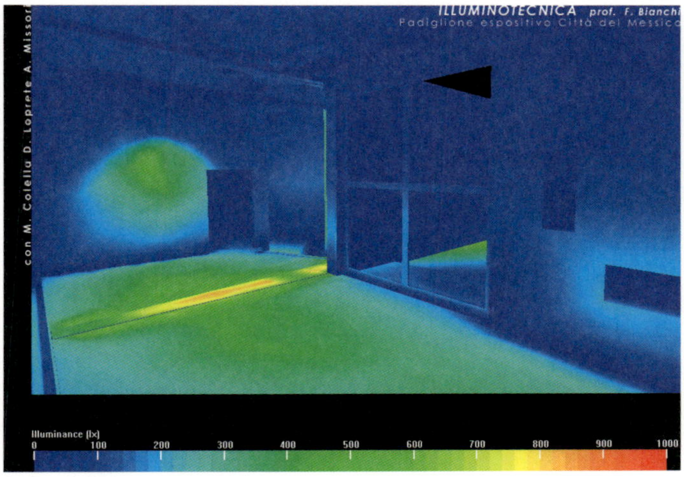

310 ○ 484
Lightscape *(Autodesk)*. [Piero Rasicci]

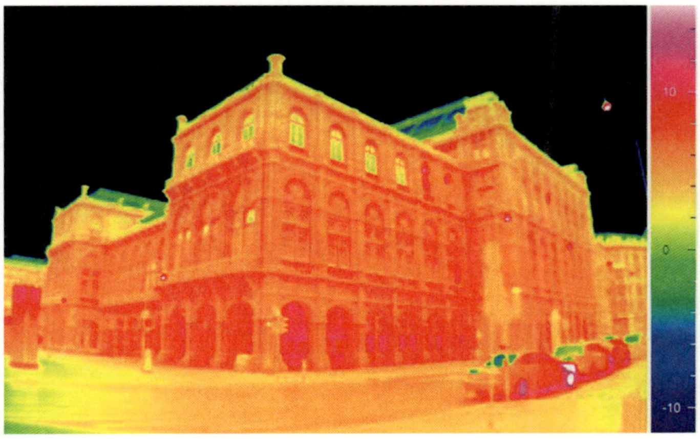

311 ○ 484
Energy simulation. [Filos e.U. Wien]

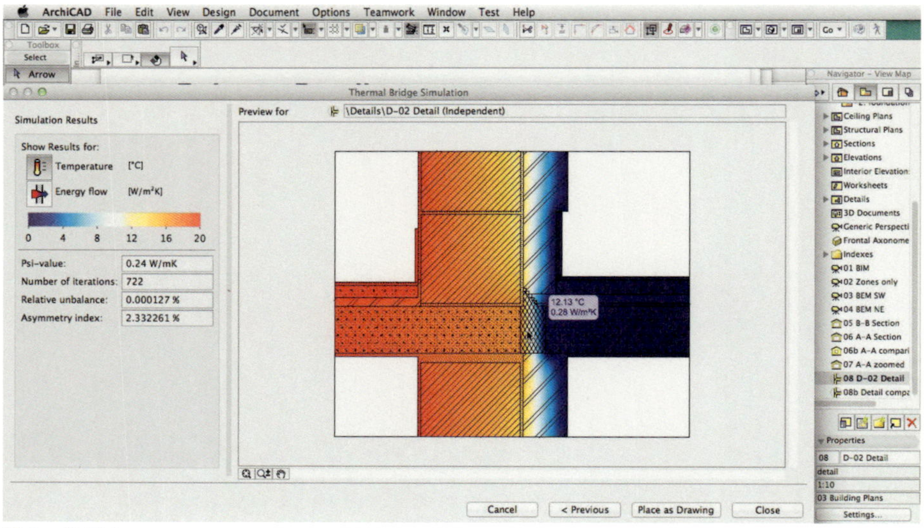

312 ○ 484
Software sample: *Graphisoft EcoDesigner Star* (see also *ArchiPhysik*). [Graphisoft]

313A ○ 485
CFD simulation used for the prediction of peak wind loads on the skin of a high rise building

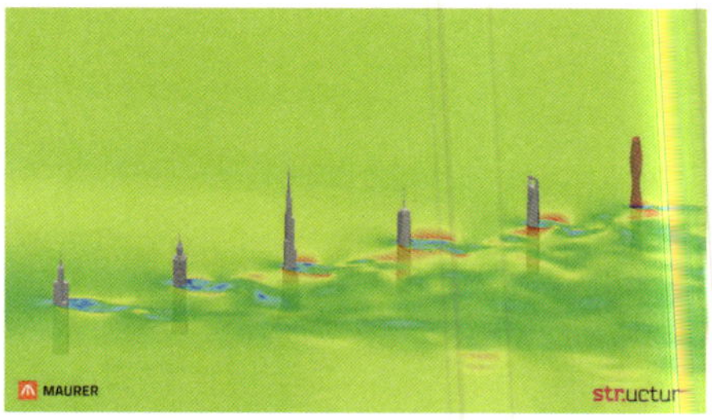

313B ○ 485
Realistic assessment of wind phenomena on different tall buildings (natural wind boundary conditions). [313A + 313B: str.ucture]

314 ○ 485
Aerial picture of Herrenberg. [Gabriel Holom]

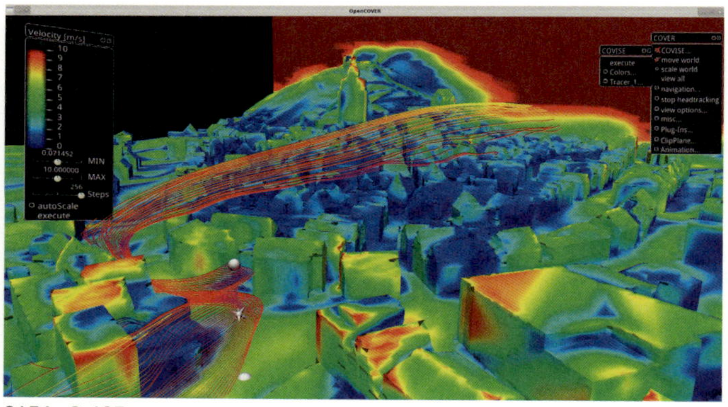

315A ○ 485
Representation of air flow.
[Series315A–315F: Uwe Wössner – HLRS Stuttgart]

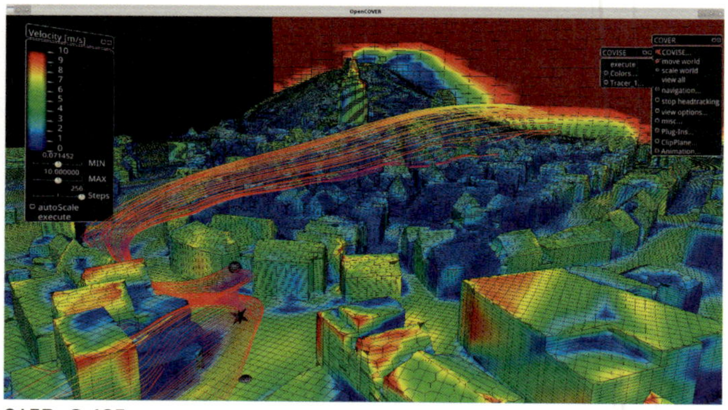

315B ○ 485
Representation of computational grid and air flow.

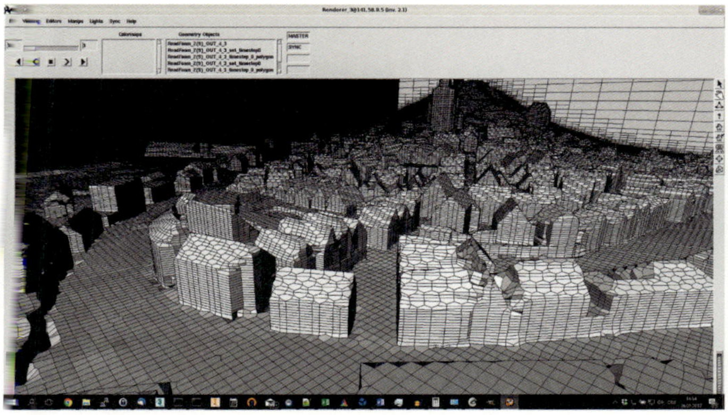

315C ○ 485
Representation of computational grid.

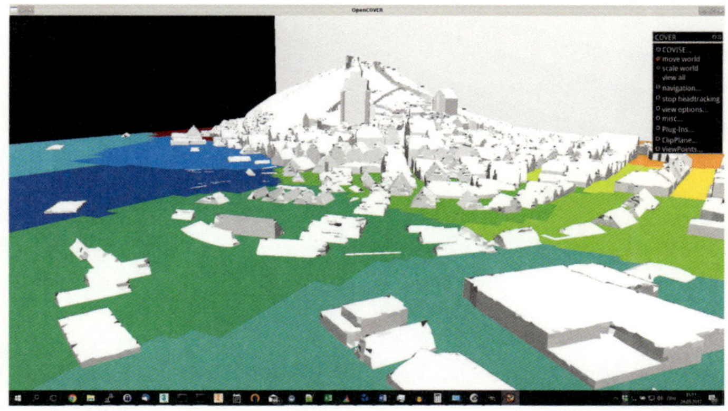

315D ○ 485
Segmentation in computational areas.

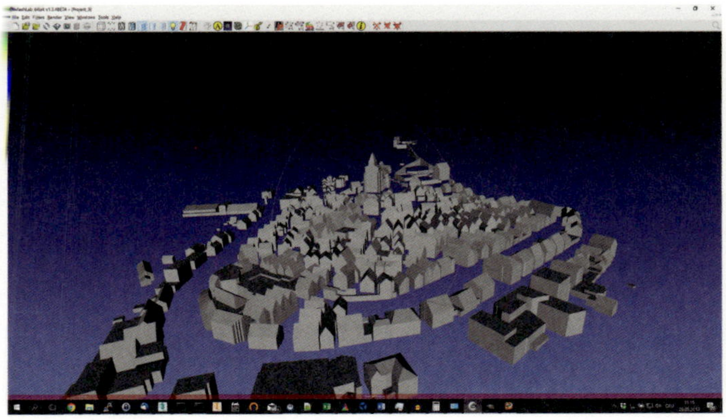

315E ○ 485
Town model of Herrenberg.

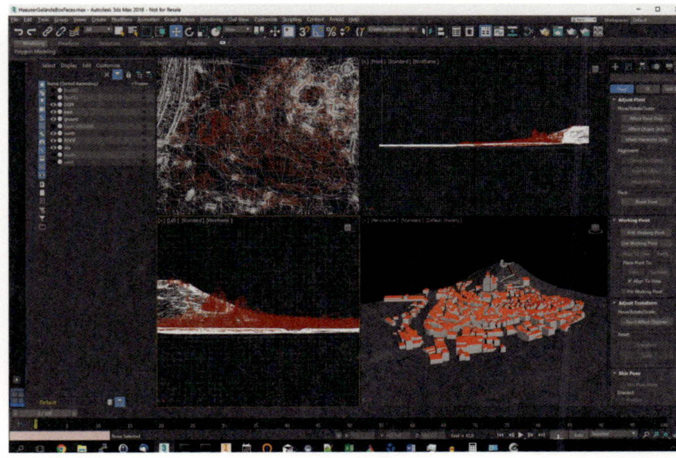

315F ○ 485
Linking the town model to the terrain model.

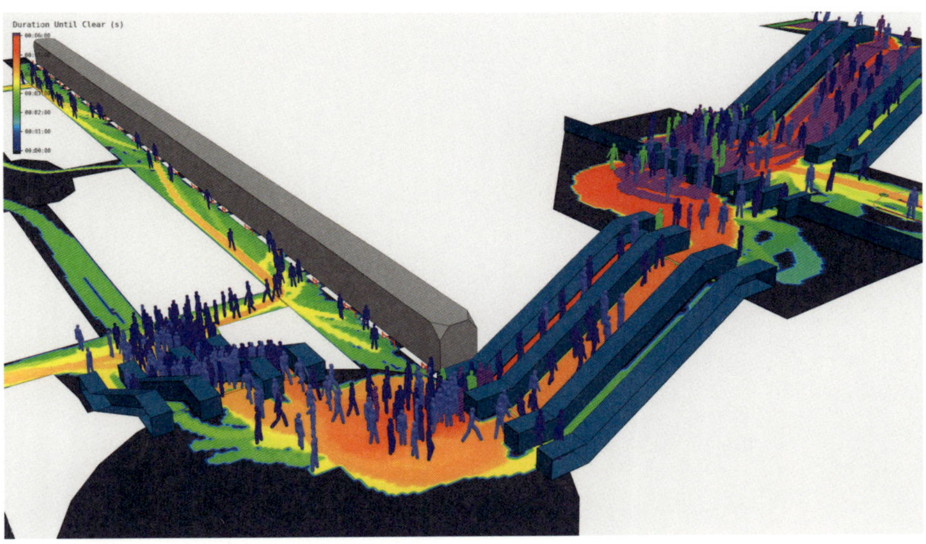

316 ○ 485
Evacuation simulation. [Oasys / MassMotion]

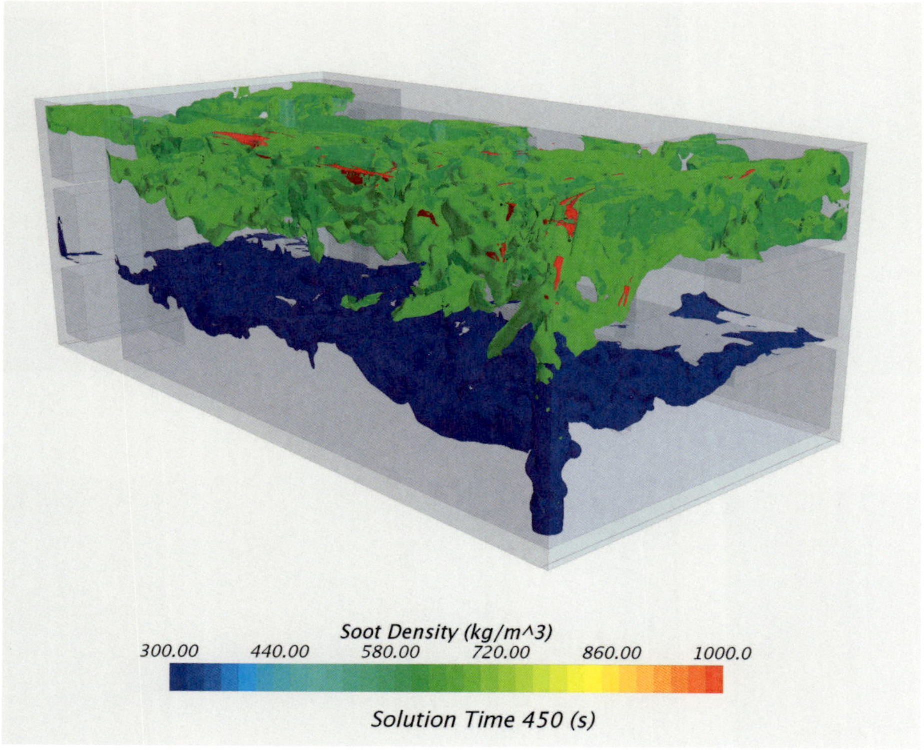

317 ○485
Fire simulation. [Christian Laemmle, Combustion and Flow Solutions GmbH]

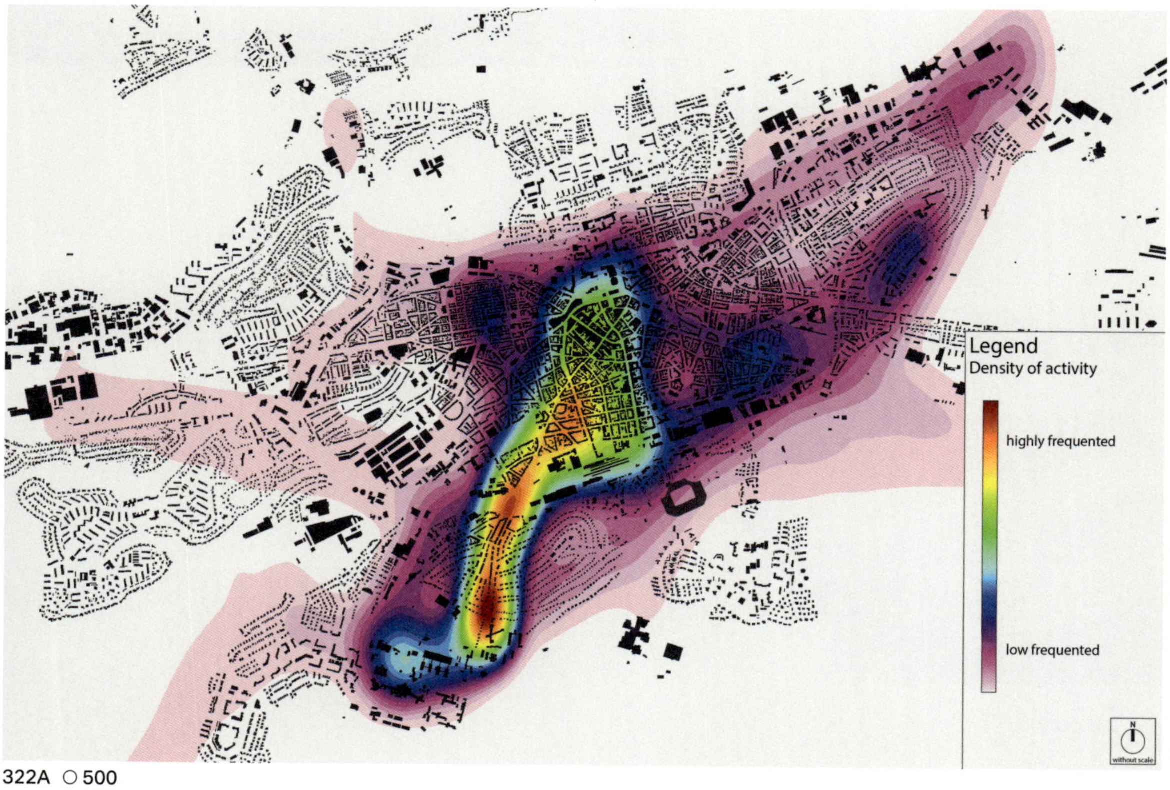

322A ○500
'Heatmap' showing areas of Kaiserslautern visited by the researchers and the frequency with which they did so. [Series 322A–322C: *Track Me if You Plan!*]

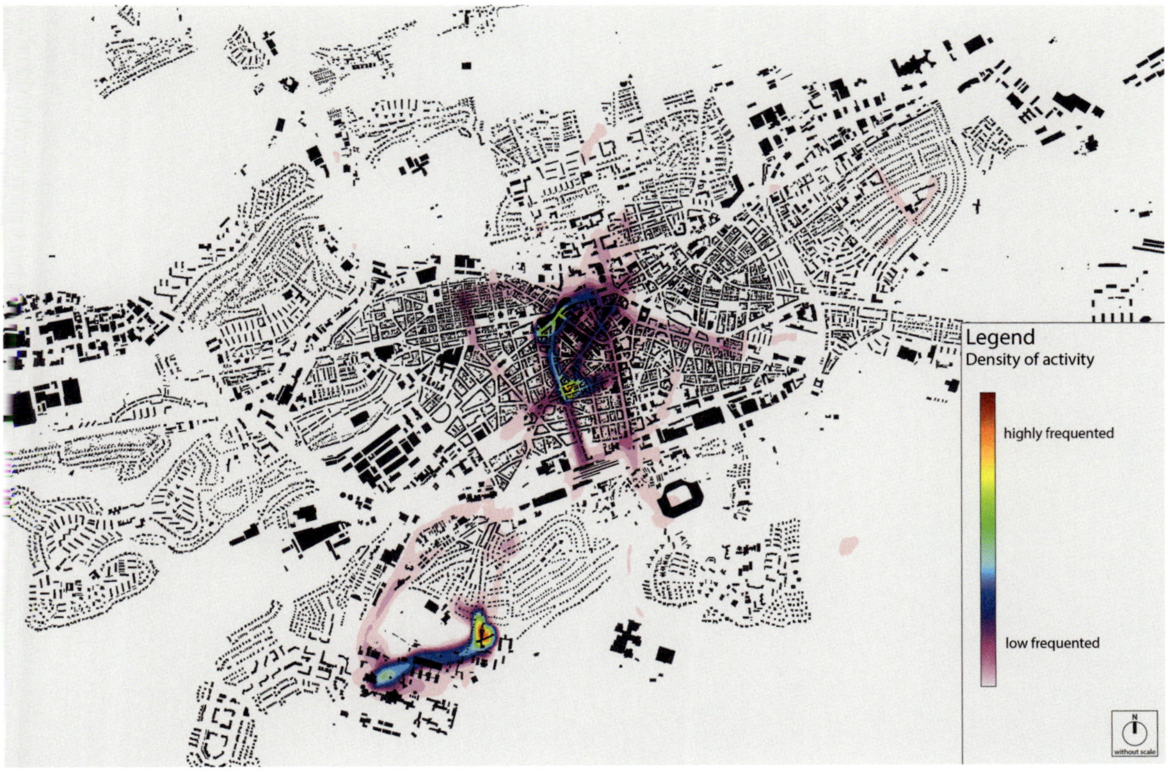

322B ○ 500
'Heatmap' detail: high to low frequency paths taken in the centre of town.

322C ○ 500
Time spent in various locations.

Being a 'Brand' 593
The Internet of Things (IoT) 613
Collaboration 629
Privacy & Security 643

COEXISTENCE
The Interfaces and Modes of Collaboration Between Information Technology and Architects

VI

Robert Venturi: *Complexity and Contradiction in Architecture*, 1966
Rem Koolhaas: *Junkspace. October No. 100: 175–90*, 2002
Bjarke Ingels: *Yes Is More: An Archicomic on Architectural Evolution*, 2009
Teuvo Kohonen: *Self-Organized Formation of Topologically Correct Feature Maps*. Biological Cybernetics 43 (1): 59–69, 2009

Being a 'Brand'

Diana Alvarez-Marin and Miro Roman

Articulating Identities Amidst The Big Plenty

In our chapter on Visualisation we note the extent to which iconic architecture is experienced not as three-dimensional structures in the physical world, but as imagery of those structures, and how much of that imagery is encountered online. This is one of the main factors that make architecture iconic in the first place: we keep coming across it, seeing it represented, expressed in pictures. And the more imagery there is, the more the architecture is talked about: in books, in articles, in academic papers, in journals. The more architecture is talked about, the more it is taken seriously and considered important, and the more important it is considered to be, the more people go and visit it. Entire cities have been lifted from comparative obscurity, and their flagging economies revived, on the back of iconic architecture, and that would scarcely be the case if the architecture itself were not comprehensively medialised.

352 ○ 680

Representing architecture in pictures and words is obviously not new. Since the beginnings, writing about architecture and illustrating it has served as a way not only of talking about the built-up environment around you – whether or not you're an architect – but very specifically also as a platform for architects to explain themselves, to put forward ideas, their rationale, their vision. Hand in hand with this goes the desire, and to quite some extent the need, to promote themselves: in some countries – the USA until the 1970s and India to this day, for example – architects were or still are not allowed to advertise or market their work directly through traditional channels. So publishing and being published allows you to make yourself heard, to enter an exchange with the world of architecture; to formulate your own style, and to make yourself and your work a recognisable entity: what today, a little loosely perhaps, we tend to think of as a 'brand'.

The idea alone of 'being a brand' may not come naturally, or sit so easily, with us, but it's nevertheless of growing significance. Ask any hundred people in the street of any European city what they think of Charles-Édouard Jeanneret-Gris, and you're likely to get as many blank stares. Ask them, on the other hand, what they think of 'Le Corbusier', and a fair number among them are likely to have an opinion, or at least know who you're talking about. The Swiss-French architect, designer, and urban planner Le Corbusier (1887–1965) is as known for his distinctive ideas as he is for his 'brand'. He is, in fact, possibly the first architect to more or less invent himself deliberately as a brand. Long before star architects systematically thought of themselves as concepts, he latched on to the fact that being someone in architecture was at least partly a case of making yourself unmistakably you.

Considering how influential Le Corbusier became, it is perhaps surprising to learn that neither he, nor his equally famous contemporary, the Welsh-American architect and designer Frank Lloyd Wright (1867–1959), nor indeed the German-American □ ↖285
architect Ludwig Mies van der Rohe (1886–1969), who together (though not, it has to be said, exclusively) shaped the modernist post-war architecture of the 20th century, had any formal training as architects. What marks them out so much is that, apart from being gifted and inspired designers, they were all exceptionally good at articulating themselves and their architecture.

So in this chapter on Being a 'Brand' we very □ ↖593
specifically want to ask this particular question: how do you, as a young architect setting out on your path today, *articulate* yourself in the digital world. We make the point often in this *Atlas* that this is a radically different one to the pre-digital world. And here, as elsewhere, we want to emphasise that we are not thinking so much of the *essence* as radically different, or let alone new – as we've just seen, and as we see throughout this *Atlas*, architects have, in one way or another, been asking themselves this question always – nor is it even the case that thinking of articulation as a form of 'marketing' is wholly new or unique to our era. When the 'product' you are selling is really, through your work, you, then 'marketing' immediately takes on an abstract dimension; that is, the dimension of you expressing yourself *about* your work in articles, texts, professional literature, interviews, lectures. After all, depending on what area of architecture you focus on, each and any of your objects may only ever be 'marketed' to one set of clients. And as we also remind ourselves repeatedly in this *Atlas*, these sets of clients can be quite complex in their make-up, and correspondingly demanding. Still, the need to articulate yourself is not what's new. What is new is the quantity and quality (as in character or type) of the images and words about architecture that abound in the world in which you express yourself.

Your challenge as a young architect today is how to be you, amidst this seemingly limitless wealth of indexes. Because here lies the great difference to where we were before, and the significant change that digitality has brought about: in the past – in the pre-digital era – we articulated ourselves through books and references which were, in a sense, 'curated' and certainly went through some kind of editorial process, whereby publishers, magazine or journal editors, and other gatekeepers would assess and approve or reject work, based on their understanding of the work (or lack thereof) on the one hand, and to quite some extent, as always, based also on the level of recognition a given author might be enjoying at the time. Today we have a situation which was famously and astutely (though perhaps not entirely accurately) foretold by the American artist Andy Warhol (1928–1987), in a programme note for a show of his works in Sweden in 1968: "In the future, everyone will be world-famous for 15 minutes."

Whether that is strictly true or not, what is certainly the case is that today we have an abundance of indexes, and everyone can (and a great many people do) promote themselves. You could argue, therefore, that up until about the 1980s to early 1990s, information had a more explicit meaning: it was largely imbued with an interpretation and put in a context that made some sort of sense, to someone. As the sheer volume of information has grown, so, in a way, has its 'meaninglessness'; or, to look at it from another, perhaps more positively phrased perspective, what has grown is the potential of information to have *any* 'meaning' we ■ ↖565 assign to it. At the same time, information is now so plentiful, and the means to express, share, and store it so omnipresent and affordable, that getting 'the message' out there (whatever that message may be) is really no longer a problem. Getting it heard among the din, let alone understood, on the other hand, has become more difficult than ever: the level of entropy in digital content has, as it must, only gone up.

If you look at this rich – some would argue excessive – stream of information, and you realise that you will need to be a part of its flow, you may be forgiven for losing heart. The challenge is formidable. And it is now not so much about making sense of it all, as it is about learning how to handle it and how to formulate a response to it; in other words: master it. Because what is the alternative? There isn't one as such. A possible counter-reaction might be to shy away from it in fear. Or to slam down the brakes and cry: '*Enough!* We can't handle this undisciplined mess. Let's regulate, curtail, *forbid* it.' We, as the authors and editors of this *Atlas* don't, as you know, advocate such a stance. What we suggest instead is that we approach the deluge – which is so vast now, we can't even measure it with normal metrics any more – with an open and curious mind: embrace its complexity completely.

Doing so affords us great new freedoms: we can be anyone we like to be, we can invent ourselves. We can be humans, mutants, we can be aliens. We are all present in this great mix, there is distance between individual elements, and there are relationships, and through these relationships – not through being the same! – we find affinity with each other, and that is also how we escape the given structures and how we are able to shape new ones; we are really curating – we know the term is overused right now, but here it fits – the way we want to be seen, and we are choosing our 'masks' that we wear at this feast of realities: we articulate ourselves.

In articulating ourselves, we are not only choosing what we want to say and how we want to say it, we are also deciding who we want to be talking to, and when. That means we also enter the realm of encryption and decryption: when previously it was a matter mainly of structuring the selective information there was, today it is as much about sifting through the unlimited information we have, and choosing what we want to be seen and heard, by whom. As we've moved from books, via magazines, to online forums and blogs, we are no longer figures in a linear narrative, we are quantum citizens. We can be in two or several places or nowhere, all at the same time, and how and whether you see us depends entirely on how you look at us: your act of observation changes the nature of the observed, and in this case that's us.

ARCHITECTURE ONLINE

Since the beginning of the 21st century, architects – along with other creative professionals and artists, and everybody else – have been moving their 'presence' online. And since the capacity for an online presence is not really restricted by any obvious physical factors, this move has entailed an unprecedented proliferation of words and images; but also of new representational 'species', so to speak. The digital space is inhabited not only by traditional text and picture material that is now simply hosted and made accessible online – although that evidently too – but also by avatars, bots, crypto-currencies; entities that behave, and enable us to behave, in new ways. Blogs, micro-blogs, image collections, comments, conversations: the presentational world is saturated with content, and much of that content is immediate or extremely quick in coming about. Ironically, it may then be much longer lived than much of the content that previously was much longer in preparation but really had the shelf life, for most of the reading public, of the magazine or journal it appeared in only. Apart from some collectors' reference and library copies, most printed content would simply disappear after a while. A little different perhaps with books, where certainly those that made an impact would stand a good chance of survival over several generations or possibly, and in rare cases, over centuries, or even millennia.

Digital content may also disappear or go under, but then again, it may not, and often it doesn't or doesn't for a long time. Rather, it remains indexed and therefore searchable, and it doesn't fade, disintegrate or perish with time but stays stable and accessible, at least for as long as data storage is available and intact. Which is one of the main reasons why such great efforts are now being made to digitise existing analogue materials, adding yet more to the volume that is generated fresh every day. And with this volume comes the other new challenge. Not only: 'how do I behave in a medially saturated world?' But also: 'how do I deal with it in order to get what I need or want out of it?'

And so, while online publications have not done away with printed books, magazines and journals (this *Atlas* attests to that), their numbers, both in terms of their readership and the volume of content they are able to produce, outstrip by far those of traditional means of publication. And in some respects they bring that content closer to us. Digital formats encapsulate all other media, and because they are so immediate and dynamic, they facilitate a deeper, more intimate, and more layered interaction with the content, and through it with its creators, than any traditional format. And they enable us to easily become content creators and thus signal generators ourselves. (When we say 'easily', we still refer only to the process of putting material online. Getting that material noticed is, once more, a different matter.)

MORE, MORE, MORE

When Mies van der Rohe put down his metaphorical flag in the new territory of post-war, minimalist architecture in 1947, he resolutely declared "less is more," not so much coining as borrowing the phrase and turning it into something of an architectural manifesto. Nearly twenty years later, in 1966, the American architect Robert Venturi (1925–2018) delivered his bold response: "Less is a bore," only to be met, after another couple of decades, with a deliberate provocation by American architect Philip Johnson (1906–2005), who in 1984, at the age of 78, echoed it by simply declaring: "I am a whore." It didn't end there. Dutch architect and urbanist Rem Koolhaas (b. 1944) got back impatiently in 2001 with "more is more," just two years after Danish architect Bjarke Ingels (b. 1974) had already taken the, for his era tellingly commercial, stance: "yes is more." Consider yourself invited to contribute your own variation on the theme whenever you feel ready to do so...

Mies van der Rohe obviously did not refer to data or content, but to an architectural approach. It's nevertheless fascinating to note the progression from an ideal of minimalism, formulated at a time when it was not only possible but desirable to think of architecture and art in terms of reduction, simplification, and essentially the weeding out of anything that could be considered surplus to requirement, to an acceptance that there simply *is* more. Of everything. More pictures, more words, more ideas, more people, more cities, more people in cities, more people in cities using words and pictures to talk about people in cities. The thought of stemming the flow now seems absurd: we find ourselves in a baroque voluptuousness of content and data: a global feast of everything. Today we inhabit a galaxy of uncharted paths, and we behave in patterns of potential states and connections.

353 ● 608

ANOTHER DIMENSION

What happens to us – to our memory, our archives, our sense of time – in the digital world? Do we experience time as linear, or as circular, or as something else? If past, present, and future collapse into one narrative, where 'pre-', 'post-', and 'neo-' become self-referential meaninglessnesses, what *are* we dealing with? The more we dive into this ocean of indexes, the more we realise that our attempts at categorising, canalising, 'managing' it, remain essentially a search *for* dimensions.

And so we can differentiate our challenge and formulate it further. Not only is it one of defining our own behaviour in a world of plenty, and one of mastering the plenty, it is also one of scanning – in our case especially architectural – universes across time (and beyond dogma) in order to get some 'useful' or at least 'interesting' or 'relevant' distillations. It's a question of how to look through different lenses simultaneously so that we can tap into the richness of these indexes, without getting lost in our endeavour.

A NEW PUBLIC SPACE

This challenge is one we face in a new public space, and that's yet another reason why it calls for new methods. Once upon a time, not so very long ago, the public space was defined by what we, as individuals, mostly in a compact with society and its institutions – the authorities – agreed and declared to be public. The 'default' setting, so to speak, was 'private' for our personal lives, especially at home, and 'public' for what we did outside the house (there would, necessarily, be overlaps and exceptions). This made it comparatively easy to know whether you were in the public or in the private space, because all you had to do to move from one to the other was leave the house or go back home.

This is no longer the case. Much of what was once our private sphere is now visible and accessible to third parties, sometimes with, often without our knowledge or express permission. A the same time, much of what we think of as public space is in fact privately owned and we can be there only because we are 'tolerated', as long as we behave as if we were in someone else's front garden. Much, if not indeed most, of our public space is under constant surveillance, and to this we add everything we freely and voluntarily share online about some of our most intimate actions, thoughts, and adventures.

We are able to create and maintain complete new and artificial identities, and yet in reality we present ourselves online mostly as we are off. Our social network profiles and our picture streams may portray us as perhaps a little happier, more interesting, better travelled, and more successful than we really are, but anyone who has ever used a dating or hookup app will know that nineteen times out of twenty what you see is more or less exactly what you get: we are remarkably ourselves, no matter which reality we choose to operate in. Or perhaps: we turn ourselves into versions of ourselves much in the same vein, whether that is in the virtual or in the physical life. Both are real. (And, here too, exceptions apply.)

What we can and do do is blur or extinguish some of our traces and make them selective, perhaps super-selective. We do not, by and large, want everyone to have access to our bank details. So we use encryption: there is still a private sphere, even if it is located and maintained differently to where it once was.

So let us explore then how we, as architects, as digital citizens, today can behave in this space, and how we can begin to articulate ourselves in a world where everything is available and anything is possible.

A NEW METHOD

Perhaps if we want to position ourselves in a world of abundance, find or define our identities, and learn to articulate ourselves as ourselves in it – whatever we happen to decide 'ourselves' to be – it may help us to embrace the Plenty and welcome it into our thinking.

One way we can do so – and this is the approach we are proposing to adopt for the purposes of this exercise – is by emulating the methods used by the big digital 'players', such as Google, Facebook, or Amazon: we will use **crawlers** and bots to search and collect data, and we will use **machine learning** – **Self-Organising Map (SOM)** algorithms and information visualisation techniques – to organise and cluster this data into word and image clouds. (There are many other methods available, within both machine learning

■
■ ↖551 654↘
■ ↖572

☐ ↖549

and information visualisation, since these are very popular and growing fields. We discuss both in more detail in our chapter on Big Data & Machine Learning.)

What we want to emphasise though is that the data we collect and the way we present it does not reflect the world as it is, but *us in the world,* and how we see ourselves in it. This is an important distinction to make. And there are two major facets to this that we need to always be aware of. Firstly: no data, no game. The 'game' we're about to play through, by way of illustration, is a data hungry one. So it not only allows us to deal with large quantities of data, it presupposes that we have data at our fingertips in the first place. Secondly, and this is perhaps even more significant: through the act of selecting what data we are going to use, and deciding in which way we are going to use it, we are leaving behind the world where there is a clear delineation between 'objective' and 'subjective', and entering a world in which these boundaries are blurred to the point where they cease to exist.

So now, rather than explain to you in detail what a crawler is or how to code a bot, we want to show you what we mean, by playing through an example of how this can work. It's a fictional 'scenario' that illustrates more than anything an approach or, even more fundamental than that, a way of thinking. We eschew the idea of recipes, and so this is not meant as an example of what to do and how to do it in order to achieve a particular result, it is really first and fore-most a figure, a gesture, from which you can draw your own conclusions and decide to what extent, if any, it may be 'useful' to you.

An Encounter With Plenty, in Two Acts

I think, I read, I draw, I take pictures. I share. I mess around with things that seem like objects, but I'm nowhere ready to build. I make a model, I change it. I don't have a style yet, as far as I know; I have no commission. I have ideas, I nearly have projects. I have an ambition, sure, but I'm not sure what it is. I look around and wonder: now what? Now actually, genuinely, just what? *I search for inspiration, but I don't 'search' so much as I gaze; I graze the imagery, I nibble at the words...*

PICTURES THAT TALK

I say to myself, all right then, show me. Show me what there is, and maybe that can be a start. It's certainly not going to be the end. There isn't a destination, as such, of that I am pretty certain. But let me get a feel for what is out there in architecture: what is around. How people think, and what they see; what they build. Let me get an introduction to the world of architecture, as it presents itself today. The Internet is an obvious place to start. Architectural blogs: the pictures and words people post on architecture.

I opt for *Dezeen* and *ArchDaily* (at dezeen.com and archdaily.com). There are many other relevant blogs on architecture, but today I am interested in these two. Why? It's a personal, random choice. I know they're both influential, they're both respected and taken note of, and so they interest me. My choosing them makes them my universe, for the time being.

I decide to start with pictures; and to get a feel for the size of my 'universe', I want to find out just how *many* pictures there are, never even mind what kind, or what they actually depict.

I write a few lines of code and run it, and the numbers I get are, as expected, impressive:

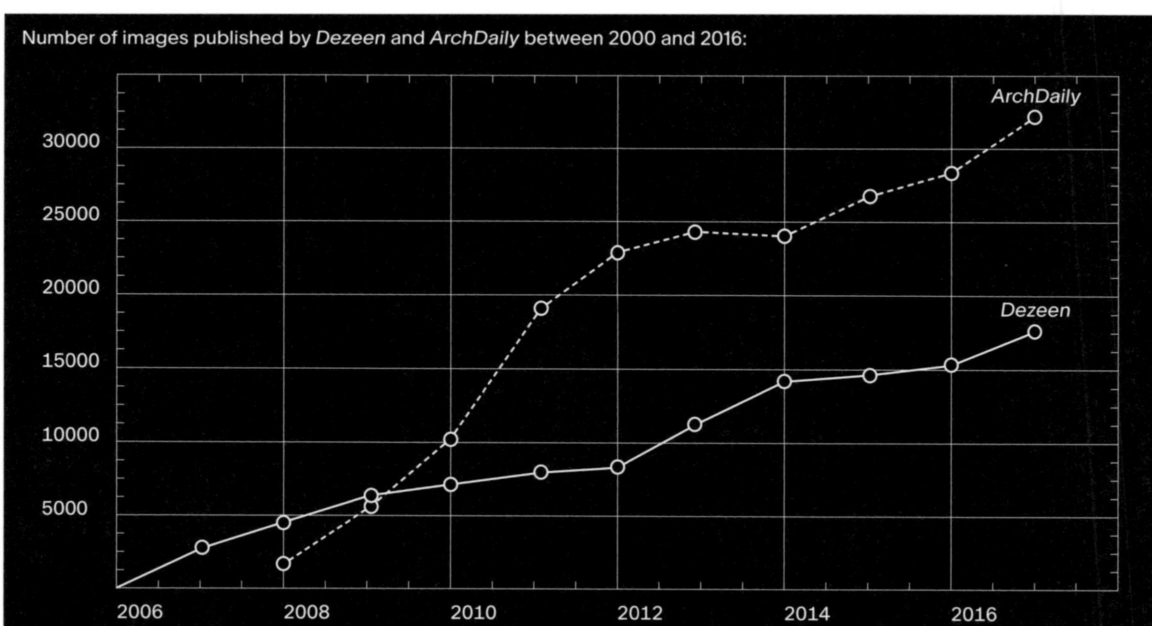

Number of images published by *Dezeen* and *ArchDaily* between 2000 and 2016:

What also doesn't come as a surprise is that they have steadily gone up over the last ten years or so. On *ArchDaily*, they've done so on a steep curve with a bump, on *Dezeen* in a more gentle incline. But both platforms publish many times as many pictures today as they did ten years ago, *ArchDaily* tickling the 30,000 mark, *Dezeen* roughly half. That's new images posted *each year.* There is no sign of this flood of imagery abating, if anything I expect that there will be more. So I now wonder: how do I collect, mediate, and measure all these images? How do I even *look* at them?

Obviously, I can't take them all in by just browsing them, as I would a website. I can't examine them all in detail, analyse them, form an opinion on them, and draw any conclusions about where architecture is at today, let alone how mine might fit in or complement or contradict or rebel against it. But that doesn't stop me.

In fact the opposite, it spurns me on: I go for it and decide I want to have everything. Everything they have ever published in terms of picture material. To me, that's not unreasonable: it's called online *publishing* after all; it's all publicly available. So I do what Google does, but I'm not a big global corporation, I am an individual, a private person active in a new public space; literate in a new way in the Quantum City, so I use its tools.

I write another small piece of code, a short script, a crawler. It's not very long, three dozen lines that look like this:

ArchDaily crawler as a 23-line 'poem':

```
ADpages[page_] := Module[{source, pos, links},
  source = Import[page, "Source"];
  pos = StringPosition[source,"<span itemprop='url'>" ~~ Shortest[__] ~~ "</span>"];
  links = "http://" <> StringDrop[StringDrop[StringTake[source, #], 28], -7] & /@ pos]

ADimages[link_] := Module[{source, strings, image, imagelink, images, imagelinks, pos, dateY,
  name},
  source = ToString@Import[link, "Source"];
  pos = StringPosition[source, "<li class=\"theDate\">" ~~ Shortest[__] ~~ "</li>"];
  dateY = StringTake[StringDrop[StringTake[source, pos], -5], -4];
  strings =
   Flatten[DeleteDuplicates[StringCases[StringSplit[ToString[source]],
       "data-src='https://images.adsttc.com/media/images/" ~~ __ ~~ ".jpg"]] /. {} -> Nothing];
  strings = StringDrop[strings[[#]], 10] & /@ Range[Length[strings]];

  If[ Length[strings] > 2, {
    strings = Delete[strings, {{-1}}];
    If[ Length[strings] > 12, {strings = Take[strings, 12], Flatten[strings]}];
    {image = Import[#, "Graphics"], name = StringJoin[{dateY, "_", StringTake[#, -10]}], #}
      & /@ strings
   }, {Print["article does not have enough images"]}]]

input = "http://www.archdaily.com/page/"; startpage = 1; stoppage = 1;
pagelinks = input ~~ ToString[#] & /@ Range[startpage, stoppage]; links = Flatten[ADpages[#]
  & /@ pagelinks];
Column@links

article = 1;
imgAD = ADimages[links[[article]]][[1]];
ImageResize[imgAD[[#, 1]], 300] & /@ Range[Length[imgAD]]
```

It's almost poetic in its succinct simplicity, and it finds all the articles' **URLs**, like this: ■ ↖188 623↘

ArchDaily – links published in one day:

```
http://www.archdaily.com/895216/the-2018-venice-biennale-winners,
http://www.archdaily.com/895115/warwick-street-squire-and-partners,
http://www.archdaily.com/895237/casa-terra-bernardes-arquitetura,
http://www.archdaily.com/895174/conference-hotel-de-botanica-jeanne-dekkers-architctuur,
http://www.archdaily.com/895191/architecture-for-wellness-the-space-for-body-and-soul,
http://www.archdaily.com/894805/wang-jing-memorial-hall-dna,
http://www.archdaily.com/894780/ais-contact-center-development-and-training-arena-
  plan-architect,
http://www.archdaily.com/894979/neri-oxman-and-mit-develop-programmable-biocomposites-
  for-digital-fabrication,
http://www.archdaily.com/894976/eva-franch-i-gilabert-on-the-meaning-of-architecture,
http://www.archdaily.com/893808/chucao-house-abestudio,
http://www.archdaily.com/895077/tensile-structures-11-edgy-images-under-strain,
http://www.archdaily.com/893996/bbva-headquarters-herzog-and-de-meuron,
http://www.archdaily.com/894678/this-instagram-is-dedicated-to-stunning-walls-from-across-
  the-world,
http://www.archdaily.com/894378/why-the-world-needs-more-architecture-memes,
http://www.archdaily.com/895041/housing-bo-lrarchitectes,
http://www.archdaily.com/894856/shanghai-modern-art-museum-atelier-deshaus,
http://www.archdaily.com/895064/juraku-ro-geneto,
http://www.archdaily.com/894877/aia-announces-2018-housing-awards-winners
```

Now, before I do anything else, I experimentally pull down the pictures from *one single* article only:

354A ○ 680

354B ○ 680

354C ○ 680

354D ○ 681

354E ○ 681

354F ○ 681

That's seven, out of hundreds of thousands. With these, I get a feel at a glance which ones, if any, appeal to me; and what, if anything, they mean, or evoke, or do for me. All it takes is one look for me to identify the colour schemes, the patterns, the things that I'm interested in. That's not a problem: so far, so good.

This having been so easy and worked so well, I now cast the net and grab them all. By the time my crawler has pulled down about 300,000 pictures from *ArchDaily* and *Dezeen* (depending on my computer and my Internet connection, this may take anything from a few hours to a few days) and put them together into a composite: different story. Now that question of how to look at them really becomes relevant as a practical issue. Because if they are to play a part in this informational game and have any kind of meaning in it, these images now need new 'identities', and here is where my new means of curation, mediation, and measurement come into play. The images need to be equipped with numbers: informationally encoded. They have to become vectors that point me in one direction or another. But what is the unit of measure?

I'm going to have to define my own metrics. These are not objective, standard units of measure, such as kilos, or grams, or metres, and so I don't expect to get an objective, or universally applicable, result of which I can say it is definitely 'useful' or let alone 'true'. Yes, there are some objective parameters, but what these mean to me is mostly up to me. (A lot of people can agree whether or not something is blue, or whether a line is straight or curved. But how they feel about it, what it signifies to them, that's a matter of personal taste and cultural coding.)

And so what these pictures are going to tell me depends on me: that's the interesting thing. It's my choice of what I'm looking at – and how I look at it – that defines my articulation. I'm in the world of data, and this generic, informational 'material' can be articulated in an infinite number of ways. None of them are good or bad, right or wrong: they just sit at different points on a spectrum, and so terms such as 'consistency', 'beauty', 'sophistication', or 'branding' all become part of this spectral constitution that I am the master of.

With this in mind, I take my next step, and I start looking for colours and edges:

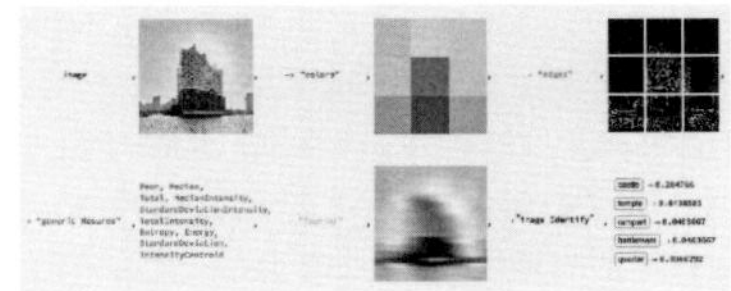

355 ○ 681

Like I say: this is just one way of defining 'units of measure' for an image. There can be many other ways. But each provides me with a set of numbers, my vector. And here it is; an informational face of an image; one of many possible ones:

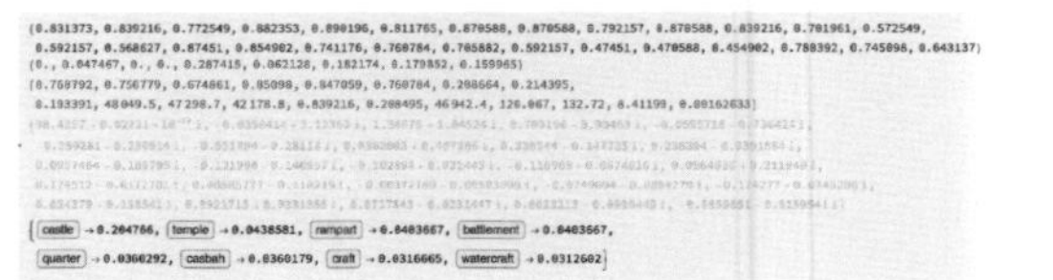

356 ○ 681

And now the spectacle can really begin. In the same way as I've just encoded this one image, I can encode *all* the images, give all of them informational faces.

Here they all are, 300,000 images, assembled from *Dezeen* and *ArchDaily*:

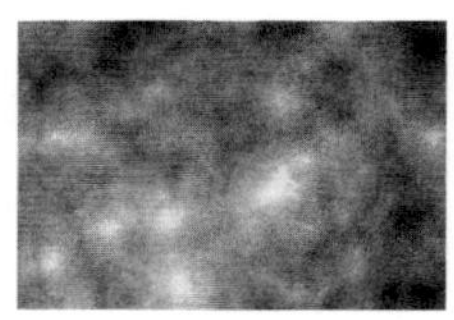

357 ○ 682

It's like a mood cloud of ten years of architecture: an impression, a face, a rendering.

But what does it tell me? Can this really be a trend barometer, a fashion gauge, or a brand checker? Let alone a 'machine' to help me articulate my own personal brand? Maybe not directly. What it does show me is the kind of pictures – in terms of composition, colour, mood – that have been used to represent architecture over the last ten years. And that, if nothing else, is a flavour.

A flavour is exactly what I'm after, and now I can dip into this mix and collect some samples, to get a taste for what I like and what I don't like, what agrees with me and what doesn't.

Textured objects, with a solidity and lightness, earthy elements and stones. They appeal to me, they taste like an old malt whisky:

358 ○ 682

Unlike these lonely solids, heavily placed in a white, abstract space; this I don't like, for me, they are the artificial mixer in a cocktail, too sweet, too sterile:

359 ○ 682

Or the 'new chic': interiors, soft shadows, floors, and ceilings that merge to celebrate the materiality of an object; a dry crisp wine, perhaps?

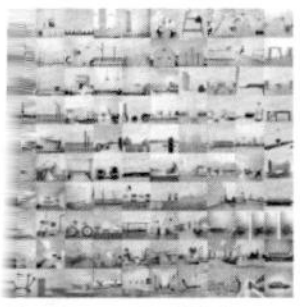

360 ○ 682

Or patterns: I like these, they can be and become anything, they are abstract enough to be free:

361 ○ 682

And houses (let's not forget houses...) with their strict and unequivocal lines; vertical, diagonal:

362 ○ 682

I like the calm of horizontals, garnished with a dash of green...

363 ○ 682

I could go on forever, but now I think I am onto something: I'm beginning to project my own taste, my palate onto the cloud. I am finding my own formula, my own selection of flavours, I am making my own label; my – dare I say it – own 'brand'.

So I specify the kinds of images I like, and they become my filter. Pictures that resemble them should pass, the others don't:

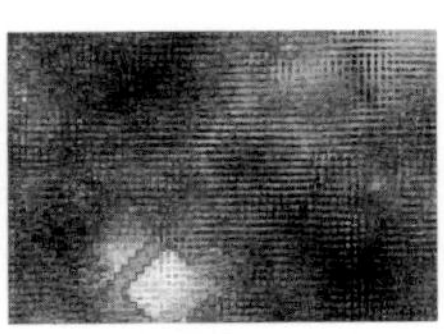

364 ○ 683

I try this out with 20 new images, just to test it:

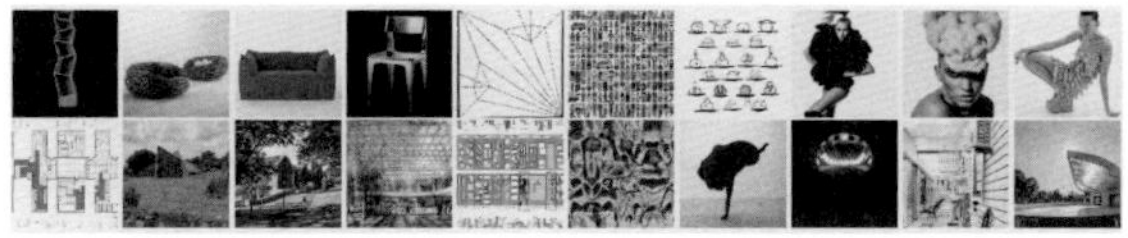

365 ○ 683

It's working! Not perfectly, but I can adjust the filter, and in any case, this is just for today; tomorrow I may want to change it all again, depending on my mood. Here are the images that pass:

366 ○ 683

And here is my personal 'portrait of the day' on the cloud of *ArchDaily* and *Dezeen*:

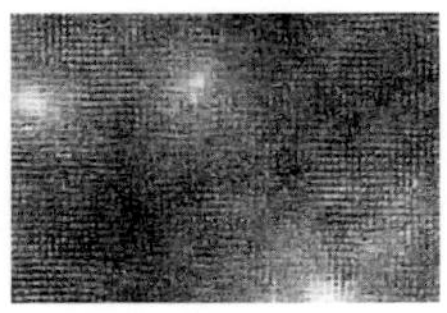

367 ○ 684

It's unique. To me, and to the way in which I've arrived at it today. Tomorrow, my personal 'portrait of the day' may look very different, with different individual images giving it different hues, different patterns, a different feel. And as with any portrait, the real characteristics that give it its 'personality' may be quite subtle: I may have to look closely to see what gives this picture its specific power.

This has been a success. But I'm only halfway there: I now have a distillation of the wealth of images and made it my own; and in their own way these images are telling me a story, they're certainly talking to me about themselves and about their constellation, but there is a part missing still that is just as important: the words. I'm hearing the stories pictures can tell, I now want to also see what pictures words can paint...

TEXTS THAT DRAW

What happens with words? What do words do for architects, what do they do for me? They are, after all, how we express what we think, not only, but certainly also not least, about architecture.

What do architects say? What language do they use? What would they say to each other, at a dinner table? I set about to find out, and my method is not dissimilar to the one I used for pictures. I sit them down at an imaginary table, and since I can make the table as big or as small as I want, I decide on a simple round figure for my guests. It could be a thousand, it could be a dozen; I decide on a hundred.

100 architects from the 20th and 21st century:

> 51N4E, AAA, Adam Caruso, Aldo Rossi, Alejandro Aravena, Alejandro Zaera-Polo, Álvaro Siza, AmidCero9, Andres Jaque,

Anne Holtrop, Achim Menges, Assemble, Atelier Bow Wow, Benjamin Dillenburger, Bernard Cache, Bernard Khoury, Bernard Tschumi, Bjarke Ingels, Carlo Ratti, Christ Gantenbein, Christian Kerez, COBE, DAAR, Daniel Libeskind, David Chipperfield, David Kohn, E2A, Ecosistema Urbano, Fake Industries AA, Forensic Architecture, Frank Gehry, Glenn Murcutt, Greg Lynn, Hans Hollein, Herzog & de Meuron, HWKN, JDS, Jean Nouvel, Johnston Marklee, Juhani Pallasmaa, Junya Ishigami, Kuehn Malvezzi, Lacaton & Vassal, LAN, Lebbeus Woods, Liam Young, Li Xiadong, Made In, MAD, Maio, Marc Fornes, MASS Design Group, Metro, Michael Hansmeyer, MOS, Nameless, Neri Hu, Neri Oxman, Norman Foster, Office KGDVS, Ole Scheeren, OOPEAA, Patrik Schumacher, Peter Eisenman, Peter Zumthor, Philip Johnson, Philippe Rahm, Pier Vittorio Aureli, Plan B, RAAAF, Rafael Moneo, RCR, Rem Koolhaas, REX, Robert Venturi, Rojkind, Sam Jacob, SANAA, SeArch, SelgasCano, Serie Architects, Smiljan Radic, Snøhetta, Eduardo Souto de Moura, Sou Fujimoto, Standard, Steven Holl, Supermachine Studio, Sverre Fehn, Tadao Ando, Team Mazzanti, Tham & Videgård, Thomas Heatherwick, Thom Mayne, Toyo Ito, Urban Think Thank, Valerio Olgiati, Wang Shu, WOHA, Zaha Hadid.

Young architects of today will talk to people who have influenced – maybe inspired – them, about anything I decide. But just as I can't expect myself to plough through hundreds of thousands of pictures, so I don't have the capacity or the time to read dozens of texts by a hundred architects each, to orchestrate this conversation. And I don't have to. All I have to do is tap into the repository of knowledge and opinion that is available online and specify what the conversation should be about: I'm the host and I not only send out the invitations, I also set the topic. And I am, of course, the 101st person at the table. I don't just sit back and observe, I take part: my stance, too, has value, and so as I add my voice to the conversation, I am projecting myself onto this conceptual 'spirit' I'm about to conjure up.

I like to think of my table as a 'space of similarity', rather than one of sameness. The similarity stems – this is an assumption – from the shared starting point of all the guests: they all have an architectural background. But I want to discover something beyond that, and dig deeper into what makes us all feel at home in architecture.

But before I ask my guests anything at all, just like at any dinner party, I let them mingle; reveal themselves and what's important to them, in their own words:

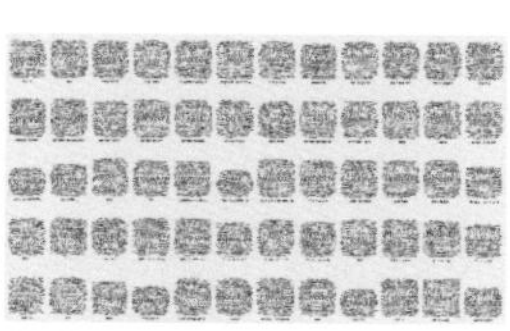
368 ● 608

The words that stand out are words I can assume matter to them, and I am not surprised to find, in this 'space of similarity' that I have prepared for them, some similarities: they talk about their 'work', their 'project', what they 'build' in the 'city', and obviously they talk about 'architecture'. This is exactly what I want to hone in on now. *How* do they talk about 'architecture'. What do they actually have to say about it? And here I'm taken with the spectrum they cover: yes, the most used words – the keywords – are much as expected, but they are surrounded now by soft clouds of personal vocabulary.

And so, already, instead of having to listen to a professor or two, telling me what architecture is (what it is to them), I can ask my guests to tell me, in their own words. I want to listen more closely. They don't talk, after all, in disjointed words: like anyone who has anything to say, they formulate themselves in sentences.

One after the other, my guests start speaking, and they do so in clusters of affinity; like a ripple of thoughts, where the first statement I hear is as far as it can be from the last person at the table, but as close as is possible to its immediate neighbour. We have ourselves another spectrum, one of positions on architecture:

HANS HOLLEIN
To me architecture is not primarily the solution of a problem, but the making of a statement.

BERNARD TSCHUMI
I am talking about inclusive architecture; all architecture is social.

TEAM MAZZANTI
I used to say and still say that architecture is the materialisation of the concept.

JUHANI PALLASMAA
Every touching experience of architecture is multi-sensory. Qualities of matter, space and scale are measured equally by the eye, ear, nose, skin, tongue, skeleton, and muscle. Silence, Time, and Solitude. However, the most essential auditory experience created by architecture is tranquility.

ROBERT VENTURI
But architecture is necessarily complex and contradictory in its very inclusion of the traditional Vitruvian elements of commodity, firmness, and delight.

JUHANI PALLASMAA
Architecture presents the drama of construction silenced into matter and space; architecture is the art of petrified silence.

BERNARD TSCHUMI
Ongoing questioning and discussion, as well as a motivation to transgress given limits...

ROBERT VENTURI
Modern architecture is never implicit.

BERNARD TSCHUMI
...constitute part of the development of every project.

DAAR
If architecture is a weapon in a military arsenal that implements the power relations of colonialist ideologies, then architecture must burn.

PATRIK SCHUMACHER
The core competency of architecture is thus the task of articulation.

MOS
Ultimately, the problem with a truly autonomous language of architecture is there is no task to perform, no goals, there are only language games. In this mode, working within and using cultural production, architecture is a pseudodiscipline.

BENJAMIN DILLENBURGER
The resolution of architecture is a measure of the spatial density of information inherent in a building.

MASS DESIGN GROUP
I think all architecture is political of course.

BENJAMIN DILLENBURGER
But the purpose of architecture is an open notion, depending on the physical, social, economic cultural and historical background, where it is used.

CHRISTIAN KEREZ
Well, I would say: my understanding of architecture is close to the understanding of art, in the sense that I consider architecture as being a media; like music defined by noises, like culture defined by volumes, and architecture is defined by the space.

RAFAEL MONEO
Of course, the more common problem of architecture is that buildings are just plainly trivial.

STEVEN HOLL
Frank Lloyd Wright said that architecture is the mother of all arts.

JEAN NOUVEL
I would like to mention Gaudí: his architecture is so spectacular but also so natural at the same time.

MAIO
It is always a reason of joy when Spanish architecture is internationally recognised.

SELGASCANO
We believe that the most interesting architecture is precisely the type that helps you to realise that architecture isn't necessary; the type that leads you to decide not to build.

SNØHETTA
That's what architecture is about, the art of prepositions: under, in, through, in front of.

ALDO ROSSI
I have always felt that my architecture is timeless.

SOU FUJIMOTO
All architecture is, in a sense, one room.

OFFICE KGDVS
Someone could say that the minimum of architecture is a wall, and that, therefore, materials do not play an important role.

STEVEN HOLL
One of the great excitements now in architecture is that we are free!

TADAO ANDO
One thing about architecture is that the more you look at good buildings, the more love you have for them.

JDS
We believe it is now exhausted and that a new approach to architecture is urgent.

ZAHA HADID
Ultimately architecture is all about the creation of pleasant and stimulating settings for all aspects of social life.

TADAO ANDO
For me, I think architecture is one of the best professions for society.

RCR
Architecture is a very long word; can it be abbreviated?

I want to explore further their ideas in text, but not as a linguist, which I'm not; I want to go beneath the language and analyse the concepts they employ, looking for rules, structures, and grammars amongst those. So here again, just as I did with pictures, I'm choosing my lens, my measure of unit. It could be a paragraph, a sentence, a letter. I choose as my unit the word, because I want to explore contemporary architectural concepts, and the smallest unit in language that can convey meaning on its own is the word. I want to look at words now as indexes, in relation to each other; place them in their contextual environment. This means that my words, rather than functioning as units inside grammatically correct sentences, now become nodes on a network; and their relationships with the words that surround them become edges.

So what interests me now is not the definition of a word itself, but the other words it can be related to. Because by looking at these relationships, I can weight them. I don't look at words as carriers of meaning any longer, but I examine the relationships they stand in, to find some meaning or significance there.

As the brook of words begins to pour out, and the droplets that are the words connect with and relate to each other, forming a stream, my guests themselves now acquire a new informational face, which consists of the words they use and their multiple connections. My dinner table for a hundred architects turns into a banquet of characters, each one unique, each one vivid in their individual appearance. I find a new way of getting to know them, through them getting to know each other.

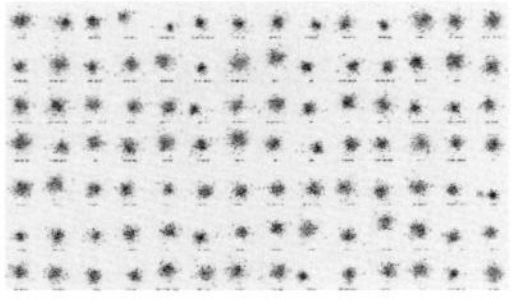

369 ● 608

Once again, I choose my method, and I don't have to justify or explain it, either to myself or to them, or to anyone else; it's just what happens to take my fancy, right now. I am, as I was when playing with pictures, master of my own story. The way I see and understand each of my guests depends on the lens through which I glance at them.

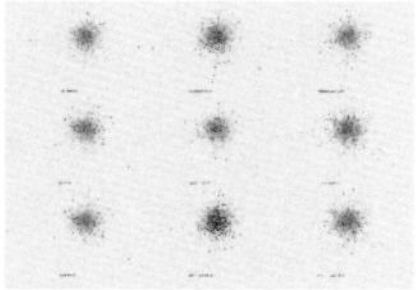

370 ● 608

Up until now, all of my guests have come with their own words and stories. But in order to make them talk to one another, rather than just iterate a multitude of monologues, I define the common space for discussion: a collective dictionary.

I'm not surprised if, as at any good dinner party, some words – some topics – turn out to be more prevalent than others. A hot topic will be in everyone's mouth, as will some basic terminology, some words that my guests will naturally use all the time; they are, after all, all architects. So in my 'dictionary' that I allow for discussion, I now declare some exclusions. There are those words I hear too often for them to reveal anything of interest to me, so I say to my guests, 'I take these terms for granted, I know you all "work" in "space," you "create" and "design." So let's leave those words out for the time being:'

{build, architecture, space, work, project, design, city, new, use, way, think, time, form, house, like, architect, person, make, different, thing, architectural, material, create, urban, idea, place, process, structure, say, mean, just, change, world, public, open, look, life, good, need, area, interest, art, year, experience, know, point, understand, allow, construction, system}

371 ● 609

There are also some words that are simply too specific: for some of my guests they are unfamiliar or irrelevant and they don't like using them, while others may not even know what they mean. I'm after a degree of clarity, and I'm also after participation, and so I make some further decisions about what I think goes too far. It's just my choice again, you would choose differently altogether, that's the beauty of it:

372 ● 609

Now that I have my space for discussion, I can really start to listen in. I can wander around my feast, like the host that I am, and eavesdrop on what my architect friends are saying to each other. It's not so much a dinner table any more, it's a masked ball where my guests choose words to obscure or reveal themselves, maybe reveal themselves with obscurity?

This is how the first words in our dictionary are experienced and weighted by each one of us:

373 ● 609

And now I can take a position. I can choose more precisely the questions I want to ask. For example, I could ask my guests how they feel about a specific word, or I can ask what these words articulate in relation to them. This is how I discover our galaxy of concepts. Here then is my first *concept map:*

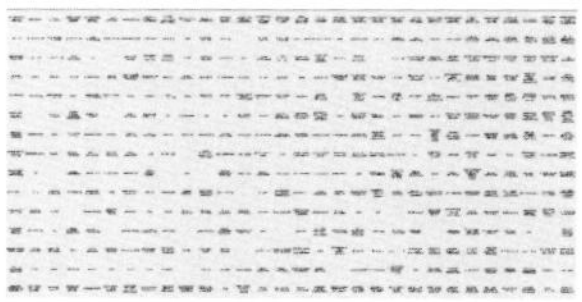

374 ● 610

Which I can zoom into to take a closer look:

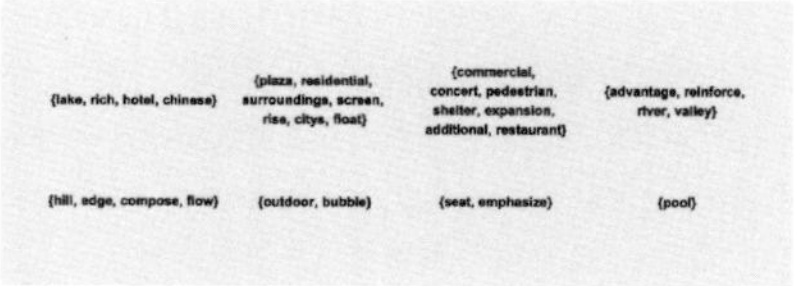

375A ● 610

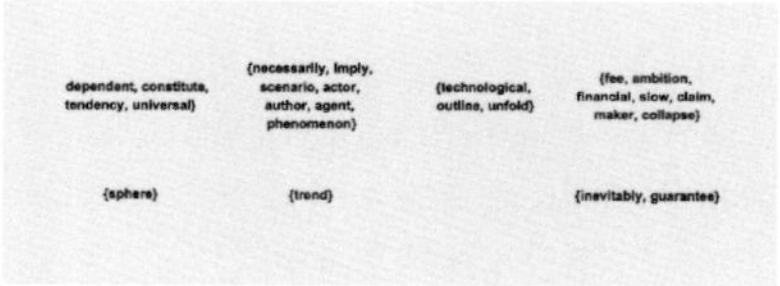

375B ● 610

The concepts can be anything that moves my guests. Some will talk about the economic activities in an urban setting, and their concepts will be, perhaps, 'commercial', 'pedestrian', 'restaurant', 'concert', 'expansion', 'hotel', 'rich'. What exactly is it they're talking about in this group? I don't know, I hear only the fragments, but I get a feel for what is important to them. Is it important to me? If it is I can pause and listen some more. I wander on and hear another group talk about 'scenario', 'actor', 'author', 'agent', 'phenomenon', 'trend': they seem to be talking about something more fundamental to architecture?

The words start drawing portraits on our conceptual canvas, my guests populate the concept map at wish. Beautiful spectrums, each one unique, yet more or less similar. Here are our first 'portraits':

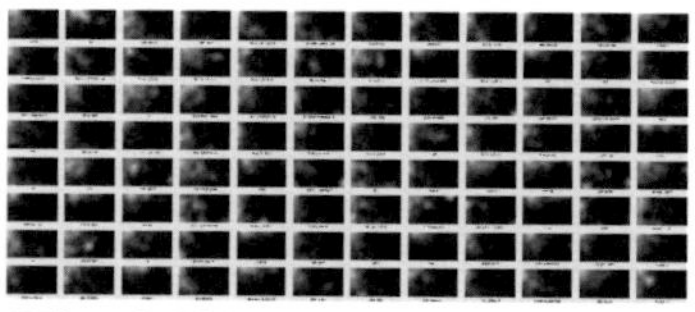

376 ○ 684

Each guest with their own look, words, style, interests. They start showing themselves – is it their mask? Is it their face? – the way *they* want to exist in this new public space.

I stumble upon Bjarke Ingels and Neri Oxman in a diagonal exchange. Bjarke likes solving problems, giving answers, responding to challenges, engaging in decisions; he is an architect of action, he wants to give precise answers to architectural problems. He cares about challenges, solutions, competitions, propositions, answers, and 'yes, yes, yes':

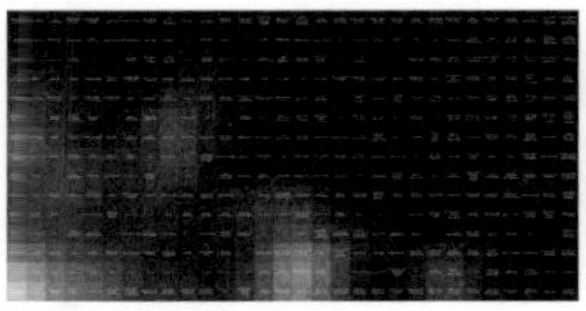
377 ○ 685

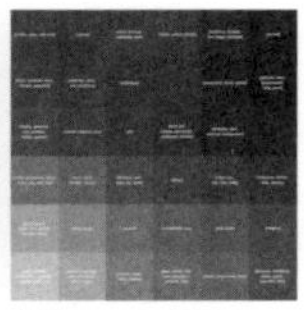
378 ○ 685

Neri seems less certain, but more intuitive. She explores concepts around morphology and fabrication; flirts with biology, mathematics, multiplicity, computation, code, applications, software, algorithms, indexes.

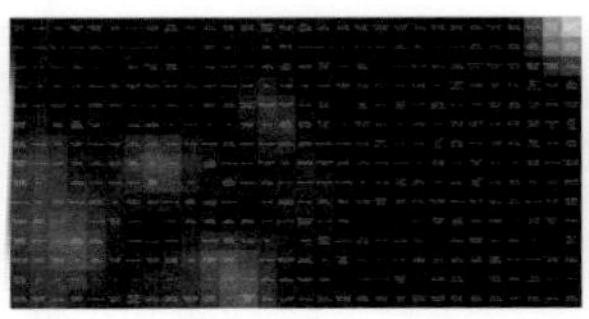
379 ○ 686

380 ○ 686

I can almost hear them, across the room:

NERI
In the Biological Age, designers and builders are empowered to dream up new, dynamic design possibilities, where products and structures can grow, heal, and adapt.

BJARKE
We architects don't control the city – we can only aspire to intervene. Architecture evolves from the collision of political, economical, functional, logistic, cultural, structural, environmental, social, and many yet unnamed and unforeseeable interests.

NERI
But striding Nature's way is far from natural. It requires a change in the way we see 'Mother Nature', from a boundless nourishing entity to one that begs nourishment by design.

BJARKE
Architecture is never triggered by a single event, never conceived by a single mind, and never shaped by a single hand. Neither is it the direct materialisation of a personal agenda or pure ideals, but rather the result of an ongoing adaptation to the multiple conflicting forces flowing through society.

NERI
As we master 'unnatural' processes at a speed and sophistication that dwarfs evolution, *Material Ecology* propels us into the age where we mother Nature by design.

I remind myself that neither of them is right or wrong. And that what I hear them say stems from the dictionary I have given them to use. With a different set of words and under a different lens, I might well find that they agree much more than they differ, or disagree even more: it's just one way of looking at them, one way of listening to them.

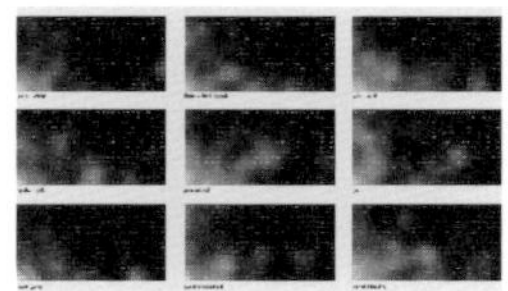
381 ○ 687

As I zoom in closely, I notice that both Bjarke and Neri have made their own circle of affinities. I have no label for them, nor any need for one; that, I think, would only negate them. As with any two individuals, their relationship with each other and their connections and relationships with people are fluid, overlapping, sometimes focusing here, sometimes there: they celebrate their similarities as well as their differences in their own way, declare their friendships on their own terms.

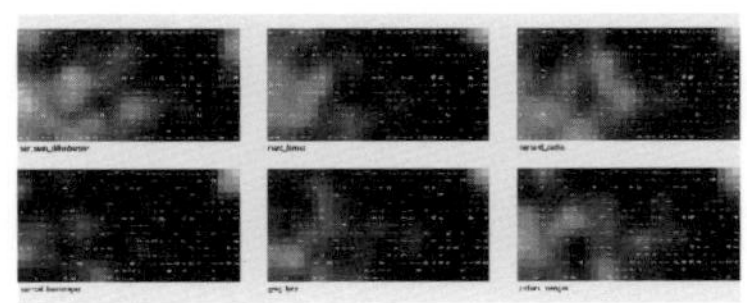
382 ○ 687

My guests, much as I hoped and anticipated, do not stand still: they change positions, they continue to mingle. They gather, but they remain borderless, porous, flexible, magnetic. They start a new conversation here and another one there, they move on from one person to the next but take with them still some of what they've been talking about: they carry concepts into the next connection.

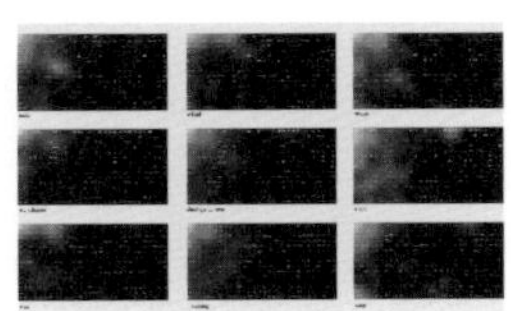
383 ○ 688

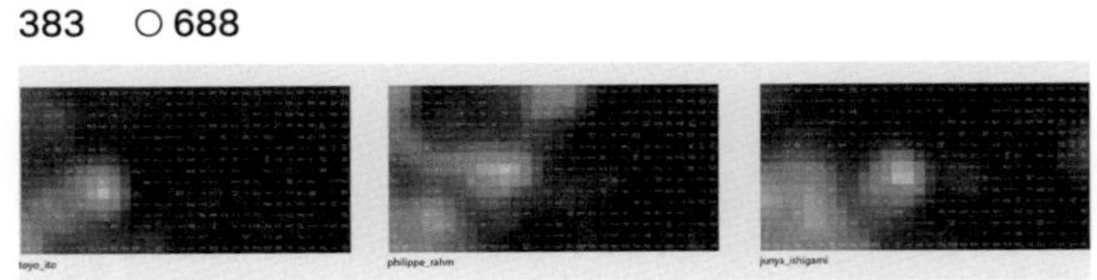
384 ○ 588

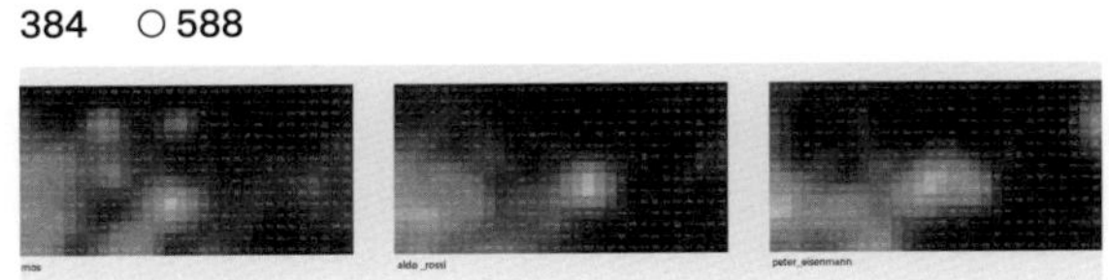
385 ○ 688

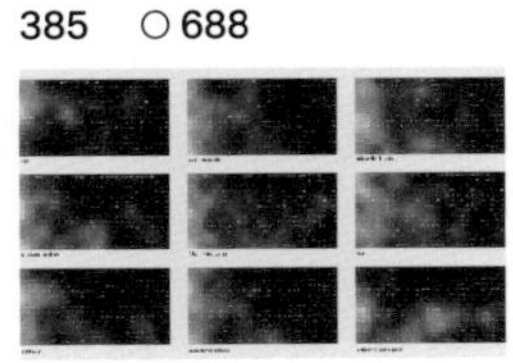
386 ○ 689

The stories, affinities and conversations I have heard tonight are not absolute. They are not an architectural truth nor a theory, just a version of many that are possible; I've said it before but I will say it again, because it is so important: it's just one way of seeing. In one world some of my guests might indulge in a love affair, in another they might repel each other and distance themselves from each other as far a space allows. I just collect a multitude of narratives of how my guests could have behaved at this party, under different circumstances, in different worlds:

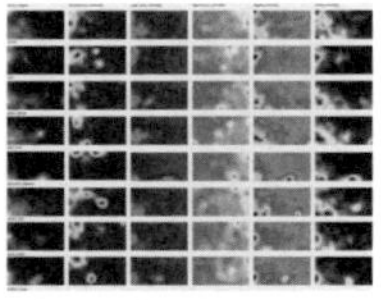

387 ○ 689

With all these different realities simultaneously in my sight, I can establish a new kind of conversation. I'm inclined to call it a 'meta-discussion', an encapsulation, where the realities talk among themselves about what my architect guests say and do. It seems like a bit of a far-fetched idea, but it's happening: the different ways of looking at my guests tell of the hidden tensions and the dynamics governing my table, or, as I should call it now, my room.

Concepts are now no longer populated by just words, but really, by the architects themselves. An architect becomes a concept, a 'brand'! Concepts encapsulate other concepts, and each time a new concept is articulated, it shows up new affinities between my guests. There is hue, there is flavour. There is proximity and colour. Proximity is attraction, affinity: my guests make friends. Hues from light green to dark purple tell me how my guests like to talk, spanning from a more common vocabulary towards more personal expressions of themselves. And now it is my turn to take a stance and ask, where should I sit at this table? Who are my friends? Who do I have an affinity with? Can I find my place, can I see myself reflected? As I explore these questions, the idea of what my 'brand' could be starts taking shape. My friends are already talking about it and I am ready to learn from them, much as they may learn from me. I find myself surrounded by Jean Nouvel, Steven Holl, Álvaro Siza, Herzog & de Meuron, Glenn Murcutt, AAA, and Plan B. Most of them are 'stars', as famous for their brand as for their architectural production.

This is the character I decide to be today, using my vocabulary and my ideas on how to present architecture. Tomorrow I can be someone else, if I want to: I may come up with different ideas and desires, different words and concepts, different guests joining me at my table. As they change, so do I, so does my 'brand', my mark. Perhaps an identity then, in this ever fluid, ever dynamic world, isn't so much a brand, a mark, fixed and burnt into my presence, any longer: it is, as I am, effervescent, organic, changeable, live.

And here now, finally, a picture of our dinner table, with me present. This is our 'selfie' of this unforgettable evening. I recognise myself, there amongst my friends and idols, and those who challenge me, feasting, talking.

This is who I can be in the world of The Big Plenty...

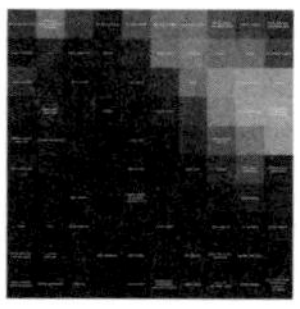

388 ○ 690

Coda

389 ○ 690

We asked at the beginning: if we think of coding as literacy and of the Internet as a new public space, then how do we as architects – more to the point, how do you as a young, aspiring architect – behave in this space? It's a space in which we have moved beyond mere formal representation; our abstractions are symbolic: figures, fugues, faces, masks, indexes, atoms, elements, characters, avatars. And so articulating ourselves has become about infusing, narrating, doping, positioning within fluid contexts.

What hasn't changed though is that articulating ourselves is about mastery. And with our 'Two Act Play' we've attempted to illustrate, in a playful way, an approach, a methodology. It is more of a game, really, but there is a reason why in English, as in German, the activity of enacting a dramatised scenario uses the same verb as the action of diverting yourself in experimentation and learning. The reason we've opted for this, rather than, say, a formal, maybe instructive way of presenting an example lies in the very 'nature' of what we are talking about (there is of course nothing 'natural' about it, it is all human-made artifice): the digital world, with its boundlessness, its voluptuousness, its outrageousness, invites us only to play. The distractions are not a few, they are overwhelming, in their billions. Just keeping your mind concentrated on one document or piece of work in front of you on your screen for longer than ten minutes has become a serious challenge. Genres, categories, disciplines are all being messed up and reconfigured, seemingly at random. The way the digital world behaves – and that's us, in the digital world – is exactly as superficially chaotic as it seems. But *of course* there are patterns. *Of course* there are dynamic relationships that influence and inform each other. And *of course* there is always more to it than meets the eye.

And none of it is frivolous. If you've ever spent an afternoon with a five-year-old or witnessed a game of rugby (or any other sport for that matter): play is dead serious. And so are we when we suggest that in order to cope with what we are calling The Big Plenty, we want to develop our thinking, that in order to orientate ourselves in the new public space we want to learn how to use the tools that are being employed in this space, that we recognise and at the same time take it upon ourselves to redefine what we want to mean by concepts such as 'identity' or, indeed, 'brand'.

Our universe is one in which we are all human beings and at the same time we are aliens, mutants, cyborgs. There is literally no defined space and so there is by definition no exact or agreed-upon time. And as we look out onto a very foreseeable future where even the binary duality that lies at the heart of digitality gives way to quantum states, there are now no real distinctions. There are blurred lines and fascinating hybrids, there are mixtures and fusions, and there is neither a pure reality nor is there a pure fiction. There is architecture. We want to be right at home here.

353 ● 597
What is 'more'? [designboom]

368 ● 602
Architects as word clouds, highlighting the most recurrent concepts.
[Word series 368–375: Diana Alvarez-Marin & Miro Roman]

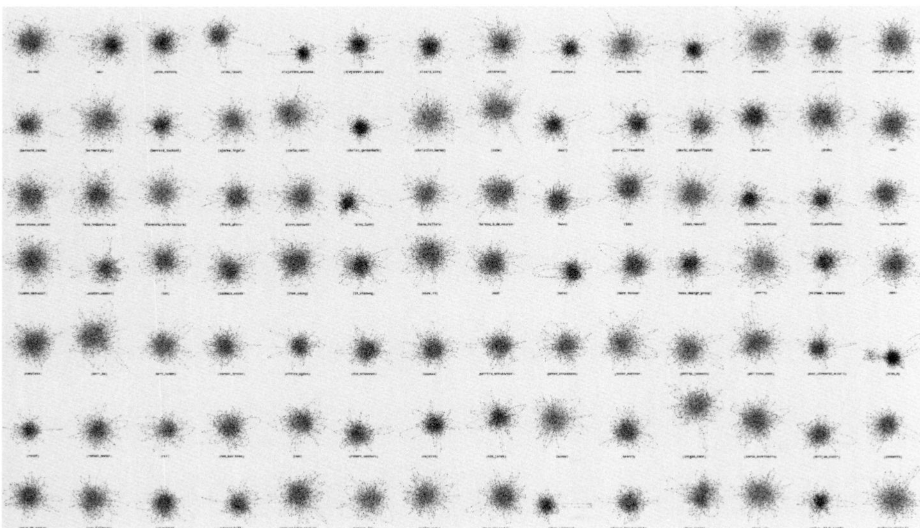

369 ● 604
Architects as bundles of relationships. [DAM, MR]

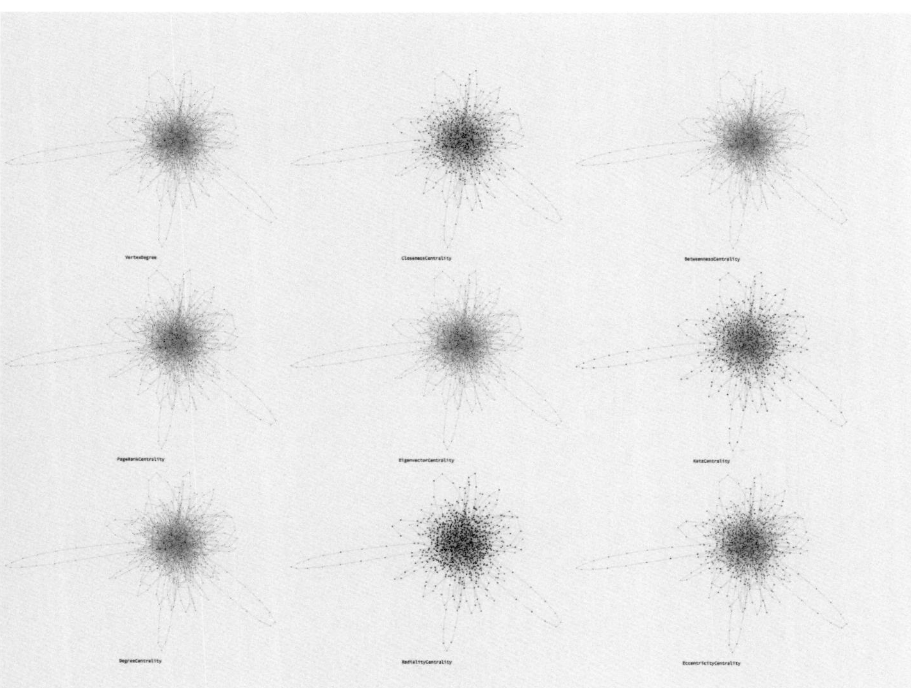

370 ● 604
Alejandro Aravena seen through different lenses. [DAM, MR]

{build, architecture, space, work, project, design, city, new, use, way, think, time, form, house, like, architect, person, make, different, thing, architectural, material, create, urban, idea, place, process, structure, say, mean, just, change, world, public, open, look, life, good, need, area, interest, art, year, experience, know, point, understand, allow, construction, system}

371 ● 604
Most recurrent words in contemporary architectural discourse. [DAM, MR]

{reframed, aperiodic, heightcontrolled, skygardens, heritagelisted, shophouses, headroom, shophouse, externalise, splay, dayak, longhouses, borneo, breezy, recombinations, hightechnology, furry, verandah, urbanistically, bonsai, padi, gully, lim, barrierfree, dampen, indooroutdoor, gazette, pebblewash, sarong, verticallystacked, beamfree, allowance, officeloftliving, buyer, watercovered, wilkie, nightlife, buzz, realitiesunited, perth, dean, wms, duxton, skyvilledawson, diamondshaped, formdefining, landlimited, whhl, elias, midseventies, malevitch, lissitzky, avantgarderadicalizing, seamlessness, willfulness, mosul, repetitiveness, lissitzkys, prouns, naum, gabos, kasimir, phaeno, miyake, erich, heydaraliyev, baku, professionally, sputnik, pizza, louchely, shoreditch, brooch, concorde, iraqi, cardiff, olympics, marseille, michigan, intrusive, crystallise, reggio, calabria, sardinia, hardworking, diligent, normalised, arty, alvin, boyarksy, syllabus, wolf, blackout, doable, waite, praemium, imperiale, heartbreaking, milton, keynes}

372 ● 604
Least recurrent or anecdotic words in contemporary architectural discourse. [DAM, MR]

373 ● 604
First 50 words in the 'architects dictionary'. [DAM, MR]

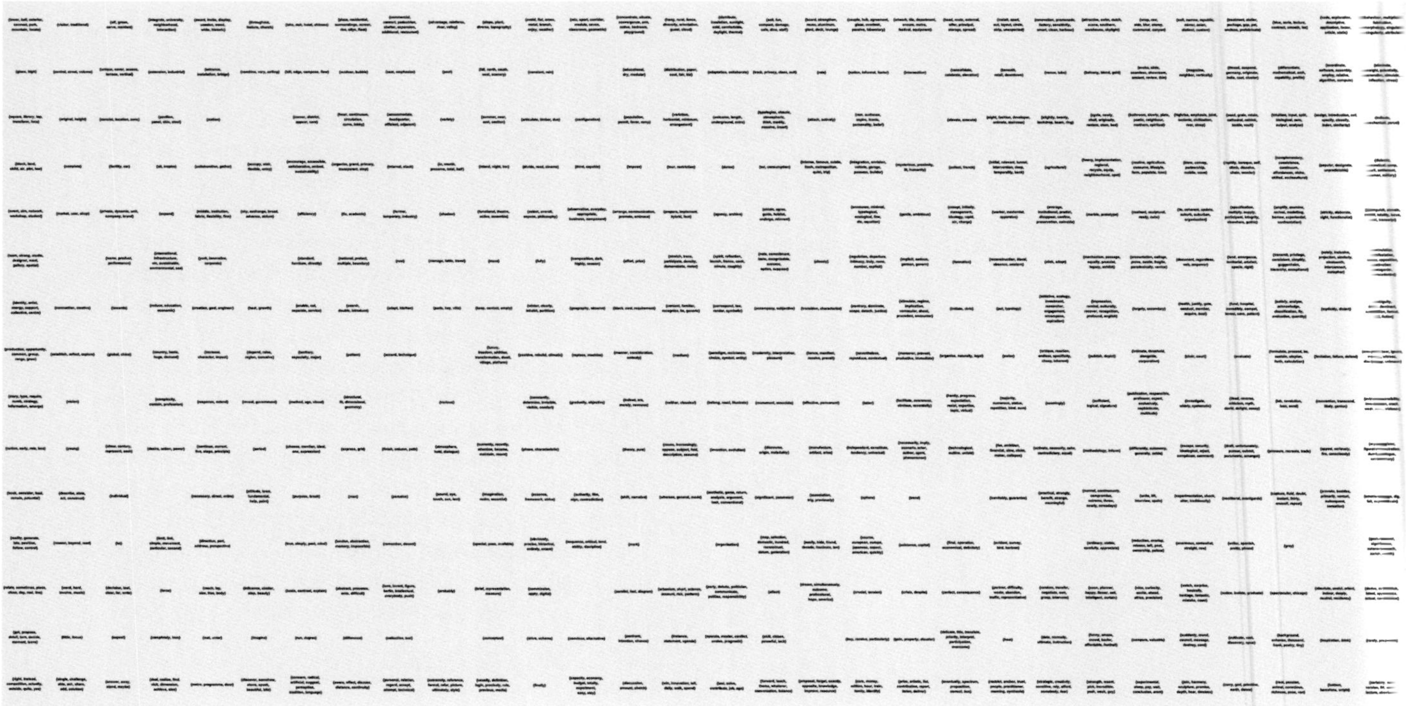

374 ● 604
Concept map. [DAM, MR]

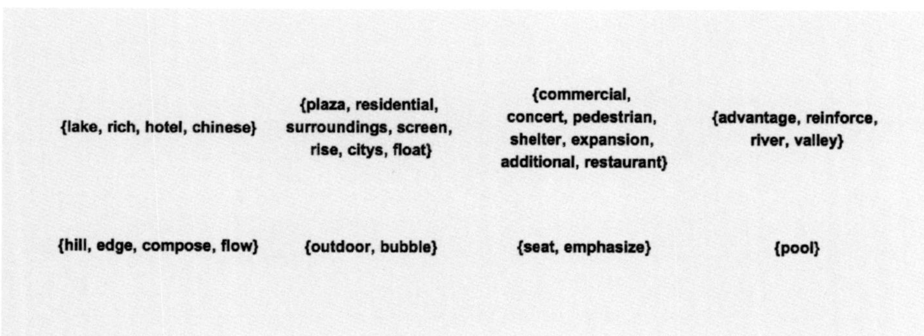

375A ● 604
Concept map zoom. [DAM, MR]

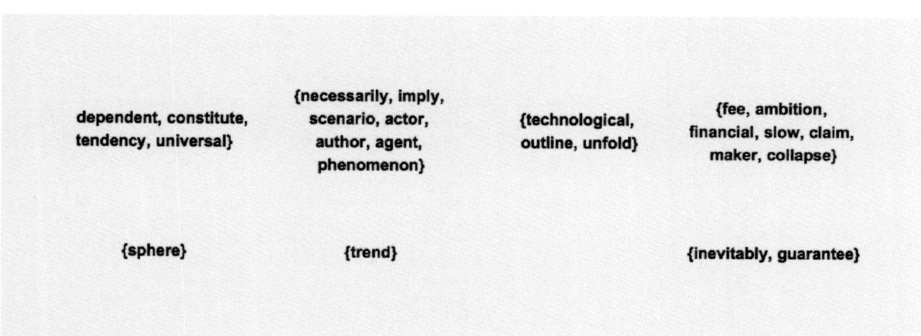

375B ● 604
A different concept map zoom. [DAM, MR]

The Internet of Things (IoT)

Kay Römer

Overview

Asked for a piece published in the *The Daily Telegraph* in May 2017, whether the anti-science stance taken by the Donald Trump administration in the United States would stifle innovation, British technology pioneer Kevin Ashton (b. 1968) replied: "It won't change anything," going on to explain that it was by now an illusion to think of America as the technology leader of the world. "That was the case in the '90s, but look at tech exports. The world leader now is China, and has been since the beginning of the Internet of Things. Number two is Germany. The US is number three, with South Korea and Singapore very close behind." To drive home the point, he then mused, maybe a little tongue-in-cheek: "Besides, the World Wide Web was invented by a British guy – Sir Tim Berners-Lee. And the Internet of Things was invented by a British guy – me."

Modesty may not be Kevin Ashton's strongest suit, and, unlike the World Wide Web, which is indeed, in terms of conception and code, largely the brainchild of British engineer and computer scientist Tim Berners-Lee (b. 1955), it is really not possible to assign credit for the 'invention' of The Internet of Things (IoT) to one single individual any more than it is possible to say who 'invented' the Internet of information that we use every day. (This not least because there are varying definitions of what the 'Internet of Things' is meant be, and different people in different parts of the world have thought pretty much along similar lines at the same time, making strides towards its realisation.) It is nevertheless interesting to hear from the man who claims to have coined the term, what the thinking was that drove him to do so, in what context, and when.

In an article of his own, published in the *RFID Journal* in June 2009, Ashton had phrased his role a little differently, more precisely, and also more humbly: "I could be wrong, but I'm fairly sure the phrase 'Internet of Things' started life as the title of a presentation I made at Procter & Gamble (P&G) in 1999." Emphasising the fact that this was now a network of *things* that could talk to each other without human input lay at the core of the consideration. Ashton recognised that the vast majority of data then handled online was at one point generated or processed by people. "The problem is, people have limited time, attention and accuracy—all of which means they are not very good at capturing data about things in the real world," he observed, and argued: "If we had computers that knew everything there was to know about things – using data they gathered without any help from us – we would be able to track and count everything, and greatly reduce waste, loss and cost. We would know when things needed replacing, repairing or recalling, and whether they were fresh or past their best." Although he was working in the context of consumer product logistics, he also knew that the scope for this was, and still is, so great, and the range of practical applications so wide, that he concluded: "The Internet of Things has the potential to change the world, just as the Internet did. Maybe even more so."

If you equip everyday objects, scientific instruments, or any other type of device with mini computers that can sense their environment and acquire – without human involvement – data and information about what's happening to and around them and decide what (if anything) they should do in response, and then connect them with each other, you turn them into nodes on a dynamic network, and that network is the Internet of Things. It ties in directly – and brings a big step closer – the notion of ubiquitous computing, a term ■ ↖561 (for which you will also find pervasive computing or ■ ambient intelligence) that is attributable to the American scientist Mark Weiser (1952–1999), who used it to ■ mean a technology environment in which computers are just there and do what they need to do without us even noticing them. This, in a vision first described in 1988, and thus just predating the World Wide Web, included all manner of devices, which Weiser originally categorised into three size groups: small, wearable 'tabs'; hand-held 'pads'; and larger, desktop mounted or elsewhere installed 'boards'. Subsequently, to these were added 'dust', which were micro-sized (perhaps down to nanometre scale) devices without any kind of display; flexible, wearable 'skin' devices; and clusters of Micro-Electronic Mechanical Systems (MEMS), ■ known as 'clay'.

What ubiquitous computing as envisioned by □ ↖613 Weiser foretold was that these devices would then no longer even be recognisable as computers, but simply fit into our existence and form a network of networks, which is why the terms *Internet of Things* (sometimes also the *Internet of Everything*) and *ubiquitous computing* are now often used interchangeably.

UBIQUITY

Technology becoming ubiquitous can be regarded as a sign of its maturity, and that in turn may be an indicator for its significance: if technology really matters to us and makes a lasting difference to the way we live, it will become part of our lives to the point where we don't notice it's there any more. Take time, for example. Before we had any technology to measure it, we orientated ourselves by the sun, nature, and our own sense of it. Then, as we invented mechanical clocks, they became a big deal: a village might have one on its church steeple, and in the city a rich person might have a fine decorative apparatus on their mantelpiece. As the technology got smaller and cheaper, it became more widely used: pocket watches appeared, then wrist watches; then, from the early 1970s onwards, digital watches; and by the mid-1980s a watch could still, but no longer had to, be a prized time piece: you could now produce one so cheaply that it could be given away as a marketing gift. Soon clocks were everywhere, and by now, we don't notice a clock, we just expect there to be one. On the computer, on the phone, on the microwave, on the oven; it doesn't surprise you to find one on your pen, or projected onto the pavement as you walk along the street – time keeping – which only a couple of generations ago was still notable enough to make for a good retirement present – has blended into our environment, and we make nothing of it.

This is replicated with many technologies: until the first half of the 19th century, a mechanical motor that could move an object or tool was something you found in a large factory. Then in big cars and locomotives. Then, with electricity, in handheld tools and domestic appliances. Obviously still in cars and trains too, but they could now be the size of a toy, and amuse your eight-year-old.

Computing, as we remind ourselves here and there in this *Atlas*, started out with machines that took up entire office floors. Today, we're not quite at the point where we have 'intelligent' dust, but we're certainly not far off. Nanotechnology is moving us close to the point where we can have computing running through our bloodstream.

'SMART HOME', 'SMART CITY', 'SMART ENVIRONMENT'

From an architect's perspective, the most relevant and therefore interesting implementation of the Internet of Things is the 'smart' or 'intelligent' built object, whether that's the home or the office, the city, the village or the town; the motorway, the bridge or the lighthouse; or the parking lot. All and any of them can, with sensor and communication technology, be partly or wholly 'intelligent'. ('Intelligent' as always in these cases meaning not that they are in a human, philosophical sense capable of actual creative consciousness and self-awareness, but simply that they are able to hold and pass on information about what and where they are, and to read, hear, sense, or otherwise register changes to their condition or their environment, and respond accordingly.)

In some contexts – prominently that of goods logistics, but also applications as diverse as cattle protection and wildlife monitoring – the communicating is done with the **RFID (Radio-Frequency Identification)** technology that Kevin Ashton was involved in developing in the 1990s. RFID chips today can be as small as an ant, contain some essential information as to their identity, purpose, and location, and communicate with an RFID reader that may be nearby or up to several hundred metres away. RFID stood at the beginnings of the Internet of Things, and it is a technology that is versatile and therefore still widely used, but it's by no means the only, or even most relevant, method of communication any more. (We will be talking in more detail about the network structure and communication protocols in use in the Internet of Things today in a moment).

In the 'smart home', the Internet of Things is often associated with the classic (and arguably now slightly worn) examples of the fridge that knows when it's time to reorder eggs and does so automatically from your supermarket, or the system that realises when you're entering the home after work and turns on the light, adjusts the heating, and lowers the blinds for you. But while these instances may seem more like nice to have add-ons that are of little actual consequence, on a city planning and urban management scale, 'intelligent' things and places can have a genuinely major impact on congestion, pollution, use of infrastructural facilities, and therefore quality of life for citizens.

A simple example of this is parking. In many urban settings, individual car users spend inordinate amounts of time searching for convenient, cheap, and above all available parking spaces. This is not merely inefficient, wasteful, and frustrating for the driver who'd rather be getting on with the meeting, the shopping, the work, or the theatre visit than be cruising around already congested streets, it also puts unnecessary pressure on the environment and uses up limited road space that needs to be shared by pedestrians, cyclists, and motorists alike. It adds to pollution for no real purpose and slows everybody down. So parking spaces that know whether they're free or not and communicate this to an app, which then directs the driver to their nearest available space, reliably and dependably, are eminently useful for the city as a whole.

Or take infrastructure maintenance: the Forth Bridge on the eastern coast of Scotland spans just over eight thousand feet (2,467 metres) across the Firth of Forth, in three elegant red arches, allowing a railway line to run south-north without lengthy detour via Stirling, and it has several claims to fame. When it opened in 1890, it had the world's longest single cantilever span (meaning the part of the bridge that is held up by one individual support of this kind), and in 2015 it was designated a UNESCO World Heritage Site. It also gave the English language the expression, 'it's like painting the Forth Bridge', to mean a job that is never done. The story that the task of painting the Forth Bridge could never be completed, because whenever a team of painters finished at one end, they immediately had to start again at the other, turns out to be sadly apocryphal, but it is true that up until 201[illegible] the maintenance crew (which still exists) included permanently employed painters who, in fact, prioritised worst affected areas, rather than going over the whole bridge evenly without end. Therein alone though lies a clue to what an 'intelligent' bridge would be good at: equipped with sensors, a structure can detect all by itself which parts of it are most affected by the strains of traffic, corrosion, and weather, and tell a maintenance system where it needs attention and when. So rather than having teams of inspectors conducting manual tests, the bridge monitors itself, and resources can be deployed precisely where they are most needed, as often and much as required, but not more.

Similarly, road tunnels: in mountainous areas, such as the Alps or the Pyrenees, road networks are punctuated with tunnels ranging in length from a few metres to several kilometres, and they all need to be safely lit. With traditional, static lighting, this means that they tend to be 'over-lit' or 'over-provisioned', simply to make sure that in all light and weather conditions the driver never goes from very bright light into a tunnel that's too dark for their eyes to adjust quickly enough to be able to see without interruption. This, replicated over miles and miles of tunnelling across Europe, uses immense amounts of energy; and it costs the tunnel and road operators a lot of money that is mostly wasted, because by equipping tunnels with light and traffic sensors both inside and outside, the lighting can be dynamically adjusted to the actual situation at any given time. So when it's dark or cloudy outside, the lighting inside the tunnel can be lowered, because drivers will already be used to driving in twilight or semi-darkness, there is no need to make the tunnel brighter than the road outside. Or little used roads, which during the night time go through several hours of virtually no traffic at all, can reduce lighting to a standby state that allows them to respond to the presence of cars when they're actually approaching.

CHALLENGES

All of these applications, whatever their context or purpose, naturally present their own challenges, and these can be formidable. Take the example of parking space monitoring above. Superficially, this would appear not too difficult a thing to accomplish: parking spaces are in the main comparatively safe and easy to access. The technology that allows for a rectangular piece of asphalt to know whether a substantial lump of metal sits above it or not is available and in itself unproblematic: it's built-in and secured, and it doesn't even have to be particularly small or lightweight, since it doesn't have to go anywhere. Even power supply, by comparison, would not appear to pose an insurmountable problem.

Yet still: parking spaces get extremely hot in the summer, something that electronics don't handle well at the best of times. In winter the reverse problem may present itself if the temperature drops to a level where it affects the hardware. The ground can get covered in snow, dust, dirt, grub, or leaves, all of which can disrupt a device's ability to function and communicate. And you need longevity: if you connect 10,000 parking spaces in your city to an intelligent network, you really want these sensors to last, because otherwise you'll be sending workers around town, continually replacing them in a very proverbially Forth Bridge sense of never-ending maintenance.

Broadly, then, the principal challenges we face with the Internet of Things are these:

1) Energy Efficiency

Any device that is connected to the network has to have an energy supply that allows it to last for months or years, without its battery needing replacement. This presents no issue where a device can be connected to a permanent power supply, such as the electricity grid. But very often that is not the case, or would be expensive and impractical to achieve. Which means that in the vast majority of cases, energy efficiency is of critical importance: the chip – that is the hardware that provides the connectivity and processes the information that is gathered – has to require as little power as possible. And this in turn limits its capabilities: the faster and more powerful a chip is, the more energy it invariably needs.

2) Computing Capability

As a direct consequence of the above, the microcomputers that turn objects into connected IoT devices have a capability that tends to be between 100 and 1000 times smaller than that of a standard laptop computer; in other words: they have a tiny fraction (between 1% and 0.1%) of a laptop's processing speed, data storage capacity, and communication bandwidth. And that means that running complex applications on them is impossible. For comparison: the *Amiga 1000* personal computer, released by Commodore International in 1985 at a retail price of USD 1,295 – excluding the monitor, which cost an extra USD 300 – was sold in Europe with a 7.09 MHz processor and 256 KB of **RAM (Random Access Memory)**, upgradeable to 512 KB. That's roughly a thousand times less powerful than a decent laptop today. You would not attempt to run most applications written for today's computers on an *Amiga 1000*; and if you did, you wouldn't get very far... ■ ↖552

3) Reliability & Security

IoT devices that form part of an urban, residential, commercial, or transport network can quickly acquire critical importance in terms of a system's integrity on the one hand, and human beings' safety on the other. London's Docklands Light Railway (DLR) for example carries 122 million passengers to and from 45 stations on seven lines each year. If this were to malfunction because of its sensors or communication devices breaking down, this would not only cause major (and costly) disruption to hundreds of thousands of people immediately, it could also potentially cost lives.

Many typical IoT installations are susceptible on the one hand to extreme temperatures and inclement weather, possibly wear and tear, and curious wildlife (also in cities); and on the other hand to deliberate acts of vandalism, sabotage, or tampering with criminal intent, and theft. The former is mostly an issue of durability and therefore reliability, the latter one of safety and security. Also a matter of concern – and, as we write this, one of the most discussed issues when it comes to the Internet of Things – is how to protect IoT networks from being hacked, infected with viruses, or otherwise compromised.

4) Self-Configuration

If, as we have posited, we think of the Internet of Things as a step towards ubiquitous computing, then over the coming years we will have tens, maybe hundreds, of billions of IoT devices, everywhere. No one person, group, or company will be responsible for all of them, but even if in your house or your company or your city you only have a few hundred, a few thousand, or a few hundred thousand of them to look after, you will not be able to treat them as you do your personal computing devices. With those, you can keep an eye on software updates and choose to install them or wait, you can (maybe have to) make decisions as to whether you want to upgrade to the latest operating system (if your machine can handle it) or not. With a laptop, a tablet, or a smartphone, this is not a problem. With three hundred domestic appliances and devices, it is already impossible. A city administration may be responsible for a few hundred thousand. This means that devices have to self-configure. They have to know what they are, what they're for, and where and when to bring themselves up to date with the latest software. All of this in view of the challenges above, particularly 1) and 2), which severely limit processing and data storage of a device.

The Components

So what are the actual elements required to make an Internet of Things possible?

DEVICES

Individual devices need three basic elements:

THE MICROCOMPUTER
When in the Internet of information computers are desktops, laptops, tablets, and smartphones, plus perhaps some wearable devices, such as watches that link up to your smartphone or similar, in the Internet of Things, the computers are mostly tiny and very basic, because their number may be vast and the functionality required of them limited and quite specific.

That notwithstanding, each of these computers will usually need to consist of three elements, to make it work as part of the Internet of Things:

■ ↖374 The **Central Processing Unit (CPU)**, which is the microchip that controls everything, what people used to call the 'brain' of the computer.

A communication capability: this can be an RFID chip, but mostly these days is some other wireless (or, occasionally, wired) connectivity that allows the device to communicate with other devices or ■ with a **base station**. (More on the structure of IoT networks, which differs significantly from the Internet of information structure, in a moment). In many cases, this element, especially if it is a wireless transceiver, is what uses most energy, which is why the management of communication is also of critical importance, as we shall see in a moment too.

One or several sensors: this is arguably the most interesting element, since it gives the device its interactive purpose. The sensor is what generates the data that is communicated to the network, and without this being somehow meaningful, the device itself cannot be a meaningful node on the network. For 'sensor' here read any means by which the device can register what is happening to or around it. Some sensors generate comparatively small amounts of data, such as a thermometer, for example: in most ordinary situations, it will simply have to read the temperature at useful intervals, maybe once every hour, and will therefore yield twenty-four very small pieces of data each day. A microphone, on the other hand, will produce potentially very large amounts of data, as may a vibration sensor – such as we hypothesised for the structural surveillance of a bridge, for example – which may have to take several readings (perhaps up to a few hundred or few thousand) *per second.* Some physical properties are more difficult to measure than others. Gas sensors that determine oxygen concentration, for example, have to be heated to more than 300 degrees celsius, which uses a lot of additional energy. And these particular instruments are often also sensitive to other gases such as nitrogen, which turns obtaining accurate readings into a complex task.

THE POWER SUPPLY
This can be a wire that feeds electricity from a mains power outlet to the microcomputer, but doesn't have to be, and in practice it very rarely is. If so, power will almost always have to be converted to a low voltage, as the majority of these chips cannot handle normal domestic voltages of between 110 and 240V, though there are some that do. But in many situations, laying wires to individual devices is not feasible or practical. A good alternative therefore can be localised energy generation, such as with solar panels or wind turbines, or even vibration-fed generators. These too can be problematic, mainly in terms of continued reliability of supply, unless there is also room and capacity for some local energy storage.

Often, therefore, the simplest and most economical solution is to equip a device with a battery; but as we also noted before, unless energy consumption sits at a level at which the battery lasts over the device's lifetime, that still makes replacing it necessary, sooner or later.

THE SOFTWARE
Much as any other computer, an IoT micro computer needs an operating system to execute one or more applications. Because these computers are tiny and have to be cheap to produce in very large numbers, they will, as we have seen, necessarily have very limited computing power compared to your average smartphone or laptop. This is the principal reason they can't run on any standard operating system, such as *OS X* for *Mac*, *Windows* for PC, or *Android* or *iOS* for smartphones and tablets. Instead you need small, compact pieces of software that require little processing power and storage, and that are capable of some basic functions that are relevant to the device and the network it is a part of.

An example of an operating system that was created specifically for IoT devices is *Contiki*, an open-source project that was originally founded by Swedish entrepreneur and programmer Adam Dunkers (b. 1978) and has since been developed by teams of collaborators and contributors at various universities, companies, and institutions, including ETH Zürich, Oxford University, and the Swedish Institute of Computer Science (among several others). According to its own website, "Contiki connects tiny low-cost, low-power micro controllers to the Internet," and thus provides, "a powerful toolbox for building complex wireless systems."

Besides which, the device has to have software – one or several applications – to its own specific purpose. Whether that purpose is being a household thermostat, or being a sensor to detect if a parking space is occupied or not; whether it is monitoring the movement of sheep or cows, or birds or badgers; or whether it is taking seismic readings: the 'thing' that is to be part of this Internet has to also do something, and do so dynamically; in other words: it has to be capable of receiving instructions and rules, and of responding to what happens to or around it in accordance with these instructions and rules. A network node that never receives nor ever sends any kind of data about anything could not be said to be a meaningful participant in that network.

IoT Node Architecture

An IoT node typically consists of a microcontroller (a processor that includes some memory and many input/output interfaces on a single chip), a power source (often a – possibly rechargeable – battery and/or an energy harvesting device such as a solar panel), a wireless transceiver to communicate with other nodes, external memory (much like a USB stick), and sensors which connect via Analogue-to-Digital Converters (ADC) to the microcontroller.

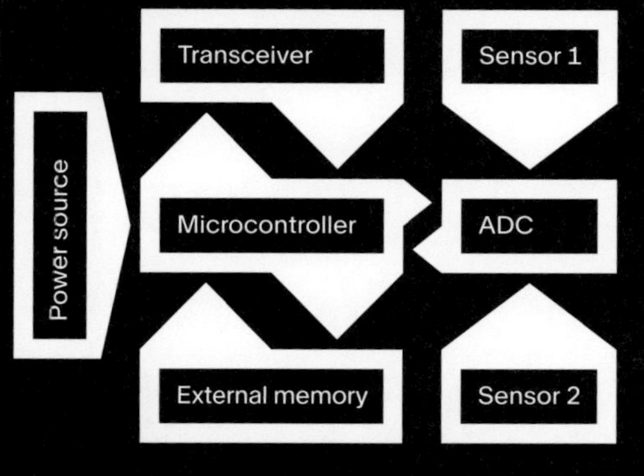

THE RANGE

We've been emphasising how cheap and therefore small these devices are, and that is certainly the case for the great majority of them. What makes the Internet of Things possible, apart from our technical ability to network devices, is our ability now to manufacture computing on a scale where we can buy it by the kilo, rather than by the unit. Think how different this is to twenty, thirty years ago. Over this period, and entirely according to Moore's law, processing speed and storage capacity for personal computers has doubled every eighteen months, while the devices themselves have more or less stayed the same size (they have become lighter and thinner, but not dramatically smaller). At this, the microcomputer end, the same principle has made it possible to reduce the size and cost of a computer with stagnant capacity every one and a half years or so by fifty percent, to the level where we are now able to treat computing as just another thing you put into your everyday object, as a matter of course.

That said, the Internet of Things does not consist exclusively of devices equipped with tiny, cheap computers that can do what a PC in the 1980s could do. A sophisticated environment observation installation, for example, may well contain sensors that cost thousands of euros apiece, if very accurate measurements are required. In general, the more accurate a sensor, the more expensive it is. And if you connect your home, your office, or your corporate headquarters to the Internet of Things, you're likely to find yourself somewhere in-between on a very broad range in terms of cost, from a few hundred euros per installation to a few hundred thousand.

MAKING YOUR OWN

What do a home made cat feeder that distinguishes between two beloved felines to dispense to each its own diet, a glove that understands sign language and translates it into voice signals, the *txtBomber* which allows graffiti artists with a message to print large font directly onto any wall, a plant with its own Twitter account, some of the instruments used at CERN to monitor the Large Hadron Collider, and several of Google's interfaces between tablets or smartphones and physical installations have in common?

They are all, as the Italian entrepreneur and designer Massimo Banzi (b. 1968), joyfully recounts in a TED Talk given in 2012, projects that used the open-source computer *Arduino*, which he, together with four of his friends, students, and colleagues, invented at the Interaction Design Institute Ivrea in Italy, in 2003.

With an *Arduino* – and we're using this as an example here; there are other, similar models available, both open-source and proprietary – anyone can build their own IoT instrument, device, gadget, or interface entirely to their own specification and requirements, from scratch, for next to nothing. Being an open-source hardware project, *Arduino* publishes the full design and specification details of its products online, so you can even build your own motherboard. If that seems too much hassle, you can buy one for (currently, as we write this in 2019), as little as EUR 8, in a range that tops EUR 62, or 80 for a complete starter kit.

The inspired user who made the cat feeder for his cats provides us with a charming example. It may not be strictly architectural, but you can easily extrapolate from it the innumerable uses you might put the thinking and approach to, if you felt so inclined, be that in a building, in a garage, on an access road, at a school or university, or in any other setting you care to think of, to whatever end you desire: Arthur (we don't know his real name, and it matters little) has two cats, Helga and Walter (we don't know their names either...), one of whom, Helga, is a little unwell. She needs specially formulated food that helps her ■ ↖558
get back to her usual, cuddlable self, whereas Walter really shouldn't be eating anything other than he usually does, let alone anything more. Arthur is a busy man, and he can't be hanging about day and night to make sure that Helga doesn't eat any of Walter's food, which is bad for her, or Walter any of Helga's, which he's prone to do, because he's a little greedy like that.

Using an *Arduino* board, a tag reader, an electronic tag sewn into each cat's collar, and a CD tray from an old computer, Arthur built himself a cat feeder that recognises which cat approaches it, and opens for it the correct tray. According to Banzi, all of this eminently useful technological wizardry was achieved using cheap ready-made, off-the-shelf, or recycled components, plus a bit of coding, the basics of which you can learn in a day. (For more on simple computer programming that allows you to create your own bespoke applications, see our chapter on Scripting.) □ ↖351
From a cat feeder to a cat flap that recognises your own cat and privileges its access to your house over other neighbourhood mogs, to a garage door that responds to your car; or, using a different kind of sensor, an automatic patio sprinkler system that waters your plants when they really need it and only ever after sundown, provided it's not freezing... — you can see a principle at work with any number of possible applications.

It would be fanciful to suggest that this particular technology would withstand the rigours of a heavy duty outdoor installation over twenty or thirty years, but what is remarkable about it is that this is the same as that used by CERN for some of its rather more advanced purposes (for collecting and analysing ambient data, it has to be said, not for colliding particles).

Telos Tmote

A famous example for an IoT node is the *Telos Tmote*, a matchbox-sized device that includes a microcontroller (a Texas Instruments *MSP430* on the bottom side), a wireless transceiver (Texas Instruments *CC2420*) with an antenna integrated in the circuit board, a very simple user interface consisting of Light Emitting Diodes (LED) and buttons, various built-in sensors, a connector to attach further sensors and actuators, and a USB connector to connect to a PCB for program upload and debugging.

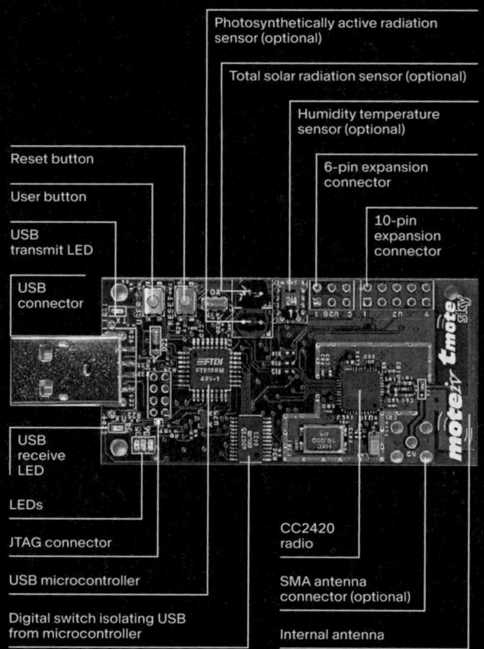

THE NETWORK

Obviously, a bunch of network enabled devices do not, in themselves, quite a network make. You also need an infrastructure that actually connects these devices and a method by which they can talk to each other.

The principal challenge here lies in making sure that the data that is being collated and sent is received at its destination correctly. In concrete terms and at its most basic: everything that has been encoded as a 0 has to arrive and be read as a 0, and everything that has been encoded as a 1 needs to arrive and be read as a 1. The reason that this is a challenge is because the radio technology that is normally used in IoT devices has a very short range indeed, 10–15 metres, owing to the limited energy supply (the longer the communication range, the more energy is required). And this means that the network has to be organised differently to the information network that is our ordinary Internet. In the Internet of information, individual devices, such as computers, smartphones and tablets, communicate with a router or modem that is perhaps ten to fifteen metres away, and that router or modem then communicates directly with a server that may be dozens or hundreds of miles away, via cable. The servers then communicate with each other over several layered network tiers that span the globe. With IoT devices (considering their short communication range, their limited power supply, their large number, and their pattern of distribution), it is often not practical to connect them all directly to a base station, which is why the Internet of Things is often structured as a mesh in which communication bounces from one device to its neighbour, and from that to the next, possibly over many instances, to a base station that then can connect to a server that can connect to the Internet.

IoT Network Architecture

The IoT builds upon the Internet backbone network, through what are known as gateways, which translate from Ethernet to the various IoT protocols (including Zigbee – IEEE 802.15.4, Bluetooth, and others.)

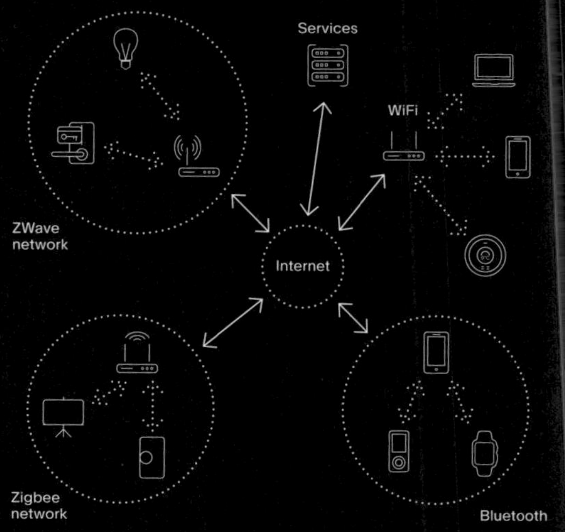

THE IEEE 802.15.4

The radio technology that is most widely in use for IoT devices today has the somewhat prosaic name *IEEE 802.15.4,* which simply denotes that it is the 4th (.4) of several Institute of Electrical and Electronics Engineers (IEEE) standards of the class 802, which is the number given to the standards dealing with Local Area Networks (LANs) and Metropolitan Area Networks (MANs), of which 15 is the working group that deals with Wireless Personal Area Network (WPAN) standards.

IEEE 802.15.4 are 'low-rate WPANs', meaning that they handle low data rates, with devices that have a very long battery life that has to last over several months or possibly years. (Other IEEE 802.15 standards include the IEEE 802.15.1 for Bluetooth, or the IEEE 802.15.3 for high-rate WPANs.)

The basic standard (there are some deviations from it) allows for a 10-metre communications range with a transfer bit rate of 250 kilobits per second. WiFi, for example, compared to IEEE 802.15.4 offers much bigger bandwidth, therefore a much higher data range, but also requires a lot more power.

The standard itself specifies a physical (PHY) layer, which handles the data transmission itself, and a data link layer, which you also see referred to as Media Access Control (MAC) layer that manages the communication of several network nodes or terminals to communicate with each other. Simply put, it is this data link or MAC layer which ensures that different IoT devices that have to talk to each other don't talk *over* each other, but await their turn and send data when the channel is free for them to do so.

IoT Network Stack

The IoT network stack follows the layered ISO/OSI model also used in the traditional Internet, but uses different protocols which are more suitable for the resource-constrained IoT.

	IETF IoT Protocol Stack	TCP/IP Protocol Stack
Application Layer	IETF COAP	HTTP, FTP, DNS, SSH, SMTP, NTP, ...
Transport Layer	UDP	TCP, UDP
Network Layer	IPv6, IETF RPL	IPv4, IPv6
Adaption Layer	IETF 6LoWPAN	N/A
MAC Layer	IEEE 802.15.4 MAC	Network Access
Physical Layer	IEEE 802.15.4 PHY	

DUTY CYCLING

With these devices – and we reiterate that this is not the case necessarily for every IoT device, but for a vast majority of them – battery life is, as we have noted once or twice before, a critical issue. It is therefore not practical for the device to be 'on' all the time. Nor does it often have to be. In many cases it is absolutely sufficient for the device to turn itself on when it needs to do some work. A sensor, for example, may not actually have to be monitoring its environment continuously, it may be able to be asleep some, in some cases as much as 99%, of the time.

This creates a new challenge though: if individual nodes on the network are asleep much of the time, 'wake up' at regular intervals to 'see what's happening', and then go to sleep again, that means that their sleep and wake cycles have to be coordinated so that their short communications with each other and with the network can amount to a meaningful 'conversation'. This is called *duty cycling,* and obviously, the shorter the duty cycle (the percentage of the time that a device is 'on'), the more precisely it has to be coordinated with other relevant devices to enable their communication.

There are several multiple access protocols that are used to handle duty cycling. The task in essence is one of broadcasting a preamble from the sending node, that lasts long enough for the receiving node to wake up and realise that there is a signal coming in. As soon as that's the case and the receiver is alert and ready, the actual data package is sent. During that particular period (which may last a fraction of a second), no other node can be sending to the same receiver. So as well as waking up the receiving node, the protocol also has to 'listen out' for any other node that is within reach, to make sure the channel is clear before attempting to send.

If, by chance, two or more nodes are sending at precisely the same moment, the protocol has a code which hands over communication from one to the other. This is not unlike a walkie-talkie or Citizens Band (CB) radio conversation. Here, you use verbal codes, such as 'over', 'roger', and 'out' to tell the other party or parties whose turn it is to talk, that you have received and understood a data packet (what's been said), or that you are now done and will not be sending any more data.

Duty Cycling

The main trick to extend the battery lifetime of IoT nodes over months or years is duty cycling, which puts nodes into a power-saving sleep mode 99% or more of the time, with very short wake-up periods. A transmitter (TX) that wants to send a message periodically sends a 'strobe message' (S) until the receiver (RX) eventually wakes up, receives the message and replies with a strobe-acknowledgement message. The sender then knows that the receiver is awake and transmits the actual data message, followed by an acknowledgement of receipt, before both sender and receiver go back to sleep.

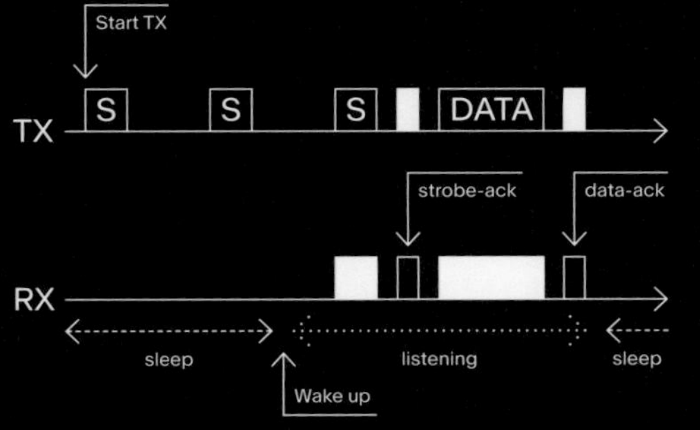

THE IPV6

If we think of network communication as structured in layers – and the industry does – then we are now, after the *physical (PHY)* layer, which provides the actual communication capability, and the *data link (or MAC) layer,* which deals with direct communication links among nodes that are within range of each other, both of which form part of the IEEE 802.15.4 standard, at a third layer, which is no longer part of that standard, but sits on top of it, so to speak.

This is called the network layer, and it deals with large networks in cases where not all nodes are within communication range of each other. The Internet Protocol (IP), which we use in the information Internet, belongs to the network layer: it is what allows you to send a message from a computer in London to one in Graz. In order to do so, the protocol has to route the data packet that constitutes your message through many intermediate computers or servers. Routing, which we'll address in more detail in just a moment, thus is also part of the network layer.

A protocol is a set of exact rules that define the grammar, syntax, and standards used by all participants in the network and allows different devices to communicate with each other, irrespective of what operating system or indeed other software (such as any applications) they might use. The task of any protocol, at any layer, is to make sure the data is encoded at one end in a way that the other end can receive and understand.

The Internet Protocol (IP) mostly in use as we write this is still what's known as *IPv4,* where *v4* simply and unspectacularly stands for *'version 4'.* But although this might suggest significant versions 1–3 that preceded it, that is not in fact really the case. None of the previous versions had any impact beyond developer stage, and it was this one, version 4, that became the first to be

650↘

deployed in the ARPANET (Advanced Research Projects Agency Network), ARPA being a US government funded body under the aegis of the US Department of Defense. Established in 1969 and finally closed in 1990, ARPANET was to all intents and purposes the forerunner of the Internet as we know it today.

During the 1990s, it became apparent that IPv4 would not, in the medium to longer term, be capable of handling the number of devices connected to the Internet, as it was conceived on the basis of allocating each device a 32-bit IP address. This allows for approximately 4.3 billion such addresses, and since each and every single device that is connected to the Internet anywhere in the world at any given time needs to have its own unique IP address, this number would soon be exhausted. In 1998 the Internet Engineering Task Force (IETF), which sets standards for the Internet, settled on a new version of the Internet Protocol, number 6, as the next one to be phased in over an extended period during which it would run in parallel with version 4. *IPv6*, as it is logically known, uses a 128-bit address base, which means that there is now 'room' for some 3.4×10^{38} IP addresses. By comparison, there are estimated to be, in the observable universe, between around 10^{23} to 10^{24} stars. So 128-bit addresses allow for a lot of devices.

This is just as well, however, because with the Internet of Things, apart from all the computers and smartphones and computer-like devices we're already owning and using, there will now be billions more that were largely unforeseen in the early days of the Internet.

128-bit addresses thus solve an immense problem, but as is always, and necessarily, the case: one solution brings with it a set of new challenges. In this case, it has once more to do with data volume. Any communication that happens between two devices needs to contain the sender and the receiver identity, there is no other way it can be directed. As with any smoke signal, letter, text message, or lover's whisper in your ear: in order for the message to make sense to you, you have to know whom it's from and whom it is for. This means that IoT devices, of which there may, in one single contextual network, be hundreds or thousands, and which may be communicating with each other at a rate of anything from several times a day to several thousand times a second, have to send and receive 256 bits of data each time just to know who's talking. Data bandwidth and energy to power transmission are both, as we've been discussing at length, limited and need to be used frugally though.

6LOWPAN

Into play comes the *6LoWPAN*. Its name stands for *IPv6 Low Power Wireless Personal Area Network*, and this is a protocol that compresses the header (containing the sender's and destination's IP addresses, among other things) to make it manageable by these very small, low powered devices. We may think of it as an adapter, metaphorically speaking, that allows us to 'plug' our devices 'into' the IPv6 protocol. While there are, as at 2019, efforts to establish 6LoWPAN as an industry standard under the name *Thread*, other, similar and competing protocols exist, such as *Z-Wave* and *ZigBee*.

ROUTING

Much as a home or office computer can't simply 'connect' to the Internet without any intermediary, so IoT devices or nodes need to have their connections 'routed'. In the Internet of information a router is normally a wireless hub supplied by the Internet service provider, which creates a local wireless network, such as a *WiFi*, and then routes the signal generated in the devices that connect to this network to the Internet.

We noted that in the Internet of Things, most nodes similarly have a range of between 10 and 20 metres, but unlike the information Internet, here it is often not practical or indeed possible to create local wireless area networks where each node can directly communicate with the hub. One, though not the only, way of dealing with this is known as mesh routing. It allows nodes to talk to each other, with one node forwarding the data it receives to the next one, until the data packet reaches its final destination within the network of nodes, or until a base station is reached, which can connect to the information Internet.

A popular standard that supports this is called Routing Protocol for Low-Power and Lossy Networks (RPL), mostly pronounced 'ripple', derived from the abbreviation RPL and because, in a way, the routing creates a 'ripple' effect. Here, in brief and in principle, is how it works:

Assuming that the network has a mesh structure, with numerous devices spaced out so that each one is within reach of five to six neighbours, a node on the network (the device) has five to six potential communication partners, that is five to six connections. Some of these connections will be better than others, for example because the neighbour is nearer, or because a neighbour is temporarily obstructed – perhaps because a person or an object has got in the way – and so RPL can establish which is the case for which node. It does so by working out how often, on average, it has to send a data packet before it arrives. The value it measures is called the Expected Transmission Count, which curiously abbreviates as ETX (rather than, as you might expect, ETC). An ETX of 1 is ideal: if on average a node has to send a data packet once for it to arrive, that means that the connection is perfect and the data arrives each time. The higher the ETX, the worse the connection.

The task of the RPL then becomes one of creating a transmission tree that leads from any node (the 'leaves', so to speak), via 'twigs' and 'branches' back to the 'trunk', which is the device that connects to the Internet. The primary communication partner a device can talk to is known as its 'parent'. But this is a dynamic tree: obstructions, interference, or a change in the weather may all affect the ETX for any given node over time, and so RPL will continuously reconfigure the routes to the trunk, using both primary 'parents' and also secondary or backup 'parents', should the main 'parent' fail.

RPL Routing Topology

RPL builds up what is known as a *Destination-Oriented Directed Acyclic Graph (DODAG)* with the gateway at the top being the destination. Every IoT node has one or more parents in this DODAG to which it can send messages wirelessly. They in turn forward the message to one of their parents, until it eventually arrives at the gateway which forwards the message via the Internet to the ultimate recipient. The rank of an IoT node indicates the distance from the gateway in terms of the number of intermediate nodes. As each node has multiple parents, RPL offers a robust routing solution which can survive node failures.

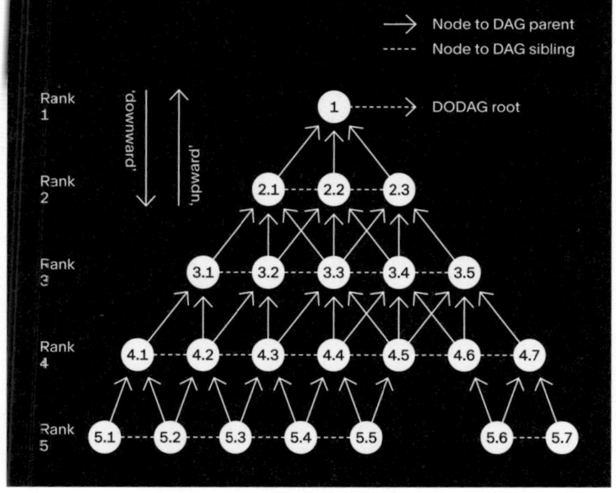

THE WEB OF THINGS

One of the chief characteristics of the Internet of Things is that it can do a lot without human intervention. And much of what the devices, nodes, sensors, or motes (as networked sensor nodes are also sometimes called) do, they can and do do autonomously. Therein lies their great strength. At one point or another, though, there will have to be some kind of link to a platform that humans can interact with, and if it is only to read the data that the sensors have registered, or the statistics that the software has compiled, or to send new instructions to part of a system for it to fulfil its purpose better or to accomplish a new task. Or, indeed, so that human beings can respond to the data the system has produced. In our example of the car park space sensors, this information – about where a parking space is available – is of scant use to the driver unless the driver is able to get hold of it, at least for as long as there are driver operated cars. (As soon as you have perfectly autonomous vehicles, the free parking space can then communicate directly with your driverless car's onboard computer and simply beckon it hither.)

Early on, we mentioned Sir Tim Berners-Lee as effectively the 'inventor' of the World Wide Web. The WWW works because Berners-Lee gave us the Hypertext Transfer Protocol (HTTP), which allows ↖344
us to access and download the content of a web page from the server on which it is hosted, through its Uniform Resource Locator (URL) address. Hence, ↖599
the typical and very familiar format of your standard webpage: https://www.w3.org/People/Berners-Lee/ (The S after HTTP stands for 'secure' and simply denotes that the communication between your computer and the website's server is encrypted; the protocol is the same.)

In the Internet of Things, as we've seen, we are dealing with multitudes of devices that are not up to handling HTTP, because HTTP was developed to be particularly user friendly, which renders it, by comparison, 'verbose': what makes it intelligible to humans are its fully spelt-out commands and tags. This presents a similar problem for IoT devices as long IP addresses: it is data intensive. For this reason, the Constrained Application Protocol (CoAP) has been developed, which is, as the name suggests, an application protocol for constrained devices, meaning devices that, owing to their size, computational capability, and low communication bandwidth, are limited in what they can do. It is, you could say, a compacted or 'light' version of HTTP. With CoAP, an IoT node is turned into a tiny web server, so that its sensor readings can be accessed and downloaded, by specifying an URL such as coap://myiotnode.com/sensors/light/ for example. In other words: CoAP connects Internet of Things nodes to the World Wide Web on the Internet of information, so that you can browse the IoT with an ordinary web browser (such as *Safari*, *Chrome*, or *Firefox*); and services that work with the WWW then also work with the 'Web of Things', as it thus becomes. Put simply, CoAP does for the Internet of Things what HTTP does for the Internet of Information, it makes it accessible to us as a 'web'.

This is of no small consequence, because ultimately, and one way or another, the 'intelligent' environment will have to be integrated into a website or smartphone app, and the data garnered and processed translated into a human readable and interpretable form. It is, after all, an app on your smartphone that allows you to quickly identify your nearest available *BikeRio* bike so you can cycle from the foot of the Sugarloaf Mountain to the Beach of Ipanema, to gaze longingly – but, as you know, vainly – at a beautiful creature who goes walking there on a regular basis, making you and everyone else he passes go *'aah'*. Or indeed the corresponding website. As the user, you would not even notice what protocol or other shenanigans have been deployed behind the scenes to make this marvellous thing possible.

Web of Things Architecture

The Web of Things builds upon the Internet of Things (networked things). In the ACCESS layer it provides methods and protocols to access IoT (sensor) data such as CoAP, a more efficient variant of HTTP. In the FIND layer, methods are provided to find IoT data and nodes. The SHARE layer includes methods to provide secure access to data such that data privacy is respected. Finally, the COMPOSE layer allows to compose multiple IoT nodes and services into complete applications, one example being IFTTT.

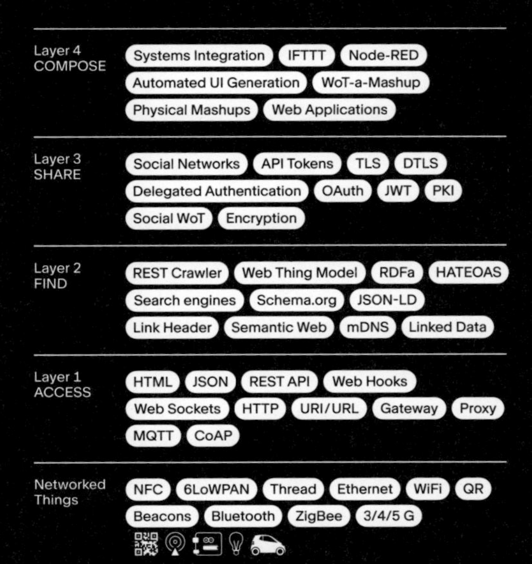

PROGRAMMING THE WEB OF THINGS

There may well be a considerable amount of sophisticated algorithm that underpins relatively simple-looking tasks in the Internet of Things, but there are also some relatively simple operations that allow the user to program useful IoT applications. It would go too far for us to enter a major discourse on programming the Internet of Things here, but a very common example is the **If This Then That (IFTTT)** system. With it, you can set a condition, such as 'if there is movement in the living room', and link it to a consequent result, 'then the lights come on'. There can be multiple conditions, such as 'if there is movement in the living room and the temperature drops below 20 degrees, then the heating comes on.' The 'if' portion of the command stems from the sensor, whereas the 'then' portion is executed by some relevant piece of equipment that is able to respond.

There is a piece of freeware called *If This Then That (IFTTT)*, which runs on the *Android* and *iOS* operating systems, that does the exact same thing for users with online services such as *YouTube*, Twitter, or eBay, allowing you to set *If* 'triggers', such as a keyword being mentioned, and *Then That* 'actions', such as a tweet being sent about it. Or *if* Adele is named as the artist of a video, *then* the video is added to your playlist, for example.

IFTTT

If This Then That (IFTTT) is a service that allows you to compose Web of Things applications by defining 'recipes'. Each recipe consists of a trigger and an action, such that the action is executed whenever the trigger fires. For example, an IoT node with an attached temperature sensor sends a CoAP notification message when temperature changes. IFTTT then checks if the temperature exceeds a threshold value given in the trigger. Actions may include sending a CoAP message to an IoT node which controls a fan.

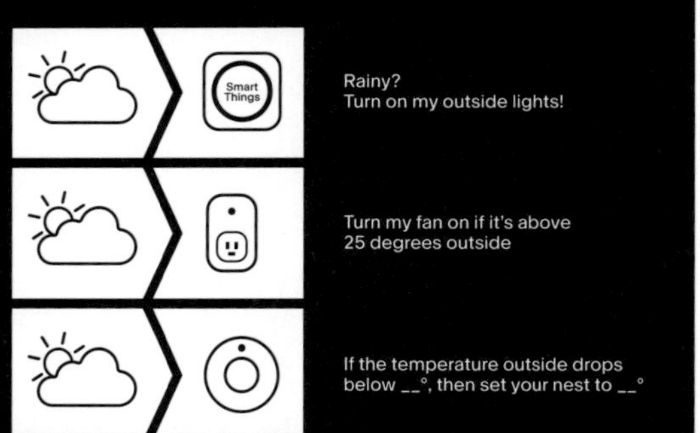

SEARCHING THE WEB OF THINGS

Most of us writing, authoring, and editing this *Atlas* are of an age group that straddles exactly the era before and since the World Wide Web. And that means we are in the privileged position to know what things were like before Google. We also remember distinctly the advent of a search engine that was better at finding relevant results than any before it. The triumph of the Internet and its resoundingly successful transition from mostly an academics' and enthusiasts' tool and plaything to the platform and driver of a whole economy in no small measure has to do with the ingenuity of the *PageRank* search algorithm, developed by Google's co-founder, American computer scientist and entrepreneur Larry Page (b. 1973) and named after himself, as well as after the principle of 'ranking' pages according to the number and, importantly, also quality of the links that exist to any given web page. In its usage, the name Google has long since eclipsed the word it originated from, the *googol*, which is the number 10^{100} – in other words: a very large number – to signify that the search engine would plough through, and throw up, a whole lot of information.

As we have seen, the new IPv6 that is being introduced to supersede the current Internet Protocol version 4, allows for not quite a googol, but very roughly a third of a googol of individual IP addresses, and that already is an extremely large number, that we are not going to reach in a great hurry. But if the number of web pages a normal Internet search engine has to go through at regular intervals to find relevant, up-to-date information is substantial, the number of 'things' on the IoT that you potentially have to search in very quick succession is seriously astronomical. Ordinary webpages may be updated once every so often: a blog might get a new entry a few times a month, perhaps even a week; a news website will get perhaps hourly updates, if there are pressing developments. An urban car park situation will be in constant flux. Cars are coming and going all the time.

If you are monitoring a colony of penguins, they may huddle in clusters for hours at a time, protecting themselves and each other against the fierce Antarctic winds. Then suddenly they may be on the move and things happen very quickly. In some parts of the IoT, things may change every few milliseconds. Granted, it is unlikely that you are ever going to scan or search the *entire* Internet of Things, since the vast majority of 'things' will not be relevant to you, but even if you concentrate on a few thousand or tens of thousand devices or sensors, and each of these sensors updates several times a second, you are quickly outpaced. Add to this the real life lag: if your app tells you there's free parking just round the corner from the cinema, but you are still ten minutes' drive away, you really don't want that information to have become obsolete by the time you get there, five minutes before the programme starts, and find all the parking spaces now taken.

For these reasons, search on the Internet of Things employs probabilistic forecasting to make predictions based on observed behaviours, and works out the likelihood of, for example, a parking space being available at a certain moment in a certain area based on known patterns. If, over a period of time, a residential street regularly has many more spaces available between Friday night and Sunday evening, then the algorithm, without knowing what that actually means, can start to predict that weekends most people here leave town and don't need their on-street parking, which means that visitors to the local restaurants and night clubs can. The search engine can then not only make this available as a fairly dependable prediction, but also use it for guidance on where to look in the first place: it can ignore all those streets where there has never been any great difference observed between week nights and weekends, and just concentrate its real time live search on the few spaces that are most likely to be available, and thus come up with remarkably accurate and current information.

The Outlook

Manufacturing electronics, put bluntly, is a print process: computer chips are literally 'printed' onto small silicon tablets. What costs money is the content, the applications, the development of technology. The actual item itself, the computer chip, is now so cheap, that – when it comes to the type of computing used in the Internet of Things – the material cost is negligible. It means that scale is everything: if you launch a technology that costs EUR 2 m to develop and that sells 10 million units, then your development costs sit at 20 cents per unit, and you stand a good chance of creating a viable business. If you sell 20,000 units, it doesn't work out.

Bearing this in mind, there is really little need for doubt that the Internet of Things will continue to take shape and play an ever bigger role in our lives, and therefore in architecture. Mostly, it will do so because it can, and because it makes sense: it's a normal, foreseeable trajectory. Not so long ago, many IoT applications had a playful, perhaps unnecessary, character. Sensors for house plants, for example, that would tell you when they needed water. At this level, you could have argued, as some people did, that there was no truly great benefit to be gained from deploying information technology to do something that you might just as well achieve by dipping your finger into the pot to see how moist the soil is.

But in many respects it is not these small, localised, applications, which yield an immediate result for the end user or consumer, that are of true significance: they are not what ubiquitous computing, and therefore the Internet of Things, is principally about. The big, game changing strides are being made in areas such as manufacturing, logistics, and research. Smart manufacture for example, of bespoke products, using industrial methods. Or energy generation, storage, and distribution: say you have a dishwasher fully loaded in the morning and you go out to work. You want this to be done by the time you get back at the end of the day, but when precisely the machine gears into action is really of no consequence to you. An IoT dishwasher that communicates with your energy provider and knows when the energy network has surplus power that it needs to get rid of can choose that particular window to do its wash cycle, at a greatly reduced tariff. This kind of situation is likely to occur much more often than it used to, as more and more energy networks are able to draw on much more volatile energy generating installations, such as wind arrays and photovoltaic solar farms. Our energy provision of the intermediate and possibly longer term future will depend to quite some extent on IoT facilitated **load shifting** (helping the network to take precisely as much energy out of the system as is being put into it), and **network solidarity**, which describes the behaviour of 'intelligent' devices, such as electric cars, air conditioning units, or fridge freezers, that are able to adjust and time their energy consumption so that the network is always perfectly balanced, because for most of these devices, it is not necessary to stubbornly draw power according to their own schedule; they very often can lean back or step up, depending on what the network happens to be capable of at any given time. This can allow for a great reduction in the amount of energy that needs to be generated purely to cover fluctuations in demand, as it evens that demand without anybody ever having to notice it.

In research and science, we see how connected sensors, arranged into small or large networks, open up entirely new perspectives by providing vast **macroscopes**: hundreds, possibly thousands or tens of thousands of nodes monitoring or observing natural phenomena, such as tectonic shifts or the migration behaviour of animal species, yielding both literal as well as metaphorical pictures on a very large scale that without this technology would just be too big or too widely dispersed to observe in a coherent way. ■

The more ubiquitous computing becomes, and the more things are connected to the Internet, the more complex and pressing become the issues of security, system integrity, and confidentiality. Any device that communicates data is potentially vulnerable to being intercepted or compromised. In October 2016, a cyber attack specifically targeted networked secondary devices, such as printers, digital cameras, and CCTV cameras, by infecting them with the *Mirai* malware that turned hundreds of thousands of them into a **botnet** – short for 'robot network' – that then flooded several global brand websites with what's known as a **Distributed Denial of Service (DDoS)** attack, making it impossible for ordinary, real life Internet users to access these websites and their services. ■ ■

Since about the mid 2010s the term **Internet of Humans** has started to surface, and while it has not strictly gained traction yet, it may point at a range of developments that bring the Internet of Things in ever closer conceptual and also physical symbiosis with us as organic, sentient beings. Augmented senses, such as better vision, hearing, smell, and touch through information technology are already a reality that can seriously improve people's quality of life, and there is a narrowing gap between standalone technology of this kind and connected technology. Both Google and Sony filed patents in 2014 for **smart eyes** or **intelligent contact lenses**, which can record, store, and play back video literally at the blink of an eye, and there is no reason to assume that it will not become feasible, quite soon, to pack into a contact lens the entire capability of Google's originally ill-fated *Google Glass* project, including full Internet connectivity and on-iris display. ■ ■ ■

Similarly, there is an ever finer line between wearable and implantable technology, and while, as we write this, there still appears to prevail a palpable level of reluctance, so as not to say squeamishness, at the thought of us turning ourselves into 'things' on the Internet, the technology to do so absolutely already exists. It is also worth bearing in mind that in other spheres, such as social networking for example, we have proven, as a species, exceptionally liberal with ourselves, voluntarily handing over data, images, ■ ■

and a constant stream of personal updates and information to the public domain and/or the relevant proprietary, profit-orientated, service providers respectively. With its roughly 2 billion active monthly users, Facebook and its subsidiaries (such as *Instagram* and *WhatsApp*) already holds, processes, mines, and monetises enough personal content from and about us to actually know us better than we know ourselves. There is little and diminishing reason to assume that we will stop just there.

- C Price, R Banham, P Barker, and P Hall: *Non Plan: An Experiment in Freedom in New Society (338)*, 1969
- John Habraken: *Supports, an Alternative to Mass Housing*, 1972
- Reyner Banham: *Alternative Networks for the Alternative Culture*, in Nigel Cross (Ed.): *Design Participation*, 1972
- Yona Friedman: *Pour une architecture scientifique*, 1975
- Alvin Toffler: *The Third Wave: The Classic Study of Tomorrow*, 1980
- Dennis Kaspori: *A Communism of Ideas: Towards an Architectural Open Source Practice in Archis*, 2003
- Kent Larson, Stephen Intille, T J McLeish, Jennifer Beaudin, and R E Williams: *Open Source Building: Reinventing Places of Living*, 2004.
- C Leadbeater: *We-think: The Power of Mass Creativity*, 2008
- M Fuller and U Haque: *Urban Versioning System 1.0 in Situated Technologies Pamphlet Series*, 2008
- N A Salingaros: *P2P Urbanism*, 2010
- R Botson and R Rogers: *What's Mine is Yours: The Rise of Collaborative Consumption*, 2010
- M Shepard (Ed): *Sentient City: Ubiquitous Computing, Architecture, and the Future of Urban Space*, 2011
- *Open Source Architecture, Domus 948 (June 2011)*
- Carlo Ratti et al: *Open Source Architecture (OSArc). Domus (948)*, 2011

Collaboration

Oliver Fritz, Urs Hirschberg, Sven Pfeiffer

Overview

AN AGE OF SHARING

Collaboration as a concept is hardly a novel idea. At the risk of stating the obvious: it's as old as architecture itself. Few indeed are the buildings in the world that have been designed and built by one person alone, and of those that have, it may be debatable whether they can be considered 'architecture' at all.

But this is an *Atlas of Digital Architecture*, and so, unsurprisingly, our focus in this chapter on Collaboration will lie on the ways in which information technology has changed – shifted, you could say – the nature of joint working, and also on the inherent significance this has on design and creative processes generally and on architecture specifically. This also entails looking at what sometimes gets referred to (and not without controversy) as an emerging 'culture of sharing'. Whether or not it is a 'culture' as such may be open to serious questioning and is well nigh impossible for us to settle just at this point; at any rate though it is a sharing *behaviour* that has become signally more prevalent, first with computing and then, second, but even more so, with the Internet.

In fact you could argue – and we do – that the way in which we collaborate today has been not just exemplified but very much precipitated by the open-source-software movement, which ideologically ties in directly (and in some respects indirectly) with the political shake-up of post-war Western society that came about through the hippie subculture or counterculture, which rejected the materialism and capitalist values of the first half of the twentieth century, perceiving them as intrinsically entwined with warfare, with the then acute and growing nuclear threat, and with an irresponsible exploitation of natural resources. This 'alternative' social and political awareness in turn is therefore inseparable from the Green, anti-nuclear, pacifist, and environmentalist movements that sprang up in the United States and in Europe towards the late 1960s and early 1970s, and it forms the cultural backdrop against which the open source idea took hold, and from which sprang many (though certainly not all) of the groundbreaking developments in shared computing and the Internet, before they were then appropriated by the commercial mainstream. (We talk in some detail about this political and cultural background to computing in our chapter on Privacy & Security.)

Because of its significance, we are treating open source here not so much as an adjunct or subset to collaboration, but as a development in information technology that may be considered integral to our ways of collaborating now: the chapter might thus almost be called Collaboration & Open Source.

SYNCHRONOUS AND ASYNCHRONOUS COMMUNICATION

We may possibly take for granted the basic practical means of communication we now all routinely employ, such as email, messaging through various channels, mobile voice, text, and data, web-based video calling and conferencing, file sharing, and of course the near-comprehensive information and knowledge resource that is the World Wide Web. Although it is absolutely worth bearing in mind that when those of us writing this book took our university degrees, we not only did *not* routinely use these means, the vast majority of people had really no concept of them, nor would most people outside the computing community have thought it likely that they would ever come about. Yet mobile phone technology and the Internet are at the core of the kind of collaboration we are talking about, and while there is certainly no need to explain them further here, it □ ↖629
is fair to say that practically everything we discuss in this chapter is predicated almost entirely on these technologies and how we use them.

What we do want to do, though, is to briefly point out the distinction that is made in information science between *synchronous* and *asynchronous communication*. This more for the sake of completeness than because it has any great bearings on what follows: it may simply help us to have the vocabulary to hand, and to be at least aware of the characteristic difference between the two.

Synchronous ways of communication are those that allow two or more people to be in a real-time exchange – be this face-to-face, over a voice or data connection, such as via phone or *Skype*, or by other, similar, means – whereby you and your interlocutor(s) are present at the same time and therefore able to respond directly and immediately to each other, much as if you were (or indeed because you are) in the same room together having a conversation. Smoke signalling is a form of synchronous communication, as is whispering sweet nothings into your lover's ear while lying next to them on a pillow, as is having an important board meeting in the important boardroom.

Asynchronous ways of communication, by contrast, are those that allow two or more people to be in an exchange that is coherent even though it happens out of time. A posted letter is a classic form of asynchronous communication, as you write your part of the dialogue first, then send it off, and then wait until the recipient has had a chance to read it, digest it, and respond to it. Email is mostly an asynchronous method, as are most forms of texting, though many a *WhatsApp* 'correspondence' effectively happens in real-time and is therefore synchronous, even though the method may have □ 643↘
been invented to be asynchronous. Sending a message in a bottle is a particularly asynchronous way of communicating, as is sending your messenger Pheidippides on foot from your battle at Marathon to Athens, to proclaim the good news of your victory, even at the risk of him dropping dead of exhaustion, having delivered the message.

Both synchronous and asynchronous modes of communication clearly have their place. Depending entirely on the situation, it may be of great advantage to be able to conduct your exchange of thoughts and ideas in a dynamic, real-time setting, and digital communication tools have obviously greatly widened our scope of these and thus made synchronous communication far more commonplace across distance than it has ever been before. On the other hand, you may be busy doing your thing. You may not be able to answer a call from your mum right now, much as you love her. Luckily, she can leave a message and you can get right back to her, as soon as your mind is not on changing the face of architecture forever. Or you may have written a fascinating paper that you need your collaborators to read, understand, and then make considered, well thought-out and fully informed comments on. This is not possible immediately. The human brain needs time to absorb, perhaps mull over, perhaps re-evaluate, and then do some additional thinking, before it can come up with in-depth feedback. So there is certainly no *value* attached to either synchronous or asynchronous communication: they're two different modes, each of which serves various purposes.

With all that acknowledged, these, then, are the ☐ ↖629 two main strands of our chapter on Collaboration: firstly, how specific digital tools and techniques, such ☐ ↖507 as Building Information Modelling (BIM), for example, make collaboration in architect practices more efficient, therefore faster, more integrated, and possibly more successful; and secondly, in a much wider, encompassing, even cultural context, how the sharing of information, software, construction plans, and ideas engenders a new quality – as in a new *kind* – of work, and what value this may add to the architecture that is being created. This is interesting to us not only as architects, but also as what, in the ☐ ↖29 Introduction to this *Atlas*, we have termed 'digital humans': (creative) citizens of a world in which we can observe the emergence of an 'evolutionary intelligence' through sharing.

We believe – and quite strongly – that the two need to be seen in relation to each other, whereby what is happening in architecture is to some large extent contingent upon what is happening in the wider context, though not necessarily vice versa. Architecture has, almost since time memorial, been a field in which strong personalities have dominated the design of new buildings and put their own, personal mark on them. This is still happening today, and it may well be the case that we are not in fact moving away from it at all. But with digitality we are adding a different element into the mix. Apart from the star designer or sole author who is realising their vision (and who still exists, though their role may have changed somewhat if they, too, adopt collaborative techniques, as many of them do), we now also get works that are really created as collaborative evolutions, with nobody taking individual credit for them; similar, perhaps, to the way in which some (though, here too, by no means all) pre-Renaissance art was far less about the artist as author, and far more about the thing that the work needed to express (which was mostly, at that time and in that culture, the exultation, in one way or another, of God).

If this is the case (and it may be too soon to tell), then that does tie in culturally and conceptually with the way 'Generation Y' is growing up: it may be difficult for most of you reading this now – as young people embarking on your careers – to imagine, but the idea that you would share *any* part of your life, let alone *every* part of it, as a continuous real-time narrative online, not confined to a small group of trusted and well-established friends, but quite open to a very loosely defined and even – depending on the platform you're using – self-selecting network of acquaintances, friends of friends, and followers whom you may or may not ever have met, is absolutely new to the twenty-first century and would simply not have occurred to people of your age only one generation ago.

Yes, some very limited and mostly slow ways of sharing existed and were also cultivated: you took pictures and you showed them to each other; you maybe even regularly got an extra set of prints of photos done, so you could give some to some people who featured in them, but that was of special occasions and trips to interesting places. You did not take a picture of your lunch, or of your dog, or of yourself, or of yourself with your dog and your friend, having lunch, and post it anywhere: there was nowhere to post it to. And if you did, you would not have expected dozens, maybe hundreds of people to like, comment on, or share this picture and circulate it further. And it wasn't just that you didn't have an Internet to curate your life on, the idea just wouldn't have crossed your mind: family pictures were for family, nights out with friends were for friends, and the notion that just about anyone entering your name in a search field might gain a comprehensive insight into how you lead your life would have horrified all but the most eccentric of individuals.

The whole concept of sharing as a *default* mode is new. Of course, people shared things they liked: everybody over the age of fifty will fondly remember the joy of making or receiving a mixtape. They were the standard way of sharing your music with someone you really liked or fancied, or needed to impress for some other reason. Or with whom you simply had an interest in music in common. People over the age of sixty-five may well remember slide show evenings with neighbours or friendly couples... – So, no, the desire to share and to maybe also obtain a degree of recognition through sharing is not new. What *is* new is the adoption of sharing as the obvious thing to do, always, and the speed and degree of proliferation with which you can do it, across the globe.

(There is a fascinating tangential thought that concerns the motivation to share. It's a topic really for a book on psychology more than on architecture, but the question to what extent we share because we want others to enjoy the things we enjoy, and to what extent we do so because we want them to find us awesome is genuinely interesting. There is a memorable moment in the Academy Award winning screenplay by American writer Tom Schulman [b. 1950] for the 1989 film *Dead Poets Society*, in which John Keating, the inspirational teacher played by American actor Robin Williams [1951–2014] asks his charge of young students why men wrote poetry. "To woo women!" he himself exclaims with relish. Today we may consider such an undifferentiated declaration presumptuous, and a real-life teacher making it in a high school environment might find themselves admonished for the lack of inclusion and the level of insensitivity it betrays towards those men who write poetry in order to woo other men, to women and those of other, non-binary gender identifications who write poetry to woo someone of any gender, and to those who write poetry to any of many possible ends, other than wooing. Still, it is not, maybe, entirely far fetched to think of software development as a twenty-first century kind of poetry that people pursue not only to make the world a better place, but also to prove to themselves and to others that they are actually here and have something to offer...)

Information technology does not invent sharing, but it is what makes sharing as a *general modus* possible. And here we say 'makes this possible' rather than 'creates this need', because it may well be entirely instinctive, human, and natural for us to share. It's just that we've never been able to do it so easily, so fast, so widely, and so dynamically before. Collaboration is a form of sharing and so it is no surprise that in an 'Age of Sharing' we are also in an 'Age of Collaboration'.

For professionals, creatives, and artists of every ilk – and therefore for architects – this may mean that we are moving away from being specialists and sole authors, to being contributors, cross-fertilisers, and collaborators much more. Here, too, it may be fanciful to make sweeping assertions and to speak in the broad brushstroke terms of generalisations. But this book is a case in point: the Working Group on Architecture and Information Technology *AK:AI (Arbeitskreis Architektur und Informatik)*, which brings you this *Atlas*, has been collaborating over a distance for years, but it is only really with the Internet and digital communication tools that a methodology like ours has become feasible at a practical level and therefore conceivable as a realistic project. 'Practical' and 'conceivable as a realistic project' are the operative terms here. Books have been written as collaborations long before ours, for certain. The French philosopher and writer Denis Diderot (1713–1784), together with his compatriot mathematician, music theorist, and physicist Jean le Rond d'Alembert (1717–1783) edited the first French *Encyclopédie*, which in turn was inspired by the *Cyclopaedia or, An Universal Dictionary of Arts and Sciences* by English writer and encyclopaedist Ephraim Chambers (c. 1680–1740).

Unlike Chambers, Diderot and his co-editor took a multi-author approach, and there are known to have contributed to their, much more expansive and ambitious, project more than 150 different individuals. Some, like French scholar and nobleman Chevalier Louis de Jaucourt (1704–1779), who employed a scribble of secretaries at his own expense to help him with his task, wrote articles in their thousands. He himself is credited with 18,000 of them, or about 25% of the whole series of tomes. Others wrote a few hundred, others just a few. Some chose to remain anonymous, others were or would become famous in their own right, like Genevan philosopher and writer Jean-Jacques Rousseau (1712–1778), whose articles covered music and political theory, or the French writer, historian, and philosopher Voltaire (1694–1778), who elucidated on history, literature, and philosophy.

All in all, the *Encyclopédie* came in 28 volumes, featuring 71,818 articles and 3,129 illustrations. Combined, its contributors wrote some 20,000,000 words: it's a collaboration. It's also something of a miracle that it ever happened. From publishing his prospectus in 1750, which announced the project and sought subscribers to finance it, to sending his by then just over 4,000 subscribers their 28th and last volume in 1772, Diderot dedicated some 21 years of his life to this *oeuvre*. During this time, he was taken to court for sedition, ridiculed, and abandoned by friends; he damaged his eyesight and struggled to keep going. In the end, he was to find out that his work had been redacted without his knowledge, or let alone consent, by his bookseller who was afraid of getting into trouble over it. Still: somehow he got it done.

Which also tells us that the *Encyclopédie* is far from commonplace: it is a highly *unusual* work, in fact it was as good as unique at the time. It took nearly a generation to complete and it was a first of its kind in the French language, so it was also a pioneering work. Others like it would follow, and none of them, for a few centuries yet, would have the benefit of the Internet, and that also is one of the reasons – possibly the most striking reason – why they were such unusual, and unusually great achievements.

390A ● 639

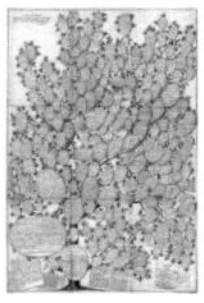
390B ● 639

An *Atlas of Digital Architecture* may pale into insignificance against such an *Encyclopédie*, but by comparison, getting this done also was an almost routine operation. And that's what's changed. Think of it: we now have twenty-five chapters provided by nearly as many academics from universities scattered all over Europe, none of whom claiming authorship, but each simply contributing their content and then not only surrendering control over it to the group, but also allowing a non-subject-expert to actually write the book. Almost all our meetings and conversations have happened on *Skype*, and the exchange of notes and documents took place by email, with large files being shared in a *Dropbox* folder or occasionally sent by *WeTransfer* link. Yes, it would also have been possible a hundred years ago, but the execution of it would have been prohibitively expensive, slow, and cumbersome. And even more to the point: as a way of writing a text book on architecture it would perhaps have been thinkable, but it would have been far from obvious and a highly challenging thing to undertake. That we were able to think it, and then carry it out within the three and a half years it ended up taking all told, at a cost that allows you to read this sentence today, mostly irrespective of how wealthy you are, is really almost entirely down to digitality.

Open Source

Unlike many other words that enter the vocabulary of their age and establish themselves by routes that quickly become untraceable in the shifting sands of cultural communication, the term *open source* can be dated and attributed precisely. It was proposed in January 1998 by one Christine Peterson at a meeting that was being held in Palo Alto, California, USA, in response to Netscape announcing the release of the source code for its *Navigator* web browser, having in effect lost the First Browser War against □ ↖351 Microsoft's *Explorer*.

From the outset, there was as much of an economical and political aspect to what became known as the *open-source-software movement*, whereby the positioning of those favouring both the term and the ethos sought to delineate themselves from the already extant free software movement, arguing that the word □ ↖439 'free', even though it explicitly referred to legally unencumbered usage, not to price, would put off players in the commercial sector who would instinctively shy away from participating in anything that did not seem to foresee any scope for a return on investment.

The precise date of its coinage notwithstanding, the principle of an 'open source' approach to what otherwise would be patented industrial or technological property nevertheless was not 'invented' in 1998. As far back as 1911, the American car maker Henry Ford (1863–1947) challenged a patent that blocked advances in the combustion engine and, by instigating the foundation of a Motor Vehicle Manufacturers Association, directly initiated the practice of sharing individually developed patents openly among members. Obviously, giving a select group of approved members of an association access to already registered patents is not quite the same as allowing anyone to become involved in the development of a new invention at any stage, and the industrial age is generally more recognisable by a desire to keep knowledge and expertise secret and proprietary than by openly sharing the fruits of your inventive work, but it is worth recognising that even in this perhaps most typically 'Digital Age' of approaches we find roots stretching far further back than we might expect.

When Christine Petersen and her colleagues were debating terminology in California some twenty years ago, the object of their attention was software, and we still readily associate with *open source* the development of a piece of software for which the source code is published openly so that anyone can use it and develop it further and make their improvements or alterations become part of the evolving code, or spawn a new branch or next generation of it. But the principle has since spread, and today the open-source model finds itself being applied to a whole spectrum of areas, including medicine, science, education, manufacturing, and, maybe most widely and most prominently, in knowledge bases such as *Wikipedia*, where, just as with the code for a piece of open-source software, absolutely anyone can access and edit pages, with changes being tracked and monitored not by any authority, but by the community of editors themselves.

In that respect, an open-source undertaking operates a bit like a self-evolving organism, in which improvements and advances are being kept, and cul-de-sac strands or deteriorations discarded. The fact that it is the community of users that controls the development is crucial to both its ethos and its success. And it is a characteristic aspect of open source working that the boundary between experts and non-experts, between providers and consumers, and between professionals and amateurs are blurred in all directions, with creativity not only being shared but also spread and, arguably, nurtured and generated.

In our chapter on Scripting you'll find us talking in some detail about the significance these programming languages have for the Internet in particular, but really for all of contemporary computing, and how extremely powerful they are as tools. Scripting has been and continues to be largely developed open source. We also mention in our chapter on 3D Printing how for a long time the evolution of this technology was arrested until the initial patent lapsed and people other than the original inventors were able to get involved and drive the technology forward. As it happens, some patents were simply ignored, some parts of the technology weren't patented at all, and in some cases the legal situation was unclear.

Generally, it is fair to say that with regard to open source, the legal situation is often not exactly clear, and that is hardly surprising, considering its genesis. Right in the first paragraph of this section and also elsewhere in this *Atlas* we mention the *'First Browser War'.* This was a legal feud between Microsoft, which in the late 1990s bundled its own *Internet Explorer* with its *Windows* operating system, effectively usurping the then leading web browser's position, Netscape's *Navigator,* and pushing it out of use on most personal computers.

Netscape ultimately won the battle, but it categorically lost the war. And so, in response to its own demise, it decided to put the source code for its browser into the public domain. While this planted the seed for the *Firefox* browser and gave rise to the meeting that brought us the term open source, the beginning of what we today consider the open-source-software movement lies nearly another couple of decades prior to this event, certainly in relation to computing. It can be anchored with some degree of justification in a specific date too: 27 September 1983.

Although, as we explained a moment ago, it would be foolhardy in the extreme to declare this the first instance of deliberately collaborative development work, it is the date when the American software developer and professor at MIT (Massachusetts Institute of Technology), Richard Stallman (b. 1953) announced to the world the GNU Project. With the term *open source* not yet coined, this was referred to as a *'free software'* project, whereby the word 'free' here – as we mentioned earlier – pertained not to the exchange of money, or any absence thereof, but to a set of basic freedom rights that were from the outset enshrined in GNU's own *General Public Licence.* These are listed on GNU's website as, "the freedom

0 to run the program
1 to study and change the program in source code form
2 to redistribute exact copies, and
3 to distribute modified versions."

The numbering may be a touch idiosyncratic, but for that it is no less logical. The same, incidentally, could also be said of the name of the project itself: GNU is a 'recursive acronym' (that is an acronym which refers to itself) meaning '*GNU's Not Unix*'. At the time Professor Stallman felt driven to initiate the making of a piece of software that was *not Unix*, but that needed to say so in its own name, *Unix* was considered to have potential as a universal operating system, owing to its modularity, adaptability, and portability. These, in turn, stemmed from what its designers, chief among them the American computer scientists Ken Thompson (b. 1943) and Dennis Ritchie (1941–2011), termed the 'Unix Philosophy', which urged themselves and their team members to:

- Make each program do one thing well. To do a new job, build afresh rather than complicate old programs by adding new 'features'.
- Expect the output of every program to become the input to another, as yet unknown, program. Don't clutter output with extraneous information. Avoid stringently columnar or binary input formats. Don't insist on interactive input.
- Design and build software, even operating systems, to be tried early, ideally within weeks. Don't hesitate to throw away the clumsy parts and rebuild them.
- Use tools in preference to unskilled help to lighten a programming task, even if you have to detour to build the tools, and expect to throw some of them out after you've finished using them.

Stallman had no beef with this philosophy or with the program itself. What he felt strongly, and what propelled him into far-reaching action, was that computer software, "differs from material objects — such as chairs, sandwiches, and gasoline — in that it can be copied and changed much more easily. These facilities are why software is useful; we believe a program's users should be free to take advantage of them, not solely its developer," as he puts it, again on the GNU website. The free software movement ('free' always being the freedom to use, reuse, add, and distribute the software without hindrance or fear of litigation) was born: Stallman set out to create an operating system that was as good as *Unix*, as adaptable, as modular, as elegant, and as robust, but that was not proprietary to anyone, not even (or perhaps least of all) to himself; one that was genuinely, resolutely, and always free. It was just like *Unix*, but not *Unix*, it was *GNU*.

LINUX

By a quirk of collaborative technology development 'fate', what started out as *GNU* is known the world over almost exclusively as *Linux*. Responsible for this oddity in no small measure is a Finn named Linus Torvalds (b. 1969) who in 1991, then aged 22 and attending the University of Helsinki, became interested in operating systems. At a time when most people didn't know what an operating system was, he went straight for the jugular and developed an operating system **kernel**, albeit for an entirely different piece of software. The kernel, as the majority of people who are not software developers themselves still don't know today, is the core or nucleus of an operating system, and thus the thing that controls everything else. Nowhere near as egomaniacal as one might think at first glance of a name that is now a globally recognisable 'brand', Linus actually wanted to call his work *Freax* (as in a slightly cool or 'street' spelling of 'Freaks' with a subtle reference to *Unix* in the x). It happened to be a volunteer system administrator for the university's FTP server who didn't like the name 'Freax' and unilaterally decided to call the project 'Linux' instead. The name stuck and Linus Torvalds did not object. Who did object, when the name started to cling not only to the developer's own kernel project on a university server, but to the whole operating system that he had started several years earlier, was *GNU's* Richard Stallman. Because the kernel young Linus had made proved so useful and usable that the free software community working on *GNU* readily adopted it as theirs and built it into the *GNU* operating system, replacing the original, heavily problematic kernel, and thus putting in place the final and by some margin most crucial piece of a complex jigsaw to actually make available a working and genuinely free *Unix*-like operating system. The Free Software Foundation, founded by Richard Stallman to propagate software such as *GNU* according to the principles of the basic freedoms associated with it, therefore calls the operating system *GNU/Linux*, arguing that *Linux* is only one, albeit an important, part of what makes the software tick, while everybody else, recognising a good name when they see one, calls it *Linux*.

The story is interesting not just because it involves fascinating characters doing extraordinary things in information technology with quite a radical ideological slant, but also because *Linux* is today the most stable operating system in the world, and also the most prevalent. It's spectacularly successful on all kinds of hardware, from NASA (National Aeronautics and Space Administration) supercomputers to notebooks, but its great distribution is due to the mobile handsets market where, as the kernel of *Android*, it is the core of the most widely used operating system in the world too. And we are, after all, always talking about a piece of software that nobody commissioned, nobody paid for, and nobody in that sense had control of. It emerged from an open source collaboration between people who did not need to see a fee first and then sat down to do some work, nor was it dreamt of as an excellent way to turn a profit for the shareholders of a corporation, and yet very big and very powerful businesses are using it to tremendous effect for their products.

COPYLEFT

One of the persistently enjoyable aspects of late 20th century computing development is its nomenclature,

and the term *copyleft* offers another fine example of what people with a keen intellect, a healthy dose of politically agitated attitude, and a wry sense of humour come up with on occasion when naming their concepts. The idea of *copyleft* as opposed to *copyright* is that you allow people to copy, use, modify, and distribute any work, such as a piece of
■ ↖407 software, music, picture, or video material, or indeed any other intellectual 'property', be it a design or an invention, stipulating only that the exact same rights be imparted on any subsequent version or derivation. This means that a 'copyleft' work is not entirely free from any type of legal restriction. By putting your creation under this type of licence, you are saying to the world: 'yes, you can use it, you can do with it essentially as you please, but you must grant everybody these exact same rights to anything that you do with my work'. This is not the same as saying: 'yes, you can use it and do with it whatever you please'. Full stop. In other words: a 'copyleft' licence provides a legal framework for sharing and therefore also for collaboration.

The *GNU General Public Licence* was the first major copyleft licence, and, currently in its 3rd version dated June 2007, remains one of the most widely used creative commons licences in the world. As are the **Creative Commons** licences. *Creative Commons* is really the name of an American not-for-profit organisation that provides a simple way of adapting the wording of a licence to the needs and wishes of an individual creator, for example by stipulating whether the work may be adapted or not, or whether or not it may be used commercially. Much of what you see on *Flickr*, watch on *YouTube* or *Vimeo*, listen to on *Bandcamp*, and virtually everything you come across or put on *Wikipedia* is made available under either an actual *Creative Commons* licence or one similar to it.

Architecture & Sharing

We are, in architecture, talking about ways of working which allow for a greater, perhaps greatest possible, collaboration, from planning to construction, so that the process of design becomes the development of a common language of all those involved. This means that knowledge, information, tools, and resources which previously were only available to select groups of experts are now made available to a broad, even public, audience as data online, so it can be continuously developed, enhanced, and expanded. And this may well be the fundamental point: by expanding the input base, you extend the volume of knowledge, expertise, and experience to the dynamic network, rather than keeping it limited and restricted to the authorised few. The network becomes the defining element.

When in the tradition of modernity the lead would come from the author, the chief architect, or the project head, in the 'digital world', architecture – like everything else – is being decentralised and democratised. And thus the impetus, so to speak, that started in the relative fluidity (so as not to say 'anarchy') of open source software development finds its way into the structured environments of large architecture practices (and, indeed, other companies); and methods that to the traditional mind simply shouldn't work – such as allowing everyone to do everything, which is the direct opposite of **Fordism** – can yield quite extraordinarily satisfying and effective results. This is significant, because here as elsewhere we witness a flattening of these structures: the engineer speaking the language of the artist, and the artist understanding the language of the IT specialist.

These are not just games that are being played: what comes out of it is – or most certainly can be – good architecture. If the hierarchies are flattened, the boundaries blurred, and the edges blunted, then that does have the effect that it frees things up: it may well also be unsettling, but it does liberate people. And so it requires a new type of architect. Not only a new type of architect: a new type of professional who is flexible, adaptable, open-minded, literate in digitality, and attuned to its methodologies.

Here, then, are a few examples of collaboration in design and architecture:

FIRMS & PROJECTS

The originally Norwegian, but now very much international design, architecture, landscaping, and brand practice Snøhetta uses the term 'transpositioning' to mean, as they state on their own website, "the working method where participants are invited to break from their professional role and switch perspectives with others in the group. By releasing ourselves from disciplinary conventions for a short period of time, we can foster a greater sense of possibility, free ourselves from habitual thinking, and build empathy for others involved in the process."

Founded in 2001 by Chilean architect Alejandro Aravena (b. 1967), *Elemental* calls itself a "Do Tank," which focuses, "on projects of public interest and social impact, including housing, public space, infrastructure and transportation." It sees its fundamental approach as based on its participatory design process, working closely with the public and end users, and it has recently published the *AutoCAD* files for four of its housing projects under a *Creative Commons* licence.

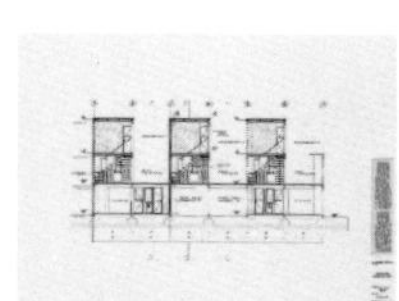

391A ● 639

391B ● 639

Assemble are a London based collective, working across disciplines in art, architecture, and design. Having started collaborating in 2010, by 2017 they had 18 members. *Assemble's* ambition, according to their own website, is to, "address the typical disconnection between the public and the process by which places are made." To this end, they, "champion a working practice that is interdependent and collaborative, seeking to actively involve the public as both participant and collaborator in the ongoing realisation of the work."

392 ● 640

The Luchtsingel, a 400-metre-long pedestrian bridge which connects three districts in the heart of Rotterdam, is an example of an alternative development strategy based on collaboration. It was initiated and designed by Rotterdam-based architects ZUS *(Zones Urbaines Sensibles)* and is the world's first piece of public infrastructure to be accomplished mostly through crowdfunding. As their 'benefit', each donor was entitled to an inscription on one plank of the bridge. These short lines of text may advertise a business, convey a message to a loved one, or simply state the donor's name.

393A ● 640

393B ● 640

Kalkbreite Zürich is a community that came about because people wanted to build their own apartment block. They got together and worked out the rules, requirements, and wishes of various sections within their own group and then commissioned some architects to execute it for them.

PLATFORMS

Opendesk, founded by a group of London creatives, is a platform for designers and furniture makers worldwide to make furniture designs available online (many, though not necessarily all, under a *Creative Commons* licence: the decision lies with the designer), so the design can be ordered by the end customer and manufactured by a carpenter or joiner local to them. The idea is to 'design globally and make locally', ideally benefitting the designer by making their work available to a wide, theoretically global audience, helping local businesses get jobs to do, and saving the consumer money because it cuts out a lot of the intermediary structure between them and the designer.

Bricks describes itself as "a collaborative design app" for architects and creatives to collect, organise, and reuse visual bricks of projects and share them with their team and the community, or, as their strap line has it: "A Hub for Open Source Architecture & Collaborative Design projects."

WikiHouse is an open source construction system that uses pieces of plywood cut by a CNC router that fit together like a giant three-dimensional puzzle to build small dwellings quickly and cost-effectively. ■

394A ● 640

394B ● 640

Paperhouses publishes open source projects developed by architects worldwide. Because they are not specific to their location, they can be easily modified and also re-shared.

SOFTWARE / CLOUD-BASED SERVICES

Unlike most collaborators involved in an architectural project who can work with quite standard technical programs, as an architect you need to have flexible software tools that support your creativity, that give you maximum freedom, and that can then be used by others in the building process later on. These tools may assist you in developing and presenting not only the design, but also the design's effects on costs and deadlines, and they can help you coordinate your work with other team members at an early stage. There are several free and commercial collaboration programs available, from parametric design software ■ ↖524
to comprehensive BIM-oriented services.

GRASSHOPPER

For those of you who are using generative algorithms to explore design, *Grasshopper* is a graphical code editor integrated within the popular 3D modelling application *Rhinoceros*. Unlike scripting languages embedded in 3D modelling applications, *Grasshopper* requires no knowledge of programming or scripting, but still allows designers to build form generators. One of the reasons for its large impact is the prolific network of users who share their work on the *Grasshopper* website at grasshopper3d.com. (We talk more about scripts and coding in our chapters on Graphs & Graphics, Writing & Code, and Scripting.)

□ ↖175
□ ↖369
□ ↖351

TRIMBLE CONNECT

Gehry Technologies – an offshoot of Gehry Partners, founded in 2002, whose principal, the Canadian-born American architect Frank Gehry (b. 1928) envisioned how a 3D computational approach to architectural design and construction documentation could transform the trillion-dollar building industry – has developed *GTeam*, a web-based 3D file management and project collaboration platform, which allows architects, designers, engineers, contractors, and subcontracts to work on projects together online, using any device of their choice, including tablets and smartphones. In 2014, Trimble, the rapidly growing software giant which has also bought 3D architectural products *SketchUp* (3D drafting), *Tekla* (3D structural engineering), *Vico* (3D project management visualisation), and *MayBim* (BIM services for mechanical/electrical/plumbing systems), announced its acquisition of Gehry Technologies.

FLUX
Flux is a web-based, paid service that allows applications such as *Grasshopper* and *Revit* to exchange data, using native plugins. *Flux* works by connecting data, rather than files, so your design preserves integrity and fidelity across different applications. Its advantages lie in the immediate feedback from your colleagues and the ability to share live and interactive visualisations via weblink. Data is pushed and pulled across your design team, with access controls and notifications.

The Outlook

Is collaboration necessarily 'The Future for Architecture'? And by 'collaboration' we mean here, of course, not the long established traditions of working with fellow architects, engineers, contractors, and clients, but the emerging digital forms of collaboration, in a spirit of openness and sharing that we've discussed in this chapter. There are good indications that it will at least play a substantial part. But there is nothing to say that this is an inevitable direction in which we all travel, from which there is no return, and which offers no alternative, or maybe as yet quite unknown branches.

After all, does everybody want to collaborate, always? It could be argued that it is in the nature of the artist – the creator of things – to be individual, to hold artistic control, to be the author of their work. If I have a fabulous vision of a magnificent thing, do I for certain want somebody else to come and spoil it with their far less fabulous but perhaps infinitely more practical idea of the same thing. Is it still the same thing if they do? Would Michelangelo's *David* be as perfect if he'd allowed the apprentices, a few non-masons, and some of his competitors in Florence at the time to chip away at it a bit? Does Bach need improvement? Would even a partnership like John Lennon and Paul McCartney have benefitted greatly from a little help from their friends, beyond that which was already in place in the structure of their band and their quite genius producer, George Martin?

These are not facetious questions. The fact alone that intensive, dynamic, and democratic collaboration and sharing are possible does not mean they are by definition a 'good thing'. You could as easily argue the opposite and say that a truly groundbreaking individual style such as that of Catalan architect Antoni Gaudí (1852–1926) would be unthinkable from a 'democratic' collaborative process. And what of the reality of constantly collaborating. Does an artist, a musician, a designer, or an architect *really* want to have people around all the time, looking over their shoulders, making suggestions, tweaking the work, or simply taking it and reinterpreting it in their own quite conceivably inferior way? And what of the reality, today, of the big, world-famous architecture firms: more often than not they have at their helm one or two founding figures who enjoy the status of rock stars and who have the charisma and power to get entire collaborative teams to rally around their vision, not just as before, but *more* than ever before.

Bearing all this firmly in mind and making no value judgment on collaboration, sharing, or open source working for its own sake, we imagine that the following developments will probably gain further momentum and may well make themselves felt much more strongly in architecture:

- The sharing and making available for download of plans for construction elements and designs, so they can be manufactured on site or locally, or reworked to the purpose of the client or user
- Participative planning methods and technologies, such as online platforms that facilitate and encourage collaboration
- Project financing through crowd funding
- Further development of planning methods, for example **design thinking** towards the solution of complex problems in relation to the collaboration among different disciplines
- Forums and blogs and social networking style platforms in the **Web 2.0** as creative touch points
- Legal frameworks for licensing models
- Open source approaches to city planning
- And ongoing debate both in theory and in practice about the respective virtues and advantages of open versus closed or proprietary software

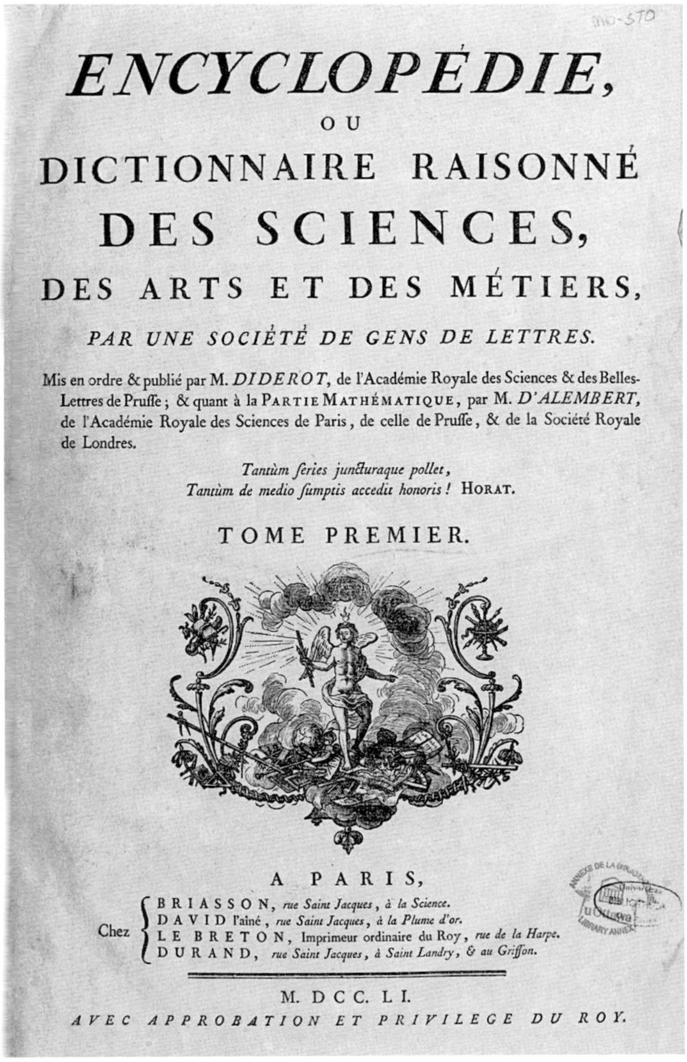

ENCYCLOPÉDIE,

OU

DICTIONNAIRE RAISONNÉ

DES SCIENCES,

DES ARTS ET DES MÉTIERS,

PAR UNE SOCIÉTÉ DE GENS DE LETTRES.

Mis en ordre & publié par M. DIDEROT, de l'Académie Royale des Sciences & des Belles-Lettres de Pruſſe ; & quant à la PARTIE MATHÉMATIQUE, par M. D'ALEMBERT, de l'Académie Royale des Sciences de Paris, de celle de Pruſſe, & de la Société Royale de Londres.

Tantùm ſeries juncturaque pollet,
Tantùm de medio ſumptis accedit honoris ! HORAT.

TOME PREMIER.

A PARIS,

Chez BRIASSON, *rue Saint Jacques, à la Science.*
DAVID l'aîné, *rue Saint Jacques, à la Plume d'or.*
LE BRETON, Imprimeur ordinaire du Roy, *rue de la Harpe.*
DURAND, *rue Saint Jacques, à Saint Landry, & au Griffon.*

M. DCC. LI.

AVEC APPROBATION ET PRIVILEGE DU ROY.

390A ● 633
The *Encyclopédie* edited by Diderot and d'Alembert, front page.

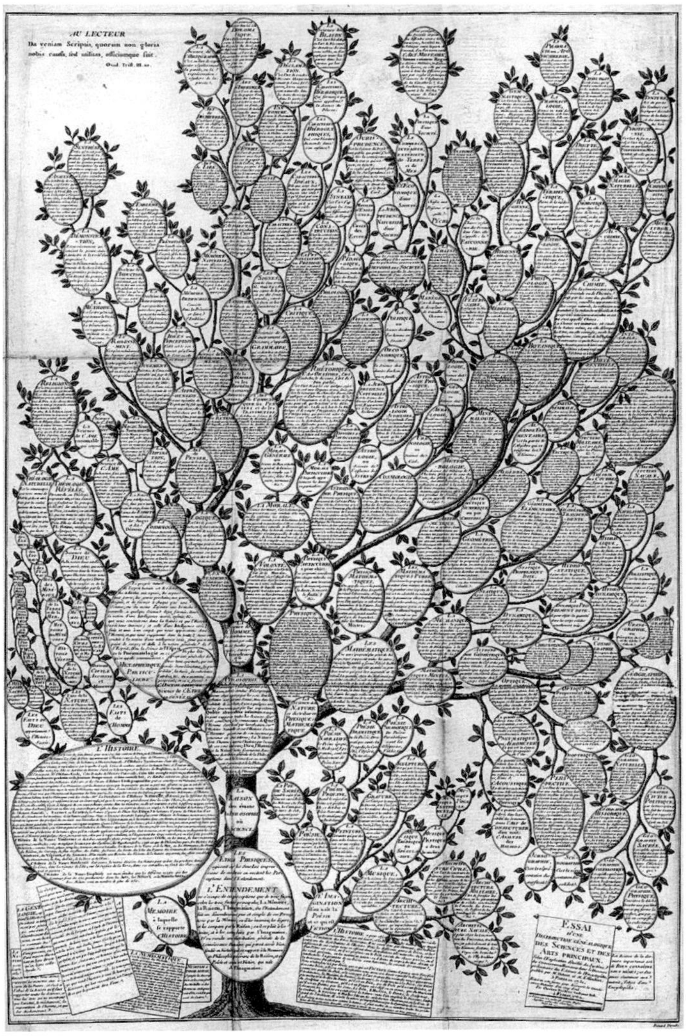

390B ● 633
An attempt at a detailed genealogy of the arts and sciences created by Chrétien Frederic Guillaume Roth for the *Encyclopédie*, 1780.

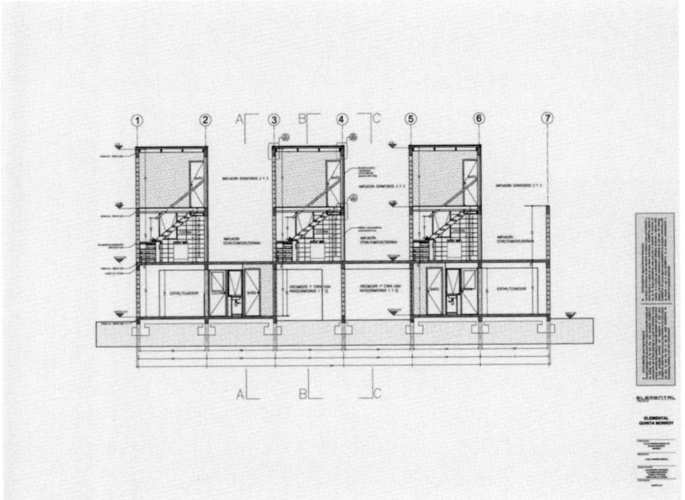

391A ● 636
Alejandro Aravena: housing project. [*Elemental*]

391B ● 636

392 ○ 637
Assemble Studio London.

393A ● 637

393B ● 637

Luchtsingel, Rotterdam, ZUS *(Zones Urbaines Sensibles)* architects. [Ossip van Duivenbode]

394A ● 637
WikiHouse. [394A+394B: *WikiHouse*]

394B ● 637

Privacy & Security

Ludger Hovestadt

Introduction

When we talk about Privacy & Security, we tend to instinctively expect to be giving a definition of what 'privacy' and 'security' respectively mean in our cultural context, possibly tied into a reflection on how this meaning has evolved over time, and then thus equipped to launch into a discourse on how they both can or cannot be safeguarded or cultivated in a way appropriate to our age, which we obviously and throughout this *Atlas* characterise as 'digital'.

But this type of pragmatic and in a sense utilitarian approach, which traditionally treats the subject matter as a 'problem', and consequently goes in search for plausible 'solutions' to address it, would be woefully inadequate in the context of both this particular topic and its context. Because identifying any type of response or policy, any set of guidelines or stance as a 'solution' to the multitude of complex and differentiated issues that come under the headings 'privacy' and 'security' would in itself be bound to end up newly oppressive and dogmatic, and therefore aid the demise, rather than serving to foster, freedom and openness.

So while in this chapter we will indeed be looking at definitions of these terms and also at their history and how their meaning has evolved over time, we want to stake out a wider horizon here and embark on an excursion that allows us to look at these concepts from different angles and through different lenses, in the hope that we may not find an answer or a stance so much, as an attitude, or a way of thinking about them.

This, then, as one or two other chapters in this *Atlas*, is not an article, or an essay, so much as a gesture. A thought journey into the realm of two apparently competing interests that have become central to our existence, even though – or perhaps precisely because – they have in their own respective ways all but disappeared from it.

We are, as a society, in pretty much uncharted territory. One where on the one hand we can gain great benefits from giving up our notion of privacy, by participating, for example, in a reputation-based economy which allows us to be the hosts and guests of complete strangers with great ease and remarkable safety, while on the other hand we are continually exposed to reputational threats to our person with hardly any effective legal protection at all: if you get caught up in the heat of a social media storm because somebody accuses you of some misdemeanour, or because you say or do something that is unwise or misguided, your name, your job, quite possibly your existence may easily be pushed to the brink of collapse long before you can take any remedial action and restore your position in society, virtually irrespective of whether an allegation is true or not, or even how grave or superficial an offence you are deemed to have caused may be.

So while on the one hand we find new kinds of comfort in new communities both virtual and real, we are also vulnerable to entirely new types of threat, from both within and outside what we perceive as 'society' or any structural framework we currently have in place for it. Taking a panoramic look at this new landscape is what with this chapter we intend to do.

□ ↖643

BIG BROTHER

On 16 September 1999, Dutch television producer John de Mol (b. 1955) unleashed on an unsuspecting world a concept and programme that at the time sensationally straddled the spheres of popular social experiment and resolutely voyeuristic entertainment: *Big Brother*. Named after the intractable figurehead of the fictional one-party state Oceania in the 1948 novel *Nineteen Eighty-Four* by English writer George Orwell (1903–1950), the franchise, which has since been broadcast in over fifty countries worldwide, saw a number of volunteer 'housemates' live under constant audio and video surveillance in a purpose-built dwelling that was otherwise isolated from the outside world. It turned on its head the notion – driven home by Orwell – that a situation where individuals would be subjected to constant 24-hour observation could only ever happen against their will and inherent instinct, at the hands of a totalitarian authority, which, presenting itself as benign and purporting to act in the interest of the people, systematically eradicated all sense of freedom, self, personal choice, or even objective truth. Here, the people being observed were not only volunteers, they were selected from large pools of available candidates, and the observer was not a central, control-obsessed authority, but the TV viewing public as a whole, who sat passing judgement over the housemates' perceived merits towards winning a substantial cash prize.

The show's creator has become fabulously rich, and although George Orwell might be turning in his grave at the realisation that he unwittingly donated the brand to a blatant trivialisation of his work, as a phenomenon, *Big Brother* anticipates by several years a reality we have manoeuvred ourselves into, whereby we voluntarily give up much of what, only a generation ago, would have been considered a closely guarded private sphere and absolutely unfit for public consumption. It exploded the notion – or perhaps myth – of an innate sense and desire for privacy residing in us all, and today we realise that we have, in very large numbers and with astonishing indifference, settled into a culture where the original 'Big Brother' as conceived by Orwell, has become virtually meaningless.

Orwell's *Nineteen Eighty-Four* was written as a dystopia, and intended as a warning of what life would be like under an all-powerful surveillance state. Conceived immediately after the Second World War and in the shadow of the excesses of totalitarianism that gave rise of the Third Reich and fascism in Europe as well as Soviet ideology, it foreshadows technology that is capable of keeping a constant eye on everything you do, say, even think. And for many decades after its publication, really right until 1984 and perhaps a little beyond, it was viewed as a brilliant, if pessimistic, science and political fiction. No more. In the roughly thirty-five years since the time of its setting, technology has outpaced and surpassed anything Orwell was able to imagine. And much as the majority of people in Oceania quietly accept their lot, the vast majority of us simply consider it normal that we are being recorded dozens, in big cities like London, New York, or Shanghai hundreds of times a day by security cameras. We accede, in the name of our own safety and security – our own 'best interests' – to extraordinary intrusions into our private sphere, and – this Orwell really did not foretell, nor could he possibly have grasped the psychology of it – we habitually post to the social networks more, and more revealing, information, pictures, and intimate details of our lives than even the most draconian government would be able to access, let alone dare openly demand, no matter how far the tentacles of its security operations might reach.

We live, to all intents and purposes, in a comprehensively observed and documented post-Orwellian world in which absolutely anything we do or say (and therefore by extension much more than we think, also, of what we think) can, and very likely does, end up on some database. Before you have attracted the attention of any secret service for any reason, you are already wholly profiled by corporations who study your online expression of yourself and your purchasing behaviour to tailor their marketing strategies to what they make you believe are 'your needs'. You, your thoughts and emotions, communicated in your comments, posts, pictures, memories, joys, grumbles, and concerns, are systematically being commodified by the providers of the platforms you use to share them: you are the product that Facebook sells to you, and they quite technically 'own' you (or at the very least your content). And this does not begin, of course, to address the issue of privacy and security in the context of secret or secretive operations, be they state-run or criminal. If you do attract the attention of the security services in any country that considers itself a significant player (and many that don't, or that do, even though they are not) you have virtually nowhere to hide. The only reason terrorist cells go unnoticed and occasionally manage to strike is that the volume of potential suspects is simply too large for the authorities to keep a close enough eye on everybody. As yet. The technology to do so is certainly there.

ROBIN HOOD

No wonder then that citizens and their states face formidable challenges and conflicts of interest that appear in many ways irreconcilable. So vast, so encompassing has been the snooping activity of the United States National Security Agency (NSA) that one of its own sub-contractors, American systems administrator Edward Snowden (b. 1983) felt compelled, in 2013, to disclose between nine and ten thousand classified documents, out of anything between 50,000 and 200,000 he had allegedly copied illegally. Publication of the leaked documents started on 5 June 2013 in *The Guardian* newspaper in the UK, swiftly followed by other international print and online media outlets, among them *Der Spiegel* in Germany, *The Washington Post* and *The New York Times* in the United States, and *Le Monde* in France. Snowden was forced to go into exile and effectively got stuck in Russia where, as we write this in 2019, he still 'enjoys' a temporary asylum, while wanted in the United States on various high ticket charges such as theft of government property and violations against the Espionage Act, each carrying maximum prison terms of up to ten years.

The high illegality of his actions stands in stark contrast to the high level of ethical legitimacy other people were just as quick to bestow on him. For some he was, and remains, a traitor to his homeland, for others he is a hero and freedom fighter in the virtual space. Some see the surveillance techniques and their pervasiveness as necessary measures the state must take to protect its citizens, others see them as a categorical, deliberate overreach: the state using technology to spy on its own citizens, simply to the end of stockpiling information on, and thus accumulate power over, them, for its own sake.

Edward Snowden is not the only 21st century renegade to have got stuck on foreign territory, unable to move, but still able to hold considerable sway over media attention. From 19 June 2012 until 11 April 2019, the Australian computer programmer and founder of *WikiLeaks*, Julian Assange (b. 1971) was living at Flat 3B, 3 Hans Crescent, Knightsbridge, London SW1. Being the address of the Embassy of Ecuador in the United Kingdom, he was technically in Ecuador, where he had been granted asylum, until this was withdrawn following a lengthy period during which his relationship with his hosts had become increasingly fractious. For all these years though he was unable to leave the premises and take advantage of the many riches London has to offer, or even step on a plane to actually visit Ecuador, because the Metropolitan Police in London held a warrant for him, following charges by the American government, also under the Espionage Act of 1917. So when Ecuador decided it had had enough and dropped Assange, the Met promptly arrived and arrested him.

Sometime between 1370 and 1390 – and so well before the Print Revolution swept across Europe and radically democratised knowledge, learning, and communication – the English poet William Langland (c. 1332 – c. 1386) sat down to write, in unrhymed alliterative verse, an allegorical narrative poem called *Piers Plowman*. This is a noteworthy piece of early Middle English literature for many reasons of its own, but it also happens to be the first known document to mention the then obviously already popular, "rhymes of Robin Hood." Robin Hood in turn is not the only, but quite possibly in the Western world the most famous outlaw who, 'robs from the rich and gives to the poor', making him, in the eyes of the establishment, a loathsome villain, in the eyes of the people though a charming rogue, being, as he is portrayed, a most excellent archer, valiant swordsman, and chivalrous protector of ladies: someone who is not in it for himself, but who breaks the law for the greater good, because the system and the social structure of the day are crooked and skewed against the common people. In other words: a good egg.

This perception – whether it is accurate or not, and whether or not it is tainted by ideology or informed by an overriding world view – prevails today as much as it did 650 years ago. If the state is or becomes corrupt, unaccountable, self-serving, then its law no longer holds any moral authority, and someone has to come along to do what is necessary to protect the interests of the citizen. There is no doubt that for a great many citizens, Edward Snowden and Julian Assange neatly fit into this tradition. Except their commodity is not gold or jewels or mere money, it is far more potent than that: it is *information*.

ALAN TURING

During the 20th Century, dominated and preoccupied by two catastrophic world wars, governments of all hues went to extreme lengths to try to protect information from falling into the hands of the enemy, while at the same time attempting to get hold of information the enemy was trying to protect from falling into theirs. This, though the inspiration for many a thrilling spy story, was not a game: on a daily basis, lives in their thousands, in the longer term in their millions, would be either lost or saved depending largely on how successful the secret services on either side of the conflict were at just this, the protected, secure channeling of information.

One name you will come across in these pages repeatedly is that of the English computer scientist, mathematician, and cryptanalyst Alan Turing (1912–1954). There are plenty good reasons for this. Mostly, when we mention him, we do so as the person who laid down much of the foundation for what today we understand as computing. Although he did not have, or make, a computer, he in 1936 invented what he himself called an *A-machine (automatic machine)*, but what the world over now is known as the Turing machine. This goes down in history as the first – even if in his lifetime purely theoretical – 'machine' capable of executing an algorithm, which makes it a milestone in the development of computing and artificial intelligence; and to this day, the accepted definition of whether or not something is computable is whether or not a Turing machine could process it. We explain in detail how it works and give a fully coded example in our chapter on Writing & Code and Writing & Code – Elaboration.

In this chapter though, we need to touch on another, similarly significant achievement of Turing's. He began to tackle it in December 1939, only a couple of months into the Second World War, which Germany started with the invasion of Poland on 1 September 1939, and which Britain entered two days later, on 3 September, honouring its alliance with Poland. The Germans had for some years used mechanical encoding machines to encrypt their communication both among their own forces, and then from 1940 onwards also between themselves and the other members of the Rome-Berlin-Tokyo Axis, which was fought by the Allied Forces, led by Britain, France, and Poland and then joined to lasting effect by the United States and the Soviet Union. The Germans called the machines they used for encoding and decoding secret communications *Enigma*, and while the machines themselves were known about and their mechanism mostly understood, the Enigma code – their encryption – was considered all but unbreakable.

Turing, soon after he arrived at the British Government Code and Cypher School (GC&CS) at Bletchley Park, began working on Enigma, in his own words, "because no one else was doing anything about it and I could have it to myself." This work proved as ingenious and groundbreaking as it was important to the Allies, employing, among others, both an electromechanical machine called *bombe* (after its Polish forerunner, the similar but less effective *bomba kryptologiczna)* and a cryptanalytic process he labelled *Banburismus:* a sequential statistical technique, which later became known as sequential analysis. ■

While most historians acknowledge that it is impossible to put an exact figure on the contribution one single person has made to what was after all a major international effort, you will read various sources suggesting that breaking the Enigma code – an achievement that can be largely attributed to the theoretical thinking of Alan Turing – not only helped the Allies win the war, but also shortened it by up to two years, thus saving very many lives.

(Speaking of privacy and security: Britain did not treat Turing – who both for his work at Bletchley Park and for his contributions to computing must rank among her most gifted sons – well during his lifetime, and afforded him neither. In 1952 he was charged with 'gross indecency', which is what the British then called homosexual acts, even when conducted in private. Turing pleaded 'guilty' and was given a choice of imprisonment or a hormonal treatment that amounted to chemical castration. He opted for the latter. On 8 June 1954, aged 41, he was found dead at his home by his housekeeper. The inquest recorded as the cause of his death suicide. It took until 2009 before the then Prime Minister Gordon Brown officially apologised for ■ ↖551
the "appalling" and "utterly unfair" treatment Turing had received at the hands of the British government; and on Christmas Eve 2013, Her Majesty The Queen signed a posthumous Royal Pardon for Alan Turing, ■ ↖551 705↘
with immediate effect. By 2017 what became informally known as the Alan Turing Law had extended this pardon to all men who were persecuted under the law that had made homosexuality illegal in Britain until 1967. On 15 July 2019, the Bank of England announced that it □ ↖369
would honour Alan Turing by featuring him on the newly □ ↖382
designed £50 note which will enter circulation in 2021.)

NUKES, DRUGS, AND CYBERNETICS

At the 48th Academy Awards held in Los Angeles on 29 March 1976, one film walked away with five Oscars in the top categories of Best Picture, Best Director, Best Actor, Best Actress, and Best Screenplay Adapted from Other Material: *One Flew Over the Cuckoo's Nest* by Miloš Forman, starring Jack Nicholson and Louise Fletcher, based on the novel of the same title by American author Ken Kesey (1935–2001). Kesey wrote it after completing a graduate fellowship in creative writing at Stanford University, and upon its publication in February 1962 it was an instant success both critically and commercially, propelling the young author into the literary limelight. ■

One of the ways he'd financed the writing of his novel (which to this day, much as the film, is considered a 20th century classic) was by participating in a programme funded by the US government, conducting research into how intelligent young people responded to mind-altering substances, such as mescaline and, more famously, Lysergic Acid Diethylamide: LSD. LSD was the "problem child" of Swiss chemist and author Albert Hofmann (1906–2008), as he himself called it in a book that appeared in 2007 when he was 101 years old, and the reason the CIA (Central Intelligence Agency) of the United States was interested in it was that after the trauma of World War II and the rise of fascism, Nazism, and communism in Europe in the first half of the 20th century, altering a new generation's minds in a controlled way so as to bring about a new world order peopled with global citizens who were not rooted in nationalism but happy to float in the general overallness of it all was not considered the stuff of science fiction or utopian delusion, but examined actively as a possible government policy.

Also on the LSD programme, codenamed *MKUltra,* was an exceptionally gifted young American mathematician called Ted Kaczynski (b. 1942), who in 1967, aged 25, became assistant professor of mathematics at the University of California in Berkeley. Two years later, in 1969, he resigned his post, and within another couple of years, in 1971, he decamped to a wood cabin he himself built in the countryside near Lincoln, Montana, there to commence a self-sufficient existence without technological aid or comfort, without electricity, or even running water. Within another seven years, starting 1978 and continuing intermittently until 1995, he had embarked on a bombing campaign that killed 3 people and hurt 23 (some of them with serious, life-changing injuries), before being arrested in 1996, following a tip-off from his estranged brother.

Known by then as the *Unabomber* (for universities and airlines, his principal targets), Kaczynski was trying to start a revolution against what he saw as a "disaster for humankind," and the orchestrated, manipulated march of technology against the human race. He believed that advances not only but particularly in information and gene technology were bound to eventually enslave human beings, and that our only escape from such a fate would be a rebellion against these advances by embracing 'wild nature', which he saw as directly pitched against technology. Arguably, Kaczynski's impotent acts of violence were his own personal impassioned, though ultimately feeble, attempt at halting the precise new world order that others were actively trying to establish.

A third character who took part in *MKUltra* was the American writer Stewart Brand (b. 1938). Not only is he credited with coining the term *Personal Computer* (according to a documentary by German director Lutz Dammbeck, entitled *The Net – The Unabomber, LSD and the Internet*), but he is also the founder of one of the first virtual communities, *The WELL (The Whole Earth 'Lectronic Link)*, in 1985, and before that of the highly influential *Whole Earth Catalog*. This listed, propagated, and sold a vast array of ecologically sound products, as well as tools and equipment that would help its customers and readers lead a more sustainable, ecologically sound existence. Among the many items featured in *The Whole Earth Catalog* over the years was not just an – according to Brand – remarkably successful handbook on how to raise and produce milk from goats, but also the assembly instructions for making exactly the kind of shed that Kaczynski built for himself in the woodlands of Lincoln, Montana.

Brand became friends with and an associate of Ken Kesey's when he, now famous and financially independent, came to live in La Honda, California. From there, Kesey in 1964 undertook an historic trip in a converted school bus painted in psychedelic colours, with a community of around a dozen artists and musicians who became known as The Merry Pranksters. The vehicle itself was named *Furthur* to reflect the idea that in order for the human race to get anywhere, we have to always go further and beyond what we already know. It would cross the entire United States from California to New York in the reverse direction of the American pioneers, with the explicit aim of pursuing, "the obliteration of the entire nation – not taken literally, of course, we won't blow up their buildings, we'll blow their minds!" This they did in parts quite successfully, liberally using and handing out LSD and marijuana wherever they went in now near-legendary 'happenings' they themselves called *Acid Tests.*

There is, on the surface, an at best tenuous – certainly no direct – link between Kesey and Brand on the one side and Kaczynski on the other side of what opens up as a very wide spectrum, where you have on the one hand those who readily, enthusiastically even, embrace not only new technology but also the idea of building a new (and implicitly better) world with a new (correspondingly better) kind of people in it using new technology, and on the other hand those who vehemently reject this new world order, which they see as obviously tied into the new technologies.

For us writing this *Atlas*, who, as an age group, are the last generation to genuinely straddle the eras before and since the Internet, it is already difficult to estimate quite how momentous, dynamic, and radical a time the 1960s were. How highly charged with both hope and fear too. For someone born after about 1985, it must seem nothing short of perplexing. But here you have a relatively short period, really from the very early 1960s to approximately the arrival of punk in the early 1970s, when just about anything seemed possible. Of both the best and the worst kind. And these possibilities were, and felt, real. You had an affluent post-war generation who considered the social, economic, and technological structures of their parents and grandparents as directly responsible for two consecutive catastrophes that couldn't have been more horrendous. The 'War to End All Wars' had done nothing of the sort and needed to be given an ordinal number when it was followed, within just over twenty years – the time it takes for a person to grow into an adult – by another, even greater cataclysm. Change was *obviously* needed.

At the same time as being made aware that an entire ethnoreligious group, together with other human beings literally labelled undesirable, had been systematically, industrially, murdered, this generation saw the effects of the nuclear bomb, which caused death and destruction on a scale that was unprecedented even with everything that had just gone before, and yet could also be reasonably argued to have hastened the end of the war. This technology then perhaps embodied exactly that same spectrum between hope and fear, between unimagined new riches and unimaginable horror. It had promised to provide cheap, clean, and forever sustainable energy in abundance, and now it also proved to be capable of destroying the planet, many times over.

In 1903, French physicist Antoine Henri Becquerel (1852–1908) shared the Nobel Prize in Physics with Polish-born French physicist Marie Curie (1867–1934) and her husband, French physicist Pierre Curie (1859–1906) for their respective and joint work that led to the discovery and understanding of radioactivity. Five years later, in 1908, New Zealand-born British physicist Ernest Rutherford (1871–1937) was awarded the Nobel Prize in Chemistry for his work on the disintegration of the elements and the chemistry of radioactive substances, and it was also Rutherford who in 1932 first realised that splitting a lithium atom in a controlled manner could release extraordinary amounts of energy.

Another six years after that, in 1938, German chemist Otto Hahn (1879–1968) discovered nuclear fission, taking his turn as a Nobel Prize winner in Chemistry in 1944. So all told, from the very beginnings of our understanding of nuclear processes to 27 June 1954, when the first nuclear power plant started to feed electricity into a grid in Obnisnk, Russia – then part of the USSR (Union of Soviet Socialist Republics) – it took just over half a century, even though Rutherford himself had considered the possibility of such a thing happening any time soon a 'moonshine' proposition. And even before then, another milestone in destruction had already been reached, when 'Little Boy' and 'Fat Man' became the two unbearably cute nicknames that were given to the deadliest weapons ever unleashed by one civilisation on another, as the United States dropped the former on Nagasaki and the latter on Hiroshima, on the 6th and 9th August 1945 respectively, obliterating both Japanese cities, indiscriminately killing approximately 200,000 people in the process.

It is no great surprise then that technology and what it could do – what it stood for, even – did not leave people cold. Or that young people who had no first hand experience of any of this, but whose entire histories had been traumatised, sought to change *everything*. And so you had 'hippy' communes trying to break free, to open their minds, and in many cases to go back to basics, to reconnect with simple, earthy, visceral pleasures, like natural food and free love, eschewing technology and any 'progress' it promised, while from exactly the same generation there also emerged a cohort who embraced the potential of technology in general and, most specifically, computers. (It may be worth noting that they mostly came from a very small group of well-educated, well-to-do, globally minded Americans and uprooted globals whose parents had come to America, often because in their own countries they would have been rounded up in concentration camps and then killed.)

Computers now, at this precise juncture start to do something they had not done before: they begin to talk to each other. And here too, there is a curious alliance between an open minded generation that is – certainly not in its entirety, but in large numbers – seeking alternatives to the establishment modes of doing things, and the American military who fund not only experiments in what are by now widely used recreational drugs, but also feed leading universities with substantial amounts of money to carry out research into, and to develop, networked computer systems.

Here we really need to bring into the 'equation', such as it is, two people who to this entire process are of immeasurable influence and therefore importance. One of these is the American mathematician and philosopher Norbert Wiener (1894–1964) who introduces the world to the concept of **cybernetics**. Wiener himself in 1948 defines cybernetics as, "the scientific study of control and communication in the animal and the machine," whereby it is generally accepted that 'animal' here means organic being and therefore includes humans. This leads directly to a *systems approach* and is therefore closely linked to the fields of systems theory, sociology, neuropsychology, behavioural psychology, philosophy, and also architecture.

Wiener's research coincides with and constitutes the title topic of no fewer than ten Cybernetics Conferences that take place in New York, under the aegis of the Josiah Macy Jr Foundation, mostly simply known as the Macy Foundation. They form part of some 160 interdisciplinary conferences held between 1946 and 1953 with the aim of establishing the foundations for a general 'science of the mind'. Other topics discussed include psychology, anthropology, how computers might learn to learn, self-regulating teleological mechanisms (feedback controlled purposes), and simulated **neural networks** ■ ↖165 emulating the calculus of propositional logic, among many others. One of several dozen leading scientists to participate in these Cybernetics Conferences is the Hungarian-American mathematician, physicist, and computer scientist John von Neumann (1902–1957), after whom the **von Neumann architecture** ■ ↖373 711↘ of computing is named, which forms the basis for some 95% of computers in use today, and whom we meet more closely in our chapter on Writing & Code. □ ↖369

The youngest member of the core group of the Cybernetics Conferences, and the man who suggested that this name be used for them (in preference to the rather longer winded *Circular Causal and Feedback Mechanisms in Biological and Social Systems* they were going to be run under) is Austrian-American physicist and philosopher Heinz von Förster (1911–2002), who becomes one of three editors of the conferences' *Proceedings* and turns himself into another highly influential figure in computer science. According to von Förster – and this seems to have proved prescient when looking at today's media world – there is no reality. There are only 'good stories'. The person who wins is the person who comes up with the most compelling story. As an example for this he cites particle theory: if you have a hole in your theory, you put in some new particles that replace the hole; particles thus are the answer to a question that cannot be answered. "In this globally functioning system of machines, all statements are correct; and that's of course what you really want; and why are they correct? Because they can be deduced from other statements." This can be continued into infinity, and it is the opposite of what had been considered to be the case before, and what had manifestly led to unimaginable ideologically-fought slaughter and destruction.

What comes about here, then, is a world view that looks at itself and talks in terms of 'open systems', but in fact still subjects itself to an absolute logic of machines and so remains in a sense tied to quite rigid thought schemes. We talk in a great deal more detail about *imperative* and *declarative programming languages* in our chapter on □ ↖369 Writing & Code, where we distinguish between the former, which are based on the von Neumann architecture, and the latter, which are based on the work of American mathematician and logician Alonzo Church (1903–1995). Our contention is that it is declarative programming which offer an alternative approach altogether. Here, the focus, we argue, lies not on *how* to do things (thinking along logical necessities in a framework of economy), but *what* we want to do: the assessment of what is possible in the sphere of the unknown, which therefore operates in a framework of politics. Computers thus are no longer tools, but become the technological basis for a new way of talking and writing: a new literacy. (See also our chapters □ ↖175 Graphs & Graphics, □ ↖549 Big Data & Machine Learning, and □ 693↘ In Conclusion – What Is Information? where we expand on this discussion.)

In architecture, a prominent figure of relevance in the larger context of technology and an emergent new perception of its role in the world is the American architect, systems theorist, inventor, and futurist Buckminster Fuller (1895–1983), who becomes one ■ ↖622 of the first and leading humanist globalists to believe in and propagate a world which has as its source of power infinitely renewable energy forms such as solar and wind, and who declares himself and his work to be "property of the universe." We ourselves would contrast this still cybernetic statement by suggesting we are rather all *'native to the universe'*.

And so to summarise and tie these perhaps at first disjointed seeming characters and thinkers and doers together: we set out from a world that, with the end of the Second World War, wakes up to a reality in which everything has been shaken up. Much has been destroyed too, and unquantifiable suffering has been unleashed and endured. In the wake of these two world wars, empires crumble, superpowers arise, and the urge to prevent anything of the kind ever being allowed to happen again gives birth to actively and deliberately global endeavours of collaboration and research, and to organisations such as the United Nations. At exactly the same time, the power balance shifts, with the Eastern Bloc countries around the Soviet Union on the one side and the Western democracies around the United States on the other finding themselves in a nuclear arms race that almost immediately turns into a Cold War of threat and counter-threat, espionage, counter-espionage, and technological competition in the civil as much as the military sphere, because, after all, the two can not be kept separate any longer: the space race and the race for technological domination on Earth are on, and they are being pursued with the full weight of the superpowers behind them.

Into this world is born a new generation of young people who are not only looking for, and opening themselves up to, new hedonistic experiences – though that certainly too – but who also seek, and believe strongly that the world needs, new structures for society, new approaches for economic endeavours, new ethics and moral principles for the species as a whole. They experiment with lifestyles, drugs, each other, and with technology, and take a radically non-commercial approach to what they do. They consider themselves to be part of a counter-culture and reject the 19th and early 20th century principles of property, possession, and top-heavy hierarchical organisation. Many, though not all, embrace new technologies, and think in new terms such as the 'gift economy', free and open access to shared information, and the common good.

This strongly feeds into the fledgling Internet. Rather than the money-dominated, principally commercial platforms of today, what you have at the beginning are the networks of universities where people freely share their content, without advertising, without data mining, and without a market place. Monetising the Internet hardly comes into play until the 1990s, when the startups which today we can't get around enter the scene: Google, Facebook, Amazon are all barely twenty years old. As Stewart Brand puts it: "The main legacy of the 1960s is the open systems approach to anything having to do with computers." And this holds true right until then, even if it no longer holds true now.

All of this is pitched against the deep reach of the American government, the American secret service, and the American military. Ironic as this may sound: the ARPANET (Advanced Research Projects Agency Network), which absolutely provides the model and basis for the Internet that we use today, was financed entirely by the eponymous ARPA (today DARPA, for Defense Advanced Research Projects Agency), a US Department of Defense branch set up in 1958 by President Dwight D Eisenhower, in direct response to the Soviet Union's successful launch of *Sputnik 1* – the first artificial satellite – the year before.

It is worth emphasising these principal motions: you have in nuclear technology a movement from scientific research towards well-intentioned civil application for the greater good, with devastating military use in-between, which then in turn escalates into a Cold War that is both fearsome in the extreme, but also credited (at least by some) with stabilising the world and preventing the exact nuclear showdown it itself enables. You have the United States emerging as the dominant superpower with its government agencies and military deploying hallucinogenic substances to carry out research on bright young minds, only for the US government subsequently to slam prohibition on recreational drug use and wage its manifestly futile 'war on drugs', in the process criminalising swathes of the same generation and over time incarcerating hundreds of thousands of people for associated offences. And you have military-funded research essentially inventing the Internet, only for these funding agencies to then simply hand over the technology to the universities and their users to be spread, propagated, and ultimately taken over by young disruptive entrepreneurs from within the next generation of computer scientists and developers.

That's the potent, heady, and at times amazingly trippy mix to which we still today owe our computers, our Internet, our lifestyles, and therefore in no small measure our architecture.

Politics

ACTIVISM 1960

For many historians, the 1960s are characterised by social reform, activism, and liberation movements. It is, to all intents and purposes, a breaking out of the confines of the hitherto traditional power structures, and people who have up until now been either actively oppressed or segregated or hidden step up to claim their place in the world: women's liberation, the sexual revolution, lesbian and gay rights, and, perhaps most dramatically, the civil rights movement in the United States demanding equality for African Americans. On 28 August 1963, the American clergyman and activist Martin Luther King Jr (1929–1968) addresses a quarter of a million people who have marched on Washington, DC, in what has become one of the seminal orations of the 20th century: departing from his written text, he repeats the phrase "I have a dream" eight times to spell out his vision of a United States that is not riven by racism and segregation, and of a fair-minded, open society: "I have a dream that my four little children will one day live in a nation where they will not be judged by the color of their skin but by the content of their character." At the same time, the emergence of the United States as the dominant power in the world outside the Eastern Bloc sees resistance movements and socialist governments in South America in particular stand up to what they see as a new imperialism of the capitalist fortress USA.

On 5 March 1960, Cuban photographer Alberto Korda (1928–2001) attended a memorial service in Havana for the victims of an explosion the day before of a French cargo ship called *La Coubre* which had at the time been in the process of unloading ammunition in the Havana harbour. He pointed his *Leica M2* camera at various guests and speakers, among them the Cuban leader Fidel Castro (1926–2016) and the French writers and philosophers Jean-Paul Sartre (1905–1980) and Simone de Beauvoir (1908–1986), and in amongst these he also snapped three frames exactly in which the Argentinian revolutionary Che Guevara (1928–1967) appears. Guevara had been attending a meeting in Havana at the time of the explosion, and on hearing about it had raced to the scene in order to help the injured: he was not only at this moment politically engaged, he had just, within the last 24 hours, been hands-on involved in the rescue of people whom the Cuban government was certain were the target of a deliberate attack on their revolution (although this has never been proven). In the first of Korda's three frames, Che Guevara is out of focus and just about recognisable behind Sartre and de Beauvoir. In the second he is flanked by a man in profile on his right and a palm tree on his left, and in the third he is on his own but somebody else's head pops up just behind his shoulder. Korda chose the second picture, cropped out the other man and the palm tree, and in doing so turned a nice-enough photograph in landscape format into one of the most iconic portraits of all time. From it has sprung an industry of reproductions in all shapes, sizes, and materials: it's the 'Che' you know from T-shirts, mugs, mouse mats, stickers, badges, and towels, and it may even now, six decades later, still hang on your or your flatmate's wall as a poster.

The reason you know this image and instantly recognise *Guerrillero Heroico*, as Korda named it, is of course not that it is a picture of a handsome man in a concentrated pose, but that it, the man it depicts, his pose, and the apparel he wears, as well as the struggle and everything he stands for, all combine to create a whole that is significantly greater than the sum of its parts: it has become a symbol of resistance, protest, revolution: liberation from oppression. It sets the tone for the decade that has barely begun.

395 ● 676

PRIVACY 1980

With 'activism' for the 1960s we were on relatively stable ground as far as terminology is concerned. But here now, with 'privacy', we encounter a term that is far more ambivalent, while tying in strongly, so our argument, with the ontologies of object-oriented programming and the development of the PC, which we examine further in our chapter on Writing & Code. □ ↖369

As a society we currently tend to conduct our discourse on the subject of privacy in the context of a legal or moral right. We have, or presume to have, or in some cases merely claim, a 'right to privacy', even describe privacy as a human right. We will be looking at the evolution, the meaning, and also the very different interpretations of the concept of privacy over time and in different languages a bit further on in this chapter, but here we want to continue our thought journey into the area of politics a little longer, because it is so relevant to our overall understanding of where we find ourselves today.

So if the 1960s were a 'Decade of Activism' – we realise this is a simplification – then arguably the 1980s stand for 'Privacy'. This is not to say, obviously, that activism did not continue right through the 1970s and into the eighties, but with the first major battles won on the platforms of civil and equal rights (by no means all, it has to be said), the focus here shifts far more from the public to the personal sphere.

On 4 May 1979, eight years after Swiss women were granted the right to vote by their menfolk in 1971, British politician Margaret Thatcher (1925–2013) becomes the first woman prime minister of the United Kingdom, and almost as much of an icon for capitalism, conservatism, and indeed her own Thatcherism as Che Guevara was a symbol of the direct opposite in every way. In a 1987 interview she tells *Woman's Own* magazine that, "there is no such thing as society," which to her may mean that people have to take responsibility for their own actions and, "look after themselves first," but has come to sum up a decade of brutal egotism and materialism, and a negation of any hint of social cohesion for an entire generation.

Right in the middle of the decade sits the Orwellian year, 1984, and for the first time surveillance technology is everywhere and unmissable. While CCTV (Closed-Circuit Television) systems had been in existence since the 1940s, it was really with the advent of VCR (Videocassette Recording) in the 1970s that video surveillance became truly widespread, because it enabled the economical capture and storage of video footage on magnetic tape. And by the 1980s these installations had become a feature of city centres, building complexes, and courtyards everywhere in the developed world. With the Cold War still far from thawing, the number of nuclear warheads held by the Eastern Bloc and NATO (North Atlantic Treaty Organization) combined threatening the destruction of civilisation as we know it, and computing no longer in the hands of the few but of the many, both genuine concerns about the continued existence of human life on Earth and a palpable sense of paranoia set the tone.

Following first strides towards LGBT rights in the 1970s, the AIDS crisis of the 80s triggers a social and political backlash, and Thatcher's conservative government in the UK, for example, finds itself emboldened to pass legislation that prohibits local authorities from "promoting homosexuality," or the teaching in schools of "the acceptability of homosexuality as a pretend family relationship." In fact, across the Western World, politicians and public figures face censure and the loss of their job if they are 'outed' by the press for instance, or declare their sexuality themselves. These are just examples: data protection generally is, for the first time, an issue that ordinary citizens care and worry about. The ideology of new conservatism may have made the individual king, but the power of information technology also makes the individual extremely vulnerable. No wonder, then, that keeping things under control becomes a major preoccupation.

396 ● 676

SECURITY 2000

We noted earlier in this chapter that we, the people writing this book, are the last generation to have first hand experience of the pre-digital world. We, who grew up in the 1970s and 80s, can only marvel at the change that we as a society have undergone with the Internet and our smartphones. It's worth reiterating: the fact that today the most intimate details are made public, by people themselves, voluntarily and actively, to us is not 'normal'. Or if it is normal now, then it certainly wasn't thirty years ago. Absolutely most people (as in everyone with perhaps a few highly individual, effectively eccentric exceptions) would have been naturally horrified at the thought that their holiday snaps would somehow be made public. Let alone the story of their breakup with their partner. Or their mental meltdown. In fact, the turnaround has been complete: today, people not only share the entirety of their lives with everyone who has access to the Internet, they also consider this to be their inalienable right. And so if we label this section about the 2000s onwards 'Security', this actually goes hand in hand with 'transparency' and stands in starkest possible contrast to the protection of privacy related priorities of the 1980s.

The notion of 'privacy' – in this age of us curating our own lives for the benefit of self-selecting onlookers – has all but evaporated. The question whether or not there is such a thing as society, too, has effectively disappeared. Of course it does, and of course it doesn't. You have a new creative commons and, for example, a *Wikipedia* where people just give of their time, their knowledge, their expertise as part of the whole, and you have corporate behemoths who sell you to yourself, and whose commercial imperative is such that they wouldn't shy away from selling you your grandmother too. The gap between the richest and the poorest is greater than ever before, but across the world there are also more people reasonably well off in a broader middle-class than ever before. The Cold War has ended with a near complete 'victory' of the West over the type of communism instituted in the former East, but new 'enemies' have replaced old ones, and we live under the spectre – both real and imagined – of terrorism and extremism as a threat both physically experienced and viscerally felt.

This turns the 2000s into a decade of 'security'. The idea that you could actually protect your private sphere has turned out to be not just impossible but also, surprisingly, irrelevant. We have – as we've seen – outdone Orwell by far: we parade our pictures, our diet, our ups and downs, our sex lives, and our professional triumphs and disasters; we talk openly about abuse, about health, about our bodies, and about our minds, and we are almost permanently on edge about something or other. Being 'offended' is par for the course, and the greatest threat – certainly in the Western world – to our freedoms of expression comes not from authoritarian regimes or dictatorial moral guardians, but from our own self-censorship and a new type of infantilisation that seeks to protect us not just from harm but from anything that might upset us, including and particularly opinions we may not agree with.

In our world, everything is possible and nothing is allowed *at the same time*, it's almost as if we have taken the concept of a quantum state of existence to a digital level of absurd, but the issue of protecting our data against breaches of security – such as keeping our bank details safe, for example – is certainly real and extraordinarily complex.

397 ● 676

THE DEMAND FOR POLITICS

If technology in the twentieth century presented us as citizens with formidable challenges, then that is even more the case for the twenty-first. When in the second half of the twentieth century we were confronted with the novelty of computers first, then with their exponentially accelerating and growing capabilities, then with the effect that these computers being networked had on our lives, our social conduct, our routines, and behaviour, the beginning of the twenty-first century has forced us to deal with digital ubiquity, permanent connectedness, and devices that 'know' and 'can do' everything.

This means we have to continuously adjust and learn, and it also means we have to continuously negotiate our relationships, both with each other, and with our environment, natural and technological. Even distinguishing between a natural and a technological world that we inhabit is no longer really possible, since technology pervades our natural space in all but the remotest regions. Architecture comes into play here more obviously than elsewhere, because architecture too has long ceased to be – if ever it was – just bricks and mortar, concrete and glass, wood and steel. Architecture is the physical manifestation and thus the body of the constitution of its day. In our day that might mean the 'body of ecology', and it is technically driven by digital code. (In our chapter on Writing & Code we discuss in detail the relationship between the phonetic alphabet as first invented by the Greeks, perspective drawing as first applied to art and architecture in the Italian Renaissance, and digital code today: a point we also arrive at in our *Conclusion* to this chapter.)

It is too simple, then, to say that technology itself is neutral and inherently innocent, that 'it's just a matter of how we deal with it'. Because the way we deal with digital technology is, at every point, charged with ethical, societal, cultural, economical, environmental impact and meaning. In the technological part that follows this overview and in the companion chapter Privacy & Security – Elaboration, we see just how breathtakingly simple it is to create exceptionally powerful tools that are, in their application, complex and far-reaching. The coding for a blockchain, for example, which allows for the unbreakable encryption of information without anyone exercising control over it, turns out to be almost banal. This presents civic society with an enormous challenge, because it means that you can effectively do whatever you like and nobody can listen or watch. With a blockchain you can bypass any bank, administration, or public order: you hand the integrity of your data over to a neutral, anonymous encryption system. The idea that we are under permanent and effective surveillance that can protect us from people who mean to abuse technology for criminal or hostile ends is once again turned on its head: the NSA may be watching and listening, but that doesn't mean it can see or hear what is happening.

This is a paradox we encounter in various places in this *Atlas*: nobody really knows how to handle, manage, or let alone control the technology. The notion that the algorithmic programming and coding is extremely difficult turns out to be wrong, it's surprisingly simple. What's increasingly complicated and therefore difficult is the *political* aspect. And this is what it boils down to: our use of technology, whether we want it to be or not, is inherently political, and the way we can, arguably must, deal with it and address its manifold challenges is with politics.

It means talking about the impact the technology has and debating where the lines are to be drawn between privacy and security, between individual freedom and civic duty, between what can be expressed and what can't, between what belongs in the private sphere and what in the public domain, between what are commercial interests, communal interests, and personal interests.

If technology allows anyone – be it the nation state, the global corporation that operates beyond national boundaries, the renegade, or organised crime – to operate completely without checks and balances, then you do have a serious situation that you can't ignore. And this situation is exacerbated by the fact that of the population – the people who vote for their politicians, and the politicians included – between 85% and 90% actually don't understand how this technology works. So how can lawmakers make good laws, when they have no real concept of what can and can't be done, how, and by whom?

In March 2018 the world was confronted with the fact that a London-based, globally active political consulting firm specialising in the mining, brokerage, and analysis of data combined with strategically tar- ☐ ↖369
geted advertising had obtained personal details – such as their location, date of birth, public profiles, and page likes – of some 87 million Facebook users. Of these, a small fraction, 270,000, had volunteered their information by using an app called *This Is Your Digital Life*, created ostensibly for research purposes. Unbeknownst to them (or at any rate certainly the vast majority of them), they were disclosing not only details about their own lives, but also granting the app access to their friends' details. Those details were then mined and analysed by Cambridge Analytica (CA), the firm in question, and used to create tailored 'advertising' and communication campaigns ☐ 661↘
to targeted groups who were considered likely to be 'influenceable'.

Cambridge Analytica had been set up in 2013 as a subsidiary of its parent company SCL Group (where 'SCL' stems from its former name Strategic Communication Laboratories). Among the main investors in Cambridge Analytica were the American billionaire computer scientist Robert Mercer (b. 1946), and his daughter Rebekah who were both heavily involved as donors – and overseeing the administration – of major right wing American political entities, such as Donald Trump's 2016 election campaign and the far-right American news network *Breitbart News*. One-time *Breitbart* executive chairman, and subsequently White House Chief Strategist to Donald Trump, Steve Bannon at one point served as vice president to Cambridge Analytica. In other words: this was not just a commercial enterprise, but one with highly enmeshed ideological and political interests.

The scandal caused a great deal of outrage and concern, and undercover reporting by British broadcaster Channel 4 showing Cambridge Analytica boast about using bribery, honey traps, and sting operations in some of their activities led to the British High Court issuing a search warrant for their premises. The company has since been wound up and its intended successor with largely the same chief personnel, Emerdata, has also been abandoned, but it is significant to note that while the affair caused Facebook – who called CA's conduct "inappropriate" and a "misuse of trust" – embarrassment and its stock price to fall, what Cambridge Analytica did as their core business was not actually illegal.

Here then is a typical example of the type of issue big data and contemporary digital technology raise: where do the boundaries lie between what is technically legal and yet would be considered by most people to be obviously unethical? And even this is a problematical statement, because: who decides what is ethical and what isn't, let alone 'obviously' so?

There is, of course, no simple answer and no quick fix solution to any of this. But there is a way to deal with this type of question, and that lies with technological literacy and political discourse. The advances in technology are so fast, and therefore the possibilities in which it can be abused before politicians latch on to them so many, that the only safeguard we have against being taken for a ride or deceived or manipulated or, in any combination of these, abused is by educating ourselves about what is possible, how things work, and what we want society to do with it. We have to know things, and we have to become literate to be able to talk, not only, but also politically.

Human and Civil Rights

■ ↖647 705↘
■ ↖597
□ ↖549

By now, we find ourselves in a world of Artificial Intelligence (AI) and machine learning. We talk in a great deal more detail about these in our dedicated chapter on Big Data & Machine Learning, but here we want to walk through an exercise in big data, to illustrate how we can use this newly available trove of information in often quite unexpected new ways. If we observe that human intelligence is fusing with machine intelligence – as it rapidly is – then this puts in our hands a powerful new instrument: suddenly we are able, for example, to make an argument in a language we don't even understand, simply by carrying out an analysis of the data: by understanding the statistical relationship of words to each other. You might consider this an exercise in how to become a digital person.

Since 2002 Google has been scanning books in the public domain (as well as providing preview excerpts of copyrighted titles where the publisher has granted permission). Originally under the codename *Project Ocean,* now known simply as *Google Books,* by 2019 it had made available to the public for free over 40 million titles. Running statistical analyses, it can now tell us the frequency of the use of any word we're interested in, in any given year, and in different languages. Without reading these books, or having to understand any of the languages in which they've been published, we can, for example, test one particular sentence that is enshrined in Article 12 of the United Nations *Universal Declaration of Human Rights*: "Privacy is a human right."

If we research this by traditional methods, we soon find that there is some confusion, or at any rate discrepancy, over an outwardly simple assertion, because what, exactly, do different cultures mean by the word 'privacy' and what by 'human right'.

Using statistical analysis, we can gain some useful insights. In the English language, the term and concept 'private' begins to establish itself around 1650, the term 'public', by contrast, a hundred years later, around 1750. In the French language, on the other hand, the term *'privée'* is relatively insignificant, whereas the term *'public'* appears to establish itself between 1550 and 1620. (We have to treat this and everything that follows with a degree of caution, because there are, in this early period, only a small number of books that form part of the statistical evaluation.)

Over the centuries, the term *'public'* remains more or less stable, with its use growing at a slow, steady rate, whereas the term *'privée'* undergoes some notable fluctuations, with a startling peak at the tail end of the 18th century, to coincide with the French Revolution.

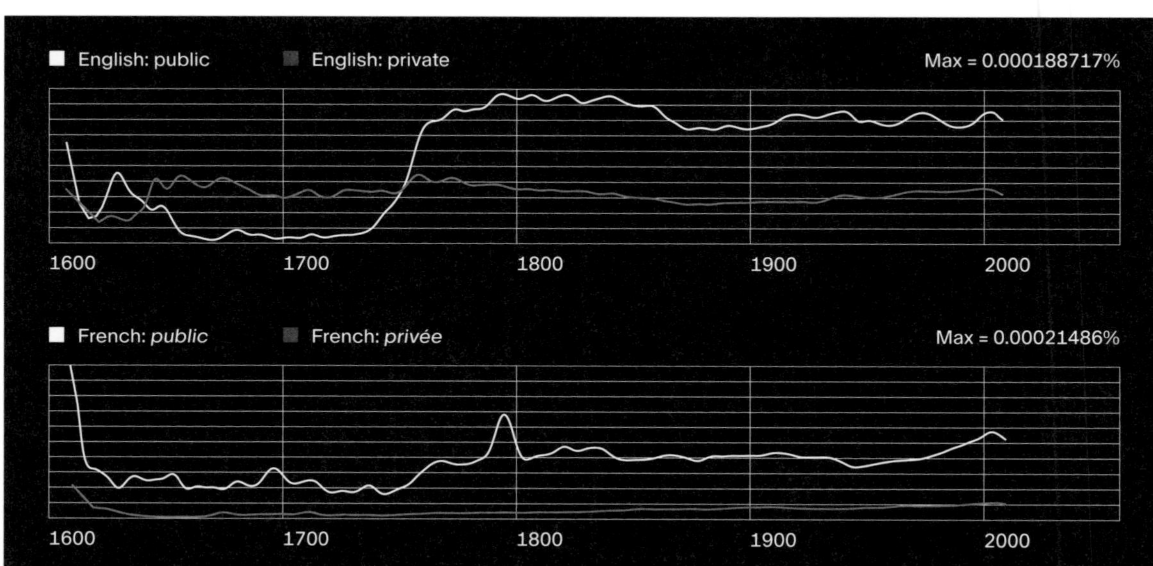

For the English term 'private', we can substitute and find the terms 'civil' and 'nature', which are of interest to us, and which refer back to the English philosopher Thomas Hobbes (1588–1679), who in his work *Leviathan or The Matter, Forme and Power of a Common Wealth Ecclesiasticall and Civil* established the idea of a social contract, specifically to overcome the violent anarchy of nature.

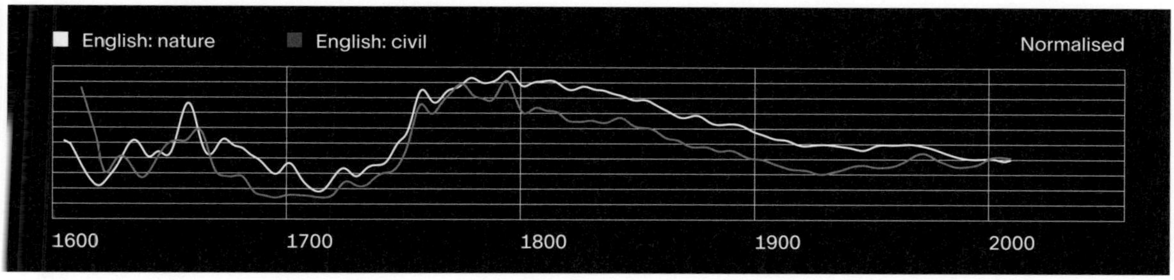

At the time of *Leviathan's* publication, in 1651, the term 'wealth' in the English language receives a spike, reaching a 0.03% usage (compared to 0.04% for 'nature', and 0.14% for 'civil'). In French literature, its equivalent *'prospérité'* takes until the time of the revolution (late 1790s) to even reach 0.005%:

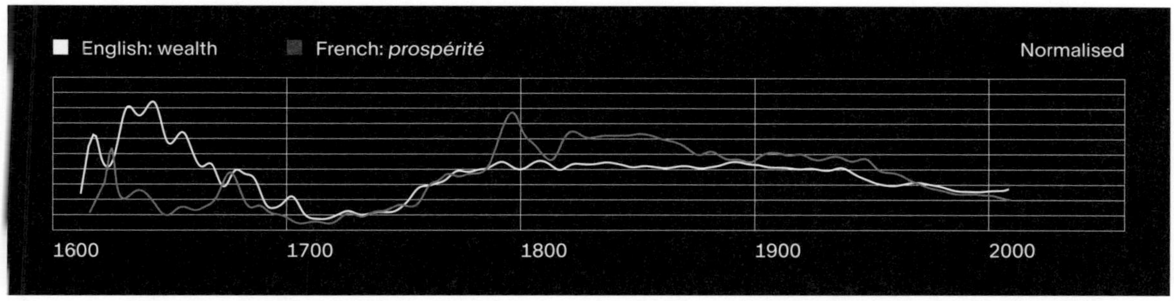

About a hundred years later, we find the term 'public' usurped by the term 'human nature', coined by the Scottish philosopher David Hume (1711–1776), and by the term 'nation', which leads us to the Scottish philosopher and economist Adam Smith (1723–1790), whereby it is interesting to note that although Adam Smith's most famous and influential work *An Inquiry Into the Nature and Causes of the Wealth of Nations*, published in 1776, did not spark a similar adoption of the term 'wealth' at the same time:

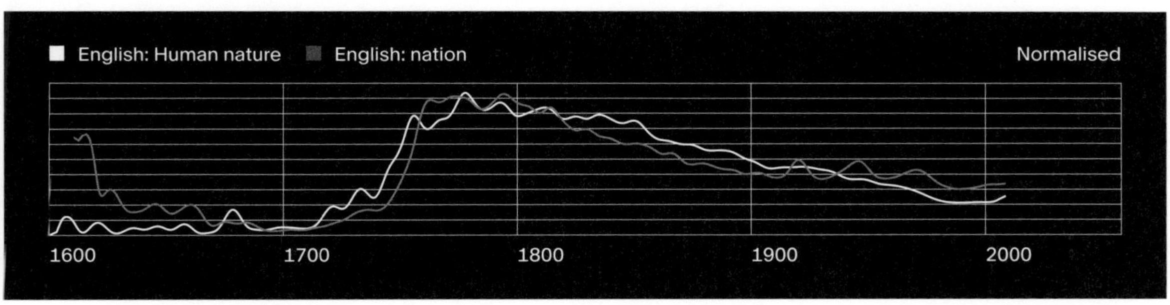

This stands in striking contrast to the term 'citizen', which in English comes into use sustainably in the second half of the 18th century and today scores just about the same as then, whereas the French *'citoyen'* unsurprisingly peaks at the time of their Revolution and then reverts to 1770s levels with just one more significant spike around 1840–50, which happens to be the aftermath of the Paris Uprising of 1832, the 'other' revolution, which French novelist Victor Hugo (1802–1885) immortalised as the backdrop for his work *Les Misérables*.

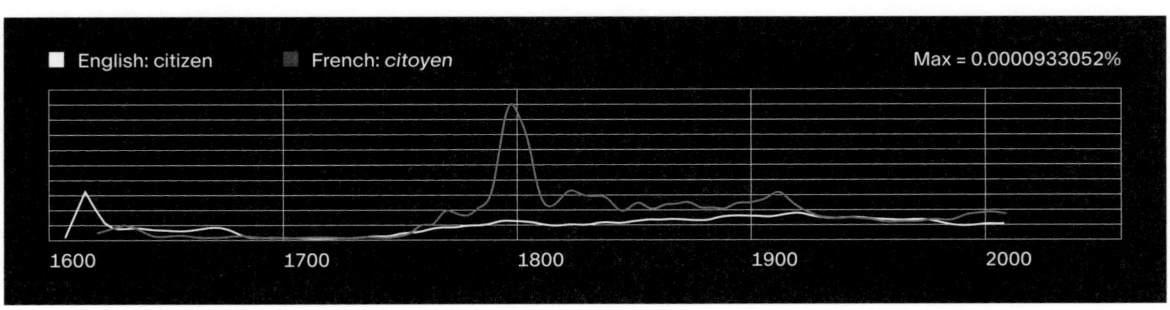

There are also some interesting differences in the use of the term 'nature'. In French, it gains significance around 1630, 1700, and 1780; in English by contrast around 1660 and 1780. By now, the use in both languages has levelled in.

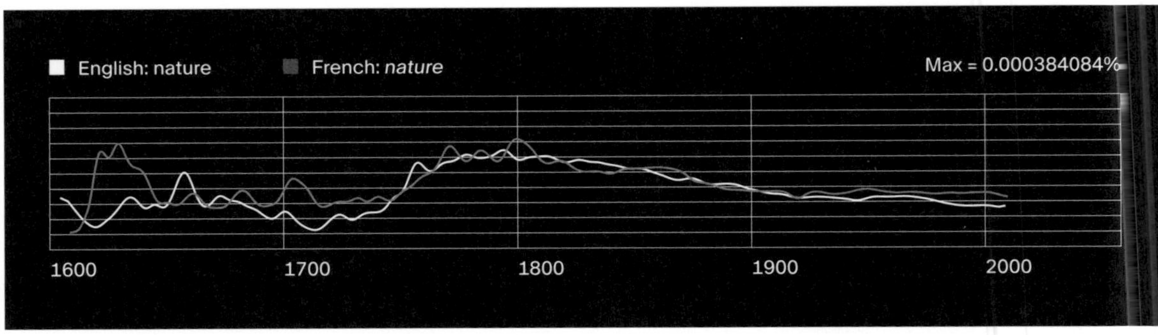

Which brings us to the difference between the terms 'civil rights' and 'human rights'.

'Civil rights' ties into the English concept of 'wealth', whereas 'human rights' are linked intrinsically to Genevan philosopher Jean-Jacques Rousseau (1712–1778) and the French Revolution. In English, the term 'human rights' does not feature until 1950, when it quickly outpaces 'civil rights' by a factor of 2:1; in French, 'human rights' become an issue at the same time, while the term 'civil rights' is practically absent from the discourse:

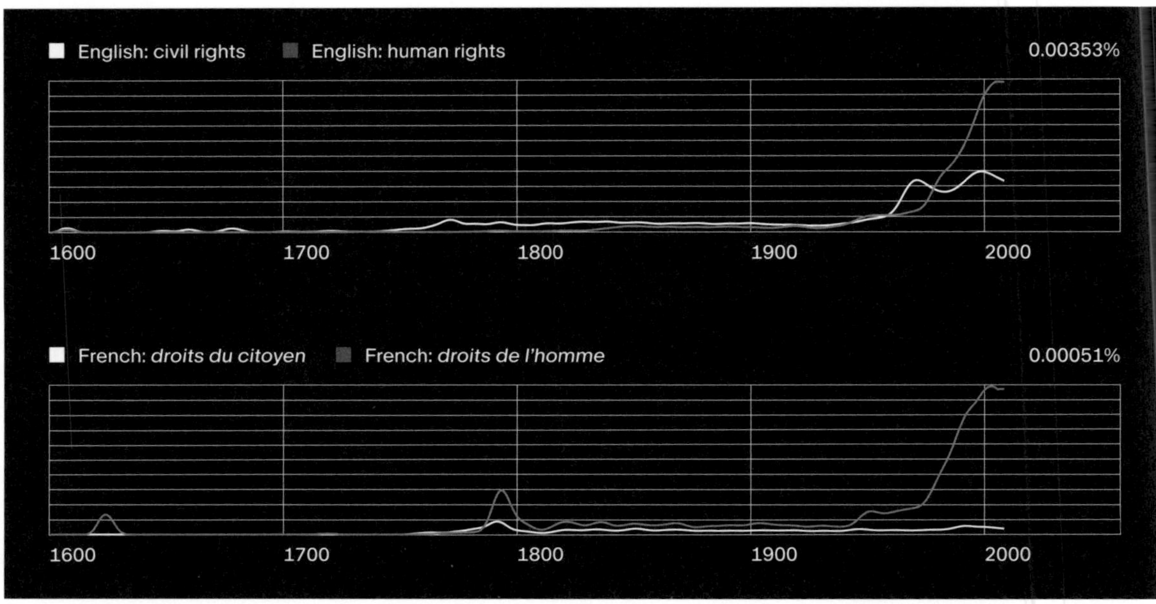

And here we find two signifiers for the French Revolution in the French language: *'égalité'* ('equality') and *'nation'*.

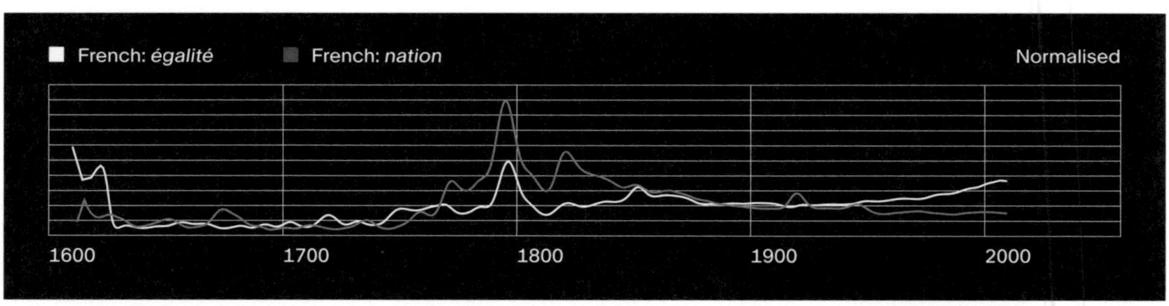

We now turn our attention to the term 'privacy': both in English and in French it comes into use in the second half of the 20th century, whereby in English it receives a first notable exposure around 1660, which seems to link it to a similar, but even more pronounced spike for 'wealth' in English at the same time. (Note that these graphs, here normalised, all have different scales: the term 'wealth' peaks at 0.03%, in 1650, whereas the term 'privacy' in English has a spike at 0.0006% in 1660: that's 50 times lower. So these observations continue to need to be treated with some caution. But the pattern is certainly perceptible.)

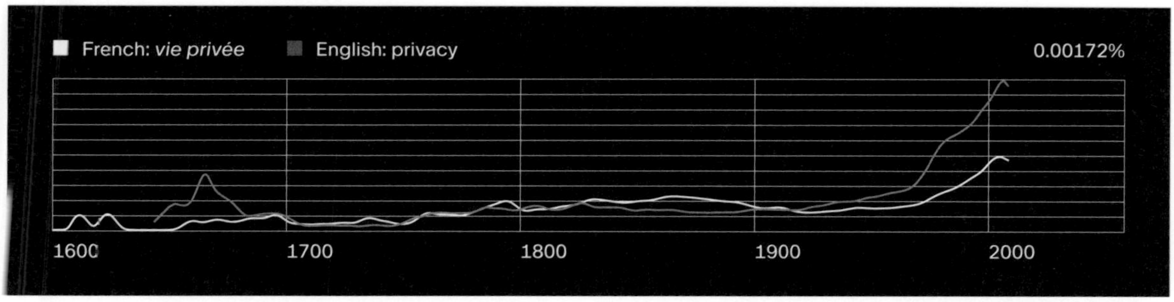

The contrast is more drastic in German, where the term *'Privatheit'* ('privacy'), and even the word *'privat'* ('private') only become relevant at all from 1950 onwards, unlike the term *'Allgemeinheit'* ('community' or 'commonality'), which points towards the German revolutions of 1848.

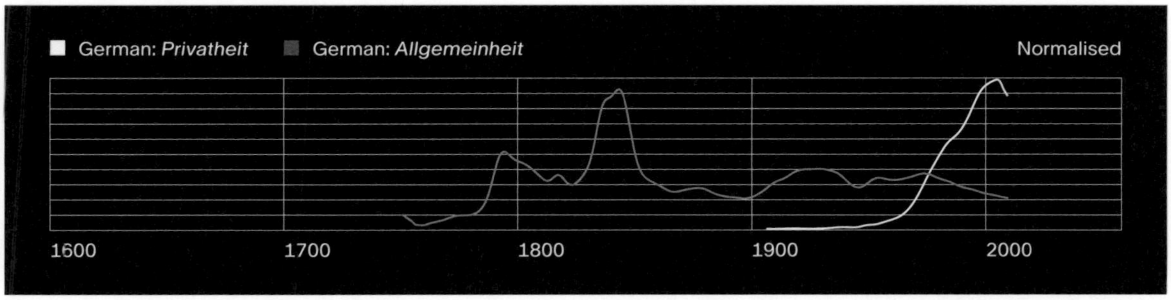

The German term *'Persönlichkeit'* ('personality') similarly points towards the 19h century revolutions in Germany, but also peaks during the Second World War. In English, the term builds almost steadily to the 1950s and then drops off, much as it does in German:

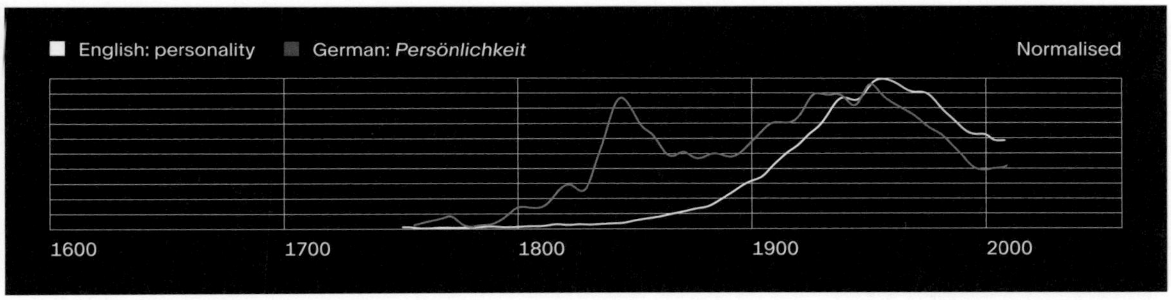

With a notable phase shift, the German term *'Gemeinsamkeit'* ('communality', 'common ground') plays an apparently restorative role after the war, whereas in French the term *'complicité'* ('complicity', 'shared guilt'), takes on a real significance just after World War II.

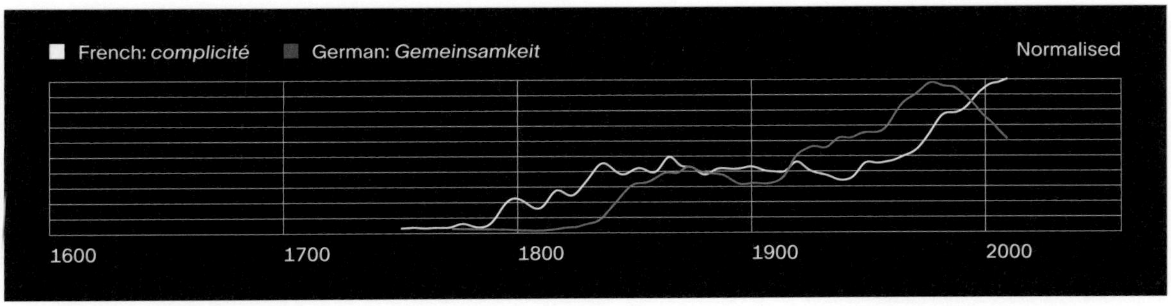

We could continue this exercise virtually without end. But let us summarise: our hypothesis was that, as stated in the UN Declaration of Human Rights, "privacy is a human right."

In German, this translates as *'Privatheit ist ein Menschenrecht'*, but *'Privatheit'* is not a German term. It is borrowed from English or French. In French, the corresponding term *'privée'* has no historical profile, whereas in English there is a parallel between 'privacy', 'civil rights', and 'nature'. 'Civil rights' originate alongside the concept of 'wealth'. The reference to 'privacy' lies with Thomas Hobbes in 1650.

By contrast, the English term 'public' has a parallel to the concepts of 'human nature' and 'nation'. There is no clear correlation to the term 'citizen', so the term 'civil rights' does not reflect the concept of 'nation'.

The reference to 'public' appears around 1750 with David Hume and Adam Smith. Meanwhile 'human rights' register as a concept in France. Parallel terms here are *'citoyen'* ('citizen') and *'égalité'* ('equality') – concepts which in English have no profile. The term 'human rights' also doesn't have any corresponding profile. There is, however, a correlation to the concept of 'wealth' *('prosperité')*. The reference to 'human rights' comes in 1780 with Jean-Jacques Rousseau and those who follow him.

The term 'nation' is ambivalent: in English, it is tied to the term 'public' – broadly speaking, it is seen as a 'public matter' – in French by contrast it is tied to the terms *'citoyen'* ('citizen') and *'égalité'* ('equality'), which, therefore, broadly speaking, makes it a 'private matter'.

So we reach the perhaps on the surface surprising conclusion that actually 'privacy' is *not* a 'human right', but rather a 'civil right'. And yes, a civil right presupposes the existence of a human being to hold such a right. But while in the end effect a 'civil right' and a 'human right' may demand similar safeguards and legislation, there is a fundamental and fascinating difference: a 'human right' is a natural right, one that is simply in place by virtue of the fact that a human being has been born. We would consider the right to life itself to be a human right, irrespective of who the person is or what they do, and in a civilised society we would expect to interpret this absolutely: even a serial killer, for example, who offends against the human right in others, still has this right inherent in their existence, without further obligation.

A 'civil right' by contrast is a civilisatory achievement that turns the human being into a citizen and therefore bestows on them also a civic duty. If you go on a march to demand civil rights for you and your particular group because you are disadvantaged or discriminated against, you are asking to be taken seriously as a citizen and given full rights as well as full duties, to be treated, and to be expected to act, as a responsible citizen in your community.

Thus far our example. The important thing to understand here is not even so much our conclusion, which may well be open to questioning, but that we were able to posit this argumentation without ever reading a book about the concepts that were discussed. With big data it is no longer a necessary requirement to read books, but simply an option: we can address a specific question and receive an idea of where we may want to read more, without actually having read the texts. This radically inverts our position towards theory, compared to what it was: when previously you were highly regarded and considered competent if you'd read books and knew answers, what is of value today is being able to articulate questions to which interesting and revealing answers can be generated automatically.

The example also serves as a metaphor for the challenge that the preservation of the private or personal sphere faces: public traces are perfectly sufficient to ask pressing questions of the private sphere. Machines do not need to know this private sphere, just as they don't need to be able to understand books in order to be able to build compelling argumentation and theory from them.

Economics, Politics, and Architecture

To get an idea of how to deal with these questions architecturally, indulge us a little further, as we visit the Old Masters and start to think about what arriving at an *adequate* architecture for today might entail.

On 30 August 1598, the then 25-year-old English nobleman Henry Wriothesley, 3rd Earl of Southampton (1573–1624) returned to London from a six-month stay in France, to marry his pregnant mistress, Elizabeth Vernon, lady-in-waiting to the Queen of England, Elizabeth I (1533–1603). The Queen was not amused. Upon hearing of the (by her) unauthorised marriage, she had the young Lady Vernon sent to Fleet Prison, where her new husband duly joined her two months later (having briefly eloped abroad once more), to await the birth of their first daughter, Penelope.

Queen Elizabeth had a complex relationship with Henry Wriothesley. He had been at times one of her favourite courtiers, at times one of her most troublesome ones; he had impressed her with his jousting and earnt her special commendation, but also offended her by getting into a brawl with one of her personal attendants at court. He'd been brought up as the warden of her chief advisor and erstwhile Secretary of State, William Cecil, 1st Baron Burghley (1520–1598), but a few years after his marriage he became directly involved in a plot to depose the Queen – the Essex Rebellion in 1601 – for which he was sentenced to death. Owing to his excellent connections, and possibly because the Queen may, after all, still have held something of a soft spot for her troubled 'nephew' (they were not directly related), his sentence was commuted into life imprisonment, which ended just as soon as the Queen herself died of natural causes in 1603 and Scotland's King James VI (1566–1625) united the crowns of the two countries and thus became King James I of England.

Although, in the latter two decades of his life, he distinguished himself as a pioneering investor, entrepreneur, property developer, and colonialist, Wriothesley never fully abandoned his fiery temperament and was involved in several more arguments and quarrels, some of which led to further short stints in gaol. In spite of all this, he is today best remembered for being not only the dedicatee of two long narrative poems by William Shakespeare (1564–1616), but much more intriguingly also for being the most likely candidate for the 'Fair Youth' to whom Shakespeare addressed 126 of his 154 *Sonnets*. Of all Shakespeare's works, they are easily the most personal body of writing, and they give insight into a passionate, at times turbulent, often heartache-inducing, jealous relationship between the poet and the young aristocrat, eleven years his junior. Going by the evidence of the *Sonnets* themselves, it's a love that runs deep and that is as physical as it is emotional, and into which – astonishingly – at times a third person steps, very possibly the mysterious 'Dark Lady' of most of the remaining *Sonnets*, to make matters just that much more complex and extraordinary.

By 1598, a man called Francis Meres publishes a collection of critical essays and articles called *Palladis Tamia*, subtitled a *Wits Treasury*, in which he refers to a "mellifluous & hony-tongued Shakespeare" and the "sugred Sonnets" that appear to be known "among his private friends." Although the *Sonnets* were almost certainly written purely for private circulation, they are first published in Shakespeare's lifetime, in 1609, but not by him, and most likely without his consent. And, when, on 3 September 1594, a pamphlet appears under the title *Willobie His Avisa*, which seems to suggest that a man known only as H.W. "betrayeth the secrecy of his disease unto his familiar friend, W.S., who, not long before, had tried the curtesy of the like passion," speculation in London runs wild as to who these two men are and what the 'disease' they have caught from what 'like passion', with whom. Even in Shakespeare and Wriothesley's world, then, certain things are still best left unspoken or at least not written about. The pamphlet was censored in 1599, possibly because it could easily be construed to be talking about none other than the Queen herself, and it was only re-released after her death in 1603. That notwithstanding and although not rated highly by critics, it proved popular enough with contemporary readers to be republished no fewer than six times by 1635.

Apart from the fact that the characters themselves could scarcely be more fascinating and that the personal stories they get themselves involved in are nothing short of riveting, what's noteworthy about this constellation, and about Henry Wriothesley as a person in particular, is the line between public and private, or rather its absence.

If you are a young Henry Wriothesley, you may be immensely privileged, but who you marry is not a private matter. The Head of State has a direct say in it. Growing up in Lord Burghley's household, young Henry is as a boy betrothed to Burghley's granddaughter, Elizabeth Vere. Henry does not like that idea, and as soon as he turns 21 and therefore comes of age and into his inheritance, which is substantial, he pays the Lady Vere £5000 *not* to marry her. Depending on how you calculate it, this equates to anything between one and two and a half million euros in 2019. To *not* marry a girl.

But he is not alone: in 16th century England (and, as we've observed, right into the middle of the 17th century), much as in continental Europe, 'privacy' as such does not only not get talked about, it really doesn't exist. You are either an important figure, or you are not. You either have a name and an estate, or you don't. Your state matters enormously, as it is directly, inseparably linked to your status, and that means your social class. If you are poor there is nowhere in your life that you can withdraw to. If you live in a city or in a town, your dwellings are small with multiple people to one room. Your family and your neighbours know everything. If you live and work on a country estate or on a farm, your employers all but own you. If you are at all wealthy, the moment any property or money comes into play, your marriage turns into an economic transaction. One of the reasons a play like the tragedy of the 'star-crossed lovers', *Romeo and Juliet*, is then and remains to this day so compelling is that it deals with a young, innocent, impassioned, and forbidden love that is purely romantic. Hardly anybody in Shakespeare's day, and for a very long time after, marries for love, including Shakespeare. Love is one thing. Your relationships are quite another. And nothing stays private.

And what, you may ask, is the point of this detour into the land of literature, poetry, and love triangles that would not be out of place in a 21st century reality TV show? We are talking about an age and examining how the concepts of privacy and security (in this case mostly privacy) do or do not come into play. We are talking, in other words, about a culture, and one that is in many ways decidedly different from ours, when in so many others it is oh so similar.

Architecture, too, is an expression – we called it a physical manifestation – of a culture, and therefore of an era. It reflects, often directly, always at least indirectly, the at the time prevailing interpretation of self, society, and human ambition.

Now, we set out in our brief *Introduction* to this chapter that with these considerations and observations that we are here making we want to steer the discourse away from categorical argumentation and instead look at our cultural context through different prisms, from different angles. All architectonic articulation is calibrated through this cultural context.

And so let us take a look at such an architectonic articulation from that same era. We set the clock back just a little, to 1567 (Shakespeare was born in 1564, Wriothesley in 1573) and swoop down on Vicenza – an easy day's ride on horseback from Verona, where Julia first espied her Romeo – to the Villa Rotonda by Italian architect Andrea Palladio (1508–1580).

Here, you have an empty centre: once in this space, you cannot hide. You are transparent, there is no privacy. All the mythological pictures around you present you with a panorama of the world: if you have access to this space, you are privileged and educated, and your education covers everything there is to know in the world. But you can't touch it: these are pictures of the world. You are connected to this world, but you are not *in* the world. And this is your economy: a world of necessities.

And then, being not in this world of necessities, you take a step out into the bright sunlight, and you make your brave point in a world of contingencies. You step outside with all your friends, the old masters of yore, the Romans and the Greeks who have led you to this point, and you constitute them in circular symmetries, celebrating the ratio of the sun in this new heliocentric world of yours...

398A ● 677

398B ● 677

A Conclusion

Your world is your culture is your architecture. As an architect, you reflect and process your world. Inherently and explicitly. You are *always* both in and of your world, and you are always shaping this world at the same time. If you want to do this well and conscientiously, consciously, and purposely, you need to master your craft. And in order to master your craft you need to attain literacy. For the Ancient Greeks this literacy is one of words and letters: the enduring and communicable articulation of the world in phonetic script, the new – and then revolutionary – alphabet.

For Palladio and his contemporaries of the Renaissance this first 'level' of literacy is in place, it can, in a way, be taken for granted. (Not for everyone, it has to be said: alphabetic literacy is still a vast privilege, but it has been around for a long time now, and it is par for the course for anybody considered important enough to get schooling.) But the new and revolutionary literacy now is the perspective drawing: the accurate and realistic visual representation of the world, its articulation in imagery.

For you today, and for all of us as digital citizens, who are saturated with imagery and with words to the point where in their abundance they have become meaningless, the new and revolutionary articulation of our world is in code. And so we have to be competent in code. Understand how it works, appreciate its power and potential, lose our ignorance and banish our fear. It does not mean that we have to all become programmers, it means we all have to become literate.

And that, in a nutshell, is the point of this chapter, as it is of much of this *Atlas*. Here, we put our focus on the complex questions of 'privacy' and 'security', but obviously we have not done so in isolation, because they can never be looked at in isolation. And while on the surface the link to architecture may at times seem tenuous, it actually really isn't. Architecture sits right in the middle of all this. And we are called upon, as architects, to own this responsibility, and enjoy it. Because think of Palladio and Shakespeare, think of the Greeks and their gods, think of Vivaldi and Händel, and think, if you like, of Lady Gaga: they don't do what they do out of a sense of duty and obligation. They know what they're doing and do what they're doing for many reasons, but certainly, among these many reasons, they do it for joy.

Elaboration

Read these examples in conjunction with the introductory texts in Privacy & Security.

Here as in the other Elaboration *sections in this* Atlas *where we play through in-depth examples and experiments in coding, we use* Mathematica, *written in the* Wolfram *programming language. This is a matter of preference, not compulsion: there are other programming languages that could do the same thing.*

ENCRYPTION – HOW TO MAKE THINGS INACCESSIBLE

CAESAR CIPHER

The *Caesar cipher* is an encryption method that dates back to the Roman emperor Julius Caesar (100–44 BCE), after whom it is named. It's a simple systematic procedure in which sender and receiver both use the same key to encode and decode.

We may characterise it as an 'encryption in space': the letters here are shifted along the alphabet by a specified number of positions and in a specified direction. The meaning of the source text is lost immediately and remains obscure until the substitution is directly reversed:

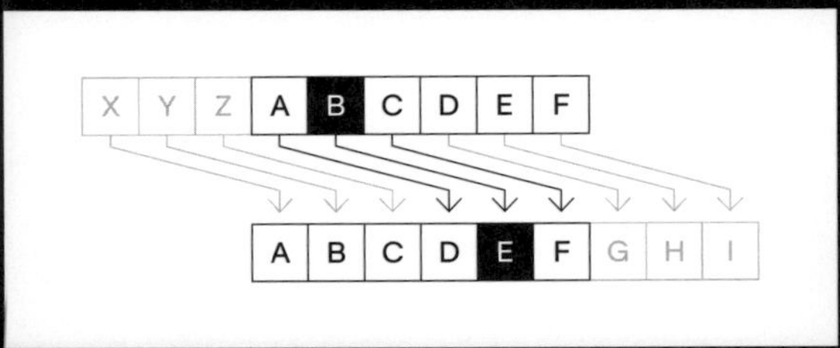

ENCRYPTION

Here is a plain text:

```
plainText="the quick brown fox jumps over
          the lazy dog";
```

These are the positions of the characters on the alphabet:

```
p1=Char2Pos@plainText
{20,8,5, ,17,21,9,3,11, ,2,18,15,23,14, ,6,15,
 24, ,10,21,13,16,19, ,15,22,5,18, ,20,8,5, ,
 12,1,26,25, ,4,15,7}
```

These are the positions of the spaces:

```
b1=Position[p1, " "]
{{4},{10},{16},{20},{26},{31},{35},{40}}
```

The list of character positions in the alphabet:

```
n1=Cases[p1,_Integer]
{20,8,5,17,21,9,3,11,2,18,15,23,14,6,15,24,10,
 21,13,16,19,15,22,5,18,20,8,5,12,1,26,25,4,
 15,7}
```

□ ↖643

This is the encryption key:

```
key=4;
```

These are the shifted character positions on an alphabetic circle:

```
n2=MOD[n1+key,26]
{24,12,9,21,25,13,7,15,6,22,19,1,18,10,19,2,
 14,25,17,20,23,19,26,9,22,24,12,9,16,5,4,3,
 8,19,11}
```

Reinsert the spaces:

```
n3=Insert[n2," ",MapIndexed[#1-#2+1&,b1]]
{24,12,9, ,21,25,13,7,15, ,6,22,19,1,18, ,10,
 19,2, ,14,25,17,20,23, ,19,26,9,22, ,24,12,
 9, ,16,5,4,3, ,8,19,11}
```

These are the corresponding characters and the encrypted text:

```
chipher=Pos2Char@n3
xli uymgo fvsar jsb nyqtw sziv xli pedc hsk
```

You can also input the spaces at even intervals, to make it more difficult to identify the encrypted words:

```
n3=Riffle[n2," ", 6];
chipher=Pos2Char@n3
xliuy mgofv sarjs bnyqt wsziv xlipe dchsk
```

DECRYPTION

Decryption of the text follows the inverse mechanics, and returns the plain text if you know the key:

```
n3=Char2Pos@chipher
{24,12,9, ,21,25,13,7,15, ,6,22,19,1,18, ,10,
 19,2, ,14,25,17,20,23, ,19,26,9,22, ,24,12,
 9, ,16,5,4,3, ,8,19,11}
```

```
n2=Cases[n3,_Integer]
{24,12,9,21,25,13,7,15,6,22,19,1,18,10,19,2,
 14,25,17,20,23,19,26,9,22,24,12,9,16,5,4,3,
 8,19,11}
```

```
n2=MOD[n2-key,26]
{20,8,5,17,21,9,3,11,2,18,15,23,14,6,15,24,
 10,21,13,16,19,15,22,5,18,20,8,5,12,1,26,
 25,4,15,7}
```

```
p1=Insert[n2," ",MapIndexed[#1-#2+1&,b1]]
```

```
{20,8,5, ,17,21,9,3,11, ,2,18,15,23,14, ,6,
 15,24, ,10,21,13,16,19, ,15,22,5,18, ,20,8,
 5, ,12,1,26,25, ,4,15,7}
```

```
plain=Pos2Char@p1
```

```
the quick brown fox jumps over the lazy dog
```

SUMMARY
This is a summary of the Caesar cipher:

```
CaesarEncryption[text_,key_]:=
 Module[{p1,b1,n1,k1,k2,n2,c1},
  p1=Char2Pos@text;
  b1=Position[p1," "];
  n1=Cases[p1,_Integer];
  n2= MOD[n1+key,26];
  c1=Insert[n2," ",MapIndexed[#1-#2+1&,b1]];
  Pos2Char@c1
]
```

```
CaesarDecryption[text_, key_]:=
 Module[{p1,k1,k2,b1,n1,n2,c1},
  c1=Char2Pos@text;
  b1=Position[c1, " "];
  n2=Cases[c1,_Integer];
  n1= MOD[n2-key ,26];
  p1=Insert[n1," ",MapIndexed[#1-#2+1&,b1]];
  Pos2Char@p1
]
```

And this is how to use it:

```
cipher=CaesarEncryption[plainText, 4]
```

```
xli uymgo fvsar jsb nyqtw sziv xli pedc hsk
```

```
CaesarDecryption[cipher,23]
```

```
aol xbpjr iyvdu mve qbtwz vcly aol shgf kvn
```

```
CaesarDecryption[cipher,4]
```

```
the quick brown fox jumps over the lazy dog
```

HOW TO CRACK THE CODE
It is fascinating to note that this method of encryption worked for more than 1500 years. You may hear people say that it is a 'simple' encryption that's easy to crack, and it is today. But it obviously wasn't during the days of Julius Caesar, and not for a long time after him, otherwise it would scarcely have endured so well. Yet people then were quite as intelligent as we are; and so this tells us a lot about the 'magic' of phonetic writing during that period. For us today it seems natural that we have a 'mechanics' of writing, and that characters are real. But it seems that in Roman antiquity, right through to the Renaissance, words were considered real, whereas characters were not. It was obviously and literally unthinkable to change the characters of a word, and so the encryption remained intact.

The code was finally solved in the 15th century by Leon Battista Alberti who in his 1467 treatise *De componendis cifris* analysed the frequency with which letters appeared. In 1987 a much older reference was discovered, namely Al-Kindi's 9th century text *On Extracting Obscured Correspondence*, which applies the same methodology. Doing so reveals which encoded cipher corresponds to which letter. But in order to be able to do this, you have to have developed a new, more abstract conception of writing. We would say: you have to leave the idea of 'letters in space' behind and learn to read 'letters in time': now the letters can move in front of the words, just as in Caesar's age words were able to move in front of things.

Here is a visualisation of the frequency with which each letter of the alphabet appears in a particular English reference text:

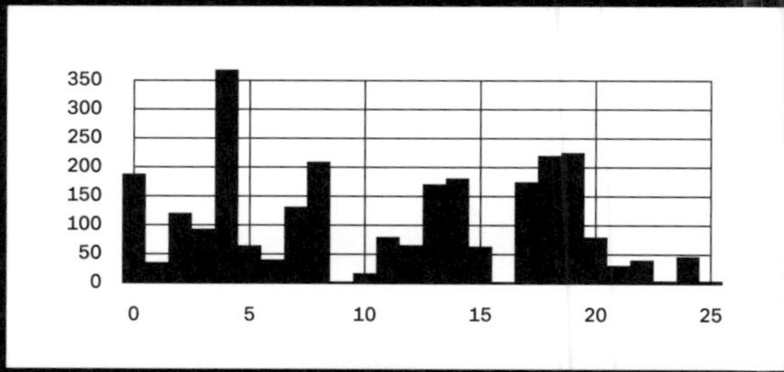

This is the encrypted text, and we do not have a key to decrypt it:

```
c1="mr gvctxskvetlc e geiwev gmtliv epws orsa
r ew geiwev w gmtliv xli wlmjx gmtliv geiwev
w gshi sv geiwev wlmjx mw sri sj xli wmqtpiwx
 erh qswx amhipc orsar irgvctxmsr xiglrmuyiw
mx mw e xcti sj wyfwxmxyxmsr gmtliv mr almgl
iegl pixxiv mr xli tpemrxibx mw vitpegih fc
e pixxiv wsqi jmbih ryqfiv sj tswmxmsrw hsar
xli eptlefix";
```

This is the histogram of the characters of this cipher:

```
h2=Select[ToCharacterCode@c1,97<=#<=122&]-97;
Histogram[h2,25]
```

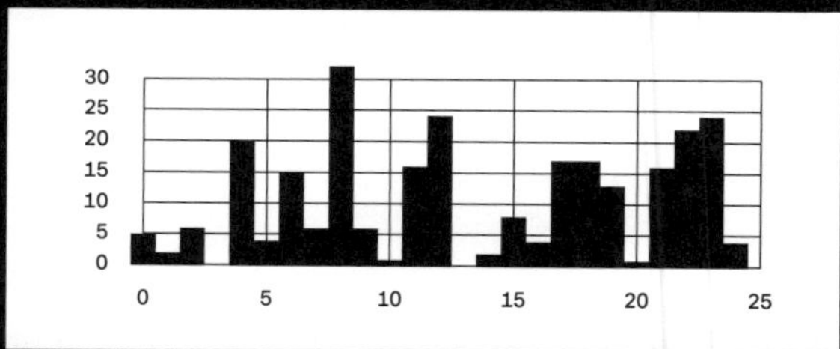

Comparing the two histograms, it is most probable that the key is an offset of 4 characters. Invert the assumed mechanic, and you get the deciphered text:

```
p2=CaesarDecryption[c1,4]
```

```
in cryptography a caesar cipher also known as
caesar s cipher the shift cipher caesar s
code or caesar shift is one of the simplest
and most widely known encryption techniques
it is a type of substitution cipher in which
each le tter in the plaintext is replaced by
a letter some fixed number of positions down
the alphabet
```

VIGENÈRE CIPHER

Once you are able to crack the Caesar cipher, and with the more abstract conception of writing in principle that is prerequisite to do so, you immediately gain access to a new system of encryption. Instead of just shifting the position of your letters on the alphabet once, which is known as **monoalphabetic substitution**, you now shift it several times and thus obtain a corresponding **polyalphabetic substitution**. We shall characterise this new procedure as 'an encryption in time'. In practice, the letters are now no longer shifted out of position in relation to each other, but rather rotated against each other in step (in rhythm, in time) with the keyword.

399 ○ 677

ENCODING

We want to illustrate a Viginère encryption schematically, as code. These are the first steps of encryption, as introduced with the Caesar cipher:

```
plainText="the quick brown fox jumps over the
 lazy dog";
p1=Char2Pos@plainText;
b1=Position[p1," "];
n1=Cases[p1,_Integer]

{20,8,5,17,21,9,3,11,2,18,15,23,14,6,15,24,10,
 21,13,16,19,15,22,5,18,20,8,5,12,1,26,25,4,
 15,7}
```

The key now is not a secret single number, but a secret word:

```
k1=Cases[Char2Pos@"vigenere",_Integer]

{22,9,7,5,14,5,18,5}
```

To encrypt, we roll out this sequence to the text; the longer the keyword, the better the encryption:

```
k2=k1[[MOD[Range@Length@n1,Length@k1]]]

{22,9,7,5,14,5,18,5,22,9,7,5,14,5,18,5,22,9,7,
 5,14,5,18,5,22,9,7,5,14,5,18,5,22,9,7}
```

Now we add both positions on the circle of the alphabet:

```
n3=MOD[n1+k2,26]

{16,17,12,22,9,14,21,16,24,1,22,2,2,11,7,3,6,
 4,20,21,7,20,14,10,14,3,15,10,26,6,18,4,26,
 24,14}
```

These are the encrypted positions written as characters:

```
c1=Insert[n3," ",MapIndexed[#1-#2+1&,b1]];
c2=Pos2Char@c1

pql vinup xavbb kgc fdtug tnjn coj zfrd zxn
```

If you look at the histogram of this encryption, there is no familiar or recognisable pattern. So whereas the Caesar encryption was 'outside of words', the Vigenère encryption is 'outside of language'.

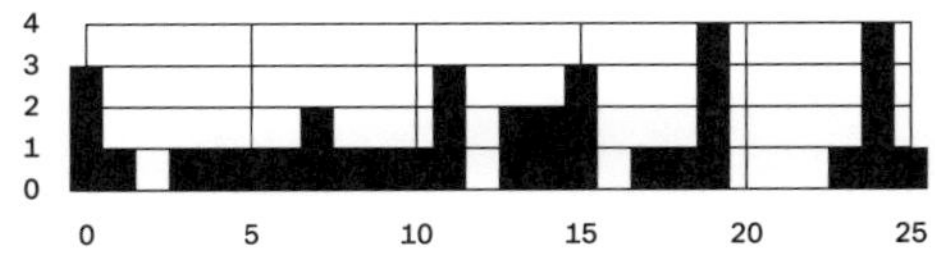

This code was cracked in 1863, by German cryptographer and archeologist (and also army officer) Friedrich Kasiski (1805–1881). And so the famous story of how the Enigma code was solved (we refer to it in the main body of this chapter) was not in fact about the encryption itself: Enigma is a polyalphabetic substitution machine, encoded according to the principles of the Viginère encryption. The extraordinary achievement of Alan Turing and his team at Bletchley Park was to find a fast mechanical decryption of the code by machine!

DECODING

To decrypt a text in the Viginère cipher we have to move our encryption machine backwards:

```
c1=Char2Pos@c2;
n2=Cases[c1,_Integer]

{14,16,10,20,4,25,11,16,20,1,8,2,15,25,14,18,
 25,16,1,20,24,7,15,25,19,8,12,6,26,5,9,12,20,
 1,12}
```

```
n1=MOD[n2-k2,26]

{20,8,5,17,21,9,3,11,2,18,15,23,14,6,15,24,10,
 21,13,16,19,15,22,5,18,20,8,5,12,1,26,25,4,
 15,7}
```

```
p1=Insert[n1," ",MapIndexed[#1-#2+1&,b1]];
plainText=Pos2Char@p1

the quick brown fox jumps over the lazy dog
```

SUMMARY

This is a summary of the Vigenère cipher:

```
VigenereEncrypt[text_,key_]:=
 Module[{p1,b1,n1,k1,k2,n2,c1},
  p1=Char2Pos@text;
  b1=Position[p1," "];
  n1=Cases[p1,_Integer];
  k1=Char2Pos@key;,
  k2=k1[[MOD[Range@Length@n1,Length@k1]]];
  n2= MOD[n1+k2,26];
  c1=Insert[n2," ",MapIndexed[#1-#2+1&,b1]];
  Pos2Char@c1,
]
```

```
VigenereDecrypt[text_,key_]:=
 Module[{p1,k1,k2,b1,n1,n2,c1},
  c1=Char2Pos@text;
  b1=Position[c1," "];
  n2=Cases[c1,_Integer];
  k1=Char2Pos@key;
  k2=k1[[MOD[Range@Length@n2,Length@k1]]];
  n1= MOD[n2-k2,26];
  p1=Insert[n1," ",MapIndexed[#1-#2+1&,b1]];
  Pos2Char@p1
]
```

This is how to encrypt:

```
plainText="the quick brown fox jumps over the
lazy dog";
cipher=VigenereEncrypt[ plainText,"vigenere"]
pql vinup xavbb kgc fdtug tnjn coj zfrd zxn
```

You don't get any meaningful text without the exact key:

```
VigenereDecrypt[cipher,"pascal"]
zps shbeo exupl jnz erdtn qmxx bvg ytbc gum
```

```
VigenereDecrypt[cipher,"vigenere"]
the quick brown fox jumps over the lazy dog
```

RANDOM – OBJECTIVE CHANCE

At the latest and current development stage, a text is no longer rotated with a secret number, or with a secret word (a rotating number), but with a secret text (a rotating word).

(You won't, incidentally, find these specific word plays in literature about coding, but to our minds they offer an accessible way for architects into what is after all a complex subject matter. Conventional representations tend to employ a very specific vocabulary, which demands extensive familiarisation, and the representations to us look too functionalist and problem orientated.)

What, then, do we mean by a 'rotating number'? You might imagine this similar to a roulette table: 12, 4, 23, 17, 8... – these numbers are there without any system, without reason, without cause. They are something about which nobody knows, which no-one can predict, which belongs to nobody. These numbers appear suddenly out of nowhere. That's the whole point of roulette: you don't know what comes up next. And that's exactly why these are not numbers, but ciphers. With numbers, you can calculate. Numbers have the primes as their cause, they come in a logical order, you can work with them. None of which is true for the ciphers of roulette. Numbers are precise and they reveal something; ciphers encrypt, and they can mean anything.

So when, using the Caesar cipher, we are rotating a text with a number, we are in our minds stepping up to a roulette table and producing a cipher with which we encrypt the text. We can summarise this as follows: with a number you can twist a text out of space. And technically we need two alphabets to do this.

The Viginère cipher goes one step further: we metaphorically go up to the roulette table again, and now we generate a sequence of ciphers – the code word – and use this to encrypt the text. We can summarise this as follows: with a sequence of numbers we can twist a text out of time. Technically, we need a movable disk with two alphabets to do this.

With today's encryption, we go yet another step further: once more, we step up to our imaginary roulette table and generate a sequence of ciphers, a secret text that encrypts each letter of the source text individually. Technically we need for this a software which automates the 'roulette table', that is in which each segment of the table plays roulette by itself and rotates around its own axis.

To illustrate, here's a simple example. Let's take an arbitrary number:

```
m=120;
```

We dissemble it into its constituent prime numbers:

```
fm=FactorInteger[m][[All,1]]
{2,3,5}
```

We now need a second number (the additive element), which is alien to the first number, meaning that it is constituted of different prime numbers:

```
c =7 11
77
```

We choose a third number (the multiplicative element). This has to be divisible by all prime factors of *m*:

```
a=(2 3 5) 2
60
```

We also need a starting value for our numbers sequence:

```
seed=20;
```

These numbers are the hidden mechanics of our software 'roulette'. They are chosen in such a way that the machine runs in the least predictable manner, and produces the most accidental results.

Using the modulor function, we now rotate the numbers with addition and multiplication, and obtain our first cipher:

```
MOD[(a+1)seed+c,m]
97
```

With this result, we can now generate the next cipher:

```
MOD[(a+1)%+c,m]
114
```

If we repeat this procedure *m* times, we obtain a sequence of all numbers up to 120, and there is no system to them. We have relieved these numbers of all their meaning. They have 'forgotten' everything they once stood for: we have taken them 'out' of time. Like a deck of cards, we've given them a good shuffle. Each number has the same probability; and probability, in this sequence of numbers, is objective. We therefore speak of an **objective probability**. Unlike probability when used as a quality to describe the interplay of separate parts, we can, with this numbers sequence, grasp this probability like an object: we can shape it, as a sculptor would shape clay.

```
rand=Rest@NestList[MOD[(a+1)#+c,m]&,seed,m]

{97,114,71,88,45,62,19,36,113,10,87,104,61,
 78,35,52,9,26,103,120,77,94,51,68,25,42,119,
 16,93,110,67,84,41,58,15,32,109,6,83,100,57,
 74,31,48,5,22,99,116,73,90,47,64,21,38,115,
 12,89,106,63,80,37,54,11,28,105,2,79,96,53,
 70,27,44,1,18,95,112,69,86,43,60,17,34,111,
 8,85,102,59,76,33,50,7,24,101,118,75,92,49,
 66,23,40,117,14,91,108,65,82,39,56,13,30,107,
 4,81,98,55,72,29,46,3,20}
```

We now have different ways of representing this meaningless sequence of numbers. For example, as a sequence of letters: our 'secret text':

```
FromCharacterCode[
 Round[26 rand/Length@rand+.5]+96]

vyptjnehycswnqhlbfwzqulofjzduxosimdgxbrvmqgkbe
vzptkneiyctwnrilcgwarulpfjaduyosjndhybswmqhkbf
vzqtkoeizdtxorimcgxarvlpgjae
```

Or in an arrangement of 120 pixels, a 'secret image':

```
Image@Partition[
 Round[2 rand/Length@rand-.5],12]
```

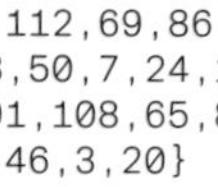

And here we see the weakness of our procedure: these are only pseudo-ciphers that we have generated. And of course they must be, because we always have, as in all encryption methods, a machine in the background. But we are thinking it in the way we've described, and so we can hide our 'roulette machine' better and better, in more and more complicated combinations of prime numbers:

```
LCG[m_,n_]:=
 Module[{fm,pr,c,a,seed},
  fm=FactorInteger[m][[All,1]];
  pr=Prime[Range@12];
  c=Times@@Complement[pr,fm];
  a=Times@@fm 2;
  seed=1;
  Rest@NestList[MOD[(a+1)#+c,m]&,seed,n]
]
```

```
n=Times@@{2,2,2,2,2,2,3,3,3,7,7,7,7};
rand=LCG[n,1000];
Image@Partition[Round[2 rand/n-.5],48]

[…]
```

[…]

ENCRYPTION OF A TEXT

Let's do the encryption again, as we did before. First, translate the text into a sequence of numbers:

```
plainText

the quick brown fox jumps over the lazy dog
```

```
p1=Char2Pos@plainText;
b1=Position[p1," "];
n1=Cases[p1,_Integer]

{20,8,5,17,21,9,3,11,2,18,15,23,14,6,15,24,10,
 21,13,16,19,15,22,5,18,20,8,5,12,1,26,25,4,
 15,7}
```

Now, with our automatic 'roulette' discussed above, we generate a key:

```
n=Times@@{2,2,2,2,2,2,3,3,3,7,7,7,7}
rand=LCG[n,Length@n1]
k1=Round[26 rand/n+.5]

4148928
{2142510,1702943,1680100,3887373,654890,
 3872011,3498048,753689,3972070,3705207,
 1766492,2932837,2497890,2867747,1114168,
 1421361,2639198,2432143,1428180,3218813,
 1912282,2878203,2002928,2285257,1389654,
 4093031,1540108,285909,1551122,1222099,
 2297640,2442209,2283790,1264959,1791812}
{14,11,11,25,5,25,22,5,25,24,12,19,16,18,7,9,
 17,16,9,21,12,19,13,15,9,26,10,2,10,8,15,16,
 15,8,12}
```

Here is the key, which is 'out of space' and 'out of time':

```
key=Pos2Char@k1

nkkyeyveyxlsprgiqpiulsmoizjbjhopohl
```

Now rotate both sequences in the alphabet, and render the results as characters:

```
n2= MOD[n1+k2,26];
c1=Insert[n2," ",MapIndexed[#1-#2+1&,b1]];
cipher=Pos2Char@c1

hsp pzhyp apapd xvg akvke hita trg vioo sws
```

TAKING THINGS OUT OF THE WORLD
AND PUTTING THEM BACK IN AGAIN

With ciphers we can 'remove' from our world texts, pictures, in fact any information at all. Once we do so, they are simply no longer there. They are encrypted, the ciphers have swallowed them. This we also want to illustrate with a simplifying example.

This is an image, a cipher. An objective probability:

```
rand=RandomInteger[1,{450,600}];
Image@rand
```

We can measure its meaninglessness: mean and standard deviation are 0.5. They are also 0.5 in any other sufficiently large section of white noise. Of course, these values vary when we zoom in: each individual element in our example is either 1 or 0 (here rendered as pixels or dots, black or white). We can conduct further analyses and they will all show that nothing of significance can be found in white noise: it is random.

```
key=Flatten[rand];
len=Length[key]
sum=Total[key];
sum/len//N
StandardDeviation[key]//N

270000
0.499304
0.5
```

With a meaningful picture, this is different:

```
eastwood=
```

```
;
```

Here now is a 'machine' that rounds up the meaning, and so in a sense eats it up: a *modulo operation* calculates the rest b of a division n by m.

```
Mod[n,m]
Mod[1, 2]
Mod[0, 2]
Mod[2, 2]

Mod[n,120]
1
0
0
```

We can modulate a list of elements:

```
Mod[{1,0,2,4,2,1,0,3},2]

{1,0,0,0,0,1,0,1}
```

Here are the first 300 elements of our picture of Clint Eastwood:

```
data=Flatten@ImageData@eastwood;
data//Short

{1,1,1,1,1,1,1,1,1,1,1,
 <<269978>>,1,1,1,1,1,1,1,1,1,1,1}
```

These are the first 300 elements of white noise:

```
key//Short

{0,1,1,0,0,0,1,1,0,0,0,
 <<269978>>,0,0,1,1,1,1,0,1,1,1,0}
```

Now, by adding the two pictures together and modulating them you get this result:

```
crypt=Mod[key+data,2];
%//Short

{1,0,0,1,1,1,0,0,1,1,1,
 <<269978>>,1,1,0,0,0,0,1,0,0,0,1}
```

```
Image[Partition[crypt,600]]
```

It's white noise. The meaning has disappeared: Clint Eastwood is no longer on this planet, he has been pushed over the entropic horizon, where meaning has faded out into nothingness and thermal death. He has been encrypted.

The only way to get him back is to reverse exactly the process of encryption with the random key image:

```
decrypt=Mod[key+ crypt, 2];
Image[Partition[decrypt,600],ImageSize → 300]
```

As long as we can keep the key – a specific instance of white noise – secret, we can take any meaningful 'thing' away from this world. It can then not be identified, by nothing and nobody. It can't be seen, or read, it just doesn't exist in this world any longer, is no longer subject to any kind of analysis. And the process really is as simple as we just described it here.

WHAT IS INFORMATION?
This raises the fundamental question: what is information? We try to approach an answer to this in the *Conclusion* to this *Atlas*, which bears the title What Is Information?, and so we won't attempt to do so here, but we are willing in this context to say that it always plays out in front of white noise.

What matters to us at this juncture is that *data* is stable. This is the case with cables, antennas, processors, databases: the engineering takes care that a 1 is always a 1 and a 0 is always a 0. It's the physics of communication, and today we think that all classical physics, all analysis, even all psychoanalysis is stable like this.

But to communicate on the basis of meaningless zeros and ones constitutes and act of will. It takes place outside of classical physics, out of nature, out of space and time. Therefore, we have to take intellectual care to keep track of the sequence of bits. In contrast to classical physics and engineering of data, we would call the meaning of the constitution of bits of data *information*.

This constitution is pure intellect, it can be freely manipulated, because it is not dependent on any structure or form; not on matter nor on energy, not on Newton's physics or Carnot's thermodynamics. So we can do with the bits whatever we want.

The *technics* used to constitute information is coding. And our coding examples of cryptography show the nature of code: it acts beyond time and space; it freely constitutes meaning; it is a quantum writing in line with quantum mechanics and quantum physics beyond classical physics. It is writing in a new world, a world we do not know.

Because we don't know this word, we first start to mimic the classical world. This is why it is so complicated to see the difference between the classical physics of data and the quantum thinking of information. But now, in 2019, we are at a stage of understanding information where we start to fake classical physics and classical reasoning. In antique Greece these 'faking people' were called *sophists*: they had become sophisticated in using the Greek language to any purpose at all, even to the point of defending the indefensible or arguing the absurd. Today, the Cambridge Analytica example we give in the main body of this chapter illustrates how you can become sophisticated in 'talking in code'. And what is at stake, now as it has always been since ancient times, is our success or failure at establishing an ethics that allows 'good fakes' but banishes 'bad fakes'. It means learning to constitute a just state of coexistence in our quantum world, much as Plato had developed it in his *Republic* (known in Greek as *Politeia*) for his world.

Programming is cryptography. Current information technology uses classical physical methods to make sure that information stays 'in this world'. With quantum computing and quantum cryptography, information technology moves towards current physics. Information itself remains cryptic, as it already is today, and programming remains cryptography: a new way of writing, as if from a different world.

SYMMETRICAL ENCRYPTION
This is how encryption works today. We differentiate between symmetrical (as in the example above) and asymmetrical processes of encryption.

☐ 693↘

Here we generate a symmetric key:

```
key=GenerateSymmetricKey[
 Method→<|"Cipher"→"AES256"|>]
SymmetricKey[
```

```
 cipher: AES256
 block mode: CBC
 key length: 256 bits
]
```

We now encrypt the image of Clint Eastwood with this key:

```
crypt=Encrypt[key, 
```

```
]
EncryptedObject[
```

```
 data length: 6.2 kB
 IV length: 128 bits
 original form: Expression
]
```

If we render the encrypted data, we get white noise:

```
Image@Partition[Flatten[
 IntegerDigits[#,2]&/@
  Normal[crypt[[1,1]]]],300]
```

With symmetric encryption, sender and receiver have the same key. The sender can use this key to get the image back:

```
decrypt=Decrypt[key,crypt]
```

The problem here always lies in the fact that the key has to be delivered at the same time as the encrypted content, and that means it can be intercepted and copied without anyone noticing.

ASYMMETRICAL ENCRYPTION
In 1976, it became possible for the first time to generate what are known as *asymmetric keys*. Here now we distinguish between a *public* and a *private* key. A public key can be used by anyone who wants to

send something to the person who has a private key: a document that has been encrypted with a public key can only be decrypted with a corresponding private key.

This is the process: the recipient, not the sender, generates an asymmetrical pair of encryption keys:

□ ↖549

```
keys=GenerateAsymmetricKeyPair[]
<|PrivateKey→PrivateKey[
    type: RSA
    public module size: 2048 bits
    private exponent size: 2048 bits
],
PublicKey→PublicKey[
    type: RSA
    public module size: 2048 bits
]|>
```

The public key is sent by the recipient of the data to the sender of the data. The sender encrypts the data with the public key:

```
package=Encrypt[keys["PublicKey"],
 "wo ist wendelin?"]
EncryptedObject[
    data length: 256 bytes
    original form: String
]
```

The data packet and the public key can both be intercepted in transit, but they are not readable:

```
Decrypt[keys["PublicKey"],package]
Decrypt::key: Key is not compatible with the
 encrypted data.
$Failed
```

Only the recipient has the private key, which they never had to give away, and so can read the message:

```
Decrypt[keys["PrivateKey"],package]
wo ist wendelin?
```

Today, 80% of communication on the Internet works with asymmetric keys. It's important to note that with comparatively short keys (in this example 256 bits) encryption is not 100% secure. But these procedures make it much, much more difficult to decrypt a text without the key. And the longer the key, the more difficult is the decryption.

TRANSPARENCY – HOW TO ACCESS THINGS

Earlier we said that encryption is a way to push things over the energetic entropic horizon; decryption we described as a way of pulling them back, which we can therefore characterise as negentropic. Information, coding, and communication is always about encryption and decryption. It jumps across the entropic horizon by nature. In this section, we want to focus on techniques, which we shall call analytic, of the 'safe' entropic ground, which we shall call nature. (More on this also in our chapter on Big Data & Machine Learning.)

THE RATIONAL AND THE REAL

This is safe to say: if you are in a world of space, you *count* different *objects* by numbers, and you bring these objects into proportions to each other according to these numbers. If you are in a world of time, you *measure* different *properties*, and you are using sets of properties to classify or construct objects in time. This is what we trust in. This is analytical science, this is engineering, this is art. It is what we know and are familiar with.

Here we want to give a very simple but comprehensive introduction to the mathematics behind this thinking.

We want to start with a typical one-dimensional sequence of numbers, which results from the measurement of a single property:

```
values={6.0,4.1,3.2,5.6,6.2,6.1,4.0,3.5,2.9,
 4.1,5.3,3.4,2.7,4.6,2.9,2.2,1.5};
```

With this sequence of numbers we have the *rationals of the measurements* in time, taken from the generic background of space. These points are not real, they are isolated indicators of something we cannot see:

```
vi = MapIndexed[{#2[[1]], #1} &, values];
Graphics[{
  RGBColor[0.3, 0.43, 0.65], PointSize[.02],
   Point@vi
 },
  PlotRange → {{0, 18}, {0, 7}}, Axes → True]
```

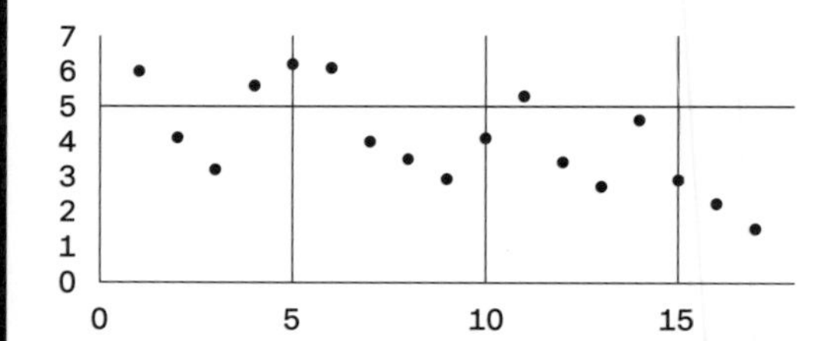

With these rationals we can *develop* an *idea* of the *kind* of thing we observed. The simplest way to do so is by the mean value:

```
v1=values[[1;;6]];
lm1 =LeastSquaresFit[v1,{1}]
5.2
```

```
vi = MapIndexed[{#2[[1]], #1} &, v1];
Graphics[{
  RGBColor[0.3, 0.43, 0.65], PointSize[.02],
  Point@vi, Line[{{0, lm1}, {Length@vi,
   lm1}}]
 },
  PlotRange → {{0, 18}, {0, 7}}, Axes → True]
[…]
```

[…]

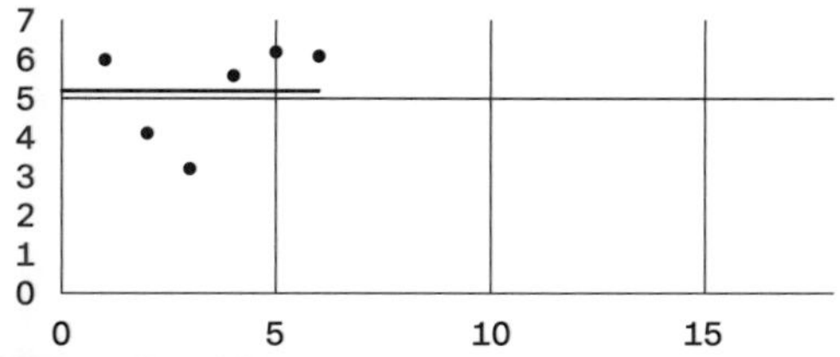

If all measurements are of the same kind, this idea will become more and more stable, the more measurements are taken. (Here too we can refer you to our discussion of the law of large numbers in our chapter on Big Data & Machine Learning.)

```
v2=values[[1;;-1]];
lm1 =LeastSquaresFit[v2,{1}]
4.01765
```

```
vi = MapIndexed[{#2[[1]], #1} &, v2];
Graphics[{
  RGBColor[0.3, 0.43, 0.65], PointSize[.02],
  Point@vi, Line[{{0, lm1}, {Length@vi,
   lm1}}]
 },
  PlotRange → {{0, 18}, {0, 7}}, Axes → True]
```

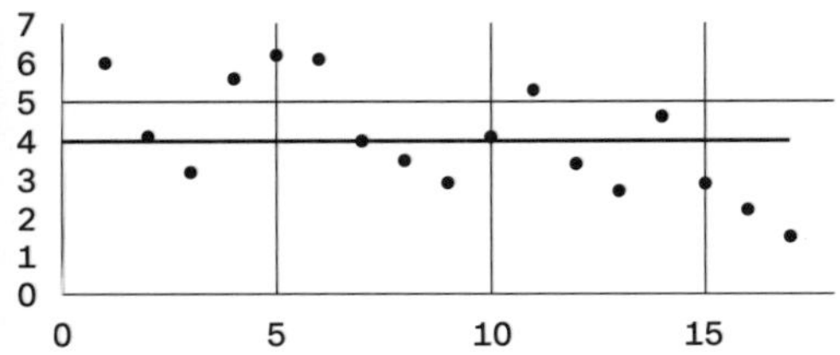

It is important to keep in mind that this line is not a ratio, like the measurements, but a fictional idea. And: we cannot see either of them, because they exist in time; what we see are only their projections in space.

Points are rationals of projections.

A line is a projection of an idea.

Now, as a next step, we can develop better ideas. This is an idea of the first order, about the kind of object we are measuring:

```
lm2 =LeastSquaresFit[values, {1,x}]
5.67206 - 0.183824 x
```

```
vi = MapIndexed[{#2[[1]], #1} &, v2];
Show[
 Plot[lm2, {x, 1, 17}, PlotStyle →
  RGBColor[0.3, 0.43, 0.65],
    PlotRange → {{0, 18}, {0, 7}},
     AspectRatio → 7 / 18],
 Graphics[{
   RGBColor[0.3, 0.43, 0.65], PointSize[.02],
    Point@vi
  },
   PlotRange → {{0, 18}, {0, 7}},
    Axes → True]
]


[…]
```

[…]

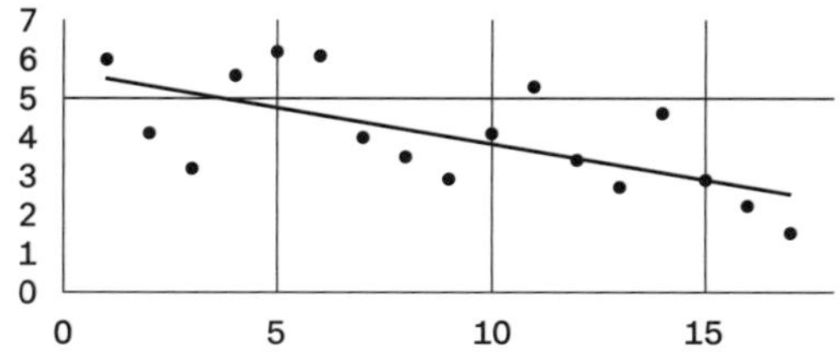

We can also have an idea of the 6th order, which fits a lot better to the rational that we measured:

```
lm6 =LeastSquaresFit[values,x^#&/@ Range[0,6]]
14.3344 - 13.1324 x + 5.80691 x^2 - 1.13476 x^3
 + 0.108631 x^4 - 0.005007 x^5 + 0.000089 x^6
```

■ ↖549

```
vi = MapIndexed[{#2[[1]], #1} &, v2];
Show[
 Plot[lm6, {x, 1, 17}, PlotStyle →
  RGBColor[0.3, 0.43, 0.65],
    PlotRange → {{0, 18}, {0, 7}},
     AspectRatio → 7 / 18],
 Graphics[{
   RGBColor[0.3, 0.43, 0.65], PointSize[.02],
    Point@vi
  },
   PlotRange → {{0, 18}, {0, 7}},
    Axes → True]
]
```

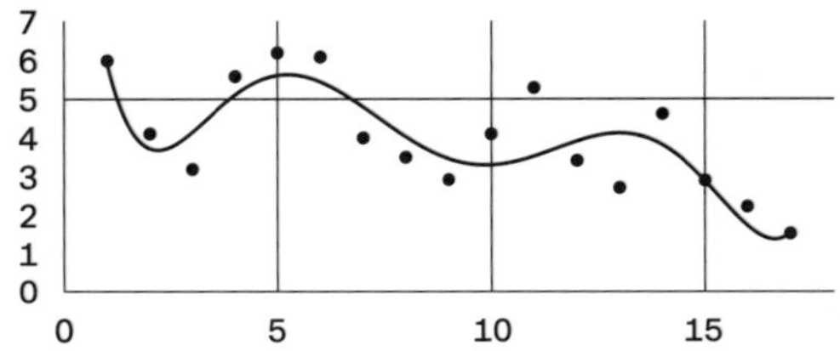

An idea can be *realised*, by using its *polynomial function*. Functions are *producing* points in between the measured ratio of things:

```
lm6/.x→2.2
3.76245
```

We can now realise our idea by the production of multiple points:

```
pts={#,lm6/.x→#}&/@Range[0,17,4/3];

vi = MapIndexed[{#2[[1]], #1} &, v2];
Show[
 Plot[lm6, {x, 1, 17}, PlotStyle →
  RGBColor[0.3, 0.43, 0.65],
    PlotRange → {{0, 18}, {0, 7}},
     AspectRatio → 7 / 18],
 Graphics[{
   RGBColor[0.8, 0.8, 0.8], PointSize[.02],
    Point@vi,
   RGBColor[0.3, 0.43, 0.65], PointSize[.02],
    Point@pts
  },
PlotRange → {{0, 18}, {0, 7}}, Axes → True]
]


[…]
```

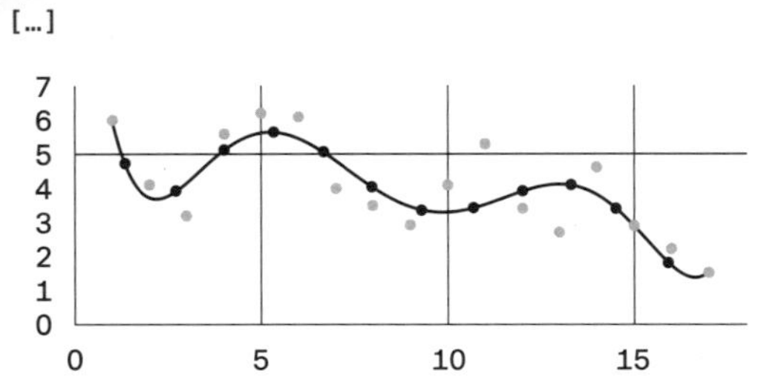

We can produce or realise an infinite number of points (here in black). These points are real, because they follow an idea, and they are *produced*, they are *systematic*. In strict contrast to the rational points measured (grey), which are just there and outside of any systematic control. They, the grey points, are elements of the ratio, not part of the realm of nature. They are rational, not real.

Measured things idealised as a line are called a *linearity* or a *dimension*.

EVERYTHING IS A PROJECTION FROM OUTSIDE OF PASSING TIME

You might think these games with numbers are just for specialists, or splitting hairs, or both. But they're not: everything we see works like that. Take for example this map of Switzerland:

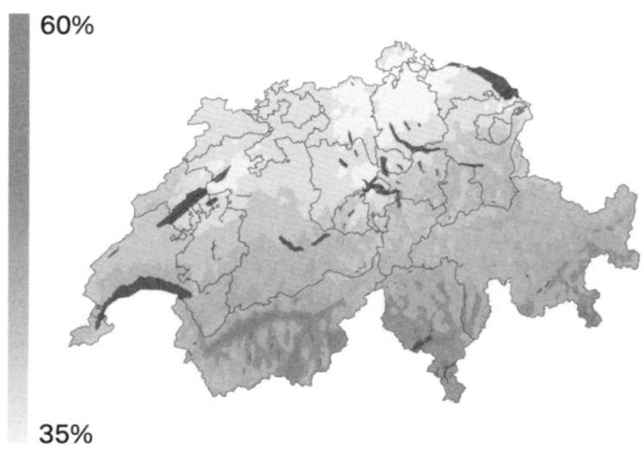

It's a two-dimensional representation of measurements of a few weather stations, used to produce a continuous field of colors all over the country. We see it, we've made things transparent, and because they are visible we in most cases trust them, intuitively.

With a temperature map of Switzerland it is more or less clear: this picture is a fiction. It is produced like the black line in the discussion of the linear function above, an interpolation between the rational weather stations, to create the impression of a continuous flow of temperature values across the country. In the scheme of our function, the grey dots are the weather stations, the map itself corresponds to the black dots: the weather stations are rational, the map is real.

Let's take a look then at the following picture: the sensor of the camera has measured a grid, not of temperature values, but of colour values. They are rational like the pixels on a computer screen, and like the grey dots in the function above. But what we see is the continuous flow of colour values of that specific view of the Amazon River, which makes the image real.

To illustrate this distinction, let's zoom in and look at the ratio of the pixels of the picture:

```
ImageResize[img, 512, Resampling→“Nearest”]
```

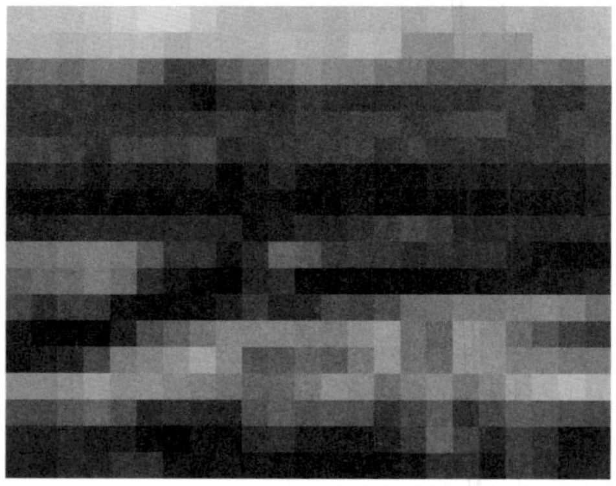

What you see on every screen and on every prin- is an interpolation between these rational points o- measurements, to yield a fictional picture of reality

```
ImageResize[img, 512, Resampling→“Gaussian”]
```

PATTERN RECOGNITION AND THE IDEA OF THINGS

We made the distinction a moment ago between rational and real points, between measured points and the ideal points of production. And there is always a difference. This is in fact what you want to know: is this rational point part of my ideal system or not? Do I control this point as part of my production or not?

This is what pattern recognition is about: is the pattern a measurement part of my system; does it share my idea, or not. Or: is it a car, a cat, or a dog. Is it healthy or not. Does it fit or not. Is it criminal, or not…

And this control becomes an important and challenging issue today: as we discussed, information is negentropic, it comes out of apparently 'nowhere', all of a sudden. Any mail, any text message, any phone call, image, film, or pop-up: there is no reason for it other than someone's decision somewhere to write a certain address, dial a certain number, or program a certain action, in space and time. We are still used to real things in nature which always have a reason that we can analyse. But things of the ratio don't and they can't be; and so they are challenging this natural game. It is not possible to control them, which is why it is of greatest importance to negotiate them.

The claim to transparency, adequate for real things in nature, turns out to be too orthodox for things in the new ratio. Tying them back to the reality of nature is not adequate. Analysis and control are important aspects of the negotiation and cultivation of the new ratio, but things become inadequate and tyrannic if they are thought of as absolute, while the categorical challenges of the new digital ratio are ignored.

And if you read the arguments above carefully, you will understand that control and not-control, transparency and non-transparency are always just two sides of the same realistic coin. The ratio is not part of the real. It is invisible to the real. And because of this you have to be very careful when reading texts on cybernetics, structuralism, or post-structuralism: very often they simplify and are therefore misleading.

So, let's have a closer look at the methods of transparency and control. For example, you can measure the distance of rational points to the linear idea and define a threshold: if the distance is less than 1, the measurement is part of the idea, if not, it is out:

```
pts={#,lm6/x→#}&/@Range[0,17,4/3];
vi=MapIndexed[{#2[[1]],#1}&,v2];
r={#,lm6/.x→#}&/@vi[[All,1]];
d=EuclideanDistance@@@Transpose[{r,vi}];
s=Select[d,#>1&];
red=vi[[Flatten[Position[d,#]&/@s]]];
Show[
 Plot[lm6, {x, 1, 17}, PlotStyle →
  RGBColor[0.3, 0.43, 0.65],
   PlotRange → {{0, 18}, {0, 7}}, AspectRatio
    → 7 / 18],
 Graphics[{
   RGBColor[0.8, 0.8, 0.8], PointSize[.02],
    Point@vi,
   RGBColor[1, 0, 0], PointSize[.02],
    Point@red
  },
   PlotRange → {{0, 18}, {0, 7}},
    Axes → True]
]
```

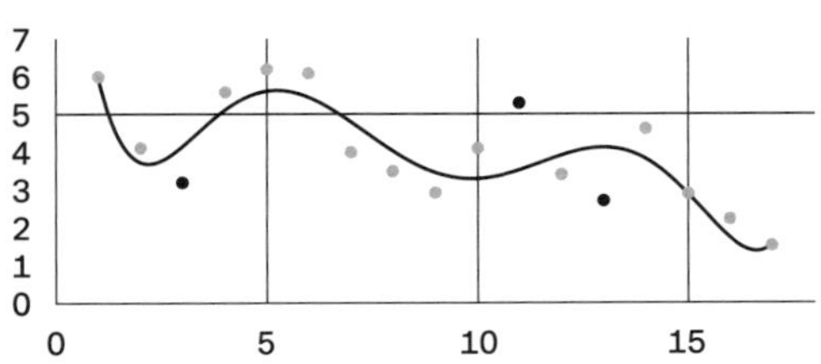

Here, for example, we are looking for turning points in a sequence of measurements:

```
max=Position[MaxDetect@values,1]
{{1},{5},{11},{14}}
```

```
vals = MapIndexed[{#2[[1]], #1} &, values];
Graphics[{
  RGBColor[0.3, 0.43, 0.65], Line@vals,
  RGBColor[0.8, 0.8, 0.8], PointSize[.02],
   Point@vals,
  Red, Point@Extract[vals, max]
 },
  PlotRange → {{0, 18}, {0, 7}}, Axes → True]
```

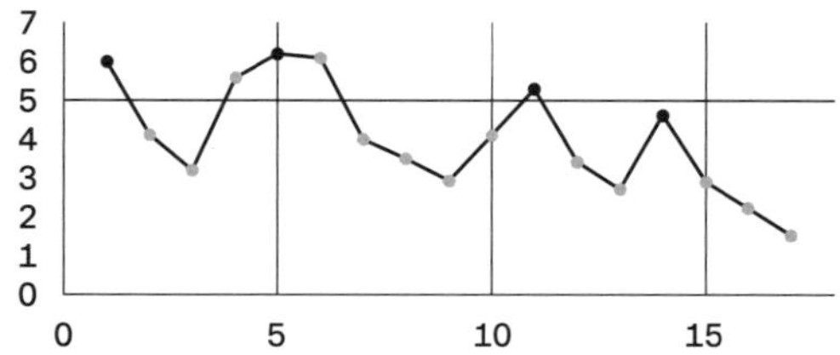

These peaks are used to detect interesting points of control in the picture of a security camera:

img=  ;

```
ImageKeypoints[img,KeypointStrength→.005];
Rasterize@HighlightImage[img,{White,%}]
```

Using comparable methods, faces can be detected…

img=  ;

```
FindFaces[img];
Rasterize@Show[img,Graphics[Rectangle@@@%]]
```

...or text characters recognised:

```
TextRecognize[
```

```
]

Ausbau der Wasserkraft
bedroht unberiihrte Tiiler

"_mmd ..- .M m _
nn an! wi :mm df' ww. mm... M Mmm".

MRI( lkll Humbul! n .In "an xhtml "hr-m
"Mlm Mmdrl *In we" Ima" "m uh bu mm ...l

I .harm |M~nm~~vnu~~n 'un
'"me ' "- m- umm'wm .ma mm

umm m .u 'uw-qu. Mm
"_ u' ~`un` nal-.- n- u-_fm- ..1
```

Here we also see the difficulties of identifying artefacts properly. The tolerance of your idea has to be adjusted properly, and you always face this conflict of interests: if you are too strict, you lose members, if you are too soft, you lose control. And in the next section we will discuss why this is so.

THE LIMITS OF LINEARITY – WHEN IDEAS DO NOT FIT

This is what happens if you refine your idea to an order as high as the number of your measurements; in other words, if you try to get 100% control over all measurements:

```
lm6=LeastSquaresFit[values,x#&/@ Range[0,17]]

-12811.3 + 41214.2 x - 56245.6 x^2
 + 43920.8 x^3 - 22179.0 x^4 + 7722.19 x^5
 - 1920.79 x^6 + 347.094 x^7 - 45.5400 x^8
 + 4.22776 x^9 - 0.25416 x^10 + 0.00637 x^11
 + 0.00041 x^12 - 0.00005 x^13 + 2.905*10^-6 x^14
 - 8.9 10^-8 x^15 + 1.5 10^-9 x^16 - 1.2 10^-11 x^17
```

```
vi = MapIndexed[{#2[[1]], #1} &, v2];
Show[
 Plot[lm17, {x, 1, 17}, PlotStyle →
  RGBColor[0.3, 0.43, 0.65],
   PlotRange → {{0, 18}, {0, 7}}, AspectRatio
    → 7 / 18],
 Graphics[{
   RGBColor[0.3, 0.43, 0.65], PointSize[.02],
    Point@vi
  },
   PlotRange → {{0, 18}, {0, 7}},
    Axes → True]
]
```

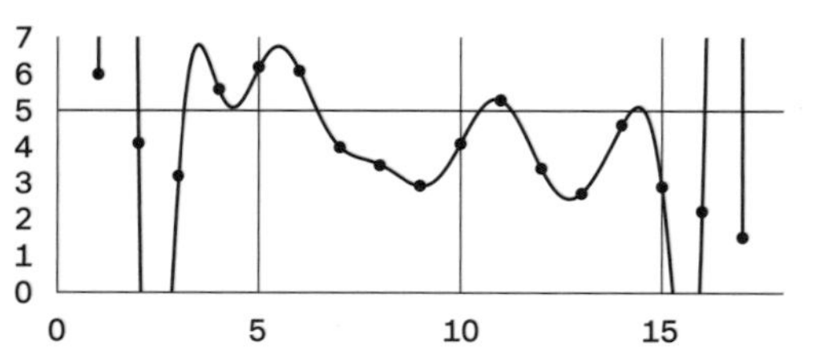

□ ↖175

We observe an interesting behaviour: on the one hand, the system meets all rational points in their locality, but, on the other hand, globally the line oscillates enormously, especially between extreme points. There principally is no way around this, other than to relax the system, lose some control, and live with divergences:

```
lm6=LeastSquaresFit[values,x#&/@ Range[0,6 ]

14.3344 - 13.1324 x + 5.80691 x^2 - 1.13476 x^3
 + 0.108631 x^4 - 0.005006 x^5 + 0.000088 x^6
```

```
vi = MapIndexed[{#2[[1]], #1} &, v2];
Show[
 Plot[lm17, {x, 1, 17}, PlotStyle →
  RGBColor[0.3, 0.43, 0.65],
   PlotRange → {{0, 18}, {0, 7}}, AspectRatio
    → 7 / 18],
 Graphics[{
   RGBColor[0.3, 0.43, 0.65], PointSize[.02],
    Point@vi
  },
   PlotRange → {{0, 18}, {0, 7}},
    Axes → True]
]
```

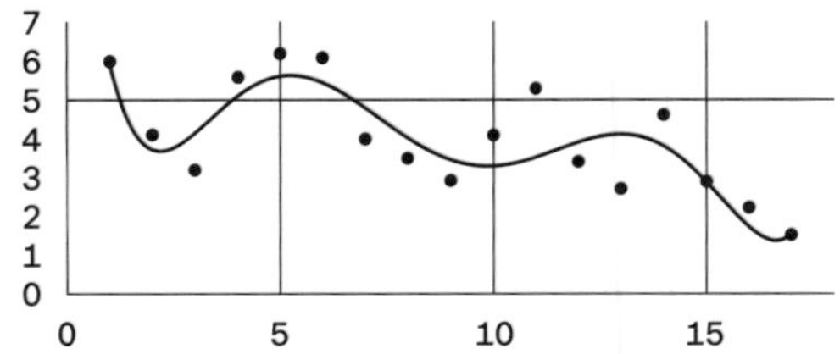

This is the fundamental problem with every system, with every type of analytics and with every kind of control: we can't get around this discrepancy between local precision and global validity of a linearity with any kind of analysis of rational values.

Why is that?

WHERE TO GO FOR THE NEXT STEP

Let us make a first principal observation: it is very common for people to say that time is the 'fourth dimension'. But this conception of time does not actually work, if you think about it: in *space* you can walk in circles; but *time* always passes. They are of totally different categories. If space exists in three dimensions, we suggest, time cannot be a dimension, but is rather a *dimensionality*. It is the ability to be projected to a dimension. This is what perspective projection of the Renaissance does: it is able to project the three dimensions of space to a two-dimensional plane, because the dimensions are thought, measured and calculated as *dimensionalities*. And because they are thought of as dimensionalities in time, these virtual objects can be moved, scaled, and rotated, and then projected to any perspective. This projection is like a snapshot into the dimensions of space of a virtual object in time, passing by in time.

The continuous line you see in Cartesian space is a projection of an idea. As we have seen, and as we discuss in detail in our chapter on Graphics & Graphics, this idea is circular, and like any circle it cannot be projected to a line without distortion. (You know this from the different maps of our spherical globe, which are always distorted, such as the widely used Mercator projection, which vastly exaggerates the size of regions around the poles.)

An idea simply does not fit space. We could leave it at that and relax our control. But we want to go an important step further, which is interesting for architects, because it opens up a new realm to model in.

What we see as points are objects in space, as we understand it in the Cartesian sense. Space is linear and infinite, and we can walk around it in circles, back and forth, again and again. Space is made of *l near circles*, which is like *talking* in our language: it goes around corners, and it passes in time.

What we see as a line is a projection of an object in *time*, an idea. And as with the stars, or a clock, you cannot grasp time. Time goes in circles and passes by (you can never get a single moment back). Time is a *circular line*. A linearity. Like *watching* with your eyes: your view is straight, and you can do it again and again.

Mathematics distinguishes between the frequency domain, which is about circular lines, and the time domain, which is about linear circles. Both domains are orthogonal to each other: *you cannot see what you hear, and you cannot hear what you see.*

We also have the different parts of numbers representing this dichotomy of line and circle, or of time and frequency domains: you have a numerator and denominator of the rational numbers, or the real and the imaginary part of a complex number in the complex plane introduced by German mathematician and physicist Carl Friedrich Gauss (1777–1855) in 1811.

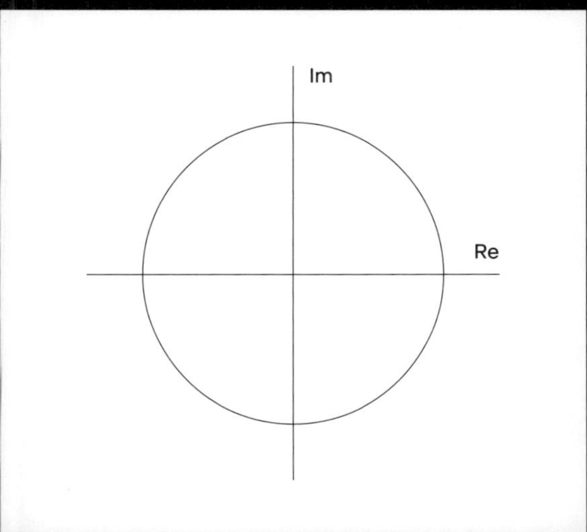

Here, the real axis (Re) is the linear circle. This is where you *watch* (sense globally) and *talk* (locally); the imaginary axis (Im) is the circular line: this is where you *listen* (sense globally) and *show* (act locally).

We are highlighting this symmetry of our senses and actions here because it gives us a lot of freedom as architects. Normally, we think of ratio as part of the real. Or we think that our mind is part of the body, and vice versa. If we do so, we are thinking on simple flat lines. But that's not what they are. They are orthogonal to each other, and they open up a plane to move on freely. If you think in flat lines, you always have to decide: are these my sensations of reality, or is this my intellect. If you think in the complex plane, you always have both, sense and intellect.

If we put our senses and actions to the complex plane, then *communication* works like a rotation: you talk (Re) – physics – someone is listening (Im) – thinking – and talks back (-Re) – physics – you are listening (-Im) – thinking – ... This notion of communication is not about control, it is about the negotiations of active subjects, respecting each other.

In the diagram below, the colouring shows a function in the complex domain. What you see is different from a polygon in Cartesian space. The points are circles represented by a spectrum of colours. This is what the points 'see'. And they are communicating not with one line, but with an infinity of curved lines. This is how they 'talk'. And every point is taking into account when another point moves or a new point is added. Thus, these points are global localities, they 'know' and they are active subjects, not passive elements you can push around.

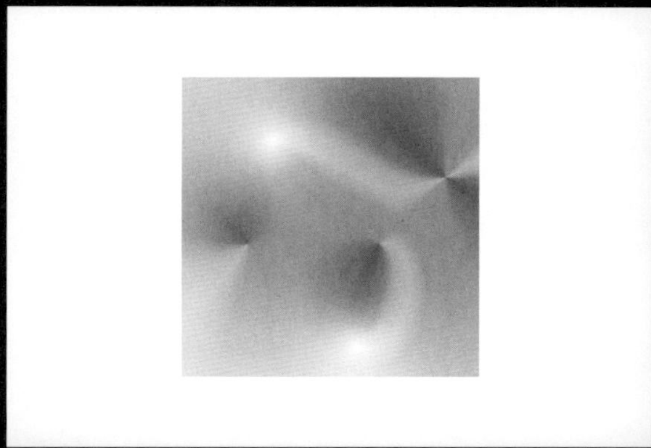

All of this looks very complex. And it is. But you are already familiar with it from splines in your CAD system, for example. A spline does not create a global linearity, but builds on local linearities for each point just with its neighbours. The resulting curve is a morphing of these logical linearities. They negotiate. And the result adapts to the measured points much better than a single global control. ↖363

The lines of linearity were systems, which were always of global control according to classical physics. This line is not a system any longer, it is a line of quantum geometry, which constitutes active points of identity, talking and negotiating with their neighbours. And you see, if you render it, that it fits much better to the local conditions. This is something which was invented in the 20th century and that can only be thought and done with computers.

```
vi = MapIndexed[{#2[[1]], #1} &, v2];
Show[
 Plot[lm6, {x, 1, 17},
  PlotStyle → Directive[Thickness@.005,
   RGBColor[0.8, 0.8, 0.8]],
    PlotRange → {{0, 18}, {0, 7}},
     AspectRatio → 7 / 18],
 Graphics[{
   RGBColor[0.8, 0.8, 0.8], Thickness@.002,
    Line@vi,
   RGBColor[0.3, 0.43, 0.65], PointSize[.02],
    Point@vi,
   Thickness@.005, BSplineCurve[vi,
    SplineDegree → 6]
  },
   PlotRange → {{0, 18}, {0, 7}},
    Axes → True]
]
```

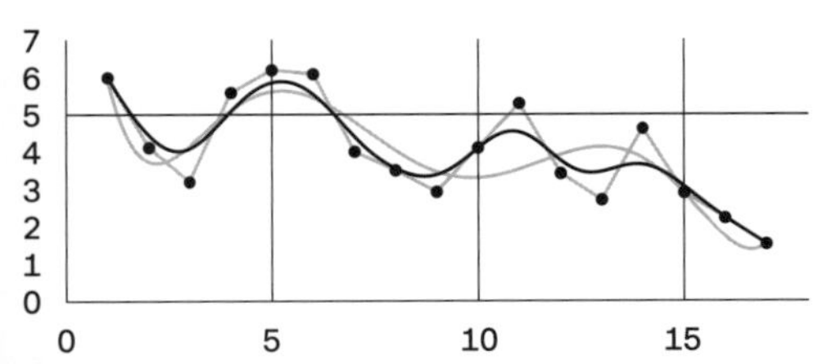

DIGITAL INTEGRITY

HASH CODES AND HOW TO KEEP YOUR DIGITAL INTEGRITY

If everything so easily can be copied, manipulated, and faked, it becomes imperative to have a tool to prove the integrity of your digital artefacts, or even your own personal integrity.

The *hash function* is a bit like a digital fingerprint of data. The algorithms (in this case 'MD2') are simple, and they work very fast. A hash more or less tumbles through the data, and in doing so fetches its particular corners and edges. It's an *integral* on the path of data: it's like a quantum physical path integral.

This is the hash of a small text:

```
Hash["wo ist wendelin?","MD2"]
143060098784512726050642901411885202350
```

This is a hash of an image:

Hash[ , "MD2"]

```
269568222515940709605433553893442396378
```

Take the following example: the text *On the Origin of Species* by the English naturalist Charles Darwin (1809–1882) contains close to 1,000,000 letters.

```
darwin=ExampleData[
 {"Text","OriginOfSpecies"}];
StringLength@darwin
Hash[darwin,"MD2"]
893121
278031923054096393219531622821406489782
```

If I change just one of these letters (letter 49), the hash becomes a totally different one, because it gets a completely different spin as it 'tumbles' through the data:

```
StringTake[darwin,90]
INTRODUCTION. When on board H.M.S. 'Beagle,' a
 s naturalist, I was much struck with certain
```

```
darwin2=StringReplacePart[darwin,"N",{49,49}]
StringTake[darwin2, 90]
INTRODUCTION. When on board H.M.S. 'Beagle,' a
 s Naturalist, I was much struck with certain
Hash[darwin2,"MD2"]
67728459143952680302004196410938531363
```

With a hash function you can confirm the identity and integrity of any kind of data.

CRYPTOGRAPHIC CONSTRUCTIONS – BLOCKCHAINS

A *blockchain* is a data bank whose integrity (protection against retroactive manipulation) is secured by saving the hash value of a data packet in the data packet that follows it. Blockchains make it possible to secure the integrity of data without having to resort to institutional authority, which is why this principle serves as the basis for cryptocurrencies, for example. Here we want to briefly explain how it works.

This is the necessary code:

```
Mine[data_]:=
 Module[{n=1},
  While[Take[IntegerDigits@Hash[
    {data, n}],{1,4}]!={1,1,1,1},n;n++];
 n]

InitChain[data_]:={{data,Mine@data}}

AddBlock2Chain[chain_,data_]:=
 Append[chain,{data,
  Mine[{Last@VerifyChain@chain,data}]}]

VerifyChain[chain_]:=
 FoldList[Hash[{{#1,#2[[1]]},#2[[2]]}]&,
   Hash@First@chain,Rest@chain]

CertifyChain[chain_]:=
 Fold[AddBlock2Chain[#1,First@#2]&,
   InitChain[],Rest@chain]
```

We initiate the chain:

```
chain=InitChain["root"]
{{root,5771}}
```

To secure data integrity, we use the hash function:

```
Hash["root"]
1393053959502318053
```

The number 5771 was supplied to check or mine the blockchain, it is called a *nonce*. The hash function for a list that consists of that data and the nonce looks like this:

```
Hash[{"root",5771}]
1111419185520659358
```

In this example we have set the mine function so that when data and mine correspond to each other, the first four digits are 1. We could also demand 6 or 12 specific digits, to make it more difficult to find a mine.

Now we can add a second datum to the chain:

chain=AddBlock2Chain[chain, ]

{{root,5771},{  ,13310}}

And again we can check the data and we see the first four 1s in the hash values:

```
VerifyChain@chain
{1111419185520659358,
 1111389736723891231}
```

For the second block in the chain we have added to the data the hash value of the preceding block, so that apart from the data also the sequence of blocks – in other words the chain itself – is checked or 'mined'. This is what the mine looks like:

```
Hash[{{1111419185520659358, },1643}]
```

```
3171587824087333123
```

Let's add another block. We can deposit any kind of data in the block chain; here, for example, a financial transaction:

```
transactions=Grid[{,
 {"23.35€","peter","an","andi",DateObject[]},
 {"12.06€","andi","an","marie",DateObject[]}
 },Frame→All]
```

23.35 €	peter	an	andi	Sat 8 Jun 2019 10:29:49 GMT+8.
12.06 €	andi	an	marie	Sat 8 Jun 2019 10:29:49 GMT+8.

```
chain=AddBlock2Chain[chain, transactions]
```

```
{{root,5771},{
```

```
,13310},
{
```

23.35 €	peter	an	andi	Sat 8 Jun 2019 10:29:49 GMT+8.
12.06 €	andi	an	marie	Sat 8 Jun 2019 10:29:49 GMT+8.

```
},8025}}
```

```
VerifyChain@chain
```

```
{1111419185520659358,
 1111389736723891231,
 1111994323789045002}
```

If we now change only one pixel in the picture in block 2 (the pixel in the top left corner), our mine function recognises this, because the data no longer correspond to the hash nonce used for verification:

```
eastwood=Image@ReplacePart[ImageData@ ,
{1,1}→ 0];
```

```
chain=ReplacePart[chain,{2,1}→eastwood]
VerifyChain@chain
```

```
{{root,5771},{
```

```
,13310},
{
```

23.35 €	peter	an	andi	Sat 8 Jun 2019 10:29:49 GMT+8.
12.06 €	andi	an	susanne	Sat 8 Jun 2019 10:29:49 GMT+8.

```
},8025}}
{1111419185520659358,
 5855733001479820530,
 4838238125888575050}
```

The first block in the chain is still intact, but the second element in the chain has obviously been manipulated, and that means that because of the interlinked hash functions all subsequent blocks of the chain are now regarded as corrupt. So from the manipulated point onwards, the nonces have to be newly calculated.

To further ensure that blockchains aren't manipulated, many of them are run in parallel on the Internet. With each new link, test values are compared and aligned. Chains which deliver a result that is different to the majority are considered corrupt and eliminated. The cryptocurrency *Bitcoin*, for example, uses approximately 5,000 chains. Every ten minutes a new block is added and the level of difficulty for calculating a test value is set such that the entire installed computing capacity of the system would take about ten minutes to work it out. This means it is virtually impossible for one individual or even a group of people to corrupt the system: its integrity is guaranteed without any central authority exercising control over it, but instead what we might call an 'absolute machine', consisting of all the computers that form part of the system.

395 ● 651
Guerrillero Heroico by Alberto Korda, 1960.

396 ● 652
“The lady’s not for turning.” Margaret Thatcher addresses the 1980 Conservative Conference, dismissing criticism and calls for a U-turn on her radical free-market policies.

397 ● 652
WikiLeaks founder Julian Assange.

398A ● 659
La Villa Rotonda, Andrea Palladio, 1571.

398B ● 659
La Villa Rotonda, Andrea Palladio, 1571.

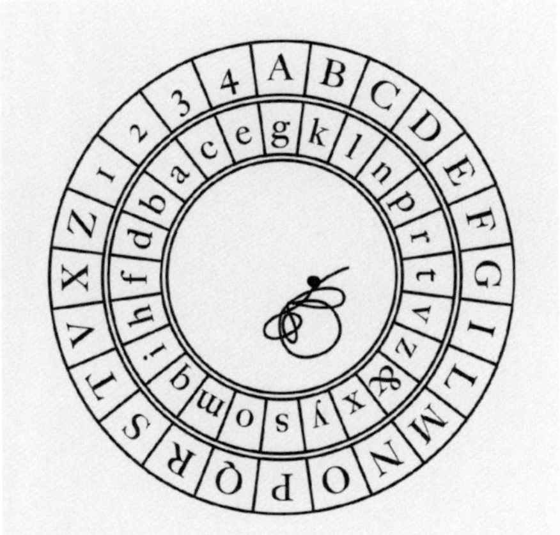

399 ● 663
A tool for the first polyalphabetic substitution, developed by Leon Battista Alberti in *De componendis cifris*, 1467.

Colour Plates

VI

P. 593–677

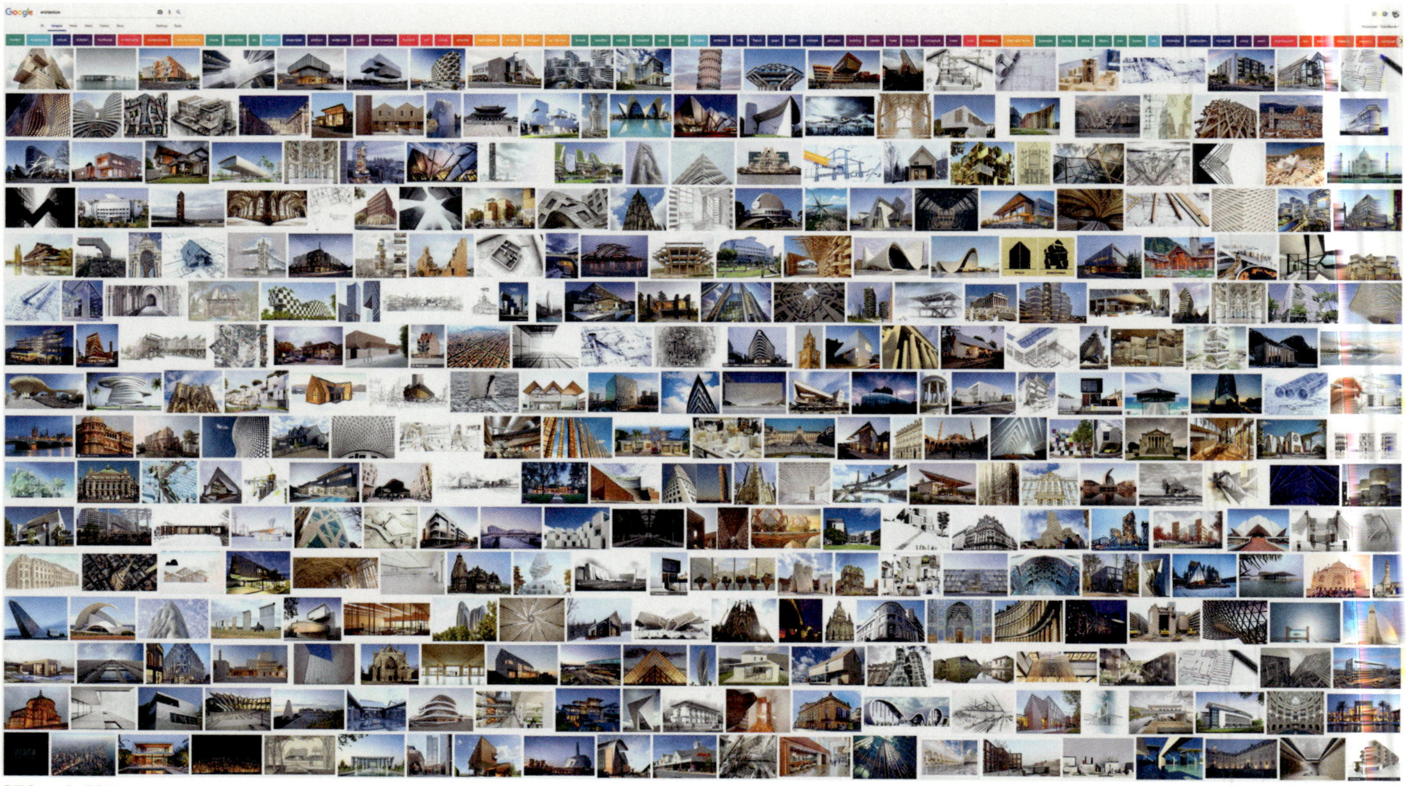

352 ○ 595
Google image search: 'architecture'. [Image collation: Diana Alvarez-Marin, Miro Roman]

354A ○ 600

354B ○ 600

354C ○ 600

ArchDaily pictures from one single article. [Series 354A–354F: *ArchDaily*]

354D ○ 600

354E ○ 600

354F ○ 600

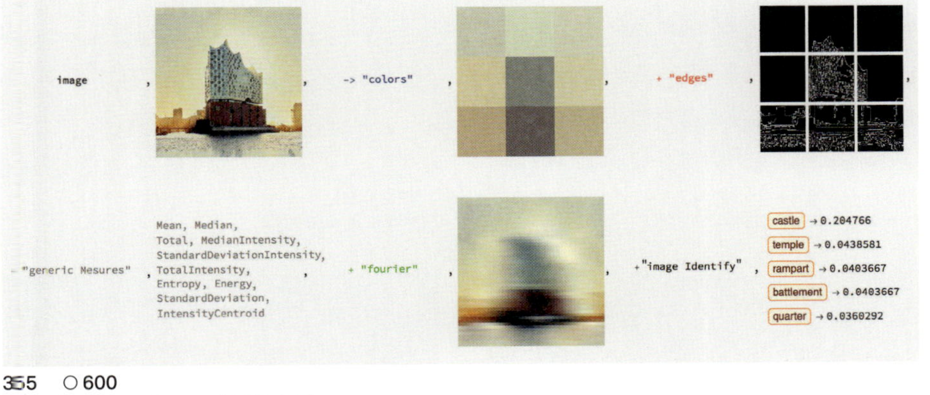

355 ○ 600
Encoding of an image. [DAM, MR]

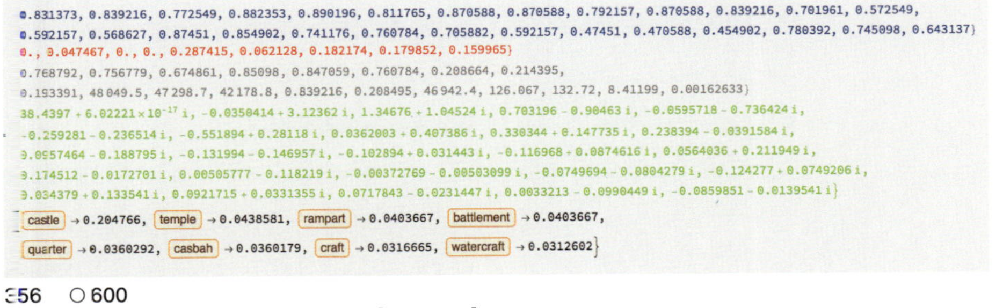

356 ○ 600
The informational face of an image. [DAM, MR]

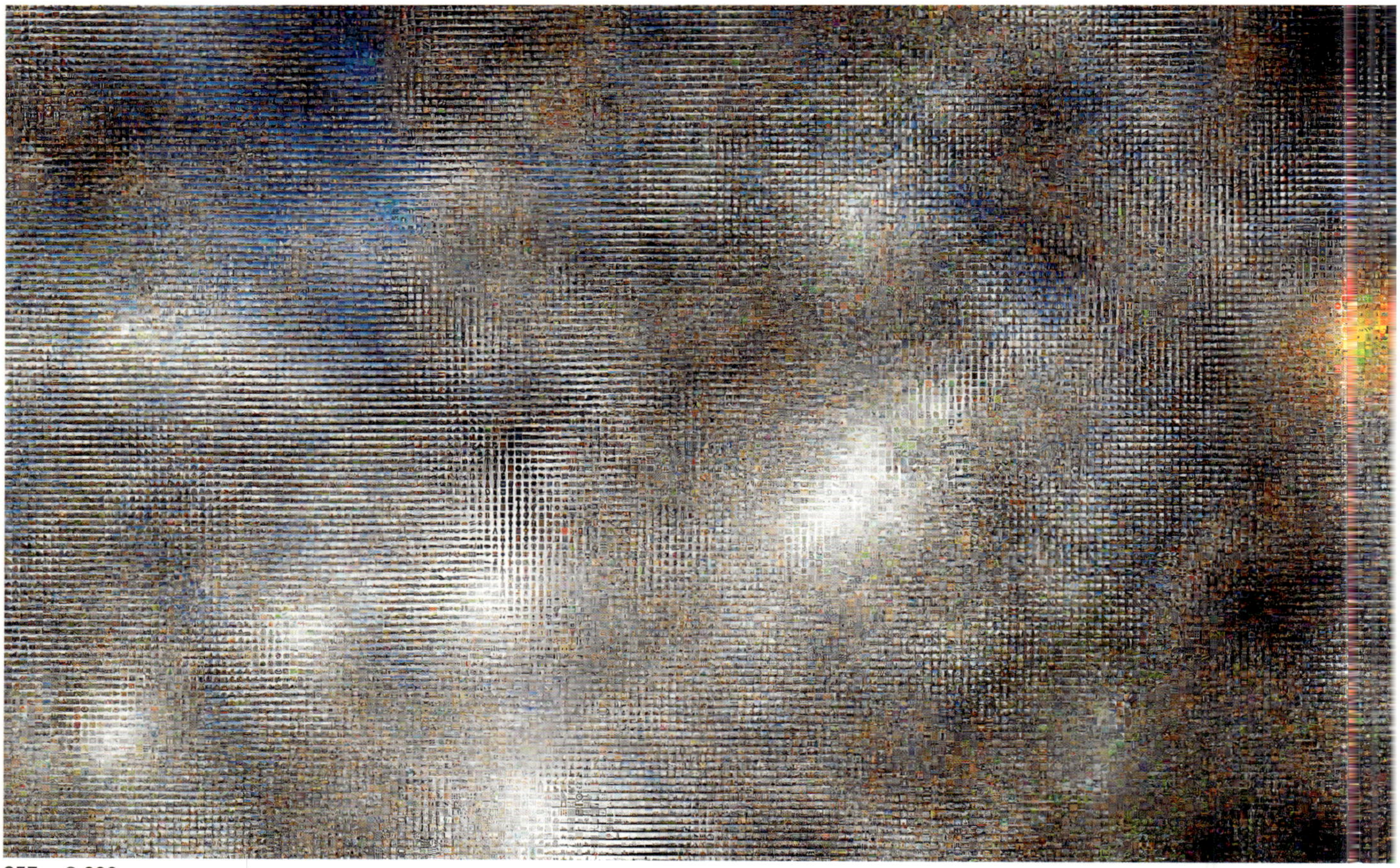

357 ○ 600
Ten years of architecture: a cloud, an atmosphere, a mood.
[Image collation series 357–367: Diana Alvarez-Marin, Miro Roman; source images: *ArchDaily*]

358 ○ 600
Flavour 1: textured objects, solid and light.

359 ○ 601
Flavour 2: lonely solids.

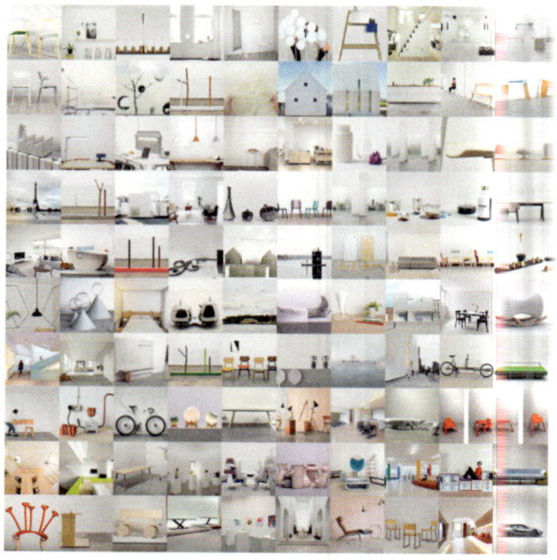

360 ○ 601
Flavour 3: new chic.

361 ○ 601
Flavour 4: patterns.

362 ○ 601
Flavour 5: vertical, diagonal.

363 ○ 601
Flavour 6: horizontal.

364 ○ 601
Personal filter. [DAM, MR]

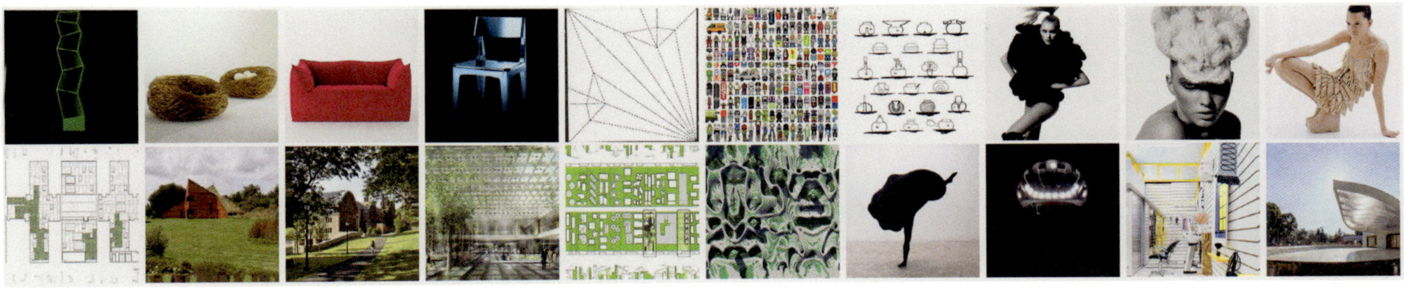

365 ○ 601
Test sample.

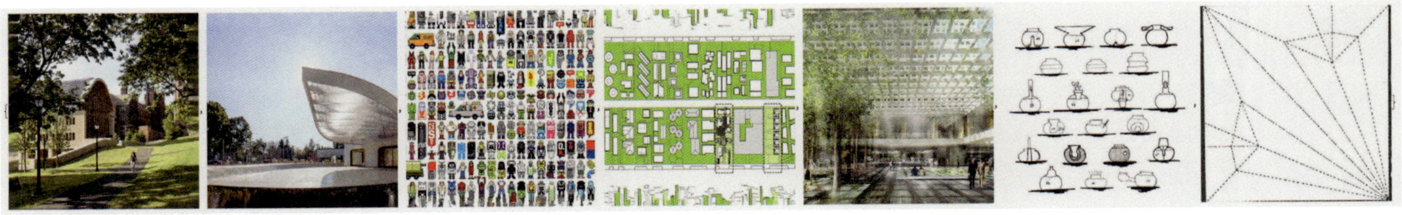

366 ○ 601
Test result.

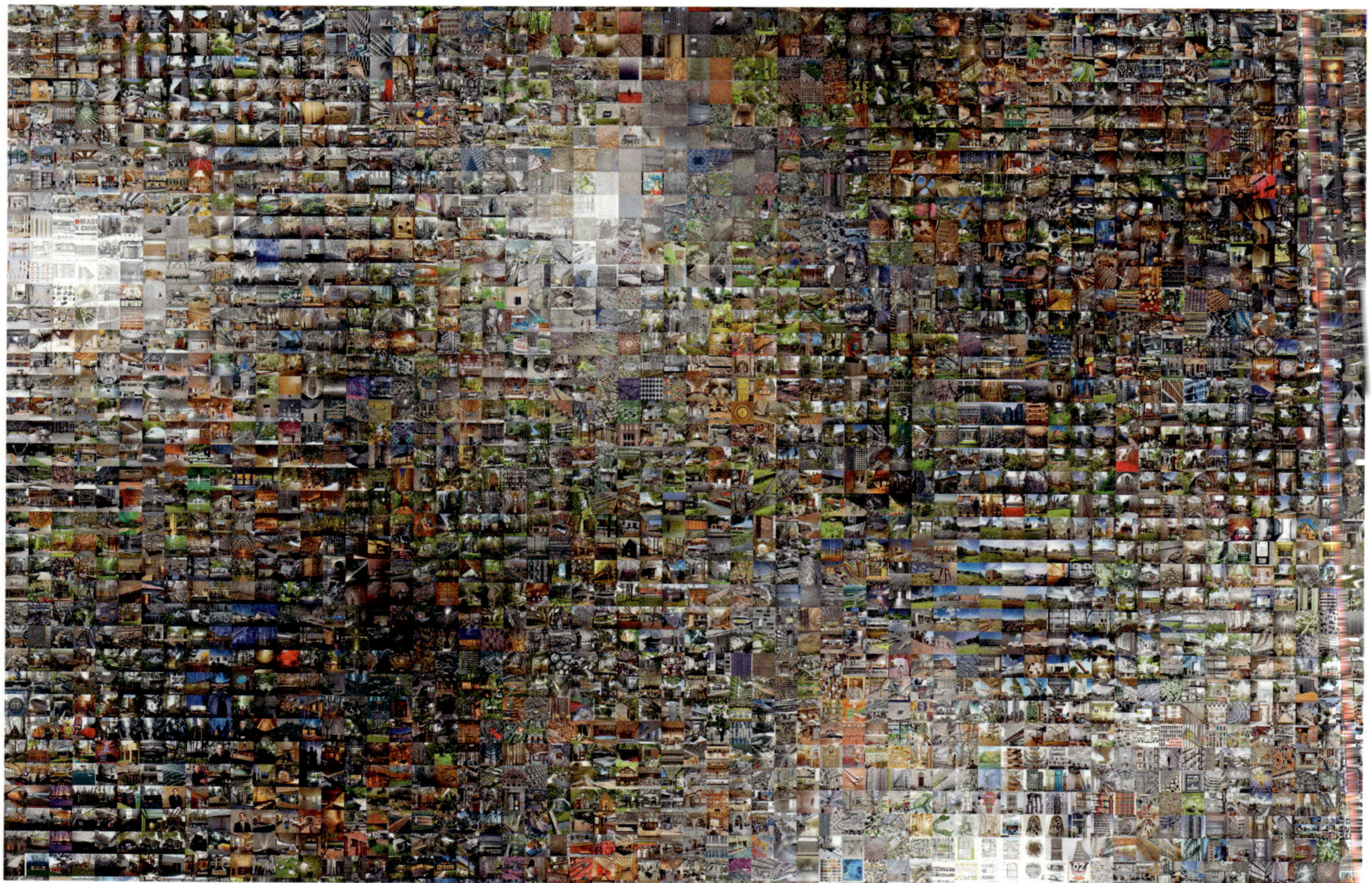

367 ○ 601
Personal mask: portrait of the day. [DAM, MR]

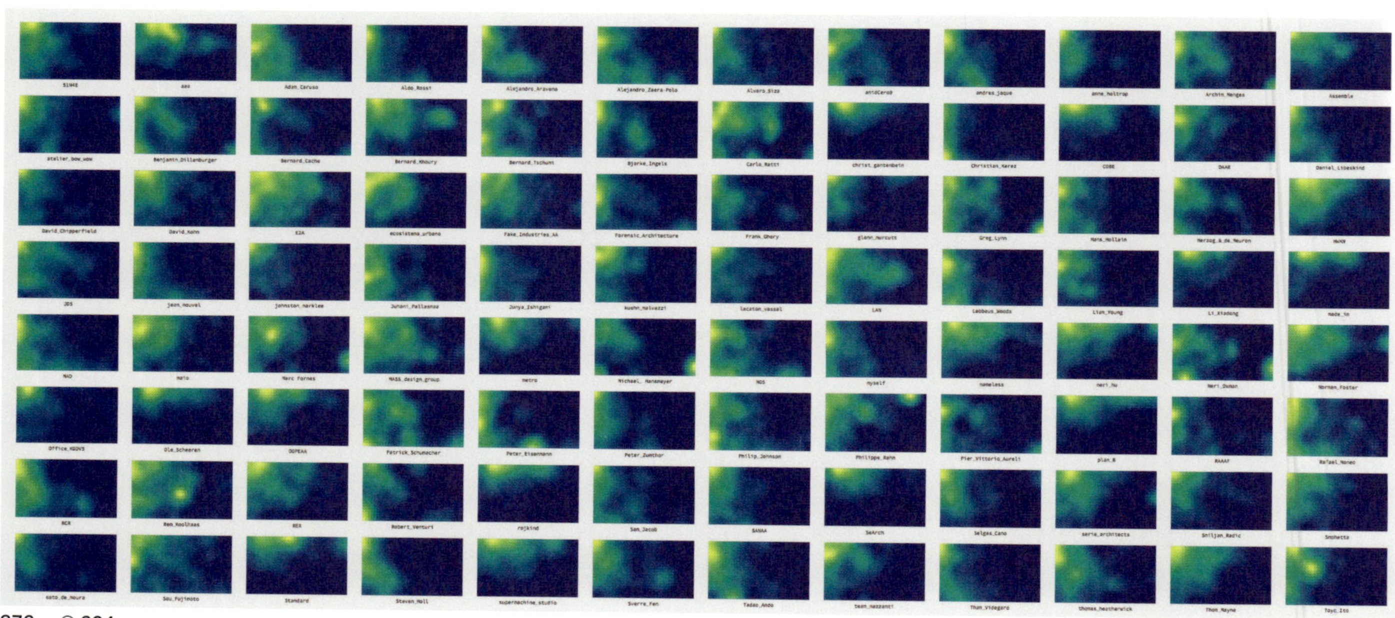

376 ○ 604
Architects wearing 'masks'. [Word collation series 376–388: Diana Alvarez-Marin, Miro Roman]

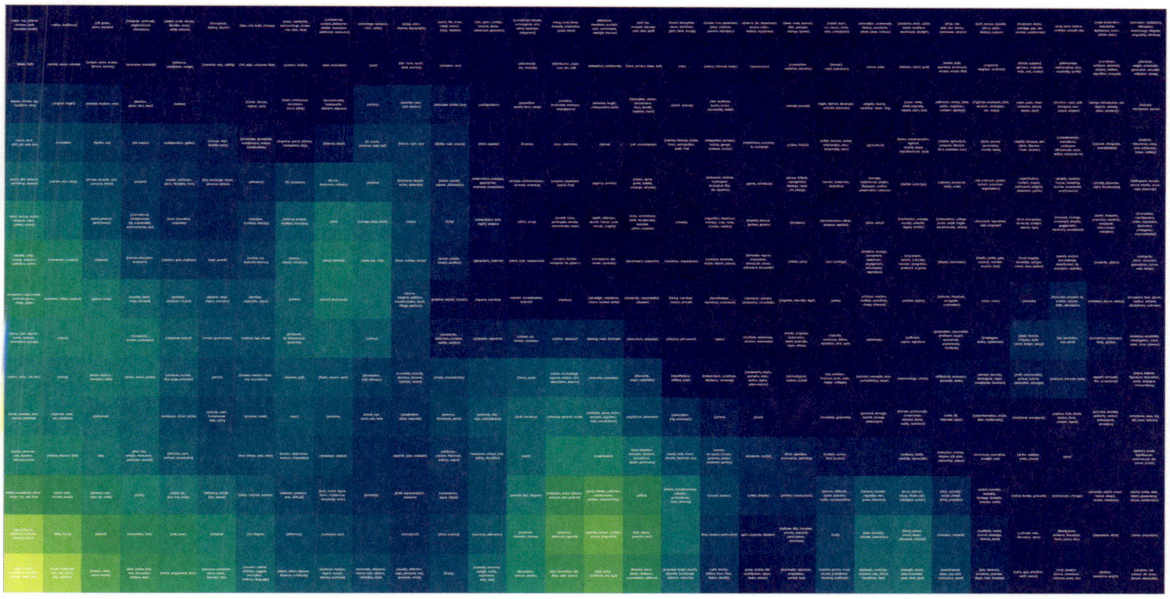

377 ○ 605
Bjarke Ingels – conceptual map. [DAM, MR]

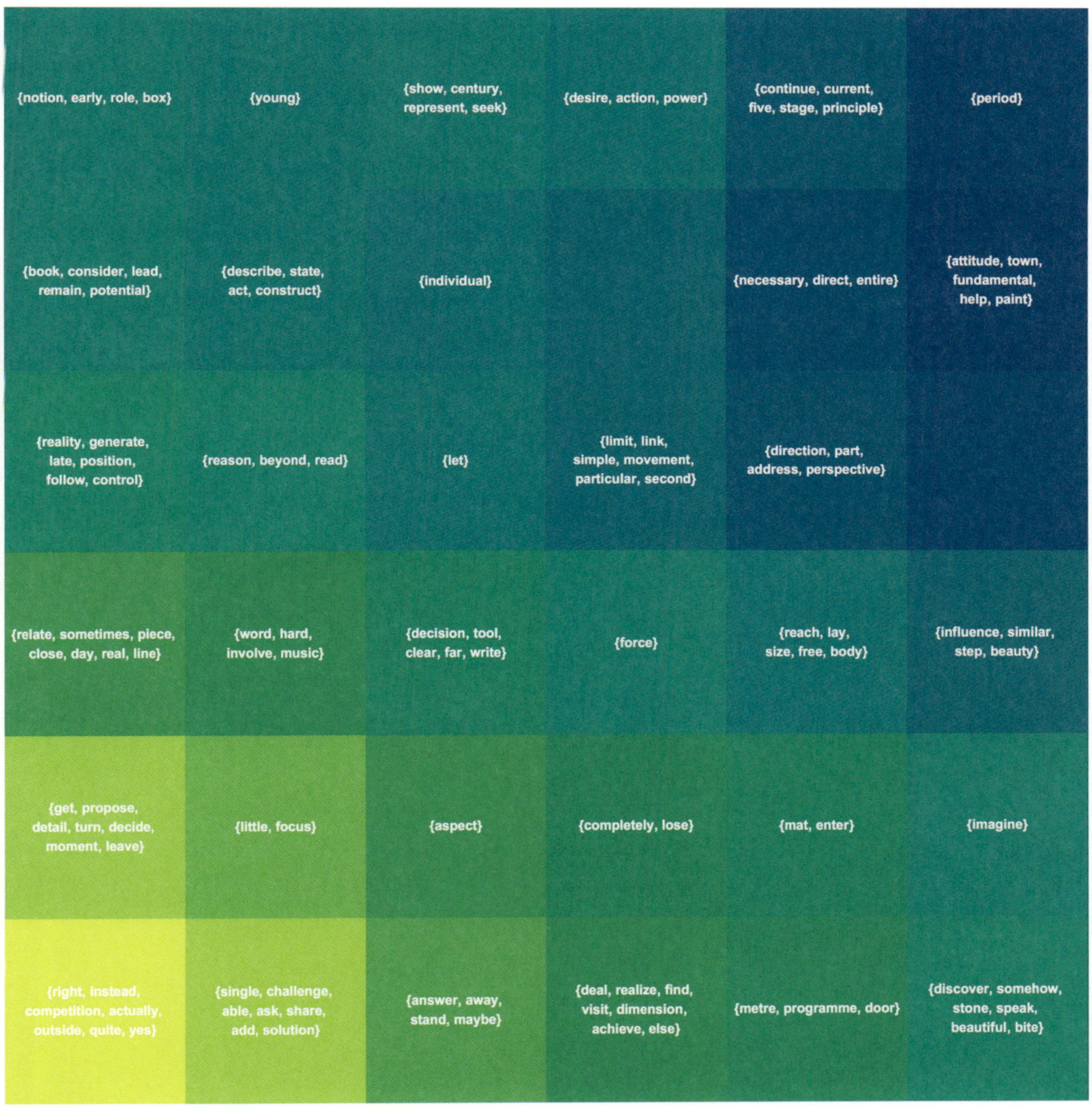

378 ○ 605
Bjarke Ingels – conceptual map, detail. [DAM, MR]

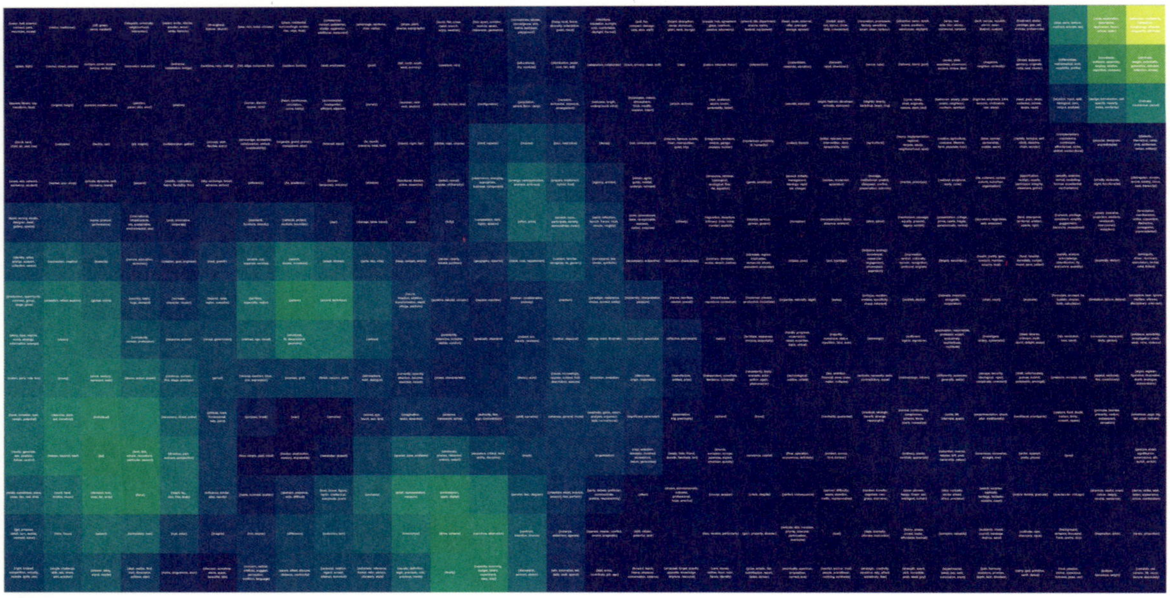

379 ○ 605
Neri Oxman – conceptual map. [DAM, MR]

380 ○ 605
Neri Oxman – conceptual map, detail. [DAM, MR]

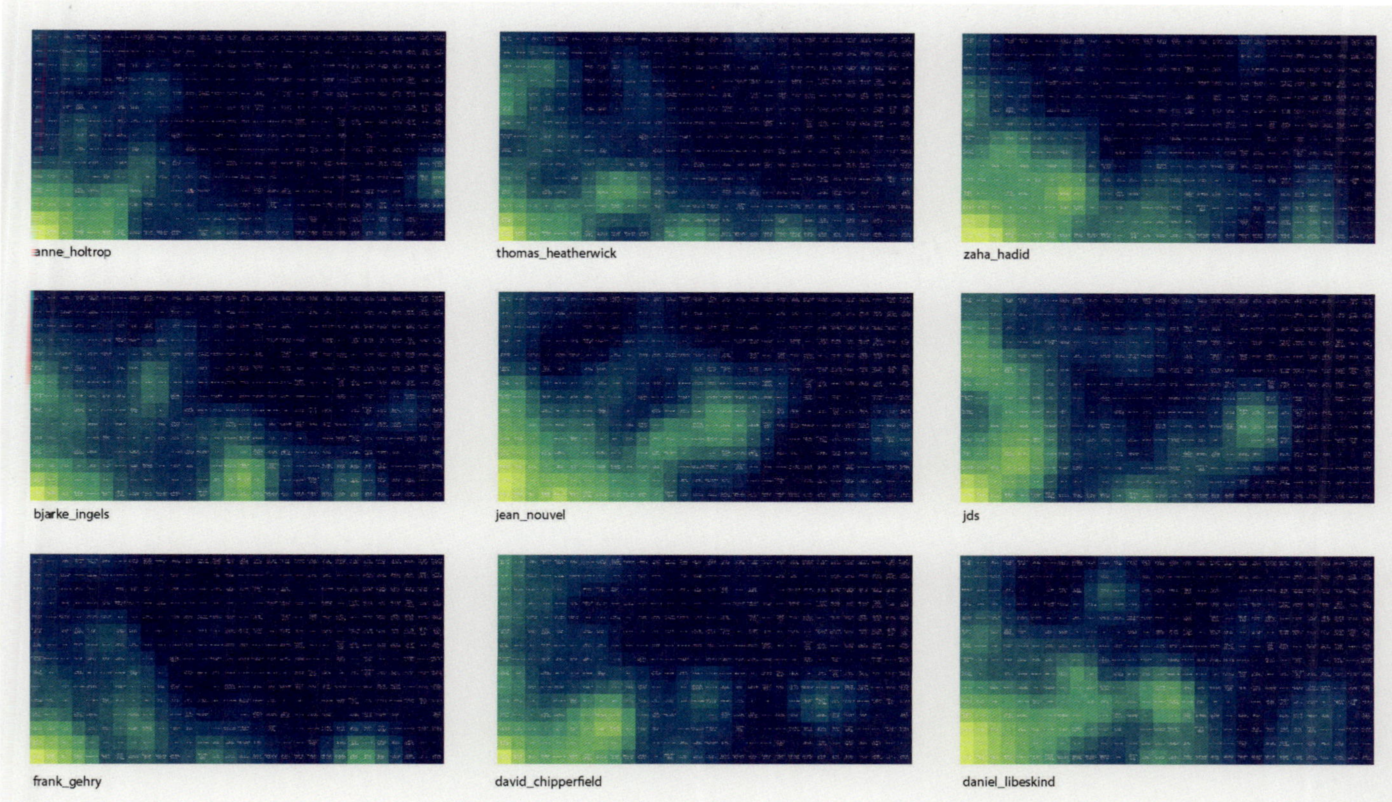

381 ○ 605
Bjarke's architectural affinities. [DAM, MR]

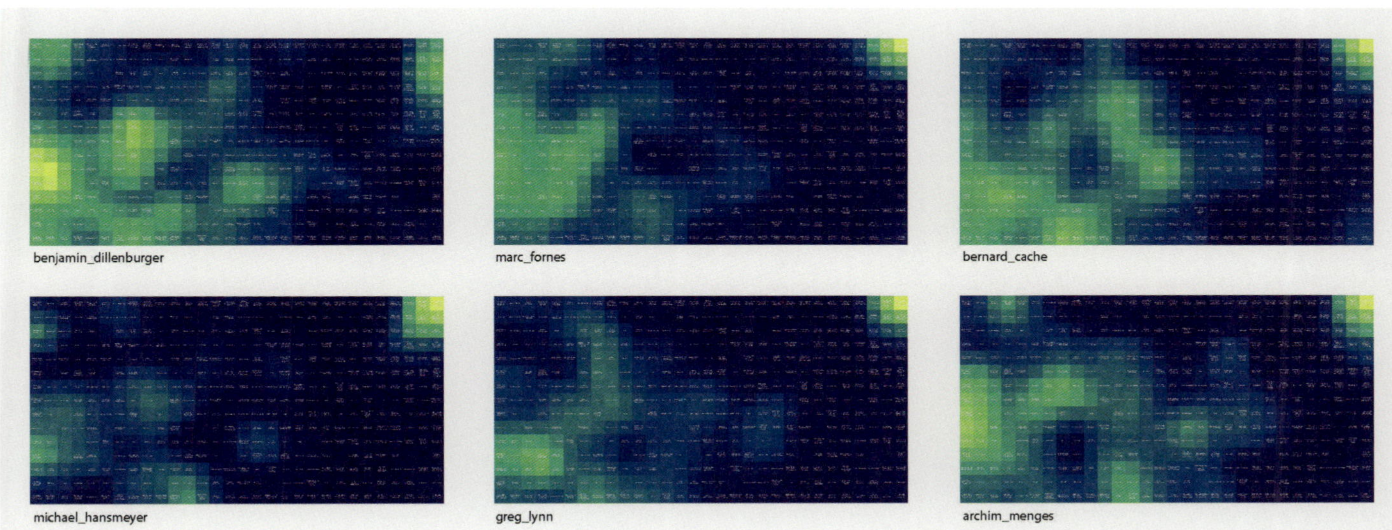

382 ○ 605
Neri's architectural affinities. [DAM, MR]

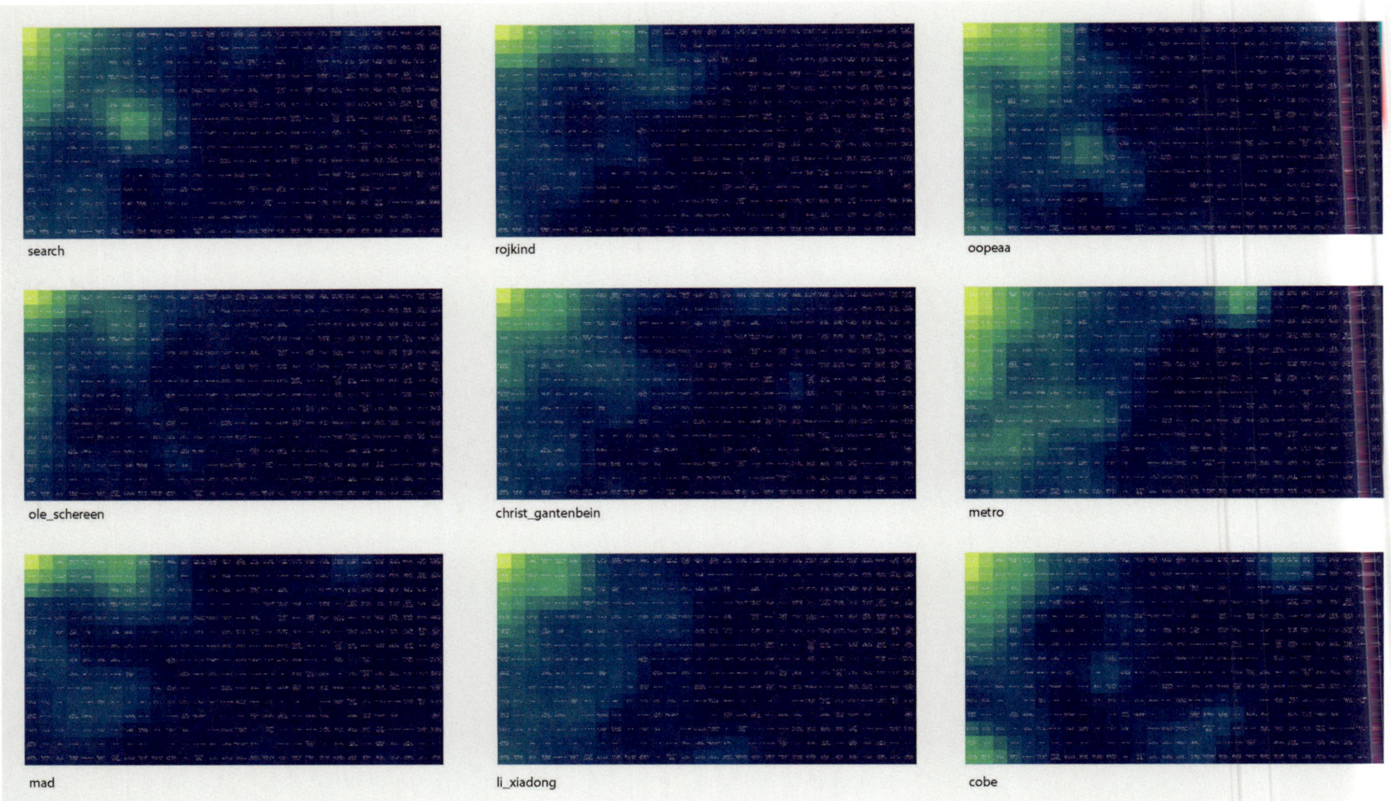

383 ○ 605
Affinities: “location, tower, connect, central, street, volume, height, access, cover, vertical, zone.” [DAM, MR]

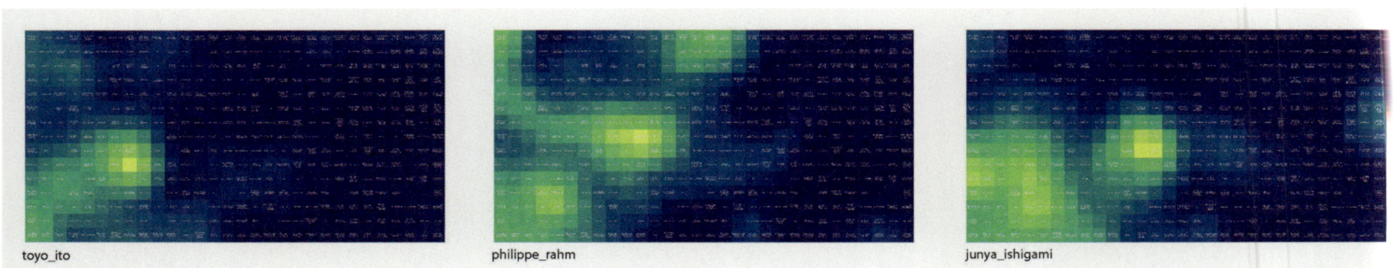

384 ○ 605
Affinities: “inhabit, observe, climatic, atmosphere, dialogue, pattern, empty, visible, invisible.” [DAM, MR]

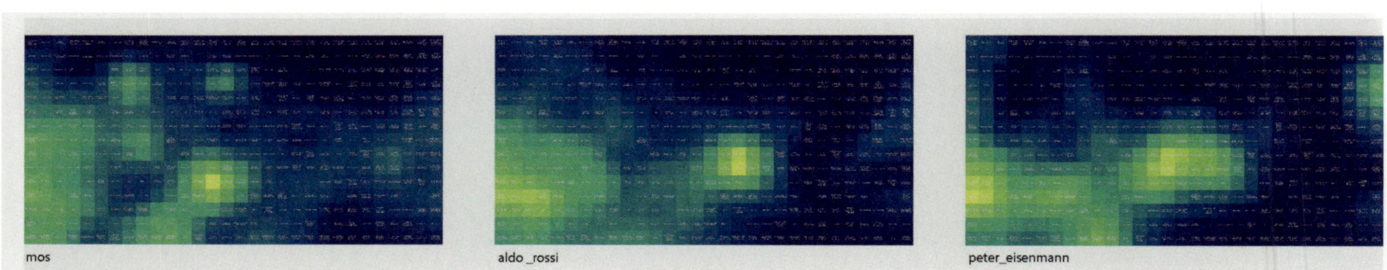

385 ○ 605
Affinities: “modern, interpretation, monument, discourse, artefact, theory, invention, classical author.” [DAM, MR]

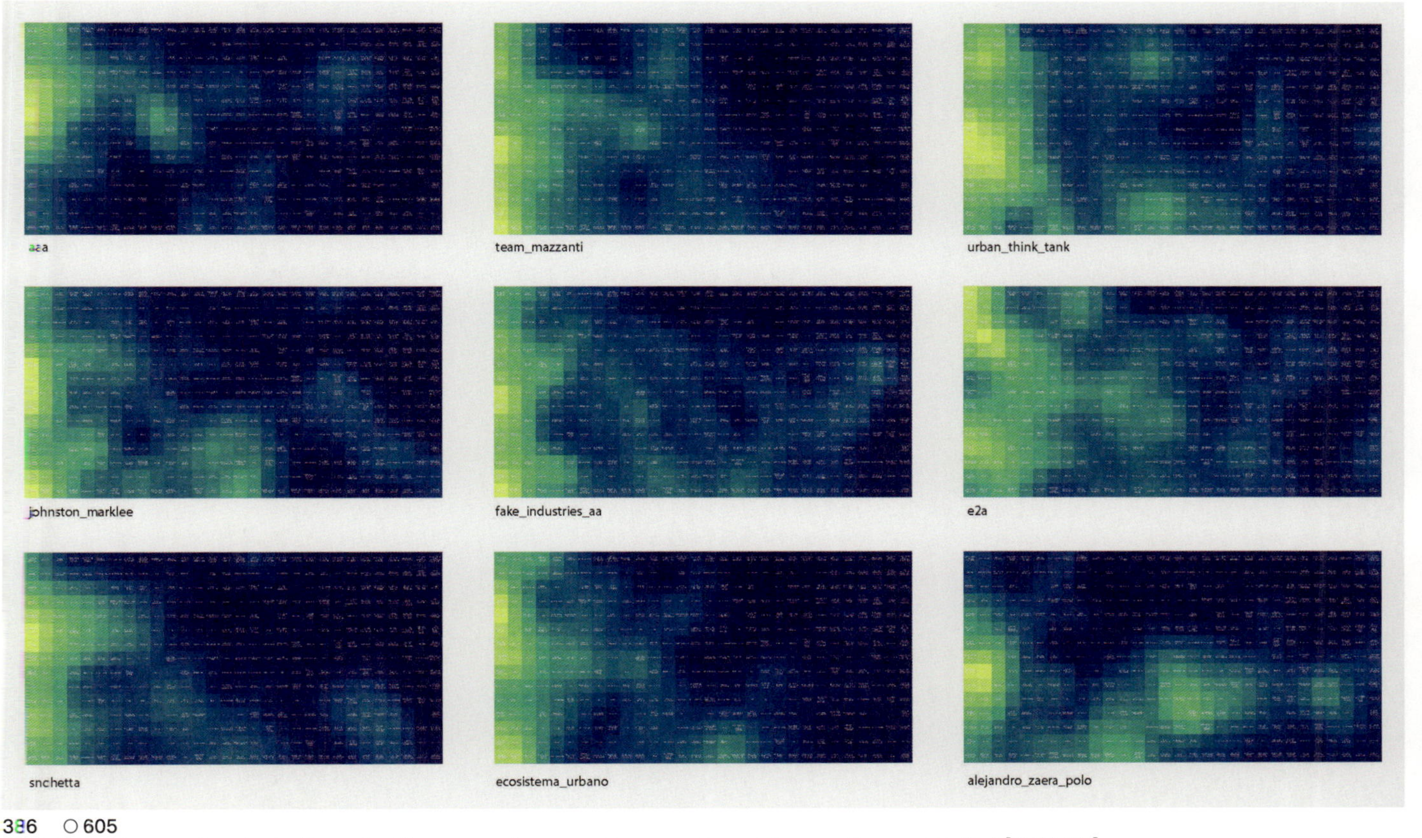

386 ○ 605
Affinities: "team, network, studio, collective, support, connection, creative, vision, reality, complexity." [DAM, MR]

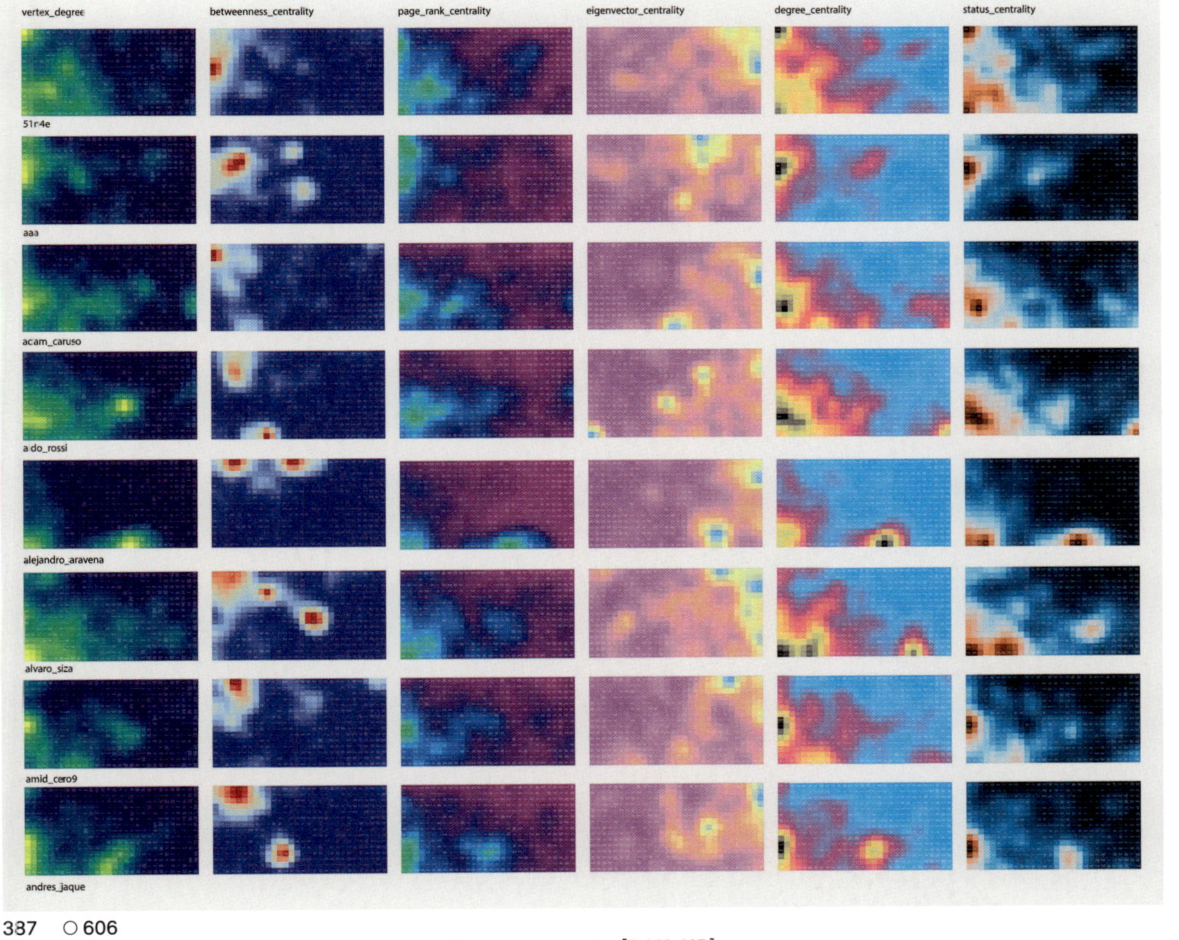

387 ○ 606
'Ways of seeing' – a multiplicity of possible table arrangements. [DAM, MR]

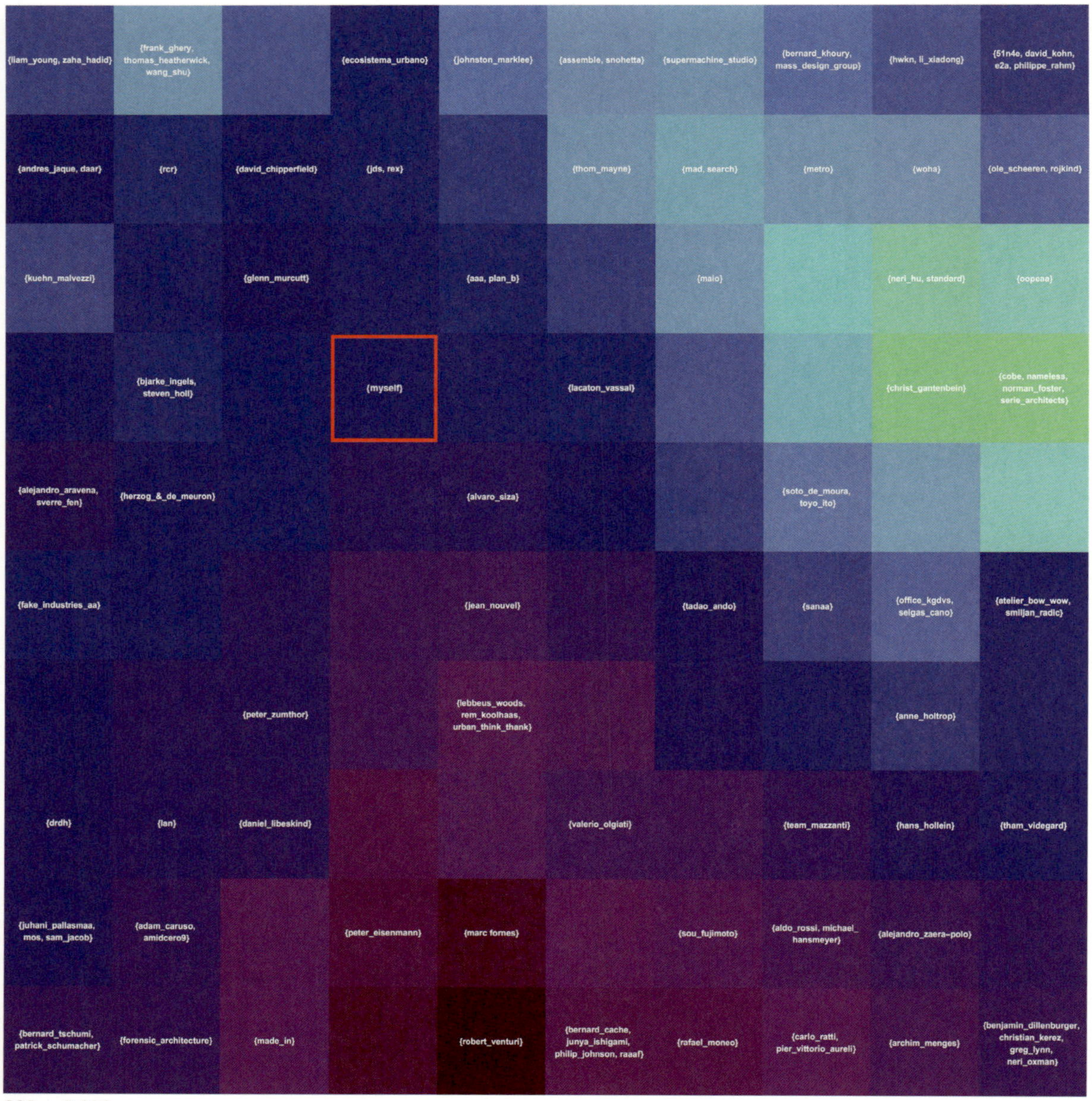

388 ○ 606
Our dinner selfie for tonight. I take a seat at the table, a position as a contemporary architect. [DAM, MR]

389 ○ 606
Takashi Murakami: *Flower Matango*, 2001–2006, Château de Versailles. [Florian Kleinefenn]

In Conclusion: What Is Information?

Ludger Hovestadt

A Quantum Phenomenon

If we are going to have an *Atlas of Digital Architecture* and accept that digitality, for want of a better word, is everything that encompasses information technology, then perhaps our starting point should be the question: what is information? We ask this in one or two places, most explicitly in Privacy & Security – Elaboration, but we think it warrants addressing in some more depth here now, by way of a conclusion. □ ↖661

If you put the word 'information' into the search field of your favourite search engine and hit enter, you're likely to come upon some fairly succinct dictionary definitions and, of course, the *Wikipedia* entry. They are worth having a look at, because information is one of those 'things' of which we may feel that we 'instinctively know' what they are, but that become a whole lot more differentiated the moment we reflect on them.

In its most general definition, so *Oxford Dictionaries*, information is a mass noun that describes, "facts provided or learned about something or someone," and specifically in relation to computing: "data as processed, stored, or transmitted by a computer."

This already validates – if that were necessary – our question. Because the two definitions have almost nothing to do with each other: the latter may or may not contain the former, and the former may or may not ever be found as the latter.

The English *Wikipedia* article on 'Information' was created in 2002 and has since been edited 2,547 times by 1,475 different editors (at the time we write this in March 2019). It has had opportunity, in other words, to settle into something of a current consensus, and states in the opening paragraph of its abstract:

> "Information is any entity or form that provides the answer to a question of some kind or resolves uncertainty. It is thus related to data and knowledge, as data represents values attributed to parameters, and knowledge signifies understanding of real things or abstract concepts."

It further observes:

> "Information can be encoded into various forms for transmission and interpretation (for example, information may

be encoded into a sequence of signs, or transmitted via a sequence of signals). It can also be encrypted for safe storage and communication."

Which similarly highlights this double layer of meanings that are actually really quite different from each other, even though they appear to refer to the same thing.

We don't want to go into a discussion now of the definitions and statements we just quoted. The point of putting them here is simply to set the scene for the landscape we are exploring with this *Atlas*, and to keep in mind what people who have given thought to the matter semantically offer as a first response when asked the question 'what is information?'

In the context of our own undertaking, *information* invariably comes coupled with *technology*, and so our focus naturally favours a perspective that looks at information with reference to computing. But not only. We are interested also in what information is *fundamentally,* and we argue that information is a *quantum phenomenon.*

The American mathematician and philosopher, and pioneer in the field of cybernetics, Norbert Wiener (1894–1964) famously postulated that information is neither matter nor energy. It is neither particle nor wave, we would say. And this opens up the discussion for us in a magnificent way. We have emphasised elsewhere

□ ↖29

in this *Atlas* (namely in the Introduction) that *'computers are not machines'* in a classical, Newtonian or da Vincian way. Similarly, if we describe information in classical terms that are rooted in traditional science and rational thought frameworks of cause and effect – that is: of classical mechanics – we shortchange ourselves. What we have to do is get used to complexity as a way of thinking, and embrace the paradoxes of quantum mechanics.

If information is a quantum phenomenon, then information technology is a quantum technology. Programs are therefore *quantum machines.*

With this as our springboard, let us then dive into a freshly filled metaphorical pool and see how we get on in this element of thought. We are, after all, interested in information as architects, and so we may grant ourselves the privilege, the luxury, even – or call it our professional right – of playing through some notions of information that may or may not be found elsewhere, but that are certainly relevant to us, in all their scope.

The way we are going to do this is not entirely orthodox. We are not, in this *Conclusion*, going to explain or elaborate much on the thought figures we are about to present. Instead, we are going to play them through and put them there, on the unclothed stage as it were, for you to do with them as you please. Not everything may therefore 'make sense' immediately. You will find us make bold statements that you can ponder and then accept or reject. They are meant here not as a through-argued thesis, but as a stimulus, as an inspiration, to send you on your way as 'digital architects', and they are to be read, of course, in the context of everything we talk about and say throughout this *Atlas*.

The Paradox of Data

The elements of mechanics, of a technique – a skilfully achieved technological accomplishment – are often paradoxical. Take a wheel, for example: along the outside of the rim it moves, and yet it stands still at the centre of its axis. Or a gnomon, the fixed part of a sundial, which takes its name from Greek γνώμων, *gnōmōn,* 'the one who knows'. It stands still, and yet its purpose is motion: it casts a moving shadow, from which we tell the time. And not only time, but also location: it captures the cosmological order specific to a single point. And each point is different under the absolute cosmological order. But it's not just there: for it to have any purpose, you have to be able to read it.

400 ● 716

Wheel and gnomon thus stand in opposition to each other: the body of the wheel moves, but the idea of the axis stands still. The body of the gnomon stands still, but the idea of its shadow moves. The body of the wheel is circular, its idea linear. The body of the gnomon is linear, and its idea circular.

In mathematics, we *count* that which is linear, and we *measure* that which is circular, just as in quantum physics we count particles and measure waves.

In practice, often – but certainly not always – a gnomon takes the shape of a triangle. In most cases this is a non-right triangle in which the length of each side is determined by the gnomon's position relative to the sun. But, for the sake of our argument, we can think of the gnomon as simply this, a practical application of a theoretical gnomon *principle,* where an angle is measured between the shadow that the gnomon throws onto the ground, the light ray from the sun that meets the gnomon on its way to the ground, and the gnomon itself. Here now, the ray from the sun describes the hypotenuse of a right triangle, the shadow describes the adjacent, and the gnomon describes the opposite, which, this being a right triangle, stands at a right angle to the adjacent.

Now, the gnomon (the 'stick in the ground') stands still, while the projected triangle on the ground moves throughout the day with the motion of the Earth around the Sun. It's the hypotenuse that determines the sundial's accuracy through its length and positioning, which is why it is here, in the hypotenuse, that the master is revealed.

In this configuration we can not only measure time, we can also measure the height of the Great Pyramid of Giza, for example, as the Greek mathematician and philosopher Thales of Miletus (c. 624 – c. 545 BCE) famously did, by calculating from the length of the shadow (the adjacent) and the angle between it and the hypotenuse (the ray of the sun) the height of the opposite (the gnomon, as imagined at the core of the pyramid from the ground to its pinnacle.

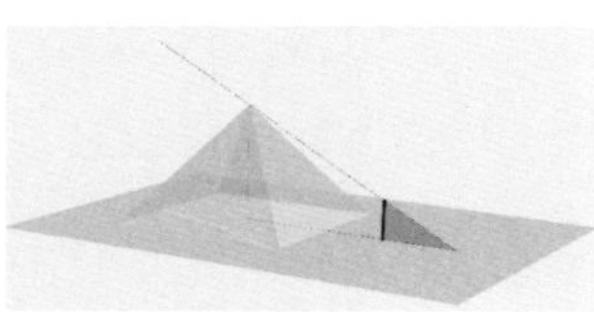

401 ● 716

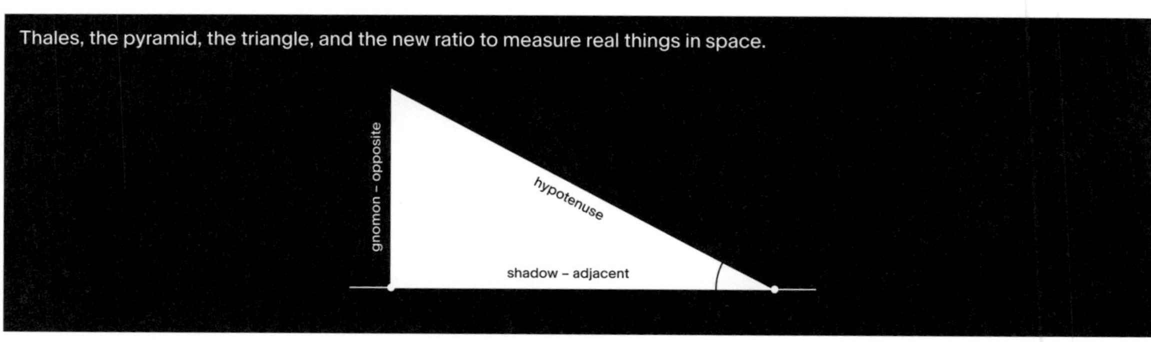

Starting our game of thought figures, we can now draw parallels from the gnomon as a principle to the principles outlined in *De architectura*, written around 30-15 BCE by the Roman architect and engineer Vitruvius (c. 80–70 BCE – after 15 BC). We encounter this, the first theoretical text on architecture to survive, at several points in this *Atlas*, and we also know that it was taken up fifteen hundred years after being written by the Italian Renaissance architect, philosopher, and cryptographer Leon Battista Alberti (1404–1472), who expanded on it in his similarly seminal work *De re aedificatoria (On the Art of Building)*, which he wrote between 1443 and 1452, and which was published posthumously in 1485.

We propose that the vertical opposite of the gnomon triangle corresponds to what Vitruvius and later Alberti describe as *orthographia* and what Alberti considered to be the elevation of a building. It is 'that which we are'. The horizontal adjacent corresponds to *ichnographia*, what today we consider the ground plan of a building: 'that which we know'. In the hypotenuse we see reflected *scaenographia*, or the perspective drawing: that which we are able to do when we learn how to do it: mastery.

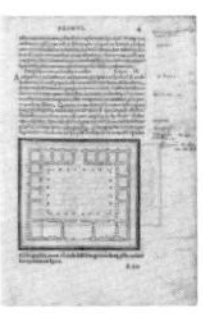
402A ● 716

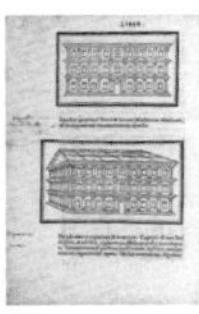
402B ● 716

And here we find the principal paradox, most clearly and evidently presented in mathematics: if we take an isosceles triangle – a triangle which has an adjacent and an opposite leg that are of equal length – and both these legs have a length of 1, then the hypotenuse is neither odd nor even, neither 2 nor 3, can, by traditional means, be neither measured nor counted; it is incalculable, infinite. It is, in a manner of speaking, 'not of this world'. Its length is in fact √2, and in our numbers system we call this an *irrational number* and express it in an infinite series of digits after the decimal point:

```
N[√2, 1000]

1.4142135623730950488016887242096980785696718753769480731766797379907324784621070388503875343276
  4157273501384623091229702492483605585073721264412149709993583141322266592750559275579995050115
  2782060571470109559971605970274534596862014728517418640889198609552329230484308714321450839762
  6036279952514079896872533965463318088296406206152583523950547457502877599617298355752203375318
  5701135437460340849884716038689997069900481503054402779031645424782306849293691862158057846311
  1596668713013015618568987237235288509264861249497715421833420428568606014682472077143585487415
  5657069677653720226485447015858801620758474922657226002085584466521458398893944370926591800311
  3882464681570826301005948587040031864803421948972782906410450726368813137398552561173220402450
  9122770022694112757362728049573810896750401836986836845072579936472906076299694138047565482372
  8997180326802474420629269124859052181004459842150591120249441341728531478105803603371077309182
  86931471017111168391658172688941975871658215212822951848847
```

In this representation, we restrict the series to 1000 decimal places. But infinite really means infinite. The series continues forever, without repeating patterns. If there are no repeating patterns and if we are to assume that this goes on forever, then any theoretically possible string of numbers will, at some point or other, be contained in the sequence. This means that, translated into digits, any piece of writing, including this one, every text message, every email, every book, every film, every genome, absolutely everything that can be encoded in any possible variation is somewhere contained in this number. It contains the world. And here we are in synch with another, more recent, paradox, that proposed by the Austro-Hungarian born American mathematician, logician, and philosopher Kurt Gödel (1906–1978) in his famous **incompleteness theorems**. We discuss these in some detail in our chapter on Big Data & Machine Learning, but in the most minuscule of nutshells, they posit that any consistent system cannot be both complete and proved to be true at the same time. It can be *either* complete, *or* it can be proved. But not both.

■ ↖556
□ ↖549

In other words: any consistent system has its limitations in a given timeframe. Or: the world is 'outside' of calculation. The gnomon and its shadow, the legs of a triangle, they are *in* the systemic and logical order of the world, they are *real*. You can see them. They are *of* nature. But the hypotenuse is not. You can't see it. So the hypotenuse and therefore *scaenographia* are not real, they are *irrational*, and beyond calculable. The hypotenuse is not of this nature, it is natural and of a new ratio.

This is a tremendous realisation and civilisatory achievement: we really cannot ever calculate the hypotenuse, no matter how long we work on it and with what levels of computing power: all the data in the universe will not suffice to do so, but we can affirm it, we can think about it, and – this is the important trick of sheer genius – we can work with it and symbolise with a small mark, like this:

$\sqrt{\;}$

In doing so, we encompass the whole world that is contained within that infinity around a centre that doesn't move. This point is the 'not everything' of our whole nature. We cannot calculate it, we cannot see it, we cannot touch it, we cannot taste it, but we can think and talk about it.

In his *Elements*, Greek mathematician Euclid (fl. 300 BCE) sets down the principles of the geometry later named after him, on which all geometry that followed is founded. *Book I* gives as the first definition: "A point is that which has no part."

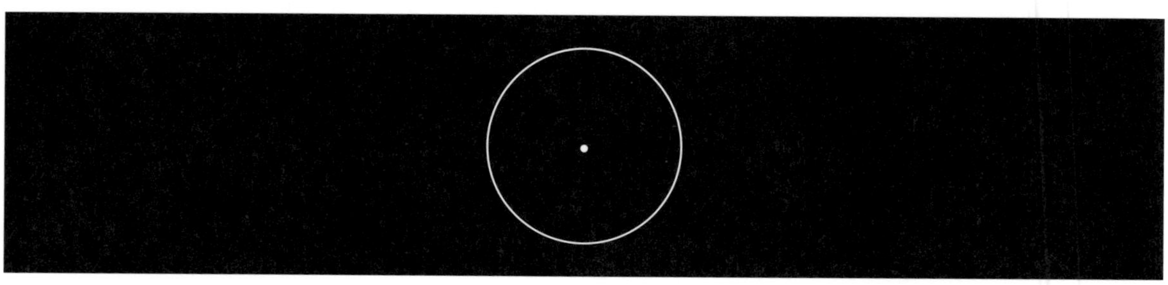

Soon we realise that with our new symbol – of which we have noted that it is 'not of this world' – we can count in a new way: $a^2 + b^2 = c^2$.

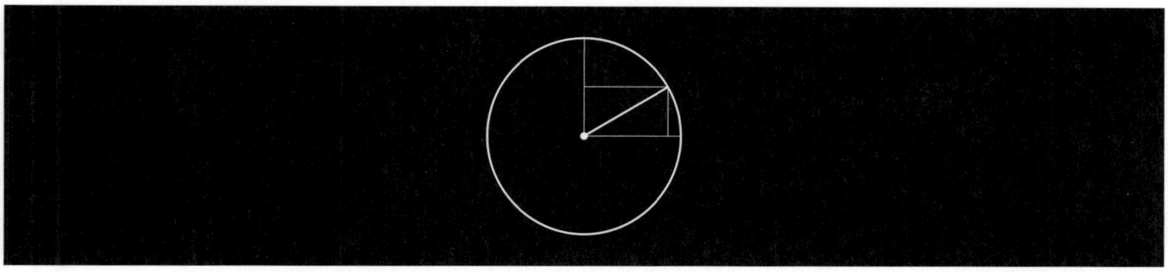

Now, the gnomon is the *axis* of a circle; we look at it straight from above and observe the circular movements of *adjacent* and *opposite*, with the *hypotenuse* a rationalised infinity, the new 1, the new *unit*. Only now can we manage the irrationality of the circle, once we have rationalised its interplay (the interplay of the triangle's real legs of nature) with the *scaenographia* of our ratio.

What we have done is set up the circle of the gnomon to make a wheel. And with it, we get a new mechanics, a new 'trick', if you like, with which we can cock a snook at the infinity of nature.

We are moving beyond the boundaries of the old world, into a new world. This is what the Ancient Greeks established, what happened again on a next level of abstraction in Italy with the Renaissance; and this is also what we are experiencing today with quantum mechanics and information technology: *information* is of the ratio and can be symbolised, and it is not of nature: it can only be established with *data,* signifying all real nature, collapsed into a single point of 'not everything'.

The Infinity of Programs

Now we go to 'the other side', so to speak: from data to programs, from symbols to signifiers, from the ciphers or characters to the numbers, from geometry to arithmetic, from 'Heaven' to 'Earth' (from 'air' and 'fire' to 'earth' and 'water' in Pythagorean terms): much as the particle or data affirms the paradox, so the wave or the program is of an infinite nature.

403 ● 717

Programs circle in an absolute, logical order; that is, they always have an unambiguous cause. Unlike data, they are not paradoxical, 'this as much as the other'. They are not 'that which has no parts', not 'not everything' in one point. Rather, they are akin to what German philosopher and mathematician Gottfried Wilhelm Leibniz (1646–1716) in his short text *Monadology* from 1714 described as, "simple substances, of which consist the things that are put together, the composita." In other words, they are 'everywhere and nowhere'.

If we said of data that they are infinite and symbolise the paradoxical, it is characteristic of programs that they are paradoxical and designate the infinite. Correspondingly, although programs work in an absolute logical order and, if they are fit for purpose and do so correctly, are founded – as is the foundation of any mathematical order – on prime numbers, these, the prime numbers, are without any order at all. In fact, there is nothing that is more disorderly than prime numbers.

Here is a sequence of the first 100 prime numbers:

```
Prime@Range@100

{2, 3, 5, 7, 11, 13, 17, 19, 23, 29, 31, 37, 41, 43, 47, 53, 59, 61, 67, 71, 73, 79, 83, 89, 97,
 101, 103, 107, 109, 113, 127, 131, 137, 139, 149, 151, 157, 163, 167, 173, 179, 181, 191, 193,
 197, 199, 211, 223, 227, 229, 233, 239, 241, 251, 257, 263, 269, 271, 277, 281, 283, 293, 307,
 311, 313, 317, 331, 337, 347, 349, 353, 359, 367, 373, 379, 383, 389, 397, 401, 409, 419, 421,
 431, 433, 439, 443, 449, 457, 461, 463, 467, 479, 487, 491, 499, 503, 509, 521, 523, 541}
```

And here is a field with the first 40,000 numbers marked as evenly spaced dots on a grid, 200 × 200. Prime numbers are rendered in white. We can identify no discernible pattern, regularity, or order: it looks not quite like, but similar to, white noise, because in essence it is. It's pure chaos.

```
tab = Table[0, 200×200];
(tab[[Prime[#]]] = 1) & /@ Range[PrimePi[200×200]];
Image@Partition[tab, 200]
```

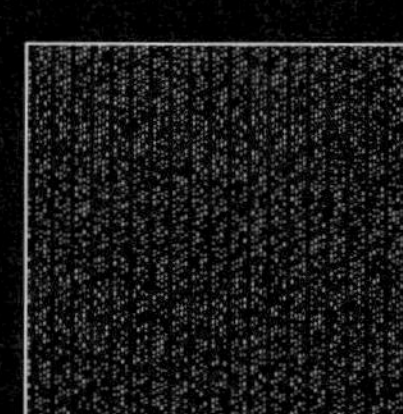

The geometric point is 'not everything'; arithmetic prime numbers are 'everywhere and nowhere': white noise.

This fundamental disorder, which lies at the basis of any mathematical order, of any analytics, of any system, of the nature of science as we understand it today, causes a principal problem that is common to all arithmetic and to any program.

The aim of all arithmetic and of any program is to create 'even steps': to count 10, 11, 12, for example, or to consider the expression '10 – 2 = 8' as algebraically equivalent to the expression '52 – 44 = 8'. And yet prime numbers, on which everything is based, only allow for any certainty at all on their own positions, which on a range from 1 to 100 are: 2, 3, 5, 7, 11, 13, 17, 19, 23, 29, 31, 37, 41, 43, 47, 53, 59, 61, 67, 71, 73, 79, 83, 89, and 97.

These, for example, are the prime numbers composing, when multiplied, the number 100:

```
pr = Flatten[Table @@@ FactorInteger[100]]

{2, 2, 5, 5}
```

If you want to get to the number 102, you need a jump:

```
pr = Flatten[Table @@@ FactorInteger[102]]

{2, 3, 17}
```

Or you build in another step of 2:

```
pr = Flatten[Table @@@ FactorInteger[104]]

{2, 2, 2, 13}
```

It is complicated...

That's why on an abacus, or on the drum of a mechanical calculating machine such as the stepped reckoner invented by Leibniz, we have these combinatorics of circular movements that we call arithmetic. And the combinatorial, circular counting that is based, as we have seen, on an absolute disorder, we call measuring. Up until modernity we measured lengths in space. With Leibniz machines and with today's programs we measure lengths in time.

Any computer program comes up against the problem of **combinatorial explosion**. We also discuss this in detail in our chapter on Big Data & Machine Learning, so we don't want to go into it here in any depth now either. Expressed in the context of prime numbers, we could illustrate it as follows:

■ ↖555
□ ↖549

We have already shown the prime numbers that constitute the number 100. They are 2, 2, 5, 5. In order to get to 100, there are several possible permutations, six to be exact:

```
Permutations@pr

{{2, 2, 5, 5}, {2, 5, 2, 5}, {2, 5, 5, 2}, {5, 2, 2, 5}, {5, 2, 5, 2}, {5, 5, 2, 2}}
```

And now we do the same thing for the number 1000: it immediately gets much more difficult to keep track:

```
Permutations@Flatten[Table @@@ FactorInteger[1000]]

{{2, 2, 2, 5, 5, 5}, {2, 2, 5, 2, 5, 5}, {2, 2, 5, 5, 2, 5}, {2, 2, 5, 5, 5, 2},
 {2, 5, 2, 2, 5, 5}, {2, 5, 2, 5, 2, 5}, {2, 5, 2, 5, 5, 2}, {2, 5, 5, 2, 2, 5},
 {2, 5, 5, 2, 5, 2}, {2, 5, 5, 5, 2, 2}, {5, 2, 2, 2, 5, 5}, {5, 2, 2, 5, 2, 5},
 {5, 2, 2, 5, 5, 2}, {5, 2, 5, 2, 2, 5}, {5, 2, 5, 2, 5, 2}, {5, 2, 5, 5, 2, 2},
 {5, 5, 2, 2, 2, 5}, {5, 5, 2, 2, 5, 2}, {5, 5, 2, 5, 2, 2}, {5, 5, 5, 2, 2, 2}}
```

■ ↖558 Directly coupled with its attendant **frame problem**, combinatorial explosion explains that in practical terms you cannot calculate problems if they are too big, and numbers if they are too large: you have to focus. You have to say: this is part of my problem, and this is not. In simplest terms, you have to be selective about what you are going to deal with and don't mess everything up with too many combinations that are too complicated.

To summarise then, we can formulate the interplay of informational concepts with an elegant symmetry: programs are a *local globality*, data are of a *global locality*. Or, to put it in a philosophical context, programs are *axiomatic*, information is *atomic*.

Information and the 'Stage of Life'

Proceeding from here, and building on the parallels we have begun to draw, we can now more clearly define the concept of information, and suggest:

Data correspond to the gnomon, the rotational axis of the wheel, the adjacent of the triangle, the *orthographia* in classical architecture, and the particle in quantum mechanics.

Programs correspond to the gnomon's shadow, the rim of the wheel, the opposite of the triangle, the *ichnographia*, and the wave.

Information corresponds to the ratio between any two elements, the turn of the wheel, the hypotenuse of the triangle, the *scaenographia*, and the quantum.

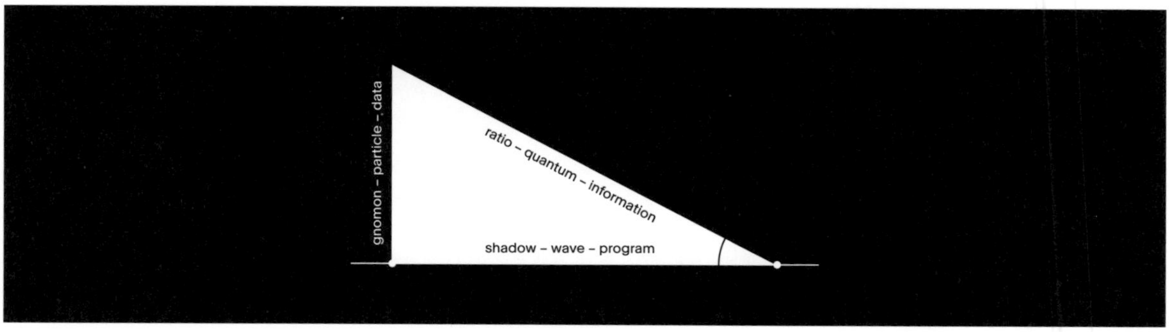

Besides which: mathematicians describe particles and waves as conjugated. In that same way we can describe data and programs – as well as 'actors' and 'plays' – as conjugated to each other. Information, by contrast, would then have to be the conjugation of the conjugated context of data and programs, much as we can describe quanta as the conjugation of the conjugated context of particles and waves.

Similarly, we can regard classical mechanics as the stage where *spatial elements* (gnomons of any 'Euclidean' mechanics of nature) move in *time*. This corresponds to the thinking of Italian polymaths Leonardo da Vinci (1452–1519) and Galileo Galilei (1564–1642), and German mathematician and astronomer Johannes Kepler (1571–1630): the Renaissance.

And so we can regard quantum mechanics as a stage where *temporal elements* (gnomons of any classical mechanics of nature) move in *'life'*. This corresponds to the thinking of German-born theoretical physicist Albert Einstein (1879–1955), French biochemist Jacques Monod (1910–1976), or English computer scientist Alan Turing (1912–1954): the age of digitality.

This is how we may imagine **artificial intelligence**: as actors, ■ ↖654
as gnomons, as 'the ones who know' everything of the old world, and are nothing in the new world. An *orthographia* in the word play of Vitruvius ('corporeal' elements on the stage of space) or Alberti (spatial elements on the stage of time). As temporal elements on the stage of 'life' today, self-contained, rotating with their own logical consistency, and incomplete: a cosmos of its own in time, a point in 'life'; or, as French philosopher Michel Serres (1930–2019) would call it, an 'active subject'.

Any single part of our nature of time is of this intelligence, it knows everything in time and casts shadows in the new world of 'life'. If we go outside, we can just say, "it thinks it rains," to quote Serres, in his book *The Incandescent* (2003). We go out, see all this and, like Thales, set our gnomon *(orthographia)*, watch the shadows under the sun *(ichnographia),* and establish a new ratio *(scenographia)*.

This might be the difference between the mechanical or artificial intelligence of nature and the natural intelligence of humans. This is the setup today and it has been the setup all along the way, at least in Western culture. Nothing new then: an invariant.

Talking About the Whole

Michel Serres – and this is the next important concept of his we want to introduce – calls the technical implementation of the quantum 'stage of life' itself 'world objects': "A satellite for speed, an atomic bomb for energy, the Internet for space, and nuclear waste for time... these are four examples of world objects."

And he talks of them as an objective force from which nothing can escape. No amount of money, no dialectic, no didactic, no contract, no culture, no research, no project, no design; not art, not goodwill; no awareness of issues, no isolation from them, no solution to any problem, and no problem can avoid running into them, there is simply no way past them. We, with our traditional methods, which are familiar to us from the 'stage of time', face this force of world objects helplessly. We are born into this new world like anew, and so we have to learn new methods of dealing with it.

Faced with 'world objects' and their all-pervasive presence we as 'digital humans' or 'digital citizens' generally, but certainly we as architects, or aspiring masters of any description in any field, have to learn to talk about the whole. Much as there is no way around these world objects, so there is no way around the need to talk about everything they're present in.

And so today – even though that may feel strange and uncomfortable – it seems that we have to learn to talk about the ancient gods again: Zeus, Hera, Ares, Hermes, Dionysus, Aphrodite, Hades. And retell the great narratives of myth and legend: the Creation, the Deluge, the Confounding of the Languages of All the Earth. Or, from our perspective today, the Big Bang.

Unsurprisingly, these ideas are omnipresent in our culture today: big companies with their branding, and major studios with their movies, they adopt this language and tell their stories in it.

404A ● 717

404B ● 717

404C ● 717

404D ● 717

405A ● 718

405B ● 718

405C ● 718

405D ● 718

And it is also reflected in the language of architects:

> "Space and light and order. Those are the things that men need just as much as they need bread or a place to sleep."
> – Le Corbusier

> "I did not want to find a monumental architecture, I did not want to find a fashionable architecture, I did not want to find a beautiful architecture, instead I always sought a 'skinless' architecture, an architecture in which the outside arises from the inside, straight out of the inner life of the men who live in it."
> – Superstudio

> "I like thinking big. I always have. To me it's very simple: if you're going to be thinking anyway, you might as well think big."
> – Rem Koolhaas

So – much as we also say in our Introduction – we can't withdraw onto a position of saying, 'our situation is particular', and moan about the bomb, about capitalism, or about the Internet, none of which we really want to have anything to do with, indulging ourselves in self-pity. If we don't take responsibility ourselves, then whom are we going to give responsibility to, for these truly awesome powers? □ ↖29

No, anyone who wants to become a master has to stand tall, and square up to these powers face to face, has to affirm and cultivate them. This is the world we are born into. It is challenging, it is immense, and it is, for all the many ways in which it might trouble us, astoundingly beautiful.

Three Geometries

Our hypothesis is that the masters of one era all think in broadly the same manner that is congruent with their time, but different from the manner of thought of the masters of any other era, and that therefore the masterpieces of any era all emerge from the same body of thought, but that the bodies of thought from different eras cannot really understand each other.

□ ↖29 In our Introduction, we say: forget about the geocentric world view, but also forget about the 'Copernican turnaround'. If we do so, we appreciate that knowledge has not spread in a geocentric manner and now lies spread out before us like a map. Rather it's like a planetary system: the celestial bodies of knowledge circle around each other and their meaning always depends on the current constellation and perspective, on how it presents itself. Which is why there is no straight line between these bodies of thought: they are in motion.

In this planetary system, everything is not relative: it has a precise mechanic and we can find constellations in it that repeat themselves. We can also find invariances with which we can stabilise ourselves and through which we can learn.

And so the most explicit and direct access we have to the mode of thinking of eras other than our own is mathematics because mathematics is not distorted by pragmatism, corrupted by politics, or diluted by opinion. It is crystalline, pure. Which is why to us mathematics is the Royal Path to Knowledge: it cuts through everything else.

As mathematics is the Royal Path to Knowledge, so architecture is the Art of Joining. Of putting elements together, in one manner or another. Our contention is that geometries are different levels of abstraction – space, time, life – and that on each of these levels of abstraction, which we consider to be the 'stage', there are different manners of 'play': comedy, satire, and tragedy.

Let us then look at the constellations that we call geometry, and describe the invariances between the two geometric events which we have inherited from history, to learn how we can characterise our constellation today.

ANCIENT GREECE AND EUCLIDEAN GEOMETRY

In antiquity, buildings were joined according to Euclidian geometry. Here, lines are spatial elements between mythical things. The elements of mathematics in antiquity are *proportionalities*, and we get to know them as arguments in *phonetic script*.

406 ● 718

407 ● 719

RENAISSANCE AND ANALYTICAL GEOMETRY

In modernity, buildings were joined according to analytical geometry. Here, lines are a temporal movement between spatial objects. The elements of mathematics in modernity are *linearities,* and we get to know them in the orbits of the planets or in *perspective drawings.*

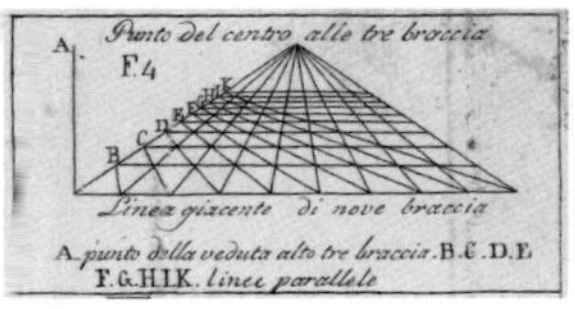

408 ● 719

409 ● 719

TODAY'S 'DIGITAL GEOMETRY'

Today, buildings are joined according to what we might call a digital geometry. Now, lines – so we postulate – are the channels of communication between temporal organisms. Naming them here as a concept, the elements of the 20th century are *categories* (mathematicians today don't really like them). We will learn to cultivate them with *code.*

410 ● 720

411 ● 720

GEOMETRY AND ART

Now look at how Italian architect Sebastiano Serlio (1475 – c. 1554) considers geometry to be the basis for the architecture of his age, in his *Seven Books of Architecture*, published in 1611:

> "The First Chapter
>
> "How needfull and necessary the most secret Art of Geometrie is for every Artificer and Workeman, as those that for a long time have studied and wrought without the same can sufficiently witnesse, who since that time have attained unto any knowledge of the said Arte, doe not onely laugh and smile at their owne former simplicities, but in truth may very well acknowledge that all whatsoever had bene formerly done by them, was not worth the looking on.
>
> "Seeing then the learning of Architecture comprehendeth in it many notable Artes, it is necessary that the Architector

> or Workeman, should first or at the least (if he cannot attaine unto any more) know so much thereof, as that hee may understand the principles of Geometrie, that he may not be accompted amongst the number of stonespoilers, who beare the name of workmen and scarce know how to make an answere what a Point, Line, Plaine, or Body is, and much lesse can tell what harmonie or correspondencie meaneth, but following after their owne minde, or other blinde conductors that have used to worke without rule or reason, they make bad worke, which is the cause of much uncut or uneven workemanship which is found in many places.
>
> "Therefore seeing that Geometrie is the first degree of a l good Art, to the end I may shew the Architector so much thereof, as that he may thereby be able with good skill, to give some reason of his worke."

What then is art, and what a work of art? For Serlio it is clear: geometry is an art. Or more radically expressed: geometry is an art form, and it falls upon the 'achitector' as 'workmaster' to create with it works of art. Serlio is unambiguous about this and talks about people "following their own minde," about "blinde conductors," "bad worke," and "much uncut or uneven workmanship," which comes about if you do not respect the art and do not learn geometry.

This is how we propose we should deal with code, which we consider to be a 'digital geometry'.

The Manners of the Architectonic Stage

If we accept these symmetries between eras, what can we learn from the ancient masters about today's architectonic stage? To us, it seems obvious that there are three manners in which these 'plays' can be 'enacted on stage'.

Taking a conceptual leaf out of the literal book by Serlio, we can frame them in theatrical terms. His highly influential work, which we quoted above, *I sette libri dell'architettura (Seven Books of Architecture*, originally and during his lifetime published as *Five Books of Architecture*, the remaining two being released posthumously), he develops the work of Alberti, who, as we saw, had written the first Renaissance text on architecture with *De re aedificatoria (On the Art of Building)* two generations earlier, in turn leaning heavily on Vitruvius' *De architettura*. But while Alberti published a purely text-based book in Latin, Serlio wrote in Italian and peppered his book with detailed and intricate illustrations.

In the second of his *Seven Books, On Perspective*, he included three drawings of theatre stage sets. They may serve us to propose this next set of parallels:

SATIRE

Satire corresponds to *ichnographia* and rhetoric. Transposed onto the digital stage, it asks: 'how does the program run?' It is the mechanics of information technology; it is a view of computers as machines. It corresponds to the imperative programming style and the **von Neumann architecture** of computing, developed in 1945 by Hungarian-American computer scientist and mathematician John von Neumann (1903–1957). It is about speed, prurience, fertility. ■ ↖649

412 ● 720

413 ● 720

TRAGEDY

Tragedy corresponds to *orthographia* and grammar. Transposed onto the digital stage, it asks: 'what do I want to express?' It is a felt mobility, the interplay, the consonance, the music of computing, but it comes together in one point (the 'not everything' we encountered earlier), that which we – somewhat romantically – call 'analogue', but which tragically collapses into the digital bit.

It is a view of computers as automata, and it corresponds to the declarative programming style and the **lambda calculus** developed by American mathematician and logician Alonzo Church (1903–1995) in the 1930s. It is about originality, truth, beauty. ■ ↖552

414 ● 721

415 ● 721

COMEDY

Comedy corresponds to *scaenographia* and dialectic. Transposed onto the digital stage, it asks: 'what is being played out?' It is the argument of information technology. It is a view of the computer as the medium of our time. It is coding in itself. It is about ability, wit, and the new.

416 ● 721

417 ● 721

Who We Are – The Digital Legacy

What marks us out as human beings? There are obviously many ways of describing what makes us human, and many thinkers have settled on many factors as most telling, most important, most defining; from our awareness of ourselves, through our capacity to formulate abstract thought, to our ability to laugh at ourselves our use of tools and materials, and our power to shape our environment, right through to our thumbs and our language.

If we listen to the big (and some of the small) narratives that are being told on our planet, through history and today, we realise that how we look at it is one thing, where we look at it from, another. Depending on how you've read this *Conclusion*, you may be inclined towards one understanding, or a very different one. We'd like to try the approach of a curious alien:

We are able, as if from the outside, to follow the traces of these new 'machines' that we have created and that aren't machines in the traditional sense, as they get to know us. While we are thinking, we can take 'pictures of our thoughts' by measuring our brain activity; we can study and observe our own species as well as any other, we can learn from the swarm behaviour of insects, or study social theories, such as the **actor-network theory**, for example, of which French philosopher Bruno Latour (b. 1947) is a principal proponent.

We can extrapolate from them that these 'machines' will soon be able to produce more neural activity than our own brains and therefore surpass us in 'intelligence'. This is the singularity put forward by American inventor and futurist Ray Kurzweil (b. 1948), who warns that from that point onward, our idea of what makes us human and our liberty as human beings will both be in grave peril. In a similar vein we can speculate that there will be a point at which 'machines' take over the world and enslave us, or at which we ourselves become immortal, because our minds will be able to exist devolved from our bodies, in a virtual space.

On the other hand we can also listen to a very different type of conversation. We can put ourselves onto the stage of this brave new world together with everybody else who is as yet an alien here, and learn the language. Do as Homer, Aristophanes, and Euripides did in antiquity. As Dante Alighieri did, or William Shakespeare, in the early modern era.

If we are all aliens in a new world that we don't know or know our way around, then the task is really obvious: we won't be able to comprehend everything at once, but we can become literate. Because literacy is what makes us capable of learning, of understanding, of adapting, and of making conscious, informed, good decisions; asking the good questions of which we speak in our Introduction, which alone can yield good answers. □ ↖29

Today, literacy means being able to read and write code. Because we have to realise that all conventional text and all conventional argument dissipates, lost in the flood of texts and arguments; that all drawings and illustrations drown in the flood of drawings and illustrations, the pictures in the flood of pictures: nothing makes sense any more. We arrive as illiterate migrants in this new world, and only code can help us begin to deal with it, to make some sort of argument. Because code is not 'afraid' of quantity.

As we explore in our chapter on Graphs & Graphics: at the heart of Google sits a code so simple, so dense, so effective, it takes up six lines. A poem. And a short one at that, half a sonnet. It invokes our image once more of the wheel and the axis: the still core of code allows the whole world of global data to spin around it, tethered by the hypotenuse of our ability. □ ↖175

And that's why we argue that here is our candidate for a new, digital, code. Not the athletic brawn of imperative von Neumann programming languages, but the intellectual brain of the lambda calculus.

We believe that this calculus today has a meaning that is not significantly different to the perspective construction 'language' of the Renaissance, as used and developed by Alberti, for instance.

The same Alberti who elaborates on Vitruvius, who breaks the cryptographic code of the ancient Romans and at the same time invents a new one with the principles of perspective drawing, builds a new architecture which doesn't supplant or replace the old, and which doesn't compete with it either. Instead, old architecture gets subsumed, newly articulated: it receives an evolved conceptualisation of its purpose, it gets new facades, literally a new face.

418 ● 722

That's how aliens arrive in a new world: they learn the language and use it to absorb and to express, to emulate and to refresh that which is already there, and fuse it with what they themselves bring to it.

You can witness this in action when you look at how immigrant populations from whichever part of the world arrive into whichever other part, there to survive and indeed thrive. Any alien, any foreigner, can become pragmatically competent in their dealings with a strange new world and attain stability, by learning the language. If you remove yourself from one culture into another, then long before you are able to understand everything and get all the nuances, have all the references (you never may get them all), and catch up with the idiom, you are able to function, to communicate, to talk; to get a sense for what's happening, to be an active subject, a citizen.

And you can assume that everything around you, all the other people, all of nature, all the trees and the birds and the cars and the buildings are in their own way 'subjects' too, they form part of the whole, they 'talk' their own 'language', they are the world. And although you can't understand them all, you can – and have to – take them seriously. Because there is in this new world (as there was in the old world, when it was new to another generation altogether) nothing other than these 'active subjects'. (How 'active' they are is possibly a matter of perception or even interpretation, but who's to say that a fountain in the square does not have as much of an impact on the people who sit by it as the people who sit by it have on each other, or that a building doesn't talk louder than its architect.) And that may surprise, entertain, even scare you. Puzzle or delight you: it's something you can talk, or joke, or laugh about, at the Queen's Garden Party...

Who are we? Here we are, looking at ourselves, feeling perhaps a little lonely, on this terribly small and distant planet, looking for ways of showing ourselves to ourselves. In Ancient Greece we find ourselves in the gods whom we create in our own image; in the Renaissance we find ourselves in the lifelike portraits that use light and perspective to such perplexing and riveting effect; today it may well be in the humanoid robot that we find ourselves reflected: in our own, home-made artificial intelligence.

"The past is a foreign country," British writer L P Hartley (1895–1972) famously wrote: "they do things differently there." This has ever been thus, and will most likely remain the case for as long as we're around, here, there, or anywhere. If we want to get along and make something of it, then we simply have to learn the language, the code, because we are all migrants native to the universe.

419 ● 722

420 ● 722

400 ● 697
The gnomon: it stands still, yet its purpose is motion under the sun.

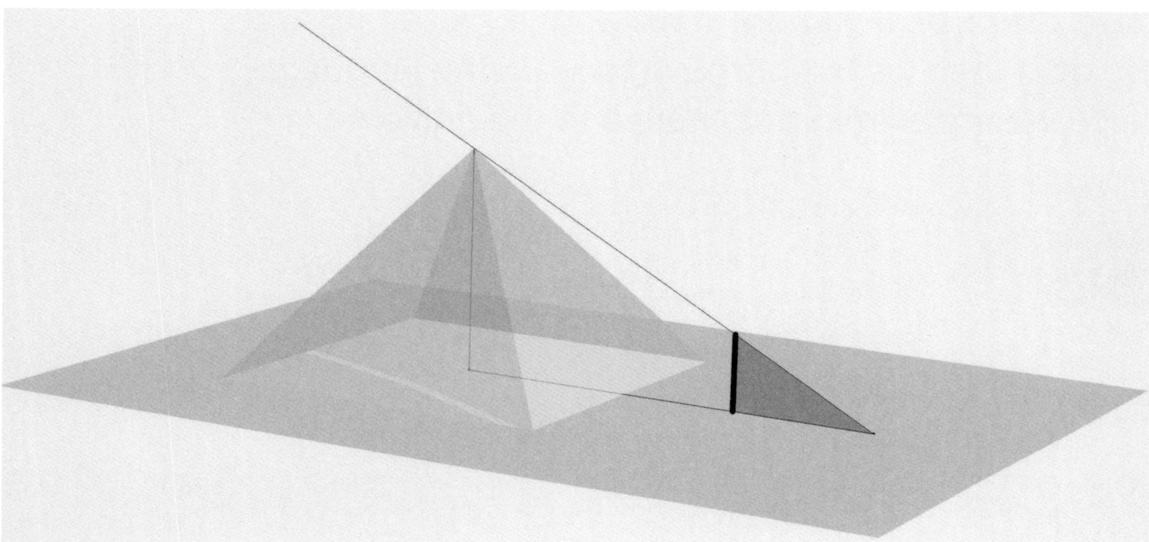

401 ● 698
Thales, the pyramid, the triangle, and the new ratio to measure real things in space.

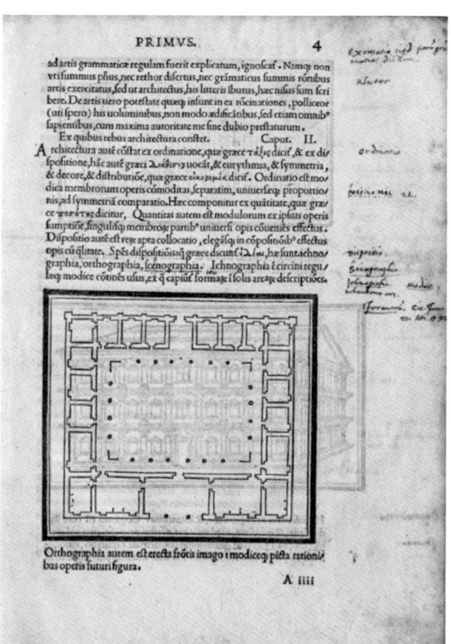

PRIMVS. 4

ad artis grammaticæ regulam fuerit explicatum, ignoscat. Namq; non vti summus phus, nec rethor disertus, nec grámaticus summis rónibus artis exercitatus, sed ut architectus, his litteris ibutus, hæc nisus sum scribere. De artis uero potestate quæq; insunt in ea rócinationes, polliceor (uti spero) his uoluminibus, non modo ædificátibus, sed etiam omnib' sapientibus, cum maxima autoritate me sine dubio prestaturum.

Ex quibus rebus architectura constet. Caput. II.

Architectura auté cóstat ex ordinatione, quæ græce τάξις dicit, & ex dispositione, hác auté græci διάθεσις uocát, & eurythmia, & symmetria, & decore, & distributióe, quæ græce οἰκονομία dicit. Ordinatio est modica membrorum operis cómoditas, separatim, uniuersæq; proportionis, ad symmetriá comparatio. Hæc componitur ex quátitate, quæ græce [illegible] dicitur, Quantitas autem est modulorum ex ipsius operis sumptióe, singulisq; membrorum partib' uniuersi opis cóueniés effectus. Dispositio auté est rerum apta collocatio, elegásq; in cópositióib' effectus opis cú qlitate. Spés dispositióis, q̃ græce dicunt ἰδέαι, hæ sunt ichnographia, orthographia, scenographia. Ichnographia é circini regulæq; modice cótinés usus, ex q̃ capiút formarum i solis arearum descriptióes.

Orthographia autem est erecta frótis imago i modiceq; picta rationibus operis futuri figura.

A iiii

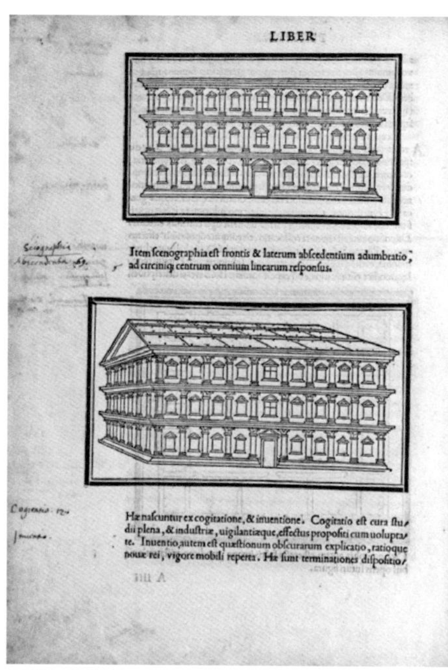

LIBER

Item scenographia est frontis & laterum abscedentium adumbratio, ad circiniq; centrum omnium linearum responsus.

Hæ nascuntur ex cogitatione, & inuentione. Cogitatio est cura studii plena, & industriæ, uigilantiæque, effectus propositi cum uoluptate. Inuentio, autem est quæstionum obscurarum explicatio, ratioque nouæ rei, vigore mobili reperta. Hæ sunt terminationes dispositio/

402A ● 699 402B ● 699
Illustrations from Fra Giovanni Giocondo on *ichnographia*, *orthographia*, and *scaenographia*, 1511.

403 ● 701
Multiple hour time lapse of a clear sky.

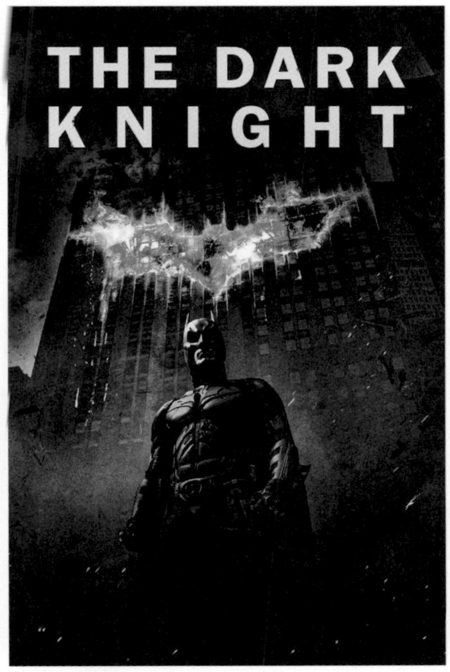

404A ● 706
The Dark Knight, 2008.

404B ● 706
Her, 2013.

404C ● 706
Assassin's Creed, 2016.

404D ● 706
Arrival, 2016.

405A ● 706
Chanel

405B ● 706
Nike

405C ● 706
Lavazza

405D ● 706
McDonald's

406 ● 708
The Oxyrhynchus Papyrus, dated 75–125 CE, featuring one of the oldest diagrams of Euclid's *Elements*.

407 ● 708
The geometry of writing in space: Temple of Concordia, 5 BCE, Sicily.

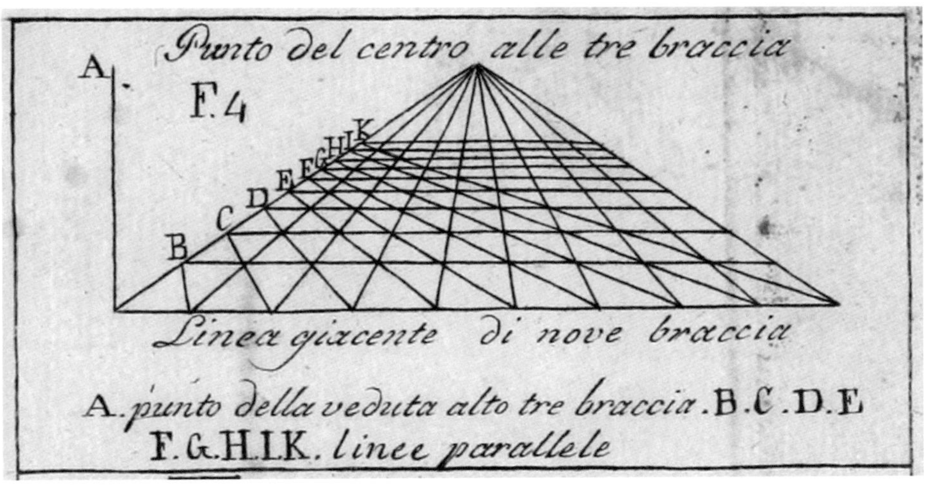

408 ● 709
Diagram by Leon Battista Alberti: perspective lines lead to a vanishing point in *Della pittura*, 1454.

409 ● 709
The geometry of drawing in time: Palladio, Villa Rotonda, 16th century, Vicenza, Italy.

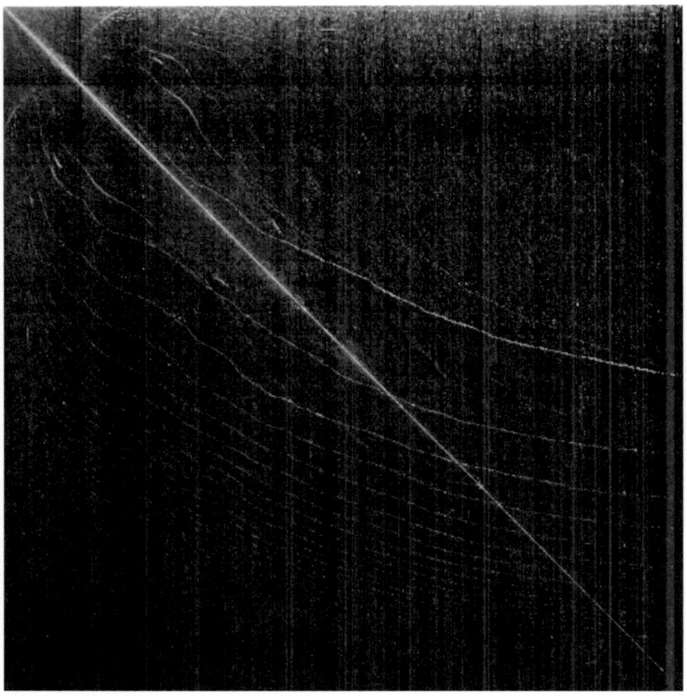

410 ● 709
Google matrix of Cambridge University network (2006).

411 ● 709
The geometry of coding in life: Le Corbusier, Villa Savoye, 20th century, Poissy, France.

412 ● 711
Satire, from Sebastiano Serlio: *Seven Books of Architecture*.

413 ● 711
McDonald's

414 ● 711
Tragedy, from Sebastiano Serlio: *Seven Books of Architecture*.

415 ● 711
Alain Ducasse

416 ● 712
Comedy, from Sebastiano Serlio: *Seven Books of Architecture*.

417 ● 712
Molecular gastronomy.

418 ● 714
Santa Maria Novella, Florence, Italy: Built on the site of a 9th century oratory, it was completed in the early 15th century by Leon Battista Alberti, drawing heavily on elements of classical architecture.

419 ● 715
Parmigianino (1504–1540): *Self-Portrait in a Convex Mirror*, 1524.

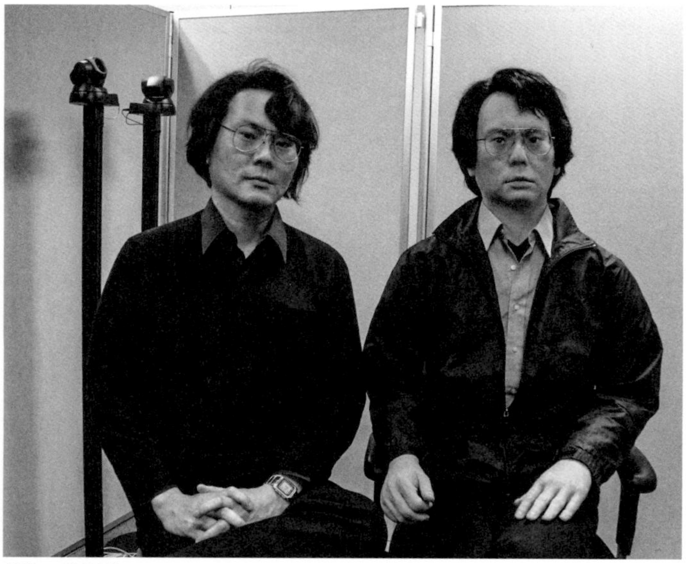

420 ● 715
Hiroshi Ishiguro (b. 1963): *Geminoid*, 2007.

Appendices

Index of Terms, Companies, Software, Publications, Institutions 727
Index of People 737
Index of Architectural Objects 741
Sources for Quotations, Citations, and Statistics 743
Sources for Images & Graphics 747
Biographies 753
Colophon 759

Index of Terms, Companies, Software, Publications, Institutions

.5D 63, 65, 134
-point perspective 265
D Modelling 470, 478, 479, 480, 509, 510, 512, 521, 524, 557
D Scanning 102, 103, 409, 445
D Studio (software) 65
D Systems (company) 411, 446
BIM (software) 519
K 236
B 113, 135, 139
LoWPAN 621, 622
5 Theses (book or paper) 372
984 63
001: A Space Odyssey (film) 554
011 Construction Strategy 511
017 Level of Specification 521

A

A 3D Bioprinting System to Produce Human-Scale Tissue Constructs With Structural Integrity (article) 443
AA (architects) 601, 606
A Files (publication) 161
Computer Animated Hand (work of art) 269
coustic simulation 480, 482
ctor-network theory 43, 712
da 376
dditive colour model 237
dditive manufacturing 407, 412
dditive shape grammar 540
ddress bus 374
djacency matrix 180, 194
dobe Acrobat Reader (software) 335
dobe Acrobat (software) 335, 336, 345
dobe Illustrator (software) 74, 336, 495
dobe Premiere Pro (software) 67
dobe Systems (company) 288, 334
dvanced Research Projects Agency (ARPA) (government agency or body) 553, 622, 650
EC *Architectes* Rotzer & Kaempfer (architects) 525
esthetics and Computation (research group or project) 359
gent-based model 160
gent-based simulation 538
gent-based system 160
I + Architecture Towards a New Approach (book or paper) 173
I (Artificial Intelligence) 64, 111, 114, 164, 182
irbnb (company) 533, 534
irborne Laser Scanning (ALS) 102
ir flow simulation 64, 477, 484, 485
ir Force Space Command (AFSC) (government agency or body) 502
JAX (Asynchronous JavaScript and XML) (standard) 394
kzidenz-Grotesk (font) 341
lbedo map 268
ldus (company) 335, 337
lgol (programming/scripting language) 376
lgorithmic urban design 539
lgorithmic urban planning 536, 538, 539, 540, 541, 542
lgorithms + Data Structures = Programs (book or paper) 156
lice's Adventures in Wonderland 469
lpha blending 296, 298
lphaGo (computer) 553
ltsys (company) 335
LU (Arithmetic Logic Unit) 374, 375, 383, 384
mazon Alexa (software) 553
mbient intelligence 615
mbient occlusion 263, 264, 268, 276
merican National Standards Institute (government agency or body) 333
merican Standard Code for Information Interchange (ASCII) 330, 331, 332, 333
miga 1000 (hardware) 617
mman (company) 412
mt für Strassen (ASTRA) (government agency or body) 341

Android (software) 551, 618, 624, 635
An Evolutionary Architecture (book or paper) 145, 164
An Improved Illumination Model for Shaded Display (book or paper) 261
An Inquiry Into the Nature and Causes of the Wealth of Nations (book or paper) 655
An Investigation of the Laws of Thought on Which Are Founded the Mathematical Theories of Logic and Probabilities (book or paper) 70, 375, 549, 551
ANN (Artificial Neural Network) 164, 553
An Outline of the Building Description System (book or paper) 524
Ansys CFD (software) 485
anti-aliasing 237, 248, 304
antiquity 35, 49, 135, 137, 139, 184, 372, 408, 425, 428, 443, 554, 662, 708, 713
Apache OpenOffice (software) 337
API (Applications Programming Interface) 235, 469, 496
Apologia (book or paper) 42
Apple (company) 63, 65, 67, 232, 233, 236, 240, 246, 333, 334, 335, 336, 337, 341, 358, 359, 400, 470, 479, 494, 496
Apple Mackintosh (hardware) 63, 232
Apple Maps (web service/app/platform) 494
AppleScript (programming/scripting language) 354
application programming 355
Applications Programming Interface (API) 469, 496
ArcGIS (software) 496, 502, 536
ArchDaily (publication) 512, 598, 599, 600, 601, 680, 682
ArchiCAD (software) 65, 134, 289, 470, 479, 519
Archimedean solid 70, 81
ArchiPhysik (software) 586
Architects' Data (book or paper) 120
Architectural Association (institution) 164
architectural geometry 360, 362
Architectural Geometry (book or paper) 57, 61
Architecture Machine Group (working group / standard body) 536
Architektur beginnt im Kopf (event/exhibition) 113
Architekturzentrum Wien (institution) 113
Arduino (hardware) 425, 619
Arial (font) 341, 342
Arithmetic Logic Unit (ALU) 374, 383, 384
ARPANET (Advanced Research Projects Agency Network) 622, 650
Arrival (film) 717
Ars conjectandi (book or paper) 569
Art+Com (company) 496
Art Forms of Nature (book or paper) 158, 170
Artificial Intelligence: A General Survey (report) 555
Artificial Intelligence (AI) 114, 182, 469, 551
Artificial Neural Network (ANN) 164, 553
Artis Engineering (company) 409
Art Nouveau 158, 170
ARUP (company) 82, 219, 409, 486, 535
ASCII (American Standard Code for Information Interchange) 238, 330, 331, 333
Assassin's Creed (film) 717
Assemble (architects) 602
Assemble (association) 637, 640
assembly language 374, 375, 376
assembly modelling 68
assymmetrical encryption 667
ASTRA-Frutiger (font) 341
Asus PC (hardware) 377
asynchronous communication 631, 632
Atelier Bow-Wow (architects) 113
Athens Charter (book or paper) 532
Audi (company) 341
Augmented Parametrics. Simulated and Expert Knowledge in Parametric Design (research group or project) 172
Augmented Reality (AR) 66, 465
Austrian Institute of Technology (institution) 545

Austrian Museum of Architecture (institution) 11
AutoCAD Architecture (ACAD) (software) 6
AutoCAD (software) 65, 13, 13
Autocode (programming/scripting language) 35
Autodesk (company) 358, 409, 41
Autodesk CFD (software) 48
Autodesk Revit (software) 470, 48
Automatically Programmed Tool (APT) 40
Automatic Sequence Controlled Calculator (ASCC) (computer) 408. See also Harvard Mark
autopoiesis 6
Avions Marcel Dassault (company) 62, 10
AWK (programming / scripting language) 7
axonometry 63, 3

B

Banburismus 6
Barneyscan (company) 23
Barneyscan XP (software) 2
base model
base station 618, 620, 6
Bash (programming/scripting language) 3
Basics of Geo-Information Systems (book or paper) 4
batch processing 35
Bauentwurfslehre (book or paper) 111, 12
Bauhaus 120, 338, 40
Bauwelt (publication) 51
beam tracing 26
Beauty Matters (event/exhibition) 22
Before Siri and Alexa There Was ELIZA (video) 55
Bentley Systems (company) 65, 409, 35
Betamax (format) 33
Bézier curve 73, 7
Bézier surface 7
BFC (BIM Collaboration Format) (format) 51
biased global illumination 26
biased rendering 26
bidirectional path tracing 26
BIG (Bjarke Ingels Group) (architects) 8
Big Brother (TV show) 64
Bilbao effect 6
BIM+ (publication) 51
BIM (Building Information Modelling) 25, 5 61, 64, 66, 67, 7
BIM Collaboration Format (BCF) (format) 51
BIMFORUM (organisation) 52
BIMServer (software) 51
BIM Vision (software) 51
BIMx (software) 51
Bing Maps (software) 49
bionics 12
Bioprinting Breakthrough: Researchers 3D Print Living Tissue for Functional Implants (article) 44
bit 124, 231, 233, 238, 23
Bitcoin 67
bitmap 232, 234, 23
Bjarke Ingels Group (BIG) (architects) 64, 84, 12
black & white photography 29
Blade Runner (film) 551, 57
Blender (software) 65, 22
Bletchley Park (government agency or body) 647, 66
Blickensderfer (company) 32
Blinn-Phong shading 261, 27
blockchain 653, 674, 67
Block research group (research group or project) 22
Bloomberg (publication) 55
Blueprint (software) 412, 47
BMVI (*Bundesministerium für Verkehr und digitale Infrastruktur*) (government agency or body) 51
bokeh 265, 276, 309, 31
Bollinger + Grohmann (company) 48
Boolean algebra 7
Boolean logic 70, 29
Boolean operation 70, 83, 199, 20
Boolean operator 7

… 565
Botnet 625
Boundary element modelling 480
Boundary Representation (BREP) model 68. See also BREP (Boundary Representaion) model; See also B-rep model
B-processor (software) 519
Breitbart News (publication) 653
BREP (Boundary Representaion) model 68. See also Boundary Representation (BREP) model; See also B-rep model
B-rep model 68. See also Boundary Representation (BREP) model; See also BREP (Boundary Representaion) model
Bricks (project or programme) 637
Brief History of BIM (article) 512
British Science and Engineering Research Council (SERC) (government agency or body) 555
BRL-CAD (software) 417
B-spline curve 73, 74
B-spline surface 74
Build 2017 (conference) 535
Building a Drawing and Drawing a Building (article) 430
Building Description System (BDS) 512, 524
Building Information Modeling (book or paper) 512
Building Information Modelling (BIM) 466, 478, 495, 496, 501, 507, 566
BuildingSMART (organisation) 501, 510, 511, 514, 521
Bump mapping 267, 268
Byte 238
Bytemark (institution) 494

C

C++ (programming/scripting language) 377, 470
CAAD (Computer Aided Architectural Design) 62, 65, 66, 67, 68, 75, 168, 172, 177
CAD (Computer Aided Design) 65, 129, 131
CAE (Computer Aided Engineering) 63, 65
Caesar cipher 661, 662, 664
Cambridge Analytica (company) 653, 654, 667
Cambridge University (institution) 180, 206, 720
CAM (Computer Aided Manufacturing) 63, 65
Canada Geographic Information System (CGIS) (system) 493, 496
Canal surface 73
Capterra (publication) 519
Carnegie Mellon University Pittsburgh (institution) 543, 556
Cartesian coordinate system 65, 66, 71, 237
Cartesian doubt 563
Cascading Style Sheets (CSS) 345. See also CSS (Cascading Style Sheets)
Case (company) 409
CASTING 413, 414
Casting Curved Shadows on Curved Surfaces (book or paper) 261
Category theory 47, 561
Catenary model 424
Cathode Ray Tube (CRT) 231, 232, 235, 236
CATIA (Computer Aided Three-Dimensional Interactive Application) (software) 62, 159, 245
Catmull-Clark subdivision-surface modelling 269, 280
CATT (Computer Aided Test Tool) (software) 481
Caustics 264
CCD (Charge-Coupled Device) camera 246, 262
CCTV (Closed-Circuit Television) 625, 652
Cellular automaton 152, 540, 545
Central Intelligence Agency (CIA) (government agency or body) 496, 648. See also CIA (Central Intelligence Agency)
Central Limit Theorem (CLT) 571
Central place theory 531
Central Processing Unit (CPU) 374, 618
CERN (international body or organisation) 619, 620
CesiumJS (software) 496
CGA shape grammar 541
CG (Computer Graphics) 257, 496
CGI (Common Gateway Interface) 356
CGI (Computer Generated Imaging) 356
CGIS (Canada Geographic Information System) (system) 493, 496
Chanel (brand) 718
channel surface 73
Chartered Institute of Building (organisation) 519
Chef's Table (TV series) 39
China State Construction Design International (CCDI) (architects) 219
Church-Turing thesis 552
CIA (Central Intelligence Agency) 496, 648. See also Central Intelligence Agency (CIA) (government agency or body)
Cinema4D (software) 65, 279
citizen participation 433, 516, 517
Citizens as Sensors: The World of Volunteered Geography (article) 494
Citizens Band (CB) radio 621
CityEngine (software) 540, 541
City Form Lab (software) 539
CityGML (standard) 501, 537
CityMapper (web service/app/platform) 104, 187, 502, 534
City of Bits (book or paper) 536
ClearType (software) 237
CLOS (Kee89) (programming/scripting language) 377
CMYK (Cyan Magenta Yellow Key) 237, 239, 304
CNC (Computer Numerical Control) 367, 408, 409, 411, 412, 413, 415
CNC router 637
CoAP (Constrained Application Protocol) 623
COBE (architects) 602
COBie (Construction Operations Building Information Exchange) (format) 519
COBOD International (company) 452
Codecademy (web service/app/platform) 353
cognitive design computing 541, 542
cognitive distance 539
colour correction 241, 265, 266, 271
colour depth 292, 297
colour profile 234, 237, 238
combinatorial explosion 379, 555, 556
Comic Sans (font) 77, 449
Comma Separated Values (CSV) (format) 500
Commodore International (company) 617
Common Data Environments (CDEs) 519
Common Desktop Environment (CDE) (software) 519, 520
Common Gateway Interface (CGI) 356
Common Lisp (programming/scripting language) 377
common sense knowledge 557
compiler 354, 375
CompuServe, company 233, 239
Computational Fluid Dynamics (CFD) 484
Computer Aided Architectural Design (book or paper) 57, 62, 177
Computer Aided Architectural Design (CAAD) 62, 65, 164, 359
Computer Aided Design (CAD) 55, 65, 129, 131, 177, 231, 259, 512
Computer Aided Engineering (CAE) 65
Computer Aided Manufacturing (CAM) 65
Computer Display of Curved Surfaces (book or paper) 260
Computer Generated Imagery (CGI) 263
Computer Graphics (CG) 257
Computer Graphics: Principles and Practice (book or paper) 255, 257, 306
Computer Hope (publication) 259
Computer Numerical Control (CNC) 408, 413, 415
Computer Vision Group (research group or project) 101
Computer Vision Lab (institution) 540
Computing Machine Laboratory (institution) 55…
Conclusiones philosophicae, cabalisticae et theologicae (book or paper) 4…
cone tracing 26…
Congrès International d'Architecture Moderne (CIAM) (conference) 53…
Constrained Application Protocol (CoAP) 62…
constrained device 62…
Construction Operations Building Information Exchange (COBie) (format) 51…
construction tree 16…
Constructive Solid Geometry (CSG) 68, 8…
context sensitive grammar 15…
Contiki (software) 61…
control polygon 7…
control unit 37…
CoolType (software) 23…
Coop Himmelb(l)au (architects) 119, 168, 40…
copyleft 635, 63…
core memory 23…
Cornell box 262, 30…
Cornell University (institution) 262, 30…
Cortana (software) 55…
Counting Palladian Plans (book or paper) 16…
Courier (font) 341, 343, 34…
CPS (Cyber Physical System) 41…
CPU (Central Processing Unit) 262, 35…
crawler 597, 598, 599, 60…
creative commons 636, 65…
Creative Commons (organisation) 407, 40… 63…
cross section 67, 121, 132, 13…
crystallography 19…
CSG model 68, 8…
C shell (programming/scripting language) 37…
CSS (Cascading Style Sheets) 34… See also Cascading Style Sheets (CSS)
CSV (Comma Separated Values) (format) 50…
CupCake CNC (hardware) 45…
Curiosity (publication) 26…
Cut 'n' Paste: From Architectural Assemblage to Collage City (event/exhibition) 31…
cybernetics 593, 647, 64…
Cybernetics Conferences (event/exhibition) 64…
Cyber Physical System (CPS) 41…
Cyclopaedia or, An Universal Dictionary of Arts and Sciences (book or paper) 63…

D

DAAR (architects) 60…
daguerrotype 25…
Daidalos (publication) 111, 12…
DARPA (Defense Advanced Research Projects Agency) (government agency or body) 55…
Dartmouth College (institution) 55…
Dartmouth Summer Research Project on Artificial Intelligence (conference) 55…
Das Japanische Haus (book or paper) 12…
Dassault Aviation (company) 40…
Dassault Systèmes (company) 62, 63, 15… 40…
data bus 37…
data link layer 62…
David (work of art) 63…
dBase IV (format) 49…
DCFL (Deterministic Context-Free Language) 15…
DCP (Digital Cinema Projection) 23…
DDoS (Distributed Denial of Service) 62…
Dead Poets' Society (film) 63…
De architectura (book or paper) 95, 12… 166, 69…
de Casteljau algorithm 7…
Decision Support System (DSS) 49…
declarative programming language 375, 65…
DecodingSpaces (company) 541, 54…
deconstructivism 11…
Deep Blue (computer) 553, 55…
deep learning 16…

DeepMind Technologies (company) 553
De harmonia mundi totius (book or paper) 118
De humani corporis fabrica libri septem (book or paper) 576
Della pittura (book or paper) 719
Denken in Modellen (event/exhibition) 427
depth buffering 259
depth of field 264, 265, 270, 271
De re aedificatoria (book or paper) 95, 699, 711
Der Spiegel (publication) 646
Der Technokrat (work of art) 125
Der Zauberlehrling (literary work) 137
Descriptio urbi Romae (book or paper) 105
descriptive geometry 132
Design by Numbers (book or paper an also programming/scripting language) 351, 359
Design File (DGN) (format) 137
design plan 132
design space 148, 149, 152, 153, 162, 164
Design Space Exploration (DSE) 162, 362, 541, 638
Design-to-Production (company) 367, 409, 412, 418
Design With Nature (book or paper) 512
Desk Top Publishing (DTP) 335, 338
Destination-Oriented Directed Acyclic Graph (DODAG) 622
Deterministic Context-Free Language (DCFL) 157
Deutsches Institut für Normung (DIN) (institution) 334
developable surface 75
Dezeen (publication) 598, 599, 600, 601
diagrammatic architecture 293
dialectic barrier 116
DIALux (software) 585
Die vier Elemente der Baukunst (book or paper) 421, 426
Die Zukunft hat schon begonnen (book or paper) 470
differential geometry 185
differential GPS 502
diffuse map 310
diffuse ray tracing 262
Digital Cinema Projection (DCP) 236
digital collage 295, 296, 297, 298, 299
Digital Equipment Corporation (DEC) (company) 556
digital fabrication 360, 405, 407, 431
digital modelling 430, 432, 433
Digital Project (software) 63
Digital Terrain Model (book or paper) 496
DIN 66001 376
Direct Ink Writing (DIW) 446, 448
Dirk Gently's Holistic Detective Agency (literary work) 554
discrete mathematics 177
discretisation 195, 200
displacement mapping 268, 280
DISTO (hardware) 97, 292
Distributed Denial of Service (DDoS) 625
distributed ray tracing 262
dividing grammar 540
DOAG (Destination-Oriented Directed Acyclic Graph) 622
Do Androids Dream of Sheep? (literary work) 551
DPI (Dots per Inch) 235
drain pipe inspection 102
Drawing (DWG) (format) 137
Drawing Exchange Format (DXF) (format) 137
drawing tablet (hardware) 233
Drohnenland (literary work) 536
Dropbox (web service/app/platform) 633
DSE (Design Space Exploration) 162, 362, 541
DTP (Desk Top Publishing) 335, 336, 337
DUS Architects (architects) 444
duty cycling 621
Dynamo (software) 159, 161

E

E2A (architects) 602
EA (Evolutionary Algorithm) 118, 121
Earth Moves: the Furnishing of Territories (book or paper) 421, 429
EarthViewer (software) 496
EASE (Enhanced Acoustic Simulator for Engineers) (software) 481
Ecosistema Urbano (architects) 602
edge 177, 178, 180, 187, 188, 189, 196, 201
Edge Design Institute (architects) 113
EDM (Electrical Discharge Machining) 413
eGovernment 534
Eiffel (programming/scripting language) 377
Electrical Discharge Machining (EDM) 413
Electrochemical Machining (ECM) 413
Electron Beam Melting (EBM) 449
Elemental (architects) 636, 639
Elements (book or paper) 700. See also The Elements (book or paper)
elevation 60, 116, 119, 699
ELIZA (software) 552, 553
Emerdata (company) 654
emergence 145, 154, 531, 561, 632, 651
EMO (Evolutionary Multi-Criteria Optimisations) 541
emotional map 535
Employer's Information Requirement (EIR) 522
Encapsulated Postscript (EPS) 327, 334, 335
Encyclopédie (book or paper) 633, 639
energy simulation 484, 513, 585
Enigma code 552, 647, 663
eParticipation 542
EPS (Encapsulated Postscript) 327, 334
ESA (European Space Agency) (international body or organisation) 493
Esri (company) 495, 496, 497, 502, 545
Essai sur l'architecture (book or paper) 125
ETH Zürich (institution) 122, 164, 168, 170, 172, 222
ETX (Expected Transmission Count) 622
Euclidean geometry 183, 184, 185, 186, 187, 189, 196, 197, 708
Euclidian vector 201
Euler's formula 69
Eurocode 483
European Space Agency (ESA) (international body or organisation) 493
Evans & Sutherland (company) 258
Evolutionary Algorithm (EA) 118, 121, 164, 541
Excel (software) 61, 519
Exif (Exchangeable Image File Format) (format) 240
Expectation-Maximisation (EM) 122
Expected Transmission Count (ETX) 622
expert system 556, 561
Explorer (software) 240, 496, 634
Exstensible Markup Language (XML) (programming/scripting language) 139, 336, 377, 394
Extensible Stylesheet Language (XSL) (programming/scripting language) 394
extension language 355, 356, 359

F

FabLab (institution) 407, 442
Facebook (company) 467, 469, 500, 535, 553, 565
facsimile 234, 246
Fake Industries AA (architects) 602
feature class 536
Ferranti Mark 1 (computer) 552
Fibonacci sequence 156
Fifth Generation Computer (project or programme) 557
film 554
Final Cut Pro (software) 67
final gather 264
Finder (software) 240, 249
finite difference time domain modelling 480
Finite Element Analysis (FEA) 483
Finite Element Method (FEM) 483
finite element modelling 480
fire and evacuation simulation 485
Firefox (software) 356, 623, 634
First Draft of a Report on the EDVAC (book or paper) 373
First Order Logic (FOL) 558
fitness function 148, 164, 165, 167
floppy disk 334
Flower Matango (Flower Matango) 690
fluid dynamics 268, 270
foam structures 70
FOL (First Order Logic) 558
font 138, 334, 335, 336, 337, 339, 340, 342, 343, 344, 345, 346, 619
foolscap folio 334
Fordism 636
Forensic Architecture (architects) 602
formal language 156, 192, 375, 554
Fortran (programming/scripting language) 375, 390
Foster + Partners (architects) 63, 216
Four Books on Human Proportion (book or paper) 421, 429, 437
Fourth Industrial Revolution 415
fractal 145, 155, 156, 158, 159, 193
frame problem 379, 558, 704
Frankenstein; or, The Modern Prometheus (literary work) 554, 559, 563
Frank Gehry and Associates (architects) 159, 362
Freax (software) 635
FreeCAD (software) 519
freeform curve 73, 74
freeform surface 88
Free Software Foundation (organisation) 635
frequency domain 673
full-surface collage 297
Functional City (concept) 532
Fused Deposition Modelling (FDM) 446, 447, 448
Fused Filament Fabrication (FFF) 446, 447, 448
Future Cities Laboratory (Singapore ETH Centre/ETH Zürich) (research group or project) 170
fuzzy logic 290
fuzzy set theory 290

G

Galileo (system) 39, 493, 705
Game of Life (software) 152, 154, 155
Garamond (font) 342
GC (GenerativeComponents) (software) 358
G-code 410, 411, 446
Gehry Partners (architects) 362, 409, 486, 537
Gehry Technologies (company) 63, 486, 537, 538
Geminoid HI-1 (work of art) 559, 722
General Public Licence 534
general purpose programming language 355
Generative Adversarial Networks (GAN) 164, 165
GenerativeComponents (GC) (software) 358
generative model 114, 117, 121
generative network 165
Genetic Algorithm (GA) 122, 145, 164, 165, 166
genotype 162, 164
Geodata Infrastructure North-Rhine Westphalia (GDI NRW) (project or programme) 501
geodesic dome 70, 83
geodesic polyhedra 70
geodesic sphere 70, 83
Geodesign (concept) 497, 529
Geodesign Technologies (company) 497
Geographic Information Systems (GIS) 491, 493, 536
Geographic Resources Analysis Support System (GRASS) (software) 496, 502
Geography Markup Language (GML) (standard) 501, 537
GeoJournal (publication) 494
geometrical room acoustics modelling 480
Geometry (book or paper) 83
Georgia Tech School of Architecture (institution) 12
Geospatial World (publication) 18
Germany Trade & Invest (government agency or body) 11

GIF (Graphics Interchange Format) (format) 233, 239
GI (Graphical Interface) 353, 358, 359
Global Illumination (GI) 262, 263, 264, 271, 287
Global Navigation Satellite System (GNNS) (system) 493, 496, 502
Global Positioning System (GPS) (system) 102, 493, 502
GLONASS (Global Navigation Satellite System) (system) 493, 496, 502
glue language 355
GML (Geography Markup Language) (standard) 501, 537
GMW Computers Ltd (company) 512
GNNS (Global Navigation Satellite System) 102, 493, 496, 502
GNU/Linux (software) 635
GNU Project 634
golden ratio 119, 120, 155, 333
Gollins Melvin Ward (GMW) (architects) 512
Good Morning America (TV show) 442
Google (company) 469, 494, 496, 500, 502
Google Books (project or programme) 654
Google Cardboard (hardware) 467, 469
Google Earth (software) 496, 500, 502
Google Glass (hardware) 625
Google Maps (software) 104, 187, 494, 502, 536
Google Now (software) 553
Google Street View (software) 536
Gouraud shading 260
Government Code & Cypher School (GCCS) (government agency or body) 647
GP104 (hardware) 395
GPS Exchange (GPX) (format) 500
GPS (Global Positioning System) (system) 102, 493, 494, 500, 502
GPU (Graphics Processing Unit) 262, 263, 271, 272
GPX (GPS Exchange) (format) 500
Grahpics Interchange Format (GIF) (format) 233, 239
graph 177, 178, 179, 180, 181, 182, 186, 187, 188, 189, 190, 192, 193, 194, 196, 202
graph distance matrix 194
Graphical Interface (GI) 353, 358, 359
Graphical User Interface (GUI) 232, 519
graphics card 131, 262, 263, 272, 470
Graphics Processing Unit (GPU) 262, 272
graphic tablet 233, 246
Graphisoft (company) 65, 134, 289, 479, 519, 586
Graphisoft EcoDesigner Star (software) 586
Graz University of Technology (institution) 9, 171, 223
Great Exhibition (event/exhibition) 426, 435
Greg Lynn FORM (architects) 63, 78, 409
Ground Penetrating Radar (GPR) 101, 103
ground plan 102, 104, 116, 119, 125, 126, 132, 133, 134, 136, 138, 141, 158
Grundlagen der Geo-Informationssysteme (book or paper) 491, 497
GTeam (software) 637
GTX 1080 (hardware) 395
Guerrillero Heroico (work of art) 651, 676

H

Haas'sche Schriftgiesserei (company) 341
hanging chain model 160, 211, 434
Harmonices mundi (book or paper) 155
Harvard Graduate School of Design (institution) 496, 497
Harvard Mark I (computer) 408
Harvard University (institution) 408, 543
hash code 674
HD (High Definition) 231, 236, 269, 298, 447
HDRI (High Dynamic Range Imaging) 258, 271
Head Mounted Display (HMD) 468, 469, 473
Helvetica (font) 341, 342
Her (film) 717
Herzog & de Meuron (architects) 122, 164, 295, 297, 315, 318, 322, 428, 481, 489, 606
heuristic 541, 555
hidden line removal 259
High Definition (HD) 231, 236, 269, 298, 447
high-level language 354, 375, 377, 390, 391, 392
high-level programming 354, 355
High Performance Computing Centre Stuttgart (institution) 485
Hochtief ViCon (company) 521
HoloLens (hardware) 469
Houdini (software) 159, 166, 221
HP (Hyperbolic Paraboloid) surface 72
HTML (Hypertext Markup Language) (programming/scripting language) 344, 345, 356, 378, 623, 672
HTTP (Hypertext Transfer Protocol) (protocol) 344, 599, 621, 623
Hundegger K2i (hardware) 417
HWKN (architects) 602
Hylozoic Soil (work of art) 458
Hypertext Markup Language (HTML) (programming/scripting language) 344, 345, 356, 378
Hypertext Transfer Protocol (HTTP) (protocol) 344, 623

I

IBM (International Business Machines) (company) 238, 341, 355, 356, 408, 552, 553, 554
IBM 701 (computer) 552
IBM Journal (publication) 552
ichnographia 699, 704, 705, 711
I-Dea (software) 65
IEC (International Electrotechnical Commission) (international body or organisation) 239
IEEE 802.15.4 (standard) 620, 621
IFC (Industry Foundation Class) (standard) 379, 501, 510, 511, 519, 520
If This Then That 624
IFTTT (If This Then That) (software) 623, 624
IJP Architects (architects) 362, 400
illumination 259, 261, 262, 263, 264, 271, 484
illumination engineering 484
Illustrator (software) 74, 336, 495
image stitching 101
imperative programming language 375
Imperial College (institution) 494, 543
incompleteness theorems 556, 700
InDesign (software) 337
induction design 157, 221, 545
Industrie 4.0 (project or programme) 511
Industry 4.0 415
Industry Foundation Class (IFC) (standard) 379, 510, 511, 519, 520
Inertial Navigation System (INS) 102
infinite image theorem 116
infinite monkey theorem 116
Inkjet head 3-Dimensional Printing (3DP) 446, 449, 452
INS (Inertial Navigation System) 102
INSPIRE (Initiative Infrastructure for Spatial Information in the European Community) (project or programme) 501
Instagram (web service/app/platform) 294, 535, 626
Institute ISMES (institution) 211
Institute of Geodesy and Geoinformatics (institution) 497
integrated processes 407, 414, 416
intelligent contact lens 625
Interaction Design Studio Ivrea (IDII) (project or programme) 619
interactive modelling 484
International Alliance for Interoperability (IAI) (international body or organisation) 501, 511
International Committee for Information Technology Standards (international body or organisation) 333
International Electrotechnical Commission (IEC) (international body or organisation) 239
International Organization for Standardization (ISO) (international body or organisation) 239
International Style 51
Internet Engineering Task Force (IETF) (working group/standard body) 621, 62
Internet Explorer (software) 356, 63
Internet of Humans 62
Internet of Things (IoT) 26, 378, 516, 53 591, 613, 615
Internet Protocol (IP) (protocol) 62
interpolation 73, 74, 184, 197, 260, 409, 67
interpreter 354, 375, 384, 386, 38
iOS (software) 618, 62
IP address 622, 623, 62
IP (Internet Protocol) (protocol) 621, 622, 62
IPV6 621, 622, 62
I quattro libri dell'architettura (book or paper) 11
IrisVR (software) 47
irradiance map 26
I sette libri dell'architettura (book or paper) 71
ISO (International Organization for Standardization) (international body or organisation) 23 334, 411, 501
isometric projection 6
isovist 53
isovist theory 53
Italy Liberated From the Goths (literary work) 11

J

Jacquard loom 407, 41
Japan Electronic Industries Development Association (JEIDA) (organisation) 24
JavaScript (programming/scripting language) 34 354, 355, 356, 357, 375, 377, 380, 38 391, 39
JCL (Job Control Language) (programming/scripting language) 35
JDS (architects) 602, 60
JEIDA (Japan Electronic Industries Development Association) (organisation) 24
JEITA (Japan Electronics and Information Technology Industries Association) (organisation) 24
Jeopardy (TV show) 55
Job Control Language (JCL) (programming/scripting language) 35
Johnston Marklee (architects) 60
Joint Photographic Experts Group (JPEG) (working group/standard body) 105, 23 24
Josiah Macy Jr Foundation (organisation) 64
Jugendstil 158, 17

K

Kaisersrot (research group or project) 12 164, 168, 17
Kalkbreite Zürich (association) 63
Kepler (software) 49
kernel 63
Kew Gardens (institution) 426, 43
Keyhole Inc (company) 49
Keyhole Markup Language (KML) (programming/scripting language) 500, 50
K-means clustering 56
KML (Keyhole Markup Language) (programming/scripting language) 500, 50
Koch curve 15
Koch snowflake 155, 156, 19
Kritios Boy (work of art) 57
Kuehn Malvezz (architects) 60
Kunstformen der Natur (book or paper) 145, 158, 17

L

Laboratory for Visionary Architecture (LAVA (architects) 121, 359, 362, 365, 36

Labours of Love (article) 431
Lacaton & Vassal (architects) 113, 602
Lagrange polynomial 184, 186
Lambda calculus (programming/scripting language) 375, 376, 380, 388
Lambertian reflectance 259
Lambert's cosine law 260
Lambert shading 259, 260
aminating 413
LAN (architects) 602
Land Information System (LIS) 496
Landscape with Pilgrim (work of art) 562, 577
LAN (Local Area Network) 620
Laplace's demon 558
Large Hadron Collider (international body or organisation) 340, 619
Large Scale Urban Modelling (LSUM) 537, 538
Laser-DISTO (hardware) 292
aser rangefinder 97, 98, 100
aser scanning 102, 103, 107, 108, 516
LaserWriter (hardware) 334
Latin square 555, 556, 567
LAVA (Laboratory fo Visionary Architecture) (architects) 121, 359, 362, 365, 366
Lavazza (brand) 718
Law of Large Numbers (LLN) 568, 669
Lawrence Berkeley National Labs (LBNL) (institution) 271
ayered texturing 270
LCD (Liquid-Crystal Display) 232, 233, 237, 238
Le carceri d'invenzione (book or paper) 468
Lego 67, 113, 134, 358, 470, 513, 524, 542
Lego Mindstorms (software) 358, 365
Leica Geosystems (company) 97
Leica M2 651
Le Monde (publication) 646
Les Misérables (play or musical) 655
Letraset 337, 449
Level of Development (LOD) 521, 522, 526
Level of Geometry (LOG) 521, 523
Level of Information (LOI) 521, 522, 523
Leviathan or The Matter, Forme and Power of a Common Wealth Ecclesiasticall and Civil (book or paper) 655
ibrary 66, 104, 134, 356, 385, 496, 512, 596
idar 102
Life Magazine (publication) 555
ight-cache 264
Lightscape (software) 308, 585
ight simulation 483, 484, 486, 585
Lightwave (software) 171
Lincoln Laboratory (institution) 231
Lincoln TX-2 (computer) 231, 244
ine of beauty 119
Linux (software) 430, 635
Lippincott's Magazine (publication) 179
Liquid-Crystal Display (LCD) 232, 233, 237, 238
Lisp (programming/scripting language) 375, 377
L'Italia liberata dai Goti (literary work) 119
LIVE Singapore! (project or programme) 491, 494
LLN (Law of Large Numbers) 568, 669
oad shifting 625
Lobster Phone (work of art) 443
Local Area Network (LAN) 620
Locational Models, Geographic Information and Planning Support Systems (book or paper) 496
Location and Land Use (book or paper) 532
oft function 73
oft surface 73, 87
LOG (Level of Geometry) 521, 523
Logic Theorist (software) 554
Logitec (hardware) 377
Logo (programming/scripting language) 358, 365
LOI (Level of Information) 521, 522, 523
Lord of the Rings (literary work) 102
ow-level programming 354
LSD-SLAM (Large Scale Direct Monocular Simultaneous Localisation and Mapping) 101
L-systems 156, 157, 159, 166

M

Mac-OS (software) 334
MacBook Pro (hardware) 236
machine code 354, 375, 410
machine learning 414, 461, 469, 470, 486, 517, 518, 535, 536, 542, 549, 551, 552, 553, 554, 556, 558, 560, 561, 564, 565, 567, 568, 571, 573, 575
machine level programming 354
MAC (Media Access Control) layer 620
macro 131, 264, 355, 444, 538
macroscope 625
MacUser (publication) 341
Macy Foundation (organisation) 649
MAD (architects) 602
Made In (architects) 602
Made in China 2025 (project or programme) 511
Magic Cube 75, 90
MAGNETOMETER 102
Mail.Ru (company) 502
mainframe 231, 355, 376, 377, 378, 379, 396, 555, 556, 561
Maio (architects) 602, 603
Maison de la publicité (work of art) 300
MakerBot Industries (company) 442
maker culture 430, 442
makerspace 430, 433
Making Sense of the New Urban Science (institution) 529, 531
Manchester Mark 1 (computer) 355, 552
manifold 36, 166, 185, 294, 486, 511, 653
MAN (Metropolitan Area Network) 620
Maperitive (software) 494, 495, 502
Maps (software) 494, 502, 536
Maps.Me (software) 502
Markov chain 188, 205, 564, 571
markup language 139, 336, 344, 377, 378, 394, 500, 501, 511, 537
Massachusetts Institute of Technology (MIT) (institution) 153, 231, 358, 407, 442, 494, 536, 552, 634
mass customisation 80, 407
MASS Design Group (architects) 602, 603
materiability (concept) 430, 437
Mathematica (software) 424, 483, 549, 551, 552, 555, 562, 563, 567, 570
Mathlab (programming/scripting language) 381
MathWorks (company) 162
MATLAB (software) 162
MATSim (software) 538
Mattel (company) 443
Maxwell Render (software) 288
Maxwell's demon 563, 564, 578
Maya (software) 65, 409
Maya/Alias (software) 65
MayBim (software) 638
McDonald's (brand) 718, 720
Media Access Control (MAC) 620, 621
mesh routing 622
metaball 160, 171, 222
meta-materiality 430
Metro (architects) 602
metropolis light transport 263
Metropolitan Area Network (MAN) 620
Michell truss 223
Microscribe (software) 106
Microsoft (company) 138, 237, 240, 334, 335, 336, 341, 348, 356, 469, 470, 494, 519, 535, 634
Microsoft MS-DOS (software) 356
MicroStation (software) 65, 137, 358
MIDI (Musical Instrument Digital Interface) 356
Mindstorms Robotics Kits (software) 358
Minecraft (software) 67, 470, 540
mipmapping 261
Mirai (malware) 625
Mixed Reality (MR) 66, 103, 431, 465, 681, 682, 683, 684, 685, 686, 687, 688, 689, 690
MKUltra (project or programme) 648
mocárabe 99
Modelica (programming/scripting language) 486
modelling 477, 481, 485, 486, 501, 502, 513, 514, 515, 516, 518, 522, 523, 537, 538, 540, 571
modelling for acoustical materials
modelling for active noise control 430
modelling for outdoor sound propagation 430
Modelling Multiple Views on Buildings – Automation in Construction (book or paper)
modernity 77, 100, 121, 197, 204, 29[illegible] 444, 636, 70[illegible]
module 120, 125, 172, 356, 40[illegible]
modulo operator
modulor function 119, 120, 155, 357
Mojang Specifications (company)
Mona Lisa (work of art) 116
Monadology (book or paper)
monoalphabetic substitution
Monotype Grotesque (font)
Monotype Typography (company)
Moore's law 558
morphogenesis 145, 155, 158, 159, 164
MOS (architects)
mote
motion capture 101, 102
Motor Vehicle Manufacturers Association (organisation)
Moves (software)
MS-DOS (software) 336, 348
Mufuti (Multifunktionstisch)
multi-image photogrammetry 97, 100, 217, 270
Multi-Jet Printing (MJP) 446, 44[illegible]
multiple access protocol
Museo Nazionale (institution)
Museum of Estonian Architecture (institution)
Musical Instrument Digital Interface (MIDI)
My Fair Lady (film and stage musical)

N

Nagata Acoustics (company) 428, 481, 48[illegible]
Nameless (architects) 602
NASA (National Aeronautics and Space Administration) (government agency or body) 231, 44[illegible] 496, 502, 63[illegible]
NASA WorldWind (software) 496, 50[illegible]
National Center for Geographic Information and Analysis (organisation) 49[illegible]
National Institute of Building Sciences in the United States (organisation) 50[illegible]
National Security Agency (NSA) (government agency or body) 646, 65[illegible]
National Technical University of Greece (institution) 53[illegible]
National Theatre (institution) 424, 51[illegible]
NATO (North Atlantic Treaty Organization) (international body or organisation) 65[illegible]
naturalised form 19[illegible]
Natural Language Processing (NLP) 551, 55[illegible], 556
Natura morta (Still Life) (work of art) 30[illegible]
Natürliche Schöpfungsgeschichte (book or paper) 15[illegible]
Navigator (software) 356, 63[illegible]
NavVis (hardware) 102, 10[illegible]
Nemetschek Allplan (software) 6[illegible]
network layer 62[illegible]
network solidarity 62[illegible]
Neue Haas Grotesk (font) 34[illegible]
Neufert (book or paper) 111, 12[illegible]
Neural Networks (NN) 16[illegible]
New York Institute of Technology (NYIT) (institution) 26[illegible]
New York University (NYU) (institution) 531, 54[illegible]
Niantic (company) 49[illegible]
Nike (brand) 71[illegible]
Nineteen Eighty-Four (literary work) 470, 64[illegible]
Ninsight (company) 48[illegible]
Nintendo (company) 467, 49[illegible]
NLP (Natural Language Processing) 551, 55[illegible], 55[illegible]
node 603, 615, 618, 619, 620, 621, 622, 62[illegible], 624, 62[illegible]

…nse 674, 675
non-Euclidian geometry 185, 186
non-standard architecture 430
Normenausschuss der Deutschen Industrie (working group / standard body) 334
Norwegian Computing Centre (institution) 377
Notes on the Synthesis of Form (book or paper) 111, 162
Numerical Control (NC) 408, 412, 446
NURBS curve 73
NURBS (Non-Univorm Rational B-Spline) 74, 134, 185, 197, 363, 489
NURBS surface 74
Nymphéas (work of art) 564, 579

O

Objectile (company) 430
objective probability 665
Oculus Rift (hardware) 467, 469, 470
Odeon (software) 481
Office KGDVS (architects) 602, 603
OGC (Open Geospatial Consortium) (working group / standard body) 501, 537
Ola (company) 493
Olivetti (company) 329, 347
Omniclass (standard) 522
On Growth and Form (book or paper) 145, 158, 170
On the Art of Building (book or paper) 95, 699, 711
On the Fabric of the Human Body in Seven Books (book or paper) 576
On the Gradual Formation of Thought Through Conversation (book or paper) 131
On the Harmony of the Whole World (book or paper) 118
On the Origin of Species by Means of Natural Selection, or the Preservation of Favoured Races in the Struggle for Life (book or paper) 145, 147
One Flew Over the Cuckoo's Nest (film & book) 647
One to One (company) 482, 489
OOPEAA (architects) 602
Opendesk (project or programme) 637
OpenFOAM (software) 485
Open Geospatial Consortium (OGC) (working group / standard body) 501, 537
OpenOffice (software) 231, 337, 519
OpenOffice Calc (software) 519
open-source model 272, 634
open source software 356, 636
open-source-software movement 634
OpenStreetMap (software) 491, 494, 495, 499, 502, 505, 536
Open Street Map Foundation (OSMF) (organisation) 494
operating system 330, 334, 335, 336, 341, 355, 356, 430, 470, 496, 617, 618, 621, 624, 635
optimisation 122, 147, 148, 152, 162, 163, 164, 167, 201, 219, 483, 487, 511, 541, 542
optimisation algorithm 162, 164
Oration on the Dignity of Man (book or paper) 29, 42
orthogonal projection 132
Orthographia 379, 380, 699, 704, 705, 711, 716
orthographic projection 60, 267
orthoimaging 101
oscilloscope 231, 287
OS X (software) 336, 618
Out of Control (book or paper) 535
Oxford Dictionaries (publication) 257, 695
Oxford University (institution) 618

P

page description language 334
PageMaker (software) 335, 337
PageRank (software) 188, 565, 624
Pages (software) 231, 337
Palladian (architecture, design) 111, 119, 126, 145, 169
Palladis Tamia (literary work) 659
Paperhouses 637
parallax mapping 267
parametric design 181, 202, 203, 204, 351, 359, 363, 401, 428, 480, 489, 637
parametric grammar 157
parametricism 64, 139, 165, 166
parametric modeller 362
parametric modelling 60, 61, 64, 361, 362, 424, 428, 480, 513
parametric object 137
parametrisation 61, 359, 361, 362
PARC (Palo Alto Research Center) (institution) 246
Pareto efficiency 163
Pareto frontier 163
Pareto optimality 163
Pareto set 163
Parsons Corporation (company) 408, 417
particle-spring systems 145, 160
particle system 159, 160, 171
Pascal (programming/scripting language) 375, 376, 390, 395
path tracing 263
PCA (Principal Component Analysis) 560
PDF (Portable Document Format) (format) 335, 336, 338, 345, 356, 359, 570
PDP-11/70 (hardware) 417
Peano curve 193
PEARL (Process and Experiment Automation Realtime Language) (programming/scripting language) 356
Penn State College of Arts and Architecture (institution) 64
perfect diffusion 259
performance capture 102
performance simulation 163, 475, 478, 480, 484
performance space 117, 118
Perl (programming/scripting language) 351, 354, 356, 358, 360
perspective projection 185, 186, 203, 292, 672
pervasive computing 615
Petri net 376
phenotype 178, 202, 203
Phong E shading 261
Phong shading 260, 261, 274, 275
photogrammetry 96, 97, 98, 100, 101, 105, 217, 270, 310, 496, 516
Photometria (book or paper) 255, 260
photometry 260
photon mapping 263, 264
Photoshop (software) 235, 241, 288, 292, 297, 300, 336, 495, 502, 519
PHP (programming/scripting language) 354, 356, 377
physical (PHY) layer 621
Piers Plowman (literary work) 646
pipe surface 73, 87
Pixar Studios (company) 269
pixel 232, 233, 234, 235, 236, 237, 238, 239, 243, 245, 259, 260, 261, 262, 267, 275, 292, 295, 296, 298, 305
PixelSense (software) 138
plain text file (TXT) 231
Plan B (architects) 602, 606
Planning Support System (PSS) 496
Plastic Jet Printing (PJP) 446, 447, 448
Platonic solid 69, 70, 80
plotter display 231
point cloud 98, 99, 100, 101, 102, 105, 106, 108, 217, 270, 310, 516
PointSense Heritage (software) 217
Pokémon Go (software) 497
pole-vertice 269
polyalphabetic substitution 663, 677
polygon mesh 445
polygon net 74
polygons (PLY) (format) 189
polynomial 184, 186, 197, 669
Portable Document Format (PDF) (format) 335, 336, 338, 345, 356, 359, 570
postmodern architecture 379
post processor 411
PostScript (software) 74, 327, 334, 335
Power of Ten (film) 1…
PowerPoint (software) 33…
PPI (Pixels per Inch) 23…
Preston Scott Cohen (architects) 40…
primitive solid 6…
Principal Component Analysis (PCA) 56…
print driver 334, 33…
Problem Solving as Information Processing (book or paper) 11…
procedural disturbances 26…
procedural geometric transformation 27…
Procedural Inc (company) 15…
procedural modelling 157, 159, 160, 221, 36…, 539, 540, 54…
procedural textures 267, 27…
Processing 478, 479, 482, 484, 516, 551, 55…, 556, 558, 57…
process map 52…
Procter & Gamble (P&G) (company) 61…
production system 64, 51…
Pro/Engineer (software) 6…
profilograph 429, 43…
Programming Language Pragmatics (book or paper) 351, 38…
projective geometry 132, 20…
Project Ocean (project or programme) 65…
project plan 13…
ProtoGeo (company) 50…
pseudo-3D 6…
PTW Architects (architects) 82, 21…
Pygmalion (play or musical) 55…
Pythagorean theorem 18…
Python (programming/scripting language) 354, 358, 359, 37…, 377, 380, 38…

Q

QGIS (software) 496, 502, 53…
quadrivium 37…
qualification problem 55…
Quantum GIS (software) 496, 53…
Quark Software (company) 33…
QuarkXPress (software) 33…
Queen's College Cork (institution) 55…
QWERTY keyboard 133, 330, 34…

R

R1 (software) 556, 55…
RAAAF (architects) 60…
Radar CH (software) 28…
Radiance (software) 27…
radiance approximation 26…
Radio Echo Sounding (RES) 10…
Radio-Frequency Identification (RFID) 61…, 61…
radiosity 262, 263, 275, 287, 30…
RAM (Random Access Memory) 55…
rapid manufacturing 40…
rapid prototyping 377, 51…
Raspberry Pi 3 Model B (hardware) 56…
raster graphics 232, 235, 237, 248, 44…
raw format 23…
ray casting 26…
ray tracing 261, 262, 287, 288, 48…
RCR (architects) 60…
Really Universal Computer Aided Production System (RUCAPS) (software) 51…
recursion 155, 156, 157, 159, 168, 39…
regular solid 69, 7…
regular surface 72, 74, 75, 28…
reinforcement learning 55…
Remington (company) 329, 33…
Renaissance 34, 35, 39, 42, 45, 49, 60, 9…, 100, 119, 120, 121, 123, 137, 139, 184, 18…, 187, 203, 204, 340, 372, 373, 379, 408, 42…, 423, 425, 428, 429, 432, 443, 467, 559, 56…, 565, 576, 653, 660, 662, 672, 699, 701, 70…, 709, 711, 714, 71…
Renaissance Man 34, 35, 95, 37…
rendering 19, 71, 100, 122, 134, 135, 15…, 160, 169, 185, 186, 190, 195, 203, 221, 22…, 387, 390, 466, 478, 481, 567, 60…
RepRap Research Foundation (institution) 44…

Retina Display 236
Revit (software) 139, 358, 523, 638
rewriting system 156, 157
REX (architects) 602
RFID Journal (publication) 615
RFID (Radio-Frequency Identification) 616, 618
RGB (Red Green Blue) 237, 239, 304
Rhinoceros 3D (software) 61, 65, 159, 181, 209, 353, 358, 359, 637
Rhinoceros Grasshopper (software) 61, 65, 159, 161, 166, 181, 209, 351, 353, 358, 359, 362, 366, 380, 480, 488, 541, 637, 638
Rhinoscript (programming / scripting language) 359
Rhino (software)
RIBA (Royal Institute of British Architects) (institution) 177
Rich Text Format (RTF) (format) 336
Riemannian geometry 185
rigid body dynamics 268
Robocasting 448
Robofold (company) 429
Rodin Centre for Transportation & Policy Management (institution) 531
Rojkind (architects) 602
RoomScan (software) 109
Rotis (font) 342
Routing Protocol for Low-Power and Lossy Networks (RPL) 622, 623
Royal Academy of Arts (institution) 524
Royal Botanic Gardens at Kew (institution) 426
Royal Horticultural Society (institution) 426
Royal Institute of British Architects (institution) 177
RPL (Routing Protocol for Low-Power and Lossy Networks) (protocol) 622
R&Sie(n) (architects) 113
RTF (Rich Text Format) (format) 336
Ruby (programming / scripting language) 354, 377
ruled surface 72, 86
R.U.R (play or musical) 414

S

saddle surface 72, 86
Salford University (institution) 480
SANAA (Sejima and Nishizawa and Associates) (architects) 88, 360, 367, 602
scaenographia 379, 380, 699, 700, 704, 712, 716
scanner 97, 102, 134, 234, 235, 238, 247, 345, 445, 553
School of the Art Institute of Chicago (institution) 429
Science, Industry and Art (book or paper) 421, 426
SCL Group (company) 653
Scott and Linton Shipbuilders (company) 409
screw surface 72, 73, 87
script 61, 67, 77, 118, 161, 354, 356, 357, 359, 360, 361, 371, 372, 373, 411, 541
scripting language 149, 354, 355, 356, 358, 377, 637
SeArch (architects) 602
Selective Laser Melting (SLM) 447, 448
Selective Laser Sintering (SLS) 446, 448
Self-Organising Map (SOM) 572
self-organising system 154
Self-Portrait in a Convex Mirror (work of art) 722
self-similarity 155
SelgasCano (architects) 602, 603
Sentiment Cocoon (installation) 535, 544
sequential analysis 647
Serie Architects (architects) 602
servomechanism 409
SETP (Standard for the Exchange of Product Model Data) (standard) 510
set theory 114, 116, 117
Seven Books on Architecture (book or paper) 709, 711, 720, 721
Seven Liberal Arts 379
Seven Wonders of the Ancient World 69
shading 131, 242, 257, 258, 259, 260, 261, 266, 269, 270, 271, 274, 275
shadow mapping 261
Shannon number 553
shapefile format 495, 496
shape grammar 64, 65, 80, 119, 145, 157, 158, 159, 540, 541, 557, 575
shell 72, 75, 222, 355, 377
Side Effects Software (company) 166
SimCity (software) 67, 537
Simula 67 (programming / scripting language) 377
Simulacra and Simulation (book or paper) 469
Simula I (programming / scripting language) 377
Simulationstechnik (event/exhibition) 223
singularity 713
sintering 414, 446, 447, 448
Siri (software) 553
Sketchpad (software) 62, 231, 244, 258, 468, 512
SketchUp (software) 65, 142, 470, 502, 522, 637
Skizoid (work of art) 173
Skype (web service / app / platform) 631, 633
slicer 446, 458
Smalltalk (programming / scripting language) 375, 377
smart city 534, 616
Smart City Wien (project or programme) 534
smart environment 616
smart eyes 625
smart home 616
SMART (Shimizu Manufacturing System by Advanced Robotics Technology) 414
Snøhetta (architects) 602, 603, 636
Snow Crash (literary work) 496
So Long, Frank Lloyd Wright 122
social sustainability 517
Soft Architecture Machines (book or paper) 229, 536
soft body dynamics 268, 270
Softimage (software) 409
Software Development Kit (SDK) 496
solar analysis 539
solid CAD model 445
solid model 68, 75
solid modeller 198, 362
solid modelling 65, 68, 159
solid transformation 70
solution space 117, 118
Some Philosophical Problems from the Standpoint of Artificial Intelligence (book or paper) 558
Some Studies in Machine Learning Using the Game Checkers (book or paper) 552
SOM (Self-Organising Map) 572
SOM (Skidmore Owings Merrill) (architects) 64, 113, 409
Sonnets (literary work) 659
Sony (company) 625
sound pixel rendering 481
source code 337, 407, 496, 634, 635
space syntax 188, 209
Space Syntax (software) 188, 539
Spartan Air Services (company) 493
Spatial Concepts in GIS and Design (event/exhibition) 497
spatial configuration 76, 540, 541
spatial economy 531
Special Interest Group 3D (SIG 3D) (working group / standard body) 501
specular highlights 260, 261, 275
spherical geometry 185
spline 65, 73, 74, 185, 186, 197, 198
Sputnik 1 650
SRI International (company) 62
Standard (architects) 602
Standard for the Exchange of Product Model Data (STEP) (standard) 510
Standard Positioning Service (SPS) 502
Stanford bunny 189, 196, 201, 210
Stanford Research Institute (SRI) (company) 62
Stanford University (institution) 189, 514, 539, 553, 647
StarOffice (software) 337
stereolithographic 3D printing 4[illegible]
stereolithography 442, 443, 446, 447, 4[illegible], 459
stereophotogrammetry 96, 97, 98, 10[illegible]
stereoscopic motion tracking 10[illegible]
STL file (format) 44[illegible]
stochastic 562, 56[illegible], 56[illegible]
stochastic grammar 15[illegible]
Stratasys Inc (company) 44[illegible]
Strava (web service / app / platform) 49[illegible], 495, 50[illegible]
Strava's Cycling App Is Helping Cities Build Better Bike Lanes (article) 50[illegible]
structural simulation 482, 48[illegible]
Structure From Motion (SFM) 10[illegible]
structure sensor 103, 104, 10[illegible]
STUDENT (software) 555
Stuttgart University (institution) 455
subdivision tree 540
subpixel rendering 23[illegible]
sub-surface scattering 268, 28[illegible]
subtractive colour model 23[illegible]
Summer Exhibition (event/exhibition) 524
Sun Microsystems (company) 37[illegible]
Sunroof (project or programme) 39[illegible]
Supermachine Studio (architects) 602
superstatistics 56[illegible]
Superstudio (architects) 70[illegible]
surface model 71, 75, 445
surface modelling 68, 26[illegible]
surface normal 71, 75, 85, 260, 267, 275
surface transformation 75, 34[illegible]
Sustainable Development Goals (book or paper) 5[illegible]
Swedish Institute of Computer Science (institution) 6[illegible]
Swift (software) 359, 40[illegible]
Sword of Damocles (hardware) 467, 46[illegible]
symbol library 134, 1[illegible]
symmetrical encryption 66[illegible]
synchronous communication 63[illegible]
synergetics 42[illegible]
Synesthesia Pharma-Huasca (work of art) 57[illegible]
synthesis barrier 11[illegible]
systems programming 35[illegible]
systems theory 47, 64[illegible]

T

tacheometer 98
tacheometry 98, 100, 21[illegible]
tachymeter 98, 10[illegible]
Tagged Image File Format (TIFF) (format) 23[illegible]
tame problem 115, 162, 163, 54[illegible]
Tango (software) 53[illegible]
tatami mat 120, 12[illegible]
Tcl (programming/scripting language) 37[illegible]
Team Mazzanti (architects) 60[illegible]
Technical University Munich (institution) 101, 54[illegible]
Tekla 63[illegible]
teleprinter 23[illegible]
teletype 33[illegible]
Ten Books on Architecture (book or paper) 166, 42[illegible]
Terravision (software) 49[illegible]
tessellation map 26[illegible]
Tetris (software) 24[illegible]
TextArt (software) 44[illegible]
texture mapping 190, 261, 266, 267, 269, 27[illegible]
TFT LCD (Thin-Film-Transistor Liquid-Crystal Display) 23[illegible]
Tham & Videgård (architects) 60[illegible]
The Algorithmic Beauty of Plants (book or paper) 14[illegible]
The Analysis of Beauty (book or paper) 11[illegible]
The Apprentice (TV show) 13[illegible]
The Architecture Machine (book or paper) 145, 536, 54[illegible]
The Ballad of East and West (literary work) 23[illegible]
The Big Bang Theory (TV sitcom) 16[illegible]
The Blind Watchmaker: Why the Evidence of Evolution Reveals a Universe without Design (book or paper) 145, 14[illegible]

The Chemical Basis of Morphogenesis
(book or paper) 145, 159
The Daily Telegraph (publication) 615
The Dark Knight (film) 717
The Delineation of Rome
(book or paper) 105
The Digital Earth: Understanding Our Planet in the 21st Century (talk) 493
The Draughtsman's Contract (film) 465, 472
The Elements (book or paper) 700
The Figthing Temeraire Tugged to Her Last Berth to Be Broken Up (work of art) 257, 306
The Flying Dutchmen (book or paper) 64
The Four Books on Architecture (book or paper) 119
The Four Elements of Architecture (book or paper) 421, 426
The Geometry of Bubbles and Foams (book or paper) 70
The Great Western Railway (work of art) 563, 578
The Guardian (publication) 431, 494, 646
The Harmony of the World (book or paper) 155
The History of Creation (book or paper) 158
The Hitchhiker's Guide to the Galaxy (literary work) 554
The Imaginary Prisons (book or paper) 468
The Incandescent (book or paper) 705
The Isolated State (book or paper) 531
The Laws of Simplicity (book or paper) 359
The Laws of Thought (book or paper) 375, 549, 551, 554
The Making of Architecture (event/exhibition) 113
The Mathematical Analysis of Logic (book or paper) 70
The Matrix (film) 469, 563, 579
The Music Lesson or Lady at the Virginals With a Gentleman (work of art) 306
The Net – The Unabomber, LSD and the Internet (film) 648
The New York Times (publication) 646
theodolite 97, 98, 99, 100, 217
Theoria musica 125
Theory of Semiotics (book or paper) 293
The Oxyrhynchus Papyrus (object) 718
The Palladian Grammar (book or paper) 111, 169
The Prisons (publication) 468
The Radiant City (book or paper) 532
The Republic (book or paper) 667
thermal imaging 101
thermography 101, 218
The Rocky Horror Show (play or musical) 559
The Shock of the New (TV series) 532
The Sorcerer's Apprentice (literary work) 137
The Tall Office Building Artistically Considered (book or paper) 179
The Technocrat (work of art) 125
The Third Man (film & book) 340
The Very Many (company) 64, 217
The Washington Post (publication) 646
Thin-Film-Transistor Liquid-Crystal Display 232
ThingMaker (hardware) 443
Thinking by Modeling (event/exhibition) 427
This Is Your Digital Life (software) 653
Thread (protocol) 622
three-quarter perspective 63
Thünen rings (concept) 531, 532
TIFF (Tagged Image File Format) (format) 239
tilt shift 241, 264, 265, 308
time domain boundary element modelling 480
Time of Flight (TOF) 103
time-sharing system 355
Times New Roman (font) 341, 342
time trace 481, 583
tipi tent 140
tone mapping 307
topological space 185
topology 159, 160, 161, 166, 168, 269, 280, 281, 283, 310, 496, 498, 499, 501, 540, 541
topology optimisation 160, 161, 166
Total City (concept) 427

Towards a New Architecture
(book or paper) 68
Toy Story (film) 263
Track Me if You Plan! (project or programme) 500, 588
transformation process 413, 532, 533
translation surfaces 72
triangulation 70, 74, 97, 200, 217, 500
trilateration 500
Trimble (company) 63, 502
Trimble Connect (software) 637
trivium 379
true colour 233, 238
Trust Network Analysis (TNA) 222
truth value 70
Turing machine 205, 329, 373, 374, 382, 384, 385, 387, 551, 552, 647
Turing test 551, 553, 559
TWAIN (working group/standard body) 235, 247
Twitter (company) 535, 619, 624
txtBomber (hardware) 619
typology 120

U

U3D (Universal 3D) 336
UAS (Unmanned Aircraft System) 102, 108
Uber (company) 493, 494, 499, 504, 533, 534, 549
Über die allmähliche Verfertigung der Gedanken beim Reden (book or paper) 131
ubiquitous computing 479, 536, 561, 615, 617, 625, 629
Udacity (company) 553
UHD (Ultra High Definition) 236
Ultimate Display (hardware) 468, 469
Ultra High Definition (UHD) 236
UML (Unified Modelling Language) 376
unbiased global illumination 263, 264
unbiased rendering 263
Underweysung der Messung, mit dem Zirckel und Richtscheyt, in Linien, Ebenen und gantzen corporen (book or paper) 212
UNESCO (United Nations Educational, Scientific and Cultural Organization) (international body or organisation) 415, 426, 532, 616
Uniclass 522
Unicode 330, 333
Unicode Transformation Format (UTF) 333
Unified Modelling Language (UML) (programming/scripting language) 376
Uniform Resource Locator (URL) 623
Unigraphics (software) 65
United States Ballistics Research Laboratory (government agency or body) 374
Unity (software) 470
Universal 3D (U3D) 336
Universal Declaration of Human Rights 654
Universal Transmercator (UTM) 502
Univers (font) 342
University College Cork (institution) 551
University College London (UCL) (institution) 494, 539, 543
University of California (institution) 497, 648
University of Cincinnati (institution) 121
University of Helsinki (institution) 635
University of Kaiserslautern (institution) 500
University of Karlsruhe (institution) 157
University of Liverpool (institution) 512
University of Michigan (institution) 288, 488
University of Oxford (institution) 147
University of Paris-Diderot (institution) 219
University of Rostock (institution) 497
University of Southern California (institution) 427
University of Utah (institution) 258, 260, 263, 269
University of Washington (institution) 101
Unix (software) 65, 356, 635
Unmanned Aircraft System (UAS) 108
Unreal Engine (software) 470
UNStudio (architects) 64, 78, 79, 409, 485

up vector 26
urban 3D model 536, 53
Urban 5: A Machine That Discusses Urban Design (book or paper) 53
urban heat island 53
urban morphological analysis 53
urban morphology 53
UrbanSim (software) 537, 53
urban simulation 537, 538, 54
Urban Think Thank (architects) 60
URL (Uniform Resource Locator) 62
US Army Construction Engineering Research Laboratory (USA-CERL) (government agency or body) 49
Utah teapot 263, 27
UTF (Unicode Transformation Format) 33
Uto Collective (company) 48
UV coordinates 26
UV mapping 71, 19
UV-unwrap 267, 26

V

VAX (hardware) 55
VCR (Videocassette Recording) 65
VDU (Visual Display Unit) 232, 35
vector algebra 6
vector displacement maps 26
vector graphics 232, 237, 24
vector monitor 232, 237, 24
Vectorworks (software) 65, 143, 47
Vers une architecture (book or paper) 6
vertex 69, 70, 177, 178, 180, 183, 187, 18 189, 196, 198, 202, 53
VGA (Video Graphics Array) 23
VGI (Volunteered Geographic Information) 49
VHS (Video Home System) 33
Vico (software) 63
Victoria University of Manchester (institution) 55
Video Indexer (web service/app/platform) 53
Vier Bücher von menschlicher Proportion (book or paper) 421, 42
viewing frustum 26
Vigenère cipher 66
Virtual Boy (hardware) 46
virtual photography 264, 293, 29
Virtual Reality (VR) 465, 466, 467, 468, 46 470, 47
Virtual Reality (VR) photography 29
Virtual Singapore (project or programme) 537, 54
Visual Display Unit (VDU) 232, 35
Visual Programming Language (VPL) (programming/scripting language) 36
Vitruvian Man (work of art) 12
Vive (hardware) 469, 47
Voigt-Kampff test 55
volumetric path tracing 26
Volunteered Geographic Information (VGI) 49
von Neumann architecture 373, 374, 64 650, 71
Voronoi diagram 16
Voronoi tessellation 16
VPL (Visual Programming Language) (programming/scripting language) 36
VR photography 29

W

W3C (World Wide Web Consortium) (working group/standard body) 34
Wang (hardware) 33
Watson (software) 55
Waymo (company) 55
WBS 70 12
Weaire-Phelan structure 7
Web 2.0 63
WebOCR (web service/app/platform) 34
Web of Things 623, 62
Web VR (software) 46
Weebly (web service/app/platform) 34
WeTransfer (web service/app/platform) 63

WGS 84 502
white space 339, 340
Whither Design Space (book or paper) 541
Whole Earth Catalogue (publication) 648
wicked problem 114, 115, 118, 162, 164, 542
WikiHouse 408, 637, 640
WikiLeaks (publication) 646, 676
Wikipedia (web service / app / platform) 12, 47, 156, 260, 353, 494, 534, 553, 560, 634, 636, 652, 695
Willobie His Avisa (literary work) 659
Windows (software) 240, 249, 334, 335, 336, 337, 341, 348, 396, 496, 510, 618, 634
Wired magazine (publication) 113, 493, 500, 535
Wireless Personal Area Network (WPAN) 620
Wissenschaft, Industrie und Kunst (book or paper) 421, 426
Wix (web service / app / platform) 345
WOHA (architects) 602
Wohnungsbauserie 70 120
Wolfram Language (programming / scripting language) 363
Wolfram Research (company) 363
Wolkenbügel (work of art) 302
Woman's Own (publication) 651
WordPerfect (software) 336, 348
WordPress (web service / app / platform) 345
Word (software) 336
World Geodetic System (WGS) 502
World Wide Web Consortium (W3C) (working group / standard body) 345, 377, 501
WPAN (Wireless Personal Area Network) 620, 622
Writer (software) 337
WYSIWYG 136, 137, 337, 344

X

xBIM (eXtensible Building Information Modelling) (software) 519
XCON (eXpert CONfigurer) (software) 556
xerography 234
Xerox Alto (hardware) 246
Xerox (company) 234, 333
XFrog (software) 157, 220
XML (Extensible Markup Language) (programming/scripting language) 139, 336, 377, 394, 537
XML Paper Specification (XPS) 336
XML standard (standard) 377
XPS (XML Paper Specification) 336
XSL (Extensible Stylesheet Language) (programming/scripting language) 394

Z

Z-buffering 259
zero-player game 152
ZigBee (protocol) 620, 622, 623
ZKM *(Zentrum für Kunst und Medien) Karlsruhe* (institution) 427
Z resolution 446
ZUS *(Zones Urbaines Sensibles)* (architects) 637, 640
Z-Wave (protocol) 259, 622

Index of People

A

Aalto, Alvar 113, 353
Adams, Douglas 554
Aicher, Otl 342
Aish, Robert 512
Alberti, Leon Battista 12, 95, 105, 117, 213, 565, 662, 677, 699, 719, 722
Alexander, Christopher 145, 162
Alexander the Great 372
Alexandrov, Gleb 222
Alighieri, Dante 713
Allen, Paul 356
Alonso, William 532
Ando, Tadao 602, 603
Appel, Arthur 261
Aravena, Alejandro 601, 608, 636, 639
Archimedes 69
Ariguzzi, Arduino 425
Aristophanes 713
Ashton, Kevin 615, 616
Assange, Julian 646, 647, 676
Aureli, Pier Vittorio 602
Austen, Jane 257

B

Bach, Johann Sebastian 44, 549, 638
Bain, Alexander 246
Bakewell, Frederick 246
Bannon, Steve 653
Ban, Shigeru 360, 412, 418
Banzi, Massimo 619
Bardi, Lina Bo 113
Batty, Michael 496, 529
Baudrillard, Jean 469
Bauersfeld, Walther 70, 427
Beaucé, Patrick 430
Beauvoir, de, Simone 651
Becker, Joe 333
Beesley, Philip 431, 458
Behnisch, Stefan 512
Behrens, Moritz 535, 544
Belin, Édouard 246
Bequerel, Antoine Henri 649
Berners-Lee, Tim 344, 378, 615, 623
Bernini, Gian Lorenzo 468, 472, 478
Bernoulli, Jacob 569
Bézier, Pierre 74
Bidwell, Shelford 246
Bill, Ralf 491, 497
Blickensderfer, George Canfield 329
Blinn, Jim 261, 267
Bloomberg, Michael 353
Blumer, Hermann 412
Bobrow, Daniel G 555
Bojár, Gabór 479
Boole, George 70, 121, 199, 374, 549, 551, 554
Borromini, Francesco 204, 213
Bowyer, Adrian 442
Brand, Stewart 648, 650
Braun, Karl Ferdinand 231
Brown, Gordon 647
Brown, Robert 570
Buchholz, Werner 238
Burghley, William Cecil 658, 659
Burkhalter, Marianne 211
Burleigh, William Cecil 658
Burrow, Andrew 216, 541
Burton, Decimus 426
Byron, Lord George Gordon 554

C

Cache, Bernard 145, 161, 166, 421, 429
Caesar, Julius 661, 662
Calatrava, Santiago 87, 121
Camilla, Duchess of Cornwall 177
Čapek, Karel 414
Caroll, Lewis 469
Caselli, Giovanni 246
Casteljau, de, Paul 74
Castro, Fidel 651
Catmull, Edwin Earl 269, 280
Cavendish, William 426
Cavendish, William George Spencer 426
Cecil, William, 1st Baron of Burleigh 658
Chaillou, Stanislas 173
Chambers, Ephraim 633
Chang, Gary 113
Chang, Jennifer 577
Charles, Prince of Wales 177
Chipperfield, Daniel 602
Chipperfield, David 602
Chomsky, Noam 43
Christaller, Walter 531
Church, Alonzo 369, 375, 376, 552, 650, 711
Churchill, Winston 257
Arthur C Clarke 554
Clark, Jack 269, 280, 553
Coast, Steve 494
Conway, John Horton 152, 153, 154, 155
Copernicus, Nicolaus 39
Costa, Lúcio 532
Curie, Marie 649
Curie, Pierre 649
Cyrus the Great 371

D

Daguerre, Louis 258
Dahl, Ole-Johan 377
d'Alembert, Jean le Rond 633
Dalí, Salvador 443
Dammbeck, Lutz 648
Dangermond, Jack 496
Dante 713
Dante Alighieri 713. See also Dante
Darwin, Charles 145, 147, 148, 158, 161, 168, 179, 674
da San Gallo, Antonio 425, 435
Davies, Alex 500
da Vinci, Leonardo 299, 340, 372, 429, 559, 705
Davison, John 512
Dawkins, Richard 145, 147
de Beauvoir, Simone 651
de Casteljau, Paul 74
Dedekind, Richard 47
de Fermat, Pierre 183
de Gastines, Jean 412, 418
de Jaucourt, Chevalier Louis 633
Deleuze, Gilles 429, 465
dell'Altissimo, Cristofano 52
de l'Orme, Philibert 118
del Villar y Lozano, Francisco Paulo 415
de' Medici, Lorenzo 42
de Meuron. See also de Meuron, Pierre
de Meuron, Pierre 122, 164, 177, 219
de Moivre, Abraham 571
de Mol, John 645
de Montaigne, Michel 432
Derrida, Jacques 43
Descartes, René 47, 65, 183, 185, 554, 563, 564
Diana, Princess of Wales 177
di Cambio, Arnolfo 425
Dick, Philip K 551
Diderot, Denis 633, 639
Dillenburger, Benjamin 603
di Pietro, Andrea 119
Dörner, Dietrich 116
Duarte, José 64, 80
Ducasse, Alain 50, 721
Dunkers, Adam 618
Durand, Jean-Nicolas-Louis 120
Dürer, Albrecht 203, 212, 259, 273, 421, 429, 437, 559
Dürrenmatt, Friedrich 123

E

Eames, Charles 155
Eames, Ray 155
Eastman, Charles 111, 512, 523
Eastwood, Clint 564, 579, 666, 667
Echter von Mespelbrunn, Julius 294
Eich, Brendan 356
Einstein, Albert 120, 432, 705
Eisen, Charles-Dominique 125
Eisenhower, Dwight D 650
Eisenman, Peter 121, 602
Elizabeth II,
Queen of the United Kingdom 515
See also Queen Elizabeth II, The Queen
Elizabeth I, Queen of England
658. See also Queen Elizabeth I
Emin, Tracey 523
Epps, Gregory 429
Euclid 119, 183, 184, 185, 70[illegible], 713
Euler, Leonhard 47, 69, 173
Euripides 713
Evans, David C 258, 260, 261, 26[illegible], 269
Evans, Robin 57, 60

F

Faletto, Joanie 263
Fancher, Hampton 551
Federer, Roger 340
Fehn, Sverre 602
Fermat, de, Pierre 183
Feurzeig, Wally 358
Fisher, Howard T 496
FitzRoy, Robert 147
Flaxman, Michael 497
Flemming, Ulrich 549, 575, 576
Fletcher, Louise 647
Ford, Henry 634
Forman, Miloš 647
Fornes, Marc 64, 302
Förster, von, Heinz 349
Frazer, John 145, 164
Freud, Sigmund 563
Friedman, Yona 113, 529
Frutiger, Adrian 327, 341, 342
Fry, Ben 351, 359
Fujimoto, Sou 602, 603
Fuller, Buckminster 70, 76, 83, 427, 437, 650

G

Gaffurio, Franchino 125
Galilei, Galileo 705
Gándara, Belén 577
Gantenbein, Christ 602
Garamont, Claude (Claude Garamond) 342
Garcia, Pablo 429, 437
Garfunkel, Art 122, 153
Gates, Bill 356
Gaudí, Antoni 73, 160, 195, 415, 419, 424, 428, 638
Gauss, Carl Friedrich 673
Gehry, Frank 62, 63, 119, 159, 177, 362, 409, 428, 454, 456, 637, 638
Gero, John S 111, 1[illegible]4
Gershenfeld, Neil 407, 4[illegible]2
Gilbert & George 5[illegible]3
Giocondo, Giovanni, Fra 7[illegible]6
Giorgi, Francesco 1[illegible]8
Gips, James 64, 145, 157, 540
Glennie, Alick 355
Glidden, Carlos 329
Gödel, Kurt 556, 70[illegible]
Goethe, von, Johan Wolfgang 137
Goodchild, Michael Frank 494, 497
Goodfellow, Ian 165
Gore, Al 493, 503
Gormley, Anthony 523
Gosper, Bill 15[illegible]
Gould, John 20[illegible]
Gouraud, Henri 260, 26[illegible]
Gray, Elisha 24[illegible]
Greenaway, Peter 465
Greene, Graham 340
Grimm, Ludwig 274, 30[illegible]
Gropius, Walter 120, 338
Guevara, Che 651
Gutenberg, Johannes 372
Guyer, Lux 113

H

Hadid, Zaha 63, 64, 78, 119, 165, 212, 363, 401, 524, 603
Haeckel, Ernst 145, 158, 159, 170
Hahn, Otto 649

[illegible], Fritz 192, 211, 427, 734
Händel, George Friedrich 660
Hansen, Theophil 482
Hansmeyer, Michael 602
Harris, Britton 496
Hartley, L P 715
Hasegawa, Itsuko 63
Hawking, Stephen 564
Hayes, Pat 558
Hearn, Alex 494
Heatherwick, Thomas 602
Hege, Walter 292
Heinsman, Hedwig 444
Hell, Rudolf 246
Herzog, Jacques 164, 177, 219, 295, 315, 318, 322
Hillenbrand, Tom 536
Hill, Fred 417
Hill, Jonathan 430
Hobbes, Thomas 554, 655, 657
Hockney, David 116
Hoesli, Bernhard 121
Hoffman, Edouard 341
Hofmann, Albert 648
Hogarth, William 111, 118, 119
Hollein, Hans 316, 602
Holl, Steven 603, 606
Holtrop, Anne 602
Homer 713
Hughes, Robert 532
Hugo, Victor 655
Hull, Chuck 442, 446
Hume, David 655, 658

I

Ingels, Bjarke 64, 84, 122, 593, 597, 605, 685
Innocent VIII, Pope 42
Ishigami, Junya 602
Ishiguro, Hiroshi 559, 576, 722
Ito, Toyo 428

J

Jacob, Sam 602
Jacquard, Joseph Marie 408
Jaquet-Droz, Pierre 559
Jeanneret-Gris, Charles-Édouard (Le Corbusier) 595. See also Le Corbusier
Jobs, Steve 432
Johnson, Boris 517
Johnson, Philip 597, 602
Jormakka, Kari 64
Joséphine, Empress 408
Julius Caesar 661, 662
Jungk, Robert 470, 471

K

Kaczynski, Ted 648
Kapoor, Anish 523
Kasiski, Friedrich 663
Kasparov, Garry 553, 558, 575
Kelly, Jude 517
Kelly, Kevin 493, 535
Kepler, Johannes 39, 494, 705
Kerez, Christian 602, 603
Kesey, Ken 647, 648
Kettler, Howard 341
Khoury, Bernard 602
Kiefer, Anselm 523
King James VI, King of Scotland and King James I, King of England 658
King, Martin Luther, Jr 651
Kinkade, Thomas 266
Kipling, Rudyard 235
Klee, Paul 59
Kleist, von, Heinrich 131, 137
Klügl, Franziska 499
Knoll, John 288
Knoll, Thomas 288
Koch, von, Helge 155
Kohn, David 602
Koolhaas, Rem 43, 63, 177, 562, 593, 597, 707
Korda, Alberto 651, 676
Koren, Benjamin 482
Korn, Arthur 246
Koslow, Tyler 443
Kubrick, Stanley 554
Kurzweil, Ray 43, 345, 551, 564, 713

L

Lady Gaga 660
Lady Georgiana 426
Laflamme, Robert Arthur 496
Lagrange, Joseph-Louis 184
Lake, Ron 501
Lambert, Johann Heinrich 255, 259, 260
Langland, William 646
Lanier, Jaron 467, 469
Laplace, Pierre-Simon 558
Latour, Bruno 43, 712
Laugier, Marc-Antoine 125
Le Corbusier 68, 119, 120, 121, 122, 155, 162, 532, 595, 707, 720
LeCun, Yan 165
Leibniz, Gottfried Wilhelm 554, 702, 703
Lennon, John 638
Lerdorf, Rasmus 356
Libeskind, Daniel 602
Lichtenberg, Georg Christoph 333
Lighthill, James 555
Lina Bo Bardi 113
Lindenmayer, Aristid 145, 156, 192
Lissitzky, El 302
Lombardi, Tullio 125
Lord Byron 554
Loudon, John Claudius 426
Lucas, John 556
Luce, Clare Boothe 287
Luckey, Palmer 469
Luther, Martin 372
Lynn, Greg 409
Lyotard, Jean-François 43

M

MacLeamy, Patrick 432, 514, 540
Macy, Josiah, Jr 649
Maeda, John 351, 359
Manneh, Carl 470
Marconi, Guglielmo 231
Markov, Andrey 571
Martin, George 638
Mavromichalis, Konstantinos 535, 544
Maximilian I, Holy Roman Emperor 340
Maxwell, James Clerk 563, 564, 578
Mayer H, Jürgen 363, 540
Mayne, Thom 602
McCarthy, John 554, 558
McCartney, Paul 638
McDermott, John P 556
McHarg, Ian 497, 512
Menges, Achim 145, 455
Mercer, Rebekah 653
Mercer, Robert 653
Mere, Francis 659
Meuron, de, Pierre 122, 164, 177, 219, 295, 297, 315, 318, 322, 428, 481, 489, 606, 736
Meydenbauer, Albrecht 96, 105
Meyer, Hannes 120
Michelangelo 421, 425, 456, 638
Mies, Edwald 316
Mies van der Rohe, Ludwig 120, 158, 316, 318, 595, 596, 597
Miller, Charles Leslie 496
Minsky, Marvin 554, 555
Mitchell, William J 57, 62, 145, 158
Moneo, Rafael 602, 603
Monet, Claude 564, 579
Monod, Jacques 705
Montaigne, de, Michel 432. See also de Montaigne, Michel
Morandi, Giorgio 309
Mordue, Stefan 519
Morrell, Paul 512
Müller, Pascal 145, 169, 540
Murakami, Takashi 690
Murcutt, Glenn 602, 6[illegible]
Muuss, Mike 41

N

Napoléon Bonaparte 408
Negroponte, Nicholas 113, 145, 229, 51[illegible], 536, 540, 54[illegible]
Neufert, Ernst 111, 12[illegible]
Neumann, Balthasar 426, 43[illegible]
Neumann, von, John 373, 374, 375, 376, 37[illegible], 395, 649, 650, 711, 71[illegible]
Newell, Martin 26[illegible]
Newman, Max 55[illegible]
Nicholas, Robin 34[illegible]
Nicholson, Jack 64[illegible]
Niemeyer, Oscar 85, 113, 114, 53[illegible]
Nitzchke, Oscar 30[illegible]
Norvig, Peter 549, 55[illegible]
Nouvel, Jean 603, 60[illegible]
Nygaard, Kristen 37[illegible]

O

O'Brien, Richard 55[illegible]
Oechslin, Werner 12[illegible]
Oguchi, Keiji 48[illegible]
Olgiati, Valerio 60[illegible]
Orwell, George 470, 645, 646, 65[illegible]
Otto, Frei 195, 427, 43[illegible]
Oxman, Neri 605, 68[illegible]

P

Page, Larry 188, 62[illegible]
Palladio, Andrea 118, 119, 158, 169, 659, 67[illegible]
Pallasmaa, Juhani 60[illegible]
Papert, Seymour 358, 36[illegible]
Pareto, Vilfredo 16[illegible]
Paré, Zaven 55[illegible]
Parmigianino 72[illegible]
Parsons, John T 408, 409, 41[illegible]
Pascal, Blaise 18[illegible]
Paulson, Boyd 514, 539, 54[illegible]
Paxton, Joseph 426, 427, 435, 43[illegible]
Peano, Giuseppe 19[illegible]
Pei, I M 81, 42[illegible]
Peirce, Charles Sanders 29[illegible]
Peoples, David 55[illegible]
Persson, Markus 47[illegible]
Peterson, Christine 63[illegible]
Pheidippides 63[illegible]
Phelan, Robert 7[illegible]
Phong, Bui Tong 260, 261, 267, 274, 27[illegible]
Picasso, Pablo 11[illegible]
Pico della Mirandola, Giovanni 29, 34, 4[illegible], 4[illegible]
Pico, Francesco 4[illegible]
Plato 69, 66[illegible]
Plutarch 42[illegible]
Poe, Edgar Allan 25[illegible]
Poliziano 4[illegible]
Pope Innocent VIII 4[illegible]
Porsér, Jakob 47[illegible]
Porstmann, Walter 33[illegible]
Pottmann, Helmut 57, 61, 35[illegible]
Prince Charles 17[illegible]
Prix, Wolf 12[illegible]
Putteneers, Joris 17[illegible]
Pythagoras 118, 119, 125, 15[illegible]

Q

Queen Elizabeth I 65[illegible]
Queen Elizabeth II, The Queen 51[illegible]

R

Radic, Smijan 60[illegible]
Rahm, Philippe 60[illegible]
Rasch, Bodo 478, 58[illegible]
Ratti, Carlo 491, 602, 62[illegible]
Ray, Phil 23[illegible]

Reas, Casey 351, 359
Reed, Carol 340
Riemann, Bernhard 185
Ritchie, Dennis 635
Rittel, Horst 115
Roche, Gus 231
Rometty, Ginni 554
Ross, Douglas T 287
Rossi, Aldo 601, 603
Roth, Chrétien Frederic Guillaume 639
Rousseau, Jean-Jacques 633, 656, 658
Rowling, J K 432
Ruffle, Simon 512
Rutherford, Ernest 649
Rutten, David 358

S

Samuel, Arthur 552, 560
San Gallo the Younger 425, 435
Sartre, Jean-Paul 651
Saunders, Patricia 341
Scheeren, Ole 602
Schinkel, Carl Friedrich 562, 577
Schock-Werner, Barbara 285, 294
Schoenberg, Jacob 74
Schulman, Tom 632
Schumacher, Patrik 57, 64, 165, 166, 602, 603
Scott, Ridley 63, 551
Sebastian Thrun 553, 554
Sedol, Lee 553
Semper, Gottfried 421, 426, 427
Sennett, Richard 431
Serkis, Andy 102
Serlio, Sebastiano 137, 190, 709, 720, 721
Serres, Michel 43, 549, 560, 705, 706
Shakespeare, William 116, 658, 659, 660, 713
Shaw, Cliff 555
Shaw, George Bernard 552
Shelley, Mary 554, 559
Shelley, Percy Bysshe 554
Sherman, Gary 496
Sholes, Christopher Latham 329
Shulman, Julius 292, 294
Shu, Wang 336, 602
Simon, Herbert A 512, 555
Simon, Paul 122, 163
Singh, Ishveena 518
Siza, Álvaro 65, 80, 606
Smith, Adam 655, 658
Snowden, Edward 646, 647
Snow, John 493, 496, 502, 504
Spavento, Giorgio 125
Sproull, Bob 468, 473
Stadler, Michael 223, 486
Stallman, Richard 634, 635
Steiner, Rudolf 524
Steinitz, Carl 497
Stephenson, Neal 496
Stiny, George 64, 119, 126, 145, 157, 169, 540
Strachey, Christopher 552, 558
Stulen, Frank L 408, 409
Sullivan, John M 70
Sullivan, Louis 70, 179
Sumi, Christian 211
Sutherland, Ivan 62, 231, 232, 244, 258, 260, 468, 469, 473, 512

T

Taylor, Dan 519
Thales of Miletus 698
Thatcher, Margaret 651, 652, 676
Thompson, D'Arcy Wentworth 145, 158, 159, 164, 170
Thompson, Ken 635
Thünen, von, Johann Heinrich 531
Tolkien, J R R 102
Tolman, F P 512
Tomlinson, Roger F 493, 496
Torvalds, Linus 635
Toulouse, Catherine 285, 291
Townsend, Anthony 543
Townsend, Anthony M 529, 531. See also Townsend, Anthony
Toyota, Yasuhisa 481, 482
Trissino, Gian Giorgio 119
Trump, Donald 615, 653
Tschumi, Bernard 602
Turing, Alan 159, 164, 329, 355, 373, 376, 468, 549, 551, 552, 647, 663, 705
Turner, J M W 257, 258, 306, 563, 578
Turner, Richard 426

U

Ungers, Oswald Mathias 114
Utzon, Jørn 70, 83, 294

V

van Berkel, Ben 78, 113
van der Rohe, Mies 120, 158, 316, 318, 595, 596, 597
van Nederveen, G A 512
Venturi, Robert 593, 597, 602
Vere, Elizabeth 659
Vernon, Elizabeth 658
Vesalius, Andreas 576
Villar y Lozano, del, Francisco Paulo 415
Vinci, da, Leonardo 299, 340, 372, 429, 559, 696, 705
Virilio, Paul 43
Vitruvius 95, 118, 119, 120, 155, 166, 425, 429, 559, 698, 699, 705, 711, 714
Vivaldi, Antonio 660
Voltaire 633
von Förster, Heinz 649
von Goethe, Johann Wolfgang 137
von Kleist, Heinrich 131, 137
von Koch, Helge 155
von Neumann, John 373, 374, 375, 376, 377, 395, 426, 435, 649, 650, 711, 713
von Thünen, Johann Heinrich 531

W

Wachowski, Andy 469
Wachowski, Lara 469. See also Wachowski, Larry
Wachowski, Larry 469
Wachowski, Lilly 469. See also Wachowski, Andy
Wachowskis, The 469
Wachsmann, Konrad 192, 210, 211, 427
Wall, Larry 351, 356
Ward-Larson, Greg 271
Warhol, Andy 595
Watanabe, Makoto Sei 157, 221, 540, 545
Watts, John 512
Weaire, Denis 70
Webber, Melvin M 111, 115
Weiser, Mark 615
Weizenbaum, Joseph 552, 555
Welles, Orson 340
Whistler, James Abbot McNeill 340
Whitted, John Turner 261, 262
Wiener, Norbert 560, 562, 649, 696
Wilhite, Steve 239
Williams, Lance 261
Williams, Robin 632
Winfrey, Oprah 432
Wirth, Niklaus 156
Wolf, Gary 493
Wolfram, Stephen 363, 382
Woodbury, Rob 541
Woods,Lebbeus 602
Woolf, Virginia 465
Wössner, Uwe 485, 586
Wright, Frank Lloyd 87, 122, 595, 603
Wriothesely, Henry, 3rd Earl of Southampton 658, 659

X

Xiadong, Li 602

Y

Yihe, Ma 444
Young, Liam 602

Z

Zadeh, Lofti 290
Zimmermann, Thomas 469
Zumthor, Peter 430, 45[illegible], 602

Index of Architectural Objects

#

20 Fenchurch Street, London 477. See also Walkie-Talkie, London
30 St Mary's Axe, London 216, 428, 524. See also Gherkin, London

A

Absolute Towers, Mississauga, Canada 84
Albert Bridge, London 477, 741, 745
Alhambra, Granada 99, 100
Aronoff Center University of Cincinnati, Cincinnati 121

B

Bankside Power Station, London 477. See also Tate Modern, London
Barricade, Dresden, temporary 426
Basílica i Temple de la Sagrada Família, Barcelona 407, 415, 419, 424. See also Gaudí Cathedral, Barcelona
Basilica of Santa Maria Novella, Florence 95, 213, 722
Battersea Power Station, London 523
Beijing National Aquatics Centre 219. See also Water Cube Aquatic Centre, Beijing
Beijing National Stadium 122, 164, 219, 297. See also Bird's Nest Stadium, Beijing
Berne Minster 294, 301
Biosphère Montreal 70
Bird's Nest Stadium, Beijing 219, 297. See also Beijing National Stadium
Bismarck National Monument, model/project/plan 316
BMW-*Vierzylinder*, Munich 85
Bologna Cathedral 425
Bosjes Chapel, South Africa 86
Brandenburg Airport, Berlin 525
Burj Khalifa tower, Dubai 478

C

Cardiff Bay Opera House, model/project/plan 63
Cathedral of Brasília 85
Centre Pompidou-Metz 412
Centre Pompidou, Paris 87, 360, 412, 418, 736
Chatsworth House, Derbyshire, England 426
Chiswick House, London 426
Coliseum, Rome 101, 106
Cologne Cathedral 89, 285, 292, 293, 294, 301, 313
Convention Hall, Chigaco, model/project/plan 318
Convertible Umbrellas, Saudi Arabia 478
Crossrail, London 513, 515
Crown Sydney 523
Crystal Palace, London 426, 427, 435, 436

E

Elbphilharmonie, Hamburg 428, 480, 481, 482, 489, 741, 745
Erechtheion, Athens 425

F

Festival Wing, model/project/plan 517
Fieramilano, Milan 88
Florence Cathedral 425
Forth Bridge, Scotland 616, 617

G

Gasometer City Vienna 95
Gaudí Cathedral, Barcelona 415. See also Basílica i Temple de la Sagrada Família, Barcelona
Gherkin, London 216, 428, 524. See also 30 St Mary's Axe, London
Goetheanum, Dornach, Switzerland 524
Great Conservatory at Chatsworth, Derbyshire, England 426, 435
Great Pyramid of Giza 69, 698
Guggenheim Museum Bilbao 64, 78, 87, 362, 363, 407, 454

H

Hauptverwaltungsgebäude München, Munich 85
Heathrow Terminal 3, London 509, 512, 525. See also Oceanic Terminal, London
Henderson Waves Bridge, Singapore 400
Heydar Aliyev Center, Baku 363, 401
Hungerburg funicular railway, Innsbruck 212
Hungerford Bridge, London 517

I

Iidabashi subway station 221

K

Kilden Performing Arts Centre, Kilden, Norway 86
Kunsthaus Bregenz, Austria 430, 457

L

Louvre Pyramid, Paris 81, 428
Luchtsingel, Rotterdam 637, 640

M

Malagueira Housing, Portugal 80
Metropol Parasol, Seville 363
Millennium Bridge, London 477, 487
Minima / Maxima World Expo 2017 Pavilion, temporary, Astana (Nor-Sultan) 217
Musée d'Orsay, Paris 95
Museum of the Human Body, Montpelier, France 122
Musikverein, Vienna 480, 482, 488

N

National Assembly Dhaka 81
National Theatre, London 424, 517

O

Oceanic Terminal, London 509. See also Heathrow Terminal 3, London
Olympic Stadium Munich, Munich 427

P

Palazzo Rucellai, Florence 95
Palm House, Kew Gardens, London 426, 435
Palm Islands, Dubai 478
Piazza Obliqua, Rome 468
Piazza Retta, Rome 468
Prophet's Mosque, Medina 582

R

Reggio Emilia Stazione Mediopadana, Italy 87
Reichskanzlei, Berlin 478
Research Pavilion of the Institute for Computational Design (ICD), temporary, Stuttgart, Germany 455
Rolex Learning Centre, EPFL, Lausanne, Switzerland 88

S

Sagrada Família, Barcelona 407, 415, 419, 424. See also Basílica i Temple de la Sagrada Família, Barcelona
San Carlo alle Quattro Fontane, Rome 213
Santa Maria Novella, Florence 95, 213, 722
Seagram Building, New York 127
Semper Opera, Dresden 42, 95, 425, 638, 722
Sir John Soane Museum, London 218
Solomon R Guggenheim Museum, New York 87
Southbank Centre, London 517
St Paul's Cathedral, London 477, 539
St Peter's Basilica, Rome 425, 435, 456, 468, 478
St Peter's Square, Rome 468, 472, 741, 745
Stuttgart, Germany 64
Sydney Opera House 70, 83, 294, 295

T

Tate Modern, London 95, 477
Teepott, Warnemünde, Rostock, Germany 36
Temple of Concordia, Sicily 719
Terminal 3 London Heathrow 509, 512, 525. See also Heathrow Terminal 3, London
Therme Vals, Switzerland 430, 457
Tower of Winds, Yokohama 428

U

Undercroft, London 517. See also Southbank Centre, London

V

Via 57 West New York, New York 84
Villa Malcontenta, Oriago, Italy 169
Villa Rotonda, Vicenza, Italy 659, 677, 719
Villa Savoye, Poissy, France 720

W

Wales Millennium Centre, Cardiff 63
Walkie-Talkie, London 477, 484. See also 20 Fenchurch Street, London
Water Cube Aquatic Centre, Beijing 82, 219
Wetzlar Cathedral, Wetzlar, Germany 96, 105
Würzburg Residence, Würzburg, Germany 435

Sources for Quotations, Citations, and Statistics

I 3D MODELLING

- Paul Klee, p 59: *Notebooks, Volume 1: The Thinking Eye*, 1956 (translated by Ralph Manheim, 1961)
- Le Corbusier, p 68: *Vers une architecture (Towards a New Architecture)*, 1923 (1927)
- John M Sullivan, p 70: *The Geometry of Bubbles and Foams*, 2011
- Buckminster Fuller, p 76: quoted in David J Darling: *The Universal Book of Mathematics*, 2004

I DIGITAL DATA ACQUISITION

- Leon Battista Alberti, p 95: variant quoted in *Enzyclopaedia Britannica*: https://www.britannica.com/topic/Renaissance-man
- Leon Battista Alberti, p 95: *De re aedificatoria (Ten Books on Architecture)*, 1485

I DIGITAL DESIGN STRATEGIES

- Oscar Niemeyer, p 113: *Centgraf, Architektur entsteht im Kopf – oder auch nicht*, in: *DBZ* April 2013, *Der Entwurf*
- Architekturzentrum Wien, p 113: https://past.azw.at/page.php?node_id=3&page_id=538
- Oswald Mathias Ungers, p 114: in conversation with Peter Neitzke in: Walter Ehlers, Gernot Feldhusen und Carl Steckeweh (Eds.): *CAD: Architektur automatisch?*, 1986
- Leon Battista Alberti, p 117–118: *De re aedificatoria (Ten Books on Architecture)*, 1485
- Philibert de l'Orme, p 118: quoted in R Wittkower: *Grundlagen der Architektur im Zeitalter des Humanismus*, 1973 München, 20, p 120.
- Gian Giorgio Trissinio, p 119: *L'Italia liberata dai Goti (Italy Liberated From the Goths)*, 1548
- Andrea Palladio, p 119: *I quattro libri dell'architettura (The Four Books of Architecture)*, 1570
- Le Corbusier, p 120: *The Modulor: A Harmonious Measure to the Human Scale, Universally Applicable to Architecture and Mechanics*, 1954, 1958
- Albert Einstein, p 120: quoted by Will Wiles in: *Modulor Man by Le Corbusier*, in *Icon*, 2009: https://www.iconeye.com/opinion/icon-of-the-month/item/3815-modulor-man-by-le-corbusier
- Werner Oechslin, p 121: *Daidalos*, 1990
- Le Corbusier and Bernhard Hoesli p 121: *Caragonne*, 1995
- *Kaisersrot*, p 122: http://www.kaisersrot.ch/kaisersrot-02/2003_National_Beijing_Olympic_Stadium_%28CN%29.html
- Paul Simon, p 122: *So Long, Frank Lloyd Wright*, on *Bridge Over Troubled Water*, 1970
- Frank Lloyd Wright, p 122: *Essay*, 1894, in: Mark Wigley: *Die Architektur der Atmosphäre, Daidalos 68/1998, Gütersloh, S. 25*
- Bjarke Ingels Group (BIG), p 122: featured at: https://big.dk/#projects
- Wolf Prix, p 123: in correspondence with Ursula Kirschner
- Friedrich Dürrenmatt, p 123: quoted in G Vollmer: *Abendstunde im Spätherbst* in: *Du – die Zeitschrift der Kultur*, 51, 1991

I COMPUTER AIDED DESIGN (CAD)

- Heinrich von Kleist, p 131: *Über die allmähliche Verfertigung der Gedanken beim Reden ('On the Gradual Formation of Thought Through Conversation')*, ca 1805–06
- Johann Wolfgang von Goethe, p 137: Der Zauberlehrling (The Sorcerer's Apprentice), 1797

I GENERATIVE METHODS

- Charles Darwin, p 147: *Notebook B*, 1837
- John S Gero, p 154: *Computers and Creative Design*, 1995: http://papers.cumincad.org/data/works/att/5580.content.pdf
- Pythagoras, p 155: frequently quoted in various versions, among others in Bertrand Russell: *A History of Western Philosophy*, 1945
- Niklaus Wirth, p 156: *Algorithms + Data Structures = Programs*, 1976
- D'Arcy Wentworth Thompson, p 158: *On Growth and Form*, 1917
- Bernard Cache, p 161: *AA Files No. 56, pp 8–19*, 2007
- Christopher Alexander, p 162: *Notes on the Synthesis of Form*, 1964
- Art Garfunkel, p 163–164: quoted by Kirstofer Bartol in: *And Garfunkel, Part III – Bridges & Waters*, 2019: https://openarticle.xyz/infotheke/and-garfunkel-p3
- Yan LeCun, p 165: quoted by Cade Metz in: *Google's Dueling Neural Networks Spar to Get Smarter, No Humans Required*, in *Wired Business*, 4 November 2017: https://www.wired.com/2017/04/googles-dueling-neural-networks-spar-get-smarter-no-humans-required/
- Patrik Schumacher, p 165: *Parametricism: A New Global Style for Architecture and Urban Design* in *Architectural Design (AD)*, 2009

I GRAPHS & GRAPHICS

- Louis Sullivan, p 179: *The Tall Office Building Artistically Considered* in *Lippincott's Magazine*, 1896
- Euclid, p 184: *Elements*, ca. 300 BCE

II IMAGE & COLOUR

- Nobel Prize citation, p 231: nobelprize.org/prizes/physics/1909/summary/
- Postmaster General, p 231: quoted in *Titanic's Wireless Connection* by the Wireless History Foundation at wirelesshistoryfoundation.org/titanics-wireless-connection/
- Rudyard Kipling, p 235: *The Ballad of East and West*, 1889

II RENDERING

- J M W Turner p 257: quoted on banknote issued by the Bank of England: bankofengland.co.uk/banknotes/polymer-20-pound-note
- J M W Turner, p 257: quoted in Donald B MacCulloch: *The Wondrous Isle of Staffa*, p 160, 1927
- J M W Turner, p 257: quoted in Eric Shanes: *The Life and Masterworks of J.M.W. Turner*, 2012
- Oxford Dictionaires, p 257: quoted on *Lexico:* https://www.lexico.com/definition/render
- *Computer Graphics: Principles and Practice*, p 257, by John F Hughes, Andries van Dam, Morgan McGuire, David F Sklar, James D Foley, Steven K Feiner, Kurt Akeley, 198[illegible]
- Edgar Allan Poe, p 258: *The Daguerrotype*, 1840: https://petapixel.com/2015/10/08/heres-what-edgar-allan-poe-wrote-about-the-birth-of-photography-in-1840/
- *Computer Hope*, p 259: https://www.computerhope.com/jargon/z/zbuffering.htm
- *Wikipedia*, p 260: https://en.wikipedia.org/wiki/Lambert's_cosine_law
- Joanie Faletto, p 261: *The Most Important Object in Computer Graphics is the Utah Teapot*, September 2017 [previously at: https://curiosity.com/topics/the-most-important-object-in-computer-graphics-is-the-utah-teapot-curiosity/]
- Thomas Kinkade, p 266: [previously featured at thomaskinkade.com]
- Oscar (Academy Award) citation, p 26[illegible]: https://www.sfgate.com/style/article/Three-Pixar-execs-get-special-Oscars-3152578.php

II VISUALISATION

- Clare Booth Luce, p 287: quoted at: https://quoteinvestigator.com/2015/04/02/simple/#note-10911-1
- Charles Sanders Peirce, p 293: quoted on *Wikipedia:* https://en.wikipedia.org/wiki/Semiotic_theory_of_Charles_Sanders_Peirce#cite_note-2
- Julius Shulman, p 294: *Visual Acoustics: The Modernism of Julius Shulman*. Directed by Eric Bricker. 2008
- Leonardo da Vinci, p 299: quoted in Irene Earls: *Renaissance Art: A Topical Dictionary*, 1987

IMAGE DATA STATISTICS ↖ 294:

- Mary Lister: *33 Mind-Boggling Instagram Stats & Facts for 2018*, WordStream, https://www.wordstream.com/blog/ws/2017/04/20/instagram-statistics
- The Top 20 Valuable Facebook Statistics – Updated January 2019, Zephoria Digital Marketing: https://zephoria.com/top-15-valuable-facebook-statistics/
- Bernard Marr: *How Much Data Do We Create Every Day? The Mind-Blowing Stats Everyone Should Read*, Forbes: https://www.forbes.com/sites/bernardmarr/2018/05/21/how-much-data-do-we-create-every-day-the-mind-blowing-stats-everyone-should-read/#3c75a0ed60ba

III TEXT, TYPOGRAPHY & LAYOUT

- Harry Lime, p 340: *The Third Man*. Directed by Carol Reed; written by Orson Welles, Carol Reed, Graham Greene, United Kingdom 1949
- Robin Nicholas, p 341: quoted in *MacUser*, 8 July 2005: flickr.com/photos/joeclark/4901460991/in/photostream/

III SCRIPTING

- Mark Burry, p 353: *Scripting Cultures: Architectural Design and Programming*, 2011

- Alvar Aalto: p 353: quoted on https://www.archisoup.com/architecture-quotes

III WRITING & CODE

- The Old Testament, p 371: *King James Bible, John 1:1*

IV MODEL MAKING

- Gottfried Semper, p 426: *Letter to Heinrich Hübsch*, January 1852: https://en.wikipedia.org/wiki/Gottfried_Semper#cite_note-5
- Jonathan Hill, p 430: *Building a Drawing and Drawing a Building*, in *Nordisk Arkitekturforskning*, 2002
- Richard Sennett, p 431: *Labours of Love*, in *The Guardian*: https://www.theguardian.com/books/2008/feb/02/featuresreviews.guardianreview14
- Philip Beesley, p 431: Foundation Telefonica VIDA, Matador Madrid, Spain, 2009

IV 3D PRINTING

- Chuck Hall, p 441: on *Good Morning America*, 30 January 1989: https://www.youtube.com/watch?v=NpRDuJ5YgoQ
- *FabLab*, p 441: https://www.fablabs.io/

V VIRTUAL & AUGMENTED REALITY

- Virginia Woolf, p 465: *Is Fiction an Art?* in *Essays III*, 1927
- Peter Greenaway, p 465: *The Draughtsman's Contract*. Written and directed by Peter Greenaway. United Kingdom, 1982
- Gilles Deleuze, p 465: *Difference and Repetition*, 1968
- Gian Lorenzo Bernini p 468: quoted in *Art Speaks: St. Peter's Square* at http://thecatholictalks.com/artspeaks_post.asp?id=6
- Ivan E Sutherland p 468: *The Ultimate Display* in *Proceedings of IFIP Congress*, 1965
- WebVR, p 469: https://webvr.info/
- Robert Jungk, p 470: *Die Zukunft hat schon Begonnen: Amerika's Allmacht und Ohnmacht*, 1952

V SIMULATION

- Albert Bridge, p 477: https://www.britainexpress.com/London/albert-bridge.htm
- Nagata and Yasuhisa Toyota, p 481: previously featured on the Nagata website at nagata-i.com; there is now a shorter but similar wording on their website at the shorter portfolio page: https://www.nagata-i.com/portfolio/elbphilharmonie-hamburg-grosser-saal/
- Keiji Oguchi, p 482: [previously featured on the Nagata website at nagata-i.com]
- Benjamin Koren, p 482: quoted by Liz Stinson: *What Happens When Algorithms Design a Concert Hall? The Stunning Elbphilharmonie* in *Wired Design*, 1 December 2017: https://www.wired.com/2017/01/happens-algorithms-design-concert-hall-stunning-elbphilharmonie/
- Yasuhisa Toyota, p 482: [previously featured on the Nagata website at nagata-i.com]
- Uwe Wössner, p 485: [previously featured at http://www.hlrs.de/covise/]
- Ninsight: p 486: [previously featured at http://ninsight.at/v3/]
- Uto Collective, p 486: https://sites.google.com/site/utotoolswiki/home

V GEOGRAPHIC INFORMATION SYSTEMS (GIS)

- Al Gore, p 493: *The Digital Earth: Understanding Our Planet in the 21st Century*, Talk given at the California Science Centre, Los Angeles, 31 January 1998: http://portal.opengeospatial.org/files/?artifact_id=6210
- Gary Wolf and Kevin Kelly, p 493, quoted by Alina Schadwinkel in *Die 10.000 Fragezeichen*, *Zeit Online*, 2015: https://www.zeit.de/wissen/gesundheit/2015-04/quantified-self-fitness-gesundheit-wissenschaft
- *LIVE Singapore!*, p 494: http://senseable.mit.edu/livesingapore/
- *Strava*, p 494: [previously featured at strava.com]
- *Strava*, p 494: correspondence
- *OpenStreetMap*, p 494: https://www.openstreetmap.org/about
- Art+Com p 496: https://artcom.de/en/project/terravision/
- *CesiumJS*, p 496: https://cesium.com/cesiumjs/
- Michael Flaxman, p 497: quoted at https://en.wikipedia.org/wiki/Geodesign (not further referenced)
- Alex Davies, p 500: *Strava's Cycling App is Helping Cities Build Better Bike Lanes*, in *Wired Gear*, 6 March 2014: https://www.wired.com/2014/06/strava-sells-cycling-data/

V BUILDING INFORMATION MODELLING (BIM)

- National Institute of Building Sciences (USA), p 509: https://www.nationalbimstandard.org/faqs
- ISO, p 510: https://www.iso.org/standard/76130.html
- *buildingSMART*, p 511, previously featured at buildingsmart.org, now quoted at https://hujb2000.gitbooks.io/ifcspecification/en/specifications/BCF_Releases.html
- *buildingSMART*, p 511: [previously featured at buildingsmart.org]
- *Germany: Industrie 4.0*, p 511: https://ec.europa.eu/growth/tools-databases/dem/monitor/sites/default/files/DTM_Industrie%204.0.pdf
- BMVI, p 511: [previously featured at bmvi.de]
- Paul Morrell, p 512, quoted by Anna Winston in *Adopt BIM or Be Betamaxed Out Says Morrell*: http://www.bdonline.co.uk/news/adopt-bim-or-be-betamaxed-out-says-morrell/5018263.article, 18 May 2011
- Stefan Behnisch, p 512: https://www.bauwelt.de/themen/interview/Digitalisierung-Stefan-Behnisch-Andreas-Hild-Bauwelt-Gespraech-3075276.html
- Vanessa Quirk, p 512: *A Brief History of BIM*: https://www.archdaily.com/302490/a-brief-history-of-bim
- Ishveena Singh, p 518: *BIM adoption and implementation around the world: Initiatives by major nations*: https://www.geospatialworld.net/blogs/bim-adoption-around-the-world/
- Dan Taylor, p 519: [previously featured on blog.capterra.com]
- *Hochtief*, p 520: https://www.hochtief-vicon.com/vicon_en/0.jhtml
- Charles Eastman, p 523: *An Outline of the Building Description System*, 1974

V DIGITAL CITIES

- Anthony M Townsend, p 531: *Making Sense of the New Urban Science*, 2015
- Robert Hughes, p 532: *The Shock of The New*, TV programme, 1980
- United Nations, p 533: *Sustainable Development Goals*, 2015
- *Wikipedia*, p 534: https://en.wikipedia.org/wiki/Smart_city
- *Smart City Wien*, p 534: [previously featured at https://smartcity.wien.gv.at/site/en/]
- Kevin Kelly, p 535: *Out of Control*, 1994
- Nicholas Negroponte, p 536: *The Architecture Machine*, 1970 and *Soft Architecture Machines*, 1976
- *UrbanSim*, p 537: [previously featured at https://urbansim.com/]
- Rob Woodbury and Andrew Burrow, p 541: *Whither Design Space*, 2006

V BIG DATA & MACHINE LEARNING

- University College Cork, p 551: [previously featured at https://www.ucc.ie/en/]
- Christopher Strachey, p 552: quoted on https://en.wikipedia.org/wiki/Christopher_Strachey
- Sebastian Thrun, p 553: quoted by Max Chafkin in *Udacity's Sebastian Thrun, Godfather Of Free Online Education, Changes Course*, in *Fast Company*, 14 November 2013: https://www.fastcompany.com/3021473/udacity-sebastian-thrun-uphill-climb
- Ginni Rometty, p 554: quoted in *Forbes*: https://www.forbes.com/sites/nicolemartin1/2019/06/27/13-greatest-quotes-about-the-future-of-artificial-intelligence/#3c63cda73bdf
- Douglas Adams, p 554: *Dirk Gently's Holistic Detective Agency*, 1987
- HAL 9000, p 554: *2001 A Space Odyssey*. Directed by Stanley Kubrick, written by Stanley Kubrick and Arthur C Clarke. United Kingdom, 1968
- John McCarthy and Marvin Minsky, p 544: *A Proposal for the Dartmouth Summer Research Project one Artificial Intelligence*, 1955: http://www-formal.stanford.edu/jmc/history/dartmouth/dartmouth.html
- John Minsky, p 555: quoted in *Life Magazine*, 1970, see: http://sitn.hms.harvard.edu/flash/2017/history-artificial-intelligence/

- Herbert Simon, p 555: quoted by Julien Simon in *Fascinating Tales of a Strange Tomorrow,* in *Towards Data Science*, 5 April 2017: https://towardsdatascience.com/fascinating-tales-of-a-strange-tomorrow-72048639e754
- Pierre-Simon Laplace, p 558: *A Philosophical Essay on Probabilities*, 1814
- Zaven Paré, p 559: quoted by Nicolas Barrial in *Zaven Paré: "Without narration the robot has no point"*, *Makery*, 6 February 2017: https://www.makery.info/en/2017/02/06/zaven-pare-sans-narration-le-robot-na-pas-dinteret/
- Dr Frank'n'Furter, p 559: *The Rocky Horror Show* (stage musical, 1973) and *The Rocky Horror Picture Show* (film, 1975) written by Richard O'Brien.
- Vitruvius, p 560: *Ten Books on Architecture, Book 1*, written ca 30–15 BCE
- *Blade Runner*, p 570: *Blade Runner*. Directed by Ridley Scott, written by Hampton Fancher and David Peoples. United States, Hong Kong, 1982
- *The Matrix*, p 575: *The Matrix*. Written and directed by The Wachowskis. United States, Australia, 1999

VI BEING A 'BRAND'

- Andy Warhol, p 595: quoted in Jeff Guinn and Douglas Perry: *The Sixteenth Minute: Life in the Aftermath of Fame*, 2005
- Mies van der Rohe, p 596: quoted (among many others) in *What did Mies van der Rohe mean by less is more?* in *Phaidon* (not dated): https://uk.phaidon.com/agenda/architecture/articles/2014/april/02/what-did-mies-van-der-rohe-mean-by-less-is-more/
- Robert Venturi, p 597: *Complexity and Contradiction in Architecture* (The Museum of Modern Art, 1966), 17.
- Philip Johnson, p 597: quoted by Kenneth Powell in *Philip Johnson – 'Godfather of American Architecture'* in *The Independent*, 28 January 2005: https://www.independent.co.uk/news/obituaries/philip-johnson-17083.html
- Rem Koolhaas, p 597: *Junkspace*, *October* No. 100 (2002): 175–90.
- Bjarke Ingels, p 597: *Yes Is More: An Archicomic on Architectural Evolution*, 2009

VI THE INTERNET OF THINGS (IOT)

- Kevin Ashton, p 615: quoted by Alex Hannaford in *The Internet of Things: Could it really change the way we live?* in *The Telegraph*, 5 May 2017: https://www.telegraph.co.uk/technology/2017/05/06/internet-things-could-really-change-way-live/
- Kevin Ashton, p 615: *That 'Internet of Things' Thing*, in *RFID Journal*, 22 June 2009: http://www.rfidjournal.com/articles/view?4986
- Contiki, p 618: http://www.contiki-os.org/

VI COLLABORATION

- John Keating, p 632: *Dead Poets Society*. Directed by Peter Weir, written by Tom Schulman. United States,1989
- GNU, p 635: https://www.gnu.org/gnu/thegnuproject.en.html
- Richard Stallman, p 635: https://www.gnu.org/gnu/thegnuproject.en.html
- Snøhetta, p 636: https://snohetta.com
- *Elemental*, p 636: https://elemntalchile.cl
- *Assemble*, p 637: https://assemblestudio.co.uk
- Bricks, p 637: [previously at https://openbricks.io]

VI PRIVACY & SECURITY

- William Langland, p 646: *Piers Plowman*, ca 1390
- Alan Turing, p 647: quoted in: A P Mahon: *The History of Hut Eight*, 1945: http://www.ellsbury.com/hut8/hut8-000.htm
- Gordon Brown: p 647: quoted in *PM apology after Turing petition* on *BBC News*, 11 September 2009: http://news.bbc.co.uk/1/hi/technology/8249792.stm
- Albert Hofmann, p 648: *LSD, My Problem Child*, 1979
- Ted Kaczynski p 648: *Industrial Society and its Future*, known as *'The Unabomber Manifesto'*, published 22 September 1995: https://www.washingtonpost.com/wp-srv/national/longterm/unabomber/manifesto.text.htm
- The Merry Pranksters, p 648: Ken Babs in *LSD Road Trip*, BBC World Service 28 July 2017: https://www.bbc.co.uk/programmes/p0253hsr
- Norbert Wiener, p 649: *Cybernetics: Or Control and Communication in the Animal and the Machine*, 1948
- Heinz von Förster, p 649 in *Das Netz (The Net – The Unabomber, LSD and the Internet)*. Documentary written and directed by Lutz Dammbeck. Germany, 2003: https://www.youtube.com/watch?v=ev7e9sfWIJo
- Buckminster Fuller, p 650: quoted on *Wikipedia:* https://en.wikipedia.org/wiki/Buckminster_Fuller (no further reference)
- Stewart Brand, p 650: in *Das Netz (The Net – The Unabomber, LSD and the Internet)*. Documentary written and directed by Lutz Dammbeck. Germany, 2003
- Martin Luther King Jr, p 651: speech delivered to the March on Washington for Jobs and Freedom, 28 August 1963: https://en.wikipedia.org/wiki/I_Have_a_Dream
- Margaret Thatcher, p 651: Interview with Douglas Keay, *Woman's Own*, 23 September 1987: https://www.margaretthatcher.org/document/106689
- UK Government (Section 28), p 652: https://en.wikipedia.org/wiki/Section_28
- Facebook, p 654: quoted in: *Data, Democracy and Dirty Tricks*, Channel 4, 2018
- United Nations, p 654: *Universal Declaration of Human Rights*, 1948: https://www.un.org/en/universal-declaration-human-rights/
- Francis Meres, p 659: *Palladis Tamia, Wits Treasury*, 1598
- John Willobie p 659: *Willobie His Avisa*, 1594

IN CONCLUSION – WHAT IS INFORMATION?

- *Oxford Dictionaries*, p 675: https://www.lexico.com/definition/information
- *Wikipedia*, p 675: https://en.wikipedia.org/wiki/Information
- Euclid, p 680: *Elements, Book I*, ca. 300 BCE
- Michel Serres, p 686: *The Incandescent*, 2003
- Michel Serres, p 685: *The Natural Contract*, 1990
- Le Corbusier, p 687: https://www.theartstory.org/artist/le-corbusier/
- *Superstudio*, p 687: http://dip9.aaschool.ac.uk/archive/superstudio-quotes/
- Rem Koolhaas, p 687: *S, M, L, XL*, 1995
- Sebastiano Serlio, p 690: *Seven Books on Architecture*, 1611
- L P Hartley, p 695: *The Go-Between*, 1953

Sources for Images & Graphics

INTRODUCTION

002 ©Adam Goldberg
http://www.alifewortheating.com/,
003 Painting by Jan van Huysum, Public Domain, Held by the National Gallery of Art, Washington
https://www.nga.gov/collection/art-object-page.96655.html
006 Painting by Cristofano dell'Altissimo, Public Domain, Held by the *Galleria degli Uffizi*, Florence
https://commons.wikimedia.org/wiki/File:Pico1.jpg

I 3D MODELLING

009 ©Greg Lynn
010A ©Zaha Hadid Architects
010B ©Zaha Hadid Architects
011A ©UNStudio
011B ©Lars Spuybroek/NOX
012A ©UNStudio
012B Photograph by Julian Herzog, Creative Commons, Source: Wikimedia
https://commons.wikimedia.org/wiki/File:Mercedes-Benz_Museum_201312_08_blue_hour.jpg
013A Photograph by Paste, Public Domain, Source: Wikimedia
https://commons.wikimedia.org/wiki/File:30_St_Mary_Axe,_%27Gherkin%27.JPG
013B ©Jonathan Massey & Andrew Weigand
013C ©Jonathan Massey & Andrew Weigand
014A ©The Very Many
014B ©NAARO
015A Courtesy of Jose Pinto Duarte
015B Courtesy of Jose Pinto Duarte
016 ©Marco Hemmerling
017 ©Marco Hemmerling
018 ©Marco Hemmerling
019A ©Marco Hemmerling
019B Photograph by John Pavelka, Creative Commons, Source: Wikimedia
https://commons.wikimedia.org/wiki/File:National_Assembly_Building_(3860418267).jpg
020A ©Marco Hemmerling
020B Photograph by Beau Wade, Creative Commons, Source: Wikimedia
https://de.wikipedia.org/wiki/Datei:Parigi-piramidi_louvre.jpg
021 ©Marco Hemmerling
022A ©ARUP (Sydney)
022B Source unknown/untraceable
023A ©Marco Hemmerling
023B Photograph by Cédric Thévenet, Creative Commons, Source: Wikimedia
https://commons.wikimedia.org/wiki/File:Biosph%C3%A8re_Montr%C3%A9al.jpg,
024A ©Marco Hemmerling
024B Photograph by Enoch Lau, Creative Commons, Source: Wikimedia
https://commons.wikimedia.org/wiki/File:Sydney_Opera_House_Sails_edit02_adj.JPG
025A ©Marco Hemmerling
025B Photograph by Sikander Iqbal, Creative Commons, Source: Wikimedia
https://commons.wikimedia.org/wiki/File:Absolute_Towers_-_20191019183707.jpg
026 ©Marco Hemmerling
027A ©Marco Hemmerling
027B Photograph by David Clay Photography, Creative Commons, Source: Wikimedia
https://commons.wikimedia.org/wiki/File:Luxury_Apartments_VIA_57_West,_Bjarke_Ingels_Group.jpg
028 ©Marco Hemmerling
029 ©Marco Hemmerling
030A ©Marco Hemmerling
030B Photograph by High Contrast, Creative Commons, Wikimedia
https://commons.wikimedia.org/wiki/File:BMW-Museum_in_M%C3%BCnchen.jpg
031A ©Marco Hemmerling
031B Photograph by Arian Zwegers, Creative Commons, Source: Wikimedia
https://commons.wikimedia.org/wiki/File:Brasilia,_Cathedral_of_Brasilia_(15309099334).jpg
032A ©Marco Hemmerling
032B Photograph by Carsten WT, Creative Commons, Source: Wikitravel
https://wikitravel.org/en/File:Kilden.JPG
033A ©Marco Hemmerling
033B ©Adam Letch
034A ©Marco Hemmerling
034B Photograph by An-d, Creative Commons, Source: Wikimedia
https://commons.wikimedia.org/wiki/File:Teepott.jpg
035A ©Marco Hemmerling
035B Photograph by Sérgio Valle Duarte, Creative Commons, Source: Wikimedia
https://commons.wikimedia.org/wiki/File:01_Solomon_R._Guggenheim_Museum_abstract.jpg
036A ©Marco Hemmerling
036B Photograph by pixabairis, Pixabay Licence, Source: Pixapay
https://pixabay.com/de/photos/centre-pompidou-paris-kunst-530069/
037A ©Marco Hemmerling
037B Photograph by Enrico Cartia, Creative Commons, Source: Wikimedia
https://commons.wikimedia.org/wiki/File:Stazione_Mediopadana_alta_velocit%C3%A0_Reggio_Emilia_(15918560268).jpg
038 ©Marco Hemmerling
039A ©Marco Hemmerling
039B Photograph by Magdalena Roeseler, Creative Commons, Source: Wikimedia
https://commons.wikimedia.org/wiki/File:Going_Your_Own_Way_(54996796).jpeg
040A ©Marco Hemmerling
040B Photograph by Michele M. F., Creative Commons, Source: Wikimedia
https://commons.wikimedia.org/wiki/File:FieraMilano,_Rho_(4422910513).jpg
041A ©Marco Hemmerling
041B Photograph by Thomas Robbin, Creative Commons, Source: Wikimedia
https://commons.wikimedia.org/wiki/File:Koelner_Dom_Innenraum.jpg
042 ©Marco Hemmerling
043 ©Marco Hemmerling
044 ©Marco Hemmerling
045A ©Marco Hemmerling
045B ©Marco Hemmerling

Vector graphics
©Marco Hemmerling,
except, ↖60: ©Marco Hemmerling, after Robin Evans

I DIGITAL DATA ACQUISITION

046 Autograph by Leon Battista Alberti, Public Domain, Source: Wikimedia
https://de.wikipedia.org/wiki/Leon_Battista_Alberti#/media/File:Autograph_von_Leon_Battista_Alberti.png
047 ©Zhonguyan Dai/McGill University, Zhongyuan Dai, Interpretation of Leon Battista Alberti's *Delineation of the City of Rome (Descriptio urbis Romae)*, 2012; constructed for the studio workshop (taught by Yelda Nasifoglu) of Prof. Alberto Perez-Gomez's history lecture course 'Architectural Intentions from Vitruvius to the Renaissance' at McGill University (https://f12arch531project.wordpress.com/).
048 Photograph by Albrecht Meydenbauer, Public Domain, Source: Wikimedia
https://commons.wikimedia.org/wiki/File:Wetzlar_Dom_81-009.jpg
049A ©Nikolaus Zieske
049B ©Nikolaus Zieske
049C ©Nikolaus Zieske
049D ©Nikolaus Zieske
050 ©Nikolaus Zieske
051 ©FARO
052 ©Nikolaus Zieske
053 ©ScanLAB Projects
054 ©Nikolaus Zieske
055 ©*Scan2BIM*
056 Source: *Businesswire*
057 ©Nikolaus Zieske, based on *Building Rome in a Day*:
https://grail.cs.washington.edu/rome/
058 ©Nikolaus Zieske
059 ©Thomas Reinold,
060 ©*Xsens*
061 ©Nikolaus Zieske
062 ©Nikolaus Zieske
063 ©Nikolaus Zieske
064 ©*NavVis*
065 ©RIEGL, www.riegl.com
066A ©Nikolaus Zieske
066B ©Nikolaus Zieske
067 ©Nikolaus Zieske, Screenshot using *RoomScan*

Vector graphic, ↖101
©Nikolaus Zieske

I DIGITAL DESIGN STRATEGIES

068 Frontispiece by Marc-Antoine Laugier, Public Domain
069 Courtesy of Ernst & Sohn
070 Wood cutting by Franchino Gaffer, Public Domain
071 Ursula Kirschner, after a description by Karl von Freckmann in *Proportionen in der Architektur*, 1965
072 ©Ursula Kirschner
073 ©George Stiny
074 ©Ursula Kirschner, after Walzer: *Das japanische Haus*
075 ©Rouven Seebo
076 Photograph by Noroton, Public Domain, Source: Wikimedia
https://commons.wikimedia.org/wiki/File:NewYorkSeagram_04.30.2008.JPG
077 ©Chris Bosse
078 ©Valentin Veroy
079 ©Chris Bosse
080 ©Ludger Hovestadt/Oliver Fritz
081 Photograph by Peter 23, edited by Ursula Kirschner, Source: Wikimedia
https://upload.wikimedia.org/wikipedia/commons/1/1e/Beijing_national_stadium.jpg

Vector graphic, ↖117
©Sven Schneider

I COMPUTER AIDED DESIGN (CAD)

082 ©Anna Fedorov,
083 Photograph by W H Jackson, Public Domain, Source: Wikimedia
https://commons.wikimedia.org/wiki/File:Shoshoni_tipis.jpg
084 Image author unknown, Public Domain, Source: Wikimedia
https://commons.wikimedia.org/wiki/File:Codex_Sangallensis_1092_recto.jpg
085 ©Oliver Fritz
086A Source: Nemetschek
086B Source: Intergraph
087 ©Oliver Fritz
088 ©Oliver Fritz

089 © Oliver Fritz, Screenshot using *SketchUp*
090 © Katrin Günther
091 © Oliver Fritz, Screenshot using *VectorWorks*
092 © Oliver Fritz, Screenshot using *VectorWorks*

Vector graphics, ↖132
© Oliver Fritz,

[illegible] GENERATIVE METHODS

093 Image by Charles Darwin, Public Domain, Source: Wikimedia https://commons.wikimedia.org/wiki/File:Darwin_Tree_1837.png
094 © *Kaisersrot* / ETH Zürich http://www.kaisersrot.ch/
095 © Urs Hirschberg / IAM TU Graz
096 © Andi Mucke, Fractal mountain surface, created with *Mandelbulb 3D* https://www.flickr.com/photos/exalk_3d/41300725661/
097A © Jan Walter Schliep
097B © Jan Walter Schliep http://www.xfrog.com/newsfeed/wp-content/uploads/xfrog_landscape_full.jpg
098A © Makato Sei Watanabe
098B © Makato Sei Watanabe https://makoto-architect.com/
099 © George Stiny, William Mitchell, *The Palladian grammar Environment and Planning B*; 1978, volume 5, pages 5–18 https://www.semanticscholar.org/paper/The-Palladian-Grammar-Stiny-Mitchell/049adf4453ffeb8e5c971a71e51b3aab81004e05
100 © Pascal Müller / Esri
101 © Singapore ETH Centre / ETH Zürich
102 Image by Ernst Haeckel, Public Domain, Source: Wikimedia https://commons.wikimedia.org/wiki/File:Haeckel_Phaeodaria_1.jpg
103 Image by D'Arcy Wentworth Thompson, Public Domain, Source: archive.org https://archive.org/download/ongrowthform00thom/ongrowthform00thom.pdf
104 © SOMA Architects http://www.soma-architecture.com/
105 Image by Tcpp, Creative Commons, Source: Wikimedia https://commons.wikimedia.org/w/index.php?curid=8041182
106A © Gleb Alexandrov
106B © Gleb Alexandrov http://glebalexandrov.com/, creativeshrimp.com
107A © Philippe Block, Block Research Group (BRG), ETH Zürich, MLK Jr. Park Stone Vault, Austin, TX, USA, 2010–2013
107B © Philippe Block, Block Research Group (BRG), ETH Zürich, MLK Jr. Park Stone Vault, Austin, TX, USA, 2010–2013 https://block.arch.ethz.ch/brg/project/mlk-jr-park-stone-vault-austin-tx-usa
108A © Michael Stadler / IAM TU Graz
108B © Michael Stadler / IAM TU Graz
108C © Michael Stadler / IAM TU Graz
109 © Milena Stavric / IAM TU Graz
110 © Jiri Pavlicek, Ioanna Simeonidou / IAM TU Graz https://iam.tugraz.at/en/research/fwf-project-augmented-parametrics-simulation-and-expert-knowledge-in-parametric-design/
111 © *Kaisersrot* / ETH Zürich http://www.kaisersrot.ch/
112 © *Kaisersrot* / ETH Zürich http://www.kaisersrot.ch/
113A © Stanislas Chaillou / Harvard GSD, *AI + Architecture Towards a New Approach*, Harvard GSD Thesis 2019
113B © Stanislas Chaillou / Harvard GSD, AI + Architecture Towards a New Approach, Harvard GSD Thesis 2019 https://issuu.com/stanislaschaillou/docs/stanislas_chaillou_thesis_
114 © Joris Putteneers, *Project Skizoid* https://jorisputteneers.tumblr.com/

Vector graphics and code samples
© Urs Hirschberg, except,
↖153: © Urs Hirschberg based on John Conway's *Game of Life*
↖154, top left: © Urs Hirschberg based on Bill Gosper's 'glider gun' in John Conway's *Game of Life*
↖154, top right: © Urs Hirschberg, after Gaetano Kanizsa
↖155: © Urs Hirschberg after Helge von Koch (Paper: *On a Continuous Curve Without Tangents, Constructible from Elementary Geometry*, 1904)
↖156: © Urs Hirschberg Przemyslaw Prusinkiewicz, Aristid Lindenmayer
↖157: © Urs Hirschberg after Gerhard Schmitt in *Architectura et Machina, Computer Aided Architectural Design und Virtuelle Architektur*
↖160: © Urs Hirschberg after Datumizer, Wikimedia: https://commons.wikimedia.org/wiki/File:Metaball_contact_sheet.png
↖163: © Urs Hirschberg after Martin Kaftan: FWF research project Augmented Architecture https://iam.tugraz.at/en/research/fwf-project-augmented-parametrics-simulation-and-expert-knowledge-in-parametric-design/
↖165: © Urs Hirschberg after Thalles Silva in *An intuitive introduction to Generative Adversarial Networks (GANs)* https://www.freecodecamp.org/news/an-intuitive-introduction-to-generative-adversarial-networks-gans-7a2264a81394/

I GRAPHS & GRAPHICS

117 Source: Haverford College http://ds-wordpress.haverford.edu/bitbybit/bit-by-bit-contents/chapter-one/1-7-pascal-and-the-pascaline/
118 Image author unknown, Creative Commons, Source: Wikimedia https://commons.wikimedia.org/wiki/File:Googlematrixwikipedia2009.jpg
119 © Transport for London
127 Software screenshot: *Rhinoceros*
131 Google Cultural Institute, Public Domain, Source: Wikimedia https://commons.wikimedia.org/wiki/File:Mosaic_floor_panel_-_Google_Art_Project.jpg
133 © Schweizer Baumuster-Centrale, baumuster.ch
135 Image author unknown, Creative Commons, Source: List of Physical Visualizations http://dataphys.org/list/gaudis-hanging-chain-models/
138 Etching by Albrecht Dürer, Public Domain, Source: Wikimedia https://de.wikipedia.org/wiki/Datei:Duerer_Underweysung_der_Messung_fig_001_page_181.jpg

Vector graphics and code samples
© Ludger Hovestadt

II IMAGE & COLOUR

141 Photograph attributed to Rømevig, Creative Commons, Source: Wikimedia https://commons.wikimedia.org/wiki/File:EDB_anlegg,_IBM-360_-_EDB003_2.jpg
142 © GIZEH *Werke*, Source: Wikimedia https://commons.wikimedia.org/w/index.php?curid=8725999
143 Creative Commons, Published by David Pape: http://resumbrae.com/ub/dms423_f08/06/
144 Photograph by Cooljeanius, Public Domain, Source: Wikimedia https://upload.wikimedia.org/wikipedia/commons/0/06/TI83tris.JPG
145 Source: Aero-Modelisme.com https://aero-modelisme.com/histoire-catia-dassault-systemes/catia-version-1-ibm/
146 Photograph by Autopilot, Creative Commons, Source: Wikimedia https://commons.wikimedia.org/wiki/File:Space_Rocks_(game).jpg
147 © Harald Gatermann
148 © Harald Gatermann
149C Photograph by Joho345, Public Domain, Source: Wikimedia https://de.wikipedia.org/wiki/Datei:Xerox_Alto_mit_Rechner.JPG
150A © Harald Gatermann
150B © Harald Gatermann
151A Photograph by Miguel Durán, Creative Commons, Source: Wikimedia https://de.m.wikipedia.org/wiki/Datei:PIC_0011_Samsung_SF100.jpg
151B © Oliver Fritz
152B Image author unknown, Creative Commons, Source: Pixabay https://pixabay.com/de/vectors/scanner-digitale-scanner-computer-146465/
152C © Oliver Fritz
153A © Harald Gatermann, Screenshot using *ScanGear*
153B © Harald Gatermann, Screenshot using *ScanGear*
154A © Harald Gatermann, *Software screenshots*
154B © Harald Gatermann, Software screenshots
154C © Harald Gatermann, Software screenshots
155A © Harald Gatermann
155B © Harald Gatermann
155C © Harald Gatermann
156 © Harald Gatermann
157A © Harald Gatermann
157B © Harald Gatermann
158A © Harald Gatermann, Software screenshots
158B © Harald Gatermann, Software screenshots
158C © Harald Gatermann
158D © Harald Gatermann
158C © Harald Gatermann
158E © Harald Gatermann
158F © Harald Gatermann
159A © Harald Gatermann, Software screenshots
159B © Harald Gatermann, Software screenshots
159C © Harald Gatermann, Software screenshots
159D © Harald Gatermann, Software screenshots
159E © Harald Gatermann, Software screenshots
159F © Harald Gatermann, Software screenshots
160A © Harald Gatermann
160B © Harald Gatermann
161A © Harald Gatermann
160B © Harald Gatermann
162A © Harald Gatermann
162B © Harald Gatermann
163A © Harald Gatermann
163B © Harald Gatermann
163C © Harald Gatermann

163D ©Harald Gatermann
164 ©Oliver Fritz
165 ©Oliver Fritz

Vector graphics and charts
©Harald Gatermann

II RENDERING

166 Painting by J M W Turner, Held by the National Gallery, London, Public Domain
167A Painting by Johannes Vermeer, Held by the Royal Collection, United Kingdom, Public Domain https://www.rct.uk/collection/405346/lady-at-the-virginals-with-a-gentleman
167B Book cover after Vermeer
168A Image by Mario Szklanny, Creative Commons, Source: Wikimedia https://commons.wikimedia.org/wiki/File:HDR_image_%2B_3_source_pictures_(Cerro_Tronador,_Argentina).jpg
168B Photograph by Uli Herrmann, Creative Commons, Source: Wikimedia https://commons.wikimedia.org/wiki/File:Admiralbr%C3%BCcke_im_Dezember_-_panoramio.jpg?uselang=de
169A Etching by Albrecht Dürer, Public Domain, Source: Wikimedia https://de.wikipedia.org/wiki/Datei:Duerer_Underweysung_der_Messung_fig_001_page_181.jpg
169B ©Ludwig Grimm, after Dürer
170 ©Ludwig Grimm
171 ©Ludwig Grimm
172 ©Urs Hirschberg
173A ©Ludwig Grimm
173B ©Ludwig Grimm
174 ©Ludwig Grimm
175A @ Urs Hirschberg
175B @ Urs Hirschberg
176A © *Lightscape*
176B © *Lightscape*
177 Image created by Dhatfield, Creative Commons, Source: Wikimedia https://commons.wikimedia.org/wiki/File:Utah_teapot_simple.png
178A ©Ludwig Grimm
178B ©Ludwig Grimm
179 ©Eszter Katona/Urs Hirschberg
180 ©Ludwig Grimm
181 ©Urs Hirschberg
182 ©Ludwig Grimm
183A ©Ludwig Grimm
183B ©Ludwig Grimm
183C ©Ludwig Grimm
183D ©Ludwig Grimm
184 ©Jay Lee, baldheretic.com
185A ©Matthias Proske, valuetech.de
185B ©Matthias Proske, valuetech.de
186 ©Ludwig Grimm
187A Painting by Jan Lievens, Held by the Rijksmuseum Amsterdam, Public Domain
187B Sophia Meeres after Giorgio Morandi
188A ©Urs Hirschberg
188B ©Ludwig Grimm
189 © *Cinema4D*
190 ©Urs Hirschberg
191A ©Ludwig Grimm
191B ©Ludwig Grimm
192 ©Ludwig Grimm
193 ©Ludwig Grimm
194 ©Ludwig Grimm
195 ©Ludwig Grimm
196 ©Ludwig Grimm
197 ©Ludwig Grimm
198A ©Ludwig Grimm
198B ©Ludwig Grimm
199A ©Ludwig Grimm
199B ©Ludwig Grimm
200A ©Ludwig Grimm
200B ©Ludwig Grimm
201 ©Ludwig Grimm
202 ©Ludwig Grimm
203 ©Ludwig Grimm
204A ©Ludwig Grimm
204B ©Ludwig Grimm
204C ©Ludwig Grimm
205A ©Ludwig Grimm
205B ©Ludwig Grimm
205C ©Ludwig Grimm
205D ©Ludwig Grimm
206 ©Ludwig Grimm
207 ©Ludwig Grimm
208 ©Ludwig Grimm
209 ©Ludwig Grimm
210A ©Ludwig Grimm
210B ©Ludwig Grimm

Vector graphics and charts:
©Ludwig Grimm

II VISUALISATION

211 Oscar Nitzchke with Hugo Herdeg, MoMA Collection, New York
212 ©Lengyel Toulouse Architects
213A ©Lengyel Toulouse Architects
213B ©Lengyel Toulouse Architects
214 ©Lengyel Toulouse Architects
215 ©Lengyel Toulouse Architects
216 ©Lengyel Toulouse Architects
217 Photomontage by El Lissitzky, Public Domain, Source: Verlag der Kunst
218 ©Philipp Schaerer
219A Photomontage by Philipp Schaerer, ©Philipp Schaerer/Herzog & de Meuron
219B Photomontage by Philipp Schaerer, ©Philipp Schaerer/Herzog & de Meuron
220 Photomontage by Hans Hollein, ©MoMA, New York
221 Photomontage by Ludwig Mies van der Rohe and Edwald Mies, ©MoMA, New York
222A Philipp Schaerer, ©Philipp Schaerer/Herzog & de Meuron
212B Philipp Schaerer, ©Philipp Schaerer/Herzog & de Meuron
212C Philipp Schaerer, ©Philipp Schaerer/Herzog & de Meuron
212D Philipp Schaerer, ©Philipp Schaerer/Herzog & de Meuron
212E Philipp Schaerer, ©Philipp Schaerer/Herzog & de Meuron
212F Philipp Schaerer, ©Philipp Schaerer/Herzog & de Meuron
212G Philipp Schaerer, ©Philipp Schaerer/Herzog & de Meuron
212H Philipp Schaerer, ©Philipp Schaerer/Herzog & de Meuron
212I Philipp Schaerer, ©Philipp Schaerer/Herzog & de Meuron
212J Philipp Schaerer, ©Philipp Schaerer/Herzog & de Meuron
212K Philipp Schaerer, ©Philipp Schaerer/Herzog & de Meuron
212L Philipp Schaerer, ©Philipp Schaerer/Herzog & de Meuron
223 Photomontage by Ludwig Mies van der Rohe, ©MoMA, New York
224A ©Philipp Schaerer
224B ©Philipp Schaerer
224C ©Philipp Schaerer
224D ©Philipp Schaerer
224E ©Philipp Schaerer
224F ©Philipp Schaerer
224G ©Philipp Schaerer
224H ©Philipp Schaerer
224I ©Philipp Schaerer
224J ©Philipp Schaerer
224K ©Philipp Schaerer
224L ©Philipp Schaerer
224M ©Philipp Schaerer
224N ©Philipp Schaerer
224O ©Philipp Schaerer
224P ©Philipp Schaerer
224Q ©Philipp Schaerer
224R ©Philipp Schaerer
224S ©Philipp Schaerer
224T ©Philipp Schaerer
225A ©Philipp Schaerer
225B ©Philipp Schaerer
226 Photomontage by Philipp Schaerer, ©Philipp Schaerer/Herzog & de Meuron
227 Photomontage by Philipp Schaerer, ©Philipp Schaerer/Herzog & de Meuron

III TEXT, TYPOGRAPHY & LAYOUT

228 Photograph by Matrobriva, Public Domain, Source: Wikimedia https://commons.wikimedia.org/wiki/File:Lettera_22_2.JPG
229 Photograph by Stefan Vorkoetter, Creative Commons, Source: Wikimedia https://commons.wikimedia.org/wiki/File:Hp35s_Calculator.jpg
230A Photograph by Arnold Reinhold, Creative Commons, Source: Wikimedia https://commons.wikimedia.org/wiki/File:Bound_computer_printout.agr.jpg
230B Source unknown/untraceable
231 ©Harald Gatermann, Software screenshot
232A ©Harald Gatermann, Software screenshots
232B ©Harald Gatermann, Software screenshots
233A ©Harald Gatermann, Software screenshots
233B ©Harald Gatermann, Software screenshots
233C ©Harald Gatermann, Software screenshots
234A Photograph by MikroLogika, Creative Commons, Source: Wikimedia https://de.wikipedia.org/wiki/Datei:Tm-u210_bondrucker_testdruck.jpg
234B ©Harald Gatermann/Onlab
234C ©Harald Gatermann/Onlab
234D ©Harald Gatermann
235 Poster by Joost Schmidt, Public Domain, Source: Wikimedia https://de.wikipedia.org/wiki/Datei:Joost_Schmidt_Bauhausausstellung_1923.jpg

Vector graphics, code sample, and tables:
↖330 top: Attributed to Denelson83, Creative Commons, Source: Wikipedia https://commons.wikimedia.org/wiki/File:KB_United_States.svg
Page 330 bottom: Image by Simo Kaupinmäki, based on Mysid, Ymulleneers, Azaghal of Belegost, adapted by Oliver Fritz, Creative Commons, Source: Wikipedia https://commons.wikimedia.org/wiki/File:ISO_keyboard_(105)_QWERTY_UK.svg
↖331+332: ©Oliver Fritz
↖333+334: ©Harald Gatermann
↖335: ©Harald Gatermann & Oliver Fritz
↖336: ©Harald Gatermann
↖338: ©Harald Gatermann, Oliver Fritz, and Onlab
↖342–345: Unattributable

III SCRIPTING

236 Software screenshot: *Logo*
237 Software screenshot: *Lego Mindstorms*
238 ©Milena Stavric/IAM TU Graz
239A ©Tobias Wallisser/LAVA
239B ©Tobias Wallisser/LAVA
239C ©Tobias Wallisser/LAVA https://www.l-a-v-a.net/
240 ©Urs Hirschberg, Screenshot using *Apple Swift*

241A ©Design-to-Production, (Fabian Scheurer)
241B ©Design-to-Production, (Fabian Scheurer) http://www.design2production.com/
241C Photograph by HP Schaefer, Creative Commons, Source: Wikimedia https://commons.wikimedia.org/wiki/File:Lausanne-sannaa-rolex-learning-center_innen.jpg
242 Photograph by Schristia, Creative Commons, Source: Wikimedia https://commons.wikimedia.org/wiki/File:Henderson_Waves,_Singapore.jpg
243 Photograph by Wertuose, Creative Commons, Source: Wikimedia https://commons.wikimedia.org/wiki/File:Right_wing_of_Heydar_Aliyev_Center,_Baku_Azerbaijan.jpg

Vector graphics, code samples, tables: ©Urs Hirschberg

III WRITING & CODE

244 Screenshot *Johnny Simulator*, Creative Commons, Source: Sourceforge https://sourceforge.net/projects/johnnysimulator/
247B Software screenshot: *Windows*
248 Software screenshot: *XCode*

Vector graphics, code samples, tables ©Ludger Hovestadt, except: ↖393: ©Ludger Hovestadt, after raywenderlich.com https://koenig-media.raywenderlich.com/uploads/2014/08/viewdebuggingscreen.png

IV DIGITAL MANUFACTURING

250 ©Wellcome Collection
251 News photograph: author and source untraceable
252 Photograph by Jeff Wallis, Pixabay Licence, Source: Pixabay https://pixabay.com/de/users/jeffwallis-2101594/
253 US Army Research Laboratory, Public Domain, Source: Wikimedia https://commons.wikimedia.org/wiki/File:Pdp11,70_640x507.jpg
254 Image author unknown, Creative Commons or Public Domain, Source untraceable
255 ©Hundegger
256 ©Shigeru Ban
257 ©Design-to-Production
258A ©Hundegger
258B ©Hundegger
258C ©Hundegger
258D ©Hundegger
259 Image author unknown, Creative Commons or Public Domain, Source: pxfuel https://www.pxfuel.com/es/free-photo-ikqcc
260A ©ICD/ITKE *Universität Stuttgart*
260B ©ICD/ITKE *Universität Stuttgart*
260C ©ICD/ITKE *Universität Stuttgart*
260D ©ICD/ITKE *Universität Stuttgart*

Vector graphic, ↖410: ©Sven Pfeiffer

IV MODEL MAKING

261 ©Milena Stavric
262 ©Denise Schmandt-Basserat
263 ©Carolina Menezes
264 Image author unknown, Source: Web Gallery of Art https://www.wga.hu/html_m/m/michelan/5archite/late/3spietr2.html
265 ©artistory390
https://www.flickr.com/photos/24364447@N05/
266 Rainer Lippert, Public Domain, Source: Wikimedia https://commons.wikimedia.org/wiki/File:W%C3%BCrzburger_Residenz,_Gartenfront.jpg
267A ©Godine
267B David Iliff, Creative Commons, Source: Wikimedia https://commons.wikimedia.org/wiki/File:Kew_Gardens_Palm_House,_London_-_July_2009.jpg
268A ©Frank Dinger https://www.flickriver.com/photos/bcmng/7327104316/
268B ©Hulton Archive
269A ©SAAI *(Südwestdeutsches Archiv für Architektur und Ingenieurbau)*
269B ©Oskar von Miller Forum
270 ©Milena Stavric
271 ©Bettina Matthiesen/Vitra Design Museum
272 Drawing by Albrecht Dürer, Public Domain
273 ©Pablo Garcia, after Dürer
274A ©Kunsthaus Bregenz
274B ©Markus Tretter
275 ©Manuel Kretzer

IV 3D PRINTING

277 ©Hannes Thalmann
278 ©Hannes Thalmann
279 Photograph by Bre Pettis, Creative Commons, Source: Wikimedia https://commons.wikimedia.org/wiki/File:MakerBot_ThingOMatic_Bre_Pettis.jpg
280 Photograph by 3DPrinthuset (Denmark), Creative Commons, Source: Wikimedia https://commons.wikimedia.org/wiki/File:The_BOD_-_3D_printed_walls_of_the_structure.jpg
281 Photograph by 3DPrinthuset (Denmark), Creative Commons, Source: Wikimedia https://en.wikipedia.org/wiki/File:BOD_printer_nozzle.jpg
282 Photograph by NotLessOrEqual, Creative Commons, Source: Wikimedia https://en.wikipedia.org/wiki/File:DD_Liberator.png
283 ©Hannes Thalmann
284 ©Open Innovation Lab HTWG
285 ©Hannes Thalmann

Vector graphics: ©Oliver Fritz

V VIRTUAL & AUGMENTED REALITY

286 Footage still from *The Draughtsman's Contract*, written and directed by Peter Greenaway; cinematography by Curtis Clark, ©British Film Institute
287 Photograph by Suttonpubcrawl, Creative Commons, Source: Wikimedia https://commons.wikimedia.org/wiki/File:Barbicanestatefromabove.jpg
288 Etching by Giovanni Battista Piranesi, Public Domain, Source: Wikimedia https://de.wikipedia.org/wiki/Datei:Piranesi-16005.jpg
289 Etching by Giovanni Battista Piranesi, Public Domain, Source: Wikimedia https://de.wikipedia.org/wiki/Datei:Giovanni_Battista_Piranesi_-_Carceri_Series,_Plate_XIV_-_Google_Art_Project.jpg
290 Chronograph by Étienne-Jules Marey, Public Domain, Source: Wikimedia https://commons.wikimedia.org/wiki/File:Chronophotographie_auf_fixer_Platte_mit_rotierendem_Spiegel_1888.jpg
291A Photographs by H Quinten Foster and Don Vickers, Courtesy of Ivan Sutherland
291B Photographs by H Quinten Foster and Don Vickers, Courtesy of Ivan Sutherland

Timeline ↖467: ©Sven Pfeiffer

V SIMULATION

292 ©Planerwissen
293 ©Bob Martens
294A ©str.ucture
294B ©str.ucture
295A ©str.ucture
295B ©str.ucture
295C ©str.ucture
296 ©Mir
297A ©Fabian Scheurer
297B ©Fabian Scheurer
297C ©Fabian Scheurer
298 ©Glen Wilcox, University of Michigan
299 ©Bob Martens
300A ©moBius Consult
300B ©moBius Consult
301A ©moBius Consult
301B ©moBius Consult
301C ©moBius Consult
302 ©moBius Consult
303A ©Bob Martens
303B ©Bob Martens
304A ©Nagata Acoustics
304B ©Nagata Acoustics
305A ©One to One
305B ©One to One
306A ©Paul Hechinger
306B ©Paul Hechinger
306C ©Paul Hechinger
306D ©Paul Hechinger
306E ©Paul Hechinger
307 ©DIAL GmbH
308 ©Max Tillberg
309 ©Greg Ward and Judy Lai, Lawrence Berkeley National Laboratory
310 ©Piero Rasicci
311 ©Filos e.U. Wien
312 ©Graphisoft
313A ©str.ucture
313B ©str.ucture
314 ©Gabriel Holom
315A ©Uwe Wössner – HLRS Stuttgart
315B ©Uwe Wössner – HLRS Stuttgart
315C ©Uwe Wössner – HLRS Stuttgart
315D ©Uwe Wössner – HLRS Stuttgart
315E ©Uwe Wössner – HLRS Stuttgart
315F ©Uwe Wössner – HLRS Stuttgart
316 ©Oasys/MassMotion
317 ©Christian Laemmle, Combustion and Flow Solutions GmbH

V GEOGRAPHIC INFORMATION SYSTEMS (GIS)

318 Map by John Snow, Public Domain, Source: Wikimedia https://commons.wikimedia.org/wiki/File:Snow-cholera-map-1.jpg
319 ©Uber/Mapbox
320A ©MIT Senseable City Lab
320B ©MIT Senseable City Lab
321 ©Peter Zeile
322A ©*Track Me if You Plan!*, Courtesy of Lisa Provo
322B ©*Track Me if You Plan!*, Courtesy of Lisa Provo
322C ©*Track Me if You Plan!*, Courtesy of Lisa Provo

Vector graphic, code sample and data visualisation:
↖495: ©Peter Zeile
↖499: ©Peter Zeile, after Franziska Klügl
↖500: ©*Track Me if You Plan!*/Peter Zeile

V BUILDING INFORMATION MODELLING (BIM)

323A ©Frank Petzold, after *Gesamtleitung von Bauten – Ein Handbuch der Projektsteuerung für Lehre und Praxis* by Paul Meyer and Manfred Huber
323B ©Frank Petzold, after *Gesamtleitung von Bauten – Ein Handbuch der Projektsteuerung für Lehre und Praxis* by Paul Meyer and Manfred Huber
323C ©Frank Petzold, after *Gesamtleitung von Bauten – Ein Handbuch der Projektsteuerung für Lehre und Praxis* by Paul Meyer and Manfred Huber
323D ©Frank Petzold, after *Gesamtleitung von Bauten – Ein Handbuch der Projektsteuerung für Lehre und Praxis* by Paul Meyer and Manfred Huber
323E ©Frank Petzold, after *Gesamtleitung von Bauten – Ein Handbuch der Projektsteuerung für Lehre und Praxis* by Paul Meyer and Manfred Huber

Vector graphics and tables:
↖510: ©André Borrmann
↖514: ©André Borrmann, after Patrick MacLeamy
↖518: ©André Borrmann
↖520: ©Jakob Beetz, André Borrmann, Petra von Both, Frank Petzold, Odilo Schoch
↖521: ©André Borrmann, after *BIM Manager*

V DIGITAL CITIES

324 ©Sebastian Michael
325A Source unknown/untraceable
325B Source unknown/untraceable
325C Source unknown/untraceable
325D Source unknown/untraceable
326 ©Virtual Singapore, Source: Five Stars and a Moon https://www.fivestarsandamoon.com/2014/12/virtual-singapore-macam-matrix/
327A ©Andrej Sluka, Serjoscha Düring, Ernst Gebetsroither, Reinhard König/Austrian Institute of Technology http://cities.ait.ac.at/site/index.php/2019/01/22/accessibility-evaluation-tool/
327B ©Andrej Sluka, Serjoscha Düring, Ernst Gebetsroither, Reinhard König/Austrian Institute of Technology http://cities.ait.ac.at/site/index.php/2019/01/22/accessibility-evaluation-tool/
328 ©Induction Cities/Induction Design Project
329 ©Reinhard König
330 ©Esri https://doc.arcgis.com/en/cityengine/
331 ©Reinhard König, Screenshot using *DeCodingSpaces*
332 ©Reinhard König, Screenshot using *Design Explorer*
333A ©Chair of Architectural Informatics, TUM, Gerhard Schubert
333B ©Chair of Architectural Informatics, TUM, Gerhard Schubert

Vector graphics and tables:
↖533: ©Reinhard König, after Global Footprint Network
↖538: ©Reinhard König, after *UrbanSim*
↖540: ©Reinhard König, after Boyd Paulson
↖543: ©Reinhard König, after Anthony Townsend

V BIG DATA & MACHINE LEARNING

334 Footage still from *Blade Runner*, directed by Ridley Scott; cinematography by Jordan Cronenweth, ©The Ladd Company/Shaw Brothers/Blade Runner Partnership
335 ©IBM
336 ©*The Atlantic*
337 Screenshot: Google
338 ©Ulrich Flemming
339 ©Ulrich Flemming
340 ©Ulrich Flemming
341 Statue attributed to Kritios, Public Domain
342 Drawing by Andreas Vesalius, Public Domain, Held by Acropolis Museum, Athens
344 ©Jennifer Chang & Belén Gándara,
345 Painting by Carl Friedrich Schinkel, Public Domain
347 Painting by J M W Turner, Public Domain, Held by the National Gallery, London
349 Footage still from *The Matrix*, written and directed by The Wachowskis; cinematography by Bill Pope, ©Warner Bros., Village Roadshow Pictures, Groucho II Film Partnership, Silver Pictures
351 Painting by Claude Monet, Public Domain

Vector graphics and code samples:
©Ludger Hovestadt, except
↖552: ©Ludger Hovestadt, after Joseph Weizenbaum

VI BEING A 'BRAND'

352 ©Diana Alvarez-Marin, Miro Roman
353 ©designboom
354A ©*ArchDaily*
354B ©*ArchDaily*
354C ©*ArchDaily*
354D ©*ArchDaily*
354E ©*ArchDaily*
354F ©*ArchDaily*
355 ©Diana Alvarez-Marin, Miro Roman
356 ©Diana Alvarez-Marin, Miro Roman
357 ©Diana Alvarez-Marin, Miro Roman
358 ©Diana Alvarez-Marin, Miro Roman
359 ©Diana Alvarez-Marin, Miro Roman
360 ©Diana Alvarez-Marin, Miro Roman
361 ©Diana Alvarez-Marin, Miro Roman
362 ©Diana Alvarez-Marin, Miro Roman
363 ©Diana Alvarez-Marin, Miro Roman
364 ©Diana Alvarez-Marin, Miro Roman
365 ©Diana Alvarez-Marin, Miro Roman
366 ©Diana Alvarez-Marin, Miro Roman
367 ©Diana Alvarez-Marin, Miro Roman
368 ©Diana Alvarez-Marin, Miro Roman
369 ©Diana Alvarez-Marin, Miro Roman
370 ©Diana Alvarez-Marin, Miro Roman
371 ©Diana Alvarez-Marin, Miro Roman
372 ©Diana Alvarez-Marin, Miro Roman
373 ©Diana Alvarez-Marin, Miro Roman
374A ©Diana Alvarez-Marin, Miro Roman
374B ©Diana Alvarez-Marin, Miro Roman
375 ©Diana Alvarez-Marin, Miro Roman
376 ©Diana Alvarez-Marin, Miro Roman
377 ©Diana Alvarez-Marin, Miro Roman
378 ©Diana Alvarez-Marin, Miro Roman
379 ©Diana Alvarez-Marin, Miro Roman
380 ©Diana Alvarez-Marin, Miro Roman
381 ©Diana Alvarez-Marin, Miro Roman
382 ©Diana Alvarez-Marin, Miro Roman
383 ©Diana Alvarez-Marin, Miro Roman
384 ©Diana Alvarez-Marin, Miro Roman
385 ©Diana Alvarez-Marin, Miro Roman
386 ©Diana Alvarez-Marin, Miro Roman
387 ©Diana Alvarez-Marin, Miro Roman
388 ©Diana Alvarez-Marin, Miro Roman
389 ©Florian Kleinefenn

Vector graphics and code samples:
©Diana Alvarez-Marin, Miro Roman

VI THE INTERNET OF THINGS (IOT

Vector graphics and charts:
©Kay Römer

VI COLLABORATION

390A Public Domain
390B Public Domain
391A ©Elemental
391B ©Elemental
392 ©Assemble Studio London
393A ©Ossip van Duivenbode
393B ©Ossip van Duivenbode
394A ©*WikiHouse*
394B ©*WikiHouse*

VI PRIVACY & SECURITY

Vector graphics and code samples
©Ludger Hovestadt

CONCLUSION

401 ©Ludger Hovestadt
402A Illustrations by Fra Giovanni Giocondo, Public Domain
402B Illustrations by Fra Giovanni Giocondo, Public Domain
404A Publicity image for *The Dark Knight*
404B Publicity image for *Her*
404C Publicity image for *Assassin's Creed*
404D Publicity image for *Arrival*
405A Publicity image for Chanel
405B Publicity image for Nike
405C Publicity image for Lavazza
405D Publicity for McDonald's
406 Ancient artefact, unauthored, Public Domain
408 Diagram by Leon Battista Alberti, Public Domain
410 Image author unknown, Creative Commons, Source: Wikimedia https://commons.wikimedia.org/wiki/File:Googlematrixwikipedia2009.jpg
412 Illustration by Sebastiano Serlio, Public Domain
413 Publicity for McDonald's
414 Illustration by Sebastiano Serlio, Public Domain
416 Illustration by Sebastiano Serlio, Public Domain
419 Painting by Parmigianino, Public Domain

Vector graphics and code samples:
©Ludger Hovestadt

Biographies

CONTRIBUTING EDITOR

Oliver Fritz

)liver Fritz is Professor for Digital Media and Archi-ectural Representation at HTWG Konstanz Univer-sity of Applied Sciences. Furthermore, he is head of the Open Innovation Lab, a cross-faculty, uni-versity-wide usable laboratory. These are publicly accessible, modern do-it-yourself workshops, in which creative new products are individually devel-oped, tested, and produced using digital tools. Furthermore, the Open Innovation Lab focuses on he innovation spaces that some large companies operate in order to quickly bring innovations to mar-ket via design thinking methods and prototypes.

Born in Berlin, Oliver studied architecture at he University of Kaiserslautern and worked there as a research assistant. He is co-initiator of the *Kai-sersrot* research network. Subsequently, he worked at ETH Zürich as Chair for CAAD, at the Liechten-stein University of Applied Sciences as Assistant Professor, and at the University of Applied Sciences Cologne, Germany, as Professor for CAD.

In addition to his professorship at HTWG Konstanz, Oliver is co-founder of the company Jser Generated Design GmbH. The team con-sists of user interface experts, interface design-ers, architects, and software developers who develop application-oriented software for design processes using scientific methods in the field of AI and parametric and evolutionary algorithms.

- Computer Aided Design (CAD) (with Harald Gatermann) ↖129
- Generative Methods (with Urs Hirschberg) ↖145
- Text, Typography & Layout (with Harald Gatermann) ↖327
- 3D Printing ↖439
- Collaboration (with Urs Hirschberg and Sven Pfeiffer) ↖629

CONTRIBUTING EDITOR

Urs Hirschberg

Jrs Leonhard Hirschberg is Professor for the Rep-esentation of Architecture and New Media and Head of the Institute of Architecture and Media (IAM) at Graz University of Technology (TU Graz). Dean of his faculty for nine years, in 2013 he was appointed Director of the TU Graz Field of Exper-tise 'Sustainable Systems', one of five interdepart-mental research fields.

Born and raised in Switzerland, he gained his architecture diploma and doctorate from ETH Zürich. Before TU Graz he served at the chair of Architecture and CAAD at ETH Zürich and at the Harvard Graduate School of Design.

Urs has worked extensively on the poten-tials of creative collaboration via networks and on digital design and fabrication. He is a founding editor of *GAM*, the *Graz Architecture Magazine*. A former president of the European Association of Architectural Education, he is a founding member of the European Architectural Research Network ARENA and a Technology Editor at *AJAR*, the *Arena Journal of Architectural Research*.

- Generative Methods (with Oliver Fritz) ↖145

- Rendering ↖255
- Scripting ↖351
- Collaboration (with Oliver Fritz and Sven Pfeiffer) ↖629

CONTRIBUTING EDITOR

Ludger Hovestadt

Ludger Hovestadt is Professor of Architecture and CAAD at the chair of Digital Architectonics, Insti-tute for Technology in Architecture, ETH Zürich.

Between 1997 and 2000 he was a visiting professor at the Department of CAAD at Uni-versity of Kaiserslautern, Germany. In 2000, he was appointed full professor at the Department of Architecture at ETH. Since 2018 he has been a visiting professor at Southeast University in Nanjing, China.

Ludger studied architecture at RWTH Aachen, Germany, and at the University of Applied Arts in Vienna, Austria. Upon completion of his diploma in 1987, he started his academic career at TU Karlsruhe with Prof Fritz Haller for whom he worked as a scientific researcher for over ten years. Under his supervision Ludger completed his doctorate at TU Karlsruhe and Carnegie Mellon in 1994, expanding Haller's school of thought of minimalist-functional mannerism into the digital domain, thereby laying the foundations for digi-tal architectonics. He is founder of several com-panies in the fields of digital fabrication, smart buildings, and the digitalisation of our energy grids. Since 2009 his focus has shifted towards basic research on architecture and information. His most important publications are: *Beyond the Grid – Architecture and Information Technology* (2009), *Printed Physics – Metalithicum Series Vol. 1* (2012), *SHEAVES – When Things Are Whatever Can Be the Case* (2013), *EigenArchitecture – Com-putability as Literacy* (2014), and *A Quantum City – Mastering the Generic* (2015).

- Graphs & Graphics ↖175
- Writing & Code ↖369
- Big Data & Machine Learning ↖549
- Privacy & Security ↖643
- In Conclusion – What Is Information? ↖693

CONTRIBUTOR

Diana Alvarez-Marin

Diana Alvarez-Marin is an architect and researcher at the chair of Digital Architectonics at ETH Zürich. She is co-author of the book *A Quantum City – Mas-tering the Generic* around which she pursues her PhD, *Atlas of Indexical Cities: Articulating Personal City Models on Generic Infrastructural Ground*. Her research explores the role of the observer in the constitution of personal city models, under the light of abundance of information and computer literacy.

Diana graduated with honours from the *Ecole Nationale Supérieure d'Architecture et de Paysage de Lille*, France. For several years she col-laborated with O.M.A. in Rotterdam and group8 in Geneva. She attended the MAS program in CAAD at ETH Zürich from 2011 to 2012. From 2013 to 2016

she was visiting researcher at the Future Cities Laboratory in Singapore.

Diana has taught several courses for archi-tecture students around her research on cities: *A Quantum City: Mastering the Generic* and *Indexical Cities: Articulating Your Own City of Indexes*. She loves writing and thinking in both natural and programming languages.

- Being A 'Brand' (with Miro Roman) ↖593

CONTRIBUTOR

Jakob Beetz

Jakob Beetz works at the chair of Computational Design, Faculty of Architecture, RWTH Aachen University, doing research in architectural and civil engineering. Within the fields of architecture and construction informatics, the focus of his past work has been on Building Information Modelling (BIM), Computer Supported Collaborative Work (CSCW), and linked data.

Jakob graduated as a *Diplom-Ingenieur* from Bauhaus University Weimar in 2003 at the chair of *Informatik in der Architektur InfAR*, under the supervision of Prof Dirk Donath. He was awarded a PhD for his work on *Facilitating Distri-buted Collaboration in the AEC/FM Sector Using Semantic Web Technologies*, supervised by Prof Bauke de Vries and Dr Jos van Leeuwen at the ISBE (Infrastructure Security for the Built Environment) Group of the Department for the Built Environment at TU Eindhoven.

He is author of more than 80 scientific peer reviewed publications and co-editor and co-author of *Building Information Modeling – Technologi-sche Grundlagen und industrielle Praxis* (2015), published in English under the title *Building Infor-mation Modeling – Technology Foundations and Industry Practice* in 2018.

He co-founded the open source collabo-ration platform *bimserver.org* and lay the foun-dations to the OWL (Web Ontology Language) representation of the Industry Foundation Classes (IFC) referred to as ifcOWL.

He has participated in numerous research projects including EU FP7 DURAARK, EU H2020 and BIM4Ren, and is active in committees for the standardisation of interoperability in information exchange for the building industry on national (DIN), EU (CEN), and international (ISO, building-SMART, W3C) levels.

- Building Information Modelling (BIM) (with André Borrmann, Petra von Both, Frank Petzold, and Odilo Schoch) ↖507

CONTRIBUTOR

André Borrmann

André Borrmann is Full Professor for Computa-tional Modeling and Simulation at the Technical University of Munich. His research interests cover the fields of Building Information Modelling (BIM), geometric design and analysis, design automa-tion, construction process simulation, and pedes-trian dynamics.

André is actively promoting the construc-tion industry's shift towards the adoption of advanced digital technology and acts as advisor for the German government concerning the broad introduction of Building Information Modelling in public construction projects. Related to this, he is pushing forward the international standardisation activities of buildingSMART, in particular in the infrastructure domain. He has published more than 200 peer-reviewed papers and won several awards, among them the Best Paper Awards of the ASCE *Journal of Computing in Civil Engineering* in 2009, the European Conference on Product and Process Modeling (ECPPM) in 2010, and the International Conference on Computing in Civil and Building Engineering (ICCCBE) in 2014. André acts as Chair of the German Association of Computing in Civil Engineering (GACCE) and is Speaker of the TUM Center of Digital Methods for the Built Environment.

■ Building Information Modelling (BIM)
(with Jakob Beetz, Petra von Both, Frank Petzold, and Odilo Schoch)
↖507

CONTRIBUTOR

Petra von Both

Petra von Both is Full Professor at the Faculty of Architecture, and Head of the Department of Building Lifecycle Management, at the Karlsruhe Institute of Technology (KIT).

Born and raised in Germany, she studied computer sciences and architecture and gained her doctorate from the University of Karlsruhe in the field of integral planning. Before her professorship at KIT she was head of corporate strategic development at Nemetschek AG, responsible for product development strategies and research in the field of collaboration, groupware, and BIM.

At KIT, Petra is working on methods and IT-based tools for integral planning. Research focuses on the implementation of technical and methodical integration approaches, for example IFC-based BIM interfaces to energy simulations or lifecycle assessment tools.

Petra is a member of numerous committees in the field of BIM, city modelling, and digitalisation and has worked as consultant for the Federal Office for Building and Regional Planning (BBR) in the area of BIM. She is the spokeswoman of the buildingSMART regional group Upper Rhine and the buildingSMART specialist group *BIM and Sustainability*.

■ Building Information Modelling (BIM)
(with Jakob Beetz, André Borrmann, Frank Petzold, and Odilo Schoch)
↖507

CONTRIBUTOR

Harald Gatermann

Harald Gatermann is Professor of Digital Media, Design and Construction at HS Bochum University of Applied Sciences and Founding Member of the BIM Institute Bochum and the Master programme Architecture Media Management. He was dean of the faculty for four years and vice president of the university for another four years.

Born in Lemgo, Germany, Harald gained his architecture diploma at the University of Stuttgart. For seven years he worked as assistant professor at Braunschweig University of Technology.

Harald has published several books on architectural design and some architecture guides. His field of research was architectural and panorama photography in combination with virtual and augmented reality. He has presented his work on several conferences organised by Caadria, Ecaade, and Sigradi. He was a member of IVAR and is a founding member of AK:AI.

■ Computer Aided Design (CAD)
(with Oliver Fritz)
↖129
■ Image & Colour
↖229
■ Text, Typography & Layout
(with Oliver Fritz)
↖327

CONTRIBUTOR

Marco Hemmerling

Marco Hemmerling is Professor of Computational Design in Architecture at Cologne University of Applied Sciences and visiting professor at *Politecnico di Milano*, School of Architecture and Urban Planning. Previously he was professor at Detmold School of Architecture and Interior Design and director of the post-graduate Master programme Computational Design and Construction at East-Westphalia University of Applied Sciences.

He studied architecture at Bauhaus University Weimar, *Politecnico di Milano*, and Bochum University of Applied Sciences. During his several years as project architect at UNStudio in Amsterdam, he was jointly responsible for the design and realisation of the Mercedes-Benz Museum in Stuttgart.

Marco is a founding partner of SPADE Studio and a co-opted member both of the Association of German Architects (BDA) and of the German Association of Craftsmen (DWB). In his work he aims to link technological advancements to spatial qualities in a human-centred design approach.

■ 3D Modelling
↖57

CONTRIBUTOR

Ursula Kirschner

Ursula Kirschner is Professor for Architecture and Digital Culture at the Faculty of Humanities and Social Sciences, Leuphana University in Lüneburg and director of the Institute for Urban and Cultural Area Research.

She holds a diploma degree in architecture from the University of Arts Berlin in 1989. Thereafter, she worked as an architect in the architectural office of Prof Winking in Hamburg and in Berlin, and as a freelance architect. She finished her PhD with a scholarship from the Dorothea Erxleben Program under the supervision of Prof Frank and Prof Winking at the University of Arts Hamburg in 2001.

Ursula is responsible for several international summer schools und exchange programmes funded by DAAD and other foundations. For many years now she has been working as a reviewer for DAAD and DFG, and been a member of the scientific committee of the Conference for Cooperative Design, Visualisation, and Engineering (CDVE). She is a founding member of the Forum Building Culture in Lüneburg.

■ Digital Design Strategies
(with Sven Schneider)
↖111

CONTRIBUTOR

Reinhard König

Reinhard König is Professor for Computational Architecture at Bauhaus University Weimar and principal scientist at the competence unit Digital Resilient Cities at the Austrian Institute of Technology (AIT) in Vienna. In addition, he acts as Co-PI in the Big Data Informed Urban Design group at the Future Cities Lab at the Singapore ETH Centre.

Reinhard studied architecture and urban planning in Munich and Kaiserslautern, completed his PhD thesis in 2009 at the University of Karlsruhe, and worked as a research assistant and appointed interim professor of the chair for Computer Science in Architecture at Bauhaus University Weimar. From 2013 to 2016 he worked at the chair of Information Architecture, ETH Zürich. In 2014 he was guest professor at the Technical University Munich.

Reinhard heads research projects on the complexity of urban systems and societies, the understanding of cities by means of urban simulation and analysis techniques, as well as the development of evolutionary design methods for architectural and urban design.

■ Digital Cities
(with Sven Schneider)
↖529

CONTRIBUTOR

Dominik Lengyel

Dominik Lengyel has been Full Professor for Architecture and Visualisation at Brandenburg University of Technology Cottbus since 2006. He has been funded by the Federal Ministry for Economic Affairs and Energy and the German Research Foundation as member of the Excellence Cluster TOPOI and of the priority programme *The Digital Image*.

Born and raised in Germany, he gained his architecture diploma from Stuttgart University, after studies in mathematics, physics, and architecture in Essen, Paris, and at ETH Zürich. Before BTU Cottbus he was full professor at the University of Applied Sciences in Cologne. Since 1999, he has been managing partner of Lengyel Toulouse Architects Berlin, an office for architecture and visualisation.

Dominik works on the visualisation of non-visual content in power engineering and of hypotheses of archaeology and building and art history. He is a member of the Koldewey Society for building history research and the European Academy of Sciences and Arts in Salzburg, Austria.

■ Visualisation
(with Philipp Schaerer)
↖285

CONTRIBUTOR

Bob Martens

Bob Martens is Professor for Spatial Simulation and (Computer Aided) Architectural Design at Vienna University of Technology (TU Wien). Next to a significant focus on design studio teaching, he has been responsible for the establishment of a full-scale experimental laboratory. Since 2005 he has also been acting as (vice-) dean for continuing education at TU Wien.

Born and raised in the Netherlands, he gained his building science diploma from TU Eindhoven and his doctoral degree from TU Wien. In addition a *venia docendi* was awarded in 1994. Before TU Wien he was affiliated to TU Eindhoven and acted as guest professor at TU Graz.

Bob has a wide range of experience in the area of simulation and conducts research activities in the field of virtual reconstruction (predominantly of destroyed Viennese synagogues). Together with Ziga Turk he initiated the Cumulative Index on CAD (CumInCAD) in 1998. Within the eCAADe-association he is acting as council member, following his presidency from 1997 to 2001.

■ Simulation
↸475

CONTRIBUTOR

Frank Petzold

Frank Petzold is Full Professor and Head of the chair for Architectural Informatics at the Department of Architecture as well as Affiliate Member of the Department of Informatics at the Technical University of Munich (TUM).

Born and raised in Germany, he studied computer sciences with a focus on architecture and civil engineering at HAB Weimar (today Bauhaus University) and gained his doctorate from Bauhaus University Weimar. Before TUM he served as research associate at the chair of Computer Sciences and as Junior Professor for Architectural Informatics at Bauhaus University Weimar.

In both research and teaching, Frank examines questions of information technology supporting the design process and the fields of activity of architects and urban planners. He is a founding member and spokesman of AK:AI, member of the GACCE (German Association of Computing in Civil Engineering Architectural Informatics), and since 2015 has held the position of Vice-President of the DARL (Association of Deans of Architecture, Urban Planning and Landscape Architecture in Germany).

■ Building Information Modelling (BIM)
(with Jakob Beetz, André Borrmann, Petra von Both, and Odilo Schoch)
↸507

CONTRIBUTOR

Sven Pfeiffer

Sven Pfeiffer is a Berlin-based architect and since 2020 Professor at the chair for Digital Design, Planning and Building at Hochschule Bochum.

He holds a professional degree in architecture from UAS Hamburg and a postgraduate architecture diploma from *Städelschule* Architecture Class (SAC) Frankfurt, with continued graduate studies at the University of Miami. From 2015 to 2017 Sven was head of the Department for Digital Architectural Production at the Technical University of Berlin. Other teaching positions include a guest professorship at the MSA Münster School of Architecture (2010–2014), and a visiting professorship for Digital and Experimental Design at the University of the Arts in Berlin (2017–2020). He has lectured and taught at several international universities, such as the KTH Stockholm and the Architectural Association, London.

His research and teaching focuses on the potential of integrating emergent simulation and fabrication technologies into the architectural design process at various scales to address complex issues of program, tectonics, and material organisation.

■ Digital Manufacturing
↸405
■ Virtual & Augmented Reality
↸463
■ Collaboration
(with Oliver Fritz and Urs Hirschberg)
↸629

CONTRIBUTOR

Miro Roman

Miro Roman is an architect and a scholar. His main focus is the overlap of information technologies and architectural articulations. Miro explores, designs, codes, and writes about architecture while playing with a lot; with 'all' the buildings, books, images; with clouds, avatars, streams, lists, indexes, and pixels. What is this abundance of information about, how to handle it, and how does it shape the way we think about the world? To navigate and surf these vast flows, Miro codes and articulates synthetic alphabets.

Miro is currently a lecturer and a postdoctoral researcher at the chair for Digital Architectonics at ETH Zürich. From 2004 to 2017 he was a part of the project *romanvlahovic*. From 2013 to 2015 he was a part of the Future Cities Laboratory, the interdisciplinary research programme of the Singapore ETH Centre for Global Environmental Sustainability (SEC).

■ Being A 'Brand'
(with Diana Alvarez-Marin)
↸593

CONTRIBUTOR

Kay Römer

Kay Römer is Professor at and Director of the Institute for Technical Informatics at TU Graz, Austria. He also heads the Field of Expertise on Information, Communication & Computing which gathers more than 100 experienced researchers at TU Graz. He obtained his doctorate in computer science from ETH Zürich where he also worked as senior scientist before joining University of Lübeck in Germany as a professor.

Kay is an internationally recognised expert on networked embedded systems. He has co-chaired leading conferences in the field, served on the editorial boards of leading ACM and IEEE Transactions, and is currently chairing the steering committee of the EWSN conference.

His research interests encompass wireless networking, fundamental services, programming models, and dependability of the Internet of Things. He coordinates the TU Graz Excellence Project *Dependable Internet of Things* and leads the research area *Cognitive Products* in the Pro2-Future research centre.

■ The Internet Of Things
↸613

CONTRIBUTOR

Hans Sachs

Hans Sachs is Professor for Computer Aided Architectural Design at the University of Applied Sciences and Arts Ostwestfalen-Lippe. He is director of the specialisation on Computational Design which is part of the international and interdisciplinary Master programme of Integrated Design. He is also an active member of the university's interdisciplinary research groups, the Construction Lab, and the Perception Lab and co-leads the strategy unit for Digital Building and Construction.

Hans is co-founder of the Responsive Design Studio, and between 2008 and 2014 he was teaching and research assistant at the former Institute of Industrial Building Production (ifib) at the Karlsruhe Institute of Technology (KIT) and the former Cologne Institute for Architectural Design (CIAD) at the Technical University Cologne. His temporary teaching activities at TH Cologne (KISD), Karlsruhe Institute of Technology, ETH Zürich, FH Düsseldorf (PBSA), as well as his expert consultancy and independently developed projects in the context of art, design, and architecture focus strongly on generative design and digital fabrication.

■ Model Making
(with Milena Stavric)
↸421

CONTRIBUTOR

Philipp Schaerer

Philipp Schaerer, born in Zürich in 1972, is a visual artist and architect and since 2014 visiting professor at ENAC, Swiss Federal Institute of Technology Lausanne (EPFL).

After graduating from there in 2000, Philipp worked as an architect and knowledge manager for Herzog & de Meuron in Basel from 2000 to 2006. During this time he created for the studio many well-known architectural illustrations that substantially influenced the visual language of today's established architectural visualisations.

Specialising in the field of digital image processing, Philipp works at the intersection of architecture, photography, and graphic design. His work has been object of multiple publications and exhibitions and is represented in several collections – among others in the MoMA New York, MoCP Chicago, the *Centre Pompidou* in Paris, and the ZKM in Karlsruhe.

■ Visualisation
(with Dominik Lengyel)
↸285

CONTRIBUTOR

Sven Schneider

Sven Schneider is Interim Professor at the chair of Computer Science in Architecture at Bauhaus University Weimar and founding partner of Decoding-Spaces GbR.

Sven studied applied computer science at TU Chemnitz and graduated in architecture at TU Dresden and BU Weimar. He completed his PhD in 2016 on the topic of automated spatial layout design from a user perspective.

His work focuses on the development of measures for evaluating the built environment regarding human-centred aspects and generative methods for supporting the design process. He was and is engaged and coordinating several state-funded research projects and has published a number of articles on generative methods for spatial layout design and spatial analysis.

■ Digital Design Strategies (with Ursula Kirschner) ↖111
■ Digital Cities (with Reinhard König) ↖529

CONTRIBUTOR

Odilo Schoch

Odilo Schoch took on the position of Head of BIM at Swiss Federal Roads Office, one of the largest infrastructure owners in Switzerland, in 2020. He is about to hand over his position as Head of Postgraduate Education on Digitalisation at ETH Zürich, where he taught computational thinking to professionals within the construction sector. He established two companies which consult infrastructure and building owners as well as government agencies in customised future proof digital solutions and value-adding BIM. Among his clients are Swiss Federal Railways, the cantons Zürich and Aargau, the City of Zürich, and retail giant Migros, and he carries out development within the Linked Data Working Group and *ifcrail* of buildingSMART International.

Odilo's interests are the critical and contextual modelling of data concepts and matching processes. This leads to the implementation of tailor-made solutions for individuals and organisations. As a principal investigator of the Swiss national Competence Centre in Digital Fabrication, *dfab.ch*, he links his expertise on data, processes, and robotic fabrication.

With a background in a family run architectural business, he studied architecture at ETH Zürich, UCL London, and RWTH Aachen. He has practised in Germany, Switzerland, and China for companies such as Ove Arup Engineers and Baumschlager Eberle architects. He was Professor for BIM at the Royal Danish Academy of Fine Arts, visiting professor at SEU South East University in Nanjing, and Tsinghua, Beijing, China.

■ Building Information Modelling (BIM) (with Jakob Beetz, André Borrmann, Petra von Both, and Frank Petzold) ↖507

CONTRIBUTOR

Milena Stavric

Milena Stavric is Associate Professor for Architectural Geometry and Digital Design at Graz University of Technology (TU Graz).

Milena completed her education in architectural engineering at Belgrade University, and since 2004 she has been working at the Institute of Architecture and Media. She was a visiting scholar at Harvard University, joining the MaP+S Group.

Milena has lectured at many universities, including Vienna, Mexico City, Istanbul, Hamburg, Novi Sad, Banja Luka, and Zagreb within the framework of research projects aimed at the implementation of digital technology in architecture and education. In addition, she continuously organises exhibitions of her students' work. The focus of her own work is on architectural geometry, digital methods, and presentation, robotics in architecture, parametric modelling, and digital fabrication.

■ Model Making (with Hans Sachs) ↖421

CONTRIBUTOR

Peter Zeile

Peter Zeile is Senior Researcher and Research Coordinator of the Department of Neighbourhood Planning, Faculty of Architecture at the Karlsruhe Institute of Technology. Among other things, he heads *arch.lab*, the platform for research in teaching at the Faculty of Architecture, and the Urban Emotions Initiative.

Born and raised in Germany, Peter obtained his diploma in spatial and environmental planning at the Technical University of Kaiserslautern, where he also completed his PhD on the topic of Real-Time Planning.

Peter's professional passion is urban sensing and geodata processing, visualisation, and simulation of complex projects in urban design, as well as geoweb and mobile solutions for spatial planning. He is editor of conference proceedings (RealCORP) as well as for journals such as *Urban Planning* and *gis.Science*, and reviewer for various publications, including *International Journal of Geo-Information*, *JoDLA – Journal of Digital Landscape Architecture*, *Urban Planning*, *Space and Culture*, and *Environment and Planning B*. He is a member of SRL (Society of Urban and Regional Planners) and national delegate of ISOCARP (International Society of City and Regional Planners).

■ Geographic Information Systems (GIS) ↖491

CONTRIBUTOR

Nikolaus Zieske

Nikolaus Zieske has been Professor of Architecture for Design and Construction in Existing Buildings at *Technische Hochschule Mittelhessen* (THM) since 2002. For many years he acted as dean and vice-dean in the Faculty of Architecture and Civil Engineering.

Nikolaus received his diploma in architecture at *Technische Universität München* (TUM) preceding his studies there and at ETH Zürich in association with Fabio Reinhart and Mirsolav Sik. Starting 1993, he has been managing an architectural office together with his wife in Erfurt and later in Gießen. In 2002 he was appointed to the Association of German Architects (BDA). He worked as an assistant at Bauhaus University in Weimar and as a visiting professor at Carnegie Mellon University CMU in Pittsburgh in 2011.

Nikolaus has a wide range of experience in surveying historic buildings, both by hand and with the help of digital tools such as tachymeters, laser scanners, and photogrammetry. His research at the moment is focused on the conversion of point clouds into digitally usable architectural plans.

■ Digital Data Acquisition ↖93

WRITER

Sebastian Michael

Sebastian Michael thinks, writes, and creates across disciplines in theatre, film, video, print, and online with a deepening interest in humans, the universe, and a quantum philosophy.

His stage plays range from contemporary relationship drama (*The Power of Love* – Southwark Playhouse) and a topical examination of religious fervour (*Elder Latimer is in Love* – Arcola Theatre), to the 'apocalyptic comedy' *Top Story* (The Old Vic Tunnels), and a celebration of Shakespeare's poetry in *The Sonneteer* (Edinburgh Fringe).

His short films and debut feature *The Hour of Living* have been screened at festivals worldwide, and he has published one novel, *Angel*, as well as a 'picture story book for grown-ups', *The Snowflake Collector*, which originated from his experimental online project *EDEN by FREI – a concept narrative in the here & now about the where, the wherefore and forever*, from which the *EDEN miniatures* paperback and ebook series has since been released and which is due for publication in hardcover in 2021.

Sebastian is co-author of *A Genius Planet* (with Ludger Hovestadt and Vera Bühlmann, 2017), contributing author to *A Quantum City* (2015) and the writer of *Your Choice* – with Christopher Peterka (2019).

Sebastian is a guest lecturer at Vera Bühlmann's chair for Architecture Theory and Philosophy of Technics at the University of Technology Vienna (TU Wien). He lives in London and works wherever his projects take him.

○ sebastianmichael.com
○ @optimistlondon